Fundamentals of Psychology in Context

third edition

Stephen M. Kosslyn
Harvard University

Robin S. Rosenberg

PEARSON

Boston   New York   San Francisco

Mexico City   Montreal   Toronto   London   Madrid   Munich   Paris

Hong Kong   Singapore   Tokyo   Cape Town   Sydney

To our parents—Bunny, Rhoda, Duke, and Stanley—
for all of life's lessons that you taught us

Editor-in-Chief: Susan Hartman
Series Editorial Assistant: Courtney Mullen
Senior Development Editor: Cheryl de Jong-Lambert
Executive Marketing Manager: Pam Laskey
Production Supervisor: Beth Houston
Editorial Production Service: Jane Hoover,
  Lifland et al., Bookmakers

Composition Buyer: Linda Cox
Manufacturing Buyer: JoAnne Sweeney
Electronic Composition: Modern Graphics, Inc.
Interior Design: Gina Hagen
Photo Researcher: Sarah Evertson, Image Quest
Cover Administrator: Linda Knowles

For related titles and support materials, visit our online catalog at www.ablongman.com.

Between the time website information is gathered and then published, it is not unusual for some sites to have closed. Also, the transcription of URLs can result in typographical errors. The publisher would appreciate notification where these errors occur so that they may be corrected in subsequent editions.

Library of Congress Cataloging-in-Publication Data
Kosslyn, Stephen Michael
    Fundamentals of psychology in context / Stephen M. Kosslyn, Robin Rosenberg.—
3rd ed.
       p. cm.
    Includes bibliographical references and indexes.
    ISBN 0-205-50757-3   ISBN 0-205-76224-7
    1. Psychology—Textbooks. I. Rosenberg, Robin S. II. Kosslyn, Stephen Michael,
Fundamentals of psychology. III. Title.

BF121.K585 2006
150—dc22

2006047809

Printed in the United States of America
10 9 8 7 6 5 4 3   Q-WC-V 10 09

● ● ● BRIEF CONTENTS

● ● ● CONTENTS

Chapter 2
THE BIOLOGY OF MIND
AND BEHAVIOR: The Brain in Action   50

Chapter 3
SENSATION AND PERCEPTION:
How the World Enters the Mind   98

Chapter 4
LEARNING: How Experience Changes Us 142

Chapter 7
EMOTION AND MOTIVATION:
Feeling and Striving   286

Chapter 8
PERSONALITY: Vive La Différence!   332

Chapter 9
PSYCHOLOGY OVER THE LIFE SPAN:
Growing Up, Growing Older, Growing Wiser   374

Chapter 10
STRESS, HEALTH, AND COPING:
Dealing With Life   424

Chapter 11
PSYCHOLOGICAL DISORDERS:
More Than Everyday Problems   472

Chapter 12
TREATMENT: Healing Actions, Healing Words   520

Chapter 13
SOCIAL PSYCHOLOGY:
Meeting of the Minds   558

Interest in gender and cultural diversity issues remains an important theme in modern psychology. These topics are treated throughout the text in an integrated fashion.

Integrated Coverage of Gender Issues

Women in history of psychology, 22–23
Sex differences in color perceptions, 106
Sex differences in color blindness, 108
Sex differences in detecting odors, 131
Female pheromones and male attraction, 132
Sex differences in sensitivity to touch, 135
Sex differences in remembering emotional stimuli, 195
Sex differences when processing phonemes, 230
Women and emotional intelligence, 260
Sex differences in intelligence, 273–274
Sex differences in nonverbal behavior, 300
Sex differences in sexual response, 321
Sex differences in hormones, 322–323
Mating preferences, 323–324, 579–580
Sexual orientation, 324–326

Freud's sex differences in psychosexual development, 336–337
Gender differences in personality, 363–365
Gender role development, 400–401
Sex differences in moral development, 410–403
Sex differences in pubertal development, 404–406
Peer relationships, 408–409
Menopause, 411
Stress and women, 429
Sex differences in hostility, 434
Gender differences in aggression, 454–455
Alcohol and sexual aggression, 458, 459
Gender and coping, 465–466
Sex differences in prevalence of depression, 489
Sex differences in prevalence of eating disorders, 507–508

Integrated Coverage of Cross-Cultural Issues

Cross-cultural differences in drawing, 112
Perception of physical beauty and culture, 120–121
Behavior modification in nutrition in the Philippines, 165–166
Cultural differences when processing phonemes, 230
Linguistic relativity hypothesis, 236–237
Cultural differences in use of heuristics, 249
Group differences in intelligence, 269–271
Bias in intelligence testing, 271
Race and basic emotions, 290–291
Cultural differences in happiness, 298–299
Emotional expression and culture, 300
Achievement in individualist versus collectivist cultures, 313–314
Food preferences (taste) and culture, 317

Culture and personality, 365–367
Attachment in different cultures, 399
Teenage pregnancy and culture, 409
Psychoneuroimmunology and culture, 436
Coping and culture, 466
Abnormal behavior and culture, 476–477, 478–479
Depression and culture, 488–489
Khmer refugees and panic attacks, 492
Culture and schizophrenia, 504
Eating disorders and culture, 508–509
Treatment and culture, 549–550
Cognition, prejudice, and culture, 568
Attraction and culture, 577–578
Culture and conformity, 585

PREFACE

How can we write a briefer book that engages students and provides them with an *integrated* introduction to the field of psychology? That is what we asked each other as we began writing this textbook. One of us is a cognitive neuroscientist and the other a clinical psychologist. In writing collaboratively, we began to see how our different areas of psychology were dovetailing. Our teaching experience convinced us that the different areas of psychology really are facets of the same whole—and we were inspired to try to bring this view to a larger audience. We also wanted to show students how to apply the results of psychological research to make learning and remembering easier—not just for this course, but for any course, from economics to art history, and for the demands of life in general. In this edition, we continue to pursue our goal of presenting an integrated view of psychology, and we've tried to make the textbook even more accessible for students—to help them better understand and retain the material they read and to help them identify gaps in their understanding.

Our Vision: Psychology in Context

Our vision has always been a textbook that better integrates the field of psychology. We do this by exploring how psychology can be viewed in terms of psychological events that occur in the context of other sorts of psychological events. The key to this approach is the idea that psychology can best be understood in terms of events that occur at different *levels of analysis*, a concept widely used in psychology and other sciences and in the real world. This approach leads us to focus on events in the brain (biological factors), the person (beliefs, desires, and feelings), and the group (social, cultural, and environmental factors). We stress that not only do all of these events occur in the physical world, where we are bathed with specific stimuli and behave in accordance with certain goals, but they also are constantly interacting.

One central idea of this book is that events at any two of the levels of analysis serve as the context for events at the remaining level. To understand fully events in the brain, we must also consider what's going on at the levels of the person and the group; by the same token, to understand events at the level of the person, we must consider the context of the brain and the group; and to understand events at the level of the group, we must consider the context of the brain and the person. No one level has a special status or is most important; any level can be the focus of our interest, leading the other levels to serve as the context. So important is this idea that we changed the title of this book—to stress that events at all three levels are always occurring and that events at any two levels serve as the context for understanding events at the third level.

For example, our brains are affected by our beliefs (just think of how worrying can make our bodies become tense, which is a direct result of events in the brain), and our social interactions both shape and are affected by our beliefs. In fact, as we discuss in this book, social interactions can actually cause the genes in our brain cells to operate differently. All psychological phenomena—from group interactions to psychological disorders, memory, and creativity—can best be understood by considering events at all three levels and how they interact, both with the world and with each other.

This view of psychology is exciting because it offers a way to organize a diverse range of theories and discoveries. The different areas of psychology are interconnected, although they are not often presented this way in textbooks. We wrote this book because no other textbook, in our opinion, was able to succeed in connecting the diverse areas of psychology.

Text Organization

Most brief psychology textbooks have anywhere from 14 to 16 chapters; ours has 13. Market research has shown that when using brief textbooks with more chapters, introductory psychology instructors often end up either skipping chapters or parts of a chapter in the interest of time or requiring students to read multiple chapters per week. Neither option is ideal, and both are likely to result in students having only a superficial grasp of the field as a whole. Introductory psychology is intended to be a survey of the entire field, and we believe that a book with 13 chapters allows students to sample all the areas of psychology. We have carefully chosen core and cutting-edge concepts, theories, and findings, to give students a thorough understanding of the field.

We have combined several topics that we think are best covered in a more integrated manner. For example, Chapter 1 includes both an introduction to the field of psychology and an overview of the methods used in psychological research. To understand any science, students need to learn about the kinds of questions that are asked and the methods for answering them. The appendix on statistics further enhances this coverage and can be assigned at any time in the course.

The topics of language, thinking, and intelligence are covered in a single chapter (Chapter 6), allowing students to see the connections among these topics. In fact, "intelligence" is not a single thing; rather, it draws on language and thinking—among other abilities.

To make a compact and manageable textbook for courses needing a brief text, we integrated the topic of sleep into the stress, health, and coping chapter (Chapter 10), focusing on how stress can affect sleep and how sleep deprivation can affect health and coping. In addition, the coverage of drugs and alcohol has been integrated into that chapter, as the abuse of such substances is often related to a maladaptive coping strategy.

Enhanced Pedagogical Features

Within each chapter of this third edition of *Fundamentals of Psychology in Context*, we have chunked the material into smaller and thus easier-to-retain units of information to help students more readily learn it. This means an increased number of headings at all levels. Furthermore, the headings themselves are written to provide concise overviews of the material covered in the text sections, which allows students to use these headings both as a roadmap to the chapter and as an aid while studying. For easier studying and remembering, we have also grouped appropriate material into bulleted or numbered lists. In addition, the running foot of each right-hand page of a spread lists all the major sections within the chapter. The section in which material on that page is included is highlighted in purple, so students are never lost—they see where they are, where they've been, and what lies ahead.

Chapter Story

We begin each chapter with a story about a person or group. The story is then elaborated on throughout the chapter, providing a framework for the chapter's discussion of relevant psychological theories and research. These stories serve several purposes. They allow students to see how the psychological material covered in the chapter might apply to people outside of a psychological laboratory. They also make the material more interesting and applicable to students' lives, thus facilitating learning and remembering. In addition, each story integrates the various topics addressed within a chapter, creating a coherent thematic whole to further enhance students' understanding. Finally, the story itself provides retrieval cues to help students remember the material.

For example, the story in Chapter 7 (Emotion and Motivation) follows Mohandas Gandhi on his long journey of peaceful activism for social justice. As students learn more about Gandhi (or any of the other people in the chapter stories) over the course of a chapter, they also learn more about psychological findings

---

chapter **7**

Emotion and Motivation
Feeling and Striving

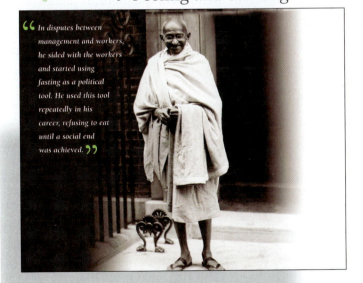

" In disputes between management and workers, he sided with the workers and started using fasting as a political tool. He used this tool repeatedly in his career, refusing to eat until a social end was achieved. "

CHAPTER OUTLINE

Emotion: I Feel, Therefore I Am

Types of Emotion: What Can You Feel?

What Causes Emotions?

Expressing Emotions: Letting It All Hang Out?

Perceiving Emotions: A Form of Mind Reading

Motivation and Reward: More Than Feeling Good

Getting Motivated: Sources and Theories of Motivation

Needs and Wants: The Stick and the Carrot

Hunger and Sex: Two Important Motivations

Eating Behavior: The Hungry Mind in the Hungry Body

Overeating: When Enough Is Not Enough

Dieting

Sexual Behavior: A Many-Splendored Thing

Sexual Orientation: More Than a Choice

Let's Sum It Up

THE PEOPLE CALLED HIM "MAHATMA," OR "GREAT SOUL." AS AN ADULT, Mohandas Karamchand Gandhi was described as follows: "Quiet dark eyes. A small, weak man, with a thin face and big ears. Wearing a white cap as headgear, clothed in rough white material, barefoot. He feeds on rice and fruits, drinks only water, sleeps on the floor, rests little, works all the time. Nothing about him strikes more than an expression of great patience and great love. . . . Such is the man who has incited to revolt three hundred million men, has shaken the British Empire and launched the most powerful movement in the politics of mankind for almost two thousand years" (Rolland, 1924, cited in Markovits, 2003, p. 18). This physically slight man cast a giant shadow across the 20th century, not only changing the face of India but also inspiring Martin Luther King, Jr., and the American civil rights movement.

In spite of his saintly reputation, Gandhi was a man of flesh and blood, possessed of raw emotions and strong motivations, just like the rest of us. The personal history of Gandhi provides us with a case study of the nature of emotion and its role in motivation.

By all reports, Gandhi was a shy, ordinary child, who was perhaps a little more stubborn than his peers, but this tendency was noticeable only through the keen lens of hindsight. As a young man, he decided to become a lawyer, following in the footsteps of his father and grandfather before him. At age 19, he went to England to study

287

and principles and their applications. Because students are likely to remember the biographical information about these interesting individuals, they will also remember a lot about the content of the chapter. The chapter story is referred to or continued at the beginning of each section. This fosters integration with the rest of the chapter and introduces each section's topic in an applied context.

Looking at Levels

Within each chapter, we take one aspect of the content—a theory or a psychological phenomenon—and consider it from the three levels of analysis: the brain, the person, and the group, as well as the interactions among events at each level.

Looking at Levels

Attachment

In our closest relationships, we develop deep attachments to other people. However, people differ in their *attachment style*—their way of relating to significant others. Before we can analyze the nature of attachment, we must consider some key facts about it. One crucial finding is that an adult's attachment style with a partner stems from the way that the adult interacted with his or her

For instance, in Chapter 8 (Personality), we examine the concept of attachment from the level of the brain (what happens biologically and how attachment might be linked to temperament), the person (how feelings of attachment affect a person's sense of security and self-worth), and the group (how attachment style, which begins as a social event between infant and primary caretaker, in turn, influences an individual's interactions with other people throughout life). Each Looking at Levels feature serves to integrate knowledge about the brain, personal beliefs, desires, and feelings, and group interactions. Moreover, we show how events at each level can be the point of focus, with events at the other two levels serving as the context; we show that no one level of analysis is the most important, and no one level alone is sufficient to understand psychological phenomena. We integrate these diverse types of knowledge within each chapter, rather than relegating such information to one or two separate chapters. The Looking at Levels features also forge bridges that reach across chapters, leading to more effective learning and remembering.

Looking Ahead: Learning Objectives

LOOKING AHEAD: *Learning Objectives*

1. *How are memories reconstructed?*
2. *What role do cues play in retrieving stored memories?*

A set of learning objectives, in the form of questions, is placed at the beginning of each major section of a chapter. These questions serve to focus the student on the section's key points. Answers in summary form are provided in a Looking Back feature at the end of each major section.

Looking Back: Review

LOOKING BACK: *Review*

1. *How are memories reconstructed?* Recognition is the determination that presented information is familiar or that it occurred in a particular context; recall is the retrieval of required information from LTM. Both recognition and recall rely on activating collections of fragments stored in LTM. If the appropriate fragments are not present, you cannot distinguish among similar alternatives and will have difficulty recalling information.

At the end of each section are summaries that answer the learning objective questions posed in the Looking Ahead feature at the section's beginning. These answers review the most important aspects of the material.

Looking Beyond: Critical Thinking

LOOKING BEYOND: *Critical Thinking*

Can you think of any advantages to storing fragments and later reconstructing memories as opposed to storing mental photographs or other complete sets of information? We generally find recognition easier than recall; can you think of any way to convert a recall task into a recognition task? Can you think of any ways to help you generate what might turn out to be useful cues?

A set of critical thinking questions—called Looking Beyond—is provided at the end of each major section of the chapter. These questions ask students to apply the material to real-world settings or to the chapter-opening story, requiring them to think deeply about the material. Such active processing enhances memory. And the location of these questions encourages students to immediately analyze and apply the information they have just acquired.

Let's Sum It Up

We have fully revised the end-of-chapter review elements to help students further grasp and consolidate what they have learned.

Summary: A section-by-section outline of the chapter's material is provided in the Let's Sum It Up section. These outlines highlight key points that students should know after a thorough reading of the material. They help consolidate the core material even further into memory.

Key Terms: Each end-of-chapter review also contains a list of key terms, including page references, to aid students in mastering key psychological vocabulary. The key terms are highlighted in the text, and their definitions are provided in a marginal glossary that runs throughout each chapter, as well as in an alphabetized end-of-book glossary.

LET'S SUM IT UP

I. The Science of Psychology: Getting to Know You

A. Psychology is the science of mental processes and behavior.

B. The goals of psychology are to describe, explain, predict, and control mental processes and behavior.

C. Psychology can best be understood by studying events at different levels of analysis: the levels of the brain, the person, and the group.

D. The level of the brain is where we examine the activity of certain brain systems, structural differences in people's brains, and effects of genes and chemicals (such as hormones) on mental processes and behavior.

E. The level of the person is where we study the content of mental processes, not just the mechanisms that give rise to them. Our beliefs, goals, and feelings are part and parcel of who we are.

F. The level of the group includes all our social interactions, past and present.

G. Events at the different levels are interdependent and are always interacting. They are also influenced by the physical environment.

II. Psychology Then and Now

A. Psychology began as the study of mental processes, such as those that underlie perception, memory, and problem solving.

B. The structuralists tried to identify the elements of consciousness and the rules by which these elements are combined into mental structures. The primary method of the structuralists was introspection ("looking within").

C. The functionalists rejected the goal of identifying mental processes and how they operated in favor of seeking explanations for thoughts, feelings, and behavior. The functionalists were interested in how mental processes adapt to help people survive in the natural world.

D. The Gestalt psychologists reacted against the structuralists' emphasis on breaking mental processes into distinct elements. The Gestaltists studied the way the brain organizes material into overall perceptual patterns.

E. Freud shifted focus to events at the level of the person. His psychodynamic theory explains how thoughts and feelings affect a person's behavior.

Practice Test: There is a practice test consisting of 15 multiple-choice questions at the end of each chapter, with answers provided at the end of the test. We ask both factual and conceptual questions to help students assess their knowledge of the chapter material, identify topics that may need additional study, and further consolidate the material in memory.

Hands On Features

In most chapters we have included at least one demonstration of psychological phenomena for students to try alone or with others. These brief exercises will (1) provide students with another way to learn about the phenomenon—experiencing it, not merely reading about it; (2) make the material more vivid, thereby enhancing students' attention and memory; and (3) put psychological principles into a concrete context, showing students that the principles really can affect how we think, feel, and behave.
     The mini demonstrations include:

Introspection (p. 10)
Simulated participation in a research study (pp. 34–36)
Measured neural conduction time (p. 55)
Transduction in the retina (p. 104)
Dark adaptation (p. 105)
Finding your blind spot (p. 105)

Seeing afterimages (p. 107)
Ambiguous figures (p. 110)
Motion cues (p. 113)
Recognition and identification (p. 115)
Pop-out (p. 118)
The Stroop Effect (p. 118)
Kinesthetic sense (p. 134)

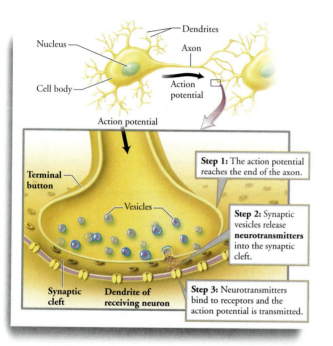

Step 1: The action potential reaches the end of the axon.

Step 2: Synaptic vesicles release **neurotransmitters** into the synaptic cleft.

Step 3: Neurotransmitters bind to receptors and the action potential is transmitted.

New!
Enhanced Art Program and Graphics Display

This edition includes an entirely new art program that features high-quality and appropriately colorized illustrations. The style and color schemes are carried throughout the book, so students don't encounter a hand-rendered fuchsia brain on one page and a grainy green brain photograph on another. Scrupulous adherence to one art style should help students develop and reinforce their own consistent mental images of important content material.

Many illustrations continue to highlight, in step-by-step fashion, some of the most important studies covered in the book. Examples are Watson's famous experiment with Little Albert (p. 149), Bandura's Bobo doll experiment (p. 178), Schachter and Singer's experiment on cognitive influences on emotion (p. 296), a study on alcohol and sexual aggression (p. 459), and Festinger's and Carlsmith's cognitive dissonance study (p. 563). These visual presentations not only complement the in-text descriptions, they enhance learning in several ways:

- The panels walk students through each study, allowing them to understand its details more fully.

- The clear, uncomplicated illustrations use perceptual principles to convey information effectively (these principles are described in detail in Kosslyn, 1994a, 2006).

- This dual-mode format promotes both verbal and visual learning; students can recall either the words in the text or the illustrations when they remember the study.

Initially, Little Albert did not show a fear of animals, but he did exhibit fear if a loud noise was made behind his back (a hammer striking a steel bar).

Then the researchers presented a white rat (CS) and made the loud noise (US).

After five presentations of the CS and US, Albert developed a phobia of rats—he began whimpering and withdrawing (the conditioned emotional response) and trying to avoid the rat. After two more presentations of the CS and US, he immediately began crying on seeing the rat. "He . . . fell over on his left side, raised himself . . . and began to crawl away so rapidly that he was caught with difficulty before reaching the edge of the table" (Watson & Rayner, 1920, p. 5).

- Working through these illustrations leads to active processing—and better remembering.

We have also added many new photos to illustrate particularly important or interesting facts or research findings. The photo captions convey information pertinent to the section, and the photos themselves are hooks that students can use to anchor their understanding of the material.

What's New in the Third Edition?

Every chapter is full of discussion of cutting-edge research, accessibly presented with engaging real-world examples that make the material relevant and interesting to readers. Examples of the key changes in the third edition are listed below by chapter.

Chapter 1: Psychology: Yesterday and Today
- Revised and expanded explanation of the unique levels-of-analysis approach
- Clear definition and discussion of psychodynamic theory
- Expanded discussion of cognitive neuroscience, which continues to draw on the skill of Tiger Woods to illustrate the concept
- Two new sections, entitled "The State of the Union: Psychology Today" and "The Changing Face of Psychology," to highlight new developments in the field and the increasing role of women
- Discussion of the burgeoning field of neuroethics in a new section called "New Frontiers: Neuroethics"
- New text and illustrations to explain the steps of the scientific method
- Revised table summarizing the different research methods used in psychology

Chapter 2: The Biology of Mind and Behavior: The Brain in Action
- Expanded coverage of glial cells and how they work in conjunction with neurons
- Revised discussion of the central nervous system
- Revised Looking at Levels feature, "The Musical Brain"
- New photos to illustrate key concepts
- Discussion of magnetoencephalography (MEG) and its uses
- New figure illustrating how features of the environment can select among variations of characteristics, called natural selection

Chapter 3: Sensation and Perception: How the World Enters the Mind
- Expanded discussion of color vision, newly formatted to make it easier for students to understand
- Reorganization of the section on visual perception for improved readability and understanding
- Expanded discussion of bottom-up and top-down processing
- New discussion of decibels, with an illustration to clarify the concept
- New illustration of dichotic listening
- Expanded discussion of pheromones and the behavior they elicit

Chapter 4: Learning: How Experience Changes Us
- Explanation of how habituation occurs
- Division of the main section on classical conditioning into smaller units for improved readability and understanding

- New photos and figures to highlight key concepts
- New coverage on conditioning and chemotherapy
- Revised discussion of operant conditioning
- Revised Looking at Levels feature, "Facial Expressions as Reinforcement and Punishment"
- Expanded discussion of observational learning

Chapter 5: Memory: Living With Yesterday
- Revised chapter organization and introduction
- Revised coverage of types of memory stores
- Revised discussion of how we make memories
- New photos, tables, and figures to illustrate key concepts
- New section about automatic versus controlled processing
- Expanded discussion of stress and its effect on memory
- Revised coverage of memory retrieval
- New section about hypnosis and memory
- Discussion of new research findings related to false memories
- New section about intentional forgetting
- Expanded coverage of amnesia
- Expanded coverage of repressed memories
- Revised section on tools and tricks that aid memory

Chapter 6: Language, Thinking, and Intelligence: What Humans Do Best
- New illustrations and tables to demonstrate key concepts
- Coverage of inductive and deductive reasoning
- Expanded coverage of the availability heuristic
- Expanded coverage of factor analysis
- Expanded discussion of fluid and crystallized intelligences
- New figures and tables to demonstrate key concepts
- Detailed discussion of Carroll's Three-Stratum Theory of Cognitive Ability
- Expanded discussion of twins and the effects of the prenatal environment
- Revised and expanded discussion of group differences in intelligence
- Expanded coverage of biological factors and sex differences in intelligence
- New Looking at Levels feature, "Stereotype Threat"

Chapter 7: Emotion and Motivation: Feeling and Striving
- New opening story on Mohandas Gandhi
- Expanded discussion of theories of emotion
- Expanded discussion of fear
- Revised discussion of happiness
- New section, "Positive Psychology: More Than a State of Mind"
- New section, "Perceiving Emotions: A Form of Mind Reading," discussing cues that help us interpret emotions, such as body language, tone of voice, and facial expressions
- Expanded Looking at Levels feature, "Lie Detection"
- New introduction to the section on motivation and reward
- New discussion of androgen insensitivity syndrome

Chapter 8: Personality: Vive la Différence!
- New chapter organization
- Revised treatment of personality traits
- Reorganization of the discussion of the effect of situation on personality
- Expanded discussion of personality dimensions (superfactors)
- New sections, "Sensation Seeking: What's New?," "Biologically Based Theories of Personality," and "Behavioral Activation and Inhibition Systems"

- Revised discussion of Eysenck's theory
- Expanded discussion of Cloninger's and Zuckerman's theories of personality
- New introduction to genes and their influence on personality
- Expanded discussion of the behavioral and sociocognitive aspects of personality
- Expanded coverage of the relationship between culture and personality
- New Looking at Levels feature, "Attachment"

Chapter 9: Psychology Over the Life Span:
Growing Up, Growing Older, Growing Wiser

- New chapter organization
- Expanded discussion of the effects of teratogens on a fetus
- Expanded discussion of the effect of a positive environment on a fetus
- Coverage of sensory perception in babies
- Revised discussion of brain development and memory
- Expanded coverage of language development with a new introduction to the section
- Discussion of changes in information processing with cognitive development
- Expanded discussion of attachment
- Expanded section on gender roles
- Expanded coverage of adolescent cognitive development
- Coverage of the aging brain

Chapter 10: Stress, Health, and Coping: Dealing With Life

- New section, "From Stressor to Allostatic Load: Multiple Stressors and Their Time Course"
- New section on cognitive appraisal of stimuli
- New table outlining different theories of why we dream
- Discussion of new research findings related to sleep apnea
- Discussion of MDMA (also known as ecstasy or "e")
- New introduction to mind–body interventions
- Revised Looking at Levels feature, "Voodoo Death"

Chapter 11: Psychological Disorders:
More Than Everyday Problems

- Increased emphasis on looking at psychological disorders from the three levels of brain, person, and group, as well as on considering how events at the different levels interact
- Expanded discussion of the advantages and disadvantages of the *DSM*
- Revised discussion of major depressive disorder
- Reorganization of the section "Explaining Mood Disorders" for improved readability and understanding
- Revised discussion of how events at the various levels interact with each other to lead to depression
- Revised coverage of phobias, obsessive-compulsive disorder, and posttraumatic stress disorder
- Revised and reorganized discussion of schizophrenia
- Expanded discussion of how eating disorders can be explained at the level of the person
- Expanded cautionary note about the diagnosis of psychological disorders

Chapter 12: Treatment: Healing Actions, Healing Words

- New chapter organization
- New introduction, with information about historical influences on psychotherapy
- New section, "Evaluating Insight-Oriented Therapies"
- Expanded section, "Techniques Based on Classical Conditioning"

- Expanded and revised coverage of psychopharmacology
- New coverage of how the placebo effect can lessen depression
- Revised discussion of self-help treatments
- Expanded discussion of therapy protocols
- New Looking at Levels feature, "Treating Obsessive-Compulsive Disorder"

Chapter 13: Social Psychology: Meeting of the Minds
- Expanded discussion of persuasion
- Expanded coverage of social cognitive neuroscience
- Discussion of prejudice and the ways it influences behavior

Instructor and Student Resources

Fundamentals of Psychology in Context, Third Edition, is accompanied by the following teaching and learning tools.

Instructor Supplements

New! *Fundamentals of Psychology in Context,* **Instructor's Classroom Kit and CD-ROM, Volumes I and II**   Our unparalleled classroom kit includes every instructional aid an introductory psychology professor needs to excel in the classroom. We have made our resources even easier to use by placing all of our print supplements in two convenient volumes. Organized by chapter, each volume contains the Instructor's Manual, Test Bank, Grade Aid Study Guide, and slides from the PowerPoint presentation. Electronic versions of the Instructor's Manual, Test Bank, PowerPoint presentation, and images from the text, all searchable by key terms, are made easily accessible to instructors on the accompanying Classroom Kit CD-ROMs.

- **Instructor's Manual** This robust teaching resource can be used by first-time or experienced instructors. Included are numerous handouts, detailed chapter outlines, lecture material, suggested reading and video sources, teaching objectives, and classroom activities and demonstrations.
- **Test Bank** Featuring more than 100 questions per chapter, the Test Bank includes multiple-choice, true/false, short answer, and essay items, each coded with a difficulty rating, page reference, and answer justification. The Test Bank is also available in TestGen 5.5 computerized version for use in personalizing tests.
- **PowerPoint™ Presentation** The PowerPoint presentation for *Fundamentals of Psychology in Context* pairs key topics with images from the book to encourage effective lectures and class discussions. The PowerPoint presentation is included on the Instructor's Classroom Kit CD-ROM and can also be downloaded from the Instructor Resource Center at www.ablongman.com/irc.

MyPsychLab   This interactive and instructive multimedia resource can be used to supplement a traditional lecture course or to administer a course entirely online. It is an all-inclusive tool, a text-specific e-book plus multimedia tutorials, audio, video, simulations, animations, and controlled assessment to completely engage students and reinforce learning. Fully customizable and easy to use, MyPsychLab meets the individual teaching and learning needs of every instructor and every student. Visit the site at www.mypsychlab.com.

New! Printed Appendix on Industrial/Organizational Psychology   Available for the first time with this edition, this appendix provides students with a valuable overview of the growing field of industrial and organizational (I/O) psychology. In this guide, students can see how the psychological concepts presented in the textbook are applied in the real world in any professional workplace. Regardless of the careers students pursue, they may be affected by the work of I/O psychologists, in anything from the description of a position they wish to obtain to the interview and evaluation processes to the way the work environment is designed.

Insights into Psychology Video or DVD, Vols. I–IV   These video programs include two or three short clips per topic, covering such topics as animal research, parapsychology, health and stress, Alzheimer's disease, bilingual education, genetics and IQ, and much more. A Video Guide containing critical thinking questions accompanies each video. Also available on DVD.

The Blockbuster Approach: A Guide to Teaching Introductory Psychology With Video   The Blockbuster Approach is a unique print resource for instructors who enjoy enhancing their classroom presentations with films. With heavy coverage of general, abnormal, social, and developmental psychology, this guide suggests a wide range of films to use in class and provides questions for reflection and other pedagogical tools to make the classroom use of film more effective.

New! Interactive Lecture Questions for Clickers   These lecture questions will jump-start exciting classroom discussions.

Allyn and Bacon Digital Media Archive for Psychology, 4.0 This comprehensive source includes still images, audio clips, Web links, animations, and video clips. Highlights include classic experimental psychology footage from Stanley Milgrim's *Invitation to Social Psychology*, biology animations, and more—with coverage of such topics as eating disorders, aggression, therapy, intelligence, and sensation and perception.

Introduction to Psychology Transparency Package   The Transparency Kit includes approximately 230 full-color acetates to enhance classroom lecture and discussion—including images from all of Allyn and Bacon's introductory psychology texts.

Course Management   Use these preloaded, customizable, content and assessment items to teach your online courses. Available in CourseCompass, Blackboard, and WebCT formats.

Student Supplements

MyPsychLab, Student Version   This interactive and instructive multimedia resource is an all-inclusive tool, a text-specific e-book plus multimedia tutorials, audio, video, simulations, animations, and controlled assessment to completely engage users and reinforce learning. Easy to use, MyPsychLab meets the individual learning needs of every student. Visit the site at www.mypsychlab.com.

Grade Aid Study Guide With Practice Tests—Now Included in MyPsychLab or Available for Separate Purchase   This is a comprehensive and interactive study guide. Each chapter includes: "Before You Read," with a brief chapter summary and chapter learning objectives; "As You Read," a collection of demonstrations, activities, and exercises; "After You Read," containing three short practice quizzes and one comprehensive practice test; "When You Have Finished," with Web links for further information and crossword puzzles using key terms from the text. An appendix includes answers to all practice tests and crossword puzzles.

Research Navigator™—Now Included in MyPsychLab or Available for Separate Purchase   The easiest way to start a research assignment or research paper. Research Navigator™ helps you quickly and efficiently make the most of your research time and write better papers. The program provides extensive help with the research process and includes three exclusive databases of credible and reliable source material: EBSCO's ContentSelect Academic Journal Database, *The New York Times* Search by Subject Archive, and Allyn and Bacon's "Best of the Web" Link Library. www.ablongman.com/researchnavigator

ACKNOWLEDGMENTS

We want to give a heartfelt thanks to the many reviewers who read earlier versions of one or more chapters, sometimes the entire book, and helped shape this third edition. This is by far a better book for their efforts.

Nancy Adler, University of California, San Francisco

Michael Todd Allen, University of Northern Colorado

Marlene Behrmann, Carnegie Mellon University

Bernard J. Baars, The Neurosciences Institute

Lisa Feldman Barrett, Boston College

Sara C. Broaders, Northwestern University

Ekaterina V. Burdo, Wright State School of Professional Psychology

Howard Casey Cromwell, Bowling Green State University

Charles S. Carver, University of Miami

Patrick Cavanagh, Harvard University

KinHo Chan, Hartwick College

Jonathan D. Cohen, Princeton University

Virginia Ann Cylke, Sweet Briar College

Richard J. Davidson, University of Wisconsin, Madison

Mark Davis, University of West Alabama

Pamela Davis-Kean, University of Michigan

Douglas R. Detterman, Case Western Reserve University

Wendy Domjan, University of Texas, Austin

Dale V. Doty, Monroe Community College

Nicholas Epley, University of Chicago

Joseph R. Ferrari, DePaul University

Albert M. Galaburda, Harvard Medical School

Peter Gerhardstein, Binghamton University

David T. Hall, Baton Rouge Community College

Argye Hillis, Johns Hopkins School of Medicine

Herman Huber, College of Saint Elizabeth

Alan E. Kazdin, Yale University School of Medicine

Andrea Rittman Lassiter, Minnesota State University, Mankato

Angela Lipsitz, Northern Kentucky University

Jon K. Maner, Florida State University

Michele Mathis, University of North Carolina, Wilmington

Stuart McKelvie, Bishop's University

Richard J. McNally, Harvard University

Steven E. Meier, University of Idaho

Robin K. Morgan, Indiana University Southeast

Eric S. Murphy, University of Alaska, Anchorage

Lynn Nadel, University of Arizona

Margaret Nauta, Illinois State University

Jason Nier, Connecticut College

Matthew K. Nock, Harvard University

Kevin Ochsner, Columbia University

Kathy R. Phillippi-Immel, University of Wisconsin, Fox Valley

Brad Pinter, Pennsylvania State University, Altoona

Robert Plomin, Institute of Psychiatry, London

Frank J. Provenzano, Greenville Technical College

Scott Rauch, Harvard Medical School

Patricia Sampson, University of Maryland, Eastern Shore

Lisa M. Shin, Tufts University

Jennifer Siciliani, University of Missouri, St. Louis

William C. Spears, Louisiana State University

Larry R. Squire, University of California, San Diego

Robert Stickgold, Harvard Medical School

Lisa Valentino, Seminole Community College

Tor Wager, Columbia University

J. Celeste Walley-Jean, Spelman College

Meg Waraczynski, University of Wisconsin–White Water

Daniel T. Willingham, University of Virginia

Karen L. Yanowitz, Arkansas State University

Marvin Zuckerman, University of Delaware

We also want to thank the reviewers who helped shape previous editions: They helped create the foundation on which this new edition is built. Their comments were invaluable. (Note that the institution given below as the affiliation for each reviewer was accurate at the time of the review; some affiliations may have changed since then.)

Second Edition Reviewers

Joel Alesancer, Western Oregon University

Mark Bardgett, Northern Kentucky University

Mark Baxter, Harvard University

Marlene Behrmann, Carnegie Mellon University

Joseph Bilotta, Western Kentucky University

Sarah Bing, University of Maryland, Eastern Shore

Galen Bodenhausen, Northwestern University

Douglas Cody Brooks, Denison University

Greg Buchanan, Beloit College

Michelle Butler, U.S. Air Force Academy

Laura Cartensen, Stanford University

Patrick Cavanagh, Harvard University

Paul Costa, National Institute of Aging, NIH

Joseph Davis, San Diego State University

Perri Bruen, York College

Lorin Elias, University of Saskatchewan

Delbert Ellsworth, Elizabethtown College

Merrill Garrett, University of Arizona

Michael Garza, Brookhaven College

Peter Gerhardstein, State University of New York—Binghamton

Harvey Ginsburg, Southwest Texas State University

Jordan Grafman, National Institute of Neurological Disorders and Strokes

Dana Gross, St. Olaf College

Larry Hawk, State University of New York—Buffalo

Julie Hoigaard, University of California—Irvine

Dan Horn, University of Michigan

Stephen Hoyer, Pittsburgh State University

Kathy Immel, University of Wisconsin—Fox Valley

Alan Kazdin, Yale University

Melvyn King, State University of New York—Cortland

Joseph LeDoux, New York University

Matthew Lieberman, University of California, Los Angeles

Serry Loch, Paradise Valley Community College

Linda Lockwood, Metropolitan State College

Eric Loken, University of Pittsburgh

Michal Markham, Florida International University

Bruce McEwen, Rockefeller University

Marcia McKinley, Mount St. Mary's College

Marisa McLeod, Santa Fe Community College

Richard McNally, Harvard University

Todd D. Nelxon, California State University

Jacqueline Pope-Tarrence, Western Kentucky University

Beth Post, University of California, Davis

Celia Reaves, Monroe Community College

Gregory Robinson-Riegler, University of St. Thomas

Bennett Schwartz, Florida International University

Alan Searleman, St. Lawerence University

Paul Shinkman, University of North Carolina—Chapel Hill

Larry Squire, Veterans Affairs Medical Center, San Diego

Robert Stickgold, Harvard Medical School

Irene Valchos-Weber, Indiana University

John Wiebe, University of Texas, El Paso

First Edition Reviewers

Sharon Akimoto, Carleton College

Jeff Anastasi, Francis Marion University

Joe Bean, Shorter College

James Benedict, James Madison University

James F. Calhoun, University of Georgia

Brad Carothers, Evergreen Valley College

James Carroll, Central Michigan University

M. D. Casey, St. Mary's College of Maryland

Dave Christian, University of Idaho

George A. Cicala, University of Delaware

Gerald S. Clack, Loyola University of New Orleans

Verne C. Cox, University of Texas, Arlington

Nancy Dickson, Tennessee Technical College

William O. Dwyer, University of Memphis

Valeri Farmer-Dougan, Illinois State University

William Ford, Bucks County Community College

Mary Gauvain, University of California, Riverside

Dan Gilbert, Harvard University

Peter Graf, University of British Columbia

Peter Gram, Pensacola Junior College

Karl Haberlandt, Trinity College

Richard Hackman, Harvard University

Richard Haier, University of California, Irvine

Marjorie Hardy, Eckerd College

Bruce Henderson, Western Carolina University

James Hilton, University of Michigan

Rich Ingram, San Diego State University

John H. Krantz, Hanover College

Richard Lippa, California State University, Fresno

Walter J. Lonner, Western Washington University

Michael Markham, Florida International University

Pam McAuslan, University of Michigan, Dearborn

David G. McDonald, University of Missouri

Rafael Mendez, Bronx Community College

Sarah Murray, Kwantlen University College

Paul Ngo, Saint Norbert College

Thomas R. Oswald, Northern Iowa Area Community College

Carol Pandey, Los Angeles Pierce College

Robert J. Pellegrini, San Jose State University

Dorothy C. Piontkowski, San Francisco State University

Brad Redburn, Johnson County Community College

Cheryl Rickabaugh, University of Redlands

Alan Salo, University of Maine, Presque Isle

Jim Schirillo, Wake Forest University

Michael Scoles, University of Central Arkansas

Michal Shaughnessy, Eastern New Mexico University

Nancy Simpson, Trident Technical College

Linda J. Skinner, Middle Tennessee State University

Michael Spiegler, Providence College

Don Stanley, North Harris College

Bruce B. Svare, State University of New York at Albany

Thomas Thielan, College of St. Catherine

Paul E. Turner, Lipscomb University

Lori Van Wallendael, University of North Carolina, Charlotte

Frank J. Vattano, Colorado State University

Rich Velayo, Pace University

Rich Wesp, East Stroudsburg University

We also profited enormously from conversations with our friends and colleagues, particularly Nalini Ambady, Mahzarin Banaji, Mark Baxter, Alain Berthoz, John Cacioppo, David Caplan, Alfonso Caramazza, Patrick Cavanagh, Verne Caviness, Christopher Chabris, Jonathan Cohen, Suzanne Corkin, Francis Crick, Richard Davidson, Susan Edbril, Jeffrey Epstein, Michael Friedman, Al Galaburda, Giorgio Gain, Jeremy Gray, Anne Harrington, Marc Hauser, Kenneth Hugdahl, Steven Hyman, Jerome Kagan, Julian Keenan, Denis Le Bihan, Fred Mast, Amy Mayer, Richard McNally, Merrill Mead-Fox, Ken Nakayama, Kevin O'Regan, Alvaro Pascual-Leone, Steven Pinker, Susan Pollak, Scott Rauch, Kim Rawlins, Melissa Robbins, Robert Rose, Steven Rosenberg, Margaret Ross, Daniel Schacter, Jeanne Serafin, Lisa Shin, Dan Simons, Edward E. Smith, Elizabeth Spelke, David Spiegel, Larry Squire, Eve van Cauter, Laura Weisberg, and Edgar Zurif. We thank Maya and Alain Berthoz, Maryvonne Carafatan and Michel Denis, Josette and Jacques Lautrey, Christiane and Denis Le Bihan, Bernard Mazoyer, and Nathalie Tzurio-Mazoyer for their hospitality during our year in France, which made it possible and enjoyable to work productively there. We also thank the staff at the Collège de France for their help, in too many ways to list. And to our parents (Bunny, Stanley, Rhoda, and the late Duke) and our children (Nathaniel, David, and Justin), a huge thanks for your patience with our work-filled weekends and evenings, and for your love, support, and good humor. You have sustained us.

Other people have been instrumental in making the first draft of this book, and thus this third edition, a reality. These include Andrea Volfova (for her good-humored assistance and incisive comments), Jennifer Shepard, Bill Thompson, David Hurvitz, Steve Stose, Cinthia Guzman, Nicole Rosenberg, and Deborah Bell for their patience and willingness to help us dig out references and check facts, especially via long-distance communication during the year we were in France. The idea for the book developed over years of working with the Sophomore Tutors and Assistant to the Head Tutor, Shawn Harriman, at Harvard

University, and we want to thank them all; helping them grapple with the concepts of levels of analysis led us to make this book clearer. We are particularly indebted to two of the tutors, Laurie Santos and Jason Mitchell, who read an early draft of the book and offered copious and wise comments. Finally, we wish to thank Christopher Brunt, an undergraduate who used the first edition of the book and spotted an ambiguity in one of the figures; we fixed the figure and appreciate his feedback. Dr. Suzanne M. Delaney, Dr. James H. Geer, and students Katherine Geier and June Ha took the time to share with us ways in which the second edition could be improved, and we greatly appreciate their observations and suggestions. We welcome with open arms feedback from all who read this book and have ideas about how to improve it.

Last but definitely not least, we want to thank the crew at Allyn and Bacon for their vision, support, good humor, and patience. Many special thanks to Susan Hartman, Editor-in-Chief for Psychology, who kept a steady hand on the tiller, helping us navigate through the inevitable shoals; Pamela Laskey, Executive Marketing Manager, whose vision and enthusiasm for the book inspired us; Beth Houston, Production Supervisor, whose diligence and great eye made this edition look so good; Jane Hoover, copy editor extraordinaire, whose eagle eye and depth of processing of our words continually impress us; Sharon Geary, Director of Development, for reading first pages so carefully; Lara Torsky and Deb Hanlon, the editorial assistants who facilitated many important projects, including the commissioning of all the reviews; Kristin Vickers, who oversaw the accuracy of the test questions; Liz Dimenno, Associate Editor, for her help with the supplements; and editorial intern Mekea Harvey, who helped put some vital, final pieces of this project together. We also thank Editorial Director Jason Jordon, for his good listening abilities and creative solutions; Roth Wilkofsky, President of Allyn and Bacon/Longman, for his support and understanding; Sandi Kirschner, President of Addison Wesley Higher Education, and Bill Barke, CEO of Addison Wesley Higher Education, for their continuing support and participation in the project. Finally, and most importantly, our development editors on this edition, who have given so much of themselves to this project: Lisa McLellan, Development Editor, for her sage advice, and Cheryl de Jong-Lambert, Senior Development Editor, who coordinated the myriad processes necessary to bring this edition to life. Thank you all.

● ● ● *ABOUT THE AUTHORS*

Stephen M. Kosslyn

Stephen M. Kosslyn is Chair of the Psychology Department and John Lindsley Professor of Psychology in Memory of William James at Harvard University, as well as Associate Psychologist in the Department of Neurology at Massachusetts General Hospital. He received his B.A. from UCLA and his Ph.D. from Stanford University, both in psychology. His research has focused primarily on the nature of visual mental imagery and visual communication, and he has published six books and over 250 papers on these topics. For ten years he was "head tutor," supervising graduate students teaching year-long introductory psychology courses using levels of analysis. While actively engaged with writing and academic pursuits, Dr. Kosslyn is currently on the editorial boards of many professional journals.

Robin S. Rosenberg

Robin S. Rosenberg is a clinical psychologist in private practice and has taught psychology at Lesley University and Harvard University. She is certified in clinical hypnosis and is a member of the Academy for Eating Disorders. She received her B.A. in psychology from New York University, and her M.A. and Ph.D. in clinical psychology from the University of Maryland, College Park. Dr. Rosenberg did her clinical internship at Massachusetts Mental Health Center, had a postdoctoral fellowship at Harvard Community Health Plan, and was on the staff at Newton-Wellesley Hospital's Outpatient Services. Dr. Rosenberg specializes in treating people with eating disorders, depression, and anxiety.

chapter 1

Psychology
Yesterday and Today

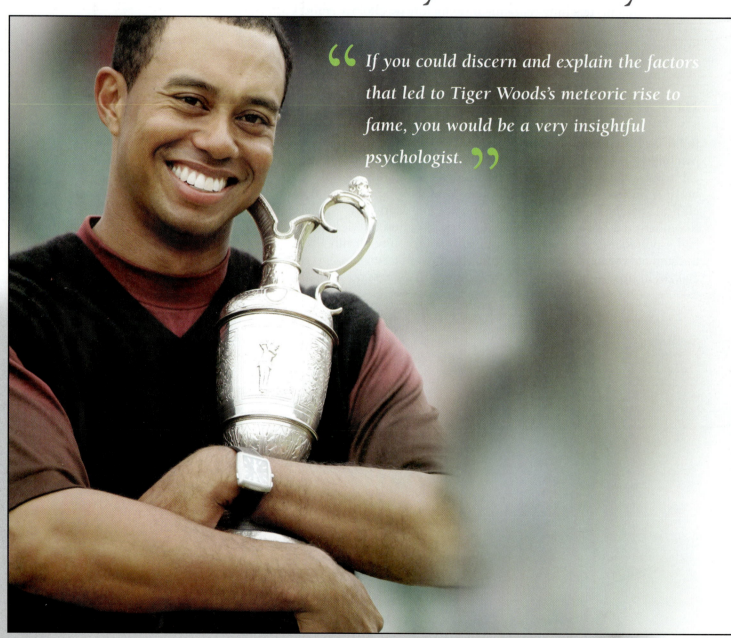

If you could discern and explain the factors that led to Tiger Woods's meteoric rise to fame, you would be a very insightful psychologist.

CHAPTER OUTLINE

O N A BALMY APRIL DAY IN 2002, A YOUNG MAN WAS PLAYING GOLF. NOTHING unusual about that. But when this young man sank his final putt, the watching crowd let out a roar, and he looked for his parents and embraced them, fighting back tears. The occasion was the PGA Masters Tournament, and the young man was Tiger Woods.

Think of the magnitude of his victory: At 26, Woods was the youngest three-time winner of the Masters. And golf's reigning champion, in a sport that had long been effectively closed to all but Whites, was of Asian, Black, White, and Native American ancestry. Tiger Woods dominated the sport of golf like no one before him or perhaps to come— all at a very young age. Before he came on the scene, golf was truly "the White man's sport," and the only place for a minority was as a caddy. After he burst into our collective awareness, he not only opened the sport to minorities, but also brought it into the mainstream—golf courses nationwide have become more crowded since Woods's rise to prominence.

If you could discern and explain the factors that led to Tiger Woods's meteoric rise to fame, you would be a very insightful psychologist.

But where would you begin? You could look at Woods's hand-eye coordination, his concentration and focus, and his ability to judge distances and calculate factors of wind, temperature, and humidity.

You could look at his personality—his reaction to racist hate mail (as a college student at

Stanford University, he even kept one particularly vile letter taped to his wall), his religious beliefs (he was raised in his mother's faith, Buddhism), his demeanor during play, and his discipline in training.

You could look at his relationships with the social world around him—his family, his competitors, his fans.

Is this psychology? Indeed it is. Psychologists ask and, in scientific ways, attempt to answer questions about why and how people think, feel, and behave as they do. Because we are all human and so have much in common, sometimes the answers are universal. But we are also, like snowflakes, all different, and psychology helps to explain our uniqueness. Psychology is about mental processes and behavior, both exceptional and ordinary. In this chapter, we show you how to look at and answer such questions by methods used in current research and (because the inquiry into what makes us tick has a history) how psychologists over the past century have approached these questions.

The Science of Psychology: Getting to Know You

Virtually everything any of us does, thinks, or feels falls within the sphere of psychology. You are dealing with the subject matter of psychology when you watch people interacting in a classroom or at a party, or notice that a friend is in a really terrible mood. The field of psychology aims to understand what is at work when you daydream as you watch the clouds drift by, when you have trouble recalling someone's name, even when you're asleep.

LOOKING AHEAD: Learning Objectives

1. *Psychology can illuminate all aspects of your life, but what is psychology?*
2. *What is the concept of levels of analysis, and how can you use it to understand psychology?*

What Is Psychology?

Although it may seem complex and wide-ranging, the field you are studying in this textbook can be defined in one simple sentence: **Psychology** *is the science of mental processes and behavior.* Let's look at the key words in this definition.

First, *science:* From the Latin *scire,* "to know," science avoids mere opinions, intuitions, and guesses and instead strives to nail down facts—to *know* them—by using objective evidence to answer questions like these: What makes the sun shine? Why does garlic make your breath smell strong? How is Tiger Woods able to execute his swings so superbly? A scientist uses logic to reason about the possible causes of a phenomenon and then tests the resulting ideas by collecting additional facts, which will either support the ideas or refute them, and thus nudge the scientist further along the road to the answer.

Psychology: The science of mental processes and behavior.

What Is Psychology?

Science

Mental Processes

Behavior

Second, *mental processes*: **Mental processes** are what your brain is doing not only when you engage in "thinking" activities such as storing memories, recognizing objects, and using language, but also when you feel depressed, jump for joy, or savor the experience of being in love. How can we find objective facts about mental processes, which are hidden and internal? One way, which has a long history in psychology, is to work backward, observing what people do and inferring from outward signs what is going on "inside." Another, as new as the latest technological advances in neuroscience, is to use brain-scanning techniques to take pictures of the living brain that show its physical changes as it works.

Third, *behavior*: By **behavior**, we mean the outwardly observable acts of a person, either alone or in a group. Behavior consists of physical movements, voluntary or involuntary, of the limbs, facial muscles, or other parts of the body. A particular behavior is often preceded by mental processes, such as a perception of the current situation (how far the golf ball must travel) and a decision about what to do next (how forcefully to swing the club). A behavior may also be governed by the relationship between the individual and a group. Tiger Woods might not have performed the way he did in 2002 had he been playing in 1920, when many in the crowd would not have wanted a non-White person to win. So there are layers upon layers: An individual's mental processes affect his or her behavior, and these processes are affected by the surrounding group (the members of which, in turn, have their own individual mental processes and behaviors).

When you think about a friend's "psychology," you might wonder about his or her motivations ("Why would she say such a thing?"), knowledge ("What does she know that led her to make that decision?"), or goals ("What is she trying to accomplish by acting like that?"). In all cases, you are trying to *describe* (such as by

Mental processes: What the brain does when a person stores, recalls, or uses information or has specific feelings.

Behavior: The outwardly observable acts of an individual, alone or in a group.

inferring what your friend knows or believes) and *explain* (such as by inferring your friend's motivations) your friend's mental processes and behavior. Most people try to describe and explain other people's psychology on the basis of "common sense" or generalizations they've heard (such as the idea that some people are grouchy in the morning). The field of psychology is dedicated to helping us understand each other by using the tools of science. But more than that, psychology's goals are not simply to describe and explain mental processes and behavior, but also to *predict* and *control* them. As an individual, you'd probably like to be able to predict what kind of person would make a good spouse for you or which politician would make sound decisions in crisis situations. As a society, we all would greatly benefit by knowing how people learn most effectively, how to control addictive and destructive behaviors, and how to cure mental illness.

Levels of Analysis: The Complete Psychology

The areas you might explore to answer questions about Tiger Woods's success— his coordination and focus, his beliefs and attitudes, his relationships with his parents and his audience—can be understood in terms of three types of events, each of which provides a field for analysis. Think for a moment about a computer. How can we understand what it does?

1. First, we can ponder the machine itself. The computer is a *mechanism*. One event causes another. You enter a Save command, it saves a file to a disk; you enter a Print command, it sends the file to the printer, and so forth. Each input triggers a specific event—cause and effect. The computer program is like a mental process; it specifies the steps the mechanism takes in particular circumstances.

2. Second, we can ask about the *content* of the computer—the specific information it contains and what's being done to it. The mechanism behaves exactly the same way if you type a research paper, a love letter, or directions to a barbecue. Nevertheless, the differences in content obviously matter a great deal. The content relies on the mechanism (for instance, if the computer is not turned on, you cannot type in any content), but the mechanism and content are not the same.

3. Third, we can hook the computer into a network. We now focus on how different computers *affect each other and the network itself*. What happens when you type in a query to Google? Your computer (both the mechanism and the particular content you type) interacts with others that relay the query and finally send back information in response.

These three *levels of analysis* (to use the most widely accepted terminology) build on one another, with each level adding something new to our understanding of computing. Specifically, the content relies on the mechanism (as anyone knows who has tried to use a computer with a broken hard drive or malfunctioning power supply), and the network depends on both the content (such as the particular commands or requests you enter) and the mechanism (a functioning computer). Do we really need to consider these three levels of analysis? To see why we do, suppose you log onto the Internet and your computer suddenly freezes. Why? It could be that your hard drive has crashed (mechanism); or perhaps you entered an invalid command (content); or perhaps the network itself is down (network). To consider all of the possible reasons for your computer's malfunction, you need to contemplate disruptions at each level of analysis.

Now let's see how this analogy applies to humans.

Three Levels of Analysis in Psychology

At any moment in Tiger Woods's day, or yours, events are happening at the same three levels we just considered in our computer analogy. Considering psychological phenomena from these three levels reveals much that would be hidden were we to look at only one level.

In humans, the *mechanism* is the brain and all of the biological factors that affect it. At this **level of the brain**, psychologists consider not only the activity of the brain but also the structure and properties of the organ itself—brain cells and their connections, the chemical soup in which they exist (including the hormones that alter the way the brain operates), and the genes that give rise to them. At the level of the brain, a psychologist might want to design an experiment to study how Tiger Woods can adjust the force of his swing so exquisitely well for driving, chipping, and putting and might speculate that the parts of his brain that control hand-eye coordination are especially well developed.

At the next level, consider how we use the information that our brains store and process. At this **level of the person**, psychologists focus on the *content* of mental processes, not just the internal mechanics that are the focus at the level of the brain. Unlike the level of the brain, we no longer talk about the characteristics of brain areas or how they operate to process information; rather, we talk about mental contents such as beliefs (including ideas, explanations, expectations), desires (such as hopes, goals, needs), and feelings (fears, guilts, attractions, and the like). Although the brain is the locus and vehicle for content, the two are not the same—any more than a computer and a love letter written on it are the same. Rather, the brain is in many ways a canvas on which life's experiences are painted. Just as we can discuss how aspects of a canvas (such as its texture) allow us to paint, we can discuss how the brain supports mental contents. But just as we can talk about the picture itself (a portrait, a landscape, and so on), we can talk about mental contents. To do so, we must shift to another level of analysis. At the level of the person, a psychologist who is studying Tiger Woods might want to investigate the factors—among them, possibly, his Buddhist faith—behind the inner calm he displays under pressure.

And third, just as computers in a network affect each other, people affect one another. "No man is an island," the poet John Donne wrote. We all live in *social environments* that vary over time and space and that are populated by our friends and professors, our parents, the other viewers in a movie theater, the other drivers on a busy highway. Our lives are intertwined with other people's lives, and from birth to old age, we take our cues from other people around us. The relationships that arise within groups make them more than simply collections of individuals. Psychologists not only study isolated individuals, but also investigate the mental processes and behavior of members of groups. Members of street gangs and political parties both have distinct identities based on shared beliefs and practices that are passed on to new members as *culture*, which has been defined as the "language, beliefs, values, norms, behaviors, and even material objects that are passed from one generation to the next" (Henslin, 1999). Thus, at the **level of the group**,

Level of the brain: Events that involve the structure and properties of the organ itself—brain cells and their connections, the chemical soup in which they exist, and the genes.

Level of the person: Events that involve the nature of beliefs, desires, and feelings—the *content* of the mind, not just its internal mechanics.

Level of the group: Events that involve relationships between people (such as love, competition, and cooperation), relationships among groups, and culture. Events at the level of the group are one aspect of the environment; the other aspect is the physical environment itself (the time, temperature, and other physical stimuli).

psychologists consider the ways that collections of people (as few as two, as many as a society) shape individual mental processes and behavior. At the level of the group, a psychologist might want to examine the role of a supportive and enthusiastic audience in helping Tiger Woods birdie instead of bogey.

Events that occur at every level of analysis—brain, person, and group—are intimately tied to conditions in the physical world. All our mental processes and behaviors take place within and are influenced by a specific *physical environment*. A windy day at the golf course changes the way Tiger Woods plays a shot. The group is only part of the world; to understand the events at each level of analysis, we must always relate them to the physical world that surrounds all of us.

All Together Now

Many people seem delighted to discover that their brains are not, in fact, computers. We noted above that the computer acts the same way when it is used to write a love letter or directions to someone's house. The human brain does not. When you feel an emotion (at the level of the person), that experience is accompanied by changes in how your brain operates (Davidson, 2004; Sheehan et al., 2004). In humans, unlike computers, events at the different levels are constantly interacting. For example, as you sit in a lecture hall, the signals among your brain cells that enable you to understand the lecture, and the new connections among your brain cells that enable you to remember it, are happening because you decided to take the course (perhaps because you need it to graduate): That is, events at the level of the person (your interests or perhaps knowledge of your school's requirements) are affecting events at the level of the brain. But, as you listen to the lecture, your neighbor's knuckle cracking is really getting to you, and you're finding it hard to concentrate: Events at the level of the group are affecting events at the level of the brain. Because you really want to hear this stuff, you're wondering how to get your neighbor to cut it out, and you decide to shoot a few dirty looks his way: Events at the level of the person are affecting events at the level of the group (which, as we've seen, affect events at the level of the brain). And all of this is going on within the physical environment of the room, where the sunlight that had seemed warm and welcoming is now pretty hot, and you're getting drowsy, and you're *really* irritated, and you finally change your seat. . . . And round and round. Events at the three levels of analysis, in a specific physical context, are constantly changing and influencing one another. To understand fully what's going on in any life situation, you need to look at all three.

The concept of levels of analysis has long held a central role in science in general (Anderson, 1998; Nagel, 1979; Schaffner, 1967) and in the field of psychology in particular (Fodor, 1968, 1983; Kosslyn & Koenig, 1995; Looren de Jong, 1996; Marr, 1982; Putnam, 1973; Saha, 2004), and for good reason: This view of psychology not only allows you to see how different types of theories and discoveries illuminate the same phenomena, but it also lets you see how these theories and discoveries are interconnected—and thus how the field of psychology as a whole emerges from them.

In each of the rest of the chapters of this book, in a feature called Looking at Levels, we will consider one aspect of psychology in detail, showing how it is illuminated when we investigate events at the three levels of analysis and their interactions. Moreover, we shall draw on the different levels continually as we encounter different aspects of the field throughout the book. The fact that interactions of events at the different levels of analysis are always present is one thread that holds the different areas of psychology together, that makes the field more than a collection of separate topics.

LOOKING BACK: *Review*

1. *Psychology can illuminate all aspects of your life, but what is psychology?* Psychology is the science of mental processes and behavior. Science is a way of answering questions that relies on, first, using logic to reason about the possible causes of a phenomenon and, then, collecting new facts to test the resulting ideas. Psychology focuses on both the internal events that underlie our thoughts, feelings, and behavior and the behavior itself.

2. *What is the concept of* levels of analysis, *and how can you use it to understand psychology?* Any psychological phenomenon can best be understood by considering events at three levels of analysis: the brain (its functioning and its structure), the person (his or her beliefs, desires, and feelings), and the group (social interactions and cultural influences). All these events occur in the context of the physical world. Events at the different levels are constantly interacting, and thus it is impossible to explain mental processes or behavior adequately in terms of only a single level of analysis.

LOOKING BEYOND: *Critical Thinking*

In your own life, can you identify instances where events at the different levels of analysis were clearly at work?

How would you react if it could be shown conclusively that all criminals have an abnormal structure in a certain part of their brains? If this were true, what should we do with this knowledge? Or, what if it could be shown that criminals have perfectly normal brains, but they all had weak parents who didn't give them enough discipline when they were children? Neither of these single-perspective views is likely to be correct, but what if one level of analysis turns out to be more important than the others?

Psychology Then and Now

How do you think psychologists 50 or 100 years ago might have interpreted Tiger Woods's performance? Would they have focused on the same things that psychologists do today? One hallmark of the sciences is that rather than casting aside earlier findings, researchers use them as stepping stones to the next set of discoveries. Reviewing how psychology has developed over time helps us understand where we are today. In the century or so during which psychology has taken shape as a formal discipline, the issues under investigation have changed, the emphasis has shifted from one level of analysis to another, and events at each level have often been viewed as operating separately or occurring in isolation.

LOOKING AHEAD: *Learning Objectives*

1. *How did psychology develop over time?*
2. *What do today's psychologists actually do?*

The Evolution of a Science

In one form or another, psychology has probably always been with us. People have apparently always been curious about why they and others think, feel, and behave the ways they do. In contrast, the history of psychology as a scientific field is relatively brief, spanning little more than a century. The roots of psychology lie in *philosophy* (the use of logic and speculation to understand the nature of reality, experience, and values) on the one hand and *physiology* (the study of the biological workings of the body, including the brain) on the other. From philosophy, psychology borrowed theories of the nature of mental processes and behavior. For example, the 17th-century French philosopher René Descartes focused attention on the distinction between mind and body and the relation between the two (still a focus of considerable debate). John Locke, a 17th-century English philosopher (and friend of Sir Isaac Newton), stressed that all human knowledge arises from experience of the world and from reflection about it. Locke argued that we only know about the world via how it is represented in the mind. From physiology, psychologists learned to recognize the role of the brain in giving rise to mental processes and behavior and acquired tools to investigate these processes. These twin influences of philosophy and physiology remain in force today, shaped and sharpened by developments over time.

Early Days: Beginning to Map Mental Processes and Behavior

The earliest scientific psychologists were not much interested in why we behave as we do. Instead, these pioneers typically focused their efforts on understanding the operation of perception (the ways in which we sense the world), memory, and problem solving—events at what we now think of as the level of the brain. But even at the beginning, psychologists focused on events at several levels of analysis.

Structuralism. Wilhelm Wundt (1832–1920), usually considered the founder of scientific psychology, set up the first psychology laboratory in 1879 in Leipzig, Germany. The work of Wundt and his colleagues led to ==structuralism==, the first formal movement in psychology. The structuralists sought to identify the "building blocks" of consciousness (*consciousness* is the state of being aware). Part of Wundt's research led him to characterize two types of elements of consciousness. The first comprised sensations, which arise from the eyes, ears, and other sense organs; the second consisted of feelings, such as fear, anger, and love. The goal of structuralism was to describe the rules that determine how particular sensations or feelings may occur at the same time or in sequence, combining in various ways into mental *structures*. Edward Titchener (1867–1927), an American student of Wundt, broadened the structuralist approach to apply it to the nature of concepts and thinking in general.

The structuralists developed and tested their theories partly with objective techniques, such as measures of the time it takes to respond to different sensations. Their primary research tool, however, was ==introspection==, which means literally "looking within." Here is an example of introspection: Try to recall how many windows and doors are in your parents' living room. Are you aware of "seeing" the room in a mental image, of scanning along the walls and counting the windows and doors? Introspection is the technique of noticing your mental processes as, or immediately after, they occur. Insofar as the structuralists' theories were about the structure of consciousness, they addressed the mechanisms of mental processes—and hence considered events at the level of the brain. But they also considered the contents of consciousness itself, at the level of the person.

Had the structuralists been asked to analyze Tiger Woods's golf success—how, for example, he perceives distances, fairway terrain, and wind direction—

Margaret Floy Washburn was not only Edward Titchener's first graduate student to receive a Ph.D., but was also the first woman to earn a Ph.D. in psychology (at Cornell in 1894).

Structuralism: The school of psychology that sought to identify the basic elements of experience and to describe the rules and circumstances under which these elements combine to form mental *structures*.

Introspection: The process of "looking within."

they probably would have trained him to use introspection to describe his mental processes. However, there was a major problem with such uses of introspection. Let's say that although you are able to use mental imagery as a tool to recall the numbers of windows and doors in your parents' living room, your best friend doesn't seem to be able to do the same. How could you prove that mental images actually exist and objects can indeed be visualized? For the early psychologists, this was the core of the problem. Barring the ability to read minds, there was no way to resolve disagreements about the mental processes that introspection revealed.

Functionalism.   Rather than trying to chart the elements of mental processes, the adherents of **functionalism** sought to understand how our minds help us to adapt to the world around us—in short, to *function* in it (Boring, 1950). Whereas the structuralists asked *what* mental processes are and *how* they operate, the functionalists wanted to know *why* humans think, feel, and behave as we do. The functionalists had less interest in events at the level of the brain than did the structuralists and greater interest in events at the level of the group. The functionalists, many of whom were Americans, shared the urge to gather knowledge that could be put to immediate use. Sitting in a room introspecting simply didn't seem worthwhile to them. The functionalists' interest lay in the methods by which people learn and in how goals and beliefs are shaped by environments. As such, their interests spanned the levels of the person and the group.

The functionalists were strongly influenced by Charles Darwin (1809–1882), whose theory of evolution by natural selection stressed that some individual organisms in every species, from ants to oaks, possess characteristics that enable them to survive and reproduce more fruitfully than others. The phrase "survival of the fittest," often quoted in relation to natural selection, doesn't quite capture the key idea. (For one thing, these days "the fittest" implies the muscle-bound star of the health club, whereas in Darwin's time it meant something "fit for" or "suited to" its situation.) The idea of natural selection is that certain inborn characteristics make particular individuals more fit for their environments, enabling them to have more offspring that survive, and those in turn have more offspring, and so on, until the characteristics that led the original individuals to flourish are spread through the whole population. Darwin called the inborn characteristics that help an organism survive and produce many offspring *adaptations*. (Chapter 2 covers Darwin's theory more fully.)

Wilhelm Wundt (the man with the long gray beard standing behind one table) in his laboratory.

The functionalists sought to apply knowledge of psychology and helped to improve education in the United States.

Functionalism: The school of psychology that sought to understand how the mind helps individuals *function*, or adapt to the world.

The functionalists applied Darwin's theory to mental characteristics. For example, William James (1842–1910), who set up the first psychology laboratory in the United States at Harvard University, studied the ways in which consciousness helps an individual survive and adapt to an environment. The functionalists likely would have tried to discover how Tiger Woods's goals and beliefs enable him to press on in the face of adversity, such as losing an important match or receiving hate mail.

The functionalists made several enduring contributions to psychology. Their emphasis on Darwin's theory of natural selection and its link between humans and nonhuman animals led them to theorize that human psychology is related to the psychology of animals. This insight meant that the observation of animals could provide clues to human behavior. The functionalists' focus on social issues, such as improving methods of education, also spawned research that continues today.

Gestalt Psychology.   Although their work began in earnest nearly 50 years later, the Gestalt psychologists, like the structuralists, were interested in consciousness, particularly as it arises during perception (and thus, they too focused on events at the levels of the brain and the person). But instead of trying to dissect the elements of experience, **Gestalt psychology**—taking its name from the German word *Gestalt*, which means "whole"—emphasized the overall patterns of thoughts or experience. Based in Germany, Max Wertheimer (1880–1943) and other scientists noted that much of the content of our thoughts comes from what we perceive and, further, from inborn tendencies to structure what we see in certain ways.

Have you ever glanced up to see a flock of birds heading south for the winter? If so, you probably didn't pay attention to each individual bird but instead focused on the flock. In Gestalt terms, the flock was a *perceptual unit*, a whole formed from individual parts. The Gestalt psychologists developed over 100 perceptual laws, or principles, that describe how our eyes and brains organize the world. Most of the Gestalt principles illustrate the dictum that "the whole is more than the sum of its parts." When you see the birds in flight, the flock has a size and shape that cannot be predicted from the size and shape of the birds viewed one at a time. To Gestalt psychologists, just as the flock is an entity that is

We do not see isolated individual musicians, but a marching band. In the words of the Gestalt psychologists, "the whole is more than the sum of its parts."

more than a collection of individual birds, our patterns of thought are more than the simple sum of individual images or ideas. Gestaltists would want to know how Tiger Woods can take in the overall layout of each hole, or even an 18-hole course, and plan his strategy accordingly.

Today, the study of perception is no longer the province of Gestalt psychology alone but rather a central focus of psychology, as well it should be. Perception is, after all, our gateway to the world; if our perceptions are not accurate, our corresponding thoughts and feelings will be based on a distorted view of reality. The research of the Gestaltists addressed how the brain works, and today Gestaltism has become integrated into studies of the brain itself.

Gestalt psychology: An approach to understanding mental processes that focuses on the idea that the whole is more than the sum of its parts.

Psychodynamic Theory: More Than Meets the Eye

Sigmund Freud (1856–1939), a Viennese physician specializing in neurology (the study and treatment of diseases of the brain and nervous system), developed a detailed and subtle theory of how thoughts and feelings affect our actions. We consider Freud and theorists who followed in his footsteps in Chapter 8; here we touch briefly on key points of this theory.

Freud stressed the notion that the mind is not a single thing, but in fact has separate components. Moreover, some of these mental processes are <mark>unconscious</mark>; that is, they are outside our awareness and beyond our ability to bring to awareness at will. Freud believed that we have many unconscious sexual, and sometimes aggressive, urges. Moreover, Freud also believed that a child absorbs his or her parents' and culture's moral standards, which then censor the child's (and, later, the adult's) goals and motivations. Thus, he argued, we often find our urges unacceptable and so keep them in check, hidden in the unconscious. According to Freud, these unconscious urges build up until, eventually and inevitably, they demand release as thoughts, feelings, or action.

Freud developed what has since been called a <mark>psychodynamic theory</mark>. From the Greek words *psyche*, or "mind," and *dynamo*, meaning "power," the term refers to the continual push-and-pull interaction among conscious and unconscious forces. Freud believed that it was these interactions that produced abnormal behaviors, such as obsessively washing one's hands until they crack and bleed. According to Freud, such hand washing might be traced to unacceptable unconscious sexual or aggressive impulses bubbling up to consciousness (the "dirt" perceived on the hands) and that washing symbolically serves to remove the "dirt." What would followers of psychodynamic theory say about Tiger Woods? A Freudian would probably ask Woods about his earliest memories and experiences and try with him to analyze the unconscious urges that led to his intense interest in golf. This theory focuses on the level of the person but addresses mental processes and behavior at all three levels of analysis: The theory of mental mechanisms is at the level of the brain, but an individual's experience affects events at the level of the person, and the nature of one's upbringing is to be understood at the level of the group. Freud developed an extraordinarily ambitious theory, which attempted to reach into all corners of human thought, feeling, and behavior.

Rather than deriving from objective scientific studies, however, the guiding principles of psychodynamic theory rest primarily on subjective interpretations of what people say and do. Moreover, psychodynamic theory became so intricate and complicated that it could usually explain any given observation or research result as easily as the opposite result, and thus became impossible to test—obviously a serious drawback.

Nevertheless, the key idea of psychodynamic theory—that behavior is driven by a collection of mental processes—had a crucial influence on later theories. In addition, the idea that some mental processes are hidden from conscious awareness has proven invaluable. Furthermore, psychodynamic theory focused attention on novel kinds of observations, such as the interpretation of slips-of-the-tongue and the analysis of dreams. These observations sparked much subsequent research. Psychodynamic theory led to entirely new approaches to treating psychological problems, which have since been modified and refined (see Chapter 12).

Behaviorism: The Power of the Environment

By the early part of the 20th century, a new generation of psychologists calling themselves behaviorists began to question a key assumption shared by their

Sigmund Freud, the father of psychodynamic theory.

<mark>Unconscious:</mark> Outside conscious awareness and not able to be brought to consciousness at will.

<mark>Psychodynamic theory:</mark> A theory of how thoughts and feelings affect behavior; refers to the continual push-and-pull interaction among conscious and unconscious forces.

THE FAR SIDE® By GARY LARSON

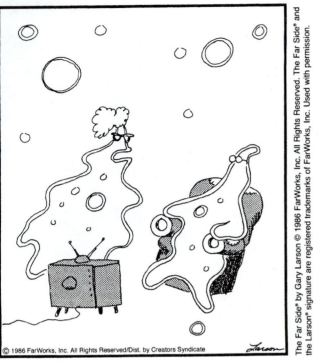

"Stimulus, response! Stimulus, response! Don't you ever *think*?"

Behaviorism: The school of psychology that focuses on how a specific stimulus (object, person, or event) evokes a specific response (behavior in reaction to the stimulus).

predecessors, that psychologists should study hidden mental processes. Because they found the theories of mental processes so difficult to pin down, American psychologists such as Edward Lee Thorndike (1874–1949), John B. Watson (1878–1958), and Clark L. Hull (1884–1952) rejected the idea that psychology should focus on these unseen phenomena. Instead, these followers of **behaviorism** concluded that psychology should concentrate on understanding directly observable behavior.

Later behaviorists, especially B. F. Skinner (1904–1990) and his followers, acknowledged that mental processes probably exist, but argued that it was not useful for psychology to focus on them. Instead, Skinner and his followers held that to understand behavior, we should study behavior. For instance, rather than trying to study the nature of "affection" so as to understand why someone treats dogs well ("affection" being an unobservable mental process), these behaviorists would look at when and how a person approaches dogs, protects them from harm, pets them, and otherwise treats them well. Such a scientific investigation would be aimed at discovering how particular responses came to be associated with the stimulus of perceiving a dog. Because of their concern with the content of the stimulus–stimulus and stimulus–response associations, the behaviorists focus on events at the level of the person.

The behaviorists have had many important insights, among them the fact that responses usually produce consequences, either negative or positive, which in turn affect how the organism responds the next time it encounters the same stimulus. Say you put money in a vending machine (a response to the stimulus of seeing the machine) and the machine dispenses a tasty candy bar; chances are good that you will repeat the behavior in the future. If, on the other hand, the machine serves up a stale candy bar with a torn wrapper, you will be less inclined to use this or another machine like it again (see Chapter 4 for a detailed discussion of how consequences affect learning).

How might the behaviorists explain Tiger Woods's success? A key idea in behaviorism is *reinforcement*, any consequence that results from a given behavior and strengthens or supports the behavior. A reward, such as payment for a job, is a common type of reinforcement. If the consequence of a behavior is reinforcing, we are likely to repeat the behavior. Conversely, if a behavior produces an undesirable outcome ("punishment"), we are less likely to do it again. From his earliest days, Tiger Woods received an extraordinary amount of reinforcement for playing well, at first from his father and then from an increasingly larger affirming public. It was this reinforcement, the behaviorists would argue, that spurred him to repeat those acts that brought desirable consequences, while shunning behaviors (including ineffective golfing techniques) that did not help him play well.

The behaviorists have developed many principles that describe the conditions in which specific stimuli lead to specific responses, many of which have stood up well in later investigations (as you will see in Chapter 4). Moreover, the behaviorists' emphasis on controlled, objective observation has had a deep and lasting impact on psychology. Today, even studies of mental processes must conform to the level of rigor established by the behaviorists. Behaviorist insights also have improved psychotherapy and education. On the other hand, as we will see, many of the behaviorists' objections to the study of mental processes have been refuted by subsequent research.

Humanistic Psychology

Partly as a reaction to the theories of the Freudians and behaviorists, which viewed people as driven either by the content of their mental processes or by external stimuli, a new school of psychological thought emerged in the late 1950s and early 1960s. According to humanistic psychology, people have positive values, free will, and deep inner creativity, which in combination allow them to choose life-fulfilling paths to personal growth. The humanistic approach (focused on the level of the person) rests on the ideas that the "client" (no longer the "patient" as in psychodynamic approaches) must be respected as equal to the therapist and that each person has dignity and self-worth.

Psychologists such as Carl Rogers (1902–1987) and Abraham Maslow (1908–1970) developed therapies based on the humanistic approach. Rogers's *client-centered therapy* incorporated Maslow's theory that people have an urge to *self-actualize*—that is, to develop to their fullest potentials—and that, given the right environment, this development will, in time, occur. Rather than serving as an expert in a position of authority, the client-centered therapist provides a "mirror" in the form of an unconditionally supportive and positive environment. How might humanistic psychologists explain Tiger Woods's success? No doubt they would point to him as someone who is striving to reach his full potential. They might question, however, whether in the long run his intense focus on golf will prove entirely satisfying, especially if he ignores other aspects of life.

Although humanistic psychology never had the impact that the other schools had, it is important in part because it represented a renewed interest in mental processes. This school continues to attract followers today, but it is not a major force in the field. Nevertheless, many of the therapies now in use reflect the influence of humanistic thinking (as we discuss in Chapter 12).

The Cognitive Revolution

The tension between approaches—on the one hand, structuralism, functionalism, and psychodynamic psychology, which studied unobservable mental processes, and on the other hand, behaviorism, which considered only directly observable behavior—was resolved by a new arrival on the scene, the computer. The computer led to the *cognitive revolution* of the late 1950s and early 1960s; its proponents looked to the computer as a model for the way human mental processes work. This movement came into full flower in the mid-1970s, led by, among others, psychologists/computer scientists Herbert A. Simon and Alan Newell (Simon went on to win a Nobel Prize, in part for this work) and linguist Noam Chomsky. (Gardner [1985] provides a detailed history of the cognitive revolution.)

We saw earlier in the chapter how useful computer metaphors can be, but the cognitive revolution focused not on the levels of analysis we have discussed, but rather solely on a new way to conceive of mental processes. This perspective gave birth to cognitive psychology, which attempts to characterize the nature of human *information processing*, that is, the way information is stored and operated on internally (Neisser, 1967). In this view, mental processes are like computer software (programs), and the brain is like the hardware (the machine itself).

Humanistic psychology: The school of psychology that assumes people have positive values, free will, and deep inner creativity, the combination of which leads them to choose life-fulfilling paths to personal growth.

Cognitive psychology: The approach in psychology that attempts to characterize how information is stored and operated on internally.

Computers provided a new way to conceptualize mental processes and to develop detailed theories about them.

Computers showed, once and for all, why it is important that there be a science of the unobservable events that take place in the head, not just a science of directly observable behavior. Consider, for example, how you might react if your word-processing program produced *italics* whenever you entered the command for **boldface**. Noticing the software's "behavior" would be only the first step in fixing this error: You would need to dig deeper in order to find out where the program had gone wrong. This would involve seeing what internal events are triggered by the command and how those events affect what the machine does. So, too, for people. If somebody is acting odd, we must go beyond the essential step of noticing the unusual behavior; we also need to think about what is happening inside and consider what is causing the problem. Indeed, the cognitive revolution led to new ways of conceptualizing and treating mental disorders, such as depression.

The theories and research methods developed by cognitive psychologists have also proven crucial in the development of <mark>cognitive neuroscience</mark>, which blends cognitive psychology and neuroscience (the study of the brain). Cognitive neuroscientists argue that "the mind is what the brain does" (Gazzaniga, 2004; Kosslyn & Koenig, 1995) and hope to discover the nature, organization, and operation of mental processes by studying the brain. One of the goals of cognitive neuroscience is to distinguish among different sorts of mental processes. For example, after Tiger Woods began to lose consistently, he was asked how he felt—and was upbeat in his response. It seems unlikely that this is how he actually felt, but he may have believed he had to "put on a happy face" and try to deceive the reporters. Researchers have found that the particular mental processes used in deception depend on whether a person draws on previously rehearsed and memorized stories or on new stories made up on the spot; brain scanning has revealed that there is more than one way to tell a lie, with separate neural systems being used in the different sorts of lying—which in turn differ from the neural systems used when one tells the truth (Ganis et al., 2003). This is one of the most exciting areas of psychology today, in part because brain-scanning technologies have allowed us, for the first time in history, to observe human brains at work.

The cognitive neuroscience approach considers events at the three levels of analysis, but with a primary focus on the brain. Cognitive neuroscientists seeking to explain Tiger Woods's golfing achievements would likely investigate how different parts of his brain function while he plays golf, looking to discover the way his brain processes information. For example, how does the visual input he receives standing at the tee allow him to judge distance to the pin? They would also compare Woods's brain function with that of less accomplished golfers and would even program computers to mimic the way his brain works during play.

Evolutionary Psychology

One of the most recent developments in the field, evolutionary psychology, first made its appearance in the late 1980s. This school of thought has a heritage—with a twist—in the work of the functionalists and their emphasis on Darwin's

Cognitive neuroscience: A blending of cognitive psychology and neuroscience (the study of the brain) that aims to specify how the brain stores and processes information.

theory of natural selection. Central to **evolutionary psychology** is the idea that certain cognitive strategies and goals are so important that natural selection has built them into our brains. But instead of proposing that evolution has selected any specific behaviors as such (as earlier evolutionary theorists, including Charles Darwin himself, believed), these theorists believe that general cognitive strategies (such as using deception to achieve one's goals) and certain goals (such as finding attractive mates) are inborn. This approach addresses events at all three levels of analysis and is being developed by researchers such as Lida Cosmides and John Tooby (1996), David Buss (1994, 1999), and Steven Pinker (1994, 1997) and reviewed by others (Barkow et al., 1992; Plotkin, 1994, 1997; Schmitt, 2002). For example, these theorists claim that we have the ability to lie because our ancestors who could lie had an advantage: They could trick their naïve companions into giving up resources. These more devious ancestors had more children who survived than did their nonlying contemporaries, and their lying children had more children, and so on, until the ability to lie was inborn in all members of our species. Notice that lying is not a specific behavior; it is a strategy that can be expressed by many behaviors, all of them deceitful.

Evolutionary psychologists also compare human abilities with those of animals, particularly nonhuman primates (Hauser, 1996). For example, by studying the way animals communicate, researchers try to infer which abilities formed the basis of human language. By studying animals, researchers hope to discover the abilities of our common ancestors and, from those data, develop theories about the way those abilities may have been refined over the course of evolution. When asked about what might underlie Tiger Woods's achievements, an evolutionary psychologist might note that although our species did not evolve to play golf, the abilities that arose via natural selection for hunting game and avoiding predators can also be used in other ways—in playing sports, for example.

But evidence of the universality of certain behaviors among humans or of shared abilities in nonhuman animals and humans does not tell us *why* those characteristics are present. Are they really adaptations? Evolutionary theories are notoriously difficult to test because we don't know what our ancestors were like and how they evolved. Just because we are born with certain tendencies and characteristics does not mean that these are evolutionarily selected adaptations. As Stephen Jay Gould and Richard Lewontin (1979) pointed out, at least some of our modern characteristics are simply by-products of other characteristics that

Evolutionary psychology: The approach in psychology that assumes that certain cognitive strategies and goals are so important that natural selection has built them into our brains.

Probably the best source of evidence for theories in evolutionary psychology is *cultural universals*, behaviors or practices that occur across all cultures, including playing music, dancing, lying, telling stories, gossiping, expressing emotions with facial expressions, fearing snakes, giving gifts, and making medicines (Brown, 1991).

Table 1.1 Schools of Psychological Thought

Name	Landmark Events	Key Ideas
Structuralism	Wundt founds first psychology laboratory, 1879.	Use introspection to discover the elements of mental processes and rules for combining them.
Functionalism	James's *Principles of Psychology*, published 1890.	Study why thoughts, feelings, and behavior occur, how they are adaptive.
Gestalt psychology	Wertheimer's paper on perceived movement, 1912.	Focus on overall patterns of thoughts or experience; "the whole is more than the sum of its parts."
Psychodynamic theory	Freud publishes *The Ego and the Id*, 1927.	Conflicts among conscious and unconscious forces underlie many thoughts, feelings, and behaviors.
Behaviorism	Watson's paper *Psychology as the Behaviorist Views It*, 1913; Skinner's *The Behavior of Organisms*, 1938.	Behavior is the appropriate focus of psychology, and it can be understood by studying stimuli, responses, and the consequences of responses.
Humanistic psychology	Maslow publishes *Motivation and Personality*, 1954.	Nonscientific approach; belief that people have positive values, free will, and deep inner creativity.
Cognitive psychology	Neisser's book *Cognitive Psychology* gives the "school" its name, 1967.	Mental processes are like information processing in a computer.
Cognitive neuroscience	First issue of the *Journal of Cognitive Neuroscience* appears, 1989.	"The mind is what the brain does."
Evolutionary psychology	Barkow, Cosmides, and Tooby edit *The Adapted Mind*, 1992.	Mental strategies and goals are often inborn, the result of natural selection.

Note: Dates prior to Maslow based on Boring (1950).

were in fact selected. Your nose evolved to warm air and detect odors; and once you have a nose, you can use it to hold up your eyeglasses. But just as nobody would claim that the nose evolved to hold up glasses, nobody should claim that all the current functions of the brain resulted from natural selection.

The various schools of psychological thought are summarized in Table 1.1.

The State of the Union: Psychology Today

Although schools of psychology gave rise to other schools over time, the original schools did not simply fade away. Rather than being replaced by their descendents, the parent schools often continued to develop and produce new and important discoveries. Moreover, the different schools began to influence each other. Today, we have a rich mix of different sorts of psychology, which are cross-fertilizing and interacting with one another in fascinating ways. For example, techniques in cognitive neuroscience (most notably brain scanning) are being used to test hypotheses about the effects of social context on reasoning and to test behaviorist principles about stimulus–response relations (Blakemore et al., 2004), and research in cognitive psychology is having an impact on many questions that motivated the functionalists, particularly in the area of improving methods of education (Kozhevnikov et al., 2005). In addition, behaviorist techniques have been used to train animals to respond only to certain visual patterns, which then has allowed scientists to discover how interactions among individual brain cells give rise to some of the Gestalt laws of organization (Merchant et al., 2003). Moreover, psychodynamic theory has influenced questions being asked in cognitive psychology and cognitive neuroscience, such as those concerning the nature of forgetting (Anderson et al., 2004). Similarly, evolutionary psychology is making intriguing points of contact with modern behaviorist theories, most notably regarding the idea that behaviors may obey economic laws (for example, by maximizing gain while minimizing expended effort).

All of these varied approaches to psychology not only co-exist but feed off one another. The result is that we are learning about mental processes and behavior at an ever-increasing clip. If you are interested in psychology, these are truly exciting times in which to live!

The Psychological Way: What Today's Psychologists Do

If you read that Tiger Woods had seen a psychologist, would you think that he had a personal problem, or that he was suffering from too much stress? Neither guess is necessarily true; psychologists do much more than help people cope with their problems. As the field of psychology developed, different schools of thought focused on different aspects of mental processes and behavior; their varying influences are felt in what today's psychologists do. And just what is that?

Here we consider three major types of psychologists: those who help people deal with personal problems or stress, those who teach and usually also study the science of mental processes and behavior, and those who seek to solve specific practical problems, such as helping athletes perform better.

Clinical and Counseling Psychology: A Healing Profession

Andrea is a **clinical psychologist** who specializes in treating people with eating disorders. Many of Andrea's clients have a disorder called *anorexia nervosa*, characterized by refusal to maintain a healthy weight. Others, who have a disorder called *bulimia nervosa*, eat and then force themselves to vomit or take laxatives immediately afterward. Andrea sees such patients once or twice a week, for 50 minutes per session. During these sessions, Andrea's job is usually to discover why behaviors that are so destructive in the long run seem so desirable to the patient in the short run. She then helps her patients phase out the destructive behaviors and replace them with more adaptive behaviors—for instance, responding to anxiety after eating by taking a quick walk around the block instead of vomiting. Depending on the setting in which Andrea works (probably a private office, clinic, or hospital), she will spend varying portions of her day with patients; meeting with other psychologists to discuss how to be more helpful to patients; supervising psychotherapists in training; going out into the community, perhaps lecturing about eating disorders at high school assemblies; and doing paperwork, including writing notes on each patient, submitting forms to insurance companies for payment, and reading professional publications to keep up with new findings and techniques.

Andrea has been trained to provide **psychotherapy**, which involves helping clients learn to change so that they can cope with troublesome thoughts, feelings, and behaviors. She also administers and interprets psychological tests, which can help in diagnosis and in planning the appropriate treatment. *Clinical*

Clinical psychologist: The type of psychologist who provides psychotherapy and is trained to administer and interpret psychological tests.

Psychotherapy: The process of helping clients learn to change so they can cope with troublesome thoughts, feelings, and behaviors.

There are many kinds of psychotherapy, and different training prepares therapists in different ways. Psychiatrists, for example, typically would not treat families, but clinical psychologists and social workers—as well as other mental health professionals—might.

neuropsychologists are clinical psychologists who work specifically with tests designed to diagnose the effects of brain damage on thoughts, feelings, and behavior and to indicate which parts of the brain are impaired following trauma. Other clinical psychologists work with organizations, such as corporations, to help groups function more effectively; for example, a psychologist might advise a company about reducing stress among workers in a particular unit or might teach relaxation techniques to all employees. Some clinical psychologists have a Ph.D. (doctor of philosophy) degree, awarded by a university psychology department; these graduate programs teach students not only how to do psychotherapy and psychological testing, but also how to conduct and interpret psychological research. Other clinical psychologists have a Psy.D. (doctor of psychology), a graduate degree from a program with less emphasis on research. In some states, clinical psychologists can obtain additional training and be granted the right to prescribe drugs (the first state to grant this privilege was New Mexico, in 2002).

If Andrea had been trained as a **counseling psychologist**, she would have learned to help people deal with issues we all face, such as choosing a career, marrying, raising a family, and performing at work. Counseling psychologists often provide career counseling and vocational testing to help people decide which occupations best suit their interests and abilities. These professionals sometimes provide psychotherapy, but they may have a more limited knowledge of therapeutic techniques than do clinical psychologists. They may have a Ph.D. (often from a program that specifically trains people in this area) or often an Ed.D. (doctor of education) degree from a school of education.

Andrea could also have become a **psychiatrist**. If she had gone this route, her training and area of competence would have differed from those of the other mental health professionals. First, as a physician with an M.D. (doctor of medicine) degree, a psychiatrist has extensive medical training and can prescribe drugs, whereas, in general, psychologists cannot. Second, as a medical doctor, a psychiatrist (unlike a clinical psychologist) has typically not been trained to interpret and understand psychological research or psychological research or psychological testing.

There are two other types of clinical mental health practitioners who are not psychologists. Her interest in clinical work might have led Andrea to choose either of those professions: social work or psychiatric nursing. If she had earned an M.S.W. (master of social work) degree, as a **social worker**, she would typically focus on using psychotherapy to help families and individuals, and she also would teach clients how to use the social service systems in their communities. A **psychiatric nurse** holds a master's degree (M.S.N., master of science in nursing) as well as a certificate of clinical specialization (C.S.) in psychiatric nursing. A psychiatric nurse provides psychotherapy, usually in a hospital or clinic or in private practice, and works closely with medical doctors to monitor and administer medications; in some cases, a psychiatric nurse can prescribe medications.

Counseling psychologist: The type of psychologist who is trained to help people with issues that naturally arise during the course of life.

Psychiatrist: A physician who focuses on mental disorders; unlike psychologists, psychiatrists can prescribe drugs, but they are not trained to administer and interpret psychological tests, nor are they trained to interpret and understand psychological research.

Social worker: A mental health professional who uses psychotherapy to help families (and individuals) and teaches clients to use the social service systems in their communities.

Psychiatric nurse: A nurse with a master's degree and a clinical specialization in psychiatric nursing who provides psychotherapy and works with medical doctors to monitor and administer medications.

Academic Psychology: Teaching and Research

James is a professor of psychology at a large state university. Most mornings he prepares lectures, which he delivers three times a week. He also has morning office hours, when students can come by to ask questions about their program of courses in the department or their progress in one of James's classes. Once a week he has a noontime committee meeting; for example, the committee on computer technology may discuss how best to structure the department computer network. His afternoons are taken up mostly with research. If he worked at a smaller college, he might spend more time teaching and less time on research; alternatively, if he worked at a hospital, he might spend the lion's share of his time doing research and very little time teaching. In fact, if John worked in a research institute (perhaps affiliated with a medical school), he might not teach at all, but instead would make discoveries that others could teach; if he worked in a small college, he might not do research, but instead would dedicate himself to teaching the accumulated knowledge of the science of psychology. James's specialty is *developmental psychology*, the study of how thinking, feeling, and behaving develop with age and experience. His research work takes place at a laboratory preschool at the university, where he and his assistants are testing the ways children become attached to objects such as dolls and blankets. James also must find time to write papers for publication in professional journals, and he regularly writes grant proposals requesting funding for his research, so that he can pay students to help him test the children in his studies. He also writes letters of recommendation, grades papers and tests, and reads journal articles to keep up with current research in his and related fields. James tries to eat lunch with colleagues at least twice a week to keep up-to-date on departmental events and the work going on at the university in other areas of psychology.

Developmental psychologists often take special care to prevent their presence from affecting the child's behavior in any way.

Although the activities of most **academic psychologists** are similar in that most teach and many also conduct research, the kinds of teaching and research vary widely. Different types of academic psychologists focus on different types of questions. For example, if James had become a *cognitive psychologist* (one who studies thinking, memory, and related topics), he might ask, "How is Tiger Woods able to hit the ball with the appropriate force in the correct direction?" but not, "What is the role of the audience at a major golf tournament, and would it have been different 50 years ago?" If he had become a *social psychologist* (one who studies how people think and feel about themselves and other people and how groups function), he might ask the second question, but not the first. And in neither case would he ask, "What aspects of Tiger Woods's character help him deal with the extreme stress he faces?" That question would interest a *personality psychologist* (one who studies individual differences in preferences and inclinations).

Because psychology is a science, it rests on objective tests of its theories and ideas. It is through research that psychologists learn how to diagnose people's problems and how to cure them; it is through research that they determine what kind of career will make good use of a particular person's talents; it is through research that they discover how to present material so that students can understand

Academic psychologist: The type of psychologist who focuses on teaching and conducting research.

Applied psychologist: The type of psychologist who studies how to improve products and procedures and conducts research to help solve specific practical problems.

and remember it most effectively. Theories about such issues can come from anywhere, but there is no way to know whether an idea is right or wrong except by testing it scientifically, through research.

There are at least as many different types of academic psychologists as there are separate sections in this book. In fact, this book represents a harvest of their research. Thousands of researchers are working on the topics covered in each chapter, and it is their efforts that allow a book like this one to be written.

Applied Psychology: Better Living Through Psychology

Maria is an applied psychologist; more specifically, she is a *human factors psychologist*, a professional who works to improve products so that people can use them more intuitively and effectively. In general, applied psychologists use the principles and theories of psychology in practical areas such as education, industry, and marketing. An applied psychologist may have a Ph.D. or, sometimes, only a master's degree in an area of psychology (in North America, a master's degree typically requires two years of postgraduate study instead of the four to six for a Ph.D.). Applied psychologists not only work on improving products and procedures but also conduct research aimed at solving specific practical problems.

Applied psychologists have many roles, one of which is to help attorneys decide which potential jurors are likely to be sympathetic or hostile to the defendant.

Working in applied psychology, a *developmental psychologist* may be employed by or consult with the product development department of a toy company. Using her knowledge of children, she can help design toys that will be appropriate for particular age levels; she then brings children to a playroom at the company to see how they play with the new toys. A *physiological psychologist* studies the brain and brain–body interactions and may work at a company that makes drugs or brain-scanning machines. A *social psychologist* may help lawyers decide which potential jurors should be rejected. A *personality psychologist* may design a new test to help select suitable personnel for a job. An *industrial/organizational (I/O) psychologist* focuses on using psychology in the workplace; he or she might help an employer create a more comfortable and effective work environment so as to increase worker productivity or might redesign work spaces to promote more effective employee communication. A *sport psychologist* works with athletes to help them improve their performances, by helping them learn to concentrate better, deal with stress, and practice more efficiently (Tiger Woods has consulted a sport psychologist). An *educational* or *school psychologist* works with educators (and sometimes families), devising ways to improve the cognitive, emotional, and social development of children at school.

The occupations of the various types of psychologists are summarized in Table 1.2.

The Changing Face of Psychology

Mary Whiton Calkins, the first woman president of the American Psychological Association (1905).

You may have noticed a lack of female names when we reviewed the history of psychology, and for good reason. In earlier times, few opportunities were available for women to make major contributions to this field; however, in spite of the barriers of those days, a few women did make their mark on psychology, such as Margaret Floy Washburn, who was Edward Titchener's first student to earn a Ph.D. (in 1894), and Mary Whiton Calkins, the first woman to become president of the American Psychological Association (in 1905).

Table 1.2 What Psychologists Do

Clinical psychologist	Administers and interprets psychological tests; provides psychotherapy.
Clinical neuropsychologist	Diagnoses effects of brain damage on thoughts, feelings, and behavior, and diagnoses the locus of damage.
Counseling psychologist	Helps people with issues that arise during everyday life (career, marriage, family, work).
Developmental psychologist	Researches and teaches the development of mental processes and behavior with age and experience.
Cognitive psychologist	Researches and teaches the nature of thinking, memory, and related aspects of mental processes.
Social psychologist	Researches and teaches how people think and feel about themselves and other people, and how groups function.
Personality psychologist	Researches and teaches individual differences in preferences and inclinations.
Physiological psychologist	Researches and teaches the nature of the brain and brain/body interactions.
Human factors psychologist	Applies psychology to improve products.
Industrial/organizational psychologist	Applies psychology in the workplace.
Sport psychologist	Applies psychology to improve athletic performance.
Educational or school psychologist	Applies psychology to improve cognitive, emotional, and social development of schoolchildren.

As shown in Figure 1.1, the situation is changing—increasing numbers of women, such as Anne Treisman, Ursula Bellugi, Susan Carey, and Elizabeth Spelke, are making major contributions in all areas of psychology (we will review fruits of their labors in the pages to come). In fact, in the last major survey (National Science Foundation, 2001), fully 77% of college graduates with psychology majors were women. Thus, we can expect to see increasing representation of women in the field at large.

*L*OOKING BACK: *Review*

1. *How did psychology develop over time?* Wundt, Titchener, and the other structuralists aimed to understand the elements of mental processes and how they are organized; this approach relied largely on introspection ("looking within"), which turned out to be not very reliable and not always valid—people often have no idea how their mental processes work, at least not in ways they can easily report. The functionalists rejected this approach as disconnected from real-world concerns and focused instead on how mental processes adapt to help us survive in the natural world; their pragmatic concerns led them to apply psychology to education and other social activities. In contrast, the Gestalt psychologists, who reacted to the attempt to dissect mental processes into isolated elements, studied the way the brain organizes material into overarching patterns. Freud shifted attention primarily to the level of the person; his psychodynamic theory was concerned largely with the operation of unconscious mental processes and primitive impulses (often related

Figure 1.1 **Women Winning the APA Award for Distinguished Scientific Contributions**

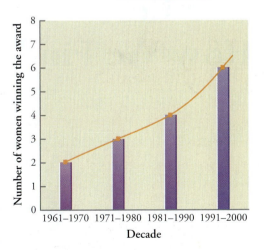

Women are playing an increasingly prominent role in scientific psychology. In 1997, two-thirds of all Ph.D. degrees in psychology were earned by women (American Psychological Association, www.apa.org/pi/wpo/wapa/final.html).

to sex) in dictating what people think, feel, and do. The behaviorists denounced the assumption, shared by all their predecessors, that mental processes should be the focus of psychology; they urged us to stick with what we could see—stimuli, responses, and the consequences of responses. But this view turned out to be too limiting. The humanists, in part reacting against the scientific approach, developed psychotherapies that relied on respect for individuals and their potentials. Elements of the various strands came together in the cognitive revolution, and many researchers who study cognition today conceive of mental processes as "what the brain does." Evolutionary psychology treats many cognitive strategies and goals as adaptive results of natural selection.

2. *What do today's psychologists actually do?* Clinical and counseling psychologists administer diagnostic tests and help people with their problems; academic psychologists teach and do research; and applied psychologists trained in various areas of psychology seek to solve specific practical problems, such as making better products and improving procedures in the workplace.

LOOKING BEYOND: *Critical Thinking*

If Tiger Woods were to be studied by adherents of a single school of psychological thought, which one would be least likely to produce useful insights? Most likely? When asked to account for his remarkable skill, Woods professes to have no conscious knowledge about how he plays so well. How would this report affect the approaches taken by the different schools?

Would the President be more effective if he had a chief psychologist? If so, which sort of psychologist would be most helpful? (Don't assume it would necessarily be a clinical psychologist.) Why?

The Research Process: How We Find Things Out

You could probably speculate for hours about how Tiger Woods came to be such a superb golfer. Let's say, however, that you want to *know* why some people like him are able to perform at high levels in spite of extraordinary pressure. How could you find out for sure? You would need to investigate in a careful and systematic way to reach a conclusion.

LOOKING AHEAD: *Learning Objectives*

1. What is the scientific method, and how is it used to study psychology?
2. What scientific research techniques are commonly used in psychology?
3. What are key characteristics of good scientific studies in psychology?
4. How are ethical principles applied to scientific studies in psychology?

The Scientific Method

Psychology is a science because it relies on a specific type of method of inquiry, and this method, in principle, allows psychologists to discover characteristics that predict human behavior. The **scientific method** is a way to gather facts that will lead to the formulation and validation of a theory. It involves *specifying a problem, systematically observing events, forming a hypothesis of the relation between variables, collecting new observations to test the hypothesis, using such evidence to formulate and support a theory, and finally, testing the theory*. Let's take a closer look at the scientific method, one step at a time.

Step 1: Specifying a Problem

What do we mean by "specifying a problem"? Science tries to answer questions, any one of which may be rephrased as a "problem." Despite the way the word is often used in ordinary conversation, a problem is not necessarily bad: It is simply a question you want to answer or a puzzle you want to solve. For example, a scientist might note that even as a child, Tiger Woods's abilities and discipline made him stand out from his peers. Why? Was there something different about his brain or the way he was being raised?

Step 2: Observing Events

After the problem is specified, it is investigated by "systematically observing events." Scientists are not content to rely on impressions or interpretations. They want to know the facts, as free from any particular notions of their significance as possible. Facts are established by collecting **data**, which are numerical measurements or careful observations of a phenomenon. Properly collected data can be obtained again in a **replication** of a study; that is, they can be collected again by the original investigator or someone else. Scientists often prefer quantitative data (numerical measurements), such as how many words on a list a person can learn in a given time. In addition to collecting numerical data, scientists rely on systematic observations, which simply document that a certain event occurs. But unless the data include numbers, it is often difficult to sort the observation from the interpretation. The data are just the facts, ma'am, nothing but the facts—when data are collected, the interpretation must be set aside, saved for later.

What do we mean by "events"? An event in the scientific sense is the occurrence of a particular phenomenon. Scientists study two kinds of events: those that are themselves directly observable (such as how many times in an hour a mother speaks to her infant) and those that, like thoughts, motivations, or emotions, can only be inferred. For example, when people smile without really meaning it (as they often do when posing for photographs), the muscles they use are not the same ones used to produce a sincere smile (Ekman, 1985). It is possible to observe directly which set of muscles is in use. But a researcher's interest goes beyond the directly observable muscle contractions to the link with inner (and invisible) thoughts and feelings. By studying what's observable (the muscles), researchers can learn about the unobservable (the mental state of the smiler).

But observations are just the beginning; they typically can be interpreted in more than one way. For example, a smile could mean happiness, agreement, politeness, or amusement.

Scientific method: The scientific method involves specifying a problem, systematically observing events, forming a hypothesis of the relation between variables, collecting new observations to test the hypothesis, using such evidence to formulate and support a theory, and finally testing the theory.

Data: Objective observations.

Replication: Collecting the same observations or measurements and finding the same results as were found previously.

Step 3: Forming a Hypothesis

What about "forming a hypothesis of the relation between variables"? First, by the term **variable**, researchers mean an aspect of a situation that is liable to change (or, in other words, that can vary); more precisely, a variable is a characteristic of a substance, quantity, or entity that is measurable. A **hypothesis** is a tentative idea that might explain a set of observations. Say you are inspired by Tiger Woods and decide to take golf lessons. On the course, you notice a particularly good player and ask her for tips. She says that when she's off the course, she often practices her swings mentally, imagining herself whacking the ball straight down the fairway or out of a sand trap; she assures you that the mental practice has improved her game. Well, maybe there's a connection here between two variables: between time spent visualizing swings and golf score. The idea appeals to you, in part because it means that you can practice at night, or whenever you are bored, or when the course is covered with snow. But it's a hypothesis only. Before you go to the trouble of imagining yourself swinging a club, over and over and over, you ought to test the hypothesis to find out whether it's correct.

Step 4: Testing the Hypothesis

Thus, you must go about "collecting new observations to test the hypothesis." The first thing you need to do is create operational definitions of the key concepts, which make them concrete enough to test. An **operational definition** specifies a variable by indicating how it is measured or manipulated. For example, "improvement" could be defined in terms of the number of putts sunk or the distance the ball is driven. In fact, much research has been conducted on mental practice, and many studies have documented that it actually does improve performance, measured in various ways. In a typical study, people are divided into two groups, and the performance of both groups is assessed. One group then uses mental practice for a specified period, while the other makes no preparation. Then the performance of both groups is assessed again. Usually, the people who engage in mental practice show greater improvement (Doheny, 1993; Driskell et al., 1994; Druckman & Swets, 1988; White & Hardy, 1995; Yagueez et al., 1998).

Step 5: Formulating a Theory

Now consider "using such evidence to formulate and support a theory." A **theory** consists of an interlocking set of concepts or principles that explains a set of observations. A theory does not appear out of thin air; rather, a theory is formulated on the basis of empirical findings that were obtained before the theory existed. Unlike a hypothesis, a theory is not a tentative idea and doesn't focus on possible relationships among variables. Instead, theories are rooted in an established web of facts and concepts and focus on the *reasons* for established relationships among variables. In our example, the idea that mental practice leads to better performance is a hypothesis, not a theory. A theory might explain that mental practice works because the brain activity that allows you to perform an action is also induced when you practice mentally; thus, when you engage in the actual behavior later, after practicing it mentally, the appropriate processes are more efficient.

Hypotheses and theories both produce **predictions**, which are new hypotheses. These hypotheses are expectations about specific events that should occur in particular circumstances if the original theory is correct. The new hypotheses can then be put to the test.

Variable: An aspect of a situation that can vary, or change; specifically, a characteristic of a substance, quantity, or entity that is measurable.

Hypothesis: A tentative idea that might explain a set of observations.

Operational definition: A definition of a variable that specifies how it is measured or manipulated.

Theory: An interlocking set of concepts or principles that explain a set of observations.

Prediction: An expectation about specific events that should occur in particular circumstances if the theory or hypothesis is correct.

Figure 1.2 The Scientific Method

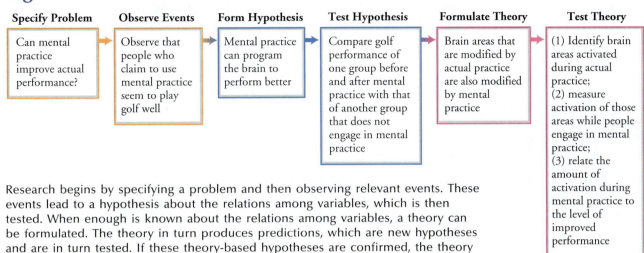

Research begins by specifying a problem and then observing relevant events. These events lead to a hypothesis about the relations among variables, which is then tested. When enough is known about the relations among variables, a theory can be formulated. The theory in turn produces predictions, which are new hypotheses and are in turn tested. If these theory-based hypotheses are confirmed, the theory is supported; if they fail to bear fruit, then the theory must be altered and the whole process repeated.

Step 6: Testing the Theory

Finally, what do we mean by "testing the theory"? The history of science is littered with theories that turned out to be wrong. Researchers evaluate a theory by testing its predictions. As illustrated in Figure 1.2, once a theory has been formulated, it plays a key role in the process of formulating hypotheses. Each prediction of the theory is, in fact, a new hypothesis to be tested. The theory of mental practice predicts that the parts of the brain used to produce a behavior—in our example, swinging a golf club—are activated by merely imagining the behavior. This prediction has also been tested by using brain-scanning techniques to observe what happens in the brain when an individual imagines making certain movements. And, in fact, parts of the brain used in controlling actual movements have been found to be activated when the movements are only imagined (Jeannerod, 1994, 1995; Kosslyn et al., 1998; Parsons, 1987, 1994; Parsons & Fox, 1998).

Each time a theory makes a correct prediction, the theory is supported, and each time it fails to make a correct prediction, the theory is weakened. If enough of its predictions are unsupported, the theory must be rejected and the data explained in some other way. A good theory is *falsifiable*; that is, it makes predictions it cannot "squirm out of." A falsifiable theory can be rejected if the predictions are not confirmed. Part of the problem with astrology, for example, is that its predictions are so vague and general that they are difficult to disprove.

Putting the Steps Together

Now that you understand all the steps of the scientific method, you could use it to investigate other questions. Say you've heard that putting a crystal under your bed will focus cosmic energies and improve your athletic ability. Should you believe this? First, you specify the problem, phrasing it as a question: Can crystals under your bed improve performance? Second, you systematically observe events: Perhaps you notice that on days after the members of a golf team place crystals under their beds, they do perform better. Third, from those data, you form a

Would putting a crystal under his bed make him play better?

hypothesis: Something about the crystals themselves—not the beliefs of the players who use them or any other factors—is responsible for the improvement. Fourth, you test the hypothesis: Before some of Tiger Woods's games, you sneak a crystal under his bed, making sure he never knows when it is there and when it isn't; then you observe whether he plays better on days after the crystal was present. Fifth, if the hypothesis is supported and Woods does play better on those days, you need a theory to explain how the crystal works (for example, you might hypothesize that it somehow alters the magnetic field of the earth). Finally, you test the theory: You might put the crystal in a magnetically shielded box and see whether its being under Woods's bed still raises his level of play.

The Psychologist's Toolbox: Techniques of Scientific Research

Although all sound psychological investigations rely on the scientific method, researchers working in the different areas of psychology often pose and answer questions differently. Psychologists use a variety of research tools, each with its own advantages and disadvantages.

Descriptive Research: Just the Facts, Ma'am

Although the scientific method is always described in terms of testing hypotheses, this isn't quite the whole story. Not all research is sparked by specific hypotheses. Some research is devoted simply to describing "things as they are." It's no accident that "observing events" is a key part of the scientific method: Theorizing without facts is a little like cooking without ingredients.

Naturalistic Observation.
For the scientist, facts are *not* intuitions, impressions, or anecdotes. Essential to the scientific method is careful, systematic, and unbiased observation that can be repeated by others, and some researchers specialize in collecting such data from real-world settings. For example, researchers observed caregivers interacting with young children, and noted that the caregivers changed their language and speech patterns, using short sentences and speaking in a high pitch. This modified way of speaking is known as *child-directed speech* (Morgan & Demuth, 1996; Snow, 1991, 1999).

Although naturalistic observation is an essential part of science, it is only a first step. The discovery of child-directed speech does not tell us whether caregivers use it in order to help children understand them, or to entertain the children, or simply to imitate other caregivers they have heard. It is difficult to test specific interpretations of a finding using only naturalistic observation (although not impossible, as any astronomer will tell you). The problem is that to test your hypothesis, you must seek out a specific situation where nature has set the relevant variables in just the right way. In science, observing an event is typically only the first step.

Some scientists observe animals in the wilds of Africa; others observe sea life in the depths of the ocean; and others observe humans in their natural habitats.

Case Studies.
Sometimes nature or human affairs produce unique situations, which change an independent variable in a novel way. A case study focuses on a single instance of a situation, examining it in detail. For example, a researcher might study a single professional athlete, looking closely at her life and circum-

Case study: A scientific study that focuses on a single instance of a situation, examining it in detail.

stances in an effort to formulate hypotheses about the psychological underpinnings that allow someone to succeed at that level. Many neuropsychologists study individual brain-damaged patients in depth to discover which abilities are "knocked out" following certain types of damage (in Chapter 2, you will read about a young soldier who, after suffering brain injury, had bizarre visual impairments). A psychologist who studies abnormal behavior might study a reported case of multiple personalities to discover whether there's anything to the idea (books such as *Sybil* and *The Three Faces of Eve* describe such cases in great detail); a cognitive psychologist may investigate how an unusually gifted memory expert is able to retain huge amounts of information almost perfectly; a personality psychologist might study in detail how aspiring professional athletes remain motivated through years and years of hard work with no guarantee that they will ever enjoy major success.

However, we must always be cautious about generalizing from a single case; that is, we must be careful in assuming that the findings in the case study extend to all other similar cases. Any particular person may be unusual for many reasons and so may not be at all representative of people in general.

Surveys. A survey is a set of questions put to a number of participants about their beliefs, attitudes, preferences, or activities. Surveys are a relatively inexpensive way to collect a lot of data fairly quickly, and they are popular among psychologists who study personality and social interactions. Surveys provide data that can be used to formulate or test a hypothesis. However, the value of surveys is limited by what people are capable of reporting accurately. You could use a survey to ask people how much they like golf, but not to ask people how their brains work or to ask them to report subtle behaviors, such as body language, that they may engage in unconsciously. Moreover, even if they are capable of answering, people may not always respond honestly; as we note in Chapter 7, this is especially a problem when the survey touches on sensitive personal issues, such as sex. And even if people do respond honestly, what they say does not always reflect what they do. Finally, not everyone who is asked to respond does, in fact, fill in the survey. Because a particular factor (such as income or age) may incline some people, but not others, to respond, it is difficult to know whether the responses obtained are actually representative of the whole group that the survey was designed to assess.

Survey questions have to be carefully worded so that they don't lead the respondents to answer in a certain way and yet still get at the data of interest. Similarly, the nature of the response scale (for example, the range of values presented) affects what people say, as does the order in which questions are asked (Schwarz, 1999).

Correlational Research: Do Birds of a Feather Flock Together?

Researchers use another method to study the relations among variables, a method that relies on the idea of correlation. A correlation is a relationship in which changes in the measurements of one variable are accompanied by changes in the measurements of another variable. For example, height is correlated with weight: Taller people tend to be heavier than smaller people. A **correlation coefficient** (often simply called a *correlation*) is an index of how closely related two measured variables are. Figure 1.3 illustrates three predicted correlations between variables.

Brain damage following an accident can cause someone to fail to name fruits and vegetables while still able to name other objects (Hart et al., 1985). A case study would examine such a person in detail, documenting precisely what sorts of things could and could not be named.

Survey: A set of questions, typically about beliefs, attitudes, preferences, or activities.

Correlation coefficient (or correlation): An index of how closely interrelated two sets of measured variables are, which ranges from −1.0 to +1.0. The higher the correlation (in either direction), the better we can predict the value of one type of measurement when given the value of the other.

Researchers have found that the lower the level of a chemical called monoamine oxidase (MAO) in the blood, the more the person will tend to seek out thrilling activities (such as sky diving and bungee jumping; Zuckerman, 1995). Thus, there is a negative correlation between the two measures: As MAO levels go down, thrill seeking goes up. But we don't know whether MAO level causes the behavior or vice versa—or whether some other chemical, personality trait, or social factor causes the levels of both MAO and thrill seeking to vary together.

In Figure 1.3a, we see a positive correlation, a relationship in which increases in one variable (height) are accompanied by increases in another (weight); a positive correlation is indicated by a correlation value that falls between 0 and 1.0. In Figure 1.3b, we see a negative correlation, a relationship in which increases in one variable (age) are accompanied by decreases in another (health); a negative correlation is indicated by a correlation value that is between 0 and −1.0. Finally, in Figure 1.3c, we see a zero correlation, which indicates no relationship between the two variables (height and aggressiveness); they do not vary together. The closer the correlation is to 1.0 or −1.0, the stronger the relationship; visually, the more tightly the data points cluster around the line, the higher the correlation.

Correlational research involves measuring at least two things about each of a number of individuals or groups (or measuring the same individuals or groups at a number of different times), and looking at the way one set of measurements goes up or down in tandem with another set of measurements; correlations always compare one pair of measurements at a time. The main advantage of correlational research is that it allows researchers to compare variables that cannot be manipulated directly. The main disadvantage is that correlations indicate only that two variables tend to vary together, not that one *causes* the other. For ex-

Figure 1.3 Strength of Correlation

POSITIVE CORRELATION
BETWEEN 0 AND 1.0

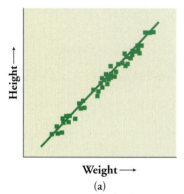

Weight ⟶
(a)

Here, increases in one variable (height) are accompanied by increases in another (weight); this is a positive correlation, indicated by a correlation value that falls between 0 and 1.0.

NEGATIVE CORRELATION
BETWEEN 0 AND −1.0

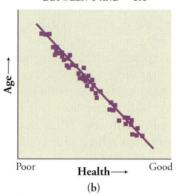

Poor   **Health** ⟶   Good
(b)

Here, increases in one variable (age) are accompanied by decreases in another (health); this is a negative correlation, indicated by a correlation value that is between 0 and −1.0.

ZERO CORRELATION

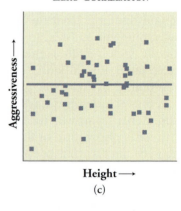

Height ⟶
(c)

A zero correlation indicates no relationship between the two variables, height and aggressiveness here; they do not vary together. The closer the correlation is to 1.0 or −1.0, the stronger the relationship; visually, the more tightly the data points cluster around the line, the higher the correlation.

ample, evidence suggests a small correlation between poor eyesight and intelligence (Belkin & Rosner, 1987; Miller, 1992; Williams et al., 1988), but poor eyesight doesn't cause someone to be smarter! Remember: *Correlation does not imply causation.*

Experimental Research: Manipulating and Measuring

Much psychological research relies on conducting *experiments*, controlled situations in which variables are manipulated. Experiments provide the strongest way to test a hypothesis, in that they can provide evidence that one event causes another.

Independent and Dependent Variables. The variables in a situation—for example, "time spent mentally practicing" and "golf score"—are the aspects of the situation that can vary. In an experiment, the investigator deliberately alters one aspect of a situation, which is called the **independent variable**, and measures another, called the **dependent variable**. In other words, in an experiment, the value of the dependent variable depends on the value of the independent variable. For our mental practice of golf example, the amount of time partici-

Figure 1.4 Relationship Between Independent and Dependent Variables

INDEPENDENT VARIABLE: Amount of time the person practices mentally	DEPENDENT VARIABLE: Subsequent performance on the golf course

The independent variable is what is manipulated—in this example, the amount of time participants spend mentally practicing. The dependent variable, what is measured, is in this case their golf score.

pants in the experiment spend mentally practicing is the independent variable (it is deliberately varied), and their golf score is the dependent variable (it is measured); see Figure 1.4. By examining the link between independent and dependent variables, a researcher hopes to discover exactly which factor is causing an **effect**, which is the difference in the dependent variable that results from a change in the independent variable. In our mental practice example, the effect is the degree of improvement in participants' golf score from the first assessment of their performance (before mental practice) to the second assessment (after mental practice).

Once researchers have found a relation between two variables, they need to test that relation to rule out other possible explanations for it; only by eliminating other possibilities can they know whether a hypothesized relation is correct. In our example, say we had tested only one group, the one that used mental practice. The fact that these players improved would not necessarily show that mental practice can improve actual golf performance. Perhaps simply practicing during the first assessment (before mental practice) is enough to cause an improvement at the second assessment. Or perhaps people are simply more relaxed at the time of the second assessment, and that is why they perform better.

A **confound**, or *confounding variable*, is any other aspect of the situation (such as the anxiety that accompanies a test) that has become entangled with the aspects that the researcher has chosen to vary. Confounds thus lead to results that are ambiguous, that do not have a clear-cut interpretation (see Figure 1.5).

Experimental and Control Groups and Conditions. One way to disentangle confounds is to use a control group. The **experimental group** receives the complete *treatment*, that is, the complete procedure that defines the experiment. A

Independent variable: The aspect of the situation that is intentionally varied while another aspect is measured.

Dependent variable: The aspect of the situation that is measured as an independent variable is changed; the value of the dependent variable depends on the independent variable.

Effect: The difference in the dependent variable that is due to the changes in the independent variable.

Confound (or confounding variable): An independent variable that varies along with the ones of interest, and could be the actual basis for what you are measuring.

Experimental group: A group that receives the complete procedure that defines the experiment.

Figure 1.5 Confounding Variables in Everyday Life

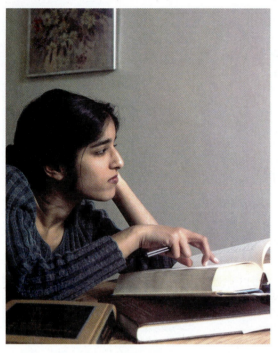

Professor Jones has made a startling observation: Students with poor posture are more intelligent than those who stand up straight. He plans to alert the college admissions office to this finding, and urge them to require applicants to supply full-body photos. But is it intelligence that accompanies poor posture? Perhaps a strong motivation to do well leads to more intense poring over books, with hunched posture. Or is it that shy people both tend to hunch and to be more comfortable spending time alone studying? Can you think of other possible confounding variables that should make Professor Jones take pause?

Control group: A group that is treated exactly the same way as the experimental group, except that the one aspect of the situation being studied is not manipulated for this group. The control group holds constant—"controls"—all of the variables in the experimental group except the one of interest.

Random assignment: The technique of assigning participants randomly, that is, by chance, to the experimental and the control groups, so that no biases can sneak into the composition of the groups.

control group is treated identically to the experimental group except with regard to the one variable that is the focus of study; a good control group holds constant—or controls—all of the variables in the experimental group except the one of interest. In the mental practice experiment, the experimental group does mental practice, the control group does not. If the kinds of people assigned to the two groups differ markedly, say, in age, gender, or learning ability (or any combination of the three), those factors could be confounds that would mask a clear reading of the experiment's results; any difference in the groups' golf scores could have been caused by any of those elements. In a properly conducted experiment, therefore, the researchers rely on **random assignment**: Participants are assigned randomly, that is, by chance, to the experimental and the control groups, so that no confounds can sneak into the composition of the groups.

Similarly, you can use an **experimental condition** and a **control condition**, either for a group of people or a single person. Instead of testing a separate control group, you test the same group another time, keeping everything the same as in the experimental condition except for the single independent variable of interest. To avoid confounding the order of testing with the condition (experimental versus control), you would test half the participants in the control condition before testing them in the experimental condition and would test the other half of the participants in the experimental condition before testing them in the control condition.

Quasi-Experimental Design

One element of a true experiment is that the participants are assigned randomly to the different groups. But in the real world, it is not always possible or desirable to achieve randomness, and so sometimes research designs must be quasi-experimental (*quasi* means "as if" in Latin). A *quasi-experimental design* includes independent and dependent variables and assesses the effects of different values of the independent variable on what is measured. However, participants are not randomly assigned to conditions, and the conditions typically are selected from naturally occurring variations in situations (not created by the investigator's manipulating the independent variable). For instance, let's say that you want to discover whether the effects of mental practice are different for people of different ages, and so you decide to test four groups of people: teenagers, college students, middle-aged people, and elderly people. Obviously, you cannot assign people to the different age groups randomly. Rather, you select groups from what nature has provided. When composing the groups, you should control for as many variables—such as health and education level—as you can in order to make the groups as similar as possible. Similarly, if you want to track changes over time, it is not possible to assign people randomly to the groups as time goes by because you are taking measurements only from people you have measured before. In quasi-experiments, participants are not assigned randomly to groups; instead, such studies rely on comparing multiple groups or multiple sets of measurements, attempting to eliminate potential confounds as much as possible. Unfortunately, because the groups can never be perfectly equated on all characteristics, you can never be certain exactly what differences among groups are responsible for the observed results. The conclusions you draw from quasi-experiments cannot be as strong as those from genuine experiments.

Table 1.3 Summary of Research Methods

Method	Key Characteristic(s)	Advantage(s)	Disadvantage(s)
Naturalistic observation	Observed events are carefully documented.	Forms the foundation for additional research by documenting the existence of an event or situation	Cannot control for confounding variables or change the variables to discover the critical factor in a particular mental process or behavior
Case study	A single instance of a situation is analyzed in depth.	Can provide in-depth understanding of the particular situation	Cannot assume that the findings extend to all other similar cases
Survey	A number of participants answer specific questions.	Relatively inexpensive way to collect a lot of data fairly quickly	Limited by how the questions are stated and by what people can and are willing to report
Correlational research	Relations among different variables are documented.	Allows comparison of variables that cannot be manipulated directly	Cannot infer causation
Experimental design	Participants are assigned randomly to groups, and the effects of manipulating one or more independent variables on a dependent variable are studied.	Allows rigorous control of variables; is able to establish causal relations between independent and dependent variables	Not all phenomena can be studied in controlled laboratory experiments (in part, because not all characteristics can be manipulated).
Quasi-experimental design	Similar to an experiment but participants are not assigned to groups randomly and conditions are often selected, not created.	Allows the study of real-world phenomena that cannot be studied in experiments	Cannot control relevant aspects of the independent variables

Table 1.3 summarizes the basic research methods used in psychology, along with their relative strengths and weaknesses. When thinking about the various methods, keep in mind that even though experiments are the most rigorous, they cannot always be performed—particularly if you are interested in studying large groups or if it is difficult (or unethical) to manipulate the variables. In addition, keep in mind that different combinations of the methods are often used. For example, observational methods are used as part of correlational research, and observational, correlational, or experimental research can be conducted with single individuals (case studies).

Meta-Analysis

Science is a communal effort. Usually many people are studying the same phenomenon, each one painting additional strokes onto an emerging picture. Meta-analysis is a technique that allows researchers to combine results from different studies. This is particularly useful when results have been mixed, with some studies showing an effect and some not. Meta-analysis can determine whether there is a relationship among variables that transcends any one study, a strand that cuts across the entire range of findings.

Sometimes results that are not evident in any individual study become obvious in a meta-analysis. Why? Studies almost always involve observing or testing a

Experimental condition: A part of a study in which the participant receives the complete procedure that defines the experiment. Usually this is accompanied by a control condition, with the same participants receiving both experimental and control conditions.

Control condition: A condition administered to the same participants who receive the experimental condition; this effectively makes the participants both the experimental and the control group.

Meta-analysis: A statistical technique that allows researchers to combine results from different studies, which can determine whether there is a relationship among variables that transcends any one study.

sample from a population; the **sample** is the group that is measured or observed, and the **population** is the entire set of relevant people or animals (perhaps defined in terms of age or gender). The crucial fact is that there is always variation in the population. Just as people vary in height and weight, they also vary in their behavioral tendencies, cognitive abilities, and personality characteristics. Thus, samples taken from the population will vary, and if a sample is relatively small, the luck of the draw could obscure an overall difference that actually exists in the population. For example, if you stopped the first two males and first two females you saw on the street and measured their heights, the females might actually be taller than the males. The problem of variation in samples is particularly severe when the difference of interest—the effect—is not great. If men averaged 8 feet tall and women 4 feet tall, small samples would not be a problem; you would quickly figure out the usual height difference between men and women. But if men averaged 5 feet 10 inches and women averaged 5 feet 9 inches (and the heights of those in both samples differed by up to 6 inches), you would need to measure many men and women before you were assured of finding the difference. Meta-analysis is a way of combining the samples from many studies, which allows you to detect even subtle differences or relations among variables (Rosenthal, 1991).

Be a Critical Consumer of Psychology

No research technique is always used perfectly, so you must be a critical consumer of all science, including the science of psychology. Metaphorically speaking, there are no good psychologists on salt-free diets—we take everything with at least a grain of salt! But this doesn't mean that you should be cynical, doubting everything you hear or read. Rather, whenever you read a report of a psychological finding in a newspaper, a journal article, or a book (including this one), look for aspects of the study that could lead to alternative explanations. You already know about the possibility of confounds; here are a few other issues that can cloud the interpretation of studies.

Reliability: Count on It!

Not all data are created equal; some are better than others. One way to evaluate data is in terms of reliability. **Reliability** means consistency. A reliable car is one you can count on to behave consistently, starting even on cold mornings and not dropping random parts on the highway. A reliable set of measurements is one that can be replicated, that is, obtained again if the study is repeated. When you read about the results of a study, find out whether they have been replicated; if so, then you can have greater confidence that the measurements were reliable.

Validity: What Does It Really Mean?

Something is said to be valid if it is what it claims to be; a valid driver's license, for example, is one that was, in fact, issued by the state and has not expired (and thus does confer the right to drive). In science, **validity** means that a method provides a true measure of what it is supposed to measure. A study may be reliable but not valid, or vice versa. Table 1.4 lists four of the major types of validity (Carmines & Zeller, 1979).

To understand the concept of validity, let's see what it's like to be a participant in a study. So, before reading further, try this exercise. Table 1.5 contains a list of words. Decide whether the first word names a living object or a nonliving one

Sample: A group that is drawn from a larger population and measured or observed.

Population: The entire set of relevant people or animals.

Reliability: Data are reliable if the same results are obtained when the measurements are repeated.

Validity: A measure is valid if it does in fact measure what it is supposed to measure.

Table 1.4 Four Major Types of Validity

Type	Description	Example
Face validity	Design and procedure appear to assess the variables of interest.	Sample essay as part of an entrance exam for journalism school.
Content validity	Measures assess all aspects of phenomenon of interest.	Test of knowledge of research methods that covers all methods.
Criterion validity	A measure or procedure is comparable to a different, valid measure or procedure.	A paper-and-pencil test of leadership ability correlates highly with poll results of leadership of actual leaders.
Construct validity	Measures assess variables specified by a theory.	A theory defines "fatigue" in terms of lack of alertness, and the measure assesses this lack.

(circle the word "living" at the right if it is living; otherwise move to the next word); then decide whether the second word begins with the letter t (circle the words "begins with t" if it does; otherwise move to the next word); then decide whether the third word names a living or a nonliving object, whether the fourth word begins with the letter t, and so on, alternating judgments as you go down the list. Please do this now.

Table 1.5 What's in a Word?

Circle the word or phrase on the right if the word on the left has the named property; otherwise, move on to the next word. After you finish the list, read on.

salmon	living	trout	living
tortoise	begins with *t*	donkey	begins with *t*
airplane	living	teapot	living
toad	begins with *t*	house	begins with *t*
guitar	living	table	living
goat	begins with *t*	terrain	begins with *t*
truck	living	tiger	living
automobile	begins with *t*	rosebush	begins with *t*
snake	living	bacteria	living
tent	begins with *t*	carpet	begins with *t*
toast	living	staple	living
television	begins with *t*	tricycle	begins with *t*
wagon	living	lawn	living
tarantula	begins with *t*	ocean	begins with *t*
toadstool	living	tuna	living
elephant	begins with *t*	terrier	begins with *t*

When you have finished marking the list, take out a piece of paper and (without looking!) write down as many of the words as you can. How many words from the list were you able to remember?

The standard result from this kind of study is that people will remember more words after making a living/nonliving judgment than after making a t/non-t judgment (for example, see Craik & Tulving, 1975). This result is usually interpreted to mean that the more we think about (or "process") the material, as we must in order to make the living/nonliving decision, the better we remember it; for the t words, we only need to look at the first letter, not think about the named object at all. In fact, if we are forced to think about something in detail but don't consciously try to learn it, we end up remembering it about as well as if we did try to learn it (we discuss this curiosity more in Chapter 5).

Does this demonstration of differences in memory following differences in judgment really support this interpretation? What if you remembered the words you judged as living/nonliving better because you had to read the whole word to make the required judgment, but you only looked at the first letter of the other words to decide whether they began with t? If this were the case, your better memory of words in the living/nonliving category would have nothing to do with "thinking about it more." Therefore, the experiment would not be valid—it would not be measuring what the investigator designed it to measure.

When you read a result, always try to think of as many interpretations for it as you can; you may be surprised at how easy this can be. And, if you can think of an alternative interpretation, see whether you can think of a control group or condition that would allow you to tell who was right, you or the authors of the study.

Bias: Playing With Loaded Dice

Sometimes beliefs, expectations, or habits alter how participants in a study respond or affect how a researcher sets up or conducts a study, thereby influencing its outcome. This leaning toward a particular result, whether conscious or unconscious, is called **bias**, and it can take many forms. One form of bias is **response bias**, in which people have a tendency to respond in a particular way regardless of their actual knowledge or beliefs. For example, many people tend to say "yes" more than "no," particularly in some Asian cultures (such as that of Japan). This sort of bias toward responding in "acceptable" ways is a devilish problem for survey research. For example, consider the difference between these two versions of a question: "Do you support using public funds to build golf courses, which will increase recreational options?" versus "Do you support using public funds to build golf courses, which will encourage people to exercise and be healthier?" Given the way the second question is phrased, you would be hard-pressed to say "no."

Another form of bias is **sampling bias**, which occurs when the participants or items are not chosen at random but instead are selected so that an attribute is over- or underrepresented—which leads to a confound. For example, say you wanted to know the average heights of male and females, and you went to shopping malls to measure people. What if you measured males outside a toy store (and so were likely to be measuring little boys), but measured females outside a fashion outlet for tall people (and so were likely to find especially tall women)? Or, what if the words in the living/nonliving category in Table 1.5 were interesting words such as "centipede" and "boomerang," and the words in the t/non-t category were bland words such as "toe" and "broom"? Or, perhaps the living/

Bias: When beliefs, expectations, or habits alter how participants in a study respond or affect how a researcher sets up or conducts a study, thereby influencing its outcome.

Response bias: A tendency to respond in a particular way regardless of respondents' actual knowledge or beliefs.

Sampling bias: A bias that occurs when the participants or items are not chosen at random, but instead are chosen so that one attribute is over- or underrepresented.

nonliving words were more emotionally charged than the t/non-t words, or were more familiar. What if only language majors were tested, or only people who read a lot and have terrific vocabularies? Could we assume that all people would respond the same way? Take another look at Table 1.5; can you spot any potential sampling bias?

Sampling bias isn't just something that sometimes spoils otherwise good studies. Do you remember the U.S. Presidential election of 2000? Albert Gore and George W. Bush were in a dead heat, and the election came down to the tally in a few counties in Florida. Based on surveys of voters exiting their polling places, the TV commentators predicted that Gore would be the winner. What led them astray? Sampling bias. The news organizations that conducted the surveys did not ask absentee voters how they cast their ballots. In such a close election, this was an important factor because the absentee voters included many members of the armed services, who tend to be Republicans. Thus, sampling only from those who voted on election day produced a biased view of how the entire population voted—and the TV commentators had to eat their words.

Experimenter Expectancy Effects: Making It Happen

Clever Hans, a horse that lived in Germany in the early 1890s, apparently could add (Rosenthal, 1976). When a questioner (one of several) called out two numbers to add, for example, "6 plus 4," Hans would tap out the correct answer with his hoof. Was Hans a genius horse? Was he psychic? No. Despite appearances, Hans wasn't really adding. He seemed to be able to add, and even to spell out words (with one tap for the letter a, and an additional tap for each letter in the alphabet), but he responded only if his questioner stood in his line of sight and knew the answer. The questioner, who expected Hans to begin tapping, always looked at Hans's feet right after asking the question—thereby cuing Hans to start tapping. When Hans had tapped out the right number, the questioner always looked up—cuing Hans to stop tapping. Although, in fact, Hans could neither add nor spell, he was a pretty bright horse: He was not trained to do this; he "figured it out" on his own.

The cues offered by Hans's questioners were completely unintentional; they had no wish to mislead (and, in fact, some of them were probably doubters). But unintentional cues such as these lead to **experimenter expectancy effects**, which occur when an investigator's expectations lead him or her (consciously or unconsciously) to treat participants in a way that encourages them to produce the expected results. Such effects can occur in all types of research, from experiments to surveys—in all cases, the investigator can provide cues that influence how participants behave. For instance, if you were polling voters about their choice for President, your own views could color what they say; if you smile whenever they mention your candidate and frown when they mention the other candidate, they may try to please you by saying what they think (perhaps unconsciously) you want to hear.

At least for experiments, it's clear how to guarantee that experimenter expectancy effects won't occur: In a **double-blind design**, not only is the participant "blind" to (unaware of) the predictions of the study and hence unable consciously or unconsciously to serve up the expected results, but the experimenter is also "blind" to the condition assigned to the participant and thus is unable to induce the expected results. What would have happened if a questioner of Clever Hans had not known the answer to the question?

Experimenter expectancy effects: Effects that occur when an investigator's expectations lead him or her (consciously or unconsciously) to treat participants in a way that encourages them to produce the expected results.

Double-blind design: The participant is "blind" to (unaware of) the predictions of the study (and so cannot consciously or unconsciously produce the predicted results), and the experimenter is "blind" to the condition assigned to the participant (and so experimenter expectancy effects cannot produce the predicted results).

Dogbert (Dilbert's dog) is thinking scientifically about astrology. He proposes a relationship among seasonal differences in diet, sunlight, and other factors and personality characteristics. These variables can be quantified, and their relationships tested. If these hypotheses are not supported by the data but Dogbert believes in astrology nevertheless, he's crossed the line into pseudopsychology.

Psychology and Pseudopsychology: What's Flaky and What Isn't?

Are you a fire sign? Do you believe that your Zodiac sign matters? So many people apparently do that the home page for *Yahoo!* will automatically provide your daily horoscope. But astrology—along with palm reading and tea-leaf reading, and all their relatives—is not a branch of psychology; it is pseudopsychology. **Pseudopsychology** is superstition or unsupported opinion pretending to be science. Pseudopsychology is not just "bad psychology," which rests on poorly documented observations or badly designed studies and, therefore, has questionable foundations. Pseudopsychology is not psychology at all. It may look and sound like psychology, but it is not science. Unfortunately, advice to be found in some self-help books falls into this category. For instance, at one point we were told that screaming would "let it all out," and so was good for us—but there was absolutely no evidence that such screams did any more than annoy the neighbors. (This is why it is a good idea to check whether the advice dispensed in a self-help book you are contemplating buying is supported by research.)

Appearances can be misleading. Consider extrasensory perception (ESP). Is this pseudopsychology? ESP refers to a collection of mental abilities that do not rely on the ordinary senses or abilities. Telepathy, for instance, is the ability to read minds. This sounds not only wonderful but magical. No wonder people are fascinated by the possibility that they, too, may have latent, untapped, extraordinary abilities. The evidence that such abilities really exist is shaky, as discussed in Chapter 3. But the mere fact that many experiments on ESP have come up empty does not mean that the experiments themselves are bad or "unscientific." One can conduct a perfectly good experiment, guarding against confounds, bias, and expectancy effects, even on ESP. Such research is not necessarily pseudopsychology.

Let's say you want to study telepathy. You might arrange to test pairs of participants, with one member of each pair acting as "sender" and the other as "receiver." Both the sender and receiver would look at hands of playing cards that contained the same four cards. The sender would focus on one card (say, an ace) and would "send" the receiver a mental image of the chosen card. The receiver's job would be to guess which card the sender is focusing on. By chance alone, with only four cards to choose from, the receiver would guess right about 25% of the time. So the question is, can the receiver do better than mere guesswork? In

Pseudopsychology: Theories or statements that at first glance look like psychology, but are in fact superstition or unsupported opinion pretending to be science.

this study, you would measure the percentage of times the receiver picks the right card, and compare this to what you would expect from guessing alone.

But wait! What if the sender, like the questioners of Clever Hans, provided visible cues (accidentally or on purpose) that have nothing to do with ESP, perhaps smiling when "sending" an ace, grimacing when "sending" a two. A better experiment would have sender and receiver in different rooms, thus controlling for such possible confounds. Furthermore, what if people have an unconscious bias to prefer red over black cards, which leads both sender and receiver to select them more often than would be dictated by chance? This difficulty can be countered by including a control condition, in which a receiver guesses cards when the sender is not actually sending. Such guesses will reveal response biases (such as a preference for red cards), which exist independently of messages sent via ESP.

Whether ESP can be considered a valid, reliable phenomenon will depend on the results of such studies. If they conclusively show that there is nothing to it, then people who claim to have ESP or to understand it will be trying to sell a bill of goods—and will be engaging in pseudopsychology. But as long as proper studies are under way, we cannot dismiss them as pseudopsychology.

Ethics: Doing It Right

Let's say that Tiger Woods wants to learn how to overcome pain so that he can practice hard even when he is hurt, but that practicing when injured might cause long-term damage to his body. Would it be ethical for a sport psychologist to teach Woods—or anyone else—techniques for continuing to work out even in the presence of damaging pain? Or, what if Woods developed a "block" that impaired his playing? Would it be ethical for a therapist to treat him with new, unproven techniques?

Ethics in Research

Following World War II, people were horrified to learn that the Nazis had performed ghastly experiments on human beings. The war trials in Nuremberg led directly to the first set of rules, subscribed to by many nations, outlawing those sorts of experiments. Sometimes the actions of psychologists also call for a set of rules, especially when participants' rights conflict with a research method or clinical treatment. Certain methods are obviously unethical: No psychologist would cause people who participate in experiments to become addicted to drugs to see how easily they can overcome the addiction or beat people to help them overcome a psychological problem. But many research situations are not so clear-cut.

Research With People: Human Guinea Pigs?   In 1996, some New York psychiatrists were tapping the spines of severely depressed teenagers at regular intervals in order to see whether the presence of certain chemicals in the spinal fluid could predict which particular teens would attempt suicide. As required by law, the youths' parents had given permission for the researchers to draw the fluids. However, this study was one of at least ten that a court ruling brought to a screeching halt on December 5, 1996 (*New York Times*, page A1). The New York State Appeals Court found that the existing rules for the treatment of children and mentally ill people in experimental settings were unconstitutional because they did not properly protect these participants from abuse by researchers. However, the researchers claimed that without these studies they would never be able to develop the most effective drugs for treating serious impairments, some of which

Informed consent: The requirement that a potential participant in a study be told what he or she will be asked to do and be advised of possible risks and benefits of the study before agreeing to take part.

Debriefing: An interview after a study to ensure that the participant has no negative reactions as a result of participation and understands why the study was conducted.

might lead to suicide. Do the potential benefits of such studies outweigh the pain they cause?

New York was more lax in its policies than many other states. California, Connecticut, Massachusetts, and Illinois allow researchers to conduct experiments in which the pain outweighs the gain or experiments that have risks but do not benefit participants directly *only* when the participants themselves (not someone else for them) provide **informed consent**. Informed consent means that before agreeing to take part, potential participants in a study must be told what they will be asked to do and must be advised of the possible risks and benefits of the procedure. They are also told that they can withdraw from the study at any time without being penalized. Only after an individual clearly understands this information and gives consent by signature can he or she take part in a study. But not all states have such rules, and there are no general federal laws that regulate all research with human participants.

Nevertheless, a study that uses funds from the U.S. government or from most private funding sources must be approved by an institutional review board (IRB) at the university, hospital, or other institution that sponsors or hosts the study. The IRB monitors all research projects at that institution, not just those of psychologists. An IRB usually includes not only scientists but also physicians, clergy, and representatives from the local community. The IRB considers the potential risks and benefits of each research study and decides whether the study can be performed. These risks and benefits are considered from all three levels of analysis: Effects on the brain (for example, of drugs), the person (for example, through imparting false beliefs), and the group (for example, from embarrassment or humiliation). In many universities and hospitals, researchers are asked to discuss their proposed studies with the board, to explain in more detail what they are doing and why.

Concerns about the ethical treatment of human participants lead most IRBs to insist that participants be **debriefed**, that is, interviewed after the study about their experience. The purpose of debriefing is to ensure that participants are having no negative reactions as a result of their participation and that they have understood the purposes of the study. Deceiving participants with false or misleading information is allowable only when the participants will not be harmed and the knowledge gained clearly outweighs the use of dishonesty.

Research With Animals. Animals are studied in some types of psychological research, particularly studies that focus on understanding the brain. Animals, of course, can't give informed consent, don't volunteer, and can't decide to withdraw from the study if they get nervous or uncomfortable. But this doesn't mean that animals lack protection. Animal studies, like human ones, must have the stamp of approval of an IRB. The IRB makes sure the animals are housed properly (in cages that are large enough and cleaned often enough) and that they are not mistreated. Researchers are not allowed to cause animals pain unless that is explicitly what is being studied—and even then, they must justify in detail the potential benefits to humans (and possibly to animals, by advancing veterinary medicine) of inflicting the pain.

Is it ethical to test animals at all? This is not an easy question to answer. Researchers who study animals argue that their research is ethical. They point out that although there are substitutes for eating meat and wearing leather, there is no substitute for the use of animals in certain kinds of research. So, if the culture allows the use of animals

In large parts of India, animals are not eaten (some are even considered sacred). Many in that culture may believe that animal research is not appropriate.

for food and clothing, it is not clear why animals should not be studied in laboratories if the animals do not suffer and the findings produce important knowledge. This is not a cut-and-dried issue, however, and thoughtful people disagree. As brain-scanning technologies improve (see Chapter 2), the need for some types of animal studies of the brain may diminish.

Ethics in Clinical Practice

Imagine a Dr. Smith who has developed a new type of therapy that she claims is particularly effective for patients who are afraid of some social situations, such as public speaking or meeting strangers. You are a therapist who has a patient struggling with such difficulties and not responding to conventional therapy. You haven't been trained in Smith therapy, but you want to help your patient. Should you try this therapy? According to the American Psychological Association guidelines (see Table 1.6), the answer is clear: No. If you have not been trained appropriately or are not learning the therapy under supervision, you have no business delivering it.

This sort of ethical decision is relatively straightforward. But the process of psychotherapy sometimes requires careful stepping through emotional and ethical minefields. Psychologists are bound by their states' laws of confidentiality and may not communicate about a patient without specific permission from the patient, except in certain extreme cases, as when a life or (in some states) property is at

---

Table 1.6 General Ethical Principles and Code of Conduct for Psychologists

Principle A: Beneficence and Nonmaleficence	"Psychologists strive to benefit those with whom they work and take care to do no harm. . . . Because psychologists' scientific and professional judgments and actions may affect the lives of others, they are alert to and guard against personal, financial, social, organizational, or political factors that might lead to misuse of their influence."
Principle B: Fidelity and Responsibility	"Psychologists uphold professional standards of conduct, clarify their professional roles and obligations, accept appropriate responsibility for their behavior, and seek to manage conflicts of interest that could lead to exploitation or harm."
Principle C: Integrity	"Psychologists seek to promote accuracy, honesty, and truthfulness in the science, teaching, and practice of psychology. In these activities psychologists do not steal, cheat, or engage in fraud, subterfuge, or intentional misrepresentation of fact. Psychologists strive to keep their promises and to avoid unwise or unclear commitments."
Principle D: Justice	"Psychologists recognize that fairness and justice entitle all persons to access to and benefit from the contributions of psychology and to equal quality in the processes, procedures, and services being conducted by psychologists."
Principle E: Respect for People's Rights and Dignity	"Psychologists respect the dignity and worth of all people, and the rights of individuals to privacy, confidentiality, and self-determination. . . . Psychologists are aware of and respect cultural, individual, and role differences, including those based on age, gender, gender identity, race, ethnicity, culture, national origin, religion, sexual orientation, disability, language, and socioeconomic status and consider these factors when working with members of such groups."

Note: This is a direct quote with portions abridged; a complete description can be found at http://www.apa.org/ethics/code2002.html.

stake. Therapists have gone to jail rather than reveal personal information about their patients. Indeed, difficult cases sometimes cause new laws to be written. A patient at the University of California told a psychologist at the student health center that he wanted to kill someone and named the person. The campus police were told; they interviewed the patient and let him go. The patient then killed his targeted victim. The dead woman's parents sued the university for "failure to warn." The case eventually wound its way to California's highest court. One issue was whether the therapist had the right to divulge confidential information from therapy sessions. The court ruled that a therapist is obligated to use reasonable care to protect a potential victim. More specifically, in California (and in most other states now), if a patient has told his or her psychologist that he or she plans to harm a specific other person, and the psychologist has reason to believe the patient can and will follow through with that plan, the psychologist must take steps to protect the targeted person from harm, even though doing so may violate the patient's confidentiality. Similar guidelines apply to cases of potential suicide.

Further, a therapist cannot engage in sexual relations with a patient or mistreat a patient physically or emotionally. The American Psychological Association has developed many detailed ethical guidelines based on the principles listed in Table 1.6.

New Frontiers: Neuroethics

As research in psychology continues to progress at an increasing pace, new issues have emerged that would have been in the realm of science fiction a few years ago. To address one set of these issues, a new branch of ethics, called *neuroethics*, is focusing on the possible dangers and benefits of research on the brain. Still in its infancy, this field is already a hotbed of debate (a recent Google search on

The Center for Cognitive Liberty and Ethics (www.cognitiveliberty.org) asserts that two fundamental principles should form the core of neuroethics: First, individuals should never be forced to use technologies or drugs that interact with their brains. Second, individuals should not be prohibited from using such technologies or drugs if they so desire, provided that such use would not lead them to harm others.

"neuroethics" turned up more than 140,000 hits). So far, however, neuroethicists have more questions than answers. For example, Is it ethical to use brain-altering drugs to force prisoners to be docile? To scan people's brains to discover whether they are telling the truth? To require young children to take medication that makes them pay attention better in school?

Some scholars have been particularly concerned about the use of neuroscience to predict and control individual behavior (see Markus, 2002). For example, suppose that the brains of murderers could be shown conclusively to have a distinctive characteristic (perhaps one region that is much smaller than normal). Should we then scan people's brains and watch them carefully if they have this characteristic? Should this characteristic be used as a criterion for parole for prisoners?

Looking at Levels

Graph Design for the Human Mind

Scientists, such as those who study the effects of mental practice, often need to consider (and show others) complex findings. Graphs are a way to convey a lot of information without overwhelming the user. But what kind of graph should be used? It depends on what message needs to be conveyed. For example, Jeffrey Zacks and Barbara Tversky (1999) found that bar graphs are better than line graphs when you need to make or illustrate comparisons between discrete data points (such as specific numbers of Democratic versus Republican voters in various regions), whereas line graphs are better when you need to understand or illustrate trends (such as changes in the numbers of Democratic and Republican supporters in different parts of the United States over time). Bars end at discrete locations, and thus it's easy to compare data points simply by comparing the heights of the bars. In contrast, bars are not as useful for conveying trends because the reader needs mentally to connect the tops of bars, creating a line in order to determine visually whether there is a trend. Hence, if that's what you want to convey, it's better to give the reader the line in the first place. But if the reader needs to compare discrete data points, a line isn't so good: Now the reader must "mentally break down" the line into specific points, which requires effort (Kosslyn, 1994a; 2006).

Think about this finding from the levels-of-analysis perspective: When designing a graph, you need to respect the way the human perceptual and conceptual systems work (level of the brain). If you choose an inappropriate graph, you will force the reader to work hard to understand your message—which he or she may not be willing to do. But that's not all there is to it. Researchers who focus on the level of the group argue that people use graphs not only to communicate, but also to impress others. "For example, the use of gratuitous graphics [for example, adding the third dimension] may allow presenters to demonstrate their mastery of state-of-the-art technology, or their 'professionalism'; they may demonstrate the extra effort they have put into setting up the presentation or show their care about the contentment of their audience. Thus, social considerations in organizations are likely to promote self-presentation behavior in the context of information presentation" (Tractinsky & Meyer, 1999; p. 401; material in square brackets added for clarification).

In addition, researchers have studied events at the level of the person, such as the qualities of graphs that presenters prefer. One finding is that a presenter's preferences depend in part on the quality of the data. Tractinsky and Meyer (1999) asked participants to choose a display to present data; they found that participants preferred visually elaborate three-dimensional graphs when the graphs were presenting bad results. Why might this be? Perhaps because the graph obscures the data? Or perhaps because a fancy graph might partly compensate for poor results?

As usual, events at the three levels interact: Depending on the graph you choose for a specific purpose, you will affect the readers (level of the group) more effectively if the readers do not have to work hard to understand the display (level of the brain), and the particular message (level of the person) may not only influence the type of graph you choose but also how motivated the readers are to understand it. Not only do events at the different levels interact, but also these events *themselves* often must be understood at the different levels. For example, what occurs in the brain when someone is "impressed"? Trying to impress someone is clearly a social event, but it relies on events at the other levels of analysis. Similarly, "communication" is more than a social event—it also involves conveying content to readers (level of the person) and, ultimately, engaging their brains. Any psychological event can be understood fully only by considering it from all three levels.

LOOKING BACK: *Review*

1. *What is the scientific method, and how is it used to study psychology?* The scientific method is a way to gain objective knowledge that involves specifying a problem, systematically observing events, forming a hypothesis of the relation between variables, collecting new observations to test the hypothesis, using such evidence to formulate and support a theory, and, finally, testing the theory.

2. *What scientific research techniques are commonly used in psychology?* Psychologists use naturalistic observation, involving careful documentation of events; case studies, which are detailed analyses of a single instance of a situation; surveys, in which participants are asked sets of specific questions; correlational research, in which the relations among variables are documented but causation cannot be inferred; experimental designs, assigning participants randomly to groups and studying the effects of one or more independent variables on a dependent variable; and quasi-experimental designs, which are similar to experimental designs except that participants are not randomly assigned to groups. Finally, psychologists also use meta-analysis, in which the results of many studies are considered in a single overall analysis.

3. *What are key characteristics of good scientific studies in psychology?* The measures taken must be reliable (repeatable), valid (assess what they are supposed to assess), unbiased, and free of experimenter expectancy effects (leading participants to respond in specific ways). The studies must be well designed (eliminating confounds and having appropriate controls), and results properly interpreted (alternative accounts are ruled out).

4. *How are ethical principles applied to scientific studies in psychology?* For humans, informed consent is necessary before a person can participate in a study (informed consent requires that the person appreciate the potential risks and benefits); in the vast majority of cases, studies must be approved in advance by an Institutional Review Board (IRB); and participants must be debriefed after the study, to ensure that they have no negative reactions and to confirm their understanding of the purpose of the study. Animals must be treated humanely; animal studies must be approved in advance by an IRB; and animals cannot be caused pain or dis-

comfort unless that is what is being studied (even then, researchers must justify the potential benefits to humans or animals). Although guidelines vary across states, in general, strict confidentiality is observed unless a specific person may be harmed, suicide appears to be a real possibility, or (in some states) another's property may be damaged. Therapists must not take advantage of their special relationships with patients in any way. A new branch of ethics, called neuroethics, is focusing on the potential benefits and dangers of research on the brain.

● LOOKING BEYOND: *Critical Thinking*

If you wanted to know whether Tiger Woods's upbringing played a crucial role in leading him to become a professional golfer, how would you go about studying this? Don't assume that it has to be a case study. Which specific questions would you ask? What are the best methods for answering them?

What characteristics and qualities do you think a pro golfer should have? Do you think psychology should prevent anyone from trying to enter this profession who does not have these characteristics and qualities? Why and why not?

LET'S SUM IT UP

I. The Science of Psychology: Getting to Know You

A. Psychology is the science of mental processes and behavior.

B. The goals of psychology are to describe, explain, predict, and control mental processes and behavior.

C. Psychology can best be understood by studying events at different levels of analysis: the levels of the brain, the person, and the group.

D. The level of the brain is where we examine the activity of certain brain systems, structural differences in people's brains, and effects of genes and chemicals (such as hormones) on mental processes and behavior.

E. The level of the person is where we study the content of mental processes, not just the mechanisms that give rise to them. Our beliefs, goals, and feelings are part and parcel of who we are.

F. The level of the group includes all our social interactions, past and present.

G. Events at the different levels are interdependent and are always interacting. They are also influenced by the physical environment.

II. Psychology Then and Now

A. Psychology began as the study of mental processes, such as those that underlie perception, memory, and problem solving.

B. The structuralists tried to identify the elements of consciousness and the rules by which these elements are combined into mental structures. The primary method of the structuralists was introspection ("looking within").

C. The functionalists rejected the goal of identifying mental processes and how they operated in favor of seeking explanations for thoughts, feelings, and behavior. The functionalists were interested in how mental processes adapt to help people survive in the natural world.

D. The Gestalt psychologists reacted against the structuralists' emphasis on breaking mental processes into distinct elements. The Gestaltists studied the way the brain organizes material into overall perceptual patterns.

E. Freud shifted focus to events at the level of the person. His psychodynamic theory explains how thoughts and feelings affect a person's behavior.

F. The behaviorists rejected the assumption that psychology should focus on mental processes; they urged us to stick with what we could see—stimuli, responses, and the consequences of responses.

G. The humanists, in part reacting against Freud's theory, were interested in developing treatments of psychological problems that relied on respect for individuals and their potentials.

H. Elements of the various strands came together in the cognitive revolution, which began by thinking of the mind by analogy to a computer program; in this view, mental processing is information processing.

I. Cognitive neuroscientists study the relation between events at all three levels of analysis, with an emphasis on how the brain gives rise to thoughts, feelings, and behavior.

J. Evolutionary psychology treats many cognitive strategies and goals as adaptations that are the results of natural selection.

K. The three major types of psychologists are distinguished by their training, work settings, and types of work.

L. Clinical and counseling psychologists administer and interpret psychological tests, provide psychotherapy, offer career and vocational counseling, and help people with specific psychological problems.

M. Academic psychologists teach and do research, in addition to helping to run their universities, colleges, or institutions.

N. Applied psychologists use the findings and theories of psychology to solve practical problems.

III. The Research Process: How We Find Things Out

A. The science of psychology relies on the scientific method, which involves specifying a problem, systematically observing events, forming a hypothesis of the relation between variables, collecting new observations to test the hypothesis, using such data to formulate and support a theory, and testing the theory.

B. Psychologists test hypotheses and look for relations among variables using a variety of tools, including naturalistic observation, case studies, surveys, correlational studies, experiments, quasi-experiments, and meta-analyses.

C. Naturalistic observation involves careful observation and documentation of events.

D. Case studies are detailed investigations of a single instance of a situation.

E. In surveys, participants are asked to answer sets of specific questions.

F. In correlational studies, the relationship between the values of pairs of variables is assessed, showing how the values of one go up or down as the values of the other increase (but not showing that changes in the values of one variable *cause* changes in the other).

G. In an experiment, the effect of manipulating one or more independent variables on the value of a dependent variable is measured, and participants are assigned randomly to groups.

H. Quasi-experiments are like experiments but participants are not assigned to groups randomly and conditions are selected from naturally occurring variations.

I. In a meta-analysis, researchers combine results from different studies in order to identify a relationship among variables that transcends any one study.

J. When reading reports of studies, you should be alert for the following: (1) evidence that the data are reliable, (2) evidence that the data are valid, (3) biases, including the tendency to respond in particular ways to everything (response bias) and the nonrandom selection of participants or experimental materials (sampling bias), and (4) experimenter expectancy effects.

K. Pseudopsychology differs from psychology not necessarily in its content, but in how it is supported by data.

L. Research with humans or nonhuman animals at universities, hospitals, and most industrial settings requires approval from an Institutional Review Board (IRB).

M. For research with humans, the IRB will insist that the participants provide informed consent, which means that they must be given information in advance about the possible risks and benefits of participation.

N. The IRB will also require debriefing, which is an interview after the study to ensure that the participant had no negative reactions and did, in fact, understand the purpose of the study.

O. The IRB will also rule out any deceiving of participants, unless the deception is harmless and absolutely necessary.

P. For research with animals, the IRB requires that the animals be treated well (for example, housed in clean cages) and that pain be inflicted only if that is what is being studied and it is justified by the benefits from the research.

Q. In clinical practice, psychotherapists have clear ethical guidelines to follow, which include maintaining confidentiality unless a specific other person (or, in some states, property) is clearly in danger, or suicide is an imminent genuine concern.

R. In addition, therapists cannot use techniques that they have not been trained to use or engage in inappropriate personal behavior with patients.

S. A new branch of ethics, called neuroethics, is focusing on the possible dangers and benefits of research on the brain.

Key Terms

academic psychologist, p. 21
applied psychologist, p. 22
behavior, p. 5
behaviorism, p. 14
bias, p. 36
case study, p. 28
clinical psychologist, p. 19
cognitive neuroscience, p. 16
cognitive psychology, p. 15
confound, p. 31
control condition, p. 32
control group, p. 32
correlation coefficient, p. 29
counseling psychologist, p. 20
data, p. 25
debriefing, p. 40
dependent variable, p. 31
double-blind design, p. 37
effect, p. 31
evolutionary psychology, p. 17

experimental condition, p. 32
experimental group, p. 31
experimenter expectancy effects, p. 37
functionalism, p. 11
Gestalt psychology, p. 12
humanistic psychology, p. 15
hypothesis, p. 26
independent variable, p. 31
informed consent, p. 40
introspection, p. 10
level of the brain, p. 7
level of the group, p. 7
level of the person, p. 7
mental processes, p. 5
meta-analysis, p. 33
operational definition, p. 26
population, p. 34
prediction, p. 26
pseudopsychology, p. 38

psychiatric nurse, p. 20
psychiatrist, p. 20
psychodynamic theory, p. 13
psychology, p. 4
psychotherapy, p. 19
random assignment, p. 32
reliability, p. 34
replication, p. 25
response bias, p. 36
sample, p. 34
sampling bias, p. 36
scientific method, p. 25
social worker, p. 20
structuralism, p. 10
survey, p. 29
theory, p. 26
unconscious, p. 13
validity, p. 34
variable, p. 26

LOOKING ONLINE: *Enhance Your Learning*

MyPsychLab is an interactive and instructive multimedia resource that can be used to supplement a traditional lecture course or as an online course. It is an all-inclusive tool with a text-specific e-book plus multimedia tutorials, videos, simulations, animations, and controlled assessment to completely engage students and reinforce learning. MyPsychLab meets the individual learning needs of every student. Visit *www.mypsychlab.com* for more information!

Practice Test

For each of the following items, choose the single best answer.

1. Why is psychology a science?
   a. It relies on popular opinion and intuition.
   b. It examines psychological questions.
   c. It uses logic to reason about phenomena and then tests the resulting ideas by collecting additional facts.
   d. It is not a science, although, when it becomes more mathematical, it may develop into one.

2. At the level of the person, the psychologist focuses on
   a. events that involve the nature of beliefs, desires, and feelings.
   b. events that involve the structure and properties of the brain—brain cells and their connections, the chemical soup in which they exist, and the genes.
   c. events that involve relationships between people, relationships among groups, and culture.
   d. physiological variables that differentiate among people (such as weight, height, shoe size, and eye color).

3. How are conditions in the physical environment related to events at the three levels of analysis?
   a. Conditions in the physical environment are not related to events at any of the levels of analysis.
   b. Conditions in the physical environment are intimately tied to events that occur at every level of analysis.
   c. Conditions in the physical environment relate to events occurring only at the level of the brain.
   d. Conditions in the physical environment influence only occasional events at the level of the person.

4. Who is usually considered the founder of scientific psychology?
   a. Max Wertheimer
   b. Sigmund Freud
   c. Edward Titchener
   d. Wilhelm Wundt

5. An approach to understanding mental processes that focuses on the idea that the whole is more than the sum of the parts is
   a. Gestalt psychology.
   b. psychodynamic theory.
   c. functionalism.
   d. structuralism.

6. Which school of psychology assumes that people have positive values, free will, and deep inner creativity?
   a. psychodynamic theory
   b. evolutionary psychology
   c. functionalism
   d. humanistic psychology

7. What type of psychologist provides psychotherapy and is trained to administer and interpret psychological tests?
   a. an applied psychologist
   b. a physiological psychologist
   c. a clinical psychologist
   d. a cognitive psychologist

8. Properly collected data can be replicated, meaning that
   a. objective observations were collected.
   b. an aspect of a situation that is liable to change was described.
   c. a control group was included.
   d. if the same observations or measurements are collected again, they will yield the same results as found previously.

9. A tentative idea that might explain a set of observations is called
   a. data.
   b. a hypothesis.
   c. replication.
   d. an operational definition.

10. An independent variable that varies along with the ones of interest and that could be the actual basis for what you are measuring is
    a. a dependent variable.
    b. a control group.
    c. a hypothesis.
    d. a confound.

11. Suppose Dr. Knight reported a correlation of .02 between height and income. This correlation indicates that
    a. taller people are very likely to have greater income, relative to shorter people.
    b. greater height causes greater income.
    c. height and income are not closely related.
    d. Dr. Knight used a quasi-experimental design.

12. Suppose Dr. Blaine has been told that he needs to improve the face validity of his study. To do so, he ought to make sure that his
    a. design and procedure appear to assess the variables of interest.
    b. measures assess all aspects of the phenomenon of interest.
    c. measure or procedure is comparable to a different, valid measure or procedure.
    d. measures assess variables specified by a theory.

13. What is a double-blind design?
    a. one in which both participants and experimenters wear blindfolds
    b. one in which experimenter expectancy effects will influence the results unless deception is used to obscure the actual purposes and predictions of the study
    c. one that is based on pseudopsychology
    d. one in which the participant is unaware of the predictions of the study and the experimenter is unaware of the condition assigned to the participant

14. An interview that takes place after a study to ensure that the participant has no negative reactions as a result of participation and understands why the study was conducted is called
    a. informed consent.
    b. debriefing.
    c. behaviorism.
    d. unconscious.

15. Suppose Dr. Smith has developed a new type of therapy that she claims is particularly effective for patients who are afraid of some social situations. You have a patient struggling with such difficulties and not responding to conventional therapy. You haven't been trained in Dr. Smith's therapy, but you want to help. Should you try Dr. Smith's therapy?
    a. yes
    b. only if your patient wants to
    c. no
    d. It depends on how long Dr. Smith's therapy takes to work

● ●

Answers: 1. c 2. a 3. b 4. d 5. a 6. d 7. c 8. d 9. b 10. d 11. c 12. a 13. d 14. b 15. c

chapter 2

The Biology of Mind and Behavior

The Brain in Action

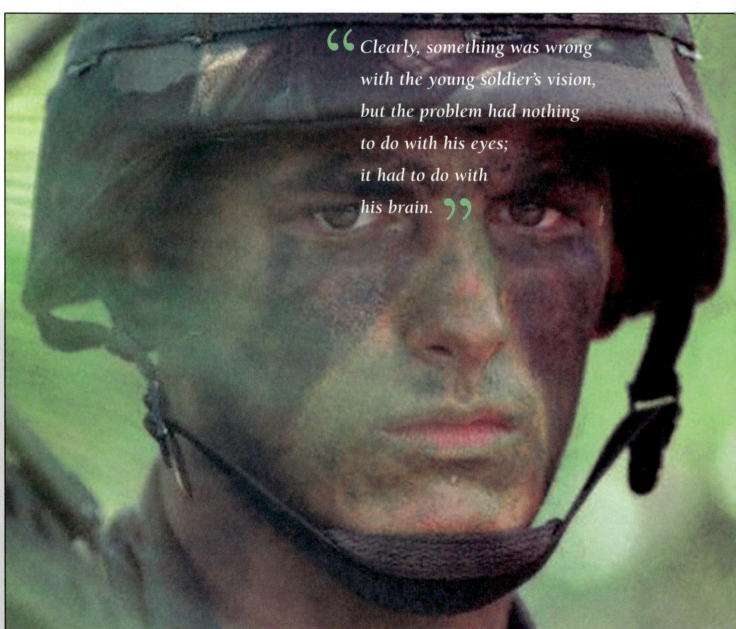

"Clearly, something was wrong with the young soldier's vision, but the problem had nothing to do with his eyes; it had to do with his brain."

Chapter Outline

AS THE HARD JETS OF WATER MASSAGED THE 25-YEAR-OLD SOLDIER WHILE HE SHOWERED, colorless and odorless fumes of carbon monoxide, which are known to cause brain damage, slowly seeped into the stall. Unaware that he was gradually being poisoned, the soldier continued his routine until he eventually passed out.

After the soldier was discovered and revived, doctors examined him. The young man could get around with ease, but he presented a host of bizarre symptoms. He was unable to name objects by sight, but as soon as he touched them, he could say what they were. He could identify things by smell and sound, he could name colors or identify a color named by someone else by pointing to it, and he had no difficulty recognizing familiar people when they spoke. But he couldn't identify these same people by sight alone. In fact, when he looked at his own face in the mirror, he thought he was looking at his doctor. When he was shown a rubber eraser, he identified it as "a small ball"; when shown a safety pin, he said it was "like a watch or nail clipper." When the doctors asked the soldier to inspect a picture of a nude woman and show where her eyes were, he pointed to her breasts (Benson & Greenberg, 1969).

Clearly, something was wrong with the young soldier's vision, but the problem had nothing to do with his eyes; it had to do with his brain. He couldn't acquire knowledge by way of his sense of sight. Why? Though he retained some aspects of his vision, he had lost others—he

51

seemed unable to recognize what he clearly could see. The fumes the soldier had inhaled had affected his brain, but how? What, exactly, had gone wrong? To consider these questions, you need to understand essential facts about how the brain works.

As you have seen, events at the level of the brain can influence many aspects of behavior, in ways not immediately apparent. If you broke your hand, you would have trouble holding a pencil: The effect of the accident would be direct and mechanical. If you were in any doubt before your mishap about the role of muscle and bone in grasping and holding, you would be in no doubt afterwards, when those abilities would be distinctly impaired because muscles were torn and bones fractured. But, although it is a physical organ like muscle and bone, the brain is unique: It is also a *psychological* organ, ultimately responsible for our moods of despair and elation, our sense of well-being and our sense that something's wrong, our perception of the outside world and our awareness of its meaning. The effects of damage to the brain are no less real than those of a broken hand, but the path by which they arise is less obvious (indeed, until recently was unobservable). It is this path, through a thicket of sometimes difficult names and processes, that we must trace if we are to gain a meaningful understanding of who we are and why we behave as we do.

So, how does it work, this mysterious brain? What is it made up of; what are its building blocks? Can we ever see the brain at work? How could we find out exactly which parts of the soldier's brain were damaged? Do all of our brains respond the same way to the same environmental influences? Or, do different people, with different genetic makeups and life experiences, respond differently? Let's start finding out.

Brain Circuits: Making Connections

1 The carbon monoxide fumes that the soldier breathed interfered with his brain's ability to use oxygen, causing him to pass out. Unfortunately, he inhaled enough of these fumes that some brain cells probably died; ordinarily, brain cells begin to succumb after a few minutes without oxygen. But just saying that brain cells "died" isn't much of an explanation—that would be a little like saying that a building fell down because its molecules were rearranged. Why did the death of those cells have the effects it did?

LOOKING AHEAD: *Learning Objectives*

1. *How do neurons work?*
2. *How do chemicals allow neurons to communicate?*

The Neuron: A Powerful Computer

2 The brain is "the psychological organ"; it gives rise to the mind, that is, to mental processes (such as perception, memory, and language) and mental experiences. The brain is arguably the most complex object in the known universe, and to begin to grasp its general outlines, we start small (with brain cells) and then move to large (brain structures). We could easily write a book about each of these topics; we present here just what you will need to know to understand material in

the remainder of this book (for example, the actions of drugs that treat psychological disorders).

3   All brain activity hinges on the workings of brain cells, or **neurons** (Kandel et al., 2000). There are three types of neurons. Some, the **sensory neurons**, respond to input from the senses; others, the **motor neurons**, send signals to muscles to control movement; finally, **interneurons** stand between the neurons that register what's out there and those that control movement—or they stand between other interneurons. Most of the neurons in the brain are interneurons, and most interneurons are connected to yet other interneurons.

4   Neurons would not be much good if they did not affect other neurons or the rest of the body—how useful would the Internet be if only one computer were connected to it? **Brain circuits** are sets of neurons that affect one another. When one neuron in a circuit is triggered by another neuron, it in turn triggers others, and so on, causing a chain reaction. Neurons often receive and put together many inputs at the same time. The result can be the awareness that a sumptuous dessert is on the table, a command to the muscles to turn up the volume of a stereo, a sudden memory of an assignment due yesterday, a flash of feeling for an attractive classmate—anything we perceive, think, feel, or do.

Structure of a Neuron: The Ins and Outs

To understand psychological events, you need to know a few facts about the structure of the neuron. As you can see in Figure 2.1, each neuron has certain parts.

5   The central part of a neuron is called the **cell body**. Like all cells, it has a nucleus, which regulates the cell's functions, and a **cell membrane**, which is the skin of the cell. The sending end of the neuron is the **axon**, the long, cablelike structure extending from the cell body, along which signals travel to other neurons, muscles, or bodily organs. Although each neuron has only a single axon,

Neuron: A cell that receives signals from other neurons or sense organs, processes these signals, and sends the signals to other neurons, muscles, or organs; the basic unit of the nervous system.

Sensory neuron: A neuron that responds to input from sense organs.

Motor neuron: A neuron that sends signals to muscles to control movement.

Interneuron: A neuron that is connected to other neurons, not to sense organs or muscles.

Brain circuit: A set of neurons that affect one another.

Cell body: The central part of a neuron (or other cell), which contains the nucleus.

Cell membrane: The skin of a cell.

Axon: The sending end of the neuron; the long cablelike structure extending from the cell body.

Figure 2.1 Major Parts of a Neuron

Dendrites receive information from other neurons or from the environment.

The **cell body** controls the cell's metabolic activities and integrates inputs.

Terminal buttons release chemicals into the space between neurons when their neuron has been triggered.

Terminal buttons

Cell membrane

Nucleus

An **axon** conducts the nerve impulse away from the cell body.

A neuron has many parts. The major ones are labeled here, but much of the action occurs internally where a complex dance of chemicals occurs.

most axons divide into many branches, called *terminals*, so that a neuron can send a message to more than one place at a time. At the ends of the terminals are **terminal buttons**, little knoblike structures that release chemicals into the space between neurons when the neuron has been triggered. Most neurons communicate this way, releasing chemicals that affect other neurons, usually at their receiving end. (A few neurons, such as some of those in the eye, communicate directly via electrical impulses, but this direct electrical communication is rare.)

Each neuron has only one sending end—that is, only one axon—but a neuron may have many receiving ends. These are the **dendrites**; their name is derived from the Greek word *dendron*, meaning "tree," which makes sense when you look at their shape. The dendrites receive messages from the axons of other neurons. Although axons sometimes connect directly to the cell body of another neuron, the connection is usually made from axon to dendrite.

Neural Impulses: The Brain in Action

Neurons are not always firing. When at rest, they maintain a negative charge within; this negative charge is called the **resting potential**. This potential arises because of how ions are distributed inside and outside the cell; **ions** are atoms that are positively or negatively charged. During rest, more positively charged ions (called *cations*, and consisting mostly of sodium ions) are outside the neuron than inside it, and more negatively charged ions (called *anions*) are inside the neuron than are in the surrounding fluid. The membrane covering the axon has very small holes, or pores, called *channels*. The channels open and close: When particular channels are open, particular ions either flow into the cell from the surrounding fluid or flow from inside the cell to the surrounding fluid. When a neuron receives enough stimulation from other neurons (when a specific *threshold* is exceeded), some of the channels in the cell membrane open, allowing a complex exchange of ions that changes the charge in the axon. This exchange works its way down to the end of the axon, finally causing the terminal buttons to release chemicals that will affect other neurons. When this occurs, the neuron is said to "fire." The shifting change in charge that moves down the axon is known as an **action potential**. This process, the basis of the neural communication that permits us to live in the world and respond to it, is illustrated in Figure 2.2.

Notice that the action potential obeys an **all-or-none law**. If enough stimulation reaches the neuron, it fires. In other words, the sequence of shifting charges sends the action potential all the way down the axon, releasing chemicals from the terminal buttons. Either the action potential occurs or it doesn't. Many neurons can fire hundreds of times a second because chemical reactions reset them so that they can fire again if they receive adequate stimulation.

Nevertheless, neurons require a measurable amount of time to work; to convince yourself that this is so, gather some friends and try the simple exercise described in Figure 2.3 (developed by Rozin & Jonides, 1977).

Neurons would operate substantially more slowly were it not for the fact that most axons are covered with **myelin**, a fatty substance that helps impulses travel down the axon more efficiently. Myelin is a bit like the insulation around copper wires, which allows them to transmit current more effectively. *Multiple sclerosis (MS)* is one of several disorders that illustrates the importance of myelin. In MS, the myelin has deteriorated, which makes impulses "stumble" as they move down the axon. People with MS experience impaired sensation in their limbs, loss of vision, and paralysis (Zajicek, 2004). Could myelin loss have caused the young soldier's problem? Probably not: His visual problem was selective, whereas myelin loss creates overall problems in seeing.

Terminal button: A structure at the end of a branch of an axon that, when the neuron is triggered, releases chemicals into the space between neurons.

Dendrite: The treelike part of a neuron that receives messages from the axons of other neurons.

Resting potential: The negative charge within a neuron when it is at rest.

Ion: An atom that has a positive or negative charge.

Action potential: The shifting change in charge that moves down the axon.

All-or-none law: States that if the neuron is sufficiently stimulated, it fires, sending the action potential all the way down the axon and releasing chemicals from the terminal buttons; either the action potential occurs or it doesn't.

Myelin: A fatty substance that helps impulses travel down the axon more efficiently.

Figure 2.2 Ion Flow That Produces an Action Potential

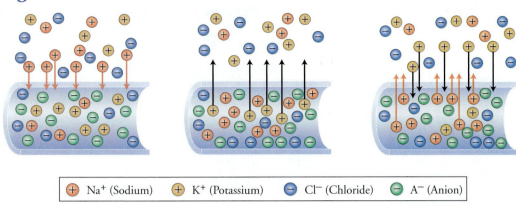

+ Na⁺ (Sodium) + K⁺ (Potassium) – Cl⁻ (Chloride) – A⁻ (Anion)

Na⁺ channels open after the neuron is stimulated, and Na⁺ ions rush into the cell; the inside of the cell then becomes positively charged. (Note: Ions are not drawn to scale, but relative proportions are correct.)

The Na⁺ channels close, K⁺ channels briefly open, and K⁺ ions go outside the cell. (The K⁺ ions are pushed out because of the addition of the positively charged Na⁺ ions.)

After this, Na⁺ pumps actively push Na⁺ ions back outside and K⁺ ions are drawn inside, until the inside and outside concentrations are returned to their original levels.

When the ion exchanges reach the end of the axon, they cause chemicals to be released from the terminal buttons.

Direction of action potential → | Chemicals released

Figure 2.3 Measuring Neural Conduction Time

In the fastest neurons, impulses travel only about 120 meters per second, compared with 300,000,000 meters per second for the speed of light. Even compared with the impulses traveling in a computer, our neurons are extremely slow. You can actually measure the speed of neural processing. Here's how.

Sit in a row with some friends, with each person using his or her left hand to grasp the ankle of the person on his or her left. The person at the head of the line, the leader, says "Go" and starts a stopwatch at the same time he or she squeezes the ankle of the person to his or her left; as soon as that person feels the squeeze, he or she squeezes the ankle of the next person to the left; and so on. When the last person feels the squeeze, he or she says "Done." The leader records the time.

Now repeat the exercise, but each of you should grasp not the ankle but the shoulder of the person to your left. Less time is required for the squeezes to make their way down the row when shoulders are squeezed than when ankles are squeezed. Why? Because the impulses have farther to travel when the ankle is squeezed. By subtracting the difference in times and estimating the average distance from ankle to shoulder for each person you can actually estimate neural transmission time! This exercise should be done several times, first ankle, then shoulder, then shoulder, and then ankle; this procedure helps to control for the effects of practice in general.

Figure 2.4 The Synapse

Impulses cross between neurons at the synapse. Chemicals released at the terminal buttons cross the synaptic cleft, where they bind to receptors and trigger events in the receiving neuron.

Step 1: The action potential reaches the end of the axon.

Step 2: Synaptic vesicles release **neurotransmitters** into the synaptic cleft.

Step 3: Neurotransmitters bind to receptors and the action potential is transmitted.

Synapse: The place where an axon of one neuron can send signals to the membrane (on a dendrite or cell body) of another neuron.

Synaptic cleft: The gap between the axon of one neuron and the membrane of another, across which communication occurs.

Neurotransmitter: A chemical that carries a signal from the terminal button on one neuron to the dendrite or cell body of another.

Neuromodulator: A chemical that alters the effect of a neurotransmitter.

Endogenous cannabinoids: Neuromodulators released by the receiving neuron that then influence the activity of the sending neuron.

Neurotransmitters and Neuromodulators: Bridging the Gap

How do neurons actually communicate? What are the connections between them like? The site where communication between neurons occurs is the **synapse**, where an axon of one neuron sends a signal to the membrane of another neuron. The sending and receiving neurons do not actually touch each other, but rather are separated by a gap called the **synaptic cleft**, shown in Figure 2.4.

Chemical Messages: Signals and Modulators

As their name suggests, the chemicals that carry signals, crossing from the terminal buttons across the synaptic clefts, are the **neurotransmitters**. Other chemicals, called **neuromodulators**, alter the effects of the neurotransmitters. Here's an analogy: Imagine that you are using a pair of tin cans with a string between them as a walkie-talkie. When you speak into one can and your friend holds the other up to her ear, sound waves transmit the message. The gap from your mouth to one of the cans, and from the other can to her ear, is crossed by these waves, which carry the message. Neurotransmitters play the same role as the sound waves, allowing the message to cross the gap. In contrast to the neurotransmitters, neuromodulators would produce the effect of tightening or loosening the string connecting the cans. When the string is drawn tight, the message is transmitted more effectively from one can to the other; when it is slackened, the sound must be louder to be heard.

Other substances (which are not, strictly speaking, called neuromodulators) can affect what happens at the gap itself, for example, by affecting how quickly the neurotransmitters are removed from the synaptic cleft. Imagine that the room holding the linked tin cans has very thin air, with fewer molecules to vibrate. In this case, a louder sound would be needed to cause the bottoms of the tin cans to vibrate. On the other hand, if the air pressure were greater, a softer sound could convey the signal.

Researchers have discovered many substances that act as neurotransmitters or neuromodulators in the brain, including some unexpected ones such as nitric oxide and carbon monoxide (Barañano et al., 2001). Table 2.1 summarizes key properties of the major neurotransmitter substances.

Not all neuromodulators are released at terminal buttons. Notably, **endogenous cannabinoids** are chemicals released by the *receiving* neuron that then influence the activity of the *sending* neuron (Wilson & Nicoll, 2002). This signaling system is one of the most important in the brain; cannabinoids affect precise locations on neurons, which allows them to fine-tune activity underlying learning, memory, pain perception, and attention (Katona et al., 2000; Kreitzer & Regehr, 2001b; Sanudo-Pena et al., 2000). Marijuana contains cannabinoids, but it affects neurons indiscriminately and promiscuously and thereby overwhelms

Table 2.1 Major Neurotransmitter Substances

Summary of the most important neurotransmitters and neuromodulators, distinguishing features, major associated disorders, and typical drugs that modulate their effects. The disorders are discussed in later chapters of this book. A question mark indicates that the substance may be involved in the disorder, but conclusive evidence has yet to be obtained.

Name	Distinguishing Features	Related Disorders and Symptoms	Drugs That Alter
Acetylcholine (ACh)	Transmitter at the neuro-muscular junction (causes muscles to contract); memory; used in autonomic nervous system	Alzheimer's disease, delusions (shortage); convulsions, spasms, tremors (excess)	Physostigmine (increases, used to treat Alzheimer's disease); scopolamine (blocks)
Dopamine (DA)	Motivation, reward, movement, thought, learning	Parkinson's disease, depression, attention deficit/hyperactivity disorder (ADHD) (shortage); aggression, schizophrenia (excess)	Amphetamine, cocaine (causes release); chlorpromazine (blocks at receptors); methylphenidate (Ritalin, blocks reuptake)
Noradrenaline (NA) (Norepinephrine, NE)	Dreaming, attention	Depression, fatigue, distractability (shortage); anxiety, headache, schizophrenia (excess)	Tricyclic antidepressants such as Elavil (keep more available at the synapse)
Serotonin (5-Hydroxytryptamine; 5HT)	Primary inhibitory neurotransmitter regulating mood, sleep	Obsessive-compulsive disorder, insomnia, depression (shortage); sleepiness, lack of motivation (excess)	Fluoxetine (Prozac), tricyclic antidepressants (keep more present at the synapse)
GABA (Gamma-aminobutyric acid)	Inhibits sending neuron	Anxiety, panic (?), epilepsy, Huntington's disease (shortage); sluggishness, lack of motivation (excess)	Sedatives (such as phenobarbital), alcohol, benzodiazepines (such as Valium, Halcion) mimic effects
Endogenous cannabinoids	Memory, attention, emotion, movement control, appetite	Chronic pain (shortage); memory and attention problems, eating disorders, schizophrenia (?) (excess)	R141716A (blocks effects of); THC (mimics effects of)

our exquisitely tuned neural systems—disrupting memory and attention, as well as other cognitive functions (Ashton, 2001; Schneider & Koch, 2002). As Barinaga (2001) put it, the chemicals introduced by marijuana eliminate the fine-tuned "local activity patterns . . . just as spilling a bottle of ink across a page obliterates any words written there" (p. 2531).

Receptors: On the Receiving End

⌐ What do the neurotransmitters do once they cross the gap? That depends. Each neuron has **receptors**, specialized sites on the dendrites or cell body that respond to specific neurotransmitters or neuromodulators. The receptor sites are the places where "messenger molecules" of the released chemicals—neurotransmitters or neuromodulators—attach themselves. A good analogy here is an ordinary lock set:

Receptor: A site on a dendrite or cell body where a messenger molecule attaches itself; like a lock that is opened by one key, a receptor receives only one type of neurotransmitter or neuromodulator.

The lock is the receptor, which is opened by the keylike action of a particular neurotransmitter or neuromodulator.

18   When neurotransmitters or neuromodulators become attached to receptors, they are said to *bind* (see Figure 2.5). After binding, they can have one of two general types of effects. They can be *excitatory*, making the receiving neuron more likely to fire an action potential, or they can be *inhibitory*, making the receiving neuron less easily triggered. Because the typical axon divides into many branches and each neuron has many dendrites, there are many binding sites; thus, the neuron can receive thousands of different inputs from different sending neurons at the same time. The exciting and inhibiting inputs to each receiving neuron add up or cancel one another out, and their sum determines whether and when the neuron fires an action potential down its axon.

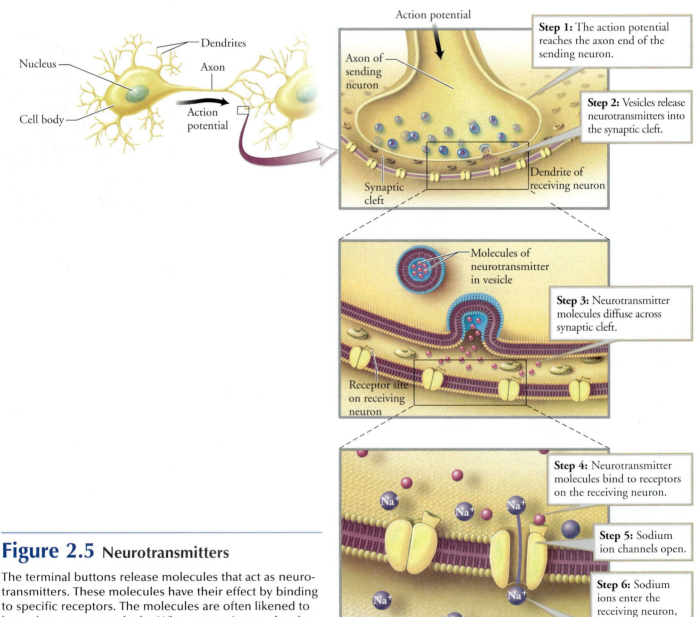

Step 1: The action potential reaches the axon end of the sending neuron.

Step 2: Vesicles release neurotransmitters into the synaptic cleft.

Step 3: Neurotransmitter molecules diffuse across synaptic cleft.

Step 4: Neurotransmitter molecules bind to receptors on the receiving neuron.

Step 5: Sodium ion channels open.

Step 6: Sodium ions enter the receiving neuron, which can lead to an action potential.

Dendrites
Nucleus
Axon
Cell body
Action potential

Action potential
Axon of sending neuron
Synaptic cleft
Dendrite of receiving neuron

Molecules of neurotransmitter in vesicle
Receptor site on receiving neuron

Figure 2.5 Neurotransmitters

The terminal buttons release molecules that act as neurotransmitters. These molecules have their effect by binding to specific receptors. The molecules are often likened to keys, the receptors to locks. When transmitter molecules bind to receptors, the receiving neuron may be stimulated or inhibited.

19 Not all of a given neurotransmitter released by the terminal buttons is taken up by receptors; some of it remains in the gap. Special chemical reactions are required to reabsorb—or **reuptake**—the excess neurotransmitter back into the *vesicles* (which store neurotransmitters) of the sending neuron.

Unbalanced Brain: Coping With Bad Chemicals

20 By piecing together the story of how neurons communicate, scientists are not only developing a clear picture of how the brain works but are also learning how its functioning can go awry and how they can use drugs to repair it. Drugs that affect the way the brain works either increase or decrease the effectiveness of neural activity. Some of these drugs are **agonists**, which mimic the effects of a neurotransmitter substance by activating a particular type of receptor. Other drugs may actually increase the amount of a neurotransmitter, sometimes by slowing down its reuptake. Depression, for example, is currently treated by several types of drugs that affect neurotransmitters, including **selective serotonin-reuptake inhibitors (SSRIs)**, which block the reuptake of the neurotransmitter serotonin. (Prozac, Zoloft, and Paxil are all SSRIs.) Still other drugs interfere with the effect of a neurotransmitter. Some of these drugs are **antagonists**, which block a particular receptor. (As a memory aid, think of an "antagonist" at a party who is "blocking you" from meeting a charmer across the room.)

21 The connection between neurotransmitter substances and behavior is also evident in the devastating effects of *Parkinson's disease*, a classic brain disorder. Named after the British physician James Parkinson, who first described the disorder in 1817, Parkinson's afflicts about half a million Americans. The hands of people with Parkinson's disease shake; they may move sluggishly, with a stooped posture and shuffling walk; their limbs often seem frozen in position and resist attempts to bend them. All of these changes, physical and behavioral, are caused directly or indirectly by the death of cells that produce dopamine. When patients take L-dopa, a drug that helps produce dopamine, their symptoms decrease (Marini et al., 2003), often for a long period of time. However, L-dopa becomes less effective with continued use (and sometimes produces side-effects), and thus researchers are developing new dopamine agonists to treat this disorder (Barone, 2003; Jenner, 2002).

22 Could the young soldier whose vision was so strangely disrupted have had malfunctioning neurotransmitters or neuromodulators? Could such a disturbance have produced the highly selective impairments he experienced after inhaling the carbon monoxide fumes? It's possible, if just the right combinations of chemicals were disrupted. However, this scenario is unlikely. Because most neurotransmitters and neuromodulators are used widely throughout the brain, not solely in the parts of the brain involved in visual perception, we would expect their disruption to create more widespread difficulties, such as in hearing, understanding language, walking, and other functions.

Glial Cells: More Than the Neurons' Helpmates

23 The average human brain contains about 100 billion neurons, plus about ten times as many **glial cells** (the name comes from the Greek word for "glue"). Researchers have long known that glial cells help neurons to form appropriate connections while the brain is developing during gestation and childhood, and thereafter participate in the "care and feeding" of neurons. The traditional view

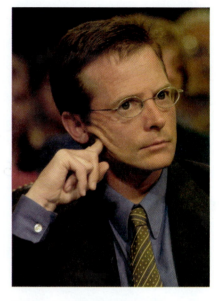

Parkinson's disease apparently can strike anyone and can interfere with a wide variety of careers. However, as actor Michael J. Fox showed, at least in some cases, medical or surgical procedures can help keep symptoms in check.

Reuptake: The process by which surplus neurotransmitter is reabsorbed back into the sending neuron so that the neuron can effectively fire again.

Agonist: A chemical that mimics the effects of a neurotransmitter by activating a type of receptor.

Selective serotonin-reuptake inhibitor (SSRI): A chemical that blocks the reuptake of the neurotransmitter serotonin.

Antagonist: A chemical that interferes with the effect of a neurotransmitter (often by blocking a receptor).

Glial cell: A type of cell that surrounds neurons, influences the communication among neurons, and generally helps in the "care and feeding" of neurons.

was that glial cells physically cushion neurons, clean up the remains of dead neurons, dispose of extra neurotransmitters and ions in the fluid surrounding neurons, and provide nutrients to neurons. This view is correct, as far as it goes. But recent research has revealed that this view doesn't go far enough; glial cells are much more than just the neurons' helpmates.

Neurons and Glia: A Mutually Giving Relationship

24 Neurons and glial cells influence each other in complex ways. On the one hand, neurons have synapses not just with other neurons, but also with glial cells—and they stimulate glial cells to release specific chemicals. On the other hand, glial cells can directly regulate how strongly one neuron affects another. Researchers now believe that glial cells might coordinate the activity of vast networks of neurons. In addition, glial cells can prod neurons to form additional synapses (Pfrieger, 2002). Although neurons can form synapses even in the absence of glial cells, they form about seven times as many when glial cells are present (Ullian et al., 2001). This occurs because some glial cells produce a type of cholesterol that stimulates neurons to produce more synapses (Mauch et al., 2001).

Glial Networks: Another Way to Think and Feel?

25 Glial cells do not produce action potentials; you will never hear about a glial cell "firing." Instead, these cells communicate by passing chemicals directly through their walls to adjoining glia or by releasing (into brain fluid that surrounds the cells) molecules that affect both neurons and other glia. Chemicals released by one glial cell can induce other glial cells to release chemicals, and so on, "like ripples on a pond" (Fields & Stevens-Graham, 2002). Researchers do not yet understand exactly what these glial networks do, but they have found that glia are important in a remarkably wide range of brain functions (Blalock et al., 2003; Cotter et al., 2001; Lonky, 2003; Watkins et al., 2001).

LOOKING BACK: *Review*

1. *How do neurons work?* Neurons receive input from other neurons (which themselves may be connected to a sense organ), on either their dendrites or their cell bodies. If the sum of all the inputs is strong enough, the neuron fires, sending a rapid exchange of ions across the cell membrane. This exchange works its way down the axon, until the terminal buttons release a neurotransmitter (which sends a signal) or a neuromodulator (which alters the effect of a signal). This chemical crosses the synaptic cleft to the dendrites or cell bodies of other neurons.

2. *How do chemicals allow neurons to communicate?* Neurons have receptors, which are like locks that can be opened by certain keys; the keys are the neurotransmitters and the neuromodulators. Depending on the properties of the particular receptors, these chemicals can excite the neuron to fire or inhibit it from firing. Agonists mimic the action of neurotransmitters or neuromodulators, whereas antagonists block their effects.

LOOKING BEYOND: *Critical Thinking*

Say you are a health-care provider who specializes in helping patients who have suffered brain damage. What would you try to do to help the young soldier? Are there any special strategies that you could teach him that might help him? Can you think of jobs that he could be trained to do in spite of his damage?

The Nervous System: An Orchestra With Many Members

26 Consider some additional problems experienced by the young soldier who was poisoned while taking a shower. When researchers showed him a blue page on which white letters were printed, he thought he was looking at a "beach scene"—the blue was water and the white letters were "people seen on the beach from an airplane." He could visually pick out objects when they were placed in front of him, but only if they were of a similar color and size. His doctors found that he could be trained to name a few everyday objects by sight as children are taught to recognize words by sight on *Sesame Street* without actually reading them, but this training broke down when the color or size of the objects changed. The young man learned to name a red toothbrush as "toothbrush," but he couldn't properly name a green toothbrush, and when he was shown a red pencil, he called it "my toothbrush."

27 The results of the entire series of tests made it clear that the soldier could see and understand color and size, but not shape. He had *some* sense of shape, though; he didn't call the pencil a "shoe" or a "basketball" but a "toothbrush." To understand what had gone wrong in the soldier's brain, we need to go beyond the essentials of how neurons work and how they affect each other via neurotransmitters and neuromodulators. You are ready to examine how neurons work within different brain structures and how their functioning can break down. To understand the root causes of the soldier's problems, you need to know what the different parts of the nervous system do.

The nervous system has two parts: the peripheral nervous system and the central nervous system. We will start with the simpler peripheral nervous system, which is crucial for getting information into and out of the brain.

LOOKING AHEAD: *Learning Objectives*

1. *What two parts comprise the peripheral nervous system, and what role does each part play?*
2. *How do the brain and spinal cord work together?*

The Peripheral Nervous System: A Moving Story

28 The **peripheral nervous system (PNS)** links the brain to the organs of the body. As shown in Figure 2.6 (on p. 62), the PNS has two parts: the autonomic nervous system and the sensory-somatic nervous system.

The Autonomic Nervous System

29 The **autonomic nervous system (ANS)** controls the smooth muscles in the body and some glandular functions. Smooth muscles, so called because they look smooth under a microscope, are found in the heart, blood vessels, stomach lining,

Peripheral nervous system (PNS): The autonomic nervous system and the sensory-somatic nervous system.

Autonomic nervous system (ANS): Controls the smooth muscles in the body, some glandular functions, and many of the body's self-regulating activities, such as digestion and circulation.

Figure 2.6 Major Parts of the Nervous System

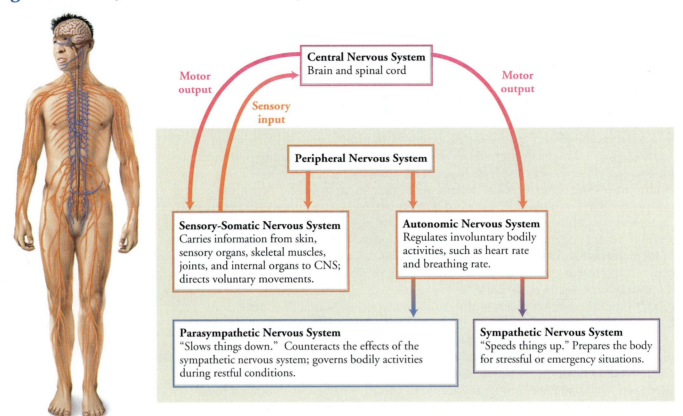

Central Nervous System
Brain and spinal cord

Motor output

Sensory input

Motor output

Peripheral Nervous System

Sensory-Somatic Nervous System
Carries information from skin, sensory organs, skeletal muscles, joints, and internal organs to CNS; directs voluntary movements.

Autonomic Nervous System
Regulates involuntary bodily activities, such as heart rate and breathing rate.

Parasympathetic Nervous System
"Slows things down." Counteracts the effects of the sympathetic nervous system; governs bodily activities during restful conditions.

Sympathetic Nervous System
"Speeds things up." Prepares the body for stressful or emergency situations.

The peripheral nervous system (PNS) comprises the sensory-somatic nervous system (SSNS) and the autonomic nervous system (ANS). The two major branches of the ANS are the sympathetic and parasympathetic nervous systems. In general, the sympathetic nervous system prepares the body to fight or flee, and the parasympathetic dampens down the sympathetic nervous system.

and intestines. Many of the activities that the ANS controls, such as digestion and circulation, are self-regulating and are usually not under conscious control (Goldstein, 2000). The ANS has two branches—which are often referred to as "nervous systems" in their own right—the sympathetic and parasympathetic nervous systems.

The Sympathetic Branch of the ANS. The **sympathetic nervous system** readies an animal (including you and the authors) to cope with an emergency. This system usually comes into play in response to a threat in the environment, perhaps a near-accident when you are driving in heavy traffic. The sympathetic system speeds up the heart, increases the breathing rate to provide more oxygen, dilates the pupils for greater light sensitivity and thus sharper vision, produces a small amount of sweat (giving your hand a better grip), decreases salivation, inhibits stomach activity, and relaxes the bladder. If your heart is pounding and your palms are sweaty, but your mouth is dry, it's a good bet that your sympathetic system has kicked in. The overall effect of these changes is to prepare your body to react—to fight or to flee. More oxygen flows into your muscles, your vision is improved, and the rest of your body is ready to support physical exertion.

Fight-or-flight situations are not the only conditions that activate the sympathetic nervous system. This system also operates in circumstances that may be less

Sympathetic nervous system: Part of the ANS that readies an animal to fight or to flee by speeding up the heart, increasing breathing rate to deliver more oxygen, dilating the pupils, producing sweat, decreasing salivation, inhibiting activity in the stomach, and relaxing the bladder.

extreme but nonetheless threatening, such as getting ready to give an important speech, having a conversation with an irritable authority figure, or rushing to avoid being late for an important meeting. People prone to excessive amounts of anxiety tend to have sympathetic nervous systems that overshoot the mark and get the body too revved up. They might hyperventilate (that is, breathe in too much oxygen), sweat profusely, or experience a pounding heart when there is no apparent threat. These and other unpleasant physical symptoms of anxiety occur whenever the sympathetic nervous system responds too strongly.

The Parasympathetic Branch of the ANS. The other branch of the ANS is called the **parasympathetic nervous system**; this system lies, figuratively, "next to" the sympathetic system (*para* is Greek for "next to" or "alongside") and tends to counteract its effects (see Figure 2.6). The sympathetic system speeds things up, and the parasympathetic system slows them down. Heart rate slows, pupils contract, salivation increases massively, digestion is stimulated, the bladder contracts. Whereas the sympathetic system tends to affect all the organs at the same time and can be thought of as increasing arousal in general, the parasympathetic system tends to affect organs one at a time or in small groups. The sympathetic and parasympathetic systems don't always work against each other. For example, an erection is caused by the parasympathetic system, but the sympathetic system controls ejaculation.

The Sensory-Somatic Nervous System

A brain living in a vat wouldn't be of much use to anyone—it would be like a computer with no keyboard or monitor. To do its job, the brain needs both to receive inputs from the body and the outside world and to be able to act on these inputs. To understand the brain's job, then, you must see what it receives and how it in turn can move the body. The other part of the PNS is the **sensory-somatic nervous system (SSNS)**. This system includes the input–output connections themselves: neurons in our sensory organs (such as the eyes and ears) that convey information to the brain, as well as neurons that trigger muscles and glands.

The SSNS also includes the **skeletal system**, which consists of nerves that are attached to muscles that can be triggered voluntarily; these muscles are also known as striated muscles because under a microscope they appear *striated*, or striped. If you clench your fist and "make a muscle," you are using this system.

The Central Nervous System: Reflex and Reflection

The largest conduit for information going to and from the brain is the **spinal cord**, the flexible rope of nerves that runs inside the backbone, or *spinal column*. In fact, so intimately connected is the spinal cord to the brain that the two together are called the **central nervous system (CNS)**.

The Spinal Cord: Getting Inside the Backbone

At each of 31 places, spinal nerves emerge from the spinal cord in pairs, one on the left and one on the right. Through these nerves, the spinal cord plays a key role in sending the brain's commands to the body (along the front side of the cord) and, in turn, allowing the brain to register information about the state of the body (along the rear side of the cord). The spinal cord also allows us, through our sense of touch, to gain information about the world.

Parasympathetic nervous system: Part of the ANS that is "next to" the sympathetic system and that tends to counteract its effects.

Sensory-somatic nervous system (SSNS): Part of the PNS that consists of neurons in the sensory organs (such as the eyes and ears) that convey information to the brain, as well as neurons that actually trigger muscles and glands.

Skeletal system: Consists of nerves that are attached to striated muscles.

Spinal cord: The flexible rope of nerves that runs inside the backbone, or spinal column.

Central nervous system (CNS): The spinal cord and the brain.

36 The spinal cord isn't simply a set of cables that relays commands and information between brain and body. The spinal cord itself can initiate some aspects of our behavior, such as reflexes. A **reflex** is an automatic response to an event, an action that does not require thought. Even a simple reflex requires hundreds of neurons. How do reflexes work? When sensory neurons in the skin detect a sharp thorn, for example, they send signals that stimulate sensory neurons in the spinal cord. These neurons in turn are connected to interneurons in the spinal cord. When you jerk away from something that pricks you, interneurons have sent signals to motor neurons, which then cause the muscles to jerk, pulling your finger away from the source of pain. This arrangement allows you to respond immediately, bypassing the brain—it wouldn't be efficient or safe to have to think through what to do every time you encountered a noxious stimulus.

37 If the point of reflexes is to get things done in a hurry, why aren't the sensory neurons directly connected to motor neurons? Why the intermediary? Because interneurons provide a particular benefit: They allow the brain to send signals to *prevent* a reflex response. Perhaps you are handing a beautiful red rose to a good friend as a gift and accidentally prick your finger. Instead of flinging the rose away, you grit your teeth and continue to hold it. You are able to do this because the part of your brain that is involved in formulating goals and intentions knows not to flub this gesture and sends a signal to the interneurons to stop the motor neurons from firing.

The Visible Brain: Lobes and Landmarks

38 To understand the range of human abilities, you need to turn to the other part of the central nervous system, the brain itself. Imagine that you could see through someone's hair and scalp, even through the skull itself. The first thing you would see under the skull are the **meninges**, three protective layered membranes that cover the brain (*meningitis* is an inflammation of these membranes). Under these lies a network of blood vessels on the surface of the brain itself. Viewing the brain from above—looking down through the top of the head—you can see that the brain is divided into two halves, left and right, separated by a deep fissure down the middle. Each half-brain is called a **cerebral hemisphere** (*cerebrum* is Latin for "brain") because each is shaped roughly like half a sphere. Curiously, each hemisphere receives information from, and controls the muscles of, the opposite side of the body. For example, if you are right-handed, your left hemisphere controls your hand as you write.

39 Each hemisphere is divided into four major parts, or **lobes**: the *occipital* lobe, at the back of the brain; the *temporal* lobe, which lies below the temples, in front of the ears, where sideburns begin to grow down; the *parietal* lobe, in the upper rear portion of the brain, above the occipital lobe; and the *frontal* lobe, behind the forehead (see Figure 2.7). The two halves of the brain are connected by the **corpus callosum**, which contains somewhere between 250 and 300 million nerve fibers (some other smaller connections exist between the two halves of the brain, but they are less important).

40 Now, peer deeper. Immediately under the network of blood vessels on the surface of the brain is the convoluted, pinkish-gray outer layer of the brain itself: This is the **cerebral cortex** (*cortex* means "rind" or "shell" in Latin). This is where most of the brain's mental processes take place. Although the cerebral cortex is only about 2 millimeters thick, it is brimming with the cell bodies of neurons, giving the cortex its characteristic color and its nickname, "gray matter." Looking directly at the surface of the brain, you can see that the cortex has many creases and bulges, as shown in Figure 2.7. The creases are called **sulci** (the singular is

Reflex: An automatic response to an event.

Meninges: Membranes that cover the brain.

Cerebral hemisphere: A left or right half-brain, shaped roughly like half a sphere.

Lobes: The four major parts of each cerebral hemisphere—occipital, temporal, parietal, and frontal.

Corpus callosum: The large band of nerve fibers that connects the two halves of the brain.

Cerebral cortex: The convoluted pinkish-gray outer layer of the brain, where most mental processes take place.

Sulcus: A crease in the cerebral cortex.

Figure 2.7 The Lobes of the Brain

Parietal lobe
Central sulcus
Frontal lobe
Lateral sulcus
Occipital lobe
Temporal lobe

Corpus callosum
Right hemisphere
Left hemisphere

FRONTAL VIEW

The brain is divided into four major lobes—occipital, temporal, parietal, and frontal. These lobes are named after the bones that cover them. The same major sulci (creases) and gyri (bulges) are evident on most brains.

sulcus), and the areas that bulge up between the sulci are the **gyri** (singular, *gyrus*). The cortex, so vital to our functioning, is crumpled up so that more of it can be stuffed into the skull. **Subcortical** ("under the cortex") **structures** of the inner brain also contain gray matter and are very similar to structures in the brains of many nonhuman animals.

Most of your brain is water; the average brain weighs about 3 pounds, but if the water were removed, it would weigh only 10 ounces. This material (which includes proteins and fats, as well as various types of ions) comprises the parts of the neurons, glial cells, and everything else that gives the brain a structure.

LOOKING BACK: *Review*

1. *What two parts comprise the peripheral nervous system, and what role does each part play?* The peripheral nervous system (PNS) has two parts: the autonomic nervous system (ANS) and the sensory-somatic nervous system (SSNS). The ANS controls the smooth muscles (like those of the heart) and some glands. The ANS has two branches: the sympathetic and parasympathetic nervous systems. The sympathetic nervous system readies an animal to cope with an emergency, whereas the parasympathetic nervous system brings an animal back to its normal state after having been aroused. In contrast, the SSNS deals with inputs from the world and voluntary control of muscles.

2. *How do the brain and spinal cord work together?* The brain and spinal cord together compose the central nervous system (CNS). The spinal cord is the largest conduit for information going to and from the brain. The neural fibers on the front side of the spinal cord convey the brain's commands to the body and thus allow us to move in coordinated ways. The neural fibers on the rear side of the spinal cord convey information about the state of the body to the brain. The spinal cord also produces reflexes, which are triggered automatically when specific stimuli are present; however, signals from the brain often can inhibit these reflexes.

Gyrus: A bulge between sulci in the cerebral cortex.

Subcortical structures: Parts of the brain located under the cerebral cortex and beneath the ventricles.

The fight-or-flight response was no doubt useful to our ancestors. Is it necessarily as useful to us today? Do you think it would be a good idea if we could voluntarily dampen down the autonomic nervous system? Do you think it would be a good idea if we could voluntarily amplify its activity, at least in selected situations?

If you could choose some thoughts or feelings to be reflexive responses to specific stimuli, what would they be and why?

Spotlight on the Brain: How It Divides and Conquers

41 Testing revealed that the soldier did not have a problem with his PNS. His cranial nerves all functioned properly, and the impulses delivered by his eyes were sent on to his brain. His problem was more subtle and could be diagnosed only by considering the specific jobs performed by different parts of the brain. Even an ability such as vision, which intuitively might seem to be a single thing, is performed by a set of brain structures, not a single structure. The brain is a master at the strategy of divide-and-conquer; it takes all complex activities and breaks them into a set of relatively simple tasks, and a different brain structure usually tackles each task. The soldier's problem reflected damage to only some of the parts of the brain, which disrupted only some of the overall processing required to identify objects by sight. To understand what went wrong after his accident, we need to delve into the brain in more detail, marveling at how it divides and conquers the challenges of daily life.

○ *LOOKING AHEAD:* *Learning Objectives*

1. *What are the major regions of the cortex, and what do they do?*
2. *How do the functions of the two sides of the brain differ?*
3. *What parts of the brain lie under the cerebral cortex? What do these subcortical structures do?*
4. *What are the neuroendocrine and neuroimmune systems, and what do they have in common?*

The Cerebral Cortex: The Seat of the Mind

The cortex of each of the four lobes of the brain serves different functions, but always remember that the lobes do not function in isolation; they usually work in concert with one another.

Occipital Lobes: Looking Good

42

The occipital lobes are concerned entirely with different aspects of vision, and most of the fibers from the eyes lead to these lobes (Brewer et al., 2002; Simos, 2001). If somebody were to hit you in the back of the head with a brick (an ex-

Occipital lobe: The brain lobe at the back of the head; concerned entirely with different aspects of vision.

periment we do not recommend), the "stars" you would likely see would appear because of the impact on this area. The occipital lobes contain many separate areas that work together to specify visual properties such as shape, color, and motion. Damage to these lobes results in partial or complete blindness. Because each half of the brain receives sensory information from the opposite side, if a surgeon has to remove the left occipital lobe (perhaps to take out a brain tumor), the patient will not be able to see things to his or her right side when looking ahead.

43   Because some of the neurons in the occipital cortex are highly active, they require more oxygen than other neurons—which makes them particularly vulnerable to poisoning by carbon monoxide. Carbon monoxide displaces oxygen but cannot be used in metabolism; thus, if someone breathes enough carbon monoxide, neurons in the occipital lobes are suffocated to death. However, not all the neurons typically die, and thus the unfortunate person is not completely blind but rather has highly degraded vision. Our young soldier probably suffered damage to the occipital lobes, perhaps in addition to injury to other parts of the brain. Such damage often affects visual perception, making the entire world seem fuzzy and making it difficult to organize information. Still, this probably does not sufficiently explain all of the soldier's vision problems; if this were all there was to it, why would he confuse white letters with sunbathers on the beach?

Temporal Lobes: Up to Their Ears in Work

44 The **temporal lobes**, which lie in front of the ears and roughly where sideburns start, play a key role in processing sound, entering new information into memory, storing visual memories, and comprehending language (Hart et al., 2003; Sekiyama et al., 2003; Witter et al., 2002). The soldier may have had damage in either one or both temporal lobes, or in the connections from the occipital lobes to the temporal lobes. If the connections were damaged, only a small amount of information might reach the part of the temporal lobes where visual memories of shapes are stored and compared to visual input (allowing you to recognize stimuli). This diagnosis would go a long way toward explaining his problem. For example, in order to see a letter, he would have to look at one segment at a time (a vertical line, then a curved line, and so on), which isn't good enough to recognize the shape of a letter as a whole. The world might look to the soldier like the images in Figure 2.8.

Figure 2.8 Shattered Vision

| (a) | (b) | (c) | (d) |

Answers: a. telephone receiver b. scissors handle c. table leg d. baseball hat

Some forms of brain damage may lead the victims to be aware of only small fragments of objects at a time, as shown here. If all you were aware of were fragments of an object, how easily do you think you could identify it? To get a sense of what such a deficit would be like, try to identify these common objects when all you have to go on are individual parts.

Temporal lobe: The brain lobe under the temples, in front of the ears, where sideburns begin to grow down; among its many functions are visual memory and hearing.

Figure 2.9 The Organization of the Somatosensory Strip

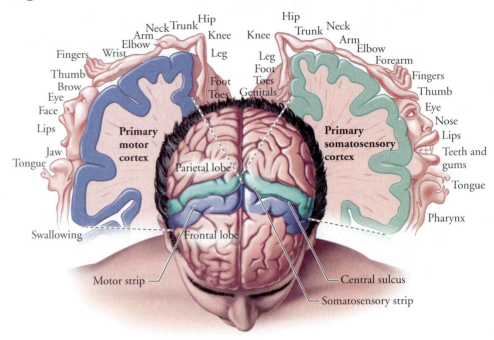

The somatosensory strip is organized so that different parts of the body are registered by adjacent portions of cortex; the size of the body part indicates the amount of brain tissue dedicated to that part.

Parietal Lobes: Inner Space

45 When you recall where you left your keys, how to drive to a friend's house, or what's over your left shoulder, your **parietal lobes** are at work (Siegel et al., 2003). Right now, your parietal lobes are playing a role in allowing you to define the distance between your face and the book and to shift attention to each of these words; they are even helping control your eye movements. The parietal lobes are also involved when you do arithmetic.

46 Part of each parietal lobe, right behind the central sulcus (see Figure 2.9), is the **somatosensory strip**. This area registers sensation on your body. In fact, sensations from each part of your body are registered in a specific section of this strip of cortex. Tickling your toes, for example, activates neurons in the cortex next to the area devoted to stimulation from your ankle, as you can see in Figure 2.9. Larger areas of the cortex correspond to areas of the body that are more sensitive (notice the amount of space devoted to lips and hands).

Frontal Lobes: Leaders of the Pack

47 Probably the most dramatic difference between the appearance of a human brain and a monkey brain is how much the human brain bulges out in front. The size and development of the **frontal lobes**, in conjunction with their plentiful connections to other areas, are features of the brain that make us uniquely human (Goldberg, 2001). The frontal lobes are critically involved in speech, the search for specific memories, reasoning (including the use of memory in reasoning), and emotions. These crucial lobes also contain the **motor strip** (also called the *primary motor cortex*), which is located in the gyrus immediately in front of the central sulcus. The motor strip controls fine movements and, just like the so-

Parietal lobe: The brain lobe across the top part of the brain behind the ears, which is involved in registering spatial location, attention, and motor control.

Somatosensory strip: The brain area, located immediately behind the central sulcus, that registers sensation on the body and is organized by body part.

Frontal lobe: The brain lobe located behind the forehead; the seat of planning, memory search, motor control, and reasoning, as well as numerous other functions.

Motor strip: The brain area, located immediately in front of the central sulcus, that controls fine movements and is organized by body part; also called *primary motor cortex*.

matosensory strip, is organized in terms of parts of the body. Relatively large areas of this strip of cortex are dedicated to those parts of the body that we control with precision, such as the hands and mouth.

48   Hints about the functions of the frontal lobes, as well as other parts of the brain, have emerged from studies of patients with brain damage. Phineas Gage, the foreman of a gang of workers building a railroad in Vermont late in the 19th century, is perhaps the most famous case of a patient with damage to the frontal lobes. Gage's unfortunate loss was psychology's gain, as researchers were able to observe the consequences of damage to this vital area of the brain. The story began when Gage became distracted as he was packing blasting powder into a hole in a rock. When the metal bar he was using to pack in the powder accidentally hit the rock, it created a spark, which set off the powder. The metal bar, like a spear shot from a cannon, went right through the front part of his head, flew high in the air, and landed about 30 meters behind him. Miraculously, Gage lived, but he was a changed man. Previously, he had been responsible and organized; he now led a disorderly life. He couldn't stick to any decision; he had little self-control, and his formerly decent language became laced with profanity (Macmillan, 1986, 1992). Like Phineas Gage, other people with damage to the frontal regions of the brain have difficulty reasoning, may have trouble controlling their emotions, and may have changed personalities.

A computer-reconstructed picture of the path taken by the metal bar as it passed through Phineas Gage's skull.

The Dual Brain: Thinking With Both Barrels

The cortices of the two cerebral hemispheres, left and right, play distinct roles in cognition. What do the hemispheres do differently?

50 Split-Brain Research: A Deep Disconnect

The most compelling evidence to date that the two half-brains perform distinct functions has come from looking at the effects of severing the connection between the two hemispheres. When this is done, neuronal impulses no longer pass from one hemisphere to the other. Patients who have undergone this surgery are called **split-brain patients** (Zaidel & Iacoboni, 2003). Why would such drastic surgery be performed? This procedure has been used to help patients with severe, otherwise untreatable epilepsy. *Epilepsy* is a disease that causes massive uncontrolled neuronal firing in parts of the brain, leading to bodily convulsions; in severe form, it prevents sufferers from leading a normal life. When the epilepsy engages the entire brain and is so severe that drugs cannot control it, surgeons may cut the corpus callosum. This operation prevents the spasm that originates in one hemisphere from reaching the other hemisphere, and thus the whole brain does not become involved in the convulsions—and their severity is thereby lessened.

Although it is easy to see how cutting the corpus callosum would decrease the severity of epileptic convulsions, the full effects of this procedure on mental processes cannot be understood without discussing vision. As shown in Figure 2.10 (on p. 70), the left half of each eye is connected directly to the left hemisphere, but not to the right hemisphere; similarly, the right half of each eye is connected directly, and only, to the right hemisphere. (Note, it's not that the left eye is connected only to the left hemisphere, and the right only to the right.) Thus, if you stare straight ahead, objects to the left are seen first by the right brain, and those to the right are seen first by the left brain. If the corpus callosum is cut, the input stays in the hemisphere that receives the information; in normal people, it also crosses over to the other hemisphere.

Split-brain patient: A person whose corpus callosum has been severed for medical reasons, so that neuronal impulses no longer pass from one hemisphere to the other.

Figure 2.10

The Eyes, Optic Nerves, and Cerebral Hemispheres

Eye

Optic nerve

Visual cortex

The inside, rearmost parts of the eyes are actually parts of the brain pushed forward during development; the left half of each eye is connected only to the left cerebral hemisphere, whereas the right half of each eye is connected only to the right cerebral hemisphere.

51 What are the practical effects of the division of the brain into two hemispheres? One way to find out is to present pictures or words to the left or right side of a split-brain patient (fast enough so that the participant can't move his or her eyes to look directly at them). In a classic study of this type, illustrated in Figure 2.11, Gazzaniga and LeDoux (1978) presented a picture of a snow scene to the right hemisphere (which controls the left hand) and, at the same time, a picture of a chicken's claw to the left hemisphere (which controls the right hand and, usually, speech). The split-brain patient was then shown several other pictures and asked to choose which of them was implied by the stimulus. The patient used his right hand (controlled by the left hemisphere) to select a picture of a chicken, and his left hand (controlled by the right hemisphere) to select a picture of a shovel. The investigators then asked the patient what he had seen. "I saw a claw, and I picked a chicken," he replied. Because the left hemisphere controls almost all speech, it described what the left hemisphere saw. The patient continued, "And you have to clean out the chicken shed with a shovel." The left hemisphere did not actually know what the right hemisphere had seen, so it made up a story. The left hemisphere, in right-handed people (and most left-handed people), not only controls most aspects of language but also plays a crucial role in interpreting the world, in making up stories, and in many forms of reasoning (Gazzaniga, 1995; LeDoux et al., 1977).

Hemispheric Specialization: Not Just for the Deeply Disconnected

It's often said that the left brain is analytical and verbal, whereas the right brain is intuitive and perceptual. In fact, these generalizations must be made with caution. For example, the left brain is actually better than the right at some types of

Figure 2.11 Gazzaniga and LeDoux Experiment

The right hemisphere of split-brain patients is capable of understanding and responding to simple stimuli, but not speaking about them. Thus, the left hemisphere will sometimes make up stories to explain actions controlled by the right hemisphere.

perception (such as determining whether one object is above or below another; Hellige & Michimata, 1989; Kosslyn et al., 1989; Laeng et al., 2003), and the right brain is better than the left at some aspects of language (such as making the pitch of the voice rise at the end of a question or understanding humor; Bihrle et al., 1986; Brownell et al., 1984; Ellis & Young, 1987). Moreover, the abilities of the two hemispheres often differ only in degree, not in kind (Hellige, 1993; Hugdahl & Davidson, 2003). A major exception to this generalization is language. As you will see in Chapter 6, many aspects of language are carried out by a single hemisphere, usually the left.

52   The young soldier with difficulties in visual recognition could have suffered a functional deficit in his right hemisphere that prevented him from being able to see the overall shapes of objects. The right temporal lobe, in particular, appears to play a key role in recognizing overall shapes (Ivry & Robertson, 1998). After such damage, he would have had to rely on his left hemisphere, which tends to register details only, not overall shape.

Beneath the Cortex: The Inner Brain

53   The *subcortical* parts of the brain, situated deep beneath the cortex, carry out many crucial tasks that affect every moment of our lives. For example, although the examiners of the young soldier did not mention it, the soldier probably became lethargic after his accident—as is typical of people who have suffered brain damage. But why would brain damage cause someone to be less vigorous? The answer lies in the connections between the cortex and inner parts of the brain that are concerned with motivation and emotion. The most important of these subcortical areas are illustrated in Figure 2.12. Together with the cortex, most of these structures are considered to be part of the **forebrain** (so called because in four-legged animals such as cats and rats, these areas are at the front); but given their great variety of function, this traditional category is not very useful.

Forebrain: The cortex, thalamus, limbic system, and basal ganglia.

Figure 2.12 Key Subcortical Brain Areas

Cerebrum
Corpus callosum
Forebrain
Midbrain
Pons
Thalamus
Hypothalamus
Pituitary gland
Cerebellum
Hindbrain
Reticular formation (also in the midbrain)
Medulla

Many of the parts of the brain needed for day-to-day living are located beneath the cortex, such as those illustrated here.

Figure 2.13 The Limbic System

54

Cingulate cortex

Thalamus

Hypothalamus

Hippocampus

Amygdala

These are the key structures that make up the limbic system, which plays a role in emotions and other psychological events.

Thalamus: A subcortical structure that receives inputs from sensory and motor systems and plays a crucial role in attention; often thought of as a switching center.

Hypothalamus: A brain structure that sits under the thalamus and plays a central role in controlling eating and drinking and in regulating the body's temperature, blood pressure, and heart rate.

Hippocampus: A subcortical structure that plays a key role in allowing new information to be stored in the brain's memory banks.

Thalamus: Crossroads of the Brain

The **thalamus** is often compared with a switching center but could also be likened to an airline hub where planes converge and then take off for far-flung destinations. The sensory systems, such as vision and hearing, and the motor systems that control muscles have neural connections to the thalamus, which routes their signals to other parts of the brain. The thalamus is also involved in attention; as a matter of fact, at this very second, your thalamus is allowing you to fix your attention on each word you read. The thalamus is also involved in sleep control. The thalamus plays such a critical role in daily life that if it is badly damaged, the patient will die, even if the cortex remains untouched. Partial damage to the young soldier's thalamus might account for some of the symptoms the doctors observed.

Hypothalamus: Thermostat and More

55 The **hypothalamus** sits under the thalamus, as illustrated in Figure 2.13. The small size of this structure shouldn't fool you: It is absolutely critical for controlling many bodily functions, such as eating and drinking; keeping body temperature, blood pressure, and heart rate within the proper limits; and governing sexual behavior (Swaab, 2003). The hypothalamus also regulates hormones, such as those that prepare an animal to fight or to flee when confronted by danger. If visual recognition is impaired, as in the case of our young soldier, the hypothalamus will not receive the information it needs to function properly. If confronted by an enemy in the field, the soldier would not be able to register the information required to cause the right chemicals to flow into his bloodstream to marshal the body's resources for fight or flight.

Hippocampus: Remember It

56 The **hippocampus** is a structure that looks something like a seahorse (at least to some people), and hence its name, from the Greek *hippokampos*, a mythological "seahorse" monster. This structure plays a key role in allowing us to enter new information into the brain's memory banks (Gluck & Myers, 2000; Squire & Schacter, 2002). The role of the hippocampus was vividly illustrated by the case of H.M., who had his hippocampus (and nearby brain structures) removed in an effort to control his epilepsy. After the operation, his doctors noticed something unexpected: H.M. could no longer learn new facts (Milner et al., 1968). His memory for events that occurred a year or so before the operation seemed normal, but he was stuck at that stage of his life. Each day began truly anew, with no memory of what had occurred earlier—in fact, he could not even remember what had happened a few minutes ago, let alone hours or days. Later, more careful study revealed that he also could not remember events that had occurred within the year or so before the operation (Squire, 1987). H.M. does not seem particularly aware of his deficit, and when one of the authors of this book interviewed him years after the operation, he was in good spirits and remarkably comfortable with himself. When asked about the meanings of words that were coined after his operation, he gamely offered definitions, suggesting, for example, that a *jacuzzi* is

a "new kind of dance." He didn't seem to notice what was missing in his life. (Perhaps this is a case of the left hemisphere telling stories to fill in gaps, as we noted when discussing the Gazzaniga and LeDoux study of a split-brain patient.)

Patients such as H.M. led researchers eventually to discover that although the hippocampus itself does not contain stored memories for extended amounts of time, it triggers processes that store new information elsewhere in the brain (as we shall discuss in Chapter 5). If the young soldier had damage to the occipital or temporal systems that register visual input, these areas would not feed the proper information to the hippocampus—and thus he would not be able to store in memory the stimuli he saw.

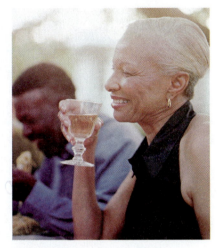

The *nucleus accumbens*, which is sometimes considered part of the basal ganglia, plays a crucial role in the brain's response to reward (Hall et al., 2001; Tzschentke & Schmidt, 2000) and its anticipation of reward (Knutson et al., 2001; Pagnoni et al., 2002). Indeed, drugs such as cocaine, amphetamines, and alcohol have their effects in part because they engage the nucleus accumbens (Dackis & O'Brien, 2001; Robbins & Everitt, 1999; Vinar, 2001). The neurotransmitter dopamine is central to the operation of this structure.

Amygdala: Inner Feelings

57 The **amygdala** is an almond-shaped structure (its name means "almond" in ancient Greek) near the hippocampus. The amygdala plays a special role in emotions such as fear and anger (Morris & Dolan, 2002) and even affects whether one can read emotions in facial expressions (Adolphs et al., 1996). The hypothalamus and amygdala play crucial roles as bridges between the CNS and the PNS. Indeed, both are key components of the **limbic system**, shown in Figure 2.13. The limbic system has long been thought of as being involved in the basics of emotion and motivation: fighting, fleeing, feeding, and sex. But each of the structures in this "system" is now known to have distinct roles that do not involve these functions (for example, the hippocampus is crucially important in storing new memories); further, other brain structures, outside this set, also play a role in emotion. For these reasons, some researchers regard the very concept of a "limbic system" as out of date (LeDoux, 1996).

Basal Ganglia: More Than Habit-Forming

58 The **basal ganglia**, positioned on the outer sides of the thalami, are involved in planning and producing movement (Iansek & Porter, 1980). People with Parkinson's disease often have abnormal basal ganglia; the functioning of these structures depends crucially on dopamine.

The basal ganglia also play a critical role in a particular type of learning: forming a habit. When you learn to put your foot on the brake automatically at a red light, the basal ganglia are busy connecting the stimulus (the light) with your response (moving your foot). As discussed in Chapter 4, this system is distinct from the one used to learn facts (the one, that, presumably, is at work right now, as you read this page).

Brainstem: The Brain's Wakeup Call

59 As illustrated in Figure 2.12 (p. 71), at the base of the brain are structures that feed into, and receive information from, the spinal cord. These structures are often collectively called the **brainstem**. The **medulla**, at the lowest part of the lower brainstem (see Figure 2.12), is important in the automatic control of breathing, swallowing, and blood circulation. The brainstem also contains a number of small structures, together called the **reticular formation**, which has two main parts. The "ascending" part, the *reticular activating system (RAS)*, plays a key role in keeping you awake and making you perk up when something interesting happens. The RAS produces neuromodulators (as do several other specialized structures deep in the brain) that affect the operation of many other parts of the brain. Neurons of the RAS have long axons that reach into other parts of the brain and alter the functioning of distant neurons. The soldier who suffered carbon monoxide poisoning

Amygdala: A subcortical structure that plays a special role in fear and is involved in other sorts of emotions, such as anger.

Limbic system: A set of brain areas, including the hippocampus, amygdala, and other areas, that have long been thought of as being involved in fighting, fleeing, feeding, and sex.

Basal ganglia: Subcortical structures that play a role in planning and producing movement.

Brainstem: The set of neural structures at the base of the brain, including the medulla and pons.

Medulla: The lowest part of the lower brainstem, which plays a central role in automatic control of breathing, swallowing, and blood circulation.

Reticular formation: A collection of small structures in the brainstem, organized into two main parts: the "ascending" part plays a key role in keeping a person awake and alert; the "descending" part is important in producing autonomic nervous system reactions.

would have been sluggish following damage to these structures. The "descending" part of the reticular formation receives input from the hypothalamus and plays a key role in producing autonomic nervous system reactions. It is also involved in conducting impulses from muscles not under voluntary control to those under voluntary control (such as those used in swallowing and speech).

The **pons** is a bridge (*pons* is Latin for "bridge") connecting the brainstem and the cerebellum; it is involved with a variety of functions, ranging from sleep to control of muscles used to form facial expressions.

Cerebellum: Walking Tall

60 The **cerebellum** is concerned in part with physical coordination. If your cerebellum were damaged, you might walk oddly and have trouble standing normally and keeping an upright posture. If you ever see an aging prizefighter, look at his walk. Too many blows to the head may have damaged his cerebellum, leading to a condition aptly described as being "punch-drunk." In addition, however, damage to some parts of the cerebellum might disrupt your ability to estimate time or to pay attention properly (Ivry & Spencer, 2004). The surface area of the cerebellum is nearly the same as that of the entire cerebral cortex, and hence it will not be surprising if this structure turns out to be involved in many cognitive functions (Manto & Pandolfo, 2001). The medulla, pons, cerebellum, and parts of the reticular formation are often grouped together as the **hindbrain** because they lie at the rear end of the brain of a four-legged animal; the other brainstem structures form the **midbrain**, which lies between the hindbrain and the forebrain (see Figure 2.12, p. 71).

The Neuroendocrine and Neuroimmune Systems: More Brain–Body Connections

61 Some of the subcortical structures we just considered play another important role: They allow the brain to communicate with the body. The brain has a total of four mechanisms for influencing the body, and these in turn provide feedback, affecting the brain itself.

- *Skeletal system.* As you now know, the sensory-somatic nervous system affects the body by moving muscles voluntarily, via the skeletal system.
- *Autonomic nervous system.* The brain can influence the ANS, which— among other things—regulates involuntary muscles (such as those in the heart).
- *Hormones.* In addition, the brain produces hormones and controls the production of hormones elsewhere in the body.
- *Immune responses.* Finally, the brain affects our immune systems, making us more or less able to fight off the onslaught of disease.

Let's consider these last two mechanisms now, which rely in part on the deep brain structures just discussed.

The Neuroendocrine System: It's Hormonal!

Some structures in the brain affect the body by producing (or causing to be produced) certain chemicals. For example, something happens during puberty that

Pons: A bridge between the brainstem and the cerebellum that plays a role in functions ranging from sleep to control of facial muscles.

Cerebellum: A large structure at the base of the brain that is concerned in part with physical coordination, estimating time, and paying attention.

Hindbrain: The medulla, pons, cerebellum, and parts of the reticular formation.

Midbrain: Brainstem structures that lie between forebrain and hindbrain, including parts of the reticular formation.

62 changes a child's body into an adult's and changes the child's behavior as well. Charming boys and sweet girls may become sullen and rebellious, moody and impulsive. That "something" is hormones. **Hormones** are chemicals that are produced by glands and can act as neuromodulators. The CNS hooks into the **neuroendocrine system**, which makes hormones that affect many functions. The CNS not only regulates this system, but also receives information from it—which in turn alters the way the CNS operates.

63 Figure 2.14 shows the locations of the major *endocrine glands*; endocrine glands secrete substances into the bloodstream, as opposed to other glands, such as sweat glands, that excrete substances outside the body. Some hormones affect sexual development and functioning. Among these, **testosterone** causes boys to develop facial hair and other external sexual characteristics, as well as to build up muscle, and **estrogen** causes girls to develop breasts and is involved in the menstrual cycle. Some hormones affect the levels of salt and sugar in the blood, and others help the body cope with stressful situations. The outer layer of the adrenal glands produces **cortisol**, which helps the body cope with the extra energy demands of stress by breaking down protein and fat and converting them to sugar; the sugar provides energy to the body, increases blood flow, and allows the person to respond more vigorously and for a longer period of time. Cortisol production is triggered even by the sight of angry faces (van Honk et al., 2000).

A part of the brain called the **pituitary gland** is particularly interesting because its hormones actually control the other endocrine glands; for this reason, it has sometimes been called the "master gland." But, master or not, this gland is still controlled by the brain, primarily via connections from the hypothalamus. If information from the world isn't interpreted properly by the young soldier's cortex, it won't have the normal effect on the hypothalamus, which in turn will not produce the normal hormonal response.

64 ## The Neuroimmune System: How the Brain Fights Disease

The brain also helps our bodies fight disease. In particular, the hypothalamus, the pituitary gland, and the adrenal glands form the **hypothalamic-pituitary-adrenal (HPA) axis**, which allows us to respond effectively to infections; this system is so important that we would soon die without it. Psychological stress and pain also activate the HPA axis; in fact, the brain can regulate the adrenal glands via neural connections (Bornstein & Chrousos, 1999). Crucially, stress is often "in the mind of the beholder"; what counts as stress for you (for instance, being on a roller coaster) might be fun for someone else. Mental processes interpret a situation, and the result affects the immune system. Thus, being stressed-out can make you more likely to catch a cold (Glaser & Kiecolt-Glaser, 1998) and more vulnerable to bacterial infections (Bailey et al., 2003). Your body affects your mind, and vice versa.

Figure 2.14 The Major Endocrine Glands

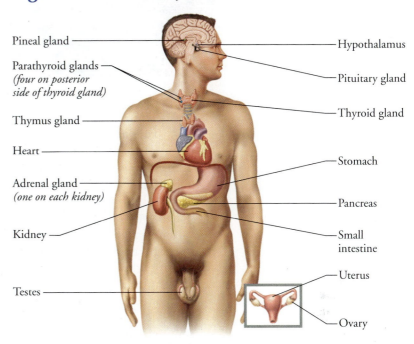

Pineal gland — Hypothalamus
Parathyroid glands (*four on posterior side of thyroid gland*) — Pituitary gland
Thymus gland — Thyroid gland
Heart — Stomach
Adrenal gland (*one on each kidney*) — Pancreas
Kidney — Small intestine
Testes — Uterus
— Ovary

The locations of major endocrine glands in the body.

Hormone: A chemical that is produced by a gland and can act as a neuromodulator.

Neuroendocrine system: The system, regulated by the CNS, that makes hormones that affect many bodily functions and that also provides the CNS with information.

Testosterone: The hormone that causes males to develop facial hair and other sex characteristics and to build up muscle volume.

Estrogen: The hormone that causes breasts to develop and is involved in the menstrual cycle.

Cortisol: A hormone produced by the outer layer of the adrenal glands that helps the body cope with the extra energy demands of stress by breaking down and converting protein and fat to sugar.

Pituitary gland: The "master gland" that regulates other glands but is itself controlled by the brain, primarily via connections from the hypothalamus.

Hypothalamic-pituitary-adrenal (HPA) axis: The hypothalamus, pituitary gland, and adrenal glands, which work together to fight off infection.

Looking at Levels

The Musical Brain

All human cultures have music. Does this imply that music is deeply embedded in the human brain, and we can understand everything interesting about it simply by looking at the brain? Not at all! As usual, we need to consider events at the different levels of analysis and how they interact.

First, the brain. Just as there is no single "language center" or "vision center," there is no single "music center" in the brain. Rather, a large network of different brain areas is activated when people listen to or play music (Baeck, 2002). Meister and colleagues (2004) monitored brain activity while music students either played the right-hand piano part of a classical music piece or simply imagined playing the piece while keeping still. These researchers found very similar activation in a large part of the frontal and parietal lobes (in both hemispheres) during both actual playing and imagery. But only during actual playing was primary motor cortex activated, and the posterior parietal lobes were more active during actual playing (which reflects their role in programming movements).

Different parts of the activated network of brain areas play different roles. For example, damage to the superior temporal lobes, which process sound, can prevent patients from distinguishing consonant from dissonant sounds (Peretz et al., 2001). Damage to the left temporal-parietal region can disrupt rhythm while leaving perception and production of melody intact (Di Pietro et al., 2004). Other researchers (Griffiths et al., 2004) found that damage to the amygdala and a related brain area (the *insula*) led a patient to lose his emotional reactions to music; pieces that previously had sent a "shiver down his spine" no longer did so.

Music also affects events at the level of the person. For example, music can reduce arousal (Pelletier, 2004) and can even calm people who have experienced trauma and help them to be better oriented to events around them (Baker, 2001). It can also improve the mood of people who have had brain damage (Magee & Davidson, 2002). Although playing music does relax people, which in turn can improve their feelings of well-being (Winkelman, 2003), that's not all there is to it; listening to music they like can actually energize older people (Hirokawa, 2004). However, these effects depend in part on the nature of the music. One study, for example, found that listening to Mozart relaxed people more than did listening to New Age music (Smith & Joyce, 2004).

Further, music has powerful effects at the level of the group. Perhaps the most impressive of such effects occur in the context of *music therapy*, which uses structured musical exercises to help people improve their emotional state and daily functioning (Wigram et al., 2002). Music therapy is not just sitting around listening to music; rather, a therapist organizes exercises for the patient, based on the patient's background, preferences, and goals. Moreover, the therapist evaluates how well the patient responds and adjusts the therapy accordingly. Music therapy can include creating new music, producing music (singing and playing instruments), and listening and responding to music. Music therapy has been used to help people not only to relax and express their emotions, but also to improve their attention spans, manage pain, and develop new ways to communicate with others. Researchers have shown that music therapy can even help people with severe problems (Schmid & Aldridge, 2004) and that such therapy can help patients with brain damage to interact socially (Wheeler et al., 2003).

Finally, events at the different levels clearly interact when it comes to making music. For example, if you are motivated (level of the person) to play music, perhaps because a teacher inspired you (level of the group), this activity will actually change your brain! Researchers have examined how playing music may change the brain. Part of the motor strip in the right half of the brain controls the fingers of the left hand, and this part of the brain is larger in orchestra members who play stringed instruments than in nonmusicians (Elber et al., 1995; Münte et al., 2001; Schlaug et al., 1995). In fact, professional keyboard players have more gray matter in auditory and visual-spatial areas than do either amateur musicians or nonmusicians (Gaser & Schlaug, 2003)—and the more people practice, the larger the relevant areas tend to be. Moreover, such differences are not restricted to variations in size: Conductors of professional orchestras actually become better able to localize sounds in the periphery, those heard from the "corner of the ear," so to speak (Münte et al., 2001). Furthermore, when you learn a particular instrument, your brain develops to allow you to hear its particular tonal quality (Pantev et al., 2001). Apparently, brain areas that are used often grow larger and come to function more effectively, probably because of the formation of additional connections among neurons.

Consider these findings from the levels perspective: The size and functionality of brain areas—the physical structure and workings of your brain—depend in part on what you do. If you have musical talent and interest (characteristics at the level of the person) and have the opportunity to develop musical ability, your brain can be altered by the experience. And if your playing is smiled upon by others (the level of the group), you will be even more motivated to continue practicing—further changing your brain. And, once your brain is altered, your playing may improve—leading to more praise from others.

LOOKING BACK: *Review*

1. *What are the major regions of the cortex, and what do they do?* The major cortical regions are organized into four sets of lobes. The occipital lobes are the first part of the cortex to process visual input in detail. The temporal lobes receive inputs from the occipital lobes and are the seat of visual memories. They are also involved in language comprehension and hearing, storing new memories, and some aspects of consciousness. The parietal lobes register location in space and are also involved in arithmetic, attention, and motor control. Each parietal lobe includes part of the somatosensory strip, which registers sensation from parts of the body. Different regions of the somatosensory strip register input from different parts of the body, with larger areas being devoted to more sensitive parts of the body. The frontal lobes are involved in producing speech, searching for memories, reasoning, and making decisions. These lobes contain the motor strip, which controls fine motor movements. The motor strip is organized so that larger areas are devoted to parts of the body that we can control more precisely.

2. *How do the functions of the two sides of the brain differ?* The left hemisphere plays a larger role in language, and the right hemisphere plays a larger role in spatial attention and nonverbal functions. The left brain appears to play a critical role in inventing stories to make sense of the

world and in many forms of reasoning. However, these differences are usually matters of degree, and both hemispheres often can perform all functions to some extent. A major exception to this generalization is that most aspects of language are restricted to a single hemisphere (typically the left).

3. *What parts of the brain lie under the cerebral cortex? What do these subcortical structures do?* The thalamus is often thought of as a switching center; it handles connections to and from distinct parts of the brain. Attention depends on the thalamus. The hypothalamus controls many bodily functions, such as eating, drinking, and sex. It is also critically involved in regulating hormones. The hippocampus plays a key role in storing new memories in the brain, and the amygdala is involved in fear and other emotions. The hippocampus, amygdala, and other subcortical structures make up the limbic system, which is essential for fighting, fleeing, feeding, and sex. The basal ganglia are important in planning and producing movements, as well as in learning new habits. The brainstem contains a number of structures, many of which are crucial for alertness, sleep, and arousal; damage to these structures causes sluggishness. The cerebellum is noteworthy because its surface area is about as large as that of the cerebral cortex, and thus it may prove to have important roles in cognitive processes. This structure is involved in motor control, timing, and attention.

4. *What are the neuroendocrine and neuroimmune systems, and what do they have in common?* The CNS regulates the neuroendocrine system, which in turn produces hormones. Hormones are chemicals that can act as neuromodulators; some affect sexual development. Stress triggers the release of the hormone cortisol, produced by the outer layer of the adrenal glands. The CNS also regulates the neuroimmune system, which helps us fight disease. Stress also affects this system. The neuroendocrine and neuroimmune systems, along with the skeletal system and the autonomic nervous system, are the means by which the CNS influences the body (and they in turn send information back to the brain).

LOOKING BEYOND: *Critical Thinking*

Clearly, the organization of the brain has a lot to do with why brain damage produces one disorder and not another. It is possible that some parts of the brain receive information that is not available to the parts that control language. If so, can you think of types of behaviors that might reveal that the information was "in there"?

Can you think of a way by which you could have tried to find out whether the soldier had a problem with attention or whether his paying attention to a small area was just a strategy? That is, perhaps he believed that by focusing on details he would see better, and thus he did so even though he was in fact able to pay attention to overall shapes. What difference, if any, would it make whether his problem was due to a faulty strategy or to something that was not under his control?

More careful examination of the soldier might have suggested that his problem was not confined to visual processing. What would you think if it could be shown that his personality was particularly unemotional? What if he had little interest in eating or sex?

Probing the Brain

Having toured the major parts of the brain and noted their major functions, you can make a pretty good guess about what areas of the brain were damaged when the soldier suffered carbon monoxide poisoning. We cannot know for sure, given the limitations of the tests available at the time of his accident, in 1966. Today, however, doctors can obtain impressive high-quality images of a living brain. These images can show damage to particular brain structures and can record brain activity, or the disruption of it, in specific areas.

*L*OOKING AHEAD: *Learning Objectives*

1. *What can researchers learn about the brain's function by studying behavior following brain damage?*
2. *What techniques allow researchers to record the activity of neurons in the brain as they function?*
3. *What is neuroimaging?*
4. *How can different parts of the brain be stimulated to see whether they are working properly?*

The Damaged Brain: What's Missing?

The first evidence that different parts of the brain do different things came from *natural experiments*, accidents in which people suffered damage to the brain. Such damage typically produces a region of impaired tissue, called a **lesion**. The most frequent source of damage is a **stroke**, which occurs when blood, with its life-sustaining nutrients and oxygen, fails to reach part of the brain (usually because a clot clogs up a crucial blood vessel), causing neurons in the affected area to die. In such cases, researchers study the patients, seeking to learn which specific abilities are disrupted independently of others when particular brain structures are damaged.

Researchers also study the effects on behavior of removing specific parts of the brains of animals. But, because animals are not people, we must be cautious in generalizing from animal brains to human brains.

Although strokes are a more common cause of brain damage, some people have suffered such damage from riding on roller coasters. One woman had trouble remembering things she just heard, could no longer see clearly, and even blacked out sporadically (S. Gilbert, 2002). A few people have died after such injuries (Brasiek & Roberts, 2002).

Recording Techniques: The Music of the Cells

Rather than having to rely on the indirect evidence supplied by damaged brains, researchers can make use of several methods to record the activity of normal brains. To some extent, brain activity can be measured by making an electromagnetic recording. In one version of this technique, a machine called an **electroencephalograph** records electrical current produced by the brain, as shown in Figure 2.15 (on p. 80). When neurons fire, they produce electrical fields. When many neurons are firing together, these fields can be detected by electrodes (small metal disks that pick up electrical activity) placed on the scalp. Researchers can record electrical activity in response to a particular stimulus, or they can record the activity over time; the result is a tracing of the "brain

Lesion: A region of impaired tissue.

Stroke: A source of brain damage that occurs when blood (with its life-giving nutrients and oxygen) fails to reach part of the brain, causing neurons in that area to die.

Electroencephalograph: A machine that records electrical current produced by the brain.

Figure 2.15 The Electroencephalograph

 Relaxed/rest

 Task performance

The top image shows an EEG during relaxed rest, whereas the bottom image shows an EEG during performance of a task; clearly, the brain is more active when an individual is performing a task than when he or she is relaxed.

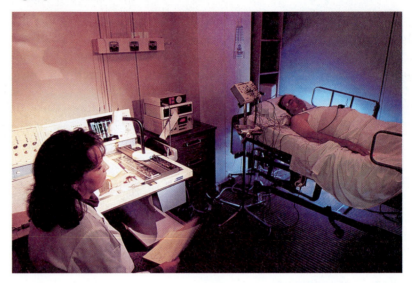

This equipment allows researchers to record electrical activity on the scalp, which reflects electrical activity in the brain.

waves" of electrical fluctuation called an **electroencephalogram (EEG)** (see Figure 2.15). Psychologists have used this technique to learn much about the brain. It is through EEGs, for example, that they learned that people go through distinct stages of sleep marked by different types of brain activity (see Chapter 10 for a detailed discussion of these stages).

Another, more recent, technique, **magnetoencephalography (MEG)**, records magnetic waves from outside of the head (without electrodes). Just as running a current through a wire produces a magnetic field, neural firings produce a magnetic field. Very fast changes in neural firing can be detected with this technique. However, neither EEG nor MEG is very sensitive to subcortical activity.

In a more direct and sensitive technique, *single-cell recording*, tiny probes called **microelectrodes** can be placed in individual cells in the brain and used to record the firing rates of neurons. A typical microelectrode is at most only 1/10 as wide as a human hair (and some are only 1/100 as wide!). Usually researchers hook up the wires from microelectrodes to amplifiers and speakers rather than to a screen, so they can hear neuronal activity (as clicking sounds) rather than watch a monitor; their eyes are then free to guide the placement of the electrodes. Microelectrodes are sometimes put in human brains before brain surgery in order to find out what a part of the brain does before it is cut. Studies with microelectrodes have yielded some fascinating results. For example, when people look at words, some neurons respond to specific words but not others (Heit et al., 1988).

Neuroimaging: Picturing the Living Brain

Today, if you had an emergency like the young soldier's, you would probably be rushed to a hospital and immediately have your brain scanned. Your doctors would order the procedure to determine both the structural damage (which areas were physically affected) and the functional deficits (which areas were performing below par). Because they yield an actual picture of neuronal structure and func-

Electroencephalogram (EEG): A recording from the scalp of electrical activity in the brain over time, which produces a tracing of pulses at different frequencies.

Magnetoencephalography (MEG): A technique for assessing brain activity that relies on recording magnetic waves from outside of the head.

Microelectrode: A tiny probe inserted into the brain to record the electrical activity of individual neurons.

tion, scanning techniques are referred to as **neuroimaging**. It is fair to say that neuroimaging techniques have transformed psychology, allowing researchers to answer questions that were hopelessly out of reach before the mid-1980s (Cabeza & Nyberg, 2000; Cappa & Grafman, 2004; Poldrak & Wagner, 2004; Posner & Raichle, 1994).

Visualizing Brain Structure

68 The oldest neuroimaging techniques involve taking pictures of brain structures using X rays. The invention of the computer allowed scientists to construct machines for **computer-assisted tomography (CT,** formerly CAT). In this technique, a series of X rays builds up a three-dimensional image, slice by slice (*tomography* comes from a Greek word meaning "section"). More recently, **magnetic resonance imaging (MRI)** makes use of the magnetic properties of different atoms to take even sharper pictures of the structures of the brain.

Visualizing Brain Function

69 CT scans and MRIs give amazing views of the physical structure of the living brain; but for images that reflect the brain in action, researchers need other types of brain scans, those that track the amount of blood, oxygen, or nutrients moving to particular parts of the brain.

One of the most important techniques for measuring blood flow or energy consumption in the brain is **positron emission tomography (PET)**. Small amounts of a radioactive substance are introduced into the blood, which is then taken up into different brain areas in proportion to how hard the neurons in each area are working (see Figure 2.16). The amount of radiation emitted at different parts of the head is recorded, and a computer uses this information to build three-dimensional images of the brain.

On the left, a computer-assisted tomography (CT) scan, and on the right, a magnetic resonance imaging (MRI) scan. MRI provides much higher resolution images of structures of the brain.

Neuroimaging: Brain-scanning techniques that produce a picture of the structure or functioning of neurons.

Computer-assisted tomography (CT, formerly CAT): A neuroimaging technique that produces a three-dimensional image of brain structures using X rays.

Magnetic resonance imaging (MRI): A technique that uses magnetic properties of atoms to take sharp pictures of the structures of the brain.

Positron emission tomography (PET): A neuroimaging technique that uses small amounts of a radioactive substance to track blood flow or energy consumption in the brain.

Figure 2.16 Positron Emission Tomography

Hearing words

Seeing words

Speaking words

Reading words

A positron emission tomography (PET) machine like that shown on the left allows researchers to observe brain activity while participants perform various tasks.

Brighter colors indicate regions of greater blood flow in the brain while the participant performed a particular task.

70 Probably the most popular type of neuroimaging today is **functional magnetic resonance imaging (fMRI)**. The most common sort of fMRI reveals function by detecting the amount of oxygen that is being brought to a particular place in the brain while a person performs a task.

The most recent technique for visualizing brain activity is *optical imaging*, which relies on shining lasers through the skull. These lasers are very weak, but use frequencies of light (near infrared) to which the skull is transparent. It turns out that blood with oxygen in it absorbs different frequencies of light than does blood in which the oxygen has been consumed. Thus, by observing how much light of different frequencies is reflected back from the brain, researchers can track blood flow (Hochman, 2000; Hoshi et al., 2000; Villringer & Chance, 1997).

It is worth emphasizing that *all* of the neuroimaging techniques we have discussed suffer from a fundamental problem: They produce evidence for *correlations* between performing a task and activation of a specific brain region. They do not establish that activated brain regions play a *causal* role in producing the behavior. To make this connection, we must turn to other techniques.

Stimulation: Tickling the Neurons

71 To come closer to discovering how neuronal activity actually gives rise to thoughts, feelings and behavior, researchers can also stimulate neurons and observe the results. Two kinds of stimulation studies have been used to find out what parts of the human brain do.

In one technique, mild electricity is delivered to parts of the participant's brain, and the person is then asked to report what he or she experiences. Wilder Penfield and his colleagues (Penfield & Perot, 1963; Penfield & Rasmussen, 1950) pioneered this method with patients who were about to undergo brain operations. Penfield reported that people experience different images, memories, and feelings depending on the area in the brain that is stimulated. A problem with this method, however, is that researchers cannot be sure whether actual memories are activated or whether the participants are making up stories. In other stimulation studies, instead of asking for reports, researchers observe which activities are disrupted when current is applied (Ojemann, 1983; Ojemann et al., 1989). However, even this method is limited because stimulating particular neurons can lead to the activation of remote neurons, and these other neurons could produce the observed effects. Nevertheless, recent advances in *microstimulation* of non-human animals have allowed researchers to alter the activity of a few neurons at a time and observe the direct consequences on an animal's perceptions, decisions, and actions (Cohen & Newsome, 2004).

In another recently developed method, **transcranial magnetic stimulation (TMS)**, researchers stimulate the brain by putting a wire coil on a person's head and discharging a large current through the coil, thus creating a magnetic field. This magnetic field is so strong that it causes a large cluster of neurons within it to fire. Using this technique, researchers can make a person's fingers move by shifting the coil over the parts of the brain that control the fingers (in the motor strip) and producing on/off magnetic pulses (Pascual-Leone et al., 1997; Pascual-Leone et al., 1998; Walsh & Pascual-Leone, 2003). Similarly, if such pulses are directed to the occipital lobe, perception can be temporarily impaired (Walsh & Pascual-Leone, 2003). This technique can show that a brain area plays a causal role in the performance of a particular task, as opposed to merely being stimu-

Functional magnetic resonance imaging (fMRI): A type of MRI that usually detects the amount of oxygen being brought to a particular place in the brain while a task is performed.

Transcranial magnetic stimulation (TMS): A technique in which the brain is stimulated from outside by putting a wire coil on a person's head and delivering a magnetic pulse. The magnetic fields are so strong that they make neurons under the coil fire.

lated by some other area that is actually doing the work. However, it is not always clear exactly which neurons have been affected by TMS.

In closing this section, we need to emphasize that each of these techniques for studying the brain has different strengths and weaknesses. Some techniques can detect activity in well under a second but cannot pinpoint where the activity originates; other techniques are slower but more discriminating. Some techniques establish correlations among far-flung parts of the brain and behavior but cannot establish causal relations, whereas other techniques establish causal relations between specific individual brain regions and behavior but have limited scope. Some are expensive, and some are relatively inexpensive. Recognizing these tradeoffs, researchers are increasingly using combinations of techniques, taking advantage of the strengths of each while compensating for their weaknesses. For example, PET scanning has revealed that the occipital lobe of the brain is activated even when people visualize with their eyes closed, and TMS has shown that this brain activity plays a causal role in mental imagery; when the occipital lobe is temporarily disrupted, so is the ability to visualize (Kosslyn et al., 1999).

LOOKING BACK: *Review*

1. *What can researchers learn about the brain's function by studying behavior following brain damage?* By looking at altered performance after brain damage has occurrred, researchers can gain hints about what functions are carried out by the particular parts of the brain that have been damaged.

2. *What techniques allow researchers to record the activity of neurons in the brain as they function?* Electroencephalography (EEG) records "brain waves"—fluctuations of electrical fields from the brain. This technique relies on electrodes placed on the skull to record electrical activity in response to a stimulus or over a period of time. Magnetoencephalography records magnetic waves from outside of the head. Researchers can also use microelectrodes to record neural activity directly, in both humans and animals.

3. *What is neuroimaging?* Neuroimaging techniques allow researchers to visualize the structure and function of the brain. At present, four major techniques are used: computer-assisted tomography (CT), which uses X rays to obtain images of the structure of the brain; magnetic resonance imaging (MRI), which uses the magnetic properties of different atoms to produce sharp pictures of the brain; positron emission tomography (PET), which relies on small amounts of a radioactive substance to track neural activity; and functional magnetic resonance imaging (fMRI), which detects the amount of oxygen brought to a particular place in the brain as a task is performed. Finally, optical imaging uses weak lasers to track blood flow, and thus activity, in the brain.

4. *How can different parts of the brain be stimulated to see whether they are working properly?* Electric current can be applied to parts of the brain or, with microstimulation, to just a few neurons, and effects on perception or behavior can then be observed. Transcranial magnetic stimulation (TMS) can be used to stimulate clusters of neurons by pulsing magnetic fields into the brain.

● LOOKING BEYOND: *Critical Thinking*

● *Dr. Scannering has invented an improved type of brain-scanning technique, which shines very dim lasers through your head and projects an image of brain activity as it is happening. His machine will be sold for less than the price of a personal computer, is very portable, and is easy to use. What would you do with such a machine? What uses can you think of for education or psychotherapy?*

Genes, Brain, and Environment: The Brain in the World

Why was the brain of the young soldier vulnerable to such damage from carbon monoxide fumes? Could he have done anything in advance to prepare his brain to survive such an event? Could he have done anything after the accident to speed his recovery? Let's consider the factors of environment and heredity that shape our brains so that they operate in particular ways and not in others, and the degree to which parts of the brain can change their functions if need be.

●LOOKING AHEAD: *Learning Objectives*

1. *How do genes and the environment interact as the brain develops and functions?*
2. *What does* heritability *mean?*
3. *How has evolution shaped the functions of the brain?*

Genes as Blueprints: Born to Be Wild?

Our genes affect us from the instant of conception and continue to affect us at every phase of our lives. The story of genetics begins in 1866, when Gregor Mendel, an Augustinian monk living in what is now the Czech Republic, wrote one of the fundamental papers in all science. In it he formulated the core ideas of what is now known as **Mendelian inheritance**, the transmission of characteristics by individual elements of inheritance, each acting separately. Two ideas are key: (1) For each trait, an offspring inherits an "element" from each parent; and (2) in some cases, one of the elements dominates the other, and that is the one whose effect is apparent. If an element is not dominant, it is recessive: The effect of a recessive element is evident only when the offspring receives two copies of it, one from each parent. Mendel, through careful experimentation and record-keeping, traced these patterns of inheritance for a number of organisms (such as pea plants), but he never knew their mechanism. That great biochemical discovery, that the mysterious "elements" are genes, was not made until the early part of the 20th century. Figure 2.17 illustrates the **deoxyribonucleic acid**, or **DNA**, molecule that contains our genes. A **gene** is a stretch of DNA that produces a specific protein (which may be an enzyme). The sum total of your particular set of genes is your **genotype**. In contrast, the **phenotype** is the observable structure and behavior of an organism.

Mendelian inheritance: The transmission of characteristics by individual elements of inheritance (genes), each acting separately.

Deoxyribonucleic acid, or DNA: The molecule that contains genes.

Gene: A stretch of DNA that produces a specific protein.

Genotype: The genetic code within an organism.

Phenotype: The observable structure and behavior of an organism.

Figure 2.17 The Secret of DNA

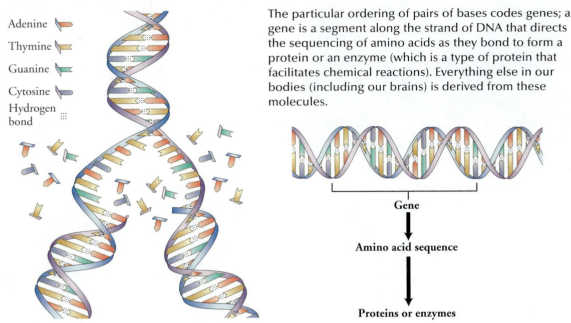

Adenine

Thymine

Guanine

Cytosine

Hydrogen bond

The particular ordering of pairs of bases codes genes; a gene is a segment along the strand of DNA that directs the sequencing of amino acids as they bond to form a protein or an enzyme (which is a type of protein that facilitates chemical reactions). Everything else in our bodies (including our brains) is derived from these molecules.

Gene

↓

Amino acid sequence

↓

Proteins or enzymes

What, exactly, is a gene? Let's begin with a chromosome, which is a tightly coiled molecule of deoxyribonucleic acid, or DNA, contained in the nucleus of all cells. Every cell of the human body (except for sex cells) has 23 pairs of chromosomes. The two strands in the DNA molecule are linked sequences of bases that are bridged by pairs of four types of bases. The base adenine (A) always hooks up with thymine (T), and guanine (G) always hooks up with cytosine (C). Thus, if the helix is unzipped down the middle, extra bases floating about will hook up correctly to form two complete copies of the original molecule. This is how this amazing molecule is able to reproduce itself.

Many genes express their effects only in combination with other genes. When this occurs, we see quantitative variations in characteristics, such as differences in height or intelligence, not qualitative variations, such as attached versus unattached ear lobes. In general, when a characteristic varies continuously over some range, it reflects ==complex inheritance==, the joint action of combinations of genes working together, rather than Mendelian inheritance, which describes the effects of individual elements of inheritance (Plomin & DeFries, 1998; Plomin et al., 2003).

73 Genetic Programs: The Genes Matter

Did you ever wonder which came first, the chicken or the egg? The answer is now clear: the egg. A mutation modified the genes of an ancestor of the chicken, and these genes produced a novel egg—which, when hatched, developed into a novel bird, the chicken we all know and love. Genes not only produce obvious traits—such as eye color, height, and other physical features—but also, by affecting our brains, affect our behavior.

Genes sometimes affect the behavior of other species in especially striking ways. Consider a startling result reported in late 1996 by Ryner and her colleagues. These researchers identified a single gene that can change the sexual behavior of fruit flies. Usually, fruit flies engage in a "courtship dance" before they mate. The male follows the female, uses his forelegs to tap her body, produces a "song" by vibrating his wings, then licks her genitals, curls his abdomen, and tries

Complex inheritance: The joint action of combinations of genes working together.

The far-reaching power of relatively small genetic differences can be seen dramatically by comparing chimpanzees with humans: About 99% of the genetic material in both species is identical (Wildman et al., 2002).

to mate with her (Ferveur et al., 1995; Hall, 1994 [cited in Ryner et al., 1996]). By altering one gene, scientists produced male fruit flies that performed this courtship dance for other males. In fact, when a group of males with this gene were together, they lined up in a long chain, each male both being courted by and courting other males. The gene that controls this behavior affects only about 500 of the 100,000 neurons in the insect's head. A small genetic change, affecting a relatively small number of neurons, had a big effect. The affected neurons apparently coordinate many other neurons, which in turn produce the behavior.

Tuning Genetic Programs: The Environment Matters   79

When it comes to physical, mental, and behavioral characteristics, what you see is not necessarily what you get in the genes: The phenotype may not simply be a read-out of the underlying genotype. There can be no question that genes play a major role in shaping our abilities, but it is critical to point out that genes *cannot* program the structure of the brain entirely in advance. Your brain contained far more connections at birth than it does now. As you interacted with the environment, certain neural connections were used over and over again, while others were used hardly at all. Connections between neurons in parts of the brain that are used frequently are retained, while others, which are not used frequently, are pruned away (Huttenlocher, 2002). **Pruning** is a process whereby certain neural connections are eliminated (Cowan et al., 1984; Huttenlocher, 2002): As the saying goes, "Use it or lose it." The genes define the range of possibilities for brain circuits, but interactions with the environment lead some connections to persist and others to disappear.

Pruning is only one of the ways in which your brain changes as you experience the world. Such changes are part and parcel of the brain's **plasticity**, its ability to change with experience. (Like plastic, the brain can be molded by external forces.) Connections are also added. In fact, researchers have found that if rats are raised in enriched environments, with lots of toys and things to do, their brains actually become heavier than those of rats raised in average environments. The additional weight comes about in part because more blood flows to the cortex (Jones & Greenough, 1996) and in part because new connections are formed (Black et al., 1998; Comery et al., 1995; Diamond et al., 1972; Greenough & Chang, 1985; Greenough et al., 1987; Nelson, 1999; Turner & Greenough, 1985). The environment not only helps to select among connections established by the genes; it can also cause new connections to form.

Plasticity of the human brain is most evident in four circumstances: (1) during infancy and childhood, when the brain is being shaped by interactions with the environment; (2) when the body changes, so that the sensory input changes; (3) when we learn something new, or store new information; and (4) as compensation after brain damage—even healthy portions of the young soldier's brain probably changed after his injury but, unfortunately, not as much as they probably would have if he had still been a child (Payne & Lomber, 2001). However, even adult brains are capable of dramatic reorganization. We now know that adult brains can create new neurons, at least in some regions (Gould et al., 1999; Kempermann et al., 2004).

Thus, genes are not destiny; they don't fix our characteristics forevermore. The genes determine the range of what is possible (humans can't grow wings),

Pruning: A process whereby certain connections among neurons are eliminated.

Plasticity: The brain's ability to be molded by experience.

but within those limits interactions with the environment can alter both the structure and the function of the brain.

Genes and Environment: A Single System

How do interactions with the environment alter the brain? Some people think of genes as blueprints for the body, providing the instructions on how to build organs, but this notion captures only part of the genes' role. For one thing, rather than being filed away in a dusty drawer once their instructions have been followed, many genes keep working throughout your life. Their action is the reason some people go bald, others develop high cholesterol, and still others get varicose veins. Even more important, genes are not simply time bombs that are set at birth and ready to explode at the proper hour. Many genes change their operation constantly, sometimes producing proteins and sometimes not. Psychiatrist Steven Hyman (personal communication) suggested the following illuminating example: Say you want bigger biceps, and so you go to the gym and start lifting weights. After the first week, all you have to show for your time and sweat is aching arms. But, after a few weeks, the muscles begin to firm up and soon may even begin to bulge. What has happened? When you first lifted weights, you actually damaged the muscles, and the damage caused the release of certain chemicals. Those chemicals then—and this is the important part—*turned on* genes in the muscle cells. Here, "turned on" means that the proteins coded by the genes were produced. These proteins were used to build up the damaged muscles. If the damage stops, so do the chemicals that signal the genes to turn on, and the genes will no longer produce those extra proteins. So, you need to lift increasingly heavier weights to keep building more muscle. No pain, no gain.

The important point to remember is that many genes are constantly being turned on and off, as needed, to produce specific substances. As you read this, for example, terminal buttons of some of your axons are releasing neurotransmitters that enable you to understand the printed words. Genes are turned on to replenish the buttons' supply of neurotransmitters. Similarly, genes regulate the flow of neuromodulators, and they also initiate new connections among cells during learning of new material.

Just as interacting with the environment by lifting weights can lead to bulging muscles, interacting with the environment in various ways can set your brain to operate more or less efficiently. And depending on how your brain is working, you behave differently. By regulating the brain, genes affect behavior.

It is commonplace today for scientists to stress that both genes and environment are important. This is true, but, stated in that way, it misses the mark. Genes and environment cannot really be considered as separate factors; they are instead *different aspects of a single system*. In much the same way as you can focus separately on the brushstrokes, perspective, composition, and colors of a painting, you can discuss genes and the environment as discrete entities. But, as with a painting, to appreciate the "whole picture," you must consider genes and environment together (Gottlieb, 1998).

Environment and Genes: A Two-Way Street

Genes can affect the environment, and the environment can affect the genes. Remember, we are talking about a single system here. Plomin and colleagues (1997), Scarr and McCartney (1983), and others distinguish three ways that genes and environment interact. First, <mark>passive interaction</mark> occurs when genetically shaped tendencies of parents or siblings produce an environment that is passively received by the child. An example: Parents with higher intelligence

Some songbirds learn the songs of their particular species only by hearing other birds sing them. Mello and colleagues (1992) showed that the process of learning a song begins when certain genes are turned on as the bird first hears the song, which in turn regulates the effects of other genes that actually produce the learning.

If you lift heavy weights, you will damage your arm muscles, which in turn causes the release of certain chemicals that *turn on* genes in the muscle cells. These genes then produce proteins, which build up the muscles. Dwayne (The Rock) Johnson has managed to turn on many of these genes, but all of us turn on genes in our brains when we expend mental effort.

Passive interaction: Occurs when genetically shaped tendencies of parents or siblings produce an environment that is passively received by the child.

Passive interaction

Evocative interaction

Active interaction

Men with a particular gene (for which they can be tested) are likely to become alcoholics if they drink at all (Goedde & Agarwal, 1987). Having this gene presents no downside, however, for men who obey the norms of a strict Muslim or Mormon culture, in which alcohol is forbidden. Genes are merely one element in a larger system, which includes the environment.

tend to read more, and thus have more books in the house. Given that parents with higher intelligence tend to have children with higher intelligence, this means that children with higher intelligence will tend to be born into environments with more books (Plomin, 1995). Second, **evocative (or reactive) interaction** occurs when genetically influenced characteristics draw out behaviors from other people. We might call this the "blondes have more fun" effect. Having blonde hair is (often, anyway) a genetic trait, one that can elicit varying responses. Some people react to blondes more positively than they do to brunettes. Others, however, may think blondes are less substantial people than are brunettes. Third, genes and environment interact when people deliberately choose to put themselves in specific situations and aggressively avoid others. Such **active interaction** occurs when people choose, partly based on genetic tendencies, to put themselves in situations that are comfortable for them or to avoid situations that are uncomfortable (or to modify existing situations in ways that make them comfortable for existing genetic tendencies). A timid person, for instance, may avoid loud parties and amusement parks, instead seeking out peaceful settings and quiet pastimes.

Evocative (or reactive) interaction: Occurs when genetically influenced characteristics draw out behaviors from other people.

Active interaction: Occurs when people choose, partly based on genetic tendencies, to put themselves in specific situations and to avoid others.

Behavioral genetics: The field in which researchers attempt to determine the extent to which the differences among people are due to their genes or to the environment.

Behavioral Genetics

Researchers in the field of **behavioral genetics** try to determine the extent to which the differences among people's behaviors and abilities are due to their different genetic makeups or to differences in their environments. The environment varies at different times and places, so this is a difficult question indeed. Throughout this book, we talk about the relative contributions of genes and the environment to differences in mental processes or behavior. Here we need to stress a crucial point: Any conclusions about the relative contributions of genes and environment can apply only to the specific circumstances in which they were measured. You've just seen that genes are turned on in different circumstances, and, depending on which genes are turned on in a given environment, the brain will work more or less effectively. Statements about relative contributions of genes and environments, therefore, apply only to the situation at hand and may have no bearing on different circumstances.

Heritability, Not Inheritability

Researchers in behavioral genetics focus on estimating the heritability of various characteristics, ranging from intelligence to personality, as they occur in specific environments. **Heritability** is a potentially confusing term. It does not indicate the amount of a characteristic or trait that is inherited, but rather how much of the *variability* in that characteristic in a population is due to genetics. Height in Western countries is about 90% heritable. This statement means that 90% of the variability among the heights of people in these countries is genetically determined, not that *your* height was determined 90% by your genes and 10% by your environment. In fact, the possible differences in height owing to diet may actually be greater than the differences owing to genes; but *in a specific environment* (for example, one in which diet is constant), heritability indicates the contribution of the genes to variations. If the environment were different, the heritability might be different, too.

About 90% of the *variation* in height is controlled by the genes, and thus height is about 90% heritable. Heritability estimates assume that the environment is constant; if the environment varies (perhaps by providing a better or poorer diet), environmental factors can overshadow even very high heritability.

Twin Studies: Only Shared Genes?

In **twin studies**, researchers assess the contribution of genes to variations in a trait or characteristic by comparing identical and fraternal twins. Identical twins start life when a single, fertilized egg divides in two; these twins are **monozygotic** (like many scientific terms, this comes from Greek: *monos*, meaning "single," and *zygotos*, meaning "yoked," as occurs when a sperm and egg are joined). Monozygotic twins have identical genes. In contrast, fraternal twins grow from two separate eggs that are fertilized by two different sperm; these twins are **dizygotic**. Fraternal twins share only as many genes as any other pair of brothers or sisters—on average, half. By comparing identical twins and fraternal twins, we get a good idea of the contribution of the genes, if we assume that the environment is the same for members of both sets of twins. Such studies have shown that the amount of gray matter in the brain (where neural cell bodies exist) is very similar in identical twins, which suggests that the amount of gray matter is, in part, under genetic control (Thompson et al., 2001; summarized and commented on by Plomin & Kosslyn, 2001). This similarity is particularly pronounced in the frontal lobes and in a part of the temporal lobe involved in language comprehension. So what? Well, the amount of such gray matter is correlated with scores on intelligence tests—and (as we will see in Chapter 6) identical twins tend to have similar levels of intelligence, perhaps for this reason.

Adoption Studies: Separating Genes and Environment?

An even better way to gather evidence for the relative contributions of genes and environment is to compare characteristics of children adopted at birth to those of their adoptive parents or siblings versus their biological parents or siblings. Called

Heritability: The degree to which variability in a characteristic is due to genetics.

Twin study: A study that compares identical and fraternal twins to determine the relative contribution of genes to variability in a trait or characteristic.

Monozygotic: From the same egg and having identical genes.

Dizygotic: From different eggs and sharing only as many genes as any pair of brothers or sisters—on average, half.

an **adoption study**, this type of investigation is particularly powerful when twins who have been separated at birth, or shortly thereafter, grow up in different environments. Even in these cases, however, it is difficult to separate genetic from environmental influences. If the twins are cute, for instance, caregivers in both households will treat them differently than if they seem tough and fearless; if they are smart and curious, both sets of parents may be inclined to buy books and read to them. So findings from studies of twins separated at birth are fascinating, but even they don't allow us to separate genetic from environmental effects with confidence. The most we can say is that genes contribute a certain amount to differences among people in particular environments, and that environments contribute a certain amount to such differences when people have particular genes.

Evolution and the Brain: The Best of All Possible Brains?

The loss of consciousness and brain damage suffered by the young soldier occurred because he breathed toxic fumes and was deprived of oxygen. However, not all species would be affected by that situation the way this member of our human species was. Sperm whales, for instance, do just fine if they take a breath every 75 minutes or so. Why don't our brains give us this extra protection? This question leads to thoughts about **evolution**, the gene-based changes in the characteristics of members of a species over successive generations.

Natural Selection: Reproduction of the Fittest

A major driving force of evolution is **natural selection**, which was first described in detail in 1858 by Charles Darwin and, independently, by Alfred Russel Wallace. Inherited characteristics that contribute to survival in an environment are those that will come to be widespread in a population. Why? Because the individuals with those characteristics are the ones that live long enough to have many offspring. In turn, those offspring, equipped with the favorable characteristics inherited from their parents, will survive to have more offspring. In this way, the "selection" of the survivors is made by "nature." An inherited characteristic that results from such selection is called an **adaptation**. The oft-used phrase "survival of the fittest" is perhaps unfortunate; the key point is that some characteristics lead some organisms to have more offspring, who in turn have more offspring, and so on—until their inheritable characteristics are spread throughout the population. Plomin and colleagues (1997) point out that the principle might better have been expressed as "reproduction of the fittest."

Evolution via natural selection tends to mold the characteristics of a group of organisms to the requirements of their environment. If a certain animal lives near the North Pole, those individuals with warm fur will tend to have more babies that survive, and those individuals that are white (and thus harder for predators to spot in the snow) will tend to have more babies that survive. If these characteristics are useful enough in that environment, eventually the species as a whole will have warm white fur.

Here's a contemporary analogy of the way natural selection works. There were two Chinese brothers; one settled in Louisiana and the other in Ohio. They both opened Chinese restaurants and began with identical menus. After the first month, the brother in Louisiana noticed that his blander dishes were not selling well, so he dropped them from the menu; in Ohio, they were doing fine, so they remained. In Louisiana, the chef one day accidentally knocked a jar of chili pow-

Adoption study: A study in which characteristics of children adopted at birth are compared to those of their adoptive parents or siblings versus their biological parents or siblings (often twins). These studies often focus on comparisons of twins who were raised in the same household and twins raised in different households.

Evolution: Gene-based changes in the characteristics of members of a species over successive generations.

Natural selection: Changes in the frequency of genes in a population that arise because genes allow an organism to have more offspring that survive.

Adaptation: A characteristic that increases an organism's fitness for an environment.

Figure 2.18 The Menu Model of Natural Selection

LOUISIANA   OHIO

Entrees
(all entrees served with fried rice)

Louisiana		Ohio	
Orange Chicken	5.50	Orange Chicken	5.50
Sesame Beef	5.50	Sesame Beef	5.50
Beef with Black Bean	5.50	Beef with Black Bean	5.50
Sweet & Sour Pork	6.40	Sweet & Sour Pork	6.40
~~Baked Duck~~	~~6.40~~	Baked Duck	6.40
~~Sweet & Sour Chicken~~	~~5.50~~	Sweet & Sour Chicken	5.50
Kung Pao Chicken	4.80	~~Kung Pao Chicken~~	~~4.80~~
Honey Garlic Pork	5.50	Honey Garlic Pork	5.50
Fire Shrimp	6.40	~~Fire Shrimp~~	~~6.40~~
Spicy Chicken	*5.50*	*Corn Chowder Chicken*	*4.80*
Chili Spring Rolls	*4.80*	*Egg Pasta*	*5.50*
Hunan Pork	*5.50*	*Shrimp with Snow Peas*	*5.50*

Evolution by natural selection is illustrated when accidental variations change the menus, and features of the environment (the diners' tastes, in this metaphor) "select" some of these changes. In living beings, over generations such selection results in changes in genes.

der into a pot of chicken he was simmering. He found he liked the taste, so this new dish became the special of the day. It sold so well that it became a standard on the menu. Hearing the tale, the brother up north in Ohio tried the chili dish, but it didn't sell well. This chef bought a lot of corn, which was on sale. He tried adding it to a traditional dish and called it the special of the day. The Ohio chef wasn't trying to achieve a particular taste, he was just experimenting. That corn dish did not sell well, and so was dropped. But when he added corn to another recipe, the result was an instant hit. Both chefs continued with new elements in their cooking, with varying degrees of success on different occasions. As shown in Figure 2.18, after two years, the brothers' menus had little in common.

Two important principles of evolution are illustrated here. First, the "environment"—the hungry restaurant patrons—"selected" different aspects of the menus: The diners in Louisiana, for example, apparently liked spicy food better than did those in Ohio. Second, variation is at the heart of the process. Without the accidents and substitutions, the process would not have worked—the menus would not have evolved over time. Natural selection in the evolution of the two menus depended on random variation, which provided the "options" that proved more or less adaptive.

The same is true in the evolution of species, but in this case the "menu" is the set of genes different organisms possess. Genes that lead an organism to have offspring who have still more offspring stay on the menu, and those that do not lead to this result eventually get dropped.

So, back to the question of why we humans don't have the sperm whale's ability to go without breathing for many minutes. If our ancestors had had to go for long periods without breathing in order to survive, then only those who could do so would have survived and had offspring—and we lucky descendants would have inherited this ability. And the story of our young soldier might have had a happier ending.

Not Just Natural Selection: Accidents Do Happen

A word of warning: Always exercise caution when trying to use the idea of natural selection to explain our present-day characteristics. Just because a characteristic exists doesn't mean that it is an adaptation to the environment or that it is the result of natural selection. Natural selection may or may not be the reason, for example, why some people are more prone than others to alcoholism. For one thing, as human brains and bodies evolved, the environment also changed: People created not only furniture, houses, and cities, but also automobiles, guns, computers, and candy. Our brains may not be ideally suited for what they are doing now.

Furthermore, natural selection is not the only way that evolution works. Accidents can happen. Sometimes characteristics piggyback on other characteristics. For example, *sickle-cell anemia*, a blood disease that is common among Black Americans, is an unfortunate side-effect of protection from malaria. (The gene that causes the anemia codes for a protein that destroys cells infected with the malaria-causing parasite, which is useful in the parts of Africa where malaria is common.) And sometimes characteristics appear because the original adaptation can be put to good use in a new role that has nothing to do with the original adaptation; the nose originally evolved to warm air and direct scents, but once you have one, you can use it to hold up your glasses (Gould & Lewontin, 1979). As another example, once we had the brain machinery to see lines and edges, abilities that probably helped our ancestors to discern prey, the brain could allow us to learn to read.

In short, some of our abilities, personality types, social styles, and so forth may have arisen from natural selection because they are useful, and others may have been accidental. It is not easy to sort out which is which, and we should not assume that there is a sound evolutionary reason for everything people do.

LOOKING BACK: *Review*

1. *How do genes and the environment interact as the brain develops and functions?* When the brain is developing, there are more neural connections than are later used; the process of pruning eliminates connections that are not useful. In addition, neurons grow more connections with use. The genes govern not only how neurons grow, but also how they function internally. Many genes are constantly being turned on and off, and the brain functions more or less efficiently depending on which genes are turned on and hence which proteins are produced.

2. *What does* heritability *mean?* Heritability refers to how much of the *variability* in a characteristic in a population is due to genetics—given a specific environment. A different environment might produce a different heritability.

3. *How has evolution shaped the functions of the brain?* Evolution has shaped the functions of the brain through both the process of natural selection (of characteristics that are adaptive) and accidents (including when one characteristic piggybacks on another).

Did natural selection change the human brain so that it is vulnerable to damage such as that sustained by the soldier's brain? Does it make sense that different areas of the brain are responsible for vision versus hearing and language? Which parts of the human brain would you expect to find in other animals, and why?

Can you think of any human abilities that seem likely to be adaptations? How about abilities that could be evolutionary accidents? How could you tell whether a characteristic is present because of natural selection?

LET'S SUM IT UP

You've seen ample evidence that carbon monoxide fumes damaged the soldier's brain—but exactly how? We could narrow down our explanation for his problems to the following three aspects of brain function: First, many—but not all—neurons in the occipital lobes died because of a lack of oxygen and nutrients. This damage caused him to have fuzzy vision. Second, the parietal lobes, thalamus, or some other area used in attention was also damaged so that he had a narrow range of attention and thus could not perceive the context in which a shape appeared. Hence, he only saw small details. Third, alternatively, or perhaps additionally, he only saw small details because the temporal lobe in his right hemisphere was damaged, an area that typically registers overall shapes; or, possibly, the connections to the right temporal lobe from the occipital lobes were damaged. But his left hemisphere, particularly his left frontal lobe, apparently was intact enough to allow him to make up a story based on what he saw, allowing him to try to make sense of the stimulus. Thus, he saw details in isolation and tried to think what they might be.

I. Brain Circuits: Making Connections

A. The neuron is the key building block of the brain. The cell body receives inputs from the dendrites (or, sometimes, directly from axons of other neurons) and sends its output via the axon (which is connected to the dendrites of other neurons or, in some cases, their cell bodies).

B. The axon is covered with myelin, a fatty insulating material that makes neural transmission more efficient. The axon branches into separate terminals. The terminal buttons at the end of the terminals contain chemical substances that are released by an action potential. These substances are either neurotransmitters or neuromodulators.

C. Neurotransmitters cross the synaptic cleft (the gap between the end of the axon and the receiving neuron) to affect another neuron. Neuromodulators can be released into this space, or they can be distributed more diffusely in the fluid surrounding neurons. Both neurotransmitters and neuromodulators affect receptors, which are like locks that are opened by the right key. Once opened, the receptor causes a chain of events inside the neuron.

D. Some neuromodulators are not released from terminal buttons. Endogenous cannabinoids, for example, are released by the receiving neuron and inhibit sending neurons.

E. When the total input to a neuron is sufficiently excitatory, the neuron "fires"—that is, chemical reactions work their way down the axon. After a neuron has fired, surplus neurotransmitter is reabsorbed back into the cells. Some drugs block this reuptake mechanism.

F. Glial cells not only control the creation of synapses and support neurons, but also help to regulate neurotransmitters and can affect neurons directly. Moreover, glial cells themselves may play a role in information processing.

II. The Nervous System: An Orchestra With Many Members

A. The nervous system has two major parts: the peripheral nervous system (PNS) and the central nervous system (CNS).

B. The PNS consists of the autonomic nervous system (ANS) and the sensory-somatic nervous system (SSNS). The ANS is in turn divided into the sympathetic and parasympathetic nervous systems, the first of which is critically involved in the "fight or flight" response. The SSNS includes the skeletal system, which connects to muscles that can be moved voluntarily.

C. The CNS consists of the spinal cord and the brain itself. In addition to sending commands from the brain to the body and passing along sensory input to the brain, the spinal cord is responsible for some reflexes. Reflexes depend on the action of interneurons, neurons that hook up to other neurons.

D. The brain itself is organized into lobes and is covered by the cerebral cortex, a thin layer of neurons.

E. The cerebral cortex contains many bulges (gyri) and creases (sulci), which allows a lot of cortex to be crammed into a relatively small space.

III. Spotlight on the Brain: How It Divides and Conquers

A. The four major lobes in each hemisphere are occipital, temporal, parietal, and frontal. The occipital lobe processes visual input. The temporal lobe is the seat of visual memories and is also involved in language comprehension, hearing, storing new memories, and some aspects of consciousness. The parietal lobe registers size, three-dimensionality, and location in space and is also involved in arithmetic and motor control; each parietal lobe includes part of the somatosensory strip, which registers sensation from parts of the body. The frontal lobe is involved in speech production, searching for memories, reasoning (and using memory to help in reasoning), emotions, fine motor control (governed by the motor strip), and making decisions.

B. Each lobe is duplicated, one on the left and one on the right. The left hemisphere, which plays a larger role in language, appears to be critical to the ability to invent stories to make sense of the world. The right hemisphere plays a larger role than the left in recognizing overall shapes and in some nonverbal functions.

C. Split-brain patients have had the two brain hemispheres surgically disconnected, through severing of the corpus callosum. This rare surgery is done only for medical reasons.

D. Under the cortex, many subcortical areas play crucial roles in the brain's function. The thalamus manages connections to and from distinct parts of the brain; the hypothalamus regulates hormones, which are important in controlling bodily functions such as eating, drinking, and sex; the hippocampus is involved in the storage of new memories; and the amygdala plays a role in fear and other emotions.

E. The hypothalamus, hippocampus, amygdala, and other structures constitute the limbic system, which is involved in fighting, fleeing, feeding, and sex.

F. The basal ganglia are used in planning and producing movements, as well as in learning new habits. The brainstem contains structures involved in automatic functions (such as breathing), alertness, sleep, and arousal; and the cerebellum is involved in motor control, timing, and attention.

G. The neuroendocrine system produces hormones, which not only affect the body but also affect the brain itself (by, for example, altering moods).

H. The neuroimmune system produces substances that affect our immunity to infection.

IV. Probing the Brain

A. The earliest method used to discover what the various parts of the brain do involved observing the effects of brain damage on behavior. Scientists also investigate the effects of removing parts of animal brains.

B. Scientists can record electrical activity produced by the firing of neurons while people and animals perform specific tasks, using either electrodes placed on the scalp or microelectrodes inserted in neurons; they find more vigorous activity in areas involved in the task than in those that are not involved. Researchers can also record magnetic fields produced by neurons when they fire.

C. Various neuroimaging techniques include the following: computer-assisted tomography (CT), which uses X rays to obtain images of the structures of the brain; magnetic resonance imaging (MRI), which makes use of magnetic fields to produce very sharp pictures of the brain; positron emission tomography (PET), which relies on small amounts of a radioactive substance to track blood flow or energy consumption in the brain; functional magnetic resonance imaging (fMRI), which tracks changes in oxygen level in a part of the brain as a person performs a task; and optical imaging, which measures how much light of different frequencies is reflected by the brain while a person performs a task.

D. Neurons can be electrically or magnetically stimulated (using transcranial magnetic stimulation, or TMS) to fire and the effects on behavior observed.

V. Genes, Brain, and Environment: The Brain in the World

A. Individual genes can affect the brain and behavior (via Mendelian inheritance), or sets of genes working together can have these effects (via complex inheritance). The genes lay down the basic structure of the brain, but the environment can mold both its structure and its function.

B. Genes influence how people and other animals respond to environmental effects.

C. During brain development, the environment affects brain structure and function through the pruning of connections that are not being used; it also causes the brain to form new connections in response to new stimuli.

D. The genes place limits on what is possible (for example, people can't grow wings), and even small genetic changes can sometimes exert significant effects on the brain, mental processes, and behavior.

E. However, many of your genes are under the control of the environment and are turned on and off depending on what you are doing; specific genes cause the manufacture of neurotransmitters or neuromodulators and can even cause neurons to hook up in new ways.

F. Behavioral genetics attempts to discover how much of the variability in a behavior or ability is due to the genes versus the environment, but such estimates apply only to the environment in which the behavior or ability is measured.

G. The relative contributions of genes and environment are sometimes investigated by comparing twins (identical versus fraternal) and by studying people who have been adopted.

H. We have our present sets of genes because of evolution, partly as a consequence of natural selection (genes are retained in the population when they produce characteristics that lead to more surviving offspring who in turn have surviving offspring) and partly as a consequence of accidents.

Key Terms

action potential, p. 54
active interaction, p. 88
adaptation, p. 90
adoption study, p. 90
agonist, p. 59
all-or-none law, p. 54
amygdala, p. 73
antagonist, p. 59
autonomic nervous system (ANS), p. 61
axon, p. 53
basal ganglia, p. 73
behavioral genetics, p. 88
brain circuit, p. 53
brainstem, p. 73
cell body, p. 53

cell membrane, p. 53
central nervous system (CNS), p. 63
cerebellum, p. 74
cerebral cortex, p. 64
cerebral hemisphere, p. 64
complex inheritance, p. 85
computer-assisted tomography (CT, formerly CAT), p. 81
corpus callosum, p. 64
cortisol, p. 75
dendrite, p. 54
deoxyribonucleic acid, DNA, p. 84
dizygotic, p. 89
electroencephalogram (EEG), p. 80
electroencephalograph, p. 79
endogenous cannabinoids, p. 56

estrogen, p. 75
evocative (or reactive) interaction, p. 88
evolution, p. 90
forebrain, p. 71
frontal lobe, p. 68
functional magnetic resonance imaging (fMRI), p. 82
gene, p. 84
genotype, p. 84
glial cell, p. 59
gyrus, p. 65
heritability, p. 89
hindbrain, p. 74
hippocampus, p. 72
hormone, p. 75

LOOKING ONLINE: *Enhance Your Learning*

MyPsychLab is an interactive and instructive multimedia resource that can be used to supplement a traditional lecture course or as an online course. It is an all-inclusive tool with a text-specific e-book plus multimedia tutorials, videos, simulations, animations, and controlled assessment to completely engage students and reinforce learning. MyPsychLab meets the individual learning needs of every student. Visit *www.mypsychlab.com* for more information!

Practice Test

For each of the following items, choose the single best answer.

1. A neuron that sends signals to muscles to control movement is called
   a. a brain circuit.
   b. a glial cell.
   c. an interneuron.
   d. a motor neuron.

2. Each neuron has a receiving end, a sending end, and a part in the middle. The part is the middle is called
   a. the cell body.
   b. the axon.
   c. the dendrite.
   d. the resting potential.

3. If a neuron is sufficiently stimulated, it fires, sending an action potential all the way down the axon and releasing chemicals from the terminal buttons; either the action potential occurs or it doesn't. This fact is best reflected by
   a. the shifting change in charge that moves down the axon.
   b. the loss of myelin.
   c. the all-or-none law.
   d. the resting potential.

4. How do neurons typically communicate?
   a. They don't communicate.
   b. They are always hooked up physically.
   c. They use sound waves.
   d. The axon of one neuron sends a signal to the membrane of another neuron; communication between neurons occurs in the synapse.

5. Chemical M is an agonist. What does this mean?
   a. Chemical M blocks the effect of a neurotransmitter.
   b. Chemical M mimics the effects of a neurotransmitter.
   c. Chemical M is used solely in the parts of the brain involved in visual perception.
   d. Chemical M helps produce dopamine.

6. What links the central nervous system to the organs of the body?
   a. the spinal cord
   b. the reflex
   c. the peripheral nervous system
   d. The central nervous system is not linked to the organs of the body.

7. What system usually comes into play in response to a threat in the environment, perhaps a near-accident while you are driving in heavy traffic?
   a. the sympathetic nervous system
   b. the synaptic cleft
   c. the spinal cord
   d. the parasympathetic nervous system

8. The occipital lobes are concerned entirely with
   a. processing sound, entering new information into memory, and comprehending language.
   b. different aspects of vision.
   c. registering spatial location, attention, and motor control.
   d. the somatosensory strip.

9. Many aspects of language are carried out by
   a. a single hemisphere, usually the right.
   b. both hemispheres.
   c. a single hemisphere, usually the left.
   d. the somatosensory strip.

10. What brain structure sits under the thalamus and plays a central role in controlling eating and drinking and in regulating the body's temperature, blood pressure, and heart rate?
   a. the hypothalamus
   b. the hippocampus
   c. the amygdala
   d. the basal ganglia

11. Natural experiments
   a. record the activity of normal brains.
   b. are accidents in which people suffer damage to the brain.
   c. use brain-scanning techniques that produce a picture of the structure or functioning of neurons.
   d. detect the amount of oxygen being brought to a particular place in the brain.

12. In general, when an inherited characteristic varies continuously, it reflects
   a. Mendelian inheritance.
   b. deoxyribonucleic acid.
   c. complex inheritance.
   d. pruning.

13. What statement best reflects current understanding of how genes interact with the environment?
   a. Genes don't interact with the environment; genes are destiny.
   b. Genes determine the range of what is possible, but within those limits interactions with the environment can alter both the structure and the function of the brain.
   c. Many genes stay constantly on or off.
   e. Genes and the environment can really be considered separate factors.

14. Changes in the frequency of genes in a population that arise because the genes allow an organism to have more offspring that survive are a result of
   a. acquired characteristics.
   b. monozygotic.
   c. heritability.
   d. natural selection.

15. Evolution via natural selection
   a. is the only way evolution works.
   b. is never the way evolution works.
   c. tends to mold the characteristics of a group of organisms to the requirements of its environment.
   d. means that there is a sound evolutionary reason for everything people do.

Answers: 1. d 2. a 3. c 4. d 5. b 6. c 7. a 8. b 9. c 10. a 11. b 12. c 13. b 14. d 15. c

chapter 3

Sensation and Perception

How the World Enters the Mind

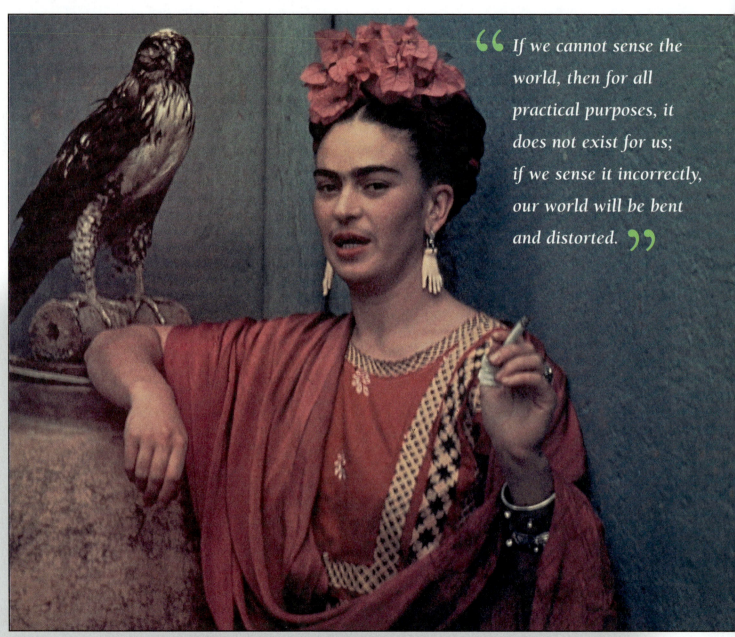

❝ *If we cannot sense the world, then for all practical purposes, it does not exist for us; if we sense it incorrectly, our world will be bent and distorted.* ❞

CHAPTER OUTLINE

THE MEXICAN PAINTER FRIDA KAHLO (1907–1954) DID NOT SIMPLY PAINT WHAT SHE saw—she painted what she felt and understood. Kahlo's style of painting is classified as *surrealist* because she took liberties in portraying what her eyes registered, distorting objects in order to reveal the feelings, desires, and longings that welled within her as she perceived the world (Lowe, 1995). Kahlo often injected her physical and emotional pain into her paintings.

As an adult, Kahlo was an old hand at managing pain. She contracted polio at the age of 6, which left her right leg thin and weak. During childhood, Kahlo embarked on an intensive program of exercise and athletics to help that leg recover its strength. When she was 18 years old, she was in a horrendous bus accident. She spent most of the next year in bed, during which time she began to paint.

Four years after the accident, Kahlo married the famed Mexican mural painter Diego Rivera. They shared passions for politics, art, music, Mexican culture, and food. Their relationship gave her great joy, but also great pain; Rivera was often unfaithful to her. They divorced, and then remarried each other about a year later.

Frida Kahlo was a person who delighted in her senses: She loved watching Rivera paint his giant murals; she enjoyed hearing the songs of street musicians in the local plaza; she reveled in the smells and tastes of Mexican food; she took pleasure in her husband's caresses. The act of sensing and perceiving stimuli of

Kahlo's label as a surrealist painter comes, in part, from her use of "X-ray" images, allowing the viewer to see what cannot normally be perceived. This painting, *The Two Fridas*, was painted in 1939 as Kahlo was getting divorced from Diego Rivera; the Frida on the left is, literally, heartbroken.

any kind, whether a song, a color-soaked canvas, or a soft caress, encompasses a remarkable series of events at the levels of the brain, the person, and the social group, all happening within the context of the physical world. The processes of sensation and perception lie at the root of our experience of being alive, serving as the foundation for most of what we know and do. If we cannot sense the world, then for all practical purposes it does not exist for us; if we sense it incorrectly, our world will be bent and distorted. To understand mental processes and behavior, therefore, we must understand how our senses allow us to make contact with the world.

Despite Kahlo's medical problems, her fundamental ability to receive and interpret the array of colors, shapes, sounds, and other sensations that whirled around her remained intact. How do our brains register that something is "out there"? And what of the other senses through which we register this amazing world—how do we smell, and hear, and taste; how are we able to be aware of our bodies? And, is there a perception beyond these—a perception that is literally "extra-sensory"—that some, if not all, of us possess? To a psychologist, the investigation of these questions provides fruitful clues in the search for knowledge of human mental processes and behavior.

Vision: Window on the World

Frida Kahlo learned new ways to see the world from her father, Guillermo Kahlo, who was a photographer and an amateur painter (Herrera, 1983). Kahlo's experiences watching her father work no doubt led her to develop skills that would later serve her in good stead, when she herself took up the brush to become a professional painter. Could such experiences literally have changed the way Kahlo saw?

LOOKING AHEAD: Learning Objectives

1. *What is sensation, and how does it differ from perception?*
2. *What is the nature of light, and how do we see color?*
3. *How are we able to separate figure from ground and see the world as a stable collection of objects?*
4. *How do we make sense of what we see?*

Phases of Vision

Vision is not accomplished in one fell swoop, but in two broad phases. First, visual sensations are evoked by an object or event. Psychologists define **sensation** as the registration of properties of an object or event that occurs when a type of receptor (such as those at the back of the eye, in the ear, on the skin) is stimulated. Sensations arise when enough physical energy strikes a sense organ, so that receptor cells send neural impulses to the brain. As discussed in Chapter 2, receptors in general are like locks, which are opened by the appropriate key; for

Sensation: The awareness of properties of an object or event that occurs when a type of receptor (such as those at the back of the eye, in the ear, on the skin) is stimulated.

sensory receptors, the appropriate physical energy or molecule serves as the key. In the study of vision, the entire cell that responds to physical stimulation is called a *receptor*, not just the parts that register the input. It is the signals sent by these receptors that cause you to become aware of the outside world. Visual sensation arises in the eye and in the parts of the brain that first register visual input.

Second, you actually perceive the stimulus; **perception** occurs when you've organized and interpreted the sensory input as signaling a particular object or event. Perception itself relies on two phases of processing (Marr, 1982; Nakayama et al., 1995):

1. *Organization into coherent units.* You don't see isolated blobs and lines, you see surfaces and objects. At the outset, you must organize patches of color, texture, edges, and other basic visual elements into coherent units, which usually correspond to surfaces and objects. As part of this process, you need to register the sizes and locations of objects.

2. *Identifying what and where.* But these surfaces and objects don't have meaning; they are just surfaces and forms. The processes that organize the input are a prelude to the final task of perception, which is to recognize and identify what you see, to realize you are seeing a house and not a hill. In addition to identifying what the object is, you need to identify where in space the object is—so you can get into your car when it's parked, but avoid cars when crossing the street.

Visual Sensation: More Than Meets the Eye

In everyday experience, you may think you have direct contact with the world—but you don't. You know the world only as it is filtered through your senses, and your senses are not always accurate. Your senses are your windows on the world, but sometimes the glass is not entirely transparent. The examples in Figure 3.1 show how far off base your perception can be.

Scientists have developed careful methods for discovering the relation between what's actually out there and what we sense and perceive; this field is known as psychophysics, and we explore its concepts and methods next.

Psychophysics: A World of Experience

Well over a hundred years ago, scientists began trying to discover the relation between the properties of events in the world and people's sensations and perceptions of them. German scientist Gustav Theodor Fechner (1801–1887) founded the field of **psychophysics**, which studies the relation between physical events and the corresponding experience of those events. Researchers in psychophysics made a series of discoveries, which apply to all the senses.

Thresholds: "Over the Top."   Have you ever wondered how far away something can be and still be seen, or how low you can turn down the sound before it

Figure 3.1 Visual Illusions

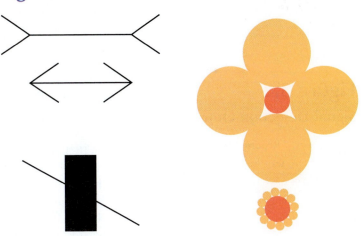

The visual system is not like a camera that accurately captures the world, as illustrated by these visual illusions. The two lines with the arrow heads and tails are in fact the same length; the diagonal line that cuts across the vertical bar is straight, not jagged; and the circles in the center of the two "flowers" are actually the same size.

Perception: The act of organizing and interpreting sensory input as signaling a particular object or event.

Psychophysics: The study of the relation between physical events and the corresponding experience of those events.

Threshold: The point at which stimulation is strong enough to be noticed.

Absolute threshold: The smallest amount of a stimulus needed in order to detect that the stimulus is present.

Just-noticeable difference (JND): The size of the difference in a stimulus property needed for the observer to notice that a change has occurred.

Weber's law: The rule that a constant percentage of a magnitude change is necessary to detect a difference.

Signal detection theory: A theory explaining why people detect signals independently of bias; the theory is based on the idea that signals are always embedded in noise, and thus the challenge is to distinguish signal from noise.

Sensitivity: In signal detection theory, the threshold level for distinguishing between a stimulus and noise; the lower the threshold, the greater the sensitivity.

Bias: In signal detection theory, a person's willingness to report noticing a stimulus.

Figure 3.2

Signal Detection Outcomes

Four types of responses are possible when a person is asked to report whether a signal was present. Signal detection theory uses the relative frequencies of these reports to compute a measure of how sensitive an observer is to a signal and a measure of how willing the observer is to report the signal.

becomes inaudible? Much as you cross a doorway when going from one room to the next, stimuli cross a **threshold** when a physical event becomes strong enough to be noticed. An **absolute threshold** is the smallest amount of a stimulus needed in order to notice that the stimulus is present at all. The absolute threshold is defined as the magnitude of the stimulus needed to make it noticeable to the observer half the time. In establishing absolute thresholds, you are distinguishing between the background and the stimulus, and the stimulus must have enough of its defining quality that you are, in fact, able to notice it. If a warning light isn't bright enough, you won't notice that it's on—which could be a serious deficiency if the light is meant to indicate that your car's radiator is about to boil over.

Sometimes you don't need simply to detect the presence of a stimulus, but rather to distinguish among stimuli. For example, suppose Kahlo were painting while the sun was setting; at what point would she notice that it had gotten darker in the room, and she should either adjust the way she was painting patterns of light or call it quits for the day? A **just-noticeable difference (JND)** is the size of the difference in a stimulus property (such as the brightness of light) needed for the observer to notice a difference. A JND is a kind of threshold. The change in light level might be so slight that sometimes you notice it, and sometimes you don't. This change would be defined as a JND if you noticed the difference half the time.

The size of a JND depends on the overall magnitude of the stimulus. If you are a thin person, a weight gain of 5 pounds would probably be noticeable at a glance, but if you are on the hefty side, a 5-pound gain might not be detected by anyone but you. Similarly, turning up the light the same amount is much more noticeable when the dimmer starts at a low setting than when it starts at a high setting. Why is this? Psychophysicists have an answer. **Weber's law** (named after another German researcher, Ernst Weber) states that a constant percentage of a magnitude change is necessary to detect a difference. So, the greater the magnitude of the light (or the thickness of the waist, or the volume of the sound), the greater the extra amount must be to be noticed. Weber's law is remarkably accurate except for very large or very small magnitudes of stimuli.

Detecting Signals: Noticing Needles in Haystacks. In World War II, radar operators sometimes "saw" airplanes that did not exist and sometimes missed airplanes that did. The simple fact that people make these kinds of errors led to a new way of thinking about thresholds. **Signal detection theory** seeks to explain why people detect signals in some situations but miss them in others. The key idea is that signals are always embedded in noise, and thus the challenge is to distinguish signal from noise. Noise, in this case, refers to other events that could be mistaken for the stimulus. Two key concepts explain how signals are detected or missed: sensitivity and bias. Greater **sensitivity** means a lower threshold for distinguishing between a stimulus (the "signal") and the background (the "noise"). For example, on a radar screen, the signal dots indicating enemy aircraft would not need to be very large or bright compared with the noise composed of random-appearing specks. **Bias** is the willingness to report noticing a stimulus (such as the willingness of a radar operator to risk identifying random specks as aircraft). You change your bias by adjusting your *criterion*—how strong the signal needs to be before you say you've detected it. Sensitivity and bias can be assessed by comparing the occasions when people *say* a stimulus is or is not present with the occasions when the stimulus is *in fact* present or not (Figure 3.2; Busemeyer, 2004; Green & Swets, 1966; MacDonald & Balakrishnan, in press).

How Do Objects Enter the Mind?
Let There Be Light

What is the bridge from objects in the world to images in the mind (the connection between the "physics" and "psycho" of visual psychophysics)? The Greek philosopher Plato, who some 2,400 years ago theorized about many aspects of existence, psychological and otherwise, offered an interesting explanation of how humans see. Plato believed that the eyes produce rays that illuminate objects and that these rays are the basis of sight. Plato was no fool, and he was reasoning based on what he perceived. He isn't the only intelligent person to come to the wrong conclusions based on observable facts: Surveys of college students reveal that a surprisingly high proportion of them—fully one third—believe the same thing! The percentage of students accepting this explanation actually doubled (to 67%) when participants were shown a computer-graphic illustration of the concept (Winer & Cottrell, 1996; Winer et al., 1996). Furthermore, two thirds of the college students who believe in such rays also believe that a person whose rays fail will go blind (Winer et al., 1996). These misconceptions are remarkably difficult to change (Gregg et al., 2001; Winer et al., 2002, 2003).

To set the record straight, there are no rays that shine from your eyes; in fact, the process works the other way. Rather than producing rays, the eye registers light that is reflected from, or is produced by, objects in the line of sight. Similarly, the ear registers vibrations of air, and the skin responds to an object when pressure from it stimulates nerves.

Light is a form of electromagnetic radiation. All of us swim in a sea of electromagnetic radiation. This sea has waves: some large, some small, some that come in rapid succession, some spaced far apart. The height of a wave is its **amplitude**, and the number of waves arriving each second is the **frequency**. With higher frequency, the peaks of the waves arrive more often. When more peaks arrive per second, there is less distance between them, and hence the light is said to have a shorter **wavelength**. The distance between waves is measured in *nanometers*, or millionths of a meter. In the electromagnetic spectrum, which ranges from the terrifically long alternating currents and radio waves to the very short gamma rays and X rays, there is a narrow band of radiation perceived as visible light. An almost uncountable number of colors are conveyed in this light; the traditional seven we readily distinguish are red, orange, yellow, green, blue, indigo, and violet. The lower frequencies (and longer wavelengths—more nanometers) are toward the red end of the spectrum; the higher frequencies (and shorter wavelengths) are toward the violet end, as illustrated in Figure 3.3, which also illustrates the properties of light.

Christopher Columbus had an intuitive grasp of signal detection theory. He offered a reward to the first sailor to spot land, but then sailors started mistaking low clouds for land. The reward not only increased sensitivity, but lowered the criterion. To adjust the criterion, Columbus announced that sailors who made false sightings would forfeit the reward. Columbus applied this higher criterion to himself and didn't wake the crew on the night he first saw a glimmer of light on a distant island.

Figure 3.3 The Range of Electromagnetic Radiation

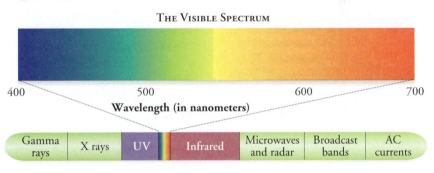

Note that only a small portion of the range comprises visible light and that the hue depends on the wavelength.

Amplitude: The height of the peaks in a light wave.

Frequency: The number of waves per second that move past a given point.

Wavelength: The distance between the arrival of peaks of a light wave (measured in nanometers); shorter wavelengths correspond to higher frequencies.

Figure 3.4 Anatomy of the Eye

The many parts of the eye either focus an image on the retina or convert light into neural impulses that are sent to the brain.

Transduction: The process whereby physical energy is converted by a sensory neuron into neural impulses.

Pupil: The opening in the eye through which light passes.

Iris: The circular muscle that adjusts the size of the pupil.

Cornea: The transparent covering over the eye, which serves partly to focus the light onto the back of the eye.

Accommodation: Occurs when muscles adjust the shape of the lens so that it focuses light on the retina from objects at different distances.

Retina: A sheet of tissue at the back of the eye containing cells that convert light to neural impulses.

Fovea: The small, central region of the retina with the highest density of cones and the highest resolution.

Rods: Rod-shaped retinal cells that are very sensitive to light but register only shades of gray.

Cones: Cone-shaped retinal cells that respond most strongly to one of three wavelengths of light; the combined outputs from cones that are most sensitive to different wavelengths play a key role in producing color vision.

Optic nerve: The large bundle of nerve fibers carrying impulses from the retina into the brain.

The Brain's Eye: More Than a Camera

The eye converts the electromagnetic energy that is light into nerve impulses; this conversion process is called **transduction**. Light enters the eye through an opening called the **pupil**; see Figure 3.4. Surrounding the pupil is a circular muscle called the **iris**. The iris changes the size of the pupil to let in more or less light. The light is focused mostly by the **cornea**, the transparent covering over the iris and pupil, and then focused even more by the lens. Unlike a camera lens, the lens in a human eye flexes. In fact, muscles can adjust the lens into a more or less round shape to focus light from objects that are different distances away. **Accommodation**, the automatic adjustment of the eye for seeing at particular distances, occurs when muscles change the shape of the lens so that it focuses light on the retina from near or far away objects. The world appears sharp and clear because we are constantly moving our eyes, and what we choose to look at can quickly be brought into focus. With age, the lens thickens and becomes less flexible (Fatt & Weissman, 1992), often causing older people to have trouble seeing nearer objects, such as reading material.

Transduction: From Photons to Neurons. The critical step in the transduction process occurs at the **retina**, a sheet of tissue at the back of the eye that is about as thick as a piece of paper (Wässle, 2004). The central part of the retina contains densely packed cells that transform light to nerve impulses, and this region—called the **fovea**—gives us the sharpest images. We are not usually aware of how fuzzy our world looks. Most of the time we notice only the images that strike the fovea, which are sharp and clear, but much of what we see is, in fact, not very sharply focused. Take a moment to look up and focus on a single spot on the other side of the room; don't move your eyes, and notice how blurry things look even a short distance to either side of that spot.

Two kinds of cells in the retina are particularly important for converting light to nerve impulses: rods and cones. Oddly, as shown in Figure 3.5, these cells are at the very back of the eye, which requires light to pass through various other types of cells to reach them. **Rods** (which actually look like little rods) are extraordinarily sensitive to light, but they only allow us to see shades of gray. Each eye contains between 100 million and 120 million rods. The **cones** (which look like, yes, cones) are not as sensitive to light as are the rods, but each of the three types of cones responds most vigorously to a particular wavelength of light, which allows us to see color. Each eye contains between 5 million and 6 million cones (Beatty, 1995; Dowling, 1992). The cones are densest near the fovea, and the rods are everywhere within the retina except in the fovea. In very dim light, there isn't enough light for the less light-sensitive cones to work, so night vision is based on the firing of the rods alone. That is why a red apple looks black and an orange cat looks gray under a moonlit night sky.

The axons from retinal cells in each eye are gathered into a single large cord called the **optic nerve**, which is about as thick as your little finger. There are no rods or cones at the place where the optic nerve exits the retina, which causes a *blind spot* in what you can see laid out in front of you. Because the brain completes patterns that fall across this blind spot, you are not aware of it as you look around every day. Look at Figure 3.6, though, and you can "see" where your blind spot is.

Dark Adaptation.   When you first enter a darkened theater, you can't see a thing. You may have noticed, though, that the risk of tripping or bumping into someone is a lot less if you wait even a brief time, because you soon can see much better. In fact, after about 30 minutes in the dark, you are about 100,000 times more sensitive to light than you are during full daylight. In ideal conditions, the rods can respond when they receive a single photon, the smallest unit of light. This process is called <mark>dark adaptation</mark>. Part of the increased sensitivity to what light there is arises because your pupil enlarges when you are in darkness; in fact, it can expand to let in about 16 times as much light as enters in full daylight. In addition, the rods actually become more sensitive as your eyes remain in the dark because your genes cause the production of a crucial chemical, called *rhodopsin*, that responds to light. Here's a hint: Because of the way the rods are arranged on the retina, if you want to see best at night, look slightly to the side of what you want to examine.

More Than Rods and Cones.   Researchers have known about rods and cones for well over 100 years, but only recently have they discovered evidence for a third kind of receptor in the eye that also registers light. Freedman and her colleagues (1999) observed that even mice whose eyes had no rods or cones still shifted their *circadian behavior* when light was shined on them. Circadian behavior is behavior that follows the daily pattern of light, such as waking and sleeping; in this case, the behavior was running, which in these mice varied depending on the time of day. But when the eyes were removed, the mice no longer adjusted their "running schedule" to the amount of light. Thus, the third kind of light-sensitive receptor must be in the eyes. Lucas and his colleagues (1999) investigated the decrease in production of a hormone called *melatonin* in the presence of light (melatonin is the hormone that some people take as a supplement to overcome jet lag). Even mice without rods or cones showed a normal decrease in melatonin production when placed in light. Clearly, light affects the brain even when there are no rod or cone sensory cells. And, in fact, Berson and colleagues (2002) found that certain *ganglion cells* (which also function as a kind of gathering station for input from rods and cones) in the retina respond to illumination in just the right ways to explain the observed effects of light on behavior. Thus, rods and cones are not the whole story: We have not two, but three kinds of cells that transduce light into neural impulses.

Color Vision: Mixing and Matching

How can you tell whether an apple is ripe? One way is to look at its color. Color also plays a key role in our appreciation of beauty in art, nature, and people. Kahlo associated certain colors with objects or feelings; for instance, she associated yellow with madness, sickness, and fear, and a reddish purple with liveliness (Herrera,

Figure 3.5 **Rods and Cones**

Cones — — Rods

Back of eyeball

Light

Nerve impulses to the brain

Two types of cells in the retina convert light into nerve impulses that produce visual sensations. The rods allow us to see with less light, but not in color; the cones allow us to see colors but are not as light-sensitive as the rods.

Figure 3.6 **Finding Your Blind Spot**

 X

Cover your left eye and stare at the X with your right eye. Now slowly bring the book closer to you, continuing to focus on the X. When the picture on the right disappears, you have found your right eye's blind spot.

Dark adaptation: The process whereby exposure to darkness causes the eyes to become more sensitive, allowing for better vision in the dark.

Trichromatic theory of color vision: The theory that color vision arises from the combinations of neural impulses from three different kinds of sensors, each of which responds maximally to a different wavelength.

1983). Color is not just a "luxury feature" of vision; for one thing, color helps us make the fundamental distinction between shadows that are cast by objects versus variations in how light is reflected from objects (Kingdom et al., 2004).

One of the remarkable aspects of human vision, which makes painting and appreciation of painting such rich experiences, is the huge range of colors that people can use and see. Indeed, colors vary in three separate ways.

- *Hue.* As noted earlier when we considered the electromagnetic spectrum, different wavelengths of light produce sensations of different colors. This aspect of color—whether it looks red, blue, and so on—is called *hue*.

- *Saturation.* The purity of the input (the amount of white that's mixed in with the color) produces the perception of *saturation*, that is, how deep the color appears.

- *Lightness.* The amplitude of the light waves produces the perception of *lightness* or (if the object, such as a TV or computer screen, produces light) *brightness*—how much light is present.

Different combinations of values on these three dimensions produce the incredibly rich palette of human color vision, which is more varied than that used by any painter. Given the large number of ways that color can vary, you might think that complicated processes underlie our ability to see these visual properties—and you would be right. Color arises through the operation of two distinct types of processes.

Color Mixing. At one point in the study of color vision, there was a debate about how humans can see such a large range of colors. One camp took its lead from observations reported by Thomas Young and Hermann von Helmholtz in the 19th century. This approach focused on phenomena such as the mixing of colors to produce new colors (for example, mixing yellow and blue paint produces green). These researchers, arguing by analogy, believed that the brain registers color by combining responses to separate wavelengths. In particular, they argued that the eye contains three kinds of color sensors, each most sensitive to a particular range of wavelengths: long, medium, and short. This view was therefore called the **trichromatic theory of color vision**.

This theory turns out to be essentially correct, but it describes processing at only some places in the eye and brain. Consistent with trichromatic theory, our perception of hue arises because most of us possess three different types of cones. One type of cone is most responsive to light in the wavelength seen as a shade of yellowish red, another to light in the wavelength seen as green, and another to light in the wavelength seen as bluish violet (Reid, 1999). The trick is that at least two of the three types of cones usually respond to any wavelength of visible light, but to different degrees (De Valois & De Valois, 1975, 1993). And here's the important part: The *mixture* of the three types of response signals is different for each of a huge range of wavelengths, and it is this mixture that is the crucial signal to the brain. The brain responds to the mixture, not the outputs from individual cones. Color television operates on this principle. Stare very closely at a color TV screen, and you will see little bubbles of three colors. Stand back, and a wide range of colors appears. Why? Because your eyes and your brain respond differently, depending on the mixture of wavelengths produced by clusters of these bubbles.

As if this weren't complicated enough, there's one more twist we must discuss, which concerns the difference between what you see on a TV screen versus what you see when you mix paints (see Figure 3.7). On the one hand, when you look at

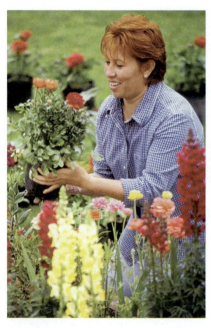

Genetic research has shown that some women possess not three, but four types of cones. As you might expect, these women see color differently from the rest of us. For example, they see more bands in a rainbow than people who have only three sorts of cones (Jameson et al., 2001). These differences in color vision arise from the same sort of mixing that underlies trichromatic theory, and thus the key ideas of that theory are correct even if—for some people—outputs from an additional type of cone are thrown into the mix.

a TV screen, each of the different wavelengths directly affects your cones. Thus, if red, green, and blue are mixed in an image, stimulating all your cones, you will see white. In this case, the hues of each contributing color are *added* together. On the other hand, when you see paints, you see the light that is *reflected* from the paints—and not all the light may be reflected. What you see is what is not *absorbed* by the paints; a yellow paint, for example, absorbs all wavelengths except that underlying our perception of yellow. This wavelength is reflected, not absorbed, and so it reaches your eyes. When you mix paints, the wavelengths absorbed by each type of paint contribute to what is absorbed by the mixture. So if you mixed red, green, and blue you would see black: The combination of paints absorbs all the visible wavelengths that give rise to the perception of hue. In this case, the hues of each contributing color are *subtracted* from the end result.

A Color Tug-of-War?   The other camp in the debate about how we see hue followed the lead of German physician Ewald Hering, who worked at the end of the 19th century and the beginning of the 20th. Hering noticed that some colors cannot be mixed: You can't make reddish green (it becomes mud) or yellowish blue (it becomes green). This and similar observations led Hering to develop the ==opponent process theory of color vision==, which states that the presence of one color of certain pairs (red/green, yellow/blue, and black/white) inhibits the perception of the other color.

And, in fact, researchers discovered that the mixtures of responses of the cones is not the whole story of color vision. If this were all there were to it, we should be able to see all mixtures of colors—but, as Hering originally observed, we can't. As the opponent process theory predicts, there's another factor at work, which will become apparent when you take a look at the strangely colored flag in Figure 3.8. Stare at the flag, and then look at the space to its right; you should see an ==afterimage==, an image left behind by a previous perception. Furthermore, the flag should look normal in the afterimage, not strangely colored as it is printed on the page. Why are the colors of afterimages different from those of the object? You need to understand more about color vision to answer that question. A key fact is that the cones feed into special types of cells in the retina and the lateral geniculate nucleus of the brain (part of the thalamus): red/green, yellow/blue, and black/white ==opponent cells==. These cells are set up to pit the colors in each pair against each other: When you gaze at a lovely green lime, for example, your opponent cells are making it difficult for you to see the red of a delicious apple. This is the sort of effect Hering predicted, and his ideas have since been developed in more detail (Hurvich & Jameson, 1957; Nayatani, 2001, 2003). This opponent process helps you to distinguish among colors that have similar wavelengths, such as green and yellow.

Figure 3.7 Mixing Color

EMITTED LIGHT   REFLECTED LIGHT

The results of mixing color depend on whether the light being perceived is emitted or reflected. When the light is emitted, from a TV screen, for example, the wavelengths of each contributing hue are added; when the light is reflected, the wavelengths of each contributing hue are subtracted.

Figure 3.8 Seeing Afterimages

Does this flag look strange to you? Stare at the dot in the center for about 60 seconds in a bright light, and then look at the blank space. You should see a brilliant afterimage of Old Glory, with red and white stripes and a blue field.

==**Opponent process theory of color vision:**== The theory that if a color is present, it causes cells that register it to inhibit the perception of the complementary color (such as red versus green).

Afterimage: The image left behind by a previous perception.

Opponent cells: Cells that pit the colors in a pair, most notably blue/yellow or red/green, against each other.

This mechanism explains why you can't see greenish red or yellowish blue: Seeing one member of a pair inhibits seeing the other. It also explains why you see afterimages like the one illustrated by staring at Figure 3.8. An afterimage occurs when one member of a pair of opponent cells inhibits the other (for example, green inhibits red) and then releases it. In the process, the previously inhibited hue (red) temporarily overshoots the mark, creating an afterimage. Think of this like a jack-in-the-box: The head is stuffed into the box (which is like one color being inhibited by its opponent color), and when the box is opened, the head springs up higher than its resting height (which is like the inhibited color over-responding when released by its opponent color).

Color Blindness. People who have <mark>color blindness</mark> are either unable to distinguish two or more hues from each other (while still being able to distinguish among other hues) or, in more serious cases, unable to see hue at all. Most color blindness is present from birth. Depending on the specific group, as many as 8% of European men but less than 0.5% of European women are born color-blind (Reid, 1999). Rather than being completely insensitive to hue, most color-blind people are unable to distinguish red from green. Researchers have found that people with the most common type of color blindness possess genes that produce similar pigments in their cones (Neitz et al., 1996), and thus the cones do not respond to wavelengths as they should—leading two hues to appear the same. A small number of people (roughly 2% of males, and a very small number of females) are actually missing a type of cone. Even more severe deficits occur when more than one type of cone is affected (Reid, 1999). Researchers have identified specific genes that lead to color blindness (Tanabe et al., 2001) and have even shown that specific genes only cause color blindness when they appear in specific places on a chromosome (Hayashi et al., 2001).

Some people only become color blind after a particular part of their brains is damaged. In Oliver Sacks's book *An Anthropologist on Mars* (1995), a color-blind artist describes how hard it is for him to eat certain foods, particularly red foods (such as apples and tomatoes), which appear to him to be a repulsive deep black. Nevertheless, in spite of not being able to experience color, at least some of these unfortunate people can still use wavelength variation to track moving objects and even to see shape; this remarkable ability appears to arise from the functioning of the color-opponent system (Cole et al., 2003).

People with normal color vision see the crayons as shown on the left. People with the most common form of color blindness—inability to distinguish red from green—would see the crayons as shown on the right. Before traffic lights were standardized so that red is always on the top, not being able to see colors made driving hazardous for people with red/green color blindness. In what other ways would such a disorder affect your life?

Color blindness: An inability, either acquired (by brain damage) or inherited, to perceive certain hues.

Phase 1 of Visual Perception: Organizing the World

Although it seems that we perceive what we see in, literally, the blink of an eye, a large number of mental steps actually occur between the moment a pattern of light strikes your eyes and the time you recognize and identify an object. At each step, different areas of the brain are crucial (Connor, 2002; Grill-Spector et al., 1998; Husain & Jackson, 2001; Olson, 2001; Sheinberg & Logothetis, 2001). We can divide the steps of visual perception into two phases (Treue, 2003). In Phase 1, the outputs from sensory processing are organized; in Phase 2, these organized units are recognized and identified. In this section, we consider Phase 1, the first step of visual perception after a stimulus has been sensed.

Take a glance at Figure 3.9. You have no trouble seeing the sailboats, the buildings, and so forth. Now take a closer look. Like pictures in a comic book, this painting is composed entirely of colored dots; no lines indicate the edges of objects or their parts. Nevertheless, you see separate objects and their parts. How? You effortlessly and unconsciously group the dots into patterns. In fact, this sort of processing is the first step of all visual perception; the edges of most objects are not specified by continuous sharp lines that set the object apart, as in a line drawing. Instead, just as you group the dots in the painting, you group the outputs from sensory processes (Marr, 1982; Nakayama et al., 1995). A crucial goal of this processing is to separate figure from ground. The **figure** is a set of characteristics (such as shape, color, and texture) that corresponds to an object, whereas the **ground** is the background, which must be distinguished in order to pick out any figure. When figure and ground are similar, the figure is said to be *camouflaged*. Animals in the desert and jungle, as well as armies the world over, have long taken advantage of this property of the perceptual system.

Perceptual Organization: Seeing the Forest Through the Trees

Separating figure from ground involves organizing regions into shapes that are likely to correspond to objects or their parts. A critical part of this process is taking fragmentary outputs from sensory processing and organizing them into edges. David H. Hubel and Torsten N. Wiesel received the Nobel Prize in 1981 for discovering that neurons in the first part of the cortex to process visual input (the *primary visual cortex*, in the occipital lobe) are arranged into columns, and the neurons in each column fire selectively to sections of edges that have a specific orientation. These columns are in turn arranged into sets that are driven by input from either the left eye or the right eye, and these sets are arranged into a *hypercolumn*. The neurons in each hypercolumn respond to input from a single spot on the retina (Hubel &

Can you see which animals are present? The coloring of the horses blends nicely with the background. Why might animals look like their surroundings?

Figure 3.9 Inserting Edges

Even though this painting has no lines indicating the edges of objects and their parts, we readily see them. Why? Because we organize the elements—colored dots, in this case—into perceptual groups.

Figure: In perception, a set of characteristics (such as shape, color, texture) that corresponds to an object.

Ground: In perception, the background, which must be distinguished in order to pick out figures.

Tootell and colleagues (1982) produced this remarkable illustration of topographic organization in the monkey brain. The animal looked at the figure on the left while radioactive sugar was being ingested by the brain cells. The dark lines on the right show which brain cells in the primary visual cortex were working hardest when the animal viewed the figure (shown here is the left-hemisphere area, which processed the right side of the display). The spatial structure of the figure is evident on the surface of the brain.

Wiesel, 1962, 1974). In addition, hypercolumns in the visual areas of the occipital lobe are *topographically organized*—that is, the pattern falling on the retina is spatially laid out on the cortex (Engel et al., 1997; Tootell et al., 1982). This arrangement helps the brain to delineate the edges of objects.

Gestalt Laws of Organization. We often view objects when they are partly covered by other objects. (Look around the room right now: What do you actually see?) Nevertheless, even when you view an object behind a bush, you don't see isolated lines, dots, and so on, but rather overall patterns. How are fragments of edges and other visual features (such as patches of color) forged into patterns? Gestalt psychologists, who were introduced briefly in Chapter 1, discovered a set of laws that describe how the brain organizes the input from the eyes (Koffka, 1935; Wertheimer, 1923). The most important of these **Gestalt laws of organization** follow:

- *Proximity*: Marks that are near one another tend to be grouped together. So, for example, we see XXX XXX as two groups and XX XX XX as three groups, even though both sets have the same total number of X marks.
- *Continuity* (also called *good continuation*): Marks that fall along a smooth curve or a straight line tend to be grouped together. So, for example, we see _ _ _ _ as a single line, not four separate dashes; and we see _ _ _ _ - - - - as two separate lines because all eight of the dashes do not fall on the same plane.
- *Similarity*: Marks that look alike tend to be grouped together. So, for example, we see XXXxxx as two groups. Whether the elements are the same or different colors also affects similarity; this is another reason color vision is so important.
- *Closure*: We tend to close any gaps in a figure, so a circle with a small section missing will still be seen as a circle.
- *Good Form*: Marks that form a single shape tend to be grouped together. So, for example, we see [ ] as a single shape, but not [_ .

Figure 3.10 Ambiguous Figures

In the left panel, you can see either two silhouetted faces or a vase, depending on what you pay attention to as the figure; in the right panel, you can see an old or a young woman, depending on how you organize the figure.

Gestalt laws of organization: A set of rules describing the circumstances—such as proximity, good continuation, similarity, closure, and good form—under which marks will be grouped into perceptual units.

Ambiguous Figures. Sometimes a figure can be organized and perceived in more than one way. Figure 3.10 shows two classic *ambiguous figures*. As these figures show, sometimes you can voluntarily organize visual patterns in different ways. But, even when you organize such patterns automatically, you organize them not only on the basis of their physical properties but also as a result of learning. For example, have you ever thought about becoming a professional "chicken sexer"? Before you dismiss this possible career path out of hand, consider the fact that even during the Great Depression members of this profession prospered. Why? Chicken farmers didn't want to send female chickens to be cooked in someone's pot—they were for laying eggs. It was the males who were sent to market. However, just looking at the pattern of bumps and indentations on a baby chick's bottom, it's very difficult to distinguish a male from a female. Traditionally, experts required years of practice before they could make this distinction accurately. Biederman and Shiffrar (1987) analyzed the problem and were able to teach people to make the discrimination by observing whether a particular part of the chick's bottom was convex versus concave or flat. However, even after training, these participants were not the same as the experts. The participants in the study had to look carefully and think about exactly what they were trying to do. Experts can identify a chick's sex with extraordinary accuracy after glancing at the chick for half a second, without even being aware of what they are doing. After extensive practice, the visual system becomes tuned so that you can automatically organize what you see in a new way (Crist et al., 2001; Olson & Chun, 2002; Vuilleumier & Sagiv, 2001).

Perceptual Constancies: Stabilizing the World

Imagine strapping a camera onto your head and making a videotape as you walk. What do you think the pictures would look like? The images striking your eyes change wildly depending on your viewpoint, but the objective world you relate to seems stable. Objects in the world appear to keep their shapes, their sizes, their colors, and so on, even when you view them in very different positions or circumstances. **Perceptual constancy** is the perception of the characteristics of objects (such as their shapes and colors) as the same even though the sensory information striking the eyes changes.

- **Size constancy** occurs when you see an object (such as a car) as the same actual size even when it is at different distances, so that its image (as in a photograph) has different sizes. Because Kahlo did not strive to paint things as they actually appear, she did not always try to convey size constancy.

- **Shape constancy** occurs when you see an object as the same shape, even when you view it from different angles (again, so that its image in a photograph would be different). This stabilization occurs not in the eyes, but in the brain, and is fundamental to the ability to recognize objects and know how to interact with them.

- **Color constancy** occurs when you see colors as constant (green as green, red as red, and so on) even when the lighting changes. When Kahlo painted in her studio or bedroom, the lighting conditions were different than they are in a gallery (perhaps the light bounced off green foliage in one setting but not the other). Nevertheless, the painting will appear to have the same colors in the different conditions. Color constancy arises in part because of experience; when monkeys are raised in light of only a single hue, their color constancy is later severely impaired (Sugita, 2004). Color constancy may occur because we see the lightest thing in a scene as white and everything else relative to that color (Land, 1959, 1977, 1983).

Knowing the Distance

Because the world is three-dimensional, we need to register distances; this is necessary to appreciate how parts of an object are arranged, as well as to reach for things and navigate among them properly. This requirement poses an interesting problem: Our eyes project images onto the two-dimensional surface of our retinas, but we need to see objects in three dimensions. Given that our eyes capture images in only two dimensions, how is it that we see in three? Once again, the an-

Perceptual constancy: The perception of characteristics that occurs when an object or quality (such as shape or color) looks the same even though the sensory information striking the eyes changes.

Size constancy: Seeing an object as being the same size when viewed at different distances.

Shape constancy: Seeing objects as having the same shape even when the image on the retina changes.

Color constancy: Seeing objects as having the same color in different viewing situations.

Notice the relative sizes and spacing of the bricks in this example of a texture gradient, one cue that the street is receding into the distance.

swer lies with the brain, which uses different types of cues to derive three dimensions from the two-dimensional images on the retinas.

Static Cues. Static ("unmoving") information plays a large role in allowing us to determine how far away something is. **Binocular cues** arise from both eyes working together. Because your eyes are separated, they need to cross in order to focus on an object (so that the same image appears on the central, high-resolution fovea in each eye). The degree to which you cross your eyes is called **convergence**, and this is one cue you use to determine distance—the more crossed your eyes, the closer the object; for example, hold a finger 2 inches from your eyes and notice how crossed they are, and compare this to when you hold your finger at arm's length. In addition, your brain uses slight differences in the images striking each of your eyes to assess the distance of an object. When you cross your eyes to focus on an object, the images of other objects—those in front of or behind the one you are focused on—fall on slightly different parts of the retinas of the two eyes. This difference between the images on the two eyes is called **retinal disparity** (also called *binocular disparity*), and the brain uses the amount of disparity to determine which objects are in front of and which are behind others (Julesz, 1971; Pinker, 1997, pp. 220–233). Retinal disparity also provides information when objects are off to the side, and you are fixated elsewhere. This cue only works up to about 10 feet; after that, the disparity is too small for the brain to detect.

Monocular (or "one-eyed") **static cues** for distance can be picked up with one eye and operate even for far distances. Monocular static cues are used effectively by artists (even surrealists such as Frida Kahlo) to create the illusion of distance. One of these cues is the **texture gradient**, a progressive change in the texture of an object. Gibson (1966) described the way texture gradients signal distance. Look at the brick street in the photograph (or, for that matter, such a street in reality). The bricks that are closer to you, the observer, give rise to larger images (they are larger in the photograph), and you use this cue to determine distance.

In drawing pictures, artists also use *linear perspective*, or *foreshortening*, making the parts of objects that are farther away from the viewer smaller on the paper. Artists also use *atmospheric perspective* to convey distance, taking advantage of the fact that vapor and dust in the air scatter the light, which makes far objects look hazy. You also infer distance if one object partially covers another, indicating that the obscured object is behind the other and thus farther away; this relation is called an *occlusion cue*. And if the base of an object appears higher on the horizon than the base of another object, you take that as a cue that the higher one is farther away. Figure 3.11 provides a good example of the power of these monocular cues.

However, the way such cues are depicted in drawings sometimes relies on cultural conventions, which must be learned (Leibowitz, 1971). For instance, in some rural parts of Africa, children's books are very rare, and thus it is not surprising that young children in such areas may not initially understand all depth and perspective cues in drawings (Liddell, 1997). These children sometimes describe shading cues on faces as blemishes, and they may say that trees are on top of a house when the trees are drawn off in the distance, behind the house (Liddell, 1997). The actual drawing cues are ambiguous, and only after learning the conventions can you know what they are supposed to convey. Such problems in interpretation disappear with age, education, and experience. A number of cross-cultural studies have shown that people must learn how to interpret some cues in drawings (Crago & Crago, 1983; Duncan et al., 1973; Liddell, 1997; Nodelmann, 1988).

Binocular cues: Cues to the distance of an object that arise from both eyes working together.

Convergence: The degree to which the eyes are crossed when a person fixates on an object.

Retinal disparity (also called binocular disparity): The difference between the images striking the retinas of the two eyes.

Monocular static cues: Information that specifies the distance of an object that can be picked up with one eye without movement of the object or eye.

Texture gradient: Progressive change in texture that signals distance.

Motion Cues. **Motion cues** specify the distance of an object on the basis of its movement, and these cues work as well with one eye as with two. In fact, motion cues are so effective that Wesley Walker, blind in one eye from birth, could catch a football well enough to be the star wide receiver for the New York Jets football team (in fact, he played for them for 13 years). To notice a motion cue, try this: Hold up this book and move your head back and forth as you look at it. Note how the images of objects behind the book seem to shift. As you shift your head to the left, the distant objects seem to move to the left; as you shift to the right, they shift to the right. Now focus on the background, still holding the book, and move your head back and forth; note how the image of the book seems to shift. This time the object you aren't focusing on, the book, seems to shift in the opposite direction to the way you move your head! Objects closer than the one on which you are fixated on seem to move in the opposite direction to your movements, whereas those farther away than the fixation point seem to move in the same direction. And, depending on the distance, the objects will seem to shift at different speeds. This difference in shifting provides information about relative distance, a cue called *motion parallax*. Motion parallax is particularly important when you are moving, and thus it is unfortunate that alcohol intoxication disrupts the brain mechanisms for this sort of depth perception; at least some alcohol-related driving accidents may be traced to this problem (Nawrot et al., 2004).

Detecting Movement: Changing Places. Motion not only helps you perceive depth, but also signals that an object is changing position relative to you—and as any driver or pedestrian will tell you, perceiving an object's movements is important in its own right. You use several types of cues to perceive movement. For example, if you are moving directly toward an object, it seems to expand symmetrically around its center and thus loom closer. Likewise, if you are moving toward its right side, that side will loom closer than the other. When silent movies were first shown to the public, the movement of an on-screen train rushing toward viewers was so startling that many moviegoers panicked and fled the theaters (Seuling, 1976). Only after they had experienced watching moving objects on a screen could they distinguish between the usual motion cues and the bogus cues in films (which are a kind of illusion called the *phi phenomenon*; see Figure 3.12 on p. 114), and be able to relax and enjoy the show. Such learning was necessary because these cues are ordinarily so important. In fact, neuroimaging research with humans has revealed that special areas in the brain detect this kind of motion (Tootell et al., 1997; Zeki, 1978, 1993). Also, studies of brain-damaged patients have documented the role of particular brain areas for processing motion. For example, one patient could not pour tea into a cup: She would see the tea suddenly appear, not continuously flow; instead of motion, she saw a series of static images (Zihl et al., 1983).

Figure 3.11 Size Constancy

Even though you know that the two white bars on the rails are in fact the same size, the one that appears farther away also appears larger. This figure is interesting because it violates size constancy: To be seen as the same size when it is farther away, an object needs to cover a smaller area of the picture (or visual field); when objects cover the same area of a picture (or visual field), our visual system assumes that the one appearing further away is larger.

The woman on the left is actually taller than the boy on the right. How is this possible? The woman is farther away, but this special Ames room has been constructed to eliminate the usual monocular depth cues.

Motion cues: Information that specifies the distance of an object on the basis of its movement.

Figure 3.12 Phi Phenomenon

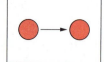

Movies are produced by a series of still photos, presented very rapidly in sequence. Why do we see movement, when there really isn't any? This sort of *apparent motion* arises from the *phi phenomenon*, a particular kind of illusion. When a stimulus appears in one location (such as in the left panel), disappears, and then appears in another location (as in the center panel), we will see it as having moved if the timing is just right (the farther the distance between locations, the greater the amount of time between removing the first stimulus and presenting the second). The phi phenomenon can produce the appearance of motion that is indistinguishable from real motion (Gregory & Harris, 1984; Shioiri et al., 2000; Wertheimer, 1912).

Figure 3.13 Two Visual Pathways

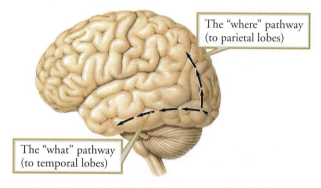

The "where" pathway (to parietal lobes)

The "what" pathway (to temporal lobes)

Visual input flows along two major pathways in the brain. The "where" pathway going up to the parietal lobes is concerned with spatial properties (such as an object's location), whereas the "what" pathway going down to the temporal lobes is concerned with properties of objects (such as their shape and color).

Phase 2 of Visual Perception: Recognition and Identification

Vision is more than organizing the world into shapes and knowing where they are, of course. If Phase 1 processing were all there was to it, how would you know whether something was good to approach (such as a useful tool or a tasty sweet) or necessary to avoid (such as a dangerous animal or an angry boss)? To answer such questions, we need to turn to the processes involved in Phase 2 of visual perception. These processes accomplish two major goals:

- *Identify shapes.* You need to assign meaning to the shapes you see.
- *Identify spatial relations.* You need to identify the spatial relations among objects (James et al., 2003; Kosslyn, 1994b; Ullman, 1996).

These two goals are attained by separate mechanisms in the brain. From the results of experiments conducted with monkeys, Ungerleider and Mishkin (1982) described two major neural pathways, which they dubbed the *what* (properties of objects) and *where* (spatial properties) *pathways* (Figure 3.13). Subsequent research has backed up this distinction (Tsao et al., 2003). Further evidence for the existence of these distinct mechanisms comes from studies of humans who have suffered brain damage. Damage in the bottom parts of the temporal lobes impairs the patient's ability to recognize objects by sight, and damage in the back parts of the parietal lobes impairs the patient's ability to register locations (James et al., 2003; Lê et al., 2002; Levine, 1982; Riddoch et al., 2004). Moreover, these separate brain areas have been found to be activated during neuroimaging studies in which normal people are asked to distinguish shapes or locations (Bar et al., 2001; Bly & Kosslyn, 1997; Flas et al., 2002; Grill-Spector, 2003; Haxby et al., 1991, 1994, 2001; Kohler et al., 1995; Rao et al., 2003; Ungerleider & Haxby, 1994). The operation of these two distinct types of processes is evident even during infancy (Mareschal & Johnson, 2003). The two pathways come together in the frontal lobes, where information about an object's identity and position is used to make decisions (Ng et al., 2001; Rao et al., 1997).

Knowing More Than You Can See

When you see an apple, the processes that underlie visual sensation respond to basic characteristics of the input, such as the wavelengths of light and changes in lightness that may signal the presence of edges. The outputs from these processes are then organized in the first phases of perceptual processing to indicate a red, shiny object of a certain shape and size that is at a certain distance. But nothing in this information tells you that inside this object are seeds and, maybe, a worm. For you to know these things, the final phases of perceptual processing must occur, which allow the visual input to activate information you've stored in memory from your prior experience. To interpret what you see, you need to compare the input to stored information. If the input matches something you've stored in memory, that information can be applied to the present case (and that's how you know that an apple *may* have a worm inside, even if you can't see one *this time*). If the object is *recognized*, it seems familiar; if it is *identified*, you know additional facts about it.

Objects are sometimes recognized as collections of parts. Irving Biederman and his colleagues (Biederman, 1987; Hummel & Biederman, 1992) have suggested that objects are represented in the brain as collections of simple shapes, with each shape representing a part of the object, such as the head, neck, body, and legs of a dog. It is clear that we can see parts of objects individually (Hoffman & Richards, 1984). But take a look at the two photographs of Britney Spears, and then turn the book around so that you can see the photos right-side up. It should also be clear that we do not always recognize or identify objects in terms of their individual parts. If that were the case, we wouldn't need to turn the book over to see how weird one of the photos is. Rather, we usually focus on the overall views of shapes and look for details only if we need them (Cave & Kosslyn, 1993). When we do look at individual features, however, they may not always be properly combined.

Look at these faces, and then turn the book and look at them right side up. One explanation for the peculiar lapse in noticing the parts is that when you view the entire face, you are attending to a single pattern—but to see the parts in detail, you need to attend to smaller pieces of the whole. Notice that if you focus on each part, you can see that some are upside down. But when you focus on the entire face, you see the overall pattern, not a collection of parts.

Informed Perception: The Active Viewer

The progression from sensation, to organization, to recognition and identification may seem to indicate a simple sequential process, but more is happening. So far, we've been discussing **bottom-up processing**, which is initiated by the stimulus. Bottom-up processing operates like a row of standing dominoes: When the neural equivalent of the first domino is tripped by the light impulses reaching your eye (or the sound vibrations reaching your ear), other neural signals are successively tripped, like falling dominoes, until you've understood what you're seeing (or hearing). As shown in Figure 3.14, bottom-up processing can sometimes trigger additional sensory experiences, as well as comprehension. In contrast, **top-down processing** is guided by knowledge, expectation, or belief. For example, go back to those ambiguous figures in Figure 3.10. Can you intentionally see the two faces or the vase? Top-down processing allows you to impose what you want to see on what is

Figure 3.14 Synesthesia

Usual appearance

Appearance to person with synesthesia

Bottom-up processing can sometimes produce remarkably complex experiences. For example, perhaps as many as 1 in 2,000 people experience *synesthesia*, where they simultaneously experience more than one perception when given certain stimuli (the term is from the Greek *syn*, which means "union," and *aisthises*, which means "of the senses"). Many of these people see letters, digits, and words that are, in fact, printed in black, as in the top row, as if they were printed in colors, as in the second row. The neural bases of this phenomenon are just starting to be understood (Rich & Mattingley, 2002).

Bottom-up processing: Processing that is initiated by stimulus input.

Top-down processing: Processing that is guided by knowledge, expectation, or belief.

actually out there. In most cases, top-down processing does not change how you see an object, but instead just makes it easier to organize or interpret it; expecting to see a particular object makes it easier to see it (van Zoest & Donk, 2004).

Bottom-up and top-down processes are often in play at the same time (Corbetta & Shulman, 2002; Humphreys et al., 1997; Kosslyn & Koenig, 1995). Here's how it works. If you turn on the TV to a random channel, you will be able to understand what appears on the screen even if it's a complete surprise: The processing is bottom up, from the stimulus alone, unaided by any expectation you might have. Your eyes and ears register what's there, and your brain processes the resulting signals. However, after the first few moments of watching this randomly selected channel, even if you seem to be just another vegetating couch potato, you are, in fact, actively anticipating what will appear next and using this information to help you see. Now you are engaging in top-down processing, which occurs when you use your knowledge of what to expect to help you look for specific characteristics and fill in missing parts of the stimulus. You can experience top-down processing at work if the TV image is really blurry and you use the sound track to provide clues to what's in the picture. For example, if the sound track makes it clear that two people are about to kiss, you will be able to make out the outlines of the faces more easily. Such top-down processing is often used to help you integrate what you see with what you hear (Ernst & Bülthoff, 2004).

Top-down processing can alter the mechanisms used in bottom-up processing (Corbetta & Shulman, 2002; Humphreys et al., 1997; Kosslyn, 1994b). In a study by Delk and Fillenbaum (1965), for example, participants were shown stimuli that were all cut from the same orangish-red cardboard, including objects that are normally red (an apple and a valentine heart) and objects that are not normally red (a mushroom and a bell). The participants were to adjust the color of a display until they thought it matched the color of the cutouts. Apparently, the knowledge of the usual color of the objects affected how participants saw the actual color; when asked to match the color of the normally red objects, they consistently selected a redder color than the one they chose to match the color of the mushroom and the bell.

Your **perceptual set** is the sum of your assumptions and beliefs that lead you to expect to perceive certain objects or characteristics in particular contexts. For example, when the bottom light on a stoplight is illuminated, you will see it as green even if it is, in fact, a bluish green. People often use context to form such *perceptual expectancies*, perceptions dependent on previous experience (Palmer, 1992a). Cues in the current context are often used to guide top-down processing during perception (Chun, 2000).

Coding Space in the Brain: More Than One Way to Identify "Where"

We have so far been focusing on the "what" pathway, but researchers have also studied the final phases of perceptual processing in the "where" pathway. The goal of this processing is to use the sum total of the distance cues (discussed earlier) to identify the distance and direction of objects, either relative to yourself or relative to other objects. Kosslyn (1987) proposed that the brain uses two different ways to code spatial relations. To get a rough sense of the idea, think of the difference between a list of directions and a map. The list relies on *categorical spatial relations*, which code relative positions with categories such as "above" or "left of" or "beside." Like all categories, these group together a set of specific examples (Laeng et al., 2003). For instance, take the simplest list of directions: Say that a friend asks you to go through the door into her bedroom and get her backpack, which she tells

Perceptual set: The sum of your assumptions and beliefs that lead you to expect to perceive certain objects or characteristics in particular contexts.

you is to the right of the bed. "Right of" is a categorical relation; it doesn't indicate a particular, specific spot, but instead gives you a whole group of possible locations—anywhere to the right of the bed, as shown in Figure 3.15.

However, categorical spatial relations are useless for the other main tasks of vision: navigation and reaching (Goodale & Milner, 1992; Milner & Goodale, 1995). Knowing that the backpack is "to the right of" (a categorical spatial relation) the bed will not allow you to walk right over to it. For instance, imagine that the electricity went out and the room was pitch black; if all you knew was that the backpack was to the right of the bed, you would have to creep carefully around, feeling your way until you happened upon it. For navigation and reaching, you need precise information about the distance and direction of objects. In contrast to categorical spatial relations, *coordinate spatial relations* specify continuous distances from your body or another object that serves as an "origin" of a coordinate space. For example, your friend might tell you that the backpack is a foot away from the right-hand corner of the head of the bed (see Figure 3.15). Knowing this, you could find it easily, even in the dark; as soon as you felt your way to the right-hand side of the bed, you would know exactly where to find the backpack.

How can we tell whether the brain does in fact use these two different ways to identify spatial relations? Kosslyn (1987) proposed that the left cerebral hemisphere may be better at identifying categorical spatial relations, which are easily named by a word or two (and thus are compatible with the left hemisphere's facility at labeling). In contrast, he proposed that the right hemisphere may be better at identifying coordinate spatial relations, which are essential for navigation (and the right hemisphere typically is better at this ability; De Renzi, 1982). Slotnick and his colleagues (2001) were able to provide particularly strong support for this hypothesis.

Figure 3.15 Coding Space

A categorical spatial relation could be used to specify that the backpack is "to the right of" the bed, which would indicate that it could be in any of the light blue region. A coordinate spatial relation would indicate that the backpack is 1 foot to the right of the back, right-hand corner of the bed, which specifies a particular spot on the floor (shown by the red arrow). Categorical and coordinate spatial relations are useful for different purposes.

Attention: The Gateway to Awareness

In order to recognize and identify an object or event, you need to engage in Phase 2 of visual perception. What determines which stimuli are given such treatment? **Attention** is the act of focusing on particular information, which allows that information to be processed more fully than information that is not attended to. For instance, if you are a movie buff, you might be fully absorbed by the latest Hollywood release—noticing every detail of how the cameras are used, of the lighting, and of other cinematic features. In order to soak up such details, you need to pay attention to the images themselves. If you are paying close attention, you will notice things that flit right by other people, such as rapid changes in camera angle. Research has shown that paying attention increases sensitivity to the attended events (Nakayama & Mackeben, 1989; Yeshurun & Carrasco, 1998, 1999). **Selective attention** allows you to pick out a particular characteristic, object, or event. For instance, you could be looking specifically for the ways that lighting is used, and thus tune yourself for this characteristic.

We are aware only of what we pay attention to. Although we focus here on visual attention, we stress that attention operates in virtually all domains of human thought and feeling, not only in visual perception; you can pay attention to a

Attention: The act of focusing on particular information, which allows it to be processed more fully than what is not attended to.

Selective attention: The process of picking out a particular quality, object, or event for relatively detailed analysis.

Figure 3.16 Pop-Out Versus Search

As shown in the left panel, basic features, such as color, are registered without the need for an item-by-item search. Is there a red T in the right panel? To find a combination of features, such as the arrangements of segments or a shape with a particular color, you must search the items one at a time.

Figure 3.17

The Stroop Effect

GREEN	RED
RED	BLUE
BLUE	GREEN
BLACK	BLACK
BLUE	GREEN
RED	BLUE
GREEN	BLACK
BLACK	RED
RED	BLUE
BLUE	GREEN

In 1935, John Ridley Stroop published a classic paper describing what is now known as the Stroop effect. Name the color of the ink used to print each word in the left column (not the color named by the word); then do the same for the words in the right column. Which is easier? You cannot help both seeing the color and reading the word, and when the meaning of the word is different from the color of the ink, you experience interference.

Pop-out: Phenomenon that occurs when a stimulus is sufficiently different from the ones around it that it is immediately evident.

particular instrument in a band, a nuance of a word, a feeling, a taste, a particular place, or the feeling of a ladybug walking over the back of your hand. We pay attention to something for one of two reasons: It grabs our attention, or we are actively searching for it.

Pop-Out: What Grabs Attention?

One reason we pay attention is that something about an event grabs us, such as a sudden change in illumination or movement. Certain qualities or features of displays, such as advertisements, automatically (via bottom-up processing) leap out—a phenomenon psychologists refer to as pop-out. For example, look at the left panel of Figure 3.16. Is a red dot present? The red dot appears to pop out; it is immediately evident without your having to search for it. Attention is immediately drawn to this "odd man out." In general, pop-out occurs when objects differ in their fundamental qualities, such as size for vision or frequency for hearing (you immediately hear a high-pitched flute in a band if all the other instruments are playing low notes). Pop-out relies on the outputs of Phase 1 processes that organize figures; separate features (such as color and orientation) are detected by the same processes, and thus having more than a single pop-out dimension does not make the odd-man-out much—if any—easier to detect than having a single distinctive feature (Krummenacher et al., 2002; Monnier, 2003).

Active Searching: Not Just What Grabs Attention

The other reason we pay attention is that we are actively searching for a particular characteristic, object, or event (via top-down processing). Have you ever wondered whether you have actually glimpsed a friend in a crowd, or heard a familiar voice in an unexpected context? In many situations, your initial perception of an event may not be very clear, and you need a "second look" or "second hear." In these cases, your first suspicions of what you might have perceived guide top-down processes to collect more information in a very efficient way: You search for distinctive characteristics, such as the shape of a particular haircut, or the pitch of a certain voice. Or, have you ever waited for a friend and anticipated her appearance with every passing stranger? *Vigilance* occurs when you are anticipating a particular event and thus maintain attention as you wait for it, which also relies on your ability to focus your attention voluntarily.

However, as shown in Figure 3.17, we cannot always use top-down processing to focus on one characteristic and shut out others. Bottom-up processing keeps us perceptually honest—we see what's there, not just what we want to see.

Seeing Without Awareness

Some people who suffer strokes that leave them blind can nevertheless report accurately when spots of light are presented—and will even know where they are. These people have no awareness of seeing the dots but rather simply "know" when they are present. Similarly, animals with damage to the visual cortex in the occipital lobe may appear to be blind at all other times, but when they are lowered onto a surface, they stick out their legs to support themselves at just the right

People suffer from *change blindness*, not seeing even large alterations of features as scenes change over time (O'Regan, 1992; Simons, 2000; Simons & Ambinder, 2005). For example, the two versions of these scenes were alternated every 640 milliseconds. In the pair of photos on the left, the railing changes, which is not of central interest. People had a difficult time noticing this change, requiring 16.2 alternations on average to spot it. In the pair of photos on the right, the location of the helicopter changes, which is of central interest. People noticed this change after only 4.0 alternations, on average (from Rensink et al., 1997).

point; some of these animals can avoid obstacles when walking, even though the primary visual cortex has been removed (Cowey & Stoerig, 1995). Such behavior has been called *blindsight* (Weiskrantz, 1986). Multiple pathways from the eye lead to many places in the brain (Felleman & Van Essen, 1991; Zeki, 1978, 1993), and some of these pathways can function even though they do not pass through brain areas that give rise to conscious experience. Thus, even when the areas crucial for consciousness, or connections from these areas, are damaged, some visual function persists.

A bird in the hand is worth two in the the bush. Did you notice anything odd about the sentence you just read? Many people miss the repeated "the"; in fact, this is said to be the hardest error for a proofreader to catch. Kanwisher (1987, 1991) has dubbed this effect **repetition blindness**, and she and many others (such as Morris & Harris, 2004) have shown that people will fail to see a second example of an object if it occurs soon after the first instance. (A similar effect, called *repetition deafness*, occurs in hearing; Soto-Faraco & Spence, 2001.) A related phenomenon is the **attentional blink**, in which attention is lost for a certain time immediately following a stimulus to which attention was paid. In contrast to repetition blindness, the attentional blink can occur for a different stimulus, not necessarily a second instance of the same or a closely related one, and the effect may actually be larger for stimuli that occur a few items after the one attended to (Arnell & Jolicoeur, 1999; Chun, 1997; Jolicoeur, 1998; Luck et al., 1996; Raymond et al., 1992). Proofreaders and copyeditors experience this unfortunate phenomenon all the time, missing obvious errors that happen to fall in the wake of

Repetition blindness: The inability to see the second occurrence of a stimulus that appears twice in succession.

Attentional blink: A rebound period in which a person cannot pay attention to one thing after having just paid attention to another.

a large error or a string of errors. Repetition blindness appears to result because the stimuli are not registered as individual events, but simply as a "type" of event (Kanwisher, 1987), whereas the attentional blink may occur because the act of registering information in detail may "lock up" certain neural processes for a brief period (within about a half-second of seeing the first stimulus), during which attention cannot easily be re-engaged (Fell et al., 2002). The attentional blink can occur even when two stimuli are presented to the separated cerebral hemispheres of a split-brain patient (see Chapter 2), which shows that the effect arises very soon after visual input begins to be processed. (Giesbrecht & Kingstone, 2004). Nevertheless, the attentional blink reflects, in part, interference in later phases of perceptual processing (Christmann & Leuthold, 2004; Vogel & Luck, 2002).

Looking at Levels

The Essential Features of Good Looks

As any painter can tell you, vision is used for more than identifying objects and registering their locations. Through the visual system, we also perceive what we call "beauty," including physical attractiveness. In fact, a specific part of the frontal lobe (the medial orbital frontal cortex, OFC, which is in the midline, behind the eyes) is activated when people look at attractive faces—and is even more strongly activated when an attractive face is smiling (O'Doherty et al., 2003). This finding is intriguing because the OFC is thought to specify the "reward value" of stimuli. However, we know that some rewards (such as food) are innate, whereas other rewards (such as money) are learned. Is the perception of attractiveness entirely inborn? To answer this, let's begin by considering exactly which features of faces are perceived to be attractive:

- *Smooth skin.* Smooth, even-colored skin is perceived as more attractive than coarser, uneven skin (Fink et al., 2001).
- *Symmetry.* Symmetrical faces tend to be perceived as attractive and as healthy (Reis & Zaidel, 2001).
- *Makeup.* Makeup has been shown to enhance attractiveness of female faces (Osborn, 1996), especially makeup that darkens the region around the eyes and the mouth; however, such makeup yields precisely the opposite reaction when applied to male faces (Russell, 2003).
- *Female hormones.* Faces that show the effects of female hormones (such as a relatively small chin, full lips, and high cheekbones) are perceived as attractive. David Perrett and his colleagues (1998) asked Asian people (Japanese in Japan) and Caucasians (Scots in Scotland) to choose the most attractive faces from a set of photographs, some of which had been altered to emphasize features that reflect high levels of male or female hormones. The researchers found that both national groups preferred women's faces with a female "hormone enhanced" look to average faces. In addition, both sets of participants found even *male* faces more attractive if they showed effects of *female* hormones. Faces that showed effects of high levels of male hormones were rated as having high "perceived dominance," as being older, and as having less warmth, emotionality, honesty, and cooperativeness (as well as other attributes). Apparently, the effects of female hormones not only made faces look younger but also softened these negative perceptions.

| Caucasian female, feminized | Caucasian female, masculinized | Caucasian male, feminized | Caucasian male, masculinized |

| Japanese female, feminized | Japanese female, masculinized | Japanese male, feminized | Japanese male, masculinized |

Facial images of Caucasian and Japanese females and males were "feminized" and "masculinized" 50% in shape. Which face in each pair do you prefer? In general, faces that reflect effects of female sex hormones are seen as more attractive.

All of these variables may reflect inborn preferences, and hence reflect events at the level of the brain. However, the correlations between people's preferences explain at most only about 25% of the differences among these preferences, and thus other factors must be at work (Thornhill & Gangestad, 1999). In fact, even the variables noted above can be modified by learning. For example, take that effect of female hormones: It was, in fact, larger for female faces within each participant's own population, a finding that was interpreted as indicating that this is a learned preference. The results of such learning operate at the level of the person, but the process of the learning itself relies on events at the level of the group. Moreover, what's perceived as attractive in one society may not be the same as what's perceived as attractive in another (Jones, 1996). At the level of the group, values and tastes develop and are taught, either explicitly (via instruction) or implicitly (via example), to the individual members of the group. These standards may evolve for different reasons.

In addition, faces are only part of the attractiveness story. For example, people find bodies with a specific weight for a specific height most attractive; but even here, learning is required to register this cue accurately when bodies are seen from different points of view (level of the person; Tovée & Cornelissen, 2001). Moreover, the preferred body shape varies in different cultures, and even subcultures (level of the group; Wetsman & Marlowe, 1999; Yu & Shepard, 1998)—as you might suspect from the art of Rubens, whose roly-poly models would never find work on today's fashion runways. For example, Ford and Beach (1951) considered what people in over 200 cultures looked at when evaluating attractiveness and found that different cultures focused on different parts and characteristics of the body (such as the size of the pelvis, pudginess, and height). Moreover, posture—which may differ even between countries such as Italy and the United States—plays a role in judgments of attractiveness (Osborn, 1996).

As usual, events at the different levels interact. Once you evaluate someone as beautiful, various expectations and beliefs come to mind. Just as once you've identified an object as an apple, you know it has seeds inside, once you classify a person as attractive, you believe that he or she is likely to be kind, nurturing, and sensitive and to have other positive attributes as well (Dion et al., 1972). Such information then affects how you interact with the person, which in turn can lead to new learning, perhaps influencing you to develop a more specialized category.

LOOKING BACK: *Review*

1. *What is sensation, and how does it differ from* perception? Sensation occurs when a physical event in the world stimulates receptors (such as those at the back of the eye, in the ear, and on the skin), which then send signals to the brain. We detect events that are over a threshold (an absolute threshold to notice that they are present at all or a just-noticeable difference (JND) to register a change), but our sensitivity to stimuli must be distinguished from our bias to classify input as signal versus noise. Perception occurs when input is organized and interpreted as indicating that a particular object or event is present.

2. *What is the nature of light, and how do we see color?* Light is made up of electromagnetic waves. These waves enter the pupil of the eye, and the lens focuses the light on the retina. Special receptors and ganglion cells in the retina transduce the light waves into neural signals, which continue along the optic nerve to the brain. Rods are receptors that are very sensitive to light but register only shades of gray. Cones are not as sensitive and respond to particular wavelengths of light, which is essential for color vision. There are three different types of cones, each most responsive to a particular color: yellowish red, green, and bluish violet. Opponent cells, on the other hand, work in pairs—yellow/blue, red/green, and black/white. The activation of one color in the opponent cell pair inhibits the other. By changing the hue, saturation, and brightness of colors, artists can lead the viewer to have an almost infinite range of color experiences.

3. *How are we able to separate figure from ground and see the world as a stable collection of objects?* We perceive figures as distinct from ground by using organizational principles, such as those described by the Gestalt laws of organization; these principles include proximity, continuity, similarity, closure, and good form. Critical constancies include size constancy (objects appear the same size in spite of differences in the images that are projected on the retina), shape constancy (objects seem to have the same shape in spite of differences in the shape of their images on the retina), and color constancy (colors appear the same in different lighting conditions). Various cues, from both eyes or only one, from static images or moving images, help establish the perceptual constancies.

4. *How do we make sense of what we see?* If we have seen an object before, information about it is stored in memory; when we see it again, we can match the input to the stored information and apply the information stored previously to the current example. We identify an object when associated information stored in memory is applied to the current stimu-

lus. Once we have identified an object, information in memory can fill in information missing from the stimulus itself. Bottom-up processing is initiated by the stimulus, whereas top-down processing is guided by knowledge, expectation, or belief. In at least some situations, we can identify objects that we are not even aware of seeing, but in most situations attention is necessary to identify objects.

LOOKING BEYOND: *Critical Thinking*

Do you think "boosted," or enhanced, sensory sensitivities would be an advantage or a disadvantage? (What if you could see the dirt in the pores on a friend's face across the room?) In what ways would such superabilities be a benefit? A drawback? What if you were able to adjust your sensory sensitivity and bias at will? Would such abilities help an artist such as Frida Kahlo? In what kinds of situations would this power be desirable?

What do you think would happen if you had been born blind and suddenly had vision at age 50? Such cases have been studied in depth (Gregory, 1974; Sacks, 1995), and even though light was being properly transduced in the eyes, these people failed to realize they were viewing a human face (that of the person who took off their bandages) until the person spoke. Why? If you had to help such a person adjust after the sight-giving operation, what would you do? Why might part of your training involve attention?

Hearing

According to Diego Rivera's daughter, Frida Kahlo loved whistles. They were sold in stands in the market: "They came in various sizes and made different sounds. She used them to call for [the different house staff], and she created quite a stir when she did" (Rivera & Colle, 1994, p. 100). How is it that Kahlo (and everyone else nearby whose hearing was intact) could *hear* the sounds of the whistles? And how could she (and we) notice that different whistles made different sounds?

LOOKING AHEAD: *Learning Objectives*

1. *How do the ears register auditory sensations?*
2. *What auditory cues allow us to organize sounds into coherent units and locate sources?*
3. *How do we make meaning out of sound?*

Auditory Sensation: If a Tree Falls but Nobody Hears It, Is There a Sound?

We know that rays don't emanate from our eyes when we see. Now for a trick question: Do you think that sound waves emanate from our ears when we hear? In 1978, researchers found that when a click is presented to someone, the ear soon produces an echo (Kemp, 1978). Not long after this discovery, researchers (Kemp, 1979; Zurek, 1981, 1985; Zwicker & Schloth, 1984) found that even when a person isn't hearing a particular stimulus, the ear sometimes actually makes a sound. In fact, about 40% of normal people emit a detectable soft humming sound from their ears, of which they are unaware. In some cases, the humming is loud enough that other people can hear it. These sounds are not like the natural sonar used by whales, sound waves bouncing off objects and returning to the ear. These sounds play no role in hearing. They are probably caused by feedback from the brain to the ear; feedback (not the sounds produced by it) helps us hear slight differences in sounds (Pickles, 1988; Zurek, 1985). As in vision, there are many feedback connections between areas of the brain that process sound, and between these areas and the ear (Felleman & Van Essen, 1991). And, as the next subsection describes, this is not the only similarity between hearing and seeing.

Sound Waves: Being Pressured

Like vision, auditory processing occurs in two major phases: sensation and perception. And, like vision, perception itself can be divided into processes used at the beginning and at the end. Hearing begins with the sensation of sound. Sound usually arises when something vibrates, creating waves of moving air that enter our ears. Sound can arise when any type of molecules—gas, liquid, or solid—move and create pressure waves. Thus, we can hear when we are surrounded by either air or water or when we put an ear to the ground, to a wall, or to another solid object. An old (but true) cliché of Western movies is listening with an ear pressed to a rail to hear whether a train is approaching. But movies sometimes get it wrong. In outer space—where there are no molecules to be moved—we could not hear anything; the loud explosion of the demolished Death Star in the original *Star Wars* movie would, in fact, have been silent as the grave.

These pressure waves go up, and then down, repeatedly; each complete up-and-down movement is called a *cycle*. Like light waves, sound waves have both frequency and amplitude. We usually hear variations in frequency as differences in pitch—how high or low the sound seems—and we hear variations in amplitude as differences in loudness. (It probably is no coincidence that people are most sensitive to the frequencies of a baby's cry, around 2,000–5,000 hertz; a hertz, or Hz, is the number of cycles per second.) Loudness is measured in decibels; a decibel (dB) is a measure of sound on a base-10 logarithmic scale (the log scale is used because we can hear an enormous range of volume). The threshold for hearing is set at 0 dB. A sound 10 times louder than the threshold sound is 10 dB; a sound 100 times louder than threshold level is 20 dB; a sound 1,000 times louder is 30 dB (the scale is based on powers of 10, so the number of zeros is indicated by the first digit in the dB measurement; a sound 10,000 times louder than threshold is 40 dB—four zeros). Figure 3.18 presents the loudness levels of some common sounds. Any sound over about 85 dB can impair your hearing if you listen to it for 8 hours straight; a sound over 140 dB can damage your hearing after a single exposure—and 160 dB will break your eardrum on the spot (National Institute for

Figure 3.18 Decibel Levels

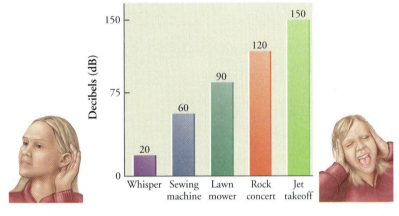

Sound is measured in terms of decibels (dB), which rely on a base-10 logarithmic scale. Any sound over 85 dB will damage hearing after 8 hours.

Pitch: How high or low a sound seems; higher frequencies of pressure waves produce the experience of higher pitches.

Loudness: The strength of a sound; pressure waves with greater amplitude produce the experience of louder sound.

Decibel (dB): A measure of loudness on a base-10 logarithmic scale; the threshold for hearing is set at 0dB.

Occupational Safety and Health, 1998). The same psychophysical concepts that apply to vision, such as absolute threshold, JND, and so on, also apply to hearing and are measured in comparable ways.

A question often asked in beginning philosophy classes is this: If a tree falls in the forest but nobody hears it, is there a sound? The answer is now clear: No. Sound is *caused* by waves of molecules (a physical event), but the waves themselves are not sound. Sound is a psychological event and hence depends on a nervous system to transduce the physical energy of the waves to nerve impulses. Without a brain to register the transduced physical energy, there can be no sound. The situation is exactly analogous to the relationships of wavelength to hue and of amplitude to lightness. Physical properties *lead* to psychological events, but they are not the events themselves. The discipline of psychophysics charts the relationship between physical events and our experiences of them.

The Brain's Ear: More Than a Microphone

The anatomy of the ear is illustrated in Figure 3.19. The ear has three parts: the outer ear, middle ear, and inner ear. The eardrum (the *tympanic membrane*) stretches across the inside end of the auditory canal, and everything between the eardrum and the auditory nerve is designed to convert movements of the eardrum to nerve impulses that are sent to the brain. Specifically, waves move the eardrum, which in turn moves three bones in the middle ear (the hammer, anvil, and stirrup; incidentally, these are the smallest bones in the human body). If you hear a loud sound, the muscles in the ear reflexively tighten, which protects against damage (Borg & Counter, 1989). These muscles also contract when you talk, which protects you from hurting your own ears. Such protection is necessary because the ear is amazingly sensitive: We can hear a sound when the eardrum is moved less than 1 billionth of an inch (Green, 1976). The three bones of the middle ear not only transfer but also amplify the vibration and cause the *basilar membrane* (which is inside the cochlea, as shown in Figure 3.19) to vibrate. The

Figure 3.19 Anatomy of the Ear

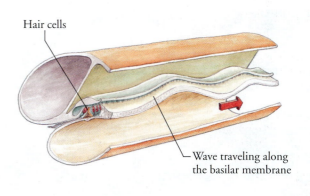

The major parts of the outer ear, middle ear, and inner ear. The semicircular canals have no role in hearing; they help us keep our balance.

If you unwound the cochlea and looked into it (as shown here), you would see the basilar membrane with its hair cells.

Figure 3.20 Place Coding of Sound Frequency

Low frequencies cause maximal vibration of the basilar membrane near one end.

Medium frequencies cause maximal vibration of the basilar membrane near the middle.

High frequencies cause maximal vibration of the basilar membrane near the other end.

Hair cells: The cells with stiff hairs along the basilar membrane of the inner ear that, when moved, produce nerve impulses that are sent to the brain; these cells are the auditory equivalent of rods and cones.

Frequency theory: The theory that higher frequencies produce higher rates of neural firing.

Place theory: The theory that different frequencies activate different places along the basilar membrane.

Nerve deafness: A type of deafness that typically occurs when the hair cells are destroyed by loud sounds.

Conduction deafness: A type of deafness caused by a physical impairment of the external or middle ear.

basilar membrane is where different frequencies of sound are coded into varying nerve impulses. Hairs sticking up from cells lining the basilar membrane are moved by the vibrations and trigger nerve impulses, which are then sent to the brain. These **hair cells** function in hearing the same way rods and cones do in vision; they produce the initial nerve impulses.

There are two main theories about the way the basilar membrane converts pressure waves to perceived sound. **Frequency theory** holds that higher frequencies produce greater neural firing. This theory cannot explain the full extent of our ability to hear: Neurons can fire only about 1,000 times a second at most, so how is it that we can hear sounds produced by much higher frequencies (Gelfand, 1981)? According to **place theory**, different frequencies activate different places along the basilar membrane, as shown in Figure 3.20. This theory appears to be correct, at least for most frequencies; it is possible, however, that the rate of vibration does help us hear relatively low tones.

Deafness: Hear Today, Gone Tomorrow

More than 28 million Americans have some sort of difficulty in hearing (Soli, 1994). One common hearing impairment is **nerve deafness**, which typically occurs when the hair cells are destroyed by loud sounds—and once a hair cell is destroyed, it is gone forever. A rock band heard at close range can produce sounds loud enough to cause this sort of damage. Nerve deafness may affect only certain frequencies; in those instances, a hearing aid can amplify the remaining frequencies, and hearing can be improved. Many researchers believe that a surgical procedure will soon be developed to make an end run around a damaged ear and allow auditory input to stimulate the auditory cortex directly (Ubell, 1995). Another form of hearing impairment, **conduction deafness**, can result from any accident or other cause that impairs the functioning of the external ear or middle ear. A broken eardrum, for example, can cause conduction deafness.

One study found that almost a third of a group of college students who went regularly to a dance club featuring loud music exhibited permanent hearing loss for high-frequency sounds (Hartman, 1982).

Phase 1 of Auditory Perception: Organizing the Auditory World

In the last year of Frida Kahlo's life, a Mexican gallery had the first-ever one-woman show of her work. The organizers scheduled a grand party on the show's opening night. Everyone wondered whether Kahlo would appear, but doubted it because she had been bedridden for some time. Friends, patrons, and well-wishers crowded into the gallery, waiting to see whether she would arrive. In the distance, they heard a siren, which got louder and louder, and finally an ambulance pulled up in front of the gallery. The ambulance staff carried Kahlo, and the four-poster bed on which she lay, out of the ambulance and into the gallery where everyone was waiting. On any other opening night, the patrons probably would not have paid much attention to the sound of a siren, but on this night they waited eagerly as they heard the sound growing louder. The processes engaged during the first phases of auditory perception allow us to organize sounds as coming from distinct objects and to locate the sources of sounds. Like vision, we can divide the steps of auditory perception into two main phases. In Phase 1, the outputs from sensory processing are organized; in Phase 2, these organized units are recognized and identified, or are used to guide movement (as occurs when you locate and turn your head to watch a particular member of a band play). In this section, we consider Phase 1, the first task of auditory perception after a stimulus has been sensed.

Sorting Out Sounds: From One, Many

In daily life, a complex jumble of many sounds usually assaults our ears, not individual sounds one at a time. To make sense of what we hear, we first need to sort out individual sounds (Carlyon, 2004). As in vision, we need to distinguish figure from ground. Bregman (1990, 1993) calls this process *auditory scene analysis*, which relies on organization very much like what occurs in vision. Indeed, the Gestalt laws apply here, too. For example, people organize sounds partly based on similarity (for example, grouping sounds with the same pitch) and good continuation (grouping the same pitch continued over time). Recognizing and identifying speech relies crucially on auditory scene analysis because the actual stimulus is continuous, with no indication of breaks to delineate the beginnings and endings of words; yet to communicate, people must identify individual words. This is the speech-segmentation problem. By analogy, *thisproblemisliketheone youarenowsolving* in vision.

In vision, we see continuous variations in the frequency of light not as continuous variations in hue, but rather as a set of distinct colors. Similarly, we hear speech sounds as distinct categories. This categorical perception groups a range of different sounds (such as those spoken by males, females, or children missing their front teeth) into the same categories, and it does so quickly and automatically (Jacobsen et al., 2004). Such processing produces categories with remarkably sharp boundaries. For example, if a computer is programmed to vary the time between the start of a syllable (the consonant being pronounced, such as b) and the "voiced" part of the syllable (the sound of the vowel being pronounced, such as a), we will hear "ba" if the voiced part starts from 0 to around 25 thousandths of a second after the consonant starts; but if the voiced part starts after a longer interval, we will hear "pa." There is very little intermediate ground; we hear one or the other (Eimas & Corbit, 1973). Infants (Dehaene-Lambertz & Pena, 2001), as well as monkeys, chinchillas, and various other animals (Kuhl, 1989; Moody et al., 1990), show categorical perception, which suggests that the perceptual system itself does this work—not the

Speech-segmentation problem: The problem of organizing a continuous stream of speech into separate parts that correspond to individual words.

Categorical perception: Identifying sounds as belonging to distinct categories that correspond to the basic units of speech.

Bats and barn owls are adept at using sound to localize objects (Konishi, 1993; Suga, 1990). The structure of the barn owl's face has developed in a way to direct sound to its ears; this maximizes location cues. Bats produce sounds and then listen for the echoes coming back. The echoes are precise enough for the bat to discern the shapes of even small objects (Simmons & Chen, 1989).

language systems of our various cultures. Indeed, the common ancestor of monkeys, chinchillas, and humans may have evolved many of the "building blocks" that were later incorporated into speech.

Locating Sounds: Why Two Ears Are Better Than One

In vision, our brains use slight differences in the images striking the two eyes to assess the distance of an object. Similarly, hearing makes use of differences in the stimuli reaching the two ears to assess the distance of a sound source (Yost & Dye, 1991). For example, a *difference in loudness* at the two ears is used as a cue. In addition to all of their other functions, our heads are useful because they block sound, and thus the amplitude of sound waves is smaller when it reaches the ear on the side of the head away from the sound source. This cue is particularly effective for high-frequency sounds.

As in vision, we use many different cues to assess from the sound it makes where an object is. Some cues depend on only one ear, not two. For example, by moving our heads and bodies, we can compare the relative volume of a sound from different vantage points, which helps us locate its source.

Phase 2 of Auditory Perception: Recognition and Identification

Phase 2 of auditory perception allows us to use sound in many ways. In addition to interpreting speech and music, we also recognize that the snap of a green bean indicates freshness, that a knock on a door means someone wants to come in, that a cat's meowing may mean she wants to be fed. As in vision, sounds become meaningful when they are matched to information already stored in memory, which is the job of Phase 2 of auditory perceptual processing.

More Than Meets the Ear

Frida Kahlo's biography recounts an incident when she and Diego Rivera were to meet outside a movie theater, but crowds prevented them from seeing each other. In trying to find each other, "Diego whistled the first bar of the *Internationale*. From somewhere in the crowd came the second; it was unmistakably Frida. After this, the task no doubt seemed easier, and the whistling continued until the couple found each other" (Herrera, 1983, p. 308). Why would hearing the whistle over the noise of the crowd seem easier once they knew to listen for their whistled tune? Just as in vision, you can adjust your criterion for "detecting a signal," and this adjustment will be based on what you expect to hear. But also, as in vision, what you expect to hear actually influences what you do hear. A demonstration of such an effect was reported by Warren and Warren (1970), who asked people to listen to a tape-recorded sentence after part of a word had been replaced with the sound of a cough. Although part of the word was actually missing, all the participants claimed that they actually heard the entire word and denied that the cough covered part of it. In fact, the listeners were not exactly sure at what point the cough occurred. This effect, more obvious for words in sentences than for words standing alone, is called the *phonemic restoration effect* (a phoneme is the smallest segment of spoken speech, such as "ba" or "da"). This filling-in effect occurs not only with speech sounds but also with musical instruments. In fact, if you see someone bowing the strings of a cello at the same time as you hear the strings being plucked, the sight is enough to distort the sound you hear (Saldaña &

Rosenblum, 1993). Neuroimaging studies have shown that vision can modify how sound is processed in the brain (Thesen et al., 2004).

Hearing Without Awareness

As happens with vision, we pick up some auditory information without being aware of it. Perhaps the most common experience of perception without awareness is the **cocktail party phenomenon**. At an event like a large party, you may not be aware of other people's conversation until someone mentions your name—which you hear immediately (Cherry, 1953; Conway et al., 2001). But in order to become aware of the sound of your name, you must have been tracking the conversation all along (using bottom-up processing); you simply were not aware of the conversation until that important word was spoken. In experiments she performed as an undergraduate, Treisman (1964a, 1964b) showed that when people listen to stimuli presented separately to the two ears (through headphones) and are instructed to listen to only one ear, a procedure known as **dichotic listening** (Hugdahl, 2001), they still register some information—such as whether the voice is male or female—from the ignored ear (see Figure 3.21). To ensure that participants listen to only one voice, they often are asked to repeat it aloud—a practice known as *shadowing*.

This discovery spawned an industry that proclaimed that people can learn in their sleep, simply by playing tapes (purchased at low, low discount prices). Unfortunately, it turns out that unless a person is paying attention, not much gets through. And even when information does get through, it is retained very briefly; when tested hours later, people remember virtually none of the information presented outside their awareness (Greenwald et al., 1991).

Figure 3.21   **Dichotic Listening**

If you are asked to pay attention to this ear, you will not hear most things through the other ear.

But you will hear some aspects of the speech from the ignored ear, such as whether it's a male or a female voice.

Dichotic listening occurs when different messages are provided to the two ears, and the person is asked to listen only to one. Even so, some information from the ignored ear is processed.

LOOKING BACK: *Review*

1. *How do the ears register auditory sensations?* Normally, pressure waves move the eardrum, which in turn causes the bones of the middle ear to move, creating movement of the hair cells of the basilar membrane, which transduce the waves into neural impulses. The frequency of the waves determines the pitch of the sound, and the amplitude determines its volume. Frequency theory may explain the conversion of pressure waves to sound at low frequencies, and place theory explains it at most frequencies, especially high ones. Nerve deafness occurs when the hair cells do not function properly; conduction deafness occurs when the external or middle ear is impaired.

2. *What auditory cues allow us to organize sounds into coherent units and locate their sources?* We use similarity of sounds and other Gestalt principles to organize sounds into units. In addition, categorical perception allows us to hear some types of sounds—particularly those from speech—as distinct units, not as continuous variations. We use a variety of cues to localize the sources of sounds, some of which hinge on differences in the way sound is registered by the two ears.

Cocktail party phenomenon: The effect of not being aware of other people's conversations until your name is mentioned, and then suddenly hearing it.

Dichotic listening: A procedure in which participants hear stimuli presented separately to the two ears (through headphones) and are instructed to listen only to sounds presented to one ear.

3. How do we make meaning out of sound? As in vision, sounds become meaningful when they are matched to information already stored in memory. Both bottom-up and top-down processes are at work in audition. Top-down processes, which produce phenomena such as the phonemic restoration effect, can fill in fragmentary information. Some auditory recognition and identification take place outside awareness and can guide attention.

LOOKING BEYOND: *Critical Thinking*

Will wearing a motorcycle helmet affect your ability to recognize sounds and your ability to localize them to the same extent? Why or why not? If one side of the helmet were made of thicker plastic than the other, which sound cues would be most affected?

Do you think that the way a musician looks or behaves when he or she is performing could influence the way the music sounds? How could this occur?

Sensing and Perceiving in Other Ways

Left to his own devices, Diego Rivera did not bathe frequently—and Frida Kahlo was not fond of his body odor. She bought him bath toys in hopes that they would motivate him to bathe more often (apparently she was successful). Kahlo's sense of smell wasn't the only other sense of which she was keenly aware; she was very aware of tastes. During several lengthy visits to the United States, Kahlo consistently complained about the blandness of American food (although she did like applesauce and American cheese). Kahlo was also aware of the senses in her body; unfortunately, she experienced much pain, and gangrene in her right foot led to its eventual amputation. What have researchers discovered about these and other senses?

LOOKING AHEAD: *Learning Objectives*

1. *How does the sense of smell work?*
2. *How does the sense of taste work?*
3. *How do we sense our bodies?*
4. *Do a magnetic sense and extrasensory perception (ESP) exist?*

Smell: A Nose for News?

Smell and taste are often grouped together as the **chemical senses** because both, unlike the other senses, rely on registering the presence of specific chemicals. People differ widely in their sense of smell, or *olfaction*. Some people are 20 times more sensitive to odors than are other people (Rabin & Cain, 1986); Kahlo may simply have had a better sense of smell than Rivera, and hence was more sensitive to the odor when he hadn't bathed. Most people are remarkably poor at identifying odors, even though they often think they are good at it (de Wijk et al., 1995). Cain (1979) found that people could correctly identify only about half of

Chemical senses: Taste and smell, which rely on sensing the presence of specific chemicals.

80 common scents; although we may know that an odor is familiar—that is, we recognize it—we may be unable to identify it. In general, women are better than men at detecting many types of odors (Cain, 1982). Women are particularly sensitive to smell when they are ovulating—unless they take birth control pills, in which case their abilities do not fluctuate over the course of the month (Caruso et al., 2001; Grillo et al., 2001). In addition, younger adults are better at detecting odors than either children (up to 14 years old) or middle-aged adults (between 40 and 50 years old) (Cain & Gent, 1991; de Wijk & Cain, 1994; Murphy, 1986). For many of the years of her marriage, Kahlo was probably at the peak of her olfactory sensitivity.

Distinguishing Odors: Lock and Key

The best theory of odor detection can be described using the lock-and-key metaphor. Molecules have different shapes, and the olfactory receptors are built so that only molecules with particular shapes will fit in particular places on the receptors (see Figure 3.22). The molecules are like keys, and the receptors like locks. When the right-shaped molecule arrives at a particular receptor, it sends a signal to the brain, and we sense the odor. Just as there is not a single type of cone for each color we can see, there is not a single receptor for each odor we can smell (see Figure 3.23); rather, the overall pattern of receptor activity signals a particular odor (Freeman, 1991; Friedrich, 2004; Hallem et al., 2004). Two Americans, Linda Buck and Richard Axel, won the Nobel Prize in 2004 for their work in identifying the genes that produce the individual odor receptors (for example, Buck & Axel, 1991). They found that about 1,000 different genes (which is about 3% of the total that we have) are devoted to this task.

Two major neural pathways send signals about odor into the brain. One, passing through the thalamus, is particularly involved in memory; the other, connected to the limbic system, is particularly involved in emotions. Moreover, neuroimaging studies have shown that the right cerebral hemisphere plays a special role in memory for odors, and the left cerebral hemisphere plays a special role in emotional responses (Royet & Plailly, 2004). The two hemispheres are connected by massive numbers of fibers, and these connections explain why odors often tap emotionally charged memories—remember

Figure 3.22 Lock-and-Key Mechanism of Smell

Floral odor molecule

Receptor site

The shape of a molecule is like a key, and the shape of the corresponding receptor is like a lock. But when this key fits in this lock, the result is not a door opening but instead a neural signal sent to the brain—which gives rise to the experience of smell.

Figure 3.23 The Olfactory System

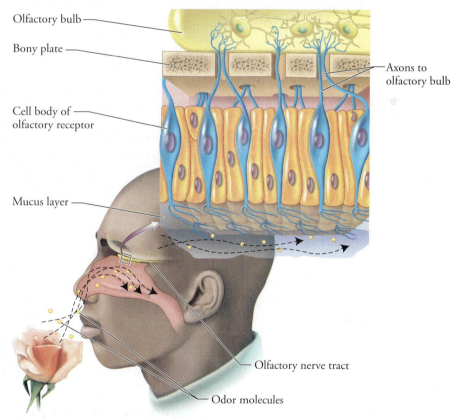

Olfactory bulb

Bony plate

Cell body of olfactory receptor

Mucus layer

Axons to olfactory bulb

Olfactory nerve tract

Odor molecules

Depending on which olfactory receptor cells are stimulated, different messages are sent to the olfactory bulb, the first part of the brain to process such signals.

the way you felt when you unexpectedly smelled a girlfriend's perfume or a boyfriend's aftershave?

Olfaction Gone Awry: Is It Safe to Cook Without Smell?

Have you ever wished you could not smell? Maybe that would be a relief once in a while, but losing your sense of smell completely is not a good idea. Smell serves to signal the presence of noxious substances; our brains are wired so that odors can quickly activate the fight-or-flight response. It would not be wise to ask a friend who has no sense of smell to cook dinner on a regular basis: Smell is often the only signal that meat or other food is spoiled. Relatively few people have no olfactory sense, a deficit that can arise from brain damage or a virus (Doty et al., 1991).

Pheromones: Another Kind of Scents?

Airborne chemicals released by female animals in heat arouse the male of the species. These are an example of ==pheromones==, chemical substances that serve as a means of communication. Like hormones, they modulate the functions of various organs, including the brain. Unlike hormones, pheromones are released *outside* the body, in urine and sweat. Much to the delight of perfume manufacturers over the world, studies have shown that female pheromones can attract men. In one study (McCoy & Pitino, 2002), university women began by recording seven social/sexual behaviors for 2 weeks (the baseline period) and then mixed a substance into their perfume and continued to record those behaviors; the substance was either a clear, odorless pheromone or an identically appearing but medically inactive substance (a placebo, for the control group). The study used a double-blind design; neither the investigator nor the participant knew whether a given participant received the pheromone or placebo. Participants who wore perfume containing the pheromone reported having more petting (which included affectionate behavior in general), sexual intercourse, sleeping next to a partner, and formal dates—but did not report that more men had approached them or that they had more informal dates or an increase in masturbation. Many more of the group receiving the pheromone reported increases in three or more of the four behaviors that were affected. All four of the affected types of behaviors require intimate interaction with someone else, whereas none of the other three do.

However, before male readers start to bemoan the uneven advantage female pheromones might confer, they will be interested to learn that another substance (derived from the human sex steroid compound 4,16-androstadien-3-one, known as AND, for short) not only increases positive mood and decreases negative mood in women, but also appears to arouse them—while at the same time apparently relaxing men (Bensafi et al, 2004). Although this substance had such effects only at high concentrations, it might have a future role in male colognes or after-shave lotions. If this finding and those about female pheromones hold up with repeated testing, do you think that people who use such substances should warn their dates?

Pheromones: Chemicals that function like hormones but are released outside the body (in urine and sweat).

Taste buds: Microscopic structures on the bumps on the tongue surface, at the back of the throat, and inside the cheeks; different types of taste buds are sensitive to sweet, sour, salty, and bitter tastes and to glutamate.

Taste: The Mouth Has It

When scientists discuss taste, they are talking about sensing via receptors located solely in the mouth. ==Taste buds== (see Figure 3.24) are microscopic structures mounted on the sides of the little bumps you can see on your tongue in a mirror. You have taste buds in other places in your mouth as well, such as the back of the throat and inside the cheeks (Smith & Frank, 1993). Your taste buds die and are replaced, on average, every 10 days (McLaughlin & Margolskee, 1994). Humans have more taste buds than some species, such as chickens, but fewer than others; some fish have taste buds spread all over their skin (Pfaffmann, 1978). Children have more sensitive taste buds than adults, and thus flavors are presumably stronger for them than for adults—which may account for children's notoriously strong likes and dislikes of foods. Nevertheless, even adults can be remarkably sensitive to slight differences in taste. When wine tasters speak of wine as having a flavor of mushrooms or cloves, they may not be speaking metaphorically. Depending on the composition of the soil in which the vines grow, grapes acquire different tastes.

Sweet, Sour, Salty, Bitter

You've seen how a wide range of colors arises from three types of cones and how patterns of odors arise from the combinations of receptors being activated. The brain uses this same mixing-and-matching trick for taste. Traditionally, the tastes of all foods have been regarded as being made up of combinations of four tastes: sweet, sour, salty, and bitter (Bartoshuk & Beauchamp, 1994; Scott & Plata-Salaman, 1991). In addition, another taste, called *umami*, has been identified. This taste is stimulated by the most abundant amino acid, glutamate, which is present in many high-protein foods (such as meat and seafood). Pure glutamate produces this taste, just as pure salt produces its distinctive tang. The umami taste is registered by two additional detectors, both of which respond to monosodium glutamate (MSG)—often used as a "taste enhancer" in Chinese restaurants (Chaudhari et al., 2000; Ruiz et al., 2003). Moreover, free nerve endings in the mouth appear to be irritated by spicy foods (Lawless, 1984), which provides another source of information about taste, one that is not directly related to the taste buds. Different parts of the mouth and tongue are more or less sensitive to different tastes; you can detect bitter flavors best in the back of your mouth (Shallenberger, 1993). However, these different sensitivities are a matter of degree: All kinds of taste buds are found in most locations on the tongue. Curiously, there is a "taste hole" in the middle of the tongue, an area where there are no taste buds at all.

Taste and Smell

Most people think that the flavor of food arises from its taste (Rozin, 1982), but, in fact, much of what we think of as taste is actually smell, or a combination of smell and taste. For example, aspartame (NutraSweet) tastes sweeter if you are simultaneously smelling vanilla (Sakai et al., 2001). In rats, the two types of information converge on a region of the frontal lobes that is critical for the perception of flavor (Schul et al., 1996). Next time you have a stuffy nose, notice the flavor of your food, or lack thereof—particularly when you close your eyes and eliminate top-down processing to fill in your perception of the flavor. Researchers have found that people have a much harder time detecting most flavors when smell is blocked (Hyman et al., 1979). Kahlo might have liked the idea of not being able to smell her husband's body odor, but not smelling at all would ruin the taste of everything from chocolate to chili peppers.

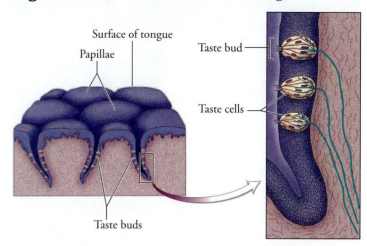

Figure 3.24 Taste Buds on the Tongue

The taste buds on the tongue line the sides of the *papillae*, the visible bumps.

Somasthetic Senses: Not Just Skin Deep

The vestibular and kinesthetic senses often work together. These people would be out of a job (or worse) if either sense failed. The vestibular sense lets them know how their bodies are oriented relative to gravity, and the kinesthetic sense lets them know where their limbs are relative to their bodies.

The traditional five senses—sight, hearing, smell, taste, and touch—were listed and described by Aristotle more than 2,000 years ago. It would be a sad commentary on the value of science if we couldn't do better after all this time. Today, we are able to argue that there are at least nine senses, perhaps ten: sight, hearing, smell, taste, and then a collection of five (or six) senses that together are called **somasthetic senses**. These senses all have to do with perceiving the body and its position in space: kinesthetic sense (awareness of where the limbs are and how they move), vestibular sense (sense of balance), touch, temperature sensitivity, and pain. There may be a sixth somasthetic sense, magnetic sense. And, finally, some researchers have argued that there is possibly an eleventh sense: extrasensory perception, or ESP.

Kinesthetic Sense: A Moving Sense

Read this, and then close your eyes and hold out your left arm in an odd position. Now, keeping your left arm in place, touch your left hand with your right hand. You shouldn't have any trouble doing this because you know where your hands are without having to see them. You know because of your **kinesthetic sense**, which registers the movement and position of the limbs. Two types of specialized cells sense this information: One type is in the tendons (the material that connects muscles to bones) and is triggered by tension; the other is in the muscles themselves and is triggered by whether the muscle is stretched out or contracted (Pinel, 1993).

Vestibular Sense: Being Oriented

The inner ear is used not only for hearing, but also for balance. The **vestibular sense**, which provides information about how your body is oriented relative to gravity, relies on an organ in the inner ear that contains three *semicircular canals* (illustrated in Figure 3.19, on p. 125). If these structures are disrupted, say by infection or injury (or by spending too much time in weightlessness in outer space, as happens to astronauts), people have a difficult time keeping their balance.

Touch: Feeling Well

Here's another trick question: What's your body's largest organ? The lungs? The intestines? The answer is the skin. As well as protecting our bodies from the environment (such as dirt, germs, flying objects, changes in temperature), making crucial vitamins, and triggering the release of various hormones, the skin is also a massive sensory organ. Millions of receptors in the skin produce impulses when stimulated in specific ways. Moreover, the same mechanism used by the other senses is at work here: It is the particular combination of receptors being stimulated that produces a specific sensation. The mix-and-match principle is at work here, too: We can feel many more types of sensations than we have types of receptors. Receptors in the skin in different parts of the body send impulses to different parts of the somatosensory cortex (see Chapter 2); in general, the more cortex devoted to a particular area of the skin, the more sensitive that area is (Weinstein, 1968).

Somasthetic senses: Senses that have to do with perceiving the body and its position in space—specifically, kinesthetic sense, vestibular sense, touch, temperature sensitivity, pain sense, and possibly magnetic sense.

Kinesthetic sense: The sense that registers the movement and position of the limbs.

Vestibular sense: The sense that provides information about the body's orientation relative to gravity.

Women tend to be more sensitive to touch than are men (Weinstein, 1968). Moreover, women are especially sensitive (relative to men) on some parts of their bodies, such as their backs and stomachs.

Temperature

The skin has separate systems for registering hot and cold; indeed, there are distinct spots on your skin that register *only* hot or *only* cold. These spots are about 1 millimeter across (Hensel, 1982). If a cold spot is stimulated, you will feel a sensation of cold even if the stimulus is something hot. This phenomenon is called **paradoxical cold**. People are not very good at telling exactly where a hot or cold stimulus is located, particularly if it is near the skin but not touching it (Cain, 1973).

Pain

Despite the discomfort, even the agony, pain brings, the inability to feel pain is even worse in the long run than the inability to smell odors. Sternbach (1978) described children who could not feel pain normally and who picked off the skin around their nostrils and bit off their fingers because they didn't notice what they were doing. Pain serves to warn us of impending danger, and it is crucial to survival.

The sensation of pain arises primarily when two different kinds of nerves are stimulated. These nerves have fibers that differ in size and in the speed with which they transmit impulses. Thus, we can feel **double pain**: The first phase, of sharp pain, occurs at the time of the injury; it is followed by a dull pain. The two kinds of pain arise from different fibers sending their messages at different speeds (Rollman, 1991).

One of the ways we deal with pain is by producing substances in our brains, called **endorphins**, that have painkilling effects. Some drugs, such as morphine, bind to the same receptors that accept endorphins, which explains how those drugs can act as painkillers (Cailliet, 1993). However, pain involves more than simple bottom-up processing. In fact, a **placebo**—which relies on your belief that a medically inert substance in fact has medicinal value—activates some of the same brain structures as do drugs such as morphine (Petrovic et al., 2002). In addition, although the parts of the brain that are activated when we feel pain are distinct from the parts that are activated when we *anticipate* feeling pain, the two sets of areas are very close (Ploghaus et al., 1999), which suggests that anticipating pain could interact with the real thing. And, in fact, top-down processing can directly inhibit the interneurons that regulate the input of pain signals to the brain (Gagliese & Katz, 2000; Melzack & Wall, 1982; Wall, 2000). This mechanism, called **gate control**, may explain how hypnosis can influence pain (Kihlstrom, 1985); indeed, hypnosis can selectively alter our experience of the unpleasantness of pain without affecting how intense it feels. Hypnosis thus may alter processing in only some of the brain areas that register pain (Rainville et al., 1997). Inhibitory impulses from the brain to neurons that send signals from the body may also occur when pain is reduced by a *counter-irritant*—a painful stimulus elsewhere in the body (Willer et al., 1990).

People differ widely in the amount of pain they can withstand; Rollman and Harris (1987) found that some people could put up with as much as eight times as much pain as others. And women at certain phases of the menstrual cycle have a lower threshold for pain (Hapidou & De Catanzaro, 1988). MacGregor and colleagues (1997) found that the threshold for pressure-based pain was highly correlated among twins, but this correlation was equally high for both identical and fraternal twins. Because identical twins share all their genes but fraternal twins

Acupuncture, the placing of small needles to treat pain, may work because the needles are a counter-irritant; this idea makes sense according to the gate control theory of pain (Carlsson & Sjoelund, 2001; Chapman & Nakamura, 1999).

Paradoxical cold: The sensation of cold that occurs when certain nerves in the skin are stimulated by something hot.

Double pain: The sensation that occurs when an injury first causes a sharp pain, and later a dull pain; the two kinds of pain arise from different fibers sending their messages at different speeds.

Endorphins: Painkilling chemicals produced naturally in the brain.

Placebo: A medically inactive substance that is presented as though it has medicinal effects.

Gate control (of pain): The top-down inhibition of interneurons that regulate the input of pain signals to the brain.

share only half their genes, the finding of the same correlation suggests that there is no substantial genetic component to pain thresholds. Instead, this correlation is more likely a result of a common family environment.

Other Senses

Two additional senses are more controversial. One of these—magnetic sense—may not exist in humans, and one—extrasensory perception—may not exist at all.

Magnetic Sense: Only for the Birds?

Many birds migrate long distances each year, guided in part by the magnetic field of the earth. Tiny bits of iron found in crucial neurons of these birds apparently play a role in this sense (Gould, 1998; Kirschvink et al., 2001). Researchers have not only documented that at least some mammals (in particular, mole rats) also have this ability, but they have zeroed in on the crucial part of the brain that underlies it (a subcortical structure called the *superior colliculus*; Nemec et al., 2001). There is evidence that humans have a weak form of this sense (Baker, 1980), but the phenomenon has not yet been studied in enough detail to conclude with certainty that we all possess it. Magnetic fields have been shown to disrupt spatial learning in mice, at least for brief periods of time (Levine & Bluni, 1994). This is a sobering finding because the magnetic fields used in these studies were weaker than those commonly used in magnetic resonance imaging (MRI) machines.

Extrasensory Perception (ESP)

The ability to perceive and know things without using the ordinary senses is often referred to as **extrasensory perception (ESP)**, but also sometimes called *anomalous cognition* or *psi*. Many forms of ESP have been asserted, including *telepathy*, the ability to send and transmit thoughts directly, mind to mind; *clairvoyance*, the ability to know about events directly, without using the ordinary senses or reading someone else's mind; and *precognition*, the ability to foretell future events. In addition, *psychokinesis* (PK), the ability to move objects directly, not by manipulating them physically, has also been reported (this ability is not a form of ESP, since it does not involve perception or knowing).

Most psychologists are skeptical about ESP and PK, for at least the four following reasons (Alcock, 1987, provides additional ones):

- *Failure to replicate*. The effects of ESP and PK studies are difficult to repeat. To be fair, some ESP researchers have argued that such failures to replicate occur because the phenomena depend on personality, details of the setting, and other variables (Brugger et al., 1990; Honorton, 1997; Watt & Morris, 1995). But as more such qualifications are added, the harder it becomes to disprove the claims, and the field is thus nudged further away from science.

- *Lack of brain mechanism*. It is not known how the brain could possibly produce or pick up ESP signals or produce PK signals.

- *Lack of signals*. No "ESP signals" have been measured, and it is not known what form these signals might take. For example, physical energy (such as

Extrasensory perception (ESP): The ability to perceive and know things without using the ordinary senses.

magnetic or electrical waves) typically declines in strength with increasing distance from the source, but there is no hint that the same is true for ESP or PK signals.

- *Alternative explanations.* Finally, there is the specter of alternative explanations, which rely on known facts about mental processing and behavior. Although many recent ESP studies are well-designed, many still leave open possible avenues for the influence of other factors.

In spite of many years of hard work by many dedicated scientists, this field remains highly controversial (Bem & Honorton, 1994; Child, 1985; Thalbourne, 1989).

LOOKING BACK: *Review*

1. *How does the sense of smell work?* We are able to smell when molecules are the right shape to fit into specific olfactory receptors, which in turn send impulses to the brain. As with colors, the range of possible smells arises from the combinations of outputs from different receptors; we do not have a different receptor for every possible odor we can distinguish.

2. *How does the sense of taste work?* Taste arises from five types of taste receptors (which produce the taste sensations of sweet, sour, salty, and bitter and respond to glutamate) and from nerves that respond to irritation; combinations of outputs from these receptors produce taste. However, what we commonly think of as taste, in fact, relies in part on our sense of smell.

3. *How do we sense our bodies?* We sense the positioning of our bodies via the kinesthetic and vestibular senses. The kinesthetic sense lets you know the positions of your limbs and identify whether your body has moved. An impairment of the vestibular sense can cause problems with keeping one's balance. When stimuli trigger receptors on the skin, you experience the sensation of pressure, temperature, or pain.

4. *Do a magnetic sense and extrasensory perception (ESP) exist?* Some birds definitely can sense magnetic fields, but it has yet to be solidly established whether humans also have this ability. In addition, although there is some evidence for some forms of ESP, these findings are difficult to replicate. It is not clear how the brain would register ESP signals or how ESP signal transmission would work.

LOOKING BEYOND: *Critical Thinking*

Say your uncle is a food fanatic, loving every morsel and seeking out only the best. Should you recommend that he blow his nose before each meal and not waste his money going to fancy restaurants when he has a bad cold? Why or why not?

Should researchers spend time studying ESP instead of studying the nature of learning, reasoning, or the traditional five senses? What are the potential pros and cons of studying ESP rather than abilities that clearly are used by everyone every day?

LET'S SUM IT UP

I. Vision: Window on the World

A. Sensation is the immediate registration of basic properties of an object or event, such as its color, whereas perception is the organization and interpretation of the sensory input as signaling a particular object or event.

B. You detect sensory stimuli when they exceed some threshold, but the level of that threshold depends in part on how hard you try to detect the stimuli. In addition, you can adjust your criteria so that you are more or less willing to guess.

C. Vision begins with light, which consists of physical energy of certain wavelengths.

D. The retina, a thin sheet of tissue at the back of the eye, contains types of cells that convert light to nerve impulses. These signals are sent to the brain and initiate the processes of visual sensation and perception.

E. Rods are sensitive to light but do not register color, whereas cones register color but are not as sensitive to light. Ganglion cells also transduce physical energy into neural signals, but these signals do not produce an image of the stimulus.

F. The operation of the three types of cones (each tuned to be most sensitive to a different wavelength of light), in combination with the opponent cells, underlies our ability to see color.

G. The trichromatic theory of color vision focused on the ways that responses to different wavelengths of light are combined, whereas the opponent process theory focused on the ways that different colors can inhibit perception of other colors.

H. Visual perception can be divided into two phases. The first takes the outputs from sensory processing and organizes them into sets of perceptual units that correspond to objects and surfaces.

I. The Gestalt laws of organization (such as similarity, proximity, continuity, good form, and closure) describe how the visual system organizes lines, dots, and other elements into perceptual units.

J. The distance, size, and shape of figures are also specified in ways that do not vary when the object is seen from different viewpoints.

K. The second phase of visual perception involves making the input meaningful.

L. "What" and "where" are identified by separate neural pathways during the second phase of visual perception. In the "what" pathway, the input is matched to information already stored in memory, which allows you to know more about the stimulus than you can see at the time. In the "where" pathway, locations are coded, using either spatial categories or spatial coordinates.

M. Perception relies on a combination of bottom-up processes, which are initiated by properties of the stimuli affecting receptors, and top-down processes, which are guided by knowledge, expectation, or belief.

N. Attention can be guided both by stimulus properties (bottom-up) and by personal knowledge, expectation, and belief (top-down).

O. When simple features are embedded in other simple features (like a red light in a sea of green lights), the stimulus "pops out" and attention is not necessary for easy detection.

P. Finally, some information can be identified outside visual awareness.

II. Hearing

A. Auditory sensation arises when you register sound waves—pressure waves that move molecules (usually in air, but also in liquids and solids).

B. Sounds differ in pitch (which reflects variations in frequency) and loudness (which reflects variations in amplitude).

C. For most frequencies, the ear uses the position of maximal activity on the basilar membrane to specify the frequency, but for low frequencies the rate of vibration of the basilar membrane may also indicate frequency.

D. Hair cells along the basilar membrane, when stimulated, produce nerve impulses, which are sent to the brain. Hair cells that respond to specific frequencies can be impaired by exposure to loud sounds.

E. Auditory perception begins with processes that organize sound into units and specify the locations of those units in space. Sounds are organized using Gestalt principles (such as similarity in pitch) and are localized using a combination of cues that rely on the two ears (such as differences in loudness) and cues that rely only on a single ear (such as changes in loudness resulting from movement).

F. Auditory perception occurs when input matches information stored in memory. Top-down processing can actually fill in missing sounds, as occurs in the phonemic restoration effect.

G. Not only can you understand speech sounds by accessing the appropriate stored memories, you can also understand environmental sounds (such as the meaning of a siren).

III. Sensing and Perceiving in Other Ways

A. The senses of smell and taste are considered to be the chemical senses because they detect the presence of particular molecules.

B. Both smell and taste involve mechanisms in which the right molecule triggers a specific receptor, which in turn sends neural signals to the brain. Both smell and taste rely on combinations of receptors being activated.

C. Pheromones can influence some types of emotional reactions and sexual behavior.

D. Instead of the traditional five senses, you have at least nine, and possibly ten: In addition to sight, hearing, smell, taste, and touch, you have a kinesthetic sense, a vestibular sense, temperature sensitivity, the ability to feel pain, and possibly a magnetic sense.

E. These additional senses all inform you about the state of your body (where limbs are located, how the body is positioned or located, what is touching you or otherwise affecting your skin).

F. Each part of the skin is mapped out on the somatosensory cortex, with the amount of brain surface reflecting the relative sensitivity in that region.

G. Pain is registered by two different systems, which can produce the feeling of double pain. Top-down processing can affect interneurons involved in pain, allowing your beliefs and desires to affect the degree to which you feel pain.

H. Finally, some researchers have argued that an eleventh sense, extrasensory perception (ESP), exists. However, the evidence for ESP is shaky, and there has yet to be a reliable demonstration that any form of it actually exists.

Key Terms

LOOKING ONLINE: *Enhance Your Learning*

MyPsychLab is an interactive and instructive multimedia resource that can be used to supplement a traditional lecture course or as an online course. It is an all-inclusive tool with a text-specific e-book plus multimedia tutorials, videos, simulations, animations, and controlled assessment to completely engage students and reinforce learning. MyPsychLab meets the individual learning needs of every student. Visit *www.mypsychlab.com* for more information!

Practice Test

For each of the following items, choose the single best answer.

1. When enough physical energy strikes a sense organ, its receptor cells send neural impulses to the brain. What is the result?
   a. Sensations arise.
   b. Perception occurs.
   c. Psychophysics is invalidated.
   d. None of the above statements is true.

2. Weber's law is
   a. always accurate.
   b. never accurate.
   c. remarkably accurate except for very large or very small magnitudes of stimuli.
   d. rarely accurate except for very large or very small magnitudes of stimuli.

3. Why does the world around us appear sharp and clear?
   a. The lens in a human eye cannot flex.
   b. We are constantly moving our eyes, and what we choose to look at can quickly be moved into focus.
   c. The iris changes the size of the pupil to let in more or less light.
   d. Light is a form of electromagnetic radiation.

4. When you first enter a darkened theater, you can't see a thing; if you wait even a brief time, you can see much better. This occurs because

   a. there are no rods or cones at the place where the optic nerve exits the retina.
   b. night vision is based on the firing of the cones alone.
   c. circadian behavior changes when light is shined on the eyes.
   d. your pupil enlarges and the rods actually become more sensitive.

5. The trichromatic theory of color vision
   a. contends that if a color is present, it causes cells that register it to inhibit the perception of the complementary color.
   b. was developed by Ewald Hering.
   c. contends that color vision arises from the combinations of neural impulses from three different kinds of sensors, each of which responds maximally to a different wavelength.
   d. is not accurate because most of us possess four types of cones.

6. The Gestalt law of organization known as _____ states that marks that form a single shape tend to be grouped together.
   a. proximity
   b. good form
   c. similarity
   d. continuity

7. Given that our eyes capture images in only two dimensions, how is it that we see in three?

a. The Gestalt laws of organization enable us to create a third dimension.

b. Perceptual constancies stabilize the world.

c. The brain uses different types of cues to derive three dimensions from the two-dimensional images on the retinas of the eyes.

d. If an object is *recognized*, it seems familiar; if it is *identified*, you know additional facts about it.

8. Movies are produced by a series of still photos, presented very rapidly in sequence. Why do we see movement, when there really isn't any?

a. If you are moving directly toward an object, it seems to expand symmetrically around its center and thus loom closer.

b. Progressive changes in texture signal distance.

c. Your brain uses slight differences in the images striking each of your eyes to assess the distance to an object.

d. The phi phenomenon, a particular kind of illusion, can produce the appearance of motion that is indistinguishable from real motion.

9. Bottom-up processing

a. is guided by knowledge, expectation, or belief.

b. cannot be in play at the same time as top-down processing.

c. can sometimes produce remarkably complex experiences, such as synesthesia.

d. explains how you know that an apple *may* have a worm inside, even if you can't see one *this* time.

10. Relative to the right cerebral hemisphere, the left cerebral hemisphere

a. may be better at specifying categorical spatial relationships, which are easily named by a word or two.

b. may be better at specifying coordinate spatial relations, which are essential for navigation.

c. is not involved in specifying spatial relations.

d. is always relatively poor at registering information about space.

11. In general, pop-out

a. is a top-down process.

b. occurs only in visual perception.

c. is the only reason we pay attention.

d. occurs when objects differ in their fundamental qualities.

12. About 40% of normal people emit a detectable soft humming sound from their ears, of which they are unaware. These sounds

a. are like the natural sonar used by whales, sound waves bouncing off objects and returning to the ear.

b. play a crucial role in hearing.

c. are probably caused by feedback from the brain to the ear; feedback (not the sounds produced by it) helps us hear slight differences in sounds.

d. can never be heard by other people.

13. If a tree falls in the forest but nobody hears it, would psychologists say that there is a sound?

a. yes, always

b. no

c. yes, but only if the sound is caused by waves of molecules

d. yes, but only if there are no molecules to be moved

14. The hammer, anvil, and stirrup

a. reflexively loosen if you hear a sound.

b. expand when you talk.

c. are the smallest bones in the human body.

d. produce nerve impulses that are sent to the brain.

15. In general, women are

a. 20 times more sensitive to odors than are men.

b. particularly sensitive to smell if they take birth control pills.

c. better at detecting odors the older they get.

d. particularly sensitive to smell when they are ovulating—unless they take birth control pills.

• •

Answers: 1. a 2. c 3. b 4. d 5. c 6. b 7. c 8. d 9. c 10. a 11. d 12. c 13. b 14. c 15. d

chapter 4

Learning
How Experience Changes Us

" Learning how to sleep standing up was probably the most useful thing that school ever taught me. "

CHAPTER OUTLINE

J ACKIE CHAN, ACTOR, DIRECTOR, MARTIAL ARTS CHOREOGRAPHER, AND STUNTMAN, begins his autobiography, *I Am Jackie Chan* (Chan & Yang, 1999), at the moment he is 45 years old and about to jump from the 21st floor of an office building in Rotterdam, the Netherlands, for his movie *Who Am I?* The stuntmen on the film had only done the jump from the 16th floor, and Chan never asks his stuntmen to do stunts that he himself would not do. Jackie Chan did, in fact, jump from the 21st floor and land safely.

Chan had begun kung fu training in early childhood: His father woke him up each morning before sunrise and required him to work out for hours as the sun rose progressively higher into the sky. His father came from a long line of Chinese warriors and believed that "pain gives you discipline. Discipline is at the root of manhood. And so, to be a real man, one must suffer as much as possible" (Chan & Yang, 1999, p. 10).

Chan's early childhood years were spent living in the French embassy in Hong Kong, where his father was the cook and his mother the housekeeper and laundress; the ambassador's youngest daughter was his friend, and he spent all day at home. When Chan was around 6 years old, he went to 1st grade, but had a hard time sitting still in the classroom. He was always making jokes and getting into trouble, often being forced to stand in the hallway, holding a desk over his head. Chan writes in his autobiography: "Sometimes I'd have to wear a sign around my neck, explaining the nature of my crime. Like, 'This is a noisy, ill behaved boy.' Or, 'This boy lost all of his books.' Or, 'This boy has not done his homework.' Sometimes it would just say, in a couple of [Chinese] characters, 'Useless!' " Chan describes standing out in the hall as "peaceful." "And, if no one was looking," he says, "I'd gently put the desk down, lean against the wall, and catch a few winks. Learning how to sleep standing up was probably the most useful thing school ever taught me" (p. 16).

Jackie Chan found the process of learning to read and write tedious, boring, and difficult. He was not promoted to 2nd grade and did not return to school the following year, remaining at home all day with his parents. Shortly thereafter, his parents brought him to visit Yu Jim-Yuen's Chinese Drama Academy, a residential school that trained students in the ancient art of Chinese opera. However, this school was not like any acting or martial arts school with which you might be familiar. In fact, schools like this no longer exist in Hong Kong because the training methods are now considered abusive, with the children rising at 5 a.m., training in martial arts, singing, and drama, for more than 12 hours, then doing chores and perhaps receiving a couple of hours of traditional "school" a few evenings a week. The children went to sleep at midnight, on the hard wooden floor with only a blanket, in the same room in which they trained during the day. Their "day" was 19 hours long, 365 days each year. School discipline included being hit repeatedly with a cane, often past the point where blood was drawn.

Jackie Chan has undertaken many dangerous stunts in his career. Why does he put himself at such risk (so great, in fact, that no insurance company will provide insurance on his films!)? According to Chan, the answer is that he wants to please his fans; their approval is very important to him. Both Chan's ability to make the type of films he does and the fact that the audience's approval is important to him reflect the capacity to learn—to learn skills and goals toward which to strive.

To learn is to discover, and the need to discover compels us from birth to the end of our days. Learning helps us both to survive and to realize our deepest dreams. It underlies virtually all of our behavior: what we eat and the way we eat it, how we dress, how we acquire the knowledge contained in books like this one, and how we live in a society with other people. And yet not all learning is positive in its results: Sometimes we "learn" to do things that either may not be good for us (as when Chan does his own death-defying stunts) or may not be what we wished to learn (as when Chan came to live out his father's view that manhood equals suffering). We can learn to do things that hurt as well as help.

Whereas many fields focus on the content of what people learn (historians, for example, add to their knowledge by finding out more facts about history), psychologists interested in the field of learning focus on the *process* of learning as well as the content. How does learning occur? To discover this, researchers have investigated both humans and animals, and, in this chapter, we look at some of the principles their research has revealed.

What did Chan learn from Master Yu Jim-Yuen's beatings? How did he learn to do martial arts so successfully? How did the audience's response to his early movies influence Chan's subsequent movies and his public behavior? Psychologists attempt to answer questions like these, in part, through theories of learning.

Psychologists define **learning** as a relatively long-term change in behavior that results from experience. When, for example, you have mastered tying

Learning: A relatively permanent change in behavior that results from experience.

your shoelaces, you will likely be able to secure your shoes properly for the rest of your life. This durability is true of all learned behavior, in virtually every domain of life, from riding a bicycle to participating in a conversation.

But, what about the following case? Suppose you watch someone write your name in Chinese characters: Having seen it done, can you claim that you have learned how to do it? What if you are able to duplicate the characters successfully? Can you legitimately say that you have learned to write your name in Chinese?

In the first instance, unless you have a photographic memory and excellent drawing ability, the answer is probably no. Merely watching someone do something complex and unfamiliar on a single occasion is usually not enough to allow you to learn it. In the second instance, even if you copy the characters correctly, the answer is still likely to be no. Just performing an action once is not enough; unless you can do it repeatedly and without assistance, you cannot claim that you have really learned to do it. You may have learned some elements of the task, but not the entire pattern, and so you cannot claim to have mastered it.

Learning can take place in a variety of ways. The simplest form of learning is *non-associative learning*, which occurs when repeated exposure to a stimulus alters an organism's responsiveness; ==habituation== occurs when repeated exposure decreases responsiveness. For instance, if you are walking in a city and hear a car horn honk nearby, you may well be startled; if other horns chime, you will not startle as much (if at all). Here's another example: When a wild animal, such as an elk, comes into contact with a human hiker (who does not scare the elk or try to harm it), that elk will habituate to humans; the next time a peaceful hiker comes by, the elk will likely allow the hiker to come even closer before it runs away.

When repeated exposure to a stimulus *increases* responsiveness, *sensitization* occurs. For example, suppose you are trying to go to sleep and your neighbor is playing music relatively quietly (you may not have even noticed). All of a sudden, his stereo blasts for a few seconds, then quiets down to the same level it was before. You now notice the music—at this quiet level—more than you did originally. You are sensitized to it.

Many other types of learning are by association—relating one object or event with another object or event. This general phenomenon is what psychologists call *associative learning*. This chapter will explore different types of learning. For all types, the criterion for learning is that we demonstrate a relatively long-term change brought about by experience.

Let's begin by exploring the model of associative learning investigated not quite a hundred years ago—classical conditioning.

Habituation: The learning that occurs when repeated exposure to a stimulus decreases an organism's responsiveness to the stimulus.

Classical Conditioning

Unfortunately, Jackie Chan's early life was filled with adversity, often in the form of physical punishment. Within a few weeks of living at the Chinese Drama Academy, Chan received his first caning:

> *Master pushed me down to the ground and told me to lie flat on my belly. I closed my eyes and gritted my teeth. I felt my pants being roughly drawn down to my knees, as my belly and thigh collapsed on the polished wooden floor. Then a whistle and a crack, a*

Classical conditioning: A type of learning that occurs when a neutral stimulus becomes paired (associated) with a stimulus that causes a reflexive behavior and, in time, is sufficient to produce that behavior.

Unconditioned stimulus (US): A stimulus that elicits an automatic response (UR), without requiring prior learning.

Unconditioned response (UR): The reflexive response elicited by a particular stimulus.

sound that I registered in my brain just a flash before the pain raged from my buttock up my spine. (Chan & Yang, 1999, p. 38)

That whistling sound came to elicit fear in Chan; *elicit* means that the response (fear) is drawn out of the organism (in this case, Chan). When a student received a caning (in front of the rest of the students), the entire class would cringe on hearing the sound. This fear response (and the cringe) is a complex example of classical conditioning.

In its simplest form, classical conditioning is a type of learning in which a neutral stimulus becomes associated, or paired, with a stimulus that causes a reflexive behavior and, in time, is sufficient to produce that behavior.

In Chan's case, the whistling sound of the fast-moving cane became paired with the extreme pain of the beating, thereby eliciting the fear and the cringe. The simplest example of the way classical conditioning works is found in the famous experiments that established the principle: the work of Pavlov and his dogs.

LOOKING AHEAD: *Learning Objectives*

1. *What is classical conditioning? How was it discovered?*
2. *How are conditioned responses eliminated?*
3. *What are common examples of classical conditioning in daily life?*

Pavlov's Experiments

Classical conditioning is also sometimes called *Pavlovian conditioning* because Ivan Pavlov (1849–1936), a Russian physiologist, was the first person to investigate systematically the variables associated with classical conditioning. Pavlov's work on conditioning began by accident. As part of his work on the digestive processes, which won him a Nobel Prize, Pavlov studied salivation in dogs. To measure the amount of saliva that dogs produced when given meat powder (food), Pavlov collected the saliva in tubes attached to the dogs' salivary glands (see Figure 4.1). Pavlov and his colleagues noticed that even though salivation usually occurs during rather than before eating, his dogs were salivating before they were fed: They would salivate simply on seeing their food bowls or on hearing the feeder's footsteps.

The Three Phases of Classical Conditioning

Intrigued, Pavlov pursued the issue with more experiments. His basic method is still in use today (see Figure 4.2). Pavlov would sound a tone on a tuning fork just before the food was brought into the dogs' room. After hearing the pairing of the tone with the food several times, the dogs would salivate on hearing the tone alone. Because food by itself elicits salivation, Pavlov considered the food the **unconditioned stimulus (US)**—that is, a stimulus that elicits an automatic response that does not depend on prior learning. The dogs' salivation is termed the **unconditioned response (UR)**, the reflexive or automatic response elicited by a US. The UR

Figure 4.1 **Pavlov's Apparatus for Measuring Salivation**

Ivan Pavlov started out measuring saliva production in dogs as part of his research on the digestive system. He went on to use this same saliva collection technique with his investigations into classical conditioning.

Figure 4.2 The Three Phases of Classical Conditioning

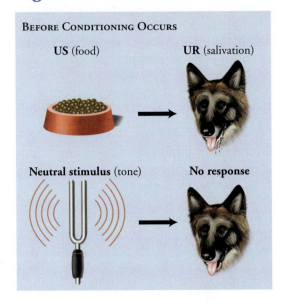

BEFORE CONDITIONING OCCURS

US (food) → UR (salivation)

Neutral stimulus (tone) → No response

CONDITIONING OCCURS

CS (tone) + US (food)

Then the CS is paired with the US—here, the tone is sounded and then the food is presented.

CONDITIONING IS COMPLETE

CS (tone) → CR (salivation)

Classical conditioning is complete when the CS elicits the conditioned response—here, the dog salivates after hearing the tone.

Before conditioning occurs, the CS does not lead to a conditioned response, but the US does.

does not require learning, but it does depend on certain circumstances. For example, if an animal has just eaten and is full, it will not salivate when presented with food. In Pavlov's experiment, the tone is the ==conditioned stimulus (CS)==—that is, an originally neutral stimulus that acquires significance through pairing(s) with a US. After hearing the tuning fork a number of times before they were fed, the dogs began to associate the tone with food. Thereafter, whenever the dogs heard the tone, even when presented by itself, they salivated. Salivation in response to the tone alone is thus a ==conditioned response (CR)==, a response that depends (is conditional) on pairings of the CS with a US (Pavlov, 1927). Not surprisingly, psychologists call the initial learning of the conditioned response ==acquisition==.

Variations of the Procedure

In an attempt to discover what factors might affect the process of conditioning, Pavlov and researchers after him altered the variables involved in creating a conditioned response. Initially, researchers thought that to create a conditioned response, the US (the food) must immediately follow the CS (the tone) in a procedure called *forward conditioning*, which occurs when the CS begins before the US begins.

After studying forward conditioning, Pavlov tried the reverse order, called *backward pairing*, where the US comes first, followed quickly by the CS: He fed the dogs first and presented the tone 10, 5, or 1 second later. He found no conditioning; the dogs did not salivate when hearing the tone after eating the food. Although Pavlov did not achieve backward conditioning with his dogs, other researchers have since found that such conditioning can occur in some animals (Chang et al., 2003). Presenting the US and CS simultaneously, called *simultaneous conditioning*, does not usually lead to a conditioned response (Hall,

Conditioned stimulus (CS): An originally neutral stimulus that acquires significance through pairings with an unconditioned stimulus (US).

Conditioned response (CR): A response that depends, or is conditional, on pairings of the conditioned stimulus with an unconditioned stimulus; once learned, the conditioned response occurs when the conditioned stimulus is presented alone.

Acquisition: In classical conditioning, the initial learning of the conditioned response (CR).

1984), although such conditioning is possible (Albert & Ayres, 1997; Barnet et al., 1991). Generally, in order for conditioning to occur, the US (food, in this example) should follow the CS (tone) immediately; however, there are exceptions, including certain food aversions, in which there may be a longer interval between the presentation of conditioned and unconditioned stimuli. As we will see, a food aversion is one of the rare examples where strong conditioning can occur when there is a long interval between the presentation of the CS and the US.

Classical Conditioning: How It Works

Researchers studying classical conditioning have discovered a good deal about how organisms (human or otherwise) engage in this form of learning. Some conditioned responses remain with us all of our lives; others fade or even disappear altogether.

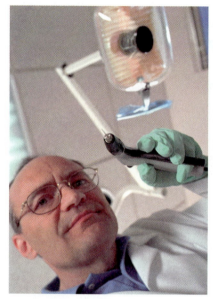

Does avoidance learning explain why some people put off going to the dentist for many years?

Another Russian researcher, Vladimir Bechterev (1857–1927), also conducted conditioning experiments. Here the US was a shock, and the UR was a dog's withdrawal of its foot. When a neutral stimulus such as a bell (CS) was paired with the shock, the dog learned to withdraw its foot (CR) after the bell but before the shock, thus successfully learning to avoid pain. Bechterev's findings were an important extension of Pavlov's work in that he extended the conditioned response to motor reflexes. Bechterev also established the basis for **avoidance learning** (Viney, 1993)—classical conditioning with a CS and an unpleasant US that leads the organism to try to avoid the CS.

Conditioned Emotions: Getting a Gut Response

If you saw a cane like the one used to beat students at the Chinese Drama Academy leaning against a chair, chances are that it would not make you cringe or show any other signs of fear. The cane is a *neutral* stimulus. However, for Jackie Chan and his schoolmates, the cane that Master Yu held in his hand was no longer a neutral object or stimulus. Repeated beatings with it created a specific type of conditioned response called a **conditioned emotional response (CER)**—an emotionally charged conditioned response elicited by a previously neutral stimulus.

A landmark study by John B. Watson, the founder of behaviorism (see Chapter 1), and his assistant Rosalie Rayner (Watson & Rayner, 1920) illustrates how classical conditioning can produce a straightforward conditioned emotional response of fear, and how fear can lead to a **phobia**, an irrational fear of a specific object or situation. Watson and Rayner classically conditioned fear and then a phobia in an 11-month-old infant—Albert B.—whom they called "Little Albert" (see Figure 4.3). Through the use of classical conditioning, Watson and Rayner created in Albert a fear of rats; on seeing a white rat, Albert would cry and exhibit signs of fearfulness. This study could not be done today because of the rigorous ethical principles that now govern psychological research (see Chapter 1) but did not exist at the time the study was undertaken. Neither Watson nor Rayner followed up on what happened to Albert after the study because the boy and his mother moved away.

Preparedness and Contrapreparedness

Although it was initially thought that any response could be conditioned by any stimulus (Kimble, 1981), this supposition is not entirely true. Organisms seem to have a **biological preparedness**, a built-in readiness for certain conditioned stimuli to elicit particular conditioned responses (Domjan et al., 2004), so less condi-

Avoidance learning: In classical conditioning, learning that occurs when a CS is paired with an unpleasant US that leads the organism to try to avoid the CS.

Conditioned emotional response (CER): An emotional response elicited by a previously neutral stimulus.

Phobia: An irrational fear of a specific object or situation.

Biological preparedness: A built-in readiness for certain conditioned stimuli to elicit particular conditioned responses, so less conditioning (training) is necessary to produce learning.

Figure 4.3 Classical Conditioning of a Phobia: Little Albert

Initially, Little Albert did not show a fear of animals, but he did exhibit fear if a loud noise was made behind his back (a hammer striking a steel bar).

Then the researchers presented a white rat (CS) and made the loud noise (US).

After five presentations of the CS and US, Albert developed a phobia of rats—he began whimpering and withdrawing (the conditioned emotional response) and trying to avoid the rat. After two more presentations of the CS and US, he immediately began crying on seeing the rat. "He . . . fell over on his left side, raised himself . . . and began to crawl away so rapidly that he was caught with difficulty before reaching the edge of the table" (Watson & Rayner, 1920, p. 5).

tioning (training) is necessary to produce learning. For instance, you may learn to avoid a certain kind of cheese if the first time you eat that variety you become nauseated. The fact that it takes only one pairing of the cheese and the nausea for you to develop an aversion to that food is an example of biological preparedness. Similarly, research has shown that it is easier to condition a fear response to some objects than to others. Öhman and colleagues (1976) used pictures as the CS and shock as the US. They found that the fear-related response of sweaty hands is more easily conditioned, and less easily lost, if the CS is a picture of a snake or a spider than if it is a picture of flowers or mushrooms. Snakes, rats, and the dark are typical objects of phobias. Some have argued that the fear response to these makes sense from an evolutionary perspective—sensitivity to the presence of such possibly dangerous elements in the environment could help an organism survive (Seligman, 1971).

Contrapreparedness is a built-in disinclination (or even an inability) for certain conditioned stimuli to elicit particular conditioned responses. For example, Marks (1969) described a patient he was treating as an adult. When this woman was 10 years old, she was on a car trip and had to go to the bathroom. Her father pulled off the road so that she could relieve herself in a ditch. As she stepped out of the car, she saw a snake in the ditch—and at that moment

Contrapreparedness: A built-in disinclination (or even an inability) for certain conditioned stimuli to elicit particular conditioned responses.

her brother accidentally slammed the door on her hand. At 43, she was still deathly afraid of snakes, but she was not afraid of car doors, which had actually done the damage. Similarly, Bregman (1934) failed—with 15 different infants—to replicate Watson and Rayner's experiment when, instead of a rat as the CS, she used various inanimate objects, such as wooden blocks and pieces of cloth. There was no evidence of conditioning when the US was a loud noise and the CS was an inanimate object. These two examples highlight the point that certain stimuli, such as a car door and a wooden block, do not make successful conditioned stimuli.

Figure 4.4 Acquisition, Extinction, and Spontaneous Recovery in Classical Conditioning

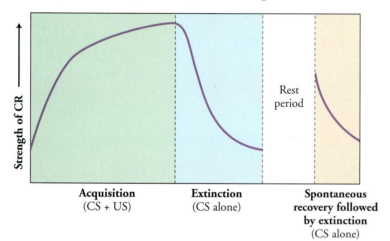

When the CS and US are paired, the organism quickly acquires the CR (left panel). However, when the CS occurs without the US, the CR quickly weakens (blue panel). After a rest period, the CR returns in response to the CS alone, but this is followed by extinction (right panel).

Extinction: In classical conditioning, the process by which a CR comes to be eliminated through repeated presentations of the CS without the presence of the US.

Spontaneous recovery: In classical conditioning, the event that occurs when the CS again elicits the CR after extinction has occurred.

Extinction and Spontaneous Recovery in Classical Conditioning: Gone Today, Here Tomorrow

The good news is that even after a conditioned response (such as a fear of snakes) is acquired, it is possible to diminish such a response significantly in the presence of the CS. This does not happen because of forgetting, which occurs simply with the passage of time. Rather, the process involved is called **extinction**, in which the CR is gradually eliminated, or *extinguished*, by repeated presentations of the CS without the US. How would this work with Pavlov's dogs? If the tone continues to be presented, but is not followed by the presentation of food, after a while the dogs will no longer salivate at the tone: The CR will be extinguished. This process is graphed in Figure 4.4.

However, after a conditioned response has been extinguished and the animal does not encounter the CS for some period of time (in an experiment, referred to as a "rest period"), when the CS is later presented, it will again elicit the CR—although sometimes not as strongly as before extinction. This event is called **spontaneous recovery** (see Figure 4.4). Let's go back to those dogs: As just noted, after the tone has been presented several times without any food forthcoming, the dogs' salivation response will be extinguished, and they will stop salivating to the tone alone. However, if the tone is not presented for a period of time before it is presented again, the previously learned conditioned response of salivation will return on simply hearing the tone. The dogs have spontaneous recovery of the response, but they may not salivate as much as they did when they were first classically conditioned to the tone.

Once classical conditioning has occurred, the connection between the CS and the US apparently never completely vanishes. After extinction occurs, the organism can be retrained so that the CS again elicits the conditioned response; in this case, learning takes place more quickly than it did during the original training period. It is much easier to condition again, after extinction, than it is to condition in the first place.

In his work on extinction and spontaneous recovery, Bouton (1993, 1994, 2000) showed that what occurs during extinction is not the forgetting of old learning, but rather the production of new learning that exists along with the old learning and interferes with the previous classically conditioned response (Bouton, 2002). Thus, according to Bouton's work, if Little Albert's fear of rats had been extinguished (that is, if the rat had been presented without the loud noise often enough that it failed to elicit the CR), Albert's association between the rat and the noise would *not* have disappeared, but rather new learning would have occurred "on top of" his previous learning. Thus, the CS (rat) would no longer signal that the US (noise) was about to occur, at least not in that context—not in Watson's testing room (Bouton, 2000).

Generalization and Discrimination in Classical Conditioning: Seen One, Seen 'Em All?

Watson and Rayner wrote that, 5 days after the conditioning of Little Albert, a rabbit, a dog, a fur coat, cotton, and a Santa Claus mask all elicited the conditioned response of fear in him. This is an example of **stimulus generalization**, a tendency for the conditioned response to be elicited by neutral stimuli that are like, but not identical to, the conditioned stimulus; in other words, the response generalizes to similar stimuli. Moreover, because of a *generalization gradient*, the more closely the new stimulus resembles the original CS, the stronger the response. Stimulus generalization can be helpful for survival because often a dangerous stimulus may not occur in exactly the same form the next time. Without stimulus generalization, we might not know to be afraid of lions as well as tigers.

In addition to stimulus generalization, organisms are also able to distinguish, or discriminate, among stimuli similar to the CS and to respond only to the actual CS; this ability is called **stimulus discrimination**. Stimulus discrimination can be extremely helpful for survival; consider that one type of mushroom may be poisonous, but another type is food. If Albert had been shown a pile of cotton balls without a loud noise occurring (but continued to be presented with a rat paired with the loud noise), only the rat would have elicited fear. Albert would have been able to discriminate between the two similar stimuli.

Cognition and the Conditioned Stimulus

Although strict behaviorists might not agree that thoughts play a role in classical conditioning, research suggests otherwise (see Chapter 1 for an explanation of behaviorism). The context in which classical conditioning occurs and the expectations that arise following classical conditioning influence the learning (Hollis, 1997; Kirsch et al., 2004). For example, Rescorla (1967) presented rats with a tone (CS) immediately before delivering a shock (US); these rats quickly learned a fear response to the tone. However, another group of rats heard the tone and were shocked, but sometimes the tone was presented after the shock. As Pavlov had found years earlier, backward pairing does not produce conditioning: This group did not come to fear the tone.

Apparently, the CS provides information by signaling the upcoming US (and therefore UR), and conditioning occurs because the animal is learning that relationship: Our current understanding is that the CS is a signal that the US will occur, at least in the particular context in which the conditioning took place. Even a placebo's effect can involve cognitive elements: The placebo signals the probability of a future event, and thus the animal (which can be a human) comes to *expect*—consciously or not—that the placebo will lead to a particular response (Kirsch, 2004; Stewart-Williams & Podd, 2004).

Kamin (1969) provided more evidence that mental processes lie between stimulus and response during conditioning. He conditioned rats by pairing a tone with a brief shock; the rats developed a conditioned fear response to the tone. But when he added a second CS by turning on a light with the tone, the rats did not develop a conditioned fear response to the light alone. Kamin hypothesized that

Stimulus generalization: A tendency for the CR to be elicited by neutral stimuli that are like, but not identical to, the CS; in other words, the response generalizes to similar stimuli.

Stimulus discrimination: The ability to distinguish among stimuli similar to the CS and to respond only to the actual CS.

the original pairing of tone and shock was blocking new learning. The light did not add new information and was therefore of no consequence and not worth their attention. The tone was enough of a signal, and the rats didn't seem to view the light as a signal. Thus, Kamin concluded that classical conditioning takes place only if the pairing of CS and US provides useful information about the likelihood of occurrence of the US.

In keeping with this way of interpreting conditioning, researchers have found that even a mental image of an object—what you see in your "mind's eye" when you visualize something—can play a role in classical conditioning, as either a CS or a US. For instance, imagining food can lead to salivation in humans (Dadds et al., 1997): Visualize the most scrumptious dessert you've ever eaten (was it a banana split? baked Alaska? ice cream drowning in chocolate sauce?). Imagine it in vivid detail. If the image is vivid enough, you may start salivating—the image is an unconditioned stimulus, the salivation is an unconditioned response.

Dissecting Conditioning: Mechanisms

The brain generally operates by a divide-and-conquer approach: Different neural structures confer different aspects of an ability. Classical conditioning is no exception. Not only are different neural structures used in different aspects of conditioning, but also different sorts of classical conditioning rely in part on different regions of the brain. Here we will consider fear conditioning (the best understood type) in detail, but also briefly see key differences with eye-blink conditioning and other sorts.

Learning to Be Afraid

Consider the case of a driver who has been honked at by a huge truck as it roars by and has barely missed being crushed. At the time of the incident, the driver experienced fear. As a result of this close encounter, when he later hears the sound of a horn and sees a truck drive by, he feels a twinge of fear—even if that truck, in fact, poses no danger. Such conditioned responses are acquired via the joint actions of the following neural mechanisms.

1. *The information registers in the brain.* When the driver later hears the sound of a horn and sees a truck drive by, the images and sounds are processed in the visual cortex and the auditory cortex, respectively.

2. *The amygdala reacts.* After the information is registered, a specific part of the amygdala reacts to the sounds and sights and plays a crucial role in storing the stimulus-response associations that underlie fear.

3. *The hippocampus helps store associations with context.* The hippocampus allows us to associate a conditioned stimulus with a particular context (such as the place where that truck barreled by the driver; Bast et al., 2003; Hall et al., 2001; Trivedi & Coover, 2004).

4. *Another part of the amygdala kicks in.* Next, another part of the amygdala triggers the behaviors that *express* fear and conditioned fear—for example, wincing when an 18-wheeler rumbles by (Cardinal et al., 2002).

5. *Other parts of the brain contribute to the outward display of fear.* Finally, yet other parts of the brain play a role in actually producing the behaviors that accompany fear. For example, Maschke and colleagues (2002) presented tones

In one study, some rats were allowed to exercise and others were not. Both groups then heard tones, which were followed by shocks. The rats that exercised showed stronger conditioning to the particular context in which the shocks occurred. Why? Exercise enhances the functioning of the hippocampus and, in so doing, makes rats better able to distinguish the context in which a shock was delivered (Baruch et al., 2004).

followed by electric shocks to humans, and they found that normal people were soon conditioned—their heart rate slowed down when they heard the tone (a decreased heart rate is related to "freezing" behavior seen in other animals—which may conserve energy and reflect focused attention). But this behavior was not induced in patients who had suffered damage to the cerebellum, which suggests that this part of the brain is important for regulating heart rate in a conditioned fear response.

6. *Sets of neurons become linked.* The result of conditioning is that sets of neurons become linked. With the honking truck, conditioning causes brain cells that register the stimulus to fire in tandem with cells in the amygdala that trigger the fear response. Activity in the two sets of neurons becomes hooked together, so that whenever the stimulus occurs, the amygdala automatically triggers the response. A crucial finding is that this linked activity never disappears entirely: Even after conditioning has been extinguished, linked neural activity remains, making it very easy for an animal (or person) to relearn a conditioned response.

Learning When to Blink

Have you ever heard a gun being fired at close range? If you have, you may have noticed that you blinked. And after this experience, simply seeing someone nearby on the verge of pulling the trigger may cause you to blink. Such eye-blink conditioning has been studied extensively, usually by using a tone (the CS) to signal an air puff to the eye (the US), which in turn evokes a blink (the UR). After conditioning, the tone alone will produce a blink (which is now a CR). Such conditioning has been shown to rely partly on neural structures different from those that underlie fear conditioning. For example, eye-blink conditioning relies on the cerebellum not just to express behavior, but also to form and store the conditioned associations themselves. Humans with brain damage to the cerebellum do not learn the association of tone and air puff as well as normal people do (Gerwig et al., 2003).

However, as we saw with fear conditioning, eye-blink conditioning does not arise from the actions of a single brain structure; the hippocampus, basal ganglia, and amygdala (among other brain structures) also contribute (Christian & Thompson, 2003). In fact, different parts of the cerebellum play different roles in eye-blink conditioning (Bao et al., 2000; Thompson et al., 1997).

Eye-blink conditioning may not be as inherently interesting as fear conditioning (learned fear is more important in daily life), but researchers have used eye-blink conditioning to study more general issues. For example, it is known that eye blinks are not as easily conditioned in old rats as in young rats. Researchers hypothesized that antioxidants in the diet can enhance brain function, and particularly that of the cerebellum. To investigate this idea, they fed some elderly rats spinach-enriched chow, which was high in antioxidants. And sure enough, the elderly rats that ate their spinach acquired eye-blink conditioning faster than did other elderly rats that ate a normal diet (Cartford et al., 2002). Popeye the sailor was onto something!

Finally, yet other brain areas may be crucial for other sorts of conditioning, such as the conditioning of pain (Kung et al., 2003), and for discriminating among stimuli (Cardinal et al., 2003).

In short, classical conditioning is a complex activity, which relies on many different neural structures working together. Moreover, different forms of conditioning rely, to some degree, on different parts of the brain.

Classical Conditioning Applied

If the investigation of classical conditioning had ended with the study of dogs' salivation, the great psychological importance of this kind of learning might not have been recognized. But other studies of classical conditioning showed that emotional responses, such as the fear response, can be conditioned, and emotional responses exert a powerful effect on people's lives. If a friend slaps you hard on the back every time you see him, you are likely to wince even as he lifts his arm to begin his greeting, and in time classical conditioning will affect how you feel about him. Classical conditioning can play a role in the effectiveness of medicines, in the operation of our immune systems, and in other aspects of health and illness (as you will see in Chapter 10). Even without our awareness, it contributes to our feelings about events and objects, including ourselves (Baccus et al., 2004; Bunce et al., 1999; Núñez & de Vincente, 2004), and to our sexual interests (Lalumiere & Quinsey, 1998).

Drug Use and Abuse

Classical conditioning plays a role in deaths caused by drug overdoses. A user who generally takes a drug in a particular setting—the bathroom, for instance—develops a conditioned response to that place (Siegel, 1988; Siegel et al., 2000; Siegel & Ramos, 2002). Here's what happens. Because of classical conditioning, as soon as the user walks into the bathroom, his or her body begins to compensate for the influx of drug that is soon to come—a *conditioned compensatory response* (Siegel & Ramos, 2002). This conditioned response is the body's attempt to counteract, or dampen, the effect of the drug. When the user takes the drug in a new setting, perhaps a friend's living room, this conditioned response does not occur. Because there is no conditioned response to the new setting, the user's body does not try to counteract the effect of the drug. The net result is a higher effective dose of the drug than the user can tolerate, leading to an overdose.

Similarly, classical conditioning also helps explain why people addicted to cocaine experience drug cravings merely from handling money (Hamilton et al., 1998). Part of the experience of using cocaine is buying it, often just before using it. Thus, handling money becomes a CS. In the same way, among cigarette smokers certain environmental stimuli can elicit a desire for a cigarette (Lazev et al., 1999), and virtual reality simulations of heroin-related cues can elicit a craving for the drug in heroin addicts (Kuntze et al., 2001). So, classical conditioning explains why some smokers automatically reach for a cigarette when they get a phone call or have a cup of coffee, often without realizing what is happening.

Therapy Techniques

Classical conditioning also serves as the basis for a number of psychotherapy techniques, including systematic desensitization, which has been used to treat phobias (this therapeutic technique and others are discussed in more detail in Chapter 12). (According to classical conditioning principles, phobias are conditioned emotional responses.) *Systematic desensitization* is the structured and repeated presentation of a feared conditioned stimulus in circumstances designed to reduce anxiety. Systematic desensitization works to extinguish the phobic response by teaching people to be relaxed in the presence of the feared object or situation, such as an elevator for those with an elevator phobia. With systematic desensitization, the CS no longer elicits the CR (fear); extinction has occurred.

Advertising

John B. Watson revolutionized the advertising industry when he formalized its use of behavioral principles while working for an ad agency. For instance, the use of "sex appeal" to sell products stems from Watson's ideas. Sex isn't the only unconditioned stimulus that can work to produce a desired response; Razran (1940) did a study showing that political slogans (CS), when paired with the eating of food (US), were viewed more favorably by participants. Classical conditioning continues to be used in advertising to promote consumers' positive attitudes about products (Grossman & Till, 1998; Kim et al., 1998; Till & Priluck, 2000). This is referred to as *evaluative conditioning*: The goal is to change your liking, or evaluation, of the conditioned stimulus—the product the advertisers want you to buy (De Houwer et al., 2001).

Through the obvious sex appeal of this man and woman, Polo Sport® is trying to get you to buy its swimwear. If you find the ad to have sex appeal, then classical conditioning principles suggest that your mild arousal or pleasure on seeing the ad (and thereafter on seeing the product itself, following its pairing with the attractive couple) would lead you to buy the product.

Food and Taste Aversion

When animals or people have an unpleasant experience during or after they eat or even just taste a particular food (leading them to try to avoid that food), they may develop a <mark>food</mark> or <mark>taste aversion</mark>. This type of classical conditioning usually involves learning after only a single experience of the CS–US pairing. Generally, the US is a nausea- or vomiting-inducing agent, and the CS is a previously neutral stimulus that was paired with it, such as the sight or smell of the food. The UR is nausea or vomiting, and so is the CR.

If you have ever had food poisoning, you may have developed a classically conditioned food aversion. A likely scenario is that the food that made you sick had some unhealthy and unwanted ingredient, such as salmonella bacteria. The bacteria are the US, and the ensuing nausea and vomiting are the UR. If the salmonella was in your dinner of broiled trout, trout might become a CS for you; whenever you eat it (or perhaps another fish similarly prepared), you become nauseated (the CR). Rather than put yourself through this experience, you are likely to avoid eating broiled trout, and a food aversion is born.

Garcia and colleagues (1966) accidentally discovered the existence of taste aversion when studying the effects of radiation on rats. The rats were exposed to high enough doses of radiation that they became sick. The researchers noticed that the rats drank less water from the plastic water bottle in the radiation chamber than from the glass water bottle in their "home" cage. Although this preference could have been due to many factors, it turned out that the water in the plastic bottle had a slightly different taste, thanks to the plastic, than did the water in the glass bottle. The researchers shifted their focus to discover *why* the rats drank less from the plastic than the glass bottle. Was it because the taste of the water in the plastic bottle had become associated with the radiation that made the rats sick, and thus become a CS? If so, then the radiation was the US, the taste of the water from the plastic bottle was the CS, getting sick was the UR, and the aversion to the water from the plastic bottle would be the CR. The researchers tested this hypothesis and found that it was

Food aversion (taste aversion): A classically conditioned avoidance of a certain food or taste.

Figure 4.5 Taste Aversion Conditioning

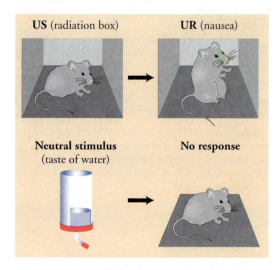

US (radiation box) → UR (nausea)

Neutral stimulus (taste of water) → No response

THE CS IS PAIRED WITH THE US.

CS (taste of water) + US (radiation box)

CS (taste of water) → CR (nausea)

Did Garcia and Koelling (1966) inadvertently create a classically conditioned taste aversion, where the US was the radiation, the CS was the taste of water in the plastic bottle in the radiation chamber, the UR was the rat getting nauseated, and the CR was the rat's taste aversion?

correct: The taste of water in the plastic bottle was a CS, causing the CR of the rats' taste aversion (see Figure 4.5).

Garcia and Koelling's research led to another important discovery. (As often occurs in science, following up on a curious result can lead to unexpected but interesting and important discoveries.) Continuing with experiments on conditioned taste aversion, Garcia and colleagues (1966) found that rats avoided novel-tasting water even if the nausea didn't occur until several hours after that water was presented. This further research showed that, at least in this case, the US doesn't need to come immediately after the CS. These findings stirred considerable controversy because they described exceptions to the "rules" of classical conditioning.

Classical conditioning is adaptive, whether it involves an animal's (including a human's) ability to learn which foods are poisonous or which animals or objects in the environment (such as predators or guns) to fear and avoid. The more readily an organism learns these associations, the more likely that organism is to survive. Learned food aversions based on one exposure can be particularly adaptive: Animals who readily learn what not to eat will probably live longer and have more offspring.

Conditioning and Chemotherapy

Cancer patients undergoing chemotherapy may experience intense nausea and vomiting as side effects of the treatment. But some patients develop *anticipatory nausea*, a classically conditioned response to chemotherapy triggered by a previously neutral CS (Burish & Carey, 1986; Carey & Burish, 1988; Davey, 1992). Such a stimulus might be as innocuous as a florist's shop seen en route to the hospital. For others undergoing chemotherapy, just thinking about the hospital where the treatment is received can produce nausea (Redd et al., 1993).

What is happening? The activity of neurons that feed into the patient's immune and autonomic nervous systems, stimulated by the US (the chemotherapeutic drugs) that induces the UR (nausea), becomes paired with the activity of neurons that register certain sights or sounds, for example, the sight of the florist shop, which becomes the CS. After enough such pairings, the two groups of neurons become functionally connected, and activity in one group triggers activity in the other (producing a CR).

However, some patients are more likely than others to develop anticipatory nausea. Some people are generally more reactive than others; that is, they have a tendency toward a stronger autonomic response to given levels of stimulation. Such people who become chemotherapy patients are more likely to develop anticipatory nausea (Kvale & Hugdahl, 1994), which can lead to a sense of helplessness and can cause them to stop the treatment altogether (Siegel & Longo, 1981). Fortunately, behavioral interventions such as relaxation training can help control anticipatory nausea, as can anti-nausea medications (Vasterling et al., 1993).

Conditioning the Immune System

Suppose you worked day and night for a week, hardly taking the time to eat or sleep, and so severely weakened your immune system that you became very sick. During that exhausting work-filled week, you spent all of your waking hours with a laptop computer on your bed, which is covered by a bright red bedspread. Do you think that, after your recovery, simply sitting on that same bedspread could cause your immune system to weaken? Ader and his colleagues (Ader, 1976; Ader & Cohen, 1975) have shown that this kind of conditioning does in fact happen in rats. Ader and Cohen paired saccharin-flavored water with injections of cyclophosphamide, a drug given to organ transplant donors that suppresses the immune system and has a side effect of nausea. Ader had intended to use this drug not for its immune-suppressing qualities, but as a way to induce nausea in a study of taste aversion. He wanted to see how long the taste aversion would last once injections of cyclophosphamide stopped, but the rats continued to drink sweetened water (the CS).

A few rats died on day 45 of the experiment, and more died over the next several days. Ader was confused; he had done similar experiments before with a different nausea-inducing drug and none of those animals had died. He eventually showed that the taste of the sweetened water was triggering not just the nausea, but a suppression of the immune system (as the actual drug would do), causing the eventual death of the rodents. Each time the rats drank the sweetened water, their immune systems were weakened—even without the immune-suppressing drug! The taste of the saccharin-sweetened water was acting as a CS, and this water was in essence a placebo. The rats' bodies responded to the CS as if it were cyclophosphamide.

Ader's accidental discovery and his follow-up studies were noteworthy for two reasons: First, they showed that a placebo response (which is sometimes referred to as a *placebo effect*) could be induced in animals, not just humans; second, they showed that the organism doesn't have to believe that the placebo has medicinal properties in order to produce a placebo response. Although Ader and Cohen could not ask the rats what they believed would happen when they drank the sweet water, we have no reason to think that they "believed" it would impair their immune systems (Dienstfrey, 1991). Ader and Cohen have reported a number of follow-up studies, all trying to rule out other explanations of their results, and their hypothesis about the conditioning of the immune system has stood up well. Indeed, another study with rats showed that the immune response could be boosted by conditioning (Gorcynski, cited in Dienstfrey, 1991). There is evidence that the placebo effect may be a conditioned immune response that occurs in humans (Voudouris et al., 1985).

Classical conditioning explains why some people undergoing chemotherapy develop anticipatory nausea Previously neutral stimuli—such as the sight of a florist shop on the way to the hospital—after being paired with nausea-inducing chemotherapy, can come to elicit nausea. Fortunately, treatments exist to prevent or minimize such conditioning.

LOOKING BACK: *Review*

1. *What is classical conditioning? How was it discovered?* Pavlov discovered classical conditioning through his studies of dogs' salivation. This phenomenon involves the pairing of a conditioned stimulus (CS, such as a tone) with an unconditioned stimulus (US, such as food). The US reflexively elicits an unconditioned response (UR, such as salivation), and with repeated US–CS pairings, the CS will come to elicit a conditioned response (CR, salivation).

2. *How are conditioned responses eliminated?* Extinction, the "unpairing" of the CS and US, is achieved by repeatedly presenting the CS without the US. If extinction is followed by a rest period, the CS may again elicit the classically conditioned response; this is known as spontaneous recovery. In stimulus generalization, a similar but nonidentical stimulus elicits the CR. In stimulus discrimination, the organism learns to distinguish among similar stimuli so that only a particular stimulus will elicit the CR.

3. *What are common examples of classical conditioning in daily life?* Classical conditioning is used in advertising and behavior therapy and is the

mechanism underlying food or taste aversions and conditioned immune responses (as can occur with a placebo effect).

⬤ LOOKING BEYOND: *Critical Thinking*

Dog obedience classes suggest that the following procedure will train a dog to stop barking. When the dog starts to bark, squirt water (from a water bottle) into its face. Right before you squirt, say, "Don't bark!" The dog startles because of the water and stops barking. Is this classical conditioning? If so, identify the US, CS, UR, and CR. If not, why not? What learning process has occurred if the dog stops barking only when you give the command in a particular tone of voice?

Operant Conditioning

Classical conditioning is not the only way that Jackie Chan learned. At times Master Yu would give some of the students special rewards—extra food or a meal in a restaurant—or special punishments. Chan's classmates were also sources of rewards and punishments: Younger classmate Yuen Baio (who later acted in several of Chan's films) was a friend, providing support, camaraderie, and sometimes snacks from his parents' weekly gift of food. Moreover, Chan was honored with the most powerful reward at the school—a much desired place in the Seven Little Fortunes, a troupe of seven students who performed nightly in front of a paying audience (the income from the performances, however, went to Master Yu to pay for the running of the school).

How did the food treats come to be such a powerful force in Chan's life? And, how did the possibility of being picked to perform in the Seven Little Fortunes exert such a powerful influence on Chan and the other students, motivating them to practice even harder and more intensely than they otherwise would have? The answer might lie in another kind of learning, **operant conditioning**, the process whereby a behavior becomes associated with its consequences.

⬤ **L**OOKING AHEAD: *Learning Objectives*

1. *What is operant conditioning? How does it occur?*
2. *What is the difference between reinforcement and punishment?*
3. *How are complex behaviors learned? How are these new behaviors maintained?*
4. *What is the role of dopamine during operant conditioning?*

The Roots of Operant Conditioning: Its Discovery and How It Works

If your behavior is followed by a positive consequence, you are more likely to repeat that behavior in the future; if it is followed by a negative consequence, you are less likely to repeat it. For instance, suppose you are swamped with schoolwork, and the day before a paper is due, you ask the professor for an extension (the behavior). If the professor gives you an extension (positive consequence), you will probably be more likely to ask for an extension in the future. In contrast, should

Operant conditioning: The process by which a behavior becomes associated with its consequences.

the professor refuse you and get angry (negative consequence), you will probably be less likely to ask for an extension in the future. This basic observation about behaviors and their consequences underlies the mechanism of operant conditioning. Unlike classical conditioning, in which the organism is largely passive, operant conditioning requires the organism to "operate" in the world, to do something. Operant conditioning is also called *instrumental conditioning*, because behavior is required to produce the effect. Whereas classical conditioning usually involves involuntary reflexes, such as cringing in response to hearing the whistling of a cane whipping through the air, operant conditioning usually involves voluntary, nonreflexive behavior, such as singing a song, assuming a kung fu stance, or eating with chopsticks or a fork.

Thorndike's Puzzle Box

At about the same time that Pavlov was working with his dogs, American psychologist Edward L. Thorndike (1874–1949) was investigating a different kind of learning. Thorndike created a puzzle box, a cage with a latched door that a cat could open by pressing down on a pedal inside the cage (see Figure 4.6). Food was placed outside the cage door. Although the cat took a while to get around to pressing down the pedal, once it did (and the door opened), the cat was quicker to press the pedal in its subsequent sessions in the box: It had learned that pressing the pedal opened the door and enabled it to get the food (see Figure 4.7). Thorndike called this type of learning "trial-and-error learning." His finding led to his famous formulation of the **Law of Effect** (Thorndike, 1927), which lies at the heart of operant conditioning: Actions that subsequently lead to a "satisfying state of affairs" are more likely to be repeated (Thorndike, 1949, p. 14).

The Skinner Box

B. F. Skinner (1904–1990), the 20th century's foremost proponent of behaviorism, is important in the history of psychology not only because he most fully developed the concept of operant conditioning, but also because he showed how conditioning could explain much of our daily behavior. Working mostly with pigeons and wanting to minimize his handling of the birds, he developed an apparatus that is now often referred to as a *Skinner box*. The box (see Figure 4.8, on p. 160) could both feed the animals and record the frequency of their responses, making it easy to quantify the responses (this enormously helpful feature was, in fact, an unintended bonus of the box's design; Skinner, 1956). If a rat is put in a Skinner box, it learns to associate pressing the lever or bar with the likelihood of a food pellet's appearing. Here, the lever is the stimulus, pressing the lever is the response, or behavior, and receiving the food pellet is the consequence.

Figure 4.6 Thorndike's Puzzle Box

Thorndike placed a hungry cat inside the box and a piece of fish just outside the door, within the cat's sight. The cat tried many behaviors to get out of the box and to the fish, but only pressing the pedal would open the door. Eventually, the cat pressed the pedal, and the door opened. When the cat was put back inside the box, it pressed the pedal more quickly, improving each time.

Figure 4.7 The Phases of Operant Conditioning

Unlike classical conditioning, operant conditioning requires the organism to produce the desired behavior (the response). That behavior is then followed by a positive or negative consequence.

Law of Effect: Actions that subsequently lead to a "satisfying state of affairs" are more likely to be repeated.

Figure 4.8 Skinner Box and Cumulative Recorder

In a Skinner box, a hungry rat presses a lever (or a pigeon pecks a key). As with Thorndike's cat, the rat will emit random behaviors, eventually pressing the lever, causing a food pellet (reinforcement) to come down the chute into the food dish, increasing the likelihood of the response in the future. The rat presses the lever again, and another food pellet appears. It presses the lever (and eats) more frequently—it has learned that pressing the lever will be followed by the appearance of a food pellet. On the outside of the box is a cumulative recorder, a device that records each lever press and the time interval between presses.

Principles of Operant Conditioning

Operant conditioning involves an association between a stimulus, the response to the stimulus (a behavior), and its consequence. (In classical conditioning, the association is between a neutral stimulus and an unconditioned stimulus.) Operant conditioning relies on **reinforcement**, the process by which consequences lead to an increase in the likelihood that the response will occur again. To be most effective, the reinforcement should be contingent on a desired response. Not surprisingly, this relationship between the response and the consequence is called **response contingency**; it occurs when a consequence is dependent on the organism's producing the desired behavior. In contrast to the responses that are elicited in classical conditioning, responses in operant conditioning are *emitted*; the responses are voluntarily produced.

An example of operant conditioning occurred in Jackie Chan's life when, as a young adult, he and many other martial arts experts were seeking work as stuntmen in the Hong Kong film industry. There were more junior (young, inexperienced) stuntmen than there were jobs, and Chan desperately needed the work in order to pay his bills. One day, a director wanted a stunt done; it was deemed so unsafe by the stunt coordinator that he refused to have any of his stuntmen do it. Chan volunteered to do it, figuring that this was the only way he'd be likely to get work. He did the dangerous stunt (twice) and *did* get more jobs after that—he shifted from being a junior stuntman to a full-fledged stuntman with regular work. What Chan learned from this experience was that trying very dangerous stunts (behavior) would get him work (the reinforcement).

A **reinforcer** is an object or event that comes after a response and that strengthens the likelihood of its recurrence. In Thorndike's puzzle box and in the Skinner box, the reinforcer, or consequence, is food. Which reinforcer works best for people? The answer to this question is tricky: What one person considers a "reward" might leave another person cold. Reinforcement, therefore, is in the eyes of the recipient. For instance, for one person, a night at the ballet might be a wonderful reinforcer for doing well on a test. To another, a night at the ballet might seem like punishment.

As an illustration of this fact about reinforcers, consider an account Chan provides of the filming of his first *Rush Hour* movie, when he was already considered a "star" in America:

> The studio [spared] nothing to make me feel like I'm a star. I have a beautiful rented mansion, a luxurious trailer on the set, a personal trainer, and a car standing by at all times. Even my stuntmen have their own private rooms. In my Hong Kong movies, we squeeze together, share what we have to, and eat lunch together, all out of the same big pot. I do everything and anything I want to—I'm the director, the producer, the cam-

Reinforcement: The process by which consequences lead to an increase in the likelihood that the response will occur again.

Response contingency: The relationship that occurs when a consequence is dependent on the organism's emitting the desired behavior.

Reinforcer: An object or event that comes after a response and that changes the likelihood of its recurrence.

eraman, the prop guy, the janitor. Anything. Here, they won't let me do anything except act. They won't even let me stand around so they can check the lighting—they have a stand-in, my height, my color, wearing my clothes, come in, and they check the lighting off of him while I sit in my trailer. (Chan & Yang, 1999, p. 303)

The producers apparently thought that this "star treatment" would reinforce Chan for acting in American movies—but, in fact, he didn't like it and was itching to be more involved between scenes.

Parents who give stickers to their child for good behavior might conclude that behavioral programs don't work if the child makes no effort to win the stickers. They'd be wrong: The problem is that their child doesn't view stickers as a reward. The parents simply need to find a reinforcer that will work, increasing the likelihood that their child will repeat a particular behavior. For instance, when the authors of this book were toilet training their children, they used reinforcers whenever the children tried to use the potty. They had asked each child to name a reinforcer, and one of the children requested black olives. This is a reminder that the proof is in the pudding—the degree to which an object or event is a reinforcer is determined by its effect on the individual organism. Just calling something a reinforcer doesn't make it so.

Like classical conditioning, operant conditioning involves cognitive processing. Simply telling people about the contingency between a behavior and reinforcement can lead to behavior change (Kirsch et al., 2004), as occurs when parents or teachers explain sticker programs to children or when supervisors announce upcoming opportunities for employees to earn bonuses through improved performance.

Reinforcement: Getting Your Just Desserts

There are two types of reinforcement, positive and negative. In **positive reinforcement**, a desired reinforcer is presented after a response, thereby increasing the likelihood of a recurrence of that response (see the first row in Figure 4.9, on p. 162). The food for Thorndike's cat and black olives for the authors' toddler are examples of positive reinforcement. Food is the usual positive reinforcer for animals; for humans, toys, money, and intangibles such as praise and attention can also be positive reinforcers, as was Jackie Chan's acceptance into the Seven Little Fortunes. Chan also describes how, when he was about 6 years old, using kung fu against other kids could produce positive reinforcement: He would fight other kids who were "stupid enough to get in my way. . . . I found out quickly that fighting was fun—when you won anyway—and it soon became one of my favorite hobbies, next to eating" (p. 12).

Sometimes we inadvertently reinforce certain behaviors by paying them too much attention (positive reinforcement); this can happen when patients with coronary heart disease receive attention when talking about their symptoms, which leads them to talk even more about their symptoms (Itkowitz et al., 2003). Scolding children is another example: If the only time a child receives any attention at all is when he or she misbehaves, then even "bad attention," such as a scolding, can be a positive reinforcer. Chan did not view having to stand outside his 1st-grade classroom with a sign around his neck as punishment for his classroom antics. Therefore, he did not learn what his teachers wanted him to learn. In the workplace, increased pay can be reinforcing for some people, whereas increased recognition or flexible hours are more likely to be reinforcing for others (Rynes et al., 2005). Again, reinforcement is particular to each individual.

In contrast, **negative reinforcement** is the removal of an unpleasant event or circumstance following a behavior, thereby increasing the probability of the behavior's occurring again (see Figure 4.9, second row). If a rat is being mildly shocked in

Positive reinforcement: Occurs when a desired reinforcer is presented after a behavior, thereby increasing the likelihood of a recurrence of that behavior.

Negative reinforcement: Occurs when an unpleasant event or circumstance that follows a behavior is removed, thereby increasing the likelihood of a recurrence of the behavior.

Figure 4.9 Positive and Negative Reinforcement and Punishment

POSITIVE REINFORCEMENT

Chan's behavior (a correct landing from a flying side kick) is positively reinforced; after he does the behavior correctly, he receives a treat.

NEGATIVE REINFORCEMENT

In contrast, the same behavior is negatively reinforced: the Master has a frown as Chan is going into the move (an aversive stimulus), but the aversive stimulus is removed when Chan lands from the flying side kick correctly. The Master's goal is the same in both examples—to maximize the likelihood that the behavior (a perfect flying side kick landing) will occur again.

POSITIVE PUNISHMENT

Chan's behavior (falling when landing from a flying side kick) is being positively punished: The Master gives an unpleasant consequence (a caning) so as to minimize the likelihood that the behavior (an incorrect flying side kick landing) will occur again.

NEGATIVE PUNISHMENT

Chan's behavior (falling when landing from a flying side kick) is being negatively punished: The Master removes a pleasant event (his smile at Jackie) so as to minimize the likelihood that the behavior (an incorrect flying side kick landing) will occur again.

its cage, and the shocks stop when it presses a bar, then bar pressing is negatively reinforced. Or consider the student whose neighbor is blaring music, song after blasting song. This unpleasant event ends when the student knocks on the neighbor's door and asks the neighbor to turn down the volume—and the neighbor complies.

Figure 4.10 Positive Reinforcement and Negative Reinforcement

This couple has been positively reinforced for buying a lottery ticket—they have received a large amount of money.

The nonsmoker has been negatively reinforced for pointing out the "No smoking" sign to the smoker—the aversive cigarette smoke disappears.

Asking to have the volume lowered has been negatively reinforced. Yet another example of negative reinforcement in action is when people use substances, such as alcohol, to decrease their anxiety (Hohlstein et al., 1998; Samoluk & Stewart, 1998); because it reduces the aversive state of anxiousness, using alcohol is negatively reinforced.

Both positive and negative reinforcement are described as reinforcing because they increase the likelihood that a behavior will be repeated. (See Figure 4.10.) Negative reinforcement is *not* the same thing as punishment. Let's see why.

Positive punishment: Occurs when a behavior leads to an undesired consequence, thereby decreasing the likelihood of a recurrence of that behavior.

Punishment

A punishment is an unpleasant stimulus or event that occurs as a consequence of a behavior. Punishment *decreases* the probability of the recurrence of a behavior, in contrast to reinforcement (both positive and negative), which *increases* the likelihood of recurrence. Although punishment is commonly confused with negative reinforcement, they are not the same: Punishment decreases the probability of a recurrence of a behavior; negative reinforcement increases the probability of a recurrence of a behavior by removing an unpleasant event or circumstance after the desired behavior (see Figure 4.11).

Just as there are positive and negative forms of reinforcement, there are also positive and negative forms of punishment. Positive punishment occurs when a behavior leads to an undesired consequence, thereby decreasing the probability that the behavior will occur again (see Figure 4.9, third row). For ex-

Figure 4.11 Negative Reinforcement Versus Punishment

NEGATIVE REINFORCEMENT

Wow, what a surprise! It's nice of you to have cleaned the kitchen—and without my asking. How about if you don't have to do any more chores this week?

PUNISHMENT

I didn't ask you to clean the kitchen, did I? Now I won't be able to find things when I need them. You're grounded the rest of the weekend, young man!

The boy performed the exact same behavior in both these cases, but the consequences of his behavior are different. With negative reinforcement, he is more likely to repeat the behavior. In contrast, with punishment, he is less likely to repeat the behavior.

ample, a student may be positively punished with a failing grade for not spending a lot of effort writing a term paper. If this punishment is effective, she will be less likely to blow off the paper next time. **Negative punishment** is the removal of a pleasant event or circumstance following a behavior, thereby decreasing the probability that the behavior will occur again (see Figure 4.9, fourth row). Consider a boy who misbehaves: His parents negatively punish him by temporarily taking away his MP3 player.

Chan and his classmates were required to do handstands for at least half an hour at a time, despite distressing physical experiences as a result of remaining upside-down for so long: "after fifteen minutes, our arms would grow limp, our blood would rush to our heads, and our stomachs would begin to turn flip-flops. But we couldn't show any weakness at all. A limb that moved would receive a whack from the master's rattan cane" (Chan & Yang, 1999, p. 43). This was an example of positive punishment: Moving a limb led to a whack of the cane.

Punishment is most effective if it has three characteristics:

- *Punishment should be swift*, occurring immediately after the undesired behavior. The old threat "Wait till you get home!" undermines the effectiveness of the punishment.

- *Punishment must be consistent*. The undesired behavior must be punished each and every time it occurs. If the behavior is punished only sporadically, the person or animal doesn't effectively learn that the behavior will be followed by punishment, and so doesn't decrease the frequency of the behavior as consistently.

- *Punishment should be aversive* but not so aversive as to create problems such as high levels of fear or anxiety, injury, or new, undesired behaviors.

We must note several cautionary points about the use of punishment. First, although punishment may decrease the frequency of a behavior, it doesn't eliminate the capacity to engage in that behavior. Your little sister may learn not to push you because your mother will punish her, but she may continue to push her classmates at school because the behavior has not been punished in that context. She has learned not to push when she will be punished for it. Moreover, sometimes people are able to avoid punishment but continue to exhibit the response, as when your little sister figures out that if she hits you but then apologizes, she will not get punished.

Second, physical punishment, such as a spanking, may actually increase aggressive behavior in the person on the receiving end (Haapasalo & Pokela, 1999; Straus, 2000; Straus et al., 1997). Although punishment provides an opportunity for operant learning, seeing others use physical violence also creates an opportunity for learning by watching the behavior of others. Such learning could account for the finding that abusive parents (and physically aggressive juvenile delinquents) tend to come from abusive families (Conger et al., 2003; Kwong et al., 2003; Straus & Gelles, 1980; Straus & McCord, 1998).

A third problem created by punishment is that, through classical conditioning, the one being punished may come to fear the one doing the punishing. This may happen even if the punishment is infrequent. If the punishment is severe, a single instance may be enough for the person being punished to learn to live in fear of the punisher, as Chan and his classmates lived in fear of Master Yu. Constantly living in fear can make people and animals chronically stressed, and it can lead to depression (Pine et al., 2001).

Punishment alone hasn't been found to be as effective as punishment used in combination with reinforcement. This is because punishment doesn't convey information about what behavior should be exhibited in place of the undesired,

Negative punishment: Occurs when a behavior leads to the removal of a pleasant event or circumstance, thereby decreasing the likelihood of a recurrence of the behavior.

punished behavior. Consider a preschool-age boy who draws on the wall. You don't want him to ruin the wallpaper so you punish him, and he learns not to draw on the wall. But, at a later time, when he's feeling creative, he might draw on the floor or the door instead. However, if you punish him for wall or floor drawing and then provide him with paper and reinforce him for drawing on the paper, he can be artistically creative without inviting punishment. Because of the disadvantages of punishment, many training programs for parents emphasize positive reinforcement for good behavior; if children don't feel their parents are noticing and appreciating their efforts at good behavior, the incentive to keep it up may diminish.

Primary and Secondary Reinforcers

There are different levels of reinforcers: **Primary reinforcers** are events or objects that are inherently reinforcing (such as food, water, and relief from pain). At the Chinese Drama Academy, the children barely had enough to eat, and food became a much sought-out and fought-over item. Master Yu rewarded the Seven Little Fortunes with a trip to a restaurant after a particularly good performance. **Secondary reinforcers**, such as attention, praise, money, a good grade, and a promotion, are learned reinforcers and do not inherently satisfy a physical need. The theme park Sea World uses food as a primary reinforcer for its dolphins. It also uses secondary reinforcers such as squirting the dolphins' faces with water. Secondary reinforcers are generally not instinctually satisfying.

Simply punishing someone does not provide that person with appropriate alternative behaviors. This mother clearly states an appropriate alternative to biting someone when angry—using words to express feelings.

When Chan was at the Academy, his secondary reinforcers included being picked to be part of a troupe performing in public and the kind words and deeds of a schoolmate. In his adult life, Chan received very powerful secondary reinforcers for making movies that were his own creation: 4.2 million Hong Kong dollars and control over how the movies were made—the new studio would not require him to get their final approval over budgets or ideas.

Behavior modification is a technique that brings about therapeutic change in behavior through the use of secondary reinforcers. Programs involving mentally retarded children and adults, psychiatric patients, and prisoners have made use of secondary reinforcement. Participants in such programs earn "tokens" that can be traded for candy or for privileges such as going out for a walk or watching a particular TV show. Such tokens have also been used to reward children for desired behavior change; the tokens can be exchanged for the secondary reinforcer of watching television or playing computer games (Jason & Fries, 2004). Some behavior modification programs provide reinforcement when an interval of time has passed *without an unwanted behavior* (Conyers et al., 2003). Behavior modification techniques using secondary reinforcement have also been used in the workplace; when employees received bonus vouchers for arriving at work on time, management found a significant reduction in tardiness (Hermann et al., 1973).

An unusual use of behavior modification with secondary reinforcers was undertaken in the rural Philippines by researchers who wanted to improve nutrition among poor children (Guthrie et al., 1982). The study was designed to discover whether reinforcement would modify mothers' nutritional care of their children more than would simply giving the mothers information about health

Primary reinforcer: An event or object, such as food, water, or relief from pain, that is inherently reinforcing.

Secondary reinforcer: An event or object, such as attention, praise, money, a good grade, or a promotion, that is reinforcing but that does not inherently satisfy a physical need.

Behavior modification: A technique that brings about therapeutic change in behavior through the use of secondary reinforcers.

and nutrition for children. All of the mothers were given appropriate information. Then the health clinic provided different forms of reinforcement that were contingent on increases in the children's heights and weights. Three different villages participated in the study. In one, the reinforcement was a ticket in a clinic lottery in which the prize was food; the reinforcer used in the second village was a photograph of the child. The third village was a control group, and these people received no reinforcement for height or weight gains. One year later, children in the two villages that received reinforcement grew more and had less malnutrition than did those in the third village; no differences were observed between the first and second village.

Immediate Versus Delayed Reinforcement

The interval of time between behavior and its consequence can affect operant conditioning. In the Skinner box, for instance, if the rat receives a food pellet immediately after pressing the bar, it is receiving **immediate reinforcement**, reinforcement given immediately after the desired behavior. If the food pellet doesn't appear immediately but comes, say, 30 seconds later, the rat is receiving **delayed reinforcement**. With delayed reinforcement, the rat has some difficulty learning that bar pressing is followed by food. After pressing the bar but before receiving reinforcement, the rat may have sniffed some other section of the cage, scratched its ear, or done any number of things. It would be hard for the rat to "figure out" which behavior had produced the pellet.

Humans often work hard for delayed reinforcement. We practice kicking the soccer ball into the goal so that we'll be able to score at the next game; we study hard in college to get into graduate school or to land a good job; we put in extra hours at work to get a promotion, raise, or bonus; we push our bodies to the limit of what's possible to please an audience or receive a medal. Walter Mischel and his colleagues (1989) found that among the 4-year-olds they studied, those who would pass up a small reward now for a big one tomorrow became more socially competent and were more likely to be high achievers during adolescence.

Choosing a delayed reinforcement over an immediate one has its advantages, but the choice is not necessarily easy. A dieter trying to obtain the delayed reinforcement of looking and feeling better sacrifices immediate reinforcement (ice cream, now!) for future personal benefits. But immediate reinforcement can be very powerful, and often difficult to reject in favor of some future good. At some point, the dieter may yield to the satisfaction of eating the ice cream, or even just a normal-sized portion of dinner, instead of making yet another sacrifice for the sake of eventual slimness.

Beyond Basic Reinforcement

Operant conditioning can play a powerful role in people's lives. To see how, let's look at ways in which conditioning can be more than simply learning to respond when reinforcement is likely to result.

Generalization and Discrimination in Operant Conditioning

Just as in classical conditioning, animals (including humans) can generalize and discriminate during operant conditioning. Thus, in operant conditioning, **generalization** is the ability to emit a learned behavior in response to a similar stimulus. When a child has a runny nose, most parents teach her to wipe her nose on a tissue. She may then generalize the learned behavior of wiping her nose and begin to wipe it on similar stimuli: any available soft surface—her sleeve, her parent's shirt, her pillow.

Discrimination is the ability to engage in a learned behavior in response to a particular stimulus (wiping a runny nose on a tissue or handkerchief) but not in response to a similar one (wiping a runny nose on a shirt sleeve). The child's parents could help her make this discrimination by reinforcing her every time she wipes her nose with tissues or handkerchiefs (making sure they are readily available), and by not reinforcing her when she wipes her nose on her sleeve or on theirs.

Discrimination depends on the ability to distinguish among the different situations in which a stimulus may occur. Animals can be trained to press a bar to get food only if a tone is sounding, or only if they hear a high tone (not a low or medium tone). A **discriminative stimulus** is the cue that tells the organism whether a specific response will lead to the expected reinforcement. Experienced drivers react to a red light without thinking, automatically putting a foot on the brake pedal. In this situation, the red light is the stimulus, stopping the car is the response, and the reinforcement (negative, in this case) is avoiding a dangerous situation. But people don't stomp their right feet if they encounter a red light while walking on the sidewalk. Driving a car is the discriminative stimulus that cues the response to move the right foot.

Extinction and Spontaneous Recovery in Operant Conditioning: Gone Today, Back Tomorrow

Have you ever lost money in a vending machine? If so, does this sequence of behaviors sound familiar? You deposit coins in the machine and press the button for your selection because you have learned that the reinforcement (the food) will come down the chute. When you press the button and no food appears, you press the button again. You then have a burst of pressing the button several times (and maybe a few other buttons for good measure), and only after these responses fail to make the machine deliver the goods do you give up. As this example shows, when someone has learned a behavior through operant conditioning (putting money in a vending machine) and the reinforcement stops (the food doesn't appear), initially there is an increase in responding. After this initial burst of behavior, the response fades. This is how **extinction** works in operant conditioning.

As with classical conditioning, the original response isn't lost through extinction; what happens is that new, opposing learning takes place. In the vending machine example, the opposing learning is that dropping coins in the slot does not lead to the appearance of food. As with classical conditioning, **spontaneous recovery** occurs: If a period of time follows extinction, the old behavior will reappear. So if you don't use that vending machine for a month, you might very well put money in it again, expecting it to dispense your bag of chips.

Building Complicated Behaviors: Shaping Up

Many complex behaviors are not learned all at one time, but rather are acquired gradually. Moreover, complex behaviors may often be built on previously learned behaviors. How do the animal trainers at Sea World train the dolphins to do a high jump? The dolphins don't naturally do it, so they can't be reinforced for that behavior.

Shaping is the gradual process of reinforcing an organism for behavior that gets closer and closer to the behavior you ultimately wish to produce. It is the method that helps train dolphins to do high jumps (see Figure 4.12, on p. 168), and it is also the method by which Jackie Chan learned kung fu: The complex behaviors were gradually shaped, first by his father when he was very young, and later by Master Yu. Shaping is used when the desired response is not one that the organism would emit in the normal course of events. The process of shaping must be done in phases, nudging the organism closer and closer to the desired response. The final desired behavior is considered as a series of smaller behaviors, which become increasingly similar to the desired behavior; these smaller behaviors are called **successive approximations**. One study found that shaping

Discriminative stimulus: The cue that tells the organism whether a specific response will lead to the expected reinforcement.

Extinction: In operant conditioning, the fading out of a response following an initial burst of that behavior after the withdrawal of reinforcement.

Spontaneous recovery: In operant conditioning, the process by which an old response reappears if there is a period of time after extinction.

Shaping: The gradual process of reinforcing an organism for behavior that gets closer to the desired behavior.

Successive approximations: The series of smaller behaviors involved in shaping a complex behavior.

Figure 4.12 Shaping Dolphins at Sea World

At Sea World, training dolphins to jump requires a number of phases, each getting closer to the final goal.

First the dolphin receives reinforcement (a food treat) after touching a target on the surface of the water.

The target is raised slightly out of the water. When the dolphin touches the target, it receives food.

The target continues to be raised until eventually the dolphin's body must come out of the water for it to touch the target. The dolphin receives a treat for doing so.

procedures could train people with profound mental retardation to choose larger, but delayed reinforcement rather than smaller, immediate reinforcement. This ability to delay reinforcement is thought to be a central feature of exercising self-control (Dixon et al., 2003).

Reinforcement Schedules: An Hourly or a Piece-Rate Wage?

Skinner's work highlighted a critical element that can change the frequency of an organism's response: the schedule on which the reinforcement is delivered (Staddon & Cerruti, 2003). Reinforcement can be given every time a desired response occurs, or it can be given less frequently. When an organism is reinforced for each desired response, it is receiving <mark>continuous reinforcement</mark>. When reinforcement does not occur after every response, but only intermittently, the organism is receiving <mark>partial reinforcement</mark>. Initial learning is slower with partial reinforcement than with continuous reinforcement. For this reason, when shaping a new behavior, it is best to use continuous reinforcement until the desired behavior is stable. Thus, Sea World trainers reward a dolphin every time it touches the target on the surface of the water. An advantage of a partial reinforcement schedule, however, is that it is more resistant to extinction: The organism learns that it won't receive reinforcement after each response, so it doesn't stop doing the behavior right away when no reinforcement is given. Some partial reinforcement schedules, called <mark>interval schedules</mark>, are based on time; reinforcement is given for responses after a specified interval of time. Other schedules, called <mark>ratio schedules</mark>, are based on a specified number of the desired responses; reinforcement is given after that number of responses is emitted.

Continuous reinforcement: Reinforcement given for each desired response.

Partial reinforcement: Reinforcement given only intermittently.

Interval schedule: Partial reinforcement schedule based on time.

Ratio schedule: Partial reinforcement schedule based on a specified number of emitted responses.

Fixed Interval Schedule. On a **fixed interval schedule**, the organism receives reinforcement for a response emitted after a fixed interval of time. In a Skinner box, a rat on a fixed interval schedule of 10 minutes would receive reinforcement for the first bar press that occurs 10 minutes after the previous reinforcement was given, but not during that 10 minutes, regardless of how many times it pressed the bar. The same applies for the next 10-minute interval: The rat would receive a food pellet only for the first bar press after 10 minutes since the last reinforcement. With animals on a fixed interval schedule, the frequency of desired behavior tends to slow down right after reinforcement and pick up again right before reinforcement. A study break after every hour of studying is reinforcement on a fixed interval schedule. So is a weekly paycheck: No matter how hard you work, you will not get an additional paycheck that week. However, companies recognize that the fixed interval schedule is not necessarily the best way to reward employees, and promotions are not always available nor desirable to award. As shown in Figure 4.13 (on p. 170), responses to a fixed interval schedule produce a scalloped pattern on the graph of cumulative responses.

As a reward for working hard all week, these students see a movie every Friday afternoon; they have put themselves on a fixed interval schedule.

Variable Interval Schedule. In **variable interval schedules**, the interval is an average over time. If a rat were reinforced for its first response after 8 minutes, then after another response 12 minutes later, then 13 minutes later, then 7 minutes later, it would be on a variable interval schedule of 10 minutes. If you took a study break after approximately an hour of studying, but sometimes after 45 minutes, sometimes after an hour and 15 minutes, sometimes after half an hour, sometimes after an hour and a half, the average would be every hour, and so you would be on a variable interval 60-minute schedule. In animals, this kind of schedule creates consistent although somewhat slow responding (see Figure 4.13).

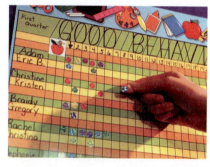

Although this teacher intends to put the appropriate star on each child's sticker chart each day, she sometimes forgets until the next day—reinforcing each child's targeted behavior on a variable interval schedule.

Fixed Ratio Schedule. **Fixed ratio schedules** provide reinforcement after a fixed number of responses. If an animal is on a "fixed ratio 10" schedule, it receives a food pellet after its 10th bar press, then again after another 10, and so on. Factory piecework is paid on a fixed ratio schedule; for example, in the garment industry, workers may be paid a certain amount for every 10 completed articles of clothing. When responses on this schedule are graphed, they assume a steplike pattern (see Figure 4.13): There is a high rate of response until reinforcement is delivered, then a lull,

The fixed ratio schedule is the schedule used to pay those doing piecework: Workers receive money for a certain number of pieces, in this case, for a certain number of tee shirts. This schedule often has the highest responding rate but can be exhausting for the workers.

followed by a high rate of response until the next reinforcement, and so on. This schedule has a higher rate of responding than a fixed interval schedule. For this reason, piecework can be exhausting, whether the work is inputting data (being paid for every 100 lines of data entered), sewing garments, or assembling machinery. On a fixed ratio schedule, workers have a good reason not to take breaks (they will not be paid for that time), but as people work long hours without breaks, efficiency and accuracy decline (Proctor & Van Zandt, 1994).

Fixed interval schedule: Reinforcement schedule in which reinforcement is given for a response emitted after a fixed interval of time.

Variable interval schedule: Reinforcement schedule in which reinforcement is given for a response emitted after a variable interval of time.

Fixed ratio schedule: Reinforcement schedule in which reinforcement is given after a fixed number of responses.

The variable ratio reinforcement schedule, often referred to as the gambling reinforcement schedule, is the most resistant to extinction. If you were playing a slot machine and didn't hit the jackpot, how long would you need to play before you might think there was a problem with the machine?

Variable Ratio Schedule. **Variable ratio schedules** present reinforcement at a variable rate. If reinforcement occurs on average after every 10th response, reinforcement could be presented after 5, 18, 4, and 13 responses, or it could presented after 24, 1, 10, and 5 responses. You never really know when the reinforcement will come. This type of schedule is often called the *gambling reinforcement schedule* because most gambling relies on such unpredictable reinforcement. Slot machines hit the jackpot on a variable ratio reinforcement schedule. If you play long enough (and spend enough money), eventually you will win; unfortunately, you might spend years, and tens of thousands of dollars, trying to hit the jackpot. The variable ratio schedule is the most resistant to extinction (which is part of the reason some people get hooked on gambling). Because you don't know exactly when you will be reinforced (but expect that eventually reinforcement will come), you keep responding. Animals on a variable ratio schedule tend to respond frequently, consistently, and without long pauses, and this kind of schedule tends to get the highest response rate; for example, Skinner (1953) found that when he shifted to reinforcing a pigeon on a variable, infrequent schedule, the pigeon continued to peck at a disk 150,000 times without reinforcement, as if still expecting reinforcement! Commission sales jobs are based on the same principle: The hope of an eventual sale (and therefore reinforcement in the form of the resulting commission) keeps salespeople pushing their wares.

Figure 4.13 Schedules of Reinforcement

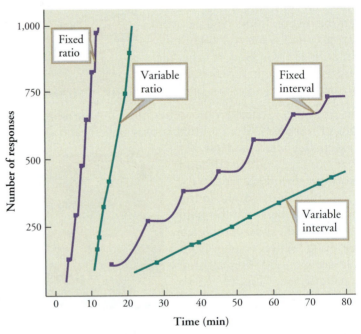

Research findings are mixed with regard to the degree of correspondence between rodents' and humans' cumulative response frequencies on the four different schedules of reinforcement. These graphs show the response patterns for rodents. Some studies with humans have found similar patterns of responding (Higgens & Morris, 1984); others have not (Lowe, 1979; Matthews et al., 1977). For both humans and rodents, however, variable reinforcement schedules induce a more consistent rate of responding than do fixed reinforcement schedules.

Variable ratio schedule: Reinforcement schedule in which reinforcement is given after a variable number of responses.

The Operant Brain

Until recently, learning theorists ignored the role of the brain in operant conditioning, focusing instead on overt behaviors. It has become clear, however, that an understanding of how the brain works can shed considerable light on this fundamental process (Montague et al., 2004).

Operant Conditioning: The Role of Dopamine

The action of the neurotransmitter dopamine lies at the core of understanding the neural events that underlie the learning of associations between stimuli, responses, and the consequences of making responses. Dopamine helps you adjust and organize your behavior so that you can achieve your goals. How does dopamine work to accomplish this? According to the most recent theories of how reinforcement alters behavior, animals plan their behaviors in advance in order to achieve certain goals, and dopamine signals the disparity between what an animal expected to happen as a result of a behavior and what actually occurred. Specifically, a burst of activity in dopamine-producing neurons (in the midbrain)—referred to as the *dopamine-based reward system*—signals that an outcome was better than expected, whereas a pause in activity of these neurons signals that an outcome was worse than expected (Fiorillo, 2004; Hollerman & Schultz, 1998; Waelti et al., 2001).

Classical Conditioning Versus Operant Conditioning: Are They Really Different?

Table 4.1 presents a comparison of operant and classical conditioning. As you can see, both classical and operant conditioning involve extinction and spontaneous

Table 4.1 Classical and Operant Conditioning Compared

	Classical Conditioning	Operant Conditioning
Similarities	• Learning is based on an association between the unconditioned stimulus and the conditioned stimulus.	• Learning is based on an association between response and reinforcement.
	• Extinction.	• Extinction.
	• Spontaneous recovery.	• Spontaneous recovery.
	• Stimulus generalization.	• Generalization.
	• Stimulus discrimination.	• Discrimination.
	• Moderating factors can affect learning.	• Moderating factors can affect learning.
Differences	• The organism is passive.	• The organism is active, "operating" on the world.
	• Responses are reflexes (limited number of possible responses).	• Responses are voluntary behaviors (limitless possible responses).
	• Responses are elicited.	• Responses are emitted.
	• "Reinforcement" is unrelated to learning the association.	• Reinforcement is contingent on the desired response.

recovery, generalization, and discrimination. In both types of conditioning, response acquisition is affected by moderating factors, especially time (in classical conditioning, the length of time between CS and US; in operant conditioning, the length of time before reinforcement, which can be immediate or delayed). Also, for both types of conditioning, biological factors influence how easily certain behaviors can be learned.

Noting these similarities, some researchers have debated whether these two types of conditioning are really so distinct after all. Perhaps they are just different procedures toward a similar end. Indeed, their differences are not so clear-cut. Some studies, for example, show that voluntary movements can be shaped via classical conditioning (Brown & Jenkins, 1968). Similarly, involuntary responses, such as learning to control tense jaw muscles to decrease facial pain, can be operantly conditioned (Dohrmann & Laskin, 1978). However, the fact that the same ends can be reached with either type of conditioning does not imply that the means to those ends are the same. After all, bats, birds, and helicopters fly, but they do so in different ways.

Perhaps the best evidence that the two kinds of conditioning are truly different is that different neural systems are used in each. Although the debate over distinguishing between classical and operant conditioning continues, recent research on the brain appears to discount the position that they are fundamentally the same. Not only do classical and operant conditioning draw on different neural mechanisms, but also classical conditioning relies on different brain structures, depending on the response being conditioned. For example, whereas classical conditioning of fear draws on the amygdala (LeDoux, 1996), classical conditioning of eye blinks relies heavily on the cerebellum (Christian & Thompson, 2003). In contrast, operant conditioning relies on neither of these brain structures, using instead the dopamine-based reward system (Montague et al., 2004; Robbins & Everitt, 1998). By providing evidence that different neural systems are used in the two types of conditioning, studies of the brain show that the two are essentially different.

Looking at Levels

Facial Expressions as Reinforcement and Punishment

Like most people, you've probably said or done something while with a family member or friend and had that person respond with a smile or a frown. Do you think that person's smile or frown affected your behavior? Research suggests that other people's facial expressions can act as reinforcement or punishment (as shown in Figure 4.9 on p. 162, where the Master's expression serves as reinforcement or punishment). Let's look at this finding from the different levels of analysis.

First, Kringelbach and colleagues (2001) asked participants to discriminate one visual stimulus from another and found that different brain areas were active when participants' performance led to an angry face (positive punishment) rather than a happy face (positive reinforcement). Perceiving different facial expressions affects the brain in different ways. Moreover, the state of the brain affects how well we perceive faces. For instance, one study found that volunteers who took diazepam (a common antianxiety medication) were less accurate in recognizing facial emotions than those who took a placebo (Coupland et al., 2003). Thus, someone taking such a drug may be less subject to the reinforcing and punishing effects of other people's expressions.

But events in the brain are not enough to explain the effects that perceiving others' facial expressions have on behavior. We must also consider events at the level of the person. For example, some people may not perceive facial expressions as accurately as others, which would affect the reinforcing and punishing effects of the expressions. In one study, researchers found that depressed patients were less likely to correctly identify mildly happy faces as happy and less likely to discriminate between mildly sad, neutral, and mildly happy faces (Surguladze et al., 2004). Thus, people with depression may be potentially deprived of positive reinforcement when others respond with mildly happy expressions. And being less sensitive to facial expressions—and thus less responsive to them—can change the interpersonal dynamic between people (level of the group) because the facial expressions don't have their desired effect.

In fact, a smile or frown can clearly alter events at the level of the group. For example, positive and negative facial expressions can affect interaction between romantic partners: An experiment by Heisel and Mongrain (2004) required couples to complete a conflict resolution task. The number of women's negative expressions during the task predicted increases in their partners' poor mood and anxiety. Also at the level of the group, many (Hall, 1978; Hall & Matsumoto, 2004), but not all (Rahman et al., 2004), studies find that women are better than men at reading facial expressions. Might this difference cause women to find smiles more reinforcing and angry faces more punishing than do men?

Also at the level of the group, Hugenberg and Bodenhausen (2003) found that White participants were more inclined to perceive anger in Black faces than in White faces. We can wonder whether people who are more likely to perceive anger in Black faces would be more likely to feel punished (by the facial expression) and to respond, in turn, to that "punishment."

Again, events at these three levels interact. For example, we cannot understand how communication among people affects the reinforcing or punishing value of facial expressions without understanding how the brain influences such communication, nor can we understand individual differences without considering their impact on the group.

LOOKING BACK: *Review*

1. *What is operant conditioning? How does it occur?* Operant conditioning is a process whereby a behavior becomes associated with the consequences of performing that behavior; in contrast to classical conditioning, these behaviors are usually voluntary. Thorndike's work with cats in a puzzle box led him to develop the Law of Effect. Skinner's work with pigeons (and later, with rats) in a Skinner box showed that operant conditioning could explain much of everyday human behavior.

2. *What is the difference between reinforcement and punishment?* Reinforcement *increases* the likelihood that a behavior will recur; punishment *decreases* that likelihood. Positive reinforcement is the *presentation* of a desired reinforcer after a particular response; negative reinforcement is the *removal* of an unpleasant stimuli after a particular response. Punishment by itself is not particularly effective. Reinforcement can be given via primary or secondary reinforcers (examples of the latter are money, praise, good grades); behavior modification programs make use of secondary reinforcers.

3. *How are complex behaviors learned? How are these new behaviors maintained?* Complex behaviors are learned through shaping, which involves reinforcing behaviors that are successive approximations toward the desired, complex behavior. Generalization, discrimination, extinction, and spontaneous recovery all occur with operant conditioning. Reinforcement schedules help maintain learned behaviors, with the variable ratio schedule producing behaviors most resistant to extinction.

4. *What is the role of dopamine during operant conditioning?* The neurotransmitter dopamine signals the disparity between what an animal expected and what actually occurred. This signal helps the animal to learn the consequences of its behavior, and reinforcement is a particularly important type of consequence.

● LOOKING BEYOND: *Critical Thinking*

You are babysitting a little girl one evening, and her parents have explicitly instructed you not to give her any more food. She whines for cookies, you say no, and she has a temper tantrum. What should you suspect about how her parents have handled her requests for after-dinner snacks in the past? If you want her to stop carrying on, what two different operant conditioning procedures could you use to try to change her behavior? (Physical or emotional violence, threats of cruelty, and yelling are not options.) Which technique do you think will be the most effective? Why? Which techniques were most effectively used by Master Yu?

Cognitive and Social Learning

Jackie Chan's first huge film success came with the film *Project A*, a pirate movie that deviated from the previously accepted formula for kung fu movies. It broke box office records in Asia. Prior to *Project A*, films starring the martial arts expert and actor Bruce Lee were all the rage, and the hero he portrayed was always a "noble" man, avenging some injustice. Chan broke the mold by having the hero of *Project A* be just a regular guy. But to understand Chan's success, we need to look beyond classical and operant conditioning to consider how he figured out what kind of movies he should make and how he learned to make them. When Chan was first given the opportunity to star in films and coordinate the stunts, he also began watching directors and film editors, observing what they did, how and why they included certain scenes and deleted others from the finished film. Chan's behavior was not being changed primarily through classical or operant conditioning, but through cognitive and social learning. Similarly, he learned how to do dangerous stunts, in part, by watching others.

● LOOKING AHEAD: *Learning Objectives*

1. *What is cognitive learning? How does it differ from classical and operant conditioning?*
2. *What is insight learning?*
3. *How can watching others help people learn?*
4. *What makes some models better than others?*

Cognitive Learning

The learning we have discussed so far focuses on behavior. In classical conditioning, the learned behavior is the conditioned response (CR); in operant conditioning, the learned behavior is the reinforced response. But even these types of learning involve the storing of new information, which guides the behavior. **Cognitive learning** is the acquisition of information that is often not immediately acted on but is stored for later use. Information acquired through cognitive learning may be used in planning, evaluating, and other forms of thinking, without producing any behavior—only, perhaps, more information to be stored. Learning how to add is an example of cognitive learning, as is learning the names of the 50 states or the meaning of a new word. You are engaged in cognitive learning right now.

These people are engaged in cognitive learning: They are storing information—directions—that they will use later.

Examples of Chan's cognitive learning include learning what underlies a successful kung fu movie and learning how to incorporate stunts into such a film. "I think that a lot of the success of *Project A* was the result of the three of us [Chan, Samo Hung, and Yuen Baio—fellow students at the Academy when they were younger] working as one. On the other hand, *Project A* was also the first film in which I did something that has since become my signature: The really, really, really dangerous stunt . . . the thrill of high risk. No blue screen and computer special effects. No stunt doubles. Real action. Real danger. And sometimes, real and terrible injury" (Chan & Yang, 1999, p. 283).

Illustrating the fact that cognitive learning is more than simple associations between stimuli and responses, Tolman and Honzik (1930a, 1930b) conducted a series of classic studies with rats. One group of rats was put in a maze that led to a food box, thus receiving a food reward for completing the maze (left panel of Figure 4.14). The other group was also put in the maze but received

Cognitive learning: The acquisition of information that often is not immediately acted on but is stored for later use.

Figure 4.14 Tolman and Honzik's Discovery of Latent Learning

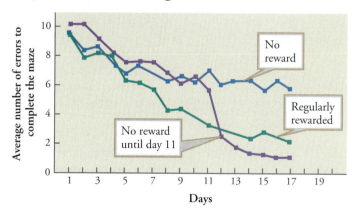

Three routes of differing lengths wind from start to finish. If two points along the most direct route are blocked, it is still possible to get to the end.

Rats that were rewarded for getting to the end of the maze made fewer "navigational" errors than rats that were not rewarded. Once rewarded (on day 11), the previously unrewarded rats made fewer mistakes than regularly reinforced rats, illustrating that the unrewarded rats had learned the spatial arrangement of the maze but did not apply that knowledge until reinforced.

no reinforcement; the rats were simply removed from the maze after a certain amount of time. Sometimes routes were blocked, and the rats had to find a different way to the end. The first group of rats, those that were rewarded with food, quickly increased their speed in the maze and decreased the number of mistakes; the speed and accuracy of the unrewarded second group did not particularly improve. This finding was consistent with what behaviorists would predict. However, when rats in the second group received a food reward on the 11th day, their speed increased and their errors decreased, both dramatically (Figure 4.14, right panel). It appears that these rats had learned how to run the maze quickly and correctly before the 11th day, but had no reason to do so.

Learning that occurs without behavioral signs is called **latent learning**. Tolman reasoned that the unreinforced rats, in their wanderings around the maze, had developed a *cognitive map* of the maze, storing information about its spatial layout. However, they did not use the map until they were motivated to do so by the reinforcement. Tolman's results, and the concept of latent learning, remind us of the important distinction between learning something and performing it. Researchers now know that latent learning depends on the hippocampus (Myers et al., 2000), which is generally used when information about new events is stored (Schacter, 1996). Note that although latent learning is a form of cognitive learning, not all cognitive learning is latent learning—you can rehearse to-be-memorized words aloud and otherwise produce observable behaviors when acquiring new information.

The study of learning focuses on the acquisition of information; in contrast, the study of memory focuses on the retention of information. By its very nature, cognitive learning relies crucially on how information is stored in memory, and most of the recent research on this topic (explored in Chapter 5) focuses on the way information is stored in memory.

Insight Learning: Seeing the Connection

Insight learning consists of suddenly grasping what something means and incorporating that new knowledge into old knowledge. It is based on the phenomenon known as the "ah-ha experience," the triumphal moment when an idea becomes crystal clear. By its very nature, insight learning, unlike other types of learning, is accompanied by a sudden flash of awareness that one has learned.

The most famous psychological experiments regarding insight learning were done by Wolfgang Köhler (1887–1967), a German Gestalt psychologist. Köhler (1925/1956) put a chimpanzee named Sultan in a cage; outside the cage, and out of reach, Köhler put fruit. Also outside the cage and out of reach, but closer than the fruit, he placed a long stick. Inside the cage, Köhler placed a short stick. Initially, Sultan showed signs of frustration as he tried to reach the food. Then he stopped. He seemed suddenly to have an insight into how to snag the fruit: He used the short stick to get the long one, and then capture the fruit. In another study, Köhler put bananas in the cage but high, out of Sultan's reach. Also in the cage were stacks of boxes. At first, Sultan tried to jump up to grab the bananas. Eventually, he looked around at the objects in the cage and again appeared to have a flash of insight; he saw that stacking the boxes and climbing on them would enable him to reach the bananas.

Latent learning: Learning that occurs without behavioral signs.

Insight learning: Learning that occurs when a person or animal suddenly grasps what something means and incorporates that new knowledge into old knowledge.

Observational Learning:
To See Is to Know

Jean Piaget (1962) described a situation in which one of his daughters watched another child have a dramatic temper tantrum, complete with writhing on the floor and howling. His daughter also saw the other child's parents react with concern. Days later, his daughter tried out this behavior, presumably to see whether she would be given the attention she thought a tantrum deserved. She did not have to engage in the behavior immediately after observing it in order to learn it. Everyone, like Piaget's daughter, has had the experience of watching someone else's behavior and then being able to reproduce it. The behavior is probably voluntary (and thus not the result of classical conditioning) and may not have been reinforced (and thus not the result of operant conditioning), but it was learned nonetheless. A group of psychologists, led by Albert Bandura, developed *social learning theory*, which emphasizes the fact that much learning occurs in a social context. This kind of learning, which results simply from watching others and does not depend on reinforcement, is called **observational learning**. Observational learning helps people learn how to behave in their families (Thorn & Gilbert, 1998) and in their cultures: By watching others, we learn how to greet people, eat, laugh, tell jokes. Observational learning has helped you figure out how to behave in your classes and on campus. Do you remember your first few days at college? By watching others, you learned how people talked to each other, what clothes were "fashionable," and how to interact with instructors.

Observational learning explains why people may not make an effort to get to meetings on time: They see that latecomers do not suffer any negative consequences.

Observational learning influenced Chan's behavior: At a basic level, he learned how to do kung fu and acrobatics largely by watching others, and then practiced. (Kung fu or acrobatics would be very difficult to learn from a book!) Later in his career, Chan learned to direct and edit through years of watching others direct and edit.

Bandura focused much of his work on *modeling*, a process in which someone learns new behaviors through observing other people. These other people function as models, presenting a behavior to be imitated. With modeling, you observe others' behaviors, and then none, some, or all of these behaviors may be learned and repeated, or modified. In one of Bandura's famous studies involving a Bobo doll, an inflated vinyl doll that pops back up when punched (Figure 4.15, on p. 178; Bandura et al., 1961), children were divided into three groups: One group watched an adult beating up a Bobo doll, one group watched an adult ignoring the Bobo doll, and the third didn't see an adult at all. After being mildly frustrated

Observational learning: Learning that occurs through watching others, not through reinforcement.

Figure 4.15 Bandura's Study on Observational Learning

Three groups of children were tested; the groups differed only in the first part of the study.

Children in one group watched an adult abuse a Bobo doll, for example, by slamming it with a mallet, kicking it, and yelling at it.

Children in a second group watched adults play with Tinkertoys and ignore the Bobo doll.

Children in a third group never saw a model (an adult) in the playroom.

In the second part of the study, all of the children played in a room with a variety of toys, including Bobo.

Children in the first group tended to imitate what they had seen, mistreating the doll (and inventing new ways to abuse it) and being more aggressive with the other toys in the room.

Children who observed the adult ignoring the Bobo doll were even less aggressive toward it than were children in the control group!

by being placed in a room with toys, but not being allowed to play with some of them, all of the children were then placed in another room with many toys, including a Bobo doll. Children who had observed the adult behaving aggressively with Bobo were themselves more aggressive. Similar studies have found similar results, including the observation that watching aggression by a live person has more of an impact than does watching a video of a person exhibiting the same behaviors. In turn, a realistic video has more of an impact than does a cartoon version of the same behaviors (Bandura et al., 1963).

Learning From Models

Learning from models has many advantages over other sorts of learning. By learning from models, you can avoid going through all the steps that learning usually requires and go directly to the end product.

Observational learning can produce both desired and undesired learning. Models may say one thing and do another, and the observer learns both, saying what the model said and doing what the model did (Rice & Grusec, 1975;

Rushton, 1975). If you are surrounded by positive models, you have the opportunity to learn a lot of positive behaviors; but if you don't have that opportunity, you may find it difficult to learn certain "skills." If adults in a family have trouble holding jobs, become explosively angry, exhibit little patience, and treat others rudely, it can be harder for the children to learn the skills involved in maintaining a job, effectively controlling anger, managing impatience and frustration, and treating others kindly. On a more positive note, Bandura and colleagues (1967) conducted a study in which preschool children who were afraid of dogs observed another child who had no fear of dogs. During eight sessions, as prearranged, the model, on each successive occasion, played more closely with a dog and for a longer time. Fearful children who watched the model play with the dog had significantly more "approach" behaviors (those oriented toward the dog) than did a control group of fearful children who did not observe the model.

Both modeling and operant conditioning are involved in learning about culture and gender. You may learn how to behave by observing others, but whether you'll actually perform those behaviors depends, in part, on the consequences that occur when you first try.

Chan recounts how he learned to minimize the number of beatings he received after arriving at the Academy: "I quickly learned to watch the other children carefully. Whenever they stood up, I stood up. If they sat down, I sat down. Whatever they said, I said, and whatever they did, I did . . . it made it less likely that Master would single me out for punishment" (Chan & Yang, 1999, p. 40).

To further understand the way modeling and operant conditioning together help children learn about culture, imagine the following family interaction in a culture that has different expectations of what constitutes appropriate play for girls and boys. A boy observes his older sister asking her parents for a new doll and sees that they buy it for her. He then asks his parents for a doll for himself and is severely punished. His request was prompted by modeling, but because it resulted in punishment, he is unlikely to make that request again. Similarly, 9th and 10th graders were more likely to get involved in community activities if their parents were involved or if their parents reinforced them for minor involvement (Fletcher et al., 2000).

Researchers have discovered that several characteristics of models can make learning through observation more effective (Bandura, 1977a, 1986). Not surprisingly, the more you pay attention to the model, the more you learn. You are more likely to pay attention if the model is an expert, is good looking, has high status, or is socially powerful (Brewer & Wann, 1998). Perhaps intuitively realizing the importance of models for children's learning through observation, and recognizing the high-status position of his office, cigar enthusiast President William McKinley refused to be photographed with a cigar (Seuling, 1978). However, tobacco companies are using the same principles toward other ends, through product placement in films—showing actors smoking on screen. Unfortunately, research suggests that such use of observational learning has some success: 9- to 15-year-olds watching films with more incidents of smoking were more likely to try smoking themselves (Sargent et al., 2001). We know that children learn by observing others, and powerful, high-status models such as presidents, athletes, or celebrities are likely to be more influential.

Children are not the only ones who learn through observation. Consider a study (Merlo & Schotter, 2003) that had college students play a complex game, where the best strategy was not immediately obvious. Players competed for small payoffs; behind each player was

Observational learning occurs frequently in everyday life: An apprentice spends large amounts of time observing a master before ever doing anything more than handing over a tool. How-to videos ranging from cooking to bike repair may be more effective than how-to books because they allow the viewer to see the desired behavior. Observational learning is the way we learn first languages, form standards of judgment, and even discover ways to solve many types of problems (Bandura, 1986).

We learn from models by seeing which of their behaviors or responses are reinforced and which are punished. We are then able to make predictions about the reactions that our own behaviors will provoke. This pattern of learning is one of the reasons many people have become increasingly concerned about the amount and type of violence, foul language, and sexuality portrayed on television. Many TV shows geared to children contain violence, which is often imitated by young viewers. Moreover, television often shows no harm to the victim as a result of violence and no negative consequences for the perpetrator.

another participant who simply observed the player's moves and decisions. At the end of the tournament, each player and observer were independently given the opportunity to play again for a larger payoff. Observers were more likely to play better, perhaps because they had been able to discern patterns that were more difficult for players—caught up in the moment—to see. In addition, those observers who had the good fortune to watch better players tended to play better themselves than those who observed worse players, which suggests that observing someone who is good at their craft will help the observer to perform better. Negotiation skills can also be learned well through observation (Nadler et al., 2003).

LOOKING BACK: *Review*

1. *What is cognitive learning? How does it differ from classical and operant conditioning?* Cognitive learning is the acquisition of information that often is not acted on immediately, but rather is stored for later use. This process contrasts with classical and operant conditioning, which focus on learning behaviors. Latent learning (such as creating a cognitive map) is an example of cognitive learning.

2. *What is insight learning?* Learning can occur following an insight, by suddenly grasping what something means and incorporating that new knowledge into old knowledge. Insight learning is based on the "ah-ha experience."

3. *How can watching others help people learn?* Observational learning allows you to acquire knowledge "second hand," without having to perform a behavior yourself. This sort of learning helps explain how children (and adults) learn their family's and their culture's rules, and the different rules that sometimes exist for men and women, boys and girls.

4. *What makes some models better than others?* Modeling is the process of learning a new behavior through observing others, and the more attention paid to the model, the more effective the learning will be. You are more likely to pay attention to a model who is an expert, is good looking, or has high status.

LOOKING BEYOND: *Critical Thinking*

Curare is a drug that so totally paralyzes an animal that a heart-lung machine is necessary to keep it alive. Although the animal can't move, it can perceive and remember normally. Imagine showing a person who has been given curare how to open a simple combination lock on a box to obtain the $1,000 inside. When the effect of the curare has worn off and the person is able to move normally, will he or she know how to open the lock to get the reward? Why or why not?

LET'S SUM IT UP

I. Classical Conditioning

A. Classical conditioning, which was first investigated systematically by Pavlov, has four basic elements:

1. The unconditioned stimulus (US), such as food, reflexively elicits an unconditioned response.

2. The unconditioned response (UR), such as salivation, is automatically elicited by a US.

3. The pairing of a conditioned stimulus (CS), such as a tone, with a US, such as food, elicits a conditioned response (CR), such as salivation. (Note that salivation can be either a conditioned or an

unconditioned response, depending on the stimulus that elicits it.)

4. The presentation of the CS alone then elicits the UR (the tone presented alone elicits the response of salivation now as a CR).

B. A conditioned emotional response is involved in the development of fear and phobias, as shown by Watson and Rayner in the case of Little Albert.

C. Extinction is the unpairing of the CS and US; spontaneous recovery is the return of a classically conditioned response after a rest period following extinction.

D. In stimulus generalization, a similar, but not identical, stimulus elicits the CR.

E. In stimulus discrimination, the organism learns to distinguish among similar stimuli so that only a particular stimulus elicits the CR.

F. Classical conditioning is involved in certain bodily responses to drug abuse, certain therapy techniques, certain types of advertising, and the acquisition of food or taste aversions.

II. Operant Conditioning

A. Operant conditioning is the process whereby a behavior (usually a voluntary one) becomes associated with the consequences of performing that behavior. Operant conditioning thus has three basic elements: stimulus, response, and consequence.

B. Both negative and positive reinforcement increase the probability of the recurrence of a behavior.

C. Both positive and negative punishment decrease the probability of the recurrence of a behavior.

D. Reinforcers can be primary or secondary.

E. Extinction, spontaneous recovery, generalization, and discrimination all occur in operant conditioning.

F. Shaping makes it possible to learn, by successive approximations, behaviors that would otherwise not be emitted.

G. Reinforcement schedules can be continuous or partial; if partial, reinforcement may be given for responses after an interval of time (interval schedule) or after a set number of responses (ratio schedule). For both these types of schedules, reinforcement can be given on a fixed or variable basis.

III. Cognitive and Social Learning

A. Cognitive learning involves the acquisition of information that may be used in planning, evaluating, and other forms of thinking, but that is not necessarily acted on immediately.

B. Latent learning, learning that occurs without behavioral signs, and insight learning, suddenly grasping what something means and incorporating that new knowledge into old knowledge, are examples of cognitive learning.

C. Observational learning is learning by watching the behavior of others. The more you pay attention to the model, the more you are likely to learn.

Key Terms

acquisition, p. 147
avoidance learning, p. 148
behavior modification, p. 165
biological preparedness, p. 148
classical conditioning, p. 146
cognitive learning, p. 175
conditioned emotional response (CER), p. 148
conditioned response (CR), p. 147
conditioned stimulus (CS), p. 147
continuous reinforcement, p. 168
contrapreparedness, p. 149

delayed reinforcement, p. 166
discrimination, p. 166
discriminative stimulus, p. 167
extinction (in classical conditioning), p. 150
extinction (in operant conditioning), p. 167
fixed interval schedule, p. 169
fixed ratio schedule, p. 169
food aversion (taste aversion), p. 155
generalization, p. 166
habituation, p. 145

immediate reinforcement, p. 166
insight learning, p. 176
interval schedule, p. 168
latent learning, p. 176
Law of Effect, p. 159
learning, p. 144
negative punishment, p. 164
negative reinforcement, p. 161
observational learning, p. 177
operant conditioning, p. 158
partial reinforcement, p. 168
phobia, p. 148

LOOKING ONLINE: *Enhance Your Learning*

MyPsychLab is an interactive and instructive multimedia resource that can be used to supplement a traditional lecture course or as an online course. It is an all-inclusive tool with a text-specific e-book plus multimedia tutorials, videos, simulations, animations, and controlled assessment to completely engage students and reinforce learning. MyPsychLab meets the individual learning needs of every student. Visit *www.mypsychlab.com* for more information!

Practice Test

For each of the following items, choose the single best answer.

1. Which of the following best expresses how psychologists define *learning*?
   a. as a relatively permanent change in behavior that results from experience
   b. when repeated exposure to a stimulus decreases an organism's responsiveness
   c. as watching someone do something complex and unfamiliar on a single occasion
   d. when a neutral stimulus becomes associated, or paired, with a stimulus that causes reflexive behavior

2. In Pavlov's experiments, food by itself elicited salivation. This means that the food was
   a. a conditioned stimulus.
   b. an acquisition.
   c. an unconditioned stimulus.
   d. an unconditioned response.

3. Presenting the unconditioned stimulus and the conditioned stimulus simultaneously
   a. leads to a very strong conditioned response.
   b. does not lead to a conditioned response.
   c. has not been investigated.
   d. results in habituation.

4. Biological preparedness is
   a. a built-in disinclination (or even an inability) for certain conditioned stimuli to elicit particular conditioned responses.
   b. an example of avoidance learning.
   c. a built-in readiness for certain conditioned stimuli to elicit particular conditioned responses, so that less learning is necessary to produce conditioning.
   d. an irrational fear of a specific object or situation.

5. Once classical conditioning has occurred, the connection between the conditioned stimulus and the unconditioned stimulus
   a. never completely vanishes.
   b. vanishes if the conditioned stimulus and the unconditioned stimulus are not paired frequently.
   c. can vanish unexpectedly through a process known as spontaneous recovery.
   d. can be eliminated through repeated presentations of the unconditioned stimulus in the presence of the conditioned stimulus.

6. When animals or people have an unpleasant experience during or after eating or tasting a particular food,
   a. the animals or people are unaffected unless the unpleasant experience occurs repeatedly.
   b. the animals or people may develop a classically conditioned aversion to that food or taste.

c. the conditioned stimulus is nausea or vomiting.

d. the animals or people go through extinction.

7. What is true about the placebo effect?

a. It can develop only in people and not in animals.

b. It can develop in people only if they believe that the placebo has medicinal properties.

c. The placebo effect is an unconditioned immune response.

d. The placebo effect can be induced in both people and animals, and the organism does not have to believe that the placebo has medicinal properties in order to produce a placebo response.

8. The Law of Effect states that

a. behavior that leads to an undesired consequence increases the likelihood of the recurrence of that behavior.

b. actions that subsequently lead to a "satisfying state of affairs" are more likely to be repeated.

c. an object or event that comes after a response changes the likelihood of its recurrence.

d. classical conditioning works best if there is a long delay between the presentation of the unconditioned stimulus and the presentation of the conditioned stimulus.

9. What do psychologists know about the use of punishment?

a. Punishment eliminates the capacity to engage in a particular behavior.

b. Physical punishment decreases aggressive behavior in the person on the receiving end.

c. Punishment alone is more effective than punishment used in combination with reinforcement.

d. None of the above statements is true.

10. If a rat receives a food pellet immediately after pressing a bar, the rat is receiving

a. delayed reinforcement.

b. behavior modification.

c. immediate reinforcement.

d. positive punishment.

11. What is discrimination in operant conditioning?

a. the ability to distinguish between the desired response and a similar but undesirable response

b. the ability to generalize to similar stimuli

c. the ability to generalize from a learned response to a similar response

d. the cue that tells the organism whether a specific response will lead to the expected reinforcement

12. In a variable interval schedule of reinforcement,

a. reinforcement is given after a fixed ratio of responses.

b. reinforcement is given for a response emitted after a fixed interval of time.

c. partial reinforcement is given based on a specified number of emitted responses.

d. reinforcement for a response is given after a variable interval of time.

13. Which statement best captures what psychologists currently know about the role of the brain in learning?

a. The neurotransmitter dopamine plays no role in any aspect of learning.

b. An understanding of how the brain works can shed considerable light on the process of learning.

c. The brain is not involved in learning.

d. Learning is a single activity.

14. What evidence best suggests that operant conditioning and classical conditioning are essentially different?

a. Only operant conditioning is subject to moderating factors that affect response acquisition.

b. Biological factors influence what can be easily learned only in classical conditioning.

c. They are not essentially different.

d. Different neural systems are used in each.

15. Learning that occurs without behavioral signs is called

a. latent learning.

b. insight learning.

c. modeling.

d. a cognitive map.

Answers: 1. a 2. c 3. b 4. c 5. a 6. b 7. d 8. b 9. d 10. c 11. a 12. d 13. b 14. d 15. a

chapter 5

Memory
Living With Yesterday

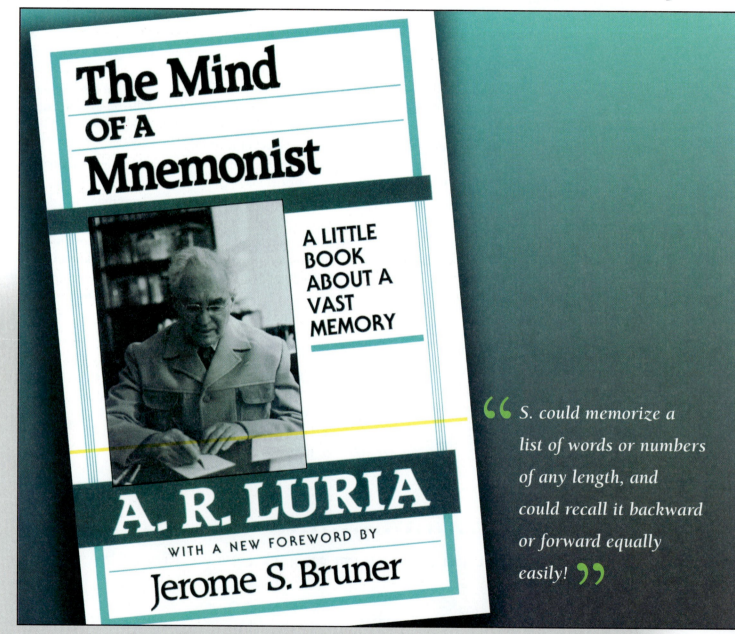

S. could memorize a list of words or numbers of any length, and could recall it backward or forward equally easily!

Chapter Outline

A LATVIAN NEWSPAPER REPORTER, KNOWN SIMPLY AS "S." (SHORT FOR S. V. Shereshevskii), had an almost superhuman memory. Each morning the editor of his newspaper would describe the day's stories and assignments, often providing addresses and details about the information the reporters needed to track down. The editor noticed that S. never took notes and initially thought that S. was simply not paying attention. When he called S. on the carpet for this apparent negligence, he was shocked to discover that S. could repeat back the entire briefing, word-perfect. When the editor quizzed S. about his memory, S. was surprised; he assumed that everyone could accurately remember what they had heard and seen. The editor suggested that S. visit the noted Russian psychologist Alexander Luria, who then studied him over the course of almost 30 years.

Luria soon discovered that S.'s memory "for all practical purposes was inexhaustible" (Luria, 1968/1887, p. 3). S. could memo-rize a list of words or numbers of any length, and could recall it backward or forward equally eas-ily! In fact, if given an item from the list, he could recall which items came immediately before it or after it. He generally made no errors. Moreover, he performed as well when he was tested years later, recalling perfectly not only the list itself but also when he learned it, where he and the exam-iner had been sitting, and even what the examiner had been wear-ing at the time.

Luria focused on unlocking the secrets behind S.'s formidable abilities. The results of this massive project are summarized in Luria's celebrated monograph *The Mind of a Mnemonist: A Little Book About a Vast Memory*. Luria found that S. recalled objects, events, words, and numbers by using mental imagery. His mental imagery was rich and complex:

> ...I recognize a word not only by the images it evokes but by a whole complex of feelings that image arouses.... Usually I experience a word's taste and weight, and I don't have to make an effort to remember it—the word seems to recall itself. (p. 28)

Sounds were accompanied by images of colored lines, puffs, splotches and splashes, and these visual images could later remind him of the sound. Moreover, S. used associations between images and concepts, which allowed the images to stand for other things. For example,

> When I hear the word green, a green flowerpot appears.... Even numbers remind me of images. Take the number 1. This is a proud, well-built man; 2 is a high-spirited woman; 3 a gloomy person (why, I don't know) ...8 a very stout woman—a sack within a sack. (p. 31)

S. could recall items in any order because he placed images along a scene and could imagine "seeing" the imaged objects in any order. For example,

> I put the image of the pencil near a fence ... the one down the street, you know. (p. 36)

S.'s ability may sound like a dream come true, especially to a student slaving away to memorize the contents of several textbooks. In fact, as attractive as S.'s abilities seem, they had a dark side: Unlike normal people, S. could not stop himself from thinking about a flood of associations that were triggered by commonplace stimuli, which could overwhelm him when he tried to read. Moreover, he could not understand poetry, metaphors, or abstract principles (such as those used in science), which always called to mind specific concrete images. A better memory is not necessarily an unmixed blessing.

As we shall see, S. was extraordinary but not supernatural. In fact, you can learn many of the tricks he used and put them to good end. S.'s memory, like yours, relied on three fundamental types of processing: **Encoding** is the process of organizing and transforming incoming information so that it can be entered into memory, either to be stored or to be compared with previously stored information. S. was a master at this process. **Storage** is the process of retaining information in memory. As we shall see, the mechanisms involved in storing information continue to operate for years after you've learned a fact. **Retrieval** is the process of digging information out of memory. For example, have you ever seen someone you know you've met before, but at first can't recall the person's name? In this situation, you get to experience the process of retrieval at work, as you struggle to bring the name to mind. S. never had such struggles, in part because his encoding and storage processing was so efficient that he could virtually always locate the information he sought in memory.

Encoding: The process of organizing and transforming incoming information so that it can be entered into memory, either to be stored or to be compared with previously stored information.

Storage: The process of retaining information in memory.

Retrieval: The process of accessing information stored in memory.

Encoding Information Into Memory: Time and Space Are of the Essence

As he learned to use his memory, S. became a master at organizing information so that he could later remember it quickly. A key part of this activity was transforming what he was given to make it memorable. For example, when given a complex (and meaningless) mathematical formula to recall, he generated a story that described each term. The first term was N, which he recalled by thinking of a gentleman named Neiman; the next symbol was a dot (indicating multiplication), which he thought of as a small hole where Neiman had jabbed his cane in the ground; next came a square-root sign, which he converted to Neiman's looking up at a tree that had that shape; and so on (Luria, 1968/1887, p. 49).

Such fancy mental gymnastics were useful for S. because they helped him encode new information into memory. In this section, we begin at the beginning and consider how information is encoded into memory.

LOOKING AHEAD: Learning Objectives

1. *What is a memory store? How do memory stores differ?*
2. *What factors affect whether we retain information in memory?*

Types of Memory Stores

S.'s tricks required him to use different sorts of memories. Until someone asks for your address, chances are you aren't consciously aware of it—or even that you have one. But, once you are asked, the information is at your mental fingertips. This difference, between memories we are aware of holding and those we are not, is one sign that different types of "memory stores" are at work. A memory store is a set of neurons that serves to retain information over time.

Although we sometimes talk as if our "hands remember" how to shoot baskets and our "fingers remember" how to play the guitar, all memories are stored in the brain. We can distinguish among three types of memory stores, which differ in the time span over which they operate and in the amount of information they can hold (Shiffrin, 1999). These three types of structures are known as *sensory, short-term,* and *long-term memory stores.* The fundamental distinctions among these types of memories were first characterized in detail by Atkinson and Shiffrin (1968, 1971) and Waugh and Norman (1965), as illustrated in Figure 5.1.

Sensory Memory: Lingering Sensations

Have you ever looked at scenery rushing past the window of a moving car and noticed that although you see literally miles and miles of landscape slipping by you,

Figure 5.1 The Three-Stage Model of Memory

The three-stage model emerged from research by Atkinson and Shiffrin (1968, 1971) and Waugh and Norman (1965). This model not only identified distinct types of memory stores, but also specified how information flows among them. Later research showed that information can, in fact, move to long-term memory without necessarily passing through short-term memory, and that rehearsal—repeating items over and over—only helps memorization if people think about the information (counter to what was initially claimed). Nevertheless, this model provided the framework for subsequent studies and theories of memory.

Memory store: A set of neurons that serves to retain information over time.

Sensory memory (SM): A memory store that holds a large amount of perceptual input for a very brief time, typically less than 1 second.

your images of the trees, signs, and telephone poles are fleeting, leaving your awareness almost as soon as you notice them? But the images linger for an instant, and even this very brief retention requires a form of memory. These rapidly fading images occur in **sensory memory (SM)**, which holds a large amount of perceptual input for a very brief time, typically less than 1 second. Sensory memory happens automatically, without effort (via bottom-up processes; see Chapter 3); sensory memory arises because of the temporary activation of perceptual areas of your brain by the stimulus.

George Sperling (1960) reported an experiment, now regarded as a classic, that demonstrated this fleeting sensory memory in vision (the visual form of SM is called *iconic memory*). When shown sets of many letters or digits very briefly, people can report only a handful afterward (see Figure 5.2). However, they claim that they can remember all the items immediately after the display is removed, but then the memory fades too quickly to "read off" all of them during recall. Sperling was able to demonstrate that this claim was, in fact, correct. He briefly showed participants rows of items, more than they could remember, and presented one of several different tones, which corresponded to specific rows. If a tone sounded *immediately* after the items were presented, the participants were able to report the corresponding row almost perfectly. Because the tonal cue was presented *after* the items were removed, the participants had to have retained some memory of all of the rows in order to perform so well. Moreover, if the cue was presented a mere second after the items were removed, performance dropped dramatically. This finding shows that iconic memory stores a large amount of information but that it fades very quickly. The sense of a fleeting memory after the stimulus has ceased holds true for hearing as well. For example, you can continue to hear the sound of a voice that has stopped speaking for the brief time it is still in auditory sensory memory (Cherry, 1953; the auditory form of SM is called *echoic memory*).

Figure 5.2 The Sperling Study

Participants saw sets of letters arranged in three rows. When the letters were flashed very quickly (for less than 0.25 second), people were able to report around 4 or 5 letters, even though they recalled seeing more.

In another part of the study, a high, medium, or low tone was presented immediately *after* the rows of letters were flashed. Participants reported the top row if the tone was high, the middle row if it was medium, and the bottom row if it was low. They could report the appropriate row almost perfectly, showing that they had briefly stored more than they could report aloud.

Short-Term Memory: The Contents of Consciousness

Whereas sensory memory retains information for the briefest time and cannot be prolonged, **short-term memory (STM,** also called *immediate memory*) holds information for several seconds and can be prolonged voluntarily (typically for about 30 seconds). When you see something you want to remember (such as the numbers on the license plate of a car involved in an accident), you can hold this information in STM by **rehearsal**, repeating the information over and over. When you dash from telephone book to telephone, repeating like a mantra the number you've just looked up, you are rehearsing. Also in contrast to SM, which can hold a large amount of information, STM holds only a handful of separate pieces of information. For instance, do you think you would be able to keep in your STM a phone number that was 20 digits long? STM overload. In fact, the lengths of telephone numbers and license plates were determined with our STM limits in mind. You are conscious only of information stored in STM. The very fact that you are aware of information is a sure sign that the information is in STM.

How Much Can You Hold in Mind? How much information can we keep in our awareness at one time—in other words, how much information can STM hold? Miller (1956) argued that STM can hold only about 7 plus-or-minus 2 (that is, from 5 to 9) "chunks" at once, but more recent research suggests that the number is more like 4 (Cowan, 2001). A **chunk** is a unit of information, such as a digit, letter, or word. Generally speaking, STM can handle somewhere between 5 and 9 items (organized into about 4 chunks); this is why telephone and license plate numbers are fairly easy to remember; for example, even though it's three digits, you will organize the area code as a single chunk. The definition of a chunk is not precise, however, and research has shown that the amount of information STM can hold depends on the types of material and the individual's experience with them (Baddeley, 1994; Broadbent, 1971; Mandler, 1967). For instance, a word is usually treated as a chunk, but you can store more one-syllable words than five-syllable ones. To get a sense of the importance of chunking, try the exercise in Figure 5.3.

Working Memory: The Thinking Person's Memory. When S. was asked to memorize a set of meaningless sounds, he would organize the information in clever ways. Researchers soon realized that rehearsal is only one process at work in STM; you operate on information in STM. Whenever you reason something out—as you do, for example, during the game Scrabble, when you mentally rearrange letters to see whether you can form words—you are using STM (Zhang & Zhu, 2001). The notion that information in STM is used in various ways led researchers to expand the conception of how this type of memory works, which led to the theory of **working memory (WM)**. The theory of WM is an advance over the original theory of STM in three ways: First, the original conception of STM specified only one type of process (rehearsal) that operated on stored information,

Short-term memory (STM) (also called *immediate memory***):** A memory store that holds relatively little information (typically 5 to 9 items) for only a few seconds (but perhaps as long as 30 seconds).

Rehearsal: The process of repeating information over and over to retain it in STM.

Chunk: A unit of information, such as a digit, letter, or word.

Working memory (WM): The system that includes two specialized STMs (auditory loop and visuospatial sketchpad) and a central executive that operates on information in them to plan, reason, or solve a problem.

Figure 5.3 Chunking in Action

A	E
7 9 1 2	5 1 8 6 1 9 2 4
8 9 8 9	7 7 7 5 5 5 8 8

B	F
1 4 2 5 9	9 6 5 2 4 6 3 7 9
2 2 4 4 1	2 2 2 2 7 7 7 7 1

C	G
9 1 3 9 2 6	1 3 8 5 2 6 2 1 7 4
4 2 4 2 4 2	3 3 5 5 9 9 4 4 2 2

D	H
6 4 1 7 6 2 8	7 2 5 8 3 1 8 4 3 2 1 6
3 3 3 8 8 5 5	2 2 5 5 8 8 1 1 6 6 3 3

Read the first row in box A, left to right, and then look up from the book and say it aloud. Check to see whether you could recall all the digits. Then read the second row in box A, left to right, and do the same. Work your way down the table, and keep going until you can't recall either of the two equal-length rows in a pair perfectly. You should find that for the shorter rows, you can remember both rows with equal ease. But for the longer ones, the second row in each pair is easier to remember than the first one. Now that you know about chunking, you know why: It's not the number of digits, it's the number of chunks that's important—and the second row of each pair is easier to organize into fewer chunks.

Figure 5.4 Working Memory

Working memory (WM) is a system that involves a central executive and two specialized short-term memory (STM) stores: one that holds pronounceable sounds (the articulatory loop) and one that holds visual or spatial patterns (the visuospatial sketchpad).

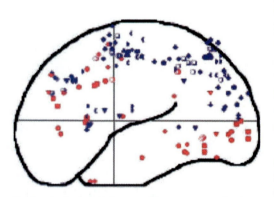

During tasks involving working memory, both the frontal lobes and perceptual areas of the brain are often activated. Different sets of areas are activated by different types of working memory tasks. The areas indicated by blue spots were activated when participants had to hold locations in mind, whereas the areas indicated by red spots were activated when participants had to hold shapes in mind (Smith, 2000).

Central executive: The set of processes that operates on information in one or another of two specialized STMs; part of working memory.

Long-term memory (LTM): A memory store that holds a huge amount of information for a long time (from hours to years).

whereas the theory of WM includes processes that interpret and transform information more generally (Baddeley, 1986; Cohen, Peristein, et al., 1997; D'Esposito et al., 1995; Smith, 2000; Smith & Jonides, 1999).

Second, as shown in Figure 5.4, the theory of WM more finely characterizes how information is stored in STM; specifically, we now know that STM includes distinct stores, which retain different kinds of information (Jonides et al., 2005). Baddeley (1986, 1992) distinguishes between an STM that holds verbally produced sounds, which he calls the *articulatory loop*, and another STM that holds visual and spatial information, which he calls the *visuospatial sketchpad*.

Third, the theory of WM includes a function known as the **central executive**, which operates on information in one or another of the two STMs to plan, reason, or solve a problem. The central executive is at work when you plan what you will say on a first date or when you think about what you would like to do tomorrow. This function of WM relies in large measure on a part of the frontal lobes that is crucially involved in managing information in order to carry out specific plans (Passingham & Sakai, 2004). WM is so important that it is sobering to learn that people who regularly used the club drug ecstasy (also known as "e") show impairments in this kind of memory for up to 2 years after they've sworn off the drug (Morgan et al., 2002).

Long-Term Memory: Records of Experience

Rehearsal is important in part because it is one way in which we move information into a third type of memory store, **long-term memory (LTM)**. (But, as we shall see, rehearsal is not the only way to transfer information into LTM.) LTM holds a huge amount of information for a very long time, from hours to years. LTM stores the information that underlies the meanings of pictures, words, and objects, as well as your memories of everything you've ever done or learned. As we noted earlier, until you are asked for your address, you are not directly aware of that information; it has to move from LTM into STM before you are conscious of it. As an analogy, think of the difference between storing a file on your hard drive versus entering it into RAM, or random-access memory, the active memory in a computer. Once information is saved on the hard drive, it can be stored indefinitely; it will not be disrupted if the power fails. If information faded rapidly from RAM (instead of being lost instantly if you close a file without clicking on "Save"), the difference between typing words into RAM and saving them on the hard drive would be much like the difference between memories held in STM versus those stored in LTM. The storage capability of LTM is so large that some researchers question whether it has a limit.

Information Flow Between STM and LTM: A Two-Way Street. Information not only goes from STM to LTM, but often moves in the other direction, from LTM to STM. In fact, the contents of working memory are typically drawn from LTM, not STM. For example, when you wrestle with a difficult decision, you draw on the fruits of your previous experiences—which are stored in LTM. Indeed, in order for a stimulus to be meaningful, information in LTM must have been activated because that is where meaning is stored. And most information in STM is *meaningful*: That is, you don't see the squiggle 6 as a curved line but as a recognizable number that conveys meaning; similarly, without conscious thought, you see the letter pattern WORD as a recognizable word. (Remember the Stroop effect, demonstrated in Chapter 3: You can't ignore the meaning of color words when you try to report the color of the ink used to print them.) So, when you look up a telephone number, you must first access LTM in order to know how to pronounce the numbers and then keep them in STM as you prepare to make the call. Hence, LTM plays a central role in perception: You recognize and identify an object only after the appropriate information is activated in LTM.

Distinguishing Between STM and LTM. The distinction between STM and LTM matters in everyday life, sometimes a great deal. If you see the license number of a car that has just hit a cyclist but then quickly lose that information from STM, it is gone forever. But, if the information has moved into LTM, you should be able to retrieve it.

Evidence for distinct short-term and long-term memory stores has been provided by many studies. The earliest of these took place over 100 years ago, when German philosopher and pioneering memory researcher Hermann Ebbinghaus (1850–1909) undertook a series of experiments to discover the factors that affect memory. Although he didn't realize it at the time, Ebbinghaus's findings were the first solid evidence that STM and LTM are distinct and operate differently. Here's what he did: To see how well he could memorize letters, digits, and *nonsense syllables* (such as *cac*, *rit*, and the like, which are not words but can be pronounced), Ebbinghaus (1885) wrote out a set of these stimuli, each on its own card. He then studied them, one at a time, and later on, assessed how many he could recall. Ebbinghaus found—as many researchers have since confirmed—that the first and last items studied were more easily remembered than those in the middle. The graph in Figure 5.5 illustrates this memory curve. The increased memory for the first few stimuli is called the **primacy effect**; it reflects the storage of information in LTM. The increased memory for the last few stimuli is the **recency effect**, which reflects the storage of information in STM.

Primacy effect: Increased memory for the first few stimuli in a set, reflecting storage of information in LTM.

Recency effect: Increased memory for the last few stimuli in a set, reflecting storage of information in STM.

Code: A type of mental representation, an internal "re-presentation" (such as in words or images) of a stimulus or event.

Figure 5.5 The Memory Curve

Memory is typically better for the first few and last few items in a set, producing the memory curve shown here.

Making Memories

Look at Figure 5.6. Do you remember which way Abraham Lincoln faces on a penny? Most people don't. Unless you've had reason to pay attention to this feature and encode it, you probably didn't store this information explicitly. In this section, we examine what it means to "store" information in memory and then look at several factors that determine whether this storage will occur.

Coding: Packaged to Store

How convenient it would be if every time you scanned a picture into a computer, the computer automatically named it and stored a brief description. With such a feature, you could easily search for the picture (by its name or its characteristics). As it happens, humans have this capacity and then some. In fact, we often register information using more than one memory system. Paivio and his collaborators (Paivio, 1971) not only showed that pictures are generally remembered better than words, but also made a convincing case that this difference occurs because pictures can be stored using *dual codes*. A **code** is a type of mental representation, an internal "re-presentation" of a stimulus or event. Just as you can print letters, draw pictures, or write the dots and dashes of Morse code on a blackboard (all of these are different representations), your brain can

Figure 5.6 Which Coin Is Correct?

Nickerson and Adams (1979) found that people perform poorly when asked to choose the correct image of a coin from a set of choices. Because we need only to distinguish pennies from other coins, not to notice which way Abe faces, we do not encode the profile information very well.

use many types of representations. Pictures can be stored with both a visual and a verbal code; that is, you can describe what you see in words as well as store it visually, so you can later recall it in your mind's eye. Research shows that illustrations improve memory for text (Levie & Lentz, 1982; Levin et al., 1987), particularly if the picture appears before the text.

Creating Verbal and Visual Codes.   As part of the encoding process, you can create new codes for storing material. For example, you can verbally describe visually perceived objects, creating a *verbal code*, or you can visualize verbally described information, creating a *visual code*. By creating and storing a verbal code when you perceive information, you don't need to use visual parts of the brain when later recalling the information. Thus, when people were asked to name from memory the colors of objects such as fire trucks and tractors that were shown to them in black-and-white drawings, the "color areas" of the brain were not activated (Chao & Martin, 1999). In this study, participants claimed not to use visual mental imagery; the associations apparently were stored verbally.

Coding in the Brain.   Portions of the frontal lobes are often active when people encode new information, an indication that organizational processing is at work (Buckner et al., 1999; Kelley et al., 1998). Indeed, the degree of activation of the frontal lobes when information is studied predicts how well it will be remembered later (Brewer et al., 1998; Wagner et al., 1998).

Consolidation and Reconsolidation

If you were ever in a play, you probably found that although you knew your lines well for the performances, a week or two after the last performance you had almost forgotten them. What happened? And how is this process of learning lines for a play different from remembering facts about your hometown, which don't evaporate even if you don't think about them for months on end?

Consolidation: Lodged in Memory.   Consider the following metaphor: Say you want to remember a path you are supposed to take in a few days. Someone shows it to you on a lawn, and, to remember it, you walk the path over and over, repeatedly tracing its shape. This is a metaphor for *dynamic memory*; if it is not continually active, it is lost. But, if you stick with a repeated route long enough, the path you're tracing becomes worn, and grass no longer covers it; this kind of memory is called *structural memory*, and, like the worn path, it no longer depends on continuing activity. When memories are stored in a dynamic form, they depend on continuing neural activity; when they are stored in a structural form, they no longer require ongoing activity to be maintained. The process of wearing a bare pathway in a lawn, of storing a memory as a new structure, is called <mark>consolidation</mark>. One goal of this book's Looking Back and Let's Sum It Up features is to help you accomplish just this process.

Many studies have shown that memories are initially stored in LTM in a dynamic form and are consolidated only after considerable amounts of time (McGaugh, 2000; Squire et al., 2001). For example, patients with major depression who receive electroconvulsive therapy—consisting of powerful jolts of electricity to the head (see Chapter 12)—experience disruption of memory for recent events, even those that are no longer in STM; however, these patients' memory for older information is unaffected (McGaugh & Herz, 1972). The hippocampus and related brain areas are crucial for consolidating memories of facts and events (Squire et al., 2001), but after consolidation they are no longer necessary for many types of memory (Corkin, 2002). Consolidation occurs not only for facts

Consolidation: The process of converting information stored dynamically in LTM into a structural change in the brain.

and events, but also for memories of sequences of movements; such consolidation involves multiple stages (Walker, Brakefield, Hobson, & Stickgold, 2003) and uses a different set of brain areas than does consolidation of factual memories (Brashers-Krug et al., 1996).

In general, memories are well along the way to being consolidated after a couple of years. However, this process is remarkably complex, and it may continue for much longer (Manns et al., 2003). In fact, the process of consolidation may occur over such a long stretch of time that some memories may never be consolidated completely (Meeter & Murre, 2004).

Reconsolidation: Can Recall Make Memories Fragile?   Have you ever wished that you could change a memory? Discoveries in numerous laboratories may suggest that such wishes may—for better or worse—someday be more than idle fantasy. In spite of the evidence that memories become increasingly consolidated over time, researchers have discovered that the simple act of recalling information can cause memories to become vulnerable to change—and to be retained, the information must be *reconsolidated*, restabilized as a stored structure. Here's a metaphor: When you encode information in the first place, it is as if you have assembled pieces into a puzzle, which you then set down on a shelf. When you later retrieve the information, you need to lift that puzzle, which puts it in danger of coming undone; before putting it back on the shelf, you have to nudge the pieces, and perhaps even reassemble parts of it (but this sort of reconsolidation is far different from consolidation, which was required to assemble the puzzle from scratch in the first place). Researchers have shown that reconsolidation is not just consolidation all over again (Alberini, 2004); notably, different proteins are critical for consolidation after information is initially encoded and for reconsolidation after a memory is activated (Lee et al., 2004).

However, reconsolidation is not necessary every time stored information is activated (Biedenkapp & Rudy, 2004; Hernandez & Kelley, 2004). Why is reconsolidation necessary at some times but not others? The length of time information has been retained in memory, the nature of the task, the degree to which the information was effectively stored and subsequently consolidated, the correspondence between what is expected and what actually occurs (Pedreira et al. 2004), and various other factors could affect the need for reconsolidation (Alberini, 2004).

Variations in Processing: Why "Thinking It Through" Is a Good Idea

If you want to remember the material in this book, you should use the Looking Back: Review features as prompts to recall the details discussed in the text, and you should take some time to reflect on the Looking Beyond: Critical Thinking questions. These features of the book have been designed to take advantage of a fundamental fact about memory: The more you think through information, the better you will remember its meaning. This finding has been interpreted in two ways, in terms of depth of processing and breadth of processing.

Depth of Processing: The Virtue of "Getting to the Bottom of It".   Craik and Lockhart (1972) hypothesized that memory improves with greater **depth of processing**, which consists of the number and complexity of the operations used when you process information. They argue that the greater the depth of processing when you first encode information, the greater the likelihood of remembering it later.

What you pay attention to plays a key role in what is encoded into memory. However, the effect is not solely a matter of the depth of processing involved: If

Depth of processing: The number and complexity of the operations involved in processing information, expressed in a continuum from shallow to deep.

you are shown words and asked which ones rhyme with "train" (which forces you to pay attention to the sounds of the words), you later will recall the *sounds* of the words better than if you were initially asked to decide which words name living versus nonliving objects. But the reverse effect occurs if you are shown words and asked later to recall their *meanings*; in this case, your later recall will be better if you initially judge whether the words named living versus nonliving objects than if you initially evaluated their sounds. The most effective processing is tailored to the reasons the material is being learned (Fisher & Craik, 1977; Morris et al., 1977; Moscovitch & Craik, 1976). Practice on one task will help you perform another to the extent that the two tasks require similar processing. In particular, you will be able to remember information more easily if you use the same type of processing when you try to retrieve it as you did when you originally studied it; this is the principle of **transfer appropriate processing** (Morris et al., 1977; Rajaram et al., 1998).

Breadth of Processing: The Virtue of "Reaching Out". Information is encoded more effectively if it is *organized and integrated* into what you already know, thus engaging greater **breadth of processing**. Encoding that involves great breadth of processing is called **elaborative encoding** (Bradshaw & Anderson, 1982; Craik & Tulving, 1975). Perhaps the most dramatic demonstration of the benefits of elaborative encoding involved an undergraduate, S.F., who after a few months' practice could repeat lists of over 80 random digits (Chase & Ericsson, 1981). This is many, many more digits than can be held in STM, so how could he do it? S.F. was on the track team and was familiar with the times for various segments of races; thus, he was able to convert the numbers on the list into times, data with which he had associations. The digits 2145, for example, might be the times (with two digits each) needed to run two segments of a particular course. But in spite of his spectacular memory for numbers, S.F. was no better than average with letters. His memory, in general, had not improved over the months of practice with lists of numbers, only his tricks for organizing and integrating information about numbers.

One of the most remarkable discoveries in the study of memory is that it barely matters how much or how hard you *try* to learn something; what matters is how well you integrate and organize the material. Bower (1972) describes experiments in which participants were asked to form a mental image connecting each pair of words in a list (for example, pairing *car* and *desk* by imagining a desk strapped to the roof of a car). In one part of the study, the participants were told to use the image to memorize the pairs of words; this kind of learning, in which you *try* to learn something, is called **intentional learning**. In another part of the study, the participants were told simply to rate the vividness of the image, and they did not try to learn the pairs of words; learning that occurs without intention is called **incidental learning**. The interesting finding was that participants who were told to rate the images did as well at recalling word pairs as those who were told to memorize them. But, this is not to say that motivation and effort aren't important. In fact, the effort that went into organizing the objects into an image appears to have helped the participants learn, even without a specific instruction. This effect has been found repeatedly, with different kinds of learning tasks (J. R. Anderson, 2000; Hyde & Jenkins, 1973).

Emotionally Charged Memories

S.'s memory was so good that the scientists who studied him found that there was no point in performing their usual memory experiments with him; such experiments typically are aimed at discovering the factors that lead to better or worse

Transfer appropriate processing: Processing used to retrieve material that is the same type as was used when the material was originally studied, which improves memory retrieval.

Breadth of processing: Processing that organizes and integrates information into previously stored information, often by making associations.

Elaborative encoding: Encoding that involves great breadth of processing.

Intentional learning: Learning that occurs as a result of trying to learn.

Incidental learning: Learning that occurs without intention.

memory. For most of us, the amount that we remember depends on specific aspects of the situation, and one important aspect is emotion: People store emotionally charged information better than they do neutral information. Bradley and colleagues (1992) showed people slides with positive, negative, and neutral images—for example, an attractive nude young man hugging an attractive nude young woman, a burned body, a table lamp. The participants later remembered the arousing stimuli, both positive and negative, better than the neutral ones.

Why Does Emotion Boost Memory? Cahill and McGaugh and colleagues (Cahill et al., 1994) have begun to answer this question in detail. They showed people photographs that illustrated a story. For some participants, the photos were all described in a neutral way (for example, "While walking along, the boy sees some wrecked cars in a junkyard, which he finds interesting"); for others, the photos at the beginning and end were described in a neutral way, but those in the middle were described as depicting a bloody accident ("While crossing the road, the boy is caught in a terrible accident which critically injures him"). An hour before seeing the photos, half of each set of participants were given a placebo, a medically inactive sugar pill; the other half were given a drug (propranolol) that blocks the action of noradrenaline (a neurotransmitter). A week later, all of the participants were given surprise memory tests. As expected, the group that received the sugar pill showed better memory for the pictures that had an emotional context, but the group that received the noradrenaline blocker failed to show this memory boost for emotional material.

Why does emotion cause more noradrenaline to be produced, which in turn causes enhanced memory encoding? Cahill and McGaugh thought that the boost in memory for emotional material reflects the activity of the amygdala, which is known to play a key role in emotion. Their hypothesis was that the amygdala, when activated, somehow enhances the operation of the hippocampus (perhaps via the plentiful direct connections between the two structures) as it encodes new information into memory. To test this idea, Cahill and his colleagues (1996) used PET scanning to examine the relation between activity in the amygdala and the degree to which people could recall emotionally arousing or neutral film clips. The amount of activity in the right amygdala when the participants viewed the clips later predicted remarkably well how many clips they could recall. Thus, the enhanced memory for emotional material relies on the activation of the amygdala, which in turn influences the hippocampus.

Flashbulb Memories. A special case of an emotionally charged memory is a **flashbulb memory**, an unusually vivid and detailed memory of a dramatic event. It is as if a flashbulb in the mind goes off at key moments, creating instant records of the events. Perhaps you have such a memory for the moment you heard about the planes crashing into the World Trade Center towers on September 11, 2001. Brown and Kulik (1977) coined the term "flashbulb memory" and conducted the first studies of the phenomena. They polled people about a number of events, counting the recollections as flashbulb memories if respondents claimed to remember details about where they were when they learned of the event, who told them about it, and how they or others felt at the time. Most of the people these researchers polled at the time had flashbulb memories of President John F. Kennedy's assassination. In contrast, although three quarters of the Black Americans interviewed had flashbulb memories for the assassination of Martin Luther King, Jr., fewer than one third of the White interviewees had such memories. Brown and Kulik suggested that only events that have important consequences for a person are stored as flashbulb memories.

Women remember emotional stimuli better than men, in part because emotion boosts the brain's memory circuits more effectively in women than in men (Canli et al., 2001). It is also possible, however, that socialization has led women to pay closer attention to emotion—and thus to encode circumstances surrounding it more effectively.

Flashbulb memory: An unusually vivid and detailed memory of a dramatic event.

Neisser and Harsch (1992) found that although people may be very confident of their flashbulb memories, these memories often become distorted over time. Moreover, this distortion becomes progressively worse with the passage of time (Schmolck et al., 2000). In fact, when researchers compared memories of a recent everyday event with those for the events of September 11, 2001 (memories initially recorded on September 12 of that year), they found that participants forgot the two events at comparable rates over time. Nevertheless, the participants' ratings of how vivid their memories were, and of how strongly they believed that the memories were accurate, did not change for their memories of September 11th but did diminish over time for the everyday memories. Although people believed that their flashbulb memories were more accurate, they weren't (Talarico & Rubin, 2003).

LOOKING BACK: *Review*

1. *What is a memory store? How do memory stores differ?* A memory store is a set of neurons that serves to retain information. Three types of memory stores have been identified: sensory memory (SM), which briefly stores a large amount of perceptual information; short-term memory (STM), which stores relatively little information for a few seconds (but for perhaps as long as 30 seconds); and long-term memory (LTM), which stores a large amount of information for a long time (hours to years). Only information in STM is in immediate awareness, and such information can be recalled faster than information in LTM.

2. *What factors affect whether we retain information in memory?* One key to effective encoding of information into memory is to organize the information well. In addition, using two kinds of codes—verbal and visual—is more effective than using only a single code. Material must be consolidated, that is, stored structurally, which can take years to complete. In general, thinking deeply about material, which requires retrieving information from memory at the time, results in more effective storage; so does breadth of processing, that is, thinking about how new material relates to previously stored material. However, the effectiveness of encoding depends on its purposes; for example, encoding the sound of a word at the time of study is more effective than encoding the meaning of a word if the memory test requires recalling sound. Finally, emotionally charged material is generally stored more effectively than emotionally neutral material.

LOOKING BEYOND: *Critical Thinking*

At first glance, the fact that memories require time to consolidate may appear to be a disadvantage. Can you think of any advantages to having to wait a while before memories are consolidated?

Why does it make sense that we have better memory for emotional events? Would this help us make decisions or lead our lives in effective ways? Can you think of ways in which this feature of memory is a drawback? Why do you think people are so confident about their flashbulb memories?

Storing Information: Not Just One LTM

S. relied heavily on mental images, but also used words and phrases as memory jogs. He eventually became a professional stage performer, and people paid to see him demonstrate his amazing memory. As part of his act, he asked audience members to produce any list or set of phrases, and he would memorize them. The audiences often tried to trip him up by giving him meaningless words or phrases. When given such verbal material to memorize, S. found it best to "break the words or meaningless phrases down into their component parts and try to attach meaning to an individual syllable by linking it up with some association" (Luria, 1968/1887, p. 43). These associations often relied on verbal knowledge, both about the meaning of words and their sounds. Unlike the single general-purpose hard drive on a computer, LTM is divided into specialized parts, as if—to continue the analogy—it has different drives for different sensory modalities (such as vision and audition), verbal information, and motor activities. S. clearly relied on many different sorts of information—and so do the rest of us. In this section, we consider these different sorts of information that are stored in memory.

LOOKING AHEAD: Learning Objectives

1. How are different types of information stored over a long period of time?
2. What role do genes play in memory?
3. How does stress affect memory?

Modality-Specific Memories: The Multimedia Brain

The fact that memory is not a single capacity becomes especially clear when we look closely at how different kinds of information are stored in LTM. For example, note what seems to happen when you decide which is the darker green, a pine tree or a frozen pea, or whether the first three notes of "Three Blind Mice" go up or down. When answering such questions, most people report recalling visual or auditory memories, "seeing" a tree and a pea or "hearing" the nursery song. S. was superb at using these kinds of memories. In fact, virtually all of his memories were rooted in images of one sort or another; even when he used elaborate verbal associations or stories, they eventually led to specific mental images. As we saw in the discussion of perception in Chapter 3, our brains store visual memories so that we may recognize previously seen objects, auditory memories to recognize environmental sounds and melodies, olfactory memories to recognize previously encountered scents (Gottfried & Dolan, 2003), and so on. These **modality-specific memory stores** retain input from a single sense or processing system (Fuster, 1997; Karni & Sagi, 1993; Squire, 1987; Squire & Kandel, 1999; Ungerleider, 1995). In addition to visual, auditory, and olfactory memory stores, we have separate memory stores for touch, movement, and language. Interestingly, nearly everyone finds visual memories easier to recall than verbal memories.

Modality-specific memory stores: Memory stores that retain input from a single sense, such as vision or audition, or from a specific processing system, such as language.

Semantic Versus Episodic Memory

In each kind of modality-specific memory store in LTM, you can retain two types of information. **Semantic memories** are memories of the meanings of words (a *pine* is an evergreen tree with long needles), concepts (heat moves from a warmer object to a cooler one), and general facts about the world (the original 13 American colonies were established by the British). For the most part, you don't remember when, where, or how you learned this kind of information.

In contrast, **episodic memories** are memories of events that are associated with a particular time, place, and circumstance (when, where, and how); in other words, episodic memories provide a *context*. The meaning of the word *memory* is, no doubt, firmly implanted in your semantic memory, whereas the time and place you first began to read this book are probably in your episodic memory. At first, a new word may be entered in both ways, but after you use it for a while you probably don't remember when, where, or how you learned its meaning. However, even though the episodic memory may be gone, the word's meaning is retained in semantic memory. Neuroimaging studies have provided evidence that semantic and episodic memories are distinct. The frontal lobes, for instance, play a key role in looking up stored information (Hasegawa et al., 1998). However, many researchers have found that the left frontal lobe tends to be activated more than the right when we recall semantic memories, but the opposite is true when we recall episodic memories. If the two types of memories were the same, the same parts of the brain should generally access both (Cabeza & Nyberg, 1997; Nyberg et al., 1996; Shallice et al., 1994).

Explicit Versus Implicit Memories: Not Just the Facts, Ma'am

When you consciously think about a previous experience, you are recalling an **explicit** (also called a **declarative) memory** (Squire, 2004). Verbal and visual memories are explicit if you can call them to mind in words or images (as you did with the pine tree and the pea). Episodic and semantic memories are explicit memories. Explicit memories are what is stored after cognitive learning occurs (see Chapter 4). When explicit memories are activated, they can be operated on in WM: You can think about the recalled information in different ways and for different purposes, and build on it with new ideas.

But think of how exhausting it would be if every time you met a friend, you had to try consciously to recall everything you knew about how people interact socially before you could have a conversation. The reason you don't have to go through such a tedious process is that you are guided through the world by **implicit** (also called **nondeclarative) memories**, memories that you are unaware of having but that nonetheless predispose you to behave in certain ways in the presence of specific stimuli or that make it easier to repeat an action you performed previously (Roediger & McDermott, 1993; Schacter, 1987, 1996; Squire, 2004). Unlike explicit memories, implicit memories cannot be voluntarily called to mind—that is, brought into WM and thus into awareness.

The first hint that memory can be either explicit or implicit arose from the dreadful accidental consequences of a brain operation. H.M., whom you met in Chapter 2, suffered before his surgery from such a severe case of epilepsy that nothing could control his body-wracking convulsions. Finally, in 1953, at age 27, he underwent surgery to remove his hippocampus (and related parts of the brain

Semantic memories: Memories of the meanings of words, concepts, and general facts about the world.

Episodic memories: Memories of events that are associated with a particular context—a time, place, and circumstance.

Explicit (or declarative) memories: Memories that can be retrieved at will and represented in STM; verbal and visual memories are explicit if they can be called to mind as words or images.

Implicit (or nondeclarative) memories: Memories that cannot be voluntarily called to mind, but nevertheless influence behavior or thinking.

in the front, inside part of the temporal lobe; Corkin, 2002). His doctors, whom H.M. had met many times, were pleased that the operation lessened his epileptic symptoms, but they were bewildered when he seemed not to recognize them. He could not remember ever having met them, and every time he saw them, he introduced himself and shook hands. To discover just how thorough this memory loss was, one of the doctors is said to have repeated an experiment first reported by Claparède in 1911: The doctor concealed a pin in his hand and gave H.M. a jab at the handshake. The next day, H.M. again behaved as if he had never seen the doctor before, but, as he reached out to shake hands, he hesitated and pulled his hand back. Even though he had no conscious memory of the doctor, his actions indicated that he had learned something about him; H.M. had acquired a type of implicit memory (Hugdahl, 1995a).

Implicit memories are of five major types: classically conditioned responses, memories formed through nonassociative learning, habits, skills, and priming.

You can voluntarily recall explicit memories, such as a particularly important birthday, but you cannot voluntarily recall implicit memories, such as how to ride a bike. Implicit memories guide much of our behavior, freeing up the mental processes that underlie consciousness to focus on novel or particularly important stimuli or events.

Classically Conditioned Responses

The first type of implicit memory is classically conditioned responses. For example, if you burned your feet when walking barefoot on a particular pier during the summer, you probably would shy away from walking on that pier barefoot in the future. You aren't necessarily consciously aware of the association and may not even be able to explain your aversion to the pier (see Chapter 4; Hugdahl, 1995b).

Nonassociative Learning

In addition to conditioned responses acquired through associative learning, implicit memories are also formed through nonassociative learning. For example, during habituation, a behavior changes after a stimulus is repeated over and over (see Chapter 4).

Habits

Another type of implicit memory is habits (which are sometimes called *procedural memories*). A **habit**, as the term is defined by memory researchers, is a well-learned response that is carried out automatically (without conscious thought) when the appropriate stimulus is present. Habits include the entire gamut of automatic behaviors we engage in every day. When you see a red light, you automatically lift your foot from the accelerator, shift it left, and press it on the brake (we hope!); if you think something is automatic, that's a give-away that the action is being guided by implicit memory. Even S., who relied so strongly on mental images (which are explicit memories), must have relied heavily on implicit memories. For example, S. could play the violin, and such ability is stored as implicit memories. An example of the amnesiac patient H.M.'s implicit memory was revealed by the working of habit. When one of the authors of this book examined him some years ago, H.M. was using a walker because he had slipped on the ice and injured himself. The walker was made of aluminum tubes, and several operations were needed to fold it properly for storage. H.M. did not remember falling on the ice (which would have been an explicit memory), but he could fold and unfold the walker

Habit: A well-learned response that is carried out automatically (without conscious thought) when the appropriate stimulus is present.

Controlled processing: Processing that requires paying attention to each step of an action and using working memory (WM) to coordinate the steps.

Automatic processing: Processing that allows you to carry out a sequence of steps without having to pay attention to each one or to the relations between the steps.

Priming: The result of having just performed a task that facilitates repeating the same or an associated task.

more quickly than the examiner could—thanks to the habit learned through using the device. He clearly had acquired a new implicit memory, even though he had no idea how he had come to need the walker in the first place. The intact ability to learn new habits, but not new episodic memories, is evidence that implicit and explicit memories are distinct from each other.

Skills: Automatic Versus Controlled Processing

A *skill* is like a habit, but more flexible: Skills are sets of behaviors that can be applied to a variety of stimuli within a domain, such as riding a bike. Once you've learned how to ride a bike, you coordinate balancing, pedaling, and steering—not to mention looking where you are going! When you first begin to acquire a skill, you rely on controlled processing. **Controlled processing** requires paying attention to each step of an action and using working memory to coordinate the steps. Do you remember when you first learned to ride a bike (or drive a car)? It was exhausting! In contrast, after you've become highly practiced, you can perform the action without such painstaking control. Instead, you rely on **automatic processing**, which is processing that allows you to carry out a sequence of steps without having to pay attention to each one or to the relations between the steps. According to Schneider and Chein (2003), automatic processes are distinguished from controlled processes by seven characteristics, as summarized in Table 5.1.

Priming

The fifth major type of implicit memory is **priming**, the effect that occurs when having just performed a task (such as recognizing a particular object) makes it easier to perform the same or an associated task more easily in the future (Schacter, 1987, 1996). For example, if you just saw an ant on the floor, you would be primed to see other ants and, thus primed, you would notice them in places where you might previously have missed them (such as on dark surfaces).

Table 5.1 Automatic Processes Versus Controlled Processes

Characteristics of Automatic Processes Not Shared by Controlled Processes	Example Involving an Automatic Process
Become automatic only after extended training	Reading aloud written words
Occur without awareness and two or more can take place simultaneously	Driving (for an experienced driver) and understanding speech (in a highly familiar language)
Operate effectively even when the maximal amount of effort is required	Driving during rush hour in a very busy city
Work effectively even when a person is stressed	Reading street signs when rushing a pregnant friend to a hospital to give birth
Are difficult to alter through changes in expectations, beliefs, and goals	Not reading a word when trying to see its color in a Stroop task
Are difficult to adjust via learning	Changing a tennis swing after having played for many years
Depend on the importance of a stimulus, not its context	Putting the right foot on the car brake when you see a red light, even very late at night on a deserted road

Figure 5.7 Types of Memories

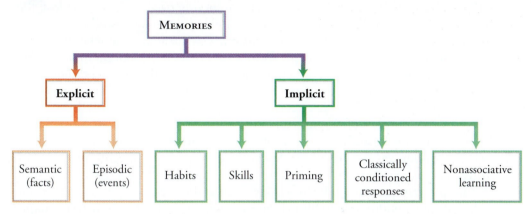

Not only are there many types of memories, as shown here, but also each type can occur in multiple stimulus modalities (visual, auditory, and so on).

Priming occurs when a preexisting memory or combination of memories is activated and the activation lingers. Priming that makes the same information more easily accessed in the future is called **repetition priming** (this is the kind of priming that enables you to see more ants). Many studies have shown that you can recognize a word or picture more quickly if you have seen it before than if it is novel. Such priming can be very long-lasting; for example, Cave (1997) found that people could name previously seen pictures faster when shown them again 48 weeks after the initial, single viewing. Your first exposure to the stimulus "greases the wheels" for your later reaction to it; in fact, after priming with a familiar object, the brain areas that perform the task work less hard when repeating it than they did initially (Gabrieli et al., 1995, 1996; Henson et al., 2000; Schacter & Badgaiyan, 2001; Squire et al., 1992).

The different major types of long-term memories are summarized in Figure 5.7.

Repetition priming: Priming that makes the same information more easily accessed in the future.

Genetic Foundations of Memory

The next time someone complains that they have a bad memory, you now know to wonder, What sort of memory? Short-term or long-term? Which modalities? Explicit or implicit? Surprisingly, in most cases, the different types of memory operate independently of one another. Evidence is emerging that different genes underlie various types of memory, serving to demonstrate further that these types are, in fact, distinct.

Knockout Mice and Blinking Rabbits

How could we tell whether different genes affect different aspects of memory? One answer comes from the study of *knockout mice*, so named because a particular gene has been "knocked out," or removed, and thus disabled. However, tracing the connection between a missing gene and a specific behavior it normally affects is easier said than done. For example, early investigators thought they had found that knocking out particular genes disrupted a mouse's ability to remember the location of a concealed platform in a pool of water (the mice wanted to swim to the platform so that they could rest, and hence were motivated to remember where it was; Morris, 1984). However, in one such study, Huerta and colleagues (1996) observed that the mice without the "remembering" gene weren't lost; they just wouldn't swim. When the researchers tickled the mice's hind feet, the animals swam and learned where the platform was located as quickly as normal mice. Their inability to find the platform wasn't caused by poor memory but by a lessened motivation to swim. (We have to wonder whether the researchers may have stumbled on a laziness gene!) One moral of this story is that removing a given gene can have multiple effects, which can cause the animal to do poorly on a test for any number of reasons (Gerlai, 1996).

Another way to study the effects of genes on memory is to observe which proteins are produced during a task. Specific genes produce specific proteins, and thus researchers can infer which genes were recently active by tracking their signature proteins. In one such study, Cavallaro and colleagues (2001) studied rabbits that were conditioned to blink their eyes when they heard a tone (see Chapter 4 for a discussion of classical conditioning). The most interesting result was that many genes decreased their production of proteins during conditioning; only a relatively few genes (for example, those that affected the cerebellum and hippocampus) were activated (allowing the results of learning to be retained, which is what memory is all about). Clearly, memory is a precise process, which involves intricate fine-tuning of that most marvelously complex of organs, the brain.

Genes and Memory Variation

The human genome project has identified human genes that play a role in memory. For example, the apolipoprotein E (apo E) gene is present in many people who develop Alzheimer's disease, which devastates memory. But this gene does more than disrupt memory; versions (different alleles) of it also affect how well the normal brain can store information. For instance, Hubacek and colleagues (2001) found that one version of this gene tends to be present more often in people who have higher education than in people who dropped out of school by age 15, and vice versa for another version of this gene.

Stressed Memories

When you are stressed, your brain sends signals to your body to prepare it for a fight-or-flight response. One of these signals increases the production of the hormone cortisol (see Chapter 2), which converts protein and fat into sugar, readying the body for rapid action. However, cortisol is a two-edged sword. Sapolsky and his colleagues have shown that in rats and baboons long-term exposure to cortisol actually kills neurons in the hippocampus (McEwen, 1997; Sapolsky, 1992). And the loss of hippocampal neurons disrupts memory.

Sapolsky studied a troop of baboons in Africa. The baboons had a well-defined social order, with some members of the troop being "on top" (getting the first choice of food, mates, and shelter), and others "on the bottom." Those on the bottom were found to have higher levels of cortisol in their blood; their social circumstances put them in a state of near-constant stress. When Sapolsky examined the brains of some of the baboons that died, he found that those near the bottom of the social order had smaller hippocampi than those higher up that were not continually stressed. And this sad state of affairs is not limited to baboons. MRI studies of the brains of people who have undergone prolonged stress during combat have shown that they have smaller hippocampi than people who were spared these experiences (Bremner et al., 1993). Similar results have been reported for victims of childhood sexual abuse who are diagnosed with posttraumatic stress disorder (PTSD; Bremner et al., 2003). Fortunately, in humans, the effects of stress on the hippocampus may be reversed if the environment changes (McEwen, 1997), and not all people who undergo stress fall prey to these effects (Pederson et al., 2004; Vythilingam et al., 2004).

In addition to disrupting the function of the hippocampus, at least some forms of stress may also disrupt other brain areas involved in storing and retrieving memories—including parts of the frontal lobe and amygdala. Researchers have found that when stress hormones disrupt storage processes in the hippocampus, they also disrupt them in a pathway connecting the amygdala and frontal lobes (Maroun & Richter-Levin, 2003). High levels of stress hormones may disrupt the processes specifically involved in memory retrieval (Roozendaal, 2003).

Looking at Levels

Autobiographical Memory

What is your first memory? How about your first memory of today? Episodic memories of events of your own life are called *autobiographical memories* (Conway & Rubin, 1993). Such memories require a kind of "time travel," where you put yourself back into a particular moment in your past and relive what you experienced at that time. To understand autobiographical memories, we must consider events at each of the three levels of analysis and their interactions.

Let's start with the brain. Are autobiographical memories different from other kinds of memories? When you reflected on those events in your own life, did you experience mental images? Did you have emotional reactions? Such characteristics might suggest that memories of events that occurred in your own life might be different from memories of events that you observed happening to someone else—and research findings support this suggestion. In one study, researchers asked participants (undergraduate students) to take photos of specific locations on campus, asking different students to photograph different places. They later brought the participants into the laboratory and showed each student some of the photos taken by others. The researchers later scanned (using fMRI) the students' brains while they looked at mixed sets of photos and decided which photos they themselves had taken (based on the memory of having done so), which had been taken by others but seen in the laboratory, and which had not been previously seen. The frontal lobe area (located in the midsection region) involved in "self-referencing" was activated more strongly by the photos that corresponded to autobiographical memories than by the other photos, as were visual regions, the hippocampus, and regions near the hippocampus (Cabeza et al., 2004). Consistent with such findings, other researchers have found that brain damage can affect people's memories of famous people and events while not affecting their own autobiographical memories (Joubert et al., 2003). From these and similar studies, it is clear that autobiographical memory holds a special place not just in our lives, but also in our brains (Greenberg & Rubin, 2003; Levine, 2004).

Studies of the brain have done more than simply show that autobiographical memories are different from other types of memories. Research at this level of analysis has also shown that autobiographical memories can be divided into two types: episodic and semantic. Specifically, Brian Levine and his colleagues (2004) asked participants to keep a record over the course of several months, tape recording both descriptions of specific events they experienced and facts they observed about the world (which correspond to episodic and semantic autobiographical memories, respectively). Later, the participants listened to these recordings while their brains were scanned using fMRI. The tape recordings would presumably trigger the corresponding memories, and in fact, the brain responded differently to descriptions of experienced events and observed facts about the world. Although both types of autobiographical memories activated the left frontal lobe (the portion in the midsection region), memories of experienced events activated this area more strongly than did memories of observed facts; this is interesting because this area has been repeatedly shown to be activated during "self-referencing," when people reflect on their own characteristics (Johnson et al., 2002; Kelley et al., 2002; Macrae et al., 2004). In addition, other brain areas were activated only during the experience-of-event condition and others only during the observation-of-fact condition. Clearly, the two kinds of autobiographical memories are distinct.

Autobiographical memories also depend on, and are affected by, events at the level of the person. What would be left if all of your autobiographical memories were erased? A large part of our personal identity hinges on our memories—memories not only of what we've done and what we know, but also of who we are. Researchers have documented this claim by showing that when people with Alzheimer's disease lose autobiographical memories, this loss is linked to distinct changes on questionnaire measures of the "self concept." Based on their results, these researchers suggest that autobiographical memories of childhood and early adulthood (which they define as the age range 16–25) are especially critical for self-identity (Addis & Tippett, 2004).

In addition, numerous events at the level of the person affect which autobiographical memories you will recall and how you will feel about them. Notably, if you felt good about an event at the time you experienced it, you are more likely to be able to recall it later. In one study, for example, people were tested on their memory for the O. J. Simpson trial. If a participant was happy about the verdict, he or she was later more likely to be able to recall details of the event (Levine & Bluck, 2004). And how you feel about autobiographical information is not determined solely by how you felt when you experienced the event—your feelings are also affected by the strategy you use during recall. In one study (Libby et al., 2005), participants were asked to recall "past social awkwardness" by taking a first-person perspective (that is, a participant's own viewpoint) or a third-person perspective (of an outside observer). Recalling events from the third-person perspective led participants to believe that they had changed more since the events had taken place. The third-person perspective apparently led participants to seek evidence that they had changed—and those who seek often will find.

Moreover, your personal characteristics also affect the recall of autobiographical material. For example, people who are anxious in social situations tend to recall more negative and shameful autobiographical memories than do people who are not socially anxious (Field et al., 2004). And people who are inclined to feel gratitude for things others have done for them tend to be biased to recall more positive than negative events from their past (Watkins et al., 2004). Finally, the flip side of the last finding has been reported: People generally are biased to forget negative affect (emotional content) associated with events more quickly than they forget positive affect—unless they are mildly depressed, in which case, this bias can evaporate (Walker, Skowronski, Gibbons, et al., 2003; Walker, Skowronski, & Thompson, 2003).

And, of course, events at the level of the group affect autobiographical memories. We are immersed in social events just as a fish is immersed in water—and like the fish, we may not be aware of the many and varied ways that such events shape our memories. Most notably, the cultures in which we live play an important role in how we remember events about our lives. For example, when Americans and Chinese were asked to recall memories of their lives, the Americans recalled more unique, one-time events than did the Chinese and reported more details of the roles they personally played in the events as well as their emotional reactions. On the other hand, the Chinese recalled more social events and downplayed their own roles while emphasizing the social interactions surrounding events (Wang & Conway, 2004).

In addition, studies have shown that the emotional impact of remembered autobiographical events can be softened if people talk about these events—and this is especially the case if you have a sympathetic listener who agrees with you (Pasupathi, 2003).

Finally, effects at the different levels interact. For example, we already noted that people tend to forget negative affect associated with autobiographical memories more quickly than they forget positive affect. This effect is enhanced for memories that are frequently discussed with others—and even more so when the person talks to many different types of people, such as friends, teachers, acquaintances, and strangers (Skowronski & Walker, 2004; Skowronski et al., 2004). The social factors that influence a person's decision to talk about autobiographical memories not only affect events at the level of the person, but also alter the way the brain functions at that moment.

LOOKING BACK: *Review*

1. *How are different types of information stored over a long period of time?*
   Each sensory modality (such as vision, audition, and touch) has a separate LTM store; separate memories also exist for motor and verbal information. In addition, each of these types of LTM can be divided into semantic memory (which is memory for meaning, concepts, and facts about the world) and episodic memory (which is memory for events that occur in the context of a specific time, place, and circumstance). In addition to explicit memories, which can be voluntarily brought to mind, implicit memories in each modality are evident only in a single context and guide our actions outside our awareness. Finally, working memory is a system that includes specialized STMs plus a central executive that operates on information stored in them; the information in the STMs has often been retrieved from LTM.

2. *What role do genes play in memory?* Some genes affect the functioning of specific parts of the brain, which can affect particular aspects of memory.

3. *How does stress affect memory?* Chronic stress increases the levels of the fight-or-flight hormone cortisol, which can kill neurons in the hippocampus. Thus, stress can disrupt the encoding of new explicit memories into LTM. In addition, stress disrupts processes involved in memory retrieval.

LOOKING BEYOND: *Critical Thinking*

S. was extraordinarily good at storing images. If he relied on this sort of storage alone, what sorts of material might be difficult for him to understand? Can you think of reasons why it makes sense that someone can be extraordinary with regard to only some types of memory? If a new drug were created that would improve one sort of memory, which sort of memory would you most prefer to improve?

Retrieving Information From Memory: More Than Reactivating the Past

S. was not simply adept at readying material to be memorized; he was also expert at later digging out material from memory. No matter how well he encoded it and retained it in memory, the information would have been useless if he couldn't later retrieve it. In this section, we explore the process of retrieving information from memory.

LOOKING AHEAD: Learning Objectives

1. *How are memories reconstructed?*
2. *What role do cues play in retrieving stored memories?*

The Act of Remembering: Reconstructing Buried Cities

It is tempting to think of memory as a collection of file drawers that contain assorted documents, all neat and complete in labeled folders, so, when we need to recall something, we simply open a drawer and take out what we need. But memory doesn't work this way. When we open that file drawer, we don't find well-organized folders, but instead a bunch of partially torn pages that are not necessarily in order. Remembering is in many ways similar to the work archaeologists do when they find fragments of buildings, walls, furniture, and pottery and reconstruct from them a long-buried city; they fit the pieces together in a way that makes sense, and they fill in the missing parts (Neisser, 1967). We store in episodic memory only bits and pieces of a given event, and we use information from episodic memories of similar situations and from semantic memories of general facts about the world to fit the pieces together and fill in the gaps.

Recognition Versus Recall

All remembering involves tapping into the right fragments of information stored in long-term memory. We remember information in two ways. **Recall** is the intentional bringing to mind of explicit information or, put more technically, the transfer of explicit information from LTM to STM. Once information is in STM, you are aware of it and can communicate it. **Recognition** occurs when you match an encoded stimulus to one that has been stored in memory. When you match the input stimulus to a stored memory, you not only know that the stimulus is familiar, but also may have access to stored associations; for example, you may know that the stimulus occurred in a particular context, such as on a list (as used by memory researchers, the term *recognition* also implies identification; see Chapter 3). A *recognition test* occurs when you are given a set of stimuli and asked to pick out the ones you previously were given. Essay tests demand recall; the essay writer must retrieve facts from memory. Multiple-

Recall: The act of intentionally bringing explicit information to awareness, which requires transferring the information from LTM to STM.

Recognition: The act of encoding an input and matching it to a stored representation.

choice tests call for recognition; the test-taker must recognize the correct an-swer among the options.

All else being equal, tests that require you to recognize information are easier than tests that demand recall. But recognition can become difficult if you must discriminate between similar choices. The more similar the choices, the harder it is to recognize the correct one. Similar objects or concepts have more character-istics in common than do dissimilar ones. If the choices are dissimilar, you can pick out the correct one on the basis of just a few stored features. But if the choices are similar, you must have encoded the object or concept in great detail in order to recognize the correct answer. Professors who want to make devilishly hard multiple-choice tests put this principle to work. If the alternative answers for each question have very similar meanings, the test-taker must know more details than if the choices are very different. In general, the more distinctive properties of a stimulus you have stored in memory, the better you can recognize it.

Of course, you do not always know in advance which details you will need to remember. Suppose S. witnessed a theft and later was asked to pick the thief from a police lineup. S., unlike the rest of us, typically remembered exactly what he saw. In the lineup, suppose both the thief and another man in the group of six are tall, a bit overweight, and have brown hair. The major difference between them is that the thief has a scar on his left cheek. S. would have probably noticed and remembered the thief's scar and would be able to identify him. But the rest of us might not have encoded this detail at the time, and thus would be hard pressed to identify the culprit. Both recog-nition and recall rely on activating collections of fragments stored in LTM. If the appropriate fragments are not present, you cannot distinguish among simi-lar alternatives, and you will have difficulty re-calling information.

Cues: Stimuli that trigger or enhance remembering; reminders.

The Role of Cues: Hints on Where to Dig

How does an archaeologist know where to dig to find the right bits of pottery to reconstruct a water jug? A logical place to start might be in the ruins of a kitchen. The archaeologist digs, finds bits of a typical kitchen floor from the period, and then is encouraged to con-tinue digging in the same area. Similarly, a good cue directs you to key stored fragments, which then allow you to remember. **Cues** are stimuli that help you remember; they are re-minders of an event.

Imagine running into an acquaintance in a bookstore and trying to remember his name. You might recall that when you met him, he reminded you of someone else with the same name who had a similar hairline. Here the hairline is a cue, reminding you of your friend Sam and allowing you to greet this new Sam by name. A helpful cue matches fragments of information stored in LTM, as illustrated in Figure 5.8 (Barclay et al., 1974).

Figure 5.8 What Makes Something a Good Cue?

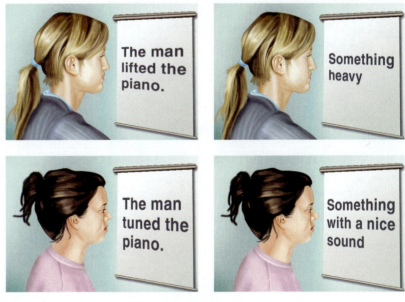

Participants were asked to memorize two sets of sentences. (What sort of mental images come to mind when you read the examples at the left?) The participants then received cues intended to help them recall the word *piano*. The top cue on the right would be more effective if the par-ticipant read the top sentence, and the bottom cue on the right would be more effective for the bottom sentence.

When participants were cued verbally to recall an event while at the same time smelling a common odor, the memory was more emotional than when no odor was present (Herz & Schooler, 2002).

Supplying Your Own Cues

Some cues are internally generated.

State-Dependent Retrieval: The Right Frame of Mind Helps.   We remember information better if we are in the same mood or psychological state (such as being hungry or sleepy) when we try to remember it as when we first learned it. If you were hungry when you studied material, you will remember it better if you are hungry at the time of recall than if you are stuffed. This can be a sobering thought if you are preparing for an exam: If you drink alcohol while studying, you will later recall the information better if you are drinking when you try to remember it. This effect is called **state-dependent retrieval** (Eich, 1989): Information is better remembered if recall is attempted in the same psychological state as when the information was first encoded. A closely related effect occurs with mood: If you are in a happy mood at the time you learn something, you may remember it better when you are feeling happy than when you are feeling sad (Bower, 1981, 1992). The effects of mood are not always very strong, however, and they can be overshadowed by other factors, such as how well the information is organized (Eich, 1995). Neither your psychological state nor your mood appears to be a very powerful retrieval cue.

Hypnosis and Memory.   S. had very vivid mental images, which apparently allowed him to recall information with ease. If someone hypnotized you and told you that your images were especially vivid, would that boost your recall? Possibly. Hypnosis sometimes improves memory of prior events. In 1976 in Chowchilla, California, a school bus was hijacked, and all of the children within kidnapped. The bus and all those inside were buried and held for ransom. When freed, the bus driver remembered the car driven by the assailants but no other details. In a hypnotic trance, he was able to recall the car's license plate, which ultimately led to the arrest of the kidnappers.

In many—if not most—cases, however, hypnosis increases people's confidence in their recollections but not their accuracy (Sheehan, 1988; Worthington, 1979). Indeed, studies have found no overall differences in accuracy of memory between witnesses who were hypnotized and those who were interviewed using techniques based on cognitive strategies such as those summarized earlier (Geiselman et al., 1985). In addition, hypnosis may actually lead people to believe that suggested events happened, rather than simply help them to recall actual events (e.g., Barber, 1997; Bryant & Barnier, 1999; Green et al., 1998). Thus, after hypnosis you might not, in fact, recall better than before, but you would probably be more confident that you did. Recognizing these problems, courts in many states will not consider testimony based on recall during hypnosis.

People who feel better about themselves in general recall more positive memories, even when they are in a bad mood, than do people who do not have a high self-regard. Both groups, however, are in a better mood after they've recalled positive memories (Setliff & Marmurek, 2002).

LOOKING BACK: *Review*

1. How are memories reconstructed? Recognition is the determination that presented information is familiar or that it occurred in a particular context; recall is the retrieval of required information from LTM. Both recognition and recall rely on activating collections of fragments stored in LTM. If the appropriate fragments are not present, you cannot distinguish among similar alternatives and will have difficulty recalling information.

State-dependent retrieval: Recall that is better if it occurs in the same psychological state that was present when the information was first encoded.

2. *What roles do cues play in retrieving stored memories?* Memories are retrieved when they are triggered by specific stimuli, thoughts, or goals. Such events serve as cues, or reminders, which are effective to the extent that they match material stored in LTM. At the time of retrieval, a cue will be most effective if you organize and interpret it in the same way that you organized and interpreted the material at the time of encoding. To aid memory, you can supply your own cues by thinking about the context in which the information was encoded, such as the time of day or the physical environment.

LOOKING BEYOND: *Critical Thinking*

Can you think of any advantages to storing fragments and later reconstructing memories as opposed to storing mental photographs or other complete sets of information? We generally find recognition easier than recall; can you think of any way to convert a recall task into a recognition task? Can you think of any ways to help you generate what might turn out to be useful cues?

When Memory Goes Wrong— and What to Do About It

S. had a near-perfect memory. When he made an error, it almost always was a "defect of perception," a result of the specific images he formed. For instance, he once forgot the word "egg" in a long list. He reported, "I had put it up against a white wall and it blended in with the background. How could I possibly spot a white egg up against a white wall?" (Luria, 1968/1887, p. 36). His memory was so good that he had a problem many of us might envy: He could not forget even when he wanted to. This became a problem when he performed on stage because material from a previous session could spring to mind unbidden, confusing him about the current list. He initially tried to imagine erasing the blackboard or burning sheets of paper on which the information had been written, but he could just as easily imagine undoing these acts or seeing the writing on the charred embers—and thus the memories persisted. Finally, S. realized that the key to forgetting was simple: He just had to want the information not to appear, and if he did not think about it, it would not return. For S., this technique worked. Was S. like the rest of us in how his memories competed with each other? Could, for the rest of us, such interference cause losses and failures of memory? How accurate are our memories?

LOOKING AHEAD: *Learning Objectives*

1. *How can actual memories be distinguished from false ones?*
2. *Is a forgotten memory necessarily gone forever, or is it still stored but difficult to retrieve?*
3. *Are memories ever repressed?*
4. *How can you improve your memory?*

Figure 5.9 Memories of Alien Abduction

Some people claim to remember being abducted by space aliens. Such people display the same bodily reactions when asked to remember the abduction as when they imagine more mundane stressful events; people who do not report memories of abduction do not react as strongly when asked to imagine an alien abduction (McNally et al., 2004). Does this mean that the memories of alien abduction are genuine?

Figure 5.10 False Memory

Please read this list of words. Now go to Figure 5.11 on page 212.

candy   caramel
soda pop   chocolate
honey   cake
pie   icing
fudge   cookie
cotton candy

False memories: Memories of events or situations that did not, in fact, occur.

False Memories

Not everything we remember actually happened. **False memories** are memories of events or situations that did not, in fact, occur. An extreme example of this sort of "memory" is illustrated in Figure 5.9.

Implanting Memories

Deese (1959) and Roediger and McDermott (1995) showed that people regularly make errors of the sort illustrated by Figures 5.10 and 5.11. (If you weren't fooled, read the list of words to a friend and wait 5 minutes before testing him or her; this will increase the likelihood of an error.) We associate the idea of "sweet" with all of the words listed, so its representation in LTM becomes activated and associated with the context of the list, and we misremember having seen it. Here is the critical point: In general, we do not necessarily remember what actually happened but rather what we *experience* as having happened.

Lest you think that misremembering only occurs when associated material is stored, consider this disturbing study reported by psychologist Elizabeth Loftus (1993). In a study with a pair of brothers, she asked the older brother to tell his younger, 14-year-old brother about the time the younger brother had been lost in a shopping mall when he was 5 years old. This story was told as if it were fact, but it was entirely fiction. The youngster later gave every indication of having genuine memories of the event, adding rich detail to the story he had been told. For example, the boy claimed to remember the flannel shirt worn by the old man who found him, his feelings at the time, and the scolding he later received from his mother. When this study was repeated with many participants, about one quarter of them fell victim to the implanting of such false memories (Loftus & Pickrell, 1995). Moreover, these participants clung steadfastly to their false memories, refusing even on debriefing to believe that they had been artificially created.

Similar results have been obtained many times (Loftus, 2004). Lindsay and colleagues (2004) reported especially striking results, finding that fully 65.2% of their participants could be led to believe that they had put Slime (a gooey concoction sold as a toy) in their teacher's desk when they were in 1st or 2nd grade. These researchers combined the usual memory-inducing suggestions (of the sort used by Loftus) with showing the participants an actual photo of their class, which boosted the number of false memories to record levels (perhaps because they were able to imagine a plausible scenario more concretely). And there was no doubt that the participants came to harbor false memories; the participants often expressed surprise and shock upon learning the truth after the study, saying things such as "No way! I remember it! That is so weird!" and "If you didn't tell me it was a false event, I would have left here thinking I did this" (p. 153). However, some false memories are easier to create than others. Pezdek and colleagues (1997) found that whereas some participants did acquire false memories of being lost in a shopping mall, none acquired false memories of having been given a rectal enema during childhood. People may have an intuitive grasp of the role of emotion in memory, which leads us to know that we would be sure to remember such an incident if it had actually happened. (The ethics of carrying out such studies might be an interesting topic for discussion.)

Distortions of memory have practical—and often quite serious—implications. After a crime is committed, for instance, witnesses are interviewed by the police, read newspaper stories about the crime, perhaps see TV reports. This information can interfere with the witnesses' actual memories. Moreover, during a trial, the way a question is asked can influence a witness's faith in his or her recollection, or even change the testimony altogether. Lest you think that such findings are merely of academic interest, reflect on the fact that several years ago the 100th person, Larry Mayes of Indiana, was released from prison because DNA evidence proved that he was innocent; these people were almost invariably convicted because witnesses had faulty memories (Loftus, 2004).

Distinguishing Fact From Fiction

Does any aspect of false memories distinguish them from real memories? Daniel Schacter and his colleagues (1996) performed the "sweet" experiment (presented in Figures 5.10 and 5.11), using similar words, while the participants' brains were being scanned. The participants were then asked which words were on the list and which words were merely implied by those listed. The hippocampus, which plays a key role in encoding new information into memory, was activated both when participants recognized actual words listed *and* when they identified associated words not on the original list. Crucially, when words actually on the list were correctly recognized, brain areas in the temporal and parietal lobes that register the sound and meaning of spoken words also were activated. In contrast, these areas were *not* active when people encountered words not on the list. Apparently, the construction of memory activates the representations of the perceptual qualities of stored words. Because the false words were not actually heard when the original list was read, this information was not activated. This cue of a "missing perception" may not be used all the time, but it clearly operates in many situations (Johnson et al., 1997).

The same principle applies to remembering a real versus an imagined event. Johnson and her colleagues (Johnson & Raye, 1981; Johnson et al., 1993) found that people often confuse actually having seen something with merely having imagined seeing it (which may be the basis of some false memories; Garry & Polaschek, 2000). Indeed, Dobson and Markham (1993) found that people who experience vivid mental images are more likely to confuse having read a description of an event with having seen it (similar findings have also been reported by Eberman & McKelvie, 2002). S., once again, is an extreme example; his "vivid images broke down the boundary between the real and the imaginary" (Luria, 1968/1887, p. 144). He commented, "To me there's no great difference between the things I imagine and what exists in reality" (p. 146).

Reality monitoring is the ongoing awareness of the perceptual and other properties that distinguish real from imagined stimuli. Reality monitoring can be

A twin sometimes has a false memory of an event that actually occurred to the other twin, such as being sent home from school for wearing a skirt that was too short. The same thing can happen (although less frequently) to non-twin siblings who are close in age, and even among same-sex friends (Sheen et al., 2001). Roediger and his colleagues (2001) describe a kind of "social contagion," where one person's recounting of memories can lead another to adopt them.

Reality monitoring: An ongoing awareness of the perceptual and other properties that distinguish real from imagined stimuli.

Figure 5.11 True or False?

Did all of these words, including *candy, chocolate,* and *sweet,* appear on the list you read in Figure 5.10 on page 210? Are you sure? In fact, the word *sweet* does not appear. If you think it did, you are not alone; most people do. This exercise shows how easily a false memory can be implanted in your brain.

candy	chocolate
soda pop	cake
honey	sweet
pie	icing
fudge	cookie
cotton candy	

Remember when you shook Mickey's hand during a childhood trip to Disneyland? Even if this never happened, seeing an advertisement that leads you to imagine this happy event will later make you more confident that it actually occurred. Researchers found the same held true even when an ad led participants to imagine that they had shaken hands with Bugs Bunny at Disneyland, which could never have happened (Bugs is not a Disney character)—and thus the ad could not have activated an actual memory (Braun et al., 2002).

Forgetting curve: A graphic representation of the rate at which information is forgotten over time: Recent events are recalled better than more distant ones, but most forgetting occurs soon after learning.

Encoding failure: A failure to process to-be-remembered information well enough to begin consolidation.

improved greatly if people are led to pay attention to the context in which stimuli occur (Lindsay & Johnson, 1989). Mather and colleagues (1997) and Schacter and colleagues (Norman & Schacter, 1997; Schacter et al., 2001) found that when people are asked to pay attention to the amount of perceptual detail in their memories (as would occur if they tried to notice the texture of objects, other nearby objects, and shadows), they are better able to distinguish actual memories from false memories. In fact, people generally experience fewer false memories for visual material than auditory material (Cleary & Greene, 2002; Kellogg, 2001). However, there is a limit to how well people can use such cues to distinguish real from false memories; false memories produced in the "sweet" experiment, for example, are remarkably persistent, even when people are warned in advance about the possibility of such memories (McDermott & Roediger, 1998). However, not all people fail to take advantage of such advance warning: People who have more effective working memories can use advance warning much better than those with less effective working memories (Watson et al., 2005).

Forgetting: Many Ways to Lose It

Once S. stored information in memory, it apparently was there for good; his recall was as accurate years later as it was immediately after learning. As first shown in 1885 by Hermann Ebbinghaus, the rest of us recall recent events better than more distant ones, and most forgetting occurs soon after learning. However, as time goes on, people lose less and less additional information from memory (Wixted & Ebbesen, 1991, 1997). Ebbinghaus discovered the **forgetting curve**, illustrated in Figure 5.12, which shows the rate at which information is forgotten over time.

Encoding Failure: Lost in Translation

Why do people lose information from memory? Sometimes the information was not well encoded in the first place. Remember the path traced over and over again through the grass? If the walker abandons the path before it is completely worn through to bare dirt, the pattern of the path is not stored structurally. Similarly, you must not "abandon" information—you must actively think about it if it is to be encoded effectively in LTM. An **encoding failure** results if you do not process information well enough to begin consolidation (Schacter, 1999).

An encoding failure causes information to be lost shortly after learning, which may be one reason for the sharp drop at the beginning of the forgetting curve. But, even if information is properly encoded, it can be lost later. Why? For many years, memory researchers hotly debated the fate of information that was once stored but then forgotten. One camp argued that once memories are gone, they are gone forever. The memory decays and disappears, just as invisible ink fades until nothing is left. The other camp claimed that the memories themselves are intact but cannot be "found." The ink hasn't faded, but the message has been misfiled. In fact, both camps had put their finger on important aspects of forgetting.

Decay: Fade Away

The invisible ink theory proposes that memories **decay**; that is, they degrade with time. The relevant connections between neurons are lost. What evidence supports this theory? In the sea slug, *Aplysia*, which has a relatively simple nervous system, it has been possible to document that the strength of the connections between neurons established by learning fades away over time (Baily & Chen, 1989). If human neurons are similar, as seems likely, memories may, in fact, decay over time. Indeed, researchers have produced evidence not only that certain genes promote stronger connections among neurons, but also that other genes prevent such connections and, hence, block memory (Abel et al., 1998). When these "memory suppressor genes" are turned on, they could cause the decay of connections that store memories.

Evidence refuting the decay theory seemed to come from dramatic findings described by Penfield (1955). Before performing brain surgery, neurosurgeons such as Penfield sometimes put small electrodes on the exposed cortex of awake patients and stimulated neurons electrically. A few patients reported vivid images and memories of long-forgotten events. For example, on having a particular area of the brain stimulated, one patient said, "Yes, sir, I think I heard a mother calling her little boy somewhere. It seemed something that happened years ago." However, at least some of these reports may not have been memories but images created on the spot (Squire, 1987; Squire & Kandel, 1999). There is no strong evidence that all memories stay stored forever. In fact, these oft-cited results occurred for only a minority of patients, and later work failed to reveal compelling evidence that memories are stored permanently.

Figure 5.12 Ebbinghaus's Forgetting Curve

Elapsed time between learning syllables and memory test

The forgetting curve shows that information becomes harder to recall over time, but that most forgetting occurs relatively soon after learning.

Interference: Tangled Up in Memory

The view that a mix-up in memory often explains forgetting has long been supported by strong direct evidence. If every summer you work with a group of kids as a camp counselor, you will find that learning the names of the current crop impairs your memory of the names of last year's campers. This is an example of interference. **Interference** is the disruption of the ability to remember one piece of information by the presence of other information. Two types of interference can plague your memories: retroactive and proactive.

Retroactive interference is interference that disrupts memory for something learned earlier. Learning the names of the new campers can interfere with your memory of the names of the previous group. **Proactive interference** is interference by something already learned that makes it difficult to learn something new. Your having learned the names of previous groups of kids may interfere with your learning the names on this summer's roster, particularly if some of the new names are similar to old ones.

Why does interference occur? The capacity of LTM is not the problem. You are not overloading a "memory-for-people" box in your brain; some politicians, after all, can remember the names of thousands of people with little or no difficulty. Interference probably occurs because the retrieval cues for various memories are similar, and thus a given cue may call up the wrong memory. The more similar the already-known and to-be-remembered information, the more interference you get (Adams, 1967).

The first president of Stanford University, David Starr Jordan, apparently worried that he might eventually fill up his memory if he learned too much. (But you shouldn't worry; we now know that the capacity of LTM is so vast that it hasn't yet

Decay: The fading away of memories with time because the relevant connections between neurons are lost.

Interference: The disruption of the ability to remember one piece of information by the presence of other information.

Retroactive interference: Interference that occurs when new learning impairs memory for something learned earlier.

Proactive interference: Interference that occurs when previous knowledge makes it difficult to learn something new.

even been measured.) President Jordan was an ichthyologist, an expert on fish who knew the names and habits of thousands of underwater species. At the beginning of each year, he met the new students and politely smiled as they were introduced, but ignored their names. One bold student asked President Jordan if he had heard the name clearly, and then repeated it. Jordan listened and realized that he had now learned the student's name. He slapped himself on the forehead and exclaimed, "Drat, there goes another fish!"

Intentional Forgetting: Out of Mind, Out of Sight

Given that interference is one reason we forget, you might wonder whether you could improve your memory by getting rid of useless information that might interfere with important facts. Was S. onto something when he tried to clear his cluttered mind by willing himself to forget unneeded information? Can we intentionally forget? Psychologists have studied this question by asking participants to learn a list of words or other stimuli, and then telling them to forget the list. Later the participants are given a surprise memory test, and their memory for the list is compared to that when they (or other people) were not told to forget it. Robert Bjork (1972) found that people have trouble later recalling information they were told to forget.

However, such information is not truly forgotten if it was successfully encoded; rather, it becomes not easily accessible (Bjork & Bjork, 2003). Indeed, when participants were asked to keep specific information out of mind, their frontal lobes became more active *and* their hippocampi became less active than when they were not trying to do this (Anderson et al., 2004). In contrast, if you decide not to remember something immediately after you perceive it, your left frontal lobe will not work as hard to encode it as it does when you try to remember (Reber et al., 2002). Clearly, the frontal lobes have a lot to do with the memory strategies we use, including those involved in trying to forget.

Drew Barrymore, as the lead character in the movie *50 First Dates*, appears to suffer from retrograde amnesia. If so, this would be a very unusual case—most such patients cannot retain information for an entire day, as she was able to do.

Amnesia: A loss of memory over an entire time span, resulting from brain damage caused by accident, infection, or stroke.

Amnesia: Not Just Forgetting to Remember

Even S., if he received a strong blow to the head, might not recall anything that had happened to him after that incident. Why? Neither normal decay nor interference accounts for such unusual losses of memory. Instead, such memory failure is an example of amnesia, a loss of memory over an entire time span, typically resulting from brain damage caused by accident, infection, or stroke. Amnesia is not like normal forgetting, which affects only some of the material learned during a given period. Moreover, there are two broad sorts of amnesia: *Organic amnesia* arises after the brain has been damaged, by stroke, injury (including during surgery), or disease; *functional amnesia* typically arises after psychological trauma (Kritchevsky et al., 2004), and there is no obvious problem in the brain itself (although changes in the brain ultimately must underlie even this variety). In spite of its usefulness as a plot twist in novels and TV dramas, functional amnesia is very rare—and you would be wise to take the portrayals of amnesia in movies with more than a single grain of salt. For example, Baxendale (2004, p. 1480) notes, "*50 First Dates* maintains a venerable movie tradition of portraying an amnesiac syndrome that bears no relation to any known neurological or psychiatric condition." Moreover, other events portrayed in such movies—such as a second bump on the head hitting a "reset button" and curing the amnesia—have no basis in fact. (However, Baxendale notes that the main character in *Momento* and Dory the fish in *Finding Nemo* both do a reasonable job of portraying known forms of amnesia.) Functional amnesia is particularly difficult to study because, at least in some cases, it may actually be *malingering*, intentional faking of the disorder.

Organic amnesia often seems to affect episodic memories while leaving semantic memories almost entirely intact (Warrington & McCarthy, 1988). Most people who have an accident that causes organic amnesia have no idea what they were doing immediately before the accident, but they can remember semantic information such as their names and birth dates. However, such selective forgetting reflects not the distinction between episodic and semantic memory, but instead the fact that most information in semantic memory was learned long ago—and hence is fully consolidated. Episodic memories of long-ago events are not disrupted by amnesia (Bayley et al., 2003). However, organic amnesia sometimes has the opposite effect, impairing mostly semantic memories. For example, De Renzi and colleagues (1987) report a patient who forgot the meanings of words and most characteristics of common objects. Nevertheless, she remembered details about key events in her life, such as her wedding and her father's illness. Researchers have found that semantic memories are more likely to be impaired by amnesia if they are recent (for example, memories for new words that have entered everyday usage, such as "Segway" for the lawn-mower-like scooter; Manns et al., 2003).

Amnesia may be retrograde or anterograde (Mayes & Downes, 1997; Parkin, 1987). **Retrograde amnesia** disrupts previous memories (Fast & Fujiwara, 2001). This is the sort of amnesia often popularized in soap operas and movies. Most of us are affected by a special form of retrograde amnesia called *infantile amnesia* or *childhood amnesia* (Newcombe et al., 2000): We don't remember much about our early childhood experiences, although some people apparently do remember very significant events (such as the birth of a sibling) that occurred when they were less than 2 years old (Eacott & Crawley, 1999). **Anterograde amnesia** leaves already consolidated memories intact but prevents the learning of new facts. It affects all explicit memories—that is, memories of facts that can be brought to consciousness voluntarily—and produces massive encoding failure. Its manifestation is well presented in an old joke: A man runs into a doctor's office, screaming, "Doc! I've lost my memory!" The doctor asks him, "When did this happen?" The man looks at him, puzzled, and says, "When did what happen?" However, it is no joke for people with anterograde amnesia, who live as if frozen in the present moment of time. H.M. had a form of anterograde amnesia.

What happens in the brain to produce amnesia? Often, as in the case of H.M., the cause involves damage to the hippocampus or its connections to or from other parts of the brain (Spiers et al., 2001). In addition, sometimes amnesia can result when areas of the cortex that serve as memory stores become degraded. All memories are a result of changes in the interactions among neurons, and most neurons involved in memory are in the cortex. In cases of Alzheimer's disease, the amnesia typically begins with small memory deficits, which become progressively worse. In the later stages of the disease, people with Alzheimer's cannot remember who they are, where they are, or who their relatives and friends are. Alzheimer's disease not only affects the hippocampus but also degrades other parts of the brain that serve as memory stores. Depending on which other parts of the brain are affected, Alzheimer's patients can have greater amnesia for one form of information or another; for example, some patients have worse spatial memory than verbal memory, and others show the opposite pattern (Albert et al., 1990).

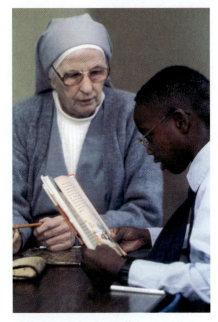

Approximately 4.5 million Americans are afflicted with Alzheimer's disease, and some experts estimate that this disease will affect over 13 million Americans by 2050 (Hebert et al., 2003). But not everybody is equally susceptible. In one study, nuns who had better linguistic ability, as judged from autobiographical essays they wrote in their 20s, were less likely than nuns with poorer linguistic ability to develop Alzheimer's disease (Snowdon et al., 2000).

Retrograde amnesia: Amnesia that disrupts previous memories.

Anterograde amnesia: Amnesia that leaves consolidated memories intact but prevents new learning.

One possible treatment for Alzheimer's disease may come from a surprising source: tea. Both green tea and black tea may enhance memory (Okello et al., 2004). Both beverages inhibit the enzyme acetylcholinesterase (AChE) from breaking down acetylcholine, which plays a key role in storing new memories.

Repressed Memories: Real or Imagined?

Recent years have witnessed many dramatic reports of suddenly recollected memories. Some people claim to have suddenly remembered that they were sexually molested by their parents decades before, when they were no more than 3 years old. One person claimed that as a child he had been strapped to the back of a dolphin as part of a bizarre devil worship ritual. Are these false memories, or are they **repressed memories**, real memories that have been pushed out of consciousness because they are emotionally threatening, as Freud believed? (When repressed information is later recalled, this is called a *recovered memory*.) Whether or not repressed memories exist is perhaps the most heated issue in memory research today (Fivush & Edwards, 2004; Madill & Holch, 2004; McNally, 2003, 2004; Ost, 2003; Pope, 1996; Rubin, 1996; Wessel & Wright, 2004).

On the one hand, there are plenty of examples where recovered memories turned out to be false, ranging from a memory of having been abducted by space aliens (McNally & Clancy, 2005) to one about someone's having committed murder. For example, Eileen Franklin-Lipsker suddenly remembered that her godfather raped Veronica Cascio and her father then murdered Ms. Cascio. However, her father's attorneys discovered that the semen found on the victim could not have come from either her godfather or her father, and that her father was definitely at a union meeting when the murder was committed (Curtius, 1996).

On the other hand, there is also evidence that traumatic memories can truly be repressed. For example, Williams (1994) interviewed 129 women 17 years after each had been admitted during her childhood to a hospital emergency room for treatment of sexual abuse. Thirty-eight percent of the women had no memory of an event of sexual abuse; in fact, 12% claimed that they had never been abused. These results suggest that some people may forget traumatic memories. Could this finding simply reflect infantile amnesia, the forgetting of events that occurred in early childhood? Not likely, for two reasons: First, whereas 55% of the women who had been 3 years old or younger at the time of abuse had no recall, fully 62% of those who were between 4 and 6 years old at the time had no recall; if the forgetting were due to infantile amnesia, the women abused at a younger age should have had the poorer recall. Second, more of the women who were abused by someone they knew, as determined from independent evidence, claimed to have forgotten the incident than did the women who were abused by a stranger. Again, this difference should not have occurred if the forgetting simply reflected infantile amnesia. Indeed, a review of 28 studies of memory for childhood sexual abuse found robust evidence that such memories can be forgotten and later recalled (Scheflin & Brown, 1996). In some cases, people who suddenly remembered being abused as children then proceeded to track down the evidence for the event (Schacter, 1996).

There is a mystery here. As noted earlier, highly charged, emotional information is typically remembered *better* than neutral information. So, why should this particular kind of emotionally charged information be recalled poorly, or forgotten for decades? Schacter (1996) suggests that, in these cases of forgetting, the person has not really unconsciously pushed the memories out of awareness. Instead, it is as if the individual were "someone else" during the abuse and thus has few retrieval cues for later accessing the memories. Nevertheless, the memories may be stored and may, under some circumstances and with appropriate cues, be retrieved. If so, it seems that people sometimes forget emotionally charged events, but after long periods of time, they can come to remember them. Clancy and col-

Repressed memories: Real memories that have been pushed out of consciousness because they are emotionally threatening.

leagues (2000) found that people who experience recovered memories of childhood abuse are more likely to mistakenly remember words such as "sweet" when asked to remember a previously presented list of words naming sweet things (as in the experiment demonstrated in Figures 5.10 and 5.11). This finding might suggest that these people are unusually sensitive to stored fragments of information. Leavitt (1997) has shown that people who recover such memories are not especially prone to making up information when given suggestions, which indicates that they are not simply more likely to form false memories.

Improving Memory: Tricks and Tools

No matter how hard you try, you probably will never develop a memory as good as S.'s. He apparently was born with something special, which he later learned to cultivate. However, you can use what you've learned in this chapter about the mechanics of memory to improve both your storage and later retrieval of information. Among normal people, the crucial difference between having a "good" memory and a "bad" one lies largely in the strategies used when storing and retrieving information. The fact that memory is so dependent on such strategies explains why it has among the lowest heritabilities (see Chapter 2) of all specific cognitive abilities. Even if a number of people in your family have fabulous memories, their gifts probably won't help you much, if at all (Nichols, 1978).

Enhancing Encoding: New Habits and Special Tricks

One way to improve your memory is to learn to encode information effectively. If you encode the information, you've won half the battle. The research results you've read about in this chapter show that you can improve your memory for information if you train yourself to engage in the following activities when you study.

Organize It!   In order to make a habit of improving your memory, you should *organize* material so that you *integrate* it, making connections between what you want to remember and what you already know.

- *Chunk it!* The first part of the organizational process requires you to form chunks, to organize the material into units. If an orange is so large that you cannot get your mouth around it, you'll pull it apart into bite-size pieces. So too with to-be-learned material. Figure out the individual facts and ideas; it is much easier to take in information after you have divided the material into easily digestible morsels. Each chapter in this book is organized into chunks by means of appropriate subheadings and paragraph breaks.

- *Make it hierarchical!* After you identify the units of material, the key is to organize them in such a way that they are tightly bound to each other. If you succeed in this, then when you recall one fact, the others will follow. *Hierarchical organization* is an especially effective way to improve learning and memory (Bower and colleagues, 1969). For example, you might memorize the errands you need to do by organizing your tasks in the same way you organize your trip: Break the trip down into separate segments and then organize the events in each segment separately. Think about which tasks need to be done at one end of town or in one part of the store, which need to be done at another specific location, and so on. The key is to think of ways to organize the material hierarchically, so that the big task breaks down into smaller ones, which themselves may break down into yet smaller ones; the goal is to group together relatively small sets of material.

This book's end-of-chapter summaries, called Let's Sum It Up, are intended to help you see the hierarchical organization of the material.

Process It! Organization is often only the first step to improved memory; how you process that organized information makes a big differences.

- *Think it through!* To be sure that you understand material (such as that presented in this book), the principles of *depth and breadth of processing* imply that you need to think about the meanings and implications of facts and ideas. For instance, you can think of ways in which facts are similar and different. (Remember those compare-and-contrast essays you had to do in high school? They weren't such a bad idea.) In addition, you should think of examples that demonstrate statements made in the text (or, conversely, think of examples that seem to refute these statements).

- *Transfer it!* In order to succeed on tests, you should try to find out what kind of test the instructor will give: If it is an essay test, you would be better off figuring out the connections between the various facts you have read and asking yourself "why" questions about them (Pressley et al., 1995); this sort of studying will be much more helpful than simple memorization, both for success on the test and for lasting understanding. For a multiple-choice or true-false test, however, simple memorization might do as well as the more complicated strategies designed to integrate and organize the material, but even here you probably will retain more of the relevant information if you process it deeply so that you understand it well.

- *Distribute practice!* Just as two thin coats of paint are better than one thick coat, you will remember better if you study in distributed sessions—repeatedly, in relatively short sessions, spread out over time. Each time you study, you encode new retrieval cues and you have more chances to integrate the information into what you already know—and both factors will improve later memory. Moreover, the encoding specificity principle suggests that you study in conditions similar to what you will experience when you take the test.

Cramming is a good way to learn material for an exam, right? Wrong. Research has shown that people remember material much better if they rely on *distributed practice*, which takes place over a period of time, than if they rely on *massed practice*, which is crammed into one or two intense sessions.

Mnemonic Tricks: Going the Extra Mile. In addition to developing new habits of thinking and studying, you can improve your memory by using many of the same tricks S. developed. These tricks will improve your memory—perhaps dramatically so. A recent search on "memory AND improvement" in the online bookstore Amazon.com came up with over 500 books—all of which provide tips on how to improve your memory, and many of which emphasize memory tricks. The use of **mnemonic devices**, or strategies that improve memory (*mnemonic* is derived from the Greek word for "memory"), requires extra effort but is often well worth it: These mnemonics can easily double your recall. Using mnemonic devices not only helps you learn something in the first place, but, should you forget it, helps you relearn it more effectively.

- *Visualize interacting objects: Images that play together, stay together.* Probably the single most effective mnemonic device is the use of *interactive images*. As discussed earlier, forming images of objects interacting will improve memory even without any effort to learn the material

Mnemonic devices: Strategies that improve memory, typically by using effective organization and integration.

(Bower, 1972; Paivio, 1971). Such interacting images can help you remember the sequences of events in a history class, the associations between meanings and sounds for foreign vocabulary, and most other types of associations. For example, if you want to learn someone's first name, visualize someone else you already know who has the same name, and imagine that person interacting with your new acquaintance in some way. You might envision them hugging, or arguing, or shaking hands. Later, when you see the new person, you can recall this image, and thus the name.

- *Visualize "in location": Putting objects in their place.* A related mnemonic device was discovered by the ancient Greek orator Simonides. He was attending a banquet one evening when he was called out of the room to receive a message. Shortly after he left, the ceiling collapsed, mangling the guests' bodies so badly that they were difficult to identify. When asked who had been at the feast, Simonides realized that he could remember easily if he visualized each person sitting at the table. This led him to develop a technique now called the *method of loci* (*loci*, the plural of *locus*, means "places" in Latin). To use this method, first memorize a set of locations. For example, you could walk through your house and memorize 12 distinct places, such as the front door, the computer desk, the potted plant near the big window, and so on. Later, when you want to memorize a list of objects, such as those on a shopping list, or a list of foreign language words you need to memorize, you can imagine walking through your house and placing an image of one object in each location. For instance, you might visualize a lightbulb leaning against the front door, a box of tissues on the computer desk, a can of coffee beside the plant, and so on. When you want to recall the list, all you need to do is visualize the scene and walk through it, "looking" to see what object is at each place.

To use the method of loci, pick out a set of locations in your house, and visualize each to-be-remembered object in a different location as you mentally walk through the house. To recall, later repeat this mental walk and "see" what's in each location.

- *Peg it: Numbered images.* The *pegword system* is similar to the method of loci, except that instead of places, you first memorize a set of objects in order. For example, you might memorize a list of rhymes, such as "One is a bun, two is a shoe, three is a tree, four is a door," and so on. Then you can treat the names of the memorized objects (bun, shoe, tree, and door) in the same way as the locations in the method of loci. You could associate the first item on your grocery list, for example, with a bun, the second with a shoe, and so on. In this case, when you want to remember the list, you remember each of the pegwords (*bun* and so on) in order and "see" what is associated with it. This method can be used to memorize all manner of lists, including those that you often find in tables in a textbook.

    When Henry Roediger (1980) asked people to use different mnemonic devices to remember sets of words, he found that these three methods—interactive imagery, the method of loci, and the pegword system—were the most effective. However, as you know, there are many types of memory, and people differ in how well they can use various techniques. You might find some other mnemonic devices more useful.

- *Try other mnemonic devices.* We can use many different sorts of tricks to improve our memories, not just the three discussed so far. For example, rhyming words provide a simple method for keeping concepts straight. For instance, the rhyme "rhyming priming rhyming" might help you remember that priming makes the same processing (like the same word repeated) easier to repeat in the future.

    Acronyms are pronounceable words made from the first letters of the important words in a phrase, such as NOW for National Organization for

Women; *initialisms* are made up of the initial letters but are usually not pronounceable words, such as LSU for Louisiana State University. Initialisms may be easier to make up for most situations; the idea in both cases is to create a single unit that can be unpacked as a set of cues for something more complicated.

In short, the key to mnemonics is figuring out a way to organize information so that you can link something new with something you already know. For example, to remember that *mnemonic* means "a memory aid," think of trying to remember something by putting a name on it: putting a NEM-ON-IC.

You can use mnemonics for material throughout this book, setting up mental connections or associations from one thing to another, perhaps with the use of imagery. For example, to remember that the word *suppression* means "voluntarily forcing unwanted thoughts back into the unconscious," you might visualize SUPerman PRESSing down demons that are bursting out of someone's head, shoving them back inside. When you form the image, you need to remember that the first part of Superman's name and what he's doing (pressing) are critical, so make sure that the S on his cape is very vivid and visible and that he is clearly pressing with his hands. Showing you a drawing of such a scene would work almost as well, but challenging you to make up your own image has the added advantage of forcing you to process the information more thoroughly, which in and of itself improves memory.

In addition, you can remember information by stringing it into a story. For example, if you wanted to remember that Freud came before the cognitivists, you can make up a story in which Freud wishes he had a computer to help him bill his patients but gets depressed when he realizes it hasn't been invented yet. Making the story a bit silly or whimsical may actually help memory (McDaniel & Einstein, 1986; McDaniel et al., 1995) and certainly makes the information more fun to think about!

One of the fundamental facts about learning is that you will learn better if you are actively involved. Instead of just reading, try to find connections across areas and try to think of your own mnemonics. You won't go wrong if you simply form a visual image, make up an association, invent a rhyme or a joke. You will be better off if you try to be an active learner. Although such studying involves more time and energy in the first place, you'll need less studying to brush up on the material before a final exam—and, in general, will be less likely to forget the material.

Enhancing Memory Retrieval: Knowing Where and How to Dig

S.'s ability to remember what he saw and heard was so good that he didn't need to notice patterns in the stimuli. For example, memorizing a table of numbers that were arranged in order was no easier for him than memorizing a table of random numbers. For us, however, once we notice such a pattern, we can store it—which will help us later to reconstruct the material. However, sometimes we need to remember things that we didn't expect to need or didn't have the opportunity to store effectively. Police officers are regularly faced with the effect of this unexpected demand on witnesses' memories. The need for accurate witness statements has been one impetus for developing methods to help people remember after the fact. Fisher and colleagues (Fisher & Geiselman, 1992; Fisher et al., 1989) used the results of laboratory studies to develop a method to help witnesses and victims of crimes recall what actually happened. Detectives trained in using their method were able to lead witnesses to recall 63% more information than was obtained with the standard police interview format. This method made use of the following memory principles and techniques:

- *Remember the context.* Recall is better when you mentally reinstate the environment in which information was learned. If you want to remember something, try to think of where you were when you learned it, what the weather was like, how you felt at the time, and so on.

- *Focus.* Searching for information in LTM requires effort and is easily disrupted by other stimuli. To remember well, focus on the task, shutting out distractions.

- *Keep trying.* The more times you try to remember something, the more likely you are eventually to retrieve it (Roediger & Thorpe, 1978).

- *Seize fragments.* If you cannot recall something immediately, try to think of characteristics of the information sought. Fisher and colleagues, in their 1989 study, advised detectives that if a witness could not remember a criminal's name, he or she should try to remember its length, first syllable, ethnic origin, and so on. These bits of information can serve as retrieval cues.

- *Structure the environment.* For certain kinds of memory retrieval, you can arrange your environment in such a way that you are reminded about what to remember. In other words, use external cues as mnemonic devices. If you are prone to forgetting your backpack, leave it by the door; if you forget to check the weather forecast before you leave home in the morning, put an umbrella on the door handle.

Arranging your world properly can aid memory. In this case, the pill holder makes it easy to recall whether or not you've taken your medication each day.

If you can find a method for improving retrieval that is fun and easy and that works for you, you are more likely to use it, and benefit by it. As in the case of mnemonic devices, try various methods and see which suits you.

LOOKING BACK: *Review*

1. *How can actual memories be distinguished from false ones?* At least under some circumstances, real memories include perceptual information from the modality in which a fact was learned—perhaps by seeing it, hearing it, reading it—whereas false memories do not include this sort of information. In many circumstances, however, it is difficult to distinguish between actual and false memories.

2. *Is a forgotten memory necessarily gone forever, or is it still stored but difficult to retrieve?* Memories may be lost by decay, probably because the relevant connections between neurons are lost. However, many "forgotten" memories are, in fact, still present, just difficult to retrieve. Memories become difficult to retrieve because of retroactive interference, in which new learning disrupts previously acquired knowledge, or because of proactive interference, in which previous knowledge impairs the ability to learn something new.

3. *Are memories ever repressed?* Memories have been thought to be repressed as a defense against trauma—threatening information is forced into the unconscious. But little evidence backs the existence of such a mechanism. Nevertheless, at least in some situations, encoding failure or a failure to encode information that can later be used as retrieval cues could result in poorer memory for traumatic events. In general, however, strong emotion enhances, not reduces, memory.

4. *How can you improve your memory?* Tricks for improving memory typically involve either visualizing objects interacting with other objects or

forming organized units where none previously existed. In addition, you can improve memory retrieval by mentally recreating the situation in which learning occurred, focusing attention on retrieving the information, repeatedly trying to recall, and generating new cues based on partial recall. It is also possible to arrange the world—your immediate circumstances—in such a way that you are reminded of what to do.

● LOOKING BEYOND: *Critical Thinking*

If effective methods for implanting false memories are demonstrated conclusively, should they be outlawed? In general, or only in certain circumstances (such as their being used by advertisers who want you to "remember" how much you like their products)? Can you think of any circumstances under which implanting a false memory might be a good idea? Explain. Can you think of anything about having amnesia that might be an advantage in some way?

Suppose a friend of the family is to be the principal of a new high school in your area. She's mentioned wanting to help students learn and remember more effectively. She asks your opinion. Do you think memory improvement techniques should be taught in school? If so, in which courses? Can you think of any reason not to teach such techniques? Why do you think that many people don't use memory improvement techniques, even after they've discovered for themselves how effective these techniques are?

LET'S SUM IT UP

I. Encoding Information Into Memory: Time and Space Are of the Essence

A. Encoding is the act of organizing and transforming incoming information so that it can be entered into memory. Effective encoding depends in part on what is perceived to be important.

B. There are three types of memory stores: sensory memory (SM), short-term memory (STM), and long-term memory (LTM). The memory stores differ in the amount of information they can retain and how long they can retain it.

C. Working memory (WM) is the use of STM to reason or to solve problems. Working memory involves specialized STMs and a central executive, which is a set of processes that manipulates information in these temporary storage structures.

D. Memory is improved as more time is spent thinking about the material to be stored and how it relates to current knowledge. Memory is most effective if the learner focuses on the properties of the material that will be relevant later. Depth of

processing involves thinking about the more complex properties of objects.

E. Elaborative encoding involves thinking of relations and associations of material to be stored. It takes time to consolidate information to be stored, converting it from a dynamic form to a structural form.

F. Strong emotion typically amplifies memory, not diminishes it.

G. Flashbulb memories are unusually vivid and accurate. Although people may be very confident of these memories, they become progressively more distorted over time.

II. Storing Information: Not Just One LTM

A. There are multiple types of LTMs, which store information for different sensory modalities, such as visual and auditory.

B. Some of the information in LTM is semantic, pertaining to the meanings of words, concepts, and facts about the world. Other information stored in

LTM is episodic, pertaining to events that occurred at a specific time, place, and circumstance.

C. Some memories in LTM are explicit (stored so that the information can be retrieved voluntarily). Other memories in LTM are implicit (stored as tendencies to process information in specific ways). Implicit memories include classical conditioned responses, responses acquired through nonassociative learning (as occurs in habituation), habits (automatic responses to appropriate stimuli), skills, and priming (which makes it easier to repeat a process in the future).

D. The process of storing new memories depends on the actions of specific genes.

E. Stress can impair memory, in part because it increases production of the hormone cortisol, which in turn impairs the functioning of the hippocampus.

III. Retrieving Information From Memory: More Than Reactivating the Past

A. Memory retrieval depends on a constructive process; you must retrieve the right pottery fragments to build a complete jug. Recognition is often easier than recall, but the ease of recognition depends on the choices you must distinguish among; the more attributes the choices have in common, the harder it is to distinguish among them.

B. Effective retrieval depends on having cues, or reminders, that match part of what is in memory, allowing you to reconstruct the rest.

C. Hypnosis typically does not improve memory retrieval.

IV. When Memory Goes Wrong—and What to Do About It

A. False memories occur when a person stores information about an event that did not happen, or that did not happen in the way that is "remembered." False memories may not include information about the perceptual features of the stimuli involved, which may allow the person to distinguish them from actual memories. Reality monitoring can be used to check for perceptual features in memory.

B. Forgetting occurs in various ways: Encoding failure prevents information from being stored. Decay results when neural connections are weakened to the point where they are no longer functional. Interference (either retroactive or proactive) prevents the digging out of stored information.

C. Intentional forgetting, which can be effective, relies in part on the operation of the frontal lobes.

D. In contrast to ordinary forgetting, amnesia wipes out explicit memory for a span of time, not just isolated aspects of memories.

E. Memories of abuse may sometimes be "repressed" if the person was "someone else" when experiencing the abuse.

F. Organizing information via chunking or hierarchical organization can make the information easier to remember.

G. Extensive processing of information, especially through distributed practice, aids memory.

H. Some mnemonic devices that can help you store information effectively include interactive images, the method of loci, the pegword system, rhyming words, and acronyms and initialisms. Mental imagery is generally very effective when it is used to organize information in a meaningful way.

I. Several tricks have been shown to help people dig out information previously stored in LTM. One technique is to provide effective retrieval cues by having people think about where they were and how they felt at the time. Another major factor is effort: It is important to focus and keep trying. If information is still difficult to recall, then people are asked to try to recall its characteristics or associated information (which in turn can serve as retrieval cues). Finally, sometimes just arranging external cues as reminders can be helpful.

Key Terms

LOOKING ONLINE: *Enhance Your Learning*

MyPsychLab is an interactive and instructive multimedia resource that can be used to supplement a traditional lecture course or as an online course. It is an all-inclusive tool with a text-specific e-book plus multimedia tutorials, videos, simulations, animations, and controlled assessment to completely engage students and reinforce learning. MyPsychLab meets the individual learning needs of every student. Visit *www.mypsychlab.com* for more information!

Practice Test

For each of the following items, choose the single best answer.

1. Which of the following statements is true?
   a. Information can flow to long-term memory without necessarily passing through short-term memory.
   b. Rehearsal—repeating items over and over—always helps memorization.
   c. Atkinson and Shiffrin proposed the four-stage model of memory.
   d. Some memories are not stored in the brain.

2. The visual form of sensory memory
   a. is called echoic memory.
   b. stores a small amount of information but holds that information for a long time.
   c. explains why you can continue to hear the sound of a voice that has stopped speaking for a brief time.
   d. stores a large amount of information, but the information fades very quickly.

3. How much information can short-term memory hold?
   a. 4 items
   b. 4 numbers
   c. 5–9 items organized into about four chunks
   d. 5–9 chunks organized into about four items

4. Long-term memory
   a. contains information of which you are directly aware.
   b. holds a small amount of information for a long time.
   c. can be thought of as analogous to your computer's RAM.
   d. is divided into specialized parts.

5. The primacy effect
   a. is increased memory for the last few stimuli in a set.
   b. reflects the storage of information in long-term memory.
   c. reflects the storage of information in short-term memory.
   d. None of the above statements is true.

6. Interestingly, nearly everyone
   a. finds verbal memories easier to recall than visual memories.
   b. uses short-term memory to retain information about the meanings of words.
   c. finds visual memories easier to recall than verbal memories.
   d. remembers when, where, and how semantic memories were learned.

7. Neuroimaging studies have
   a. provided evidence that semantic and episodic memories are distinct.
   b. found that when people recall visual versus auditory information from LTM and store it temporarily in STM, different perceptual areas of the brain are activated.
   c. revealed that when we recall semantic memories, the left frontal lobe tends to be activated more than the right, but vice versa when we recall episodic memories.
   d. All of the above statements are true.

8. Which of the following is an implicit memory?
   a. an episodic memory
   b. a semantic memory
   c. a habit
   d. a declarative memory

9. Researchers have increasingly studied how genes affect memory. Which of the following statements is true?
   a. Genes do not affect memory.
   b. Removing a given gene always has a single effect on the organism.
   c. Genes can disrupt memory but do not affect how well the normal brain stores information.
   d. Evidence is emerging that different genes underlie different types of memory.

10. In humans, the effects of stress on the hippocampus
    a. may be reversed if the environment changes.
    b. result in a larger hippocampus.
    c. lead to better memory.
    d. are not at all similar to the effects of stress on the hippocampus in baboons.

11. When people encode new information,
    a. portions of the frontal lobes are often active.
    b. the degree of activation of the frontal lobes does not predict how well the information will be remembered later.
    c. the memories are consolidated immediately.
    d. None of the above statements is true.

12. Depth of processing refers to
    a. processing that organizes and integrates information into previously stored information, often by making associations.
    b. reliance on massed practice.
    c. learning that occurs as a result of trying to learn.
    d. the number and complexity of the operations involved in processing information.

13. Certain emotions affect noradrenaline production and memory by causing
    a. less noradrenaline to be produced, which in turn causes enhanced memory encoding.
    b. more noradrenaline to be produced, which in turn causes enhanced memory encoding.
    c. less noradrenaline to be produced, which in turn causes decreased memory encoding.
    d. more noradrenaline to be produced, which in turn causes decreased memory encoding.

14. How accurate are our memories?
    a. Misremembering occurs only when associated material is stored.
    b. Everything we remember actually happened.
    c. In general, we do not necessarily remember what actually happened but rather what we *experience* as having happened.
    d. False memories do occur, but they persist for only two days.

15. An encoding failure results
    a. because all memories are stored forever.
    b. because long-term memory has only a limited capacity.
    c. if the retrieval cues for various memories are similar.
    d. if you do not process information well enough to begin consolidation.

• •

Answers: 1. a 2. d 3. c 4. d 5. b 6. c 7. d 8. c 9. d 10. a 11. a 12. d 13. b 14. c 15. d

chapter 6

Language, Thinking, and Intelligence

What Humans Do Best

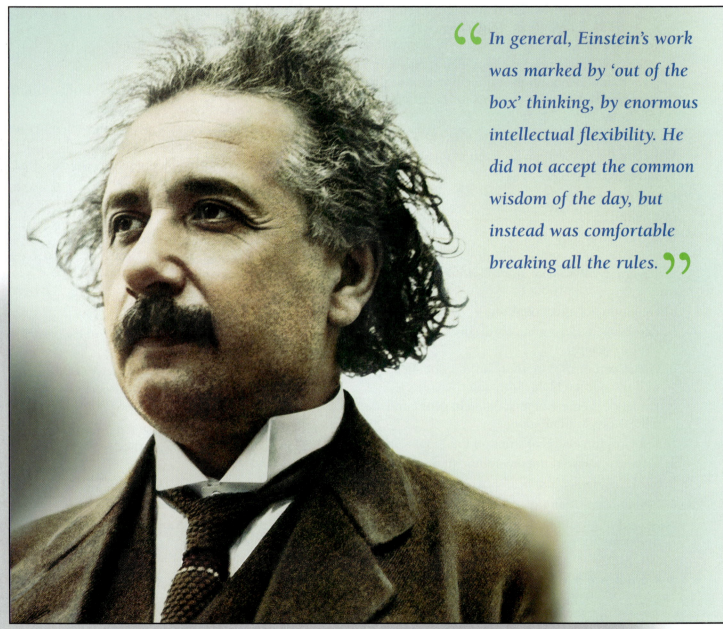

" In general, Einstein's work was marked by 'out of the box' thinking, by enormous intellectual flexibility. He did not accept the common wisdom of the day, but instead was comfortable breaking all the rules. "

CHAPTER OUTLINE

ALBERT EINSTEIN HAD ONE OF THE MOST REMARKABLE MINDS IN HISTORY. HE DIDN'T simply revolutionize physics, he changed the way the human species looks at the world. Einstein is often thought of today as he was in his later years—a saintly figure, patient and benevolent, his head framed by a white halo of hair. However, as a young man, he had a rebellious streak. He hated his experiences in the rigid and authoritarian German schools (experiences so alienating that he renounced his German citizenship when he was 17 years old and remained stateless until he was granted Swiss citizenship 5 years later). Einstein's father wanted him to have a practical career, and so insisted that young Albert apply to study electrical engineering. He failed the entrance exam, probably intentionally. He did attend university, but he regularly missed classes—staying home either to play his violin or to study physics on his own. When he did show up, he managed to annoy so many of his teachers that they shunned him after graduation, and he had great difficulty finding a job. Indeed, because of these personal characteristics, Einstein held only temporary teaching positions until he was 23 years old, when a friend's father helped him land an entry-level job at the Swiss patent office. He worked in the patent office for 7 years.

Even though he was cut off from universities and good libraries, Einstein later recounted that he was very lucky to be working in the patent office at that point in his life (Clark, 1971). In those days in Switzerland, hopeful inventors had to supply physical models along with their patent applications. Einstein became adept at studying such models and drawings, discerning the underlying principles; his job was to rewrite the often vague and muddled descriptions, cleaning them up so that they could be protected by law. Einstein learned to abstract clear-cut principles that explained how devices worked. He later noted that this was good training for discerning the laws of nature. In his spare time, he thought long and hard about the fundamental properties of the universe, and he published a series of papers that shook the world.

In general, Einstein's work was marked by "out-of-the-box" thinking, by enormous intellectual flexibility. He did not accept the common wisdom of the day, but instead was comfortable breaking all the rules. He correctly reasoned not only that light waves are bent when they pass near a strong source of gravity (such as a star), but also that time isn't constant and that light transfers mass. Moreover, he put together what had previously been viewed as distinctly different—for example, showing how mass and energy are, in fact, different facets of the same thing.

Einstein's insights often arose only after years of thought and intense work. For example, he labored for 10 years to produce his famous Special Theory of Relativity (which showed why the laws of physics apply only in the context of specific frames of reference, except that the speed of light is always constant). But don't think of Einstein as a kind of supercomputer, working through problems methodically and systematically, a step at a time. Einstein's methods of thinking often resembled those of an artist. He said, "When I examine myself and my methods of thought, I come to the conclusion that the gift of fantasy has meant more to me than my talent for absorbing positive knowledge" (Clark, 1971, p. 88).

What is thinking? How do people solve problems and reach decisions? Can you learn to think more effectively? What does it mean to be intelligent? Why are some people apparently more intelligent than others? In this chapter, we consider some of the most fundamental ways in which we humans tower over the other animals—namely, in our language, thinking, and intelligence.

Language: More Than Meaningful Sounds

Albert Einstein did not begin to talk until he was 3 years old, and he wasn't entirely fluent even by the time he was 9 (Clark, 1971, p. 10). His language skills were so poor that his parents worried that he might be mentally retarded! Nevertheless, he eventually learned to speak not only his native German, but also French and English. However, he mixed German with his French, and his English, learned later in life, never became fluent—as countless satirists have noted, he made grammatical mistakes and had a heavy German accent. If we judged him by his language alone, we wouldn't be impressed. Clearly, using language to communicate relies on at least some abilities that are not used in reasoning and problem solving.

LOOKING AHEAD: *Learning Objectives*

1. *What are the essential characteristics of all languages?*
2. *Are first and second languages used in different ways?*

The Essentials: What Makes Language Language?

Language accomplishes its role in communication via a two-pronged process of sending and receiving. **Language production** is the ability to speak or otherwise use words, phrases, and sentences to convey information. Perhaps the most remarkable thing about language production is that it is *generative*. We create, or generate, new sentences all the time; we don't simply retrieve and repeat stored sentences. The number of new sentences we can produce is astounding. Psychologist Steven Pinker (1994, p. 86) estimates that we would need at least 100 trillion years to memorize all the sentences any one of us can possibly produce. **Language comprehension** is the ability to understand the message conveyed by words, phrases, and sentences. We humans are endowed with the extraordinary ability to comprehend even fragments of speech, mispronounced words, and scrambled syntax. For example, you can probably extract the general meaning from the following: "Me speech badly with grammar, but words use appropriately." We can understand the speech of the very young, speech flavored with foreign or regional accents, and lisping speech, even though the actual sounds made in each of these cases are very different. Even Albert Einstein, who spoke French and English with difficulty, could make himself understood in those languages. To put things in perspective, even today's most sophisticated speech recognition devices can decode only a fraction of what a competent 5-year-old can do effortlessly.

So, if language involves a process of sending and receiving information, what about when your dog whines when it is hungry, barks to go for a walk, and sits when told to? Your pet can send and receive information, all right, but is it using language? The intuitive answer is no, and the intuitive answer is right—there's more to language than that (Pinker & Jackendoff, 2005). Language units are built from simple building blocks that can be combined in many ways, but only according to specific rules. Four types of units, and the rules for combining them, distinguish language from other communicative sounds such as whines. These units and rules provide the key to both language production and language comprehension, and they make up the phonology, syntax, semantics, and pragmatics of a language. Let's look at each of these aspects of language in turn.

Phonology: Some Say "ToMAYto"

Phonology is the structure of the sounds of the words in a language. Linguists Roman Jakobson and Morris Halle (1956) provided evidence that the sounds of any language are built up from sets of **phonemes**, which are the basic building blocks of speech sounds (Halle, 1990). The words *boy* and *toy* differ in one phoneme.

Language production: The ability to speak or otherwise use words, phrases, and sentences to convey information.

Language comprehension: The ability to understand the message conveyed by words, phrases, and sentences.

Phonology: The structure of the sounds that can be used to produce words in a language.

Phoneme: The basic building block of speech sounds.

Curiously, the left cerebral hemisphere is primarily activated when males process phonemes, but both hemispheres are strongly activated when females process phonemes (Shaywitz et al., 1995); perhaps this is one reason females tend to be better with language than males (Halpern, 1997).

Humans can produce about 100 phonemes, but no single language uses all 100; English, for instance, uses about 45. Back-of-the-throat, soft French *r*'s do not exist in the world of hard American *r*'s, and Japanese has no *r*'s at all. One of the reasons French is difficult to learn for people who learned English as their native tongue is that the two languages use some different phonemes (such as those for *r* and *u*).

In English, some sounds in each word are accented (given extra emphasis). Some people say "toMAYto," and others say "toMAHto," but in both cases the second syllable is stressed. Some other languages do not usually stress only one of the syllables in a word. In French, for example, each sound typically is given equal emphasis. Linguist Lisa Selkirk (personal communication, 2002) suggests that this difference explains why French rock and roll often sounds bland: French rock artists can't synchronize the "beats" in the language with the rhythm of the music.

Syntax: The Rules of the Road

Every language has building blocks of sound and rules for cementing them together into words. Similarly, all languages include rules for how words can be organized into sentences. Sentences in any language contain an internal structure, an acceptable arrangement of words called **syntax**. The syntax of a sentence is determined by a set of rules (grammar) for combining different categories of words, such as nouns, verbs, and adjectives. For example, in English, this is not an acceptable sentence: "Kicked girl ball the blue." The basic units of syntax are parts of speech, not the individual words that fall into each category. A sentence in English needs a noun phrase (which must at a minimum have a noun—a word that names a person, place, or thing) and a verb phrase (at a minimum a single verb—a word that describes an action or a state of being). Thus, the shortest possible sentence in English has only three letters: "I am."

Ask a friend to help you perform the following experiment, which should help you understand the syntactic structures that underlie sentences: At night, turn on the lights and shut all the blinds in a room. Read aloud from any book. Ask your friend to turn off the lights at some random point. You should find that you can keep saying the words leading up to the next major syntactic boundary (usually indicated by a verb, a conjunction, or a comma, period, or other punctuation mark). Fluent readers take in entire parts of the syntactic structure, one part at a time—and you can usually identify those units by seeing what you've already taken in, when the lights are turned off.

Semantics: The Meaning Is the Message

Syntax: The internal structure of a sentence, determined by a set of rules (grammar) for combining different parts of speech into acceptable arrangements.

Semantics: The meaning of a word or sentence.

Morpheme: The smallest unit of meaning in a language.

Language is, of course, more than sounds and sentence structures (Pinker & Jackendoff, 2005). To do its job, language must convey meaning. The **semantics** of a word or sentence is its meaning. Just as the sounds of words are represented by smaller elements (phonemes) and the syntactic aspects of a sentence are represented by its elements (parts of speech), semantics is represented by **morphemes**, the smallest units of *meaning* in a language. The word *wet* includes but a single morpheme, but the meanings of many words are determined by more than one morpheme. Prefixes and suffixes are obvious examples of morphemes used in combination with other morphemes. For example, adding the morpheme *-ing* to a verb, as in *walking, talking,* or *flirting,* creates a word expressing a continuing state, whereas adding the morpheme *-ed* to a verb indicates a completed state. Just as the other elements of language are combined according to rules, so, too, with combining morphemes. We cannot add *-ing* at the front of a word, or *mis-* (another morpheme) to the end. Ambiguous words (words with more than one meaning) have more than one set of morphemes; thus, *park* as in "park the car" has different morphemes than does *park* meaning "place with benches and pigeons." Many jokes rely on the fact that words can have more than one meaning. For example, "Energizer Bunny arrested—charged with battery." Different parts of the brain tend to be involved in processing syntax and semantics.

How Is Meaning Assigned?   Meanings are often assigned arbitrarily to different sounds or written words; *dog* (both the combination of sounds and the written set of letters) could easily have been assigned to that feline we keep as a pet and *cat* to the animal that likes to gnaw on bones and slippers. Specific events in the past have a lot to do with how particular words have come to have their meanings. For example, early medieval Scandinavian warriors wore bearskin shirts, for which the Old Norwegian word was *berserkr;* the ferocity of the Vikings' frenzied attacks in battle thus led to the English expression "going berserk." Sometimes the meanings of words seem to reveal deeper aspects of a culture: The Chinese character for *crisis* is composed of two other characters, one signifying "risk" and the other "opportunity."

How Does Semantics Differ From Syntax?   The meaning of a sentence and its syntax are to a large extent distinct. For example, Chomsky (1957) pointed out that the sentence "Colorless green ideas sleep furiously" has an acceptable English syntax but is meaningless. On the other hand, "Fastly dinner eat, ball-game soon start" has the opposite properties: It is syntactically incorrect but understandable. The wise alien Yoda of the *Star Wars* movies often uttered such sentences, probably in part to remind the audience that he was not an ordinary person. Nevertheless, although syntax and semantics are distinct, they do interact; for example, sentences are easier to understand when named objects appear in the same order in the sentence as they do in the corresponding event (O'Grady & Lee, 2005).

How Does Semantics Allow Us to Express Assertions?   Just as morphemes are combined into representations of the meanings of words, the representations of words in turn are combined into *propositions.* **Propositional representations** are mental sentences that unambiguously express the meanings of assertions. The same sets of words can express different propositions, depending on how they are organized (see Figure 6.1, on p. 232).

Propositional representations are not the same thing as sentences in a language such as English. Most importantly, propositional representations cannot be ambiguous; a propositional representation specifies the meaning that underlies the particular sense of a statement. Many studies have shown that people typically store not the literal words used in sentences, but rather the propositions that specify the meaning. For example, Sachs (1967) had participants in a study listen to paragraphs and then tested their memories for specific sentences. The participants had to indicate whether each test sentence had been presented in a paragraph as stated or was an altered version of one that had been presented. The participants remembered the meanings of sentences well, but not the particular wordings (Bransford and Franks, 1971, report comparable results).

Propositional representation: A mental sentence that expresses the unambiguous meaning of an assertion.

Figure 6.1 The Same Words Can Express Different Propositions

To understand the nature of propositional representation, consider this anecdote: An English professor wrote the words "Woman without her man is a savage" on the blackboard and directed his students to punctuate the sentence. The men and women used different punctuation; as you see, the punctuation organizes the words in different ways to express different propositions.

Pragmatics: Being Indirect

At least in German, Einstein was perfectly able to understand the semantics of words (he understood morphemes and how they are combined into words) and sentences (he understood how the meanings of words are combined into phrases and sentences and their underlying propositional representations); but he sometimes failed at another aspect of meaning. Utterances have not only a literal meaning but also an *implied* meaning. For example, Einstein once sat through a series of vicious attacks on his theory of relativity by Nazis, who claimed the theory was part of a plot to disrupt the proper thought processes of the German people (Clark, 1971). Einstein laughed and apparently had a great time listening to the diatribes, oblivious to the barely concealed threats beneath them. The **pragmatics** of a language is concerned with the way the words and sentences imply meaning. Have you ever asked a 13-year-old, "Do you know where the restroom is?" and got back the response "Yes"? This question can be interpreted literally, as an inquiry about your knowledge of, say, the layout of a large building, or indirectly, as a request for directions. In some contexts, as when parents are dropping off their children at an auditorium by themselves, the question might really be meant literally. But in most instances, we would understand that the questioner has a need for the facilities. This understanding depends on our grasp of pragmatics, which often involves knowledge of the world as well as of the particular language and its specific conventions about how to communicate (Grice, 1975; Lindblom, 2001).

Understanding Metaphors and Humor. Pragmatics plays a key role in understanding metaphors; a *metaphor* is a direct comparison of two things in which one is described as being the other (Bowdle & Gentner, 2005; Gentner & Bowdle, 2001). To say that somebody's lawyer is a shark means that the attorney is vicious—but it doesn't mean that he or she can breathe under water or has pebbly skin. To understand a metaphor, we actively inhibit the irrelevant aspects of the meaning (Glucksberg et al., 2001). The fact that understanding metaphors involves different mechanisms than those used for other aspects of language is attested to by the role of the right cerebral hemisphere. Other language abilities

Pragmatics: The way in which words and sentences in a language convey meaning indirectly, by implying rather than asserting.

depend primarily (in right-handed people) on the left hemisphere, but the ability to understand metaphors, as well as humor, depends crucially on the brain's right hemisphere. Patients who have suffered damage to the right hemisphere might understand a metaphorical question such as "Can you lend me a hand?" as asking literally for a hand on a platter. Indeed, in normal people, the right hemisphere is particularly active (as measured by PET) when they are interpreting metaphors (Bottini et al., 1994).

Rinaldi and colleagues (2004) showed that patients with damage to the right cerebral hemisphere not only make more errors when comprehending metaphors than do patients with damage to the left hemisphere, but also are particularly prone to make errors when the metaphors involve spatial information. This finding may suggest that mental imagery is sometimes used to understand such metaphors. However, other studies have shown that patients with left-hemisphere damage have more difficulty than do patients with right-hemisphere damage in other aspects of pragmatics, such as producing the proper emphasis when they speak (for example, by raising pitch at the end of a question; Gandour & Baum, 2001). Pragmatics is not a single process, and different aspects of pragmatics rely on different parts of the brain.

Patients with left-hemisphere damage that disrupted their ability to comprehend speech nevertheless could detect lies better than normal people (Etcoff et al., 2000). Apparently, the meanings of words can obscure other telltale features of deception, such as changes in intonation or facial expression.

Interlocking Mechanisms. It's worth underscoring that the various aspects of language interact and are not entirely independent. For example, although speech production and comprehension at first may seem entirely different, they actually draw on many of the same mechanisms. Similarly, we learn phonological production through phonological perception, and the mechanisms that produce syntactically correct utterances also help us comprehend them. Moreover, the semantic representations that underlie our ability to speak coherently also allow us to comprehend; propositional representations express ideas, both our own (which we can express by speaking) and those of others (which we have decoded from their speech). Finally, we use the principles of pragmatics both when producing speech (guiding our patterns of intonation and use of metaphor and humor) and when comprehending speech.

Bilingualism: A Window of Opportunity?

All normal people learn a language, and most of the people in the world learn a second language at some point in life (Fabbro, 2001). Is learning a second language the same as learning a first one? Using fMRI, Kim and his colleagues (1997) scanned the brains of two groups of bilingual people while the participants thought about what they had done the previous day, using each of their two languages in turn. One group had learned their second language as young children, the other as adults. A brain area crucially involved in comprehension (located in the back part of the left temporal lobe) was activated in the same way with both languages and in both groups. But a brain area involved in grammar and speech production (located in the left frontal lobe) showed a different pattern: If the participants had learned the second language as young children, the same part of this frontal lobe area displayed activity for both the first and the second languages. If they had learned the second language after childhood, however, activity for that language appeared in a different part of the left frontal lobe—in a part used in working memory. One theory is that if you learn grammar early enough, it becomes procedural memories, which are mediated in part by subcortical structures; if you don't learn grammar early enough, it is stored as explicit memories—which you need to think about to recall (Ullman, 2001). In any case, second (and third) languages rely primarily on the left hemisphere, as do first languages (Paradis, 1990, 1992).

In spite of the fact that languages learned as an adult generally are not as well learned as those acquired during childhood, it is remarkably easy to learn some aspects of second languages. Dupuy and Krashen (1993) asked third-semester college students who were taking French to read five scenes from a script of a French movie, after having seen the first five scenes to get the story line. The scenes that were read contained many highly colloquial words that the students were unlikely to have seen or heard before. A surprise vocabulary test after reading showed that participants were learning almost five words per hour, without trying! This rate is remarkably close to the learning rates of children who are reading in their native languages.

Unfortunately, because there is a critical period in childhood for learning grammar and phonology (as we will discuss in Chapter 9), it is not so easy to learn the grammar or sound pattern of a second language as an adult. Indeed, the vast majority of people who learn a second language after puberty will make grammatical errors and will speak with an accent. However, some people can learn to pronounce words in another language almost flawlessly (Marinova-Todd et al., 2000; Snow, 2002).

In addition, "one-size teaching" of second languages may not fit all: Loori (2005) found that when learning English as a second language, males preferred using logical and mathematical thinking, whereas females preferred learning activities that relied on self-reflection. In general, the more formal education you have and the younger you are when you start, the better you will be at learning a second language (Hakuta et al., 2003). People differ greatly (perhaps even genetically?) in how easily they can acquire second languages.

LOOKING BACK: *Review*

1. *What are the essential characteristics of all languages?* All languages have four key characteristics. First, they have phonology. Phonemes are the basic units of speech, and they are arranged in sequences to form words. Second, languages have syntax, a set of rules (grammar) that governs how different words can be combined according to their parts of speech. Third, languages have semantics, which specifies meaning. The semantics of a word arises from its morphemes, small elements of meaning. Fourth, languages have pragmatics, the indirect or implied aspects of meaning. Pragmatics plays a key role in understanding whether a question is actually a request, and whether a statement ending with a rising pitch is actually a question. Pragmatics is also involved in understanding metaphor.

2. *Are first and second languages used in different ways?* Depending on your age when you learn it, a second language functions in the brain either in the same way as the first language or in a different way. At least for people of college age, acquiring vocabulary in a second language is remarkably easy. However, mastering the grammar and sound patterns (phonology) of a second language after puberty is very difficult.

Would it be technically correct to say that Einstein could speak French and English? In these languages, his phonology and grammar were faulty, and he never mastered the pragmatics of any language. Is there a difference between speaking a language imperfectly and not speaking it at all? At what point would you decide that a person's command of one or more of the aspects of language was so poor that you would no longer say that he or she could use language? Can you think of a way to decide when a student studying a new language has reached the point of "speaking the language"?

Some forms of representation play critical roles in pragmatics. Consider this joke: A man showed up for work one day with huge bandages over each ear. A coworker asked him what happened. He replied, "I was ironing and was lost in thought. The phone rang, and without thinking I lifted my hand to answer it." The coworker was aghast, but then asked, "But what about the other ear?" "Oh," he replied, "then I had to call the doctor." This is a visual joke, and people who do not form mental images well don't seem to get it. Can you think of other such jokes?

Thinking: Understanding the World and Guiding Behavior

Einstein was a theoretical physicist. He didn't perform experiments; he didn't collect new data. Instead, he tried to put together known facts and to synthesize specialized principles into larger and simpler overarching theories. At first glance, these abilities and skills might suggest that Einstein reasoned at a very abstract level, using complex mathematical symbols to manipulate arcane ideas. But Einstein denied thinking in that way. Instead, he said that he relied on mental imagery, playing with images of objects and events, "seeing" what would happen in certain circumstances. In fact, the initial insight that led to his Special Theory of Relativity came when he imagined himself chasing a beam of light, matching its speed, and "seeing" what it would look like. He reported, "Conventional words or other signs have to be sought for laboriously only in a secondary stage, when the mentioned associative play is sufficiently established and can be reproduced at will" (Einstein, 1945, pp. 142–143).

Thinking involves manipulating information in your head. Sometimes it involves solving problems; sometimes it involves simply determining what is implied by or associated with the information at hand. We do think partly by using language, but this isn't always the case. In fact, as Einstein noted, language may come into play rather late in the thinking game. Both inner speech ("talk" we direct to ourselves) and images are manipulated in working memory, and thus they play a key role in thinking (as discussed in Chapter 5, working memory operates on stored information to allow us to perform a task). However, although language and images help us to think, they cannot themselves be the only means by which we think. To see why, let's consider each in turn, and then look at another way in which information is specified in the mind.

LOOKING AHEAD: *Learning Objectives*

1. *Does language mold our thoughts?*
2. *Can we think with mental images?*

3. *What is a concept?*
4. *What methods can we use to solve problems?*
5. *Do people reason logically? Why do we commit reasoning errors?*

Words: Inner Speech and Spoken Thoughts

Many people, if asked, would say that they think with words. And, at first glance, that seems plausible: After all, to communicate with someone, we usually have to express ourselves in words, so why not use words when thinking?

Putting Thoughts Into Words

There are at least three problems with the idea that thinking is just talking to yourself, as was claimed by the founder of behaviorism, John B. Watson (1913):

1. If this were true, why would you ever have trouble "putting a thought into words"? If thoughts were already formed in language, expressing them in language should be child's play.

2. Words are often ambiguous, but thoughts are not. If you are thinking about "the port," you don't wonder whether you are thinking about a wine or a harbor.

3. Anyone who has owned a dog or a cat has sensed that at least some animals can think, and yet they don't use language. In fact, there is ample evidence that many animals can not only think, but can also solve problems—remember Köhler's work with the chimpanzee Sultan, discussed in Chapter 4.

Even though the Dani have only two words for color, *light* and *dark*, they can perceive and learn shades of color as easily as people who speak languages with many terms for color.

Linguistic relativity hypothesis: The idea that perceptions and thoughts are shaped by language, and thus people who speak different languages think differently.

Does Language Shape Thought?

Even if thought is not the silent equivalent of talking to yourself, many people have been fascinated by the possibility that our perceptions and thoughts are shaped by the particular language we speak. This idea, known as the linguistic relativity hypothesis, was championed by Benjamin Lee Whorf (1956). For example, some have suggested that because the Inuit of northern Canada have many words for the different types of snow they recognize, they can see and think about subtle differences in snow better than speakers of English can, with their paltry single word for the white stuff. If this idea is correct, then people who speak languages with lots of color words should be able to perceive more distinctions among colors than people who speak languages with few such words. Rosch (1973, 1975) tested this idea by studying the Dani, a remote tribe living in Papua New Guinea. The Dani use only two words for color, corresponding to *light* and *dark*. However, they perceive variations in color and are able to learn shades of color as readily as people who speak languages with words that label many colors.

Nevertheless, even if language does not entirely determine how we can think, it does influence some aspects of thought and memory. For example, Roberson and colleagues (2004) found that linguistic distinctions affect how well people can remember shades of color. They studied speakers of the Himba language of Africa; this language makes fewer distinctions among colors than does English. For instance, red, orange, and pink are named with the same word. The Himba speakers made memory errors when they had to recall different colors that were named with the same word in Himba; in contrast, English speakers performed better in naming those colors, because their language helped them to draw the necessary distinctions. In addition, in some cases, we appear to use words as a crutch to help us think, particularly when working memory is involved. In such circumstances, we often perform relatively slow, step-by-step reasoning—for example, memorizing a series of directions and recalling them one at a time, holding them in working memory long enough to turn the right way and continue to the next landmark. Furthermore, language can enhance memory. For example, you can remember the shapes of clouds better if you come up with a distinctive characterization for each (such as "a rabbit sticking out of a tube" or "a face without a chin") than if you use a single label for them all (Ellis, 1973). Also, the written version of a language may affect thought. For example, speakers of English tend to think of time as if it were horizontal, but speakers of Mandarin Chinese think of time as if it were vertical ("Wednesday is lower than Tuesday"; Boroditsky, 2001). However, the existence of relationships among language, memory, and perception does not imply that language determines the nature of our thoughts.

Mental Imagery: Perception Without Sensation

If language is not the basis of thinking, what might be? Virtually all the great thinkers who applied themselves to this question in the past, including Plato and Aristotle, and later John Locke and other British philosophers, identified thought with a stream of mental images (Kosslyn, 1980). **Mental images** are representations like those that arise during perception, but they arise from stored information rather than from immediate sensory input. Visual mental images give rise to the experience of "seeing with the mind's eye," an experience you probably will have if someone asks you, for example, whether the Statue of Liberty holds the torch in her left or right hand. To "get" some jokes you need to form an image, for example: "Corduroy pillows are making headlines." (Hint: think about what your cheek would look like if you slept on a corduroy pillow all night.) Auditory mental images give rise to the experience of "hearing with the mind's ear," as is likely to happen if you try to decide whether the first three notes of "Row, Row, Row Your Boat" change in pitch. Because visual imagery is the most common form of imagery (Kosslyn et al., 1990, 2001, 2006; McKellar, 1965), we focus on it here.

Mental Space

There are many types of mental images (Kosslyn, 1994b); the most common seems to occur in a kind of "mental space." This space has three properties: spatial extent, limited size, and grain (the equivalent of resolution on the screen of a TV or computer monitor). Let's investigate these properties in turn.

Spatial Extent. First, visualize your living room, and count the number of windows. Does it feel as if you are scanning the walls? As illustrated in Figure 6.2 (on p. 238), the greater the extent of your scan, the longer it takes to do the job; these results show that when you visualize something, its mental representation has a definite *spatial extent* (Denis & Kosslyn, 1999).

Mental images: Representations like those that arise during perception, but based on stored information rather than on immediate sensory input.

Figure 6.2 Scanning Visual Mental Images

Participants memorized a map like this one, paying special attention to the locations of the seven objects.

Even though their eyes were closed, the farther the participants had to scan from the first object to the second, the longer it took.

Later, the participants were asked to close their eyes and focus on one location (such as the hut) and then to scan to another named location if it was on the map; they were to press one button if they found the second object and another if they could not (and the time was recorded). Participants scanned between every possible pair of objects.

Limited Size. Second, how large can an object in a mental image be? When you mentally counted the windows in your living room, you scanned across each wall one by one because you couldn't "see" all four walls at once; you have only a limited field of view in a mental image. Now imagine you are walking toward an elephant, mentally staring at the center of its body. Imagine walking closer and closer to it, keeping your mental gaze fixed on its center. Most people doing this exercise report that when they are at a certain distance from the elephant, its edges seem to blur, to "overflow" their field of vision—that is, their mental space. Note the distance at which the edges of the elephant seem to blur. Now try the same exercise with a rabbit. Fixate on its center, and imagine seeing it loom up as you get closer and closer to it. When you imagine walking toward the rabbit, can you get closer to it than you could to the elephant before the edges seem to blur? When this study was done carefully, the larger the object, the farther away it seemed to be in the mental image when it began to overflow (Kosslyn, 1978). This result is as expected if mental space has a *limited size*: Bigger objects must be "seen" from farther away to fit within it.

Grain. Third, try this: Imagine stretching out your arm and looking at a butterfly perched on your fingertip. Can you see the color of its head? Many people find that they have to "zoom in" mentally to answer that question. Now move the butterfly to your palm and gently bring it to within 10 inches from your eyes; this time, zooming probably isn't necessary to "see" its head. Studies have shown that people require more time to "see" properties of objects that are visualized at small sizes than those visualized at larger sizes (Kosslyn, 1975, 1976). It is as if the imagery space has a *grain*. If you look at a TV screen close up, you will see that the picture is made up of many small dots. The dots form the grain of the screen; if an object is too small, there will not be enough dots to define the details, and thus the details will be blurred.

In short, objects in images have many of the properties of actual objects; thus, images can "stand in" for objects. You can think about an absent object by visualizing it, and you can manipulate the image. For example, if you mentally rotate the letter N 90° clockwise, is it another letter? Most people can do such tasks, but more time is required to rotate imagined objects by greater amounts (Shepard & Cooper, 1982).

The Visualizing Brain

Visual images rely on most—as much as 90%—of the same parts of the brain as are used in visual perception (Ganis et al., 2004; Kosslyn et al., 2001), and we can understand the properties of mental imagery in part because images arise in brain areas used in vision.

The scans in the top row are from the front parts of the brain. It is evident from these scans that activation was virtually identical in imagery and perception, even though the participants had their eyes closed during imagery. The scans in the bottom row are from the back parts of the brain. As is evident, these parts of the brain were more strongly activated during perception than during imagery. The greater activation during perception may be one way we know whether we are seeing or imaging.

Understanding Spatial Extent. How can we explain the fact that objects in images have spatial extent? Many of the areas of the brain that process visual input are organized so that images on the retina are laid out on the cortex in what are called *topographically organized areas* (from the Greek *topos*, "place"). As shown in Chapter 3 (see p. 110), there are literally "pictures in the brain" in these areas. Many researchers have found that when people visualize with their eyes closed, these areas are active (Kosslyn & Thompson, 2003; Kosslyn et al., 1995, 1999, 2001; LeBihan et al., 1993). Moreover, if these areas are temporarily impaired by the effect of strong magnetic pulses, visual mental imagery is disrupted (Kosslyn et al., 1999).

Understanding Limits on Size. Let's consider why there are limits on the spatial extent of objects in images, why they seem to overflow if they loom too large. The brain needed to evolve only to process input from the eyes, and we don't see behind our heads. Objects in images overflow at about the same size that actual objects seem to become blurred in perception (Kosslyn, 1978). Like TV or computer screens, topographically organized areas have definite boundaries, and images cannot extend beyond them. Of course, these areas do not function literally as screens: No hidden observer in the brain looks at them—rather, the areas organize and process signals, which are sent to other areas in the brain.

Understanding Grain.   Characteristics of topographically organized brain areas can also explain why images have grain. The neurons in topographically organized visual areas of the brain attempt to inhibit the activity of nearby neurons. During mental imagery, these neurons are not very strongly activated (Ganis et al., 2004), and thus when each neuron receives inhibitory input from many other nearby neurons, it may not be able to resist. If so, then some neurons would become deactivated, which would blur fine details (Kosslyn et al., 2006).

Other types of images, such as the sense you have of where things are around you at any given moment, do not depict surfaces but rather specify locations; such spatial images, which even blind people can have, do not activate topographically organized areas of the brain (Mellet et al., 1998). In addition, in at least some tasks for some people, it is possible that images arise on the basis of memories that were originally formed by topographically organized areas but that no longer rely on such areas (Behrmann, 2000). Finally, we can manipulate objects in images by imagining that we physically manipulate them, which actually engages parts of the brain involved in physical movement (Grèzes & Decety, 2001; Jeannerod & Frak, 1999; Kosslyn et al., 1998; Lamm et al., 2001; Wraga et al., 2003). In all of these cases, key properties of mental imagery arise from the fact that it relies on brain mechanisms used for other purposes, specifically perception and movement control.

Limitations of Mental Images as Vehicles of Thought

But images have limitations that prevent them from being the only tools of the mind, even in combination with words. For one thing, images cannot represent abstract concepts. Take justice, for example. How would you represent "justice" with an image? You might choose a blindfolded woman holding a pair of scales. But how would you know if that image represented the familiar statue or was supposed to stand for the abstract concept of justice? Another problem is that images are often ambiguous. An image of a box seen from the side could just as easily be an image of that side alone, detached from the box. Furthermore, not everybody can produce good images; perhaps 2% of the population have poor visual imagery (McKellar, 1965). Yet another problem is, how do you "decide" which images to form? Some other process must pick out which images are likely to be useful. Like language, imagery can contribute to our thought processes, and like language, it cannot be the only means by which we think.

Concepts: Neither Images nor Words

A **concept** is a grouping of a set of objects (which may include living things) or events (which can specify relations between things, such as "falling" or "on"). A concept is an unambiguous internal representation that may be abstract (such as the concept of truth or justice). Concepts may be *expressed* by images and words, but they are not the same as either (Kosslyn, 1980; Pinker, 1994). Thought arises from the manipulation of concepts, but words and images are used to express thoughts and further expand on them in working memory. Words and images play much the same role that a notepad does when you are planning a shopping

Concept: An unambiguous, sometimes abstract, internal representation that defines a grouping of a set of objects (including living things) or events (including relationships).

trip; they not only help you work through and organize your thoughts, but also provide a way to store them.

The oldest idea of the nature of concepts was proposed by Aristotle in the 4th century B.C. According to this view, a concept can be defined by a set of features. For example, for the concept "bird," the features might be "wings, feathers, a beak, and the ability to fly." The features not only describe perceivable characteristics (such as wings and beak), but also specify appropriate activities (such as flight). A modern adaptation of this view is to assume that such features are actually stored and constitute the representation of the concept. In this case, the morphemes that underlie the meaning of the word *bird* would capture each of the defining properties. Some concepts are captured by the meanings of words, but others require a phrase or two to be fully expressed. Like the meanings of words, concepts are unambiguous.

Prototypes: An Ostrich Is a Bad Bird

According to Aristotelian theories, the features that underlie our representation of a concept must be both necessary and sufficient. A *necessary* feature is one that all members of the group must have; a *sufficient* feature is one that is enough—that *suffices*—to put an entity into a given category (having feathers is a sufficient feature for "birdness"; if it has feathers, it's a bird). A category is a grouping in which the members are specific cases of a more general type. But Aristotle's formula doesn't always work: Although "the ability to fly" is a feature of birds, it is also a feature of insects and bats; but they're not birds, so flying is not sufficient for "birdness." And an ostrich is a bird, but it can't fly, so flying is not a necessary feature of birds.

In addition, adapting Aristotle's notion to a theory of how concepts are represented leads us to make wrong predictions. For example, according to this theory of how concepts are specified, if an object has the required properties, it is a member of the concept, period; all members of a concept have equally good standing. But Rosch (1978) showed that some objects are actually "better" members of their concept category than others. How good an example of its category an object is depends on its typicality—that is, how representative it is of that type of thing. As illustrated in Figure 6.3, people name objects that are typical members of a

Figure 6.3 Name These Animals

Research has shown that you will name the animal in the center most readily; and, in fact, the mutt is most typical for the category "dog."

Category: A grouping in which the members are specific cases of a more general type.

Typicality: The degree to which an entity is representative of its concept category.

concept category faster than objects that are not typical members. Typicality affects not only the time it takes you to identify an object, but also your confidence in naming the object as an example of a specific concept (Garrard et al., 2001; Smith & Medin, 1981).

Most responses related to how typical an object is for a category can be explained if a concept corresponds to a set of features that describe the **prototype** of the category—that is, its most typical member—but only a *percentage* of those features need to be present in any particular member. That is, the more features that apply above the bare minimum, the faster you can name the object—and more prototypical members of a concept have more such distinguishing features (Rips et al., 1973). Thus, people take longer to name ostriches as birds because fewer bird features apply to them (they cannot fly; they are not the size of the standard bird); on the other hand, robins are named faster because more of the features of birds, in general, apply to them.

However, at least some concepts that are not collections of features may be stored as prototypes, such as the prototype of the concept "an odd number between 1 and 10" (Armstrong et al., 1983). Quick, think of an odd number between 1 and 10. Most people select 3, and on that basis 3 can be considered as the most typical member of this category. But such concepts are unusual in that, by definition, they require selecting a single example, and so these special cases may be represented by a single example stored individually. In fact, some researchers have made the case that not all concepts are stored as prototypes, but rather some concepts rely on storing sets of examples of the category (Medin & Schaffer, 1978; Smith & Medin, 1981). For example, your concept of a chair might correspond to representations of a collection of chairs (rocking chair, desk chair, easy chair, and so on), not a single prototype. In addition, concepts of movement or action, such as those labeled by verbs, may largely rely on functional features (for instance, whether an object can be lifted; Bird et al., 2000). At least some concepts may be stored in multiple ways or using combinations of methods, and different representations may be used in different situations (Anderson & Betz, 2001; Medin et al., 2000; Rips, 2001; Smith et al., 1998).

How Are Concepts Organized?

Many concepts can be applied to any given object. We can name an object with words that correspond to concepts at different levels of specificity: "Granny Smith apple" is very specific, "apple" is more general, and "fruit" more general still. How are different concepts organized?

Look at the objects in Figure 6.4, and name them as fast as you can. It's very likely that you name them "apple," "tree," and "dog." You probably didn't name the apple a "fruit" or a "Granny Smith" or call the tree an "oak" or the dog a "mammal" or an "animal." People consistently name objects at what Rosch and her colleagues (1976) have called the **basic level**. The basic level is like the middle rung of a ladder, with more general concepts above it and more specific concepts below it. So "apple" is the basic level; "fruit" is on a rung above it, and "Granny Smith" on a rung below. Each more general concept includes a number of more specific concepts; for example, "apple" includes "Granny Smith," "Delicious," "McIntosh," and many more.

At each level of specificity, there are prototypes for the concept. For example, apple might be the prototypical fruit, and McIntosh might be the prototypical apple. The basic level indicates the level of specificity with which we are likely to apply a concept to an object. Rosch offered several ways to identify the basic level. For example, one way is based on shape: At the most specific level, if we compare

Prototype: The most typical example of a concept category.

Basic level: A level of specificity, which is usually the most likely to be applied to an object.

Figure 6.4 Basic-Level Names

Name these objects as fast as you can. It is remarkable that most people choose the same three names, a feat no computer vision system can match.

individual Delicious apples with other Delicious apples, their shapes are very similar. Moving up a rung of generality, if we compare Delicious apples with McIntosh apples, Cortland apples, and so on, their shapes are pretty similar. But, moving up another rung, if we compare apples with other fruits, such as bananas, watermelons, or grapes, their shapes are not similar at all. The basic-level category is the one that is as general as possible, while still being limited to objects having similar shapes.

How to Solve Problems: More Than Inspiration

Einstein never shied away from proposing radically new concepts, such as the idea that light consists of both particles and waves. But formulating concepts is only a small part of what we do while thinking. Once we form concepts, we use them in various ways, such as in solving problems. A **problem** is an obstacle that must be overcome to reach a goal. Problems come in many types and can often be solved in many ways. Let's consider some of the tools at your disposal for solving a diverse range of puzzles and predicaments.

Solving the Representation Problem: It's All in How You Look at It

The first step to solving any problem is figuring out how to look at it. This fundamental challenge is called the **representation problem**. If you hit on the right way to represent a specific problem, the solution can be amazingly simple. Consider the example of the hiking monk in Figure 6.5 (on p. 244; based on Duncker, 1945). You have to decide whether, *at any one time of day*, the monk would be at precisely the same spot on the path, both on the day he went up and on the day he came down. At first glance, this problem may seem difficult. If the

Problem: An obstacle that must be overcome to reach a goal.

Representation problem: The challenge of how best to formulate the nature of a problem.

Figure 6.5 The Hiking Monk Problem

A monk leaves the bottom of a mountain every Monday at 5:00 A.M. and walks up a twisty path, climbing at a rate of 1.5 miles an hour, until he reaches the top at 4:00 P.M., having taken off a half-hour for lunch. He meditates on the mountain until sundown. At 5:00 the next morning, he departs and walks down the path, going 3.5 miles an hour, until he reaches the bottom. Is there *any* point in the two journeys when he is at precisely the same location on the path at precisely the same time of day? You don't need to say what that time is, just whether there would be such a time.

Functional fixedness: When solving a problem, getting stuck on one interpretation of an object or one part of the situation.

Strategy: An approach to solving a problem, determined by the type of representation used and the processing steps to be tried.

Algorithm: A set of steps that, if followed methodically, will guarantee the solution to a problem.

Heuristic: A strategy that does not guarantee the correct answer to a problem but offers a likely shortcut to it.

precise specifications of departure times, speed, and so on lure you into trying to use algebra, you may work on it for hours. But if you hit on the right representation, it's easy: Imagine a mountain with a monk leaving from the top at the same time that another monk leaves from the bottom. It is clear that the two monks must pass each other at a particular point on the path—and the same will be true if instead of two monks leaving at the same time on the same day, a single monk goes up on one day and goes down on another day (provided that he departs at the same time in the morning for both treks). And so the answer is simply yes.

Finding the right representation for a problem can be tricky because once you think of a problem in a certain way, you may find it difficult to drop this view and try out others (Smith & Blankenship, 1989, 1991). For example, consider the problem in Figure 6.6 (adapted from Duncker, 1945); after you think about it, look at its solution in Figure 6.7 (on p. 246). At first, you probably thought of the box simply as a container, and not as a potential part of the solution. Becoming stuck on one interpretation of an object or aspect of a situation is called **functional fixedness** (Behrens, 2003). Even members of the Shuar, who live in the Ecuadorian Amazon, fall into functional fixedness—in spite of the fact that most of their artifacts are intended to have multiple functions. German and Barrett (2005), in reporting this finding, suggest that functional fixedness may be a result of how semantic memory operates. In fact, neuroimaging studies have shown that extra brain activity is required when you need to inhibit one kind of performance and switch to another (Konishi et al., 1999).

Algorithms and Heuristics: Getting From Here to There

To solve a problem, you need a **strategy**, an approach to solving a problem determined by the type of representation used and the processing steps to be tried. There are two types of strategies: algorithms and heuristics. Let's say you hear about a fantastic price being offered on a new music CD you covet by an independent record store, but you don't know the name of the store. You could try to find it by calling every relevant listing in the yellow pages. This process involves using an **algorithm**, a set of steps that, if followed methodically, will guarantee the right answer. But you may not have time to call every store. Instead, you might guess that the record store is in a part of town where many students live. In this case, having reduced the list of candidates to those located near the campus, you might find the store after calling only a few. This process reflects use of a **heuristic**, a strategy that does not guarantee the correct answer but offers a likely shortcut to it. One common heuristic is to divide a big problem into parts and solve them one at a time.

Solving Problems by Analogy: Comparing Features

Another way to solve problems requires you to compare the features of two situations, noticing what they have in common and what's different (Gentner &

Figure 6.6 The Candle Problem

Participants are asked to use the materials provided to mount the candle on the wall so that it can be lit. Some participants are given the materials as shown on the left; others, as shown at the right. Participants given the materials as shown at the right are more likely to solve the problem.

Gunn, 2001; Hummel & Holyoak, 1997). Let's begin with the following problem (based on Duncker, 1945): A surgeon has to remove a cancerous tumor from deep within a patient's brain. The use of a scalpel would cause permanent brain damage. An alternative is to use a beam of X rays to demolish the cancerous cells. However, the beam will also kill healthy cells in its path. Is there a way to reach only the cancerous cells and spare the healthy ones?

The solution is to split the beam into several minibeams, each aimed from a different angle but crossing at the location of the tumor. Each minibeam is so weak that it will not hurt the healthy tissue, but their combined impact will destroy the tumor. Gick and Holyoak (1980, 1983) found that most people do not realize this solution. However, if they are first presented with an analogous problem and are told to think about how it relates to the second problem, success rates skyrocket. In this case, they first read about a problem faced by a general who wants to attack a fortress. If he advances all of his troops along a single road, mines will blow them to pieces. But smaller groups could travel on various approach roads without exploding the mines. The solution is to divide the army into smaller parties and have each take a separate road to the fortress. Once people see this solution and know it is relevant, the solution to the tumor problem becomes much easier (in fact, close to 80% get the problem right). If the participants are not told that the army problem is relevant to the tumor one, however, thinking about the solution to the former does not help them much with the latter. At first glance, the two problems are unrelated. One involves soldiers and a fortress; the other, beams of radiation and a tumor. But beneath these surface differences, the problems have the same structure: Something too big is broken into parts, the parts are delivered separately, and then they are recombined. To see how a previous experience can be applied to a present case, you must recognize the similarities in the structure of the situations.

Various approaches to problem solving are summarized in Table 6.1 (on p. 246).

Table 6.1 Approaches to Problem Solving

Approach	Definition	Example
Address the representation of the problem	Change the way the problem is represented, or formulated	Use an image of two monks starting to walk the path at the same time, one from the top and the other from the bottom
Use an algorithm	Series of steps that is guaranteed to produce a solution	Check every music store in the phone book to find the lowest price on a CD
Use a heuristic	Short-cut strategy that may or may not be effective	Check music stores in the part of town where most of the students live to find the lowest price on a CD
Use an analogy	A type of heuristic that relies on finding points of correspondence with previously solved problems	Realizing that a particular medical problem is like a previously encountered military problem

Figure 6.7

Solution to the Candle Problem

When the box is presented as a container, functional fixedness often prevents people from imagining the box as a shelf.

Mental set: A fixed way of viewing the kind of solution being sought.

Overcoming Obstacles to Problem Solving

You can improve your ability to overcome obstacles to solving problems if you keep the following points in mind (Ellis & Hunt, 1993; Newsome, 2000):

1. A major challenge is to represent the problem effectively. One way to meet this challenge is to make sure that you really understand the problem. Explain the problem to somebody else; sometimes, the simple act of explaining leads to a representation that immediately implies a solution.

2. Keep your eye on the ball: Don't lose sight of what actually constitutes the problem. People sometimes tend to transform the problem—resist this. If the problem is "how to get to Hawaii for spring break," don't redefine the problem as "how to talk my parents into subsidizing the trip." This advice also applies to debates and arguments; you'll be surprised at how much more effective you'll be if you keep the pertinent issue in mind and don't allow yourself to be drawn off on tangents.

3. Don't get locked into viewing your resources in only one way, which is a form of functional fixedness. See whether you can come up with more than one strategy for approaching the problem. Einstein noted, "I am enough of an artist to draw freely upon my imagination. Imagination is more important than knowledge. Knowledge is limited. Imagination encircles the world" (as cited in Viereck, 1929).

4. Don't get stuck with a certain ==mental set==, a fixed way of viewing the kind of solution you seek. It's okay to begin by focusing on one possible solution, but recognize that there may be more than one happy outcome. Be willing to consider alternatives. (Southern California is a great spring break destination, too.)

5. If you do get stuck, walk away from the problem for a while. A fresh look can lead to new ways of representing it or new strategies for solving it.

Logic, Reasoning, and Decision Making

How do we humans—Einstein included—reason logically? And why do we sometimes reason incorrectly?

Are People Logical?

Not all thinking consists of figuring out how to overcome obstacles; sometimes thinking is considering what follows from what, evaluating alternatives, and deciding what to do next. Decision making requires us to evaluate possible outcomes and choose one alternative or course of action over the others. Let's review the ways people reason and then consider some common errors in reasoning.

How People Reason. **Logic** is the process of applying the principles of correct reasoning to reach a decision or to evaluate the truth of a claim. "Hector is a man; all men are human; therefore Hector is a human" is correct logic. But note that "Hector is a man; all men are Martians; therefore Hector is a Martian" is *also* correct logic. The first two statements in each case are the *premises*, and the only question in logic is whether the final statement, the *conclusion*, follows from the premises. The *content*—the actual meaning of the premises—is irrelevant to logic; only the *form*, the sequence of what-implies-what, counts in logic. If you accept the premises, then the rules of logic dictate that you must also accept the conclusion. In this process of **deductive reasoning**—that is, reasoning from the general to the particular—the rules of logic are applied to a set of assumptions stated as premises to discover what conclusions inevitably follow from those assumptions.

Reasoning can be inductive as well as deductive. The opposite of deductive reasoning, **inductive reasoning** works toward a conclusion by moving from the particular case to a generalization. Induction uses individual examples to figure out a rule that governs them. If you ate two green apples and each was sour, you might induce that green apples in general are sour. However, your conclusion would be faulty: You ignored the evidence of Granny Smiths (which are sweet). That inductive reasoning works at all is something of a miracle—nevertheless, it often does (Prasada, 2000), and much of scientific discovery relies on just this kind of reasoning. Figure 6.8 schematizes the difference between deductive and inductive reasoning. Much of our reasoning involves a combination of deductive and inductive processes.

Logical Errors. Much research has shown that humans—even extraordinary ones such as Albert Einstein—are not entirely logical. For example, people often make the error of **affirming the consequent**—that is, assuming that a specific cause is present because a particular result has occurred. Here is a cause–effect relation: "If it is sunny out, Hector wears a hat." If you see that Hector is wearing a hat, can you assume that it is sunny out? Not necessarily. Maybe Hector's on his way to a ballgame and has put on a hat with his team's logo. Maybe after checking The Weather Channel, he has put on a rain hat. Maybe he simply thinks a particular hat looks good with his outfit. Maybe—well, there

Figure 6.8 Deductive Versus Inductive Reasoning

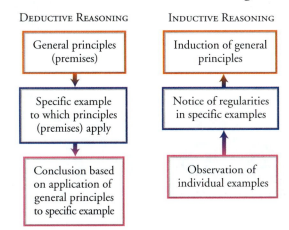

To remember the difference between deductive and inductive reasoning, try these mnemonics: To DEduce is to move DOWN FROM something larger; to INduce is to move INTO something larger.

Logic: The process of applying the principles of correct reasoning to reach a decision or evaluate the truth of a claim.

Deductive reasoning: Reasoning that applies the rules of logic to a set of assumptions (stated as premises) to discover whether certain conclusions follow from those assumptions; deduction goes from the general to the particular.

Inductive reasoning: Reasoning that uses examples to figure out a rule that governs them; induction goes from the particular (examples) to the general (a rule).

Affirming the consequent: A reasoning error that occurs because of the assumption that if a result has occurred, a specific cause must also be present.

might be any number of reasons, including that it is, in fact, sunny out. Affirming the consequent occurs because we incorrectly work backward, from result to cause. Armed with this knowledge, you can now tell what's wrong with the following reasoning:

1. Japanese do not eat much fat and have fewer heart attacks than the Americans and British.
2. The French eat a lot of fat and have fewer heart attacks than the Americans and British.
3. Japanese do not drink much red wine and have fewer heart attacks than the Americans and British.
4. Italians drink large amounts of red wine and have fewer heart attacks than the Americans and British.
5. Conclusion: Eat and drink what you like. It's speaking English that causes heart attacks.

Figure 6.9

Wason and Johnson-Laird's Card Task

Here is the rule presented along with these cards: "If a card has a vowel on one side, then it will have an even number on the other side." How many and which of these cards must be flipped over to decide whether this rule is true?

Wason and Johnson-Laird (1972) devised a task that laid bare another of our reasoning frailties. Look at Figure 6.9: What would you do? The answer is that both A and 7 must be flipped. People tend to flip A, to see whether an even number is on the other side; if not, the rule would be wrong. If there is an even number on the reverse of A, most people assume the rule is confirmed. Very few think to turn over the 7: If there is a vowel on the other side, then the rule is wrong no matter what's on the reverse of A. Most people do not think about what it would take to *disconfirm* the rule. A **confirmation bias** occurs when people seek information that will confirm a rule but do not seek information that might refute it.

Heuristics and Biases: Cognitive Illusions?

If the laws of logic lead to inescapable conclusions, why do people make errors in reasoning? The answer is implied in the question: because people do not always use the laws of logic, but rely instead on sets of heuristics. While often useful, these heuristics, or short-cut strategies, sometimes steer us to the wrong conclusions (Kahneman, 2003). Amos Tversky and Daniel Kahneman performed the ground-breaking studies of such errors—which earned Kahneman a Nobel Prize in 2002 (Tversky unfortunately did not live to see his work so honored).

Representativeness. The **representativeness heuristic** assumes that the more similar something is to a prototype stored in memory, the more likely it is that the thing belongs to the category of the prototype. Tversky and Kahneman (1974) asked participants to read this passage:

Jack is a 45-year-old man. He is married and has four children. He is generally conservative, careful, and ambitious. He shows no interest in political and social issues and spends most of his free time on his many hobbies, including home carpentry, sailing, and mathematical puzzles.

Confirmation bias: A tendency to seek information that will confirm a rule and not to seek information that is inconsistent with the rule.

Representativeness heuristic: The heuristic that the more similar something is to a prototype stored in memory, the more likely it is to belong to the prototype's category.

The participants were then told that Jack was selected at random from a group of 100 people, all of whom were either lawyers or engineers. Here's the trick: Half of the participants were told that 70 members of the group were lawyers and 30 were engineers; the other participants were told that 30 members of the group were lawyers and 70 engineers. Pause for a moment and imagine that there are 100 balls in a jug, 70 red and 30 black, randomly mixed up. Imagine shutting your eyes and drawing out one ball. Do you think you would be more likely to pluck out a red one than a black one? Sure. Now reverse the colors, so that 70 are black and 30 red. Now you would be more likely to pull out a black one. However, when asked to decide whether Jack, who was selected at random from the group, was a lawyer or an engineer, the great majority of all participants, no matter what they had been told about the constitution of the group, said he was an engineer. The description of Jack, especially his interest in mathematical puzzles, fit the participants' ideas about the characteristics of engineers better than it fit their ideas about lawyers, and thus they labeled Jack "engineer" because he matched the prototype.

The participants in Tversky and Kahneman's study used their knowledge—or assumptions—about typical properties of people in different professions to make their decision, ignoring the ==base-rate rule==. This rule states that if something is chosen at random from a set, the chances of that thing's being a particular type are directly proportional to the percentage of that type in the larger set. Our failure to appreciate the working of this rule can be thought of as a *cognitive illusion*.

Gigerenzer, however, argues that people do not often have true cognitive illusions, but instead simply have trouble understanding descriptions of probabilities. Gigerenzer and his colleagues (1988) performed an experiment that ensured that the participants understood the information about the proportions of different professions included in the larger set under consideration. The researchers took 10 slips of paper and on each one wrote a description of a person and the person's profession. Seven slips had one profession written on them, and three had another; the slips were folded and put in an urn. Each participant drew out a single slip and read the description (but not the profession), and then guessed the profession. In this situation, the participants did well, proving themselves able to keep in mind the relative proportions of the two professions. According to Gigerenzer and colleagues, in earlier experiments, such as the one with Jack, participants did not understand the proportions of the two professions well enough to override their prior knowledge about types of people; they categorized Jack based on prior knowledge, not probability (additional support for this conclusion is provided by Goodie & Fantino, 1996).

However, research results suggest that when people cannot use prior knowledge about how often events occur (for example, in thinking about events that only happen once, such as the destruction of the World Trade Center), they use reasoning heuristics such as representativeness. The bottom line is that people use different strategies in different situations—sometimes heuristics, sometimes relative frequencies, and sometimes other kinds of information (Ayton & Wright, 1994; Gigerenzer, 1996; Gigerenzer & Goldstein, 1996; Kahneman & Tversky, 1996; Teigen, 1994; Vranas, 2000).

Culture affects the heuristics people use to anticipate changes over time. Americans tend to think that things will continue as they have, whereas Chinese tend to think that situations regularly change over time. For example, when shown a graph that illustrated a trend (such as global economic growth over several years) and asked to extrapolate this trend into the future, Americans tended to preserve the direction and rate, whereas Chinese often changed the direction and rate (Ji et al., 2001).

Availability. Another shortcut is the ==availability heuristic==, which is the tendency to judge objects or events as more likely, common, or frequent if they are easier to bring to mind. For example, Tversky and Kahneman (1974) asked people to judge the relative proportions of English words that begin with the letter *k* and words with *k* in the third position. What do you think? Most of the participants in the study thought that *k* occurred more often as a first letter than a third letter, but in fact almost three times as many words have *k* in the third position as

Base-rate rule: The rule stating that if something is chosen from a set at random, the chances that the thing will be of a particular type are directly proportional to the percentage of that type in the larger set.

Availability heuristic: The tendency to judge objects or events as more likely, common, or frequent if they are easier to bring to mind.

If you have ever budgeted time to work on a paper and then run out of hours way too soon, you may have fallen victim to the *planning fallacy*: the tendency to underestimate the time it takes to accomplish a task. This error may arise because the completion of similar tasks is more available in your memory than is their duration. Thus, the availability heuristic can lead to the planning fallacy. The good news is that the planning fallacy can be reduced by thinking carefully about how long past projects actually took to complete (Buehler et al., 1994).

in the first one. Why this error? Because it is much easier to bring to mind words starting with *k* than words that have *k* in the third position. Similarly, when given a list of names of famous men and not famous women, people later will mistakenly remember that there were more men than women on the list (or vice versa, if given names of famous women and not famous men; McKelvie, 2000). The availability heuristic may also explain why people tend to think that infrequent but highly memorable events, such as murders and plane crashes, are more common than they really are, and that more frequent but mundane killers, such as stomach cancer and stroke, are less common.

The availability heuristic affects how we evaluate many sorts of information. For instance, researchers have found that the final phases of a painful experience are likely to be most available to memory, which leads to a counterintuitive prediction: In some situations, normal people will prefer more pain to less, provided that the pain tapers off at the end. In one study, participants put their hands into 14°C water, which they endured for 60 seconds. In another condition, after 60 seconds of immersion at this temperature, the water was gradually warmed to 15°C (which is still uncomfortable) over the course of 30 seconds. The participants were then asked which condition they would prefer to repeat. Most said they would prefer to have their hands in uncomfortably cold water for a longer duration than a shorter duration (thus objectively suffering more total pain), provided that the final 30 seconds were less painful in the longer session (Kahneman et al., 1993).

These findings are not just a laboratory curiosity: In a subsequent study, instead of measuring responses to ice water, researchers asked patients to judge the pain of a colonoscopy, a medical procedure in which a monitoring instrument is inserted through the anus to observe the intestines (Redelmeier & Kahneman, 1996); consistent with the findings from the ice water study, the amount of pain the patients judged for the entire procedure depended largely on how they judged the final 3 minutes. As aversive as it may sound, a colonoscopy is a crucial test for those over 50 years old; it can detect colon cancer soon enough to prevent it from spreading. Knowing that patients are more likely to return for a later checkup if a procedure was less painful in the final 3 minutes, should doctors inflict a few minutes of additional (but diminished) pain after the procedure is actually complete? True, this added pain would be less severe than what came before, but it's still added pain. And is it appropriate to distort intentionally a patient's judgment of the overall amount of pain?

Emotions and Decision Making: Having a Hunch

Einstein was once upset with himself for being "provoked into making a caustic reply." His emotions apparently got the better of him (Clark, 1971, pp. 263–264), and he vowed not to let that happen again. *Star Trek*'s Mr. Spock and Albert Einstein seemed to agree: Emotion clouds reason and distorts our ability to be objective. Doesn't it? Well, not exactly. Researchers have found that sometimes emotion can actually help reasoning (Martinez-Miranda & Aldea, 2005). Bechara and colleagues (1997) found that people played a gambling game better once they had "hunches," even though they were not aware of the bases of the hunches. Evidence of a hunch was detected by the researchers as a skin-conductance response. Such a response occurred when the brain signaled the body that certain choices were risky before the participant consciously realized it.

Emotional responses such as hunches may underlie what we mean by *intuition*. having an idea that is not easy to express. These responses appear to be based on implicit memories (see Chapter 5) and nudge conscious decision making. Without such nudges, people do not choose wisely. However, Einstein and Mr. Spock weren't all wrong about emotion and reasoning: It is true that negative emotion can sometimes disrupt reasoning (Goel & Dolan, 2003; Gray, 1999). For example, in 1997, the world champion chess player, Garry Kasparov, was challenged to play a match against a new, improved computer. The fate of the human species seemed to be on the line, and the world watched closely. In the second game, Kasparov became shaken by the unexpectedly strong performance of the computer and resigned when he still could have managed a draw (Chabris, personal communication, 1999).

LOOKING BACK: *Review*

1. *Does language mold our thoughts?* Although some researchers have claimed that language shapes thought, the evidence does not support this view. Thinking cannot rely entirely on words; for example, words are ambiguous, but thoughts are not, and people sometimes have difficulty putting thoughts into words. Nevertheless, some thinking does make use of language, and it is clear that being able to name something makes that object or idea easier to remember.

2. *Can we think with mental images?* Objects in images can "stand in" for the actual objects, as evidenced by the facts that they have spatial extent, occur in a mental space with a limited extent, and have grain. Many studies have found that areas of the brain used in vision are activated when people form mental images, and the properties of these areas may explain the characteristics of images. Nevertheless, thinking cannot rely entirely on mental images; such images are difficult to use to represent abstract ideas and, like words, can be ambiguous.

3. *What is a concept?* A concept is a grouping of a set of objects or events (including relations, such as the concept of one object's being "on" another object). This grouping often can be accomplished by sets of unambiguous features that specify key characteristics of the concept, but only a percentage of the features must apply in any given instance. Members of concepts that have more of the key features are "better" (more typical) examples of the concept. A member that has the most specifying features is a prototype. Some concepts may be specified by prototypes that are not collections of features; others may be specified by sets of examples of the concept. Concepts are organized according to levels of specificity.

4. *What methods can we use to solve problems?* The first step is to discover how best to specify the problem, how to represent it to yourself. If you find the proper representation, the solution is sometimes obvious. To solve a problem, you can use an algorithm or a heuristic. One common heuristic is to divide a problem into a set of smaller problems and then tackle those subproblems one at a time. In addition, you can search for correspondences with other situations and then use analogical thinking to solve a problem.

5. *Do people reason logically? Why do we commit reasoning errors?* In deductive reasoning, logic is applied to determine what specific conclusions must follow from a set of general premises. People often make errors in this kind of reasoning, for example, by affirming the consequent or by having a confirmation bias. Inductive reasoning goes in the

other direction, from particulars to a generalization. Inductive reasoning is also prone to errors because it is not always obvious what general principle is suggested by a set of examples. We often use heuristics in reasoning, which can lead to specific types of errors. The representativeness heuristic, for example, can lead us to ignore the base-rate rule. The availability heuristic can lead to the planning fallacy, which arises because different aspects of an event are more or less easy to recall. Finally, emotion can nudge reasoning in a positive direction or disrupt reasoning, depending on the type of emotion and the circumstances.

⬤ LOOKING BEYOND: *Critical Thinking*

In what ways do the human weaknesses in logic and decision making reflect other mental processes that actually help us? Can you think of how to use any of the material you just learned to be a better debater?

Do you think the general human weakness in using logic adversely affects world politics? Why or why not?

Intelligence: Is There More Than One Way to Be Smart?

Einstein did not always act intelligently. For example, when offered a job at the new Institute for Advanced Study at Princeton, he was asked what he would need to live and work there. His request for salary and support was so unrealistically low that it was turned down, and the administrators asked his wife for a more reasonable estimate. Nevertheless, this same man derived equations that explained a previously inexplicable slippage in the orbit of Mercury. When his equations produced the correct result, he was satisfied but not exuberant, noting that "I did not for one second doubt that [my calculations] would agree with observation. There was no sense in getting excited about what was self-evident" (Clark, 1971, p. 206).

What does it mean to say that someone is or is not intelligent? Intelligence is certainly not a concrete entity that can be quantified, like the amount of water in a jug; rather, it is a concept. Psychologists have offered many definitions of intelligence, and there is considerable disagreement about what intelligence is and whether it can be accurately measured (Gardner, 2002; Gardner et al., 1996; Sternberg, 1986b, 1990; Sternberg & Detterman, 1986). What most researchers in psychology mean by "intelligence" is pretty close to the standard dictionary definition: Intelligence is the ability to solve problems well and to understand and learn complex material. Researchers also typically stress that a key aspect of intelligence is the ability to adapt to the environment (Sternberg, 2000). Intelligence is often associated with mental quickness, but this need not be so; sometimes, still waters do run deep. However, researchers typically assume that "solving problems well" implies "in a reasonable amount of time." There is a limit to how much time you could take when solving a problem or learning complex material and still be considered "intelligent." Virtually all tests of intelligence rely on the assumption that intelligent people can solve problems and understand and learn complex material relatively easily, and thus quickly as well.

Intelligence: The ability to solve problems well and to understand and learn complex material.

1. What is IQ?
2. Is intelligence a single characteristic or a complex set of characteristics?

Measuring Intelligence: What Is IQ?

Let's look at exactly what IQ is.

A Brief History of Intelligence Testing

IQ is short for **intelligence quotient**, a test score used in Western countries as a general measure of intelligence. To understand the meaning of IQ scores, it will be helpful to see how intelligence testing has evolved over time.

Binet and Simon: Testing to Help. The original test from which modern IQ tests derive had a more specific and different purpose than the modern tests. Responding to a call from the French government, which had recently enacted universal elementary education, a French physician named Alfred Binet (1857–1911) and his collaborator, Theodore Simon (1873–1961), devised the first intelligence test between 1904 and 1911 (Matarazzo, 1972). Their aim was to develop an objective way to identify children in the public schools who needed extra classroom help. They started with the idea that intelligence shows itself in a wide variety of abilities, a perspective that led them to construct a test consisting of many sorts of tasks. Among other things, children were asked to copy a drawing, repeat a string of digits, recognize coins and make change, and explain why a particular statement did not make sense. Binet and Simon assumed that the children's performance on the tests reflected educational experience, and thus that special classes could help those who did poorly.

To assess performance, Binet and Simon first gave the test to a group of normal children of various ages. They noted which problems were solved by most of the 6-year-olds, by most of the 10-year-olds, and so forth; then they compared the performance of other children of the same age with those "normal" scores. So, if a child could solve all of the problems solved by most 9-year-olds, but failed those passed by most 10-year-olds, the child's *mental age (MA)* was said to be 9. Children with a mental age lower than their *chronological age (CA)* were considered relatively slow.

Terman and Wechsler: Tests for Everyone. Binet and Simon's test was quickly adapted to suit new purposes. In 1916, Lewis Terman and his colleagues at Stanford University developed the Stanford-Binet Revision of the Binet-Simon test, which is still used to test people from age 2 to adulthood. To refine the testing further (especially for adults, by expanding the range at the "top"), to test a wider range of abilities, and to improve the method of scoring and interpreting results, David Wechsler (1958) developed another set of intelligence tests, the **Wechsler Adult Intelligence Scale (WAIS)** and the *Wechsler Intelligence Scale for Children (WISC)*. Today, the WAIS-III and the WISC-III ("III" denoting the third major versions) are the most widely used IQ tests in the United States.

Believing that Binet's test relied too much on verbal skills, Wechsler divided his test into two major parts, summarized in Table 6.2 (on p. 254). The *verbal subtests* assess the ability to understand and use language by testing vocabulary, comprehension, and other aspects of verbal skill. The *performance subtests* consist of nonverbal tasks such as arranging pictures in an order that tells a story and

Intelligence quotient (IQ): A score on an intelligence test, originally based on comparing mental age to chronological age, but later based on norms and used as a measure of general intelligence.

Wechsler Adult Intelligence Scale (WAIS): The most widely used intelligence test; consists of both verbal and performance subtests.

The WISC-III is administered to children individually by a trained examiner.

Table 6.2 WAIS-III Subtests With Simulated Examples of Questions

I. Verbal Subtests

- *Vocabulary:* Written and spoken words, which must be defined; the words are ordered in terms of increasing difficulty.
  Example: "What does *trek* mean?"

- *Similarities:* Questions that require explaining how the concepts named by two words are similar.
  Example: "How are an airplane and a car alike?"

- *Arithmetic:* Problems, all but one presented orally (one involves using blocks); the test is timed.
  Example: "If 2 men need 4 days to paint a house, how long would 4 men need?"

- *Digit Span:* Lists of digits, 2–9 numbers long, are presented. The test-taker repeats the digits, either in the same or reverse order.
  Example: "6, 1, 7, 5, 3."

- *Information:* Questions that draw on literature, history, general science, and common knowledge.
  Example: "Who was Martin Luther King, Jr.?"

- *Comprehension:* Questions that require understanding of social mores and conventions.
  Example: "Why are there taxes?"

II. Performance Subtests

- *Picture Completion*: Drawings of common objects or scenes, each of which is missing a feature. The test-taker must point out what's missing.
  Example:
  What is missing?

- *Digit Symbol-Coding:* The test-taker learns a symbol for each of the numbers 1–9 and then sees numbers and must write their appropriate symbols; the test is timed.
  Example:

Shown:					Fill in:			
1	2	3	4		4	1	3	2
+	−	×	÷		—	—	—	—

- *Block Design:* Problems that require the test-taker to arrange blocks colored on each side—white, red, or half white and half red—to reproduce a white-and-red pattern in a fixed amount of time.
  Example:
  Assemble blocks to match this design:

- *Matrix Reasoning:* Items that require the test-taker to study a progression of stimuli in a sequence from which a section is missing. The test-taker must choose which of 5 given possibilities completes the sequence.

- *Picture Arrangement:* Sets of cards that must be arranged to tell a story.
  Example:
  Put the pictures in the right order.

This version is intended for people aged 16 to 89. Three additional tests are included as "spares," to be used if there are problems in administering the basic set summarized here.

spotting the missing element in a picture. Because the performance subtests do not focus on the ability to use and manipulate words, they probably rely less heavily than do the verbal subtests on the test-taker's education or cultural experiences.

Scoring IQ Tests: Measuring the Mind

Modern IQ tests have been modified from earlier versions both in the nature of their tasks and in the way they are scored. Binet and Simon were satisfied with simply knowing whether a child was below or at par for his or her age, but later researchers wanted a more precise measure of the degree of intelligence. Early in the 20th century, William Stern, a German psychologist, developed the idea of an *intelligence quotient (IQ)*, computed by dividing mental age (MA) by chronological age (CA) and multiplying by 100 to avoid fractional scores:

$$IQ = (MA/CA) \times 100$$

Thus, a score of 100 meant that a child's mental age exactly matched the child's chronological age. Computing IQ scores using the MA/CA ratio presents a major disadvantage, however: Because mental age does not keep developing forever, whereas chronological age marches on, test-takers cannot help but appear to become less intelligent as they age. For example, if your mental age is 25 and you are 25 years old, you would be average; but if your mental age is the same in 5 years, your IQ would drop from 100 to 83, even though you are just as smart at 30 as you were at 25. And at 40, your IQ would be about 62. But people do not actually become stupider with age. Therefore, today's IQ tests are scored not by using the MA/CA ratio but by specifying how a test-taker's performance stands relative to that of other people of the same age. A score of 100 is set as the average score.

Interpreting IQ Scores: Standardized Samples and Norming. Although the average IQ score is set at 100, most people do not score at this precise level. How can we interpret the meaning of scores above or below this benchmark? IQ test scores are based on a large **standardized sample**, a random selection of people from the appropriate population. In this sense, a *population* is defined as a group of people who share one or more specific characteristics, such as age, sex, or any other relevant attributes. Almost always, scores are spread along a normal distribution, illustrated in Figure 6.10 (on p. 256). When the distribution of scores follows a normal distribution, most scores fall near the middle, with gradually fewer scores toward either extreme. After the test has been given to a standardized sample of people, the developers "norm" the test to make it easy to interpret the meaning of any one test-taker's score relative to the others. **Norming** a test involves setting two measures: The first is the mean, or average; the mean score for an IQ test is set at 100. The second is the standard deviation, which indicates the degree to which the individual scores deviate from the mean. The greater the number of standard deviations from the mean, the farther above or below the score is from the mean (see the Appendix for more details about statistical terms and procedures). If the scores fall into a normal distribution, a certain percentage of them occur within each standard deviation from the mean, as shown in Figure 6.10 (each marked unit on the bottom corresponds to one standard deviation).

For the WAIS-III IQ test, scores are adjusted so that a standard deviation is 15 points. As shown in Figure 6.10, about two thirds of all people have IQs from 85 to 115 points (that is, within one standard deviation above or below the mean), but only a bit more than a quarter have IQs either between 70 and 85 or between 115 and 130 (within the second standard deviation above or below the mean). Only 4.54% of IQ scores are above 130 or below 70.

Standardized sample: A random selection of people, drawn from a carefully defined population.

Norming: The process of setting the mean and the standard deviation of a set of test scores, based on results from a standardized sample.

Figure 6.10 The Normal Curve and WAIS-III IQ Scores

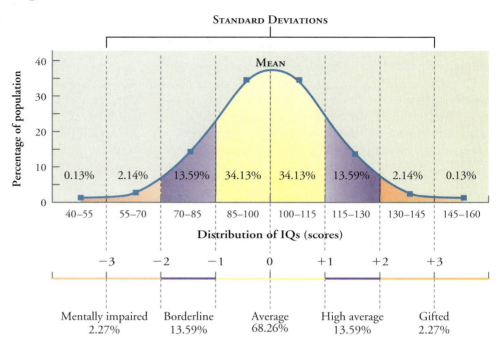

Because of its shape, the normal curve is also known as the *bell curve*. In nature, most characteristics clump around the midpoint, and progressively fewer have very high or very low measures. This diagram indicates the percentage of people who have scores on the WAIS-III IQ test that fall within different regions of the distribution.

Reliability and Validity. For IQ scores to be meaningful or useful, the test must be *reliable*. A reliable test produces consistent results; that is, if you test the same group of people on two occasions, the two sets of scores will be highly positively correlated. The WAIS-III has been shown to be highly reliable. In addition, a useful test must be *valid*. A valid test measures what it is supposed to measure. Do IQ tests really measure intelligence; do they measure the ability to solve problems well and to understand and learn complex material? One way to find out whether IQ tests actually measure intelligence is to see whether scores on these tests are related to measures of performance for other tasks that seem to require intelligence, which we consider next.

IQ and Achievement: IQ in the Real World

More than likely, IQ scores would have ceased to interest us long ago if they did not somehow relate to performance in the real world. In the United States, people with higher IQ scores, particularly on the verbal subtests, earn higher grade point averages overall in high school and college (Cronbach, 1990; Jensen, 1980; Snow & Yalow, 1982). IQ also predicts job success to some extent (Cronbach, 1990; Wagner, 1997). People with higher IQs tend to land higher-prestige jobs and make more money; they are also more likely to enjoy stable marriages and to stay out of jail (Herrnstein & Murray, 1994). In fact, measures of intelligence taken at age 11 predict how old people will be when they die—and even whether they will succumb to heart disease or some forms of cancer (Deary et al., 2004).

Although IQ does, in fact, predict success on the job, this does not mean that everybody who is successful at work has a high IQ; nor are all people with high IQs necessarily successful. Correlations between IQ and job performance show that, at most, only about a quarter of the variation in job success can be predicted by IQ (Hunter, 1983; Jensen, 1980; Schmidt & Hunter, 2004; Streufert & Swezey, 1986). This means that the lion's share of that variation reflects something else. For example, the personality traits of conscientiousness and integrity also (in addition to IQ) predict success on the job (Schmidt & Hunter, 2004). Moreover, motivation, ambition, education, and other factors may figure into the mix (Lubinski, 2000, 2004), but such factors probably play less of a role than you might think (Gagné & St. Père, 2001). However, culture clearly plays a role. For example, Asian cultures, with their strong family bonds and emphasis on hard work, foster achievement (Stevenson et al., 1986), and IQ scores underpredict job success among Japanese and Chinese Americans (Flynn, 1991, 1999a, 1999b).

Achievement is only partly determined by intelligence; motivation is also important. Subcultures differ in the degree to which they value education, and thus the degree to which their members are strongly motivated to obtain education.

Analyzing Intelligence: One Ability or Many?

As we just noted, in the United States, a high IQ score predicts, to some degree, success in school and in life. To interpret these findings, we need to know more about what, precisely, IQ tests measure. Is there some general ability, some basic intelligence, that determines IQ score? And do IQ tests tap everything meant by "intelligence"?

Psychometric Approaches: IQ, g, and Specialized Abilities

How do researchers determine whether IQ scores reflect some basic, overall type of intelligence or a collection of various cognitive abilities, such as the ability to identify patterns or make use of previously learned information? Psychologists who have investigated this question have used a *psychometric approach*; they have designed tests to measure psychological characteristics and have devised ways to use correlations and other statistical techniques to analyze the results from such tests.

Spearman's g Factor. Today's IQ tests include a variety of subtests, such as the picture completion, vocabulary, block design, and arithmetic subtests included in the WAIS-III. It turns out that people who do well on one subtest tend to do well on others; that is, scores on these different types of tests are positively correlated (Deary, 2000; Gottfredson, 1997; Jensen, 1998). This finding has led researchers to infer that there is a single form of intelligence that cuts across the various subtests. Early in the last century, British psychologist Charles Spearman (1927) argued that the positive correlations among scores on different types of mental tests indicate the existence of a single underlying intellectual capacity, which he labeled **g**, for "general factor." Spearman developed a new statistical tool to analyze sets of test scores, called factor analysis. **Factor analysis** is a method that uncovers the particular attributes (factors) that make scores more or less similar. A factor analysis of the correlations among different measures of performance shows, for example, that speed of processing

g: "General factor," a single intellectual capacity that underlies the positive correlations among different tests of intelligence.

Factor analysis: A statistical method that uncovers the particular attributes (factors) that make scores more or less similar; the more similar the scores, the more strongly implicated are shared underlying factors.

is one important factor in many tasks, and the amount of information that can be held in working memory (see Chapter 5) is another. When he analyzed the correlations among various test scores, Spearman found that the first, and most important, factor underlying test performance was g. Subsequently, researchers have found that estimates of g taken from different sets of tests reflect the same underlying common ingredient; these separate estimates are almost perfectly correlated with each other (Johnson et al., 2004).

But if intelligence is simply g, then all of the scores from the different subtests should be correlated to the same degree. This is not the case: Spearman also noted a wide variation in the sizes of the correlations, which he took to reflect the influence of "specific factors," or s. When you perform a task, according to Spearman, you are drawing on g as well as on a particular type of ability, s, specific to that task. For example, spelling draws on a specialized ability, which is largely independent of other abilities. Some tasks, such as being able to analyze Shakespeare, rely more on g than on s; others, such as discriminating musical tones, rely more on a particular s than on g. Factor analysis documented the existence of these specific factors and also showed that they are less important than g for predicting performance. In Spearman's view, IQ scores depend mostly on g; how smart you are overall depends on how much of this general intellectual capacity you have.

Thurstone's Primary Mental Abilities.   A second perspective on what IQ scores reflect came from Louis L. Thurstone (1938). Thurstone devised a battery of 56 tests and then analyzed the correlations of scores on these tests using Spearman's method of factor analysis. Thurstone found that how well you can do arithmetic has little if anything to do with how well you can notice whether a scene has changed or how well you can figure out the best way to get home when traffic is heavy (Thurstone & Thurstone, 1941). Instead of believing in a single general capacity, such as g, Thurstone found evidence that intelligence consists of seven separate primary mental abilities, fundamental abilities that are the components of intelligence and that are not outgrowths of other abilities. Verbal comprehension and spatial visualization are two of Thurstone's primary mental abilities.

In the decades since Thurstone proposed his list of primary abilities, other researchers seeking to discover the facets of intelligence have analyzed and reanalyzed similar sets of test scores with varying results. Some (such as J. P. Guilford, 1967) have reported finding more than a hundred distinct factors that underlie intelligence.

Cattell and Horn's Fluid and Crystallized Intelligences.   One especially influential alternative to Thurstone's approach was proposed by Raymond B. Cattell (1971), and then developed further by his student and collaborator John Horn (1985, 1986, 1989, 1994; Horn & Cattell, 1966; Horn & Noll, 1997). These researchers suggested that instead of possessing a single general capacity, g, people possess two general types of intelligence: fluid and crystallized. Fluid intelligence is the ability to reason without relying heavily on previously learned knowledge or procedures ("a person's mental horsepower, the ability to solve cognitive problems on the spot"; Gottfredson, 2003a, p. 350). Fluid intelligence would be used to figure out novel solutions, such as how to write when a pen or pencil isn't available (one creative songsmith scribbled the lyrics to a new rock tune using the heads of burnt matches). Fluid intelligence can be measured with tests that do not rely on language, and thus some researchers have argued that it may reflect a fairer, less culturally bound measure of intelligence (Athanasiou, 2000; Braden, 2000). In contrast, crystallized intelligence relies on using previously learned information and procedures to reason [it is the "very general skills (e.g., language) that have been developed—crystallized—from exercising fluid g

s: "Specific factors," or aspects of performance that are particular to a given kind of processing—and distinct from g.

Primary mental abilities: According to Thurstone, seven fundamental abilities that are the components of intelligence and are not outgrowths of other abilities.

Fluid intelligence: According to Cattell and Horn, the kind of intelligence that underlies the creation of novel solutions to problems.

Crystallized intelligence: According to Cattell and Horn, the kind of intelligence that relies on knowing facts and having the ability to use and combine them.

in the past"; Gottfredson, 2003a, p. 350]. This is the sort of intelligence that develops as you become an expert in an area. If you make good use of your college experience, you should boost your crystallized intelligence.

A variety of factors affect fluid and crystallized intelligence differently. For example, as we age, crystallized intelligence does not suffer much, if at all, whereas fluid intelligence deteriorates; we are still able to maintain our expertise in areas of strength, but the ability to shift gears quickly to solve new problems tends to decrease (Horn, 1985, 1986, 1994; Horn & Noll, 1994; Salthouse, 1996). In addition, the two forms of intelligence develop at different rates during childhood, appear to rely on different brain structures, and are not equally heritable (Horn & Masunaga, 2000; Horn & Noll, 1997); also, different facets of academic achievement are predicted by the two forms of intelligence (Evans et al., 2002). These sorts of findings provide evidence that the two types of intelligence are, in fact, distinct; if there were only a single form of intelligence, such factors should show the same effects on the two proposed sets of abilities. After the discovery of crystallized and fluid intelligences, Cattell and Horn provided evidence for a number of other "broad" factors (Jensen, 1998). Key characteristics of fluid and crystallized intelligences are summarized in Table 6.3.

For the veteran angler, fishing consists of well-worn routines (such as putting the bait on the hook, casting the line in the water, knowing when to yank and when to wait, reeling in the fish, and so on), and thus it relies on crystallized intelligence. But what would happen if you didn't have bait, a hook, line, and sinker? You would need fluid intelligence to figure out how to catch fish.

Table 6.3 Fluid Versus Crystallized Intelligence

Fluid Intelligence	Crystallized Intelligence
Ability to reason about novel situations and to solve novel problems	Ability to reason using previously learned procedures
Ability to abstract concepts on the basis of new information or procedures	Ability to use factual knowledge acquired through education and experience
Ability to use reasoning that does not depend primarily on learning and acculturation	Ability to use reasoning that is based on learning and acculturation
Ability to manipulate abstract concepts, rules, and generalizations and to use logical relations	Ability to use language to communicate

Carroll's Three-Stratum Theory of Cognitive Ability. John B. Carroll produced a landmark book in 1993, in which he reanalyzed massive amounts of test data (from over 450 high-quality studies). He found that the relations among test scores are neatly structured into a three-tiered hierarchy (of the sort developed earlier by Gustafsson, 1984). At the top of the hierarchy is g, and immediately under it are eight broad cognitive abilities (which include fluid and crystallized intelligences). Each of these broad abilities is infused with g, and each of the broad abilities is, in turn, drawn on by several narrow abilities.

We must stress that explaining performance in any specific task requires citing factors in all three tiers. For example, Deary (2000, drawing on the work of Carroll, 1993) discusses the ability to produce ideas. A test of this ability might require you to name as many red things as possible in a few minutes. To understand why different classmates name different numbers of red objects (that is, to understand the variation in performance), you would need to understand the roles of *g* (which has been shown to account for about half the variation in performance in this task), of the broad factor of general retrieval ability, and of the narrow factor of ideational fluency (which is specific to this simple task).

The hierarchical structure of intelligence in Carroll's *three-stratum theory* is a grand synthesis of the earlier theories, fitting them all into a single framework. For example, this structure allows us to understand fluid and crystallized intelligences by noting that they are somewhat—but not entirely—distinct. Because they have unique aspects, factors such as aging can affect them differently; but because they also both draw on *g*, they are highly correlated. Many subsequent studies have supported Carroll's theory (Deary, 2000). However, two areas of debate persist. (1) Horn and his colleagues continue to maintain that fluid and crystallized intelligences sit at the top of the hierarchy, not a single *g*, as Carroll maintains. (2) Lubinski (2004), Snow (1994, 1996), and others have argued that the broad cognitive abilities of the middle tier can be specified in fewer categories, namely, quantitative, spatial, and verbal abilities.

Emotional Intelligence: Knowing Feelings

Another approach to understanding what makes us smart posits additional sorts of intelligence, which are not tapped by the standard tests. Let's consider one example of another sort of intelligence—emotional intelligence.

Have you ever seen someone you *know* is smart do something incredibly dumb—for instance, unintentionally or uncontrollably make a remark that infuriates a friend or boss? Salovey and Mayer (1990) believe that whether you act intelligently often depends in large part on how well you understand both your own emotions and the effects your actions have on others. Salovey and Mayer refer to the ability to understand and regulate emotions effectively as **emotional intelligence (EI)**.

EI has two major facets. One facet involves intelligence, as usually defined. This facet of EI is typically defined as having the four "branches" listed in Table 6.4, which are thought to form a hierarchy, with managing emotions being the most general dimension and perceiving emotions being the most specific. The tests for this facet of EI rely on asking test-takers to make objective decisions about emotion-laden situations, and the decisions are scored as right or wrong (Mayer et al., 2000, 2001a, 2001b, 2003).

The other facet of EI involves subjective experiences and inclinations. The tests for this facet of EI require test-takers to rate themselves subjectively regarding relevant characteristics, such as their degree of assertiveness, empathy, tolerance for stress, and optimism (Bar-On et al., 2000). A meta-analysis revealed that the objective measures of EI are more highly correlated with *g* (but nevertheless share only about 10% of the variation in performance with it) than the subjective measures (which are almost entirely distinct from *g*); the subjective measures are more highly correlated with measures of personality (Van Rooy et al., 2005b).

In recent years, EI has been the subject of intense research interest (Bar-On & Parker, 2000; Ciarrochi et al., 2001; Matthews et al., 2002; Roberts et al., 2001), and researchers are reporting many intriguing findings. For example, women tend to score higher than men on some dimensions of EI (Carrothers et al., 2000; Van Rooy et al., 2005a), particularly those that relate to social skills (Petrides & Furnham, 2000). Nevertheless, men may (falsely) believe that they have higher EI than women do (Petrides & Furnham, 2000). In addition, members of minority groups tend to score higher than Whites, and older people tend to score higher than college students (Van Rooy et al., 2005a). Moreover, people

Emotional intelligence (EI): The ability to understand and regulate emotions effectively.

Table 6.4 The Four-Branch Model of Emotional Intelligence

The four branches of emotional intelligence are ordered here from least to most general.

Branch	Description	Example
1. Perceiving emotion	Ability to identify emotions on the basis of perceptual cues	Noticing a slight frown when a friend hears someone's name, and realizing that it signals jealousy
2. Facilitating thought with emotion	Ability to harness emotional information to enhance thinking	Thinking through a planned comment to your friend, and changing the plan to avoid an anticipated rocky outcome
3. Understanding emotion	Ability to comprehend emotional information about relationships, transitions from one emotion to another, and verbal information about emotion	Understanding that your friend is jealous of someone else because of your previous relationship with that person
4. Managing emotion	Ability to manage emotions and emotional relationships	Noticing that you are becoming annoyed at your friend, and being able to take a deep breath, count to 10, and then respond calmly

who can more accurately read variations in other people's moods tend to be better adjusted socially (Engelberg & Sjöberg, 2004).

Although the subjective measures of EI appear, in part, to assess aspects of personality (Dawda & Hart, 2000), these tests can make predictions above and beyond what is possible with personality tests (Petrides & Furnham, 2003; Van Rooy et al., 2005b). Recent objective tests of EI also explain behavior that is not explained by measures of personality or of verbal or fluid intelligence (Lopes et al., 2003; Lopes et al., 2005). The newest such test provides separate scores for each of the four dimensions summarized in Table 6.4.

In short, this is an exciting and promising area of research, but it is still in its infancy. The research results have not yet charted the utility and limits of EI for understanding human behavior.

Multiple Intelligences: More Than One Way to Shine?

Instead of trying to add another form of intelligence to the standard sort, some researchers have proposed sets of multiple intelligences. Although controversial, these alternative perspectives have proven attractive to many, particularly to those who work in education. Let's briefly consider the two most influential of these theories.

Gardner's Theory of Multiple Intelligences: Something for Everyone. Howard Gardner (1983/1993b, 1995, 1999) developed a novel view of intelligence, called the **theory of multiple intelligences**, which holds that there are eight distinct forms of intelligence and another, tentative, form, as summarized in Table 6.5 (on page 262).

By far the best support for Gardner's theory comes from the very findings and phenomena that inspired it in the first place. Specifically, Gardner reflected on the fact that brain damage often results in the loss of a certain ability while

Theory of multiple intelligences: Gardner's theory of eight distinct forms of intelligence, which can vary separately for a given individual.

Table 6.5 Gardner's Multiple Intelligences

Form of Intelligence	Definition	Examples of Professions in Which the Form Is Important
Linguistic	The ability to use language well	Journalism, law
Spatial	The ability to reason well about spatial relations	Architecture, surgery
Musical	The ability to compose and understand music	Audio engineering, music
Logical-Mathematical	The ability to manipulate abstract symbols	Science, computer programming
Bodily-Kinesthetic	The ability to plan and understand sequences of movements	Dance, athletics
Intrapersonal	The ability to understand yourself	Ministry
Interpersonal	The ability to understand other people and social interactions	Politics, teaching
Naturalist	The ability to observe aspects of the natural environment carefully	Forest conservation
Existential (tentative; Gardner, 1999)	The ability to address "the big questions" about existence	Philosophy

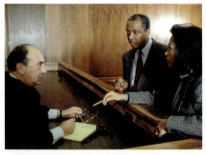

Linguistic intelligence is the ability to use language well, as relied on by journalists and lawyers.

Spatial intelligence is the ability to reason well about spatial relations, as relied on by architects and surgeons.

leaving others relatively intact. For example, language can be disrupted but the patient can still sing, or vice versa; mathematical ability can be disrupted but the patient can still speak, or vice versa; social skills can be disrupted while ordinary reasoning is unimpaired, or vice versa. Gardner reasoned that if abilities can be disrupted independently, then they arise from distinct brain systems—and hence reflect specific types of intelligence. In addition, he considered other kinds of data. He noted, for example, that although everybody learns their first language in a few years, very few people master complex mathematics so easily. If two abilities develop at different rates during childhood, he reasoned, they must rely on different underlying processes. He also observed that some abilities, such as music and mathematics, can be extraordinarily well developed in child prodigies, whereas these same children perform at average levels in other areas. This coexistence of the extraordinary and the ordinary, Gardner believes, suggests that some intellectual capacities, such as those related to music and mathematics, may be psychologically distinct from others.

According to Gardner, most professions require combinations of different types of intelligence; to be a novelist, for example, you need linguistic, intrapersonal, and interpersonal intelligence—but you don't need bodily-kinesthetic intelligence. Each person can be characterized by a *profile of intelligences*, with some types of intelligence being relatively strong and others relatively weak (Connell et al., 2003; Walters & Gardner, 1985).

As appealing as Gardner's theory of multiple intelligences is to many, it has not been embraced by many researchers in the field. One severe problem is that neither Gardner nor anyone else has developed a way to measure all of the separate intelligences, which makes the theory impossible to test rigorously (Hunt, 2001); however, people can rate themselves and others on each type of intelligence, which is a first step (Furnham et al., 2002). Another problem is perhaps even more fundamental: Some question whether the word *intelligence* should be applied so liberally; many of Gardner's types, they say, have more to do with talents and skills than with intelligence as most of us understand the concept.

Sternberg's Analytic, Practical, and Creative Intelligences. Robert Sternberg (1985, 1988b) has also developed a theory of multiple intelligences, which he calls the *Triarchic Theory of Successful Intelligence*. According to this theory, there are three types of intelligence: analytic, practical, and creative.

1. *Analytic intelligence*, the ability to learn to write clearly, do math, and understand literature, is critical for academic performance. Einstein had a high level of this analytic intelligence. Knowing about the distinctions among different cognitive abilities in Carroll's three-stratum theory, you might wonder whether this category is too broad.

2. *Practical intelligence* involves knowing how to do such things as fix a car or sew on a button, and it sometimes relies on implicit memories, learned responses and skills that guide our actions without our being aware of them (see Chapter 5); "street smarts" are a form of practical intelligence. Again, you might ask whether this type of intelligence is too broadly defined.

3. *Creative intelligence*, which seems closely related to Cattell and Horn's fluid intelligence, is the ability to formulate novel solutions to problems.

How do these three types of intelligence relate to IQ? Analytic intelligence is what IQ tests measure. However, according to Sternberg and his colleagues (Sternberg & Wagner, 1993; Sternberg et al., 1993, 2001), measures of practical intelligence are better predictors of how well someone will do on the job than are standard measures of IQ, and practical intelligence is largely distinct from analytic intelligence. But these claims have proven highly controversial: Other researchers have found that IQ predicts on-the-job performance better than measures of practical intelligence do (Kuncel et al., 2004). In fact, some experts argue that even Sternberg's own data provide only weak support, if any, for his theory (Brody, 2003a, 2003b; Gottfredson, 2003a, 2003b); however, Sternberg (2003a, 2003b) maintains his views in the face of this criticism. Finally, although creative intelligence is distinct from IQ, people do need a certain level of IQ to be able to find creative solutions to problems or to create novel products that have specific uses (Guilford, 1967; Runco & Albert, 1986; Sternberg, 1985).

Table 6.6 (on p. 264) summarizes six prominent views about the nature of intelligence.

LOOKING BACK: *Review*

1. *What is IQ?* IQ (intelligence quotient) is a score on an intelligence test. IQ originally was a comparison of mental age to chronological age, but now IQ scores relate individual performance to a norm. The most common tests, the Wechsler Adult Intelligence Scale (WAIS) and the Wechsler Intelligence Scale for Children (WISC), consist of two main parts, one that assesses verbal performance and one that assesses nonverbal performance. The scores are normed so that 100 is the mean, and each standard deviation is 15 points.

2. *Is intelligence a single characteristic or a complex set of characteristics?* Intelligence has many facets. Although intelligence probably involves, as Spearman theorized, a single general intellectual ability (symbolized as *g*), virtually all theorists agree that it also includes many specialized abilities. These abilities may be strong or weak, independently of *g*. Thurstone, for example, proposed that intelligence consists of seven

Table 6.6 The Nature of Intelligence: Six Views

Theorist	Key Ideas
Spearman (1927)	• *g* (generalized ability, contributes to all intellectual activities) • *s* (specialized abilities, such as spelling or distinguishing among tones) • IQ mostly reflects *g*.
Thurstone and Thurstone (1941)	• Seven primary mental abilities, such as verbal comprehension and spatial visualization • No *g*
Cattell (1971) and Horn (1985, 1986, 1989)	• Fluid intelligence (producing novel solutions to problems, such as by using burnt match heads to write) • Crystallized intelligence (using previously acquired knowledge appropriately, such as when doing arithmetic)
Gardner (1983/1993b, 1999)	• At least eight multiple intelligences (including such nontraditional forms as bodily-kinesthetic and interpersonal intelligences) • Based on a wide variety of types of data (such as effects of brain damage, and areas in which child prodigies excel)
Sternberg (1985, 1988b)	• Analytic intelligence (the kind of reasoning relied upon in academic studies) • Practical intelligence (the kind of reasoning used to solve everyday, real-world problems) • Creative intelligence (the kind of reasoning needed to invent new things or to solve problems in new ways)
Carroll (1993)	• Three-stratum theory • *g* at the top, 8 broad abilities (including fluid and crystallized intelligences) in the middle tier, and 69 specific abilities (such as ideational fluency) at the bottom

primary mental abilities. Cattell and Horn initially theorized that instead of one general capacity, g, people possess two types of intelligence—crystallized and fluid—and then later expanded this list to include abilities like those identified by Thurstone. Carroll derived aspects of intelligence that are arranged in three levels, with g at the top, 8 broad abilities in the middle, and 69 specific abilities at the bottom. Gardner, in his theory of multiple intelligences, suggests at least eight basic forms of intelligence ranging from linguistic, to logical-mathematical, to interpersonal. According to Sternberg, the different types of intelligence boil down to three: analytic, practical, and creative. Finally, emotional intelligence may affect the operation of all other types.

● LOOKING BEYOND: *Critical Thinking*

For what purposes does it make sense to have only a single overall IQ score? For what purposes might it be better to have separate scores for the subtests? Can you think of ways in which making all high school students take an IQ test would be potentially harmful? Potentially helpful?

If you were designing the ideal school, how would you organize it so that different forms of intelligence were properly nurtured? Can you imagine teaching methods that would allow students to use their specific cognitive strengths to learn any subject matter? Do you think such methods are theoretically possible?

What Makes Us Smart?
Nature and Nurture

Albert Einstein was born on Friday, March 14, 1879. Was his brilliance evident at birth? Hardly. He had a misshapen head and odd physical proportions, which greatly distressed his family. (Fortunately, a few weeks after birth, the shape of his head approached normal, and he no longer looked so strange.) And he wasn't born into an extraordinarily gifted family. His father, Hermann, was not a successful businessman and spent much of his time trying to keep the family financially afloat. But Einstein's family did influence him in major ways. For example, the independence of mind he exhibited so often as an adult may have been a result of his parents' encouraging him to be independent, to the point of allowing him to cross streets alone when he was only 4 years old (Brian, 1996). Moreover, Uncle Jakob excited young Albert about math, for example, by couching algebra problems in terms of a hunt for an animal called X, which they could name after it was bagged.

Thus, various influences were at work in young Einstein's life. He was not the child of geniuses, but did have the good fortune to have intelligent, caring parents. He was not coddled, but was stimulated with interesting ideas and encouraged to fend for himself. How do such varied and multifaceted influences affect intelligence?

LOOKING AHEAD: Learning Objectives

1. *How do environment and genetics contribute to intelligence?*
2. *How can we interpret group differences in IQ?*
3. *What are the extremes of intelligence, high and low?*

Smart Genes, Smart Environment:
A Single System

Intelligence must be related—in one way or the other—to the way the brain functions; it is the brain, after all, not the kidney or the big toe, that underlies reasoning and learning. But there's no reason to think that intelligence *must* be related to the genes. Could Einstein have had a certain level of *g*, and high levels of some specific abilities but not others, because of the genetic deck of cards he was dealt by his parents? Or were his *g* and specific abilities mostly (or entirely) a result of his particular experiences?

Genetic Effects: How Important Are Genes for Intelligence?

Because intelligence has many facets, we would not expect it to be determined by a single gene, or even a small number of genes. And, in fact, researchers have had trouble identifying individual genes that are related to *g* (Hill et al., 1999, 2002; Plomin & Spinath, 2004). Studies (for instance, Fisher et al., 1999) have shown that multiple genes contribute to intelligence and do so in different ways. For example, a portion of DNA has been found to be associated with one type of spatial ability (Berman & Noble, 1995) but not with g (Petrill, Plomin, et al., 1997), and two different genes have been shown to predict performance aspects (but not verbal aspects) of IQ (Tsai et al., 2002, 2004).

Shared Genes Versus Shared Environment: What Predicts IQ?   How can we begin to sort out the relative contributions to intelligence of the genetic component and of other factors? How strong is the genetic influence? The most common method of assessing the contribution of genes to a characteristic is to observe correlations of that characteristic among people who share different proportions of their genes (see Chapter 2).

One way that researchers have tried to sort out the effects of genes versus environment is through *adoption studies*. In these studies, the scores of adopted children are compared to those of their adoptive and their biological relatives. In some of these studies (for example, Bouchard et al., 1990), tests are given to twins who were separated soon after birth and adopted into different families. Because these twins were reared in different homes, any similarities between them are thought to reflect their common genetics. What do adoption studies find? The correlation of IQs for adult identical twins who were raised apart is higher than both that for fraternal twins and that for nontwin siblings raised together (Bouchard & McGue, 1981; Bouchard et al., 1990; Plomin, 1990). In addition, an adopted child's IQ correlates higher with the biological mother's IQ than with the adoptive mother's IQ. Moreover, although the IQs of an adopted child and the biological children in a family are positively correlated, by the time the children grow up, virtually no correlation remains (Plomin, 1990; Plomin, Fulker, et al., 1997; Scarr & Weinberg, 1983). These findings provide clear evidence that genes affect IQ.

Other studies have tried to find out exactly how large a role genes play in determining IQ by comparing IQs of people with different numbers of genes in common. The results clearly show that the more genes in common, the higher the correlations. The usual estimate is that the heritability of IQ is around .50, which means that about half the variation in IQ can be attributed to heredity (Chipuer et al., 1990; Loehlin, 1989). (Heritability estimates indicate what proportion of observed variability in a characteristic within a population is caused by inherited factors [Bell, 1977; Lush, 1937]; see Chapter 2 for further discussion of heritability.) Keep in mind that heritability estimates have no bearing on how much of *your* personal intelligence is the result of your genes. A number that denotes heritability refers to the proportion of variation within a population, not to the proportion of the characteristic that is inherited by an individual.

Brain Similarities, Genetics, and Intelligence.   Researchers have begun combining twin studies with neuroimaging studies to discover whether the sizes of specific brain areas are under genetic control (Gray & Thompson, 2004). Thompson and colleagues (2001) found that the amount of gray matter (neurons' cell bodies) in various portions of the frontal lobes and in rear portions of the left temporal lobe (which play crucial roles in language comprehension) is substantially more similar in identical twins than in fraternal twins—the hallmark of high heritability. In addition, the IQ scores of the twins were highly correlated with the amount of gray matter in the frontal lobes. Note, however, that the amount of gray matter need not be the *cause* of intelligence: Both the amount of gray matter and the IQ scores could *result* from other factors. For example, genes that affect the efficiency of neural transmission could also have contributed to the amount of gray matter. Or perhaps some twins tend to be peppy and others lethargic, which leads them to engage in more or less stimulating activities—and these activities cause neuron growth in key brain areas (Chapter 2) and increase IQ. (In fact, 3-year-olds who tend to seek out stimulation score higher on IQ tests at age 11 [Raine et al., 2002], and the personality trait known as openness to experience is correlated with intelligence [McCrae & Costa, 1997a].) Such differences in temperament could themselves be genetically determined or could depend on the environment. The environment and genes engage in an intimate and intricate dance, as we consider in more detail next.

Environmental Effects: More Real Than Apparent?

It is clear that the environment affects intelligence as assessed by IQ. The observed relationship between IQ and achievement, noted earlier, can also act in the opposite direction: People who achieve more can develop higher IQ scores (for example, see Kohn & Schooler, 1973; Neisser et al., 1996). Perhaps the best evidence for this comes from studies of the effects of formal schooling. For example, when poor black children moved from the rural South to Philadelphia in the 1940s, their IQs increased by a bit more than half a point for each year they spent in their new schools (Cahan & Cohen, 1989; Ceci, 1991; Ceci & Williams, 1997; Lee, 1951).

Consider some factors that make it difficult to interpret heritability estimates based on studies of twins and relatives.

Shared Prenatal Environment: On Being Wombmates. Twins share much the same environment in the womb before birth and are subject to most of the same pluses and minuses of that residence. The fetus suffers when the mother has a bad diet, takes drugs or alcohol, smokes, or experiences a great deal of stress; the fetus profits when the mother eats well, takes vitamins, and doesn't drink, smoke, or take drugs. Aspects of this common environment affect later IQ (Devlin et al., 1997; Jacobs et al., 2001), and they are shared even by identical twins separated at birth and raised apart (Phelps et al., 1997). In addition, about two thirds of identical twins share the same placenta and amniotic sac in the uterus (Phelps et al., 1997; see Figure 6.11). At first glance, you might think that sharing the same placenta and amniotic sac would make the twins more similar, but the opposite turns out to be true: These twins compete for resources; one identical twin will be in the favored position and will obtain more of the nutrients—and whatever else is in the mother's blood—than the other. Thus, these identical twins have larger disparities in weight and length at birth than do fraternal twins, and their early environment may make them less similar than their genes would dictate.

Figure 6.11 Fraternal and Identical Twins

Twins can have separate placentas and separate amniotic sacs or can share a single placenta and sac; sharing results in greater environmental similarity prior to birth. Virtually all fraternal twins are in separate sacs (left), whereas about two thirds of identical twins are in the same sac (right).

In short, it is difficult to know how the shared prenatal environment experienced by identical twins versus that experienced by fraternal twins affects the magnitude of the correlations between their IQs.

Adoptive Households. It is not clear just how different the early environmental influences on twins raised in different homes really are. Families that seek to adopt a child share many characteristics, and these similarities are further enhanced by the fact that adoption agencies frown on placing children in deprived conditions. The households in which separated twins are placed are thus often fairly similar. When Stoolmiller (1999) mathematically corrected for the small variations among adopting families, he estimated the effects of environment on IQ to be 57%. It is not clear, however, whether this estimate applies only to the special case of twins raised apart or can be taken as a general estimate.

Microenvironments: Here, There, Everywhere.

A person's genes can help shape aspects of his or her environment. The **microenvironment** is the environment you create by your very presence. For one thing, identical twins may have more aspects of their environments in common than fraternal twins because much of the environment includes social interactions, and people respond to us in part because of the way we look and behave. So if both twins are physically appealing, they will be treated very differently than if both are homely, and ditto for twins who are sluggish and overweight versus athletic and trim. Also, to the extent that children have similar inborn tendencies, their behavior may shape their environments in similar ways. For example, children who enjoy being read to will reinforce adults for this activity, leading the adults to buy or borrow more books—thereby providing more opportunity for stimulating interactions.

In addition, depending on their personalities, people select aspects of the environment that appeal to them (perhaps, initially, for genetic reasons), and thus what appear to be different environments may in fact function pretty much the same for two people with similar inclinations. For example, two homes may differ in the number of books they contain, but a child who likes to read may seize on whatever is available and end up reading as much in a home with fewer books as a child who lives in a home with many books. In short, identical twins share many characteristics that define their microenvironments, and so they live in more similar microenvironments than do other siblings. Even twins separated at birth may create similar microenvironments, and so it is not clear exactly how different the environmental influences on these twins are.

 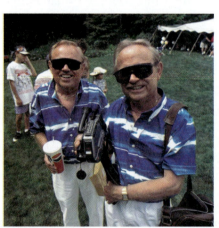

We create a part of our environments simply by the way we look and act, which influences how others treat us. This *microenvironment* is similar for twins, and their shared characteristics may, in part, reflect common aspects of their microenvironment, not the direct effects of the genes.

Perceived Reality: It's What's Inside That Counts.

Researchers have also observed that only about a quarter or a third of the variability in *g* can be explained by shared environment, or aspects of the family setting that are present for all siblings in a household, such as the number of books in the house (Plomin, Fulker, et al., 1997). If genes account for about half the variability in intelligence and shared environment for less than half of what remains, what accounts for the rest? Some aspects of the environment don't have the same effect on all children growing up in the household; the same event can be a very different experience for different people. Watching TV can be the mindless pastime of a couch potato, or it can be made into a stimulating experience by a child with an active imagination. Even when the environment of two siblings appears to be identical, its influence depends in part on each child's predispositions and inclinations, which may be partly innate (Kagan, 1989b; Turkheimer & Waldron, 2000). A shy child, for example, will be pleased to be left alone to find solitary amusements; but the same treatment would be a punishment for an outgoing, gregarious child. The *perceived* environment, not the objective environment, is the important one.

Microenvironment: The environment created by a person's own presence, which depends partly on appearance and behavior.

Selecting the Environment. In general, a shared family environment produces positive correlations among the IQ scores of all children who grow up in the same house, but these effects wear off by adulthood, and genetic influences become increasingly evident with age (McCartney et al., 1990; McGue et al., 1993; Plomin, 1990). Why? One theory is that, as people age, they are increasingly able to select their environments, and genetically determined properties, such as temperament, lead people to select certain environments over others. For example, if you are temperamentally shy, you will not take a job in sales; if you are outgoing, you might enjoy managing a hotel. Thus, as you grow older and have more choices about how to live, the effects of your environment are increasingly related to the effects of genes (Neisser et al., 1996). This does not mean, however, that the environment is not playing a crucial role in helping you function well (Cleveland et al., 2000).

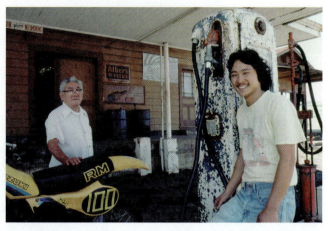

Our genes determine the range within which the environment can mold us. For example, Japanese youth are typically much taller than their parents. Why? Same genes, but different environment (especially nutrition)—which led the genes to operate differently. Similarly, genes for intelligence define a range of possible intelligences, and an individual's intelligence level embodies just one instance from the range of possibilities offered by the genes.

Group Differences in Intelligence

How would you feel if you were told that you are a member of a group that is genetically stupid? Many groups have faced such labeling, often with far-reaching consequences. The Immigration Act of 1924 aimed to minimize immigration to the United States of "biologically weak stocks," a term that was defined to include Italians and Jews of southern and eastern Europe. During congressional testimony, supporters of the bill pointed to the results of intelligence tests, on which recent immigrants scored less well than established Americans with northern European roots. There is debate about the extent to which this testimony mattered (Snyderman & Herrnstein, 1983), but no debate over the catastrophic effects of this bill less than 20 years later, during World War II, when Jews attempting to escape Nazi Germany were severely restricted from immigrating to the United States.

Contemporary studies comparing IQ scores find that some groups have lower average scores than others; for example, Jews of European descent in Israel score about 15 points higher than Jews of North African descent. What do such findings mean?

Within-Group Versus Between-Group Differences

If, as most experts have concluded, about 50% of the differences in IQ can be accounted for by differences in genes, is it reasonable to say that differences in IQ scores between groups are largely genetic? Absolutely not. The genetic contribution to intelligence *within* a given group cannot say anything about possible genetic differences *between* groups (Block, 1995; Lewontin, 1976a, 1976b; Plomin, 1988). To see why not, imagine that you have two orchards with the same kind of apple trees. You make sure that each orchard receives exactly the same amounts of sunlight, fertilizer, water, and so on. If you succeed in making the environments identical, then any differences in the sizes of apples from the two orchards should reflect genetic differences among the trees. However, say the two orchards have overall different conditions, that one gets more sunshine and water than the other (see Figure 6.12). *Within* each orchard, differences in the sizes of the

Figure 6.12 Within-Group Differences Do Not Explain Between-Group Differences

The state of an organism is a result of interactions between genes and environment. The two groups of trees could have the same genes, but differences in the environment cause the genes to produce different characteristics. Differences among trees in the *same* environment may reflect differences in genes, but this says nothing about differences among trees in different environments.

apples would reflect genetic differences (assuming that the environment is exactly the same throughout the orchard). But those differences say nothing about the differences *between* the orchards. The disadvantaged environment puts the trees in one orchard in a generally lower part of the range of possibilities due to the genes than those benefiting from the advantaged environment in the other orchard. It is even possible that the differences within the "advantaged" orchard reflect the operation of one set of genes, whereas the differences within the "disadvantaged" orchard reflect the operation of another set that allows the trees to make the most of skimpy amounts of sunshine or water. No question about it: Differences within one group cannot be used to explain differences between groups or within another group.

Researchers have shown that this analogy is not simply theoretical. For example, Eric Turkheimer and colleagues (2003) compared the IQs of identical and fraternal twins from both affluent and impoverished backgrounds. They found that genetics accounted for the bulk of the variations in IQ of the affluent twins (with a heritability of 72%), and that the shared environment accounted for little variation (15%). In striking contrast, the story was exactly the reverse for the impoverished twins: In this group, the shared environment accounted for the bulk of the variations in IQ (58%), and heritability accounted for little variation (10%)! This result is clear evidence that the environment plays a more important role in affecting IQ scores for impoverished children than do the genes—which makes perfect sense if we think of each pair of twins as a mini-orchard, getting different amounts of sun and water.

When you see an apple, all you have to go on is its present size, which reflects the actions of genes in a specific environment. You have no way of knowing the range of possible sizes for that type of apple. Further, heritability only tells you about the effects of genes in a *certain environment*; it says nothing about their possible effects in *other environments* (Hirsch, 1971, 1997).

Race Differences

When you see an apple, you know that it's not a tomato or an orange. But when you see a person, you cannot classify his or her race so easily. As Charles Darwin long ago pointed out, the races meld seamlessly into one another, and the very concept of race is difficult to define. In fact, some researchers believe that this concept is a social invention, not a biological reality. Today, the idea that different races exist is highly controversial; this controversy is addressed, for example, in the pages of a special issue of the journal the *American Psychologist*, edited by Anderson and Nickerson (2005).

Nevertheless, many researchers have grouped people into different races, using various criteria (including simple self-identification), and differences among these groups have been documented—and now must be explained. Here we consider some key differences and explanations.

To begin, researchers have repeatedly shown that Asian Americans tend to score higher on IQ tests than do White Americans, who in turn tend to score higher than Black Americans (Neisser et al., 1996; Rushton, 1995; Suzuki & Valencia, 1997); Hispanic Americans tend to score between White and Black Americans. For decades, the relatively low IQ scores of Black Americans have attracted attention, and controversy has flared over the claim that their scores, and their poorer achievement, are rooted in their genes. A firestorm of debate raged when Richard Herrnstein and Charles Murray (1994) published *The Bell Curve*, in which they argued that IQ not only predicts many aspects of life and performance, but also that differences in IQ are largely genetic. However, as discussed earlier, it's not easy to disentangle effects of the environment (particularly the microenvironment) and the genes. Although we focus on White and Black Americans in the following discussion, as has most of the research literature, keep in mind that the same issues also apply to all groups that generally score relatively poorly on IQ tests.

What do we make of the finding that the average IQ score of White Americans is 10 to 15 points higher than the average among Black Americans? Does this gap necessarily imply genetic differences? Before leaping to that conclusion, we must consider numerous other accounts (Block, 1995; Nisbett, 1996).

Test Bias?   Some have argued that the disparity in test scores simply reflects the fact that the tests were designed for a White middle-class culture and thus are biased against Black Americans, who have a different set of common experiences. This sort of ==test bias==, features of test items or design that are not appropriate for all members of the population, could apply to the verbal and general information parts of the IQ test, but what about the performance parts? The race difference in IQ scores is present even here. So a simple "biased testing" explanation is probably not correct (Glutting et al., 2000; Neisser et al., 1996; Sackett et al., 2001).

Test Anxiety?   Taking IQ tests isn't simply a matter of flexing your intellectual muscles. As you no doubt know from experience, taking a test of any kind, whether an achievement test (such as the SAT) or a midterm exam or an IQ test, can be anxiety provoking. Test stress may manifest itself in distinct physical symptoms, such as a speeded-up heart rate and sweaty palms. And as you feel literally "put to the test," your thinking may become clouded by a variety of distracting thoughts. Thus, factors unrelated to intelligence may affect IQ scores and other test scores.

Test bias: Features of test items or design that lead a particular group to perform well or poorly and that thus invalidate the test.

African children who are accustomed to using wire to make their own playthings, such as this toy car, are more adept at using wire models in pattern reproduction tests.

It is also possible that people with different backgrounds are more or less comfortable taking various sorts of tests. Indeed, Serpell (1979) found that Zambian children could reproduce patterns better using wire models (which they often used to make their own toys) than using pencil and paper, but the opposite was true for English children from the same social class (who were used to pencil and paper but not to wire models).

Bad Environments?   Others have argued that the observed IQ difference between White and Black Americans is caused by environmental differences. The people who are best off in U.S. society tend to score higher on IQ tests, and so do their children. Black Americans typically make less money than do Whites, and this factor could cause environmental differences that lead them to score lower than Whites. Some orchards get less sun and water than others, and thus the trees tend to bear smaller fruit. Flynn (1999b) points out that IQ differences between White and Black Americans can be accounted for if "the average environment for [Blacks] of 1995 matches the quality of the average environment for Whites in 1945" (p. 15).

Inferior Schooling?   Another possibility is that Black Americans tend to have inferior schooling. Fryer and Levitt (2004) found that there is no difference in intelligence among Black and White children when they begin kindergarten (provided that certain variables are controlled, such as age, birth weight, and number of children's books in the home). However, after 2 years of school, Blacks score notably worse than Whites. Fryer and Levitt considered a number of possible explanations for this finding, but only one received any support: Blacks tend to attend lower quality schools than do Whites.

The possibility that Blacks attend inferior schools might help to explain Lynn's (1998) report that the difference in Black and White intelligence scores had not changed over the years 1972–1996. Lynn assessed intelligence by looking at scores on a 10-item vocabulary test, and Blacks consistently fared worse than Whites. However, Fagan and Holland (2002) showed that Blacks do just as well as Whites on vocabulary tests *provided that they've had the opportunity to learn the words*. These researchers argue that Blacks simply haven't had "equal opportunity" to learn many of the words that are typically on vocabulary tests—which is consistent with the hypothesis that they tend to attend inferior schools.

Nevertheless, the quality of schools is probably not the whole story. For example, one study found that parents on welfare talk to their children less than working-class and professional parents do—and when welfare parents do talk to their children, they use a smaller vocabulary (Hart & Risley, 1995/2002). Most of the welfare parents in this study were Black. However, as intriguing as these sorts of findings are, they cannot explain why Black children adopted into White families have lower IQ scores by the time they reach adolescence than do their White siblings (Scarr & Weinberg, 1983). These Black and White children attended the same schools, and so schooling alone—or family environment alone—cannot explain the difference in their scores.

Effects of the Microenvironment?   Some have argued that the microenvironment plays a key role in IQ score differences. Black Americans have darker skin, which is part of their microenvironment; in the United States, this cue may elicit some kinds of negative treatment from the White majority. What would happen in a society in which the majority did not respond this way? Consider this example: Eyferth (1961) studied the IQs of German children who were fathered by White or Black American servicemen right after World War II. If the Black American fathers had lower IQs than the White fathers, which is not known but is likely given the group averages, and if this difference is due to genes, then the children of the Black soldiers should have had a lower average IQ. But they didn't. Both groups of children had the same average IQs. At that time, there were very few Blacks in Germany, and the majority Whites may not have had negative stereotypes about them. Thus, the children may not have experienced negative environmental influences because of their racial background.

Finally, whatever the explanation of the observed group differences in IQ scores may turn out to be, it is crucial to realize that the distributions of scores between races overlap; plenty of Black Americans have higher IQs than plenty of Whites. Group differences do not necessarily apply to any particular individual.

Sex Differences

Group differences in intelligence are often considered only in the context of race differences, but consider another possible group difference that would affect fully half the population. Are there sex differences in IQ scores? Although some findings may suggest very small sex differences in IQ (Dai & Lynn, 1994; Held et al., 1993; Lynn & Irwing, 2004), these effects are not always found (Aluja-Fabregat et al., 2000; Jensen, 1998). Instead, researchers typically find that males are better at some tasks than are females, and vice versa (McGillicuddy-De Lisi & De Lisi, 2002). In general, males tend to be better than females at tasks that require spatial reasoning, whereas females tend to be better than males at tasks that require verbal reasoning. Such differences have been found in at least 30 countries (Beller & Gafni, 1996; Halpern, 1992, 2000; Vogel, 1996).

Some theorists have tried to explain sex differences in spatial ability by appealing to the roles attributed to our primitive ancestors (D. M. Buss, 1995; Eals & Silverman, 1994; Geary, 1996). The men, in this view, were out hunting, which required the ability to navigate and recall where the home cave was, whereas the women stayed home, picking berries, weaving baskets, and tending children. But we really don't know much about what our male and female ancestors actually did, and even if these role descriptions are accurate, it isn't clear that women engaged in fewer spatial tasks. Gathering berries requires remembering where they are likely to grow and how to return home, and weaving baskets certainly requires spatial processing (Halpern, 1997).

Biological Factors and Sex Differences. At least some of the sex differences arise from the effects of sex hormones (Fitch & Bimonte, 2002; Hines, 2004; Kimura, 1994). One study examined women who were about to have a sex-change operation. As part of the procedure, the women received massive doses of male hormones, specifically testosterone. Within 3 months of this treatment, these people's spatial abilities increased and verbal abilities decreased (Van Goozen et al., 1995). Researchers have even found that a woman's spatial abilities shift during the course of her monthly cycle, as the balance of hormones changes (Hampson, 1990; Hampson & Kimura, 1988; Hausmann et al., 2000). Similarly, the level of male hormones shifts during the course of the day and over the seasons, and researchers have found that American males have poorer spatial abilities in the fall, when their levels of male hormones are highest, than in the spring. These hormones do not produce a more-is-better pattern, but apparently one like an upside-down U: Too little or too much is worse than intermediate amounts (Kimura, 1994). Elderly men have low levels of male hormones, and interestingly, testosterone supplements can boost their scores on spatial tests (Janowsky et al., 1994). However, these relationships between hormone levels and behavior are not always found (Halari et al., 2005; Liben et al., 2002; Wolf et al.,

Participating in activities that utilize spatial abilities means that the neural systems that underlie those activities are exercised. Subrahmanyam and Greenfield (1994) showed that spatial abilities could be improved by having children play certain video games, and boys and girls in these studies improved the same amount. However, sex differences in spatial abilities are evident even in early childhood, and so are unlikely to be totally the result of learning (Reinisch & Sanders, 1992; Robinson et al., 1996).

2000), and the effects observed probably depend on a variety of other currently unknown factors.

Sociological Factors and Sex Differences. Sex differences in cognitive abilities are not due solely to biological differences (Wigfield et al., 2002). To begin, some researchers argue that systematic differences in men's and women's health have muddied the waters. For example, men tend to drink more alcohol and to exercise more often than do women, and women tend to have more depressive symptoms than do men (Jorm et al., 2004). When health factors were controlled statistically, the male superiority in performance on certain cognitive tasks disappeared—and the female superiority on other tasks actually became greater. As the researchers put it, "better health and health habits in males can account for their better performance on some tests, but such factors cannot account for better female performance on other tests" (p. 16)

In addition, at least part of the sex differences may arise from how boys and girls are treated in our society. Boys and girls are encouraged to take part in "sex appropriate" activities (Lytton & Romney, 1991). This is important in part because if you do not perform activities that utilize spatial abilities, those abilities do not develop (Baenninger & Newcombe, 1989). And traditionally, girls have not been encouraged to participate in as many activities that require spatial skills, such as climbing trees and playing ball, as have boys.

Finally, keep in mind that many females are better at spatial reasoning than many males, and many males are better at verbal reasoning than many females. Here, too, differences in the group averages say nothing about differences among particular individuals.

Looking at Levels

Stereotype Threat

Researchers Claude Steele and Joshua Aronson (1995) conducted a study to investigate the possible effects of negative racial stereotypes on the test-taking performance of Black Americans. They asked Black and White American college students to take a test that included the most difficult items from the verbal portion of the Graduate Record Examination (GRE), a test like the SAT but used for admissions to graduate school. Some students, both Blacks and Whites, were told that the test assessed intellectual ability; another mixed group was told that it was for a study conducted by the laboratory. Blacks and Whites performed comparably when they were told that the test was simply a laboratory experiment, but Black students did much worse than Whites when they thought the test measured intelligence. In another study, Steele and Aronson (1995) asked half the participants of each race simply to list their race immediately before taking the test. The test was always described as a laboratory study, not a test of intelligence. Blacks and Whites performed the same when they did not list their races, but the simple act of being asked to list race drastically reduced the Black students' scores.

According to Steele (1997), asking Blacks about race activates information in long-term memory about negative stereotypes, such as that Blacks are not smart. If you believe that a negative stereotype addresses characteristics that are important to you, then the mere possibility that others will see you as conforming to that stereotype is threatening, even if you do not believe that you have those characteristics. Steele terms this phenomenon *stereotype threat*.

These sorts of findings have been replicated by many others (Croizet & Claire, 1998; Keller & Dauenheimer, 2003; Mayer & Hanges, 2003; Smith & White, 2002) and have been shown to apply not only to race but also to sex (women perform worse on math tests when the negative stereotype about female math ability is activated; Cadinu et al., 2003; O'Brien & Crandall, 2003; Schmader, 2002), old age (older people have poorer memories after the negative stereotype about older adults' memory is invoked; Hess et al., 2003), homosexuality (gay men have greater anxiety when interacting with preschoolers after the stereotype is activated; Bosson et al., 2004), and even athletic ability (activating the stereotype that Whites have poorer "natural athletic ability" than Blacks led Whites to practice less before a sports test; Stone, 2002).

These studies dramatically illustrate the interactions of events at the levels of the brain, the person, and the group. At the level of the brain, when you are threatened, a number of neurotransmitters (including dopamine and norepinephrine) are released; these neurotransmitters play crucial roles in the fight-or-flight response (see Chapters 2 and 10). When confronted by an emergency, you want to act quickly and decisively, and not be lost in thought. But what may be a good response in an emergency is not good for taking a test: These substances not only facilitate subcortical systems involved in the fight-or-flight response, but also disrupt the operation of the parts of the frontal lobes involved in working memory (Arnsten, 1998). Moreover, acute stress results in the release of a substance called *protein kinase* C, which also disrupts working memory—and may cause a person to become distractible and impulsive and to have impaired judgment (Birnbaum et al., 2004; Tan et al., 2004). Croizet and colleagues (2004) found clear evidence of such a stress response when participants took a nonverbal intelligence test while experiencing stereotype threat, and Schmader and Johns (2003) found that stereotype threat does, in fact, disrupt working memory.

At the level of the person, stereotypes are all about the beliefs you hold. Stereotype threat disrupts performance more severely if a person strongly identifies with the negatively stereotyped group, thus allowing the threat to activate stored information about group membership (Marx et al., 2005; McFarland et al., 2003; Ployhart et al., 2003; Schmader, 2002). Moreover, the effect is larger if you feel that the stereotyped ability is important (Cadinu et al., 2003) or you feel personally stigmatized by the stereotype (Brown & Pinel, 2003). In addition, characteristics at the level of the person can reduce the effects of stereotype threat; for example, stereotype threat is less disruptive for people who use humor to cope with their anxiety (Ford et al., 2004).

At the level of the group, not only does social interaction implant stereotypes in the first place, but such interaction activates stored stereotypes. By the same token, a social interaction can alleviate the effects of stereotype threat. For example, in one study, women did much better on a challenging math test if they first read about four successful professional women (McIntyre et al., 2003). In fact, Aronson and colleagues (2002) report that coaching Black students to see intelligence as "a malleable rather than fixed capacity" helped them to earn higher grades than students in control groups who were not led to adopt this perspective.

However, researchers do not always find that activating a negative stereotype disrupts performance on relevant tasks (Cullen et al., 2004; McKay et al., 2002; Stricker & Ward, 2004). In fact, interactions among events at the various levels appear to be responsible for whether the effect occurs at all (Davies et al., 2005; Major & O'Brien, 2005; Ryan & Ryan, 2005). Some of these interactions may be subtle: Activating a negative stereotype about women's math abilities impaired performance more for women who had relatively high levels of testosterone than for women who had relatively low levels of this sex hormone (Josephs et al., 2003). Thus, a social invention—stereotypes about groups—can become part of an individual's knowledge (level of the person). And that knowledge in turn can be activated by social situations. When activated, the knowledge produces events in the brain (as well as in the body—pounding heart, sweaty palms, and so on), which in turn disrupt performance. And the disrupted performance can then reinforce the stereotypes.

Diversity in Intelligence

Einstein is often regarded as *the* example of genius, largely based on his astonishing creativity—his ability to think "outside the box" and see things in a new light. In this section, we consider the extreme levels of intelligence, high and low. We also consider the bases of perhaps the highest form of intelligence, creativity.

Mental Retardation: People With Special Needs

For want of a better definition, people with an IQ score of 70 or lower (that is, who fall more than two standard deviations below the mean; see Figure 6.10 on p. 256) have traditionally been considered to be <mark>mentally retarded</mark>. The American Association for Mental Retardation (1992) specifies two additional criteria:

1. "significant limitations" in two or more everyday abilities, such as communication, self-care, and self-direction, and

2. the presence of the condition since childhood.

Although estimates vary widely, at least 4 million Americans are mentally retarded (Larson et al., 2001), and possibly as many as 7 million (Fryers, 1993). Mental retardation (also called *intellectual disability*) affects about 100 times more people than does total blindness (Batshaw & Perret, 1992). One out of every 10 families in the United States is directly affected by mental retardation (American Association for Mental Retardation, 1992). The good news is that mild mental retardation appears to be on the decline (Howard, 2001). However, the bad news is that the norms for IQ tests are periodically adjusted—and thus somebody who has not been considered to be retarded one day can wake up the next day to discover that he or she has been reclassified as retarded! This renorming of IQ tests can disrupt a person's life, for instance, by having him or her fall below the bar for admission to the U.S. military (Kanaya et al., 2003).

Retardation does not imply an inability to learn. Mildly retarded people can learn to function as well as normal adults, and behavioral techniques that involve explicit shaping and reinforcement (see Chapter 4) can allow even severely retarded people to master many tasks.

Mental retardation results when the brain fails to develop properly, which can happen in the womb or during childhood. Although hundreds of causes have now been identified, the causes of about one third of all cases are still mysteries. However, it is clear that both genetic and environmental factors can lead to retardation.

Mentally retarded: People who have an IQ of 70 or less and significant limitations in at least two aspects of everyday life since childhood.

Genetic Influences: When Good Genes Go Bad. Mutations in over 280 separate genes have been found to lead to mental retardation (Inlow & Restifo, 2004). The most common type of mental retardation (occurring in about 1 in 1,000 births) is known as Down syndrome, first described by British physician J. Langdon Down in 1866. Down children have an average IQ of 55, but the degree of retardation varies widely—and may disrupt everyday activities less severely than other forms of mental retardation (Chapman & Hesketh, 2000). The most frequent form of Down syndrome is not inherited, but it is caused by a genetic problem—the creation of an extra chromosome (number 21) during conception. This genetic abnormality apparently prevents neurons from developing properly, so that action potentials (neural firings) do not operate normally (Galdzicki et al., 2001). Down syndrome is more likely to occur in births to older mothers, whose eggs have been dormant for many years. Another relatively common cause of mental retardation is *fragile X syndrome*, so named because the X chromosome of these individuals tends to break when examined under laboratory conditions. (The X chromosome is the female sex chromosome; the Y chromosome is the male sex chromosome. Females have two X chromosomes, whereas males have one X and one Y chromosome.)

Environmental Influences: Bad Luck, Bad Behavior. Drinking and driving don't mix; neither do drinking and pregnancy. If the mother drinks heavily during pregnancy, her child can be born with fetal alcohol syndrome. Part of this syndrome is mental retardation (Streissguth et al., 1989, 1999). Indeed, many environmental factors can lead to mental retardation. If a pregnant woman experiences malnutrition, rubella, diabetes, HIV infection, high doses of X rays, or any of a number of infections, her child may be born with mental retardation. Streissguth and colleagues (1989) found that taking antibiotics and even aspirin during pregnancy also can adversely affect the developing baby's brain. People whose retardation is due to such environmental factors tend not to have retarded children themselves.

Mental retardation can also arise if the birth is unusually difficult and the infant's brain is injured. Premature birth and low birth weight put a child at risk for retardation. In addition, some childhood diseases, such as chicken pox and measles, can sometimes cause brain damage, as can ingesting lead, mercury, or poisons. Vaccines and other medical treatments greatly reduced the incidence of mental retardation in the latter part of the 20th century (Alexander, 1991; Croen et al., 2002). Both genetic and environmental factors are summarized in Table 6.7 (on p. 278).

The Gifted

There is no hard-and-fast way to determine whether a person is gifted (Robinson et al., 2000); the term is sometimes used to refer to people who have IQs of at least 135, but more commonly denotes the 150–180 range (Winner, 1997). Much of the research on the gifted has focused on people with very high IQs, above 150, and that is the criterion we apply here. It is not known how genes and the environment, including the environment in the womb, contribute to the condition. However, gifted boys tend to have lower testosterone levels than nongifted boys, whereas gifted girls may actually have higher amounts of testosterone than nongifted girls (Dohnanyiova et al., 2001; Ostatnikova et al., 2000, 2002); these findings hint at biological factors that could predispose some people to become gifted.

As expected from the idea that intelligence has a number of facets, children can be gifted in some domains while not being gifted in others (Winner, 2000a, 2000b). Prodigies, children with immense talent in a particular area, may be

If a mother drinks alcohol heavily during pregnancy, her child can be born with fetal alcohol syndrome (FAS)—one aspect of which is mental retardation and another aspect of which is the type of facial characteristics shown here.

Down syndrome: A type of mental retardation that results from the creation of an extra chromosome during conception; it is a genetic problem but not inherited.

Fetal alcohol syndrome: A condition that includes mental retardation and is caused by excessive drinking of alcohol by the mother during pregnancy.

Gifted: People who have IQs between 150 and 180.

Prodigies: Children who demonstrate immense talent in a particular area, such as music or mathematics, but who are normal in other areas.

Table 6.7 **Causes of Retardation: Common Examples**

Genetic conditions

- Down syndrome
- Fragile X syndrome

Problems during pregnancy

- Use of alcohol or drugs
- Malnutrition
- Rubella
- Glandular disorders and diabetes
- Illnesses of the mother during pregnancy
- Physical malformations of the brain
- HIV infection in the fetus

Problems at birth

- Prematurity
- Low birth weight

Problems after birth

- Childhood diseases such as whooping cough, chicken pox, and measles, which may lead to meningitis and encephalitis, which can in turn damage the brain
- Accidents such as a blow to the head or near drowning
- Lead and mercury poisoning

Poverty and cultural deprivation

- Malnutrition
- Disease-producing conditions
- Inadequate medical care
- Environmental health hazards

perfectly normal in other areas; for example, mathematically gifted children often are not gifted in other domains (Benbow & Minor, 1990). Achter and colleagues (1996) found that over 95% of the gifted children they tested had sharply differing mathematical and verbal abilities.

According to some researchers (such as Jackson & Butterfield, 1986), gifted children do the same kinds of processing as average children but simply do it more effectively. As Winner (1997) notes, however, some children "as young as three or four years of age have induced rules of algebra on their own (Winner, 1996), have memorized almost instantly entire musical scores (Feldman & Goldsmith, 1991), and have figured out on their own how to identify all prime numbers (Winner, 1996)" (p. 1071). Such intellectual feats suggest that the cognitive processes of gifted children may be qualitatively different from those of other people. Specifically, Winner suggests that gifted children may be exceptionally able to intuit solutions to problems and may be driven by an extraordinary passion to master tasks.

The gifts are sometimes bestowed with a price. Gifted children are at times socially awkward and may be treated as "geeks" and "nerds" (Silverman, 1993a, 1993b; Winner, 1996). In addition, they may tend to be solitary and introverted (Silverman, 1993b). They have twice the rate of emotional and social problems as nongifted children (Winner, 1997).

If you aren't gifted as a child, does this mean you have no hope of becoming a gifted adult? Not at all. Many distinguished adults—Charles Darwin, for example—showed no signs of being gifted as children (Simonton, 1994); furthermore, most gifted children grow up to be rather ordinary adults (Richert, 1997; Winner, 2000a, 2000b).

Many eminent adults had the help of able mentors at critical phases of their lives (Bloom, 1985; Gardner, 1993a). Having an apprentice relationship with an appropriate role model can make a huge difference. That is one reason why grad-

Prodigies are children who have a gift in one particular area. For example, a child may be an extraordinary violinist but not so outstanding in other areas.

uate education in the sciences in the United States is based on apprenticeship: Students in Ph.D. programs in the sciences learn at the elbows of their supervisors, not simply from reading books or listening to lectures.

Creative Smarts: Not Just Inspiration

Creativity lies at the heart of many forms of intelligence. **Creativity** is the ability to produce something original of high quality or to devise an effective new way of solving a problem. Creativity necessarily involves the ability to recognize and develop a novel approach, the ability to consider a problem from multiple angles and to change points of view repeatedly, and the ability to develop a simple idea in different ways. Creative thought can be applied to practical problems (such as raising money), intellectual tasks (making new connections in a term paper), or artistic work (writing a novel).

Creativity involves an interplay between two types of thinking, *divergent* and *convergent* (Guilford, 1967; Mumford, 2001). With divergent thinking, you come at a problem from a number of different angles, exploring a variety of approaches to a solution before settling on one (Mednick, 1962; Reese et al., 2001). With convergent thinking, you stay focused on one particular approach to a problem and work through a series of steps to arrive at a solution. Convergent thinking also plays a role in setting up a problem in the first place and in cutting back the lush jungle of ideas created by divergent thinking.

How many uses can you think of for a brick? Divergent thinking might lead you to consider bricks as doorstops, supports for bookshelves, or bookends.

What Makes a Person Creative?

Creative people may tend to think differently than the rest of us. Amabile (1983, 1998) found that creative people keep options open, do not make snap decisions about the likely outcome of an effort, and are good at seeing a problem from a new vantage point. Similarly, when Guilford used factor analysis to discover which underlying abilities are tapped by various tests of creativity, he found that flexibility and the ability to reorganize information were key (similar conclusions were drawn by Aguilar-Alonso, 1996, and Eysenck, 1995). Martindale (1989, 2001) stresses that creative people tend to think in terms of analogies, tend to have high intelligence, have wide interests, don't like traditional dogmas, have high self-esteem, and like to work hard. In addition, creative people are often highly motivated and persistent, driven to create (Sulloway, 1996). Amabile (2001) emphasizes the role of hard work and strong motivation in creativity, and Heilman and colleagues (2003) underscore the importance of knowledge about the relevant domain and having the skills to be able to work with that knowledge.

Are creative people born that way? Although researchers are beginning to study and theorize about the neural bases of creativity (Dietrich, 2004; Heilman et al., 2003; Ione, 2003; Zeki, 2002), we do not yet know how the brains of creative people are special. However, we do know that—in sharp contrast to differences in IQ—differences in creativity are not strongly related to genetic differences, if at all. Furthermore, and also in contrast to IQ, shared aspects of the home (such as exposure to cultural resources, home libraries, or parents' mechanical or artistic hobbies) strongly affect creativity (Canter, 1973; Nichols, 1978; Simonton, 1988).

Are highly creative people mentally unstable? It has long been believed that certain mental disorders promote creativity (Kraepelin, 1921). Manic-depressive (bipolar) mental illness (see Chapter 11) can result in shifts between very "high" energetic moods and very "low" depressed ones. Kay Redfield Jamison and her colleagues (Goodwin & Jamison, 1990; Jamison, 1989; Jamison et al., 1980), as

Creativity: The ability to produce something original of high quality or to devise an effective new way of solving a problem.

In some ways, creativity is like pitching in baseball. Cy Young was the pitcher with the greatest number of wins in baseball history. The pitcher with the most losses? Cy Young. People who produce large numbers of creative works are also likely to produce large numbers of mundane works.

well as Hershman and Lieb (1988, 1998), have argued that a "loosening" of thought that occurs during the manic phase of this disorder enhances creativity. If so, the manic phase may spur creativity by increasing the number of possible solutions a person can formulate during the first stage of the creative process (Barrantes-Vidal, 2004). Isaac Newton, Charles Dickens, and Kurt Cobain apparently suffered from this disorder, and Andreasen (1987) found that almost half the visiting faculty in the University of Iowa Writers' Workshop, an intensive course for creative writers, had experienced it. Jamison (1989) reports similar findings, particularly for poets.

Although some have claimed that mental illness is associated with increased creativity, others have claimed that mental illness is independent of creativity; these claims are consistent with analyses by Dennis (1966) and Simonton (1984, 1997), who showed that the quality of a creative person's work tends to be constant over their productive years; in years when a large number of particularly good works are produced, a correspondingly large number of inferior works are also produced.

LOOKING BACK: *Review*

1. *How do environment and genetics contribute to intelligence?* In general, approximately 50% of the variability in IQ scores can be attributed to variations in genes. At least some of these effects may, in fact, reflect the way that the environment is regulating the genes or the way that genes in turn affect the environment (including by influencing appearance and temperament, which affect the microenvironment).

2. *How can we interpret group differences in IQ?* Although group differences definitely exist, it is impossible to sort out the relative contributions made by genes and the environment in creating such differences. Findings about the genetic contribution to within-group differences do not apply to between-group differences. In addition, all distributions of abilities within any group overlap those of other groups; for this reason, group differences cannot be applied to particular individuals.

3. *What are the extremes of intelligence, high and low?* Mental retardation is usually defined as having since childhood an IQ of 70 or less and having significant limitations in two or more everyday abilities. Researchers have identified hundreds of causes of mental retardation. Some types are caused by genetic abnormalities; others are caused by environmental events, such as childhood diseases. Gifted people are defined as those having high IQs, typically between 150 and 180. It is not clear how the genes and environment interact to produce such high IQs. Finally, creative people are not born that way, but rather have learned certain cognitive strategies. Although creative people are typically highly motivated and driven to create, their creativity is not a by-product of mental instability.

LOOKING BEYOND: *Critical Thinking*

Do you think tests should be designed so that there are no differences between men and women or between other groups? What are the pros and cons of such an approach?

What implications, if any, would group differences in IQ scores have for the way schools should be organized? Can you think of factors that might make group differences in IQ shrink?

LET'S SUM IT UP

I. Language: More Than Meets the Ear

A. Both comprehension and production rely on four aspects of language: phonology (proper speech sounds), syntax (rules that govern how different types of words can be combined to form sentences), semantics (meanings of words, phrases, and sentences), and pragmatics (meaning that is indirect or implied).

B. Adults can learn semantics and pragmatics of a new language as well as children can, but unless people learn a second language early in life, they probably will never use it as well or as automatically as they do their first language.

II. Thinking: Understanding the World and Guiding Behavior

A. When thinking, we use words and images as a way of keeping track of thoughts and storing them effectively, like making notations on a pad of paper. Language does not determine thought but may influence it in subtle ways.

B. Objects in visual mental images preserve many of the properties of actual objects, such as spatial extent and relative size; at least some of these properties may arise from characteristics of the brain areas that give rise to imagery.

C. Thinking cannot rely solely on words or images: Both types of representations are ambiguous, and thoughts are not. If thoughts were based only on words, we would never have difficulty figuring out how to put our thoughts into words; if thoughts were based only on images, we would have trouble thinking about abstractions (such as truth and justice).

D. Thoughts arise from manipulations of concepts, which specify groupings of objects or events.

E. Representations of concepts are unambiguous and can be concrete (such as "bird") or abstract (such as "justice"). Some examples of a concept category are better (more typical) than others.

F. Concepts are organized according to how specific or general they are.

G. If a problem is not specified appropriately from the outset, it will be difficult to solve.

H. People can solve problems by using heuristics (short-cut strategies that do not guarantee a correct answer) and algorithms (sets of steps that are guaranteed to produce the answer). People can also use analogies in solving problems.

I. Knowing about the obstacles to problem solving can help you to overcome them.

J. Reasoning involves both deduction (going from premises to implied conclusions) and induction (going from particular instances to generalizations), as well as making decisions at pivotal points. Decision making requires you to evaluate possible outcomes and choose one alternative or course of action over the others.

K. People are not, strictly speaking, logical; for example, we fall prey to biases, such as affirming the consequent and the confirmation bias.

L. We often rely on heuristics, such as the availability heuristic, when making decisions. Heuristics often lead us to the correct conclusion faster than we could get there with a step-by-step algorithm; however, they also sometimes lead to errors.

M. Although many people consider emotion a weakness when reasoning, in fact, emotion often helps us to develop useful hunches and useful intuitions.

III. Intelligence: Is There More Than One Way to Be Smart?

A. The most common measure of intelligence is the score on an intelligence test, called the intelligence quotient, or IQ. IQ scores are a composite of many different underlying abilities, and the same IQ score can arise from different mixtures of relative strengths and weaknesses.

B. The most common IQ tests, the Wechsler Adult Intelligence Scale (WAIS) and the Wechsler

Intelligence Scale for Children (WISC), consist of two sets of subtests, one that assesses verbal performance and one that assesses nonverbal performance.

C. When first devised, IQ was a measure of mental age compared to chronological age. Today, IQ scores are based on standardized norms for large samples, which are updated periodically so that the mean score on the WAIS or the WISC is always 100 and a standard deviation is 15.

D. Scores on IQ tests are positively correlated with achievement in school and on the job; they are also correlated with many aspects of success in life, such as staying out of prison or having an enduring marriage.

E. There are many theories of intelligence, most of which posit a single overarching "general intelligence" (g) and a set of specific abilities. According to one theory, g may be broken down into fluid and crystallized intelligence. Performance in a wide range of occupations is well predicted by g, and barely—if at all—by specific abilities.

F. Emotional intelligence is not assessed by standard IQ tests, but it may turn out to be important in daily life.

G. Some researchers believe that there are many aspects of intelligence; the theory of multiple intelligences posits a number of forms of intelligence. However, this theory has yet to be tested, and many researchers question whether all of the abilities are, in fact, forms of intelligence.

IV. What Makes Us Smart? Nature and Nurture

A. Although about 50% of the variability in scores on IQ tests can be explained in terms of genetic factors, this number is an average and does not apply to individuals.

B. Variations in intelligence probably reflect an intimate dance between the genes and the environment.

C. Group differences in IQ have been well documented; it is impossible to sort out the relative contributions of genes and environment to such differences. Some group differences in some abilities, such as sex differences in spatial ability, may reflect biological differences, for example, in hormone levels. However, other group differences—in IQ scores of Black and White Americans, for example—may arise in part from the ways in which environments affect individuals. Group differences may also reflect the way in which individuals' characteristics create their microenvironments and influence the reactions of others to them.

D. All distributions of abilities within any group overlap those of other groups, and hence group differences have no applicability to particular individuals in a given group.

E. Environmental effects can also occur at the time an IQ test is administered; when this happens, test scores are not valid indicators of ability.

F. Mental retardation is traditionally defined on the basis of overall IQ score *plus* significant difficulty with two or more everyday tasks, with both conditions existing since childhood. By this definition, someone who is retarded cannot be gifted; giftedness is defined by a very high IQ score (typically between 150 and 180).

G. Mental retardation can arise for many reasons, some genetic and some environmental. Not all of the genetic reasons reflect inherited defects; some reflect accidents during conception or environmental damage to genes.

H. Creativity leads to the production of original works or to innovative effective solutions to problems.

I. Creative people have many characteristics, including the tendency to make loose associations, engage in divergent thinking, keep options open, avoid snap decisions, be flexible, organize information well, and see problems from many points of view. Creativity has a very low heritability and is strongly influenced by shared environment.

Key Terms

LOOKING ONLINE: *Enhance Your Learning*

MyPsychLab is an interactive and instructive multimedia resource that can be used to supplement a traditional lecture course or as an online course. It is an all-inclusive tool with a text-specific e-book plus multimedia tutorials, videos, simulations, animations, and controlled assessment to completely engage students and reinforce learning. MyPsychLab meets the individual learning needs of every student. Visit *www.mypsychlab.com* for more information!

Practice Test

For each of the following items, choose the single best answer.

1. Sentences in any language contain an internal structure, an acceptable arrangement of words called
   a. syntax.
   b. phoneme.
   c. phonology.
   d. aphasia.

2. A mental sentence that expresses the unambiguous meaning of an assertion is
   a. a morpheme.
   b. a propositional representation.
   c. an aspect of pragmatics.
   d. found only in the English language.

3. Learning a second language is
   a. exactly the same as learning a first language.
   b. easier if you have less formal education.
   c. an ability in which people differ greatly.
   d. easier the older you are when you start.

4. What is wrong with the idea that thinking is just talking to yourself?
   a. Words are often ambiguous, but thoughts are not.
   b. If thoughts were already formed in language, expressing them in language should be easy.
   c. At least some animals can think, and yet they don't use language.
   d. All of the above statements identify problems with this idea.

5. The most common type of mental image seems to occur in a kind of mental space, which has the property of
   a. spatial extent.
   b. limited size.
   c. grain.
   d. Mental space has all three of the above properties.

6. Visual images
   a. do not have any of the properties of perceptions of actual objects.
   b. rely on many—about two thirds—of the same parts of the brain that are used in visual perception.

   c. can be the only means by which we think, at least when we are thinking about objects and events we have actually seen.
   d. All of the above statements are true.

7. The basic level at which people name objects is a
   a. representation of the most typical example of a category of things.
   b. collection of concepts that specify necessary and "optional" aspects of the particular situation.
   c. level of specificity that is usually the most likely to be applied to an object.
   d. grouping of objects in which the members are specific cases of a more general type.

8. You can improve your ability to solve problems if you
   a. represent the problem effectively.
   b. don't get locked into viewing your resources in only one way, which is a form of functional fixedness.
   c. don't get stuck with a certain mental set, a fixed way of viewing the kind of solution you seek.
   d. All of the above describe ways that will help improve your ability to solve problems.

9. The reasoning error called affirming the consequent
   a. is rarely made by humans.
   b. occurs because of the assumption that if a result is present, a specific cause must also be present.
   c. occurs when people seek out information that will confirm a rule but do not seek information that might refute it.
   d. assumes that the more similar something is to a prototype stored in memory, the more likely it is that the entity belongs to the category of the prototype.

10. The intelligence quotient was originally computed by
    a. dividing mental age by chronological age and multiplying by 100.
    b. dividing chronological age by mental age and multiplying by 100.
    c. subtracting mental age from chronological age and multiplying by 100.
    d. subtracting chronological age from mental age and multiplying by 100.

11. The mean and standard deviation for the WAIS-III IQ test are, respectively,
    a. 100 and 10.
    b. 110 and 15.
    c. 100 and 15.
    d. 100 and 12.

12. According to Raymond Cattell and John Horn, people possess
    a. one type of intelligence, g, for "general factor."
    b. two types of intelligence: crystallized and fluid.
    c. seven separate primary mental abilities.
    d. eight basic forms of intelligence.

13. Robert Sternberg has proposed three types of intelligence. According to Sternberg's theory, which of the following statements is true?
    a. Analytic intelligence is what IQ tests measure.
    b. Measures of practical intelligence are better predictors of how well someone will do on the job than are standard measures of IQ.
    c. Practical intelligence is largely distinct from analytic intelligence.
    d. All of the above statements are true.

14. Intelligence
    a. is determined by a single gene.
    b. is affected by multiple genes; the heritability of IQ is around .50.
    c. is clearly not affected by genes.
    d. None of the above statements is true.

15. What do researchers know about sex differences in intelligence?
    a. At least some sex differences arise from the effects of sex hormones.
    b. In general, females tend to be better than males at tasks that require spatial reasoning.
    c. In general, males tend to be better than females at tasks that require verbal reasoning.
    d. There are very large sex differences in IQ.

Answers 1.a 2.b 3.c 4.d 5.d 6.b 7.c 8.d 9.b 10.a 11.c 12.b 13.d 14.b 15.a

chapter 7

Emotion and Motivation
Feeling and Striving

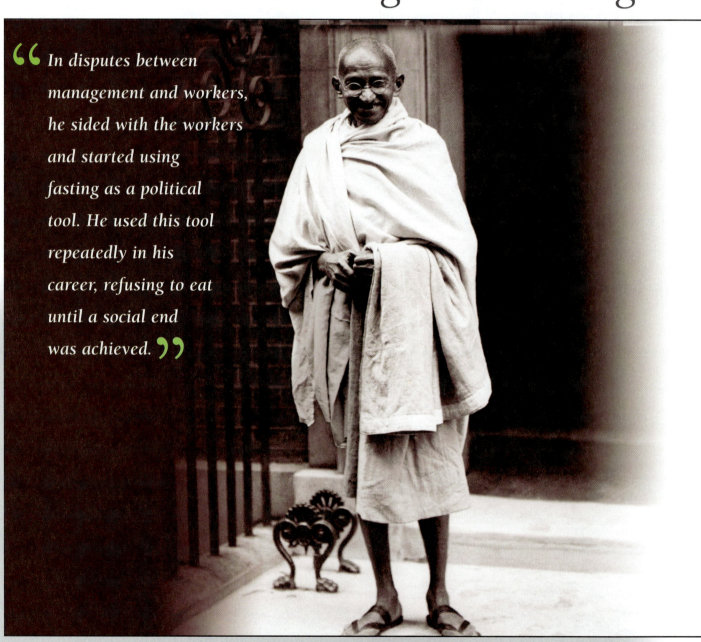

In disputes between management and workers, he sided with the workers and started using fasting as a political tool. He used this tool repeatedly in his career, refusing to eat until a social end was achieved.

CHAPTER OUTLINE

THE PEOPLE CALLED HIM "MAHATMA," OR "GREAT SOUL." AS AN ADULT, Mohandas Karamchand Gandhi was described as follows: "Quiet dark eyes. A small, weak man, with a thin face and big ears. Wearing a white cap as headgear, clothed in rough white material, barefoot. He feeds on rice and fruits, drinks only water, sleeps on the floor, rests little, works all the time. Nothing about him strikes more than an expression of great patience and great love. . . . Such is the man who has incited to revolt three hundred million men, has shaken the British Empire and launched the most powerful movement in the politics of mankind for almost two thousand years" (Rolland, 1924, cited in Markovits, 2003, p. 18). This physically slight man cast a giant shadow across the 20th century, not only changing the face of India but also inspiring Martin Luther King, Jr., and the American civil rights movement.

In spite of his saintly reputation, Gandhi was a man of flesh and blood, possessed of raw emotions and strong motivations, just like the rest of us. The personal history of Gandhi provides us with a case study of the nature of emotion and its role in motivation.

By all reports, Gandhi was a shy, ordinary child, who was perhaps a little more stubborn than his peers, but this tendency was noticeable only through the keen lens of hindsight. As a young man, he decided to become a lawyer, following in the footsteps of his father and grandfather before him. At age 19, he went to England to study law, over the objections of his mother. She relented when he promised not to touch alcohol, women, or meat, but other members of his caste (hereditary social class) were not so flexible: They viewed crossing the ocean as a form of "contamination" and excommunicated him for this act. Knowing this consequence in advance did not deter him, so determined was he to reach his goal.

When he first arrived in England, Gandhi bent over backward to adapt. He adopted English dress and manners, and even studied ballroom dancing and took French lessons so that he could have the same social skills as his British classmates. He soon realized the folly of trying to pretend to be something he was not, and he began to re-explore his roots in the Hindu faith—which provided spiritual sustenance for him in this foreign land.

Gandhi returned to India after obtaining his law degree, but was a miserable failure as a lawyer in Bombay. When rising to argue his first case in court, he was overcome with anxiety and froze, tongue-tied and speechless. Following this humiliating experience, he was happy to accept a job in South Africa, helping a group of Indian merchants with a lawsuit. This was in the waning days of the 19th century, when the social climate in South Africa was hostile to Indians, who were treated as second-class citizens—or worse, resident aliens. Gandhi's emotional and intellectual reactions to the insults—and even beatings—he experienced gave rise to an unusually strong sense of social justice, which was to stay with him the rest of his life.

Gandhi's countrymen asked him to stay in South Africa and help them fight against discrimination. He agreed, and the shy lawyer gradually evolved into a charismatic leader. As part of this evolution, he abandoned Western clothes and began to dress as an Indian peasant. He reduced his needs and simplified his life, doing his own laundry, cleaning his own chamber pots (this was before flushing toilets were available), and even learning to be a midwife so that he could deliver his fourth (and last) son. He founded a residential community based on spiritual ideals, where the residents did all the work. Every member of the community—no matter what his or her social class—had to help with even the most menial tasks, such as cleaning, and all had to learn a craft. Gandhi learned to make sandals.

Gandhi organized the Indian expatriates of South Africa to use nonviolent resistance to oppose oppressive new tax laws, as well as a Supreme Court ruling that invalidated all Hindu and Muslim marriages—which had the effect of making all Indian wives into concubines. After he prevailed, he sent a gift to his main adversary, General Jan Christian Smuts—a pair of sandals he had made while in jail for leading demonstrations and civil actions. Twenty-five years later, the general wrote, "I have worn these sandals for many a summer since then even though I may feel that I am not worthy to stand in the shoes of so great a man" (Nanda, 1987).

After 20 years in South Africa, Gandhi returned to India in 1915, when it was still a colony ruled by Great Britain. He became the first Indian national leader in its history (all previous leaders had been regional), spending much time with peasants and focusing on teaching them to overcome the many fears that grow from powerlessness and poverty. In disputes between management and workers, he sided with the workers and started using fasting as a political tool. He used this tool repeatedly in his career, refusing to eat until a social end was achieved (such as resolution of a dispute or an end to violence).

What emotions did Gandhi feel when confronted with the social realities of his day? How did his emotions and motivations affect him? What these two forces have in common is their power to move us. (The root of both English words—*emotion* and *motivation*—comes from the Latin *movere*, "to move.") Our motivations and emotions are intimately interwoven: We are often motivated to do something because we are feeling an emotion, as when love leads us to hug someone; or we are motivated because we look forward to changing an emotion, as when we work on an overdue project in the expectation of replacing guilt with pride. Our emotions and motivations are not always obvious; they may confuse us or compel us to do things that surprise us. In this chapter, we consider first the nature of emotion and how it affects our behavior. This analysis leads us to consider motivation—what makes us act. Finally, we focus on two of the most important motivations: hunger and sex.

Emotion: I Feel, Therefore I Am

Soon after his return to India, Gandhi called for nonviolent demonstrations to protest repressive laws. But the disobedience soon spun out of control, sparking arson and violence—and the British reacted by killing many Indian protestors. Gandhi admitted that he had made a "Himalayan blunder" (referring to the highest mountains in the world) because he had initiated a social movement before he understood how to lead it. The peasants had trouble grasping Gandhi's ideas about nonviolence, and they questioned whether he was serious about these ideas—or was talking about them just to confuse the British. Gandhi's views stemmed from his spiritual convictions; he believed that if people could learn to control and overcome their "internal violence" (their destructive impulses, thoughts, and goals), "external" violence would not occur. But most people did not have his self-control, and their inflamed emotions sometimes got the better of them.

What, specifically, are emotions? An **emotion** has four components: (1) a positive or negative subjective experience, (2) bodily arousal, (3) the activation of specific mental processes and stored information, and (4) characteristic behavior. Emotions not only help guide us to approach some things and withdraw from others, but they also provide visible cues that help other people know key aspects of our thoughts and desires.

LOOKING AHEAD: *Learning Objectives*

1. *What are the different emotions?*
2. *What causes emotion?*
3. *How do we express and regulate our emotions?*
4. *How do we perceive emotions in others?*

Types of Emotion: What Can You Feel?

Think of the emotions you have experienced in your life. Fear? Guilt? Guilt tinged with fear? Love? Love mixed with joy? The range of human emotions is huge. Some researchers who have studied emotions have argued that the brain

Emotion: A psychological state with four components: (1) a positive or negative subjective experience, (2) bodily arousal, (3) the activation of specific mental processes and stored information, and (4) characteristic overt behavior.

produces many gradations and types of these experienced reactions by combining sets of simple signals (Plutchik & Kellerman, 1980). Just as all colors can be produced by mixtures of three primary colors, researchers have claimed that all emotions, even the most complex, arise from combinations of a simple set we all possess, which, like primary colors on an artist's palette, lie ready for us to blend, experience, and present to the world.

Basic Emotions

Charles Darwin (1872/1965), for one, believed that many emotional behaviors—the outward acts that arise from our emotions—are inborn. He noticed that people of many races and cultures appear to use very similar facial expressions to signal similar emotional states. Moreover, blind people show those same expressions, even if they have never had the chance to observe the way others look when they have particular emotional reactions. Are we all born with a built-in set of emotions? If so, these emotions would be an essential part of what we call "human nature," constituting a defining characteristic of what it means to be human in every time and culture.

Ekman and Friesen (1971) described the results of experiments that were designed to investigate this possibility (see Figure 7.1). They wanted to know

Figure 7.1 Recognition of Basic Emotions

Ekman and Friesen told the participants a story, and then presented three pictures of faces displaying different emotions. The participants chose the face that showed the appropriate emotion for the story.

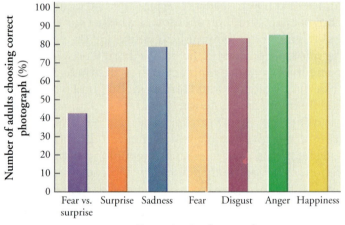

Participants could distinguish all of the emotions, except they tended to confuse fear and surprise. (Note that chance performance would be 33.3%.)

Happiness   Sadness   Fear   Anger   Surprise   Disgust

The six basic emotions that Ekman and others identified and studied. In the Ekman and Friesen study (1971), however, all the faces were Caucasian.

whether people who had never seen White faces could identify the emotions underlying facial expressions in photographs of such faces. The researchers visited a New Guinea tribe, the Fore, who had rarely, if ever, seen White people in person or in images. Nonetheless, the Fore were able to identify expressions of happiness, anger, sadness, disgust, fear, and surprise in photos. The one difficulty they had was in distinguishing the expression of fear from that of surprise, probably because the two are very similar emotions. Also, it is possible that in Fore culture the two often go together: Most surprises in the jungle, such as the unexpected wild boar, are life-threatening, fear-inducing ones.

Ekman (1984) concluded that surprise, happiness, anger, fear, disgust, and sadness are **basic emotions**, emotions that are innate and shared by all humans. Other theorists have proposed slightly different lists of basic emotions. For example, Tomkins (1962) identified surprise, interest, joy, rage, fear, disgust, shame, and anguish. Some of the apparent disagreements may be simply a matter of word choice; *joy* and *happiness*, for example, may label the same emotion (LeDoux, 1996) or versions of it (perhaps joy is more intense than happiness, or comes and goes more quickly). Based on research with nonhuman animals, Panksepp (1998, 2005) offers a set of "emotional systems," which guide behavior (such as sexuality–lust, nurturance–care, and joy–play). And other specific emotions, such as pride, have been proposed for the list of basic emotions (Tracy & Robins, 2004).

But the idea that there is a fixed set of basic emotions has proven controversial. One challenge rests on the finding that some of these basic emotions are not simple. For example, Rozin and colleagues (1994) distinguish among three types of disgust, each of which is signaled by a different facial expression. A nose-wrinkling expression of disgust is associated with bad smells (and, sometimes, bad tastes); an open mouth with the tongue hanging down is associated with foods perceived as disgusting (the "yech" reaction); and a raised upper lip accompanies feelings of disgust, such as those associated with death and filth. Similarly, positive emotions can be divided at least into five types (amusement, desire, happiness, love, and interest; Keltner & Shiota, 2003).

Another challenge focuses on the role of culture in shaping emotion. Some researchers have argued that although some emotions are basic, in the sense that they have a consistent "signature" across cultures, other emotions are shaped by the social practices and norms of a culture (Keltner & Haidt, 2001). In fact, the perception of basic emotions in others turns out not to be entirely innate; learning also plays a role. Hillary Anger Elfenbein and Nalini Ambady (2002) carried out a meta-analysis of studies on the perception of emotion, looking carefully at the effects of many variables. First, they found that although people can recognize basic emotions of members of other racial groups better than you would expect by chance alone, they generally recognize emotions in their own group better than in other groups. Moreover, Elfenbein and Ambady found that some members of a minority group may actually recognize emotions on faces of members of the majority group better than they do on faces of their own group. This finding is a clear testament to the role of learning.

Thus, even with "basic" emotions, the contribution of the genes (which produce inborn tendencies) cannot be considered in isolation from events at the levels of the person (such as learning) and the group (such as whether one is a member of a specific culture).

Separate but Equal Emotions

Have you ever watched a movie that was a four-star tear-jerker and found yourself racked with sobs *and* rolling with laughter? Or, have you ever found yourself enjoying a luscious dessert and simultaneously feeling disgusted because

Basic emotion: An innate emotion that is shared by all humans, such as surprise, happiness, anger, fear, disgust, or sadness.

you are being such a glutton? There is evidence that positive and negative emotions are not really opposite sides of the same coin. Rather, positive and negative emotions can occur at the same time, in any combination (Bradburn, 1969; Cacioppo et al., 1997; Diener & Emmons, 1984; Goldstein & Strube, 1994; Larsen et al., 2001).

The notion that positive and negative emotions are independent is supported by what happens in the brain when people experience emotions. Davidson and his colleagues have provided several types of evidence that there are separate systems in the brain for two general types of human emotions: *approach* emotions (such as love and happiness) and *withdrawal* emotions (such as fear and disgust; Davidson, 1992a, 1992b, 1993, 1998, 2002; Davidson et al., 2000a; Lang, 1995; Solomon & Corbit, 1974). In general, approach emotions are positive, and withdrawal emotions are negative. EEG recordings show that the left frontal lobe tends to be more active than the right when people have approach emotions, whereas the right frontal lobe tends to be more active when people have withdrawal emotions (Simon-Thomas et al., 2005). Moreover, people who normally show more activation in the left frontal lobe tend to have a rosier outlook on life than do people who show more activation in the right frontal lobe. And brain scanning has shown that clinically depressed patients have lower activity in the left frontal lobe than do people who are not depressed (Davidson, 1993, 1994a, 1998; Davidson et al., 1999). However, these effects may be very transient; they are not reliably found in studies that use fRMI (which can only register changes over several seconds, whereas EEG can register changes that occur in a fraction of a second) (Wager et al., 2003).

What Causes Emotions?

Distinguishing among different emotions is interesting, but it doesn't tell us what emotions are for, or why particular emotions arise when they do, any more than a theory of color perception can explain how Leonardo da Vinci painted the *Mona Lisa*. Gandhi was not a placid person; he wrote virulent critiques of Western civilization, disparaging its values and creations (for example, he detested the scale of modern cities and the ugliness of many of their buildings). Why did he feel anger? What possible good would such an emotion do him? The major theories of emotion provide insight into these questions.

Theories of Emotion: Brain, Body, and World

It seems both obvious and logical that emotion would work like this: You are in a particular situation; that situation induces a specific emotion; that emotion leads you to behave in a certain way. The British used violence to try to trigger this process in Indian demonstrators: They would become afraid and therefore run. Although this process may seem to make sense intuitively, research has shown that it's not quite right. Each of the following theories has succeeded in capturing at least a grain of truth about how emotions actually operate.

James–Lange Theory. More than 100 years ago, William James (1884) argued that the intuitively plausible relation between emotion and behavior is exactly backward. James believed that you feel emotions after your body reacts (see Figure 7.2). For example, if a soldier raised his gun the moment he saw you coming, James would say that you would first run and then feel afraid, not the other way around. The emotion of fear, according to James, arises because you sense your bodily state as you are fleeing. You are aroused, and you sense your heart speeding up, your breathing increasing, and other signs that your sympathetic nervous system is being activated (see Chapter 2). According to his theory, different emotions arise from different sets of bodily reactions, and that's why emotions feel different (Reisenzein et al., 1995). Carl Lange (1887), a Danish physiologist, independently developed a similar theory, and thus the theory has come to be called the *James–Lange theory* (Lang, 1994). Damasio's (1994) *somatic marker hypothesis* is in many ways a contemporary version of the James–Lange theory, as it hinges on the role of bodily signals (that is, somatic markers) in producing emotions.

Cannon–Bard Theory.   Walter Cannon (1927) claimed that the James–Lange theory focused too much on noticing bodily signals, such as heart and breathing rates. He raised a telling criticism of the James–Lange theory—that it takes many seconds for the body to become aroused and yet emotions are usually experienced before this happens. Instead, he claimed, the brain itself is all that matters. You perceive the threat of being shot, and the results of that perception marshal the body's resources for fleeing or fighting *at the same time* as they generate an emotion. According to the *Cannon–Bard theory* (see Figure 7.2), formulated by Cannon and another physiologist, Philip Bard, bodily arousal and the experience of emotion arise in tandem.

Cognitive Theory.   *Cognitive theory* holds that an emotion arises when you interpret the situation. Although some of these theorists focus solely on how people interpret the situation, without regard for bodily states, most of them consider the situation as a whole—the bodily state in the context of everything that surrounds it. According to this theory, you don't react to a stimulus and then feel an emotion after the reaction, as the James–Lange theory holds, and you don't have separate bodily and emotional reactions, as the Cannon–Bard theory has it. Rather, your reactions and the general situation together form the basis of emotions. For example, the act of running and the accompanying arousal can equally well be associated with the emotion of joy (as you rush to embrace someone you love), fear (as you flee a pursuing soldier), or excitement (as you join the crowd on the field to celebrate a football victory). The difference is not in the bodily state, but in how you interpret it at the time it occurs. Richard Lazarus, Stanley Schachter, and Magda Arnold were pioneers in developing this view. In general, the cognitive theory of emotion rests on the idea that, as Lazarus puts it, emotion "cannot be understood solely in terms of what happens in the person or in the brain, but grows out of ongoing transactions with the environment that are evaluated" (Lazarus, 1984, p. 124). This statement clearly embodies our by now familiar approach of looking at events at the levels of brain, person, and group.

The Emerging Synthesis.   The study of emotion is particularly exciting today because researchers are synthesizing a new theory from the best parts of what has come before. Let's briefly consider two elements of the emerging view. First, Joseph LeDoux (1996) modified the cognitive theory in an important way through

Figure 7.2 Four Theories of Emotion

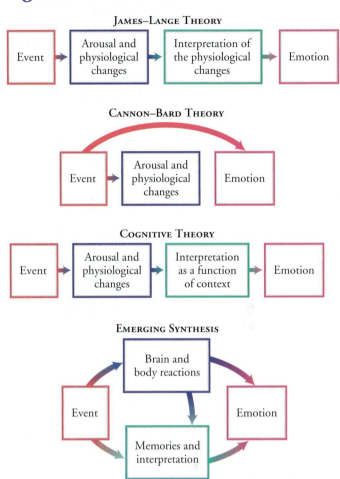

Theories of emotion differ in how they view the relationship between body reactions and interpretations of events.

his claim that there are different brain systems for different broad categories of emotions. Some of these systems operate as reflex pathways do, *independent* of thought or interpretation, whereas others *depend* on thought and interpretation. Fear, for example, relies on activation of the amygdala, a small brain structure located at the front inside part of the temporal lobes (see Chapter 2), without need for cognitive interpretation. But other emotions, such as guilt, rely on cognitive interpretation and memories of previous similar situations. Thus, the emotions we feel at any moment arise from a mixture of (1) brain and body reactions and (2) interpretations and memories pertaining to the situation. Second, other researchers are focusing on exactly how people interpret brain and body reactions. Some researchers claim that these reactions produce *core affect*, which consists of the "simplest raw feelings" that differ in the degree to which they are positive or negative and the degree to which they are strongly or weakly activated (Barrett, 2006; Russell, 2003). Changes in core affect are then *categorized*, much as ambiguous stimuli are categorized (Barrett, 2006). By analogy, to a farmer trying to gather his cows at dusk, a passing shadow may be seen as a cow; the farmer is categorizing the stimulus, not simply registering what is there. Similarly, context and previous experience may lead us to categorize types of core affect in ways that fit the situation, leading us to feel and express different emotions.

Which theory comes closest to the mark? To find out, let's take a closer look at the nature of emotion.

Physiological Profiles: Are Emotions Just Bodily Responses?

Gandhi stressed the importance of inner control, which includes controlling emotions. Suppose that one of his followers was so anxious about participating in a civil action that he meditated for hours in advance—which allowed him to keep his heart from pounding and otherwise prevented his sympathetic nervous system from becoming fully activated. Would he still have felt fear after the soldiers started shooting? Yes, he probably would have. Let's see why.

Perhaps the strongest evidence against James's idea that emotions arise when people interpret their own bodily states is the finding that even people with spinal cord injuries so severe that they receive no sensations from their bodies still report having emotions (Bermond et al., 1991). However, it is possible that these patients experience emotions differently than do people with intact spinal cords. For example, one such patient described in this way what it felt like when a lit cigarette fell onto his bed: "I could have burned up right there, but the funny thing is, I didn't get all shook up about it. I just didn't feel afraid at all, like you would suppose." Speaking about another common emotion, he said, "Sometimes I act angry when I see some injustice. I yell and cuss and raise hell, because if you don't do it sometimes, I've learned people will take advantage of you, but it doesn't have the heat to it that it used to. It's a mental kind of anger" (Hohman, 1966, pp. 150–151). These quotations suggest that this man's emotions were largely rational evaluations, rather than feelings in reaction to events. Nevertheless, he did express emotions.

The James–Lange theory implies that we feel different emotions because each emotion corresponds to a largely distinct bodily state. The Indian demonstrator's heart would probably begin pounding and his palms become sweaty when he heard the guns begin to roar and his compatriots cry out in pain, and these events would probably play a key role in the emotions he felt. The lag in time for these bodily events to arise after the violence began could explain why the demonstrator would continue to feel fear even after he escaped the British soldiers. In contrast, the Cannon–Bard theory implies that our bodies are aroused similarly in different arousing situations. According to this view, arousal is arousal; it occurs not only if you are mugged, but also if you win the lottery. But physiological evidence challenges both of these theories (Barrett et al., in press).

On the one hand, the James–Lange theory has not fared well in the face of research results. For example, a meta-analysis did not reveal clear patterns of bodily responses that distinguish the different emotions (Cacioppo et al., 2000). Moreover, meta-analyses of neuroimaging data have shown a similar finding about the brain: In general, different emotions evoke overlapping patterns of brain activation, not distinct areas (Murphy et al., 2003; Phan et al., 2002, 2004; Wager et al., 2003). The James–Lange theory does not require an absolute correspondence between brain or body reactions and specific emotions, but there should be a strong correlation between them—which has not been found.

On the other hand, the Cannon–Bard theory is challenged by the finding that *some* emotions (but not all) are accompanied by distinct patterns of heart rate, body temperature, sweating, and other reactions. For example, when you feel anger, your heart rate increases and so does the temperature of your skin; and when you feel fear, your heart rate increases, but your skin temperature decreases (Levenson et al., 1990). Although the James–Lange theory is not correct in general, distinct bodily reactions do occur in response to challenge and threat (Quigley et al., 2002; Tomaka et al., 1997) and, furthermore, in response to positive versus negative emotions (Cacioppo et al., 2000). In addition, evidence of a relationship between brain states and emotion is provided by neuroimaging data: Fear is associated with activation of the amygdala (but not uniquely, as we discuss shortly), and sadness activates the front part of the upper midline area of the frontal lobe (called the *anterior cingulate*; Phan et al., 2002).

It is also possible that a particular emotion corresponds to another bodily state, one that is not defined in terms of autonomic reactions. At least 20 muscles in your face do nothing but vary your facial expressions (Fridlund, 1994). When you move these muscles, your brain receives feedback from them. According to the **facial feedback hypothesis**, you feel emotions in part because of the way your muscles are positioned in your face (Izard, 1971; Tomkins, 1962). Presumably, reflexive neural systems and cognitive categorization systems first produce the facial expression, which then prompts the conscious experience of the emotion.

There is evidence that "putting on a happy face" is more than a phrase from a catchy song; it can actually make you feel happier. Following up on other studies (Duclos et al., 1989; Laird, 1974, 1984), Ekman and colleagues (Ekman, 1992; Ekman et al., 1990) tested this idea by leading participants to shift parts of their faces until they held specific expressions—for example, lifting the corners of the mouth until a smile and other signs of happiness were formed. The participants maintained these configurations while they rated their mood. If their faces were posed in a positive expression, they tended to rate their mood more positively than if their faces were posed in a negative expression.

However, putting on a happy face does not get our brains into exactly the same state as when we are genuinely happy (Ekman & Davidson, 1993). Thus, although facial feedback may affect emotions, our smiles, frowns, and glowers are not the only causes of our emotional experiences. Similarly, although there may be some bodily differences that accompany different emotions, there is no evidence that a distinct bodily state underlies each of our emotions.

Stick a pencil sideways (not point first) in your mouth, so that as you bite down on it, the corners of your lips turn up. Simply making this motion will actually make you feel happier (Strack et al., 1988). For more dramatic results, try to make a big smile, raising your cheeks.

Facial feedback hypothesis: The idea that emotions arise partly as a result of the positioning of facial muscles.

Figure 7.3 The Schachter–Singer Experiment

Participants received an epinephrine injection.

Confederates acted very differently while the participants waited.

The participants reacted very differently to the drug, depending on what the confederate was doing.

Cognitive Interpretation

Bodily factors are not enough to explain the range of feelings we have. What's missing? Our interpretations of events and the context in which events occur, both of which affect our feelings (Barrett et al., in press).

The classic experiment in this area was reported by Stanley Schachter and Jerome Singer in 1962; it is illustrated in Figure 7.3. The participants, who believed that they would be taking part in a test of vision, received an injection of what they were told was a vitamin supplement. The injection was really a shot of epinephrine, a neurotransmitter that causes general arousal. Each participant then waited in a room before beginning the "vision test." Also waiting in the room was a *confederate*—that is, someone who is posing as a participant but is, in fact, cooperating with the investigators to set up the conditions of the experiment. The experiment consisted of having the confederate act in different ways during the "waiting period" and recording the effects of his behavior on the participant. In one condition, the confederate was manic, playing with a hula hoop, tossing paper airplanes, and generally acting silly. In another condition, the confederate was sullen and irritable; he tried to make the participant angry, and eventually stormed out of the room. The participants who had waited with the manic confederate reported that they felt happy, whereas the participants who had waited with the irritable confederate reported that they felt angry.

Although these participants had the same bodily arousal induced by the drug, they experienced this arousal very differently, depending on the context in which it occurred; and this difference apparently led them to attribute different explanations for the arousal. In contrast, when participants were told in advance about the drug and its effects, they did *not* feel differently in the different contexts; it was only when they interpreted the arousal as arising from the context that their feelings differed. In addition, participants in a control group, who did not receive an injection, experienced no effects of context. It is worth noting that this study took place more than 40 years ago; giving participants drugs without their knowledge is now considered unethical and impermissible.

If you interpret signs of bodily arousal incorrectly, making a cognitive error called <mark>misattribution of arousal</mark>, you may experience emotions that ordinarily would not arise in the particular situation. For example, in one study, male participants were given false feedback about their own internal responses (Valins, 1966). They had been asked, while looking at slides of partially nude women, to listen to what they were told was their own heart beating. The heartbeats the men heard were, in fact, not their own; they were sometimes faster and sometimes slower than the men's actual heart rates. When the participants later were asked to rate the attractiveness of each woman, their ratings were based not just on what they saw but also on what they had heard: If they had associated a rapid heartbeat with a picture, they rated the woman as more attractive. It is clear that our interpretation of bodily feedback depends on the situation—and how we interpret the situation depends at least in part on bodily feedback (Palace, 1999).

To the extent that different bodily reactions occur for different emotions, then, categorization of core affect is supplemented by less ambiguous internal stimuli; it is as if that farmer gathering his cows could hear a cowbell as well as see the passing shadow. Emotion is a complex mixture that arises when the "whispers and shouts" of the body are filtered through the expectations and interpretations of the mind.

Fear: The Amygdala and You

Because it is one of the best-understood emotions, fear has become a testing ground for theories of emotion. Fear causes changes in the brain, in the autonomic nervous system, in hormones, and in behavior. When people are afraid, they tend to freeze (to be "paralyzed by fear"), and they have an increased tendency to be startled, a tendency called *fear-potentiated startle* (Davis, 1992; Lang, 1995; Vrana et al., 1988). For example, as Indian demonstrators approached a line of armed soldiers, the unfolding tableau probably made them susceptible to being startled, so that they were more likely to be thrown off balance when the first gunshots rang out.

Researchers have discovered four important facts about fear from studying the brain systems that produce it:

1. After you have learned to fear an object, fear can well up later as a kind of "emotional reflex," with no thought, or cognitive interpretation, at all (LeDoux, 1996). The amygdala plays a crucial role in producing the reactions you have when you are afraid. It sends signals to other brain areas and structures, such as the hypothalamus, that cause your heart to speed up, your muscles to freeze (as Gandhi's apparently did, when he rose to plead his first case in court), and all the other autonomic reactions associated with fear. In fact, conscious awareness is not needed for a stimulus to trigger the amygdala into producing fear-related responses (Öhman, 2002).

2. There is evidence that once you learn to associate fear with an object or situation, you will always do so. Fear is a classically conditioned response, and even after its extinction, the neurons that were linked by the conditioned association still fire together (see Chapter 4). Although extinction can block whether you express the emotion, the underlying connections are still there. This is one reason why it is so easy to reinstate conditioned fear. Even though you are not aware of the association, it is never fully lost (LeDoux, 1996).

3. In spite of its reflexive nature, fear interacts with mental processes. For example, if you merely visualize yourself in a scary situation, you become susceptible to being startled (Cook et al., 1991; Lang et al., 1990; Vrana & Lang, 1990); the parts of the brain involved in cognition play a key role in "setting you up" to be easily startled. Moreover, you can acquire fear associations merely by watching someone else be conditioned to fear a specific stimulus (Olsson & Phelps, 2004)!

4. In spite of its role in regulating fearful behaviors, the amygdala does not play a direct role in producing the emotional "feel" of fear; patients with damaged

In an fMRI study, pictures of faces with angry expressions were shown so briefly to participants that they were not aware of having seen the expressions. Even so, their amygdalae responded (Whalen et al., 1998). In addition, people who have a particular variant of a gene (SLC6A4, the human serotonin transporter gene) that affects serotonin levels show increased activation of the amygdala when they see emotional stimuli (Hariri et al., 2002).

amygdalae report experiencing positive and negative emotions (such as fear) as often and as strongly as normal people do (Anderson & Phelps, 2002).

What does all this tell us about emotion in general?

- There are distinct biological events that are associated with feelings of fear, a finding that is consistent with the James–Lange theory. However, these states are not just bodily reactions; they also involve specific brain systems.

- The events that lead to fear appear to produce both the experience and the bodily reaction at the same time, which fits the Cannon–Bard theory. However, the experience and the reaction are not entirely separate; rather, the person's interpretation of the event can affect both.

- Although cognitive interpretation is not always necessary for feeling fear, it is clear that mental events do interact with emotion. Thus, aspects of cognitive theory are supported.

- In spite of the distinct events that underlie fear, particular emotions cannot be identified with the activation of a single brain area (Barrett, 2006; Barrett et al., in press; Phan et al., 2002, 2004; Wager et al., 2003). For example, fear is typically the strongest emotion, and some researchers have suggested that the amygdala may be responding when we perceive or feel strong emotions in general—not just fear in particular (Davis & Whalen, 2001). In fact, researchers have found that the amygdala responds when people experience both positive and negative emotions (Aalto et al., 2002), when they read words that name positive and negative emotions (Hamann & Mao, 2002), and even when they think they've won or lost a simple game (Zalla et al., 2000). Thus, the study of fear is revealing the inner workings of emotion more generally.

In short, the three older theories of emotion all contain a grain of truth. However, the sum total of the findings is most consistent with the emerging synthesis, which includes roles for both brain-based, reflexive reactions and the categorization of bodily states in particular contexts.

Positive Emotions: More Than Feeling Good

Lest you think that psychologists have a morbid fascination with the dark side, we must note that much has also been learned about positive emotions (Biswas-Diener et al., 2004; Diener, 2000; Fredrickson, 2001; Lyubomirsky, 2001; Myers, 2000; Peterson, 2000; Ryan & Deci, 2000).

Happiness. Fear and happiness differ in fundamental ways. For one, fear narrows the scope of attention and tends to restrict behavior to the small set of fight-or-flight responses; in contrast, happiness leads people to broaden the scope of attention and to be open to novel courses of action (Biswas-Diener et al., 2004). Moreover, whereas fear is a momentary state, which is easy to study in the brain, happiness is a more chronic state, bearing on the tenor of your life—this makes the brain mechanisms underlying happiness much more difficult to study. Instead, happiness has been studied largely from the levels of the person and the group.

What makes us happy? There are several answers to this question.

- Not surprisingly, a survey of happiness in 40 countries found that money *can* sometimes buy happiness, at least to some extent: Money generally can buy happiness for those in poverty and deprivation; people tend to be happier when they are living in better economic conditions (Diener & Biswas-Diener, 2002; Schyns, 1998). However, once a person has risen above the level of poverty and deprivation, additional material resources make little—if any—difference in happiness. Although we are happier immediately after getting a big raise or winning a prize in a lottery, the blip in happiness is short-lived; before long, we are no more or less happy than we were before (Brickman & Campbell, 1971).

- Immediate life circumstances, such as how we are treated by those around us and time pressure at work, clearly affect our happiness (Kahneman et al., 2004).

- Moreover, our attitudes have a lot to do with how happy we are: In general, happy people have adjusted their desires to be consistent with their resources and abilities (Crawford Solberg et al., 2002).

- One possible additional contributor to feelings of happiness is *social support*, the degree to which you feel that other people are willing and able to listen and help (Myers, 2000). In China, the strongest predictor of happiness was a measure of social support (Lu, 1999; Lu et al., 1997).

- It is also clear that personality affects happiness. For example, at least in Western countries, assertive people tend to be happier than nonassertive people (Argyle & Lu, 1990). And extraverted (outgoing) people tend to be happier than introverted people. But more than that, happy people tend to perceive the world through rose-colored glasses; they construe situations to "maintain and even promote their happiness and positive self views" (Lyubomirsky, 2001, p. 241).

Researchers have found that in 16 of 17 countries they examined (the exception was Northern Ireland), marriage is linked to greater happiness than is either being single or living with someone to whom you aren't married. This increase in happiness was comparable for both men and women (Ross, 1995; Stack & Eshleman, 1998; Weerasinghe & Tepperman, 1994). Apparently, most of the effects of marriage on happiness are indirect: increasing satisfaction with household finances and improving perceived health. However, this is not all there is to it; the simple fact of being married, all by itself, contributes to happiness.

Although not much has been learned about the neural bases of happiness, some progress has been made. We have already noted that people with more activation in the left frontal lobe (not only during a particular task, but in general) tend to be happier than people with more activation in the right frontal lobe (Davidson, 1992a, 1992b, 1993, 1994, 1998, 2002). But why do people differ in these ways? One possibility lies in their genetic make-up. At least 50% of the variability in happiness may arise from heredity (Lykken & Tellegen, 1996). Does this mean that if you are unhappy, you should just adjust because you can't change? Not at all! As we discussed in Chapter 2, genes are not destiny.

Positive Psychology: More Than a State of Mind. Being happy is one focus of what has come to be known as *positive psychology* (Seligman & Csikszentmihalyi, 2000; Seligman & Pawelski, 2003). Researchers have shown that positive states of mind can promote *resilience*, which is the ability to bounce back from adversity, to keep an even keel (Bonanno, 2004, 2005; Tugade & Fredrickson, 2004). But more than that, maintaining a positive attitude can promote personal growth (Linley & Joseph, 2004). In fact, positive emotions can literally boost the immune system and help us cope with disease (Rosenkrantz et al., 2003; Tugade et al., 2004). Because positive emotions broaden attention and lead people to become more open and receptive, such emotions often promote effective coping strategies. And effective coping, in turn, creates more positive emotions, which produces an "upward spiral" (Fredrickson & Joiner, 2002).

Expressing Emotions: Letting It All Hang Out?

Emotions occur in the social context of family, friends, and culture. Like Gandhi's emotions, many of our emotions arise from social interactions, both positive (Gandhi's exhilaration when he attains a victory for social justice) and negative (his fear after having been beaten by a train conductor for refusing to give up his seat to a White person). Not only do social stimuli trigger emotions, but emotions also serve social roles; these roles range from communicating to providing connections among people.

Culture and Emotional Expression: Rules of the Mode

In many ways, emotional experience is a private affair, inaccessible to others. But emotional expression is crucial for our daily interactions with other people. According to Ekman (1980), each of us learns a set of **display rules** for our culture that indicate when, to whom, and how strongly certain emotions can be shown. For example, he notes that in North America people will find it suspicious if a man's secretary seems more upset at his funeral than his wife does. In the display rules for North American culture, the closer the relation to the deceased, the more emotion may be displayed. Display rules are partly a function of habit (individuals do differ in their styles), but they largely reflect "the way things are done" in a particular region, class, or culture.

Ekman (1984) described a fascinating test of his theory that all people share the same basic emotions but their expression of emotions sometimes differs because of display rules. He challenged the stereotype that Asians are less emotional than Westerners. Americans in Berkeley and Japanese in Tokyo were shown the same films, one positive (scenery) and one negative (a surgical procedure). Participants viewed the films either alone or in the company of a white-coated scientist. Both national groups showed the same range of emotional expression when they viewed the films in individual screenings, one person at a time, but the Japanese participants were notably more restrained when they were in company. Ekman analyzed slow-motion videotapes of the participants as they watched. The tapes revealed that a Japanese participant watching alone reacted in the same way as the Americans. But a Japanese watching in company would begin showing an emotional reaction, then quickly squelch it. According to Ekman, the initial Japanese reaction reflected the basic, innate emotions; then display rules came to the fore, and the participant regulated the show of emotions accordingly.

Body Language: Broadcasting Feelings

Nonverbal communication isn't really language (see Chapter 6), but it is a form of communication that is particularly effective at conveying emotions.

Body language is undoubtedly shaped in part by the display rules of a culture, and it plays many roles. One important role is in conveying sexual interest. For example, studies have shown that men and women hold their bodies differently in the presence of someone of the opposite sex if they are interested in that person than if they are not interested. However, interest is not conveyed in exactly the same way by men and women. Grammer (1990) found that interested men had "open postures" (with the legs relaxed and open) and watched the women, whereas interested women avoided eye contact, presented their body rotated slightly to the side (so that their breasts were seen in profile), and uncrossed their arms and legs. For both males and females, a closed posture conveyed lack of interest.

Display rule: A culture-specific rule that indicates when, to whom, and how strongly certain emotions can be shown.

Emotion is conveyed not only by facial expression, but also by tone of voice and body movements. People can sense happiness more accurately than other emotions from facial expressions—but they sense happiness least accurately from tone of voice. In contrast, of all the emotions, anger is most easily sensed from the tone of voice, and it is less well sensed from the face (Elfenbein & Ambady, 2002). Nonverbal information is not entirely conveyed by facial expression, so it's wise to pay attention to all sources of information.

At least some of our body language may result from innate factors. Although there has yet to be a good rigorous study of this, one anecdote is highly suggestive. In reviewing 30 studies of identical twins who were separated and raised apart, Faber (1981) wrote: "As with voice, the way the twins held themselves, walked, turned their heads, or flicked their wrists was more alike than any quantifiable trait the observers were able to measure. . . . If one twin had a limp, moist handshake, so did the other. If one had a spirited prance, so did the partner" (pp. 86–87).

Emotion Regulation

Gandhi helped many ordinary people overcome fear. His techniques of collective action built on the Indian tradition of yoga, which emphasizes self-control. The very fact that display rules exist implies that we have at least some voluntary control over our emotional expressions. Researchers have shown that we also have at least some control over how our brains respond emotionally. For example, in one study, participants saw neutral or negative pictures while their brains were being scanned using fMRI. The participants were told either simply to view the pictures or to maintain their initial emotional responses to the pictures. In fact, when they maintained negative emotions, their amygdalae continued to be activated over a longer period of time. Moreover, the more strongly the participants rated their negative reaction to the picture, the more strongly their amygdalae were activated (Schaefer et al., 2002).

Regulating the Emotional Brain. Can people voluntarily dampen down the mechanisms that underlie emotion? Gandhi assumed that the answer is "yes," and apparently trained himself to keep his emotions in check. And his assumption was justified (Ochsner & Gross, 2005). In one neuroimaging study, researchers showed male participants erotic videos and asked them to respond normally or to try to inhibit sexual arousal (Beauregard et al., 2001). When the men were reacting normally, various brain areas involved in emotion were activated, such as the amygdala and hypothalamus. When the men were inhibiting their reactions, parts of the frontal lobe became activated—and the brain areas normally activated by those reactions no longer were.

Consequences of Emotion Regulation. Emotion regulation is important for at least three reasons:

1. Difficulty in controlling negative emotions could be a source of violent aggression, perhaps in part because of the frustration at having to keep feelings under wraps (Davidson et al., 2000b).

2. If you try to control emotions by suppressing your overt behavior, you will impair your memory for the surrounding events (Bonanno et al., 2004; Richards & Gross, 2000), impede your ability to reason (Baumeister et al., 1998) and your ability to communicate clearly (Butler et al., 2003), and even raise your blood pressure (Butler et al., 2003). You can avoid these negative consequences if you regulate your emotions by reinterpreting the situation and your role in it (Gross, 2001, 2002; Richards, 2004; Richards et al., 2003).

3. Being able to regulate emotion is also important because emotion affects cognition (especially working memory; J. R. Gray, 2001). Positive emotions facilitate verbal tasks but interfere with spatial tasks (such as remembering an object's location or recognizing faces); negative emotions have the opposite effects. (Could these findings say something about how you might

prepare to study for an English versus a geometry test?) The different effects of positive and negative emotions on cognition may arise from the fact that positive emotion activates the left frontal lobe during a verbal task, whereas negative emotion activates the right frontal lobe during a spatial task (J. R. Gray et al., 2002).

Perceiving Emotions: A Form of Mind Reading

Emotions play a role in moving us to behave in certain ways, and they also cue others about our internal states and likely behaviors. In some cases, people may direct an emotional expression toward another person, as a deliberate form of communication; but in many cases, an emotional expression may simply be a sign, produced unconsciously, of an internal state (Russell et al., 2003); in either case, emotional expressions invite us to engage in a form of "mind reading." Just as we know that a dog is feeling hot when it pants and its tongue lolls out, we can read even unintentional expressions and draw inferences about a person's emotional state.

Reading Cues

We are remarkably good at reading cues about emotion, acquiring information from even minimal cues. For instance, Dittrich and colleagues (1996) attached 13 small lights to the bodies of each of two professional dancers and had them perform dances that conveyed fear, anger, grief, joy, surprise, and disgust. Undergraduate students who later watched videotapes of the dances were able to recognize the intended emotions, even in the dark when only the lights were visible.

The ability to read nonverbal communications is at least partly determined by experience. For example, children who watch more television tend to be better at judging emotional expressions (Feldman et al., 1996). Moreover, culture affects not only how willing you are to express emotion in specific situations, but also how sensitive you are to the emotional expressions of others (Stephan et al., 1996). When a culture makes emotions difficult to detect through more stringent display rules, it almost seems as though its members compensate by developing better abilities to detect emotions. For example, although display rules in China call for more emotional restraint than those in Australia, Chinese children can detect basic emotions more accurately than Australian children can (Markham & Wang, 1996).

Perceiving by Imitating: Making the Match

"Smile and the whole world smiles along with you." Could this be more than a well-worn adage? In fact, researchers have found that when we perceive an emotional expression, we imitate it, at least somewhat (Adolphs, 2002; Niedenthal et al., 2001); such imitation can occur even when people are not consciously aware of having seen a face displaying a specific emotion (Dimberg et al., 2000). Do these findings mean that if you were totally paralyzed, you couldn't recognize emotions? Probably not. Such findings are consistent with the idea that we categorize what we see, which involves retrieving information about similar situations that occurred in the past and our responses to them (Barrett & Niedenthal, 2004).

Looking at Levels

Lie Detection

Gandhi was lied to often in his long and turbulent career. In South Africa, for example, General Smuts tried to lull Gandhi with agreements that he had no intention of honoring, much to the later disappointment and chagrin of the Mahatma. Gandhi no doubt would have appreciated knowing whether others were lying to him. Are there good methods for detecting lies? Although lie detector tests are not admissible evidence in court, they are still used in various investigations. What do they really "detect"?

If distinct brain and body states accompany at least some emotions, researchers have reasoned, then there might be distinct biological "signatures" of the feelings of guilt and fear when someone is caught at some wrongdoing. This idea underlies a long history of attempts to detect deception objectively. One result has been machines called **polygraphs**, known misleadingly as "lie detectors." These machines don't "detect lies" directly; they monitor the activity of the sympathetic and parasympathetic nervous systems—in particular, changes in skin conductance, breathing, and heart rate.

The polygraph relies on asking a person questions and comparing the verbal responses to the bodily responses. But how should questions be asked? The most basic technique used with a polygraph is the *relevant/irrelevant technique* (*RIT*; Larson, 1932). Suppose you are trying to determine whether the suspect in a crime is telling the truth. When the RIT technique is used, the suspect is asked crime-related questions ("Did you break into Mr. Johnson's house last night?") and neutral questions ("Do you live at 43 Pleasant Street?"). The bodily responses accompanying the answers to the two types of questions are then compared. However, there is clearly a large difference in the emotional weight of the two types of questions. Thus, a greater bodily response to a crime-related question may reflect not guilt but simply the fact that the idea posed by the question is more arousing. To avoid this possibility, the *control question technique* (*CQT*; Reid, 1947) includes comparison questions that should have an emotional weight roughly equivalent to that of the crime-related questions. For example, in addition to the two questions above, the suspect might be asked, "Did you ever do anything you were ashamed of?"

A more recent technique is the *guilty knowledge test* (*GKT*; sometimes called the *concealed information test*), developed by Lykken (1959, 1960). In contrast to the RIT and the CQT, the GKT does not rely on asking direct questions about the crime. Instead, this test uses indirect questions that presumably only the guilty person would be in a position to answer correctly. In addition, the GKT relies on multiple-choice questions. So the suspect might be asked, "Was the color of the walls in Mr. Johnson's bedroom white? Yellow? Blue?" Someone who has never been in the room should have comparable responses to each of the choices, whereas someone who has guilty knowledge should respond selectively to the actual color. A modification of this approach is the *guilty actions test* (Bradley & Warfield, 1984; Bradley et al., 1996), which observes responses when people are given statements about actions that they may have committed.

Do these techniques work? Ben-Shakhar and Furedy (1990) report that in the laboratory the CQT on average correctly classifies 80% of the guilty and 63% of

Polygraph: A machine that monitors the activity of the sympathetic and parasympathetic nervous systems, particularly changes in skin conductance, breathing, and heart rate, in an attempt to detect lying.

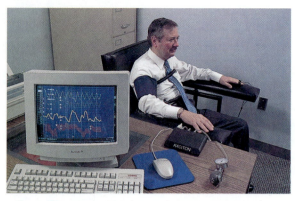

Polygraphs are used to detect changes in autonomic nervous system activity, which may signal that the person being interviewed is lying.

Table 7.1

Some Common (Although Not Entirely Reliable) Signs of Deception

- Frequent eye blinks
- Sideways glances
- Downcast eyes
- Stiff body posture combined with direct eye contact
- Larger pupil size
- Rising pitch of voice
- Exaggerated facial expressions
- Increased grammatical errors
- Slower and less fluent speech than normal
- Repetition of words and phrases

the innocent. Thus, this technique unfortunately leads too often to the classification of honest responses as lies. The GKT has a better track record; the guilty were detected 84% of the time, and the innocent 94%. However, the range of accuracy in the reviewed studies was from 64% to 100% for detecting the guilty and from 81% to 100% for detecting the innocent. Many other researchers have reported comparable results (DeClue, 2003). (You are probably getting a sense as to why polygraph evidence is not admitted in courts of law.) More recent techniques that measure electrical activity in the brain can sometimes have accuracy as high as 95%, but there is still enough variability to cast doubt on the examiner's ability to classify individual answers as untruthful (Allen & Iacono, 1997).

Also at the level of the brain, neuroimaging studies are beginning to illuminate just why it is so difficult to detect lies. For example, Ganis and colleagues (2003) found that unlike a rose, a lie is not a lie is not a lie. From the brain's point of view, there is more than one way to lie. Specifically, when people lied spontaneously, making up responses "on the fly," parts of the brain involved in working memory and in monitoring errors were very active; but when people lied on the basis of a well-learned "alternative reality" scenario (for example, saying that they drove to the mountains on vacation when in fact they flew to the coast), areas of the brain involved in retrieving memories were activated instead. Moreover, as other researchers have found (Kozel, Padgett, & George, 2004; Kozel, Revell, et al., 2004), the specific pattern of brain activation in each condition varied for different people, which makes interpreting the results even more complicated.

At the level of the person, we can ask whether some people are particularly gifted at detecting lies. DePaulo and her collaborators (1997) reported a meta-analysis of studies on the relation between an individual's confidence that he or she has spotted a lie and the level of the person's accuracy, and they found essentially no relation between the two (a correlation of essentially zero). Similarly, in another study, police officers viewed videotapes of an interview with a man who was lying about a murder (which he later confessed to committing); these officers correctly classified 70% of the true statements but only 57% of the lies (Vrij & Mann, 2001). Many other researchers have reported similar results (Elaad, 2003; Garrido et al., 2004; Granhag & Strömwall, 2001; Vrij, 2004). However, other evidence suggests that *some* people can distinguish truth from lies extraordinarily accurately, particularly some (but not all) of those who have been trained in law enforcement or in clinical psychology with an interest in deception (Ekman et al., 1999). A few rare people are intuitively able to pick up telltale cues of deception, but scientists have yet to isolate those cues.

At the level of the group, we can ask what cues people use to detect whether someone is lying. Researchers have discovered that we detect lies by registering *microexpressions*, flickers of expressions—such as frequent eyeblinks, quick sideways glances, or downcast eyes for as little as a tenth of a second (DePaulo et al., 2003; Ekman, 1985; Ekman & Friesen, 1975). We recognize different types of nonverbal information and can detect lies when inconsistent information arises from different sources, such as a stiff body posture combined with trusting, direct eye contact. We are also sensitive to a variety of telltale cues, summarized in Table 7.1. However, many of these cues are not highly reliable (Mann et al., 2004; Strömwall et al., 2003; Vrij & Mann, 2001).

How can we best understand lie detection? The goal of lie detection is to assess a particular social interaction in which one person is trying to mislead another person. Perhaps the greatest problem with the polygraph is that it really detects guilt or fear (the level of the person). If the person being tested lies but does not *feel* guilty or afraid, the palms won't become sweaty, heart rate won't increase, and so forth; the brain does not produce the autonomic responses associated with the feeling. And because the interviewer does not have any basis for detecting the lie, this lack of biological response in turn may alter how the person is being treated during the interview (a social interaction), and that treatment in turn can affect the person's reactions to the questions. Moreover, if the person being interviewed feels comfortable, he or she may be less likely to produce the microexpressions that some people can readily detect (without any need for the machine). Thus, in order to understand lie detection, we need to consider all three levels of analysis: The activity in the brain that produces the autonomic signals and observable behavior; the personality differences that could lead a person to feel guilty or afraid; and the rules of the society, together with the person's understanding of them, which would lead the person to feel guilty under certain circumstances.

LOOKING BACK: *Review*

1. *What are the different emotions?* Ekman and his collaborators offered much evidence that six emotions are "basic"—happiness, anger, sadness, disgust, surprise, and fear—but the last two are more easily confused with each other than are any of the others. Emotions can be categorized as approach or withdrawal emotions.

2. *What causes emotion?* The James–Lange theory states that emotion follows bodily reactions; the Cannon–Bard theory holds that emotions and bodily reactions occur at the same time, not in the order claimed by James and Lange; cognitive theory holds that emotions arise when bodily states are interpreted in the context of the specific situation; and, most recently, an emerging synthesis of previous theories maintains that some emotions arise reflexively from specific brain activity, whereas others depend on thought and interpretation. All the theories have captured a facet of how emotions work. As the James–Lange theory predicts, emotions may be caused in part by differences in internal bodily state (such as heart rate and breathing rate) and in facial expression. As the Cannon–Bard theory predicts, some emotions are reflexes that simultaneously produce both the experience and the bodily reaction. As cognitive theory predicts, how you interpret the causes of your bodily states influences which emotion you will feel. But as the emerging synthesis predicts, some emotions (in some circumstances) rely more on cognitive interpretation than others. Environmental events also play a key role in emotion; a person's happiness, for example, depends in part on his or her economic and cultural context.

3. *How do we express and regulate our emotions?* We express our emotions through overt behavior—such as changes in facial expression, tone of voice, and posture—as well as through speech. However, our outward expression does not always reflect our inner feelings. Cultures have different display rules, which determine when and to what degree emotions are shown. In addition, we can voluntarily regulate not only our emotional expression, but also emotions themselves. The most effective way to regulate emotions relies on reinterpreting the situation and our role in it.

4. How do we perceive emotions in others? We can read even minimal cues—such as subtle differences in body language—to infer emotion. When a culture has stringent display rules, its members appear to compensate by becoming more sensitive to emotion cues. In addition, when we perceive an emotion, we often imitate it, and the act of imitation provides feedback that allows us to perceive the emotion better.

LOOKING BEYOND: *Critical Thinking*

Would the world necessarily be a better place if people could control their emotions perfectly?

If scientists eventually come to understand fully the nature and causes of emotions, in what ways could this information be used in the real world? Would it be helpful for politicians? Diplomats? Advertisers? Would it be a good idea to include the information in everyone's education, so that people's emotions could not be easily manipulated?

What would be the advantages and disadvantages of a machine that always detected lies and never mistook the truth for lying? If your school offered a course in reading "body language," would you take it? Why or why not?

Motivation and Reward: More Than Feeling Good

Gandhi eventually proved exceptionally successful as a lawyer in South Africa. Not only did he make an unusually good living, but he also had White employees—a sign of status for an Indian lawyer (Markovits, 2003). This success may have shown him the limits of what money could do and also endowed him with a measure of self-confidence, which allowed him to behave unconventionally. For example, he adopted the dress of an Indian peasant, and eventually wore only a loincloth. Why? His appearance disconcerted his upper-crust British opponents, who often had trouble reconciling his fluent English and obvious intelligence with his garb. But his motivation for dressing as he did was not simply to disconcert other people. Gandhi wanted to promote hand-spinning and hand-weaving in India, to eliminate the dependence on imported cloth that largely came from England. For him, establishing economic independence was a central part of helping India establish its dignity. But he was also motivated to help India attain political independence and develop spiritually.

LOOKING AHEAD: *Learning Objectives*

1. *What are the sources of motivation?*
2. *What is the difference between* needs *and* wants, *and what factors affect them?*

Getting Motivated: Sources and Theories of Motivation

Motivation: The set of requirements and desires that lead an animal (including a human) to behave in a particular way at a particular time and place.

Motivation is the set of requirements and desires that lead an animal (including a human) to behave in a particular way at a particular time and place. There is

Many different goals motivate us, ranging from getting good grades, to needing to keep warm, to being the object of others' attention. What goals motivate you most strongly?

no single, widely accepted theory that can explain all of human motivation. There are motives based on biological needs (for example, the desire for primary reinforcers such as food to quell hunger) and motives based on learning (for example, the desire for secondary reinforcers such as a promotion), motives rooted in the internal state of a person (such as hunger) and motives sparked by the external world (such as exploration), motives based on a current situation and motives based on an expected future situation. Psychologists have analyzed, classified, and identified human motives in numerous ways, developing a variety of theories of motivation. Let's look at the key concepts in these theories and find out what each has to offer as an explanation of human behavior.

Instincts: My Genes Made Me Do It

Why do birds fly south for the winter and spiders make certain kinds of webs? Instinct. For many animals, instincts provide the main motivation for behaviors. An **instinct** is an inherited tendency to produce organized and unalterable responses to particular stimuli. For several decades at the beginning of the 20th century, some psychologists tried to explain human motivation in terms of instincts (for example, McDougall, 1908/1960); their approach is termed *instinct theory*. Much of Freud's theory, for example, hinges on ideas about how we grapple with our sexual urges, which he considered to be instinctive (these ideas are discussed in Chapter 8). But unlike many other animals, we humans are remarkably flexible in the way we can respond to any stimulus, so it is difficult to assign an important role to instincts in human motivation.

Evolutionary psychology has offered an alternative to instinct theory. Instead of proposing that a behavior itself is "hard-wired" (part of our inherited make-up), these theorists believe that goals that motivate us (such as finding attractive mates) and general cognitive strategies for achieving goals (such as deception) are inborn (Barkow et al., 1992; Buss, 1998; Cosmides & Tooby, 1996; Pinker, 1997, 2002; Plotkin, 1997). However, evolutionary theories of motivation are notoriously difficult to test because we can never know for sure what our ancestors were like and how they evolved. Moreover, some goals are unlikely to be a result of heredity. For example, Gandhi valued punctuality and was almost obsessively on time; in fact, a large gold watch was the only thing of value he owned at the time of his death. Nevertheless, evolutionary thinking can be a source of novel hypotheses that can be tested in their own right (Pinker, 1997).

Instinct: An inherited tendency to produce organized and unalterable responses to particular stimuli.

Drives and Homeostasis: Staying in Balance

Instinct theory and evolutionary theory focus on specifying particular innate behaviors or goals and strategies. In contrast, *drive theory* focuses on the mechanisms that underlie such tendencies, whether or not they are innate. A **drive** is an internal imbalance that pushes you to reach a particular goal, which in turn will reduce that imbalance. Drives differ in terms of the goals to which they direct you, but all are aimed at satisfying a requirement (decreasing an imbalance). For example, hunger is a drive that orients you toward food; thirst is a drive that impels you toward drink; being cold is a drive that nudges you toward a source of warmth. Gandhi added a woolen shawl to his loincloth when he visited Buckingham Palace, in response to the raw London weather. Some drive theories link drives with reinforcement: Something is reinforcing if it reduces an imbalance. According to this theory, if you are hungry, food is reinforcing because it reduces the imbalance experienced when you have the hunger drive; if you are not hungry, food is not reinforcing.

What is the nature of the imbalance that is quelled by reinforcement? In 1932, Walter B. Cannon published a ground-breaking book titled *The Wisdom of the Body*, in which he pointed out that for life to be sustained, certain characteristics and substances of the body must be kept within a certain range, neither rising too high nor falling too low. These characteristics and substances include body temperature and the amounts of oxygen, minerals, water, and food taken in. Bodily processes such as digestion and respiration work toward keeping the levels steady. The process of maintaining a steady state is called **homeostasis**. Homeostasis works not simply to keep the body in balance, but to keep it in balance in the range in which it functions best. The usual analogy to homeostasis is a thermostat and furnace: The thermostat turns the furnace on when the temperature drops too low and turns it off when the temperature reaches the desired level. But Cannon pointed out that in living creatures, homeostasis often involves active behavior, not simply the passive registering of the state of the environment. To stay alive, you must nourish yourself by obtaining and taking in food and water, and you must maintain body temperature by finding shelter and wearing clothing. If the homeostatic balance goes awry, an imbalance results—and you are motivated to correct the imbalance. In fact, emotion may play a role in anticipating "homeostatic challenges before the fact" (Watt, 2005, p. 84), and thereby be a key factor in motivating us. For example, a moment's thought about how you would feel if you go outside in shirtsleeves during the dead of a Massachusetts winter would lead you to put on a coat before venturing out.

Arousal Theory: Avoiding Boredom, Avoiding Overload

People are also motivated to maintain another kind of balance, one that has nothing to do with physiological homeostasis: Simply put, we don't like stimuli that are either too boring or too arousing; instead, we seek to maintain an intermediate level of stimulation. Berlyne (1960, 1974) showed that people like random patterns, paintings, or music best when they are neither too simple nor too complex, but rather somewhere in the middle. What is classed as "simple" or "complex" depends partly on the person as well as the nature of the stimulus. For example, children find patterns complex that to adults are less so.

These findings conform to what is now known as the *Yerkes–Dodson law* (Figure 7.4), named after the researchers who first described a similar principle. This law states that we perform best when we are at an intermediate level of arousal. If we are underaroused, we are sluggish; if we are overaroused, we can't focus and sustain attention. Intermediate levels of arousal may occur when

Drive: An internal imbalance that motivates animals (including humans) to reach a particular goal that will reduce the imbalance.

Homeostasis: The process of maintaining a steady state, in which bodily characteristics and substances are within a certain range.

we are challenged not too much and not too little. For example, if you have to speak before a large group, you may become tongue-tied because of overarousal; if you are rehearsing the speech alone in your room, you may be understimulated and give a lackluster presentation. Indeed, people adapt to a constant set of stimuli, become bored, and then seek additional stimulation (Helson, 1964). We are apparently drawn to moderate stimulation. As intuitive as this idea may seem, not all studies have supported it (for example, Messinger, 1998), perhaps because it is difficult to define precisely levels of stimulation and how they vary.

Incentives and Reward: Happy Expectations

Homeostasis is a useful concept for understanding thirst, hunger, and certain other drives (such as those for salt, oxygen, and temperature control), and arousal theory helps explain why people select certain activities and situations and reject others. However, neither principle helps to explain other motivations, such as for sex (Beach, 1956). Your body doesn't actually need sex in the way you need food and oxygen; you can't die from celibacy. Moreover, sex is an example of an activity that invokes high arousal, not the intermediate levels we apparently prefer in other contexts. Much of what motivates us is best understood in terms of <mark>incentives</mark>, which are stimuli or events that draw us to achieve a particular goal in anticipation of a reward. Sex is a good example of a behavior that results from incentive-related motivation; so, too, is any money-making activity. To see the difference between a drive and an incentive, consider the fact that hunger is a drive, which is often long gone before dessert—but dessert can nevertheless still be an incentive to keep eating (as exploited by countless parents, who use dessert as an incentive to get their kids to eat their spinach).

The notion that much of motivation can best be understood in terms of incentives has led theorists to think about some aspects of motivation in terms of *expectations* of reinforcement (Wise, 2004). We tend to behave in ways that experience has shown us will produce a desirable outcome (see Chapter 4), either a positive consequence of the behavior (positive reinforcement) or the removal of a negative condition (negative reinforcement). If working 20 hours a week in a store has led to a regular paycheck, you will likely want to keep working (assuming that the check is large enough!).

Classical conditioning may play a role in determining what is an incentive by making a previously neutral stimulus desirable (Bindra, 1968; see Chapter 4). Patients with damage to the lower midline portion of the frontal lobe seem unable either to draw on the results of such learning or to set up new emotional associations that can guide them to make good decisions in the future (Bechara et al., 2000). In general, because we have all had different experiences, and hence learned different things, it's hard to know for sure what stimuli will serve as incentives for a given person. Consider, for example, the fact that, for Gandhi, prison was "more a luxury than a punishment. He could devote more time to prayer, study and spinning than he could outside" (Nanda, 1987).

Figure 7.4 The Yerkes–Dodson Law

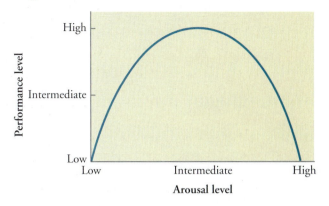

People perform best at intermediate levels of arousal.

Rewarding a child merely for performing an activity can undermine *intrinsic motivation*—it can make a child less likely to engage in that activity for its own sake (Deci et al., 1999; Lepper et al., 1973). But this need not occur. For example, praise can increase intrinsic motivation, provided that it has a number of characteristics, including being perceived as sincere, focusing on personal competence and positive traits (but not by relying on social comparisons), and helping the recipient feel autonomous (Cialdini et al., 1998; Eisenberger & Cameron, 1996; Henderlong & Lepper, 2002).

Incentive: A stimulus or event that draws animals (including humans) toward a particular goal in anticipation of a reward.

Figure 7.5 The Classic Learned Helplessness Experiment

An animal is placed in a cage and shocked. Initially, the animal tries to escape, but it can do nothing to avoid or prevent the shocks.

The animal eventually gives up.

When the animal is moved into a new cage in which only a small barrier separates the side where shocks are delivered from the side where no shocks occur, it does not try to escape the shock, even when the shock is signaled by a tone.

Learned Helplessness: Unhappy Expectations

People not only can learn new strategies for coping with problems, but they also can learn to give up trying. Martin Seligman and his colleagues first described **learned helplessness**, which occurs when an animal has an aversive experience in which nothing it does can affect what happens to it, and so it simply gives up and stops trying to change the situation or to escape (Mikulincer, 1994). As shown in Figure 7.5 (Overmeier & Seligman, 1967), when dogs were put in a cage in which they could not escape shocks, they eventually gave up responding and just huddled on the floor and endured—and they continued to do so even when they were moved to a new cage in which it was easy to escape the shocks. This condition can also afflict humans who experience a lack of control over negative events: If nothing you do seems to make an abusive spouse stop tormenting you, you may eventually just give up and stop trying. Learned helplessness can lead to depression and a range of stress-related problems.

Needs and Wants: The Stick and the Carrot

Different things motivate different people: Gandhi was not motivated to make money; the typical entrepreneur is not motivated to give away all earthly possessions and lead a social and political revolution. Moreover, you are not motivated by the same forces day in and day out; rather, your motivations often shift over the course of the day (or year or life span). A particular motivation comes to the fore when you have a *need* or *want*. A **need** is a condition that arises from the lack of a requirement. Needs give rise to drives, which push you to reach a particular goal that will reduce the need. A low level of nutrients creates a need; hunger is a drive that will lead you to fill that need. In contrast, a **want** is a condition that arises when you have an unmet goal that will not fill a requirement. A want causes the goal to act as an incentive. You might *need* to eat, but you don't *need* a fancier car, although you might desperately *want* one—and the promise of a

Learned helplessness: The condition that occurs after an animal has an aversive experience in which nothing it does can affect what happens to it, and so it simply gives up and stops trying to change the situation or to escape.

Need: A condition that arises from the lack of a requirement; needs give rise to drives.

Want: A condition that arises when you have an unmet goal that will not fill a requirement; wants turn goals into incentives.

new car for working hard over the summer would be an incentive for you to put in long hours on the job. You are not necessarily aware of your needs or wants. Gandhi may not have been consciously aware of the motives that led him to imitate British dress and manners when he went to law school in London, but they affected him nonetheless.

Is There More Than One Type of Reward?

For all needs and wants, attaining the goal reinforces the behaviors that lead to it. But what makes attaining the goal rewarding? What is "reward"? Even the strongest regulatory needs, creating drives such as hunger and thirst, arise from the brain—and those needs are satisfied not by what we do directly, but rather by the effects of our actions on the brain. To understand why something is rewarding, we must look more closely at the brain's response to events in the world. By looking at the brain mechanisms underlying reward, we find support for the distinction between needs and wants.

Olds and Milner (1954) found that rats who received electrical stimulation in a certain brain area acted as if they desired more of it. These researchers thought that they had identified a "pleasure center" in the brain. Later research showed that they had stumbled on a brain system that underlies reward when an animal has been deprived of the reinforcer. **Deprived reward** is reward that occurs when a biological need is met. Such reward arises from the brain pathway that runs from certain parts of the brain stem, through the hypothalamus, on up to specific parts of the limbic system and the frontal lobes (Baxter et al., 2000; Kalivas & Nakamura, 1999; Rolls & Cooper, 1974; Wise, 1996). Many of the neurons in this circuit use, or are affected by, the neurotransmitter dopamine (Wise, 2004).

There is good evidence that the brain has a second system, which operates for **nondeprived reward**, reward that occurs when the rewarding stimulus or activity is not something that is necessary—in other words, when you had a want but not a need. For example, when ending a fast (which he often used as a political tool), even Gandhi probably felt pleasure in eating: Such pleasure is mediated by brain circuits used in deprived reward, which rely on dopamine. In contrast, if Gandhi ate one last juicy piece of fruit at the end of the meal, even though he was no longer hungry, he was eating even though he was nondeprived (it's an open question how often Gandhi actually did eat in such circumstances—but probably not often). Although dopamine plays a crucial role in producing the rewarding effects of a stimulus or activity that fills a deprivation, it does not play a role when you are not deprived. A key part of the brain involved in nondeprived reward is in the brain stem. Damage to this area knocks out the system that registers reward when an animal is not deprived, but leaves intact the system for deprived reward (Bechara & Van der Kooy, 1992; Berridge, 1996; Nader et al., 1997).

Do we usually eat dessert simply because we *like* the taste? Possibly, but *wanting* something is not the same thing as *liking* it (Berridge, 2003, 2004). For example, you can like a particular tree, bridge, or sunset very much without wanting it—and most of us can even like chocolate very much but not always want it. In fact, distinct neural circuits underlie liking something (receiving pleasure from perceiving it or thinking about it) and wanting it (Berridge, 2003, 2004; Cardinal et al., 2002; Robinson & Berridge, 2001; Wyvell & Berridge, 2000). Nevertheless, liking the taste of something can motivate you to eat it, and the nondeprived reward system will make the experience gratifying even if you aren't hungry.

The existence of different brain systems for deprived and nondeprived reward is grounds for drawing a psychological distinction between needs and wants, between motivation that arises when a requirement must be filled and motivation

Deprived reward: Reward that occurs when a biological need is met.

Nondeprived reward: Reward that occurs not when a need is being met, but rather when a want is being satisfied.

Figure 7.6 Needs and Wants

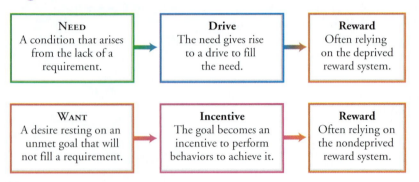

Need	Drive	Reward
A condition that arises from the lack of a requirement.	The need gives rise to a drive to fill the need.	Often relying on the deprived reward system.

Want	Incentive	Reward
A desire resting on an unmet goal that will not fill a requirement.	The goal becomes an incentive to perform behaviors to achieve it.	Often relying on the nondeprived reward system.

Needs and wants typically trigger different sorts of events.

What sorts of needs do you suppose motivated President Franklin Delano Roosevelt? During FDR's entire presidency (from 1933 to 1945), he could not walk without the use of metal braces or crutches (he contracted polio in 1921 and was paralyzed thereafter). However, this did not stop him from getting around the White House on his own by using his hands to crawl from one room to another.

Need for achievement (nAch): The need to reach goals that require skilled performance or competence to be accomplished.

that arises when a goal that is not a requirement is desired. Figure 7.6 summarizes the relation between these different facets of motivation.

Types of Needs: No Shortage of Shortages

There are psychological as well as bodily needs, and these needs can be organized within a hierarchy.

Psychological Needs. Researchers have proposed that our psychological needs include a need to be competent, to be autonomous (Sheldon et al., 1996), to have social approval, to be dominant or in control (Kim & Kim, 1997), to be affiliated with others, to be powerful (McClelland et al., 1989), to reach closure (Kruglanski & Webster, 1996; Taris, 2000), to understand, to maintain self-esteem, and even to find the world benevolent (Stevens & Fiske, 1995). Many studies have examined individual differences in such needs. These individual differences probably arise from differences in inherited temperament (Kagan, 1994) and differences in personal experiences, such as interactions with peers (Harris, 1998) and family (Sulloway, 1997).

A classic example of a psychological need is the **need for achievement (nAch**; McClelland & Atkinson, 1953), which is the need to reach goals that require skilled performance or competence to be accomplished. There is a large body of research assessing the consequences of differences in this need (for example, Neel et al., 1986; Spangler, 1992). People who have a high need for achievement tend to assume that their successes are due to their personal characteristics, whereas their failures are due to environmental circumstances (Nathawat et al., 1997; Weiner & Kukla, 1970). In a meta-analysis, Spangler (1992) found that measures of "implicit" (that is, not conscious) need for achievement predict actual success better than measures of "explicit" (or conscious) need for achievement, obtained from questionnaires filled in by participants.

Maslow's Hierarchy of Needs. Abraham Maslow (1970) created a hierarchy of physical and emotional needs, illustrated in Figure 7.7. Lower-level needs are considered more essential to life and must be met before needs further up the hierarchy can be addressed and satisfied. Needs toward the top of the hierarchy are considered less basic because they arise less frequently and, if not met, do not seriously impair the quality of life. You can live without understanding the world, but not without air or food. According to Maslow's theory, once a need is met, it becomes less important, and unmet, higher-level needs become more important. During a crisis (such as loss of a home due to a fire), lower-level needs take precedence, and higher-level needs are put on hold.

Maslow's hierarchy of needs has had an enormous impact on how people think about motivation, particularly in the business world (Soper et al., 1995). But is it right? Research has produced mixed evidence, at best, for the idea that needs are organized into a hierarchy (Wahba & Bridwell, 1976). There is no good evidence that unmet needs become more important and that met needs become less important. In fact, Hall and Nougaim (1968) found that the more consistently a need was met, the more important it became. Furthermore, this theory fails to explain various phenomena—for example, why people voluntarily go to war and put themselves in the line of fire (Fox, 1982).

Figure 7.7 Maslow's Hierarchy of Needs

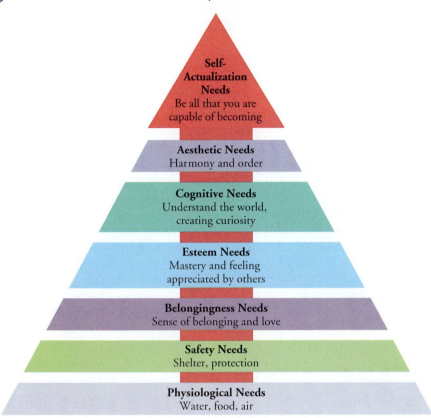

According to Maslow's theory, needs lower in the hierarchy must be met before needs higher up become the focus of concerns.

Achievement in Individualist Versus Collectivist Cultures

Many of the goals that motivate us are clearly provided by groups, and the structure of a society determines what sorts of activities will be reinforced. Cultures can be divided into two general types that affect achievement motivation differently (although these differences may often be matters of degree and may vary for subgroups within a culture; Oyserman et al., 2002). Individualist cultures, such as that of the United States, emphasize the rights and responsibilities of the individual over those of the group. Collectivist cultures, such as that of China, emphasize the rights and responsibilities of the group over those of the individual. Such cultural differences have been shown to affect achievement goals. For example, Anglo-Australians (from an individualist culture) have been found to be focused more on personal success than on family or groups, whereas Sri Lankans (from a collectivist culture) are oriented more toward their families and groups (Niles, 1998). Similarly, Sagie and colleagues (1996) found that Americans had higher achievement motivation (as measured by scales that emphasize individual achievement) than did Japanese or Hungarians, members of collectivist cultures. Thus, growing up in one or the other type of culture influences a person's needs and wants. The effects of growing up in an individualist culture are not without a cost: Tafarodi and Swann (1996) found that Americans like themselves less than do Chinese. Why? Tafarodi and Swann believe that collectivist cultures tend to de-emphasize competition among individuals, which leads them to like each other more. This may lead to greater

Individualist culture: A culture that emphasizes the rights and responsibilities of the individual over those of the group.

Collectivist culture: A culture that emphasizes the rights and responsibilities of the group over those of the individual.

self-liking if we assume that self-liking is increased if others like us. In individualist cultures, on the other hand, members are raised to strive for freedom and independence, which tends to produce competition and conflict. In such cultures, there are more feelings of self-competence, but fewer of self-liking.

LOOKING BACK: *Review*

1. *What are the sources of motivation?* Motivation arises for many reasons, including evolutionarily shaped instincts, drives, the maintenance of homeostasis, a desire to have an intermediate level of arousal, and incentives.

2. *What is the difference between* needs *and* wants, *and what factors affect them?* Needs arise when a requirement (physiological or psychological) is not met, which leads to a drive to fill the requirement (for example, a need for water leads to a drive to drink). Needs may be related to a system in the brain that provides a reward when a deprivation is satisfied. In contrast, wants arise when an animal has an unmet goal that will not fulfill a requirement, which causes the goal to act as an incentive; wants may be related to a system in the brain that provides a reward when you achieve a desired goal but are not deprived. There are many types of needs and wants, and the importance of any given one depends partly on your culture—for example, on whether it is individualist versus collectivist.

LOOKING BEYOND: *Critical Thinking*

If you were designing a school for young children, how would you organize it so that the children were motivated as strongly as possible to learn? How can you find out what motivates a particular child?

You could argue that wants are never satisfied for very long. If this is correct, does it make sense to try to fulfill them at all? How could you tell if a motivation is a need or a want?

Do you think it might be useful to develop a drug that blocks the deprived reward system? The nondeprived reward system? Why might such a drug be dangerous? Beneficial?

Hunger and Sex: Two Important Motivations

Gandhi's diet centered around fresh fruit, and the amount that he ate would have broken the budget of a typical middle-class Indian household. Reflecting on his diet, a financial backer once quipped that it cost Gandhi's friends "a great deal of money to keep him in poverty" (Markovits, 2003, p. 89). However, in spite of his love of such food, Gandhi fasted many times in his life, using the threat of his starvation to force the hands of his adversaries. What led him to want to eat and allowed him to stop eating voluntarily?

In addition to having unusual eating habits, Gandhi had unusual attitudes toward another major source of motivation—sex. Gandhi felt that sex for pleasure was morally wrong, that sex should be engaged in only for procreation. In his later years, he urged sexual abstention so that "sexual energy" could be preserved and channeled into social causes (Markowitz, 2003, p. 94).

Hunger and sex are two of the drives that are best understood, and they represent strikingly different kinds of motivation. Hunger is the classic drive that relies on the deprived reward system; by definition, to be hungry is to be deprived of food. If you don't eat, you will eventually die. Sex does not rely on this system; if you follow Gandhi's advice and don't have sex, you won't die. In spite of their differences, hunger and sex—and their satisfaction—share many characteristics and affect many aspects of our lives, social and experiential, as well as physiological.

LOOKING AHEAD: *Learning Objectives*

1. *What makes us hungry and leads us to eat particular foods at particular times?*
2. *How is your weight kept relatively constant, and why do some people become obese?*
3. *What is the nature of the sexual response cycle?*
4. *What determines whether we are attracted to the same sex or the opposite sex?*

Eating Behavior: The Hungry Mind in the Hungry Body

Your life is sustained by your body's **metabolism**, the sum of the chemical events in each of your cells, events that convert food molecules to the energy needed for the cells to function. Eating is necessary to maintain your metabolism. What factors determine what and when we eat?

Is Being Hungry the Opposite of Being Full?

Although you might think of hunger as a continuum from starvation to satiety, hunger in fact arises from the action of two distinct brain systems. One system leads you to feel a need to eat; the other leads you to feel satiated (Davis & Levine, 1977; Yeomans & Gray, 1997).

The feeling of a need to eat arises when your brain senses that the level of food molecules in your blood is too low. The brain registers the quantities of two major types of food molecules: *glucose* (a type of sugar) and *fatty acids* (Friedman, 1991; Friedman et al., 1986). In contrast, "feeling full" does not depend on the level of food molecules in the blood: You feel full well before food is digested and food molecules enter the bloodstream. If you suspect that feeling full has something to do with the state of your stomach, you're on the right track. If food is removed with a flexible tube from the stomach of a rat that has just eaten to satisfaction, the rat will eat just enough to replace the loss (Davis & Campbell, 1973). But a full stomach is not enough to tell an animal to stop eating. Filling an animal's stomach with saltwater does not diminish appetite as much as filling it with milk, even if the fluids are placed directly into the stomach so that the animals cannot taste them (Deutsch et al., 1978). The stomach contains detectors that register the food value of its contents, and this information is transmitted to the brain. People know when to stop eating largely because of signals sent by sensory neurons in the stomach to the brain. Similar

Metabolism: The sum of the chemical events in each of the body's cells, events that convert food molecules to the energy needed for the cells to function.

The brain system that regulates eating is surprisingly complex, as is revealed when it is disrupted by a stroke. For example, a person can develop what is known as *gourmand syndrome*, a neurological disorder that is characterized by an obsession with fine food. Such people do not report being hungry all of the time, and they may not overeat—but their entire lives become centered on food.

signals are also sent by other organs, including the upper part of the small intestine and the liver.

What part of the brain detects these signals? It appears to be an area in the hypothalamus. When neurons in the lateral hypothalamus (*lateral* means "side") are destroyed, hunger *is* reduced more than most other drives (Dunnett et al., 1985; Stricker et al., 1978). The ventromedial hypothalamus (*ventromedial* means "lower midline") appears to affect other brain regions that allow stored food molecules to be released; thus, when it is damaged, the animal has no choice but to keep eating (Weingarten et al., 1985). Humans and other animals thus have some neurons in the brain that signal when nutrient levels are low and others that signal when stored food molecules should be released (Shiraishi et al., 2000). These neurons act not so much like buttons or switches as like sensors that provide information that guides attention and behavior. In fact, learning plays a role in how an animal interprets such signals; only after prior experience that eating reduces hunger signals and drinking reduces thirst signals do young rats intentionally seek out food or drink (as appropriate) when they are food deprived or dehydrated (Changizi et al., 2002).

Appetite: A Moving Target

The early phases of eating depend on the taste of food. When you take the first bites of a meal or snack, you probably experience the *appetizer effect*; if those first bites taste good, your appetite is stimulated. This effect is driven in part by *opioids* in the brain; as you might suspect from their name, opioids are chemicals that behave like opium-derived drugs and cause you to experience pleasure. The opioids are released when you first eat food that tastes good (Yeomans & Gray, 1997).

As you continue to eat, your responses to food-related stimuli change. After eating some fresh-baked cookies, the smell of them doesn't seem quite as heavenly as it did before you ate them. If people have had their fill of a certain food, they rate its odor as less pleasant than they did before eating it (Duclaux et al., 1973). However, when the flavor, texture, color, or shape of a food is changed, people will eat more of the same food (Rolls et al., 1981b). After you've eaten a few chocolate chip cookies, you might find yourself not interested in more cookies, but happy to have some fresh-baked bread.

Not surprisingly, these changes in your appetite are linked to events in the hypothalamus. Neurons in the lateral hypothalamus initially fire when an animal sees or tastes a food and then reduce their firing after the animal has eaten its fill of that food (Burton et al., 1976). These neurons are selective: After they stop responding to one food, they can still be stimulated by another (Rolls et al., 1981b). But appetite, like most psychological phenomena, is governed by a complex set of brain areas. In one study, participants' brains were scanned as they ate their fill of chocolate, and then, at the request of the investigators, kept on eating and eating (Small et al., 2001). As they ate beyond the point when the candy was appetizing, activity changed in parts of the frontal lobes and the *insula* (an area of the cerebral cortex that registers bodily sensations).

And appetite isn't just about the brain. To understand why you eat the amount you do, you need to consider events at the different levels of analysis. When alone, you vary the size of a meal depending on the size and length of time since your last meal—for example, by eating less for dinner if you had a late lunch

(Woods et al., 2000). But this biological mechanism doesn't work so well when you eat with others (De Castro, 1990; Herman et al., 2003). When people eat in groups, they do not vary the size of their meals to reflect their degree of hunger. Moreover, the amount people eat depends on the amount others eat. In some circumstances, people not only eat more when with company, but report eating a greater amount when more people are present for a meal. Part of this effect may simply reflect the fact that when more people are present, the meal takes longer to complete. In other circumstances, people will actually eat less when eating in a group than they would when alone. You might call this the "not wanting to look like a pig" effect! It is clear that eating with other people can lead you to eat more or less than you would when alone, but the precise ways in which others exert their influence are not yet known (Herman et al., 2003).

At the level of the person, men want chocolate (and report that they enjoy it more) when they are in a good mood, for example, after they've watched films that make them happy (such as *When Harry Met Sally*; Macht et al., 2002). Moreover, anything that reminds you of good food you've eaten on a previous occasion—an event at the level of the person—can increase hunger. As usual, events at the different levels interact. For example, you get hungry when reminded of good food in part because your body responds both to perceptions of food and to thoughts of food by secreting insulin. **Insulin** is a hormone that stimulates the storage of food molecules in the form of fat. Thus, insulin reduces the level of food molecules in the blood, which may increase hunger.

Why Does It Taste Good?

What about preferences for specific foods? Some of our tastes clearly are a consequence of beliefs that develop with experience. Some people develop disgust reactions to certain foods (Rozin & Fallon, 1986), and the very idea of that food then keeps them away from it. Such *cognitive taste aversion* is apparently long-lasting and can be formed without classical conditioning (for instance, without being nauseated after eating the food; see Batsell & Brown, 1998). Rozin and his colleagues have shown that people apparently believe that "once in contact, always in contact." If a neutral food was in contact with an aversive food, the aversive properties seem to transfer. Suppose someone dunked a sterilized, dead cockroach briefly in your glass of water. Would you want to take a sip? The answer is probably a resounding no. Similarly, if a morsel of premium chocolate fudge were molded into the shape of feces, the shape alone would make it unappealing. Rozin and his colleagues have also shown that Americans harbor exaggerated beliefs about the harmful effects of some foods; in fact, many incorrectly believe that salt and fat are harmful even at trace levels (Rozin et al., 1996).

Beliefs also play another role in determining what we want to eat: Perhaps unconsciously, people believe that "you are what you eat." Nemeroff and Rozin (1989) asked people to rate qualities of people who "ate boar" and those who "ate turtle." The boar eaters were believed to be more likely to have boarlike qualities, such as being bearded and heavy-set.

Insulin: A hormone that stimulates the storage of food molecules in the form of fat.

Culture plays a key role in shaping our tastes in food: The French would never give up their beloved snails or frogs; Koreans find pickled snakes delicious; Filipinos enjoy unhatched chicks in the shell; the Germans savor stuffed pig intestines; and Chileans eat a kind of sea anemone whose looks would qualify it to star in a science-fiction movie.

Overeating: When Enough Is Not Enough

We humans like the taste of fatty foods, which is bad news because eating too much fat can lead to a variety of diseases, such as diabetes, cardiovascular disease, cancer, high blood pressure, and gallbladder disease (Schiffman et al., 1999). Diet books and cookbooks are best-sellers. Does this seem ironic to you? Do we

Set point: The particular body weight that is easiest for an animal (including a human) to maintain.

want to lose weight so that we can eat more? Or does our love of eating make us need to diet? Our culture places a premium on being thin. Nonetheless, some of us overeat, and according to the Centers for Disease Control and Prevention (2004), 31% of Americans are obese and another 34% are overweight—but why?

Set Point: Your Normal Weight

If you lose weight, fat cells become less likely to give up their stored energy. In addition, receptors in your brain that are sensitive to low levels of fat then become active and make you hungry; you eat more, and thus you end up gaining weight. This mechanism reminded researchers of the way a thermostat turns on the heater when the room is too cold, bringing it back to a constant temperature. This analogy led to the notion that animals, including humans, settle at a particular body weight that is easiest to maintain; this weight is called the **set point**. For many years, researchers thought of the set point as relatively constant, kept that way by homeostatic mechanisms (Nisbett, 1972; Stunkard, 1982). However, more recently, some researchers have argued that the body doesn't maintain the set point the way a thermostat maintains room temperature (Berthoud, 2002; Levine & Billington, 1997). Rather, although your body weight is relatively stable, it can change if your environment changes (for example, so that you are tempted by more and fattier foods), your activities change (for example, you walk to work and thus exercise more often), or your emotional state changes (for example, you become depressed and listless).

Why would you ever eat more than your body needs? Cognitive systems in the brain are connected to, and apparently can "overpower," the hypothalamic systems that underlie hunger (Berthoud, 2002). Thus, we sometimes eat not because we're hungry, but because we're bored or lonely, or simply because we think we ought to eat (perhaps because the clock says it's lunchtime). If you eat when your body doesn't need the energy, you are "overeating"; if you overeat for a prolonged time, the number of fat cells in your body increases to store the additional energy. Thus, you gain weight. In contrast, when you lose weight, each fat cell decreases in size, but you don't lose fat cells. This may explain why it's generally easier to gain weight than to lose it. Regular, moderately vigorous exercise can speed up your metabolism, leading your cells to need more energy even when you are not exercising. This is the best method of changing your balance of energy input and output, and thereby of losing weight.

Obesity

An obese person is defined as one who is more than 20% heavier than the medically ideal weight for that person's sex, height, and bone structure. By this standard, almost one third of Americans are obese. But why? Consider three theories.

Fat Personalities? Do obese people have weak characters that make them slaves to food? No. The personality characteristics of obese and nonobese people are similar (Nilsson et al., 1998; Poston et al., 1999). Indeed, President William Howard Taft (president from 1909 to 1913) was a grossly obese man, weighing over 300 pounds. He was so overweight that, after getting stuck in a White House bathtub, he had a new tub constructed that would hold four average-sized men. However, his size did not deter him from achieving the highest office in the land.

So, why are some people obese? Some explanations have grown out of psychodynamic theory. According to one such explanation, obese people eat when they feel stress, as a kind of defense. The evidence for this explanation is mixed:

Obese people have the same "will power" to resist eating junk food as nonobese people.

Obese people do not always overeat when they feel stress and may instead tend to overeat when aroused, positively or negatively (Andrews & Jones, 1990; McKenna, 1972). Overeating is not the same thing as an eating disorder (see Chapter 11); people don't necessarily overeat because they have a psychological problem.

Fat Genes?   There is good reason to believe that at least some forms of obesity have a genetic basis—and may not be connected to how much a person actually eats. If one identical twin is obese, the other probably is too; variations in weight may be as much as 70% heritable (Berthoud, 2002; Ravussin & Bouchard, 2000). In fact, 58 distinct genes and portions of all chromosomes but chromosome Y (the male sex chromosome) have been related to obesity (Rankinen et al., 2002). Claude Bouchard, a researcher in this area, notes that genes may affect weight in numerous ways: "Some affect appetite, some affect satiety. Some affect metabolic rate" (quoted in Gladwell, 1998, p. 53). Thus, the genetics of obesity will not be simple to unravel, but some highlights have already been noted. For example, the neurons in certain brain areas involved in registering satiety appear to rely on the neurotransmitter serotonin (Blundell, 1977, 1984, 1986; Blundell & Halford, 1998), and mutant mice that lack specific receptors for this neurotransmitter will keep eating until they become obese (Tecott et al., 1995). The notion that humans may act the same way is supported by the finding that people gain weight if they take medication that happens to block these receptors (Fitton & Heel, 1990); moreover, people who take drugs that activate these receptors report being less hungry, and they actually lose weight while on the medication (Sargent et al., 1997).

Genes can make a big difference. Researchers found that by altering a single gene, they could increase the production of substances that make a mouse obese.

Fat Environment?   Genes determine the range of possibilities for a particular characteristic, and the environment sets individuals within that range (Chapter 6). Some people have a propensity to become fat, but do so only in certain environments (Ravussin & Bouchard, 2000). Overeating is encouraged by many aspects of the American environment: Food is relatively cheap, fast foods are high in fat, snacking is all too easy and acceptable, and portions have grown larger in the United States (but not in many parts of Europe). At the same time, people exercise less not only because most of us drive or ride to work, but also because many of our amusements, such as watching television and surfing the Web, are sedentary. Moreover, whereas in earlier eras many people were paid for work that involved significant exercise, most now have to pay (in both cash and leisure time) to exercise (Philipson & Posner, 2003). Hill and Peters (1998) suggest three approaches to "curing the environment," which is currently the basis of a virtual epidemic in obesity:

1. Educating people to eat smaller portions,
2. Making foods that are low in fat and calories more available, and
3. Encouraging more physical activity.

Some obese people are capable of losing large amounts of weight and keeping the weight off (Tinker & Tucker, 1997). These people are able to adopt healthier eating and exercise habits. Note, however, that changes in the environment can be effective only if the genes define a relatively wide range of possible weights. If the range of possible weights set by the genes that control obesity is narrow, then people who have those genes may not have much choice in determining how heavy they are.

Dieting

Even Gandhi, famous for his fasts, liked to eat. None of us especially relishes diets that require us to eat less, and we are receptive to diets that promise weight loss while allowing us to eat like we always do. A study of four popular diets found that overweight or obese people lost modest amounts of weight when following any of the diets, that the diets were equally effective, and that at least a third of people who began a diet did not stick with it (Dansinger et al., 2005). Low-carbohydrate diets (such as the Atkins) do not lead obese people to shed more pounds than standard diets, such as that advocated by Weight Watchers (Foster et al., 2003).

The science of dieting is clear: If you want to lose weight, eat fewer calories (Freedman et al., 2001) and exercise more. The most commonly recommended diet for obese people requires them to cut their normal food intake in half (Stallone & Stunkard, 1994).

Sexual Behavior: A Many-Splendored Thing

People engage in sexual relations for two general reasons: to have babies (*reproductive sex*) and for pleasure (*recreational sex*). The vast majority of sexual acts, around 98% of them (Linner, 1972), are for pleasure, as opposed to procreation. Sex leads to some of the most intense of all positive emotions, and hence it is valued highly by members of our species. The earliest known attempts at contraception were developed 4,000 years ago by the Egyptians; they thought dried crocodile dung would do the job.

Alfred Kinsey began the first systematic surveys about human sexual behavior in the late 1940s. He and his colleagues interviewed thousands of Americans about their sex lives. Kinsey found that people frequently reported engaging in sexual practices then considered rare or even abnormal. However, attempts to study sexual behavior ran into some unique problems. As Freud wrote (1910, p. 41), "People in general are not candid over sexual matters, they do not show their sexuality freely, but to conceal it wear a heavy overcoat of a tissue of lies, as though the weather were bad in the world of sexuality." Psychologists have had difficulty seeing through this "tissue of lies," and even today there is debate about whether we have reliable information about many facets of human sexuality.

Most studies of sexual behavior rely on surveys. But would you volunteer to be in a study of sexual behavior? How about filling in a questionnaire about your most intimate moments? Researchers have found that not everybody is equally willing to participate in studies of sexual behavior, and thus the data are likely to come from a biased sample. Bogaert (1996), for example, found that the undergraduate males who volunteered for a study on human sexuality differed in many ways from males who volunteered for a study on personality: The former group had more sexual experience, were more interested in sexual variety, were more inclined to seek out sensation and excitement, and were less socially conforming and less likely to follow rules (Trivedi and Sabini [1998] reported similar findings). In addition, people from different cultures may respond differently when asked about their sexual and reproductive behavior: Researchers found that Hispanic American women reported less sexual activity when their interviewers were older, but Black American women did not display this bias as strongly (Ford & Norris, 1997). The researchers suspected that this bias arose because the Hispanic culture has traditionally frowned on premarital sex for women, leading

Alfred Kinsey's life and work have received renewed interest—and generated controversy—as a result of the 2004 movie about him.

the Hispanic women to underreport their sexual activity to older women who might disapprove.

In short, interview data about sex are suspect. Sampling bias as well as response bias can distort the results.

Sexual Responses: Step by Step

William Masters and Virginia Johnson (1966) were the first researchers to systematically study actual sexual behavior, not just reports or descriptions of it, with a large sample of participants. Their effort was the first that provided a look behind the "tissue of lies" about sex. Over the course of many years, Masters and Johnson brought thousands of men and women into their laboratory and devised ways to measure what the body does during sex. The outcome was a description of four stages the human body—male or female—passes through during sexual activity:

1. *Excitement* (during the initial phases, when the person becomes aroused),
2. *Plateau* (a full level of arousal),
3. *Orgasm* (accompanied by muscle contractions and, in men, ejaculation), and
4. *Resolution* (the release of sexual tension).

These stages meld into one another, with no sharp divisions separating them (Levin, 1980, 1994). The mountain of research they conducted led Masters and Johnson to reach four general conclusions, summarized in Table 7.2.

Others have built on Masters and Johnson's research and have developed a comprehensive description of the **sexual response cycle**: *Sexual attraction* leads to *sexual desire*, *sexual excitement* (arousal), and possibly *sexual performance* (which involves becoming fully aroused, reaching orgasm, and then experiencing resolution followed by—for men—a refractory period).

Why do we have sexual responses at the times, and with the partners, we do? Not unexpectedly, events at all three levels of analysis play crucial roles in our sexual behavior.

Table 7.2 **Masters and Johnson's Conclusions**
• Men and women are similar in their bodily reactions to sex.
• Women tend to respond more slowly than men, but stay aroused longer.
• Many women can have multiple orgasms, whereas men typically have a *refractory period*, a period of time following orgasm when they cannot become aroused again.
• Women reported that penis size is not related to sexual performance, unless the man is worried about it.

The Role of Hormones: Do Chemicals Dictate Behavior?

In 1849, German scientist Arnold Berthold wondered why castrated roosters acted like hens. They stopped crowing, mating with hens, fighting, and engaging in other typical rooster behaviors. So, he castrated some roosters and then put the testes into their abdominal cavities. Shortly thereafter, the roosters started behaving like roosters again. Berthold reasoned that the testes produced their effects not because of nerves or other physical connections, but because they released something into the bloodstream. We now know that what the testes release is the male hormone *testosterone*.

Hormones are chemicals that are secreted into the bloodstream primarily by endocrine glands and that trigger receptors on neurons and other types of cells (see Chapter 2). Hormones are controlled in large part by the pituitary gland, the brain's "master gland." The pituitary gland in turn is controlled by the hypothalamus, which plays a major role in emotion and motivation and is affected by hormones produced elsewhere in the body.

Sexual response cycle: The stages the body passes through during sexual activity, including sexual attraction, desire, excitement, and possibly performance (which includes full arousal, orgasm, and resolution).

Androgens: Sex hormones that cause many male characteristics such as beard growth and a low voice.

Estrogens: Sex hormones that cause many female characteristics such as breast development and the bone structure of the female pelvis.

Sex Hormones. When you are sexually aroused, hormones from the gonads (the testes and ovaries) act on the brain and genital tissue. **Androgens** are usually referred to as "male hormones" (such as testosterone), which cause many male characteristics such as beard growth and a low voice. **Estrogens**, usually referred to as "female hormones," cause many female characteristics such as breast development and the bone structure of the female pelvis. The presence of the different hormones is not all-or-none between the sexes. Both types of hormones are present in both males and females, but to different degrees. Although they exert direct effects on physical characteristics, hormones don't directly dictate behavior. Rather, they lead to a tendency to *want* to behave in certain ways in the presence of particular stimuli. That is, they modify motivation. For example, giving young women a dose of testosterone later caused their heart rates to speed up when they saw angry faces. This response could indicate that the women were more ready to "fight or defend status in face-to-face challenges" (van Honk et al., 2001, p. 241). Testosterone does more than influence sexual behavior.

Insensitivity to Sex Hormones. Not everyone responds to sex hormones in a normal way. For example, people who have *androgen insensitivity syndrome* have an X chromosome (the female sex chromosome) and a Y chromosome (the male sex chromosome) and a genetic mutation that does not allow receptors for the "male hormone" androgen to develop. Thus, the lock is missing for the hormonal key, and the hormone has no effects either during development or afterward. These people, who should have been boys, grow into girls, but with testes tucked up in the belly and no uterus or ovaries. In some cases, the vagina is too shallow and must be surgically altered later in life. In spite of their genetic identities as males, the failure of male hormones to have an effect does not allow the genes to influence these individuals' sexuality. In fact, although they sometimes require appropriate female hormone supplements, people with androgen insensitivity syndrome look like women, often marry, and have normal female sex lives (which include normal orgasms during intercourse).

Ovulation and Eroticism. Sex hormones also influence our interest in sex. In fact, changes in the level of sex hormones over the course of a woman's menstrual cycle affect the degree to which she is inclined to become sexually aroused. And when women are ovulating, they prefer "ruggedly handsome" male faces more than when they are not ovulating (Penton-Voak & Perrett, 2000). Moreover, women are more likely to be interested in men who are not their partners while they are ovulating (Gangestad et al., 2002). However, the effects of shifting hormone levels are only tendencies, affecting different people to different degrees (Regan, 1996).

Testosterone and Intimacy. The relationship between hormones and motivation runs in both directions. In a famous study, a researcher who signed his paper "Anonymous" (1970) reported the effects of his building anticipation of female companionship after sustained periods of enforced celibacy. This man was a scientist who worked on a small island and only occasionally visited the mainland, where he would have brief periods of contact with the opposite sex. He ap-

Although single and married men have the same levels of testosterone in the morning, by the end of the day married men have less than unmarried men (testosterone normally decreases over the course of the day, but does so more sharply for married men; P. B. Gray et al., 2002). This is true whether or not the men have children.

parently had time on his hands when he was alone, as he decided to measure his beard growth every day by weighing his beard clippings after shaving. He found that his beard grew thicker as his visits to the mainland approached. Just thinking about the visit apparently caused increases in his levels of androgens, which in turn caused increased beard growth. Researchers have also documented the reverse effect.

Oxytocin and Motherly Love. The so-called sex hormones aren't the only ones that affect our sex lives (Carter, 2004; Meston & Frohlich, 2000). *Oxytocin* is a hormone (produced by the pituitary gland) that increases dramatically in women immediately after they give birth, and probably helps to forge the mother–infant emotional bond (Insel, 2000). Oxytocin is also released after orgasm and may bond sex partners—perhaps even if they consciously don't like each other. Could oxytocin explain why "love is blind"? Future research will tell us.

Sexual Motivation

People use sex to satisfy different psychological needs. Cooper and colleagues (1998) showed that motivations for having sex can be thought of in terms of the two dimensions illustrated in Figure 7.8, which range from avoidance to approach (the horizontal dimension) and from social connection to self-oriented independence (the vertical dimension). The importance of these dimensions varies for different people and in different contexts—for instance, for people in stable relationships, exclusive relationships, or relationships that are both stable and exclusive.

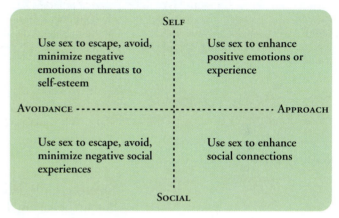

Figure 7.8 Motives for Having Sex

People engage in sex for many reasons, which Cooper and colleagues (1998) characterize as falling along two dimensions.

Mating Preferences

Think about it: What sort of person would be your ideal mate? Or just a good date for tomorrow night? Evolutionary psychology has offered theories of what makes someone seem desirable as a potential mate. Some of these theories derive from Trivers's (1972) influential theory of *parental investment*. He argued that males, who typically invest less than do females in the nurturing and raising of children, should be more interested in short-term sex and less particular about mates; females, who typically are very invested in nurturing and raising children, should have opposite preferences. However, when Pedersen and colleagues (2002) tested this idea, they found that 98.9% of men and 99.2% of women hoped to have a long-term stable relationship. Very few of either gender were motivated by the prospect of continued short-term sex. In addition, the two genders spend comparable amounts of time and money in "short-term mating," such as trying to meet someone at a party (Miller et al., 2002).

Another evolutionary theory relies on the observation that because fertilization occurs in the privacy of a woman's fallopian tubes, a man can never be absolutely certain that a baby carries his genes; thus, according to this theory, men should be particularly alert to their mates' possible sexual infidelity. In contrast, because women value a man who will devote time, energy, and resources to her children, women should be particularly alert to their mates' becoming emotionally involved with someone else. When asked which would be more upsetting, their mates' falling in love with someone else or having sex with someone else, most men chose the latter and most women chose the former (Buss et al., 1992; Cramer et al., 2001–2002). However, these preferences may not be observed

Adolescents apparently model their behavior after that of their friends, and hence are more likely to have sexual relations early if their friends are having sexual relations early (DiBlasio & Benda, 1990). However, such social interactions can be mediated by biological events—including whether the adolescent has certain genes (Miller et al., 1999).

when participants use a continuous scale to specify their reaction to each event (DeSteno & Salovey, 1996) or when they are asked to reflect about actual experiences (Harris, 2002). Moreover, other researchers have found that men and women value remarkably similar characteristics in a potential mate (Miller et al., 2002). To avoid methodological problems (such as the tendency to respond in ways that are considered socially desirable) that arise when participants are asked to make these kinds of judgments, some researchers have recorded bodily reactions to such questions (Buss et al., 1992; Grice & Seely, 2000). One particularly careful study of such reactions was conducted by Harris (2000). She asked participants to imagine different scenarios while she recorded their blood pressure, heart rate, and skin conductivity. Men did show greater reactions to imagining their mate having sex versus being emotionally involved with someone else. But they showed the same reactions when they imagined *themselves* having sex versus being emotionally involved with their mate. Moreover, women who had been in a committed sexual relationship showed reactions very much like those of the men—clearly counter to the predictions of evolutionary theory.

Does all of this mean that evolution had no role in shaping mate preferences? Not necessarily. However, these findings do show that mate selection, like all other human behavior, does not arise solely from events at a single level of analysis.

Sexual Orientation: More Than a Choice

People who are sexually attracted to the opposite sex are termed **heterosexual**; people attracted to the same sex are termed **homosexual**; people attracted to both sexes are termed **bisexual**. Sexuality might best be regarded as a continuum, with most people being primarily heterosexual, and somewhere between 4% and 10% of the U.S. population being primarily homosexual in their behavior (Fay et al., 1989). Studies of bisexual men have shown that many of them tend to become more homosexually oriented over time (Stokes et al., 1997).

For many years, homosexuality was considered either a personal choice or the result of being raised a certain way (for instance, with a weak father and an overly strict mother). However, programs to train homosexuals to prefer the opposite sex have failed, even those that relied on extreme techniques such as electric shock to punish homosexual thoughts or behavior (Brown, 1989, offers a personal account).

The Biology of Homosexuality

There is now evidence that people do not choose to be homosexual or heterosexual, nor are homosexuals or heterosexuals created by the ways their parents treat them as young children. Rather, biological events appear to play a major role in determining sexual orientation.

A Gay Hypothalamus? LeVay (1991) studied the brains of homosexual men and found that a small part of the hypothalamus, about as large as an average-

Heterosexual: A person who is sexually attracted to members of the opposite sex.

Homosexual: A person who is sexually attracted to members of the same sex.

Bisexual: A person who is sexually attracted to members of both sexes.

sized grain of sand, was about half the size of the same part in heterosexual men (Allen & Gorski, 1992, report related evidence). This was interesting because others had previously found that this same structure typically is smaller in women than in men. However, all of the brains LeVay studied came from men who had died of AIDS, and it is possible that the disease had something to do with the structural abnormality. But when this same structure was surgically disrupted in monkeys, they displayed atypical sexual behavior (Slimp et al., 1978). These and similar data may suggest that there is a biological predisposition for some people to become homosexual (LeVay & Hamer, 1994). However, keep in mind that correlation does not prove causation: In theory, there could be something else about being homosexual that causes these parts of the brain to change.

Other Biological Differences.   Other differences between heterosexual and homosexual people point toward biological differences. Consider, for example, the sound that is emitted from the ears of some people in some circumstances (see the discussion in Chapter 3). In some cases, the sound is a response to a heard click, although the ears of some people emit sound even without such a trigger event. It turns out that this response to a click is less frequent and weaker for homosexual and bisexual women than for heterosexual women—and men in general have less frequent and weaker ear responses than do heterosexual women (McFadden & Pasanen, 1999). Apparently, parts of the ear are different in women with different sexual orientations. However, no such difference appears among heterosexual, bisexual, and homosexual men. Thus, these results not only show a biological difference for homosexual and bisexual women, but may also hint at different biological bases for male and female homosexuality.

In the Genes?   The findings of biological differences between homosexual and heterosexual people do not indicate whether the causes are hereditary (that is, genetic), the result of experiences in the womb, or the result of experiences during early childhood. Hamer and his colleagues (1993) studied 114 families that included a homosexual man and found that inheritance of homosexuality seemed to be passed from the mother. This result led them to examine the X chromosome, which is the sex chromosome from the mother (females have two X chromosomes, one from the mother and one from the father; males have one X chromosome, from the mother, and one Y chromosome, from the father). These researchers concluded that a small portion of the X chromosome is related to homosexual preference and behavior. However, not all studies have supported this view (McKnight & Malcolm, 2000). Moreover, although Bailey and Pillard (1991) conducted a study with twins that supported the idea that homosexuality is at least partly inherited, a later study failed to find this effect (Rice et al., 1999).

The mixed findings from genetic studies may mean that there is more than one way homosexuality can arise. One intriguing possibility is suggested by the finding that homosexual men are more likely than heterosexual men to have older brothers (Blanchard, 2001; Ellis & Blanchard, 2001). In fact, the sexual orientation of about 15% of gay men appears to arise from the fact that they had older brothers (Cantor et al., 2002). Why? It appears that the mother's body somehow "remembers" the number of boys she bore (possibly by building up specific antibodies; Ellis & Blanchard, 2001) and alters the level of testosterone accordingly. Boys with older brothers receive proportionally more testosterone during gestation, which appears to increase the likelihood that they will be homosexual.

One intriguing—if preliminary—bit of evidence for this theory relies on the fact that prenatal levels of maternal testosterone regulate genes (called *Homeobox*, or *Hox*, *genes*; Kondo et al., 1997) that not only determine how the genitals develop, but also regulate testosterone levels in the fetus and dictate the relative lengths of the ring and index fingers. Some researchers have in fact found that, on average, the relative lengths of the ring and index fingers differ for homosexual and heterosexual men (Robinson & Manning, 2000). Additional research with a large number of participants suggests that this relation only occurs for gay men who have older brothers (T. J. Williams et al., 2000).

LOOKING BACK: *Review*

1. *What makes us hungry and leads us to eat particular foods at particular times?* Hunger occurs when the brain determines that the level of glucose or fatty acids in the bloodstream is too low. Hunger is not the opposite of being full; different mechanisms determine whether you feel hungry or full. Being sated depends in large part on having nutrients in your stomach. At the beginning of a meal, taste plays an especially important role in determining whether you eat. As a meal progresses, changes in the type of food will keep your appetite up, and tastes (as well as thoughts) that cause insulin to be released will increase hunger. Beliefs about the history of a food item (such as whether it was ever in contact with something repulsive) and even associations linked to the shape of a food affect how appealing it is.

2. *How is your weight kept relatively constant, and why do some people become obese?* The set point operates to keep your weight constant. However, your weight can change if your environment, activity level, or emotional state changes. At least some obese people are genetically predisposed to becoming obese.

3. *What is the nature of the sexual response cycle?* According to research on sexual activity, people first experience sexual attraction, next desire, and then excitement (arousal), which may be followed by sexual performance; sexual performance involves becoming fully aroused, reaching orgasm, and finally experiencing resolution (followed by a refractory period for men). Hormones play a role in sexual behavior by biasing people to behave in certain ways.

4. *What determines whether we are attracted to the same sex or the opposite sex?* Biological events, either caused by the genes or occurring in the womb or during childhood, appear to play a key role in determining sexual orientation.

LOOKING BEYOND: *Critical Thinking*

In what ways do advertisements (and not just those for food) indirectly or directly affect your eating habits? Do you think you are always aware of such influences?

Do you think researchers should be trying to find a gene (or genes) for homosexuality? What positive uses could such knowledge have? What negative uses? Would it be ethical to try to alter such genes either before conception or in the womb?

LET'S SUM IT UP

I. Emotion: I Feel, Therefore I Am

A. Ekman identified six basic emotions: surprise, happiness, anger, fear, disgust, and sadness. Research results have shown that surprise and fear are more easily confused with each other than they are with any of the other basic emotions.

B. Culture and experience influence how easily emotions can be read; although humans can read emotions from any other human at better than chance levels, they do better with members of familiar cultures.

C. Each of several widely known theories of emotion has captured a grain of the truth. The James–Lange theory holds that you feel emotion after your body reacts to a situation. The Cannon–Bard theory holds that emotions and bodily reactions occur at the same time. Cognitive theory claims that emotions arise when you interpret your bodily reactions in the context of the specific situation. The emerging synthesis of views on emotion proposes that some emotions arise from brain responses that do not involve cognitive interpretation, whereas others depend on such interpretation.

D. As the James–Lange theory predicts, some emotions may arise in part from changes in bodily reactions, such as heart rate, breathing rate, and facial expression. As the Cannon–Bard theory predicts, some emotions, such as fear, are reflexes that produce the emotional experience and the bodily reaction simultaneously. As cognitive theory predicts, how you interpret the causes of your bodily reactions does in fact influence which emotion you feel. The emerging synthesis puts all of these discoveries together, recognizing that an emotion arises from a mixture of different mechanisms operating at the same time.

E. Fear may often be the strongest of our emotions, and the amygdala may play a role in strong emotions in general. Environmental events influence emotion; our happiness, for example, depends in part on our economic and cultural context. In addition, the emotions we feel depend on how we construe a situation; happy people tend to remain happy, in part because of how they view the world.

F. Culture shapes people's emotional reactions. It also influences how effectively they can read body language to determine another person's emotion.

G. We can control our emotions, both by prolonging them over time and by suppressing them; this control is directly reflected in the activation of brain mechanisms. Culture affects the display rules we use, the rules that determine when and how we express emotion.

H. Lies cannot be reliably detected by current methods, although some individuals are particularly adept at spotting deception.

II. Motivation and Reward: Feeling Good

A. Some of our motivations arise from evolutionarily shaped instincts, sex being an obvious example. Other motivations are drives, such as thirst; some drives are designed to maintain homeostasis (when we are cold, we seek warmth). Still other motivations center on a preference for an intermediate level of arousal.

B. We are often motivated by incentives, such as the potential rewards (including money) for engaging in a behavior.

C. Animals (including humans) can learn to be helpless if their behavior fails to reduce punishment.

D. A need is a condition that arises when you lack a requirement, which in turn gives rise to a drive to acquire specific rewards to fulfill the requirement. A want is a condition that arises when you have an unmet goal that will not fulfill a requirement, which in turn causes the goal to act as an incentive.

E. Needs may be related to a brain system that provides an internal reward when a deprivation is satisfied (for example, by eating when you are hungry). In contrast, many wants may be related to a system that provides a reward when you are not deprived but you achieve a desired goal.

F. There are many types of needs; the importance of at least some needs depends partly on your culture, particularly on whether the culture is individualist or collectivist.

G. Maslow proposed a hierarchy of needs, but the evidence for his highly influential theory is mixed.

III. Hunger and Sex: Two Important Motivations

A. We eat for many reasons: for pleasure, for nutrition, as a social activity. The brain senses when the level of nutrients in the blood is too low and causes you to feel hungry. We often eat until signals from the stomach (and other digestive organs) indicate that we've consumed enough food.

B. The hypothalamus plays a particularly important role in hunger and thirst. At the beginning of a meal, taste plays an especially important role in determining whether you want to eat. As a meal progresses, changes in the type of food you are eating will keep your appetite up, and tastes (as well as thoughts) that cause insulin to be released will increase hunger.

C. Beliefs about the history of a food item (for example, whether it was ever in contact with something repulsive) and even associations with the shape of the food affect how appealing it is.

D. Overeating can cause your body weight to increase, and the increase is often difficult to lose. However, weight is determined by many factors that affect metabolism and behavior, including your set point, environment, types of activities, and emotional state. Cognitive mechanisms in the brain can override the hypothalamic mechanisms, leading us to eat when we aren't actually hungry.

E. Obese people do not have "weak characters" but rather may be genetically predisposed to becoming obese. Many genes are likely to affect body weight in different ways. Dieting alters cognition, emotion, and personality in obese people.

F. Sexual attraction leads to sexual desire, sexual excitement (arousal), and possibly sexual performance (which involves becoming fully aroused, reaching orgasm, and then experiencing resolution followed, for men, by a refractory period).

G. Hormones play a key role in sexual development and modify motivation toward sexual behavior. Fluctuations in sex hormones affect cognition and emotion.

H. Mating preferences may be influenced by evolutionary characteristics, but they are not determined by them.

I. There is evidence that male homosexuals differ from heterosexuals in certain brain structures and that female homosexuals and bisexuals differ from heterosexuals in the operation of certain neural systems (involved in hearing). Such biological differences, and homosexuality itself, are probably caused either by genes or by events in the womb or during childhood.

Key Terms

androgens, p. 322

basic emotion, p. 291

bisexual, p. 324

collectivist culture, p. 313

deprived reward, p. 311

display rule, p. 300

drive, p. 308

emotion, p. 289

estrogens, p. 322

facial feedback hypothesis, p. 295

heterosexual, p. 324

homeostasis, p. 308

homosexual, p. 324

incentive, p. 309

individualist culture, p. 313

instinct, p. 307

insulin, p. 317

learned helplessness, p. 310

metabolism, p. 315

misattribution of arousal, p. 296

motivation, p. 306

need, p. 310

need for achievement (nAch), p. 312

nondeprived reward, p. 311

polygraph, p. 303

set point, p. 318

sexual response cycle, p. 321

want, p. 310

LOOKING ONLINE: *Enhance Your Learning*

MyPsychLab is an interactive and instructive multimedia resource that can be used to supplement a traditional lecture course or as an online course. It is an all-inclusive tool with a text-specific e-book plus multimedia tutorials, videos, simulations, animations, and controlled assessment to completely engage students and reinforce learning. MyPsychLab meets the individual learning needs of every student. Visit *www.mypsychlab.com* for more information!

Practice Test

For each of the following items, choose the single best answer.

1. Which of the following statements is true?
   a. Our emotions are not always obvious.
   b. Emotions help guide us to approach some things and withdraw from others.
   c. Emotions provide visible cues that help other people know key aspects of our thoughts and desires.
   d. All of the above statements are true.

2. There is widespread agreement that
   a. there are precisely five basic emotions.
   b. humans have a set of built-in emotions that express the most basic types of reactions.
   c. damage to the brain cannot selectively disrupt the ability to detect another person's fear and sadness without disrupting the ability to discern other emotions.
   d. blind people do not show the same facial expressions of emotion as do people with sight.

3. Davidson and his colleagues have provided evidence that there are separate systems in the brain for two general types of human emotion. In general,
   a. approach emotions are negative, and withdrawal emotions are positive.
   b. the right frontal lobe tends to be more active than the left when people have approach emotions.
   c. clinically depressed patients have relatively diminished activity in the left frontal lobe.
   d. positive and negative emotions are really opposite sides of the same coin and cannot occur at the same time.

4. Theories of emotion differ in the relationship they assume between bodily events, interpretations of events, and distinct brain systems. Which of the following statements best represents this relationship according to the Cannon–Bard theory?
   a. Different emotions arise from different sets of bodily reactions.
   b. An emotion arises when you interpret the situation as a whole—your bodily state in the context of everything that surrounds it.
   c. The emotions we feel at any moment arise from

(1) a mixture of brain and body reactions and
(2) interpretations and memories pertaining to the situation.
   d. Bodily arousal and the experience of emotion arise in tandem.

5. According to the facial feedback hypothesis, "putting on a happy face"
   a. is just a catchy song lyric.
   b. leads our brains to be in exactly the same state as when we are genuinely happy.
   c. tends to result in more positive ratings of mood than when the face is posed in a negative expression.
   d. has an effect that suggests that emotions are defined only in terms of autonomic reactions.

6. In their classic experiment, Schachter and Singer found that
   a. bodily factors are sufficient to explain the range of feelings we have.
   b. participants who were told in advance about the drug used in the experiment and its effects felt differently in the different contexts.
   c. participants in the control group, who did not receive an injection, experienced a strong effect of context and made a cognitive error called the misattribution of arousal.
   d. None of the above statements is true.

7. From studying the brain systems that produce fear, researchers have discovered that
   a. conscious awareness is needed for a stimulus to trigger the amygdala into producing a fear response.
   b. once you learn to associate fear with an object or situation, you will always do so.
   c. people who have a gene (SLC6A4, the human serotonin transporter gene) that affects serotonin levels show decreased activation of the amygdala when they see emotional stimuli.
   d. the amygdala does not play a role in perceiving that *other* people feel fear.

8. Emotion is conveyed not only by facial expression, but also by tone of voice and body language. Researchers studying nonverbal communication have determined that

a. there are no gender differences in the ability to decode nonverbal cues.

b. people can sense happiness less accurately than other emotions from facial expressions.

c. the ability to *read* nonverbal communications is at least partly determined by experience.

d. of all the emotions, anger is least easily sensed from tone of voice.

9. What happens in the brain when people try voluntarily to dampen down the mechanisms that underlie emotion?

a. Nothing happens; people cannot voluntarily dampen down these mechanisms.

b. Various brain areas involved in emotion are activated, such as the amygdala and hypothalamus.

c. Parts of the frontal lobe become activated—and the brain areas normally activated during emotional responses are no longer activated.

d. None of the above statements is true.

10. Deprived reward

a. occurs when you fill a biological need.

b. arises from the brain pathway that runs from certain parts of the brain stem, through the lateral (side) hypothalamus, on up to specific parts of the limbic system and the frontal lobes.

c. arises from a brain circuit in which many of the neurons use, or are affected by, dopamine.

d. All of the above statements are true.

11. According to Abraham Maslow's hierarchy of physical and emotional needs,

a. higher-level needs are considered more essential to life.

b. needs lower in the pyramid must be met before needs higher in the pyramid become the focus of concerns.

c. once a need is met, its level of importance does not change.

d. during crises, higher needs advance to an even higher level and lower-level needs are put on hold.

12. Which of the following statements best explains why you "feel full" when you eat?

a. Feeling full depends on the level of food molecules in the blood.

b. A full stomach is enough to tell an animal to stop eating.

c. You feel full after food is digested.

d. You know when to stop eating largely because of signals sent by sensory neurons in the stomach to the brain.

13. When you take the first bites of a tasty meal or snack,

a. you probably experience the appetizer effect.

b. opioids are released.

c. neurons in the lateral hypothalamus fire.

d. All of the above statements are true.

14. Estrogens

a. are present in both males and females.

b. cause many male characteristics such as beard growth and a low voice.

c. directly dictate behavior.

d. are released after orgasm and probably help to forge the mother–infant emotional bond.

15. Which of the following did Masters and Johnson *not* find in their research on sexual behavior?

a. Young people enjoy sex more than middle-aged people do.

b. Men and women have similar bodily reactions to sex.

c. Women stay aroused longer than men do.

d. Many women can have multiple orgasms.

Answers: 1. d 2. b 3. c 4. d 5. c 6. d 7. b 8. c 9. c 10. d 11. b 12. d 13. d 14. a 15. a

chapter 8

Personality
Vive la Différence!

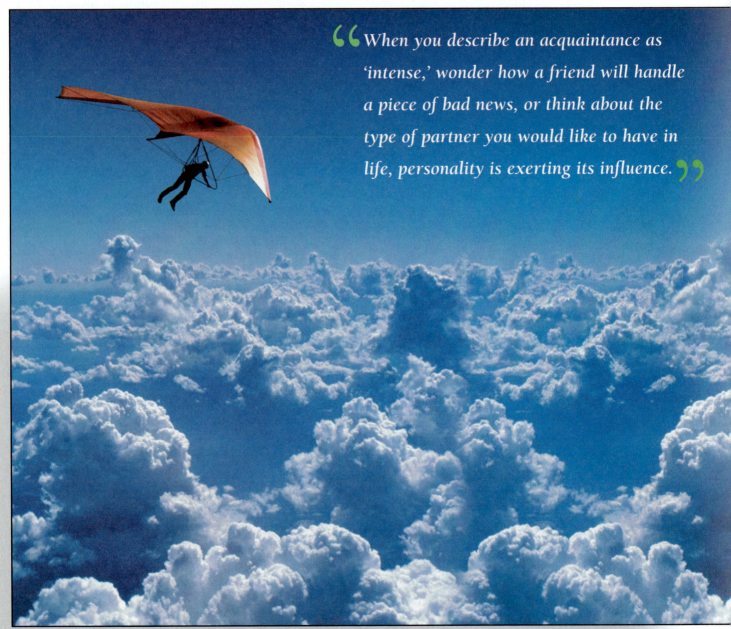

"When you describe an acquaintance as 'intense,' wonder how a friend will handle a piece of bad news, or think about the type of partner you would like to have in life, personality is exerting its influence."

CHAPTER OUTLINE

TINA AND GABE MET IN THEIR INTRODUCTORY PSYCHOLOGY CLASS. THEY WERE IMMEDIATELY attracted to each other and started studying together. After a few conversations, they were pleased to discover that they had similar values and political views. Predictably, they began going out together. On their fourth date, though, Tina began to realize that she and Gabe weren't as much alike as she had thought; she was surprised by this because their views on so many issues were so similar. Tina sometimes had trouble "reading" Gabe because he was shy and emotionally steady, without many highs or lows—his manner was "mellow." She wondered why he wasn't more enthusiastic when she proposed activities she thought would be fun to do together, such as in-line skating, bungee-jumping, or biking. "Well, opposites attract, I guess," she thought. And although Gabe enjoyed Tina's spirit, her emotional vibrancy, and her interest in trying new things, now and then he asked her why she was so emotional and always in such a hurry. Tina began to worry that, even though they were strongly attracted to each other, a long-term relationship might reveal persistent differences between them that would be difficult to deal with.

Do these differences reveal something fundamental about Tina and Gabe as people? Do they reflect their personalities? And if so, are personalities set in stone?

The concept of personality infuses daily life. When you describe an acquaintance as "intense," wonder how a friend will handle a piece of bad news, or think about the type of partner you would like to have in life, personality is exerting its influence. What exactly is this quality, which is part and parcel of each of us? **Personality** is a set of behavioral, emotional, and cognitive tendencies that people display over time and across situations and that distinguish individuals from each other. This chapter explores the idea of personality, the perspectives of a number of different theorists who have sought to describe and explain it, and the ways in which psychologists measure it. It also considers historical views of personality, the genetic influence on personality development, the influence of learning experiences, motives, and thoughts on personality, and the effects of the social environment on personality.

Personality: Historical Perspectives

Tina wanted to understand why Gabe was the way he was—or, put another way, why he had the personality he did. Gabe studied a lot and could do it for much longer than Tina; Tina learned a lot when she studied with him, but lately when they studied together, he'd have a big bag of pistachio nuts and sit there cracking and eating nuts while they read. It was driving Tina, well, nuts. She couldn't understand how he could just sit there hour after hour, cracking and crunching nuts while studying. And he'd leave the shells lying around on the table, creating a mess. She wanted to ask him about it—why didn't he just buy shelled nuts, and wasn't he distracted by the shelling process? But she didn't feel comfortable asking him. Why are Tina and Gabe so different? How do our personalities develop, and why do they develop differently? Among the notable theories that attempt to answer these questions are the psychodynamic theory of Sigmund Freud and the humanistic theories of Carl Rogers and Abraham Maslow.

LOOKING AHEAD: *Learning Objectives*

1. *What is the Freudian view of personality?*
2. *What is the main emphasis of humanistic theories?*

Freud's Theory: The Dynamic Personality

Sigmund Freud viewed personality as a bubbling cauldron, rocked by unconscious, irrational forces at war with one another, competing for expression and preventing the individual's exercise of free will. He believed in **psychological determinism**, the view that all behavior, even something as mundane as forgetting someone's name or being late for an appointment, has an underlying psychological cause. Freud proposed that two major drives, sex and aggression, are the primary motivating forces of human behavior. Tension occurs when these drives are not given opportunity for expression.

The Structure of Personality

In order to understand Freud's view of the structure of personality, it is necessary first to understand his view of consciousness. Freud proposed that consciousness is not one thing, but rather can be thought of as divided into three levels (see

Personality: A set of behavioral, emotional, and cognitive tendencies that people display over time and across situations and that distinguish individuals from each other.

Psychological determinism: The view that all behavior, no matter how mundane or insignificant, has an underlying psychological cause.

Figure 8.1). The topmost level is normal awareness, or the *conscious*, which includes thoughts, feelings, and motivations of which you are aware. The second level, the *preconscious*, holds subjective material that you can easily bring into conscious awareness but are not aware of most of the time. For example, your telephone number is in your preconscious until someone asks you what it is, and at that point, it moves into your conscious awareness. The final level is the *unconscious*, which houses the thoughts, feelings, and motivations that you cannot bring into consciousness but which nevertheless influence you. A much greater proportion of your thoughts, feelings, and motivations are in the unconscious than are in the conscious.

As part of the dynamic nature of personality (not consciousness), Freud proposed three personality structures—the id, superego, and ego (see Figure 8.1). These are not physical structures, but abstract mental entities. The **id**, which exists from birth, houses the sexual and aggressive drives, physical needs such as the need to sleep or eat, and simple psychological needs such as the need for comfort; these needs and drives constantly vie for expression. The id lives by the *pleasure principle*, wanting immediate gratification of its needs by a reduction in pain, discomfort, or tension, regardless of the consequences. Because of this insistent urge for immediate gratification, the id is sometimes compared with a demanding infant. Freud proposed that when the id's instincts threaten to erupt, anxiety can develop. When that anxiety reaches a sufficiently high level, abnormal behavior and mental illness can result.

A second personality structure, the **ego**, also develops in childhood. The ego tries to keep the id under control and ensure that rational thought governs behavior. The ego is guided by the *reality principle*, which leads it to assess what is realistically possible in the world. According to Freud's theory, the ego is also responsible for cognitive functions such as problem solving and reasoning. Although he believed that the ego develops out of the id, Freud (1937/1964) wrote fairly late in his life that the ego's characteristics may be determined by heredity (Nye, 1992).

A third personality structure, the **superego**, forms during early childhood, but after the id and ego; this entity houses the child's (and later the adult's) sense of right and wrong. The superego tries to prevent the expression of the id's inappropriate sexual and aggressive impulses. The child learns morality by internalizing—that is, taking in—the values of the parents and of the immediate culture. The superego is the home of the conscience, and depending on the parents' way of teaching right and wrong, it can be more or less punishing. If your superego is very harsh, you experience much anxiety and strive for perfection. The superego can cause feelings of *guilt*, an uncomfortable sensation of having done something wrong, which results in feelings of inadequacy. The superego's morality is responsible for the *ego ideal*, which provides the ultimate standard of what a person should be (Nye, 1992).

With the appearance of the superego, the ego has to work very hard to balance the demands of the id and the superego. The ego tries to give the id enough gratification to prevent it from making too much trouble, while at the same time making sure that no major moral lapses lead the superego to become too punishing. The ego must also make sure that the actions of both id and superego, as well as its own actions, don't create problems for the person in the real world.

Figure 8.1 Freud's View of Personality Structure

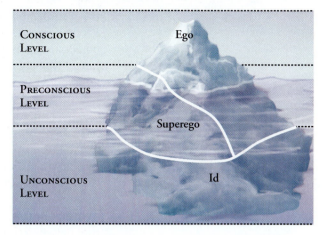

In Freud's view, only part of the mind is available for inspection and provides normal awareness (conscious); some of it is occasionally conscious (preconscious), and some is hidden, not available for observation (unconscious). Repressed thoughts, feelings, and wishes are hidden from awareness.

Id: A personality structure, proposed by Freud, that exists at birth and houses sexual and aggressive drives, physical needs, and simple psychological needs.

Ego: A personality structure, proposed by Freud, that develops in childhood and tries to balance the competing demands of the id, superego, and reality.

Superego: A personality structure, proposed by Freud, that is formed during early childhood and houses the sense of right and wrong, based on the internalization of parental and cultural morality.

Personality Development: Avoiding Arrest

Freud viewed childhood as central in determining the formation of personality. He proposed five distinct phases, or stages, of development, each having an important task requiring successful resolution for healthy personality development. Four of Freud's five stages involve specific erogenous zones, areas of the body (mouth, anus, and genitals) that can provide satisfaction of instinctual drives. Freud believed that each zone demands some form of sexual gratification, with a different zone being prominent during each stage. For this reason, Freud's stages are called **psychosexual stages**: oral, anal, phallic, latency, and genital (see Table 8.1).

If a child does not satisfy the needs of a given stage, he or she will develop a *fixation*, a state in which energy is still focused on an earlier stage of development even as the child moves on to the next stage. A fixation results from incomplete resolution of an earlier stage. In times of stress, Freud argued, the person will regress to the thoughts, feelings, and behaviors of the fixated stage. Such arrested development could create a **neurosis**: an abnormal behavior pattern relating to a conflict between the ego and either the id or the superego. According to Freud (1938), conflict between the ego and reality results in *psychosis*, a break from reality.

One of Freud's provocative ideas involves the phallic stage (see Table 8.1): Freud proposed that children in this stage are preoccupied with the discovery that girls don't have penises, a discovery that creates jealousy of the male's penis in girls and fear of castration in boys. Freud took inspiration from the ancient Greek story of Oedipus, who unknowingly killed his father and married his mother. Freud believed that boys in this stage jealously love their mothers and view their fathers as competitors for their mothers' love; so they both fear and hate their fathers. Freud called this dynamic the *Oedipus complex*. A boy fears that, as punishment for loving his mother and hating his father, his father will cut off his penis, the primary zone of pleasure; this concern leads to the boy's **castration anxiety**. For successful resolution, a boy must renounce his passionate love for his mother and make peace with his father, choosing to identify with him and accept

Psychosexual stages: Freud's developmental stages based on erogenous zones; the specific needs of each stage must be met for its successful resolution.

Neurosis: An abnormal behavior pattern relating to a conflict between the ego and either the id or the superego.

Castration anxiety: A boy's anxiety-laden fear that, as punishment for loving mother and hating father, his father will cut off his penis (the primary zone of pleasure).

Table 8.1 Freud's Psychosexual Stages

Psychosexual Stage	Age of Stage (years)	Locus of Pleasure	Developmental Task of Stage
Oral Stage	0–1	Mouth (sucking and biting)	Successful weaning from mother's breast or bottle
Anal Stage	1–3	Anus (retaining and expelling feces)	Successful toilet training
Phallic Stage	3–6	Clitoris or penis	Successful identification with same-sex parent
Latency Period	6 to puberty	No particular locus of pleasure; sexual impulses are repressed	Successful transformation of repressed sexual urges into socially acceptable activities
Genital Stage	Puberty onward	Vagina or penis	1. Successful formation of mature sexual love relationship 2. Successful development of interests and talents related to productive work

his position instead of viewing him as a competitor. In doing so, the boy "introjects," or internalizes, his father's morality as part of his superego.

Girls' personality development at this stage, according to Freud, is different from that of boys; girls' version of the Oedipus complex has been labeled the *Electra complex*, after a Greek myth about a girl who avenges her father's murder, committed by her mother and her mother's lover, by persuading her brother to kill their mother. Girls at this stage experience *penis envy*, a sense of being ineffectual owing to the lack of a penis, accompanied by a desire to have a penis. Girls also struggle with feelings of anger and jealousy toward the mother: anger for neither providing a penis for her daughter nor having one herself, and jealousy because of the mother's relationship with the father. Girls ambivalently identify with their mothers. As a product of the Victorian era, Freud justified women's inferiority to men by explaining that they only partially resolved this stage. Because they do not experience castration anxiety, he wrote, they are not motivated to resolve fully this ambivalent identification with their mothers. They remain fixated at this stage and, as a result, have a less well-developed superego, less ego strength, and less ability to negotiate between reality and the id.

Defense Mechanisms: Protecting the Self

The ego's job of handling threatening material is made easier by its use of **defense mechanisms**, unconscious psychological means by which a person tries to prevent unacceptable thoughts or urges from reaching conscious awareness, thereby decreasing anxiety (see Table 8.2). Freud proposed a number of

Defense mechanism: An unconscious psychological means by which a person tries to prevent unacceptable thoughts or urges from reaching conscious awareness.

Table 8.2 Common Defense Mechanisms

Defense mechanisms are used by the ego to prevent threatening thoughts from entering awareness.

Denial

Threatening thoughts are denied outright. *Example*: You have a drinking problem but deny that it is a problem (and truly believe this).

Intellectualization

Threatening thoughts or emotions are kept at arm's length by thinking about them rationally and logically. *Example*: While watching a frightening part of a horror movie, you focus on the special effects, make-up, camera angles, and other emotionally nonthreatening details.

Projection

Threatening thoughts are projected onto (attributed to) others. *Example*: You accuse your partner of wanting to have an affair rather than recognizing your own conscious or unconscious wish to have one yourself.

Rationalization

Creating explanations to justify threatening thoughts or actions. *Example*: In response to watching a football game instead of studying, and subsequently doing poorly on an exam, you say, "Oh, I can make up for it on the final exam."

Reaction Formation

Unconsciously changing an unacceptable feeling into its opposite. *Example*: You harbor aggressive impulses toward your boss, but instead you experience warm, positive feelings toward him, transforming your anger about his obnoxious behavior into an appreciation of "his fairness as a manager."

Repression

Anxiety-provoking thoughts, impulses, and memories are prevented from entering consciousness. *Example*: After failing an exam, you keep forgetting to tell your parents about it.

Sublimation

Threatening impulses are directed into more socially acceptable activities. *Example*: You sublimate your unacceptable aggressive urges to engage in physical fights by playing ice hockey.

Undoing

Your actions try to "undo" a threatening wish or thought. *Example*: After having the thought of eating several slices of chocolate cake, you go to the gym and work out for an hour.

Repression: A defense mechanism that occurs when the unconscious prevents threatening thoughts, impulses, and memories from entering consciousness.

defense mechanisms; these were further developed by his daughter, Anna Freud (1895–1982), herself a noted psychoanalyst. The most important defense mechanism is repression, a process that occurs when the unconscious prevents threatening thoughts, impulses, and memories from entering consciousness. An example of repression might be "forgetting" to go to a dreaded dentist appointment. According to Freud, overreliance on particular defense mechanisms may lead to the development of neuroses.

Freud's Followers

Freud attracted many followers, a number of whom modified his theory of personality or added ideas of their own. Among those who expanded on Freud's work, termed *neo-Freudians*, were Carl Jung, Alfred Adler, and Karen Horney, all of whom de-emphasized sexuality (see Figure 8.2).

Critiquing Freudian Theory: Is It Science?

Psychoanalytic theory remains fascinating a century after Freud first conceived it, and legions of people worldwide—psychologists, writers, filmmakers, and others—have seen truth in its observations about personality. But as fascinating as Freud's theory may be, is it grounded in good science? First, as you saw in Chapter 1, a scientific theory must be testable, but many aspects of Freud's theory are difficult to test. Some key concepts were not concretely defined, some changed over time, and often the interpretation of concepts was left open. Freud

Figure 8.2 Neo-Freudians: Jung, Adler, and Horney

Carl Jung (1875–1961) was a former student of Freud's whose own theory of personality focused on the *collective unconscious*—the unconscious storehouse of ideas and memories common to all humankind.

Alfred Adler (1870–1937) focused on the importance of feelings of inferiority and helplessness in personality formation. Feelings of inferiority fuel the striving for superiority; but, if inferiority feelings become too severe, they can lead to an *inferiority complex*, which hampers such strivings.

Karen Horney (1885–1952) emphasized the importance of parent–child interactions, proposing that parents should show warmth, respect, and consistent interest in their children. Horney also proposed that girls did not have penis envy, but *privilege envy*, the desire for the privileges that go along with having a penis.

believed that many actions and objects have symbolic meanings. For example, long thin objects are *phallic symbols*—they stand for a penis. However, when Freud was asked about the meaning of his sucking on a cigar, he replied, "Sometimes a cigar is only a cigar." Maybe so, but a good theory would tell us when it is and when it isn't "only a cigar."

A second criticism of Freud's theory is that it is so complicated that it can explain, or explain away, almost anything. When there is an apparent contradiction within someone's personality, it is almost always possible to appeal to a defense mechanism to explain that contradiction. If Gabe had had a difficult time with toilet training, resulting in frequent constipation, we could predict that he would have an *anal-retentive personality*. According to Freud, such people are more likely to delay gratification and to be neat, methodical, miserly, and stubborn. But, if so, then how would we explain that Gabe is often generous and so messy with the pistachios? Freud might say that Gabe's generosity and messiness are an undoing of his desire to be selfish and orderly.

Third, Freud developed his theory by analyzing patients, mostly women, and by analyzing himself. And Freud's views of women, of proper parenting, and of appropriate development were all biased by his sensibilities and surroundings, as we are biased by ours. He and his patients were upper-middle-class or upper-class products of late 19th-century Vienna; their sensibilities were not necessarily representative of other classes, times, or cultures. Applying a theory based on a particular group of people at a particular time and place to other people at another time or place raises issues of validity.

However, some aspects of Freud's theory have received support from contemporary research (see Westen, 1998, 1999). For example, the type of attachment we have to our parents predicts the type of attachment we will have to a partner and to our own children (Shaver & Hazan, 1994). Although not supporting Freud's specific psychosexual stages, such findings support the general idea that relationships with parents can affect aspects of later development. Moreover, research on defense mechanisms as coping styles has supported some aspects of Sigmund and Anna Freud's views on those mechanisms (Bond et al., 1983; Mikulincer & Horesh, 1999; Newman, Duff, & Baumeister, 1997; Silverman, 1976). More generally, research on conditioned emotional responses (see Chapter 4), implicit memory (see Chapter 5), and aspects of thinking (see Chapter 6) supports the broad idea that some mental processes can be unconscious—that is, occurring without awareness. Despite the difficulty in evaluating most of Freud's theory, many aspects of it have endured because it offers a truly comprehensive, and sometimes insightful, view of people and of personality.

Humanistic Psychology: Thinking Positively

Partly as a reaction to Freud's theory, which in many ways draws a pessimistic picture of human nature and personality formation, the humanistic psychologists have focused on people's positive aspects—their innate goodness, creativity, and free will. Rather than being driven by forces outside of their control, as the Freudians claimed, people can create solutions to their problems. A cornerstone of humanistic theories is that we all have a drive toward **self-actualization**, an innate motivation to attain our highest emotional and intellectual potential. The

Self-actualization: An innate motivation to attain the highest possible emotional and intellectual potential.

work of two psychologists, Abraham Maslow and Carl Rogers, represents the humanistic perspective on personality.

Abraham Maslow

The personality theory developed by Abraham Maslow (1908–1970) is really a theory of motivation based on a hierarchy of physical and emotional needs (see Chapter 7). Lower-level needs, said Maslow, must be met before needs further up the hierarchy can be satisfied; moreover, during crises, higher-level needs are put on hold while lower-level ones take priority. Maslow proposed that the need for self-actualization is at the highest-level; this need leads people to strive to develop their full potential. People who are self-actualizing have these qualities: a true perception of reality, an acceptance of themselves and their environments, an appreciation of the ordinary, a focus on cultural rather than personal problems, few but deep personal relationships, and what Maslow called "oceanic feelings," a sense of oneness with nature that transcends time and space. Maslow regarded oceanic feelings as *peak experiences,* moments with intense clarity of perception (Privette & Landsman, 1983), a suspended sense of time, and a feeling of wonderment at the experience. Various researchers have studied Maslow's theory, particularly as it relates to motivation on the job. In the end, many of Maslow's concepts are difficult to test, and the validity of his theory remains questionable (Fox, 1982; Soper et al., 1995; Wahba & Bridwell, 1976).

Carl Rogers

Carl Rogers (1902–1987) is noted for his formulation of client-centered therapy (see Chapter 1) and his notions of personality and its development. Like Maslow, Rogers viewed humans as possessing a need for self-actualization. But rather than viewing the satisfaction of a hierarchy of needs as the driving force behind personality, he believed that the *self-concept*—our sense of ourselves and of how others see us—is central to personality development. Rogers proposed that our feelings about ourselves are in part a reflection of how others see us. Thus, we have a basic need for ==unconditional positive regard==, acceptance without any conditions. Receiving unconditional positive regard, according to Rogers, is crucial for the development of a healthy self-concept. Of course, it is impossible to receive or provide unconditional positive regard all the time, and the socialization process requires that adults praise children for behaving in accordance with societal rules. This praise for specific behaviors leads children to learn *conditions of worth,* or "what it takes" to be treated as worthwhile. According to Rogers, people whose lives revolve around meeting such conditions of worth will not achieve their full human potential. In order to prevent such obstruction of potential, yet meet society's need for children to learn what is generally considered appropriate behavior, Rogers advised parents to make the distinction between a child's inappropriate *behavior* and his or her *worth* as a human being.

Humanistic theories appeal to many because of their emphasis on the uniqueness of each person and on free will. According to this view, how you live your life is determined not by unconscious forces but by using your conscious awareness and your freedom to choose your experiences. Critics of humanistic theory point out that, as with Freud's theory, many of the concepts are difficult to test and have received little research support. Moreover, the uplifting, positive view of human nature seems too idealistic to many people in light of the amount of violence and evil in the world.

Good or bad child? Rogers argues that a child may at times behave unsuitably, but that does not mean he or she is a bad child. Labeling children as "bad" may affect their developing self-concept or self-worth (Kamins & Dweck, 1999).

==Unconditional positive regard:==
Acceptance without any conditions.

1. *What is the Freudian view of personality?* There are three different levels of consciousness (unconscious, preconscious, and conscious) and three structures of personality (id, ego, and superego), in a dynamic relationship with each other. Freud proposed five psychosexual stages (oral, anal, phallic, latency, and genital) and theorized that when resolution of a psychosexual stage is incomplete, a person's development is arrested, often creating a neurosis. Moreover, sexual and aggressive impulses can create anxiety, prompting the use of defense mechanisms. Neo-Freudians—including Carl Jung, Alfred Adler, and Karen Horney—added to or altered aspects of Freud's theory. Although Freud's theory is comprehensive and intriguing, many aspects of it are difficult to test scientifically.

2. *What is the main emphasis of humanistic theories?* Humanistic theories—such as those of Abraham Maslow and Carl Rogers—celebrate each person's uniqueness and stress positive qualities of human nature and free will. They also emphasize self-actualization. Although uplifting, humanistic theories have many aspects that are difficult to test scientifically.

LOOKING BEYOND: *Critical Thinking*

If you used Freudian theory to understand a historical figure's personality and motivations, do you think you could be sure about the validity of your analysis? Why or why not? Could you use a humanistic theory to understand such a person? What would you need to know about him or her?

What Exactly *Is* Personality?

As Tina got to know Gabe, she began to make certain assumptions about him, about who he was as a person. He studied hard and did well on psychology exams and quizzes, so Tina figured he was smart, hard-working, and conscientious. (Tina did well on her psychology exams and quizzes, too, but she didn't study much. She considered herself smart, but not particularly hard-working.) She was a bit surprised to discover that Gabe's apartment was a disaster area—she had assumed he would be as orderly and neat in his personal space as he was in his approach to schoolwork. She started to wonder whether his "personality," as she thought of it, was altogether consistent. Tina also noticed that, on dates, Gabe preferred to get together for dinner and a movie, not for lunch or an afternoon break ("Too much studying," he said). If she suggested going to a party together, Gabe invariably declined; he didn't like parties. Tina attributed this reluctance to his shyness.

The very concept of personality implies that people have enduring, stable qualities such as, say, talkativeness and curiosity. These qualities are called personality traits, relatively consistent characteristics exhibited across a range of situations. But notice the "relatively" in the preceding sentence. Let's see just what that means.

LOOKING AHEAD: *Learning Objectives*

1. *Does such a thing as a consistent personality really exist, or do our behaviors, thoughts, and feelings depend primarily on the situation?*

Personality trait: A relatively consistent characteristic exhibited in different situations.

2. How do psychologists group personality traits into sets of personality types?

3. *What methods do psychologists use to measure personality?*

The names of Snow White's seven dwarves fit their personalities. Imagine the personalities of dwarves named Dirty, Hungry, Shifty, Flabby, Puffy, Crabby, Awful, Doleful, all of which were on Disney Studios' list of possible names (Seuling, 1976). The final choices work so well because we view their personalities as consistent with their names; but what if Grumpy were, in fact, upbeat and easy-going?

Personality: Traits and Situations

Traits exist on a continuum (for example, from extremely quiet to extremely talkative). Gabe's shyness and Tina's adventurousness can be considered traits. Many personality psychologists believe that personality is built on traits. Moreover, these psychologists accept that each person can be placed at different locations within the same set of traits.

Gordon Allport (1897–1967) proposed that some personality traits can be grouped as *central traits*, which are traits that affect a wide range of behavior; however, the particular traits that are central will vary from individual to individual (Allport, 1937). Whether or not traits are viewed as causing behavior, they certainly aren't always accurate in *predicting* behavior (witness Gabe's domestic messiness). The situations in which we find ourselves can exert powerful influences on behaviors, thoughts, and feelings.

The Power of the Situation

People are not necessarily consistent across situations. You may get angry in some situations, but be totally mellow in others. Someone seeing you when you're angry may infer that you're an angry person, whereas someone seeing you only in situations in which you are mellow will infer that this is your disposition. Which is the "real" you? It has been argued that if much of our behavior depends on the situation in which we find ourselves, then perhaps there aren't consistent personality traits at all. In a now-classic study that illustrates the importance of the situation on behavior, Mischel and Peake (1982) observed college students and recorded 19 different behaviors reflecting the trait of conscientiousness, defined by how regularly they attended class, how promptly they completed assignments, how neatly they made their beds, and how neatly they recorded class notes. These researchers found that the students were likely to be consistent in similar situations, but not across different types of situations.

In later research, Mischel (1984) found that inconsistency across situations is pervasive; he found this not only with the traits of honesty and conscientiousness, but also with other traits, such as aggression and dependency. Furthermore, different measures of what should be the same trait often were only weakly correlated, or not related at all. For instance, two people could score high on measures of aggression, but express their aggression differently—one through put-downs and verbal abuse, the other through physical abuse (Mischel, 2004). Such findings led to the theory of *situationism*, which holds that a person's behavior is mostly governed by the particular situation, not by internal traits.

Situationism recognizes that, in part, we create our own situations, not necessarily by our actions but simply by who we are. In other words, characteristics such as age, sex, race, religion, ethnicity, and socioeconomic status can influence other people's behavior toward us, often in culturally determined ways, creating

342 **CHAPTER 8: Personality**

a different "situation," which can in turn lead to differences in our behavior (see the discussion of microenvironments in Chapter 6).

Interactions Between Situation and Personality

Nineteen-year-old Tina behaves very differently with Gabe—drinking from his cup, calling him after midnight—than she does with her 52-year-old female economics professor. In each case, Tina's age, sex, and status relative to the other person might be said to influence her behavior. If you knew Tina only from economics class, you might be surprised by how different her "personality" seems when she is with Gabe. However, we can guess that Tina's way of interacting with her economics professor will be similar to how she interacts with other professors. And how she interacts with Gabe is probably similar to how she's interacted with past boyfriends. That is, there is an interaction between the person and the situation, and in situations that are psychologically similar, the person will behave in similar ways (Magnusson, 2003; Mischel, 2004; Mischel & Shoda, 1995). Specifically, when different individuals are in the same situation, they will differ in what they pay attention to, how they encode and process the stimuli they perceive, what emotions are associated with those stimuli, and then how they respond. These differences reflect an interaction between the person and the situation—*interactionism*. But what is psychologically important in a given situation will differ from person to person (Shoda & LeeTiernan, 2002). Thus, Tina's behavior is consistent in that she responds similarly to all academic authority figures, and she responds to boyfriends in a different, but consistent, way.

In short, over long periods of time and over many similar situations, people are fairly consistent, and personality traits become reliably evident (Funder, 2001; Funder & Colvin, 1991; Kenrick & Funder, 1988; Roberts et al., 2001). Moreover, the more precisely a trait is defined, the more accurate it is in predicting behavior (Wiggins, 1992). Thus, saying that someone is sociable will not predict his or her behavior at a party nearly as well as saying that the person appears at ease in interactions with new people. This is the tradeoff: The more narrowly a trait is defined, the better it predicts behavior, but the fewer situations there are to which it can be applied. However, even when a trait is narrowly defined, there is not necessarily a one-to-one correspondence between a person's assessed level of that trait and the person's behavior. Rather, several traits may interact, along with situational factors, to influence the person's behavior (Ahadi & Diener, 1989).

Finally, although situations do influence the characteristic behaviors that people exhibit, personality also affects situations, and does so in three major ways. First, personality will influence how people perceive, encode, remember, and respond in any given situation. Second, people often can choose their situations—their jobs, their friends, their leisure activities. And, insofar as they are able, people tend to choose environments that fit their personalities. It's up to you, for instance, to decide whether to go bungee-jumping or sunbathing at the beach when you have a day off. Third, people also find opportunities to create their environments. An aggressive person, for instance, will create a tense situation by words or deeds (A. H. Buss, 1995), and others will react accordingly.

Asian Americans tend to show lower levels of assertiveness than do White Americans on personality tests. However, Zane and colleagues (1991) found that this is true only when the people involved are strangers. Thus, it isn't accurate to describe Asian Americans as "low on the assertiveness trait"; in general, a better characterization would be the more specific "unassertive when among strangers."

Factors of Personality: The Big Five? Three? More?

How many personality traits are there? The answer depends on how specific you want to be about a given trait. You could be very specific, narrowing all the way down to a "shy-so-only-goes-on-dates-to-dinner-and-a-movie-but-not-to-parties" trait. Narrowing traits to this level of precision, however, poses certain problems. Each trait explains only particular patterns of thoughts, feelings, and behaviors in very specific instances. For example, you could consider sociability—which personality psychologists call "extraversion"—a trait. Or you could say that extraversion is really a combination of the more specific traits of warmth, gregariousness, and assertiveness—each of which exists on a continuum. In this case, you could say that extraversion is a *personality dimension*, a set of related personality traits. Using the statistical technique of factor analysis (see Chapter 6), some researchers have sought to discover whether specific traits are in fact associated and, together, constitute a more general personality dimension; such a personality dimension is sometimes called a *superfactor*. An early proponent of factor analysis to determine personality factors was Raymond Cattell (1905–1998); he proposed 16 personality factors (listed in Figure 8.3) (Cattell, 1943), although further factor analyses lead to fewer factors (which are in turn less predictive of specific behaviors). Personality dimensions, or superfactors, may be a useful way of conceptualizing personality, but they have a disadvantage: They predict behavior less well than do the traits on which they are built (Paunonen, 1998; Paunonen et al., 2003). Moreover, two people can score high on the same dimension, yet attain their high scores by being extreme on different traits that are part of that dimension. In such cases, they score high on the dimension for different reasons and through different mechanisms (Cervone, 2005).

Many factor analytic studies have revealed that personality traits can be reduced to five superfactors, which are listed along with their included traits in Table 8.3 (Digman, 1990; McCrae & Costa, 1987); each superfactor or trait is on a separate continuum, with the name of the superfactor or trait identifying one end of that continuum. Thus, for example, at the other end of the continuum for the superfactor neuroticism is emotional stability. These five superfactors are sometimes referred to as the *Five-Factor Model*, or the **Big Five** (Goldberg, 1981): extraversion (versus introversion), neuroticism (also called *emotionality*, versus emotional stability), agreeableness (versus disagreeableness), conscientiousness (also called *dependability*, versus irresponsibleness), and openness to experience (versus incuriosity or unimaginativeness) (Costa et al., 1991). To remember these factors, which are supposed to "plumb the depths" of personality, use the mnemonic OCEAN (Openness, Conscientiousness, Extraversion, Agreeableness, and Neuroticism).

Psychologist Hans Eysenck identified not five but three superfactors, or, as he labeled them, personality dimensions: extraversion, neuroticism, and psychoti-

Figure 8.3 Personality Profiles and Employment

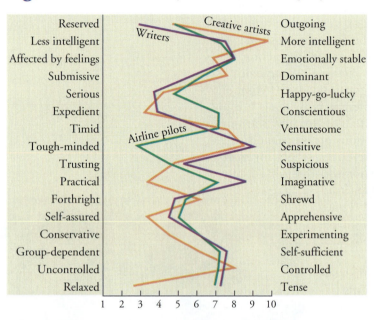

Completed personality inventories provide personality profiles of different traits. According to Cattell's personality inventory (the 16PF for its 16 personality factors), writers, creative artists, and airline pilots show different profiles.

Big Five: The five superfactors of personality—extraversion, neuroticism, agreeableness, conscientiousness, and openness—determined by factor analysis.

Table 8.3 The Big Five Superfactors and Their Traits

Superfactor	Traits
Extraversion (also called *sociability*)	Warmth, gregariousness, assertiveness, activity, excitement seeking, positive emotions
Neuroticism (also called *emotionality*)	Anxiety, hostility, depression, self-consciousness, impulsiveness, vulnerability
Agreeableness	Trust, straightforwardness, altruism, compliance, modesty, tender-mindedness
Conscientiousness (also called *dependability*)	Competence, order, dutifulness, achievement striving, deliberation, self-discipline
Openness	Fantasy, aesthetics, feelings, actions, ideas, values

cism. Eysenck's first two dimensions resemble the Big Five's superfactors of the same names, but the third—psychoticism—was originally thought to measure a propensity toward becoming psychotic, that is, toward loss of touch with reality, as occurs in schizophrenia (Eysenck, 1992). It is true that people with schizophrenia score high on this dimension; however, psychoticism as defined by Eysenck also contains traits related to social deviance (such as criminality and the inclination toward substance addiction) and to a lack of conventional socialization (such as disrespectfulness for rules and disregard for the feelings of others) (Costa & McCrae, 1995). For this reason, Eysenck's psychoticism includes some of the traits listed under the Big Five's superfactors of agreeableness and conscientiousness (or lack thereof) (Draycott & Kline, 1995; Saggino, 2000).

Instead of the term *psychoticism*, some psychologists have suggested using a broader term, such as *nonconformity* or *social deviance*, in order to highlight the traits of creativity and nonconformity that are also part of this dimension. Artists, for example, tend to score higher on this personality dimension than people who are truly psychotic (Zuckerman et al., 1988). The Big Five's superfactor of openness has no direct counterpart in Eysenck's scheme.

Measuring Personality: Is Grumpy Really Grumpy?

Psychologists, employers, teachers, and parents—indeed, all of us—might want to be able to understand and predict the behavior of others by discovering as much as possible about their personalities. Various techniques and tests for assessing personality attempt to do just that. Most personality assessments focus on measuring overt behaviors that psychologists believe to be manifestations of a given trait, inferring the strength of a trait from an individual's behavior. The use of behavior to infer personality traits is at the heart of all methods of personality assessment discussed here.

When "meeting" in cyberspace (for example, through a dating service), people commonly try to "assess" a potential mate's personality by looking at his or her Web site or finding other information on the Internet. Such information becomes the basis for inferring personality, much as we infer personality after viewing someone's bedroom or apartment (Vazire & Gosling, 2004). However, there are standardized ways to assess personality.

Two of the methods used to assess personality are *observation*, observing others' behavior and inferring their personality traits, and *interviews*, asking questions and inferring personality traits from the responses. Other assessment methods are inventories and projective tests.

Inventories: Check This

Perhaps the most common method of personality assessment is a **personality inventory**, a paper-and-pencil test that requires those being assessed to read statements and indicate whether each is true or false about themselves (only two choices) or how much they agree or disagree with each statement along a multi-point rating scale (three or more choices). Personality inventories usually assess many different traits and contain a great number of statements, often more than 300, so as to include statements that cover different aspects of each trait. This comprehensiveness ensures an inventory's validity.

Rather than producing a single indicator of personality (such as "friendly" or "seeks excitement"), the results of a personality inventory provide information about a number of traits in the form of a *personality profile*, a summary of the different traits that constitute someone's personality (see Figure 8.3). Personality inventories are used in a variety of settings and for a variety of purposes: by mental health professionals to assess mental illness, by research psychologists to assess how personality traits are related to other variables, and by employers to assess how personality characteristics are related to aspects of the job (Borman et al., 1997).

One of the key advantages of personality inventories is that they are easy to administer; a major drawback is that responses can be biased in several ways. Some people are more likely to check off "agree" than "disagree," regardless of the content of the statement. This response style, called *acquiescence*, can be reduced by wording half the items negatively. For example, the item "I often feel shy when meeting new people" would be reworded as "I don't usually feel shy when meeting new people." Another source of bias is **social desirability**: answering questions in a way that you think makes you "look good," even if the answer is not true. For instance, some people might not agree with the statement "It is better to be honest, even if others don't like you for it," but think that they should agree, and so respond accordingly. To compensate for this bias, many personality inventories have a scale that assesses the respondent's propensity to answer in a socially desirable manner. This scale is then used to adjust or, in the language of testing, to "correct" the scores on the part of the inventory that measures traits.

One personality inventory is Raymond Cattell's 16PF (Cattell et al., 1970; see Figure 8.3). People's responses on this inventory are categorized into Cattell's 16 personality factors. Another, the **Minnesota Multiphasic Personality Inventory-2 (MMPI-2)**, is commonly used to assess psychopathology (Butcher & Rouse, 1996). It has 567 questions that the test-taker checks off as either true or false, it usually takes 60–90 minutes to complete. (There is a short form consisting of 370 questions.) In contrast to the MMPI-2, which primarily assesses psychopathology or maladaptive extremes of personality, the *NEO Personality Inventory (NEO-PI-R)* is designed to assess 30 personality traits from the Five-Factor Model (N for Neuroticism, E for Extraversion, O for Openness—three of the Big Five superfactors—and R for Revised). There are both self-report and other-report (by spouse or roommate, for example) versions of this inventory.

Personality inventory: A pencil-and-paper method for assessing personality that requires the test-takers to read statements and indicate whether each is true or false about themselves.

Social desirability: A source of bias in responding to questions on personality inventories that occurs when people try to make themselves "look good" even if it means giving untrue answers.

Minnesota Multiphasic Personality Inventory-2 (MMPI-2): A personality inventory primarily used to assess psychopathology.

As with the MMPI-2, the NEO-PI-R has been used extensively and is considered to be both valid and reliable.

Projective Tests: Faces in the Clouds

A **projective test** presents the respondent with an ambiguous stimulus, such as a shapeless blot of ink or a drawing of people, and asks the respondent to make sense of the stimulus. The respondent is asked to provide the story behind the stimulus: What does the inkblot look like? What are the people in the drawing doing? The theory behind projective tests is that people's personalities can be revealed by what they project onto an ambiguous stimulus as their minds impose structure on it. This is the reasoning behind the **Rorschach test** (see Figure 8.4). Developed by Herman Rorschach (1884–1922), this commonly used projective technique has 10 cards, each with a different inkblot. The ambiguous shapes of the inkblots allow people to use their imaginations as they decide what the shapes might represent or resemble (for example, a bat or a butterfly) and what features of the inkblot made them think so.

A common complaint about the use of projective tests (and the Rorschach in particular) is that their validity and reliability are questionable. For instance, an individual taking the test on different days may answer differently, leading to different assessments of the person's personality (Anastasi, 1988; Entwisle, 1972). To increase the Rorschach's reliability and validity, a comprehensive and systematic scoring method was developed (Exner, 1974), which has been extensively tested and normed on different populations. Some (Exner, 2002; Meyer, 2002; Meyer & Archer, 2001), but not others (Lilienfeld et al., 2000; Wood, Lilienfeld, et al., 2001), view this scoring method as reliable and valid. Also controversial is how truly representative those norms are, and whether someone free of psychological disorders would appear to have psychopathology in comparison to those norms (Garb et al., 2002; Wood, Nezworski, et al., 2001).

The **Thematic Apperception Test (TAT)**, developed in the 1930s by Henry Murray, relies on the same concept as the Rorschach but uses detailed black-and-white drawings, often with people in them. Several criticisms are leveled at the TAT: (1) Although systematic scoring systems exist, only 3% of clinicians actually use a scoring system to interpret the TAT, preferring to rely on intuitive interpretations of participants' responses (Pinkerman et al., 1993). (2) From a person's response to the cards, the test administrator cannot distinguish between how the person actually thinks, feels, and would behave versus how the person *wishes* to think, feel, and behave (Lilienfeld et al., 2000). Defenders of the TAT and the Rorschach point out that the tests' abilities to predict future behavior depend not only on the test administrator's experience, but on the specific behavior(s) that the tests are being used to predict (Karon, 2000).

Figure 8.4 The Rorschach Test

This inkblot is similar to those used in the Rorschach test, in which people are asked to decide what the inkblot resembles or represents and to tell why they think so.

Projective test: A method used to assess personality and psychopathology that involves asking the test-taker to make sense of an ambiguous stimulus.

Rorschach test: A projective test consisting of a set of inkblots that people are asked to interpret.

Thematic Apperception Test (TAT): A projective test consisting of a set of detailed black-and-white drawings, various elements of which people are asked to explain.

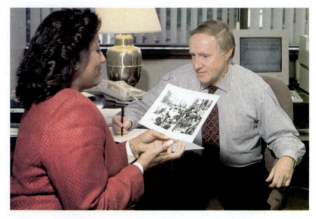

People are shown a drawing like this one from the Thematic Apperception Test (TAT) and asked to explain what is happening in the picture, what led up to it, what will happen later, and what the characters are thinking and feeling.

1. **Does such a thing as a consistent personality really exist, or do our behaviors, thoughts, and feelings depend primarily on the situation?** Trait theorists argue that personality is composed of enduring traits that lead people to behave in specific ways. Situationist theorists argue that there are no enduring personality traits; rather, behavior depends on the situation. Theorists who posit interactionism propose that some enduring personality traits do exist, and the interaction of traits with situations determines thoughts, feelings, and behavior.

2. **How do psychologists group personality traits into sets of personality types?** The Big Five superfactors are described by the Five-Factor Model of personality, which was derived through the statistical technique of factor analysis of personality inventories. The five superfactors are openness to experience, conscientiousness, extraversion, agreeableness, and neuroticism (represented as OCEAN). Each superfactor is composed of a number of specific traits. Eysenck proposes three rather than five personality dimensions (his term for superfactors): extraversion, neuroticism, and psychoticism.

3. **What methods do psychologists use to measure personality?** There are four major ways to assess personality: observation; interviews; inventories, such as Cattell's 16PF, which yields a personality profile; and projective tests, such as the Rorschach test and the Thematic Apperception Test (TAT). Psychologists most commonly use inventories to assess personality.

LOOKING BEYOND: *Critical Thinking*

Suppose you were interested in dating someone and wanted to assess his or her personality before getting too involved. Which assessment method would you choose? Why would you choose that particular method? If you could assess a prospective employer's personality, would you use the same method or a different one? Would you be able to predict your future employer's behavior if you knew his or her scores on the Big Five? Why or why not? Why might it change the accuracy of your predictions if you knew the person's scores on the specific traits that make up the five superfactors?

Biology's Influences on Personality

As their relationship progressed, Tina began to notice a host of ways in which she and Gabe were different: She loved in-line skating, biking, dancing, and skiing, he liked to read outdoors (weather permitting), go on long walks, and watch movies. She liked to meet new people or hang out with her friends and generally didn't enjoy being alone; Gabe had a few close friends but was happy spending time by himself. Tina was fairly straightforward and, up to a point, flexible; Gabe seemed less direct and more rigid. Tina was spontaneous and a bit anxious; Gabe was not spontaneous and never seemed anxious, depressed, or worried. Tina could be impatient, sometimes even snappish; Gabe was always kind and gentle. When Tina was finally able to drag Gabe to a party (he kept forgetting he had agreed to go), she was surprised by his reaction: He stayed in a corner talking to one person for half an hour, then announced that he'd had enough and was ready to leave. Tina, on the other hand, felt like the party was just beginning. Taken together, the differences between them left Tina increasingly puzzled and wondering why they were attracted to each other.

Some aspects of personality are biologically based, so personalities are partly born, not entirely made. Is Gabe shy and mellow because of his biology? Is Tina outgoing and a bit anxious because of her genes or hormones? Let's explore how biology contributes to personality.

LOOKING AHEAD: Learning Objectives

1. *What exactly is temperament?*
2. *What do the biologically based theories of personality have in common?*
3. *What does the field of behavioral genetics say about the genes' effects on personality?*

Temperament: Waxing Hot or Cold

Psychologists use the term **temperament** to refer to innate, biologically based inclinations to engage in a certain style of behavior. Arnold Buss (1995) views temperament as having more influence on behavior than personality traits or factors, affecting not just *what* people do, think, and feel, but *how* they act, think, and feel. Such inborn tendencies can appear at an early age and persist throughout adulthood. Longitudinal studies have found that children's temperaments at age 3 are

Your temperament (such as your preferred level of vigor for activities) and personality traits will likely determine whether your idea of a good time at the beach (assuming you like beaches) will lead you to be physically active or inactive.

correlated with their personalities, as assessed by a personality inventory, at age 18 (Caspi, 2000; Chess & Thomas, 1996). A study of 21-year-olds also linked temperament with health-risk behaviors such as unsafe sex, alcohol dependence, violent crime, and dangerous driving (Caspi et al., 1997).

Just as psychologists have proposed different ways of classifying personality, so too with temperaments: Different personality theorists propose different sets of temperaments as fundamental. Arnold Buss and Robert Plomin (1984; A. H. Buss, 1995) propose four dimensions of temperament:

- **Sociability**: a preference for being in the company of others rather than alone (similar to the Big Five's extraversion)
- **Emotionality**: an inclination to become aroused in emotional situations, but only when the emotion of distress, fear, or anger is involved (similar to neuroticism)
- **Activity**: the general expenditure of energy, which has two components: *vigor* (the intensity of activity) and *tempo* (the speed of activity)

Temperament: Innate inclinations to engage in a certain style of behavior.

Sociability: A temperament dimension characterized by a preference for being in other people's company rather than alone.

Emotionality: A temperament dimension characterized by an inclination to become aroused in situations in which the predominant emotion is distress, fear, or anger.

Activity: A temperament dimension characterized by the general expenditure of energy, which has two components: vigor (intensity of the activity) and tempo (speed of the activity).

- **Impulsivity**: a tendency to respond to stimuli immediately, without reflection or concern for consequences

Let's look at a couple of specific, well-studied temperaments in detail.

Shyness: The Wallflower Temperament

Are you shy, or do you know someone who is? Have you ever wondered what causes one person to be shy and another outgoing? Is shyness innate? Kagan and his colleagues (1988) have found that some babies are more reactive, or sensitive, to environmental stimuli and thus are more fussy than other babies. These "high-reactive" infants are more likely than "low-reactive" babies to respond to a recording of a woman's voice or to a colored toy with crying, general distress, and increased motor activity. Such infants tend to have faster heart rates and higher levels of the stress hormone cortisol. Kagan and his colleagues have shown that babies with a fast heart rate in the womb are more likely later to become inhibited, fearful children who startle more easily; in fact, the heart activity of even 2-week-old infants can predict later inhibition (Snidman et al., 1995). These children's sympathetic nervous systems are more easily aroused, leading to a preference for situations less likely to create high arousal. As these inhibited children get older, they are usually the ones who hide behind their parents in a room full of adults.

Some of these inhibited children become shy teenagers and adults—and are often extremely self-conscious, so much so that they may painfully and ruthlessly analyze their behavior after a social interaction, an unhappy process that leads them to avoid interactions with others in the future. They become preoccupied with their shyness and its effects ("I can't stop imagining what they're thinking about me"). These preoccupying thoughts can occur in response to autonomic nervous system reactions (a pounding heart), to behavior (what to do with the hands), and to thoughts ("No one wants to talk to me"). Fear and distress in social situations are common feelings for highly inhibited people.

But not all inhibited toddlers are still inhibited at age 7, and not all inhibited children become shy adults (Kagan, 1989a). The environment can play a role either in diminishing the effects of shyness or in maintaining shyness into adulthood. Children can develop a more varied repertoire of responses to novel social situations and so may become less inhibited as they get older (Fox et al., 2005). However, children who are very inhibited or very outgoing are the least likely to change over time (Kagan et al., 1988; Zhengyan et al., 2003). Fox (cited in Azar [1995]) found that the home environment, specifically the parents, can help inhibited children by recognizing their temperament and supporting the children—by encouraging them to learn new responses to social situations and doing so in a way that promotes mastery rather than leads them to feel overwhelmed (Fox et al., 2005; Rubin et al., 2002; Wood et al., 2003). As one previously inhibited 7-year-old explained, "My parents introduced me to new things slowly" (Azar, 1995).

Having an easily aroused autonomic nervous system may produce a bias toward shyness, but the view taken by the family and culture toward such behavior will determine how a person thinks and feels about himself or herself. American culture tends to favor outgoing people, a social bias that puts shy people at a disadvantage. Their self-image as social beings is more likely to be negative, and this negative self-concept increases the likelihood of an autonomic reaction in social situations, thereby perpetuating the cycle.

Sensation Seeking: What's New?

Another well-studied temperament is that of *sensation seeking*: the pursuit of novelty, often in high-stimulation situations, such as sky diving, fast driving, or drug and alcohol use, or occupations, such as working in a hospital emergency room (Zuckerman, 1979). High sensation seekers are more likely to send flaming e-mails (Alonzo & Aiken, 2004), to surf (versus play golf, Diehm & Armatas, 2004), and to listen to punk music (Weisskirch & Murphy, 2004). High sensation seekers view a given situation as less risky than do low sensation seekers (Horvath & Zuckerman, 1993). A study of personality predictors of driving accidents found that those drivers who had had car accidents or traffic violations were more likely than those who didn't to be thrill seekers and risk takers (Trimpop & Kirkcaldy, 1997). Tina appears to have a sensation-seeking temperament, and Gabe, who actively shies away from adventurous activities, doesn't. Sensation seeking is associated with lower levels of the chemical monoamine oxidase-B (MAO-B) in the blood. MAO-B helps break down neurotransmitters for storage, affecting the amounts of those neurotransmitters that are available (Zuckerman & Kulhman, 2000), at least in males (Shekim et al., 1989).

Biologically Based Theories of Personality

Although the Five Factor Model identifies and describes traits and superfactors, it does not take the crucial next step—it does not attempt to explain *why* these personality differences exist. For this exploration, we turn to theories of personality that involve biological systems, which focus on how various aspects of biology—genes, neurotransmitters, brain areas—influence temperament and personality.

Behavioral Activation and Inhibition Systems

Jeffrey Gray (1982, 1987, 1991) proposes two underlying biological systems that explain aspects of personality. One system, the *behavioral activation system (BAS)*, is a mechanism based on activation, or reward. This system is associated with extraversion (both the Big Five superfactor and Eysenck's dimension), and people in whom the BAS is easily activated are more sensitive to, and more easily conditioned by, reward; in contrast, introverts are more sensitive to, and more easily conditioned by, punishment. The BAS triggers positive feelings (such as elation or hope), but it also underlies impulsivity, and people with an easily activated BAS tend to respond readily to even minor incentives and rewards (Meyer et al., 2005). People in whom the BAS is easily activated are also likely to have problems with substance abuse (Johnson et al., 2003).

The other system proposed by Gray, the *behavioral inhibition system (BIS)*, is a mechanism based on inhibition, or punishment. This system is associated with neuroticism (again, both the Big Five's and Eysenck's). Whereas the BAS is activated by incentives and rewards, the BIS is activated by threat-related stimuli, which trigger anxiety and inhibit behavior. People with an easily activated BIS become distressed when confronted with even minor threats; in contrast, those with an insensitive BIS are not distressed by most threats and are only somewhat distressed when confronted with significant threats (Carver & White, 1994; Carver et al., 2000; Heponiemi et al., 2003; Meyer et al., 2005). Many people in whom

People who engage in highly stimulating hobbies such as hang gliding, downhill skiing, or snowboarding are more likely to be sensation seekers.

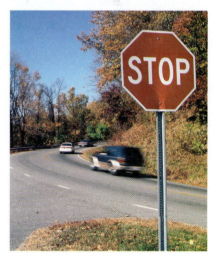

People who are more sensitive to, and motivated by, reward are more likely to violate traffic rules than are people less sensitive to reward (Castellà & Pérez, 2004).

the BIS is easily activated are also anxious and depressed (Johnson et al., 2003; Kasch et al., 2002).

Gray and others (Davidson, 1992a, 1992b; Fox et al., 2005; Zuckerman, 2003) argue that the properties of these systems arise from characteristics of specific brain structures, neurotransmitters, and neuromodulators, and research supports this view.

Eysenck's Theory

Eysenck also proposed that biological mechanisms underlie his three personality dimensions. Eysenck conceived of a hierarchy, where the personality dimensions (at the top of the hierarchy) are composed of more specific traits, which in turn are composed of automatic responses (habit responses), which are themselves based on specific, learned associations between a stimulus and response. As you will see, there is support for some aspects of Eysenck's theory (Matthews & Gilliland, 1999; Zuckerman, 2003). Let's consider Eysenck's three dimensions in more detail.

Research suggests that extraverts are more easily conditioned by reward (such as winning money), whereas introverts are more easily conditioned by punishment (such as losing money). These differences may be related to differences in brain structure or function (Gray, 1987).

Extraversion. Eysenck believed that the cerebral cortex of extraverts is less easily aroused than that of introverts (Haier et al., 1984). His view was that it takes more stimulation to arouse or to overstimulate extraverts (Eysenck & Eysenck, 1967). This may at first seem an unlikely claim, but consider what it means: Because of this higher threshold, extraverts seek out activities that are more stimulating and arousing (recreational activities such as hang gliding or occupations such as espionage). Moreover, introverts and extraverts have different biological responses to caffeine, nicotine, and sedatives (Corr & Kumari, 1997; Corr et al., 1995; Stelmack, 1990), as this theory predicts. And researchers have also found differences between introverts and extraverts in skin conductance and EEG recordings (Eysenck, 1990a; Matthews & Amelang, 1993). In spite of such support, however, studies of cortical arousal—which are at the heart of Eysenck's theory—have yielded mixed results (Zuckerman, 2003).

Neuroticism. Those who score high on the dimension of neuroticism are easily and intensely emotionally aroused and so are more likely to experience conditioned emotional responses—that is, emotional responses elicited by previously neutral stimuli (see Chapter 4; Eysenck, 1979). Thus, someone high on this dimension who is stuck in an elevator is more likely to develop a fear of elevators than is someone low on this dimension.

Neuroimaging data confirm that extraversion and neuroticism are associated with different types of brain activation. Canli and colleagues (2001) used fMRI to monitor brain activity while women looked at positive pictures (such as puppies playing, a happy couple) and negative pictures (such as people crying, a cemetery). The investigators then looked at the relation between the women's extraversion and neuroticism scores and their brain activity in several regions. Extraversion scores were correlated with activation in one set of brain areas when the women looked at the positive pictures (compared with negative ones); in contrast, neuroticism scores were correlated with activation in another set of brain areas when the women looked at negative pictures (compared with positive ones). These findings indicate that the two personality dimensions are not only distinct, but also related to different brain systems. However, research has not yet produced a detailed biological explanation for Eysenck's neuroticism dimension (Zuckerman, 2003).

Psychoticism. Eysenck viewed those high on psychoticism as having less control over their emotions and therefore as more likely to be aggressive or impulsive. Similarly, Zuckerman (1989, 1991, 2003) suggests that those high on psychoticism have difficulty learning not to engage in particular behaviors. Both tendencies could lead to criminal behavior. In fact, Eysenck (1990b) claimed that 50–60% of the variability in such tendencies is inherited. This does not mean that some people are born crooks, but rather that some are born with autonomic and central nervous systems whose underarousal indirectly leads them to seek risks—and some of these risks, given exposure to certain environmental influences, may be associated with criminal behavior (Eysenck, 1977). Low arousal may occur in part because of low levels of activity of the neurotransmitter serotonin in the central nervous system, a condition that has been associated with impulsive behavior (Klinteberg et al., 1993; Linnoila et al., 1983). Indeed, Raine and colleagues (1990) showed that underarousal at age 15 (as assessed by three different measures of autonomic and central nervous system activity) predicted criminality at age 24 in 75% of cases.

Although showing an impressive link between biology and criminality, these findings do not prove that biology is destiny, in this or most other areas. By analogy, our biology leads us all to need to eat, but how, what, and when we eat are determined in large part by the way we are raised. Environmental factors play a strong role in the development of criminality (Eysenck & Gudjonsson, 1989; Henry et al., 1996). Indeed, twin studies document the influence of environmental factors in criminality (Caspi et al., 2004; McGuffin & Gottesman, 1985; Plomin et al., 1997).

Cloninger's Theory

Cloninger and his colleagues (1993) propose that people differ on four basic personality dimensions:

- *Reward dependence* (motivated by a warm attachment to others, its opposite is pragmatism and tough-mindedness)
- *Harm avoidance* (pessimism, shyness, and a fear of uncertainty, an inhibition of approach behaviors and an increase in escape behaviors)
- *Novelty seeking* (an excited response to new situations; it is related to Gray's BAS)
- *Persistence* (the tendency to continue to seek a goal in the face of obstacles or resistance)

Cloninger further proposes that each of these dimensions corresponds to some combination of Big Five superfactors and is associated with a distinct biological system. For example, novelty seeking is similar to sensation seeking (Zuckerman & Cloninger, 1996), which in turn corresponds to a combination of a high score on extraversion and a low score on conscientiousness in the Big Five (Zuckerman, 2003). Ebstein and colleagues note that people who score higher than average on novelty seeking are "impulsive, exploratory, fickle, excitable, quick-tempered, and extravagant, whereas those who score lower than average tend to be reflective, rigid, loyal, stoic, slow-tempered, and frugal" (1996, p. 78). Cloninger and his colleagues hypothesized that the novelty-seeking dimension is related to the dopamine-based reward system (Hansenne et al., 2002; Reif &

Lesch, 2003; Wiesbeck et al., 1995; Zuckerman & Cloninger, 1996). Earlier studies with animals had shown that dopamine is involved in exploratory behavior, and a lack of dopamine in people with Parkinson's disease leads to a low level of novelty seeking (Cloninger et al., 1993).

Zuckerman's Theory

Like Cloninger, Zuckerman has proposed a classification system of personality dimensions that is rooted in biological mechanisms; this system is known as the *alternative five*:

- *Sociability*, which is similar to extraversion
- *Neuroticism-anxiety*, which is similar to neuroticism
- *Impulsive sensation seeking*, which is a tendency to act impulsively. This dimension is a reconceptualization of Eysenck's psychoticism and is related to sensation seeking and Gray's BAS; it is at the opposite end of the Big Five's conscientiousness superfactor (Zuckerman, 1989; Zuckerman et al., 1999). Impulsive sensation seeking is the most studied of the alternative five; it is more typical of men than women and is associated with a diminished sensitivity to punishment or loss of reward (Zuckerman & Kuhlman, 2000). This dimension has a high heritability estimate (Fulker et al., 1980; Hur & Bouchard, 1997).
- *Activity*, which is reflected in a need for activity, a high energy level, a preference for challenges, and difficulty in relaxing
- *Aggression-hostility*, which is a tendency toward antisocial behavior, verbal aggression, and vengefulness. Aggression-hostility is the opposite of the Big Five's agreeableness (Zuckerman, 1994).

Comparing the Biologically Based Theories

Although the names of the personality dimensions used in the four biologically based theories differ, there seem to be correspondences across the theories (see Table 8.4). All four theories have a dimension related to sociability and a dimension related to anxiety or emotionality. The theories differ in the breadth of these dimensions and in the specific traits associated with them (Ball, 2002). In addi-

People with higher numbers of tattoos score higher on measures of sensation seeking (Roberti et al., 2004).

Table 8.4 Biologically Based Theories of Personality

Gray	Eysenck	Cloninger	Zuckerman
Behavioral activation system (BAS)	Extraversion*	Reward dependence	Sociability
Behavioral inhibition system (BIS)	Neuroticism	Harm avoidance	Neuroticism-anxiety
	Psychoticism	Novelty seeking**	Impulsive sensation seeking**
		Persistence	Activity
			Aggression-hostility

*Extraversion is also inversely related to BIS levels.
**Novelty seeking and impulsive sensation seeking are also related to BAS levels.

tion, Cloninger's novelty seeking and Zuckerman's impulsive sensation seeking are closely related, and Cloninger's persistence and Zuckerman's activity are moderately related (Zuckerman & Cloninger, 1996).

Genes and Personality: Born to Be Mild?

Ebstein and colleagues (1996) found that the personality dimension of novelty seeking can be influenced by a single gene, which is a biological factor. This finding raises a question: Are all personality differences genetically determined? Behavioral geneticists seek to ascertain the influence of heredity on behavior and, in so doing, investigate a wide range of psychological phenomena, including personality. One way these researchers try to tease apart the effects of heredity and those of the environment is to compare twins separated at birth and raised apart with twins raised together (see Chapter 2). Also compared are identical and fraternal twins who share an environment but have exactly the same genes (the identical twins) or on average only half their genes in common (the fraternal twins). If the identical twins are more similar than the fraternal twins, that difference is usually attributed to effects of the genes.

The largest study of twins reared apart (identical and fraternal), the Minnesota Study of Twins Reared Apart (MISTRA), was undertaken in 1979 at the University of Minnesota. For this study, the researchers located 59 pairs of identical twins, 47 pairs of fraternal twins, and four sets of triplets adopted into different families at some point after birth (Bouchard, 1994). Once enrolled in the program, adult twins spent 6 days taking personality (including the MMPI) and intelligence (including the WAIS) tests, undergoing medical and dental exams, and answering a total of 15,000 written questions (Rosen, 1987; Segal, 1999). In addition, about 24,000 pairs of twins raised together were studied. The results of MISTRA indicate that both extraversion and neuroticism have substantial heritability (the fraction of observed variability of a characteristic that arises from inherited factors; see Chapter 2).

Heritability of Personality

It is worth stressing that, although personality traits—as well as work interests and social attitudes—may be partly caused by your genes, even among twins not all traits are found to be equally heritable, as shown in Figure 8.5 on p. 356 (Bouchard, 2004; Heath & Martin, 1990; Loehlin, 1992; Pederson et al., 1988). Similar results have been found when twins rate themselves and when others rate them (Angleitner et al., 1995).

The method of using twins to obtain heritability estimates has been criticized on both statistical and methodological grounds (Joseph, 2001; Stoolmiller, 1999), and studies of adoptive families have not found such high correlations (Loehlin et al., 1981). Critics have pointed out that the adoptive homes for the twins reared apart were more similar to each other than a random selection of homes would be and that some of the twin pairs reared apart lived together through infancy or saw each other sporadically throughout childhood. Both of these factors would increase the correlations among the twin pairs, but not because of genetics.

Heritability of Specific Behaviors

Despite such criticisms, some researchers propose a genetic origin for very specific behaviors (Bergeman et al., 1990; Kendler et al., 1992; Lyons et al., 1993):

Figure 8.5 Heritability of Personality

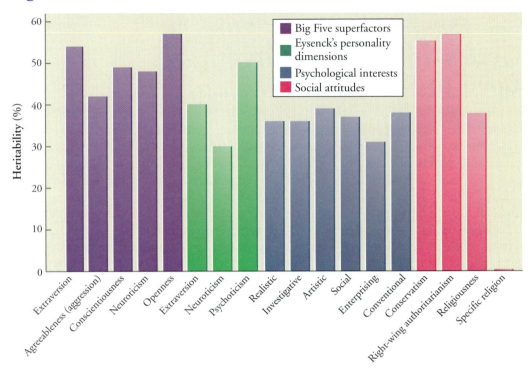

Heritability of the Big Five superfactors, Eysenck's three dimensions of personality, psychological interests, and social attitudes, based on research with twins.

from the amount of time spent watching television (Prescott et al., 1991) and the number of childhood accidents (Phillips & Matheny, 1995) to a tendency to marry (Johnson et al., 2004) or divorce (McGue & Lykken, 1992) and even religious attitudes (Bouchard, 2004; Waller et al., 1990). Genes apparently influence the way people respond to specific situations (Lensvelt-Mulders & Hettema, 2001a). Similarly, Lykken and colleagues (1993) found a heritability estimate of .50 for work and leisure interests in a twin study, and they estimate that a subjective sense of well-being (what some might call happiness) has a heritability between .44 and .80 (Lykken & Tellegen, 1996)! Other researchers have found that the subjective sense of well-being has a higher heritability in women (.54) than in men (.46) (Roysamb et al., 2002); a particularly interesting result of this study was a suggestion that different genes may underlie variations in happiness for men and women.

Of course, nobody claims that the amount of time you spend watching television is explicitly coded in your genes. What some researchers do claim, however, is that the genes may influence characteristics such as how easily your autonomic nervous system is aroused (Lensvelt-Mulders & Hettema, 2001b; Tesser et al., 1998)—and such factors in turn influence personality traits. Indeed, even physical traits—such as how attractive and athletic you are—may indirectly allow your genes to influence your personality (Olson et al., 2001). If, for instance, your activity level is both

These identical twins were separated in infancy and adopted by different working-class families. In school, neither liked spelling, but both liked math; as adults, both worked as part-time deputy sheriffs, vacationed in Florida, had first wives named Linda, second wives named Betty, and gave their sons the same names. They both drove Chevys and liked carpentry (Holden, 1980). Moreover, their medical histories were remarkably similar, including the onset of migraine headaches at age 18. Are these similarities a result of coincidence or of the twins' shared genetics? How many similarities would any two random people have if they compared such detailed information?

"low vigor" and "low tempo" (based on Buss and Plomin's temperament) and you tend to be shy, you are more likely to spend time alone in sedentary pursuits (such as watching television) than if you are a gregarious person who likes vigorous, fast-paced activities. It is also important to note that simply because some aspects of personality have a genetic component, this does not mean that personality is fixed from birth to death. All researchers agree that other factors, such as personal experience, also shape personality. Even Eysenck (1993), who argued that much of behavior is biologically determined, conceded that the environment makes a difference in whether someone high in psychoticism will become a creative, productive researcher or artist or will be disabled by schizophrenia. As we have seen throughout this book, the environment can affect the body and the brain, in turn, leading to psychological changes (Davidson, 2001).

Genes and the Family Environment

The MISTRA study did not generally find the family environment to be a large contributor to personality traits. The exceptions are *social closeness*, that is, the desire for intimacy with others (Tellegen et al., 1988), and *positive emotionality*, a trait "characterized by an active engagement in one's environment" (p. 1037). The relatively small influence of a shared family environment on other personality traits may simply reflect the fact that adoptive families are more similar to each other than are families in general, thereby diminishing the correlation for shared family environment (Stoolmiller, 1999). Moreover, many important aspects of the family environment are not really shared. The same family event, such as a divorce, will be experienced differently by children of different ages and cognitive abilities (Hoffman, 1991). In addition, parents do not treat each of their children exactly the same. Children create aspects of their own environments based on their temperaments at birth, leading parents to develop a different pattern of interaction with each of their children and different expectations of each child (Graziano et al., 1998; Jenkins et al., 2003; Plomin & Bergeman, 1991; Scarr & McCartney, 1983; see Chapter 6). It is also possible that there are individual differences in the susceptibility to environmental forces during personality development (Holden, 1980). Genes not only have direct effects, but indirect ones as well—and these can alter the environment, which, in turn, can alter the operation of the genes. As we discussed earlier (Chapters 2 and 6), genes and environment are best regarded as aspects of a single system.

How Do Genes Exert Their Influence?

Unlike eye color, most aspects of personality aren't affected by a single gene. Rather, sets of genes, exerting their influence in concert, affect personality (Bouchard, 2004). Also, variations in a single gene, interacting with other genes, may affect more than one aspect of personality (Ebstein et al., 2002; Livesley et al., 2003).

Scientists are trying to identify some of the genes that affect personality. Although some studies find that a particular gene is associated with a particular trait or superfactor, variations of a single gene account for less than 10% of the genetic influence (Lesch, 2003; Reif & Lesch, 2003). Moreover, studies investigating the relationships between a particular gene and a trait or superfactor often yield inconsistent results (Livesley et al., 2003).

In addition to wanting to find the genes that influence personality, researchers want to know the mechanisms by which genes affect personality. Recent research has focused on neurotransmitters and their activities. However, the process of discovering the relationships of genes to neurotransmitters and of neurotransmitters to personality traits and superfactors has just begun. Correlational studies sometimes find relationships between levels of a neurotransmitter by-product (in the blood, urine, or saliva) and a personality trait, but subsequent studies often fail to replicate these results. The most common explanation for such inconstancies is that neurotransmitters affect personality in complex ways, both direct and indirect (Zuckerman, 2003).

LOOKING BACK: *Review*

1. *What exactly is temperament?* Temperament refers to an innate style of behavior. Four temperament dimensions are activity (which has two components, vigor and tempo), sociability, emotionality, and impulsivity.

2. *What do the biologically based theories of personality have in common?* All four biologically based theories of personality (those of Gray, Eysenck, Cloninger, and Zuckerman) include a personality dimension related to sociability and another one related to anxiety or emotionality.

3. *What does the field of behavioral genetics say about the genes' effects on personality?* Based on twin studies, behavioral geneticists propose that some dimensions of personality are up to 50% heritable, depending in part on the trait or factor being assessed. Despite this high heritability, environmental factors still play an important role in personality development.

LOOKING BEYOND: *Critical Thinking*

Imagine that you know a family in which both parents are highly extraverted, emotionally stable, not particularly creative, and very conscientious. Would you predict that their child would have the same personality features? Why or why not? If their child is very shy (one of Kagan's inhibited children), would that mean that the child will always be shy, or might he or she become like the parents? (Hint: Think about what you have learned about temperament.)

Might Gabe have been one of Kagan's inhibited children? Explain your answer.

Learning and the Cognitive Elements of Personality

Tina's and Gabe's personalities may have been shaped partly by biology, but their unique experiences also shaped their beliefs, expectations, and goals. For instance, Tina's past positive experiences with thrilling activities lead her to get excited about new stimulating activities. Similarly, Gabe may hesitate about going to parties because of previous experiences where socializing in groups was awkward and uncomfortable. How does experience build on the biological framework of our personalities, affecting our beliefs, motivations, and views of ourselves?

LOOKING AHEAD: *Learning Objectives*

1. *How do behavioral factors influence personality?*
2. *What is the sociocognitive view of personality?*

Learning to Have Personality: Genes Are Not Destiny

Early learning theorists (see Chapter 4), particularly Skinner (1971) and Watson (1924), viewed personality as sets of behaviors that are acquired through experience. These theorists argued that an individual's inclination to behave in consistent ways arises from his or her conditioning history; no mental processes (or biologically based temperaments) are involved. According to this view, people may spontaneously produce a specific behavior once or twice, but they will continue to engage in the behavior only because they have been conditioned to do so. As discussed in Chapter 4, learning influences personality by creating:

- *classically conditioned behaviors*, such as a phobia (leading to a persistent avoidance of a stimulus),
- *operantly conditioned behaviors*, such as engaging in highly stimulating activities because of past reinforcement (or avoiding parties because of past "punishment" for attending), and
- *behaviors learned though observation* (such as avoiding a particular behavior after hearing about or witnessing a sibling's severe punishment for that behavior).

Although a strict behaviorist view of personality is not supported by research, behavioral factors do exert an influence on personality. For example, behaviorally inhibited children tend to have poor assertiveness skills (Rubin & Borwick, 1984), and other children's reactions to them—such as laughing at them or making them the butt of pranks—will affect their social behavior (and as we discuss shortly, also their thoughts about themselves; Fox et al., 2005). And as we noted in discussing genetics and personality, personality does not develop in isolation, but through interaction with the environment (Caprara et al., 2003, 2004; Lickliter & Honeycutt, 2003a, 2003b), which reinforces and punishes various behaviors.

The Sociocognitive View of Personality: You Are What You Expect

The sociocognitive approach to personality emphasizes that the development of personality is affected by people's thoughts, which in turn are shaped by social interactions—including those that are part and parcel of the surrounding culture. The key idea is that social interactions affect your thoughts, feelings, and behaviors—and consistent thoughts, feelings, and behaviors (consistent in a given situation at least) create personality. Thus, personality affects which stimuli are attended to or ignored, how stimuli are interpreted, and how emotions influence those interpretations. In turn, these perceptions and interpretations affect expectations, goals, and behaviors (Mischel & Shoda, 1995). For example, people high in neuroticism are more likely to search for threatening stimuli (and to remain focused on such stimuli) than those who score lower on that dimension (Derryberry & Reed, 2002; Eisenberg et al., 1995; Fox et al., 2001, 2002). Such stimuli may include body language and facial expressions.

The sociocognitive view acknowledges the influence of biological factors on personality, but emphasizes the role of the person's experiences (including social

Figure 8.6 How Biology, Learning, Cognition, and Culture Influence Personality

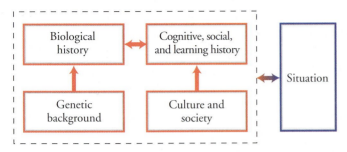

As part of their personality, people bring to any situation their genetic background and their biological, cognitive, learning, and social histories; their culture also has an influence on those elements. In turn, situations exert an influence on biology, cognition, and learning, as well as on the expression of some genes.

experiences), of consistent patterns of cognitive processing, of the view of self, and of behavior. Moreover, this view—as indicated by the "socio" part of its name—stresses that your society and culture contribute to your experiences, and ultimately even affect your biology (see Figure 8.6; Mischel & Shoda, 1995). For instance, levels of neuroticism among Americans have increased from 1963 to 1993 (Twenge, 2000), as cultural changes have led to an increase in crime and other dangers.

Expectancies

One aspect of the sociocognitive view of personality development is the idea of **expectancies**: What you *expect* to happen has a powerful influence on your thoughts, feelings, and behaviors and, in turn, on your personality. Expectancies about the outcomes of behaviors, often based on past experiences, can explain why operant conditioning works. You learn that a certain stimulus signals a likely outcome if you behave in a certain way, so you come to expect certain outcomes from particular behaviors in certain situations. Perhaps Gabe doesn't like parties because, from his previous experience of them, he expects that he will have a miserable time and feel socially isolated (in the language of conditioning, his prior unhappy experiences constituted punishment for attending a party; see Chapter 4). Such expectancies have a powerful influence on many types of social behavior. Collins and Feeney (2004) found that how people perceive their partners' attempts to provide emotional support was influenced by their beliefs and expectancies about intimate relationships. Based on their past experiences, shy children may come to *expect* to have a bad time at parties or be teased by others. People interpret ambiguous situations according to their expectancies.

One type of personality difference related to expectancy focuses on **locus of control**, the source we perceive as exerting control over our life events—that is, determining the outcomes (Rotter, 1966). People who have an internal locus of control, called *internals*, are more likely to see control over events as coming from within themselves when the situation is ambiguous; that is, they feel personally responsible for what happens to them. Gabe's responsible approach to studying would indicate that he has an internal locus of control. In contrast, *externals* are people with an external locus of control; these people are more likely to see control as coming from outside forces, and they feel less personal responsibility. Because Tina does well in her classes without studying much, she chalks up her good grades to easy tests. She feels less personally responsible for her academic success than does Gabe and seems to have more of an external locus of control. Research examining locus of control among college students between 1960 and 2002 found that, over time, college students are becoming increasingly external in their locus of control; that is, they tend to feel that their lives are out of their personal control. An average college student in 2002 had a more external locus of control than did 80% of college students in the 1960s (Twenge et al., 2004).

Internals and externals have different responses to success and failure. Internals are more likely to increase their expectancies in response to success and to lower their expectancies in response to failure. Externals are likely to do the opposite, lowering their expectancies after success and raising them after failure; externals apparently reason that the present situation may change in the future—for better or worse. Thus, what you believe about a situation depends on whether you

Expectancies: Expectations that have a powerful influence on thoughts, feelings, and behaviors and, in turn, on personality.

Locus of control: The source a person perceives to be exerting control over life's events.

attribute the consequences you experience to your own behavior or to outside forces. As an internal, Gabe has lowered expectations about future parties because of what he sees as his failures at past ones. Tina, as an external, doesn't fully expect to maintain her high grades because she doesn't feel completely responsible for them in the first place.

Self-Efficacy

People also differ with respect to **self-efficacy**, the sense of having the ability to follow through and produce desired behaviors (Bandura, 1977b). Those with high self-efficacy believe that they will be able to behave in a specific way if they want to do so (Ajzen, 2002). Self-efficacy is distinct from locus of control, which focuses on internal or external causes. (Note, however, that the two types of expectancies appear to have in common our self-evaluations and beliefs about our behaviors; Judge et al., 2002.) Albert Bandura (2004) hypothesized that self-efficacy helps people believe in themselves and in their ability to change or per-

According to the sociocognitive concept of *self-regulation*, self-administered reinforcement or punishment allows us to regulate our own behavior (Bandura, 1976, 1977a). This student is treating herself to an afternoon of surfing as a reward for studying so diligently for a final exam.

form behaviors previously viewed as difficult or impossible. Those with high self-efficacy persist more than others when working on difficult problems (Brown & Inouye, 1978). Both Gabe and Tina have high self-efficacy, a correspondence that partly accounts for the initial sense they had of being a lot alike. Bandura (2001) also proposed another important cognitive element of personality: *self-reflectiveness*, the tendency to reflect on yourself and determine whether your behaviors are appropriate and your thoughts (such as predictions and expectations) are accurate.

LOOKING BACK: Review

1. *How do behavioral factors influence personality?* Personality can be viewed as a set of behaviors that are acquired through experience. Classical and operant conditioning, as well as observational learning, help provide the experiences on which such behaviors are based.

2. *What is the sociocognitive view of personality?* The sociocognitive approach stresses the effects of expectancies on people's thoughts, feelings, and behaviors: What you expect to happen will influence personality development. Expectancies arise from locus of control, the source we perceive as exerting control over our life events, and they are affected by self-efficacy, the sense that we have the ability to follow through and produce the behaviors we would like to perform.

LOOKING BEYOND: Critical Thinking

Imagine two people who have been together as a couple for a number of years. Whatever their personalities might have been like when they started dating each other, how would learning theorists explain their current personalities? What would be the limits or weaknesses of such an explanation? What would someone taking a sociocognitive view say about how their personalities have developed? What would be the limits of that explanation?

Self-efficacy: The sense of being able to follow through and produce specific desired behaviors.

Sociocultural Influences on Personality

Tina wondered whether some of the differences between Gabe and herself might reflect the different environments in which they had grown up. Gabe was an only child; Tina was the youngest of three, with two older brothers. Gabe grew up in a rural part of the United States and, before college, had lived in the same town his whole life. Tina, an Air Force "brat," had lived in half a dozen countries before she was 12.

Although personality is influenced by genetic and biological factors, the environment clearly plays a role. For example, our family environments and the ways in which we are raised contribute substantially to the personality traits of social closeness and positive emotionality (Tellegen et al., 1988). Other environmental influences on personality that psychologists have investigated include birth order, gender differences, and culture.

LOOKING AHEAD: Learning Objectives

1. To what extent does birth order shape personality?
2. Do social factors produce gender differences in personality?
3. Do different cultures produce different types of personalities?

Birth Order: Are You Number One?

The neo-Freudian Alfred Adler (1964), himself a younger sibling raised in the shadow of a high-achieving brother, was one of the early personality theorists who proposed that birth order affects personality. In the past, research has not shown clear-cut evidence for the impact of birth order on personality development (Ernst & Angst, 1983), but more recent reviews of birth order research, using meta-analytic procedures, have found consistent and interesting results.

Science historian Frank Sulloway (1996) used meta-analyses to support his proposal that at least one aspect of personality, openness to experience (one of the Big Five superfactors), is shaped by birth order. But Sulloway was careful to point out that birth order acts along with other factors, such as the number of children in a family and the level of conflict between each child and his or her parents. Moreover, a person's sex (and that of his or her siblings), the number of years between siblings, temperament, social class, and loss of a parent can also affect this aspect of personality.

Sulloway developed his theory in an effort to understand why, throughout history, some people have supported scientific and political revolutions, whereas others have insisted on maintaining the status quo—and especially why such opposite views occur within the same family. From available information about the lives of historical figures, Sulloway proposed that, in general, firstborns, because of their place in the birth order, are more likely to support parental authority, see things as their parents do, and be less open to new ideas and experiences. Younger siblings, because they must find a different niche in the family and in the world around them, are more likely to be open to new ideas and experiences. In their personalities, "only" children are similar to firstborn children.

Table 8.5 The Effects of Birth Order on Personality

Firstborns and Only Children	Middle-Borns	Later-Borns
• More responsible, ambitious, organized, academically successful, energetic, self-disciplined; conscientious • More temperamental, more anxious about their status • More assertive, dominant (Sulloway, 1996)	• More rebellious and impulsive • Less closely identified with family • Less conscientious • Less likely to ask for parental help in an emergency • Less likely to report having been loved as a child • Compared with siblings, more likely to live farther from parents and less likely to visit parents (Salmon, 1999; Salmon & Daley, 1998; Saroglou & Fiasse, 2003)	• More agreeable and warmer • More tender-minded, easy-going, trusting, accommodating, altruistic • More adventurous, prone to fantasy, attracted by novelty, untraditional • More sociable, affectionate, excitement-seeking, fun-loving • More self-conscious (Saroglou & Fiasse, 2003; Sulloway, 1996)

Although not all psychologists agree with his meta-analytic conclusions about birth order and personality development (Modell, 1996), and not all subsequent research has supported his views (Freese et al., 1999; Skinner, 2003), some studies have supported some aspects of Sulloway's theory (Michalski & Shakelford, 2002; Zweigenhaft, 2002). Sulloway (1999) has extended and replicated his results with over 5,000 adults and across different countries (Rohde et al., 2003). And other researchers have also contributed to this research. For example, Salmon's work (1998, 1999; Salmon & Daly, 1998) has focused on middle-born children and found that middle-borns are less close to their families than are their elder or younger siblings. For instance, when hearing political speeches, middle-borns responded more positively to the speeches when the speakers used the term *friends* than when they used the terms *brothers* and *sisters*. In contrast, firstborns and last-borns responded more positively to speeches in which family terms were used (Salmon, 1998). Further, when asked to define themselves, middle-borns were least likely to define themselves by their last names, that is, their family names (Salmon & Daly, 1998). One study found middle-borns to be more rebellious and impulsive and less conscientious than their siblings (Saroglou & Fiasse, 2003). Some research results are summarized in Table 8.5.

In sum, birth order does appear to exert an influence on personality. However, its specific effects have not been found consistently across all studies, suggesting that other factors may temper the ways in which it shapes a given individual.

Sex Differences in Personality: Nature and Nurture

In general, personality differences between females and males are not very great, especially when compared with the large differences among people within each sex (Costa et al., 2001). In fact, some have proposed that it is counterproductive to look for sex differences in personality, arguing that the context in which behavior takes place has a larger role in personality development (Lott, 1996). For example, there are no notable sex differences in social anxiety, locus of control, impulsiveness, or reflectiveness (Feingold, 1994).

Nonetheless, some consistent sex differences have been found (Feingold, 1994). Women tend to score higher on traits reflecting *social connectedness*, which is a focus on the importance of relationships (Gilligan, 1982). In contrast, men tend to score higher on traits reflecting *individuality* and *autonomy*, with a focus on separateness from others, achievement, and self-sufficiency. Women tend to be more empathic than men (Lennon & Eisenberg, 1987) and to report more nurturing tendencies (Feingold, 1994). In addition, women assess emotion in other people better than do men (Hall, 1978, 1987; McClure, 2000). For example, women are better than men at spotting when their partners are deceiving them (McCornack & Parks, 1990).

Males and females also differ in their degree of neuroticism, with men scoring lower, on average (Costa et al., 2001; Goodwin & Gotlib, 2004; Lynn & Martin, 1997; Zuckerman et al., 1988). However, women generally score lower on anger and aggression (Archer, 2004; Shields, 1987) and on assertiveness (Costa et al., 2001; Feingold, 1994). However, the sex difference in assertiveness is diminishing (Twenge, 2001a).

These findings are consistent with stereotypes about men and women, but the fact that sex differences exist doesn't tell us *why* they exist—what the roles of biological or cultural factors might be (sex differences caused by cultural factors are sometimes referred to as *gender differences*).

Sociocultural Explanations

Several cultural and social theories attempt to explain personality differences between men and women. *Social role theory* proposes that boys and girls learn different skills and beliefs. For example, some computer games specifically targeted at girls emphasize social interactions and concern for others and portray getting along as more important than winning. This emphasis is in contrast to the more typical genre, which involves killing the enemy, capturing others' territory, and defending against capture or death. These two types of computer games invite the users to cultivate different skills and lead to different moral lessons. Expectancy effects can also play a role in gender differences in personality; through direct interaction with their environments, boys and girls come to have different expectancies about likely responses when they exhibit behaviors that are seen as appropriate or inappropriate for typical gender roles (Henley, 1977). An additional sociocultural explanation for gender differences in assessing others' emotions is the difference in power between men and women. Traditionally, women have been less likely to hold positions of power. Being able to read the emotions of others allows women who lack power to make rapid assessments of a situation and thus confers some advantage in maintaining personal safety (Snodgrass, 1985; Tavris, 1991).

The importance of context, or situation, has raised the question of whether examining sex differences in personality is valid; in fact, different situations can produce contradictory findings (Eagly, 1987, 1995; Lott, 1996). For example, Moskowitz (1993) found differences between men and women when participants interacted with same-sex friends (males were more dominant, and females were more friendly), but those differences disappeared when the interactions were between opposite-sex strangers. Thus, although differences between men's and women's personalities have been observed, they do not necessarily hold in all situations. Moreover, a large, 26-country meta-analysis using results from the NEO-PI-R found that, in general, differences between men and women are not as large as differences within each sex. If sex (or gender) exerts a large role on personality, then more differences between men and women than the usual ones in individ-

One sociocultural explanation for gender differences in personality is that as boys between the ages of 3 and 5 realize they are a different sex than their mothers, they lose their identification and connection with her and come to experience themselves as more autonomous than do girls (Choderow, 1978).

uality and social connectedness should have been observed. However, this was not the case (Costa et al., 2001).

Biological Explanations

In spite of the evidence that culture and context shape gender differences, we must also note that there are biological explanations for these differences. Biological explanations for sex differences include attributing them to the effects of the "male" hormone testosterone (see Chapters 2 and 7) (Berenbaum, 1999; Dabbs et al., 1997, 2001), as well as suggesting that men and women have evolved differently because of differences in mate selection and parenting strategies (D. Buss, 1995). According to this evolutionary view, women have a greater investment in their offspring because they cannot have as many children as men can. This greater investment, along with their caretaker role, supposedly causes women to become more strongly attached to their children, which has an evolutionary advantage: Highly attached mothers are more likely to have children who survive into adulthood and have children themselves.

From what we know of Tina and Gabe, we cannot say with certainty that any of the personality differences between them are explained by sex differences. Although he prefers to be alone more often than she does, Gabe has close friends, and we can't say whether their contrasting preferences reflect a difference in gender, in social connectedness and individuality, in temperament, or in their learning histories.

Culture and Personality

We can see the influence of the environment on personality in two additional ways: Psychologists have found consistent differences in people's personality traits and superfactors over time and across countries.

Personality Changes Within a Culture, Over Time: The Times They Are A-Changin'

We noted earlier that researchers have found that, over time, college students are increasingly reporting an external locus of control (Twenge et al., 2004). Similarly, the prevalence of other personality traits has also changed over time. As anxiety and neuroticism have increased significantly from 1963 to 1993, the average anxiety reported by American children in the 1980s was equivalent to the amount reported by children who were psychiatric patients in the 1950s (Twenge, 2000). In addition, the degree of extraversion has increased over time (Twenge, 2001b), and personality traits typically considered consistent with gender roles have decreased for both sexes (Twenge, 1997). Such changes are thought to reflect certain cultural shifts over the last half of the 20th century: increasing fear of crime, terrorism, and other dangers (leading to increased anxiety, neuroticism, and external locus of control), increasing valuation of traits related to extraversion, and decreasing emphasis on personality traits related to sex roles (Twenge, 1997, 2000, 2001a, 2001b; Twenge et al., 2004).

Consistent Personality Differences Across Cultures: Different Strokes for Different Countries

It is more difficult to compare personalities across cultures than you might think. Although it is possible to translate personality assessment measures into other languages, some concepts don't translate very well, even if the words themselves can be rendered in different languages. For example, it is possible to translate the phrase *self-esteem* into French, but the concept of self-esteem as Americans understand it has not been generally familiar in France, and so a simple translation of the words from English to French doesn't convey the meaning of the idea.

Translating Traits Across Languages and Cultures. Personality measures have been carefully translated in an effort to compensate for the problems that can arise with respect to the meaning of concepts, and such tests reveal the same Big Five personality superfactors in many, although not all, cultures (Katigbak et al., 1996, 2002; McCrae & Costa, 1997b; McCrae, Costa, et al., 1998; Paunonen & Ashton, 1998; Paunonen et al., 2000). Personality measures developed in the native language of a culture, rather than translated into it, may be more accurate for that culture, depending on the behaviors of interest (Katigbak et al., 2002). For example, Chinese college students were asked to rate other people on qualities described by Chinese adjectives (not English adjectives translated into Chinese); five personality factors were identified, but they were not the same as the Big Five found with English-language tests (Yang & Bond, 1990).

Individualist and Collectivist Personalities: Yours, Mine, and Ours. In general, personality differences have been found between collectivist and individualist cultures (see Chapter 7). Collectivist cultures often rank the needs of the group as more important than those of the individual; for instance, these cultures tend to value humility, honoring the family, and efforts to maintain the social order (Triandis et al., 1990), and people raised in them are more likely to care about others, even strangers (Hui & Triandis, 1986). Asian, African, Latin American, and Arab cultures tend to have this orientation (Buda & Elsayed-Elkhouly, 1998). In contrast, individualist cultures emphasize individual freedom, equality, and enjoyment—even at the expense of others. The United States, Great Britain, Canada, and Australia, for example, have this orientation. This distinction between cultures has been used to explain differences in crime rates, which are higher in individualist cultures: Collectivist cultures exert more social control over the individual, and criminals' actions reflect not only on themselves but also on their families. In fact, as the global economy leads collectivist cultures to shift their work habits and values to those of individualist countries, crime rates and other social ills often increase (Strom, 2000).

People in collectivist cultures tend to define themselves as part of a group, are very attached to the group, and see their personal goals as secondary to the group's goals. People from individualist cultures define themselves as individuals, are less attached to the group, and see their personal goals as more important than the group's goals (Triandis et al., 1988).

As proof of the impact of culture on personality, after Chinese immigrants move to North America, their personality profiles begin to resemble those of native-born North Americans; the longer they have lived in North America, the more similar the profiles (McCrae, Costa, et al., 1998).

Who Am I? Cross-Cultural Differences in Self-Concept. Not surprisingly, individualist cultures also differ from collectivist cultures in their citizens' self-concepts: People from individualist cultures characterize the "self" as a composite of traits, independent from the group; people from collectivist cultures see the "self" in relation to specific situations and contexts (Markus & Kitayama, 1991). That is, other people are incorporated into the definition of self in the latter type of culture. Perhaps for this reason, traits may be less useful for predicting behavior in collectivist cultures, such as that of the Philippines (Church & Katigbak, 2000).

These cultural differences also affect individuals' behaviors and views of themselves: Americans are more likely to enhance their view of themselves through individualist-oriented behaviors, whereas Japanese are more likely to enhance their view of themselves through collectivist-oriented behaviors (Kitayama et al., 1997; Sedikides et al., 2003).

Understanding Cultural Differences in Personality: How Do Differences Arise?

How might culture produce personality differences? Hofstede and McCrae (2004) propose three possible explanations:

- The responses on personality tests reflect a social desirability bias; people fill out the tests in ways that they believe are consistent with their culture's values (but which may not necessarily be accurate representations of their personality).

- Genetically influenced temperaments may differ across countries and geographic regions.

- Children in a given culture tend to be socialized according to that culture's values, and thus are more likely to exhibit personality traits valued by the culture.

Looking at Levels

Attachment

In our closest relationships, we develop deep attachments to other people. However, people differ in their *attachment style*—their way of relating to significant others. Before we can analyze the nature of attachment, we must consider some key facts about it. One crucial finding is that an adult's attachment style with a partner stems from the way that the adult interacted with his or her parent (or other primary caregiver) when he or she was an infant (Waller & Shaver, 1994). In those earliest of interactions, in the intimate choreography between parent and infant, a parent may be consistently responsive and empathic toward the infant, be neglectful or abusive, or be inconsistent. According to Bowlby (1973), these interaction patterns between parent and infant mold an internal *working model* about relationships. The working model—which continues to operate throughout life—gives rise to beliefs and expectations about relationships and influences how relationship-related stimuli are perceived, remembered, and responded to. For instance, the working model leads a person to feel, react, and behave in particular ways when a romantic partner no longer seems 100% committed. The model leads a person to appraise the situation as no big deal, to ruminate about it, to become anxious, to have a "big talk" with the partner, or to pull away.

Hazan and Shaver (1987) developed three categories of adult attachment style: *secure*, *anxious*, and *avoidant* (see Table 8.6 on p. 368). Studies suggest that a majority of Americans have a secure style (Hazan & Shaver, 1987); other studies indicate that an anxious style is more common in Japan and Israel and an avoidant style in Germany (Shaver & Hazan, 1994).

Table 8.6 Secure, Anxious, and Avoidant Attachment Styles

Adult Attachment Style	Percentage of an American Sample Having This Style	First-Person Description
Secure Attachment Style: These adults seek closeness and interdependence in relationships and are not worried about the possibility of the relationship's ending.	59%	"I find it relatively easy to get close to others and am comfortable depending on them and having them depend on me. I don't often worry about being abandoned or about someone getting too close to me."
Anxious Attachment Style: These adults want but simultaneously fear a close relationship.	11%	"I find that others are reluctant to get as close as I would like. I often worry that my partner doesn't really love me or won't want to stay with me. I want to merge completely with another person, and this desire sometimes scares people away."
Avoidant Attachment Style: These adults are uncomfortable with intimacy and closeness, and hence structure their daily lives to avoid closeness (Tidwell et al., 1996)	25%	"I am somewhat uncomfortable being close to others. I find it difficult to trust them completely, difficult to allow myself to depend on them. I am nervous when anyone gets too close, and often love partners want me to be more intimate than I feel comfortable being."

We can best understand attachment styles—how they arise and exert their influence—from a levels-of-analysis perspective. Attachment style clearly reflects events at the *level of the group*: It arises from interactions of caregivers and infants, and it affects adults' relationships with their partners. For example, infants who attend poor-quality day care, with few caregivers for many infants, are more likely to develop insecure attachments styles (Sagi et al., 2002). In childhood, consistent parental abuse or neglect is unlikely to engender a secure type of attachment (O'Conner et al., 2003). But our attachments styles are not fixed in stone: The relationships we have as adults can change our attachment style (Shaver & Hazan, 1994).

At the *level of the person*, attachment style influences what you pay attention to and how you interpret what you perceive. For instance, people differ in how they process sensory information (Jerome & Liss, 2005) and how they characteristically respond to those stimuli. Paula Niedenthal and colleagues (2002) examined the effect of attachment style on adults' perception of specific types of stimuli—small changes in facial expressions: The results of their studies indicate that people with different attachment styles process such stimuli differently, although in ways consistent with each particular attachment style.

Also at the level of the person, attachment style appears to relate to how people manage their emotions. As the word implies, people with an avoidant attachment style tend to avoid emotional aspects about relationships. Consider these findings comparing avoidantly attached people to those with other attachment styles:

- They tend to require more time to remember sad and anxious occasions (Mikulincer & Orbach, 1995).
- They pay *less* attention to emotional events (Collins, 1996; Fraley & Shaver, 1997; Fraley et al., 2000).
- Although consciously denying that they feel distressed when remembering stressful family events, bodily reactions suggest that they do in fact feel anxiety and stress during the recollections (Dozier & Kobak, 1992).

- They encode less information when listening to someone speaking about relationship issues; however, they forget what they did remember at the same rate as people with the other attachment styles (Fraley et al., 2000).

The type of attachment style also influences how people respond to the loss of a relationship: Those with an anxious attachment style are most likely to report distress, cognitive preoccupations, and anger and to use drugs or alcohol to cope; those with an avoidant style were most likely to exhibit self-reliance and distance themselves from the relationship. In contrast, those with a secure style used family and friends for support (Davis et al., 2003).

Thus, attachment style influences a variety of events at the level of the person: sensory and perceptual processing, how emotions are managed, and how people respond to relationship-related stimuli.

At the *level of the brain*, psychologists have examined whether attachment style is related to facets of temperament. Meyer and colleagues (2005) examined the relationship between attachment style and BIS and BAS in adult women: People who had an easily activated BIS tended to have an anxious attachment style, whereas people who had an easily activated BAS tended not to have an avoidant attachment style. The women with a responsive BAS preferred to confront their partners when their relationship was strongly threatened, but not when the relationship was only mildly threatened. Women who had an avoidant attachment style preferred more distance—they were more likely than women with other styles to end the relationship or to become less responsive to their partner after their relationship was threatened. The association between BIS and insecure attachment has been supported by additional research (Muris & Meesters, 2002).

In addition, researchers have found that infants tend to develop an attachment style like their mother's (Siegel, 1999). For instance, if the mother has an anxious style, her child will likely have that style as well (van IJzendoorn, 1995). It could be that her own attachment style affects her moment-to-moment interactions with her infant, which leads to the development of a particular attachment style in her infant (Edelstein et al., 2004). Another possibility is that—as we saw for personality traits that have relatively high heritability—attachment styles may be (at least partly) heritable. Studies of adult twins suggest otherwise, however. A twin study of adult attachment styles found that unique environmental factors—rather than genetic factors—have the greatest influence on adult attachment styles (Brussoni et al., 2000). Another twin study confirms the minimal influence of genes: When adult twins were tested on six scales that measured different aspects of love styles in romantic relationships, little evidence of heritability of styles was found (Waller & Shaver, 1994). Twin studies with children found similar results (Bokhorst et al., 2003). As Plomin and his colleagues (1997, p. 205) put it, "Perhaps love *is* blind, at least from the DNA point of view." Even if this literally isn't true of love, at least attachment is blind from a DNA point of view.

Events at each level are not isolated from one another: It is primarily the caregiver's behavior with the infant (level of the group) that gives rise to the infant's—and with time, the adult's—internal working model of relationships (level of the person). Nevertheless, attachment style may be partly related to BAS and BIS activity (level of the brain). Furthermore, the infant's temperament (determined in part by biological factors) interacts with the caregiver's personality (and the caregiver's attachment style; Sagi et al., 1997). These factors affect each other, as well as the internal working model of relationships that the child develops and usually carries into adulthood. In turn, the adult's attachment style affects his or her relationships (level of the group). And adult relationships can change attachment style; events at the level of the group can change events at the level of the person.

LOOKING BACK: *Review*

1. *To what extent does birth order shape personality?* From studying historical figures, Sulloway suggests that birth order, along with other factors such as the number of children in a family and the level of conflict between parents and children, can influence openness to experience. Further research has found additional differences between first-, middle-, and later-borns. Specifically, firstborns are less open to new experiences and are more conscientious, middle-borns identify less closely with family, and later-borns are more easy-going and more open to new experiences.

2. *Do social factors produce gender differences in personality?* Although men and women exhibit few broad personality differences, there are noteworthy differences in social connectedness (versus individuality) and in neuroticism (high versus low). Social explanations for these differences include social role theory and differences in power. Given the importance of context, gender may not be predictive of behavior in a given situation.

3. *Do different cultures produce different types of personalities?* There are cultural differences in personality: The native-born citizens of countries that emphasize the needs of the group tend to have personalities that reflect the collectivist orientation. In contrast, the native-born citizens of countries that emphasize individualism tend to have personalities that reflect the individualist orientation.

LOOKING BEYOND: *Critical Thinking*

What might be two possible explanations for regional personality differences that have been found between "mellow" Californians and "fast-paced" Northeasterners? (Hint: Genetic? Environmental?) How might you go about trying to determine whether either explanation is supported by research data? What type of study could you design, and what kinds of participants would you need? What would your hypothesis be—that is, what kind of results would you expect?

LET'S SUM IT UP

I. Personality: Historical Perspectives

A. People's motives, thoughts, and feelings are at the heart of Freud's psychodynamic theory, which focuses on three structures of personality (id, ego, and superego) and their dynamic relationships and three levels of awareness (unconscious, preconscious, and conscious), as well as sexual and aggressive drives, defense mechanisms, and psychosexual stages (oral, anal, phallic, latency, and genital).

B. According to Freud, when resolution of a psychosexual stage is incomplete, development is arrested, often creating a neurosis. Moreover, sexual and aggressive impulses can create anxiety, causing the use of defense mechanisms.

C. Maslow's and Rogers's humanistic theories also address motives, feelings, and the self, but they celebrate each person's uniqueness, stress positive qualities of human nature and free will, and emphasize self-actualization.

II. What Exactly *Is* Personality?

A. Personality is a consistent set of behavioral, emotional, and cognitive tendencies that people display over time and across situations and that distinguish individuals from each other.

B. People do not behave in the same manner in all situations: The context, or situation, influences the way people behave, and people can influence the situation.

C. Some researchers have found that personality traits can be statistically grouped into five superfactors (extraversion, neuroticism, agreeableness, conscientiousness, and openness) or, according to Eysenck, three personality dimensions (extraversion, neuroticism, and psychoticism).

D. Personality can be measured by observation, interviews, inventories (such as Cattell's 16PF), and projective tests (such as the Rorschach test and the Thematic Apperception Test, or TAT). Inventories are the most commonly used method.

III. Biology's Influences on Personality

A. Innate inclinations, often referred to as temperament, include sociability, emotionality, activity, and impulsivity. Two well-studied temperaments are shyness and sensation seeking.

B. Gray proposed two basic biological systems: the behavioral activation system (BAS) and the behavioral inhibition system (BIS). These systems underlie certain personality traits and dimensions.

C. Eysenck proposed that each of his three personality dimensions (extraversion, neuroticism, and psychoticism) has a corresponding biological basis. Aspects of this theory have been supported by neuroimaging and other biological research.

D. Cloninger proposed four biologically based personality dimensions, each with a distinct biological system: reward dependence, harm avoidance, novelty seeking, and persistence.

E. According to Zuckerman, there are five biologically based personality dimensions: sociability, neuroticism-anxiety, impulsive sensation seeking, activity, and aggression-hostility.

F. Some psychologists and behavioral geneticists estimate that as much as 50% of the variation in personality is inherited, although some traits appear to be more heritable than others.

IV. Learning and the Cognitive Elements of Personality

A. The influence of learning on personality occurs through classical and operant conditioning as well as through observational learning.

B. The sociocognitive view of personality focuses on the effects of expectancies on people's thoughts, feelings, and behaviors: What we expect to happen will influence our personality development.

C. Personality differences related to expectancies are exhibited in our locus of control (the source we perceive as exerting control over life events) and our self-efficacy (the sense that we have the ability to follow through and produce the behaviors we would like to perform).

V. Sociocultural Influences on Personality

A. Birth order, along with other moderating factors, such as the number of children in a family and the level of conflict between parents and children, can influence openness to experience and other aspects of personality.

B. Although there are a few broad personality differences between women and men (in social connectedness versus individuality and in high versus low neuroticism), in general, such differences tend to be small, and it is not clear whether they are due to biological or sociocultural factors. Sociocultural explanations for these differences include social role theory and differences in power. Context may predict personality better than does sex or gender.

C. Personality differences have also been found between people raised in cultures that are collectivist as opposed to individualist, with people in each type of culture tending to have personality traits that are more valued in their culture.

D. Attachment style is influenced by the person's working model of relationships; these models develop dynamically through interactions with caregivers, through temperament, and through the specific ways that children and adults perceive and process the world around them.

Key Terms

activity, p. 349
Big Five, p. 344
castration anxiety, p. 336
defense mechanism, p. 337
ego, p. 335
emotionality, p. 349
expectancies, p. 360
id, p. 335
impulsivity, p. 350
locus of control, p. 360

Minnesota Multiphasic Personality
   Inventory-2 (MMPI-2), p. 346
neurosis, p. 336
personality, p. 334
personality inventory, p. 346
personality trait, p. 341
projective test, p. 347
psychological determinism, p. 334
psychosexual stages, p. 336
repression, p. 338

Rorschach test, p. 347
self-actualization, p. 339
self-efficacy, p. 361
sociability, p. 349
social desirability, p. 346
superego, p. 335
temperament, p. 349
Thematic Apperception Test (TAT),
   p. 347
unconditional positive regard, p. 340

LOOKING ONLINE: *Enhance Your Learning*

MyPsychLab is an interactive and instructive multimedia resource that can be used to supplement a traditional lecture course or as an online course. It is an all-inclusive tool with a text-specific e-book plus multimedia tutorials, videos, simulations, animations, and controlled assessment to completely engage students and reinforce learning. MyPsychLab meets the individual learning needs of every student. Visit *www.mypsychlab.com* for more information!

Practice Test

For each of the following items, choose the single best answer.

1. Sigmund Freud believed in psychological determinism; that is, he contended that

   a. all behavior, no matter how mundane or insignificant, has a psychological cause.

   b. people have an innate motivation to fulfill the highest possible emotional and intellectual potential.

   c. people need unconditional acceptance.

   d. expectancies have a powerful influence on thoughts, feelings, and behavior, and, in turn, on personality.

2. According to Freud, what developmental task occurs during the phallic stage?

   a. Successful weaning from the mother's breast or bottle

   b. Successful identification with the same-sex parent

   c. Successful toilet training

   d. Transformation of sexual urges into more culturally acceptable, nonsexual behaviors

3. Defense mechanisms are used by the ego, Freud suggested, to prevent threatening thoughts from entering awareness. With the defense mechanism of projection,

   a. threatening thoughts are attributed to others.

   b. threatening thoughts or emotions are kept at arm's length by thinking about them logically and rationally.

   c. threatening impulses are directed into more socially acceptable activities.

   d. anxiety-provoking thoughts, impulses, and memories are prevented from entering consciousness.

4. According to Rogers, people

   a. need to satisfy lower-level needs before needs further up the hierarchy can be satisfied.

   b. whose lives revolve around meeting conditions of worth will achieve their full human potential.

   c. whose lives revolve around meeting conditions of worth will not achieve their full human potential.

   d. need to receive conditional positive regard to develop a healthy self-concept.

5. What is interactionism?

   a. A view of personality that regards behavior as mostly a function of the situation, not of internal traits

   b. A view of personality in which both traits and situations are believed to affect thoughts, feelings, and behaviors

c. The relationship among the five superfactors of personality

d. A pencil-and-paper method for assessing personality that requires test-takers to read statements and indicate whether each is true or false about themselves

6. Many factor analytic studies have revealed that traits
   a. form 16 personality factors.
   b. all form a single factor called social deviance.
   c. can be reduced to five superfactors.
   d. explain and thereby predict human behavior.

7. Someone who scores high on the personality dimension of neuroticism most likely
   a. enjoys people and social situations.
   b. is easily and intensely emotionally aroused.
   c. has difficulty learning not to engage in particular behaviors.
   d. has decreased sensitivity of the amygdala.

8. Suppose that Dr. Taft is concerned with avoiding the effect of acquiescence in his personality inventory; that is, he is worried that
   a. people will respond to questions in a way they think will make themselves look good.
   b. people will skip difficult questions.
   c. some people will be more likely to check off "agree" than "disagree," regardless of the content of the statement.
   d. the reading level of the personality inventory is not appropriate for his population of interest.

9. A projective test is a(n)
   a. personality inventory primarily used to assess social deviance.
   b. bias in responding to questions that arises because people try to make themselves "look good."
   c. observational test used by employers to measure people's behavior and infer their personalities.
   d. method used to assess personality and psychopathology that involves asking the test-taker to make sense of an ambiguous stimulus.

10. According to Buss and Plomin, temperament has the following dimensions:
    a. openness to experience, neuroticism, and extraversion.
    b. psychotism, agreeableness, and nonconformity.
    c. activity, sociability, emotionality, and impulsivity.
    d. specific response level, habit response level, trait level, and type level.

11. Gray's behavioral activation system (BAS) is most similar to
    a. Eysenck's neuroticism.
    b. Cloninger's persistence.
    c. Zuckerman's sociability.
    d. Buss and Plomin's vigor.

12. What effect does having a highly reactive autonomic nervous system have on a child?
    a. The child will necessarily become a shy adult.
    b. The child will become a shy adult only if he or she is a firstborn or only child.
    c. Having a reactive autonomic nervous system may produce a bias towards shyness, but the view taken by the family and culture toward such behavior will determine how a person thinks and feels about himself or herself.
    d. The child is most likely to prefer situations that are more likely to create high arousal.

13. How does the family environment contribute to personality traits?
    a. The family environment strongly influences personality traits.
    b. The family environment does not influence any personality traits.
    c. The family environment does not affect the personality traits of social closeness and positive emotionality.
    d. The family environment is generally not a large contributor to personality traits; the exceptions are social closeness and positive emotionality.

14. In general, what personality differences exist between females and males?
    a. Males tend to score higher on traits reflecting social connectedness.
    b. Females tend to score lower on measures of neuroticism.
    c. There are none.
    d. None of the above statements is true.

15. People in collectivist cultures tend to
    a. engage in repression.
    b. see their personal goals as more important than the group's goals.
    c. define themselves as part of a group.
    d. have no personality differences with people in individualist cultures.

Answers: 1. a 2. b 3. a 4. c 5. b 6. c 7. b 8. c 9. d 10. c 11. c 12. c 13. d 14. d 15. c

Historical Perspectives/What *Is* Personality?/Biology's Influences/Learning/Sociocultural Influences/LET'S SUM IT UP   373

9 chapter

Psychology Over the Life Span

Growing Up, Growing Older, Growing Wiser

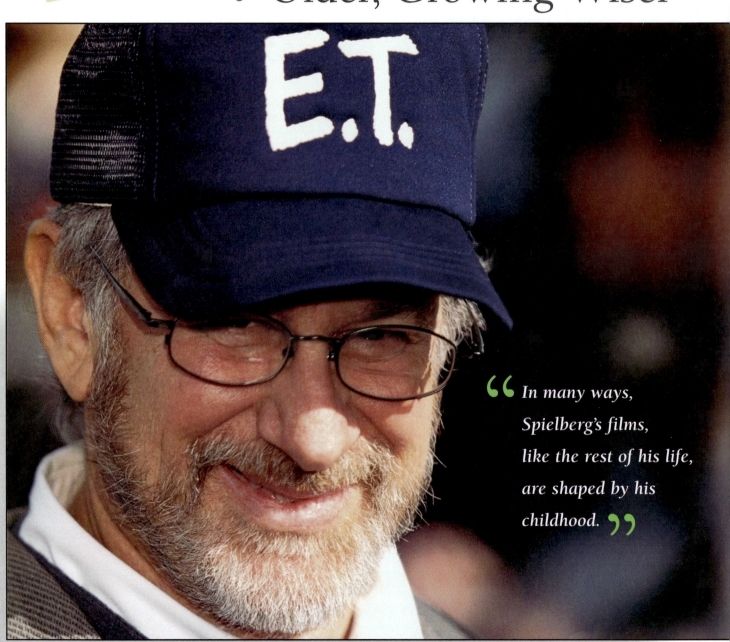

❝ *In many ways, Spielberg's films, like the rest of his life, are shaped by his childhood.* ❞

CHAPTER OUTLINE

In the Beginning: From Conception to Birth

Infancy and Childhood: Taking Off

Adolescence: Between Two Worlds

Adulthood and Aging: The Continuously Changing Self

Let's Sum It Up

SOME OF HIS CLASSMATES CALLED HIM "SPIELBUG." GIRLS THOUGHT HE WAS NERDY and unattractive. His father, Arnold, a pioneer in the use of computers in engineering, was hardly ever around and, to make matters worse, frequently uprooted his family, moving from Ohio to New Jersey, to Arizona, and finally to Northern California. Steven Spielberg was a perpetual new kid on the block. He was also, by all accounts, an unusual child, both in his appearance (he had a large head and protruding ears) and in his fearful and awkward behavior (McBride, 1999). Spielberg himself has said that he "felt like an alien" throughout his childhood. He desperately wanted to be accepted, but didn't fit in. So, at age 12, he began making films, "little 8mm things. I did it to find something that, for me, could be permanent" (quoted in R. Sullivan, 1999, p. 66). Spielberg continued to make movies as a teenager, often casting his three sisters in roles. He discovered that making movies was one way to win his peers' acceptance, as well as some small measure of power—for he sometimes induced his worst enemies to appear in his films.

When he was 16, Spielberg's parents divorced, and Spielberg blamed his father's constant traveling for the breakup. His unhappiness only deepened when his father remarried, taking for his second wife a woman Spielberg couldn't stand. At the same time that he withdrew from his father, Spielberg continued to have a close relationship with his mother, Leah, a concert pianist and artist. The split with his father lasted some 15 years.

In many ways, Spielberg's films, like the rest of his life, are shaped by his childhood. Spielberg himself has said about *E.T., The Extra-Terrestrial,* "The whole movie is really about divorce. . . . Henry's [the main character's] ambition to find a father by bringing E.T. into his life to fill some black hole—that was my struggle to find somebody to replace the dad who I felt had abandoned me" (R. Sullivan, 1999, p. 68). Many of Spielberg's other films feature children who are separated from their parents (such as the girl in *Poltergeist* and the boy in *Close Encounters of the Third Kind*). And *Back to the Future* might represent his longings to change the past, if only he could. Only when he turned 40 did he turn to adult contexts. As he matured, Spielberg's identification with oppressed people in general (not just oppressed children) led him to make movies such as *The Color Purple, Schindler's List*, and *Amistad.*

Steven Spielberg married and had a child, but eventually divorced his first wife, actress Amy Irving. His own experiences made him extremely sensitive to the effect of the divorce on his son, Max, and he made every attempt to ensure that Max did not feel abandoned. When he married again, he became deeply involved with his family (which includes seven children, some of them adopted). There was a happy development in the previous generation's father–son relationship as well: Arnold became a well-loved grandfather and a regular presence in the Spielberg household.

Spielberg's journey is one version of the universal story of human development: A skinny kid beset by fears and with few friends becomes one of the most powerful figures in the global entertainment industry; from a fragmented family life develops a man's resolve to make the best possible life for his own family; across generations, a father and a son come to like each other, now as a grandfather and a father, after 15 years of estrangement. *Developmental psychologists* study exactly these sorts of events in our lives— the fascinating and varied process of human development over the life span. In this chapter, we begin by considering prenatal development and the newborn, and we see that even here genes and environment are intimately intertwined. We next turn to infancy and childhood and observe the interplay between maturation and experience in shaping a child's physical, mental, emotional, and social development. Then we consider adolescence, a crucial time in development, bridging childhood and adulthood. And finally, we discuss adulthood and aging, gaining insights that help us understand how Arnold Spielberg could develop from a less-than-optimal father into a terrific grandfather.

In the Beginning: From Conception to Birth

Steven Spielberg has been celebrated as one of the most successful moviemakers of all time. He just seemed to have a natural bent for making movies (he never attended film school). Where did his talent come from? In this section, we begin at the beginning and think about the foundations of our skills and abilities.

Prenatal Development: Nature and Nurture From the Start

For each of us, life began with the meeting of two cells, a sperm and an egg (or *ovum*, which in Latin means "egg"). These specialized cells are sex cells, or *gametes*. The sperm penetrates the egg, and the genetic material of the sperm melds with that of the ovum. The ovum is not a passive partner in this dance of life; the sperm is drawn to the egg by chemical reactions on the surface of the egg. And when a sperm has been accepted within the egg, other reactions prevent additional sperm from penetrating. The ovum is a supercell, the largest in the human body. Even so, it is barely the size of a pinprick, and sperm are much smaller (about 1/500 of an inch). But despite their small sizes, within the ovum and sperm reside all the machinery necessary to create a new life. And, even at this earliest stage of development, *genes* (*nature*) and the *environment* (*nurture*) are intimately intertwined.

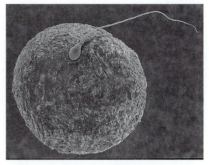

At the moment of conception, a sperm penetrates an ovum. The egg, however, is not a passive recipient; by changing its surface properties, it actively regulates the behavior of the sperm.

From Zygote to Birth: Getting a Start in Life

The genetic heritage of every normal human being is 23 pairs of chromosomes, one member of each pair coming from an egg and the other from a sperm. A *chromosome* is a strand of *DNA* (*deoxyribonucleic acid*) in the nucleus of the cell. A molecule of DNA is shaped like a twisted ladder—the famous double helix—in which the "rungs" are formed by the bonds between pairs of chemicals. Each *gene* on the chromosome is a series of particular rungs (see Chapter 2). All cells in the human body except the gametes (eggs and sperm) contain all 23 pairs of chromosomes; each gamete contains only a single member of each chromosome pair. In an egg, one of these 23 is a chromosome known as X; in a sperm, the corresponding chromosome is either an X chromosome or a shorter one called a Y chromosome.

In the Beginning. Much of early development is determined by <mark>maturation</mark>, the process that produces genetically programmed changes with increasing age. But from the very start, genes and the environment interact. Although the genes in both the sperm and the egg have a major impact on the characteristics of the person who will eventually develop, the environment plays a crucial role in whether the sperm ever reaches the egg. Sperm actually "surf" on subtle muscle contractions in the uterus; these waves usually move in the correct direction in fertile women, but they either move in the wrong direction or are weak in infertile women (Kunz et al., 1997; Lyons & Levi, 1994). In addition, the fluid in the uterus must be the right consistency and must have the right chemical composition for the sperm to complete their journey (Mori et al., 1998; Shibahara et al., 1995; Singh, 1995).

The fertilization of the egg by the sperm creates a cell called a <mark>zygote</mark>, in which the chromosomes from the egg and from the sperm pair up so that the zygote contains the full complement of 23 pairs. If the sperm contributes an X chromosome, the offspring will be female (XX); if Y, male (XY). The Y chromosome contains a gene (the *SRY* gene, for "sex-determining region of the Y

Maturation: The developmental process that produces genetically programmed changes with increasing age.

Zygote: A fertilized ovum (egg).

chromosome") that produces a chemical substance that ultimately causes the zygote to develop into a male; if this substance is not present, genes on the X chromosome will produce other substances that cause the baby to be female (Goodfellow & Lovell-Badge, 1993; Hawkins, 1994).

Dance of the Chromosomes. The two members of each pair of chromosomes (other than the XY pair in males) are similar—but they are not identical. For example, the gene for the shape of your earlobes is on the same spot on both chromosomes, but because of its particular chemical composition, the gene on one chromosome may code for an attached earlobe and the gene on the other for an unattached earlobe. The gametes are formed from specialized cells that, while themselves containing the full 23 pairs, in the course of division produce cells with half that number, with only one member of each pair. So, because the members of each pair are not identical, the genetic contents of the resulting gametes are not all the same. And there's another wrinkle, which further contributes to our wonderful human variety: In the course of cell division, the chromosomal decks of cards are shuffled so that pieces of the chromosomes in each pair in the parent cell are exchanged, as shown in Figure 9.1 to form new combinations of genes.

From Conception to Fetus: A Tale of Three Trimesters. Human development in the womb is divided into *trimesters*, three equal periods of 3 months each. The first trimester is divided into three stages: The developing baby starts off as a zygote, becomes an **embryo** when the major axis of the body is present (about 2 weeks after conception), and then becomes a **fetus** when all major body structures are present

---

Figure 9.1 The Long Road to a Zygote

SPERM DEVELOPMENT   EGG DEVELOPMENT

Original cells (46 chromosomes, in 23 pairs)

Chromosomes duplicate.

In the course of cell division, pieces of parent chromosomes in each pair are exchanged.

Gametes contain 23 chromosomes each, which recombine after conception.

CONCEPTION

Zygote with 46 chromosomes, in 23 pairs

Embryo: A developing baby from the point where the major axis of the body is present until all major structures are present, spanning from about 2 weeks to 8 weeks after conception.

Fetus: A developing baby during the final phase of development in the womb, from about 8 weeks after conception until birth.

The chromosomes in eggs and sperm are not simply copies of those of the parent, but rather unique combinations of the material in the two chromosomes in each pair of the parent's chromosomes. The sperm and egg combine to form the basis of a unique individual (or individuals, in the case of identical twins).

(about 8 weeks after conception; thereafter, the developing baby is called a fetus until he or she is born). At the end of the second trimester, the great bulk of the neurons each individual possesses are in place (Nowakowski, 1987; Rakic, 1975; Rodier, 1980), but they are not completely fixed; researchers have found that new neurons can be produced even in adult brains (Gould et al., 1999).

Learning and Behavior in the Womb

A popular—though misleading—image shows the fetus floating peacefully asleep

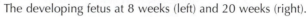

The developing fetus at 8 weeks (left) and 20 weeks (right).

in the womb. But in truth, the fetus is active nearly from the start, at first with automatic movements, such as the heart beating, and then with large-scale coordinated behaviors. As the fetus develops, the heart rate slows down (but becomes more variable), the fetus moves less often but more vigorously when it does stir, and the heart rate and movement patterns become coordinated. Some researchers have even reported sex differences in behavior in the womb, with male fetuses more active than females (Almli et al., 2001; DiPietro et al., 1996). After 20–25 weeks of gestation, the fetus is sensitive to both sound and light (Nilsson & Hamberger, 1990; Pujol et al., 1990). How do we know this? Because if a fetus is examined, as is sometimes medically necessary, by a special light-emitting instrument called a *fetoscope*, it will actually move its hands to shield its eyes. As the fetus develops, its movements become increasingly coordinated, and by 28 weeks, it responds to external stimulation. A bit later, its heart rate can change if the mother is startled (DiPietro et al., 1996; Kisilevsky & Low, 1998), and sometime between 25 and 34 weeks, a fetus can detect human speech (Cheour-Luhtanen et al., 1996; Zimmer et al., 1993). In fact, researchers have found that fetuses older than 33 weeks even pay attention to music (Kisilevsky et al., 2004).

In addition, there is evidence that fetuses can learn. In a classic study (DeCasper & Fifer, 1980), pregnant women read the story *The Cat in the Hat* aloud twice each day during the 6 weeks before their babies were born. A few hours after birth, the babies were tested. The researchers put earphones on the babies' little heads and a special pacifier-like device in their mouths. Sucking faster or slower on this device allowed the infants to hear either their mother's voice or another woman's voice reading the story. The infants sucked at the speed that produced their own mother's voice. Perhaps even more impressive, the researchers also gave the infants the opportunity to choose between hearing their mother read *The Cat in the Hat* or another story—and the infants preferred the story their mother had read aloud before they were born!

Moreover, characteristics of the fetus predict those of the child after birth. For example, fetuses that had more variable heart rates later developed into more linguistically able toddlers and demonstrated more sophisticated forms of play (Bornstein et al., 2002).

Teratogens: Negative Environment Events

A **teratogen** is an external agent, such as a chemical, virus, or type of radiation, that can cause damage to the zygote, embryo, or fetus. Because of events at

Teratogen: Any external agent, such as a chemical, virus, or type of radiation, that can cause damage to the zygote, embryo, or fetus.

different stages in the course of development, different organs are vulnerable to teratogens at different times.

Maternal Illness. Unfortunately, the central nervous system is vulnerable at virtually every phase of prenatal development. For example, the development of the brain can be disrupted if the mother catches a virus, such as chicken pox or rubella (3-day German measles); more than half the babies born to mothers who contract rubella will be mentally retarded if the developing child is in the embryonic period at the onset of the disease. In addition, a mother who is HIV-positive can pass the virus on to the baby during gestation or birth (but only about one third of these babies contract the virus). The HIV virus causes brain damage, leading to problems in concentration, attention, memory, movement control, and the ability to reason (Clifford, 2000; Grant et al., 1999).

Alcohol and Drugs. Another potential teratogen is alcohol, which can damage a woman's eggs before fertilization (Kaufman, 1997) as well as affect the developing baby throughout pregnancy, starting with the embryo phase. If the mother drinks enough alcohol during pregnancy, the baby may be born with *fetal alcohol syndrome*; part of this syndrome is mental retardation (Streissguth et al., 1989, 1999; see Chapter 6). If a mother consumes any alcohol during pregnancy, research suggests that she should take antioxidants, such as vitamins C and E, which may reduce the damage to the fetus (Cohen-Kerem & Koren, 2003). In addition, using heroin or cocaine during pregnancy can cause a host of problems: physical defects (Singer et al., 2002b), irritability, and sleep and attentional problems in the newborn (Fox, 1994; J. M. Miller et al., 1995; Vogel, 1997). Although prenatal exposure to cocaine may have only subtle effects in infancy (such as slowed language development; Lester et al., 1998), such exposure may have long-lasting consequences—some of which may become more marked in subsequent years (Chapman, 2000; Lester, 2000; Singer et al., 2002a). In addition, the problem is not restricted to mothers. Certain drugs (both prescription and illegal, such as cocaine) can affect the father's sperm and thereby affect the growing fetus and child (Yazigi et al., 1991).

Caffeine and Smoking. Major diseases and strong drugs are not the only threats to healthy prenatal development. Excessive amounts of caffeine (three cups of coffee a day, according to one study) can lead to miscarriage or low birth weight, irritability, and other symptoms (Eskenazi, 1993; Eskenazi et al., 1999). Smoking during pregnancy affects both mother and fetus; it is correlated with higher rates of miscarriage, lower birth weights, smaller head size, stillbirth, and infant mortality, and it can cause attentional difficulties in the infant (Cornelius & Day, 2000; Floyd et al., 1993; Fried & Makin, 1987; Fried & Watkinson, 2000). Smoking may even damage the fetus's genes (de la Chica et al., 2005). A mother's smoking also significantly increases the chance that her baby will die from *sudden infant death syndrome* (SIDS; Pollack, 2001). Smoking during pregnancy alters the way the infant's autonomic nervous system operates, which may contribute to SIDS (Browne et al., 2000).

Diet and Pollution. A mother's poor diet can lead her infant to have fewer brain cells than normal (Morgane et al., 1993) and can increase the risk that the child will develop a host of psychological disorders—including antisocial personality disorder (Neugebauer et al., 1999) and schizophrenia (Susser et al., 1996). (Both of these disorders will be discussed in detail in Chapter 11.) In addition, the lack of even a single important vitamin or mineral can have significant effects. For example, insufficient folic acid (a type of vitamin B) can disrupt the early development of the central nervous system (Nevid et al., 1998), and thereby cause birth defects. Most important, if the mother does not have enough folic acid, the infant can be born without the top of the skull or with *spina bifida*, which occurs when the spine does not close properly. Spina bifida requires immediate surgery and can lead to problems in bladder and bowel control (and can even prove fatal). Folic acid is also essential for producing the iron-containing protein needed to form red blood cells. (However, there can be too much of a good thing: Folic acid supplements are associated with a higher incidence of fraternal twins [Källén, 2004].)

Furthermore, if the mother eats fish with high levels of a chemical called methylmercury, this can cause the infant to be born deaf or to have visual problems; it may also impair auditory processing (Murata et al., 1999). Moreover, other environmental pollutants as well as ionizing radiation can have effects ranging from birth defects and cancer to behavioral difficulties (such as in paying attention). And, in other animals at least, these effects can be passed on to the third generation, to the offspring of the offspring (Friedler, 1996).

Maternal Stressors. The fetus is exquisitely sensitive to the mother's stress level. For example, when a pregnant woman takes a mildly stressful cognitive test (the Stroop color-word test; see Figure 3.17 on p. 118) the fetus stops moving, and its heart rate becomes more variable (DiPietro et al., 2003). Given this sensitivity, we should not be surprised that stressors in the mother's life can endanger the developing fetus. When the stress is severe enough, infants may subsequently experience attentional difficulties, be unusually anxious, and exhibit unusual social behavior (Weinstock, 1997). In fact, fetuses with mothers of lower socioeconomic status, who are often more stressed than those of higher socioeconomic status, move less often and less vigorously and show other differences from fetuses whose mothers are better-off (Pressman et al., 1998). There are several biological reasons for these effects: When the mother is stressed, more of her blood flows to parts of the body affected by the fight-or-flight response (such as the limbs and heart), and less flows to the uterus. She produces hormones such as cortisol, which slows down the operation of genes that guide prenatal development of the brain, suppressing brain growth (Brown, 1999). There is evidence that the babies born to stressed mothers have smaller heads than those born to unstressed mothers, which may be related to the poorer behavioral functioning scores observed for such babies (Lou et al., 1994). That said, you shouldn't despair about the fact that life often presents stress: There's evidence that *mild* stress may actually be good for the developing fetus (DiPietro, 2004).

A particularly powerful example of interactions among events at the different levels of analysis is the fact that social interactions with friends and family can lead to healthier babies being born to stressed mothers (McLean et al., 1993). Social support presumably helps to reduce the mother's stress, which in turn keeps her from the fight-or-flight state and its accompanying unfortunate consequences for the developing baby.

Positive Environmental Events: The Earliest Head Start

The previous paragraphs might seem to suggest that our species would be better off if maturation alone controlled development. But environmental effects are not all bad, and some prenatal experiences help the fetus. For example, researchers found that mothers who ate chocolate every day during pregnancy later rated their 6-month-old babies as having more positive temperaments than did mothers who did not eat chocolate so regularly (Räikkönen et al., 2004). However, this may say more about the effects of the candy on the mother than on her infant!

Other findings show more conclusively that the prenatal environment can play a positive role in development. Consider a study by Lafuente and colleagues (1997). Each of 172 pregnant women was assigned to an experimental or control group. The participants in the experimental group were given a waistband with a tape recorder and small speakers, on which they played tapes of violin music for an average of 70 hours, starting at about 28 weeks after conception and continuing until the birth of the baby. The researchers then tracked the development of all the babies for 6 months and found that those whose mothers were in the experimental group were more advanced than those whose mothers were in the control group. For example, they had better motor control and better vocal abilities of the sort that precede language. Steven Spielberg's mother played the piano frequently while she was pregnant; could these prenatal concerts have had long-term positive effects on him?

The Newborn: A Work in Progress

The human brain is not fully developed at birth, perhaps because the baby's head would not fit through the birth canal if he or she had a full-size adult brain. Much

human brain development continues after birth (Johnson, 2001), and thus the newborn's abilities to think, feel, and behave differ from those of older children and adults. For example, newborns cannot be classically conditioned to associate a tone with an air puff that causes them to blink (Naito & Lipsitt, 1969; Sommer & Ling, 1970); in rats, researchers have shown that this ability emerges

In many ways, the human infant compares unfavorably with the young of some other species. A kitten is able to walk on its own and explore its environment at only 6 weeks, an age when no human infant can even crawl.

only after key parts of the cerebellum have matured during infancy (Freeman & Nicholson, 2001; Rush et al., 2001).

Nevertheless, although the typical infant may seem thoroughly incompetent—capable of eating, sleeping, cooing, crying, drooling, and not much else—such an assessment is off the mark. A baby is not a blank slate, waiting for learning or maturity to descend. On the contrary, babies come equipped with a surprising range of abilities and capacities.

Sensory Capacities and Reflexes

Until about 3–4 months of age, babies produce a *rooting reflex* when their cheek is stroked lightly: They turn their head toward the stimulus and start trying to suck.

Even at the earliest phases of development, babies have the beginnings of sophisticated sensory capabilities. They are born sensitive to the range of frequencies of women's voices (Hauser, 1996) and have a relatively sensitive sense of smell. Even babies who are fed by bottle prefer the odor of a woman who is breast-feeding another infant to that of a woman who is not breast-feeding (Porter et al., 1992).

Infants also come equipped with a wide range of reflexes. A *reflex* is an automatic response to an event, an action that does not require thought. Some reflexes shown by infants, such as sucking, have obvious survival value, and some, such as the *Moro reflex* (in which the startled baby throws its arms wide, as if to grab hold of someone), may have had survival value for our ancestors. Other reflexes, such as the *Babinski reflex* (in which the baby's big toe flexes while the other toes fan out when the sole of his or her foot is stroked), are less obviously useful. Interestingly, many of the reflexes that babies have at birth disappear after a while.

Temperament: Instant Personality

A friend describing the birth of his second son expressed amazement as he realized, when handed the child immediately after birth, that the infant was *already different* from his first son, calmer and steadier. Our friend should not have been surprised. From their earliest hours, babies show the makings of individual personalities. They demonstrate differences in *temperament*, in their innate inclinations to engage in a certain style of behavior (see Chapter 8). Some babies may be inclined toward "approach," others toward "withdrawal" (Thomas & Chess, 1996). Infants who tend to show an approach response generally react positively to new situations or stimuli, such as a new food, toy, person, or place. Infants who are inclined to show a withdrawal response typically react negatively to new situations or stimuli, by crying, fussing, or otherwise indicating their discomfort (Chess & Thomas, 1987). Some babies are considered "easy" in that they do not cry often and are not demanding, whereas others are "difficult" in that they are fussy and demanding.

For temperament, like other characteristics, the story of development over the life span reveals themes of both stability and change. Some of the stability of temperament may arise not from innate predispositions, but from early nurturing experiences. Probably the most compelling evidence of this comes from research with nonhuman animals. Meaney and his colleagues (Anisman et al., 1998; Liu et al., 1997; Meaney et al., 1991; Zaharia et al., 1996) have shown that simply handling rat pups during the first 10 days after birth has enormous effects on the way the animals later respond to stressful events. As adults, these animals don't become as nervous as other rats (as reflected by fewer feces, less "freezing" responses, and more exploration) when put in a large open field, and they have lower cortisol responses (and thus are less vulnerable to the negative effects of prolonged exposure to cortisol, as discussed in Chapter 5). They are also less prone to learned helplessness (discussed in Chapter 7; Costela et al., 1995). The effects of handling occur naturally when the mother rat licks her pups and engages in nursing with an arched back (so the pups are directly under her); offspring of mothers that behaved this way later had lower amounts of the type of RNA that produces cortisol (Liu et al., 1997) and changes in the sensitivity of the hypothalamic-pituitary-adrenal axis (Weaver et al., 2004; see Chapter 2).

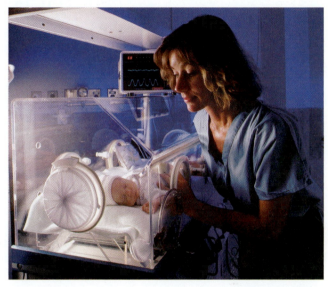

Social interactions can help babies who are born prematurely. Field and her colleagues (1986) found that premature infants who were touched three times a day (moving the babies' limbs, stroking their bodies), in 15-minute sessions, grew 50% faster, developed more quickly behaviorally, were more alert and active, and were discharged from the hospital sooner than other premature infants who were not touched three times a day.

There is good reason to believe that similar effects extend to humans: Touching infants not only can enhance growth and development, but also can reduce the EEG activation in the right frontal lobe that is associated with depression (even in 1-month-old infants!) and can boost immune function (Field, 1998; Field et al., 1986; Jones et al., 1998). Moreover, parents who perceive their infants as having a particular sort of temperament appear to influence the development of such a temperament (Pauli-Pott et al., 2003).

LOOKING BACK: *Review*

1. *How does development progress in the womb?* The genes and environment interact even in the womb. Your mother's and father's genes recombined when their gametes (eggs and sperm) were formed, leading you to have

a unique combination of alleles. Prenatal development unfolds in an orderly progression through a series of stages, or trimesters, as the zygote becomes first an embryo, then a fetus. The developing fetus is active and becomes increasingly coordinated over time. Moreover, the fetus is capable of some forms of learning and can detect human speech, preferring the mother's voice. These maturational processes can be disrupted by teratogens or enhanced by certain environmental events, such as those that reduce the level of stress experienced by the mother.

2. *What are the capabilities of newborns?* Newborns have a relatively sensitive sense of smell and are equipped with a host of inborn reflexes, such as sucking and the Moro reflex. These reflexes often disappear as the child grows and develops. However, in some infants, aspects of temperament that are present at birth may persist for many years.

LOOKING BEYOND: *Critical Thinking*

Do you think that Steven Spielberg was born with the abilities that make him so successful as a filmmaker? In what ways might his abilities have been affected by a combination of biological factors, teratogens, maternal nutrition, and appropriate stimulation (perhaps even the sounds of his mother's piano playing) during his prenatal development?

If you were going to design a program to teach newly pregnant women how best to ensure the normal development of their unborn children, what would you emphasize?

Infancy and Childhood: Taking Off

Steven Spielberg has repeatedly noted that his ability to make movies that appeal to children and to "the child inside adults" stems from the fact that he's never grown up himself. But although he may retain many childlike characteristics, the filmmaker has indeed matured. That is, his motor, perceptual, cognitive, and even social abilities have long outstripped those of even a preadolescent child. In this section, we see how this development occurs.

LOOKING AHEAD: *Learning Objectives*

1. *How does the ability to control the body develop with age?*
2. *What perceptual, linguistic, and cognitive abilities emerge over the course of development?*
3. *How do social and emotional development occur?*

Physical and Motor Development: Getting Control

Developmental psychologists have spent many years studying the precise ways in which babies' movements change as they grow. Two of the early pioneers, Arnold Gesell (Gesell & Thompson, 1938) and Myrtle McGraw (1943), described a se-

Figure 9.2 Typical Ages for Developmental Motor Milestones

2–5 months

Follow movements with eyes; lift head and chest while on stomach; hold head steady; hold an object placed in hand

6–9 months

Roll over; sit upright; pick up small objects with thumb and fingers; shift objects between hands; crawl

10–12 months

Pull to upright standing, and "cruise" (walk by supporting body against objects); turn pages of book

13–18 months

Scribble; walk unaided; feed self; point to pictures when asked; throw a ball while keeping balance

Motor abilities emerge at different times. Keep in mind, however, that the ages given in this figure are averages and may not apply to a particular child.

ries of milestones that all babies, from all races and cultures, pass in an orderly progression. Figure 9.2 presents average age ranges for major motor developments (but keep in mind that various factors, such as the opportunities to use specific muscles, affect these ages). In general, control progresses from the head down the trunk to the arms, and finally to the legs; at the same time, control extends out from the center of the body to the periphery (hands, fingers, toes). By the age of 2, the child has good control over all the limbs. However, fine motor control—of the sort needed to play piano or type on a keyboard—develops more slowly. And some of us do this better than others; Spielberg, for example, was notoriously clumsy and uncoordinated throughout his childhood.

In spite of the dramatic improvements with age, even young infants have remarkable control of their movements. For example, when reaching for a ball in order to toss it into a tub on the floor, 10-month-old infants reach more quickly than if they are going to drop the ball down a tube—which shows that they are planning the pair of movements in tandem (Claxton et al., 2003).

The early theorists believed that the consistent and universal order of motor development implies that this development is entirely maturational. However, later studies of motor control showed that this view cannot be correct (Thelen & Ulrich, 1991). For example, consider the unanticipated consequences of having infants sleep on their backs, in an effort to reduce the chances of SIDS (this is advocated by the "Back to Sleep" movement, which has helped to reduce SIDS in the United States by about 30% since 1994; Association of SIDS and Infant Mortality Programs, 2002). Ratliff-Schaub and colleagues (2001) found that premature infants who slept on their backs had more difficulty holding their heads up and lowering them with control than did infants who slept on their bellies. Moreover, other back-sleeping babies were slow to roll from their backs to bellies, to sit up, to creep, crawl, and to pull themselves to a standing position (B. E. Davis et al., 1998). However, the children walked at the same age, regardless of how they slept. In fact, since babies have begun sleeping on their backs, some never learn to crawl. "It was an occasional phenomenon before, and now about a third of babies skip the step of crawling and go right to walking," says Dr. Karen Dewling (quoted by Seith, 2000). Thus, developing some aspects of motor control involves more than maturation; it also involves learning about the body and the world (Adolph, 2000; Thelen, 1995).

Perceptual and Cognitive Development: Extended Horizons

A parent probably would not tell as elaborate a story to a 3-year-old as to a 10-year-old. The reason is obvious: The younger child not only has a shorter attention span and understands fewer concepts about objects and events, but also can grasp only simple concepts about relations between objects and events (such as that one object can physically cause another to move). Where do these concepts come from? In part from perception, the organization and identification of information received through the senses; in part from cognition, or mental processes; and in part from the social environment.

Perceptual Development: Opening Windows on the World

Along with the rest of the body, the sensory organs develop with age. For example, young infants view the world blurrily, as if through thick gauze; with age, their visual acuity increases, in part because of developments in the eye, particularly in the lens and the retina (Banks & Bennett, 1988).

Infant Visual Perception.
How do we know that infants can't see well? You obviously can't ask them, so how might you determine what babies are capable of seeing? Psychologists working in this area have developed a number of clever techniques. For example, to determine depth perception, infants are placed on a level sheet of glass that at first lies directly on a floor, but then extends over a part of the floor that has been stepped down. In this *visual cliff* experiment, researchers have found that even 6-month-old infants don't want to crawl out on the glass over the "deep end"—even when coaxed by their mothers—thus demonstrating that they can perceive depth before they can talk (Gibson & Walk, 1960).

But the visual cliff task is of no use with babies who are not yet able to crawl, so it is possible that even younger babies can see depth. How can we tell? In one study, researchers measured infants' heart rates when they were placed on the shallow or deep end of the visual cliff and found that 2-month-old babies had slower heart rates on the deep side (Campos et al., 1970); slower heart rates indicate that someone is paying closer attention, which suggests that the infants could in fact tell the difference between the two depths.

Other techniques for examining infants' visual perception measure the amount of time they spend looking at stimuli. For example, the *habituation technique* (also sometimes called the *looking time technique*), illustrated in Figure 9.3, is based on the fact that all animals—including humans of all ages—*habituate* to a stimulus: If a baby looks at a particular shape long enough, he or she will no longer find it interesting—and thus will prefer to look at something new. This technique can be used to discover what babies can see, hear, or feel as "different." If you simply added a copy of the habituated stimulus, it would be no more interesting than the original—the infant has to perceive it as different to find it interesting. By varying how two stimuli differ (in shape, distance, color, pattern of movement, and so on) and noting the circumstances in which babies prefer a new stimulus after habituating to a previous one, it is possible to discover what differences they can detect. Habituation techniques have shown that babies can detect depth between 2 and 3 months of age. In fact, 8-week-old babies can see depth as represented by sets of points flowing on a screen, the way we do when we see a spaceship whizzing through a cloud of meteors in a movie—and infants of this age can even see shapes that are depicted three-dimensionally by sets of flowing points (Arterberry & Yonas, 2000).

Babies are placed on the sheet of glass over a floor that appears to be directly under the glass. A short distance ahead, the floor drops down (although the glass remains level). If the baby can perceive depth, he or she will be reluctant to crawl on the part of the glass that is over the "deep end." This is the famous visual cliff invented by Gibson and Walk (1960).

Figure 9.3 The Habituation Technique

In the habituation task, the baby is first shown one stimulus and allowed to look at it until he or she is bored with it (has habituated to it).

After habituation, the baby is shown the original stimulus along with another stimulus. The baby prefers to look at something new. This technique can be used to determine what shape differences babies see and whether they see depth or other physical properties.

Newborns aren't very attentive companions, but they will notice if you make direct eye contact with them; in fact, even infants 2–5 days old prefer to look at faces that look directly at them rather than faces in which the eyes are averted (Farroni et al., 2002). Thus, looking time can be used not simply to assess habituation, but as a more general reflection of what an infant notices. Such techniques have shown that newborn infants only notice isolated portions of objects; within about 2 or 3 months, they can perceive overall shapes (Spelke et al., 1993) and even organize line fragments into three-dimensional forms (Bhatt & Bertin, 2001). By about 6 months of age, they can organize sets of isolated squares into horizontal or vertical stripes (Quinn et al., 2002), can visually "chunk" groups of objects into units (Feigenson & Halberda, 2004), and can mentally fill in when their view of a moving object is briefly obstructed (Johnson et al., 2003). As they grow older, babies need less stimulus information to recognize patterns. It is tempting to speculate that their enjoyment of playing "peek-a-boo" may reflect this developing ability, in that they can use top-down processing (see Chapter 3) and their knowledge about objects to infer a whole from a part.

Infant Auditory Perception.   Compared with visual perception, auditory perception appears to be more fully developed at an earlier age. For example, researchers played consonant (pleasant-sounding) or dissonant (harmonically jarring) versions of two sequences of tones to 4-month-olds. When the sequence was consonant, the infants looked longer at the audio speakers than when it was dissonant. Not only did they look away when the stimulus was dissonant, but they were more physically active. The researchers suggested that infants are innately tuned to find consonance more pleasing than dissonance (Zentner & Kagan, 1998). Apparently, to appreciate dissonant music, you must learn to overcome preferences that may be innate.

Perceptual development continues beyond the first year of life. When, for instance, toddlers (2- and 3-year-olds) are shown an array of objects and asked whether it includes a specific object, they look haphazardly from place to place (Vurpillot, 1968). But 6- to 9-year-olds will search the array systematically, left to right, then top to bottom, as if they were reading a page. In general, by about age

11, children have perceptual abilities that are similar to (although often slower than) those of adults (Lobaugh et al., 1998; Piaget, 1969; Semenov et al., 2000), but some aspects of perceptual processing (used in organizing complex patterns) probably continue to develop until late adolescence (Sireteanu, 2000).

Language Development: Out of the Mouths of Babes

One of the hallmarks of language is that normal human children will pick up the language being spoken around them, without needing to be taught. As kids, we are linguistic sponges. But what do we learn, and how do we absorb it?

How Is Language Acquired?

Why do people in France grow up speaking French, people in Japan grow up speaking Japanese, and people in Greece grow up speaking Greek? At first glance, the answer might seem obvious: They are taught by their parents and teachers, and they also absorb language from their peers. But the process is not so simple and straightforward; there has long been a debate about how language is acquired, and three different camps have emerged.

- *Behaviorist theories.* Behaviorists, following the lead of B. F. Skinner, believe that language is entirely the result of learning. According to this theory, children acquire words and combinations of words through imitation; such utterances then are reinforced, and thus language is learned according to the same principles of learning that apply to all other materials (see Chapter 4).

- *Nativist theories.* In contrast to the behaviorist view, many linguists believe that the crucial aspects of language are innate (inborn), not learned. This theory is rooted in the school of philosophy known as **nativism**, which takes the view that people are born with some knowledge. Linguist Noam Chomsky (1972) has championed the nativist approach to language acquisition, theorizing that we are all born with an internal **language acquisition device (LAD)**, which contains a set of grammatical rules common to all languages and thus allows children to learn the particular language to which they are exposed.

- *Interactionist theories.* Interactionist theories call on both learning and innate knowledge to explain how language is acquired. These theories hold that language acquisition relies on social events that draw on relatively general cognitive abilities, such as those used in motor control and perception (Dick et al., 2001; Dominey & Dodane, 2004; Elman et al., 1996). However, even these theorists assume that at least some language abilities are built in, part of our genetic heritage.

Foundations of Language: Organizing the Linguistic World. The fact that virtually all normal humans come to speak a language, even without formal instruction, is evidence that there is something special about the way our brains are constructed that allows us to acquire and use language; we humans are innately gifted with the ability to acquire language. But this doesn't mean that we acquire language all at once; many genetically influenced characteristics do not appear full-blown at birth (for example, consider baldness). Language ability develops in an orderly progression.

To help the child learn language, caregivers (typically, in Western culture, mothers) intuitively adjust their speech so that the baby receives clear messages. The language that caregivers use to talk to babies, dubbed **child-directed speech (CDS)**, is characterized by short sentences with clear pauses between phrases,

Nativism (approach to language): The view that people are born with some knowledge.

Language acquisition device (LAD): An innate mechanism, hypothesized by Chomsky, that contains the grammatical rules common to all languages and allows language acquisition.

Child-directed speech (CDS): Speech by caregivers to babies that relies on short sentences with clear pauses, careful enunciation, exaggerated intonation, and a high-pitched voice.

careful enunciation, and exaggerated intonation that is spoken in a high-pitched voice (Bornstein et al., 1992; Cameron-Faulkner et al., 2003; Cooper et al., 1997; Fernald et al., 1989). A similar pattern has been observed in the sign language caregivers use to communicate with deaf infants: They make signs more slowly, often repeat a sign, and use exaggerated movements (Masataka, 1996); babies attend more closely to such signing than to the more rapid, fluent signing used between adults.

Infants are surprisingly sophisticated in their ability to encode spoken sounds. Although adults have difficulty hearing distinctions in spoken sounds that are not used in their language (for instance, English speakers often have trouble distinguishing between two slightly different "wah" sounds used in French), babies have no such difficulty (Jusczyk, 1995). At 2–3 months old, infants can register in less than half a second that a syllable has been changed ("ga" to "ba"; Dehaene-Lambertz & Dehaene, 1994). However, after about 6 months of age, they start to ignore distinctions among sounds that are not used in the language spoken around them (Kuhl et al., 1992). At around 8 months, infants can use patterns of sound regularity to identify individual words, even when the actual sounds run together into a single continuous stream (Saffran, 2001). Moreover, by 14 months, infants pay attention to different sound distinctions in different tasks: When they are required to distinguish between speech sounds, they are sensitive to differences in the sounds that they ignore when they are learning to pair words with particular objects (Stager & Werker, 1997).

The ability of infants to discriminate and organize sounds outstrips their ability to produce them. All babies, even deaf ones, begin by babbling at around 6 months of age (Stoel-Gammon & Otomo, 1986). Initial babbling includes the sounds made in all human languages. However, as the child is exposed to speaking adults, the range of sounds narrows; at about 1 year, the child's babbling begins to have adultlike intonation patterns (Levitt & Wang, 1991). Deaf children do not develop the more advanced types of babbling, but, if they are exposed to sign language, their hand and arm motions develop in corresponding ways—beginning with a wide range of motions and eventually narrowing down to those used in the sign language they see around them (Petitto & Marentette, 1991). The first words children in all languages say grow directly out of their babbles, such as "ma-ma" and "da-da."

Getting the Words.   Most children begin to speak when they are about a year old. Two-year-olds can learn words even when the object or action being named is not present (Akhtar & Tomasello, 1996). By the time they are 6 years old, children know approximately 10,000 words (Anglin, 1993). The rate of learning differs for boys and girls, however, as shown in Figure 9.4. Children begin by understanding words far in advance of their ability to say them. Indeed, they can understand about 50 words at about 13 months of age but cannot say this many words until about 18 months (Menyuk et al., 1995).

Even 3-year-olds can often learn the meanings of words or facts about objects after hearing them only a single time (Carey, 1978; Markson &

Sign language resembles spoken language in crucial ways. For example, when communicating with infants, speakers or signers slow down and exaggerate their vocalizations or their hand and arm movements in order to communicate more clearly.

Figure 9.4

The Number of New Words Understood During the First 2 Years of Life

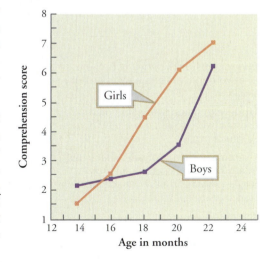

Notice the difference in comprehension rates for boys and girls.

Bloom, 1997). Which words children learn first depends partly on their culture; in Vietnam, children learn the respectful pronouns used to refer to elders before learning the words for many objects (Nelson, 1981). However, rather than learning the exact meanings of words in one fell swoop, children sometimes make **overextensions**, using words overly broadly when referring to new objects or situations. They might use "dog" to refer to a dog and a cat and a horse, and even a sawhorse. This makes sense if their initial idea of the meaning of "dog" is anything with four legs. With learning, they discover which features—in the case of a dog, more than just four-leggedness—restrict the appropriate use of the word (Clark, 1983, 1993). Overextensions may sometimes occur simply because the child has trouble recalling the appropriate word and apparently uses the next best one instead. Children sometimes also make **underextensions**, using words too narrowly. For example, a child may use "animal" to refer only to dogs. This may occur because an adult uses a superordinate term (such as "animal") when referring to a typical member of the category (a dog), and the child does not experience the term being used more broadly for other members of the category (Kay & Anglin, 1982; White, 1982). However, as knowledge of distinctions within a domain (such as dinosaurs) increases, both children and adults tend to make more underextensions and fewer overextensions (Johnson & Eilers, 1998).

Grammar: Not From School.   The heart of any language is its **grammar**, the set of rules that allows users of the language to combine words into an infinite number of acceptable sentences. Traditionally, the term *grammar* has referred to syntax and some aspects of semantics (including those aspects of word meaning that must be in agreement in a sentence, such as using a plural verb with a plural subject). However, some researchers argue that the concept of grammar should be extended to include features of all aspects of language except pragmatics (and treating pragmatics as part of grammar has been discussed by some; Hu, 1990, 1995; Payne, 1992). By looking at the patterns of sounds to which babies became habituated, Marcus and colleagues (1999) showed that even 7-month-old babies have the capacity to abstract grammarlike rules. However, it is at around 2 years of age that children start putting words together into the simplest sentences, two-word utterances such as "Go dog." These utterances are often called **telegraphic speech** because, like the telegrams of days gone by (and the text messages people send to cell phones today), they pack a lot of information into a few choice words (Bochner & Jones, 2003). By about 3 years of age, children who speak English start to use sentences that follow the sequence subject–verb–object ("Dog chase cat"). Words such as *the*, *a*, and *of* are left out. The particular sequence of the parts of speech depends on the language being learned, but all children at this stage start to make sentences with words in the appropriate order (de Villiers & de Villiers, 1992).

Adults do not teach grammatical rules to children, or even systematically correct grammatical errors (de Villiers & de Villiers, 1992; Pinker, 1994), but even 4-year-olds acquire such rules. Berko (1958) showed that most children of this age generalize grammatical rules. This is true even when sentences contain nonsense words. For example, a 4-year-old can usually provide the missing word in the following:

This is a wug. Now there is another one. Now there are two _____.

Most verbs in a language are *regular*, following an easily derived rule for changes in tense—*play* becomes *played*, *work* becomes *worked*. But the most frequently used verbs in a language are often *irregular*—for example, *eat* becomes *ate*. Children may start off using irregular verbs properly, but then begin to make mistakes such as *runned* instead of *ran*. These **overregularization errors**, mistakes caused by the misapplication of the rule for regular verb formation, occur be-

Overextension: An overly broad use of a word to refer to a new object or situation.

Underextension: An overly narrow use of a word to refer to a new object or situation.

Grammar: The set of rules that determines how words can be organized into an infinite number of acceptable sentences in a language.

Telegraphic speech: Speech that packs a lot of information into a few words, typically omitting words such as *the*, *a*, and *of*.

Overregularization error: A mistake that occurs in speech because the child applies a newly learned rule even to cases where it does not apply.

Figure 9.5 Major Milestones in Language Acquisition

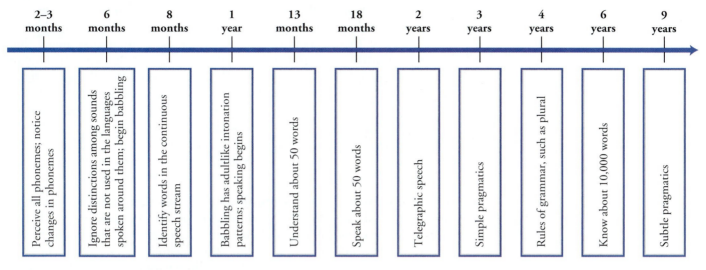

2–3 months	6 months	8 months	1 year	13 months	18 months	2 years	3 years	4 years	6 years	9 years
Perceive all phonemes; notice changes in phonemes	Ignore distinctions among sounds that are not used in the languages spoken around them; begin babbling	Identify words in the continuous speech stream	Babbling has adultlike intonation patterns; speaking begins	Understand about 50 words	Speak about 50 words	Telegraphic speech	Simple pragmatics	Rules of grammar, such as plural	Know about 10,000 words	Subtle pragmatics

Language acquisition typically progresses through a series of orderly steps, as illustrated here.

cause once a child has learned the rule, he or she begins to apply it systematically, even when it is inappropriate (Pinker, 1999). The same thing happens with plurals; a child who could use *feet* correctly last week may suddenly start saying, "Mommy, my feets are tired."

The major milestones of language acquisition are shown in the timeline in Figure 9.5. These steps occur for children exposed to any language. However, throughout history, there have been reports of children who grew up in the wild, never exposed to human language. When such cases occur, they provide a key test of the theory that language can only be learned during a narrow window of time called the ==critical period==. Careful studies have shown that children who are not exposed to language before puberty never grasp the rules of grammar fully; there does seem to be a critical period for acquiring grammar (Grimshaw et al., 1998; Pinker 1994).

Long-Term Memory Development: Living Beyond the Here and Now

As discussed in Chapter 5, we adults have both explicit and implicit long-term memories. Is the same true of infants?

Infant Explicit Memory. Many studies have documented that even 3-month-old infants can store information explicitly (Rovee-Collier, 1997). How could researchers find this out? The key idea is that recognition taps explicit memory, whereas priming taps implicit memory (priming occurs when performing a task "greases the wheels," making the same or a related task easier to perform in the future). In one study conducted to assess recognition, researchers attached one end of a ribbon to an infant's foot and the other to a mobile that hung over the crib. The mobile was decorated with plus marks of a particular size. The infants soon learned that kicking would move the mobile, which they found reinforcing—and hence they kicked at a higher rate. The researchers waited a day and then showed the infants either the identical mobile from the previous trial or one with plus marks that were either larger or smaller than on the original. The infants kicked at

Critical period: A narrow window of time when a certain type of learning or some aspect of development is possible.

Kicking moves the mobile, which the infant finds reinforcing. Infants kick more vigorously when the marks on the mobile are the same over repeated sessions, showing that they remember what happened last time they kicked, when that stimulus was present. Gerhardstein and colleagues (2000) used this sort of apparatus to study both explicit and implicit memory.

Schema: In Piaget's theory, a mental structure that organizes perceptual input and connects it to the appropriate responses.

Assimilation: In Piaget's theory, the process that allows the use of existing schemas to take in new sets of stimuli and respond accordingly.

a higher rate only when the plus marks were the initial size. This is evidence that they recalled the original mobile explicitly (Gerhardstein et al., 2000).

Infant Implicit Memory.   What about implicit memory? To test whether even 3-month-old infants have such memory, the same researchers used the kicking test but now waited 2 weeks before retesting, which is a time period longer than that for which infants can recall that kicking moves the mobile (typically only up to 6–8 days after learning). They had each infant watch while the investigator held the ribbon attached to the mobile and moved it at about the same rate that the infant had moved it before. This priming event was sufficient to reactivate the memory, leading the infants to recall the relationship between kicking and moving the mobile. However, the explicit memory was not activated: Now infants increased their kicking when they saw mobiles that had all sizes of plus marks, not just when the plus marks were the original size (Gerhardstein et al., 2000).

Memory Development.   Language-based types of memory take on increasing importance as a child gets older. For example, in one study, Simcock and Hayne (2002) asked young children to learn to operate a machine that apparently shrank the sizes of toys. Six months or a year later, the researchers tested the children's memory for this event. They found that in recalling various aspects of the event, the children used only words that they knew at the time when they initially experienced it; that is, no words learned in the intervening period were used. This finding suggested to the researchers that the "children's verbal reports of the event were frozen in time, reflecting their verbal skill at the time of encoding, rather than at the time of test" (p. 229). We noted in Chapter 5 that adults have remarkably poor memory for events that occurred during early childhood—perhaps this is one explanation.

Stages of Cognitive Development: Piaget's Theory

Thinking is more than perceiving and remembering; it also involves reasoning. It's obvious that babies don't have the mental capacity of adults; they can't even understand most problems, let alone solve them. The gradual transition from infant to adult mental capacity is known as *cognitive development*. The great Swiss psychologist Jean Piaget (1896–1980) developed a far-reaching and comprehensive theory of cognitive development. Interest in Piaget's theory helped generate other lines of research that have focused on how the gradual improvement in information processing, the maturation of the brain, and the social environment contribute to cognitive development.

Piaget was originally trained in biology, but early in his career, he worked in Paris with Alfred Binet's collaborator, Theodore Simon, helping to standardize Binet's newly developed intelligence tests for children (see Chapter 6). Piaget was curious about the types of reasoning mistakes children are likely to make. This new interest connected with his long-term fascination with biology and the nature of the mind, leading him to a general investigation of the reasoning processes of children at various ages. Piaget believed that babies begin with very simple, innate **schemas**, mental structures that organize perceptual input and connect it to the appropriate responses. For the youngest infant, such schemas trigger grasping and sucking at the nipple when the infant is hungry and in the presence of a bottle or breast. According to Piaget, the process of **assimilation** allows the infant to use existing schemas to take in new stimuli and respond accordingly.

Piaget was an extraordinarily sensitive observer of children's behavior.

For example, the schema for sucking a breast can also be used for sucking a bottle or a thumb. In contrast, the process of **accommodation** results in schemas' changing as necessary to cope with a broader range of situations. For example, an original schema for sucking may give rise to two separate schemas, one for bottles and one for thumbs, which in turn may give rise to schemas for drinking with a straw, drinking from a cup, and eating solid food.

These two processes—assimilation and accommodation—together are the engine that powers cognitive development. Piaget's theory of development hinges on what results when assimilation and accommodation work in tandem, which he claimed produces a system of rules—in Piaget's terms, a "logic"—that guides the child's thought. Depending on the available schemas, different kinds of logical operations are possible. Thus, according to Piaget, the child's thinking changes systematically over time as new schemas develop.

Piaget described four major stages, or *periods*, of cognitive development, as shown in Table 9.1; each period is governed by a different type of logic and includes many substages, with key characteristics. The periods overlap slightly, and they may occur at different ages for different children; thus, the ages given in the table are only approximate.

Sensorimotor Period.   The infant's experience begins in the *sensorimotor period*, which extends from birth to approximately 2 years of age. According to Piaget's theory, infants initially conceive of the world solely in terms of their perceptions and actions. In this period, infants lack the ability to form mental representations that can be used to think about an object in its absence (see Chapter 6). In the early stages of the sensorimotor period, the infant does not yet have **object permanence**, the understanding that objects (including people) continue to exist even when they cannot be immediately perceived. For example, a rattle dropped by an infant over the side of the high chair is quickly forgotten—and more than forgotten: Out of sight means not just out of mind but out of existence! Piaget claimed that by the end of the sensorimotor period, by about age 2, the toddler understands that objects exist even when they are no longer perceived. In addition, Piaget claimed that a second major achievement of the sensorimotor period—at around 9 months of age—is the ability to imitate.

Preoperational Period.   Once out of the sensorimotor period, the toddler enters the *preoperational period*, from roughly age 2 until age 7. Armed with the ability

Accommodation: In Piaget's theory, the process that results in schemas' changing as necessary to cope with a broader range of situations.

Object permanence: The understanding that objects (including people) continue to exist even when they cannot be immediately perceived.

Only after an infant has object permanence does he or she understand that objects continue to exist even after they are no longer being perceived.

Table 9.1 Piaget's Periods of Cognitive Development

Period	Age	Essential Characteristics
Sensorimotor	0–2 years	The child acts on the world as perceived and is not capable of thinking about objects in their absence.
Preoperational	2–7 years	Words, images, and actions are used to represent information mentally. Language and symbolic play develop, but thought is still tied to perceived events.
Concrete operations	7–11 years	Reasoning is based on a logic that is tied to what can be perceived. The child is capable of organizing information systematically into categories, and can reverse mental manipulations.
Formal operations	11 years (at the earliest)	Reasoning is based on a logic that includes abstractions, which leads to systematic thinking about hypothetical events.

Conservation: The Piagetian principle that certain properties, such as amount or mass, remain the same even when the appearance of the material or object changes, provided that nothing is added or removed.

Egocentrism: In Piaget's theory, the inability to take another person's point of view.

to form mental representations, children in the preoperational period are able to think about objects and events that are not immediately present. As a result, they can imitate actions that occurred in the past. This newfound capacity for mental representation allows the child to engage in symbolic play. Whereas the infant might play with a bar of soap in the bath by squeezing it and watching it pop up, the preoperational child, performing the same actions, might think of the soap as a submerged submarine that is breaking the surface.

A cook asks two boys who have just ordered a large pizza, "How many slices do you want me to cut your pizza into, 8 or 12?" One boy immediately answers, "Please cut it into 12 pieces, because I'm very hungry!" This is a joke for older children and adults, but not for preoperational children, whose thoughts are limited in part because they do not yet have a "logic" for manipulating, or *operating* on, mental representations. Therefore, they often reason on the basis of appearances. One of Piaget's important discoveries is that these children do not understand **conservation**, the principle that properties such as amount or mass remain the same even when the appearance of the material or object changes, provided that nothing is added or removed. Many studies have documented that preoperational children do not conserve, and so they do not realize that cutting a pizza into 12 pieces instead of 8 does not increase the total amount of pizza. A classic example, illustrated in Figure 9.6, is that preoperational children do not understand that pouring liquid from a short wide glass into a tall thin glass does not alter the amount of liquid. Similarly, they typically think that flattening a ball of clay decreases the amount of clay and that spreading the objects in a row farther apart changes the number of objects in the row.

Both sensorimotor and preoperational children show **egocentrism**, which does not mean "selfishness" in the ordinary sense of the word, but instead the inability to take another's point of view. For example, children in this period will hold a picture they've drawn up to the telephone, to "show" it to a grandparent. They mistakenly assume that others see the same things they do.

Concrete Operations Period.   By the end of the preoperational period, at about age 7, children develop the ability to take another person's perspective. This abil-

---

Figure 9.6 **Conservation of Liquids**

In the classic conservation of liquids test, the child is first shown two identical glasses with water at the same level.

The water is poured from one of the short, wide glasses into the tall, thin one.

When asked whether the two glasses have the same amount, or if one has more, the preoperational child replies that the tall, thin glass has more. This is a failure to conserve liquids.

ity is linked to the fact that they can now perform **concrete operations**, manipulating mental representations in much the same way as they can manipulate the corresponding objects. At this point, children are able to begin to classify objects and their properties, to grasp concepts such as length, width, volume, and time, and to understand various mental operations such as those involved in simple arithmetic. This *period of concrete operations* is Piaget's third period of cognitive development, which takes place roughly between the ages of 7 and 11. Concrete operations allow the child to reason logically, partly because this mode of conceptualizing is *reversible*; that is, it can be used to make or undo a transformation. For example, having seen the liquid being poured into a tall thin glass, the child can mentally reverse the process and imagine the liquid being poured back into the original container. Seeing that no liquid has been added or subtracted in the process, the child realizes that the amount in both glasses must be the same.

Concrete operation: In Piaget's theory, a (reversible) manipulation of the mental representation of an object that corresponds to an actual physical manipulation.

Formal operation: In Piaget's theory, a mental act that can be performed (and reversed) even with an abstract concept.

Formal Operations Period.   By definition, concrete operations cannot be used for reasoning about abstract concepts; children in the period of concrete operations cannot figure out, for example, that whenever 1 is added to an even number, the result will always be an odd number. To be able to reason abstractly, Piaget said, requires that the child be capable of **formal operations**, reversible mental acts that can be performed even with abstract concepts. This ability emerges roughly at the age of 11 or 12, at the onset of what Piaget termed the *period of formal operations*. Rather than simply understanding the logic of "what is," as occurs with concrete operations, the emerging adolescent is now able to imagine the possibilities of "what could be." Formal operations allow children to engage in abstract thinking, to think about "what-would-happen-if" situations, to formulate and test theories, and to think systematically about the possible outcomes of an act by being able to list alternatives in advance and consider each in turn. For example, formal operations would permit a child to think about how best to spend his or her money and to weigh the benefits and drawbacks of each possible budget decision.

The Child's Concepts: Beyond Piaget

Do children follow the stages Piaget described? When researchers use techniques different from Piaget's in order to see what children do or do not understand, they often come up with results that differ from his. Although Piaget employed very clever tasks (such as those used to assess conservation), those tasks typically assessed only easily observable aspects of behavior. When more subtle measurements are taken, evidence sometimes emerges that children can show competence well before they have reached the appropriate Piagetian stage.

Very young infants can imitate some facial expressions, as shown in these photos from Meltzoff and Moore's study.

   The capacities of infants often far exceed those claimed by Piaget. For example, Andrew Meltzoff and his colleagues (notably, Meltzoff & Moore, 1977) have found that 2- to 3-week-old infants can show true imitation, and others have found that even 2-day-old infants can imitate happy and sad facial expressions (Field et al., 1982). And there's evidence that 9-month-old infants can add and subtract (McCrink & Wynn, 2004). Moreover, given what's been learned about infant memory, you won't be surprised that other researchers have shown that babies as young as 3 months old can have object permanence—they know that previously seen objects continue to exist after they are removed from sight. This refutes Piaget's idea that object permanence does not establish itself until the child is a toddler (Baillargeon, 1993,

Figure 9.7 Early Perception of Possible Events

POSSIBLE EVENT

This panel shows a possible event: A box on top of another box is slid over to the edge, but it is still fully supported.

IMPOSSIBLE EVENT

This panel shows an impossible event: The top box is slid so far over that only 15% of it is supported, and yet it does not fall. Between 3 and 6½ months, babies realize that one box must rest on top of the other to be supported.

2004; Spelke et al., 1992). Moreover, when appropriately tested, children as young as 3 years show that they understand the conservation of amount or mass (Gelman, 1972).

Piaget's theory seems to underestimate the sophistication of young children's conceptions of the world. Infants demonstrate an understanding of some physical laws even before they have developed the kinds of perceptual-motor schemas that Piaget claimed are the foundations of such knowledge. For example, even 4-month-old infants are aware of time intervals, showing surprise when a predictable sequence of flashing lights is interrupted (Colombo & Richman, 2002). Moreover, from experiments using looking-time methods, researchers have concluded that even young infants realize that objects need to be physically supported to remain stable (Figure 9.7), that objects can't move *through* other objects, and that objects don't flit from place to place but shift along connected paths (Spelke, 1991; Spelke et al., 1992).

The finding that many abilities are evident much earlier than Piaget predicted challenges his idea that all of a given child's thought reflects a single underlying logic, a logic that changes with increasing age and development. Moreover, later research has shown that many children do not enter the period of formal operations until high school, and some individuals never enter it at all (Hooper et al., 1984; Lunzer, 1978). Nevertheless, Piaget has been proven correct in his observation that there are qualitative shifts in children's performance of specific tasks as they age. He must also be credited with discovering many counterintuitive phenomena, such as failure to conserve and egocentrism, that all subsequent theories of cognitive development must be able to explain.

Information Processing and Neural Development

Efforts to explain the findings sparked by Piaget's theory have looked at specific changes in the way children process information and at how their brains mature. The brain develops dramatically from birth to about 3 years of age, and it continues to show substantial growth until the child is about 12 years old (Tsekhmistrenko et al., 2004). But what is this enhanced brain able to do? The *information-processing approach* is based on the idea that perception and cognition rely on a host of distinct processes in the brain, not all of which necessarily develop at the same rate.

A particularly important reason why young children may perform more poorly than older children is that their *working memory*—their ability to use information held in an active state—does not stack up well against that of older children or adults. Working memory capacity increases with age throughout childhood (Case, 1977, 1978). As working memory capacity increases, a child becomes able to perform tasks that were previously beyond reach.

The finding that working memory increases with age explains many of the phenomena documented by Piaget, such as the out-of-sight/out-of-mind behavior that he interpreted as showing a lack of object permanence (Baird et al., 2002). In this case, a *quantitative* change in capacity (the increase in its size) can lead to a *qualitative* change in performance (the transition to a new stage; Case, 1992a; Pascual-Leone, 1970). By analogy, if you have a relatively small amount of RAM memory in your computer, then you will be able to run only relatively simple programs (such as basic text editing or e-mail), but not more complicated ones (such as a complex word-processing program or large slide-show presentation). If you increase the amount of memory, you will be able not only to run more complex programs, but also to run multiple programs at the same time. A quantitative change in the amount of memory underlies qualitative changes in performance.

What accounts for the improvements in a child's working memory with age? The initial immaturity of the brain may be key. The brain undergoes rapid growth spurts (Epstein, 1980) around the ages that Piaget identified as marking transitions to new periods. Some of the increase in brain weight with age may be due to *myelinization* (the laying down of myelin, a fatty substance that serves as an insulator, on the axons), which increases the speed and efficiency of neural transmission, and some may be due to larger numbers of synapses and long-distance connections (Case, 1992b; Thatcher, 1994; Thompson et al., 2000). These changes would not only increase the speed of information processing (Demetriou et al., 2002), but also would allow more information to be activated at the same time—which, in turn, would increase working memory capacity. In fact, as more white matter matures in two different parts of the frontal lobes between the ages of 8 and 18, working memory improves (Nagy, Westerberg & Klingberg, 2004).

Vygotsky's Sociocultural Theory: Outside/Inside

Appreciating the importance of events at different levels of analysis leads us to look beyond any single source to explain psychological events. Thus, it isn't surprising that at least some aspects of cognitive development reflect social interactions. Russian psychologist Lev S. Vygotsky (1896–1934) emphasized the role of social interaction during development (Vygotsky, 1978, 1934/1986). Whereas Piaget believed that the child constructs representations of the world in the course of experiencing it firsthand, Vygotsky believed that the child constructs representations of the world by first absorbing his or her culture; the culture, as represented in the child's mind, then serves to guide behavior (Beilin, 1996; Kitchener, 1996). According to Vygotsky, adults promote cognitive development by guiding and explicitly instructing children, and cultural creations, particularly language, play a crucial role in development (Cole & Wertsch, 1996; Karpov & Haywood, 1998).

It might be tempting to think that culture is one influence on cognitive development, and the brain another. But this would be an error. The two factors interact: Culture affects the brain, and vice versa. For example, culture determines which language or languages you learn, which in turn affects how your brain processes sounds. By the same token, aspects of the brain affect culture; for example, we don't have customs that require more working memory capacity than the brain provides.

Children in different cultures master different skills; for example, middle-class North Americans often master the visual-motor skills needed to play computer games, whereas street children in Brazil may master the kinds of arithmetic needed to bargain with tourists over the prices of goods (Saxe, 1988).

Social and Emotional Development: The Child in the World

The psychological development of a child includes more than the improvement in mental processing and the acquisition of knowledge and beliefs. Equally impressive development occurs in the child's social interactions, such as the ability to form relationships.

Attachment: More Than Dependency

In our closest relationships, we develop deep attachments to other people. **Attachment** is an emotional bond that leads us to want to be with someone and to miss him or her when we are separated. The tendency to form such an emotional

Attachment: An emotional bond that leads a person to want to be with someone else and to miss him or her when separated.

Baby monkeys were separated from their mothers shortly after birth and were raised with two substitute "mothers." One was wire and held the baby bottle, and each young monkey needed to climb on this one to be fed. The other was covered with terry cloth and did not provide food. Baby monkeys preferred to cling to the fuzzy "mother," even though it never provided food.

bond begins during infancy, when normal infants become attached to their primary caregivers.

Origins of Attachment.   What is the origin of the infant's attachment? Decades ago, a prominent theory—sometimes called the "cupboard theory" because it centered on food—held that infants become attached because their caregivers feed them and thus become associated with positive feelings (Sears et al., 1957). However, classic experiments by Harry Harlow and his collaborators disproved this and similar theories (for example, Harlow, 1958). These researchers found that baby monkeys became much more attached to a model "mother" that had a pleasing texture and a more realistic face than to another "mother" that lacked these characteristics, even though the latter was the only one from which the baby monkeys received food. The impulse to seek comfort from something soft is an innate rather than a learned characteristic of mammals.

British psychoanalyst John Bowlby (1969) developed a theory of attachment that has become widely accepted among developmental psychologists. According to Bowlby, children go through phases during the development of attachment. Just as in Piaget's stages, the order of the phases is thought to be determined biologically, but the precise ages of the transitions depend on experience. A major shift, usually occurring between 6 months and 2 years, is characterized by **separation anxiety**, which is fear of being away from the primary caregiver. This shift may arise on the heels of a transition in cognitive development—specifically, infants can now think about and remember objects (including the primary caregiver) for relatively long periods when the objects are no longer present.

Types of Attachment.   Not all babies become attached to their caregivers in the same way. Ainsworth and her colleagues (1978) developed a way to assess attachment using a scenario they called the *Strange Situation*. The setup involves a staged sequence of events designed to discover how a child reacts when left with a stranger or alone in an unfamiliar situation. If the child has developed secure attachment, he or she should show separation anxiety, becoming upset when the mother leaves, and should not be soothed equally well by a stranger as by the mother. Studies using the Strange Situation revealed four types of attachment:

- *Secure attachment* (seen in about 60–70% of American babies) is evident if babies venture away from the mother, are upset when she leaves and not well comforted by a stranger, but calm down quickly when the mother returns.

- *Avoidant attachment* (seen in about 15–20% of American babies) is evident if babies don't seem to care very much whether the mother is present or absent and are equally comfortable with her and a stranger; when she returns, they do not immediately gravitate to her.

- *Resistant attachment* (seen in about 10–15% of American babies) is evident if babies do not use the mother as a base of operations but rather stay close to her and become angry when she leaves; some of these babies may go so far as to hit the mother when she returns, and they do not calm down easily thereafter.

- *Disorganized/disoriented attachment* (seen in 5–10% of American babies) is evident if the babies become depressed and have periods of unresponsiveness along with spurts of sudden emotion at the end of the procedure.

Separation anxiety: Fear of being away from the primary caregiver.

However, these differences have proven to be matters of degree, not sharply defined categories (Fraley & Spieker, 2003). Various factors influence the kind of attachment an infant will show. For example, if the mother was a heavy user of cocaine or other illicit drugs while pregnant, her infant is more likely at age 18 months to have disorganized/disoriented attachment (Swanson et al., 2000). In addition, mothers who are more sensitive to their babies' moods and behaviors had more securely attached infants (Tarabulsy et al., 2005). Moreover, the children of poor Black mothers are less securely attached than those of White mothers, which may reflect the adverse effects of poverty on a mother's ability to remain highly sensitive to her child (Bakermans-Kranenburg et al., 2004).

The type of early attachment can have long-lasting effects. Infants with secure attachment who were later studied at age 11 were found to have closer friendships and better social skills than children who had not been securely attached as infants (Shulman et al., 1994). In fact, the type of attachment determines how some genes operate: At least in monkeys, certain genes that underlie aggression and excessive drinking of alcohol are only activated (and thus only have their effects) when the monkey had an insecure early attachment—not when it experienced secure attachment (Suomi, 2003). Furthermore, secure attachment can lead a child to be more comfortable with exploring, which leads to better learning and can lead to more intimate love relationships later in life (Sroufe & Fleeson, 1986; Weiss, 1986).

We know that at least some aspects of attachment are learned because infants in different cultures become attached differently. For example, American infants show less resistant attachment than do Japanese infants. In Japan, many more women are full-time caregivers for their children than in the United States, and their children are not used to being left with other adults (Takahashi, 1990).

Self-Concept and Identity: The Growing Self

A critical aspect of social development is the emerging sense of who you are and how you stand relative to other people. Psychologists use the term **self-concept** to refer to the beliefs, desires, values, and attributes that define a person to himself or herself. A key part of Steven Spielberg's self-concept as a child was his many fears, both large and small (McBride, 1999).

For young children, the self-concept is necessarily grounded in the level of cognitive development. Thus, preschoolers think of themselves in very concrete terms, in terms of behaviors and physical appearance (Keller et al., 1978). At what age do children begin to conceive of themselves as having specific characteristics? To find out, a dab of red paint was placed on babies' noses without their knowledge, and the babies then looked in a mirror. Some babies of about 15 months of age will notice the smudge and rub it off. By age 2, virtually all children have

Knowledge of your appearance is part of your self-concept.

this response (Amsterdam, 1972; Lewis & Brooks-Gunn, 1979). However, this test may in fact assess understanding of temporary changes in appearance, not self-concept (Asendorpf et al., 1996). Other researchers have argued that the roots of the self-concept are present in children much younger than toddlers. Bahrick and her collaborators (1996) found that even 3-month-olds prefer to look at the face of another child of the same age rather than at their own face, which suggests that they are already familiar with the appearance of their face. Even newborns distinguish between touching themselves and being touched by someone else, a distinction that may mark the beginning of a self-concept (Rochat & Hespos, 1997).

Self-concept: The beliefs, desires, values, and attributes that define a person to himself or herself.

Gender roles: The culturally determined appropriate behaviors for males versus females.

By 3 years of age, children begin to appreciate that they have distinct psychological characteristics, such as being happy in certain situations and not in others (Eder, 1989). Children of about 8 to 11 begin to describe themselves in terms of personality traits, perhaps as "energetic" or "musical." The oldest children in this age range also describe themselves in terms of social relations (Rosenberg, 1979), such as the relationships they have with their siblings and friends. This ability to self-label depends on reasoning abilities that develop during what Piaget described as the period of formal operations.

The Development of Gender Roles. **Gender roles** are the culturally determined appropriate behaviors for males versus females. It is one thing to identify yourself as male or female, but something else entirely to understand what behaviors are appropriate for your gender (Martin & Ruble, 2004). Gender roles vary in different cultures, social classes, and time periods; for example, a proper woman in Victorian England (or, perhaps, 19th-century America) would probably be very surprised to learn that a woman can be a senator or the president of a major corporation today. Conceptions about gender roles develop early. Indeed, by age 2, children have apparently learned about gender role differences (Caldera & Sciaraffa, 1998; Witt, 1997). Some preschool boys apparently believe that if they play with cross-gender toys (say, dishes instead of tools), their fathers will think that was "bad" (Raag & Rackliff, 1998).

Freud argued that children identify with the same-sex parent, and that this is the main way in which gender roles develop (see Chapter 8). But Eleanor Maccoby believes that identification with the same-sex parent may be the *result* of gender role development, not the cause. Her account rests on events at all three levels. At the level of the group, in Maccoby's view, peer-group interactions are key to learning gender roles. It is in the peer group, she argues, that boys first learn about how to gain and maintain status in the hierarchy and that girls develop their styles of interaction (Maccoby, 1990, 1991). Maccoby and Jacklin (1987) found that 4-year-old children spent triple the amount of time playing with same-sex peers as with opposite-sex peers, and this proportion shot up to 11

 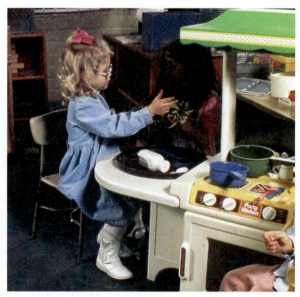

Boys and girls play in characteristic ways, partly because of biological differences.

times more when the children were 6 years old. According to Maccoby (1990, p. 514), "Gender segregation . . . is found in all the cultural settings in which children are in social groups large enough to permit choice."

Why does gender segregation occur? Maccoby (1988) suggests that part of the answer may lie in biological, particularly hormonal, differences. Boys play more aggressively than do girls, and their orientation toward competition and dominance may be aversive to many girls. However, shifting to the level of the person, Maccoby (1990) also notes that girls may not like playing with boys because they believe that boys are too difficult to influence; the polite manner in which girls tend to make suggestions apparently doesn't carry much weight with boys. Girls find this response (or lack of response) frustrating and retreat to the company of other girls.

Moral Development: The Right Stuff

A key aspect of social development is the emergence of more complex ideas of morality, which center on the ability to tell right from wrong. As children grow older, their developing cognitive abilities allow them to draw more subtle inferences. The young child may feel that a girl who knocks over a lamp and breaks it is equally to blame if she smashed it intentionally, bumped it by accident while horsing around, or fell against it accidentally when the dog jumped on her. An older child is able to make clear distinctions among the three cases, seeing decreasing blame for each in turn. Piaget was a pioneer in the study of moral as well as cognitive development. His studies often involved telling children stories in which he varied the intentions of the characters and the results of their actions, and then asking the children to evaluate the characters' morality. Lawrence Kohlberg extended Piaget's approach and developed an influential theory of moral development.

Kohlberg's Theory. Kohlberg presented boys and men with **moral dilemmas**, situations in which there are moral pros and cons for each of a set of possible actions. He asked participants to decide what the character should do and to explain why. This is the famous dilemma that confronted Heinz (Puka, 1994; see Figure 9.8):

> In Europe, a woman was near death from a special kind of cancer. There was one drug that the doctors thought might save her. It was a form of radium that a druggist in the same town had recently discovered. The drug was expensive to make, but the druggist was charging 5 times what it cost him to make the drug. He paid $400 for the radium, and charged $2,000 for a small dose of the drug. The sick woman's husband, Heinz, went to everyone he knew to borrow the money, but he could only get together about $1,000, half of what it cost. He told the druggist that his wife was dying, and asked him to sell it cheaper or let him pay later. But the druggist said, "No, I discovered the drug and I'm going to make money from it, so I won't let you have it unless you give me $2,000 now." So Heinz got desperate and broke into the man's store to steal the drug for his wife.
>
> Should Heinz have done that? Why?

Kohlberg was not so much interested in what the participants decided as in the way that they reached their decisions. What kinds of factors did they consider? Which conflicts did they identify (such as the conflict between the value of human life and the value of private property), and how did they try to resolve these conflicts? Kohlberg interviewed boys and men at length, and from their responses he identified three general levels of moral development (Kohlberg, 1969; Rest, 1979), which are ordered as follows:

Moral dilemma: A situation in which there are moral pros and cons for each of a set of possible actions.

Figure 9.8 A Moral Dilemma

Can you imagine circumstances in which breaking into a store would not only be acceptable, but would actually be the right thing to do? If you were in a situation where you had to decide whether such an action was justified, you would be facing a moral dilemma.

- The *preconventional level* rests on the idea that good behaviors are rewarded and bad ones are punished. Correct action is what an authority figure says it is. A preconventional response to the Heinz dilemma might be, "If you let your wife die, you will get in trouble" (this and the following examples are adapted from Kohlberg, 1969, and Rest, 1979).

- The *conventional level* rests on the role of rules that maintain social order and allow people to get along. For example, a child reasoning at this level wants to be viewed as a "good person" by friends and family and tries to follow the Golden Rule ("Do unto others as you would have them do unto you"). Morality is still closely tied to individual relationships ("If he lets his wife die, people would think he was some kind of heartless lizard").

- The *postconventional level* (also called the *principled level*) rests on the development of abstract principles that govern the decision to accept or reject specific rules. In the most advanced stage at this level, principles are adopted that are believed to apply to everyone. ("Human life is the highest principle, and everything else must be secondary. People have a duty to help one another to live").

Evaluating Kohlberg's Theory.   Some researchers have questioned the generality of Kohlberg's levels. For example, Carol Gilligan (1982) argued that because the theory was based on studies of boys and men, it applies only to males. She believed that females tend to focus on an *ethic of care*, a concern and responsibility for the well-being of others. In contrast, Kohlberg's higher levels of moral development focus on abstract rights and justice, which Gilligan saw as a male-oriented perspective.

However, later studies have shown that differences in how males and females reason about moral issues do not reflect fundamental differences in the way their minds work. Although there is evidence that males and females do emphasize different principles in their moral reasoning (Wark & Krebs, 1996), this difference seems more a reflection of their daily activities (and the assumptions and general orientations that result from such activities) than an enduring gender difference. For example, if people are presented with dilemmas that feature concerns about raising children, men and women reason in the same ways (Clopton & Sorell, 1993). In addition, males and females score comparably on Kohlberg's tests, and both sexes reveal concerns with both caring and justice (Jadack et al., 1995; Walker, 1995). Furthermore, it is not clear that Kohlberg's levels are like traits, which characterize a person in all situations. Rather, people may use different types of moral reasoning, depending on the details of the dilemma (Trevethan & Walker, 1989).

In addition, we must distinguish between *moral reasoning* and *moral behavior:* The fact that someone reasons in a particular way doesn't guarantee that he or she will act on this reasoning. Moral behavior may be governed not simply by reasoning, but also by various aspects of your character, such as your *conscience*— which leads you to appreciate what is morally correct and feel obligated to follow this path. A conscience may develop far earlier than sophisticated moral reasoning. For example, Grazyna Kochanska and her colleagues (1994) have found that conscience typically develops at about age 3. And conscience is not the only aspect of character that can direct moral behavior. Another is the capacity to feel *empathy*, the ability to put yourself in another person's situation and feel what they feel. Indeed, Martin Hoffman (2000) shows that by early adolescence most

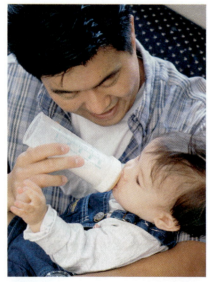

Differences in how men and women reason about moral issues may reflect the concerns that arise in their daily activities rather than inherent differences between the genders.

children have sophisticated abilities to feel and act on empathy in a wide range of moral situations. For example, the children appreciate the unfairness of another person's not receiving a just reward for his or her efforts.

In short, many factors affect how people behave in moral situations, and some of these factors develop much earlier than does the ability to reason logically about morality. Our behavior is not just a result of how we reason, but also of who we are.

LOOKING BACK: *Review*

1. *How does the ability to control the body develop with age?* In general, control progresses from the head down the trunk to the arms and, finally, to the legs; at the same time, control extends out from the center of the body to the periphery (hands, fingers, and toes). Developing motor control involves more than maturation; it also involves learning about the body and the world.

2. *What perceptual, linguistic, and cognitive abilities emerge over the course of development?* As perception develops, the child can make finer discriminations, needs less stimulus information to recognize objects, and can search more systematically. In addition, very young children learn to ignore the distinctions in sounds that are not used in their language, and young children typically overextend words and overregularize rules of grammar. Research findings suggest that to master the grammar of a language, we must learn it during a critical period, prior to puberty. Piaget proposed that during cognitive development the child moves through a series of major periods, each subdivided into stages, but researchers have since found that children have at least the rudiments of many abilities far earlier than Piaget's theory would predict. Cognitive development arises in part from improved information processing, particularly more efficient working memory, which to some degree probably reflects brain development. Finally, as Vygotsky pointed out, culture and instruction from adults also play a role in cognitive development.

3. *How do social and emotional development occur?* Children become attached to their primary caregivers, going through a series of stages, but may end up being attached in different ways. The self-concept begins to develop during very early infancy, and, in turn, probably affects many social interactions, including gender roles. People may move through a series of stages in the way they tend to reason about moral issues, and males and females may tend to reason slightly differently at the higher levels—but this divergence is mostly a function of their different concerns in daily life, and is not intrinsic to their genders per se.

LOOKING BEYOND: *Critical Thinking*

Why would you expect variation in the ages at which stages of cognitive development are reached? Do you think schools should focus on speeding up cognitive development, so that children pass through the stages more quickly? Why or why not?

Can a child experience normal emotional development if he or she spends much of the day watching television? Which aspects of emotional development do you think would be affected by watching so much television?

Adolescence: Between Two Worlds

Steven Spielberg's adolescence was different from that of many of his peers in many ways; nonetheless, the challenges he faced in those years—forming friendships, testing limits, coming to terms with a new and unfamiliar body—are essentially universal. Because his family had moved so often, none of his friends from early childhood were still with him in high school; most of his classmates, in addition, were firmly established in cliques. Spielberg craved their acceptance and used his newfound love of moviemaking and storytelling as a way of gaining it. Nevertheless, his obsession with movies and his lack of interest in the usual teenage pursuits of dating and sports continued to set him apart.

Not surprisingly, Spielberg's adolescence was not an easy time for him or, sometimes, for those around him. On one occasion, he and some friends spent 3 hours throwing rocks through plate-glass windows at a shopping mall, causing about $30,000 worth of damage (McBride, 1999, p. 88). He later said that *Poltergeist* was "all about the terrible things I did to my younger sisters" (McBride, 1999, p. 89). He fought his father's wishes for him to study math and science, declaring that someday he was going to be a famous movie director and didn't need to know those kinds of things (McBride, 1999). Extreme behavior, yes. Adolescent behavior, yes.

LOOKING AHEAD: Learning Objectives

1. *How does puberty affect the body?*
2. *How do thought processes change in adolescence?*
3. *Does adolescence always lead to emotional upheaval?*

Physical Development: In Puberty's Wake

Adolescence begins with puberty, the time when hormones cause the sex organs to mature and secondary sexual characteristics, such as breasts for women and a beard for men, to appear. These changes typically begin between ages 8–14 for girls and between ages 9–15 for boys. Adolescence is the period between the appearance of these sexual characteristics and, roughly, the end of the teenage years. Figure 9.9 summarizes pubertal events in girls and boys.

Although girls usually experience their first period (*menarche*) about 2 years after the onset of puberty, typically between 12 and 13 years of age today (Chumlea et al., 2003), various factors influence when this occurs. In fact, in the mid-19th century, girls had their first period at about 17 years of age. In recent years, the age of puberty has declined—for both girls and boys—throughout the developed and developing world, including the United States (Finlay et al., 2002; Herman-Giddens et al., 2001), Europe (de Muinck Keizer-Schrama & Mul, 2001), China (Huen et al., 1997), and Brazil (Kac et al., 2000). This may reflect a *secular trend* in society: As children receive better health care and consistently better nutrition and lead less physically strenuous lives, puberty occurs earlier. For example, in rural Brazil, girls whose fathers were unemployed and those from low-income families

Puberty: The time when hormones cause the sex organs to mature and secondary sexual characteristics, such as breasts for women and a beard for men, to appear.

Adolescence: The period between the onset of puberty and, roughly, the end of the teenage years.

Figure 9.9 Pubertal Events in Boys and Girls

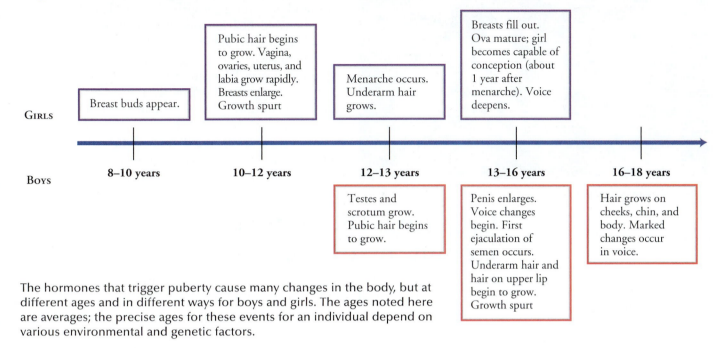

GIRLS

Breast buds appear.

Pubic hair begins to grow. Vagina, ovaries, uterus, and labia grow rapidly. Breasts enlarge. Growth spurt

Menarche occurs. Underarm hair grows.

Breasts fill out. Ova mature; girl becomes capable of conception (about 1 year after menarche). Voice deepens.

8–10 years   10–12 years   12–13 years   13–16 years   16–18 years

BOYS

Testes and scrotum grow. Pubic hair begins to grow.

Penis enlarges. Voice changes begin. First ejaculation of semen occurs. Underarm hair and hair on upper lip begin to grow. Growth spurt

Hair grows on cheeks, chin, and body. Marked changes occur in voice.

The hormones that trigger puberty cause many changes in the body, but at different ages and in different ways for boys and girls. The ages noted here are averages; the precise ages for these events for an individual depend on various environmental and genetic factors.

had their first periods later than girls from more prosperous backgrounds (Tavares et al., 2000). Another study documented that American boys of various ethnic backgrounds are taller and heavier today than in previous generations, and these boys also develop pubic hair and mature genitalia at a younger age than was previously considered the norm (Herman-Giddens et al., 2001).

Could better nutrition explain this secular trend? Studies have shown that overweight girls tend to experience their first periods before those who are not overweight (Kaplowitz et al., 2001), which suggests a link between diet and the age of onset of puberty. However, Black American girls tend to be overweight less often than White American girls, but are younger when they have their first periods (Herman-Giddens et al., 1997). Thus, diet alone cannot explain the secular trend. In addition, for at least some girls who have a certain gene, stress (especially caused by having an absent father) apparently triggers early puberty (Comings et al., 2002). Many theories have been proposed to explain the trend, ranging from the effects of additives in food (such as hormones added to animal feed and then passed on to human consumers; Teilmann et al., 2002) to various chemical pollutants in the environment (such as polybrominated biphenyls, or PBBs; Blanck et al., 2000)—but the reason or reasons underlying it are still not understood.

Physical development during adolescence also, of course, includes growth. During infancy and childhood, the body grows from the trunk outward; the upper arms grow before the lower arms, which in turn grow before the hands. At puberty, the trend is reversed: Rapid growth of the hands, feet, and legs is followed by growth of the torso (Wheeler, 1991). Do you remember when you stopped needing larger shoes but still needed larger coats? That's why. The uneven growth during adolescence can lead to an awkward, gawky look, which doesn't do wonders for a teen's sense of self-confidence.

Girls tend to mature faster than boys.

Once the sex hormones start operating in earnest, the shoulders of young boys grow large relative to their hips, and vice versa for girls. At age 11, girls typically are taller and heavier than boys because their major growth spurt starts about 2 years before that of boys. By age 14, however, boys' heights and weights have taken off, whereas girls have stopped growing or have begun to grow more slowly. American girls typically stop growing at around age 13 (some may continue to grow until about age 16), but American boys usually continue to grow until about their 16th birthdays (and some may continue growing until they are almost 18 years old; Malina & Bouchard, 1991; Tanner, 1990).

Cognitive Development: Getting It All Together

The adolescent's ability to reason can become dramatically more powerful, but nevertheless be plagued with biases and distortions.

More Reasoned Reasoning?

The major cognitive development of adolescence, achieved by some but not all adolescents, is the ability to reason abstractly. Piaget's period of formal operations covers the cognitive achievements of these adolescents. According to Piaget, formal operational thinking allows a person not only to think abstractly, but also to think systematically about abstract concepts and possible scenarios. In one of his experiments, now regarded as a classic, Piaget gave a child a set of weights, string that could be attached to the weights, and a bar to which the string could be attached, allowing the weight to swing like a pendulum. The child was asked to vary both the weight and the length of the string in order to discover what factors would make the weight swing most quickly. Adolescents in the formal operational period are not only able to figure out the possibly relevant factors (size of weight, length of string, how high the weight is raised before being dropped, force with which it is pushed), but also to understand that to discover the role of each variable, they must alter only one thing at a time. These adolescents have grasped the very essence of scientific experimentation: holding everything else constant while systematically varying one factor at a time. In short, all the cognitive machinery necessary to think scientifically can be present by about 11 or 12 years of age. But not all adolescents develop these abilities this early, and some never do.

Most adolescents in Western societies are able to grasp the rules that underlie algebra and geometry. The ability to think systematically about abstractions also allows them to think about concepts such as justice and politics, as well as about relationships and the causes of human behavior. In fact, there's evidence that the adolescent brain is better prepared to learn algebra than is the adult brain! Researchers found that adolescents and adults used parts of the frontal and parietal lobes when they first learned rules of algebra and used those rules to solve equations—but after practice, adolescents' parietal lobes stopped being activated, whereas those brain areas in adults continued to be activated (Luna, 2004; Qin et al., 2004).

How does the ability to think abstractly and logically emerge? It is tempting to conclude that it is a result of the development of working memory, which does not function at adult levels until about 19 years of age (Luna et al., 2004). Moreover, one might speculate that this ability emerges at this time because it depends on the final stages of brain maturation (and the brain does, in fact, continue to develop well into adolescence—Sowell et al., 1999). However, assuming that events at any one level alone could account for such a sweeping change would be rash indeed. Cole (1990) has found that, in many traditional African societies, even the adults cannot use the kinds of abilities described by Piaget's idea of formal operations, but there is no indication that their brains have failed to develop fully. Culture must play a role, perhaps shaping the developing child's thought, as Vygotsky theorized.

But thinking is more than using logic or knowing how to grapple with abstractions. Emotion is often involved in our reasoning, and such processing relies on the lower middle part of the frontal lobes. Evidence suggests that this brain area is not fully mature during adolescence, and thus emotions do not guide teenagers' thinking effectively (Hooper et al., 2004). It is tempting to speculate that this maturational lag may sometimes explain a lack of "common sense" during this stage of life.

Adolescent Egocentrism: It's All in Your Point of View

The enhanced cognitive abilities of adolescents allow them to take other points of view easily—in particular, to see themselves as they imagine others see them. Theorists have claimed that these improved abilities can lead to two kinds of distortions in adolescents' conceptions of how others view them (Greene et al., 2002).

First, the *imaginary audience* is a belief sometimes held by adolescents, in which they view themselves as actors and everyone else as an audience (Elkind, 1967; Elkind & Bowen, 1979). This view can lead teenagers to be extremely self-conscious and easily embarrassed; a pimple feels like a beacon, not unlike Rudolph's nose. Although many adolescents do not succumb to such cognitive distortions (Vartanian, 2001), those who do—perhaps because they believe others may be watching them—are less likely to engage in risky behaviors (Galanaki, 2001). However, some researchers argue that often there is nothing "imaginary" about the audience (echoing the old joke that even paranoids sometimes have enemies), and that adolescents have realistic concerns about others' opinions (Bell & Bromnick, 2003).

Second, some teenagers have a *personal fable*, which is a story in which they are the star and, as the star, have extraordinary abilities and privileges. Teenagers may have unprotected sex and drive recklessly because they believe that they are immune to the possible consequences (Lapsley, 1990; Lapsley et al., 1988). These tendencies, and other social behaviors, are clearly influenced by peers. However, adolescents are influenced primarily by their families with regard to basic values and goals (Brown et al., 1986a, 1986b).

Who is the imaginary audience?

Social and Emotional Development: New Rules, New Roles

A bridge between childhood and adulthood, adolescence is a time of transition. The adolescent must forge a new identity, which emerges as he or she negotiates a new place in the world (Marica, 1993). This negotiation involves not only coming to grips with changing roles in the larger society, which requires obeying new sets of rules, but also learning to live with cognitive and biological changes that affect interactions with others in many ways.

"Storm and Stress": Raging Hormones?

The notion that adolescents experience a period of "storm and stress" has waxed and waned in popularity (Arnett, 1999). Anna Freud (1958) not only believed that adolescent "angst" (anguish) was inevitable but also that "normal" behavior during adolescence was in itself evidence of deep *abnormalities* in the individual. A strong reaction to this view soon followed, and only a few years ago, many psychologists were dismissing the idea of adolescent turmoil as another popular misconception. However, additional studies have shown that there is in fact a tendency for normal adolescents to have three sorts of problems (Arnett, 1999):

1. Adolescents tend to have conflicts with their parents (Laursen et al., 1998). The *frequency* of the conflicts is greatest in early adolescence, whereas the *intensity* of the conflicts is greatest in midadolescence (Laursen et al., 1998).

2. Adolescents experience extreme mood swings (Buchanan et al., 1992; Larson & Richards, 1994; Petersen et al., 1993), and by the middle of the teen years, about one third of adolescents are seriously depressed (Petersen et al., 1993)—and such depression is associated with increased levels of delinquency (Beyers & Loeber, 2003). Adolescents also often report feeling lonely and nervous.

3. Adolescents may be prone to taking risks. Adolescents are relatively likely to commit crimes, drive recklessly, and have high-risk sex (Arnett, 1992; Gottfredson & Hirschi, 1990; Johnston et al., 1994). Such behaviors are related to problems in regulating emotions (Cooper et al., 2003), and they tend to peak in late adolescence.

Many adolescents don't have these problems; rather, as Arnett (1999) documents, such problems are simply "more likely to occur during adolescence than at other ages" (p. 317). But why do they occur at all? Many people assume that they are an unavoidable result of the hormonal changes that accompany puberty. In fact, the hormonal changes that go along with puberty do make the adolescent prone to emotional swings (Brooks-Gunn et al., 1994; Buchanan et al., 1992). But hormones only predispose, they do not cause; environmental events trigger the emotional reactions (Dodge & Pettit, 2003).

In sum, adolescents are more likely than people of other ages to experience "storm and stress," which arises in part from the workings of hormones. However, this is only a tendency, and the degree to which an adolescent will experience such turmoil depends on personal and cultural circumstances.

Evolving Peer Relationships

The adolescent's relationship with his or her parents casts a long shadow. Both young men and women who have a more positive relationship with their mothers later have more positive intimate relationships with others (Robinson, 2000). Parental and peer relationships have a major impact on self-esteem (Wilkinson, 2004). However, many kinds of life experiences affect whether a young man or woman will develop intimate relationships. For example, perhaps counterintuitively, military service can enhance the ability to form intimate relationships (for example, by helping someone learn to trust and rely on others; Dar & Kimhi, 2001). Most adolescents develop predominantly same-gender networks of friends, and women's friendships tend to be stronger than men's (Roy et al., 2000). The one exception to this generalization is gay young men—who tend to have more female than male friends; moreover, gay young men tend to be less emotionally attached to their love interests than are heterosexual young men (Diamond & Dube, 2002). In addition, as portrayed in countless Hollywood "nerd films," some adolescents can be rejected by their peers. For example, girls can effectively use indirect aggression (for example, by spreading false rumors) to exclude other girls from their circle (Owens et al., 2000). Hurt pride or lowered self-esteem is not always the only result of such rejection. Many gay or bisexual students report being victimized at school, which apparently contributes to their being at risk for suicide and substance abuse and for their engaging in high-risk behaviors (Bontempo & D'Augelli, 2002).

Teenage Pregnancy

In general, American teenage girls engage in amounts of sexual activity comparable to those of girls in other industrialized societies, but American teens do not use contraception as effectively. In 2001, 33.4% of births in the United States were to unmarried mothers. However, American teens are having fewer children; in 2001, they had 25.3 births per 10,000, compared to 27.4 in 2000—an 8% decline (Wetzstein, 2002).

Which teenagers are likely to become pregnant? Those at greatest risk are poor and do not have clear career plans—and their father is likely to be absent (Ellis et al., 2003). Maynard (1996) reports that a third of the teenagers who become pregnant drop out of school even before they become pregnant. Further, over half of teenage mothers were living in poverty when they had their children. For many of these young women, particularly Black Americans, having a baby is part of "coming of age" and is in many ways equivalent to a career choice (Burton, 1990; Merrick, 1995). Unfortunately, the adult children of teen mothers are likely to leave school early, be unemployed, and be in trouble with the law for violent offences—and they themselves tend to become parents at an early age (Jaffee et al., 2001).

However, the specific consequences of having a child depend on the mother's subsequent behavior and social group: If teenage mothers do not drop out of school, they are about as likely to graduate as girls who did not give birth, and Black Americans appear to suffer the fewest economic consequences of having given birth as a teenager. Apparently, Black American teenage mothers tend to live at home, continue school, and benefit from the assistance of members of their families (Burton, 1990, 1996; Rosenheim & Testa, 1992).

LOOKING BACK: *Review*

1. *How does puberty affect the body?* Hormones are responsible for the fact that the extremities (arms and legs) grow rapidly, with the trunk lagging behind, a pattern that can produce a gawky appearance. During this period, the body grows pubic hair and acquires other secondary sex characteristics.

2. *How do thought processes change in adolescence?* Adolescents can become capable of reasoning logically. In addition, if the adolescent reaches the period of formal operations, he or she can reason about abstract concepts systematically—and thus becomes capable of scientific thought. The enhanced cognitive abilities that appear during adolescence can lead to the distorting formulations of an imaginary audience and a personal fable.

3. *Does adolescence always lead to emotional upheaval?* Although hormones do prime the adolescent to experience more conflicts with parents as well as to have major mood swings and be prone to taking risks, these tendencies are neither certain nor necessarily severe. Many kinds of experiences and characteristics (especially gender) influence the way peer relationships develop during adolescence.

● *If you were going to design a school program that takes into account the biological changes that occur during adolescence, how would it differ from your own middle school or high school experience? What kinds of classes, activities, or schedule might make the transition to adulthood easier?*

Why was adolescence a particularly important period for Steven Spielberg? Do you think it played such a large role in your own life? Why or why not?

Adulthood and Aging: The Continuously Changing Self

Steven Spielberg was an unhappy teenager and—in some aspects of life—a spectacularly successful young adult. But being successful in his chosen career did not mean that he was successful in all aspects of life. His first marriage ended; his relationship with his father was strained; and he was concerned that he himself would not measure up as a father (several of his movies deal with difficult relationships between fathers and sons). When he had children of his own, he realized that he needed to be an adult for them; he, and his relationships, had to change, and they did.

Famous filmmaker or not, the grown-up Steven Spielberg is in a very different phase of life than his children are; he is also in a very different phase of life than his father is. This is the human condition, and we now turn to an exploration of the stages of adult development.

LOOKING AHEAD: *Learning Objectives*

1. *How do changes in the body affect us as we age?*
2. *How does aging affect perception, memory, and intelligence?*
3. *What is the course of social and emotional development during adulthood?*

The Changing Body: What's Inevitable, What's Not

By your early 20s, it is unlikely that you will grow taller, and your weight has typically stabilized for many years to come. For the next several decades, changes in your body should be relatively minor. True, you may come to need bifocals, and your hair may begin to gray or to thin. But the basic bodily systems continue to function well. However, after age 50 or so, noticeable changes in the body begin to occur (Lemme, 1995).

Aging has two aspects: changes that are programmed into the genes and changes that arise from environmental events (Busse, 1969; Rowe & Kahn, 1998). Many changes that come with aging arise not from inevitable processes, but rather from lack of adequate nutrition (such as fragile bones that result from osteoporosis-related calcium deficiency), lack of exercise (resulting in obesity in some elderly people and frailty in others, or just plain sluggishness and poor health; Brach et al., 2004), or lack of meaningful activities (which can lead to feelings of helplessness or apathy; Avorn & Langer, 1982; Langer & Rodin, 1976; Rodin & Langer, 1977; Rowe & Kahn, 1998). By the same token, environmental events—such as taking calcium supplements or lifting weights—can help to counter or diminish such problems.

One of the inevitable age-related changes in women is *menopause*, the gradual ending of menstruation that typically occurs between the ages of 45 and 55; following menopause, eggs are no longer released and pregnancy is not possible (Wise et al., 1996). Hormonal changes that accompany menopause can lead to various bodily sensations (such as "hot flashes"); the knowledge that childbearing is no longer possible, along with the decline in youthful appearance, can adversely affect a woman's self-concept and self-esteem. On the other hand, for many women, the physical discomforts are slight, if present at all, and the idea of sexual intercourse without the threat of an unwanted pregnancy provides new pleasure. Some women feel "postmenopausal zest" and are reinvigorated by this change and the freedom it represents. For men, after about age 40, sperm production begins to fall off—but, unlike the cessation of egg production after menopause, men never fully lose the ability to produce sperm. Men do experience declining vigor (strength and energy) with age, which can affect sexual performance.

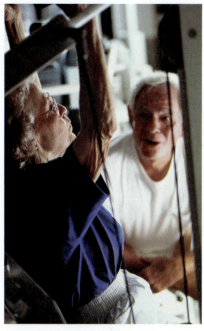

It's not just diet that can help prevent osteoporosis; behavior can also play a role. Lifting weights helps the bones retain calcium.

Perception and Cognition in Adulthood: Taking the Good With the Bad

Cognitive abilities remain relatively stable through most of adulthood, but signs of a decline in some abilities begin to appear by age 50. The good news is that aging itself probably doesn't cause neurons to die (Long et al., 1999; Stern & Carstensen, 2000), but the bad news is that aging does impair communication among neurons, possibly by disrupting neurotransmitter functioning (S-C. Li et al., 2001) or by degrading the white matter of the brain, which provides the connections among neurons (Guttmann et al., 1998). These changes in the brain will eventually catch up with you and lead you to perform more slowly and be more prone to making errors. Indeed, by age 60, people perform most cognitive tasks more slowly than do younger people (Birren et al., 1962; Cerella, 1990; Salthouse, 1991b). The harder the task, the larger the difference in the time taken by young adults and elderly ones.

Shortly before death, however, many people exhibit *terminal decline* (Kleemeier, 1962). Their performance on a wide range of cognitive tasks takes a dramatic turn for the worse (Berg, 1996). This decline appears most dramatically in those who will die from cerebrovascular diseases, such as strokes and heart attacks, and it may be related to such disease states (Small & Bäckman, 2000). Thus, terminal decline is probably not an inevitable final chapter of the book of life (Bosworth & Siegler, 2002). More common is a gradual degradation in cognitive performance in the years leading up to death (Johansson et al., 2004; Small et al., 2003).

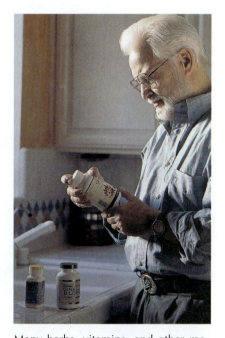

Many herbs, vitamins, and other medicinal remedies promise to reverse the negative cognitive effects of aging. For example, the herb *Ginkgo biloba* and the drug acetyl-L-carnitine have been reported to improve blood flow to the brain (Dean et al., 1993). However, much more research is necessary before we will know for sure whether such treatments work as advertised.

Perception: Through a Glass Darkly?

During early and middle adulthood, worsening vision can usually be corrected with eyeglasses. Later in life, however, more severe visual difficulties emerge. More than half of the 65 and older population has *cataracts*, a clouding of the lenses of the eyes; in older people, the pupil (the opening of the eye through which light enters) also cannot open as widely as it does in younger people. Surgery can remove cataracts and result in greatly improved vision. But when such surgery has not been prescribed, moderate optical difficulties cause many older people to need greater contrast to see differences in light (Fozard, 1990). Contrasts between lit and unlit surfaces, such as shadows caused by steps, can define differences in depth, and if older people cannot perceive such definition, they are more likely to stumble over a step. Simply providing more light will not necessarily help older people to see well; because of the clouding of the lenses, more light causes more glare. Thus, the best level of illumination is a compromise between what produces the best contrast and the least glare. However, some declines in visual perception have nothing to do with the physical condition of the eyes, but rather reflect changes in how the brain functions. For instance, the elderly do not classify the identities of faces as well as younger people do—but they can classify facial expressions as well as younger people do (Kiffel et al., 2005).

Hearing is also affected by age. After age 50 or so, people have increased difficulty hearing high-frequency sounds (Botwinick, 1984; Lemme, 1995). Because consonants (such as *k*, *c*, *p*, and *t*) are produced with higher-frequency sounds than are vowels, older people often have trouble distinguishing between words that differ by a single consonant, such as *kill* and *pill*. Older people also have more difficulty shutting out background noise, a problem that may actually be worsened by hearing aids, which boost the loudness of both irrelevant background sounds and relevant sounds.

Memory: Difficulties in Digging It Out

Parts of the brain that produce the neurotransmitter acetylcholine become impaired with age (Albert & Moss, 1996; D. E. Smith et al., 1999); this neurotransmitter is crucial for the proper functioning of the hippocampus, which plays a key role in explicit memory. The less efficient processing in this part of the brain is probably one reason why older people often have trouble with some kinds of memory (Schacter, 1996); in fact, the hippocampus and related brain structures are smaller in older adults, and the sizes of these structures are correlated with recall ability (Rosen et al., 2003).

Even so, aging affects some aspects of memory more than others. *Semantic memory* (memory for facts, words, meanings, and other information that is not associated with a particular time and place) remains relatively intact into very old age (Light, 1991), and the storing of new *episodic memories* (memory for specific events) is often relatively effective. People in their 70s and 80s do fairly well if they are given a list of words and then asked to pick out these words from a longer list that also contains other words (Craik & McDowd, 1987). Moreover, the elderly have good implicit memory (Fleischman et al., 2004), and they can recall the gist of a description and its implications at least as well as younger people (Radvansky, 1999).

However, the elderly have difficulty when they must actively recall specific episodic memories: For example, they do poorly if they are given a list of common words to remember and later asked to recall them (Craik & McDowd, 1987). Tasks that require the *recall* of specific information appear to rely on the frontal lobes to dig the information out of memory, and processes accomplished there are not as efficient in the elderly as they are in younger people.

Frontal lobe impairment is probably also responsible for difficulties the elderly have with tasks involving working memory (De Beni & Palladino, 2004). Such deficits are especially evident when elderly people

The frontal lobes are among the brain areas that lose the most gray matter in old age (Raz et al., 1997; Resnick et al., 2003), which may be one factor that affects the ability to recall information easily. In these MRI scans, the brighter the color, the more gray matter was lost with aging: *bottom*, a view from the bottom, looking up; *midline side*, a midline side view of the inside regions; *front*, a slice viewed from the front.

must hold information in mind while doing something else at the same time (Craik et al., 1995). If strategies are needed to perform a task (such as figuring out the most efficient way to move through a store to collect different items), the frontal lobe impairments of the elderly can affect their performance (Gabrieli, 1996; S-C. Li et al., 2001). As Salthouse (1985) suggests, slowed cognitive processes may also lead the elderly to use inefficient strategies, strategies composed of many steps, each relatively simple. Ironically, there is evidence that elderly people are actually more likely than younger people to use strategies that rely more on their frontal lobes, attempting to compensate for less efficient processing in other parts of the brain (Gutchess et al., 2005).

Intelligence and Specific Abilities: Different Strokes for Different Folks

It might seem likely that as you age, your accumulated life experience should add up to an increasingly important determinant of your intelligence. But this is not so. Researchers were surprised to discover that although overall level of intelligence is remarkably stable from age 11 to age 78 (Deary et al., 2004), genetic influences on general intelligence actually *increase* with age (Finkel et al., 1995; Plomin et al., 1994).

Changes in Fluid and Crystallized Intelligence.
Investigators have asked whether aging affects all types of intelligence in the same way. In particular, they have examined the effects of age on *fluid intelligence*, which involves flexibility in reasoning and the ability to figure out novel solutions, and *crystallized intelligence*, which involves using knowledge as a basis of reasoning (see Chapter 6). It might seem that crystallized intelligence, which, by definition, relies on experience, would be less influenced by age than would fluid intelligence. How could we tell? These two types of intelligence have been assessed in <mark>longitudinal studies</mark>, which test the same group of people repeatedly, at different ages. These findings suggest that *both* types of intelligence are stable until somewhere between the mid-50s and the early 70s, when both decline (Hertzog & Schaie, 1988). However, the very strength of longitudinal studies—the continuing use of the same group—also leads to a weakness: The participants become familiar with the type of testing, and this familiarity can influence their performance on later assessments. <mark>Cross-sectional studies</mark> involve testing different groups of people, with each group composed of individuals of a particular age. The key here is to ensure that the groups are equated on all possible measures other than age (such as sex, educational level, and health status). Such studies have led most researchers to believe that fluid intelligence begins to decline as early as the late 20s (Salthouse, 1991a), whereas crystallized intelligence may actually grow with age and decline only late in life (Baltes, 1987; Li et al., 2004; McArdle et al., 2002).

Changes in Specific Abilities.
Crystallized intelligence, rooted in experience, may be thought of as underlying much of what we mean by "wisdom." The ability to draw on such intelligence may explain why researchers found that older adults were rated as telling more interesting, higher-quality, and more informative stories than younger adults (James et al., 1998). This should be cheering news for Steven Spielberg, who plans to keep telling stories as long as he can.

Moreover, in some respects, old people actually reason better than young people. For example, in one study, researchers asked young and old participants to indicate their preferences when given either two or three alternatives—for

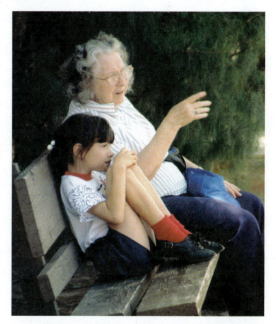

Crystallized intelligence does not decline dramatically until very late in life, which allows the elderly to tell more interesting and informative stories.

Longitudinal study: A study in which the same group of people is tested repeatedly, at different ages.

Cross-sectional study: A study in which different groups of people are tested, with each group composed of individuals of a particular age.

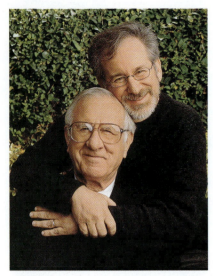

After a 15-year split, Steven Spielberg developed a new relationship with his dad.

Psychosocial development: The effects of maturation and learning on personality and relationships.

example, chocolate or vanilla ice cream versus chocolate, vanilla, or strawberry ice cream. Young people were inconsistent, perhaps choosing vanilla when only two choices were offered, but chocolate when strawberry was included. Old people were much more consistent and "logical" in their choices (Tentori et al., 2001).

Social and Emotional Development During Adulthood

The phrase "growing up" might seem to imply that psychological development is like height: After a certain age, you reach a plateau, and that's where you stay. Not so. At least in mentally healthy people, psychological development continues throughout the life span. In discussing Steven Spielberg's 15-year split with his father, an expert on father–son relationships, James Levine, commented: "In such a split, you don't recognize that under the anger is sadness. There's denial: pretending it's not important to heal the rift. But a split in the father–child relationship always has an effect" (quoted in Sullivan, 1999, p. 67). Still, as in Spielberg's case, relationships change and evolve over time.

Theories of Psychosocial Stages in Adulthood

Some theorists, Freud included, believed that personality stops developing in childhood. But Erik Erikson (1921–1994) proposed three stages of adult **psychosocial development**, due to effects of maturation and learning on personality and relationships, in addition to five stages of psychosocial development through childhood and adolescence (see Table 9.2). The adult stages were defined by issues that adults are most likely to confront and need to resolve.

Table 9.2 Erikson's (1950) Psychosocial Stages

Issue to Be Resolved	Average Age	Summary
Basic trust vs. mistrust	0–1 year	Depending on how well they are treated by caregivers, infants either develop a basic trust that the world is good or fail to develop such a basic trust.
Autonomy vs. doubt	1–3 years	The child either is allowed to choose and make independent decisions or is made to feel ashamed and full of self-doubt for wanting to do so.
Initiative vs. guilt	3–6 years	The child either develops a sense of purpose and direction or is overly controlled by the parents and made to feel constrained or guilty.
Industry vs. inferiority	6–11 years	The child either develops a sense of competence and ability to work with others or becomes beset with feelings of incompetence and inferiority.
Identity vs. role confusion	Adolescence	The adolescent either successfully grapples with questions of identity and future roles as an adult or becomes confused about possible adult roles.
Intimacy vs. isolation	Young adulthood	The young adult either develops deep and intimate relations with others or is socially isolated.
Generativity vs. self-absorption	Middle adulthood	The adult in the "prime of life" must look to the future and determine what to leave behind for future generations; failing this task leads to a sense of meaninglessness in life.
Integrity vs. despair	Old age	In reflecting back on life, a person either feels that life was worthwhile as it was lived or feels despair and fears death.

- The first stage, *intimacy versus isolation*, occurs in young adulthood. To navigate this stage of development successfully, the young adult must develop deep and intimate relations with others and avoid becoming socially isolated. Steven Spielberg had serious difficulty being intimate with people, which may be one reason why his first marriage dissolved (McBride, 1999).

- The second adult stage, characterized by *generativity versus self-absorption*, occurs during the middle adult years. The challenge here is for men and women to think about the future and decide what their contributions will be for their children or for society at large. People who are highly generative agree with the African proverb "The world was not left to us by our parents. It was lent to us by our children" (which is inscribed on a wall in the UNICEF office in New York). People who fail at the task of this stage will be faced with a sense of meaninglessness in life. Steven Spielberg not only cares for his own children but also makes it a point to help young directors who are just starting out; such altruistic behavior is another type of generativity.

- The third adult stage, characterized by *integrity versus despair*, occurs during old age. The task here is to be able to reflect back on life and feel that it was worthwhile, thereby avoiding feelings of despair and fear of death.

By performing live concerts in their sixties, Mick Jagger and fellow rockers in The Rolling Stones show that many roles are open to us as we age, despite stereotypes to the contrary!

Many theorists have picked up where Erikson left off (Gould, 1978; Havinghurst, 1953; Vaillant, 1977). Some have focused on one aspect of Erikson's theory. For example, McAdams and his colleagues developed ways to assess generativity (McAdams & de St. Aubin, 1992), and they found that adults who are concerned about providing for future generations tend to be more satisfied with their lives (McAdams et al., 1993) and to view life optimistically—believing that even bad events will eventually have a happy outcome (McAdams et al., 2001).

Continued Personality Development

We must distinguish between the changes in perspective represented by the psychosocial changes and changes in personality; evidence indicates that personality does not change substantially during adulthood (Costa et al., 2000; Johnson et al., 2005; Schaie et al., 2004). In fact, Costa and McCrae (1988) tested more than a thousand adults, both men and women, using standardized measures (not interviews) of the Big Five personality dimensions: openness to experience, conscientiousness, extraversion, agreeableness, and neuroticism (see Chapter 8). The participants ranged in age from 21 to 96 years. In addition to asking the participants to complete the measures, the researchers also asked 167 spouses to fill in the measures about the participants. Eighty-nine men and 78 women were tested twice, 6 years apart; thus, both cross-sectional and longitudinal data were collected. The results were clear: There were very few differences in any of the dimensions of personality over the years, and when such differences were found, they were very small. Moreover, Costa and McCrae found that personality was equally stable over time for men and women. They concluded that "aging itself has little effect on personality. This is true despite the fact that the normal course of aging includes disease, bereavement, divorce, unemployment, and many other significant events for substantial portions of the population" (p. 862). As a matter of fact, objective tests have shown that even when a person feels that his or her personality has changed (over the course of 6–9 years) during middle age, it really hasn't (Herbst et al., 2000).

Apparent changes in personality over time probably reflect not so much changes in the person as changes in the life challenges that he or she is confronting at the time: For many people, aging is accompanied by changes in marital status, parenting, and job-related factors. Such major life changes often become less frequent or severe as a person grows older, which could explain the finding that people become increasingly consistent in the degree to which they can be described by particular traits until around age 50, and thereafter are stable (Roberts & DelVecchio, 2000). Consistency, in this sense, refers to the relative ordering of people according to a trait—with increasing age, your ranking relative to other people will become more stable. This stability could reflect, in part, your settling into a niche in life, and thus restricting the range and variety of situations you encounter.

Mature Emotions

The poet Robert Browning wrote, "Grow old along with me! / The best is yet to be / The last of life, for which the first is made." He may have been more right than he realized. In one study, people of different ages were prompted to report their emotions at various times over the course of a week (Carstensen et al., 2000). The researchers found that as people enter old age, they tend to experience more extended periods of highly positive emotions and less enduring spells of negative emotions than do younger people. Moreover, positive emotions were evoked as regularly for the elderly as for the young. Negative emotions, on the other hand, arose increasingly less often until about age 60 (when they leveled off).

But the news is even better than this. Older people are, well, more "mature" in their emotional responses. With age, people become better able to regulate emotions (Gross et al., 1997). In fact, elderly Americans of European and Chinese ethnic backgrounds had smaller changes in heart rate when watching emotional films than did younger people (Tsai et al., 2000). But this doesn't mean that their emotions are blunted or diminished; even when heart rate changes were smaller, older participants had subjective responses comparable to those of younger participants.

At one point, approximately 2,500 people well over 100 years old were reported to be living in countries comprising the former Soviet Union. One purportedly 168-year-old gentleman, who was still walking half a mile daily and gardening, attributed his longevity to the fact that he didn't marry until he was 65 (Seuling, 1986). Second marriages are common among elderly people.

Adult Relationships: Stable Changes

Perhaps as a result of their increased ability to grapple with emotions, older people tend to change their outlook on life. Laura Carstensen and her collaborators have developed the *socioemotional selectivity theory*, which rests on the idea that older people come to focus on the limited time they have left, which in turn changes their motivations (Carstensen & Charles, 1998; Lang & Carstensen, 2002). Consistent with this theory, these researchers find that as people age, they come increasingly to value emotionally fulfilling relationships. This leads older people to prefer the company of those with whom they are emotionally close. The same findings hold true both for White and Black Americans (Fung et al., 2001).

In general, as people age, they interact with fewer people, but these interactions tend to be more intimate (Carstensen,

1991, 1992)—older people don't miss the broader social networks that they had when they were young (Lansford et al., 1998). Relationships earlier in life tend to include more friends than relatives, but with age the mix reverses, with more time spent with relatives than with friends. This pattern is even more pronounced among Latinos than Americans of European descent (Levitt et al., 1993). In later life, a relationship long dormant can be picked up and reestablished with minimal effort (Carstensen, 1992); after young adulthood, personality variables are relatively stable, which makes it easy to "know" someone again even after a long lapse.

During young adulthood, people are concerned that their relationships with friends and relatives are equitable—that neither party gives more than he or she receives (Lemme, 1995; Walster et al., 1978). As people age, such concerns recede into the background. In successful marriages, the members of the couple think of themselves as a team, not separate people who are in constant negotiations (Keith & Schafer, 1991). Because they are in it for the long haul, people trust that the balance of favors and repayment will even out over time. Thus, older couples resolve their differences with less negative emotion than do younger couples (Carstensen et al., 1995).

Looking at Levels

Keeping the Aging Brain Sharp

In old age, particularly in the years just before death, many people do not function as well mentally as they did earlier in life, even if they are physically healthy (Small & Bäckman, 2000). Is this deterioration inevitable? As people age, the brain receives less blood, which means that it is sustained by fewer nutrients and less oxygen (Ivy et al., 1992). The blood supply to the brain decreases with age because the blood vessels themselves become smaller. Why does this happen? One reason may be that the brain cells are not working as hard, so they need less blood—which in turn leads the vessels to adjust (Ivy et al., 1992). This is like Catch-22: The neurons don't work as effectively because they receive fewer blood-borne nutrients and less oxygen, but the reason they don't receive as much is that they haven't been functioning as effectively as they did before.

But focusing on the brain alone is not enough. At the level of the person (at least in the United States), the elderly have absorbed societally transmitted negative conceptions about aging—and these stereotypes apparently can undermine the will to live. In one study, young and elderly people were shown positive or negative words concerning old age; the words were presented too briefly to be seen consciously—and hence functioned as unconscious "primes." The elderly participants were more likely to say that they would reject treatment for serious illness after being primed with negative words than they were after being primed with positive words; the negative words apparently activated stored negative concepts about aging. For the young participants, the type of words used as primes made no difference (Levy et al., 1999–2000).

As usual, we must also consider events at the level of the group. Social interactions clearly affect how well older people can cope with stress (Krause, 2004), which in turn affects the stress response; and older people experience cognitive degradation when they lose social support (Aartsen et al., 2004). But more than that, it is tempting to hypothesize that if you managed to engage your elderly parents, grandparents, or other family members in more challenging tasks, you could literally increase the blood supply to their brains and improve their thinking

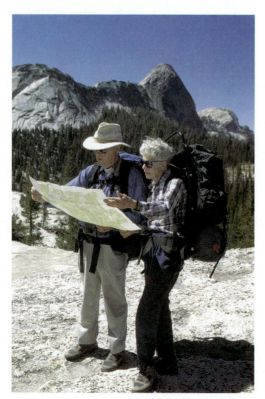

Research with mice suggests that it's not the pure amount of stimulation that boosts brain function, but rather the amount of novelty that's encountered (Kempermann & Gage, 1999). If this result generalizes to humans, travel may truly broaden the mind, even for the elderly!

abilities. This result is plausible because "mental workouts" appear to enhance cognitive function in the elderly (Rowe & Kahn, 1998); in fact, training over the course of only 10 sessions can substantially improve memory, reasoning, and speed of processing in the elderly (Ball et al., 2002). Moreover, neurons' dendrites continue to grow normally even into old age (Coleman & Flood, 1986), and as neurons die, new connections may be formed to compensate for losses (Cotman, 1990). In one study, when elderly rats were moved from their standard cages into a rat playpen full of toys and other rats, they developed heavier brains with more extensive connections among neurons. Moreover, other researchers have found that mice that live in an enriched environment (complete with lots of attractive toys, other mice to play with, and opportunities to explore and exercise) retain more neurons as they age (Kempermann et al., 1998). Indeed, simply giving animals the chance to exercise enhances neuronal growth and improves survival rates (Cotman & Berchtold, 2002; van Praag et al., 1999). Very likely the same would be true for humans who were provided with more stimulating environments (Avorn & Langer, 1982; Langer & Rodin, 1976; Rodin & Langer, 1977; Rowe & Kahn, 1998). In fact, researchers have found that the brain generally becomes smaller with aging, but that people with more education have less severe size reductions (Coffey et al., 1999).

Thus, if your otherwise healthy parents or grandparents are understimulated by their surroundings (as occurs in some nursing homes as well as in many home environments), this could affect their brains. The changes in their brains could in turn lead them to avoid mental challenge and engagement, which in turn could lead to changes in self-concept and level of self-esteem. These changes then may lead them to become lethargic and to avoid social interaction. And not interacting with others could lead to even less effective neural functioning, and so on. Clearly, there is ample opportunity for events at all three levels to interact.

However, it is unlikely that all of the functions that are impaired with age can be helped simply by getting your grandparents to use their brains more, or even by changing their conceptions of what it means to be elderly. MRI scans of more than 3,600 apparently normal elderly people (aged 65 to 97) revealed that slightly over one third had brain lesions. These were often small and usually affected subcortical structures, but some of the lesions were probably large enough to perhaps affect a specific cognitive function (Bryan et al., 1997). Damage to the white matter can also disrupt cognition in the elderly (Koga et al., 2002). Thus, possible effects of changing beliefs and of social interactions must be considered within the context of changes in the brain. As always, events at the three levels interact.

LOOKING BACK: *Review*

1. How do changes in the body affect us as we age? The adult body remains relatively stable until around age 50. At about this point, women experience menopause, and both men and women may become less vigorous. Many of the changes in the body can be treated, however, either by dietary supplements (such as calcium for bone weakness) or changes in activities (such as increased exercise).

2. *How does aging affect perception, memory, and intelligence?* With age the lens clouds and the pupils dilate less, leading to difficulty in seeing light–dark contrasts; the elderly also have difficulty hearing high-frequency sounds, including consonants. With advancing old age, working memory operates less effectively, and people sometimes have difficulty recalling information. Although intelligence declines with advanced age, fluid intelligence may be more affected than crystallized intelligence.

3. *What is the course of social and emotional development during adulthood?* Many theorists, especially Erikson, have proposed that people pass through psychosocial stages as they age; these stages may reflect particular issues that need to be resolved. Little evidence points to personality changes after age 30. Adult relationships focus on fewer people (often relatives) and tend to be stable over long periods of time.

LOOKING BEYOND: *Critical Thinking*

If you could choose several of your own abilities to protect from decaying with age, which would they be? Why? If you could choose between becoming wise or having a perfect memory, which would you choose? Why?

As you age, what factors do you think will influence whether you stay close to friends you made earlier in life?

LET'S SUM IT UP

I. In the Beginning: From Conception to Birth

A. Your mother's and father's genes recombined when their eggs and sperm were formed, and you received half of your chromosomes from your mother's egg and half from your father's sperm, leading you to have a unique combination of genes. The development of both the brain and the body relies on the activation of specific genes, which is regulated in part by environmental events.

B. Prenatal development progresses in order through a series of stages; in the first trimester (3 months), the zygote becomes an embryo, then a fetus.

C. The developing fetus is active and becomes increasingly coordinated over time. The fetus can detect human speech and prefers the mother's voice.

D. Maturational processes can be disrupted by teratogens or enhanced by certain environmental events, such as those that reduce the level of stress experienced by the mother.

E. Newborns have a relatively good sense of smell and can learn that different stimuli tend to occur together. They have the sensory capacities needed to organize sounds into words and recognize objects. Newborns are equipped with a host of inborn reflexes, such as the sucking and Moro reflexes. These reflexes often disappear during the course of development.

F. Aspects of temperament that are present at birth may persist for many years to come.

II. Infancy and Childhood: Taking Off

A. In general, motor development progresses from the head, down the trunk to the arms, and finally to the legs; at the same time, it proceeds out from the center of the body to the periphery (hands, fingers, and toes).

B. Perception develops so that the child can make finer discriminations, needs less stimulus information to recognize objects, can focus attention more deliberately, and can search more systematically.

C. Young children learn language without explicit instruction. Language is acquired gradually over time, but there seems to be a critical period for learning grammar.

D. Even 3-month-old infants have both implicit and explicit memory. Not all aspects of memory develop at the same rate. Although perceptual memory is present before verbal memory, not all aspects of perceptual memory change with age in the same way.

E. Piaget believed that each child moves through a series of major periods of cognitive development. However, these stages may not be fixed, and many abilities are evident at earlier ages than originally believed. Researchers have since found that children have at least the rudiments of many abilities far earlier than Piaget's theory would predict.

F. Cognitive development arises in part from improved information processing, particularly more efficient working memory, which probably in part reflects neural development. However, as Vygotsky stressed, culture and instruction also play a role in cognitive development.

G. Children become attached to their caregivers through a series of stages, but may end up being attached in different ways.

H. The self-concept begins to develop during very early infancy, and it probably affects many social interactions, including gender roles.

I. People may move through a series of stages in the way they tend to reason about moral decisions, and males and females may tend to reason slightly differently about such decisions—but this is most likely a function of their different concerns in daily life, not something intrinsic to their gender. The conscience governs moral behavior and may develop early in life (at around 3 years old).

III. Adolescence: Between Two Worlds

A. The extremities (arms and legs) grow rapidly during adolescence, with the trunk lagging behind, a pattern that can produce a gawky appearance. During this period, the body acquires pubic hair and other secondary sexual characteristics. Puberty occurs earlier today than it did previously.

B. If the adolescent reaches Piaget's period of formal operations, he or she can reason about abstract concepts systematically—and thus becomes capable of true scientific thought. This enhanced reasoning ability affects all aspects of thinking, including conceptions of self.

C. Enhanced cognitive capacities during adolescence allow the teenager to think about relationships in more sophisticated ways, but adolescents are also affected by their perceptions of an imaginary audience and a personal fable.

D. Although hormonal changes can lead the adolescent to experience more conflicts with parents as well as to have mood swings and to tend to take risks, these tendencies are not universal.

E. Most adolescents develop strong same-gender friendships, but these bonds tend to be stronger among young women than young men.

IV. Adulthood and Aging: The Continuously Changing Self

A. The body remains relatively stable until around age 50. At about this point, women experience menopause, and both men and women may begin to become less vigorous. Many of the changes in the body can be treated, either by dietary supplements (such as calcium for bone weakness) or with changes in activities (which can reduce obesity and strengthen bones).

B. With age, the lens of the eye clouds, and the pupil doesn't open as much as it did before, leading to difficulty in seeing contrast. The elderly also have difficulty hearing higher-frequency sounds, and their sense of smell declines.

C. With advancing old age, working memory operates less effectively, and memory retrieval becomes more difficult.

D. Although intelligence declines with advanced age, fluid intelligence may be more affected than crystallized intelligence. In some respects, the elderly can reason more logically than younger people.

E. Many theorists, especially Erikson, have proposed that people pass through psychosocial stages as they age. These stages may reflect particular issues that need to be resolved. There is little evidence that personality changes substantially during adulthood.

F. Adult relationships focus on closer involvement with fewer people (often relatives) and tend to be stable over long periods of time. The elderly tend to have greater emotional control than younger people.

G. In old age, the brain may not function as well as it did before, in part because the person is no longer being intellectually challenged; enrichment of the environment can in part reverse this decline.

Key Terms

accommodation, p. 393
adolescence, p. 404
assimilation, p. 392
attachment, p. 397
child-directed speech (CDS), p. 388
concrete operation, p. 395
conservation, p. 394
critical period, p. 391
cross-sectional study, p. 413
egocentrism, p. 394
embryo, p. 378

fetus, p. 378
formal operation, p. 395
gender roles, p. 400
grammar, p. 390
language acquisition device (LAD), p. 388
longitudinal study, p. 413
maturation, p. 377
moral dilemma, p. 401
nativism, p. 388
object permanence, p. 393

overextension, p. 390
overregularization error, p. 390
psychosocial development, p. 414
puberty, p. 404
schema, p. 392
self-concept, p. 399
separation anxiety, p. 398
telegraphic speech, p. 390
teratogen, p. 379
underextension, p. 390
zygote, p. 377

LOOKING ONLINE: *Enhance Your Learning*

MyPsychLab is an interactive and instructive multimedia resource that can be used to supplement a traditional lecture course or as an online course. It is an all-inclusive tool with a text-specific e-book plus multimedia tutorials, videos, simulations, animations, and controlled assessment to completely engage students and reinforce learning. MyPsychLab meets the individual learning needs of every student. Visit *www.mypsychlab.com* for more information!

Practice Test

For each of the following items, choose the single best answer.

1. At the moment of conception,
    a. a sperm penetrates an ovum.
    b. a zygote becomes a gamete.
    c. the ovum is a passive recipient.
    d. the egg changes its surface properties and activates the sperm.

2. Human development in the womb is divided into trimesters. At the end of the second trimester,
    a. the zygote becomes an embryo when the major axis of the body is present.
    b. the embryo becomes a fetus when all major body structures are present.
    c. the great bulk of the neurons each individual possesses are in place and are completely fixed.
    d. the great bulk of the neurons each individual possesses are in place, but they are not completely fixed.

3. As fetuses develop,
    a. their heart rates speed up.
    b. their heart rates become less variable.
    c. they move less often but more vigorously when they do stir.
    d. they become sensitive to both sound and light after 2 weeks of gestation.

4. Babies
    a. are born sensitive to the range of frequencies of women's voices.
    b. have a relatively sensitive sense of smell.
    c. prefer the odor of a woman who is breast-feeding another infant to that of a women who is not breast-feeding.
    d. All of the above statements are true.

5. Compared to infants who sleep on their bellies, those who sleep on their backs
    a. have an increased chance of sudden infant death syndrome (SIDS).
    b. are more likely to crawl at an earlier age.
    c. are more likely to walk at an earlier age.
    d. are more likely to skip the step of crawling and go right to walking.

6. At the approximate age of 2–5 months, babies can
    a. roll over, sit upright, and pick up small objects with the thumb and fingers.
    b. follow movements with their eyes, hold their heads steady, and hold an object placed in their hands.
    c. turn pages of a book and "cruise" (walk by supporting their body against objects).
    d. All of the above statements are true.

7. Infants who are 3 months old
    a. cannot store information implicitly.
    b. cannot store information explicitly.
    c. have completed their perceptual development.
    d. can see three-dimensional shapes instead of isolated line fragments.

8. An example of an overregularization error children make is
    a. saying *runned* instead of *ran*.
    b. calling a sawhorse a "dog."
    c. only referring to dogs with the word "animal."
    d. leaving out words such as *the*, *a*, and *of*.

9. According to Piaget's theory of cognitive development, during the preoperational period,
    a. the child tends to be between 7 and 11 years old.
    b. the child is not capable of thinking about objects in their absence.
    c. language and symbolic play develop, but thought is still tied to perceived events.
    d. the child can reverse mental manipulations.

10. To be able to reason abstractly, Piaget said, the child must
    a. be capable of concrete operations.
    b. be capable of formal operations.
    c. be capable of egocentrism.
    d. not understand conservation.

11. In studies using the Strange Situation, babies with resistant attachment
    a. have periods of unresponsiveness along with spurts of sudden emotion at the end of the procedure.
    b. are equally comfortable with the mother and a stranger.

c. may go so far as to hit the mother when she returns.

d. calm down quickly when the mother returns.

12. Girls

a. who are overweight tend to experience their first periods before those who are not overweight.

b. who are overweight tend to experience their first periods after those who are not overweight.

c. typically are shorter and lighter at age 11 than boys at that age because girls' major growth spurt starts about 2 years after that of boys.

d. typically stop growing at around age 18.

13. There is a normal tendency for adolescents to

a. have conflicts with their parents.

b. experience extreme mood swings.

c. be prone to taking risks.

d. All of the above statements are true.

14. After age 50 or so,

a. people tend to exhibit terminal decline.

b. people perform all cognitive tasks more slowly than do younger people.

c. people have increased difficulty hearing high-frequency sounds.

d. more than half the population has cataracts.

15. Costa and McCrae found that as adults age, dimensions of personality

a. change dramatically, with very large differences.

b. are more stable over time for men than they are for women.

c. are more stable over time for women than they are for men.

d. remain equally stable over time for men and women.

• •

Answers: 1. a 2. d 3. c 4. d 5. d 6. b 7. d 8. a 9. c 10. b 11. c 12. a 13. d 14. c 15. d

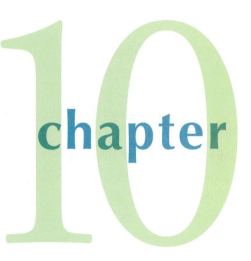

chapter 10

Stress, Health, and Coping
Dealing With Life

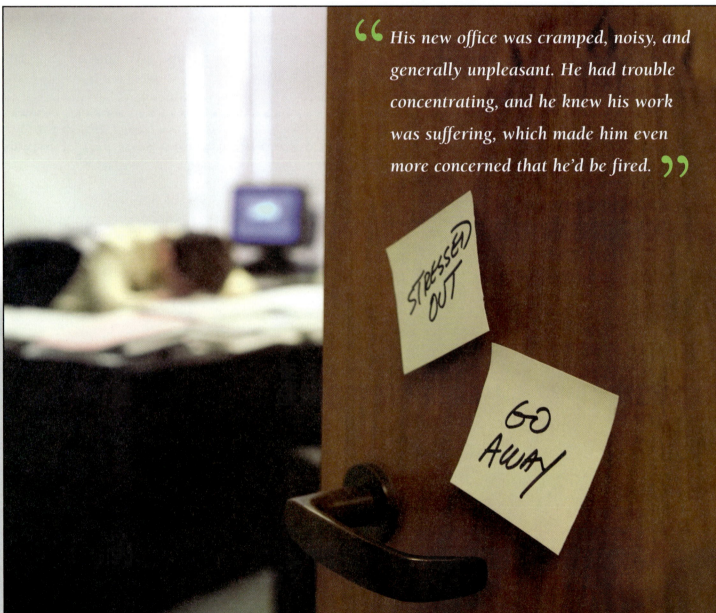

" His new office was cramped, noisy, and generally unpleasant. He had trouble concentrating, and he knew his work was suffering, which made him even more concerned that he'd be fired. "

STRESSED OUT

GO AWAY

CHAPTER OUTLINE

What Is Stress?

Stress, Disease, and Health

Strategies for Coping

Let's Sum It Up

LISA, A COLLEGE SOPHOMORE, WAS BECOMING WORRIED ABOUT HER FATHER, AL. ONLY 54 years old, he always seemed exhausted, regardless of the time of day or the amount of work he'd been doing. Whenever Lisa asked him why he was so tired, he answered in generalities: "Oh, work's crazy. That's all, honey." He'd also been coughing a lot, and when Lisa asked about this, he'd reply, "I've been sick more than usual—it's just been a bad winter."

Lisa used to look forward to her visits home and her telephone conversations with her father, but now she dreaded talking to him because he always sounded so tired and dejected. Lisa suggested that he see his doctor, exercise, maybe learn some type of relaxation technique. Al finally told her the real reason he was so tense and tired: His company had laid off several of his colleagues, and he was afraid he'd be next. The layoffs meant that Al's department was now responsible for more work with less staff. In addition, as part of the downsizing, the company had moved to smaller premises. His new office was cramped, noisy, and generally unpleasant. He had trouble concentrating, and he knew his work was suffering, which made him even more concerned that he'd be fired. There was a possibility of a job offer from another company, but at a substantially lower salary. Lisa, listening to his story, understood that he had tried to protect her by not telling her. If he was fired or took the other job, he wouldn't be able to help with her college expenses, and she was already working 25 hours a week. If Al's fears materialized, she would probably have to leave school, at least for a while, or take out very large loans. He was worried about his own situation, and worried about his daughter; Lisa understood the burden of those worries, which she now shared. She worried, too, about his persistent cough—was it just from lots of winter colds, or was it something more?

This situation produced stress in both father and daughter. Just what is "stress"? Can it affect our health? How can we deal with it? Such questions, and the search for answers, are in the domain of **health psychology**, the field concerned with the promotion of health and the prevention and treatment of illness as it relates to psychological factors.

What Is Stress?

Al began to hate going to work. Often, as he worked at his desk, he felt as if he'd just finished a race—heart beating, palms sweating, breath coming hard—but without any accompanying sense of relief or accomplishment. He was simply exhausted all of the time and felt as if his heart wasn't pumping his blood fast enough for his body's needs. He began to be seriously worried about his health, as well as his job.

In contrast, Maya, a colleague who so far had also survived at the company, didn't seem disturbed by the changes happening around them. Maya had two children and, like Al, needed her job, but she seemed to be taking this difficult situation in stride. Al didn't understand how Maya was able to stay so calm—didn't she understand what was going on?

And what about Lisa's response to pressures? She had been managing the demands of college and job well; but after her father explained his situation at work and the possible repercussions for both of them, she noticed physical symptoms in herself—sweaty palms, racing heart—even while studying or taking class notes. Al and Lisa were responding to stress.

LOOKING AHEAD: *Learning Objectives*

1. *What exactly is stress?*
2. *What is the biology of stress?*
3. *What role does the perception of control play in stress?*
4. *What are common sources of stress?*

Health psychology: The field concerned with the promotion of health and the prevention and treatment of illness as it relates to psychological factors.

Stress: The general term describing the psychological and physical response to a stimulus that alters the body's state of equilibrium.

Stress: The Big Picture

Today, even third graders complain of feeling "stressed out," and adults take evening courses in "stress management." But what exactly *is* stress? **Stress** is the general term describing the psychological and physical response to a stimulus

Table 10.1 Examples of Types of Stressors

Type of Stressor	Duration of Stressor	
	Acute	Chronic
Physical	Being injured in a car crash	Being underfed; having cancer
Psychological (level of the person)	Working against a deadline	Chronically feeling pressured by work
Social	Being humiliated	Chronic isolation; overcrowding

that alters the body's equilibrium (Lazarus & Folkman, 1984). The stimulus that throws the body's equilibrium out of balance is called a **stressor**; for instance, stepping on a piece of glass while walking barefoot and getting a puncture wound is a stressor. The body's response to a stressor is the **stress response**, also called the *fight-or-flight response*; this response consists of the bodily changes that occur to help you cope with the stressor. If you get a puncture wound, your body may produce chemicals called *endorphins* and *enkephalins*, its own versions of painkillers, and cause white blood cells to congregate at the site of the injury to fight off any infectious agents. These responses work to bring the body back to normal, to restore homeostasis.

The long list of potential stressors is categorized according to a number of criteria (Table 10.1). Stressors can be short-term (**acute stressor**) or long-term (**chronic stressor**); they can be physical, psychological (which affect events at the level of the person), or social (or, of course, some combination). Physical stressors, such as not eating for 2 days, generally apply to most people; psychological and social stressors, on the other hand, can be much more subjective. Going to a dance club for hours can be a party animal's idea of a great time or a shy person's nightmare. In general, it is our *perception* of a stimulus that determines whether it will elicit the stress response, not necessarily the objective nature of the stimulus itself.

Stress is not always a negative process, however. Stress, or more accurately, stressors, can lead to positive change and growth (Linley & Joseph, 2004). Consider that college students reported that their most stressful experience during the previous 6 months had led to personal growth (Park & Fenster, 2004).

The Biology of Stress

Austrian-born researcher Hans Selye (1907–1982), who pioneered the study of stress, established that the body responds to stressors in generally predictable ways (Selye, 1976). He called the overall stress response the **general adaptation syndrome (GAS)** and suggested that it has three distinct phases: alarm, resistance, and exhaustion (Figure 10.1, on p. 428).

The Alarm Phase: Fight or Flight

Perception of a stressor triggers the **alarm phase**, which is characterized by the fight-or-flight response. In this response, the body mobilizes itself to fight or to flee from a threatening stimulus, which can be a physical threat, such as a knife at the throat, or a psychological one, such as working against a deadline.

Stressor: A stimulus that throws the body's equilibrium out of balance.

Stress response: The bodily changes that occur to help a person cope with a stressor; also called the *fight-or-flight response*.

Acute stressor: A stressor of short-term duration.

Chronic stressor: A stressor of long-term duration.

General adaptation syndrome (GAS): The overall stress response that has three phases: alarm, resistance, and exhaustion.

Alarm phase: The first phase of the GAS, in which a stressor is perceived and the fight-or-flight response is activated.

Figure 10.1 Selye's Three-Stage Stress Response

The body mobilizes its resources to fight or flee.

The body mobilizes its resources to achieve homeostasis in the presence of the stressor.

Continued efforts to achieve homeostasis lead to exhaustion and damage of the body.

Hans Selye proposed that the body's response to prolonged stress has three stages: alarm, resistance, and exhaustion.

When you perceive a threat, your brain, via the hypothalamic-pituitary-adrenal axis (the HPA axis), responds to the threat by activating the sympathetic nervous system and inhibiting the parasympathetic nervous system (see Chapter 2). Neurotransmitters and hormonal secretions such as epinephrine and norepinephrine (also referred to as adrenaline and noradrenaline, respectively) cause breathing, heart rate, and blood pressure to increase and can alter immune system functioning (Madden, 2003). (Note that norepinephrine is considered a neurotransmitter when it is found in the brain, but a hormone when dispersed in other parts of the body.) These changes serve to bring more oxygen to the muscles as you prepare to fight or flee. In addition, these sympathetic nervous system changes cause your pupils to dilate (allowing more light to enter for greater visual acuity) and your palms to sweat slightly (for better gripping).

When the stress response is triggered, the hypothalamus secretes a substance that causes the release of **glucocorticoids**, another group of hormones. *Cortisol*, a glucocorticoid, not only increases the production of energy from glucose, but also has an anti-inflammatory effect, which makes it effective in helping restore the body's equilibrium after physical injury. In the short run, all of these changes sharpen the senses, improve some qualities of memory (Sapolsky, 1997), and make it easier to fight or flee. Cortisol also affects neurotransmitter functioning, and thus it can affect cognition and emotion (Erickson et al., 2003); the changes in neurotransmitter functioning may account for the emotional responses and changes in thinking that can occur in extremely stressful situations.

Selye proposed that the fight-or-flight response, and the GAS more generally, is the same regardless of the nature of the stressor. Research since Selye's time indicates that this aspect of his theory was off the mark: Although the general stress response occurs with all stressors, the speed of its action and the amount of each hormone that is produced can differ, depending on the particular type of stressor (Goldstein, 1995; Henry, 1977; Pacak & Palkovits, 2001; Romero & Sapolsky, 1996).

For most of us, the threats we experience do not require the kind of *physical* response required of our distant ancestors. Taking a final exam requires sitting in a chair, not running or climbing away from an enemy. Nonetheless, your body may still react to the test-taking situation with the fight-or-flight response; it can get all revved up with nowhere to go.

The Resistance Phase

Once your body is primed to fight or flee, you enter the **resistance phase** (also known as the *adaptation phase*), in which the body mobilizes its resources to achieve equilibrium despite the continued presence of the stressor. In other words, it *adapts* to the stressor.

Both the initial stress response and the resistance phase require energy, which comes from fat cells, muscles, and the liver. The increased blood flow (which results from increased heart and respiration rates) helps deliver the energy quickly and efficiently to the parts of the body that need it most. Digestion, growth, sex drive, and reproductive processes are slowed during times of stress.

Glucocorticoids: A group of hormones that are released when the stress response is triggered.

Resistance phase: The second phase of the GAS, in which the body mobilizes its resources to achieve equilibrium, despite the continued presence of the stressor; also called the *adaptation phase*.

In women, menstruation may stop or may occur irregularly in response to chronic stress; in men, sperm and testosterone levels may decrease. As a matter of survival, why waste energy on these processes when it is needed elsewhere? In addition to these changes, no new energy is stored during stress; this means that chronic stress leads to a lack of any reserve of energy to repair bodily damage, producing a sense of fatigue.

During the resistance phase, cortisol helps the body return to a more normal state in the presence of a continued stressor (McEwen & Schmeck, 1994). Cortisol levels reach their peak within 20–40 minutes after the onset of the acute stressor, and they return to baseline, on average, up to 1 hour after the acute stressor has been eliminated (Dickerson & Kemeny, 2002); however, with continued stress, cortisol levels may not return to baseline. The more extreme the stressors, the more glucocorticoids are produced in an attempt to restore equilibrium, and this process decreases the functioning of the immune system.

The Exhaustion Phase

If the stressor continues, the <mark>exhaustion phase</mark> sets in. Selye proposed that, with a continued stressor, the body becomes exhausted because its limited resources for dealing with stress are depleted. More recent research has found that rather than producing "exhaustion," the continued stress response begins to damage the body, leading to an increased risk of stress-related diseases. In addition, cortisol can damage hippocampal cells (see Chapter 5), decreasing the number of these cells as well as the amount of branching of some of their dendrites (McEwen, 2003); such changes adversely affect learning and memory (Newcomer et al., 1999; Sapolsky, 1992).

From Stressor to Allostatic Load: Multiple Stressors and Their Time Course

The term *allostasis* (from the Greek *allo*, meaning "other," and *stasis* meaning "stability") refers to the multiple biological changes that allow you to adapt to a stressor or a set of stressors in the short run, so your body functions within a comfortable range. Although adaptive in the short run, maintaining equilibrium within a comfortable range through biological changes has a cost—cumulative wear and tear, referred to as the *allostatic load*. Allostatic load is the stress carried by the body to maintain equilibrium (McEwen, 1998, 2000; McEwen & Wingfield, 2003). As the number or intensity of stressors rises, so does the allostatic load.

Here's an analogy: Say you have a wooden seesaw, of the sort you see in playgrounds the world over. If two 40-pound children are on it, there's relatively little load. But what if two 400-pound gorillas were to sit on the ends? Although the seesaw could still be in balance, it would be under much greater stress. And just as the probability that the seesaw will break increases when it is put under greater stress, so too with the body; greater allostatic load increases the risk of medical and psychological symptoms (Goldstein & McEwen, 2002). When you must fight or flee, more demands are made on your body than during calmer times; chronic demands (high allostatic load) will produce biological wear and tear, lessen the body's ability to respond appropriately, and possibly lead to disease or illness (Karlamangla et al., 2002; Seeman, Singer, et al., 1997). And just as the seesaw would be in greater jeopardy if those gorillas played on it for an hour instead of a minute, chronic stressors take more toll on your body than do time-limited stressors (Evans, 2003).

Exhaustion phase: The final stage of the GAS, in which the continued stress response itself becomes damaging to the body.

It's How You Think of It: Interpreting Stimuli as Stressors

Is a new relationship stressful? How about writing a term paper? Hearing a baby cry? Being stuck in a traffic jam? The answer to all of these is maybe, maybe not. Many psychological, social, and even physical stimuli are stressors only if you *perceive* them as stressful (Lazarus & Folkman, 1984).

Appraisal: Stressors in the Eyes of the Beholder

Physical stressors, such as a piece of glass stuck in your bare foot, are generally easy to identify, but the definition of a psychological or social stressor is more subjective. Al's colleague Maya is not bothered about the recent firings because she wants to spend more time with her children. In some respects, she wouldn't mind being out of work (and collecting unemployment) so that she could stay home for a while; between savings and her husband's paycheck, the family could get by for a few months. So, for Maya, the threat of being fired is not perceived as a stressor.

The importance of perceptions in determining whether something is a stressor was demonstrated in a classic study by Speisman and colleagues (1964). Participants were asked to watch a film of a primitive ritual involving a crude genital operation called "subincision." Participants in one group heard a "trauma" soundtrack for the film that emphasized the pain experienced by those undergoing the rite. Another group heard a "denial" soundtrack, which emphasized the positive aspects of the ritual and minimized the experience of pain. A third group heard an "intellectualization" soundtrack, which described the ceremony in a detached, clinical manner. Those in either the denial or the intellectualization group showed less of an autonomic response to the film and reported being less upset than those in the trauma group. This study demonstrated that the content of the narration about the ritual (the context, and therefore how the stimulus is perceived) affected the stress response of the participants.

As illustrated in Figure 10.2, this process of *cognitive appraisal* of a stimulus occurs in two phases. First, the stimulus is assessed for the likelihood of danger; this is the *primary appraisal*. This assessment is followed by the *secondary appraisal*, the determination of the resources available to deal with the stressor. In other words, the question "Am I in danger?" is followed by the question "What can I do about it?" (Bishop, 1994). (Note, however, that such appraisals can happen without conscious awareness; Smith & Kirby, 2000.) After the secondary appraisal comes coping; that is, the person experiencing stress takes some course of action regarding the stressor, its effects, or his or her reaction to it.

Depending on how you appraise a stimulus, you will experience different emotions and your body will react in different ways (Maier et al., 2003). For instance, should you determine that you have the resources—emotional, financial, and practical—to cope with a stressor, you will likely view the stressor as a challenge, not a threat. In contrast, should you determine that you do not have the resources to cope, you probably will view the stressor as a threat (Blascovich & Tomaka, 1996). In addition, should your cognitive appraisal lead you to conclude

Even among college students, what is considered stressful differs, depending on whether the student is traditional (went to college straight from high school) or nontraditional (took some time off between high school and college, or has multiple roles, such as student and parent or employee). Social activities have a larger impact on traditional students, whereas nontraditional students are more likely to enjoy doing homework and going to classes and to worry less about how they are doing academically (Dill & Henley, 1998).

Coping: Taking some course of action regarding the stressor, its effects, or the person's reaction to it.

Figure 10.2 Cognitive Appraisal of a Stimulus

Cognitive appraisal of a stimulus, in this case a snake, is a two-stage process: (1) determining whether a stimulus is dangerous, and, if so, (2) determining what can be done to prevent or minimize the danger.

that a stimulus is dangerous, negative emotions will be triggered—and these emotions then become a part of the problem that you must address with your coping strategies (Folkman & Moscowitz, 2004).

Perceived Control

How do you think you would feel if your boss told you to get a project finished a day earlier than you had planned: Do you think you would experience less pressure if you had decided, all by yourself, to finish the project earlier? What if your boss had actually made the decision but gave you the impression that the final decision was yours? Research has shown that actual control is not important; what is important is whether you *perceive* a sense of control (Shapiro et al., 1996). The perception of control can affect your performance. Perceived lack of control in the face of a stressor can lead to the onset of *learned helplessness* (Overmier, 2002; see Chapter 7). When animals cannot escape being shocked, they may respond with learned helplessness and depression. This is also true for humans who feel that they have no control in an aversive situation.

Cultural factors can affect people's perception of control. Western cultures, particularly that of the United States, emphasize active control of yourself and mastery of your environment. Some other cultures emphasize adaptation—accepting yourself and your circumstances (Shapiro et al., 1996), as when a train is very late.

Not everyone is equally eager to feel in control; in fact, some people experience more stress when they perceive themselves as having more control. For example, some cancer patients find that taking responsibility for and control of their medical treatment is overwhelming and stressful. Researchers looking at the role of social class in the perception of control and health found that, not surprisingly, people with lower incomes perceived less control in their lives *and* were in poorer health. Those who did have a greater sense of control, regardless of income, had better health (Lachman & Weaver, 1998).

Even for people who prefer to have more control, perceiving a lack of control doesn't always produce stress. This apparent contradiction is resolved by another factor: Many things that are beyond our control are at least *predictable*. You have no control over whether or not you take math quizzes (at least, not if you want to pass the course), but announced quizzes are likely to be less stressful than surprise quizzes. If quizzes are announced, you can relax on the days when none are scheduled; in contrast, the possibility of surprise quizzes means that the beginning of every class can be stressful as you wait to learn your fate. However, if surprise quizzes are a frequent occurrence in a course, you will habituate to them and not view them to be as great a stressor—the quizzes, unpleasant as they might be, will no longer be so unpredictable.

In general, perceived control is helpful only when you can see how much worse things could have been; then you can feel positive about what you have controlled. In the face of a catastrophic stressor, such as the diagnosis of a terminal illness, perceived control actually *increases* the stress: Things can't be much worse, and if the person given the diagnosis has perceived control, he or she may feel responsible for the catastrophic stressor (Pitman et al., 1995; Sapolsky, 1997).

Sources of Stress

Psychologists have found that certain types of stimuli are more likely to be appraised as stressful. That is, certain events and situations are more likely to lead to a stress response.

Internal Conflict

Stress can be caused by **internal conflict**, the emotional predicament people experience when they make difficult choices. The choices may involve competing goals, actions, impulses, or situations. Miller (1959) categorized three types of internal conflict. **Approach–approach conflict** results when competing alternatives are equally positive. Although this kind of conflict can be stressful, it is not necessarily experienced as unpleasant because both options are pleasing. For instance, if you had to choose between two very good job offers and wanted both jobs about equally, you would be facing an approach–approach conflict. The contrary case is **avoidance–avoidance conflict**, which results when competing alternatives are equally unpleasant. In such circumstances, making a choice can be very stressful. Faced with the choice of either taking a job you really don't want or being unemployed (and needing to pay back college loans), you would experience an avoidance–avoidance conflict. The third type of internal conflict, **approach–avoidance conflict**, occurs when a possible course of action has both positive and negative aspects and thus produces *both* approach *and* avoidance. If you were offered a job that you wanted but that would require you to move to a city in which you didn't want to live, you would experience approach–avoidance conflict.

Internal conflict: The emotional predicament people experience when making difficult choices.

Approach–approach conflict: The internal conflict that occurs when competing alternatives are equally positive.

Avoidance–avoidance conflict: The internal conflict that occurs when competing alternatives are equally unpleasant.

Approach–avoidance conflict: The internal conflict that occurs when a course of action has both positive and negative aspects.

Life's Hassles

In the 1960s, researchers began to explore the stressfulness of various life experiences. These investigations led to the idea that certain events, such as divorce or job loss, were stressful for almost everyone (Holmes & Rahe, 1967). What was perhaps more surprising was the finding that positive events, such as vacations and job promotions, could also be stressors. Subsequent research, however, has not shown these kinds of events, positive or negative, to be reliable predictors of stress-related illness. Because this original line of research focused on the events themselves and not the *perception* of the events, it was not, in fact, a valid way to measure life's stressors. More recent work has focused on life's daily hassles, rather than major changes in life circumstances, as better predicting distress and stress-related illnesses (Chamberlain & Zika, 1990; Tein et al., 2000).

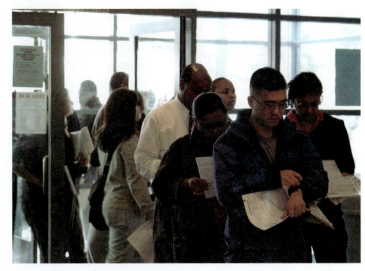

Life's daily hassles can be significant stressors, leading to psychological and physical symptoms.

All of the daily hassles—the "little things" (which are sometimes not so little but ongoing), such as concern about the health of someone in your family, having too many things to do, misplacing or losing things, trying to lose weight—add up to create stress. Those who report more daily hassles also report more psychological problems (D'Angelo & Wierzbicki, 2003; Kanner et al., 1981; Mroczek & Almeida, 2004) and physical symptoms (DeLongis et al., 1982), and they are more likely to experience problems with the immune system (Bosch et al., 1998; Martin & Dobbin, 1988; Peters et al., 2003) as well as higher cholesterol levels (Twisk et al., 1999).

Interruptions are another feature of daily life that can be a stressor. Think of how you feel when you're trying to study or write a paper and are repeatedly interrupted by phone calls or visitors. If your reaction is to feel more "stressed out," you're not alone. Interruptions during a mentally challenging task can be stressful enough to cause large increases in cortisol levels (Earle et al., 1999; Suarez et al., 1998). Note that e-mail "interruptions" may not feel as stressful because you choose—that is, control—when to check your e-mail.

Hostility

Although some work and home environments may be more stressful than others, some people seem to experience stress more than others, regardless of their circumstances. Cardiologists Meyer Friedman and Ray Rosenman (1974) studied men who had coronary heart disease and discovered a common set of traits, including a sense of urgency, competitiveness, and interpersonal hostility. Friedman and Rosenman called this constellation of traits *Type A personality*. Subsequent research was unable to obtain the same clear-cut findings relating Type A personality to the incidence of coronary heart disease, but investigators were able to refine the concept of a stressed, heart disease–prone personality (Hecker et al., 1988). The most important component of the Type A personality in predicting heart disease is

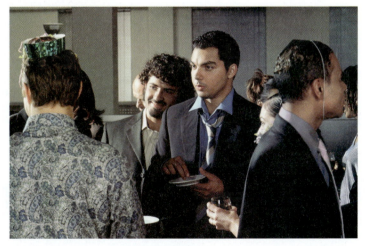

Hostile people are more likely to perceive stressors in situations in which nonhostile people do not perceive stressors (Hardy & Smith, 1988; Suarez & Williams, 1989).

Hostility: The personality trait associated with heart disease and characterized by mistrust, an expectation of harm and provocation by others, and a cynical attitude.

hostility, a trait characterized by mistrust, an expectation of harm and provocation by others, and a cynical attitude (Hart & Hope, 2004; Miller et al., 1996; Smith & Ruiz, 2002; Williams, Paton, et al., 2000). For instance, Barefoot and his colleagues (1983) found that medical students who scored in the top 20% on a hostility scale were more than four times as likely to develop heart disease 25 years later as were their low-hostility peers. Those same high-hostility doctors were seven times more likely than their low-hostility peers to die of any cause by age 50. Further research (Barefoot et al., 1989) found that, among lawyers, increased mortality was associated with an untrusting and cynical view of people, repeated negative emotions in personal interactions, and recurrent expressions of overt anger and aggression in the face of difficulties or frustrations. Other studies have found a similar link between hostility and risk factors for heart disease (Knox et al., 2004; Kop, 2003).

Men are generally more hostile than women (Miller et al., 1999; Räikkönen et al., 1999), and researchers found that even at the same level of hostility, men's blood pressure is more affected by their hostility than is women's (Räikkönen et al., 1999). When interrupted while concentrating on a task, highly hostile men had elevated heart rates, blood pressure, and cortisol production, as well as exhibiting other changes associated with a negative mood such as anger (Suarez et al., 1998). Regardless of their sex, people high in hostility are more likely to have a higher heart rate and blood pressure throughout the day, no matter what their mood. In contrast, people low in hostility showed cardiac changes only when they were in a negative mood (Davis et al., 2000; Räikkönen et al., 1999).

Hostility need not be a lifelong trait. Cognitive and behavioral programs (see Chapter 12) designed to help reduce anger levels can reduce not only hostility (Beck & Fernandez, 1998) and anger (DiGiuseppe & Tafrate, 2003), but also anger-related autonomic arousal and blood pressure increases (Gidron et al., 1999); these changes were generally maintained 1 year after the end of a 5-week program (Deffenbacher et al., 1996).

LOOKING BACK: *Review*

1. *What exactly is stress?* Stress is the general term describing the psychological and bodily response to a stimulus that alters a person's state of equilibrium. A stressor is a stimulus that throws the body's equilibrium out of balance. Stressors can be acute or chronic in duration and physical, psychological, or social in nature.

2. *What is the biology of stress?* The stress response consists of changes in the activity of the sympathetic and parasympathetic nervous systems that prepare the body for physical effort and repair injury. These include changes in heart and respiration rates and the release of epinephrine, norepinephrine, and glucocorticoids. These changes occur during the alarm phase of the general adaptation syndrome (GAS). If the stressor continues, the body tries to return to equilibrium in the resistance (adaptation) phase. During the exhaustion phase, the stress response itself begins to cause damage, leading to a risk of stress-related diseases.

3. *What role does the perception of control play in stress?* Determining whether a given stimulus is a stressor influences whether the stress response will occur; this is often called primary appraisal. Moreover, even among stimuli that are appraised as stressors, some stimuli can cause more stress than others. A perceived lack of control over the stimulus can lead to higher levels of stress.

4. *What are common sources of stress?* Certain factors likely to lead to a stress response include unpredictability, internal conflict, and daily hassles. Some people are more stress-prone than others: Hostile people are more likely than others to view social situations as stressors.

LOOKING BEYOND: *Critical Thinking*

Suppose that you have several job offers upon graduation from college. All of them have advantages, and all of them have drawbacks. Would this be a stressful situation? Why or why not? What specific factors about the job offers would make you more likely to experience the choice as stressful? What factors would make the choice seem less stressful?

Stress, Disease, and Health

Al was clearly experiencing a great deal of stress, and his being sick so often only made matters worse. He'd had to miss work some days, which didn't help his sense of control in his difficult situation. Sometimes he'd cough so much that he would have trouble sleeping, and then he'd lie awake worrying that he had lung cancer. He had started smoking again, after having quit 5 years before, so it was hard to know whether the more frequent colds and coughs were from the cigarettes or from the stress of work. He'd been having a few more drinks than usual, and he wasn't getting any exercise; he worried that if he started exercising, he'd bring on a heart attack. In short, Al wasn't doing very well, and he knew it.

The stress response is a good thing, very useful when the stressor is acute, such as a piece of glass in the foot; but there can be too much of a good thing. Too strong a stress response for too long a time—too great an allostatic load—can lead to stress-related illness.

B cell: A type of white blood cell that matures in the bone marrow.

T cell: A type of white blood cell that matures in the thymus.

Natural killer (NK) cell: A type of T cell that detects and destroys damaged or altered cells, such as precancerous cells.

LOOKING AHEAD: *Learning Objectives*

1. *Can stress affect the immune system and make illness more likely?*
2. *Are stress and cancer related?*
3. *Can stress cause a heart attack or heart disease?*
4. *What is the relationship between sleep and stress?*

The Immune System: Catching Cold

No question about it: Stress can affect the immune system, which functions to defend the body against infection. Critical to the immune system are two classes of white blood cells: **B cells**, which mature in the bone marrow, and **T cells**, which mature in the thymus, an organ located in the chest. One type of T cell is the **natural killer (NK) cell**, which detects and destroys damaged or altered cells, such as precancerous cells before they become tumors. Glucocorticoids, which are released when the stress response is triggered, hinder the formation of some white blood cells (including NK cells) or kill other white blood cells (Cohen & Herbert, 1996; McEwen et al., 1997), making the body more vulnerable to infection and tumor growth. For this reason, many studies investigating the relationship between

The immune system's job is to fend off infectious agents such as viruses or precancerous cells. The release of glucocorticoids (as occurs during stress) suppresses the functioning of the immune system, making it more difficult for the body to fight the invaders and leaving the body more vulnerable to infection. This photo shows two natural killer (NK) cells (yellow) attacking a leukemia cell (red). The NK cells have made contact and are beginning to engulf and destroy the leukemia cell.

A study of allergic responses found that, among Japanese couples who do not habitually kiss, kissing privately for up to 30 minutes increased their immune responses (Kimata, 2003). Could this be a new stress reduction technique?

stress and the immune system measure the number of circulating white blood cells, such as NK cells. People who exhibit greater sympathetic nervous system responses to stress also show the most changes in immune system functioning (Bachen et al., 1995; Manuck et al., 1991), indicating that changes in the immune system are moderated by changes in the sympathetic nervous system. Exposure to some chronic psychological stressors can increase inflammation and the risk for autoimmune disorders (G. E. Miller et al., 2002).

A field called *psychoneuroimmunology* focuses on the ways in which mental and emotional states affect the immune system. For example, researchers have found that traditional elderly Chinese are more likely to die right after the Harvest Moon festival, an important event in their culture, than just before it, whereas orthodox Jews show no difference in mortality rates during this period. However, the pattern is exactly reversed around the High Holy Days, the most important days in the Jewish year; it is now the Jews who hold on until the holidays are over and the Chinese who are unaffected (Phillips & Smith, 1990; Phillips et al., 1992). What does this have to do with the immune system? People probably live longer because their bodies are fighting off whatever ailment is killing them.

But stress can harm the immune system. Because stress can impair the functioning of the white blood cells, it can play a role in the length of time it takes a wound to heal: The wounds of women who experienced a high level of stress by caring for a relative with Alzheimer's disease took 9 days longer to heal than those of women of similar age and economic status who were not engaged in such caregiving (Kiecolt-Glaser et al., 1995). In another study, dental student participants received slight mouth wounds on two different occasions (3 days before a major test and during summer vacation). The wounds given before exams, when, presumably, the students were experiencing more stressors, took 40% longer to heal (Marucha et al., 1998). Moreover, stress can increase the risk of infection after receiving a wound (Rojas et al., 2002). Major stressors such as a natural disaster (a devastating earthquake or hurricane) or victimization (being robbed or raped) can affect the immune system. Among people living in Florida neighborhoods damaged by Hurricane Andrew in 1992, the victims who perceived their losses to be most severe experienced the most changes in number of NK cells (Ironson et al., 1997).

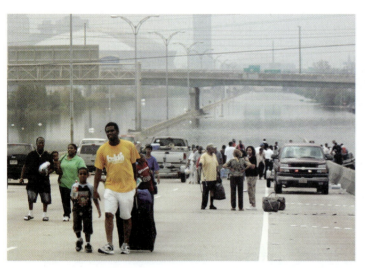

Traumatic events, such as experiencing the devastation of a hurricane, can affect the immune system, as well as produce psychological symptoms such as anxiety and depression.

But not everyone who is exposed to trauma responds the same way. Some survivors of traumatic events later (sometimes considerably later) experience *posttraumatic stress disorder (PTSD)*, a psychological disorder characterized by involuntary reexperiencing of the trauma through unwanted thoughts, sensations, and dreams, heightened arousal, and avoidance of anything associated with the trauma. (A further discussion of PTSD appears in Chapter 11.)

Cancer

Although stress can't cause cancer, there is evidence that it can affect the growth of some cancerous tumors. How can this happen?

- *If the immune system is suppressed, NK cells do not work as well to prevent the spread of tumor cells.* Levy and her colleagues (Levy et al., 1985, 1987,

1988) found a relationship among the perception of inadequate social support, feelings of distress and fatigue with little joy, and lower levels of NK cell activity. Such negative psychological experiences, by weakening the immune system, left people more vulnerable to the growth of cancerous tumors. Locke and colleagues (1984) found similar results.

- *Stress can facilitate the growth of capillaries feeding into the tumor.* When stress has a distinct physical cause, our bodies produce more capillaries to supply blood to that area. If the stressor is an injury or infection (such as would be caused by a puncture wound in the foot), capillary growth is beneficial because the vessels carry more white blood cells to the part of the body that needs them. However, if a tumor is already present in the body, the stress response will cause more blood to be supplied to the tumor, literally feeding it and supporting its growth. Stress does not appear to *cause* a tumor to develop, only to assist in its growth.

- *The perception of control can also play a role in the progression of some types of cancer.* Among cancer patients, those who did not perceive much control and felt helpless about their cancer were likely to have a recurrence sooner and to die earlier from the cancer (Andersen et al., 1994; Watson et al., 1991).

Although psychological factors can affect the immune system, these findings should be interpreted with caution. The type of cancer, and biological factors related to the progression of the disease, can outweigh psychological factors in tumor growth (Compas et al., 1998; Grossarth-Maticek et al., 2000), especially in the final stages of the disease (Cohen & Herbert, 1996). Moreover, some people may be genetically endowed with an immune system that is more effective at warding off illness. Data on twins reared together and apart suggest that, on average, identical twins have more key antibodies in common (7 out of a possible 9) than do fraternal twins (4 out of a possible 9) (Kohler et al., 1985).

Atherosclerosis: A medical condition characterized by plaque buildup in the arteries.

Heart Disease

Stress can also lead, indirectly, to heart disease. Let's examine how.

How Stress Affects the Heart

The increased blood pressure created by chronic stress, in combination with hormonally induced narrowing of the arteries, promotes <mark>atherosclerosis</mark>, or the buildup of plaque (fatty deposits) on the inside walls of the arteries (Figure 10.3). As plaque accumulates, the arteries narrow—which makes the heart work even harder to meet the body's need for nutrients and oxygen. Working harder means pumping the blood with more power, creating more damage to the arteries, and a vicious cycle is created. This chronic wear and tear on the cardiovascular system can lead to heart damage, which can lead to sudden death from inadequate blood supply to the heart muscle or from irregular electrical firing of the muscle, preventing coordinated heartbeats.

Figure 10.3 Stress on the Arteries

CUT SECTION THROUGH BRANCHING ARTERY

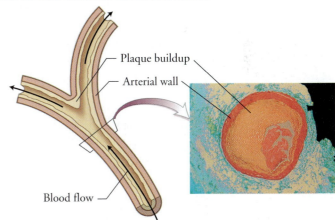

Plaque buildup

Arterial wall

Blood flow

Each time a stressor causes an increase in blood pressure, the branching points of arteries are at risk for damage. The hormones released during the fight-or-flight response also cause blood vessels to constrict, which has the net effect of increasing blood pressure even more. Thus, if someone experiences frequent stressors, his or her blood vessels take a pounding. With rapidly increased blood pressure, the circulating blood can create a slight tear of the arterial wall, creating a place for plaque to attach itself to the artery wall. Once this occurs, the artery gets narrower and narrower (as plaque builds and builds). This atherosclerosis makes the work of pumping blood through the body even harder for the heart.

When a person experiences a strong stressor, his or her body's response may cause a piece of plaque to break off (Strike et al., 2004). The loosened plaque may then block an artery going to the heart, preventing or limiting blood flow to that organ, leading to a heart attack. For someone who already has heart disease, even extremely positive states of stress, such as joy or orgasm, can precipitate this event and cause sudden death.

Some people, perhaps because of a history of heart disease or an overly responsive HPA axis, are more vulnerable to calamitous aftereffects of stress. For these people, work stress can increase the risk of a heart attack; for example, if such a person is working under a tight deadline, this can increase the risk of heart attack soon after the deadline (Moller et al., 2005), as can being stuck in traffic (Peters et al., 2004). Such stress-related heart attacks need to be distinguished from the recently identified and potentially fatal "broken heart syndrome," which has caused people to die after becoming extremely upset; this syndrome occurs when a person has a massive amount (up to 34 times the normal level) of adrenaline in response to an acute emotional stressor, along with a temporary weakening of the heart so that it cannot pump effectively (Wittstein et al., 2005).

Stress, Emotions, and Heart Disease

Stressors often elicit negative emotions such as fear, anger, sadness, and helplessness. Such emotions can produce a rise in heart rate that lasts longer than does the rise following positive emotions (Brosschot & Thayer, 2003). When the stressors are chronic, they can lead to helplessness, depression, and despair. Depression in particular appears to be associated with a greater likelihood of heart disease (Barth et al., 2004; Ferketich et al., 2000; Kiecolt-Glaser & Glaser, 2002; Rosengren et al., 2004). Consider these findings:

- Depressed people have a faster heartbeat even when at rest (Moser et al., 1998), and they tend to have high blood pressure (Carney et al., 1999).
- People who are more likely to experience negative emotions (that is, they are high in the personality dimension of neuroticism, see Chapter 8) have an increased risk of heart disease and heart attacks, perhaps from a biological hyperreactivity to stress (Habra et al., 2003).

It isn't surprising, then, that those who have had an episode of depression have a higher risk of developing heart problems, and once having had a heart attack, those who are depressed are more likely to have further health problems (Frasure-Smith et al., 1999). When the depression is treated, however, these stress-related responses subside, and heart rate and blood pressure decrease (Kolata, 1997). Anxiety is also associated with heart disease (Kubzansky & Kawachi, 2000; Kubzansky et al., 1998), possibly because it can lead to high blood pressure and changes in cardiac functioning—and also because people may attempt to cope with it by engaging in unhealthy behaviors, such as smoking or drinking.

Lifestyle Can Make a Difference

The course of heart disease can be affected by a change in lifestyle. A study of people with severe heart disease found that intensive changes in diet, exercise, stress management (such as meditation), and social support could help to halt the narrowing of the arteries, and could even reverse the atherosclerosis and minimize further damage to the heart (Ornish et al., 1998). Other studies confirm the positive effects of such intensive lifestyle changes (Lisspers et al., 2005).

Sleep

Al was having a difficult time sleeping. Could stress be affecting his sleep? In fact, stress and health problems can affect sleep—for instance, making someone unable to fall asleep once in bed with the lights out or not feel rested in the morning. In addition, not getting enough sleep—sleep deprivation—can affect your health and ability to cope. To understand this reciprocal relationship, we need to know more about sleep.

Stages of Sleep: Working Through the Night

Some people think that sleep is a single state, and you are either asleep or awake. Until the invention of the electroencephalograph (which creates recordings of brain activity called electroencephalograms, or EEGs; see Chapter 2) in 1928, that is what scientists used to think as well (Hobson, 1995). With the use of this new technology, they learned that **sleep**, a natural experience during which normal consciousness is suspended, is not a single state. By taking EEGs of brain activity during sleep, researchers discovered several different types of sleep, which occur in five stages during the night. Everyone proceeds through these stages, but people differ in how much time they spend in each stage (Anch et al., 1988).

Stage 1. This initial sleep stage, lasting approximately 5 minutes and sometimes described as **hypnogogic sleep**, marks the transition from relaxed wakefulness to sleep. In Stage 1 sleep, your breathing becomes deeper and more regular, and the EEG registers brain waves that are less regular and of lower amplitude than those that mark the waking state (see Figure 10.4). You can be awakened relatively easily from Stage 1 sleep, and if you are, you do not feel as if you have been asleep at all. In this stage, you may experience a gentle falling or floating sensation, or your body may jerk suddenly and rather violently in a movement called a *hypnic jerk*.

Figure 10.4 Brain Waves During the Stages of Sleep

Recordings show that brain waves differ in both amplitude (the height of the wave) and frequency (how often they occur). By examining individuals' EEG patterns when asleep, which differ from their EEG patterns when awake, researchers have identified five phases of sleep, each with its own unique EEG pattern.

Sleep: The naturally recurrent experience during which normal consciousness is suspended.

Hypnogogic sleep: The initial stage of sleep, which lasts about 5 minutes and can include the sensation of gentle falling or floating or a sudden jerking of the body.

REM sleep: Stage of sleep characterized by rapid eye movements and marked brain activity.

Stage 2. Once you are clearly asleep, your EEG pattern begins to record *sleep spindles*—brief bursts of brain activity (see Figure 10.4)—and single high-amplitude waves. You are now more relaxed and less responsive to your environment, although still relatively easy to awaken. But if you are awakened during Stage 2, you will most likely report that you have been asleep. This phase lasts for approximately 20 minutes.

Stages 3 and 4. Stages 3 and 4 are sometimes referred to collectively as *slow-wave sleep* (SWS) because your brain produces *delta waves*—recorded as slow, high-amplitude waves on an EEG; notice in Figure 10.4 how the waves of Stages 3 and 4 are higher and more spread out compared to those of wakefulness and Stages 1 and 2. In Stage 3, 20–50% of EEG-recorded brain activity is in the form of delta waves; in Stage 4, the proportion is greater than 50%. In Stage 3, your heart rate and body temperature decrease, and you are no longer easily awakened. By the time you reach Stage 4, you are in a very deep sleep indeed, so deep that attempts by a friend (or an alarm clock) to wake you won't readily succeed. If you do wake up directly from this stage, you are likely to be briefly disoriented. During Stage 4 sleep, your heart rate, blood pressure, breathing, and body temperature slow down; all are at their lowest ebb.

REM Sleep. About an hour after going to sleep, you begin to reverse the sleep cycle, going from Stage 4 through Stages 3 and 2. Instead of going all the way to Stage 1, though, you now enter a state of *rapid eye movement (REM)* under the lids, and, as shown in Figure 10.4, your EEG registers marked brain activity—similar to when you are awake. It is in this stage of sleep that you are likely to have dreams vivid enough to remember. During **REM sleep**, your breathing and heart rate are fast and irregular, and your genitals may show signs of arousal (men may have an erection; women may have increased genital blood flow and vaginal lubrication). These events occur in REM sleep regardless of the content of the sleeper's dreams, unless a dream is particularly anxiety-provoking, in which case the genitals may not be aroused (Karacan et al., 1966). During REM sleep, your muscles are relaxed and unresponsive; in fact, your voluntary muscles (except those in your eyes) are so paralyzed that you could not physically enact the behaviors in your dreams. However, your involuntary muscles continue to move (which allows your respiratory, vascular, and other systems to keep working).

Sleep Cycles. After a period of REM sleep, you go through at least some of the other stages, and then return to REM, as shown in Figure 10.5. Each cycle takes about 90 minutes and occurs four or five times each night. However, the time you spend in each stage varies over the course of the night, with slow-wave sleep occurring predominantly in the early hours of sleep and REM sleep occurring primarily in the later hours of sleep.

Sleep also varies over the course of a lifetime. The phrase "I slept like a baby" turns out to have more truth to it than most of us realize. Infants sleep longer than adults (13–16 hours per night in the first year) and have a higher percentage of REM sleep. They often enter REM immediately after falling

Figure 10.5 The March of Sleep Cycles

During the earlier part of the night, more time is spent in Stages 3 and 4, but later in the night, REM periods lengthen and Stages 3 and 4 shorten, eventually disappearing.

asleep and change stages often. With age, the pattern of sleep stages changes; when you enter your 40s, the amount of time spent in deep, slow-wave sleep begins to decrease (Van Cauter et al., 2000). With less slow-wave activity, your sleep is shallower and more fragmented, you wake more easily, and the sleep you do get is less satisfying (Hobson, 1995; Klerman et al., 2004). As you move from middle age to older adulthood, the amounts of lighter sleep (Stages 1 and 2) and REM sleep also decrease (Van Cauter et al., 2000). With increasing age, changes in the sleep cycle and in the production of hormones involved in the sleep process make restful sleep less common (Center for the Advancement of Health, 1998; Klinkenborg, 1997). As the quality of sleep declines, so does its restorative effect on the cardiovascular and endocrine systems.

Sleep Deprivation: Is Less Just as Good?

Al wasn't sleeping well; he rarely slept more than 6 hours a night. He wondered if his sleep deprivation was affecting his performance at work—it certainly felt like it was.

In today's world of overscheduled lives and 10-hour workdays, can anyone claim to be getting a natural amount of sleep? A 2002 survey by the National Sleep Foundation found that two out of three adults are not getting enough sleep (defined as approximately 8 hours), and one of those three gets less than 6 hours each night. Even children under the age of 11 are not getting enough sleep (National Sleep Foundation, 2004). Falling asleep in a dull class *may* signal sleep deprivation: "boredom doesn't cause sleepiness, it merely unmasks it" (Dement, as cited in Brody, 1998). What else happens when you don't get enough sleep, or miss a night's sleep entirely?

REM Rebound.   When you don't get enough REM sleep on a given night, a higher percentage of the next night's sleep will be REM sleep (Brunner et al., 1990); this phenomenon is called **REM rebound**. You can become REM deprived by not getting enough sleep at either end of the night (going to bed late or waking up early) or by using alcohol or sleep medications (depressants), which suppress REM sleep. If these substances are used habitually and then discontinued, REM rebound dreams can be so vivid, bizarre, and generally unpleasant that people resume using these substances to fall asleep, and to suppress dreaming as well. Some people who have been deeply traumatized (victims of rape or assault, for example) cite disturbing dreams or nightmares as a reason for using alcohol or drugs before sleep (Inman et al., 1990).

Sleep Deprivation: What Happens When You Skimp on Sleep?   If you have ever stayed up late, say, studying or partying, and then awakened early the next morning, you have probably experienced sleep deprivation. In fact, you may be sleep deprived right now. If so, you have company: 40% of adults claim to be so sleepy during the day that daily activities are affected (National Sleep Foundation, 2002). In trying to determine the function of sleep, a common research method is to interfere with participants' sleep in some way and see what the effects might be. What happens as a result of sleep deprivation? Young adults who volunteered for a sleep deprivation study were allowed to sleep for only 5 hours each night, for a total of 7 nights. After 3 nights of restricted sleep, volunteers complained of cognitive, physical, and emotional difficulties.

Attention and performance drop.   Cognitive and physical difficulties that result from sleep deprivation involve problems in sustaining attention and in performing visual-motor tasks. Performance on a visual-motor task declined after only 2 nights of restricted sleep. Visual-motor tasks usually require participants to

Some students may stay up all night before an exam or a paper is due, but not without a cost. Sleep deprivation decreases immune system functioning and temporarily impairs some cognitive abilities, such as maintaining prolonged attention.

There is increasing recognition that requiring medical interns and residents to stay awake for days and nights of round-the-clock duties can have detrimental effects on their cognitive processes (Landrigan et al., 2004; Lockley et al., 2004) and even cause them to be more likely to have car accidents (Barger et al., 2005). In response, some states are restricting the number of consecutive hours doctors can work.

concentrate on detecting a change in a particular stimulus, and then to respond as quickly as they can after they perceive the change by pressing a button (Dinges et al., 1997). Although you may be able to perform simple, brief mental tasks normally when sleep deprived, if a task requires sustained attention and a motor response, your performance will suffer. Driving a car is an example of such a task. In fact, in a survey by the National Sleep Foundation (1998), 25% of the respondents reported that they had at some time fallen asleep at the wheel; sleepy drivers account for at least 100,000 car crashes each year.

Emotions flare. Moods are also affected by sleep deprivation (Dinges et al., 1997; Monk et al., 1997). Those who sleep less than 6 hours each weekday night are more likely to report being impatient or aggravated when faced with common minor frustrations such as being stuck in traffic or having to wait in line, and they are more dissatisfied with life in general (National Sleep Foundation, 2002).

The body suffers. The loss of even one night's sleep can lead to increases in the next day's level of cortisol (Leproult, Copinschi, et al., 1997). As mentioned earlier in this chapter, cortisol helps the body meet the increased demands imposed by stress. However, sleep deprivation can lead to a change in cortisol level that, in turn, alters other biological functions, such as decreasing immune system functioning (Kiecolt-Glaser et al., 1995) and creating an increased risk for diabetes.

Learning decreases. Sleep deprivation is also associated with deficits in learning in two ways. First, chronically increased cortisol levels can cause memory deficits (Sapolsky, 1996). Second, as we shall see in more detail later, REM and slow-wave sleep facilitate the learning of information that was encountered during the day (Walker & Stickgold, 2004).

The Effects of All-Nighters. And, what about a series of all-nighters, when you get no sleep at all, as might occur during finals period? Getting no sleep can interfere with certain types of learning, such as making perceptual discriminations, but naps can help (Cajochen et al., 2004; Mednick et al., 2003). As for pulling all-nighters throughout exam periods, results from volunteers who have gone without sleep for long stretches (finally sleeping after staying awake anywhere from 4 to 11 days) show profound psychological changes, such as hallucinations, feelings of losing control or going crazy, anxiety, and paranoia (Coren, 1996). Moreover, going without sleep alters the normal daily patterns of changes in temperature, metabolism, and hormone secretions (Leproult, Van Reeth, et al., 1997). These changes are also seen in adult rats that are forced to stay awake. Within 2 weeks, they show major negative bodily changes. In fact, despite eating two and a half times their usual amount, they begin to lose weight. Moreover, their temperature does not stay in the normal range, and they die within 21 days (Rechtschaffen et al., 1983). Even rats deprived only of REM sleep (they are awakened each time they enter the REM stage) experience temperature regulation changes, but these changes are less extreme (Shaw et al., 1998). Results of a PET study found a different pattern of brain activation when sleep-deprived human participants were learning verbal material than when non–sleep-deprived participants were learning the material, which may reflect an attempt to compensate for the brain changes induced by sleep deprivation (Drummond et al., 2000).

Thus, sleep deprivation affects us in at least four important psychological areas: attention, physical performance, mood, and learning.

The Function of Sleep

We know that doing without sleep has adverse effects on attention, performance, mood, and learning. But why do we sleep? What purpose or purposes does it serve? Research on sleep is beginning to piece together answers to these questions.

Evolutionary Theory. One theory of the function of sleep is that it provided an evolutionary advantage—it kept our ancestors metaphorically off the streets and out of trouble. That is, sleeping removes us from potential life-threatening conflicts with predatory animals at night, when humans do not have the advantage of night vision. (Note, however, that we are also more vulnerable to prey while asleep, which is a clear disadvantage.) Another, perhaps more plausible, evolutionary account is that sleep (and its associated biological changes) allows energy conservation because the body's temperature lowers and caloric demands decline. Although interesting, such theories at present must be regarded as speculation.

Restorative Theory. Another theory of the function of sleep is that sleep helps the body repair the wear and tear from the day's events (Hobson, 1989). Support for this view comes from research on sleep deprivation and the adverse effects of lack of sleep mentioned earlier.

Facilitating Learning. Yet another theory about the function of sleep is that it facilitates the learning of material encountered during the day (Walker & Stickgold, 2004). In studies where participants were asked to discriminate among different visual stimuli, both slow-wave sleep in the first quarter of the night and REM sleep in the last quarter of the night were crucial for visual learning: Participants deprived of these phases of sleep did not remember well what they had previously learned (Stickgold, 1998; Stickgold, Whidbee, et al., 2000). Sleep is critical in laying down memories associated with perceptual and motor learning (Atienza et al., 2004; Stickgold et al., 2002; Walker, Brakefield, Seidman, et al., 2003).

Why Do We Dream?

In addition to the biological changes that occur during sleep, there is a distinct change in consciousness—that of dreaming. It is *not* true that dreams take place only during REM sleep, but it *is* true that the dreams that take place during REM sleep are more memorable than those occurring during non-REM (NREM) stages (Dement, 1974). If awakened during REM sleep, people recall dreams 78% of the time, compared with a 50% rate of recall for awakenings during NREM sleep; moreover, NREM dreams are less vivid, less storylike, and less emotional (Farthing, 1992; Nielsen, 2000).

Dreams can offer us a pleasant respite from the daily grind, bring us terror in the form of a nightmare, or leave us puzzled about their confusing or curious content. What function does dreaming serve?

Freud: Wish Fulfillment. Researchers and nonresearchers alike have long sought to know why we dream. The first modern

Dreams that occur right after you drift off to sleep may reflect events that occurred just before sleep: One study found that people who learned to play the computer game *Tetris* found themselves dreaming of elements of that game at the beginning of their sleep (Stickgold, Malia, et al., 2000).

dream theory was proposed by Sigmund Freud. Freud (1900/1958), convinced that dream content originates in the unconscious—outside our conscious awareness—dubbed dreams the "royal road to the unconscious." Further, he believed that dreams allow us to fulfill unconscious desires. Such *wish fulfillment* may not always be apparent from the **manifest content** of a dream, that is, its obvious, memorable content. We have to dig to find the **latent content** of the dream, its symbolic content and meaning, which, according to Freud, might reflect sexual or aggressive themes associated with an inner conflict. Although Freud's theory of the unconscious origin of the content of dreams has yet to be supported by solid, objective evidence, the idea of dream interpretation has both ancient appeal and current fascination—witness the large number of dream interpretation books and Web sites on the Internet. Can someone interpret your dreams? Although dream interpretation can be interesting and fun, it is unclear that any meaning inferred from the content of dreams is accurate.

Research suggests, however, that Freud may have been on to something with one aspect of his dream theory: If we try *not* to think about someone before we go to sleep, that person is more likely to appear in our dreams than if we didn't try to suppress thoughts of him or her (Wegner et al., 2004). That is, although the content of our dreams may not reflect our unconscious *desires*, the content may reflect mental processes that happen outside of conscious awareness.

Activation-Synthesis Hypothesis.

Freudians find dreams brimming over with meaningful, albeit disguised, content. The opposite view is at the heart of the **activation-synthesis hypothesis**, which contends that dreams arise from random bursts of nerve cell activity. These bursts may affect brain cells involved in hearing and seeing, as well as storing information, and the brain's response is to try to make sense of the hodge-podge of stimuli (Hobson & McCarley, 1977); however, the dreams do not disguise meaning, as Freud suggested (Goode, 1999). The brain synthesizes the sensory images and activates stored information to create the experience of a dream. This theory would explain why dreams sometimes seem so bizarre and unrelated: Stickgold and colleagues (1994) asked people to write down their dreams and then literally cut their reports in half. They asked other people to reassemble each dream, deciding which half came first. This proved a very difficult task, a result that is understandable if dreams are merely attempts to interpret random activity and have no cohesive story line.

Editing Versus Strengthening Neural Connections.

Francis Crick believed that dreams are used to edit out unnecessary or accidental brain connections formed during the day (Crick & Mitchison, 1983, 1986). Other theories of dreaming focus on the reverse notion: that dreams are used to *strengthen* useful connections. This view is supported by a study by Karni and colleagues (1994). Participants learned to discriminate between two visual stimuli before falling asleep; those who slept normally improved their performance on the task when tested the following morning. But participants who were awakened when they entered REM sleep did not improve when tested in the morning. In contrast, participants who slept but were deprived of slow-wave, Stage 4 sleep showed normal learning—which suggests that REM sleep is crucial for cementing in memory certain kinds of information gleaned during the day. However, more recent research suggests that such memories do not absolutely depend on REM; at least in some circumstances, slow-wave sleep may play a role (Stickgold, 1998; Stickgold, Whidbee, et al., 2000). It may be that REM sleep—and the dreaming associated with it—is particularly important for perceptual memories, and slow-wave sleep is important for other sorts of memory, but at present this remains an area for further research.

Manifest content: The obvious, memorable content of a dream.

Latent content: The symbolic content and meaning of a dream.

Activation-synthesis hypothesis: The theory that dreams arise from random bursts of nerve cell activity, which may affect brain cells involved in hearing and seeing; the brain attempts to make sense of this hodge-podge of stimuli, resulting in the experience of dreams.

Goals/Desires and Arousal/Inhibition. The largest and most systematic study of the neurological bases of dreaming was reported by Solms (1997), of the London Hospital Medical College. Solms interviewed more than 350 stroke patients about the changed nature of their dreams after their strokes. Solms found that dreaming was affected by damage to any number of brain areas. Perhaps Solms's most intriguing discovery was that dreaming stopped completely if a patient had damage that disconnected parts of the frontal cortex from the brainstem and the limbic system. These connections coordinate brain areas involved in curiosity, interest, and alert involvement with goals in the world (Panksepp, 1985, cited in Solms, 1997). Solms speculates that dreaming may occur in response to any type of arousal that activates brain structures involved in motivation (Goode, 1999). Alternatively, the damage that disconnected frontal

In some societies, such as the Maya, telling dreams to others can provide a way to communicate feelings or solve problems (Degarrod, 1990; Tedlock, 1992).

cortex from brainstem and limbic system may have disrupted the brain's storage and integration of memories related to needs, goals, and desires. In either case, the inhibiting mechanisms of sleep prevent us from acting on these memories, emotions, or desires, which may lead the brain to convert them into dreams.

In sum, although we cannot yet definitively answer *why* we dream, we do know something about *how* we dream. We know that dreaming is a neurological process, involving brain activity. We don't know whether dreams represent deep desires and conflicts, random bursts of nerve cell activity, the editing of unneeded neural connections, or the strengthening of neural connections. But it is interesting that all of these theories, despite their differences, agree that in some way the day's events, or the neural connections they instigate, affect dreams. These hypotheses about the purpose of dreaming are summarized in Table 10.2.

The Chemistry of Sleep: Ups and Downs

We spend about one third of our lives asleep. During that time, our brains and bodies are working away, responding to outside stimuli such as light and dark, and

---

Table 10.2 Why Do We Dream?

Purpose of Dreaming

- *Wish fulfillment* of unconscious desires (Freud)

- Attempts to *synthesize* and make sense of effects of random bursts of neural *activity* during sleep (Hobson and McCarley)

- *Changing neural connections*:

  ○ *Editing out* unneeded neural connections (Crick)

  ○ *Strengthening* useful neural connections (Karni)

- *Arousal of motivation-related brain structures*, leading to dreams associated with needs, goals, and desires (Solms)

---

releasing fluctuating levels of neurotransmitters and hormones. These chemical changes are crucial to our daily functioning.

When you are in slow-wave sleep, the brain cells that release the neurotransmitter acetylcholine are inhibited, but when you are in REM sleep, they are activated (Hobson et al., 2000; McCarley & Hobson, 1975). Your dreams of walking, flying, or falling may occur because of the increased acetylcholine during REM, which activates the motor and visual areas of your brain and may cause you to dream of a wild roller-coaster ride or other types of motion (Hobson, 1995). Moreover, the cells in parts of your brainstem that release other neurotransmitters, specifically serotonin and norepinephrine, are most active when you are awake. Sleeping pills work in part by blocking production of these two "wake-up" neurotransmitters (Garcia-Arraras & Pappenheimer, 1983).

The hormone melatonin, which is secreted by the pineal gland, plays a role in promoting sleep. The body normally begins secreting melatonin around dusk, tapering off production at dawn; this cycle appears to be regulated, at least in part, by a recently discovered type of light receptor in the eye (Brainard et al., 2001; see Chapter 3). A person who takes melatonin in pill form may soon feel drowsy and, if undisturbed, may fall asleep within half an hour. Unlike other sleep aids, melatonin appears to induce a natural sleep, with the appropriate amounts and timing of REM and NREM sleep (Zhdanova & Wurtman, 1996). Some have argued that taking melatonin at the right times can help a traveler overcome jet lag, especially when traveling east (Beaumont et al., 2004; Herxheimer & Petrie, 2002; Takahashi et al., 2002).

Circadian Rhythms

Our brain activity and internal chemistry dance in time to the daily cycling of light and dark in a pattern called <mark>circadian rhythms</mark> (*circadian* means "about a day"). Daily fluctuations governed by circadian rhythms occur with blood pressure, pulse rate, body temperature, blood sugar level, hormone levels, and metabolism. Every one of us has an internal clock that coordinates these fluctuations; this clock is regulated by a small part of the hypothalamus just above the optic chiasm, called the <mark>suprachiasmatic nucleus (SCN)</mark>, which is illustrated in Figure 10.6. Through photoreceptors in the retina, the SCN registers changes in light, which lead it to produce hormones that set the body's clock and regulate various bodily functions (Berson et al., 2002). Researchers have found a gene in mice that is responsible for the regulation of their daily clocks; tissues in the eyes and the SCN generate the signals that cue the mouse's brain as to when to sleep and when to awaken (Antoch et al., 1997). The rudiments of circadian rhythms appear in human infants as early as 1 week after birth (McGraw et al., 1999). The circadian clock is even responsible for the length of time between heart beats (Hu et al., 2004).

What happens to the human sleep–wake cycle in the absence of external cues of dark and light (except for electric light, which can be turned on and off at will) and cultural cues such as clocks? Volunteers who have lived this way as part of a research project ended up living a 24.9-hour day. In a variant of this study, in which only subdued lighting was provided, with no opportunity for stronger reading light, participants were more likely to have a 24.2-hour day (Czeisler et al., 1999).

Figure 10.6 The Suprachiasmatic Nucleus (SCN) and the Optic Chiasm

This illustration of a human brain shows the proximity of the SCN to the optic chiasm. Given the SCN's role in regulating circadian rhythms, it is not surprising that it is so close to the optic chiasm, which relays visual input about light and dark to the brain.

Circadian rhythms: The body's daily fluctuations in response to the cycle of dark and light, which occur with blood pressure, pulse rate, body temperature, blood sugar level, hormone levels, and metabolism.

Suprachiasmatic nucleus (SCN): A small part of the hypothalamus just above the optic chiasm that registers changes in light, leading to production of hormones that regulate various bodily functions.

But what about people who are completely blind and cannot detect light at all? As with the people who had no external cues, but could turn lights on and off and so create a structure to their day, completely blind people show evidence of a 24.9-hour day, with 76% of the blind people studied reporting difficulty falling asleep at their usual bedtimes, based on a 24-hour day (Coren, 1996; Miles et al., 1977). Thus, the 24-hour schedule, so ingrained in us by the daily rotation of the earth, is not hard-wired into our brains, but instead is maintained by exposure to light–dark cycles, whether natural or artificial, and by cues from mechanical instruments such as clocks and radios.

Working Against Your Rhythms. Even within the 24-hour day, however, not everyone prefers to wake up or go to sleep at the same time. As you have no doubt noticed, some people are energetic and alert early in the morning, whereas others do not perk up until late morning or afternoon. People differ in the timing of their circadian rhythms: Morning people, or "larks," experience peak body temperature, alertness, and efficiency in the morning; evening people, or "owls," peak at night (Luce, 1971). Normally you are not aware of your circadian rhythms until you try to function well at your nonpeak time. If you're a night owl, for example, how do you feel when faced with a 9:00 a.m. class? Flying across time zones is bound to make you aware of your own circadian rhythms, especially if it's a long trip. Regardless of the time of day that finds you most alert, however, most people have a late-afternoon dip in energy level. More industrial and traffic accidents occur between 1:00 and 4:00 p.m. than at any other time of day (Klinkenborg, 1997). Rest breaks can help counter fatigue and enhance performance (Tucker, 2003).

Are you grouchy on a Monday morning? If so, it might be more than simply "waking up on the wrong side of the bed." Boivin and colleagues (1997), who studied mood and circadian rhythms, found that bad moods occurred during times of day when the participants' circadian clocks said they should be asleep. These results suggest that even minor alterations in sleep schedules, relative to individual circadian rhythms, can have a noticeable effect on mood after awakening. Thus, if you go to bed later and sleep later on weekends, you may be adversely altering your circadian rhythms. You are, in a sense, putting yourself in another time zone for the weekend, so when Monday morning rolls around, you are hit with jet lag. Even 5th-grade children are affected by having to wake up earlier to go to school. Regardless of how much sleep

Many cultures have a rest time in the afternoon, perhaps related to the dip in energy during that part of the day that is part of our circadian rhythms.

they had, those children who had to be in school by 7:10 a.m. reported more daytime fatigue and poorer attention and concentration at school than those whose school day started at 8:00 a.m. (Epstein et al., 1998).

What can you do if your schedule conflicts with your natural circadian tendencies? One remedy is to sleep on a disciplined schedule 7 days a week. If, as in the case of jet lag, that isn't possible, try exposing yourself to plenty of light on Monday mornings; this may help reset your internal clock.

Troubled Sleep

Al's tiredness during the day was starting to wear him down, and drinking before bed didn't seem to help him sleep soundly. He craved a good night's sleep. Feeling tired during the day or having difficulty sleeping may be caused by insomnia or sleep apnea.

If you have insomnia, lying in bed should only be associated with actually going to sleep, not with watching television or reading when you are unable to fall asleep. The man in the photograph should sit in a chair or sofa while watching television if he can't sleep.

Insomnia.   Al probably had insomnia. **Insomnia** is characterized by repeated difficulty falling asleep or staying asleep or waking too early. If you suffer from this disorder, you are certainly not alone. Half the adults in the United States experience occasional insomnia. Temporary insomnia may be related to environmental factors such as stress related to family, school, or work (Bastien et al., 2004), which can cause increased sympathetic nervous system activity and can make sleep difficult. When sleep does not occur rapidly, the stressed person becomes frustrated. The frustration serves to increase arousal, compounding the problem.

For many Americans, insomnia is a way of life. Chronic insomnia may stem from other disorders, such as anxiety and depression, as you will see in Chapter 11. Sleeping pills (barbiturates) are the most common, but not necessarily the most effective, treatment for insomnia. They not only suppress needed REM sleep but also are addictive. Moreover, people develop tolerance to this medication, requiring larger and larger dosages to get the same effect.

What can you do if you have trouble sleeping? The following nonmedicinal techniques may help (Hobson, 1995; Lacks & Morin, 1992; Maas, 1998):

- *Restrict your sleeping hours* to the same nightly pattern. When living in the White House, both Martha and George Washington went to bed promptly at 9:00 p.m. each evening (Seuling, 1978). The Washingtons were on to something: Keep regular sleeping hours. Avoid sleeping late in the morning, napping longer than an hour, or going to bed earlier than usual, all of which will throw you off schedule, creating even more sleep difficulties later. And try to get up at the same time every day, even on weekends or days off.

- *Control bedtime stimuli* so that things normally associated with sleep are associated only with sleep, not with the frustration of insomnia. Use your bed only for sleep or sex (don't read or watch TV in bed). If you can't fall asleep within 10 minutes, get out of bed and do something else.

- *Avoid ingesting substances with stimulant properties.* Don't smoke cigarettes or drink beverages with alcohol or caffeine in the evening. Alcohol may cause initial drowsiness, but it has a "rebound effect" that leaves many people wide awake in the middle of the night. Don't drink water close to bedtime; getting up to use the bathroom can lead to poor sleep.

- *Consider meditation or progressive muscle relaxation.* Either of these techniques can be helpful (see Chapter 12). Regular aerobic exercise four times a week may be a long-term solution, but it can take up to 16 weeks for the effect on insomnia to kick in (King et al., 1997).

These techniques are often part of psychological treatment of insomnia, which focuses on the sleep-related thoughts and behaviors that can contribute to

Insomnia: Repeated difficulty falling asleep, difficulty staying asleep, or waking up too early.

insomnia (Bastien, Morin, et al., 2004); such techniques can be more effective than sleep medication (Jacobs et al., 2004).

Sleep Apnea. Snoring can be a nuisance to those sharing a room with a snorer, but it can also be a sign of a more troublesome problem. **Sleep apnea** is a disorder characterized by a temporary cessation of breathing during sleep, usually preceded by a period of difficult breathing accompanied by loud snoring. Breathing may stop for up to 70 seconds, startling the sleeper into a lighter state of sleep. This ailment, which affects 12 million Americans (National Heart, Lung, & Blood Institute, 2003), can produce many such events each hour, preventing restful sleep. Perhaps this explains the results of a research study of medical students who snore versus those who do not: 13% of nonsnorers failed their exams, compared with 42% of frequent snorers (Ficker et al., 1999). If the snorers had sleep apnea, they would not function as well because of their troubled sleep.

Sleep apnea results when muscles at the base of the throat relax and consequently block the airway. In obese patients, weight loss can help reduce the obstruction, although normal-weight people also can have sleep apnea. Sleep apnea can lead to heart problems, so treatment is essential. A device called *Continuous Positive Airway Pressure (CPAP)* can assist a person's breathing during sleep; alternatively, surgery is sometimes recommended. In addition, research suggests that a complex interplay of heart rate, functioning of parts of the nervous system, and breathing may also influence sleep apnea: Men with heart problems and implanted pacemakers who also had sleep apnea found that their apnea symptoms improved when their pacemakers increased the number of heartbeats by 15 per minute (Garrigue et al., 2002). Researchers hypothesized that because sleep apnea disrupts sleep, it should also impair memory and other cognitive abilities. To test this hypothesis, they studied the effects that surgically removing the airway obstruction had on learning, memory, and decision making in 53 people who had this disorder. They administered tests of cognitive abilities before surgery and 6 months after surgery. Happily, surgery did lead to better learning, memory, and decision-making abilities. Moreover, the researchers found that the more effective the treatment was in eliminating the apnea, the larger the improvement in these abilities (Dahloef et al., 2002).

Those with undiagnosed sleep apnea may take barbiturates to get a good night's sleep—this is unfortunate because barbiturates seriously compound the problem by depressing the central nervous system, interfering with the normal reflex to begin breathing again.

LOOKING BACK: *Review*

1. *Can stress affect the immune system and make illness more likely?* Yes. Stress increases the production of glucocorticoids, which can depress the immune system, including the formation and functioning of white blood cells such as natural killer (NK) cells. This makes the body more vulnerable to infection, tumor growth, and slowed healing.

2. *Are stress and cancer related?* Although stress does not cause tumors to develop, increased glucocorticoid production (part of the stress response) can depress the level of tumor-fighting NK cells and can increase the growth of capillaries that provide a blood supply to nourish a tumor. Conversely, decreasing the stress response leads to an increase in the NK cells' ability to fight tumors. However, not all cancers are equally affected by psychological factors.

Sleep apnea: A disorder characterized by a temporary cessation of breathing during sleep, usually preceded by a period of difficult breathing accompanied by loud snoring.

3. *Can stress cause a heart attack or heart disease?* The stress response causes blood pressure to increase and the arteries to narrow. These two events can promote atherosclerosis, the buildup of plaque in the arteries. This requires the heart to work even harder to supply blood to the body and can lead to coronary heart disease. The course of heart disease can be affected by psychological and social factors, such as stress management and social support.

4. *What is the relationship between sleep and stress?* Stress can affect the ability to get a good night's sleep by causing either temporary or chronic insomnia. Also, a lack of sleep—sleep deprivation—can create stress by impairing attention, performance, mood, and learning.

LOOKING BEYOND: *Critical Thinking*

Suppose you were caught in a thunderstorm and were soaking wet by the time you got home. Would you now be more likely to catch a cold? Why or why not? What factors might make you more or less likely to catch a cold? What if you had been out very late or instead had had a lot of sleep? Why might these factors matter, or would they not matter? Why might Al become sicker as time goes on?

Strategies for Coping

Worrying that his drinking was getting out of control and beginning to realize that he was in truly bad shape, Al finally recognized that he needed to take action. He looked around the office to see how other people were doing, how they were handling the stress of the difficult situation at work. He paid particular attention to Maya, who didn't seem ruffled by the unsettled atmosphere and the layoffs. Al was puzzled by her reaction, or apparent lack thereof, and he talked with Lisa about it. Lisa suggested that perhaps Maya had particularly effective ways of dealing with stress. She pointed out that the perception of stress depends not only on your view of a situation, but also on the conscious actions you take in response to the stressors. *Coping* is the inclusive term for the multitude of techniques that people employ to handle stress or their reactions to it. Some of these techniques may "come naturally," arising partly from temperament; others can be learned. But some coping strategies are more adaptive than others.

LOOKING AHEAD: *Learning Objectives*

1. What are the different types of coping strategies?
2. How do relationships affect stress and health?
3. What are mind–body interventions?
4. Do gender and culture play a role in coping?

Coping Strategies: Approaches and Tactics

Different people tend to use different coping strategies, and the use of a particular strategy may also depend on the situation and the emotions aroused by it (Folkman & Moscowitz, 2004). People cope in two broad ways: They rely on *reactive coping*, which involves responding to current or past stressors; and *proactive coping*, which involves responding to *potential* stressors, such as a possible upcoming medical procedure, or as is the case with Al, the possibility of a lay-off (Aspinwall & Taylor, 1997; Schwarzer & Knoll, 2003). *Proactive* means "taking action before—not in response to—events."

Problem-Focused and Emotion-Focused Coping

Another way to classify coping strategies is by considering whether they address internal or external circumstances (Carver et al., 1989). **Problem-focused coping** involves the use of strategies that alter either the environment itself or the way in which the person and the environment interact (see Table 10.3). This type of coping is more common when people believe that their actions can affect the stressor (Park et al., 2004), and it tends to be used by people with a high score on the Big Five personality superfactor conscientiousness (see Chapter 8; Watson & Hubbard, 1996). In contrast, **emotion-focused coping** involves the use of strategies that change a person's emotional response to the stressor (see Table 10.3). This type of coping usually decreases arousal. People are more likely to adopt emotion-focused coping when they do not think their actions can affect the stressor itself, and so they must alter their perception of, or response to, the stressor.

Typically, people use more than one strategy in response to a given stressor. The effectiveness of a particular strategy depends in part on a person's accuracy in assessing whether the environment can, in fact, be changed. For example, suppose Lisa assumes that if she gets straight A's in the spring term, she can probably get a scholarship to cover next year's tuition. Here she is approaching the need to pay for her education with the problem-focused coping strategy of *planning*: She is coping with a stressor by thinking about how to manage it (see Table 10.3). If she works hard all spring and carefully rations her social time, Lisa is using two problem-focused strategies: *active coping* and *suppression of competing activities*.

Problem-focused coping: Coping focused on changing the environment itself or the way the person interacts with the environment.

Emotion-focused coping: Coping focused on changing the person's emotional response to the stressor.

Table 10.3 Problem-Focused and Emotion-Focused Coping Strategies

Strategy	Description
Problem-Focused Strategies	
Active coping	Actively tries to remove or work around stressor, or to ameliorate its effects.
Planning	Thinks about how to manage stressor.
Instrumental social support	Seeks concrete advice, assistance, information.
Suppression of competing activities	Puts other activities on hold in order to concentrate on and cope with stressor.
Restraint coping	Waits to act until the appropriate time.
Emotion-Focused Strategies	
Emotional social support	Seeks encouragement, moral support, sympathy, and understanding from others.
Venting emotions	Focuses on and talks about distressing feelings.
Positive reinterpretation/growth	Reinterprets the stressor or situation in a positive way or as a challenge.
Behavioral disengagement	Reduces efforts to deal with the stressor (as occurs with learned helplessness).
Mental disengagement	Turns to other activities to distract attention from the stressor.

What Lisa doesn't know, however, is that the financial aid office awards all of next year's scholarships before the end of the spring term, so her efforts for top grades will not help her achieve her goal of a scholarship. As this example demonstrates, although it is adaptive to try to adopt problem-focused coping in the face of stressors, such an approach is effective only when applied to factors that are controllable. Accurate information and appraisal are important to determine whether this is the case.

The coping strategies people use are affected by their allostatic load—the level of stressors in their lives: The more stressors they face, the more people are likely to use avoidant coping strategies such as distraction and behavioral or mental disengagement, which aim to decrease the focus on the stressor and increase the focus on other matters (Ingledew et al., 1997). In *behavioral disengagement*, people reduce their efforts to deal actively with the stressor (Table 10.3). In its extreme form, this disengagement can lead to a sense of helplessness. In *mental disengagement*, people turn to other activities to distract their attention from the stressor. So, the more stressors that Al and Lisa experience, the less likely they are to cope actively with them.

Avoidant coping strategies can be adaptive when nothing can be done to change a stressor (Folkman & Moscowitz, 2004). Studies (with male participants) have indicated that those perceiving less control over events are less likely to use problem-focused coping strategies (which involve direct action) and more likely to use emotion-focused strategies, such as distraction and emotional support (David & Suls, 1999). Moreover, adjusting their approach in such a way can help people cope more effectively (Christensen et al., 1995; Terry & Hynes, 1998). If Al doesn't think that anything he does at work will ultimately affect whether he gets laid off, he is less likely to use active coping strategies.

Another type of emotion-focused coping strategy is venting (see Table 10.3)—that is, focusing on and talking about the stressor. James Pennebaker (1989) asked a group of college students to write for 20 minutes a day for 4 consecutive days; they were told that their writing samples would remain confidential. Pennebaker gave half of them the following instructions:

> *During each of the 4 writing days, I want you to write about the most traumatic and upsetting experiences of your whole life. You can write on different topics each day or on the same topic for all 4 days. The important thing is that you write about your deepest thoughts and feelings. Ideally, whatever you write about should deal with an event or experience that you have not talked about with others in detail.*

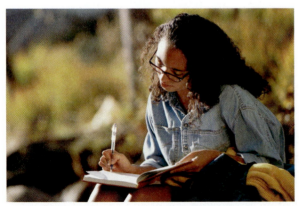

Writing in detail about upsetting or difficult experiences can enhance immune system functioning and can lead to better moods.

Another group, serving as a control, was asked to write each day about superficial topics. In this study and variants of it, students who were asked to write about an emotional topic were more likely to report negative moods immediately after writing, although their overall moods were more positive by the end of the school year (Pennebaker et al., 1990). Perhaps paradoxically, those who wrote about traumatic events were less likely to get sick (as measured by visits to the student health center) in the months following the expressive writing. Similar results were reported by Pennebaker and Francis (1996) and were found even when the writing occurred via e-mail (Sheese et al., 2004).

Writing about a traumatic event allows the writer to work through and come to terms with the experience, which in turn appears to reduce the negative effects of stress on the immune system. This interpretation is buttressed by the results of other studies that assessed the relation between writing and immune function (Petrie et al., 1995, 1998), absenteeism from work (Francis & Pennebaker, 1992), and specific medical problems (Smyth et al., 1999). It appears, however, that writing only briefly—say, just a 3-minute outline of a traumatic experience—doesn't provide enough emotional expression to confer the benefits; the participants must actively process their experiences by writing about them in detail (Páez et al., 1999).

These studies suggest that focusing on and "working through" feelings about a traumatic experience have positive effects, although it may take a while for these effects to appear. *Venting* as investigated in these studies does not mean that internal "pressure" is released, as Freud believed. Rather this process could simply help a person come to terms with an emotion—to make sense of and make peace with emotional events.

Thought Suppression

Purposefully trying not to think about something emotionally arousing or distressing is **thought suppression** (Wegner et al., 1987). Suppose Al and Lisa used thought suppression. They would try not to think about Al's work situation and all that depended on it. However, research has shown that trying *not* to think about something can have the paradoxical effect of causing that "suppressed" thought to pop into consciousness more than it does when you are not trying to suppress it. This phenomenon is referred to as a *rebound effect*. Research on the application of thought suppression to health and illness has shown that the act of suppressing emotional thoughts actually magnifies both the intensity of the thoughts and the autonomic reactions to those thoughts (Clark et al., 1991; Wegner et al., 1987). Attempts to suppress thoughts that are emotionally charged (either positive or negative) have also been associated with changes in the sympathetic nervous system (Gross & Levenson, 1997).

Some people use thought suppression more frequently than others. Such "high thought suppressors" have less success in suppressing thoughts related to a stressor when they are under a heavy allostatic load. Because of the rebound effect, the subsequent increase in thoughts about the stressor may lead to excessive focus on it and to depression (Beevers & Meyer, 2004; Koster et al., 2003; Wenzlaff & Luxton, 2003). Additional research suggests that current measures of thought suppression may assess only failed attempts at suppression—not the use of the strategy itself—and those failures then result in rebound (Rassin, 2003).

Aggression: Coping Gone Awry

For good or ill, one way to cope with stressors is through **aggression**, behavior that is intended to harm another living being who does not wish to be harmed (Baron & Richardson, 1994). Couples who were more verbally and physically aggressive with each other were more likely to report a higher number of stressful events than couples who were not as abusive (Eby, 2004; Straus, 1980). However, this is only a correlation, and thus cause and effect are unclear: It is possible that stress leads to aggression, but it is also possible that people who are abusive *create* more stressful events in their lives by their aggressive manner (see Chapters 6 and 9 for discussions of how people create their own microenvironments; McGuffin & Katz, 1993; Thapar & McGuffin, 1996; Wang et al., 2005). However, using correlational designs, which assess only whether two factors vary together,

Thought suppression: The coping strategy that involves purposefully trying not to think about something emotionally arousing or distressing.

Aggression: Behavior that is intended to harm another living being who does not wish to be harmed.

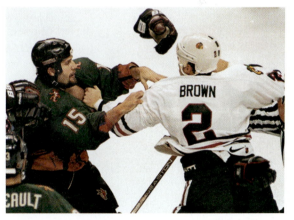

Some people are more aggressive than others. For example, the personality trait of aggressiveness (measured by a self-report paper-and-pencil test) predicts actual aggressive behavior. Hockey players who scored higher on aggressiveness before the hockey season spent more time in the penalty box for aggressive penalties, but not for nonaggressive penalties (Bushman & Wells, 1998).

not whether one causes the other—in combination with experimental ones, which can reveal causation—investigators have found a number of specific stressors that are associated with or lead to aggression.

Environmental Factors. External factors in the environment, such as noise and heat, can sometimes spark aggression (Berkowitz & Harmon-Jones, 2004), and the target is usually innocent people who happen to be in the line of fire. Depression and pain are also associated with increased aggression (Berkowitz, 1998). These unpleasant experiences have in common the ability to predispose people to make a negative appraisal of a stimulus, particularly if the potential for threat is ambiguous. For instance, if Al has a headache, he may be more likely than if he were pain-free to assume that a colleague's comment ("Hey Al, quitting early?" on a day he's going to pick up Lisa for a weekend visit) has hostile intent. Rather than taking the remark as office kidding, he might worry that he was viewed as a slacker and thus a good candidate to be laid off next.

Hostile Attribution Bias. Although external stressors such as noise and pain can clearly lead to inaccurate and negative appraisals of a stimulus, some people are more likely than others to make a negative appraisal of an ambiguous, or even neutral, stimulus, even without the presence of such stressors. The propensity to misread the intentions of others, interpreting them negatively, is referred to as the **hostile attribution bias** (Dodge & Newman, 1981; Nasby et al., 1979). Because Al doesn't have a hostile attribution bias, he would not normally interpret his colleague's comment as a threat.

Aggressive Tendencies. Many stressors lead to an unpleasant internal state and increased negative mood, which in turn can lead to the fight-or-flight response. Whether a person responds to this internal state with aggression is determined by events at the three levels of analysis: in part by the person's biology (including his or her genes, hormones, arousal levels, and central nervous system traumas or abnormalities); in part by his or her thoughts, beliefs, feelings, and expectations (which arise in part from his or her history of reinforcement and observational learning); and in part by the culture's expectations of appropriate behavior. And all of these factors interact (Berkowitz, 1998).

Clearly, however, not everyone responds to an unpleasant internal state and negative mood with aggression. Some people, whose initial response to a threat is fear, will try to "flee" by escaping or avoiding whatever or whomever instigated the negative situation. Others will respond initially with irritation, annoyance, or anger. Berkowitz proposes that this initial response is then tempered by further cognitive processing about the desired goals and expectations of punishment, reward, or harm, allowing people to make a final determination of a feeling of anger or fear (although some people fight or flee without further appraisal).

Gender Differences in Aggression. If aggression is defined by physical acts, then, as children and adults, males are more aggressive than females. The results of a meta-analysis by Eagly and Steffen (1986) found that females are less likely to be aggressive if they think the aggression will physically harm another person, backfire on themselves, or cause them to feel considerable guilt or shame. However, when considering acts of aggression that do not cause physical harm, such as hurting other people's relationships (or threatening to do so), males are not necessarily more aggressive than females. Nonphysical aggression includes threatened or actual social exclusion of a friend, gossiping, or withdrawing acceptance of another person. Because of her gender (that is, the social expectations for some-

Hostile attribution bias: The propensity to misread the intentions of others as negative.

one of her sex), Lisa may be less likely than a male fellow student to shove someone when she feels aggressive; however, she might gossip about someone or slight that person in some way. *Relational aggression* is the term for nonphysical aggression that damages relationships or uses relationships to injure others psychologically, for example, by socially excluding them (Crick & Grotpeter, 1995); relational aggression is instigated more by females than by males.

Self-Esteem and Narcissism. Not surprisingly, hostile people are more likely than others to behave aggressively (Anderson & Bushman, 1997). However, determining why some people use aggression as a coping strategy is more difficult than you may think. Conventional wisdom, at least in the United States, has been that aggression is more likely to be perpetrated by people who feel bad about themselves—that is, who have low self-esteem—and that their aggression toward others is a way of bolstering their view of themselves. Is conventional wisdom right? Research results (Baumeister et al., 1996; Bushman, 1998) indicate that the answer is a resounding no! On the contrary, most aggressors are people who think exceedingly well of themselves (that is, have high self-esteem) and experience an insult as a threat to their positive self-view. Their aggression is a response to a perceived threat (Bushman, 1998). Not *all* people with high self-esteem are likely to be more aggressive; the aggressors are a subset of this group whose positive view of themselves may be either overinflated (that is, it doesn't correspond to reality) or unstable (Baumeister et al., 1996; Morf & Rhodewalt, 2001). Such people, who are termed *narcissists*, may view a

On April 20, 1999, Littleton, Colorado's Colombine High School students Dylan Klebold and Eric Harris killed 15 people (including themselves). It was reported that Eric Harris would get enraged at the smallest slight (Lowe, 1999). Before the rampage, Harris had received several rejections, including a rejection for entry into the Marine Corps 5 days before the killings. Could this rejection have threatened an unrealistically high sense of self-esteem?

threat to their positive self-image as likely to lead to a drop in self-esteem, and thus they defend against this drop (and the ensuing negative emotions) with aggressive behavior (Bushman et al., 2001; Twenge & Campbell, 2003). Just as men are more likely to be physically aggressive, men also score higher on scales of narcissism (Bushman, 1998); they also have higher self-esteem in general.

Imagine that you agreed to participate in a psychological study and, as part of the study, wrote an essay on some topic. You get the essay back with this comment: "This is the worst essay I've ever read." Later, you are competing with the person who wrote this comment on a reaction time test, in which the winner sets the loudness and duration of a buzzer that goes off each time the other player loses. How would you respond if you won? How obnoxious would you let the sound be? Bushman (1998) hypothesized that people who score high on narcissism would be more likely to behave aggressively than those who score low, and indeed that is what he found. For these narcissists, a poor evaluation endangered their view of themselves, and was enough to elicit aggression toward the person doing the evaluating. Participants who scored low on narcissism were less likely to perceive negative evaluations of their essays as threats, and they were less aggressive. Not only was Bushman correct in his prediction, but he also found that the narcissistic participants were more likely to be aggressive *even if their essays were positively received*; a negative evaluation simply increased their aggressive behavior. For narcissists, then, it appears that *any* evaluation is a stressor that threatens their view of themselves. Further research on male narcissists reveals that they, in contrast to other men, are less likely to feel empathic toward rape victims and, when rebuffed by women, are more likely to retaliate in some way (Bushman et al., 2003).

Substance abuse: Drug or alcohol use that causes distress or trouble with functioning in major areas of life, occurs in dangerous situations, or leads to legal difficulties.

Substance dependence: Chronic substance abuse that is characterized by seven symptoms, the two most important being tolerance and withdrawal.

Tolerance: The condition of requiring more of a substance to achieve the same effect (because the usual amount provides a diminished response).

Withdrawal symptoms: The onset of uncomfortable or life-threatening effects when the use of a substance is stopped.

Depressants: A class of substances, including barbiturates, alcohol, and antianxiety drugs, that depress the central nervous system, decreasing the user's behavioral activity and level of awareness; also called *sedative-hypnotic drugs*.

Table 10.4

The Seven Symptoms of Substance Dependence

1. Tolerance.

2. Withdrawal.

3. Larger amounts of substance taken over a longer period of time than intended.

4. Unsuccessful efforts or a persistent desire to decrease or control the substance use.

5. Much time spent in obtaining the substance, using it, or recovering from its effects.

6. Important work, social, or recreational activities given up as a result of the substance.

7. Despite knowledge of recurrent or ongoing physical or psychological problems caused or exacerbated by the substance, continued use of substance.

Summing Up. We are all, at one time or another, confronted by stressors that can elicit aggression; Thornton Wilder has written, "We have all murdered, in thought." Why do only some of us act on our aggressive thoughts? Baumeister and Boden (1998) propose that the answer may lie in the difficulty aggressive people have in regulating, or controlling, themselves. In turn, the ability to control ourselves and our aggressive impulses is related to a host of factors, including community standards, the perceived likelihood of punishment, our ability to monitor our behavior, our estimate of whether it will make us feel better (Bushman et al., 2001), and a conscious decision *not* to control ourselves (as occurs when people, knowing that the likely outcome will be physical aggression, still decide to drink or use drugs).

Drugs and Alcohol

Al started out drinking to help him get to sleep. Now, however, he drinks because he feels it helps him unwind from the day, from the stress and anxiety of work. Al's drinking illustrates how substances—drugs and alcohol—are used as coping strategies. Although the use of substances may change the perception of the stressor while someone is under their influence, substance use as a coping strategy does not change the stressor, nor does it provide any lasting change in how the stressor is viewed. At what point does such a coping strategy become problematic and maladaptive?

A woman drinks heavily, but only over the weekend, and she never misses work because of it. Is she an alcoholic? How about the man who smokes marijuana at the end of the day to feel relaxed, or the student who downs four cups of caffeinated coffee each evening while studying? Have these people crossed some biological or psychological line between use and abuse? The American Psychiatric Association (2000a) has developed three main criteria for substance abuse:

1. a pattern of substance use that leads to significant distress or difficulty functioning in major areas of life (for instance, at home, work, or school, or in relationships);

2. substance use that occurs in dangerous situations (for instance, while or before driving a car); or

3. substance use that leads to legal difficulties.

Substance dependence results from chronic abuse. It is characterized by seven symptoms (see Table 10.4), the two most important of which are tolerance and withdrawal (American Psychiatric Association, 2000a). Tolerance is the condition, resulting from repeated use, in which the same amount of a substance produces a diminished effect (thus, more of the substance is required to achieve the same effect). Tolerance typically occurs with the use of alcohol, barbiturates, amphetamines, and opiates such as morphine and heroin. *Withdrawal* is the cessation of the use of a substance; withdrawal symptoms are the uncomfortable or life-threatening effects that may be experienced during withdrawal. Substance abuse presents costs to society as a whole as well as to the individual: In the United States, the costs related to crime, drug treatment, medical care, social welfare programs, and time lost from work total an estimated $67 billion per year (National Institute on Drug Abuse, 2003).

Depressants: Focus on Alcohol. The depressants, also called *sedative-hypnotic drugs*, include barbiturates, alcohol, and antianxiety drugs such as Valium. Drugs in this category depress the central nervous system and thus tend to slow a person down, decreasing the user's behavioral activity and level of awareness. Because of its prevalence and the fact that so much is known about its effects, we focus at length on alcohol here.

Approximately 60% of adults in the United States reported that they drank alcohol within the previous year (Centers for Disease Control and Prevention, 2003); 8% of adults in the United States (17 million people) are considered to have either alcohol abuse or dependence (Grant et al., 2004). The younger people are when they start drinking, the more likely they are to develop an alcohol disorder (Grant & Dawson, 1997).

Biological effects of alcohol. Alcohol is classified as a depressant because it depresses the nervous system through its inhibiting effect on excitatory neurotransmitters. Alcohol changes the structure of the neuron's cell membrane, altering neural transmission (Goldstein, 1994; Grilly, 1994). But depressants such as alcohol can also inhibit the action of inhibitory neurons, so some neurons fire that otherwise would be inhibited. Thus, in addition to depressing some neural activity, depressants also activate neurons that otherwise would not fire. This phenomenon is called **disinhibition**.

Although it takes about an hour for alcohol to be fully absorbed into the blood (as measured by blood alcohol levels), drinkers can feel an effect within a few minutes. The effects of alcohol depend on the dosage. At low doses, alcohol can cause a sense of decreased awareness and increased relaxation, and the drinker may become talkative or outgoing. At moderate doses, the drinker experiences slowed reaction time and impaired judgment—which is why drinking and driving shouldn't mix. At higher doses, alcohol impairs cognition, self-control, and self-restraint, and the drinker may become emotionally unstable or overly aggressive. "Barroom brawls" often occur because a drunk patron misconstrues a casual remark that otherwise might have passed unnoticed. As the effects of the alcohol take hold, the drinker's responses are more likely to be out of proportion to the situation. At very high doses, the drinker can have a diminished sense of cold, pain, and discomfort (which is why some people drink when in pain). At these high doses, alcohol causes dilation of the peripheral blood vessels, which increases the amount of blood circulating through the skin and makes the drinker both feel warmer and lose heat faster. Thus, heavy drinking in the cold increases the chance of hypothermia (that is, decreased body temperature) and frostbite. Such high doses can bring on respiratory arrest, coma, or death.

Psychological effects of alcohol. Steele and Southwick (1985) conducted a meta-analysis of the effects of alcohol on social behavior, specifically in "high-conflict" and "low-conflict" situations. The type of conflict considered here is within the person, between two opposing desires. Specifically, Steele and Southwick wanted to see whether the use of alcohol changes the way people behave when they experience such internal conflict. They found a pattern of what they called **inhibitory conflict**: If a person in a high-conflict situation was sober, his or her response was "both strongly instigated and inhibited"; that is, the person would both want to act and not want to act. A person might very much have wanted to engage in a particular behavior, but the consequences (moral, legal, social, or personal) were great enough to inhibit it. After drinking enough alcohol, however, the same person would not restrain his or her behavior. And the more alcohol consumed, the greater the likelihood of engaging in the behavior despite societal or other sanctions. When the conflict level

People's expectations of what will happen to them as a result of drinking alcohol can affect their behavior (Kirsch & Lynn, 1999).

Disinhibition: The inhibition of inhibitory neurons, which makes other neurons (the ones that are usually inhibited) more likely to fire and which usually occurs as a result of depressant use.

Inhibitory conflict: An internal response when a behavior is both strongly instigated and inhibited.

Alcohol myopia can make a drinker incorrectly interpret someone else's clenched fist as a threatening aggressive act, rather than as an indicator of that person's nervousness or anxiety.

Table 10.5

Summary of the Psychological Effects of Alcohol

Alcohol use can lead to:

- Difficulties in abstract thinking
- Impaired ability to conceptualize information
- Problems noticing situational cues
- Poor processing of ambiguous social situations
- Inhibitory conflict
- Alcohol myopia
- Increased aggression

Alcohol myopia: The disproportionate influence of immediate experience on behavior and emotion due to the effects of alcohol use.

Blackout: A period of time for which an alcoholic has no memory of events that transpired while he or she was intoxicated.

was low, it was still possible to inhibit the behavior; only in high-conflict situations was inhibition overcome by alcohol. This finding explains how date rape can happen: When sober, a man might want to have sexual relations but be inhibited from using force. But under the influence of alcohol, he might be more likely to act—in a high-conflict, sexually charged situation, he might have difficulty attending to the consequences that would otherwise cause him to inhibit such aggressive behavior.

The results of many studies have shown that the use of alcohol facilitates aggressive behavior (Bushman & Cooper, 1990). You have already seen one path for increased aggression with alcohol use: Alcohol can make it difficult to inhibit behavior in a high-conflict situation. Aggression can also result from misreading a situation, as in the barroom brawl example. Alcohol impairs the ability to abstract and conceptualize information (Pihl et al., 2003; Tarter et al., 1971) and to notice many situational cues (Washburne, 1956). This impairment results in **alcohol myopia**, "a state of short-sightedness in which superficially understood, immediate aspects of experience have a disproportionate influence on behavior and emotion" (Steele & Josephs, 1990, p. 923). Thus, stimuli that elicit aggression (such as someone's clenched fists or a date's refusal to have sexual intercourse) loom larger than stimuli that must be abstracted or require more thought (such as considerations that the aggressive behavior may be immoral, illegal, or unnecessary). Drinking also makes it more difficult to process ambiguous social situations, such as occasions when someone's words and body language are contradictory. For example, suppose friends have gone out drinking and all are now quite drunk. One of them might announce that he is sick, but laugh about it. The others might not understand that their friend really *is* sick and needs medical care.

Noting the fact that more than 50% of on-campus date rapes occur when men are under the influence of alcohol (Muehlenhard & Linton, 1987; Ouimette, 1997), Johnson and colleagues (2000) set out to determine exactly how drinking might be involved. They asked male volunteers to drink different levels of alcohol, then watch one of two videos of a woman on a blind date. In one video, she exhibited friendly, cordial behavior; in the other, she was unresponsive. The men were then asked how acceptable it would be for a man to be sexually aggressive toward his date (see Figure 10.7). Among the men who viewed the video with the unresponsive woman, alcohol intake made no difference in the men's answers. However, alcohol intake did make a difference for the men who viewed the video of the friendly woman: Those men who had more to drink thought that sexual aggression toward a friendly date was acceptable. The alcohol impaired the men's ability to understand that the friendliness the woman showed did not mean that it was acceptable for a man to force her to have sex. To reason about this social situation appropriately, a person needs to be able conceptualize and engage in abstract thinking—and such functions are compromised by drinking alcohol.

Table 10.5 provides a summary of the psychological effects of alcohol.

Chronic abuse: More than a bad habit Alcoholics come from all socioeconomic classes. Historically, more males than females have become alcoholics, and this pattern continues today, although the gap is narrowing (Nelson et al., 1998). Almost all cultures recognize that drinking can create both tolerance and withdrawal symptoms, although problematic alcohol use is defined differently in different cultures (Gureje et al., 1997). Chronic alcohol abuse can cause severe memory deficits, even **blackouts**, periods of time for which the alcoholic has no memory of events that occurred while he or she was intoxicated. The chronic al-

Figure 10.7 Alcohol and Sexual Aggression

Male participants were assigned to one of four alcohol consumption groups: moderate alcohol intake, low alcohol intake, placebo alcohol intake (alcohol rubbed on the rim of glasses holding nonalcoholic drinks), and control group (drank ice water). The three alcohol groups did not know the strength of their drinks.

Half of each group of men watched a video about a blind date in which the woman was very friendly; the other half of each group watched a video about a blind date in which the woman was unresponsive and cold.

Regardless of alcohol intake, the participants who watched the unresponsive date were not very accepting of the idea of sexual aggression by the man and attributed any responsibility for aggression to *him*. In contrast, there was clear alcohol myopia in those who watched the friendly date: The more alcohol they drank, the more the men accepted the idea of sexual aggression toward the woman, and the more they attributed any aggression by the man as being the *woman's* responsibility (Johnson et al., 2000).

coholic often experiences difficulty with abstract reasoning, problem solving, and perceptual motor functions. It has been difficult for researchers to sort out to what degree these memory deficits are caused by the action of the alcohol itself or by the malnutrition that often accompanies alcoholism. Alcohol is highly caloric but contains very little in the way of nutrients; consequently, many heavy drinkers are inadequately nourished.

Other depressants. Barbiturates, including Amytal, Nembutal, and Seconal, mimic the effects of alcohol in that they depress the central nervous system. Barbiturates cause sedation and drowsiness and are therefore usually prescribed to aid sleep or to reduce anxiety, but they can be lethal when combined with alcohol. In higher doses, barbiturates cause slurred speech, dizziness, poor judgment, and irritability. Users will develop both tolerance and withdrawal symptoms: Withdrawal may be accompanied by agitation, restlessness, and hallucinations (vivid mental images that seem real). Sedation and drowsiness are also effects of benzodiazepines (such as Ativan, Xanax, and Valium, sometimes prescribed because they can reduce symptoms of anxiety). Because benzodiazepines are less habit-forming than barbiturates, the former are more frequently prescribed for sleep problems (Arana & Rosenbaum, 2000).

Stimulants: Focus on Cocaine. In contrast to depressants, **stimulants** excite the central nervous system, stimulating behavioral activity and heightened arousal. Low doses of amphetamines and cocaine can lead to a perception of increased physical and mental energy, diminished hunger, and a sense of invulnerability. Because "coming down" from this state is a disappointment, stimulant users often

Stimulants: A class of substances that excite the central nervous system, leading to increases in behavioral activity and heightened arousal.

want to repeat the experience and so are at risk for continued drug use. Of all drugs, stimulants are the most likely to induce dependence.

Cocaine is commonly inhaled in its powdered form, and it has a local anesthetic effect. The user has an enhanced sense of physical and mental capacity and a simultaneous loss of appetite. Chronic users develop paranoia, teeth grinding, and repetitive behaviors and may also experience disturbances in the visual field, such as seeing snow, or the feeling that insects ("cocaine bugs") are crawling on the skin. This latter sensation arises from the spontaneous firing of sensory neurons, caused by the cocaine.

Figure 10.8 Action of Stimulants on Neurotransmitters

Cocaine and other stimulants create their stimulating effects by blocking reuptake—that is, by preventing the normal reabsorption into the terminal button—of some norepinephrine and dopamine molecules at the synaptic cleft. The net effect is that more of these neurotransmitters remain in the synaptic cleft.

Cocaine exerts its effects by inhibiting the reuptake of dopamine and norepinephrine (Figure 10.8). The increased presence of these neurotransmitters in the synaptic cleft leads to a pleasurable, even euphoric, feeling. With continued use of cocaine, the drug becomes the main trigger for activation of the reward system, leading other sources of pleasure, such as food or sex, to have little or no effect (National Institute on Drug Abuse, 1998). When cocaine and alcohol are taken together, the human liver (which metabolizes the substances) creates a third substance, called *cocaethylene*, which intensifies cocaine's effects while at the same time increasing the risk of sudden death (National Institute on Drug Abuse, 2004).

Crack. Cocaine in crystalline form, known as **crack**, is usually smoked in a pipe ("free-basing") or rolled into a cigarette. Crack is faster acting and more intense in its effect than is cocaine powder inhaled through the nostrils; however, because its effects last for only a few minutes, the user tends to take greater amounts of crack than of powdered cocaine. Crack cocaine has more potential for abuse and dependence (Cone, 1995). The user experiences a feeling of euphoria, perceived clarity of thought, and increased energy. Crack increases heart rate and blood pressure and constricts blood vessels—a potentially lethal combination. After the drug wears off, the user experiences a massive "crash," with intense depression and intense craving for more crack. Both cocaine and crack can create strong dependence, particularly if injected or smoked. The user can develop tolerance; with crack, the development of tolerance is particularly swift. Sudden death can occur even in healthy people who use the drug only occasionally.

Other stimulants. **Amphetamines** are synthetic stimulants such as Benzedrine and Dexedrine; they are usually taken in pill form or injected. With high doses, the user can suffer *amphetamine psychosis*, which is similar to paranoid schizophrenia; symptoms include delusions (entrenched false beliefs), hallucinations, and paranoia. Chronic use of amphetamines stimulates violent behaviors (Leccese, 1991) and can cause long-term neural changes associated with impaired memory and motor coordination (Volkow et al., 2001).

The stimulant *MDMA* (also known as ecstasy, or "e") causes the neurotransmitter serotonin, and to a lesser extent dopamine, to be released from certain neurons (Colado et al., 2004; Green et al., 1995). Research on animals indicates that MDMA, used even once, can permanently damage neurons that release serotonin, affecting memory, learning, sleep, and appetite (Fischer et al., 1995). Studies (Jacobsen et al., 2004; Wareing et al., 2004) with humans have not yet been able to discern MDMA's unique effects on cognition, emo-

Crack: Cocaine in crystalline form, usually smoked in a pipe (free-basing) or rolled into a cigarette.

Amphetamines: Synthetic stimulants.

tion, and behavior because these studies are generally correlational or quasiexperimental (see Chapter 1); such research designs do not lend themselves to eliminating confounds, such as the effects of other drugs that are taken along with MDMA (Green, 2004). Researchers have struggled mightily to sort out MDMA's effects on humans not only because users tend to take multiple drugs (Schifano, 2004), but also because MDMA pills may—unbeknownst to the user—also contain other substances.

Finally, *caffeine* and *nicotine* are also stimulants. Caffeine is present in coffee, tea, chocolate, and colas, among other beverages and foods. It causes increased alertness, raises pulse and heart rate, and can produce insomnia, restlessness, and ringing in the ears. There is some degree of tolerance, and chronic users will experience withdrawal headaches if they miss their customary morning coffee. Nicotine, present in cigarettes and tobacco in any form, can cause increased alertness and relaxation, as well as irritability, increased blood pressure, stomach pains, dizziness, emphysema, and heart disease. Nicotine works by triggering the release of several neurotransmitters that lead to a pleasurable sensation. Nicotine is addictive, causing some level of tolerance, as well as withdrawal symptoms when its use is stopped.

Caffeine and nicotine are both stimulants, and people who regularly smoke or drink may experience tolerance and, when they skip their usual coffee or cigarette, symptoms of withdrawal.

Narcotic Analgesics: Focus on Heroin. Certain drugs, including heroin, morphine, codeine, Percodan, Demerol, Vicodin, and Oxycodone, are called ==narcotic analgesics== because they are strongly addictive drugs that dull the senses and provide analgesia; that is, they relieve pain. These drugs affect certain endorphin receptors (see Chapter 3). Generally, drugs of this type are prescribed to relieve pain, severe diarrhea, protracted coughing, and troubled sleep. Heroin, an illegal drug, is one of the stronger narcotic analgesics. Like morphine, from which it is derived, heroin is an ==opiate== (or *opioid*), produced from the opium poppy.

Heroin can bring about a feeling of relaxation and euphoria, but these effects are very short-term and are followed by negative changes in mood and behavior. Like other opiates, heroin is a central nervous system depressant, causing a slowing of neural activity in brainstem areas responsible for respiration and coughing, as well as in other areas of the brain. When heroin is in the body, the user's pupils may constrict and he or she may experience slower breathing and lethargy. Tolerance and withdrawal symptoms occur, with the latter usually involving periods of yawning, chills, hot flashes, restlessness, diarrhea, and goose bumps on the skin, followed by up to 12 hours of sleep.

In the brain, heroin and other opiates work by activating the dopamine-based reward system and also by binding to the opioid receptors, where the body's endorphins (opioids produced in the body) usually bind. This creates a negative feedback loop, leading the body to decrease its production of endorphins, and leaving the heroin user without natural means to relieve pain. Thus, more heroin is needed to achieve the analgesic effect. When the user tries to quit, endorphins do not kick in to alleviate the withdrawal symptoms, thus heightening the discomfort—and making it difficult to quit.

Hallucinogens: Focus on LSD. A ==hallucinogen== is a substance that induces the perceptual experiences known as hallucinations. Hallucinogens include mescaline, peyote, psilocybin, lysergic acid diethylamide (LSD), phencyclidine (PCP), ketamine ("Special K"), and marijuana. In general, all but marijuana can cause visual hallucinations at moderate dosages; much higher dosages are needed before marijuana will do so.

Narcotic analgesics: A class of strongly addictive drugs, such as heroin, that relieve pain.

Opiate: A narcotic, such as morphine, derived from the opium poppy.

Hallucinogen: A substance that induces hallucinations.

LSD is a synthetic substance that produces perceptual alterations. Exactly how LSD works is not well understood, but it is known to alter the functioning of the serotonin system. Users commonly experience visual hallucinations, which often include geometric shapes, vivid colors, and violent movement. At higher doses, geometric shapes give way to quickly changing meaningful objects. Users may feel as if they are becoming part of whatever they observe. Auditory hallucinations include hearing invented foreign languages or symphonies. These symptoms may last several hours, and the user's expectations can shape the experience induced by LSD.

A creativity boost? Although some people report that they feel more creative as a result of taking LSD, research does not support this subjective experience of increased creativity (Dusek & Girdano, 1980). Actually, LSD can produce frightening experiences ("bad trips"), which may be caused by a change in dose, mood, expectations, and environment. A user may panic during a bad trip and need to be "talked down," repeatedly reminded that the frightening experience is in fact a drug-induced state that will wear off. Occasionally, suicide or murder takes place in the course of a user's hallucination. Hallucinations can recur without use of the drug; these spontaneous, perhaps alarming, ==flashbacks== can happen weeks, even years, afterward and can be triggered by entering a dark environment (Abraham, 1983).

Other hallucinogens. The most commonly used hallucinogen in America is marijuana (National Institute on Drug Abuse, 2004), whose active ingredient is tetrahydrocannabinol (THC), which is chemically similar to the naturally occurring neurotransmitters in the body called *cannabinoids* (such as anandamide). There are receptors for cannabinoid molecules throughout the body and brain, including in the hippocampus (see Chapter 2) and brain areas involved in concentration, time and sensory perception, pleasure, and movement control; cannabinoids can affect learning and memory, appetite, and pain, and they can modulate other neurotransmitters (Gruber et al., 2003; Wilson & Nicoll, 2001). The effects of marijuana depend on the user's mood, expectations, and environment: If alone, the user may experience drowsiness and go to sleep; if with others, the user may feel euphoric; some people may experience anxiety and panic after using the substance (Dannon et al., 2004; Patel et al., in press). The effects of the drug can be subtle, including perceptual alterations in which sights and sounds seem more vivid. Distortions of space and time are also common, and perceptual motor skills may be impaired, making driving unsafe (Petersen, 1977, 1979; Sterling-Smith, 1976). Although marijuana is less powerful than most other hallucinogens, every year approximately 230,000 Americans attend treatment centers in an effort to stop using it (National Admissions to Substance Abuse Treatment Services, 2001). Long-term use of marijuana can lead to withdrawal symptoms (Haney et al., 1999).

The substance *ketamine*, similar to PCP, is legally used as an anesthetic for animals. Use by humans can induce hallucinations, anesthesia, and stimulation of the cardiovascular and respiratory systems. Ketamine use is also associated with violence, a loss of contact with reality, and impaired thinking (White & Ryan, 1996). Users are likely to develop tolerance and dependence.

Coping and Social Support

==Social support==, the help and support gained through interacting with others, buffers the adverse effects of stress. Certain types of positive relationships, such as a good marriage, positive contact with friends and family, participation in group activities, and involvement in a religious organization, can lengthen life ex-

Flashback: A hallucination that recurs without the use of a drug.

Social support: The help and support gained through interacting with others.

pectancy. Just having such connections can have as much influence on mortality as being a nonsmoker or being physically active (House et al., 1988). Consider the following findings related to social support:

- In a study of over 4,000 men and women in Alameda County, California, the death rate for socially isolated people was twice that for people with strong social ties. Deaths were due not only to heart disease, but also to cancer, infectious disease, and other causes (Berkman & Syme, 1979).

- The benefits of social support can be gained simply from holding hands or making some other kind of physical contact (Sapolsky, 1997).

- For those undergoing a painful and frightening surgical procedure, just talking with their doctor the night before surgery positively affected recovery (Egbert et al., 1964).

- In a study of people with severe coronary heart disease, half of the group without social support died within 5 years, three times the rate for those who had a close friend or spouse (Williams et al., 1992). Other researchers have reported similar results (Rutledge et al., 2004).

- Among college students experiencing high levels of stress, those reporting high levels of social support were less likely to be depressed than those reporting lower levels of social support (Pengilly & Dowd, 1997).

There is a confounding variable influencing the association between social support and longevity among heart patients: Although couch potatoes report less social support, it may be their sedentary behavior, not the diminished social support, that accounts for their shorter life spans (Brummett et al., 2005).

Social support is also related to immune system functioning (Seeman et al., 1994). Looking at the relation between social support and catching a cold, researchers found that participants who had a wide range of acquaintances (friends, neighbors, relatives, work colleagues, people from social or religious groups, and so forth) were half as likely to catch a cold as those who were socially isolated (Cohen et al., 1997). The key is not the total number of supportive relationships, but rather their variety. Not just any relationship will do the trick: Demanding and critical relationships—but not positive and supportive ones—are associated with stress-related symptoms (Seeman, 2000). Bad marriages are associated with suppressed immune functioning (Kiecolt-Glaser & Newton, 2001), at least in men (Kiecolt-Glaser et al., 1988). For women, marital stress is associated with coronary heart disease at a later point in time (Orth-Gomér et al., 2000).

The person dressed in yellow is receiving enacted social support. However, she may not necessarily have the sense that support is available when she needs it (perceived social support) because these two aspects of social support are not necessarily correlated. Also, what constitutes support may differ from person to person.

Perceived social support, the subjective sense that support is available should it be needed, is distinct from the actual size and variety of your social network, and from **enacted social support**, specific support that is provided to you, such as a friend bringing you a meal when he or she knows you aren't feeling well. Research has shown that it is generally perceived support, not enacted support, that provides the buffer against stress (Cohen & Wills, 1985). Moreover, the perception of support is unrelated to actual support. For instance, researchers observed college students, some of whom perceived a high degree of social support in their lives and some of whom perceived much less, as they responded to stressors in the presence of their friends.

Perceived social support: The subjective sense that support is available should it be needed.

Enacted social support: The specific supportive behaviors provided by others.

The participants' perceptions of their friends' support was unrelated to the actual support the friends offered (Lakey & Heller, 1988). People who perceive themselves as having low social support tend to view a given social interaction more negatively (Lakey & Dickenson, 1994).

Mind–Body Interventions

<table>
<tr><td>

Table 10.6

Common Mind–Body Interventions

- Hypnosis
- Meditation
- Yoga
- Biofeedback
- Visual imagery
- Cognitive therapy
- Stress management/relaxation induction
- Prayer
- Tai chi

</td></tr>
</table>

When you receive an injection, take a pill, have surgery, or undergo a medical procedure, it doesn't much matter what you are thinking about and focusing on, as long as your body responds in the intended way to the intervention. In contrast, *mind–body interventions* seek to engage your mind in a particular way in order to influence your body's functioning. As you can see in Table 10.6, there are a number of commonly used mind–body techniques. One survey found that almost 20% of adults questioned had employed at least one type of mind–body intervention within the previous year (Wolsko et al., 2004). Mind–body techniques are used by people from many walks of life, including medical patients, athletes (Ryska, 1998), managers, teachers (Anderson et al., 1999), and first-year law school students (Sheehy & Horan, 2004). The National Institutes of Health has a special branch, the National Center for Complementary and Alternative Medicine (NCCAM), which is dedicated to the investigation of such techniques. NCCAM provides funding to researchers who study how a wide range of mind–body interventions can be used in treating specific diseases and pain and in maintaining health (Berman & Straus, 2004).

The goal of mind–body interventions is not to change a stressful stimulus, but to allow you to adapt to the stimulus—and, in doing so, to alter bodily functioning. Mind–body interventions can alter heart and breathing rates, hormone secretion, and brain activation. Researchers have found that both progressive muscle relaxation and hypnosis effectively decrease autonomic reactivity to stress and that deep abdominal breathing is somewhat effective. Even sitting quietly with your eyes closed for a few minutes decreases pulse rate (Forbes & Pekala, 1993). Some mind–body techniques, such as meditation and hypnosis, are intended to improve well-being by altering consciousness (Barnes et al., 2004; Wickramasekera et al., 1996).

The Effects of Mind–Body Interventions

Collegiate rowers were randomly assigned to either a stress management program or a control group; those in the stress management group had fewer illnesses and injuries, and fewer medical visits to the student health center, than did those in the control group (Perna et al., 2003).

Kiecolt-Glaser and colleagues (1986) studied whether different stress-reduction techniques can boost medical students' immune systems during examinations. Half of the participants were taught hypnosis and other relaxation techniques and encouraged to practice at home; the other half were taught nothing. The students in the relaxation group did in fact have better immune functioning during the exams than the students in the control group; the same benefits later were documented for highly hypnotizable medical and dental students who learned hypnotic relaxation techniques (Kiecolt-Glaser et al., 2001).

Many mind–body techniques for people who are physically ill provide specific coping strategies, relaxation training, training in meditation (to decrease arousal and increase perceived control), increased social support (Andersen, 1997), disease-related information, and a supportive environment in which to address fears about the illness. These interventions have been found to confer the following benefits:

- improved mood and immune system functioning (Fawzy et al., 1990; Zakowski et al., 1992);
- increased lung functioning in people with asthma (Hockemeyer & Smyth, 2002);
- improved control of pain (NIH Technology Assessment Panel, 1996);
- decreased levels of reported stress, emotional distress, and poor coping strategies (Tacón et al., 2004; Timmerman et al., 1998); and
- fewer subsequent heart problems (Blumenthal et al., 2002).

However, mind–body techniques do not guarantee health or stave off death (Claar & Blumenthal, 2003).

The Placebo Effect as a Mind–Body Intervention

The fact that placebos can be effective also illustrates the link between mind and body. Simply believing that you are receiving a remedy (even if it has no medicinal effects) not only can lessen your experience of pain (Wager et al., 2004), but also can affect your immune system's functioning. One neuroimaging study found that, after participants received an intensely hot stimulus, the injection of a placebo activated the same brain areas as did an injection of a fast-acting opioid painkiller. Moreover, those who were more responsive to the pain medicine were also more responsive to the placebo (Petrovic et al., 2002).

In general, properties of the placebo itself and the way it is dispensed can make it more or less effective. For example, placebo injections are more effective than placebos taken orally, capsules are more effective than pills, and more (placebo) pills work better than fewer (placebo) pills. The color of the capsule can also make a difference: Blue capsules work best as tranquilizers; yellow, pink, and red capsules work best as stimulants (Buckalew & Ross, 1981). Moreover, if the person dispensing the treatment is friendly and sympathetic and shows an interest in the patient's problems, the placebo is more likely to be effective (Shapiro & Morris, 1978). Even the clinician's own view of a placebo's effectiveness can make a difference: If the treatment provider has high expectations for the treatment, it is more likely to be effective (Shapiro, 1964). To avoid this effect, a research study with placebos often has a *double-blind design*, in which neither those dispensing the treatment nor the participants know whether a given participant is receiving a placebo or the active medication. In a review of research that reported successful results from five treatments (for three diseases) that were later proved worthless, Roberts and colleagues (1993) found that when presented enthusiastically, these placebos were 70% effective.

Gender, Culture, and Coping

Do men and women experience the same amounts of stress? Do people in different cultures experience different amounts of stress? Do they cope with stress equally well? Psychologists have begun to pose questions such as these in an effort to learn whether stressors affect different groups of people differently.

Gender Differences in Coping

There is some evidence that women in Western cultures experience more stress than men. A survey of 2,500 Swedes found that women, particularly younger women, reported feeling more hassled, depressed, anxious, and hostile (Scott & Melin, 1998). As women have entered the workforce, a number of studies have focused on the effects of their multiple roles: employee, wife, mother, daughter.

The effects of having multiple roles can be both positive and negative: Women who are parents tend to have more to do than men who are parents and also to experience more conflict among their different roles and to be less able to unwind at home (Clay, 1995). Women generally report more stress with multiple roles than do men, and women employed outside the home generally do more work than men in their "second shift" at home: cooking, cleaning, and shopping (Hochschild, 1989; Phillips & Imhoff, 1997). However, these multiple roles can also confer advantages: increased feelings of self-esteem and control (Pietromonaco et al., 1986), financial gain, social support from colleagues (Brannon, 1996), and decreased psychological stress (Abrams & Jones, 1994). Thus, although employment outside the home can be more stressful (particularly if there are children), it is not necessarily more stressful for women than for men. Having financial and familial resources and control over the job (Taylor et al., 1997; Tingey et al., 1996), as well as a sense of mastery at work (Christensen et al., 1998), can reduce the stress of multiple roles.

Husbands and wives also differ in the benefits and stressors accrued in marriage: Women experience more stress and negative health effects from marital conflicts, but they also experience more happiness from their marital relationships (Kiecolt-Glaser & Newton, 2001). Men and women also tend to have differences in how they cope: As summarized by Shelley Taylor and colleagues (2000, 2002), when under stress, women tend to seek out social support whereas men tend to be more action-oriented, directly addressing the cause of the stress (Luckow et al., 1998).

Cultural Differences in Coping

Culture can help determine what constitutes a stressor, as well as when and how a person asks for assistance in coping with stressors. Different cultures may not only lead their members to view different stimuli as stressors, but also lead them to believe that they have more or less control over particular stressors. For example, crowding is a culturally defined stressor. In different cultures, different levels of *density* (the number of people in a given space) produce the perception of *crowding* (the subjective experience created by density). Members of Asian cultures experience less stress than Westerners would in high-density living conditions; Asians have developed ways of creating a sense of privacy in the midst of density, thereby providing a sense of control (Werner et al., 1997).

Culture also plays a role in defining which coping strategies are socially appropriate, as well as defining the appropriate use of social support (Aranda & Knight, 1997; Morling et al., 2003; O'Connor & Shimizu, 2002; Patterson et al., 1998). For instance, Indian students prefer emotion-focused coping strategies more than do Canadian students (Sinha et al., 2000), and people from collectivist cultures are less likely to seek social support than those from individualist cultures (Taylor, Sherman, et al., 2004).

Looking at Levels

Voodoo Death

In some cultures, it has been reported that when a shaman (religious leader) puts a curse on someone, death sometimes ensues; this phenomenon is known as *voodoo death* (Cannon, 1942). Although there is some debate as to whether voodoo death actually occurs (Hahn, 1997), research has shown that expectations of sickness can, in fact, cause sickness. This is the **nocebo effect**, a variation of the placebo effect, but with the expectation of a negative outcome rather than a positive outcome. (*Placebo* in Latin means "I will please"; *nocebo* means "I will harm.") Voodoo death represents an extreme example of the nocebo effect. But you shouldn't think that the nocebo effect happens only in primitive cultures: Among American women enrolled in a study of the risk factors for heart disease, those who believed that they were more likely to die of a heart attack were, in fact, 3.7 times more likely to die of a heart attack than other women in the study, even after researchers controlled for known risk factors for heart disease (Eaker, Pinsky, & Castelli, 1992).

Have you ever taken a new medicine and discovered that it had unpleasant—although not dangerous—side effects? For instance, cold medications may make you feel drowsy. But some people experience side effects that do not appear to occur directly from medicinal properties; such reactions are called *nonspecific side effects*, and they can be uncomfortable enough that they lead people to stop taking the medication. The particular nonspecific side effects vary among people taking the same medication. Arthur Barsky and colleagues (2002) propose that these effects are nocebo effects and offer two accounts for them. First, expectations may play a role; people who expect negative side effects from a new medication (perhaps because they've heard of such effects from it) may then experience them. Second, some people may have nonspecific side effects because they've become classically conditioned, perhaps by their past experiences with side effects from other medicines, which then generalize.

In addition, once people take a medication, they may come to attribute any uncomfortable bodily symptoms to it. This is a problem because we all have uncomfortable aches and twinges, from time to time. In fact, a study of healthy college students found that 81% experienced at least one physical symptom within a 3-day stretch (Gick & Thompson, 1997). People who are most likely to develop nonspecific side effects attribute these transient disturbances to the medication.

Barsky and colleagues summarize various studies that support the position that nonspecific side effects are, in fact, nocebo effects:

- Patients who were told that a medicine was a stimulant (when it was, in fact, a muscle relaxant) reported more muscle tension than those who were told that the medicine was a relaxant (Flaten et al., 1999).

- Patients with food allergies received an injection (that was saline solution) and were told that it contained the substance to which they were allergic. They subsequently developed allergic symptoms (Jewett et al., 1990).

- Healthy volunteers were told that they would receive mild electric current through their heads and that such current could produce mild headaches; 70% reported headaches, even though the current was never turned on (Schweiger & Parducci, 1981).

- Approximately 20–25% (and sometimes more) of people taking placebo medications report unpleasant side effects (Dhume et al., 1975; Drid et al., 1995; Rosenzweig et al., 1993; Shepherd, 1993; Tangrea et al., 1994). Such nonspecific effects include drowsiness, nausea, fatigue, insomnia, poor concentration, and gastrointestinal problems.

How can we understand the nocebo response? At the level of the brain, classical conditioning plays a role in the development of certain nocebo—and placebo—responses. An example of a conditioned nocebo effect is anticipatory nausea before chemotherapy (see Chapter 4). In addition, some people, particularly those high in the personality dimension of neuroticism, are more likely to experience conditioned emotional responses, including these nonspecific side

Nocebo effect: A variation of the placebo effect in which the person expects a negative outcome instead of a positive outcome.

effects (Davis et al., 1995). Neuroticism is moderately heritable, and so this effect is partly an event at the level of the brain.

At the level of the person, the *expectation* of a negative outcome leads an individual to be hypervigilant for any bodily changes and to attribute such changes to the nocebo instead of to some other stimulus (Barsky et al., 2002). Expectation of a negative response can increase pain, and expectation of a positive response can diminish pain (Benedetti et al., 2003). For those people who experience frequent nonspecific side effects, events at the level of the person include their beliefs about what such symptoms mean, as well as the ways they assess whether a bodily sensation constitutes a "side effect" (Hahn, 1999).

At the level of the group, expectations about a given nocebo can arise after one person directly *tells* another about negative effects (Benedetti et al., 2003). Sometimes expectations are communicated through stories, warnings, or written prohibitions. For instance, beliefs about a medicine can be shaped by advertisements, information on the Internet, friends' recountings of their experiences with the medication, or a doctor's admonitions about side effects. In addition, each culture promotes somewhat different ideas and expectations about sickness and health (Hahn, 1995).

Events at these three levels of analysis interact. For example, culture and social interactions (level of the group) provided the context for the people whose pain responses were affected by their expectations (Benedetti et al., 2003) and for the people who experience frequent nonspecific side effects of medications. Such group-level events, in part, led these people to have beliefs about the "medication" they were taking and to be hypervigilant (level of the person) to their physical response (level of the brain). In addition, these events, as well as the individuals' past experiences with medications and side effects and their predisposition toward conditioned emotional responses, may have led to a classically conditioned nocebo response (level of the brain). In turn, all these events led people to interpret the bodily changes in particular ways (level of the person).

LOOKING BACK: *Review*

1. *What are the different types of coping strategies?* Coping strategies are the ways in which people handle stress. They can be classified into two general categories: problem-focused and emotion-focused. Problem-focused coping attempts to alter either the environment itself or the way in which the person and the environment interact; it is helpful when the person can affect the stressor. Emotion-focused coping attempts to change the emotional response to a stressor and can be particularly helpful when the stressor itself cannot be changed. Whether either type of coping strategy will be effective depends on an accurate assessment of the possibility of changing the environment. Although an ineffective strategy in the long term, substance use or abuse is sometimes used to help people cope with stressors. Substance use only temporarily changes the perception of the stressor.

2. *How do relationships affect stress and health?* Positive relationships can provide social support, which can buffer the negative effects of stress and boost the immune system. Perceived social support is effective in buffering stress, even though it can be unrelated to enacted support.

3. *What are mind–body interventions?* Some coping strategies (such as relaxation and meditation) take advantage of the mind–body interaction, using psychological tools to change psychological and bodily states.

4. *Do gender and culture play a role in coping?* Although a woman may experience more stress because of multiple roles (particularly if one of the roles is mother), these multiple roles can provide a buffer against stress and depression; the financial, self-esteem, and collegial benefits of the employee role can outweigh the increased daily stress. Culture helps determine what is perceived to be stressful and provides ways to increase a sense of control in the face of a stressor.

● LOOKING BEYOND: *Critical Thinking*

If your next-door neighbor plays music very loudly every night when you are trying to go to sleep, and you find this to be a stressor, what could you do to lower your stress response? What type of coping strategies would work best in this situation? What personality characteristics would make you less likely to feel stressed by a noisy neighbor? If you were in a non-Western culture, could the nightly serenade be less stressful? Why or why not?

LET'S SUM IT UP

I. What Is Stress?

A. Stress is the general term describing the psychological and physical response to a stimulus that alters the body's equilibrium. The stress response of the autonomic nervous system increases heart rate and blood pressure.

B. Continued stressors can lead the body's response to stress to become harmful. A higher allostatic load increases the risk for medical and psychological problems.

C. The perception of stress helps determine what constitutes a stressor. Common sources of stress include a sense of a lack of control and a lack of predictability, internal conflicts, and daily hassles.

D. The personality trait of hostility is associated with increased stress, heart rate, blood pressure, and cortisol production. Men are generally more hostile than women.

II. Stress, Disease, and Health

A. Frequent activation of the stress response can lead to changes in the immune system, which can make you vulnerable to contracting a cold or can promote the growth of existing tumors. However, stress does not cause tumors to develop.

B. Stress can create cardiovascular changes and can contribute to the development of heart disease through increased blood pressure.

C. Stress can also affect sleep, and sleep deprivation can create stress through impaired performance and mood and increased cortisol level.

III. Strategies for Coping

A. A realistic appraisal of whether your actions can affect a stressor will help you to determine what coping strategies will be effective.

B. Emotion-focused coping strategies work best when the situation can't be changed, and problem-focused strategies work best when it can.

C. Substance use is *not* effective as a long-term coping strategy because it does not change the stressor; it merely changes the person's perception of the stress while he or she is under the influence of the substance.

D. Social support (particularly perceived social support) can help decrease the experience of stress.

E. Mind–body techniques, such as relaxation training, meditation, and hypnosis, can decrease the physical effects of stress.

F. Culture can affect both the appraisal of a stimulus as a stressor and the choice of coping strategies for managing the stressor.

G. Both placebo and nocebo effects illustrate the interactions between mind and body.

Key Terms

LOOKING ONLINE: *Enhance Your Learning*

MyPsychLab is an interactive and instructive multimedia resource that can be used to supplement a traditional lecture course or as an online course. It is an all-inclusive tool with a text-specific e-book plus multimedia tutorials, videos, simulations, animations, and controlled assessment to completely engage students and reinforce learning. MyPsychLab meets the individual learning needs of every student. Visit *www.mypsychlab.com* for more information!

Practice Test

For each of the following items, choose the single best answer.

1. Perception of a stressor triggers the _____, which is characterized by the fight-or-flight response.
   a. alarm phase
   b. resistance phase
   c. adaptation phase
   d. exhaustion phase

2. With continued stressors,
   a. the body becomes exhausted because its limited resources in fighting stress become depleted.
   b. the continued stress response begins to damage the body, leading to a risk of stress-related diseases.

   c. cortisol improves learning and memory.
   d. All of the above statements are true.

3. What is the order in which coping and the phases of cognitive appraisal occur?
   a. coping, primary appraisal, and secondary appraisal
   b. secondary appraisal, primary appraisal, and coping
   c. primary appraisal, secondary appraisal, and coping
   d. coping, secondary appraisal, and primary appraisal

4. Which of the following statements about control and stress is true?
   a. Actual control is not important; what is important is whether you *perceive* a sense of control.
   b. Not everyone is equally eager to feel in control.

c. Even for those who prefer to have more control, perceiving a lack of control doesn't always produce stress.

d. All of the above statements are true.

5. High hostility is

a. a lifelong trait.

b. more likely in women than in men.

c. associated with a higher heart rate and blood pressure throughout the day.

d. associated with a decreased risk of heart disease.

6. The natural killer (NK) cell

a. is a type of T cell.

b. matures in the thymus, an organ located in the chest.

c. destroys damaged or altered cells, such as precancerous cells.

d. All of the above statements are true.

7. Which of the following statements is true about the relationship between stress and cancer?

a. Stress can cause cancer.

b. Stress cannot affect the growth of cancerous tumors.

c. Stress can facilitate the growth of capillaries feeding into a tumor.

d. The type of cancer, and biological factors related to its progression, never outweigh psychological factors in tumor growth.

8. Sleep

a. is a single state.

b. comprises five stages that alternate during the night.

c. has an initial stage, lasting approximately 5 minutes, called REM sleep.

d. All of the above statements are true.

9. During REM sleep, your

a. breathing and heart rate are fast and irregular.

b. brain shows even more activity than when you are awake.

c. muscles are relaxed and unresponsive.

d. All of the above statements are true.

10. Sleep deprivation

a. affects at least three important psychological areas: attention, mood, and performance.

b. improves mood.

c. does not affect tasks that require sustained attention and a motor response.

d. leads to decreases in the next day's level of cortisol.

11. Which of the following statements about dreams and sleep stages is true?

a. If awakened during REM sleep, people recall dreams 78% of the time, compared with 14% recall during NREM sleep.

b. NREM dreams are more vivid and more emotional than REM dreams.

c. Dreams take place only during REM sleep.

d. Dreams that take place during REM sleep are less memorable than those occurring during NREM stages.

12. Sleep apnea

a. is a disorder characterized by a temporary cessation of breathing during sleep.

b. results when muscles at the base of the throat relax and consequently block the airway.

c. can be fatal.

d. All of the above statements are true.

13. The act of trying to suppress distressing thoughts

a. decreases the intensity of the thoughts.

b. can result in a rebound effect.

c. is not associated with changes in the functioning of the sympathetic nervous system or immune system.

d. decreases the autonomic reactions to those thoughts.

14. Alcohol use

a. excites the central nervous system through its effect on excitatory neurotransmitters.

b. in high doses causes constriction of the peripheral blood vessels.

c. facilitates aggressive behavior.

d. All of the above statements are true.

15. Enacted social support

a. provides the buffer against stress.

b. is the specific supportive behaviors provided by others.

c. is the subjective sense that support is available should it be needed.

d. is closely related to the perception of support.

Answers: 1. a 2. b 3. c 4. d 5. c 6. d 7. c 8. b 9. d 10. a 11. a 12. d 13. b 14. c 15. b

chapter 11

Psychological Disorders
More Than Everyday Problems

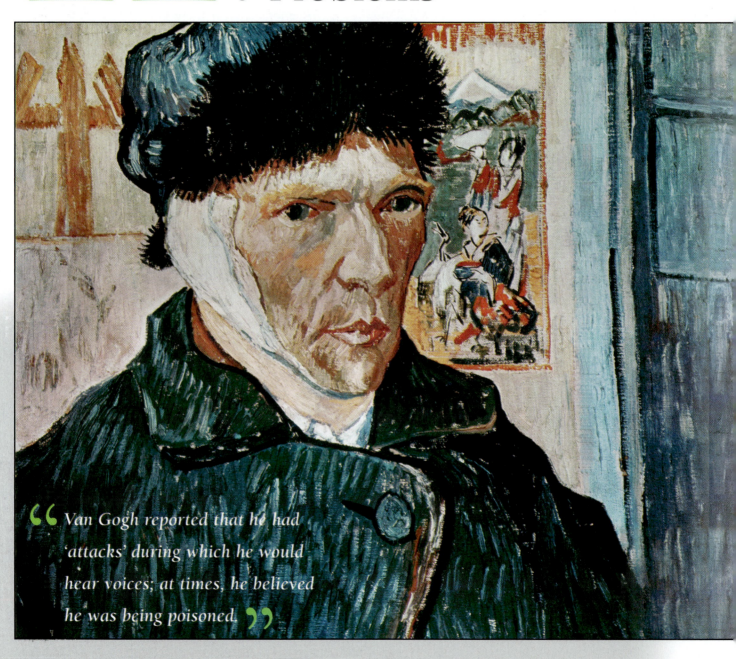

Van Gogh reported that he had 'attacks' during which he would hear voices; at times, he believed he was being poisoned.

MUSEUM-GOERS WORLDWIDE THRONG TO SEE EXHIBITS OF THE works of Vincent van Gogh. Born in Holland in 1853, van Gogh created extraordinary art and took much joy in painting, but his life is a tale of misery. The son and grandson of Protestant ministers, van Gogh was the second of six children. A memoir by his sister-in-law records, "As a child he was of difficult temper, often troublesome and self-willed" (Roskill, 1963, p. 37). According to his parents, when punished, Vincent became more "difficult." As a child he showed no particular awareness of his great gifts; however, on two occasions, once when he modeled a clay elephant and again when he drew a cat, he destroyed his creations when he felt a "fuss" was being made about them (Roskill, 1963).

When van Gogh was 16, he worked as a clerk in an art gallery, but his long, moody silences and irritability isolated him from his coworkers. After 4 years, he was transferred to the gallery's office in London, where he fell in love with his landlady's daughter, Ursula. They spent many months together, until she revealed her engagement to a previous tenant and rejected van Gogh. Feeling utterly defeated, he found it difficult to concentrate at work. He frequently argued with his coworkers and was soon fired.

Van Gogh next decided on a career in the ministry but could not master the Greek and Latin necessary for the entrance exams. Instead, he became a lay pastor, preaching to miners in the Borinage, a coal-mining area in Belgium. He went without bathing and slept in a hut on bare planks, as the miners did. But the miners feared this unkempt, wild-looking man, and the church elders dismissed him. Increasingly, van Gogh found comfort in painting and drawing.

His life continued to be marked by instability. After he left the Borinage, he lived in and out of his parents' home and wandered around the country. Whereas once his interest in religion had been intense, if not obsessional, he now turned his back on religion. He developed a relationship with a pregnant prostitute, Sien, but their liaison ended after about a year and a half. Van Gogh reported that he had "attacks" during which he would hear voices; at times, he believed he was being poisoned.

When he was 35, van Gogh convinced fellow painter Paul Gauguin to share a house with him in Arles, France. As was true for all of van Gogh's relationships, he and Gauguin frequently quarreled. According to Gauguin, after one particularly violent argument, van Gogh approached him threateningly with an open razor, but Gauguin stared him down. Van Gogh then ran to their house, where he cut off his earlobe, which he then sent to a local prostitute (not Sien). The next day he was found at home, bleeding and unconscious, and was taken to a hospital, where he remained for 2 weeks. His brother Theo spent time with him in the hospital and found Vincent in great spiritual anguish.

After his release from the hospital in January 1889, van Gogh's behavior became increasingly bizarre, so much so that within 2 months the residents of Arles petitioned that he be confined, and he again stayed for a time in the hospital. In May, van Gogh moved to the asylum at Saint-Remy, not far from Arles, where he lived on and off for the next year and a half, and where he produced many paintings. Shortly after his last release, less than 2 years after the incident with Gauguin, he purposefully ended his anguish and his life by going out into a field with a gun and shooting himself in the stomach. Yet, a few weeks before his death, he could say, "I still love art and life very much indeed" (Roskill, 1963).

Questions of art aside, van Gogh's experiences focus our attention on psychological disorders: What defines a psychological disorder? Who establishes criteria for determining what is abnormal behavior? What are the symptoms and origins of some specific disorders?

Identifying Psychological Disorders: What's Abnormal?

What distinguishes unusual behaviors from behaviors that are symptoms of a psychological disorder? Before he rejected religion, van Gogh was tormented by religious ideas and believed in ghosts. Are these signs of psychological disturbance?

What about his self-mutilation? What would you want to know about him before drawing any conclusions?

Mental health professionals face questions such as these every day. In this section, you will see how formulations of and findings about psychological disorders suggest answers to those questions.

LOOKING AHEAD: Learning Objectives

1. How is abnormality defined?
2. How are psychological disorders explained?
3. How are psychological disorders classified?

Defining Abnormality

It is difficult to give an exact definition of psychological disorders—also referred to as psychiatric disorders, mental disorders or, less systematically, mental illnesses—because they can encompass many aspects of behavioral, experiential, and bodily functioning. However, a good working definition is that a **psychological disorder** is signaled by a constellation of cognitive, emotional, and behavioral symptoms that create significant distress; impair work, school, family, relationships, or daily living; or lead to significant risk of harm. This definition takes into account three factors: distress, impairment, and danger.

Distress

People with psychological disorders may display or experience *distress*. One example of distress that is obvious to others is repeatedly bursting into tears and expressing hopelessness about the future, for no apparent reason. However, a person's distress is not always observable to others, as when people chronically worry, feel profoundly sad for long periods of time, or hear voices that only they can hear.

Impairment

People with psychological disorders may experience a *disability* or *impairment* in some aspect of life. Examples include a police officer who becomes so anxious that he cannot perform his job or an individual (such as van Gogh) whose emotional outbursts drive others away. An individual's impairment may not necessarily cause him or her distress but can be maladaptive nonetheless.

Psychological disorders can be very debilitating, and worldwide they rank second among diseases that lead to death and disability, a higher ranking than cancer (Murray & Lopez, 1996). The World Health Organization (2001) estimates that in the year 2000, 450 million people suffered from psychological disorders worldwide. According to some estimates, up to 48% of Americans have experienced 1 of 30 common psychological disorders at some point in their lives (Kessler et al., 1994), and 20% of Americans have a diagnosable mental disorder in any given year (Regier et al., 1993; Satcher, 1999). Psychological disorders can affect people's relationships, their ability to care for themselves, and their functioning on the job. For every 100 workers, an average of 37 work days per month are lost because of either reduced output or absences stemming from psychological disorders (Kessler & Frank, 1997).

Psychological disorder: The presence of a constellation of cognitive, emotional, and behavioral symptoms that create significant distress; impair work, school, family, relationships, or daily living; or lead to significant risk of harm.

Danger

Danger can occur when symptoms of a psychological disorder cause an individual to put life (his or her own, or another's) at risk, either purposefully or accidentally. For instance, depression may lead someone to attempt suicide, extreme paranoia may provoke someone to attack other people, or a parent's disorder may be sufficiently severe that children's safety is put at risk (as when Andrea Yates, who suffered so severely from depression that she lost touch with reality, drowned her five young children in 2001, thinking that she was rescuing them from Satan's grasp).

Cultural and Social Influences

Picture someone hopping on one leg, thumb in mouth, trying to sing the French national anthem during a hockey game. You would probably consider this behavior abnormal; but what if the behavior was part of a fraternity initiation ritual or a new kind of performance art? A behavior that is bizarre or inappropriate in one context may be entirely appropriate in another. To be considered "disordered," it is not enough for a behavior or a set of behaviors to be deviant from the mainstream culture. Being unconventional or different in religious, political, or sexual arenas does not qualify as abnormal. What is considered deviant changes from generation to generation, and can differ across cultures.

Consider that, in 1851, Dr. Samuel Cartwright of Louisiana wrote an essay in which he declared that slaves' running away was evidence of a serious mental disorder, which he called "drapetomania" (Eakin, 2000). Also, homosexuality was officially considered a psychological disorder in the United States until 1973, and then it was removed from the *Diagnostic and Statistical Manual of Mental Disorders* (this manual is used by mental health clinicians to classify psychological disorders). And in the last decade, the determination of abnormality has been given a new twist in the United States; as health maintenance organizations (HMOs) and other types of managed care organizations try to keep costs down, they have developed their own criteria for which symptoms and disorders they will pay to have treated—and have also regulated the frequency and duration of the treatment.

The line between normal and abnormal behavior is perhaps easiest to draw in the case of **psychosis**, which is an obvious impairment in the ability to perceive and comprehend events accurately, combined with a gross disorganization of behavior. People with psychoses may have **hallucinations**, mental images—in any sensory modality (but mainly visual or auditory)—so vivid that they seem real (such as hearing voices), or **delusions**, which are entrenched false beliefs that are often bizarre (such as that their thoughts are being controlled by aliens). However, such beliefs, even if false (or at least not susceptible to rational proof), should not be considered abnormal if they are an accepted

Van Gogh's painting of the church at Auvers is unusual because of its unconventional perspective, use of color, and brushstrokes. Do these differences reflect a psychological disorder, or just a different way of seeing or conveying the structure and its surroundings?

Mathematician John Nash (left), whose life was the basis for the movie *A Beautiful Mind*, starring Oscar-winning actor Russell Crowe (right), had delusions that aliens were communicating with him. Although the movie portrayed Nash as having both hallucinations and delusions, in real life he did not have hallucinations.

Psychosis: An obvious impairment in the ability to perceive and comprehend events accurately, combined with a gross disorganization of behavior.

Hallucinations: Sensory images so vivid that they seem real.

Delusions: Entrenched false beliefs that are often bizarre.

part of the culture. For instance, in some religious groups, such as Pentecostals, it is not considered abnormal to hear voices, especially the voice of God (Cox, personal communication, 2000). Another example is *zar*, or spirit possession, experienced in some North African and Middle Eastern cultures. Those affected may shout, laugh, hit their heads against a wall, or exhibit other behavior that otherwise would be considered inappropriate; an experience of *zar* is not considered abnormal in the cultures in which it occurs (American Psychiatric Association, 2000a).

Explaining Abnormality

Explanations for abnormal behavior have changed with the times and reflect the thinking of each culture. In ancient Greece, abnormal behaviors, as well as medical problems, were thought to arise from imbalances of the body's four fluids, or "humors": yellow bile, phlegm, blood, and black bile. Too much phlegm, for instance, made you phlegmatic, or sluggish and slow; too much black bile made you melancholic. In 17th-century New England, abnormality was thought to be the work of the devil. In the middle of the 20th century, Sigmund Freud's work was influential, and psychodynamic theory was the instrument used to understand abnormality. Currently, in order to understand psychological disorders, many psychologists and others in the field have used the *biopsychosocial model*. This model focuses on factors at the levels of the brain, the person, and the group. In this discussion, we go one step further and show how events at those three levels are not discrete but affect one another through various interactions.

The Brain: Genes, Neurotransmitters, and Brain Structure and Function

Van Gogh's family history points to a possible cause of his psychological problems. Van Gogh's brother Theo was often depressed and anxious, and he committed suicide within a year after Vincent's suicide; his sister Wilhelmina exhibited a long-standing psychosis; his youngest brother Cor is thought to have committed suicide. Does this history indicate that van Gogh inherited some vulnerability to a psychological disorder? Not necessarily, but researchers are finding increasing evidence that genetic factors frequently contribute to the development of some disorders.

Biological factors, including neurotransmitters (such as serotonin), hormones (such as adrenaline, which functions as a hormone in the body), and abnormalities in the structure of the brain, appear to play a role in the development of some psychological disorders. From a biological point of view, depression can be seen as a manifestation of an abnormal serotonin level. Similarly, the cause of an irrational fear of spiders could be the outcome of an overreactive amygdala. Although these explanations may be valid, they are only a part of the picture. *Why* are someone's serotonin levels abnormal? *Why* is someone else's amygdala overreactive to the sight of a spider? As previously noted in many contexts, our own thoughts, feelings, and behaviors, as well as our interactions with others and our environment, can affect the workings of our brains.

Thus, abnormality cannot be considered solely as a function of brain chemistry or structure. Many researchers and clinicians today believe that psychological disorders can best be explained by a **diathesis–stress model** (*diathesis* means a predisposition to a state or condition). This conceptualization, illustrated in

Diathesis–stress model: A way of understanding the development of a psychological disorder, in which a predisposition to a given disorder (diathesis) and specific factors (stress) combine to trigger the onset of the disorder.

Figure 11.1 The Diathesis–Stress Model

DIATHESIS	STRESSORS
• Genes	• Noxious physical stressors
• Abnormalities of brain structure or functioning	• Trauma, abuse, neglect
• Neurotransmitter imbalances	• Relationships—loss, turbulence
• Particular ways of thinking	• Culture-related stressors
	• Childbirth complications

Vulnerability to psychological disorders

PSYCHOLOGICAL DISORDERS

Most mental health researchers and professionals believe that both biological factors (diathesis) and environmental stressors (stress) together cause psychological disorders.

Figure 11.1, states that "for a given disorder, there is both a predisposition to the disorder (a *diathesis*) and specific factors (*stress*) that combine with the diathesis to trigger the onset of the disorder" (Rende & Plomin, 1992, p. 177). According to the diathesis–stress model, because of certain biological factors (such as genes, abnormality of brain structures, or neurotransmitters), as well as other types of factors, some people may be more vulnerable to developing a particular disorder; however, without certain environmental stressors, the disorder is not triggered. By the same token, when experiencing a stressor, people without a biological vulnerability for a disorder may not develop that disorder. From this perspective, it's the interactions among events at the different levels of analysis that are crucial; no single event or stimulus alone can cause illness, and as noted in Chapter 10, not everyone perceives a particular event or stimulus to be a stressor. Whether because of learning or biology, or an interaction of the two, some people are more likely to perceive more stressors (and therefore to experience more stress) than others. For instance, although schizophrenia appears to have a genetic component, even if an identical twin has schizophrenia, his or her twin will not necessarily develop the disorder. The diathesis–stress model proposes that it is the *combination* of biological vulnerability and some specific other factors, such as a trauma or the death of a loved one, that elicits the disorder.

The Person: Behaviors, Thoughts and Biases, and Emotions

Several factors at the level of the person also play a role in psychological disorders. One factor is classical conditioning, as in the case of Little Albert (Chapter 4), who developed a fear of white furry things based on his classical conditioning experiences with a white rat and a loud noise. Operant conditioning and observational learning can also help explain some psychological disorders. In addition, the content of mental processes, such as biases in what a person tends to pay attention to, the pattern of a person's thoughts, and the attributions that he or she makes, can also make a person vulnerable to psychological disorders. For instance, chronic negative thought patterns ("Nothing ever turns out right for me; what's the point in trying?") can lead to depressing feelings and can contribute to the development or maintenance of depression, as can attributing negative events to oneself rather than to circumstances ("I'm incompetent; I can't do anything right"). Learning, thoughts, and feelings may help explain why certain psychological disorders develop in some people. Furthermore, as we shall see, some disorders involve difficulties in regulating emotion—leading to feelings that seem too intense, an absence of feeling, or emotions that rapidly change.

When something falls, do you attribute the mishap to some outside factor or to yourself? Do you ruminate about negative things or things that make you anxious, or do you tend to put them out of your mind? Some thought patterns can create a diathesis for a particular disorder.

The Group: Social and Cultural Factors

Factors at the level of the group also play a role in triggering psychological disorders, as well as in increasing the risk of a disorder's recurrence. For example, the "stress" part of post-traumatic stress disorder (discussed in detail later in this chapter) is usually caused by other people (such as a terrorist or a rapist) or the physical environment (through natural disasters such as floods and earthquakes).

Culture can also influence the conception of psychological disorders. For a period during the 1960s, a number of mental health professionals argued that mental illness is a myth, merely a label applied to culturally undesirable behavior (Szasz, 1961). In this view, the label determines how people are treated and, in a self-fulfilling prophecy, may even play a role in how the "mentally ill" person behaves, once labeled.

David Rosenhan (1973) tested an aspect of this idea. In his study, people without a psychological disorder gained admittance to psychiatric hospitals by claiming that they heard voices. Once in the hospital, they behaved normally. But because they were given a psychiatric diagnosis—that is, they were labeled—their normal behavior was interpreted as pathological, and they were treated accordingly. For example, these "pseudopatients" took notes while they were in hospital; not furtively, but out in the open, in a normal manner. This behavior, interpreted by the staff through the lens of the diagnostic label, was attributed to their illness, even perceived as proof of their abnormality. Moreover, when the pseudopatients asked about eligibility for grounds privileges, the psychiatrists responded to such questions only 6% of the time; in 71% of the encounters, the doctors just moved on.

Rosenhan claimed that his study illustrated the power of labels and contexts. But does it tell us anything about the reality of mental disorders? The pseudopatients originally reported auditory hallucinations that were troubling enough to drive them to request admission to a mental hospital; people do not normally have such symptoms. How was the staff to know that the pseudopatients were lying when they described their "symptoms"? Similarly, the fact that the staff in Rosenhan's study labeled and treated the pseudopatients as if their symptoms were genuine does not indicate that psychological disorders with these symptoms do not exist, only that doctors did not recognize that the pseudopatients were "faking it" (Spitzer, 1975). In fact, the doctors *did* notice that something was amiss because, when the pseudopatients were discharged from the hospital, the diagnosis they were given was "schizophrenia, in remission," a rarely given diagnosis. Moreover, the generalizability of Rosenhan's findings are limited because he did not use any type of control or comparison group (Millon, 1975).

Diagnosing individuals involves making judgments that, like all judgments, are subject to error, and this is part of what Rosenhan felt his study illustrated. A systematic type of error in diagnosis is called a *diagnostic bias* (Meehl, 1960), and it often has the result that some people receive certain diagnoses based on nonmedical factors, such as race. For instance, studies of racial bias show that Black patients in the United States are more likely to be evaluated negatively than are White patients (Garb, 1997; Jenkins-Hall & Sacco, 1991; Strakowski et al., 1995) and are prescribed higher doses of medication (Strakowski et al., 1993). (Such biases occur at the level of the person, and thus we once again see interactions among events at the different levels of analysis.)

However, the reality of certain disorders—schizophrenia being one—is attested to by the fact that these disorders are recognized worldwide. Nevertheless, cultures differ in which behaviors they consider abnormal, and the symptoms, course, and prognosis of disorders may vary from culture to culture (Basic Behavioral Science Task Force, 1996).

Events at all three levels and the interactions among them must be examined to understand the various psychological disorders discussed in this chapter. Biological factors, emotions, learning, and thought patterns, familial, cultural, and environmental factors, *and the relationships among them* all play a role in explaining psychological disorders.

Categorizing Disorders: Is a Rose Still a Rose by Any Other Name?

Suppose a man comes to a clinical psychologist's office complaining that he feels he is going crazy and that he has a strong sense of impending doom. How would the clinical psychologist determine the nature of this man's difficulties and figure out how best to help him? What questions should the psychologist ask? One guide to help this psychologist and other mental health clinicians is the *Diagnostic and Statistical Manual of Mental Disorders*, known to its users simply as the *DSM*.

History of the *DSM*

In 1952, the American Psychiatric Association published the inaugural edition of the *DSM*, the first manual of mental disorders designed primarily to help clinicians diagnose and treat patients. This edition was based on psychodynamic theory. In later editions of the manual, its developers tried to avoid relying on any one theory of the causes of disorders and to base the identification of disorders on a growing body of empirical research. The fourth edition, the *DSM-IV*, published in 1994, was an attempt to refine the diagnostic criteria and make the diagnostic categories more useful to mental health researchers and practitioners.

Since the third edition, the *DSM* has described five *axes*, or types of information, that should be considered in the assessment of a patient. Clinical disorders are noted on Axis I, and personality disorders and mental retardation on Axis II. Axis III notes any general medical conditions that might be relevant to a diagnosis on Axis I or II. Psychosocial and environmental problems are identified on Axis IV, and Axis V records the patient's highest level of functioning in major areas of life within the past year. An appendix to the manual outlines aspects of the patient's cultural context that clinicians should take into account when making a diagnosis. Most of the manual, however, is devoted to describing disorders. It defines 17 major categories of psychological problems. All told, almost 300 mental disorders are specified. A revision published in 2000 and called *DSM-IV-TR* (TR stands for *Text Revision*) included more up-to-date information on incidence rates and cultural factors, but did not change the diagnostic categories nor the criteria.

Disadvantages and Advantages of the *DSM*

The sheer number of disorders included in the *DSM-IV* has provoked criticism of the manual; the breadth of the major diagnostic categories is shown in Table 11.1. As the *DSM* has evolved, it has introduced categories that define medical problems as psychological disorders, leading to a pathologizing of mental health. For example, a new diagnosis in the *DSM-IV* was "Breathing-Related Sleep Disorder" (one cause of which is sleep apnea; see Chapter 10). Thus, the *DSM-IV* created a *psychological* or *psychiatric* disorder for a medical problem. Moreover, the *DSM-IV* does not provide a discrete boundary separating abnormality from normality (Beals et al., 2004; Double, 2002; Frances, 1998); a clinician's judgment determines whether an individual's degree of impairment is "clinically significant." Another criticism leveled at the *DSM-IV* is that some of

Table 11.1 *DSM-IV-TR*'s 17 Major Categories of Disorders

Major Category of Disorders	Explanation
Disorders usually first diagnosed in infancy, childhood, or adolescence	Although disorders in this category are usually first evident early in life, some adults are newly diagnosed with one of these disorders, such as attention-deficit/hyperactivity disorder.
Delirium, dementia, and amnestic and other cognitive disorders	Disorders of consciousness and cognition.
Mental disorders due to a general medical condition not elsewhere classified	Disorders in which mental and psychological symptoms are judged to be due to a medical condition (coded on Axis III).
Substance-related disorders	Disorders of substance dependence and abuse, as well as disorders induced by a substance, such as a substance-induced psychotic disorder.
Schizophrenia and other psychotic disorders	Disorders related to psychoses.
Mood disorders	Disorders of mood or feelings.
Anxiety disorders	Disorders of anxiety.
Somatoform disorders	Disorders in which physical/medical complaints have no known medical origin (or the symptoms are not proportional to a medical condition) and so are thought to be psychological in nature.
Factitious disorders	Disorders in which the person intentionally fabricates symptoms of a medical or psychological disorder, but not for external gain (such as disability claims).
Dissociative disorders	Disorders in which there is a disruption in the usually integrated functions of consciousness, memory, or identity.
Sexual and gender identity disorders	Disorders of sexual function, the object of sexual desire, and/or of gender identity.
Eating disorders	Disorders related to eating.
Sleep disorders	Disorders related to sleep.
Impulse-control disorders not elsewhere classified	Disorders related to the ability to contain impulses (such as kleptomania).
Adjustment disorders	Disorders related to the development of distressing emotional or behavioral symptoms in response to an identifiable stressor.
Personality disorders	Disorders related to personality traits that are inflexible and maladaptive, and that cause distress or difficulty with daily functioning.
Other conditions that may be a focus of clinical attention	A problem receiving treatment for which no psychological disorder described in the manual applies or for which the symptoms do not meet the criteria for any disorder.

the disorders are not clearly distinct from one another (Blais et al., 1997), although they are often presented as if they were (Tucker, 1998).

Despite these criticisms, one advantage of the *DSM-IV* is that it is theoretically neutral; that is, it makes no assumptions about why disorders arise or about the best way to treat them. Moreover, it strives to create standards that can be used to ensure reliability in diagnosis: If two people with similar symptoms and mental health histories are seen in two different cities by two different mental health clinicians who are using the *DSM-IV* to guide their diagnosis, the odds are that those people will be diagnosed with the same disorder. In fact, the *DSM-IV* is the predominant means of categorizing psychological disorders in the United States. The discussion of disorders in this chapter uses the *DSM-IV* system of categorization.

LOOKING BACK: *Review*

1. *How is abnormality defined?* DSM-IV defines abnormality by taking into account three factors: subjective distress, significant disability or impairment, and danger to self or others. Merely being deviant from a cultural norm is not sufficient for behavior to be diagnosed as a psychological disorder.

2. *How are psychological disorders explained?* Psychological disorders can be explained as arising from events at the levels of the brain, by biological abnormalities; of the person, by objective behaviors and subjective distress; and of the group, in which abnormality is defined by the culture and context of the behaviors. The diathesis–stress model explains psychological disorders as arising from certain biological factors that make some individuals more vulnerable to developing particular disorders, which are then triggered by stressors.

3. *How are psychological disorders classified?* Psychiatric disorders are classified in the *DSM-IV* along two axes: clinical and personality disorders. Three other axes address factors affecting the disorders, the nature of the problem, and the highest level of functioning attained. Impairment in functioning at work, in school, in relationships, or in daily living are necessary to merit a diagnosis of a disorder.

LOOKING BEYOND: *Critical Thinking*

If a classmate told you in all seriousness that someone you both know is "weird" and a "basket case," how would you respond? What would you want to know about the behavior that led your friend to this conclusion? What other questions should you ask? Why?

Axis I: An Overview of Selected Disorders

What we know of van Gogh's history suggests that he met *DSM-IV*'s broad criteria for having a psychological disorder: He was greatly distressed, he was at times impaired by his psychological difficulties, and he was clearly a danger to himself and others. From what type of disorder might he have suffered? Let's examine several categories of Axis I disorders and see if we can better understand van Gogh's difficulties.

1. *What are mood disorders? What causes them?*
2. *What are the main types of anxiety disorders? What are their symptoms and causes?*
3. *What are the symptoms and causes of schizophrenia?*
4. *What are the symptoms and causes of eating disorders?*

Mood Disorders

We cannot diagnose from a distance, but we know enough about van Gogh's life and behavior to make some educated guesses about the nature of his moods and emotional turmoil. He frequently spoke of feeling sad; still, he clung to the commonality of human feeling, saying, "I prefer feeling my sorrow to forgetting it or becoming indifferent" (Lubin, 1972, p. 22). Painting was the one thing that drove away his sadness, and sometimes he painted with a frenzy. He had bouts of irritability, had difficulty concentrating, was often miserable, and was frequently quarrelsome. People described him as odd, argumentative, very sensitive, and unpredictable. He described himself as an alcoholic. He had frequent thoughts of suicide, and in the end, at the age of 37, he died after intentionally shooting himself (Lubin, 1972).

Mood disorders are disorders marked by persistent or episodic disturbances in emotion that interfere with normal functioning in at least one realm of life. Among the most common mood disorders are *major depressive disorder, dysthymia* (a less intense but longer lasting form of depression), and *bipolar disorder* (formerly known as manic-depressive disorder).

Major Depressive Disorder: Not Just Feeling Blue

When people are feeling sad or blue, they may say they are "depressed," but generally they do not mean that they are suffering from a psychological disorder. **Major depressive disorder (MDD)** is characterized by at least 2 weeks of depressed mood or loss of interest in nearly all activities, along with sleep or eating disturbances, loss of energy, and feelings of hopelessness, as described in Table 11.2 (on p. 484; American Psychiatric Association, 2000a). Thus, major depression affects a person's "ABC's":

- *affect* (mood),
- *behavior* (actions), and
- *cognition* (thoughts).

It is estimated that up to one in five people in the United States will experience MDD in their lifetimes (American Psychiatric Association, 2000a; Kessler et al., 2003; Ross, 1991), often in addition to another *DSM-IV* disorder (Kessler et al., 2003). Major depressive disorder is the most common psychological disorder in the United States (Kessler et al., 1994), and it is found among all cultural and ethnic groups (Weissman et al., 1991), as well as across the economic spectrum. In developing countries, prevalence rates are estimated to be about the same for men and for women (Culbertson, 1997), but American women are diagnosed with depression two to three times more frequently than American men (American Psychiatric Association, 2000a; Culbertson, 1997; Gater et al., 1998).

Mood disorders: A category of disorders marked by persistent or episodic disturbances in emotion that interfere with normal functioning in at least one realm of life.

Major depressive disorder (MDD): A mood disorder characterized by at least 2 weeks of depressed mood or loss of interest in nearly all activities, along with sleep or eating disturbances, loss of energy, and feelings of hopelessness.

Table 11.2 Diagnostic Criteria for Major Depressive Disorder

During a period of at least 2 weeks, five or more of the following symptoms have occurred and represent a change in functioning.

- Depressed mood most of the day, almost daily (based on subjective report or observations of others).
- Markedly diminished interest or pleasure in nearly all daily activities (based on subjective or objective reports).
- Significant weight loss, not through dieting.
- Daily insomnia or hypersomnia (sleeping a lot).
- Daily psychomotor agitation (intense restlessness) or retardation (physical sluggishness).
- Daily fatigue, or loss of energy.
- Almost daily feelings of worthlessness, or inappropriate or excessive guilt.
- Almost daily diminished ability to think or concentrate, or indecisiveness (based on subjective or objective reports).
- Recurrent thoughts of death or suicide with or without a specific plan.

Further, the overall prevalence of depression is increasing in the United States (Lewinsohn et al., 1993).

In the workplace, MDD is the leading cause of both absenteeism and "presenteeism," which occurs when a depressed person is present in body but not in mind, leading them to be less effective at work (Druss et al., 2001; Stewart et al., 2003). If current trends continue, by the year 2020, depression may well be the second most disabling disease in the United States, after heart disease (Schrof & Schultz, 1999). Some people with depression may experience only one episode; others experience recurrent episodes that may be frequent or separated by years; for some, depression may become more chronic (Judd et al., 1998). A 10-year study of over 300 people diagnosed with major depressive disorder found that more than one-third of the participants did not have a recurrence of depression (Solomon et al., 2000).

Artist Kate Monson, who experienced depression, describes her painting as a reflection of her depression.

Major Depressive Disorder From the Inside

The experience of depression is captured in words by Elizabeth Wurtzel, author of *Prozac Nation*:

> *In my case, I was not frightened in the least bit at the thought that I might live because I was certain, quite certain, that I was already dead. The actual dying part, the withering away of my physical body, was a mere formality. My spirit, my emotional being, whatever you want to call all that inner turmoil that has nothing to do with physical existence, were long gone, dead and gone, and only a mass of the most . . . god-awful excruciating pain . . . was left in its wake. (Wurtzel, 1995, p. 22)*

Elizabeth Wurtzel's description of her depression captures the essence of the painful, extremely disturbing quality of many of the symptoms. In some cases, se-

Table 11.3 Common Misconceptions of Suicide

- *If you talk about suicide, you won't really do it.* (False: Most people who commit suicide gave some clue or warning. Threats or statements about suicide should not be ignored.)

- *People who attempt suicide are "crazy."* (False: Suicidal people are not "crazy"; they *are* likely to be depressed or upset or to feel hopeless.)

- *Someone determined to commit suicide can't be stopped.* (False: Almost all suicidal people have mixed feelings about living and dying up until the last moment. Moreover, most suicidal people don't want to die; they want their pain to stop. And the suicidal impulse often passes.)

- *People who commit suicide weren't willing to seek help.* (False: Studies have shown that more than half of suicide victims sought medical help within the 6 months before death.)

- *Talking about suicide could give someone the idea, so you shouldn't talk or ask about it.* (False. Discussing suicide openly can be helpful to someone who is suicidal.)

verely depressed people also have delusions or hallucinations. Often these psychotic symptoms feature themes of guilt, deserved punishment, and personal inadequacy, such as voices asserting the individual's worthlessness.

However, members of different cultures may not experience exactly the same symptoms. Consider that people from Zimbabwe who are depressed often complain of headache and fatigue (Patel et al., 2001), as do people in Latin and Mediterranean cultures. They do not necessarily report sadness and guilt. In Asian cultures, people with major depression are likely to report weakness, tiredness, a sense of "imbalance," or other bodily symptoms (Parker et al., 2001).

Many, if not most, suicide attempts seem to be motivated by the sense of hopelessness that is often a part of depression. Approximately 30% of people with depression attempt suicide, and half of those attempters succeed. One estimate is that over 31,000 depressed people in the United States commit suicide every year, making it the 8th leading cause of death in the country (Arlas et al., 2003). Suicide prevention programs try, in part, to treat depression and alcohol use, both of which are associated with suicide (Reifman & Windle, 1995). Several common misconceptions about suicide are listed in Table 11.3. Test yourself to see whether your views of suicide are accurate.

Bipolar Disorder: Going to Extremes

In contrast to depression, **bipolar disorder** is a mood disorder marked by one or more manic episodes or by the less intense hypomania, often alternating with periods of depression. Approximately 1% of Americans have this disorder (Regier & Kaelber, 1995). A **manic episode** is a period of at least a week during which an abnormally elevated, expansive, or irritable mood persists. Being manic is not just having an "up" day. During a manic episode, the sufferer may be euphoric and enthusiastic about everything, starting conversations with strangers and making grandiose plans. People experiencing *hypomania* have less severe symptoms of mania, and their symptoms are less likely to interfere with social functioning.

Bipolar disorder: A mood disorder marked by one or more episodes of either mania or hypomania, often alternating with periods of depression.

Manic episode: A period of at least 1 week during which an abnormally elevated, expansive, or irritable mood persists.

Jamison, like many people with bipolar disorder, had difficulty recognizing that she had a psychological disorder and resisted attempts at treatment for a number of years. Manic or hypomanic episodes are often preceded or followed by episodes of depression, and the cycling of the mood usually takes place over a number of years, although some people may experience rapid cycling, with four or more mood shifts in a year. If left untreated, mood swings often become more frequent over time, leading to a poorer prognosis. The early phase of an episode, before the symptoms become acute, is termed the *prodromal phase* (a *prodrome* is a warning symptom). Some people with bipolar disorder report prodromal indicators of manic or depressive symptoms that signal that an episode will occur (Keitner et al., 1996).

Explaining Mood Disorders

Although bipolar disorder and major depressive disorder are distinct, research has characterized them as lying on a spectrum of mood disorders (Akiskal, 1996; Angst, 1998) that are related by biological and psychological factors. Mood disorders can best be understood by considering the interactions of events at the three levels of analysis: the brain, the person, and the group.

Level of the Brain in Mood Disorders. Both depression and bipolar disorder arise in part from events at the level of the brain.

Biological factors in depression. Depression tends to run in families (Weissman et al., 2005), and twin studies show that if one identical twin has major depression, the co-twin is four times more likely to experience depression than is the co-twin of an affected fraternal twin (Bowman & Nurnberger, 1993; Kendler et al., 1999). This appears to be good evidence for genetic influence. However, adoption studies have not shown the same clear-cut evidence for a genetic role (Eley et al., 1998; Wender et al., 1986). More definitive evidence that biological factors play a role in depression comes from research with depressed people whose relatives also suffer from depression: The depressed people studied had unusually low activity in one area of the frontal lobe that has direct connections to

This PET scan shows brain activity of a depressed individual. Red and yellow indicate brain areas with low activity: part of the frontal lobes (at left) and the parieto-temporal area (at right). Individuals who are not depressed show higher levels of activity in these brain areas.

many brain areas involved in emotion, such as the amygdala. This part of the frontal lobe also has connections to brain structures that produce serotonin, norepinephrine, and dopamine (Kennedy et al., 1997). Parts of this area of the frontal lobe have frequently been found to have abnormal patterns of activation in people who are depressed (Davidson et al., 2002; Liotti et al., 2002). People with depression have also been found to have smaller hippocampi, a key brain area involved in memory (Bremner et al., 2000; Sheline et al., 2003). Additional studies suggest that people with depression have increased activity in the amygdala (Drevets et al., 2002), which is involved in emotional memory; the amygdala's involvement may account for the protracted thinking about emotional events that is often part of depression (Cahill et al., 2001).

Unfortunately, it is not yet clear which neurotransmitters are most involved in depression; it is not even clear whether the problem is having too much or too little of those substances (Duman et al., 1997). What *is* clear, however, is that in people with depression, some change occurs in the activity of serotonin, norepinephrine, and possibly a more recently discovered neurotransmitter, *substance P* (Kramer et al., 1998). Depression also involves a dysfunction of the HPA axis (Hasler et al., 2004; see Chapter 2 for information about the HPA axis).

Biological factors in bipolar disorder. Among those with bipolar disorder, there is evidence that the amygdala is enlarged (Altshuler et al., 1998; Strakowski et al., 2002). The association of this disorder with some abnormality affecting the amygdala is consistent with the role of this structure in regulating mood and accessing emotional memories (LeDoux, 1996; see Chapters 5 and 7). Neuroimaging studies of people with bipolar disorder have found shifts in temporal lobe activity during manic episodes that do not occur during other mood states (Gyulai et al., 1997); these shifts may be related to activity in parts of the limbic system that are located in those lobes.

There is clear evidence for an underlying genetic relationship between bipolar and depressive mood disorders. For example, if an identical twin has bipolar disorder, the co-twin has an 80% chance of developing some kind of mood disorder (such as depression), although not necessarily bipolar disorder (Karkowski & Kendler, 1997; Vehmanen et al., 1995).

Neurotransmitters are also implicated in bipolar disorder, although the exact mechanism is unknown. There is some support for the theory that bipolar disorder involves disturbances in the functioning of serotonin (Goodwin & Jamison, 1990). Moreover, it is known that lithium, the medication usually prescribed for bipolar disorder, lowers the activity level of norepinephrine in the brain (Bunney & Garland, 1983), but just how this happens is not yet known.

Level of the Person in Mood Disorders. Much is known about how events at the level of the person contribute to depression, but relatively little is known about how such events contribute to bipolar disorder.

The person and depression. Compared with people who are not depressed, depressed people make more negative comments and less eye contact, are less responsive, and speak more softly and in shorter sentences (Gotlib & Robinson, 1982; Segrin & Abramson, 1994). Aaron Beck (1967) found evidence for a *negative triad of depression* in the thoughts of depressed people. This triad consists of: (1) a negative view of the world, (2) a negative view of the self, and (3) a negative view of the future (see Figure 11.2). Beck proposes that people with depression commit errors in their thinking, or *cognitive distortions*, based on these three sets of beliefs, and that these errors maintain an outlook on life that perpetuates depressing feelings and behaviors. These cognitive distortions may be based on early learning.

Figure 11.2
Beck's Negative Triad

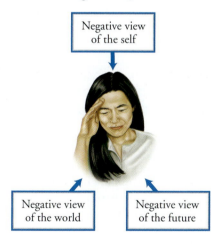

Among people who are depressed, Beck's triad of distorted, negative thinking about the world, the self, and the future add up to produce a negative view of life. However, these cognitive distortions can be corrected.

Research has found that at the beginning of a semester, college students whose attributional style led them to blame internal—as opposed to external—causes are more likely to become depressed when receiving a bad grade. These students are more likely to attribute a bad grade to their lack of ability rather than to the difficulty of the test, poor teaching, or other external factors (Peterson & Seligman, 1984).

The phenomenon of learned helplessness (see Chapter 7) also contributes to depression; when people feel that they have no control over negative aspects of their environment, they are more likely to develop depression. Of particular interest is evidence that people's views of themselves and the world can influence their risk of developing depression. A person's characteristic way of explaining life events—his or her **attributional style**—affects the risk of depression. For people who attribute blame to themselves (versus external factors), the risk of depression rises, especially after a stressful event (Monroe & Depue, 1991). Research on attributional styles and depression finds that those people who tend to attribute unfortunate events to internal causes (their own thoughts, abilities, behaviors, and the like), and who believe that these causes are stable, are more likely to become depressed. Thus, depressing thoughts (such as "I deserved to be fired . . . I wasn't as good at my job as some other people") are more likely to lead to depressing feelings. In contrast, patterns of attributing blame to external causes ("I was laid off because I didn't have enough seniority"), even if inaccurate, are less likely to lead to depression (Abramson et al., 1978).

The person and bipolar disorder. Surprisingly little is known about how events at the level of the person contribute to bipolar disorder. About all we can say with confidence is that people with bipolar disorder have a depressive attributional style when in a depressed phase of the disorder (Lyon et al., 1999; Scott et al., 2000).

Level of the Group in Mood Disorders. Again, although much is known about how events at the level of the group contribute to depression, relatively little is known about how such events contribute to bipolar disorder.

The group and depression. Events at the level of the group have also been tied to depression. Life stressors are associated with a subsequent first episode of depression (see Figure 11.3), and such stressors can influence how severe it becomes (Lewinsohn et al., 1999). Moreover, as would be expected according to the principles of operant conditioning (see Chapter 4), the less opportunity there is for social reinforcement because of decreased activity and contact with other people, the more likely it is that depressive symptoms will occur (MacPhillamy & Lewinsohn, 1974). Similarly, environments that not only lack positive reinforcements but also provide many "punishing" experiences (such as being regularly criticized) put people at risk for depression. For example, although not necessarily associated with the *onset* of depression, the family environment can be influential in *recovery* from a depressive episode. Living with unsupportive and critical relatives can increase the risk of a relapse of depression (Hooley & Licht, 1997; Miller et al., 1992). Some programs designed to help those with depression attempt to minimize the depressive symptoms and increase the frequency and quality of positive interactions with others (as well as help decrease the frequency and quality of punishing interactions; Teri & Lewinsohn, 1985).

Culture may also play a role in facilitating depression by influencing the type of events that are likely to lead to poor mood. For instance, among Malaysian students in a British university, depressed mood was more likely to follow negative social events, whereas, among British students, depressed mood was more likely to follow negative academic events (such as a poor grade; Tafarodi

Figure 11.3 Stressful Life Events and Depression Among Teenagers

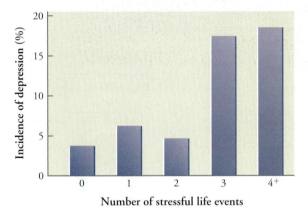

The incidence of the first episode of depression almost quadruples among those teenagers who experienced three or more stressful life events in the previous year (Lewinsohn et al., 1999). After the first depressive episode, subsequent depressive episodes are triggered more easily by fewer stressful events.

Attributional style: A person's characteristic way of explaining life events.

& Smith, 2001). These results are consistent with the different cultural values in collectivist versus individualist cultures (see Chapter 7).

In addition, at least some of the sex differences in the frequency of depression may be influenced by culture. For example, Nolen-Hoeksema (1987) offered a cultural explanation for the finding that women in developed countries experience depression more often than men. She and others (Nolen-Hoeksema & Morrow, 1993; Vajk et al., 1997) have found that people in developed countries who *ruminate* about (persistently ponder or dwell on) their depressed mood are more likely to have longer periods of depression. She proposes that boys and girls are taught to respond differently to stressors, and they carry these response styles with them into adulthood. Nolen-Hoeksema contends that boys are encouraged to deemphasize feelings and to use distraction and action-oriented coping strategies, whereas girls are encouraged to be introspective and not to take action. A ruminative response is known to promote depression (Nolen-Hoeksema, 2000); action and distraction can protect against depression. In fact, research has shown that depressed mood improves when college students learn to use strategies of distraction more often and learn to curtail their ruminations (Nolen-Hoeksema & Morrow, 1993). Other psychologists propose that the substantially higher rate of depression in women may also be due to biases in how the diagnosis is made and how depression is measured (Hartung & Widiger, 1998; Sprock & Yoder, 1997).

The group and bipolar disorder. As with depression, there is evidence that more Americans are experiencing bipolar disorder than ever before, and at earlier ages (Goodwin & Jamison, 1990). One cause may be the unnaturally lengthened day experienced in modern society due to the pervasive use of electric lights. When a patient with rapid-cycling bipolar disorder was put in an environment without electric lights (thereby experiencing 10–14 hours of darkness a night), the cycles lengthened, bringing more stability of mood (Wehr et al., 1998).

First episodes of bipolar disorder are invariably preceded by significant stressors (Goodwin & Ghaemi, 1998). And, like people with depression, those with bipolar disorder are more likely to relapse if they live with critical families (Honig et al., 1997; Miklowitz et al., 1988). Life stressors can also impede recovery after hospitalization for bipolar disorder (Johnson & Miller, 1997). On a positive note, treatment programs designed to reduce the critical behavior of families appear to be effective in reducing relapses (Honig et al., 1997).

Events at the level of the group can affect the course of bipolar disorder. Social stressors that affect biological rhythms or daily schedules, such as frequent plane travel or repeated changes in work schedules, can adversely affect the course of the disease (Johnson & Roberts, 1995; Post, 1992).

Interacting Levels: Depression Is as Depression Does. As we've seen previously, events at the three levels of analysis are not independent, but rather interact in complex and subtle ways. James Coyne (1976; Coyne & Downey, 1991) proposed an influential *interactional theory of depression*. He theorizes that the depressed person, who may be biologically vulnerable to depression (level of the brain), has thoughts and impulses (level of the person) that lead him or her to do or say things that alienate others (level of the group), who might provide support (Katz & Joiner, 2001; Nolan & Mineka, 1997). Actions that alienate others include (Katz & Joiner, 2001):

- seeking excessive reassurance,
- seeking out negative feedback, and
- interpersonal aggression.

These actions may lead others to reject the depressed person (level of the group), confirming that person's negative view of himself or herself. The depressed individual may then continue to seek out feedback from others, perhaps attempting to determine whether such negative feedback was a fluke or to elicit positive feedback from others; whatever the motivation, such rejections and criticisms increase the likelihood of negative future events (Casbon et al., 2005).

But this isn't all there is to the interactions among events at the different levels: For instance, have you ever noticed that it's no fun being with a depressed person (level of the group)? A depressed mood can be contagious, and relatives and friends of a depressed individual may find themselves feeling and acting somewhat depressed, which further limits how well they can assist the depressed person (Coyne et al., 1987). Thomas Joiner (1994) found that college students who spent time with depressed roommates over a period of 3 weeks themselves became more depressed. (Indeed, anger, anxiety, and sadness have also been found to be contagious; Coyne, 1976; Hsee et al., 1990; Joiner, 1994; Katz et al., 1999; Segrin & Dillard, 1992; Sullins, 1991.) Moreover, those who develop depression are more likely to behave in ways that create stress in those around them, which in turn can trigger the onset of depression in the other people (McGuffin et al., 1988; Rende & Plomin, 1992). Thus, your roommate's or family member's depression can lead you to feel depressed, perhaps changing your brain and bodily functioning (level of the brain).

We know that van Gogh suffered from bouts of depression, at times had poor hygiene, narrowed his activities severely, and took pleasure only in painting. MDD seems like a possible diagnosis. Van Gogh's attempted assault on Gauguin, as well as the self-mutilation of his ear might be explained by MDD with psychotic features. He said he heard voices (auditory hallucinations) that told him to kill his friend; these hallucinations might have been symptoms of depression. Although a diagnosis of MDD could explain the majority of these symptoms, it is not the only possibility. Bipolar disorder is another potential diagnosis. Perhaps van Gogh's episodes of frenzied painting were manic episodes, although they could also have been an intense restlessness that can occur with depression. His attacks, which became more frequent over time, might have been episodes of mania that became psychotic; untreated episodes of mania do become more frequent.

Anxiety Disorders

We know that van Gogh had what he called "attacks." Were these anxiety attacks? He was also considered to be nervous and had concentration problems—signs of anxiety. Can we recognize a pattern in these symptoms? Could he have had an anxiety disorder? What is an anxiety disorder?

Many people are nervous when they have to speak in public. But suppose you become *so* nervous before an in-class presentation that your mouth is dry, you feel lightheaded, your heart begins to race, and you think you're having a heart attack and going crazy at the same time. These reactions are not normal "stage jitters." They are typical signs of an anxiety disorder, a category of disorders characterized by extreme fear (a response to an external stimulus, such as a snake) and extreme anxiety (a vague but persistent sense of foreboding or dread when not in the presence of the stimulus). Many anxiety disorders are focused on a specific object or situation. However, generalized anxiety disorder involves excessive anxiety and worry that is not consistently related to a specific object or situation, and approximately 3% of people have this disorder at any given point in time (American Psychiatric Association, 2000a). Fear and anxiety are part of life, but people who have anxiety disorders experience *intense* or *pervasive* anxiety and/or fear or en-

Anxiety disorders: A category of disorders whose hallmark is intense or pervasive anxiety or fear, or extreme attempts to avoid these feelings.

Generalized anxiety disorder: An anxiety disorder whose hallmark is excessive anxiety and worry that is not consistently related to a specific object or situation.

gage in *extreme* attempts to avoid these feelings. These experiences create exceptional distress that can interfere with the ability to function normally. Four major types of anxiety disorders are panic disorder, phobias, obsessive-compulsive disorder, and posttraumatic stress disorder.

Panic Disorder

Panic attacks are episodes of intense fear or discomfort accompanied by symptoms such as palpitations, breathing difficulties, chest pain, nausea, sweating, dizziness, fear of going crazy or doing something uncontrollable, fear of impending doom, and a sense of unreality. These symptoms reach their peak within a few minutes of the beginning of an attack, which can last from minutes to hours. Often, these attacks are not associated with a specific situation or object and may even seem to occur randomly. One study of college students found that 12% of the participants experienced spontaneous panic attacks in college or in the years leading up to college (Telch et al., 1989). A person is said to have **panic disorder** if he or she endures frequent, unexpected panic attacks or fears additional panic attacks and thus changes aspects of his or her life in hopes of avoiding them. Internationally, approximately 3% of all people will experience panic disorder during their lifetimes (Rouillon, 1997). Some people may have episodic outbreaks of panic disorder, with years of remission; others may have more persistent symptoms.

Panic attacks can interfere with everyday functioning. Mob captain Tony Soprano sought professional help to keep his panic attacks under control.

Panic Disorder From the Inside

Here is one person's description of a panic attack:

My breathing starts getting very shallow. I feel I'm going to stop breathing. The air feels like it gets thinner. I feel the air is not coming up through my nose. I take short rapid breaths. Then I see an image of myself gasping for air and remember what happened in the hospital. I think that I will start gasping. I get very dizzy and disoriented. I cannot sit or stand still. I start pacing. Then I start shaking and sweating. I feel I'm losing my mind and I will flip out and hurt myself or someone else. My heart starts beating fast and I start getting pains in my chest. My chest tightens up. I become very frightened. I get afraid that these feelings will not go away. Then I get really upset. I feel no one will be able to help me. I get very frightened I will die. I want to run to some place safe but I don't know where. (Beck et al., 1985, p. 107)

People with panic disorder worry constantly about having more attacks, and in their attempts to avoid or minimize panic attacks, they may change their behavior. People may go to great lengths to try to avoid panic attacks, quitting their jobs and avoiding places (such as hot, crowded rooms or events) or activities that increase their heart rate (such as exercise, sex, or watching suspenseful movies or sporting events). Some people fear or avoid places that might be difficult to leave should a panic attack occur—for example, a plane or car; this condition is called **agoraphobia**, literally, "fear of the marketplace." Such people may completely avoid leaving home (Bouton et al., 2001) or will do so only with a close friend or relative. Agoraphobia can restrict daily life; some people have agoraphobia without panic attacks, avoiding many places because they fear either losing control of themselves in some way (such as losing bladder control) or experiencing less severe but still distressing panic symptoms.

Panic attack: An episode of intense fear or discomfort accompanied by physical and psychological symptoms such as palpitations, breathing difficulties, chest pain, fear of impending doom or of doing something uncontrollable, and a sense of unreality.

Panic disorder: An anxiety disorder whose hallmark is panic attacks or fear and avoidance of such attacks.

Agoraphobia: A condition in which people fear or avoid places that might be difficult to leave should panic symptoms occur.

Figure 11.4 Panic Disorder: Locus Coeruleus and the Alarm System

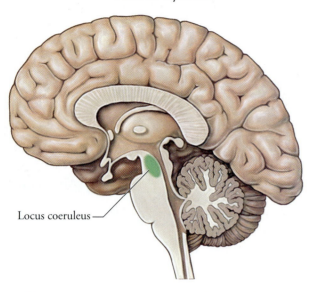

Locus coeruleus

The locus coeruleus is a group of cells in the brainstem that serves as an alarm system. When the alarm is activated, the body responds with the fight-or-flight response, including increased heart and respiration rates.

Level of the Brain in Panic Disorder. What causes panic attacks? A person can apparently inherit a biological vulnerability for panic, an event at the level of the brain (Crowe et al., 1983; Torgersen, 1983; van den Heuvel et al., 2000). Evidence of one possible route to such a vulnerability comes from animal studies, which suggest that panic attacks may arise from having an excessively sensitive *locus coeruleus*, a small group of cells deep in the brainstem (Gorman et al., 1989; see Figure 11.4). The locus coeruleus is the seat of an "alarm system" that triggers an increased heart rate, faster breathing, sweating, and other components of the fight-or-flight response (see Chapters 2 and 10), and these bodily symptoms can lead to the experience of panic. Also, people with panic disorder may be more sensitive than others to changes in carbon dioxide inhalation (Beck et al., 1999; Papp et al., 1993, 1997), which can come about through hyperventilation. Changes in carbon dioxide levels can elicit panic, perhaps through a "suffocation alarm" in the brain that has an abnormally low threshold for firing in some people (Coplan et al., 1998; Klein, 1993).

Level of the Person in Panic Disorder. How a person interprets and responds to certain signals from the body—that is, events at the level of the person—may be critical to the development of panic disorder. For instance, people who have *anxiety sensitivity*, defined as the "belief that autonomic arousal can have harmful consequences" (Schmidt et al., 1997, p. 355), are at higher risk of experiencing spontaneous panic attacks (Plehn & Peterson, 2002; Schmidt et al., 1999). People can also become hypervigilant for the signals that have led to panic in the past. Thus, in a vicious cycle, these people are more likely to experience anticipatory anxiety, which increases sympathetic nervous system activity (including increased heart rate and breathing changes), which, in turn, triggers panic.

Level of the Group in Panic Disorder. At the level of the group, although 80% of people with panic disorder reported experiencing a stressful life event before the disorder developed, the presence of such stress did not predict how severe the disorder would be, nor did it predict whether the symptoms would become chronic (Manfro et al., 1996; Rouillon, 1997).

In addition, increased dangers in the environment (rising crime rate) and fewer social connections among people have increased the baseline level of anxiety. Today's "normal" children score higher on measures of a personality trait related to anxiety than did children in the 1950s who had a psychiatric diagnosis (Twenge, 2000), suggesting that those born recently are more likely to develop anxiety disorders than those born earlier.

Culture can also influence the particular form of some panic-related symptoms. Among Khmer refugees, for example, panic attacks are associated with symptoms of *kyol goeu*, "wind overload"—a fainting syndrome that can occur when you stand up from a lying or sitting down position. Those who have experienced *kyol goeu* are more likely to be sensitive to signs of autonomic arousal in their bodies and to have negative beliefs about what the arousal means; this increased anxiety makes panic attacks more likely (Hinton et al., 2001).

Although van Gogh was anxious and irritable, we do not know enough about what happened during one of his self-reported "attacks" to know whether these episodes were panic attacks or something else. In any event, panic disorder alone would not account for his symptoms of depressed mood, irritability, and impulsiveness or for his bizarre behavior.

Phobias: Social and Specific

A phobia is an exaggerated fear of an object, class of objects, or particular situations, accompanied by avoidance that is extreme enough to interfere with everyday life. Phobias can be sorted into types, based on the object or situation that is feared. Social phobia (or *social anxiety disorder*) is the fear of public embarrassment or humiliation and the ensuing avoidance of social situations likely to arouse this

A social phobia involves fear of public humiliation or embarrassment, whereas a specific phobia involves a fear of a particular object or situation.

fear (Kessler, Stein, et al., 1998). People with this disorder might try to avoid eating, speaking, or performing in public or using public restrooms or dressing rooms. When unable to avoid these situations, they invariably experience anxiety or panic. This is one of the most common psychiatric diagnoses (major depressive disorder is *the* most common; American Psychiatric Association, 1994). Estimates are that approximately 13% of Americans currently experience social phobia (Fones et al., 1998).

A specific phobia is focused on a specific object or situation. Most people with a phobia about blood, for example, faint if they see blood and may, because of their phobia, avoid getting appropriate treatment for medical problems (Kleinknecht & Lenz, 1989). People may have phobias about flying, heights, spiders, or dental work (see Table 11.4). The fear may occur in the presence of the stimulus or in anticipation of it, despite an intellectual recognition that the fear is excessive or unreasonable. By avoiding the object or situation, the sufferer avoids the fear and the anxiety or panic that it might elicit.

Level of the Brain in Phobias.   Studies with twins suggest that phobias have a genetic component that affects events at the level of the brain (Kendler et al., 1992, 2001, 2002; D. Li et al., 2001). The genetic vulnerability may cause the amygdala, as well as other fear-related brain structures (see Chapter 7), to react too strongly in certain situations (LeDoux, 1996). However, not all identical twins

Table 11.4 Five Subtypes of Specific Phobias

Phobia Subtype	Examples (Fear of . . .)
Animal fears	Snakes, rats, insects
Blood–injection–injury fears	Seeing blood or receiving an injection
Natural environment fears	Storms, heights, the ocean
Situation fears	Public transportation, tunnels, bridges, elevators, dental work, flying
Miscellaneous fears cued by stimuli not already mentioned	Choking, vomiting, contracting an illness, falling down

Phobia: A fear and avoidance of an object or situation extreme enough to interfere with everyday life.

Social phobia: A type of phobia involving fear of public humiliation or embarrassment and the ensuing avoidance of situations likely to arouse this fear.

Specific phobia: A type of phobia involving persistent and excessive or unreasonable fear triggered by a specific object or situation, along with attempts to avoid the feared stimulus.

are phobic if their co-twin is phobic, so nongenetic factors must play a role. Humans seem biologically *prepared* to develop phobias about certain stimuli and not others (see Chapter 4). Moreover, as we saw in the discussion of personality (Chapter 8), some people may be biologically predisposed to develop a classically conditioned fear more readily than others (Lissek et al., 2005).

Level of the Person in Phobias.   Learning may play a role in the development of specific phobias. Classical and operant conditioning, in particular, could be involved in producing some phobias (Mowrer, 1939; see Chapter 4). If a stimulus such as a thunderstorm (the *conditioned stimulus*) is paired with a traumatic event (the *unconditioned stimulus*), anxiety and fear may become *conditioned responses* to thunderstorms. Furthermore, because fear and anxiety are reduced by avoiding the feared stimulus, the avoidant behavior is operantly reinforced.

Level of the Group in Phobias.   Some researchers have suggested that classical conditioning can play a role in producing a phobia, even if indirectly. When a person observes the behavior of other people who fear particular objects or situations, observational learning can lead to the development of a phobia, by indicating what should be feared (Mineka et al., 1984).

In addition, some researchers propose that specific phobias may reflect a genetic predisposition to fear naturally occurring situations or objects that were a danger to the human species (such as heights or water) and to which some people never habituate (Poulton & Menzies, 2002). Observational learning may also help explain why males and females tend to have different specific fears—boys are encouraged to interact more with potentially fearful objects and situations (such as playing with spiders or climbing into high places) and in the process may naturally be exposed to such stimuli (Antony & Barlow, 2002).

Finally, many people with social phobias may have been extremely shy as children (see Chapter 8; Biederman et al., 2001; Kagan, 1989b); thus, they do not *develop* a social phobia, but rather they never lost their discomfort in certain situations.

Obsessive-Compulsive Disorder (OCD)

Obsessive-compulsive disorder (OCD) is marked by the presence of obsessions, either alone or in combination with compulsions. **Obsessions** are recurrent and persistent thoughts, impulses, or images that feel intrusive and inappropriate and that are difficult to suppress or ignore. Obsessions are more than excessive worries about real problems, and they may cause significant anxiety and distress. Common obsessions involve:

- thoughts of *contamination* ("Will I become contaminated by shaking her hand?"),
- repeated *doubts* ("Did I lock the door? Did I turn off the stove?"),
- the need to have things in a certain *order* (a perfect alignment of cans of food in a cupboard), or
- aggressive or horrific *impulses* (such as the urge to shout an obscenity in church).

Compulsions are repetitive behaviors or mental acts that some individuals feel compelled to perform in response to an obsession. Examples of compulsive behaviors are:

- *washing* in response to thoughts of contamination (washing the hands repeatedly until they are raw),

Obsessive-compulsive disorder (OCD): An anxiety disorder marked by the presence of obsessions, and sometimes compulsions.

Obsession: A recurrent and persistent thought, impulse, or image that feels intrusive and inappropriate and is difficult to suppress or ignore.

Compulsion: A repetitive behavior or mental act that an individual feels compelled to perform in response to an obsession.

- *checking* (checking again and again that the stove is turned off or the windows closed so that it can take hours to leave the house),
- *ordering* (putting objects in a certain order or in precise symmetry, a task that may take hours until perfection is attained), and
- *counting* (counting to 100 after each obsessive thought, such as thinking about hitting one's child or shouting an obscenity).

Some people with OCD believe that a dreaded event will occur if they do not perform their ritual of checking, ordering, and so on, but the particular compulsion is not realistically connected to what they are trying to ward off, at least not in the frequency and duration with which the compulsion occurs. Approximately 2–3% of Americans suffer from OCD at some point in their lives (Robins & Regier, 1991).

Obsessive-Compulsive Disorder From the Inside

One woman with OCD describes the ordeal of grocery shopping:

> *Once I have attained control of the car, I have the burden of getting into it and getting it going. This can be a big project some days, locking and unlocking the doors, rolling up and down the power windows, putting on and off the seat belts, sometimes countlessly.... Sometimes while driving I must do overtly good deeds, like letting cars out of streets in front of me, or stopping to let people cross. These are things everyone probably should do, but things I must do.... My trip in the car may take us to the grocery store. Inside I have certain rituals I must perform. I am relatively subtle about how I do them to avoid drawing attention to myself. Certain foods must have their packages read several times before I am allowed to purchase them. Some things need to be touched repetitively, certain tiles on the floor must be stepped on by myself and my family. I'll find myself having to go from one end of an aisle to the other and back again, just to make everything all right. I fear being accused of shoplifting sometimes because of the way I behave and the way I am always looking around to see if people have noticed my actions. (Steketee & White, 1990, pp. 12–13)*

People with a hand-washing compulsion may spend hours washing their hands until they are raw.

OCD can be understood by looking at events at the three levels and their interactions.

Level of the Brain in OCD. At the level of the brain, studies of families have produced evidence for a genetic contribution, although not a straightforward link: If one member of a family has OCD, others are more likely to have some type of anxiety disorder, but not necessarily OCD itself (Black et al., 1992; Pato et al., 2002; Torgersen, 1983). Brain structures have been implicated: Obsessions and compulsions have been related to a loop of neural activity that occurs in the basal ganglia (Breiter et al., 1996; Jenike, 1984; Rauch et al., 1994). Obsessions may occur when part of this brain structure does not do its normal job of "turning off" recurrent thoughts about an object or situation before they become obsessional; carrying out a compulsion may temporarily end the obsessional thoughts (Insel, 1992; Jenike, 1984; Modell et al., 1989; Saxena & Rauch, 2000). In addition, the neurotransmitter serotonin appears to play a role in OCD symptoms; serotonin-based medications such as Prozac reduce the symptoms, although the exact mechanism of this effect is unknown (Greenberg et al., 1997; Micallef & Blin, 2001).

Level of the Person in OCD. As with other anxiety disorders, operant conditioning may play a role in OCD's emergence in an individual. Because compulsive behavior may momentarily relieve the anxiety created by obsessions, the compulsion is reinforced and thus more likely to recur. Research has found that obsessions themselves are not all that uncommon (Weissman et al., 1994)—many people experience obsessive thoughts during their lives, including thoughts about a partner during the early stages of a relationship, without developing a disorder. Salkovskis (1985; Salkovskis et al., 2000) proposes that such obsessive thoughts develop into a disorder when the person having them determines that the thoughts are about an unacceptable action (such as killing a newborn child) or interprets the thoughts as conveying something fundamentally negative about himself or herself (Ferrier & Brewin, 2005; Rachman, 1997).

Research suggests that people with OCD whose predominant compulsion is checking may be more self-aware than previously believed: Participants were given pairs of words to study and asked about their confidence in their future ability to recognize the word pairs. Those with checking-related OCD did not feel confident about their future ability to remember the word pairs (in contrast to those without OCD), and their lack of certainty was well-founded: On both recognition and recall tests, they remembered fewer pairs than other participants. However, they were not accurate in *which* particular word pairs they would have difficulty recognizing (Tuna et al., 2005). Thus, their compulsion to go back and check whether they locked the door or turned off the stove may, in part, arise both because they have more difficulty remembering whether they actually performed those behaviors previously and because they have less confidence in their ability to remember things in general.

Level of the Group in OCD. Although similar percentages of people in different countries experience OCD (Horwath & Weissman, 2000), culture plays a role in the particular symptoms displayed (Weissman et al., 1994); for example, religious obsessions and praying compulsions are more common among Turkish men with OCD than among French men with OCD (Millet et al., 2000).

In addition, research studies have shown that people with more severe OCD tended to have families who were more rejecting of them and to have experienced more kinds of family stress (Calvocoressi et al., 1995). However, the direction of causation is unclear: Were families more rejecting because their OCD relatives were more symptomatic, and therefore more difficult to live with? Or did the strong rejection by the families produce stronger symptoms of OCD in the affected relatives? Perhaps future research will be able to discover more about causation.

Posttraumatic Stress Disorder (PTSD)

Psychological symptoms can occur as a consequence of a traumatic event such as war, physical or sexual abuse, terrorism, or natural disasters. The diagnosis of posttraumatic stress disorder (PTSD) is made when three conditions are met:

1. The person experiences or witnesses an event that involves actual or threatened serious injury or death.
2. The traumatized person responds to the situation with fear and helplessness.
3. The traumatized individual then experiences three sets of symptoms:

Posttraumatic stress disorder (PTSD): An anxiety disorder experienced by some people after a traumatic event and whose symptoms include persistent re-experiencing of the trauma, avoidance of anything associated with the trauma, and heightened arousal.

a. persistent re-experiencing of the traumatic event, which may take the form of intrusive, unwanted, and distressing recollections, dreams, or nightmares of the event or may involve flashbacks that can include illusions, hallucinations, and a sense of reliving the experience;

b. persistent avoidance of anything associated with the trauma and a general emotional numbing; and

c. heightened arousal, which can cause people with PTSD to startle easily (Shalev et al., 2000), have difficulty sleeping, or be in a constant state of hypervigilance.

These symptoms do not always appear immediately after the traumatic event, but once they start, they can persist for months or even for years.

Posttraumatic Stress Disorder From the Inside

Mr. E, age 65, complained that ever since World War II he experienced extreme nervousness that was somewhat alleviated by chewing tobacco.... After this wartime nervousness—consisting of subjective feelings of anxiety, itching, and shaking—developed [it got to the point where he experienced] eight such episodes in the month before he came to the hospital.

During the war Mr. E manned a landing craft that transported soldiers to the beaches. He was particularly distraught about an experience in which he felt something underfoot on a sandy beach and discovered that he was stepping on the face of a dead GI. He also described an incident in which his ship had been torpedoed and several crewmen killed. He experienced intense survivor guilt about this incident. (Hierholzer et al., 1992, p. 819)

Some soldiers develop posttraumatic stress disorder.

The majority of people who experience trauma do not go on to develop PTSD (Breslau et al., 1998; Koren et al., 2005; Resnick et al., 1993; Shalev et al., 1998; Yehuda, 2002a), and the type of trauma makes a difference in the outcome for a given person. For example, one study found that women were more likely to develop PTSD when their traumas resulted from crimes rather than from natural disasters (Resnick et al., 1993), and other studies corroborate this finding (Breslau et al., 1998). Other factors that affect whether PTSD will arise can be found in the interactions of events at each level of analysis: the brain, the person, and the group.

Level of the Brain in PTSD. Some people may be biologically at risk for developing symptoms of PTSD after a trauma. Perhaps such a biological vulnerability occurs because of a genetic predisposition (Shalev et al., 1998; True et al., 1993) or some trauma experienced in childhood

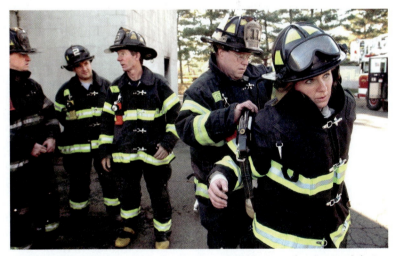

Firefighter-trainees were asked to listen to loud bursts of noise, and their tendency to be startled (indicated by blinking of the eyes) was assessed. The researchers measured this tendency before the trainees experienced any fire-related trauma in their work. The researchers later reassessed this tendency within 4 weeks after the trainees experienced such trauma. The trainees who were more reactive before a trauma were more likely to develop PTSD symptoms after a trauma (Guthrie & Bryant, 2005).

(Vermetten & Bremner, 2002). This predisposition could arise from having an overly reactive locus coeruleus, as occurs with panic disorder. In addition, the limbic system (including the amygdala) of people with PTSD appears to be more easily activated by mental imagery of traumatic events than that of non-traumatic events, possibly because part of the frontal lobe doesn't do as good a job of inhibiting the amygdala (Rauch et al., 1996, 2000; Shin et al., 1997, 2004). Researchers have also found that people with PTSD often have unusually small hippocampi, which may help to explain why they have intrusive memories (Bremner et al., 2003; Yehuda, 2002a).

In addition, people with PTSD appear to have lower baseline levels of cortisol and, when stressed, may not produce the high levels of cortisol that typically occur with the fight-or-flight response; this difference may exist before exposure to the trauma that produces the disorder (Yehuda, 2002b). Research findings further suggest that people who develop PTSD may have more glucocorticoid receptors (Yehuda et al., 2004). This would indicate that when they are stressed, any increase in cortisol level will have an amplified effect compared to people with fewer glucocorticoid receptors (Yehuda, 2003). In other words, people who develop PTSD after a traumatic experience may have a qualitatively different response to the trauma and its aftermath (Yehuda, 2002b), which leads to the unique symptoms of PTSD.

Level of the Person in PTSD.   PTSD is not simply a biological response to trauma. Events at the level of the person also influence whether a person will develop this disorder. Such events include the traumatized person's psychological characteristics before, during, and after a trauma (Ehlers et al., 1998; Ozer et al., 2003). A history of social withdrawal, depression, or a sense of not being able to control stressors increases the risk of developing PTSD after a trauma (Joseph et al., 1995). The perception that your life is at risk during the traumatic event or that you have no control over your situation can also facilitate development of PTSD, regardless of the actual threat (Foa et al., 1989). Risk of suffering the disorder rises, too, if you believe the world is a dangerous place (Keane et al., 1985; Kushner et al., 1992). Furthermore, people who have a lower IQ are more likely to develop symptoms of PTSD in the aftermath of a trauma (Macklin et al., 1998; McNally & Shin, 1995), perhaps because they have fewer cognitive resources for coping with the trauma.

In addition, the quality of thoughts differs between those who develop PTSD and those who do not. Trauma survivors who later developed PTSD were more likely to report that their intrusive thoughts of the trauma arose spontaneously and had a vivid, "here and now" quality than were trauma survivors who did not develop PTSD. Not surprisingly, such memories were more distressing (Michael et al., 2005). As in the case of phobias, classical and operant conditioning may help to explain the avoidance symptoms of PTSD. In addition, operant conditioning may be why people with PTSD are at a higher risk of developing drug abuse or dependence than those who experienced trauma but did not develop PTSD (Chilcoat & Breslau, 1998; Jacobsen et al., 2001): Substance use can lead to negative reinforcement because the symptoms of PTSD temporarily subside when the substance is taken.

Level of the Group in PTSD.   Whether trauma will lead to PTSD also depends, in part, on events at the level of the group. Support from friends, family members, or counselors immediately after a trauma may help decrease the likelihood that PTSD will develop (Kaniasty & Norris, 1992; Kaniasty et al., 1990). In the case of those exposed to trauma as part of military service, social support after coming back home can reduce the risk of PTSD (King, King, et al., 1998). Group factors play an integral role in creating the "trauma" part of the disorder, since traumatic events involving other people (violent crimes) are more likely to lead to PTSD.

Schizophrenia

In the last years of his life, van Gogh apparently had increasing difficulty distinguishing between his internal experiences and external reality. He would become disoriented and not know who he was. He had delusions of being poisoned and attacked. Gauguin claimed that van Gogh referred to himself as a ghost before cutting off part of his ear. During a period of mental clarity, when van Gogh was asked about the assault on Gauguin, he said that he was given to hearing voices, that he had heard voices telling him to kill Gauguin. Then he remembered the biblical injunction "If thine own eye offend thee, pluck it out." His ear had offended him by "hearing" the voice that suggested he kill Gauguin, so he cut part of it off as penance for his sin against Gauguin (Lubin, 1972).

These aspects of van Gogh's life and behavior suggest the possibility of schizophrenia. The word *schizophrenia* is derived from two Greek words, *schizo*, meaning "to split" or "to cut," and *phren*, meaning "mind" or "reason." Books and movies sometimes portray schizophrenia as if it meant having a split personality, but schizophrenia is characterized by a split from reality, not a split between different aspects of oneself. **Schizophrenia** is a psychotic disorder that profoundly alters affect, behavior, and cognition, particularly the pattern or form of thought.

Symptoms: What Schizophrenia Looks Like

DSM-IV divides the symptoms of schizophrenia into two groups (see Table 11.5). **Positive symptoms** involve an excess or distortion of normal functions; an example is hallucinations. They are called positive not because they indicate something desirable, but because they mark the *presence* of certain unusual behaviors. **Negative symptoms**, on the other hand, involve a *diminution* or *loss* of normal functions; an example is a restriction in speech or movement.

Table 11.5 Positive and Negative Symptoms of Schizophrenia	
Positive Symptoms	**Negative Symptoms**
• Delusions of *persecution* (beliefs that others are out to "get" you) of *grandeur* (beliefs that you are an important person) of *reference* (beliefs that normal events have special meaning directed toward you) of *control* (beliefs that your feelings, behaviors, or thoughts are controlled by others) • Hallucinations • Disordered behavior • Disorganized speech	• Flat affect (appears to be without emotion) • Alogia (brief, slow, empty replies to questions) • Avolition (inability to initiate goal-directed behavior)

Schizophrenia: A psychotic disorder in which the patient's affect, behavior, and thoughts are profoundly altered.

Positive symptom: An excess or distortion of normal functions, such as a hallucination.

Negative symptom: A diminution or loss of normal functions, such as a restriction in speech.

Positive Symptoms. Positive symptoms include *delusions* (distortions of thought) and *hallucinations*. Positive symptoms are usually more responsive than negative symptoms to antipsychotic medication (discussed in Chapter 12). Delusions can be complex, centering on a particular theme, such as the belief that someone, or some group, is out to "get" you. Hallucinations in schizophrenia are typically auditory; hearing voices is a common symptom. *Disorganized behavior* can consist of inappropriate, childlike silliness or unpredictable agitation. People with disorganized behavior may have difficulty with everyday tasks such as organizing meals, maintaining hygiene, and selecting their clothes (they might wear two overcoats in the summer). Another positive symptom is *disorganized speech*, as in the following example: "I may be a 'Blue Baby' but 'Social Baby' not, but yet a blue heart baby could be in the Blue Book published before the war" (Maher, 1966, p. 413).

Negative Symptoms. Negative symptoms include flat affect, alogia, and avolition (see Table 11.5). *Flat affect* is a general failure to express or respond to emotion. There may be occasional smiles or warmth of manner, but usually the facial expression is constant; eye contact is rare and body language minimal. *Alogia*, or "poverty of speech," is characterized by brief, slow, empty replies to questions. Alogia is not an unwillingness to speak; rather, the thoughts behind the words seem slowed down. Someone with alogia speaks less than others and doesn't use words as freely. *Avolition* is an inability to initiate or persist in goal-directed activities. Someone exhibiting avolition may sit for long periods without engaging in any behavior or social interaction.

Diagnosing Schizophrenia. Not all of the positive or negative symptoms are present in everyone affected with schizophrenia. According to the *DSM-IV*, a diagnosis of schizophrenia requires that two or more of these symptoms are displayed for at least a week and that other signs of socially inappropriate behavior are exhibited for at least 6 months. The average age of onset of schizophrenia is the 20s, although in some people (particularly women) onset does not occur until later in life. Symptoms often develop gradually, with a prodromal phase characterized by slow deterioration in functioning, including withdrawal from other people, poor hygiene, and outbursts of anger (Heinssen et al., 2001). Eventually, the disorder reaches an active phase, in which full-blown positive and negative symptoms arise.

Approximately 1% of people worldwide will develop schizophrenia in their lifetimes (Keith et al., 1991; Kulhara & Chakrabarti, 2001). The course of schizophrenia is variable: 25% of schizophrenics have only one psychotic episode and recover relatively completely, 25% improve enough to live independently, 25% improve, but not enough to live independently, 15% do not improve and are the "chronic" cases, and 10% commit suicide (Torrey, 1988).

Subtypes of Schizophrenia

People with schizophrenia, as mentioned earlier, tend to suffer from only some of the full range of possible symptoms. The symptoms of schizophrenia tend to cluster into groupings, from which mental health professionals and researchers have identified subtypes of schizophrenia. The *DSM-IV* specifies four subtypes of schizophrenia (see Table 11.6): paranoid, disorganized, catatonic, and undifferentiated.

If van Gogh did indeed suffer from schizophrenia, a diagnosis of the paranoid subtype would seem to fit him best, because his intellectual functioning and affect remained relatively intact between "attacks." But he apparently did not have extended periods of paranoid delusions, and schizophrenia would not account for his lengthy bouts of depression.

Table 11.6

Four Subtypes of Schizophrenia, According to *DSM-IV-TR*

Paranoid

Delusions of persecution are prominent; intellectual functioning and affect are relatively intact, but auditory hallucinations are common. This type has the best prognosis.

Disorganized

Disorganized speech and behavior and flat or inappropriate affect are prominent. This type has the worst prognosis.

Catatonic

Catatonic (bizarre, immobile, or relentless) motor behaviors are prominent.

Undifferentiated

Symptoms do not clearly fall into any of the above three subtypes.

Why Does This Happen to Some People, But Not Others?

With few exceptions, schizophrenia occurs at about the same rate worldwide, with about 1 in 100 people developing the disorder (Gottesman, 1991). The reason some people and not others suffer from schizophrenia involves events at the three levels of analysis and their interactions.

Level of the Brain in Schizophrenia. Biological events related to schizophrenia include genetics, abnormal brain structure and function, and hormonal and neurotransmitter activity.

Genetic factors in schizophrenia. Twin, family, and adoption studies point to the influence of genetic factors in the development of schizophrenia (Gottesman, 1991; Kendler & Diehl, 1993; Tiernari, 1991). People who have relatives with schizophrenia have an increased risk of developing the disorder; the closer the relative, the greater the risk. However, it is important to note that even for those who have a close relative with schizophrenia, the actual incidence is still quite low. More than 80% of people who have a parent or sibling diagnosed with schizophrenia do *not* have the disorder themselves (Gottesman & Moldin, 1998). Even when there is the highest level of genetic resemblance, in pairs of identical twins, the co-twin of a schizophrenic twin has only a 48% chance of developing schizophrenia. If the disease were entirely genetic, there should be a 100% correspondence in its incidence in pairs of identical twins. And a fraternal co-twin of a person with schizophrenia has only a 17% likelihood of developing the disorder (Gottesman, 1991). Although genes do play a role in the etiology (underlying causation) of schizophrenia, they are clearly not the only factor.

Structural brain abnormalities in schizophrenia. Evidence from autopsies and neuroimaging studies suggests that schizophrenia may involve abnormalities in brain structures. Someone with schizophrenia is more likely than others to have enlarged *ventricles*, cavities in the center of the brain filled with cerebrospinal fluid. Increased ventricle size means a reduction in size of the parts of the brain that contain gray matter and white matter, including the frontal cortex (Goldstein et al., 1999), which plays a central role in abstract thinking and planning. Impaired frontal lobe functioning has been the focus of a substantial amount of the research on schizophrenia.

Other brain abnormalities associated with schizophrenia include a relatively small thalamus and hippocampus, which might account for the memory problems commonly encountered by people with the dis-

Well   Affected

28-year-old males

Those with schizophrenia have larger ventricles, smaller amounts of frontal and temporal lobe cortex, and a smaller thalamus. This decreased cortical volume probably accounts for some of the cognitive deficits found in people with this disorder (Andreasen et al., 1986, 1992).

order (Schmajuk, 2001). These brain abnormalities may reflect a basic miswiring of brain circuits, so brain areas are connected to each other in abnormal ways. As a result of this faulty brain circuitry, neural activity doesn't occur in the way it is supposed to (Andreasen et al., 1999; Walker et al., 2004).

Researchers looking at different ways in which these brain abnormalities might arise have found several possible causes. One focus has been on the fetus's developing brain—specifically, on how normal brain development might go awry during pregnancy. Possibilities include:

Despite odds of one in a billion, all four of these identical quadruplets—from oldest to youngest, Nora, Iris, Myra, and Hester—went on to develop schizophrenia. The physical stressors experienced by the quads in their mother's uterus may have contributed to their developing the disorder. However, their symptoms and the onset and course of the illness differed. Hester and Iris were more disabled than were their sisters.

- maternal malnourishment during pregnancy (Brown, van Os, et al., 1999; Wahlbeck et al., 2001),

- maternal illness (Buka et al., 1999; Brown et al., 2001; Gilmore et al., 1997; Mednick et al., 1998),

- maternal stress (and higher levels of glucocorticoids; see Chapter 10) during pregnancy (Weinstock, 1997; Welberg & Seckl, 2001), and

- prenatal or birth-related medical complications that lead to fetal oxygen deprivation (Cannon, 1997; Geddes & Lawrie, 1995; McNeil et al., 2000; Zornberg et al., 2000).

Elevated levels of stress-related hormones. Children who are at risk for schizophrenia show an extreme discomfort with close relationships and exhibit relatively high levels of quirky or odd behavior. These children are also more reactive to stress and have higher baseline levels of the stress-related hormone cortisol (Walker et al., 1999; see Chapter 10). Moreover, higher levels of cortisol are associated with the severity of symptoms (Walder et al., 2000). Some researchers suggest that the increased biological changes and stressors of adolescence lead to higher levels of stress-related hormones. Prodromal symptoms of schizophrenia often begin to emerge during adolescence.

Similarly, Elaine Walker and her colleagues carefully analyzed home movies taken during the childhoods of people who were later diagnosed with schizophrenia and found that those children were different from their siblings (Grimes & Walker, 1994; Walker et al., 1993). They noted that, from infancy through adolescence, these people exhibited more involuntary movements, such as writhing or excessive movements of the tongue, lips, or arms (Walker et al., 1994). The more severe the involuntary movements, the more severe the schizophrenic symptoms in adulthood (Neumann & Walker, 1996).

Neurotransmitters. High levels of stress-related hormones are thought to affect activity of the neurotransmitter dopamine, and abnormalities in the functioning of this neurotransmitter have been implicated in schizophrenia (Walker & Diforio, 1997). Although dopamine clearly plays a role in schizophrenia, other neurotransmitters and other neural processes are also involved (Goff & Coyle, 2001; Laruelle et al., 2003; Nestler, 1997; Syvalathi, 1994; Tsai & Coyle, 2002; Walker & Diforio, 1997; Walker et al., 2004). In sum, researchers now agree that prenatal and birth complications may play a role in the development of schizophrenia, and some individuals are genetically vulnerable to the disorder. These factors may create abnormalities in brain structure, particularly in the frontal lobe, and in brain function, especially that of neurotransmitter systems.

Level of the Person in Schizophrenia. Although not part of the *DSM-IV* diagnostic criteria, people with schizophrenia may have problems in processing and responding to sensory stimuli (Green et al., 1999, 2000; Krieger et al., 2001), and these problems may lead to unusual sensory experiences (such as seeing inanimate objects move of their own accord). The individuals may feel bombarded by the myriad of stimuli around them and have trouble focusing on and making sense of those stimuli, leading to additional problems in organizing what they are perceiving and experiencing.

In addition, people with schizophrenia are likely to have difficulties with interpreting and using information in various contexts (Green et al., 2000; Kuperberg & Heckers, 2000; Walker et al., 2004). They may:

- not be able to determine the importance or relevance of new information or stimuli (Hemsley, 1994) or to distinguish relevant from irrelevant stimuli (Cornblatt et al., 1997; Nuechterlein, 1991);
- lose the "big picture," or be unable to keep track of the overall goal in a multistep task;
- have difficulty understanding social cues and therefore respond inappropriately (Penn et al., 1997); or
- not realize that they are having problems (referred to as a *lack of insight*).

These deficits also affect what these people experience, which affects their beliefs and goals.

The home movies study mentioned earlier also found that those children who went on to develop schizophrenia exhibited fewer expressions of joy than their unaffected siblings (Walker et al., 1993). (This emotional dampening may also cause other people to respond less positively to the affected person.)

Level of the Group in Schizophrenia. For someone who has been diagnosed with schizophrenia but whose symptoms have subsequently subsided, a stressful life event may act as a trigger, leading to a recurrence of symptoms (Gottesman, 1991; Ventura et al., 1989). Events at the level of the group can produce such stress. For example, almost two thirds of people hospitalized with schizophrenia live with their families after leaving the hospital, and the way members of a family express emotion can affect the likelihood of a recurrence of acute schizophrenia symptoms, although it does not *cause* schizophrenia. Families that are critical, hostile, and overinvolved are said to have <mark>high expressed emotion</mark>; they are more likely than families with low expressed emotion to include a member with chronic schizophrenia (Butzlaff & Hooley, 1998; Kavanagh, 1992; Vaughn & Leff, 1976). However, it is possible that the direction of causality runs the other way: Perhaps high expressed emotion families are responding to a relative with schizophrenia whose behavior is more bizarre or disruptive, and low expressed emotion families include someone whose schizophrenic symptoms are less extreme. Casting the social net wider, a longitudinal study of people with schizophrenia found that those who had larger numbers of nonrelated people in their social support networks before their first psychotic episode had the best rate of recovery 5 years after that episode (Erikson et al., 1998).

A higher rate of schizophrenia is found in urban areas and in lower socioeconomic classes (Freeman, 1994; Mortensen et al., 1999). Why might this be? Two factors appear to play a role: *social selection* and *social causation* (Dauncey et al., 1993). <mark>Social selection</mark>, also called *social drift*, refers to the "drifting" to lower socioeconomic classes of those who have become mentally disabled (Mulvany et al., 2001). This often happens to those who are no longer able to work and who lack family support or care (Dohrenwend et al., 1992). <mark>Social causation</mark> refers to the chronic psychological and social stressors in an urban environment, particularly for the poor. The stress from these living conditions may trigger the disorder in persons who are biologically vulnerable (Freeman, 1994).

High expressed emotion: An emotional style in families that are critical, hostile, and overinvolved.

Social selection: The tendency of the mentally disabled to drift to the lower economic classes; also called *social drift*.

Social causation: The chronic psychological and social stresses of living in an urban environment that may lead to an increase in the rate of schizophrenia (especially among the poor).

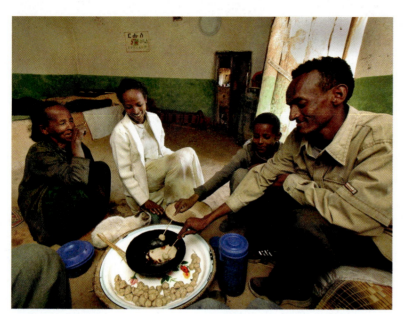

Industrialized countries generally have lower recovery rates for those with schizophrenia than do developing nations (American Psychiatric Association, 1994; Kulhara & Chakrabarti, 2001), although not all studies support this finding (Edgerton & Cohen, 1994; von Zerssen et al., 1990). If this finding is further substantiated, possible explanations include a more tolerant attitude and lower expressed emotion in extended families among people in developing countries (El-Islam, 1991).

Interacting Levels in Schizophrenia. Events at the three levels of analysis interact: As suggested by the finding that 48% of identical co-twins develop schizophrenia if their twin has schizophrenia, biological factors play a role in the development of the disorder, leading a person to be vulnerable to it. Such a biological vulnerability, in combination with environmental and social factors and with the individual's learning history, helps determine whether the disorder manifests itself. Walker and Diforio (1997) propose a specific diathesis–stress model to explain how stress can worsen schizophrenic symptoms. They note that people who develop schizophrenia do not experience more life stressors overall than people who do not develop the disorder; however, among individuals with schizophrenia, those who experience more of such stressors are likely to have more severe schizophrenic symptoms and experience more relapses (Hultman et al., 1997). And, in fact, people with schizophrenia have higher baseline levels of cortisol, an indicator of the stress response. This relationship is even more extended, since not only people with schizophrenia but also those at risk for the disorder (because of family history or evidence of some symptoms of schizophrenia) are more likely to have higher levels of cortisol. And antipsychotic medications (discussed in Chapter 12) decrease cortisol levels in people with schizophrenia.

Walker and Diforio further propose that this heightened susceptibility to stress comes about because of cortisol's effect on dopamine activity, which is to produce an overactivation of dopamine systems, which, in turn, can worsen symptoms of schizophrenia. They suggest that the negative symptoms of schizophrenia, such as social withdrawal, are attempts to reduce stress. Thus, genetic, prenatal, or birth factors increase a susceptibility to stress, and stress aggravates schizophrenic symptoms.

Van Gogh had a family history of schizophrenia, implicating a possible genetic factor, and some biographical material suggests that van Gogh's extremely strict father could be regarded as a high expressed emotion parent. And before becoming an artist, van Gogh repeatedly returned to live with his parents after leaving his various jobs. Moreover, after becoming an artist, he generally lived off money sent by his brother Theo. He was so poor that he often experienced enormous stress; for example, he often had to choose whether to spend Theo's gift of money on painting supplies or on food, and frequently chose the former (Auden, 1989).

Eating Disorders: You Are How You Eat?

At times, van Gogh ate only breakfast and a dinner of coffee and bread. And while in the hospital during the last year of his life, he would eat only meager dinners of half-cooked chick-peas or alcohol or bread and a little soup (Auden, 1989). Were van Gogh to be seen by mental health professionals now, they would undoubtedly ask more about his restricted and bizarre eating habits. Particularly if van Gogh were female, mental health professionals might wonder whether his eating habits were symptoms of an eating disorder.

In addition to the disorders in the major diagnostic categories already discussed, there are several less common Axis I disorders; some of these unfortunately are becoming more common. In this section, we consider the category of eating disorders.

Do you have a friend who's on a diet? If you do, the chances are that friend is a woman. Is her mood determined by the numbers on the scale? Does she want to lose more weight, even if she stops menstruating and others tell her she is too thin? If she eats more than she wants, does she feel that she must exercise, even if she's tired or sick? Is her view of herself on a given day dependent on whether she exercises that day? Does she eat as little as possible during the day, and then find herself "losing control" with food in the afternoon or evening? A "yes" response to these questions does not necessarily indicate the presence of a disorder, but it does indicate a preoccupation with food, body image, and weight. These preoccupations are typical of people with ==eating disorders==, disorders involving severe disturbances in eating behavior. And although more than 90% of those diagnosed with eating disorders are females, males are increasingly suffering from these disorders, too.

Anorexia Nervosa: You Can Be Too Thin

==Anorexia nervosa== is a potentially fatal eating disorder characterized by a refusal to maintain even a low normal weight. Someone with anorexia nervosa pursues thinness regardless of the physical consequences. Of those hospitalized with anorexia nervosa, 10% will eventually die of causes related to the disorder (American Psychiatric Association, 1994).

Anorexia Nervosa From the Inside

People with anorexia nervosa develop irrational and unhealthy beliefs about food, as recounted by one woman:

> Yesterday . . . I had a grapefruit and black coffee for breakfast, and for dinner I had the . . . salad I eat every night. I always skip lunch. I had promised myself that I would only eat three-quarters of the salad since I've been feeling stuffed after it lately—but I think I ate more than the three-quarters. I know it was just lettuce and broccoli but I can't believe I did that. I was up all night worrying about getting fat. (Siegel et al., 1988, p. 17)

Included in the list of symptoms required for a diagnosis of anorexia nervosa are:

- distortions of how such people see their bodies ("body image"; see Figure 11.5, on p. 506),
- an intense fear of gaining weight or becoming fat,
- a refusal to maintain a healthy weight, and
- among females, *amenorrhea* (the cessation of menstruation).

It is common for extremely anorexic women to "know" that they are underweight, yet when they look in the mirror, they "see" fat that is not there, or

Eating disorders: A category of disorders involving a severe disturbance in eating behavior.

Anorexia nervosa: An eating disorder characterized by the refusal to maintain even a low normal weight, and an intense fear of gaining weight.

Figure 11.5 Body Image Distortion

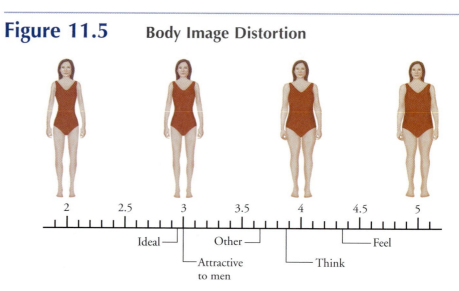

Many women, not only those with anorexia nervosa, have distorted body images. "Ideal" is the average of women's ratings of the ideal figure. "Attractive to men" is the average rating of the figure women believe is most attractive to men. "Other" is the average actual selection of the female figure that men find most attractive. "Think" is the average figure women think best matches their figure. "Feel" is the average figure women feel best matches their figure.

generally overestimate their body size (Smeets et al., 1997). They are often obsessed by thoughts of food, and these thoughts are usually based on irrational or illogical thinking (such as what are "good" and "bad" foods). They often deny that their low weight is a problem, or even that they have a problem. Some symptoms of anorexia nervosa differ from culture to culture. For example, half of young Chinese women with this disorder do not have the fear of being fat common among North Americans, but explain their restricted diet as a distaste for food or bodily discomfort when eating (Lee, 1996).

Some, but not all, people with anorexia nervosa periodically engage in *binge eating* (eating substantially more food within a certain time period than most people would eat in similar circumstances) or *purging* (getting rid of unwanted calories through vomiting or the misuse of laxatives, diuretics, or enemas), or both. Thus, there are two types of anorexia nervosa: the *binge-eating/purging type* and the classic *restricting type*, in which weight loss is achieved primarily by undereating, without purging.

Bulimia Nervosa

People with bulimia nervosa, like those with anorexia nervosa, are usually women, but they may be of normal weight or even overweight, and thus they continue to menstruate. **Bulimia nervosa** is marked by recurrent episodes of binge eating, followed by an attempt to prevent weight gain. When that attempt is made through purging (by vomiting or with the use of laxatives), the diagnosis of bulimia nervosa is further specified as *purging type*. Attempts to restrict weight gain may also occur through other methods, such as fasting or excessive exercise, and when this is the case, the disorder is the *nonpurging type*.

Some people with bulimia purge even when their eating does not constitute a binge: "If I had *one* bite of bread, just one, I felt as though I blew it! I'd stop listening to whomever was talking to me at the table. I'd start thinking, *How can I get rid of this?* I'd worry about how fat I'd look, how I couldn't fit into my clothes.

Bulimia nervosa: An eating disorder characterized by recurrent episodes of binge eating, followed by some attempt to prevent weight gain.

My head would be flooded with thoughts of what to do now. . . . I had to undo what I'd done. The night was blown. I was a mess" (Siegel et al., 1988, p. 18). Although most people with bulimia do not realize it, in the long run, purging does not usually eliminate all the calories ingested and is, in fact, a poor method for losing weight (Garner, 1997).

Explaining Eating Disorders

Why do people, most often women, develop eating disorders?

Level of the Brain in Eating Disorders. There is evidence of a genetic predisposition for anorexia. In one study, 56% of identical co-twins were likely to have anorexia if their twins did, compared to 5% of co-twins of affected fraternal twins (Holland et al., 1988). Moreover, another study found that relatives of those with anorexia nervosa had a higher incidence of obsessive-compulsive symptoms than did relatives of people with bulimia nervosa or control participants. This finding suggests that obsessive personality traits in a family may increase the risk for anorexia nervosa (Lilenfeld et al., 1998). However, learning (resulting in changes at the level of the person) can also account for this finding: People with obsessional relatives may learn to be obsessional; those with eating disorders have focused the obsession on food and weight.

The data for bulimia nervosa in twins shows a sharply different pattern: Twenty-three percent of identical co-twins were likely to have bulimia if their twins did, compared with 9% of co-twins of affected fraternal twins (Kendler et al., 1991). In bulimia, the environment, not genes, clearly plays the larger role (Wade et al., 1998).

The malnutrition and weight loss that occur with anorexia nervosa lead to changes in neurotransmitters, particularly serotonin. This neurotransmitter is also involved in obsessive-compulsive disorder, and the obsessional thinking about food and pathological eating behavior of anorexia are hypothesized to be related to alterations in serotonergic functioning (Barbarich, 2002; Kaye, 1995). Because one effect of serotonin is to create a feeling of satiety (Halmi, 1996), lower levels of serotonin may be a predisposing factor for bulimia nervosa (Pirke, 1995). The biological effects of dieting may also make women vulnerable to developing bulimia nervosa: Some, though not all, studies indicate that dieting sometimes precedes the onset of bulimia in some people (Garner, 1997). Although the research points to abnormalities or dysregulation of neurotransmitters as being involved in eating disorders, it is as yet unclear how the changes in different neurotransmitters are related; nor is it known whether these changes *precede* the development of an eating disorder, and thus may create a susceptibility to it, or instead are *consequences* of an eating disorder (Halmi, 1995).

Level of the Person in Eating Disorders. Numerous personal characteristics have been linked with eating disorders. An increased risk of developing anorexia occurs among women who are perfectionists and have a negative evaluation of themselves (Bulik et al., 2003; Fairburn et al., 1999; Tyrka et al., 2002). More generally, people with eating disorders often exhibit irrational beliefs and inappropriate expectations about their bodies, jobs, relationships, and themselves (Fairburn et al., 2003; Garfinkel et al., 1992; Striegel-Moore, 1993). They tend to engage in dichotomous, black-or-white thinking: Fruit is "good"; pizza is "bad." Moreover, as shown in Figure 11.6 (on p. 508), when examining photographs of themselves, these women spend more time looking at their "ugly" body parts than at their "beautiful" parts; in contrast, when they look at photos of other women, they spend more time looking at those women's "beautiful" body parts than at their "ugly" parts. Women who do not have an eating disorder devote equal time to looking at

Figure 11.6 Gazing at Body Parts: Women With and Without Eating Disorders

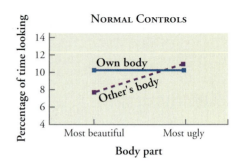

Women with eating disorders spend more time looking at their "most ugly" body parts than at their "most beautiful" parts; women without eating disorders spend equal amounts of time looking at both types of their own body parts. When looking at photos of other women, those with eating disorders look at the "most beautiful" parts more than the "most ugly" parts, and this pattern is reversed for women who do not have eating disorders (Jansen et al., 2005).

Cultural pressure on women to be thin and to attain an "ideal" body shape can contribute to eating disorders. Such pressure explains why there is a higher incidence of eating disorders now than 50 years ago, as the ideal figure has changed from the generous proportions of Marilyn Monroe to the rail-thin silhouette of today's runway models (Andersen & DiDomenico, 1992; Field et al., 1999; Nemeroff et al., 1994).

their own "beautiful" and "ugly" parts, and when looking at photos of other women, spend more time looking at their "ugly" parts than at their "beautiful" parts (Jansen et al., 2005).

Perhaps people with these personality characteristics, irrational beliefs, and inappropriate expectations are especially likely to find rewards in the behaviors associated with eating disorders. Preoccupations with food can provide distractions from work, family conflicts, or social problems. By restricting their eating, people may gain a sense of increased control—over food and over life in general—although such feelings of mastery are often short-lived as the disease takes over (Garner, 1997). By purging, people with an eating disorder may relieve the anxiety created by overeating.

Level of the Group in Eating Disorders. The family and the larger culture also play important roles in the development of eating disorders. They may contribute to these disorders by encouraging a preoccupation with weight and appearance (Crowther et al., 2002; Thompson & Stice, 2001). Children have an increased risk of developing eating disorders if their families are overly concerned about appearance and weight (Strober, 1995). Symptoms of eating disorders increase among immigrants from less weight-conscious cultures (such as the Chinese and the Egyptian) as they assimilate to American culture (Bilukha & Utermohlen, 2002; Dolan, 1991; Lee & Lee, 1996), although not all studies find this (Abdollahi & Mann, 2001). One prospective study in Fiji found that, with the advent of television (and Western television shows) in that country in 1995, Fijian girls' feelings about their bodies began to shift: Whereas before watching Western television shows, they felt comfortable having a large body—the ideal body shape in their culture—after viewing such shows, 75% of girls felt too fat or big at least some of the time (Becker et al., 2002). It is not only females who are susceptible: Eating disorders are increasing among men who regularly take part in appearance- or weight-conscious activities, such as modeling and wrestling (Brownell & Rodin, 1992).

Among U.S. women, the focus on appearance and weight may derive from a desire to meet the culture's ideal of femininity (Striegel-Moore, 1993). Westernization (or modernization) increases dieting (Gunewardene et al., 2001;

Lee & Lee, 2000), a risk factor for developing eating disorders. Culture also plays a role by promoting the idea that body shape can be changed and by determining the rationales people offer for their symptoms (Becker & Hamburg, 1996).

Van Gogh had abnormal eating habits; could he have had an eating disorder? It is unlikely; although van Gogh often ate sparingly and peculiarly, he did not appear to be preoccupied with weight gain or body image, and no information suggests that he purged in any way.

Looking at Levels

Binge Eating

You have learned what eating disorders are and explanations of why they might occur. Let's consider in detail a core aspect of bulimia nervosa—binge eating. Why do some people chronically binge eat?

At the level of the brain, food restriction is a contributor to binge eating (Nakai et al., 2001; Polivy & Herman, 1993; Stice et al., 2002). In their efforts to be "in control" of food, people with bulimia generally consume fewer calories at nonbinge meals than do nonbulimics, thus setting the stage for later binge eating because they are hungry and have food cravings (Walsh, 1993); the bingeing is thus reinforced. A binge/purge episode may be followed by an endorphin rush (and the ensuing positive feelings that it creates), further reinforcing the binge/purge cycle. As one woman with bulimia reported, "I go to never-never land. Once I start bingeing, it's like being in a stupor, like being drunk . . . I'm like a different person. It's very humiliating—but not then, not while I'm eating. While I'm eating, nothing else matters" (Siegel et al., 1988, p. 20).

At the level of the person, the dichotomous thinking typical of people with eating disorders leads them to view themselves as either "good" (when dieting or restricting food intake) or "bad" (eating "forbidden foods" or feeling out of control while eating). This thinking sets the stage for bingeing if any small amount of forbidden food is eaten; a bite of a candy bar is followed by a thought like this: "Well, I shouldn't have eaten *any* of the candy bar, but since I did, I might as well eat the whole thing, especially since I really shouldn't have a candy bar again." This line of reasoning is part of the *abstinence violation effect* (Polivy & Herman, 1993; Urbszat et al., 2002), the sense of letting go of self-restraint after transgressing a self-imposed rule about food: Once you violate the rule, why not go all the way? In addition, purging is negatively reinforcing (remember, negative reinforcement is reinforcement, not punishment; see Chapter 4): Eating too much, or eating forbidden foods, can cause anxiety, which is then relieved by purging. This reinforcement then increases the likelihood of purging in the future.

At the level of the group, if social interactions are stressful, then bingeing and purging, which are usually done alone, are reinforced by the isolation they provide. Such behaviors further serve to increase the affected person's sense of isolation and decrease his or her social interactions.

Events at the different levels interact: Cultural pressure to be thin or to eat small meals leads vulnerable individuals to try to curb their food intake. The hunger caused by this undereating may trigger a binge. The binge may also be triggered by stress, social interactions, negative affect, or viewing one's appearance as very important (Polivy & Herman, 1993; Stice et al., 2002; Vanderlinden et al., 2001); bingeing can then create positive changes (such as decreased hunger, distraction from an uncomfortable feeling or thought, and removal from difficult social interactions). This immediate reinforcement often outweighs the negative consequences that are experienced later.

LOOKING BACK: *Review*

1. *What are mood disorders? What causes them?* Mood disorders include major depressive disorder (MDD) and bipolar disorder (which may have psychotic features). Major depressive disorder is characterized by depressed mood, loss of pleasure, fatigue, weight loss, poor sleep, a sense of worthlessness or guilt, and poor attention and concentration. Bipolar disorder involves alternating episodes of mania and depression. Although these disorders appear to have a biological component, events at the levels of the person and group can play a role in onset or relapse.

2. *What are the main types of anxiety disorders? What are their symptoms and causes?* The anxiety disorders include panic disorder (with or without agoraphobia), specific and social phobias, OCD, and PTSD. Panic symptoms include breathing difficulties, nausea, dizziness, palpitations, and a fear of doing something crazy or uncontrollable. Phobias involve avoiding a feared object or situation that would cause anxiety or panic if encountered. OCD involves obsessions and often compulsions. PTSD occurs in response to traumatic events; it involves some symptoms of panic, as well as a reliving of the trauma. Anxiety disorders are caused by the interaction of events at the levels of the brain, the person, and the group.

3. *What are the symptoms and causes of schizophrenia?* Positive symptoms of schizophrenia include delusions, hallucinations, and disorders of behavior and speech. Negative symptoms include flat affect, alogia, and avolition. A biological vulnerability to schizophrenia plays a role in the development of the disease. This vulnerability can be genetic, related to prenatal maternal illness, or derived from prenatal or birth complications; all these factors may lead to brain abnormalities. The biological changes and increased stressors of adolescence can play a role in the onset of schizophrenia, and environmental factors, such as living with high expressed emotion families or being a member of a lower socioeconomic class, are associated with the risk of relapse.

4. *What are the symptoms and causes of eating disorders?* Symptoms of anorexia nervosa include a distorted body image, a fear of weight gain or becoming fat, a refusal to maintain a healthy weight, and (among females) amenorrhea. Symptoms of bulimia nervosa include recurrent binge eating, followed by purging. Eating disorders appear to be caused by an interaction of biological factors, rigid thinking about food and appearance, personal learning history, and family and cultural messages about weight.

LOOKING BEYOND: *Critical Thinking*

Suppose someone you know, someone whose sharp style of dress and confident manner you admire, starts looking unkempt and acting tired, nervous, and fidgety. Would this change suggest a psychological disorder? Why or why not? If so, what type of disorder do you have in mind and why? Would psychological impairment be the only explanation?

Axis II: Focus on Personality Disorders

By now, it should come as no surprise to know that van Gogh was more than just unconventional; his difficulties in life went beyond his attacks, his hallucinations, and his periods of depression. Van Gogh's relationships with other people were troubled, and they often followed a pattern: Initial positive feelings and excitement about someone new in his life (such as happened with Gauguin and Sien) were invariably followed by a turbulent phase and an eventual falling out. Throughout his life, he had emotional outbursts that sooner or later caused others to withdraw their friendship. His relationship with his brother Theo is the only one that endured. Does such a pattern suggest that he may have had a personality disorder?

LOOKING AHEAD: Learning Objectives

1. *What are personality disorders?*
2. *What is antisocial personality disorder?*

Axis II Personality Disorders

Axis II of the *DSM-IV* allows the possibility of a **personality disorder**, which is a set of relatively stable personality traits that are inflexible and maladaptive, causing distress or difficulty with daily functioning. A personality disorder may occur alone, or it may be accompanied by an Axis I disorder.

Whereas Axis I symptoms—those discussed up to this point in the chapter—feel as if they are inflicted from the outside, the maladaptive traits of Axis II are often experienced as parts of the person's personality. The maladaptive traits of personality disorders cause distress or difficulty with daily functioning in school, work, social life, or relationships. They can be so subtle as to be unnoticeable in a brief encounter. It is only after getting to know the person over time that a personality disorder may become evident.

As shown in Table 11.7 (on p. 512), *DSM-IV* organizes personality disorders into three clusters, with each grouping based on common symptoms:

- Cluster A—odd, eccentric behaviors
- Cluster B—emotional or dramatic behaviors
- Cluster C—anxious or fearful behaviors or symptoms

However, these clusters were not derived from research, but rather because personality disorders within a cluster appeared to have common elements (Livesley, 2001).

Some researchers argue that the combinations of traits now defined as personality disorders should not be called "disorders" at all. Doing so, they contend, either treats normal variations in personality as pathological or creates separate Axis II categories for conditions that could be part of an Axis I clinical disorder (Hyman, personal communication, 1998; Livesley, 1998). For example, the clinging, submissive behavior that *DSM-IV* categorizes as part of

Personality disorders: A category of disorders in which relatively stable personality traits are inflexible and maladaptive, causing distress or difficulty with daily functioning.

Table 11.7 Axis II Personality Disorders

Disorder	Description
Cluster A	
Paranoid personality disorder	A pattern of suspiciousness and distrust of others to the extent that other people's motives are interpreted as ill-intentioned. However, unlike the paranoid subtype of schizophrenia, there are no delusions or hallucinations.
Schizoid personality disorder	A pattern of detachment from social relationships and a narrow range of displayed emotion.
Schizotypal personality disorder	A pattern of extreme discomfort in close relationships, odd or quirky behavior, and cognitive or perceptual distortions (such as sensing the presence of another person or spirit).
Cluster B	
Antisocial personality disorder	A pattern of disregard or violation of the rights of others.
Borderline personality disorder	A pattern of instability in relationships, self-image, and feelings, and pronounced impulsivity (such as in spending, substance abuse, sex, reckless driving, or binge eating). Relationships are often characterized by rapid swings from idealizing another person to devaluing him or her. Recurrent suicidal gestures, threats, or self-mutilation, such as nonlethal cuts on the arm are common, as are chronic feelings of emptiness.
Histrionic personality disorder	A pattern of excessive attention seeking and expression of emotion.
Narcissistic personality disorder	A pattern of an exaggerated sense of self-importance, need for admiration, and lack of empathy.
Cluster C	
Avoidant personality disorder	A pattern of social discomfort, feelings of inadequacy, and hypersensitivity to negative evaluation.
Dependent personality disorder	A pattern of clingy, submissive behavior due to an extreme need to be taken care of.
Obsessive-compulsive personality disorder	A pattern of preoccupation with perfectionism, orderliness, and control (but no obsessions or compulsions, as occur with obsessive-compulsive disorder).

the dependent personality disorder of Axis II might also characterize a personality that is within the normal range. And the symptoms of avoidant personality disorder overlap those of Axis I's social phobia—only the greater severity of the anxiety and the presence of depressive symptoms in avoidant personality disorder distinguish it from social phobia (Johnson & Lydiard, 1995); the two disorders are quantitatively, not qualitatively, different. Thus, some personality disorders can be thought of as versions of Axis I disorders that differ in degree of severity.

Other researchers argue that each personality disorder is not a research-validated disorder distinct from all others (Atre-Vaidya & Hussain, 1999; Horowitz, 1998). Furthermore, the criteria for the various personality disorders do not all require the same level of dysfunction. Thus, a lesser—and, in some cases, quite mild—degree of impairment is required for a diagnosis of obsessive-compulsive, antisocial, or paranoid personality disorder (Funtowicz & Widiger, 1999).

From what is known about his life, it is not impossible that van Gogh had a personality disorder; but we have no way of knowing if he, in fact, met all of the criteria.

Antisocial Personality Disorder

The most intensively studied personality disorder is **antisocial personality disorder (ASPD)**, evidenced by a long-standing pattern of disregard for others to the point of violating their rights (American Psychiatric Association, 2000a). Symptoms include a superficial charm; egocentrism; impulsive, reckless, and deceitful behavior without regard for others' safety; a tendency to blame others for any adversity that comes along; and a lack of conscience, empathy, and remorse. People with this disorder talk a good line and know how to manipulate others, but they don't have the capacity to know or care how another person feels.

Antisocial Personality Disorder From the Inside

A common feature among people with ASPD is that they see *themselves* as the real victims. While discussing the many and horrible murders he had committed, John Wayne Gacy portrayed himself as the 34th victim:

> I was made an asshole and a scapegoat . . . when I look back, I see myself more as a victim than a perpetrator. . . . I was the victim; I was cheated out of my childhood. . . . [He wondered whether] there would be someone, somewhere who would understand how badly it had hurt to be John Wayne Gacy. (Hare, 1993, p. 43)

Antisocial personality disorder occurs three times more frequently in men than in women, and although only 1–2% of Americans are diagnosed with this disorder, 60% of males in U.S. prisons are estimated to have it (Moran, 1999). Cross-cultural studies have found a similar pattern of symptoms in both Western and non-Western cultures (Zoccolillo et al., 1999). Many people diagnosed with antisocial personality disorder also abuse alcohol and other drugs (Nigg & Goldsmith, 1994).

POLICE DEPT.
DES PLAINES, ILL.

John Wayne Gacy, convicted serial killer, saw himself as a victim; he shared this feature with other people who have antisocial personality disorder.

Understanding Antisocial Personality Disorder

What causes antisocial personality disorder? As you've seen for other psychological disorders, this one is best understood by examining events at the three levels of analysis and their interactions.

Level of the Brain in Antisocial Personality Disorder

Evidence for the contribution of biological factors (level of the brain) arises from a number of sources. Some of the data on antisocial personality disorder come from studies of certain types of criminal behavior patterns, which are related to some of the symptoms of antisocial personality disorder. These data show that the disorder runs in families (Nigg & Goldsmith, 1994). Moreover, adoption studies show that environment matters only if a child's biological parents were criminals; if they were, there was a slight increase in criminal behavior for boys adopted into

Antisocial personality disorder (ASPD): A personality disorder characterized by a long-standing pattern of disregard for other people to the point of violating their rights.

a family of law-abiding people, but there was a whopping increase in criminal behavior if they were adopted into a family of criminals. If the biological parents were not criminals, the adopted child's later criminal behavior was the same whether he or she grew up in a law-abiding or criminal family (Mednick et al., 1984). Criminal behavior provides a clear example of how genes and environment can interact: The genes predispose; the environment triggers.

Genes may produce a relatively underresponsive central and autonomic nervous system. In turn, this might lead people with such genes to seek out highly arousing, thrilling activities (Quay, 1965).

Level of the Person in Antisocial Personality Disorder

Research suggests that people with antisocial personality disorder have difficulty controlling their impulses and modulating their anger (Zlotnick, 1999). In addition, they have difficulty understanding how others feel, which engenders a lack of empathy (Kagan & Reid, 1986).

Level of the Group in Antisocial Personality Disorder

People with this personality disorder may not bond appropriately with their parents. Perhaps it is because, as children, they often experienced or witnessed abuse, deviant behavior, or lack of concern for the welfare of others by peers, parents, or others (Gabbard, 1990; Patterson, 1986; Patterson et al., 1989; Pollock et al., 1990). The behaviors of models who lack basic regard for others may later be imitated (Elliott et al., 1985).

Interacting Levels in Antisocial Personality Disorder

How might events at these levels of analysis interact? To begin with, a depressed central and autonomic nervous system (level of the brain) might leave people who develop antisocial personality disorder relatively unaffected by social rejection or mild punishment. In other words, when people have an underresponsive nervous system, the normal social and legal consequences of inappropriate behavior might not make them feel anxious (level of the person). However, a moderate level of arousal is optimal for performance (see Chapter 7). Together, these consequences of an underresponsive nervous system might produce another important result—difficulty in learning to control impulses (level of the person). In fact, Schachter and Latané (1964) found that such people have difficulty learning to avoid shocks. But when they are injected with adrenaline so that their level of arousal is increased, they learn to avoid shocks at the same rate as other people. This underresponsiveness of the nervous system may also be related to poor parental bonding, since normal stimulation provided by parents may not be enough to engage these infants. Moreover, as these individuals grow up, learning antisocial behavior from others in the immediate environment may be arousing enough to hold their interest and increase their learning (level of the person), which creates a vicious cycle. In addition, their underresponsiveness may have *caused* their caregivers to treat them differently (level of the group).

LOOKING BACK: *Review*

1. *What are personality disorders?* Personality disorders reflect relatively stable personality traits that have become inflexible and maladaptive, causing distress or difficulty with daily functioning.

2. *What is antisocial personality disorder?* The hallmark of antisocial personality disorder is a long-standing pattern of disregard for others, to the point of violating their rights. It occurs more frequently in men than in women.

LOOKING BEYOND: *Critical Thinking*

At first, your new neighbor seemed like a really nice guy—then you got to know him better. Weeks ago he borrowed money because of an "emergency," but he never repaid you. When you ask for your money back, he always has an excuse. Whenever friends come by to see you, he seems to make a point of sticking his head out the door and charming your visitors. You become increasingly frustrated because your friends can't understand why you keep complaining about him. Would you suspect that antisocial personality disorder might be in the picture? Why? If you knew that a mental health clinician had diagnosed him as having antisocial personality disorder, what could you infer about his family history? What should you not infer?

A Cautionary Note About Diagnosis

The events of van Gogh's life present an opportunity to explore the ways in which the human psyche can be troubled and the ways in which the mental health field presently classifies disorders. But that is not the same as proposing a diagnosis of someone who, while in art is very close to us, is in his person very distant in time.

No mental health clinician can really know with certainty from what, if any, specific disorder van Gogh suffered. Major depressive disorder and schizophrenia are possibilities, as is bipolar disorder (Jamison, 1993). Alternatively, his "attacks" and hallucinations might have been caused by withdrawal from alcohol (see Chapter 10); but such a diagnosis would not explain why van Gogh had attacks even during lengthy periods of sobriety (Lubin, 1972). Possibly he suffered from a form of epilepsy, and his attacks were seizures; before epileptic seizures, victims are sometimes overcome with religious feelings and delusions. The possibility of epilepsy, a neurological disorder not a psychological one, points to the importance of ensuring that a patient does not have a medical disorder that can cause psychological symptoms. Only after ruling out medical illnesses can the mental health clinician or researcher have confidence in a diagnosis of a psychological disorder.

Similarly, it may be tempting to use the knowledge you acquired in this chapter to diagnose friends, family members, or yourself, However, the information in this chapter is only a brief introduction to the topic of psychological disorders. The ability to diagnose accurately requires detailed knowledge and extensive training. You would undoubtedly not consider yourself qualified to diagnose a neuropsychological problem after reading about the brain in Chapter 2 or to diagnose a memory problem after reading Chapter 5. If you suspect that you or someone close to you may have a psychological disorder, consult with a mental health clinician. Information about finding a mental health clinician, and about treatments for psychological disorders, is discussed in the following chapter.

LET'S SUM IT UP

I. Identifying Psychological Disorders: What's Abnormal?

A. A psychological disorder is signaled by a constellation of cognitive, emotional, and behavioral symptoms that create significant distress, impairment, and danger.

B. Behaviors that are merely deviant from the mainstream culture are not considered to be "disordered."

C. Psychological disorders are best understood as arising from the interactions of events at the levels of the brain, the person, and the group.

D. The catalog of psychiatric disorders in the *DSM-IV* distinguishes among disorders on the basis of the symptoms exhibited or reported and the reported history of the symptoms. The *DSM-IV* includes both clinical and personality disorders.

II. Axis I: An Overview of Selected Disorders

Mood Disorders

A. Major depressive disorder (MDD) is characterized by depressed mood and loss of interest or pleasure, along with sleep or eating disturbances, loss of energy, and feelings of hopelessness. Bipolar disorder involves episodes of mania, which may or may not alternate with depression.

B. Some people are biologically vulnerable to developing these disorders; further, neurotransmitters are implicated in both major depressive disorder and bipolar disorder, although the exact mechanisms of their influence are not yet understood.

C. People's worldviews, thought patterns, and attributional styles, such as the negative triad of depression, also play a role in the development of major depressive disorder. Learned helplessness can also contribute to depression. Operant conditioning and the available rewards or punishments in the environment also may be related to the development of depression, and life stressors are associated with the first episode of depression and with the severity of the disorder.

D. Women in developed countries experience depression more often than do men. This difference may occur because, as children, girls are taught to be introspective and not to take action. As women, such rumination may promote depression.

E. Depressed people, through their actions, may inadvertently alienate others, who then reject those depressed people, who, in turn, view the rejection as confirmation of their negative views.

Anxiety Disorders

F. Anxiety disorders include panic disorder, specific and social phobias, obsessive-compulsive disorder (OCD), and posttraumatic stress disorder (PTSD).

G. People with panic disorder may avoid places or activities in order to minimize the possibility of additional panic attacks; when such avoidance restricts daily life, it is referred to as agoraphobia.

H. People can inherit a biological vulnerability for panic. Moreover, an anxiety sensitivity can increase the risk for panic disorder, as can a misinterpretation of certain bodily sensations.

I. People can be biologically vulnerable to developing both social and specific phobias. Although learning can also contribute, it is unclear to what extent it does so.

J. Neutral activity in the caudate nucleus is related to OCD. Compulsions may momentarily relieve the anxiety that obsessions cause, operantly reinforcing the compulsions.

K. Not everyone who experiences a traumatic event goes on to develop PTSD. The type of trauma, the response to it, and other factors can increase or decease the risk of developing PTSD.

Schizophrenia

L. Schizophrenia involves a markedly restricted range of affect, odd or disorganized thoughts, delusions or hallucinations, and behaviors; it is characterized by positive and negative symptoms. The *DSM-IV* specifies four subtypes of schizophrenia: paranoid, disorganized, catatonic, and undifferentiated, each with a different set of symptoms and prognosis.

M. Research findings on schizophrenia point to genetic and biological abnormalities in those affected.

These abnormalities include enlarged ventricles and a decrease in the frontal cortex. Such abnormalities may arise during fetal development, as a result of maternal illness, malnutrition, or stress during pregnancy, or may be due to prenatal or birth-related complications.

N. Children at risk for schizophrenia show extreme discomfort with close relationships, exhibit high levels of odd or quirky behavior, are more reactive to stress, and have higher baseline levels of cortisol.

O. Those with schizophrenia who have high expressed emotion families are more likely to suffer a recurrence. However, this finding is only a correlation.

P. Social selection and social causation are factors that may account for the higher rates of schizophrenia in urban areas and in lower socioeconomic classes.

Q. Eating disorders (anorexia nervosa and bulimia nervosa) are characterized by preoccupations with weight and body image, as well as abnormal eating (such as restriction, binges, and purges).

R. Symptoms of anorexia nervosa include a refusal to maintain a healthy weight, a fear of becoming fat, a disturbed body image, and amenorrhea (in women). Symptoms of bulimia include recurrent binge eating episodes, followed by an attempt to prevent weight gain.

S. Genetic factors are more influential in the development of anorexia nervosa than of bulimia nervosa, and environmental factors, specifically the cultural emphasis on thinness, affect the development of both eating disorders.

T. Biological factors related to dieting (food restriction) and binge eating can also lead to the development of an eating disorder.

III. Axis II: Focus on Personality Disorders

A. Personality disorders are sets of inflexible and maladaptive personality traits that cause distress or difficulty in work, school, or in other social spheres. Such traits may be unnoticeable in a brief encounter and may only reveal themselves over time.

B. In contrast to Axis I disorders, which seem to the sufferer to be inflicted from the outside, personality disorders, which are on Axis II, are experienced as part of the personality itself.

C. Antisocial personality disorder is the most intensively studied personality disorder; the key symptom is a long-standing pattern of disregard for others to the point of violating their rights.

D. Antisocial personality has a biological basis, perhaps an underresponsive central and autonomic nervous system. For those who are biologically vulnerable, the environment in which they are raised can influence whether they later develop criminal behavior.

Key Terms

agoraphobia, p. 491
anorexia nervosa, p. 505
antisocial personality disorder (ASPD), p. 513
anxiety disorders, p. 490
attributional style, p. 488
bipolar disorder, p. 485
bulimia nervosa, p. 506
compulsion, p. 494
delusions, p. 476
diathesis–stress model, p. 477
eating disorders, p. 505
generalized anxiety disorder, p. 490

hallucinations, p. 476
high expressed emotion, p. 503
major depressive disorder (MDD), p. 483
manic episode, p. 485
mood disorders, p. 483
negative symptom, p. 499
obsession, p. 494
obsessive-compulsive disorder (OCD), p. 494
panic attack, p. 491
panic disorder, p. 491
personality disorders, p. 511

phobia, p. 493
positive symptom, p. 499
posttraumatic stress disorder (PTSD), p. 496
psychological disorder, p. 475
psychosis, p. 476
schizophrenia, p. 499
social causation, p. 503
social phobia, p. 493
social selection, p. 503
specific phobia, p. 493

LOOKING ONLINE: *Enhance Your Learning*

MyPsychLab is an interactive and instructive multimedia resource that can be used to supplement a traditional lecture course or as an online course. It is an all-inclusive tool with a text-specific e-book plus multimedia tutorials, videos, simulations, animations, and controlled assessment to completely engage students and reinforce learning. MyPsychLab meets the individual learning needs of every student. Visit www.mypsychlab.com for more information!

Practice Test

For each of the following items, choose the single best answer.

1. Many researchers and clinicians today believe that psychological disorders can best be explained by
   a. a diathesis–stress model.
   b. the fact that unconventional behavior is always abnormal.
   c. biological factors alone.
   d. imbalances of the body's four fluids, or "humors."

2. Several factors at the level of the person play a role in psychological disorders. These factors include
   a. culture.
   b. genetic factors.
   c. classical conditioning, operant conditioning, and observational learning.
   d. None of the above statements is true.

3. Since the third edition, the *DSM* has described five axes. Axis III notes
   a. clinical disorders.
   b. personality disorders and mental retardation.
   c. psychosocial and environmental problems.
   d. any general medical conditions that might be relevant to a diagnosis on Axis I or II.

4. Which of the following statements is true about major depressive disorder (MDD)?
   a. Major depressive disorder is the most common psychological disorder in the United States.
   b. American women are diagnosed with depression two to three times more frequently than American men.
   c. The overall rate of depression is increasing in the United States.
   d. All of the above statements are true.

5. Consider a person suffering from bipolar disorder. If left untreated, his or her mood swings will likely
   a. stop occurring.
   b. become less frequent over time.
   c. become more frequent over time, leading to a poorer prognosis.
   d. become more frequent over time, leading to a better prognosis.

6. Mood disorders can best be understood by considering events
   a. at the level of the brain only.
   b. at the levels of the brain and person only.
   c. at the level of the group only.
   d. at the levels of the brain, the person, and the group, and their interactions.

7. The hallmark of panic disorder is
   a. a fear and avoidance of an object or situation extreme enough to interfere with everyday life.
   b. the presence of obsessions, either alone or in combination with compulsions.
   c. the experience of episodes of intense fear or discomfort accompanied by physical and psychological symptoms.
   d. at least 2 weeks of depressed mood or loss of interest in nearly all activities.

8. Which of the following statements is true about the relationship between trauma and posttraumatic stress disorder (PTSD)?
   a. The majority of people who experience trauma do not go on to experience PTSD.
   b. The type of trauma experienced makes a difference in the outcome.

c. Women are more likely to develop PTSD when their trauma results from a crime rather than from a natural disaster.

d. All of the above statements are true.

9. Avolition, a negative symptom of schizophrenia, refers to

a. brief, slow, empty replies to questions.

b. an inability to initiate or persist in goal-directed activities.

c. a general failure to express or respond to emotion.

d. inappropriate, childlike silliness.

10. If one twin has schizophrenia, the risk of the co-twin developing schizophrenia is

a. higher, but still only 48%, when the twins are identical than when they are fraternal.

b. the same, regardless of whether the twins are fraternal or identical.

c. zero when the twins are identical.

d. higher when the twins are fraternal than when they are identical.

11. Which of the following statements is true about schizophrenia?

a. Those who develop schizophrenia experience more life stressors than people who do not develop the disorder.

b. Those who develop schizophrenia have higher baseline levels of cortisol.

c. Those who develop schizophrenia have lower baseline levels of cortisol.

d. Antipsychotic medications increase cortisol levels in people with schizophrenia.

12. The nonpurging type of bulimia nervosa is characterized by

a. vomiting or the misuse of laxatives, diuretics, or enemas.

b. a failure to maintain even a low normal weight.

c. a failure to menstruate.

d. fasting or excessive exercise.

13. Which of the following statements is true about eating disorders?

a. The malnutrition and weight loss that occur with anorexia nervosa lead to changes in neurotransmitters, particularly serotonin.

b. Symptoms of eating disorders decrease among immigrants from less weight-conscious cultures as they assimilate to American culture.

c. Genes, rather than the environment, play the most significant role in both anorexia nervosa and bulimia nervosa.

d. None of the above statements is true.

14. A pattern of preoccupation with perfectionism, orderliness, and control (but without obsessions or compulsions) describes

a. avoidant personality disorder.

b. obsessive-compulsive disorder.

c. obsessive-compulsive personality disorder.

d. borderline personality disorder.

15. Antisocial personality disorder

a. occurs three times more frequently in women than in men.

b. is estimated to occur in 60% of male prisoners.

c. does not frequently co-occur with drug or alcohol abuse.

d. is characterized by a relatively overresponsive central and autonomic nervous system.

• •

Answers: 1. a 2. c 3. d 4. d 5. c 6. d 7. c 8. d 9. b 10. a 11. b 12. d 13. a 14. c 15. b

chapter 12

Treatment
Healing Actions, Healing Words

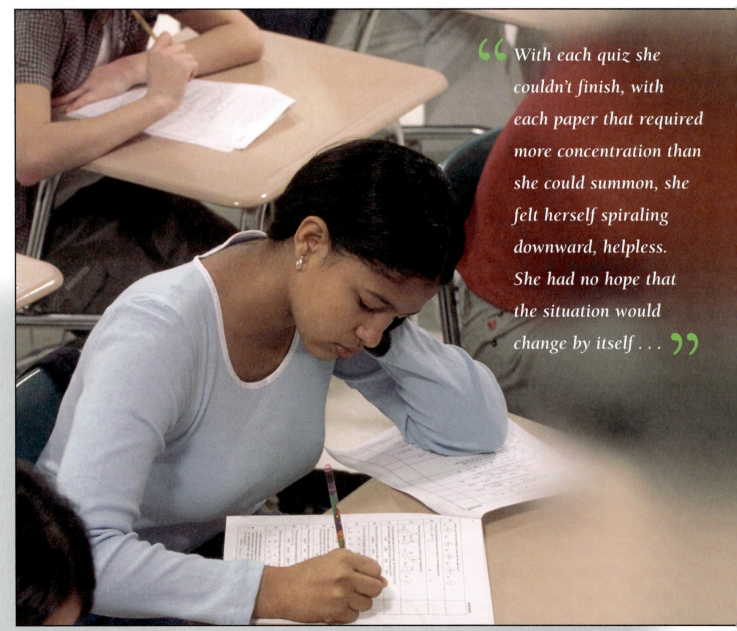

"With each quiz she couldn't finish, with each paper that required more concentration than she could summon, she felt herself spiraling downward, helpless. She had no hope that the situation would change by itself . . ."

CHAPTER OUTLINE

At 2 a.m., Beth sat hunched over her textbook and notes, studying for her midterm. Concentration was difficult; she had to struggle to make sense of the words before her eyes. She'd read the same page four times and still couldn't remember what it said. She tried to give herself a pep talk ("Okay, Beth, read it one more time, and then you'll understand it"), but her upbeat words would be drowned out by a different, negative internal monologue (*"Well, Beth, you've really screwed yourself, and there's no way out of it now. You're going to fail, get kicked out of school, never be employed, end up destitute, homeless, hopeless, talking to yourself on the street"*).

Beth was 21 years old, a junior in college. She'd already had to walk out of two exams because she couldn't answer most of the questions, although she had understood the material earlier. Her thoughts had been jumbled, and she'd had a hard time organizing her answers to the questions. She'd always been nervous before a test or class presentation, but this year her anxiety had spun out of control. Taking the first quiz of the semester, she simply drew a blank when she tried to answer the questions.

Since then, she'd become more anxious, and depressed as well. With each quiz she couldn't finish, with each paper that required more concentration than she could summon, she felt herself spiraling downward, helpless. She had no hope that the situation would change by itself, and no amount of good intentions or resolutions or even effort made a difference. She began cutting classes and spent much of her time in bed; she had no interest in doing anything with her friends because she felt she didn't deserve to have fun. She'd put off saying anything to her professors; at first she figured things would get better, and then she was too embarrassed to face them. But she knew that eventually she'd have to talk to them or else she'd definitely fail her courses.

She finally did talk to her professors. Several of them suggested that she seek treatment, or at least go to the campus counseling center, but she didn't want to do that. Taking that step, she felt, would be admitting to herself and to the world not only that something was wrong with her, but also that she was too weak to deal with it herself.

Beth was reluctant to seek help partly because when she was growing up, her mother had experienced bouts of depression severe enough to require hospitalization several times. Beth recognized that she, too, was becoming depressed, and she was afraid that if she went to see a therapist, she'd end up in the hospital.

Finally, Beth confided in a family friend, Nina, who had been the school nurse at Beth's elementary school. Nina told Beth that people with problems like hers often felt much better after psychotherapy and that her problems were not severe enough to warrant hospitalization. She also pointed out that there were many forms of therapy available to Beth that were not as readily available to her mother 20 years earlier. Modern treatments, Nina said, ranged from psychologically based approaches, such as cognitive and behavioral therapies, to biologically based treatments such as medication. Research has revealed that, for a given problem, some treatments may be more effective than others, and for Beth's problems, there were a number of potentially helpful treatments. Beth agreed to see a therapist, but didn't know where to begin to find one. The campus counseling center could be useful, Nina said, but Beth might also explore other ways to find a therapist who would be right for her needs, such as the Internet and referral organizations.

Let's make a similar exploration in this chapter, examining the different types of therapy, how they work, and what research has to say about their effectiveness. Many of the therapies discussed in this chapter rest on principles or theories discussed in previous chapters of this book. Here, we apply these principles and theories to treatment of psychological disorders (see Chapter 11). First, though, let's examine historical influences on psychotherapy.

Historical Influences on Psychotherapy: Insight-Oriented Therapies

Beth didn't know much about psychotherapy, and she made an appointment with a psychotherapist she picked from the phone book. If Beth had called an insight-oriented therapist, chances are that the therapist would ask Beth about her past, her relationships with family members, how she felt about her family, and about her feelings in general and would ask surprisingly little about her current anxiety or her depression.

Therapies that aim to remove distressing symptoms by leading someone to understand their causes through deeply felt personal insights are called **insight-oriented therapies**. The key idea underlying this approach is that once someone truly understands the causes of distressing symptoms (which often arise from past relationships), the symptoms themselves will diminish. Psychoanalysis is the original insight-oriented therapy; client-centered therapy is also considered an insight-oriented therapy because it rests on the belief that therapeutic change follows from the experience of insight.

LOOKING AHEAD: Learning Objectives

1. *What is the focus of treatment in psychodynamic therapy? What are its main techniques?*

2. *How do client-centered therapists approach treatment? What techniques do they use?*

Psychodynamic Therapy: Origins in Psychoanalysis

Developed by Sigmund Freud, **psychoanalysis** is a type of therapy directly connected to Freud's theory of personality, which holds that people's psychological difficulties are caused by conflicts among the three psychic structures of the mind: the id, the ego, and the superego. According to Freud, the id strives for immediate gratification of its needs, the superego tries to impose its version of morality, and the ego attempts to balance the demands of id, superego, and external reality. These unconscious competing demands can create anxiety and other symptoms (see Chapter 8). The goal of psychoanalysis is to help patients understand the unconscious motivations that lead them to behave in specific ways; if the motivations and feelings remain unconscious, those forces are more likely to shape patients' behavior, without their awareness. According to this theory, only after true understanding—that is, insight—is attained can patients choose more adaptive, satisfying, and productive behaviors.

In psychoanalysis, patients talk about their problems, and the analyst tries to infer the root causes. At its beginnings, this method was revolutionary because, before Freud, most European patients were treated medically for psychological problems. Freud started out using hypnosis but, over time, developed the method of **free association**, in which the patient says whatever comes into his or her mind. The resulting train of thought reveals the issues that concern the patient, as well as the way he or she is handling them. Because Freud (1900/1958) viewed dreams as the "royal road to the unconscious," another important feature of psychoanalysis is the use of **dream analysis**, the examination of the content of dreams to gain access to the unconscious. Freud did not believe that psychoanalysis was a cure, but rather that it could transform abject misery into ordinary unhappiness.

Psychoanalysis has declined in popularity over the last several decades for a number of reasons; one is the outlay of time and money required for the four to five sessions per week. The average patient engages in 835 sessions before completing psychoanalysis (Voth & Orth, 1973), which usually lasts at least 4 years.

Insight-oriented therapy: A type of therapy that aims to remove distressing symptoms by leading people to understand their causes through deeply felt personal insights.

Psychoanalysis: An intensive form of therapy, originally developed by Freud, based on the idea that people's psychological difficulties are caused by conflicts among the id, the ego, and the superego.

Free association: A technique used in psychoanalysis and psychodynamic therapy in which the patient says whatever comes to mind and the train of thought reveals the patient's issues and ways of dealing with them.

Dream analysis: A technique used in psychoanalysis and psychodynamic therapy in which the therapist examines the content of dreams to gain access to the unconscious.

Psychoanalysis usually takes place 4 or 5 days a week for a number of years. Psychodynamic therapy can take place anywhere from several times a month to twice a week. The patient lies on a couch in psycho-analysis, and the analyst sits in a chair behind the couch, out of the patient's range of sight so that the patient can better free associate without seeing the analyst's reactions to his or her thoughts. In psychodynamic therapy, the client and therapist sit in chairs facing each other.

Psychodynamic therapy: A less in-tensive form of psychoanalysis.

Some patients who begin psychoanalysis never complete it. Psychoanalysis is rarely paid for by health insurance. A second reason for the decline of psychoanalysis is that studies have not generally found this type of treatment to be effective in treat-ing various disorders, such as those discussed in Chapter 11.

A less intensive form of psychoanalysis, and one that is more common today, is **psychodynamic therapy**. Although based on psychoanalytic theory, its techniques differ in some important ways, including less frequent sessions and a de-creased emphasis on sexual and aggressive drives. A wide-spread trend in psychodynamic therapy is the use of short-term versions of psychotherapy (Bloom, 1997; Crits-Christoph, 1992; Malan, 1976; Sifneos, 1992), which might involve therapy lasting 12 to 20 sessions. However, short-term psychodynamic therapy differs somewhat in goals and focus from its longer-term counterpart, often focusing on current rather than past relationships (Greenberg & Mitchell, 1983; Kohut, 1977; Sullivan, 1953; Winnicott, 1958). At least one study found that when psychiatrists refer people for psychological treatment, they do not refer all prospective patients to psychodynamic therapy, only those who are healthier and who do not have a personality disorder (Svanborg et al., 1999). Such people, who are often seeking help for relationship difficulties, may ben-efit from the insight that can be attained through short-term therapy (Kivlighan et al., 2000).

Theory of Psychodynamic Therapy

The goal of psychodynamic therapy, like that of psychoanalysis, is to bring un-conscious impulses and conflicts into awareness. Doing so leads to intellectual and emotional insights, which are supposed to give the patient more control over these impulses. With this control, the patient can actively and consciously choose behaviors instead of acting on unconscious impulses. Both psychoanalysis and psychodynamic therapy try to link the patient's current difficulties with past ex-periences, and both forms of treatment view the patient's relationship with the therapist as an integral part of treatment. Given the importance of relationships, the therapy relationship can provide a "corrective emotional experience"—that is, a new, positive experience of relationships, which can lead to changes in symp-toms, behavior, and personality (Alexander & French, 1946).

From a psychodynamic perspective, Beth's anxiety and depression might re-flect two competing desires. On the one hand, Beth wants to be different from her mother. Doing well in school and going on to graduate school represent a path different from that taken by her mother, who, although she did well in college, elected not to pursue a graduate degree. Although her plan was not necessarily logically thought out, Beth hoped that by making different choices in her own life, she could avoid the intermittent depressions that had plagued her mother. On the other hand, Beth loves her mother, and the idea of academically passing a parent by, in essence, abandoning her, causes Beth to feel guilty about her ac-complishments. Although Beth's anxiety and depression are upsetting and debil-itating, part of her may feel relief that those symptoms prevent her from leaving her mother behind. Psychodynamic theory would say that, by gaining insight into these issues, Beth will not have to "act out" her ambivalent feelings (that is, im-pulsively or compulsively behave in a maladaptive way) and will have more con-trol over her anxiety and depression.

Techniques of Psychodynamic Therapy

Along with dream analysis and free association, psychodynamic therapists rely on **interpretation**, deciphering the patient's words and behaviors and assigning unconscious motivations to them. Through the therapist's interpretations, the patient becomes aware of his or her motives and potential conflicts within the unconscious. The patient's own interpretations are not considered as accurate as those of the therapist because they are biased by the patient's conflicts. Slips of the tongue—or *Freudian slips*—are interpreted as having unconscious meanings. For example, should Beth tell her therapist that her mother recommended that she come to therapy (instead of her mother's friend, which was the case, and what she meant to say), the therapist might interpret this as Beth's wish that her mother would take care of her by suggesting that she seek therapy.

Through interpretation, patients also become aware of their *defense mechanisms*, unconscious mechanisms used to handle conflictual and distressing thoughts and feelings (see Chapter 8). At some point in the course of psychodynamic therapy, patients are likely to experience **resistance**, a reluctance or refusal to cooperate with the therapist. Resistance can range from unconscious forgetting to outright refusal to comply with a therapist's request. Resistance can occur as the patient explores or remembers painful feelings or experiences in the past. Thus, if Beth comes late to a therapy session, a psychodynamic therapist might interpret this behavior as resistance: Perhaps Beth does not want to work on the issues currently being explored or is concerned about something that she doesn't want to share with her therapist.

Over the course of therapy, patients may come to relate to their therapist as they did to someone who was important in their lives, perhaps a parent. This phenomenon is called **transference**. If Beth began asking how the therapist is feeling, or if she began to talk less about her own distressing feelings because she worried that the therapist might become upset, Beth would be "transferring" onto her therapist her usual style of relating with her mother, in which she views her mother as fragile and needing protection. The therapeutic value of transference is that patients can talk about what they are experiencing (which they may very well have been unable to do with the parent) to heighten understanding. Moreover, the therapist's acceptance of uncomfortable or shameful feelings helps patients accept those feelings in order to choose whether to act on them. A psychodynamic therapist would likely interpret Beth's questions about the therapist's well-being as transference. Beth and her therapist would then talk about what it was like for Beth to feel so protective toward, and careful with, her mother.

Humanistic Therapy: Client-Centered Therapy

Like the humanistic approach to personality (see Chapter 8), humanistic therapy emphasizes free will, personal growth, self-esteem, and mastery. This approach is in contrast to psychodynamic therapy, which emphasizes the past, mental mechanisms, and the working through of conflictual impulses and feelings. One of the early proponents of humanistic psychology was Carl Rogers, who developed a therapeutic approach that came to be called **client-centered therapy** and that focuses on people's potential for growth and the importance of an empathic therapist. Instead of using the term "patient," which suggests treating a person with an illness (a medical term), Rogers used the term "client."

Interpretation: A technique used in psychodynamic therapies in which the therapist deciphers the patient's words and behaviors, assigning unconscious motivations to them.

Resistance: A reluctance or refusal to cooperate with the therapist, which can range from unconscious forgetting to outright refusal to comply with a therapist's request.

Transference: The process by which patients may relate to their therapists as they did to some important person in their lives.

Client-centered therapy: A type of insight-oriented therapy that focuses on people's potential for growth and the importance of an empathic therapist.

Theory of Client-Centered Therapy

Rogers believed that a person's distressing symptoms grow out of a blocked potential for personal growth. The goal of client-centered therapy is to dismantle that block so that clients can reach their full potential. Within Rogers's framework, problems arise because of a lack of a coherent, unified sense of self. An example is a mismatch, or **incongruence**, between the real self (who you actually are) and the ideal self (who you would like to be). By helping clients to become more like their ideal selves, client-centered therapy lessens the incongruence, and the clients feel better. Within the framework of client-centered therapy, Beth's problems may stem from incongruence between her real self (a self that has to work hard for good grades and feels shame and guilt about the imperfections that remind her of her mother's depression) and her ideal self (a self that always does the "right thing" and never experiences sadness, hopelessness, or anxiety). The tension between her real and ideal selves creates a fragmented sense of self, which drains Beth's time and energy; these different parts of herself are in conflict with each other and prevent her from reaching her full potential.

Techniques of Client-Centered Therapy

The client-centered therapist should be warm, able to see the world as the client does, and able to empathize with the client. The therapist does not offer analyses to the client; instead, the therapist reflects back the thrust of what the client has said. However, the therapist must not simply parrot the client's words or phrases but show accurate and genuine empathy. Such empathy lets the client know that he or she is really understood. If the therapist does not accurately reflect what the client says or is not genuinely empathic, the intervention will fail. The therapist must also provide *unconditional positive regard*; that is, he or she must convey positive feelings for the client regardless of the client's thoughts, feelings, or actions. The therapist does this by continually showing the client that he or she is inherently worthy as a human being. According to the theory, genuine empathy and unconditional positive regard allow the client to decrease the incongruence between the real and ideal selves. Although Beth was not able to take some of her exams (real self), a client-centered therapist's empathy and unconditional positive regard would allow Beth to see that she is still smart (ideal self) and that everyone sometimes has negative, uncomfortable feelings. This therapeutic approach could help Beth see her real and ideal selves in a different light and allow her to think of herself more positively.

The client-centered therapist provides both genuine empathy and unconditional positive regard by making a distinction between the client as a person and the client's behaviors. The therapist could dislike a client's behavior but still view the client as a good person. If Beth were seeing a client-centered therapist, the topic of a therapy session might be what it was like for Beth during her mother's bouts of depression. A session might include this exchange:

Beth:	I was so disappointed and ashamed when I'd come home from school and she'd still be in bed, wearing her bathrobe.
Therapist:	Yes, it must have caused you to feel ashamed, anxious, and worried when you came home and found your mother still in bed.
Beth:	And I felt that it was my fault, that I wasn't doing enough to make her feel better.
Therapist:	Although you felt that it was your fault, you did all that you possibly could. You were concerned about her. You were, and still are, a good, worthwhile person.

Being rejected by a partner can leave a person feeling bad about himself or herself. Client-centered therapy makes a distinction between the person's actions in the relationship and the fact he or she is still a worthwhile, good person.

Incongruence: According to client-centered therapy, a mismatch between a person's real self and his or her ideal self.

Beth:	And now I spend most of the day in bed and don't bother to get dressed . . . am I becoming like my mother?
Therapist:	You and your mother are two separate individuals. Although you may have some things in common, and right now that may include depression, that doesn't mean that your path in life is identical to hers.

The therapist repeatedly emphasizes the worthiness of the client until the client comes to accept this valuation and is able to reach his or her potential by making different, healthier choices and decisions. When successful, client-centered therapy can achieve its objective in a few months rather than years.

Evaluating Insight-Oriented Therapies

Psychodynamic therapies are difficult to evaluate, for several reasons. One is that there isn't much research to evaluate. Consider that for every research article on transference, there are 500 related to psychodynamic theories. Most research on psychodynamically oriented treatment has been case studies, which limits the reliability and generalizability of the findings (Roth & Fonagy, 2005). Moreover, the interpretations the therapists made in these cases have not been tested, and they may not be correct. For instance, research shows that interpretations of transference during therapy are rarely—if ever—helpful to the treatment (Henry et al., 1994). Psychodynamic therapists have tended to view treatment failures as the patient's responsibility rather than the therapist's. It is possible that this view is correct—lack of behavioral change may result from insufficient insight—but insight is not objectively measurable, at least not yet.

Psychodynamic therapy appears to work best with patients who are able to articulate their feelings and want to understand their unconscious mental processes (and who have the time and money for lengthy treatment). Some meta-analyses find that short-term psychodynamic therapy is as effective as, but not superior to, other short-term treatments (Crits-Christoph, 1992; Leichsenring, 2001; Leichsenring et al., 2004). However, some studies contradict this conclusion (Svartberg & Stiles, 1991), particularly studies with a 1-year follow-up (Barkham et al., 1999). Moreover, researchers have not extensively investigated whether short-term psychodynamic therapy can help those with specific disorders.

Although Rogers proposed the first real insight-oriented alternative to psychodynamic therapy and made the treatment amenable to research by tape-recording therapy sessions, research has not been as supportive as he might have wished. Nevertheless, almost all forms of therapy incorporate Rogers's view that the therapist's warmth, empathy, and positive regard for the client are fundamental for a working relationship between client and therapist (Lambert, 1983; Roth & Fonagy, 2005). However, most other therapies do not rest on the idea that these factors are enough to bring about change. Moreover, although client-centered therapy was the first major school of therapy to focus on assessing the effectiveness of the treatment, it can be difficult to measure which clients have achieved their potentials.

In sum, although there are differences between the insight-oriented therapies, the people most likely to benefit from these treatments are similar in that they are relatively healthy, articulate individuals who are interested in knowing more about their own motivations rather than seeking to address specific symptoms, such as those related to anxiety. Moreover, little research indicates that insight-oriented treatments are likely to be successful for most disorders. We now turn to examine treatments that have received greater support from research.

LOOKING BACK: *Review*

1. *What is the focus of treatment in psychodynamic therapy? What are its main techniques?* Psychodynamic therapy seeks to help patients become aware of their unconscious motivations, which can cause psychological symptoms. Through insight, they can choose whether to respond to those impulses. At some point in the treatment, patients typically experience transference to the therapist and resistance. Techniques include free association, dream analysis, and interpretation.

2. *How do client-centered therapists approach treatment? What techniques do they use?* Client-centered therapy focuses on helping clients experience congruence between their real and ideal selves, thereby reducing the clients' problems. The therapist should be warm, empathic, and genuine and should show unconditional positive regard toward clients. According to client-centered therapy, these elements are enough to bring about therapeutic change.

LOOKING BEYOND: *Critical Thinking*

Imagine two people, one of whom is the ideal candidate for insight-oriented therapy and one of whom is the worst possible candidate. How would you describe these two people? If a friend tells you that he or she is in insight-oriented therapy, what can you assume about his therapy? What can't you assume?

Cognitive–Behavior Therapy

Suppose Beth's therapist (chosen from listings in the phone book) starts asking questions not about her family and her relationships, but about what she currently believes about herself and her abilities. Suppose the therapist also inquires about her behaviors: What does she do before sits down to study or take an exam? What, in detail, does she do during the day? Has she ever tried any relaxation techniques? These are questions about thoughts and behaviors. Odds are that Beth has contacted a cognitive–behavior therapist.

Cognitive–behavior therapy (CBT) seeks both to change problematic behaviors and irrational thoughts and to provide new, more adaptive behaviors and beliefs to replace the old, maladaptive ones. CBT utilizes techniques from both behavior therapy and cognitive therapy; behavior therapy itself rests on learning principles discussed in Chapter 4. Let's begin by discussing behavior and cognitive therapies separately so that you can understand the unique focus of each approach.

Cognitive–behavior therapy (CBT): A type of therapy that aims to change problematic behaviors and irrational thoughts and provide new, more adaptive behaviors and beliefs to replace old, maladaptive ones.

LOOKING AHEAD: *Learning Objectives*

1. *What is the focus of behavior therapy? What are some of its techniques?*

2. *What are the goals of cognitive therapy? What techniques are used?*

Behavior Therapy and Its Techniques

Traditionally, **behavior therapy** focused on changing observable, measurable behavior. Joseph Wolpe (1915–1997) profoundly altered the practice of psychotherapy in 1958 when he published *Psychotherapy by Reciprocal Inhibition*. He was a psychiatrist, but his concern with behavior created a new form of treatment that particularly appealed to psychologists because of its emphasis on quantifiable results. In general, behavior therapy rests on well-researched principles of learning (see Chapter 4; Wolpe, 1997). Whereas Wolpe focused on applications of classical conditioning, B. F. Skinner focused on applications of operant conditioning. As noted in Chapter 4, applications of both sorts of learning can be employed more broadly: in education, marketing, sports, military training, medicine, and business. Here we consider ways in which these techniques are used to treat many of the psychological disorders discussed in Chapter 11.

Theory of Behavior Therapy

In behavior therapy, distressing symptoms are seen as the result of learning. Through the use of social learning—that is, modeling—as well as through classical and operant conditioning, clients can change unwanted behaviors by learning new ones; it is easiest to change a problematic behavior by replacing it with a new, more adaptive one. The behavior therapist is interested in the ABCs of the behavior:

- its *antecedents* (what is the stimulus that triggers the problematic behavior?),
- the problematic *behavior* itself, and
- its *consequences* (what is reinforcing the behavior?).

Behavior therapy's lack of interest or belief in an unconscious "root cause" was revolutionary. Behaviors and performance are emphasized, the therapist takes an active, directive role in treatment, and "homework"—between-session tasks for the client to work on—is an important component of the treatment. Therapists took a new look at treatment results: Did the client experience less frequent or less intense symptoms after therapy? The ABCs of Beth's anxiety are noted in Table 12.1.

Techniques of Behavior Therapy

Behavioral techniques rest on classical conditioning, operant conditioning, and social learning principles.

Behavior therapy: A type of therapy, based on well-researched learning principles, that focuses on changing observable, measurable behaviors.

Table 12.1 The ABCs of Beth's Anxiety

The possible antecedents and consequences of Beth's problematic behavior.

Antecedents	(Problematic) Behavior	Consequences
The antecedents for Beth's anxiety might include the act of sitting down to study for an exam or waiting in class to receive her exam booklet.	The behavior is the conditioned emotional response of fear and anxiety, evidenced by her sweating hands and racing heart rate and her inability to do her schoolwork.	The consequences might include negative reinforcement (the uncomfortable symptoms go away) when skipping an exam, reinforcement of related nonacademic avoidant behaviors (such as sleeping through an exam), and subsequent social isolation, leading to a loss of pleasant activities and opportunities for social reinforcement, which, in turn, can lead to depression.

Techniques Based on Classical Conditioning. One classical conditioning technique commonly used to treat anxiety disorders is <mark>exposure</mark>. It is based on the principle of habituation (see Chapter 4). Patients are asked to *expose* themselves to feared stimuli in a planned and (usually) gradual way. In general, exposure and habituation do not occur naturally because people with an anxiety disorder avoid the feared stimulus. People can be exposed to the feared stimulus in any of three ways:

Virtual reality exposure appears to work as well as in vivo (actual) exposure for fears of flying and heights (Emmelkamp et al., 2001, 2002; Rothbaum et al., 2001, 2002).

- *imaginal exposure*, where they imagine the feared stimulus;

- *in vivo exposure*, where they expose themselves to the actual stimulus; or

- *virtual reality exposure*, where they use virtual reality techniques to expose themselves to the stimulus.

Exposure, like all other behavioral and cognitive therapy techniques, is primarily directed at the levels of person and group; however, such techniques also affect events at the level of the brain. Consider a neuroimaging study of people with a spider phobia who had exposure treatment (Paquette et al., 2003). Before treatment, fMRI scans indicated that when these people saw pictures of spiders, part of the prefrontal cortex (and the parahippocampal gyrus) were activated; in contrast, when people who did not have such a phobia saw these pictures, these brain areas were not activated. After successful exposure therapy, another round of fMRI scans was done. The results were dramatically different: Now, when the people who used to have phobias saw the pictures of spiders, the key brain areas were no longer activated. Exposure had "rewired" neural circuits that apparently had been involved in the phobia.

A related technique, *exposure with response prevention*, is a planned, programmatic procedure that exposes the client to the anxiety-provoking object or situation but prevents the usual maladaptive response. For instance, clients with an obsessive-compulsive disorder (OCD) that compels them to wash their hands repeatedly would, using exposure with response prevention, intentionally get their hands dirty during a therapy session and then stop themselves from washing their hands immediately afterward. In this way, they would habituate to the anxiety. Researchers have found that exposure with response prevention is as effective as medication for OCD; moreover, such behavioral treatment can have longer-lasting benefits (Foa et al., 2005; Marks, 1997). However, not all people who have OCD are willing to use this behavioral technique (Stanley & Turner, 1995).

The technique of exposure with response prevention has also been used to treat people with bulimia nervosa. In this case, rather than induce vomiting after eating a "forbidden food," the person does not throw up (or delays it as long as possible). Before the exposure to forbidden foods, client and therapist develop strategies that the client can use while trying not to engage in the maladaptive behavior, such as taking a walk around the block or watching a movie.

Another technique, called <mark>stimulus control</mark>, involves controlling exposure to a stimulus that elicits a conditioned response, so as to decrease or increase the frequency of the response. For instance, a woman with bulimia who binges on donuts would exert stimulus control by buying only a single donut rather than a dozen.

Exposure: A therapeutic technique based on classical conditioning that rests on the principle of habituation.

Stimulus control: A behavior therapy technique that involves controlling the exposure to a stimulus that elicits a conditioned response, so as to decrease or increase the frequency of the response.

An additional technique based on classical conditioning is **systematic desensitization**, a procedure that teaches people to be relaxed in the presence of a feared object or situation. This technique, developed by Wolpe for treating phobias, grew out of the idea that someone cannot be fearful (and hence anxious) and relaxed at the same time. Systematic desensitization uses **progressive muscle relaxation**, a relaxation technique whereby the muscles are sequentially relaxed from one end of the body to the other, usually from feet to head. Although progressive muscle relaxation is used in systematic desensitization, it can be used by itself to induce relaxation (visit www.ablongman.com/kosslyn3e for instructions on progressive muscle relaxation).

When using systematic desensitization to overcome a phobia, therapist and client begin by constructing a hierarchy of real or imagined activities related to the feared object or situation—such as a fear of elevators. This hierarchy begins with the least fearful activity, such as pressing an elevator call button, progressing to the most fearful, being stuck in a stopped elevator. Over the course of a number of sessions, clients work on becoming relaxed when imagining increasingly anxiety-provoking activities.

If an alcoholic drank to excess only when in a bar, limiting or eliminating the occasions of going to a bar would be an example of stimulus control.

Techniques Based on Operant Conditioning. Techniques based on operant conditioning make use of the principles of reinforcement, punishment, and extinction, with the goal of **behavior modification**—that is, changing the behavior, not focusing on thoughts or feelings. Setting the appropriate *response contingencies*, or behaviors that will earn reinforcement, is crucial. *Extinction*, eliminating a behavior by not reinforcing it, is another important tool of the behavioral therapist.

Therapists also use behavior modification techniques in group settings, such as inpatient psychiatric units. In these facilities, it is possible to change the response contingencies for an undesired behavior as well as for a desired behavior. Behavior modification can be used to change even severely maladaptive behaviors. *Secondary reinforcers*, those that are learned and don't inherently satisfy a biological need, are used in treatment programs not only with psychiatric patients but also with mentally retarded children and adults, and even in prisons. Patients or others must earn "tokens" by behaving appropriately; these tokens then can be traded for small items such as cigarettes or candy at a "token store" or for privileges such as going out for a walk or watching a particular TV show.

These **token economies**—treatment programs that use secondary reinforcers to change behavior—can be used to mold social behavior directly by modifying what patients say to one another and to nonpatients. For instance, using a token economy, hospitalized patients with schizophrenia can learn to talk to others, answer questions, or eat more normally. Operant conditioning can also modify how patients perceive specific stimuli, such as when someone with schizophrenia begins to interpret a question as something that requires an answer. Although token economies can be effective, their use is declining because of ethical and moral questions about depriving patients and clients of secondary reinforcers (such as television, cigarettes, and walks on the grounds) if they do not earn them through behavior change (Glynn, 1990).

In addition, operant conditioning principles have led to **self-monitoring techniques**, such as keeping a daily log about instances of a problematic behavior. Such self-monitoring can help identify the antecedents and consequences of the problematic behavior, which can clarify how behavior modification may be best

Systematic desensitization: A behavior therapy technique that teaches people to be relaxed in the presence of a feared object or situation.

Progressive muscle relaxation: A relaxation technique whereby the person relaxes muscles sequentially from one end of the body to the other.

Behavior modification: A category of therapeutic techniques for changing behavior based on operant conditioning principles.

Token economy: A treatment program that uses secondary reinforcers (tokens) to bring about behavior modification.

Self-monitoring techniques: Behavioral techniques that help the client identify the antecedents and consequences of a problematic behavior.

achieved. Daily logs are used for a variety of problems, including poor mood, anxiety, overeating, smoking, sleep problems, and compulsive gambling.

If Beth used behavior modification techniques, she would seek to establish response contingencies for behaving in desired new ways: She might reward herself with a movie or a dinner out after taking an exam, or allow herself an hour's conversation with a friend after studying for 2 hours.

Techniques Based on Observational Learning. Observational learning also plays a role in behavior therapy, particularly with children and with people who have phobias, especially animal phobias (Goetestam & Berntzen, 1997). Patients observe other people interacting with the feared stimulus in a relaxed way and learn to do the same.

Cognitive Therapy and Techniques: It's the Thought That Counts

The ripples of the cognitive revolution in psychology (see Chapter 1) were felt in therapy as well as in research. Therapists began to examine the mental processes that contribute to behavior, not simply the physical stimuli that trigger it. It became clear that people's thoughts (cognitions), not just their learning histories, influence their feelings and behavior, and do so in myriad ways. Just thinking about a past positive experience with love can put you in a good mood, and thinking about an unhappy love experience can have the opposite effect (Clark & Collins, 1993). A cognitive therapist would focus on Beth's thoughts and the way in which one thought leads to another, contributing to her emotional experience of anxiety and depression.

Theory of Cognitive Therapy

The way people interpret events can affect their well-being (Chapter 10); such interpretation (involving conscious and unconscious processes) imparts meaning to what we perceive. **Cognitive therapy** aims to help clients think rationally in order to reinterpret events that otherwise lead to distressing feelings and behaviors: It is the interpretation of any experience that determines the response to that experience. Two particularly important contributors to cognitive therapy were Albert Ellis and Aaron Beck. Although both were pioneers of cognitive therapy, their treatments also rely in part on aspects of behavioral theory and therapy.

Albert Ellis (b. 1913) is a clinical psychologist who in the 1950s developed a treatment called *rational-emotive behavior therapy (REBT)*. REBT emphasizes rational, logical thinking and assumes that distressing feelings or symptoms are caused by faulty or illogical thoughts. Researchers have supported this idea, for example by showing that such faulty thinking is associated with higher scores on a measure of daily hassles (Ziegler & Leslie, 2003). People may develop illogical or irrational thoughts as a result of their experiences and never assess whether these thoughts are valid. They elevate irrational thoughts to "godlike absolutist musts, shoulds, demands, and commands" (Ellis, 1994a, p. 103). According to REBT, Beth's thought that she needs to do well in school is based on a dysfunctional, irrational belief that in order to be a lovable, deserving human being, she must earn good grades; if she does not, she believes that she will be unlovable and worthless.

Ellis (1994a) proposed three processes that interfere with healthy functioning:

1. *self-downing*, or being critical of oneself for performing poorly or being rejected;

2. *hostility and rage*, or being unkind to or critical of others for performing poorly; and

Cognitive therapy: A type of therapy that focuses on the client's thoughts rather than his or her feelings or behaviors.

3. *low frustration tolerance*, or blaming everyone and everything for "poor, dislikable conditions."

REBT focuses on creating more rational thoughts. In Beth's case, these might be, "I might be disappointed or disappoint others if I don't do well this semester, but they will still love and care about me." This more rational thinking should then dampen down the problematic behavior, allowing her to choose more rational courses of action. Part of the goal of REBT is educational, and clients should be able to use the techniques on their own once they have mastered them. Like behavior therapy, REBT is oriented toward *solving* problems as opposed to exploring them psychologically. The REBT therapist encourages self-acceptance and a new way of thinking; self-blame is viewed as counterproductive because it involves faulty beliefs. Shortcomings or failures are viewed as simply part of life, not as crimes or signs of moral weakness.

Psychiatrist Aaron Beck (b. 1921) developed a form of cognitive therapy that, like REBT, rests on the premise that irrational thoughts are the root cause of psychological problems, and that recognition of their irrationality and adoption of more realistic, rational thoughts cause psychological problems to improve. According to his theory, irrational thoughts that arise from a systematic bias, such as the belief that if you tell your friend you are mad at her she will reject you, are considered **cognitive distortions** of reality; several common distortions are presented in Table 12.2. Such cognitive distortions (or faulty thoughts, in the vocabulary of REBT) are learned and maintained through reinforcement.

Cognitive distortions: Irrational thoughts that arise from a systematic bias in the way a person thinks about reality.

Table 12.2 Five Common Cognitive Distortions

Distortion	Description	Example
Dichotomous thinking	Also known as black-and-white thinking, which allows for nothing in between the extremes; you are either perfect or a piece of garbage.	Beth thinks that if she doesn't get an A on a test, she has failed in life.
Mental filter	Magnifying the negative aspects of something while filtering out the positive.	Beth remembers only the things she did that were below her expectations and doesn't pay attention to (or remember) the things she did well.
Mind reading	Thinking you know exactly what other people are thinking, particularly as it relates to you.	Beth believes that she *knows* her professors think less of her because of what happened on the exams (when in fact they don't think less of her, but are concerned about her).
Catastrophic exaggeration	Thinking that your worst nightmare will come true and that it will be intolerable.	Beth's fear is that she'll be kicked out of school and end up homeless; a more likely reality is that she may have to take some courses over again.
Control beliefs	Believing either that you are helpless and totally subject to forces beyond your control, or that you must tightly control your life for fear that, if you don't, you will never be able to regain control.	Until talking to the family friend, Nina, Beth thought that there was nothing she could do to change the downward spiral of events and that she was either totally in control of her studying or else not in control at all.

Unlike REBT, which relies on the therapist's attempts to persuade the client that his or her beliefs are irrational, Beck's version of cognitive therapy encourages the client to view beliefs as hypotheses to be tested. Thus, interactions with the world provide opportunities to perform "experiments" to ascertain the accuracy of the client's beliefs (Hollon & Beck, 1994). Beck and his colleagues have approached treatment empirically, developing measures to assess depression, anxiety, and other problems and to evaluate the effectiveness of treatment.

Techniques of Cognitive Therapy

Some of the same techniques are used in REBT and Beck's cognitive therapy, but each approach also relies on its own distinctive techniques.

REBT Techniques. The REBT therapist helps the client identify his or her irrational beliefs, relying on verbal persuasion (Hollon & Beck, 1994), and then works through a sequence of techniques with the client. These techniques can be remembered by the alphabetical sequence ABCDEF: Distressing feelings exist because an *activating event* (A) along with the person's *beliefs* (B) lead to a *highly charged emotional consequence* (C). It is not the event itself that created the problem, but rather the beliefs attached to the event led to a problematic consequence. Thus, changing the beliefs will lead to a different consequence. This is done by helping the client *dispute* (D) the irrational beliefs and perceive their illogical and self-defeating nature. Such disputes lead to an *effect* (E; also called an *effective new philosophy*), a new way of feeling and acting. Finally, clients may have to take *further action* (F) to solidify the change in beliefs. Each session is devoted to a specific aspect of the client's problem. Often, at the outset of a session, client and therapist will determine what effect the client wants from the intervention. Beth and an REBT therapist might agree on what the effect should be when she studies—namely, less anxiety—and go through the ABCDEF procedure to achieve that effect. Figure 12.1 illustrates the ABCDEF techniques applied to Beth's anxiety.

The REBT therapist sometimes argues with the client to help him or her confront (and dispute) the faulty cognitions that contribute to his or her distress. The therapist may also use role-playing to help the client practice new ways of thinking and behaving (Ellis, 1994b). REBT can be helpful with anxiety, unassertiveness (Haaga & Davison, 1989), and unrealistic expectations; it is generally not successful with psychotic disorders.

Figure 12.1 The ABCDEF Technique Applied to Beth's Anxiety

ACTIVATING EVENT	BELIEFS	CONSEQUENCE	DISPUTE	EFFECT	FURTHER ACTION
Beth and an REBT therapist discuss the activating event: sitting down to study.	They discuss Beth's belief that if she does not do well on a test, she will be a failure as a person.	Anxiety	The bulk of their work together focuses on disputing Beth's belief, "*I must get an A*"; it is irrational and creates unpleasant feelings. The REBT therapist helps her see its more realistic counterpart, "*I prefer to get an A,*" which makes it clearer that she has some choice about the grade she sets as a goal.	Ideally, Beth feels less anxiety.	Although Beth should feel less anxiety, additional work (steps A–E) may be necessary to lessen her anxiety or consolidate the changes she has made.

Figure 12.2 Daily Record of Dysfunctional Beliefs

Situation	Emotion(s)	Automatic Thought(s)	Rational Response	Outcome
Actual event or stream of thoughts	Rate (1–100%)	ATs that preceded emotion Rate belief in ATs (1–100%)	Write rational response to ATs Rate belief in rational response (1–100%)	Rerate AT (1–100%)
1. Sit down to study	Anxious 70%	I won't be able to do as well on the test as I would like. —100% (Dichotomous thinking)	I might not be able to do as well as I want, but that doesn't mean that I will necessarily fail. —50%	Anxious 50%
2. In bed in the morning	Sad 80%	There's no point in getting out of bed—the day will be awful. I fail at everything I try. —90% (Mental filter)	Although I may not "succeed" in the goals I set for myself, it is possible that my expectations are too high, that I have too many expectations, or that I only notice the goals I don't attain, and don't notice the ones I do. —70%	Sad 6%

In a daily record of dysfunctional beliefs, clients like Beth are asked to identify the situation in which their automatic negative thoughts occurred, rate their emotional state (Emotions column), write down the automatic thoughts, their rational response to the automatic negative thoughts, and then rerate their emotional state (Outcome column).

Beck's Cognitive Therapy Techniques. Beck's cognitive therapy often makes use of a daily record of dysfunctional thoughts (see Figure 12.2). Clients are asked to identify the situation in which the automatic negative thoughts (comparable to irrational beliefs) occurred, rate their emotional state, write down the automatic negative thoughts and their rational response to those thoughts (comparable to the REBT "dispute"), and then rerate their emotional state. Clients should rate their emotional state as improved after going through this process. Although this technique appears straightforward, it can be hard to use because the client has believed the "truth" of the automatic thought for so long that it doesn't seem to be distorted or irrational. The process of helping clients shift their thinking away from automatic, dysfunctional thoughts to more realistic ones is called **cognitive restructuring**. The therapist helps clients examine and assess the accuracy of the automatic thoughts and their habitual ways of viewing themselves and the world and then helps them search for alternative interpretations for those thoughts.

Cognitive therapy also makes use of **psychoeducation**—that is, educating clients about therapy and research findings pertaining to their disorders or problems. This knowledge is then used to help clients develop a more realistic, undistorted view of their problems. Beth was afraid to seek treatment because she was afraid she would be hospitalized; a cognitive therapist might explain to her the criteria for a hospital admission so that this fear wouldn't become the basis for developing irrational automatic thoughts.

Cognitive restructuring: The process of helping clients shift their thinking away from the focus on automatic, dysfunctional thoughts to more realistic ones.

Psychoeducation: The process of educating clients about therapy and research findings pertaining to their disorders or problems.

Cognitive–Behavior Therapy

In some sense, the distinction between behavior therapy and cognitive therapy is really a matter of emphasis; they are not categorically distinct. We've already noted that cognitive therapy implicitly involves behavior change. Similarly, behavior

Table 12.3 The Focus, Goals, and Techniques of Cognitive–Behavior Therapy

Although cognitive–behavior therapy addresses clients' symptoms and focuses on symptom relief as a goal in and of itself, cognitive and behavioral techniques have different foci and goals.

Type of Techniques	Focus	Goal(s)	Specific Techniques
Behavioral techniques	Maladaptive behavior	Change the behavior, its antecedents, or its consequences	Relaxation techniques, systematic desensitization, exposure with response prevention, stimulus control, behavior modification, observational learning
Cognitive techniques	Automatic, irrational thoughts	Change dysfunctional, unrealistic thoughts to more realistic ones Recognize the relationships among thoughts, feelings, and behaviors	Cognitive restructuring (or Ellis's ABCDEF technique), psychoeducation, role playing

therapy involves changing cognitions: For instance, during exposure treatment, clients get to see that their negative automatic thoughts do not, in fact, come to pass. That is, through exposure, they learn that catastrophic events don't transpire when using an elevator or that touching dirt (for someone with OCD) won't lead to a catastrophe or fatal illness (Emmelkamp, 2004).

In the last quarter of the 20th century, therapists began to use both cognitive and behavioral techniques within the same treatment. This merging of therapies grew out of the recognition that cognitions and behaviors affect each other, and both affect feelings—and that alterations in cognitions, behaviors, and feelings are often a part of most psychological disorders. CBT combines the goals and techniques of both behavior and cognitive therapies (Table 12.3). The two sets of techniques can work together to promote therapeutic change: Cognitive techniques change thoughts, which then affect feelings and behaviors; behavioral techniques change behaviors, which, in turn, lead to new experiences, feelings, and ways of relating, which then change how people think about themselves and the world. These techniques may also be used to treat stress-related problems (see Chapter 10). CBT is appropriate for a wide range of clients and disorders and provides the opportunity for clients to learn new coping strategies and master new tasks.

LOOKING BACK: Review

1. *What is the focus of behavior therapy? What are some of its techniques?*
Behavior therapy assumes that problematic behavior is based on previous learning and focuses on changing distressing or abnormal behavior via learning principles. Behavioral therapists use techniques such as systematic desensitization, exposure with response prevention, stimulus control, behavior modification programs, and observational learning.

2. *What are the goals of cognitive therapy? What techniques are used?*
Cognitive therapy rests on the assumption that thoughts influence feelings and behaviors. According to this approach, someone experiencing distressing symptoms such as depression has irrational, automatic

thoughts that affect feelings and behavior. The goal of cognitive therapy is to reduce these irrational cognitive distortions via cognitive restructuring, disputes, and psychoeducation.

● LOOKING BEYOND: *Critical Thinking*

If you read about a study that claimed that CBT treatment effectively reduces kleptomania (compulsive stealing not done for material need), what questions would you ask about how the study was conducted? Suppose that each therapist in the study treated some clients with CBT and some with client-centered therapy. What would you need to know before agreeing with the conclusions about the superiority of CBT? Why? Would CBT be effective if a client was not motivated or had a poor memory? From what you know about her, would you recommend CBT to Beth? Explain your answers.

Biomedical Therapies

Thinking about her mother's depression led Beth to wonder whether medication might help her own anxiety and depression. Five years earlier, Beth's mother had participated in a research study in the hospital to which she had been admitted, where she was treated successfully with antidepressant medication and cognitive–behavior therapy. Although Beth's mother had tried medication many years before, it hadn't helped. Yet the new medication seemed to help a great deal. Might there be medications or other biomedical treatments that would help Beth feel better? With recent advances in knowledge about the brain have come advances in biomedical treatments of many disorders.

● LOOKING AHEAD: *Learning Objectives*

1. What are the different types of medications that can be used to treat psychological disorders?

2. What is electroconvulsive therapy, and what disorders does it help alleviate?

3. When is transcranial magnetic stimulation used as a treatment?

Psychopharmacology

The use of medication to treat psychological disorders and problems is known as **psychopharmacology**. In the last two decades, the number and types of medications for the treatment of psychological disorders have multiplied. As scientists learn more about the brain and its neurotransmitters, researchers are able to develop new medications to target symptoms more effectively and with fewer side effects. Thus, for any given disorder, there are more medication options.

Schizophrenia and Other Psychotic Disorders

The most common type of medication for the treatment of schizophrenia and other psychotic disorders is **antipsychotic medication** (also called *neuroleptic medication*), which generally reduces psychotic symptoms but does not cure the

Psychopharmacology: The use of medication to treat psychological disorders and problems.

Antipsychotic medication: Medication that reduces psychotic symptoms.

disorder. Antipsychotic drugs have long been known to have an effect on the positive symptoms of schizophrenia (see Chapter 11), such as hallucinations. Traditional antipsychotic medications include Thorazine and Haldol. However, long-term use of these medications can cause **tardive dyskinesia**, an irreversible movement disorder in which the affected person involuntarily smacks his or her lips, displays facial grimaces, and exhibits other symptoms. *Atypical antipsychotics* are a newer group of antipsychotic drugs that affect the neurotransmitter dopamine (as does traditional antipsychotic medication), as well as other neurotransmitters. For instance, the atypical antipsychotic medication Risperdal cuts down on the amount of free serotonin and dopamine available in the brain, which affects the ease with which signals cross synapses. In addition to decreasing positive symptoms, such as hallucinations, these newer drugs also counteract negative symptoms, such as apathy, lack of interest, and withdrawal, and are effective in improving cognitive functioning (Keefe et al., 1999); all of which can have the effect of allowing psychological therapies to be more effective (Ballus, 1997). These drugs also appear to have fewer side effects than traditional antipsychotic medications, and they are associated with very little decrease in gray brain matter compared to the traditional antipsychotic Haldol (Lieberman et al., 2005). Increasing amounts of data suggest that pharmacological treatment administered soon after the first psychotic episode is associated with a better long-term prognosis, compared to treatment begun later (Wyatt et al., 1997).

Mood Disorders

The number of medications to treat mood disorders continues to grow.

Medications for Depression. Effective pharmacological treatment for depression began in earnest in the 1950s with the discovery of **tricyclic antidepressants (TCAs)**, named for the three rings in their chemical structure. Elavil is an example of this class of drug. For decades, TCAs were the only effective antidepressant medication readily available, although their common side effects include constipation, dry mouth, blurred vision, and low blood pressure. These medications affect serotonin levels, and they can take weeks to work. Although another type of medication, **monoamine oxidase inhibitors (MAOIs)**, was the first antidepressant medication discovered, MAOIs have never been as widely prescribed as TCAs, for two major reasons. First, MAOIs require users not to eat or drink anything that contains the substance *tyramine* (such as cheese and wine) because of potentially fatal changes in blood pressure. Second, they are particularly effective with atypical depression involving increased appetite and hypersomnia (increased need for sleep; Prien & Kocsis, 1995) but less effective with typical symptoms of depression.

Selective serotonin reuptake inhibitors (SSRIs), such as Prozac, Zoloft, and Paxil, were developed in the 1980s. They generally have fewer side effects (they only work on *selective* serotonin receptors), and thus, people are less likely to stop taking them (Anderson, 2000); however, by 2004, researchers were finding that SSRI use among children and adolescents was associated with an increased risk of suicide (Martinez et al., 2005). This increased risk with SSRIs (compared to other antidepressants) has not been found among adults (Fergusson et al., 2005; Gunnell et al., 2005).

A common side effect of SSRIs is decreased sexual interest. In addition, many people experience a "Prozac poop-out" after a while, no longer attaining the same benefit from what had previously been an effective dose. A meta-analysis of the use of Prozac in treating depression found it to be as effective as, but not more so

Tardive dyskinesia: An irreversible movement disorder in which the person involuntarily smacks his or her lips, displays facial grimaces, and exhibits other symptoms; caused by traditional antipsychotic medication.

Tricyclic antidepressant (TCA): A type of antidepressant medication named for the three rings in the chemical structure.

Monoamine oxidase inhibitor (MAOI): A type of antidepressant medication that requires strict adherence to a diet free of tyramine.

Selective serotonin reuptake inhibitor (SSRI): A type of antidepressant medication that affects only selective serotonin receptors, with relatively few side effects.

than, TCAs (Agency for Health Care Policy and Research, 1999; Geddes et al., 2000). Researchers continue to discover ways to alleviate symptoms of depression without as many side effects and to discover additional biological mechanisms so that those who do not respond to existing antidepressants can obtain relief from medication. Some newer antidepressants (such as Serzone, Effexor, and Remeron) don't fall into the existing categories; these drugs, which affect both the serotonin and norepinephrine systems, are sometimes referred to as **serotonin/ norepinephrine reuptake inhibitors (SNRIs)**.

Antidepressant Effect as Placebo Effect? As we saw in Chapter 10, a person's beliefs and expectations about medication can affect the individual's symptoms through the *placebo effect*, the healing effect that occurs after taking a medically inactive substance that nevertheless has medicinal effects. Consider that a meta-analysis of the effectiveness of antidepressants found that about 75–80% of the effect of antidepressants can be achieved with a placebo. Only about 25% of the response to an antidepressant arises from the active ingredients in the medication. Thus, among those helped by an antidepressant, much—if not most—of the positive response arises from expectations that symptoms will get better (Kirsch & Lynn, 1999; Kirsch et al., 2002a; Kirsch & Sapirstein, 1998; Walach & Maidhof, 1999). In addition, more than half of the antidepressant studies funded by drug companies have found that medication and placebo were equally effective (Kirsch et al., 2002a; Kirsch et al., 2002b).

When the placebo has ingredients that mimic the side effects of antidepressants (so that patients think they are taking the medication and not a placebo), the difference in effectiveness between a true antidepressant and the placebo is even smaller (Greenberg & Fisher, 1989). Moreover, depressed people taking either an SSRI or a placebo medication had similar changes in brain functioning (Leuchter et al., 2002). Thus, someone's *beliefs* about what will happen after taking antidepressant medication (level of the person) affect what happens (level of the brain), which, in turn, affects the person's interactions with others (level of the group).

Note that this does *not* mean that people taking antidepressants should necessarily go off their medication. Taking a placebo is *not* the same as not taking a medication. Rather, it appears that the act of taking a placebo promotes biological changes that would not otherwise occur.

Medications for Bipolar Disorder. For bipolar disorder, mood stabilizers such as *lithium* can prevent a recurrence of both manic and depressive phases, although up to half of those with this disorder either will show no significant improvement or will be unable to tolerate the side effects, which include gastrointestinal problems, increased thirst, and trembling. These individuals can instead take a mood stabilizer such as Depakote or Tegretol to minimize the recurrence of manic episodes. During a manic episode, doctors often prescribe antipsychotic drugs or antianxiety drugs. The treatment regimen for bipolar disorder may involve lifelong use of medication.

Anxiety Disorders

For most anxiety disorders (including panic disorder, the panic symptoms of phobias, and PTSD), **benzodiazepines** are often the medication prescribed. Xanax and Valium are types of benzodiazepines, which affect the target symptoms within 36 hours and do not need to be taken for 10 days or more to build up to an effective level, as is the case with antidepressants. However, they can cause drowsiness

Studies have shown that the herbal remedy St. John's wort may be effective in treating mild to moderately severe depression (Agency for Health Care Policy and Research, 1999; Gaster & Holroyd, 2000).

Serotonin/norepinephrine reuptake inhibitor (SNRI): A newer type of antidepressant that affects both serotonin and norepinephrine neurotransmitter systems.

Benzodiazepine: A type of antianxiety medication that affects the target symptoms within 36 hours and does not need to be taken for more than a week to be effective.

and are potentially lethal when taken with alcohol. In addition, a person using benzodiazepines can develop tolerance and dependence (see Chapter 10) and can experience withdrawal reactions. For these reasons, drugs of this class are often prescribed for only short periods of time, such as during a particularly stressful period. Antidepressants (TCAs, SSRIs, or SNRIs) may be prescribed for long-term treatment of anxiety disorders, although the dosage may be lower or higher than that used in the treatment of depression, depending on the anxiety disorder (Gorman & Kent, 1999; Kasper & Resinger, 2001; Rivas-Vazques, 2001). Obsessive-compulsive disorder can be treated effectively with SSRI antidepressants such as clomiprimine, although at a higher dose than that prescribed for depression or other anxiety disorders.

Electroconvulsive Therapy

Essentially a controlled brain seizure, **electroconvulsive therapy (ECT)** was developed in the 1930s as a treatment for schizophrenia. It was based on the idea that schizophrenia and epilepsy are incompatible, and thus ECT-induced epilepsy should relieve the symptoms of schizophrenia. Although it does not cure schizophrenia, it is still a recommended treatment when medication does not work (Lehman & Steinwachs, 1998). ECT has been particularly helpful in treating certain mood disorders, such as psychotic depression and manic episodes of bipolar disorder (Maletzky, 2004). In fact, over 80% of those receiving ECT suffer from depression (Eranti & McLoughlin, 2003; Sackeim et al., 1995), often those with severe depression who have not received much benefit from psychotherapy or medication (Lam et al., 1999) or those for whom drugs are inadvisable for medical reasons. Although the treatment can be effective, the reasons are not well understood. The patient is given a muscle relaxant before each ECT treatment and is under anesthesia during the procedure; because of the anesthesia, ECT is administered in a hospital and generally requires a hospital stay. Patients may experience temporary memory loss for events right before, during, or after each treatment. After a course of 6–12 sessions, usually administered two or three times a week over several weeks (Husain et al., 2004; Shapira et al., 1998; Vieweg & Shawcross, 1998), depression often lifts; relief may come sooner for the depressed elderly (Tew et al., 1999).

ECT was considered a major biomedical treatment in the 1940s and 1950s, but the ready availability of medications in subsequent decades led to a decline in its use. Another reason for its decreased use was that some patients seemed to experience significant cognitive impairment, including memory loss. And, as it became known that it was sometimes used in understaffed institutions to produce a docile patient population (as immortalized in the book and movie *One Flew Over the Cuckoo's Nest*), ECT became politically unpopular. However, improvements in the way ECT is administered have significantly reduced the cognitive deficits and undesirable side effects, and since the 1980s, the use of ECT has increased (Glass, 2001). However, severely depressed patients helped by ECT are at risk for relapse, particularly if they do not take medication after the ECT treatments end (Birkenhäger et al., 2004; Sackeim et al., 2001). The increase in ECT's use reflects a new appreciation of its effectiveness, as well as a recognition that not all people with depression, mania, or schizophrenia can either take medication or find it helpful. In recent years, ECT has been more frequently administered to affluent patients than to those in publicly funded hospitals (Sackeim et al., 1995).

Electroconvulsive therapy (ECT): Use of an electric current to induce a controlled brain seizure in people with certain psychological disorders such as psychotic depression or those for whom medication has not been effective or recommended.

Transcranial Magnetic Stimulation

Unlike someone undergoing ECT, the person receiving transcranial magnetic stimulation is awake and does not need anesthesia.

A new treatment currently being researched is *transcranial magnetic stimulation (TMS)* (see Chapter 2), a procedure in which an electromagnetic coil on the scalp transmits pulses of high-intensity magnetism to the brain in short bursts lasting 100–200 microseconds. Although it is not yet known exactly how this magnetic field changes brain neurophysiology and neurochemistry, TMS has varying effects, depending on the exact location of the coil on the head and the frequency of the pulses. Placebo studies of TMS (in which the procedure of TMS is administered, but at an angle that does not affect the brain) have found that actual TMS is more effective than the placebo (George et al., 1999; Klein et al., 1999). Studies of people with depression who have not responded to medication have yielded positive results, with depressive symptoms decreasing after TMS (Epstein et al., 1998; Figiel et al., 1998; Klein et al., 1999). Some studies have found that severely depressed people receiving TMS respond as well as those receiving ECT (Dannon et al., 2002; Janicak et al., 2002). Should additional studies confirm these early positive results, TMS offers a number of advantages over ECT, including easier administration (it requires neither anesthesia nor hospitalization) and minimal side effects. The most common short-term side effect, experienced by 5–20% of patients, is a slight headache.

TMS has been administered to people with depression, bipolar disorder (Grisaru, Chudakov, et al., 1998), schizophrenia (Hoffman et al., 2003; Poulet et al., 2005), OCD (Alonso et al., 2001), and PTSD (Grisaru, Amir, et al., 1998). But more research, particularly on the coil's location and the stimulation's frequency, is needed before TMS can be declared a treatment of choice rather than an experimental one (Kauffmann et al., 2004; Schlaepfer et al., 2003).

LOOKING BACK: *Review*

1. *What are the different types of medications that can be used to treat psychological disorders?* Antipsychotic medication can help people with schizophrenia and other psychotic disorders; antidepressants can help those with depression and anxiety; lithium can help people with bipolar disorder; and antianxiety drugs can help individuals with anxiety disorders.

2. *What is electroconvulsive therapy, and what disorders does it help alleviate?* Electroconvulsive therapy is basically a controlled brain seizure, which may be used as a treatment for patients who remain severely depressed despite the use of other therapies.

3. *When is transcranial magnetic stimulation used as a treatment?* Transcranial magnetic stimulation, a procedure in which pulses of high-intensity magnetism are transmitted to the brain, is currently an experimental treatment. It has been used with people who have mood disorders and schizophrenia.

LOOKING BEYOND: *Critical Thinking*

Suppose your best friend's mother has bipolar disorder. What treatment would likely be given to her? Why? Suppose instead that your friend's father has schizophrenia; what treatment might he receive?

Under what circumstances might you consider ECT to be a reasonable treatment for someone?

Treatment Variations and Issues

After a number of therapy sessions, Beth began to feel better. She was going to class more often, and felt better able to handle studying and preparing for tests. She wanted to know what it was about the therapy that was helping her, and why her therapist used specific techniques at certain times. Her treatment had not included medication, and she still wondered whether she would be feeling even better—or worse—if she had taken medication. She also wondered whether her therapy would be as effective for other people in her situation. If her best friend went to see Beth's therapist for anxiety and depression, would her friend fare as well as Beth?

LOOKING AHEAD: *Learning Objectives*

1. *What are other forms, or modalities, of therapy besides individual therapy?*
2. *What are some innovations in psychotherapy?*
3. *What key issues should be kept in mind when reading research studies on psychotherapy?*
4. *What are good ways to find a therapist?*

Modalities: When Two or More Isn't a Crowd

Modality: A form of therapy.

Individual therapy: A therapy modality in which an individual client is treated by a single therapist.

Group therapy: A therapy modality in which a number of clients with compatible needs meet together with one or two therapists.

Many of the therapy approaches can be implemented in a variety of **modalities**, or forms. **Individual therapy**—therapy in which one client is treated by one therapist—is a modality. Other modalities have one or more therapists working with a family or with a group of people who share some commonality, such as a diagnosis of agoraphobia. Each theoretical orientation discussed earlier can be brought to bear in these various modalities: individual, group, or family.

Group Therapy

Clients with compatible needs who meet together with one or two therapists are engaging in **group therapy**. The course of treatment in group therapy can range from a single occasion (usually an educational session) to ongoing treatment lasting for years. Some groups are for members who have a particular problem or disorder, focusing on, for instance, recent divorce or posttraumatic stress disorder. These groups may offer emotional support, psychoeducation, and concrete strategies for managing the problem or disorder. Other groups have members who do not share any specific problem or disorder, but rather who want to learn more about maladaptive or inappropriate ways in which they are interacting with people; the therapy group provides an opportunity to learn about themselves and change their undesired patterns of behavior.

In addition to offering information, support, and (if the group has a cognitive–behavioral orientation) between-

Group therapy can help reduce shame and isolation and can provide support and an opportunity to interact in new ways with other people.

session homework assignments, group therapy provides something that individual therapy cannot: interaction with other people who are experiencing similar difficulties. The group experience can decrease the sense of isolation and shame that clients sometimes feel. In revealing their own experiences and being moved by others', clients often come to see their own lives and difficulties in a new light. Also, because some clients' problems relate to their interpersonal interactions, the group provides a safe opportunity for clients to try out new behaviors.

Family Therapy

In **family therapy**, a family as a whole, or a subset of some of its members, such as a couple, is treated. A "family" is often defined as consisting of those who think of themselves or function as a family; thus, blended families created by marriage are seen in family therapy, as are other nontraditional families. The most common theoretical orientation among those providing family therapy is **systems therapy**, which starts from the premise that no client is an island: A client's symptoms occur in a larger context, or system (the family and subculture), and any change in one part of the system will affect the rest of the system. Thus, the client is referred to as the "identified patient," although the system (the couple or the family) is considered the "patient" that is to be treated. Systems therapy was originally used exclusively with families; in fact, some of the pioneers in systems therapy would refuse to see individuals without their families. For this reason, systems therapy is sometimes referred to as "family therapy," although this is a misnomer. Some therapists treat entire families, but not necessarily from a systems approach. They may use a psychodynamic or behavioral approach. Similarly, some systems therapists see individuals without their families, but the therapy makes use of systems theory. Systems therapy can also be the theoretical framework used to treat couples in therapy.

Systems therapy focuses on a family's communication, structure, and power relationships. The theory views the identified patient's symptoms as attempts to convey a message. Initially, a systems therapist takes a family history to discover which members of the family are close to one another or angry with one another and to ascertain more generally how anger, sadness, and other feelings or issues are handled within the family. In some cases, one parent may be underinvolved and the other overinvolved; treatment would be directed to encourage the underinvolved parent to be more involved, and the overinvolved parent to be less involved. Or, the parents' relationship with each other may need strengthening, with consequences for other family members, because conflict between parents affects their children's behavior (Kitzmann, 2000). For instance, in a family in which the parents fight a lot, an adolescent boy's rebelliousness may serve to unite his parents in their anger and frustration at him. The systems therapist might explain to the family that their son is intentionally being rebellious to keep his parents united, for fear of what could happen to the parents' relationship if he wasn't causing them problems. The family therapist might praise the son for his efforts at keeping his parents together, and even urge him not to stop rebelling yet, because his parents haven't yet practiced how to relate to each other without fighting.

Self-Help Therapies

Self-help therapies are available both in groups and individually.

Helping Groups. **Self-help groups** (sometimes referred to as *support groups*) can be used on their own or as a supplement to psychotherapy and are focused on a specific disorder or event. They do not usually have a clinically trained

Family therapy: A therapy modality in which a family (or certain members of a family) is treated.

Systems therapy: A type of therapy that views a client's symptoms as occurring in a larger context, or system (the family and subculture), and holds that a change in one part of the system affects the rest of the system.

Self-help group: A group whose members focus on a specific disorder or event and do not usually have a clinically trained leader; also called a *support group.*

leader, although a mental health professional may be involved in some capacity (Shepherd et al., 1999). Alcoholics Anonymous (AA), the first self-help program, is based on 12 steps toward recovery. Most 12-step programs view a belief in a Higher Power (for most people, God) as crucial to recovery, and meta-analytic results show that weekly attendance in group meetings is associated with drug or alcohol abstinence, whereas less than weekly attendance is not (Fiorentine, 1999). People who are not religious can also benefit from attending AA meetings (Winzelberg & Humphreys, 1999) or meetings of Smart Recovery, an organization for overcoming drug or alcohol abuse that does not use a 12-step approach but is based on cognitive–behavioral principles. Another self-help group that does not use the 12-step approach is the National Depressive and Manic Depressive Association, which helps those suffering from bipolar disorder or depression and their families and friends. Self-help groups not only are valuable sources of information and support, but also can provide referrals to therapists who are knowledgeable about the particular disorder or problem. Relatives of those with a psychological disorder report that such groups are helpful in providing support and promoting self-understanding (Citron et al., 1999). As is true in group therapy, self-help groups can be invaluable in decreasing feelings of isolation and shame.

A new vehicle for self-help is the Internet, where there are chat room "support groups" and psychoeducation. However, beware: Information on a Web site may not be accurate, and people in an online support group may not be who they claim to be (Finn & Banach, 2000; Waldron et al., 2000). Some of the Web-based self-help cognitive–behavioral programs are better than no treatment (Carlbring et al., 2001), but whether they are as effective as the treatment provided by a mental health clinician awaits further study.

Helping Yourself.   Self help is not limited to groups. The last two decades have witnessed a proliferation of self-help books and tapes dealing with a wide range of problems; the use of such materials is sometimes referred to as **bibliotherapy**. Many of these materials incorporate philosophies and techniques of the therapies discussed in this chapter, and therapists often suggest that clients read particular books (Adams & Pitre, 2000; Starker, 1988). Researchers have found that such material can help with depression and anxiety (Febbraro, 2005; Floyd et al., 2004; Gregory et al., 2004), but are not as effective for helping people to eliminate habits such as smoking, drinking, and overeating. Not surprisingly, those who complied with the materials' recommendations fared better than those who did not (Gould & Clum, 1993).

Innovations in Psychotherapy

As psychologists learn more about effective treatments, treatment changes. Changes also occur as a result of technological and economic realities.

Psychotherapy Integration: Mixing and Matching

In the past several decades, many therapists have moved away from a single theoretical orientation, such as psychodynamic or behavioral. Surveys found that between 68% (Jensen et al., 1990) and 98% (Smith, 1982) of mental health professionals identify themselves as *eclectic* in orientation. A therapist using **psychotherapy integration** uses techniques from different theoretical orientations, with an overarching theory of how the integrated techniques will achieve the goals of treatment. A therapist's integrating of specific techniques *without* regard for an overarching theory is referred to as **technical eclecticism** (Beutler & Hodgson, 1993). This integrative approach involves the incorporation of new

Bibliotherapy: The use of self-help books and tapes for therapeutic purposes.

Psychotherapy integration: The use of techniques from different theoretical orientations with an overarching theory of how the integrated techniques will be used to achieve the goals of treatment.

Technical eclecticism: The use of specific techniques that may benefit a particular client, without regard for an overarching theory.

techniques based on research findings and the clinical needs of a particular client at a specific point in the treatment (Stricker, 1993). Such an approach provides the aspects of therapy that are common to all theoretical orientations (such as offering hope, a caring listener, and a new way of thinking about problems) and employs specific techniques for a given disorder, such as exposure with response prevention for people with OCD (Weinberger, 1995). Two clients with the same diagnosis may receive different integrative treatments from the same therapist, based on factors other than the diagnosis—such as family issues, a client's preference for directive versus nondirective treatment, and other concerns.

Time and Therapy: Therapy Protocols and Brief Therapy

Recent decades have also seen a rise in the use of *therapy protocols*, detailed session-by-session manuals specifying how therapy should proceed for a specific disorder from a certain theoretical orientation (such as behavior therapy for panic disorder or cognitive therapy for depression). These manual-based treatments were created, in part, to ensure that when a research study was testing the effectiveness of a given therapy (for example, CBT), all the therapists were using the same techniques in the same way. This meant, of course, that the results of the study were relevant to the treatment's effectiveness because the conditions were comparable. Some clinicians advocate the use of therapy performed without deviation from treatment manuals (Addis, 1997). However, a large study of the manual-based treatment of panic disorder found that, even when therapists adhere to the manual, each therapist, as an individual, makes his or her own unique contribution to the treatment (Huppert et al., 2001; Malik et al., 2003). Many of the protocols for manual-based therapy were developed for treatment lasting 15–20 sessions. Today, many managed care organizations in different parts of the United States will approve 3–10 sessions, and the therapist must request additional sessions, precluding the systematic use of sessions as is done in manual-based therapy. Research indicates that those with recent, focused problems in one sphere of life (such as work) receive more benefit from brief psychotherapy than those who have difficulties in multiple spheres or who have long-standing problems (Barkham & Shapiro, 1990; Klosko et al., 1990; Roth & Fonagy, 2005; Strupp & Binder, 1984).

Interpersonal therapy (IPT): A type of researched, manual-based treatment that focuses on how issues that arise in the client's current relationships can affect mood.

Manual-based treatments usually focus on specific disorders, and they tend to utilize behavioral or cognitive–behavioral techniques. For instance, there are research-based treatment manuals for behavior therapy for various anxiety disorders and for CBT for depression, anxiety disorders, and eating disorders (Elkin et al., 1989; Linden et al., 2005; Wilson & Fairburn, 2002).

Another type of researched, manual-based treatment is **interpersonal therapy (IPT)**, which focuses on how issues that arise in the client's current relationships can affect mood. This type of therapy arose from theory about the importance of interpersonal relationships (Sullivan, 1953) and was developed in the late 1970s for a research study examining various treatments of depression. The goal of IPT is to help the client's

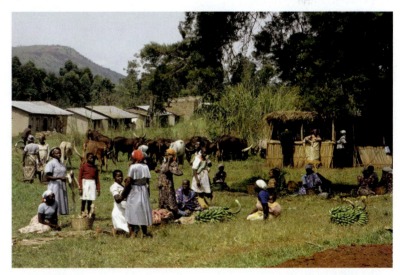

IPT for depression was adapted to a group format and administered in 30 rural villages in Uganda (which were randomly selected). Compared to depressed people in control villages, who received no treatment, those who received group IPT had a significant reduction of their depressive symptoms and were able to function better in their daily lives (Bolton et al., 2003).

High-tech gadgets such as this palm-top computer are at the cutting edge of brief CBT; they are often preprogrammed with tasks to help participants self-monitor their thoughts.

relationships work better and become more satisfying. IPT for depression rests on the assumption that if the relationships are functioning better, the depression will lessen. Therapeutic techniques include helping clients explore the consequences of their actions in their relationships and facilitating better personal communication, perhaps by encouraging clients to tell others how they feel. IPT protocols have been adapted to treat people with bulimia nervosa (Mitchell et al., 2002) and PTSD (Bleiberg & Markowitz, 2005).

Technology and Therapy: High-Tech Treatment

Computer technology is now used to facilitate brief therapy (Gega et al., 2004) through the use of personal digital assistants (PDAs) or other palmtop devices and software. The goal of using these technologies is to reduce symptoms through increased access to (computerized) treatment, lessening the amount of time spent with the therapist. Palmtop devices can be used for portable self-monitoring. For instance, a PDA may have an alarm that goes off at set or random times during the day, signaling the client to assess mood, hunger, anxiety, or some other relevant variable or to employ a previously learned technique such as muscle relaxation. Consider that research on the use of a palmtop device that was preprogrammed with cognitive–behavioral tasks found that 4 weeks of such assisted treatment (plus 8 weeks of practice with the device) was—as determined at follow-up—as effective as 12 weeks of regular CBT (Newman, Kenardy, et al., 1997). Subsequent studies have found similar results (Przeworski & Newman, 2004).

Issues in Psychotherapy Research

Hundreds of types of psychotherapy are currently available (Garfield & Bergin, 1994), but many of them do not rest on well-constructed and replicated research. Research is crucial for determining how well a new or old type of therapy treats a particular problem. It is easy to claim that a new therapy is a wonder cure, but harder to back up that claim with solid data. There are many issues to consider when evaluating findings about psychotherapy.

Research that asks whether clients feel better, function better, live more independently, or have fewer symptoms after treatment is called **outcome research**. These questions are trickier to answer than it would seem because they depend on how you define "outcome"; in research lingo, the answers to the questions depend on what you designate as the therapy's dependent variable. For example, you could have clients rate their thoughts, feelings, *or* behaviors, which are not necessarily highly correlated and might yield different outcomes (Kazdin, 1994). You must also decide how long after the end of treatment to assess outcome (Roth & Fonagy, 2005): Immediately afterward? A month later? A year later? And even if you find that clients are better after treatment, how can you know that this occurred because of the treatment itself and not simply because their symptoms improved with time? Suppose you do find that the group that received treatment fared better than a group that did not receive treatment but rather is on a waiting list for it—a *wait-list control group*. Can you attribute the improvement to the treatment itself? How can you know which elements of the treatment were the ones that led to clients' improvement? Table 12.4 lists questions that should be addressed when designing or evaluating studies of psychotherapy. These questions get at the heart of some of the challenges of conducting outcome research.

Outcome research: Research that asks whether, after psychotherapy, clients are feeling better, functioning better, living more independently, and experiencing fewer symptoms.

Table 12.4 Questions About Psychotherapy Research

1. Are the participants randomly assigned?

2. Is a specific disorder being treated?

3. Are there exclusion criteria (must participants have only one diagnosis)?

4. Are the therapists' treatments representative of their stated approaches?

5. What types of outcome measures are selected, who is the evaluator, and how is success defined?

6. Are clients more likely to drop out of some types of therapy than others?

7. Is a follow-up assessment planned, and if so, at what interval of time after the end of treatment?

Therapy, Medication, or Both?

Therapy—specifically behavior therapy—can work as well as medication to alleviate OCD. Is this general result true for other disorders? The answer to this global question is no, but the specific treatment (or treatments) that is most effective varies from disorder to disorder (Gloaguen et al., 1998; Reynolds et al., 1999; Thase et al., 1997). As we discuss specific treatments for particular disorders below, we will also note relevant comparisons with medication.

Depression

CBT and IPT have repeatedly been shown to provide relief from depression (Blatt et al., 2000). However, depression has one of the highest relapse rates among psychological disorders, and it appears that common factors—common at least among different forms of CBT and IPT—rather than specific techniques, may be key to therapeutic change with depression (Emmelkamp, 2004).

In a neuroimaging study of CBT's effects, 17 depressed adults had PET scans taken before and after 15–20 CBT sessions (Goldapple et al., 2004). As expected, symptom reduction was associated with changes in brain function. However, some brain areas were more active after treatment (such as the hippocampus and part of the cingulate cortex), whereas other areas were less active (such as regions of the frontal lobe). Thus, depression is not caused simply because some brain areas are not activated enough; at least some areas may be too active. In addition, the researchers compared these findings with those from patients who improved after they took the SSRI Paxil. This treatment produced strikingly different brain changes (see Figure 12.3): Following this drug treatment, portions of the frontal lobe became more active (not less active, as was found following CBT), and the hippocampus became less active, not more active. Thus, the two types of treatment for depression affect the brain differently. The bottom line is that

Figure 12.3

Brain Changes After Successful CBT for Depression Versus Medication

CBT and medication for depression produce different changes in brain activity, which suggests that the different therapies rely on different mechanisms. Increased activity is shown in orange, and decreased activity is shown in blue.

depression arises from a set of brain areas working in abnormal ways, and several changes in how those areas function can be associated with improvement. However, it is likely that the different brain changes produce different patterns of symptom change, but this has yet to be established.

Medication does alleviate depression for many people; why, therefore, might someone choose psychotherapy over medication? The main drawback of medication becomes apparent when you look at how people with depression fare over the long haul. When medication is discontinued, the relapse rate is high, a fact that has led some doctors to recommend continued use of medication for those at risk for additional depressive episodes (American Psychiatric Association, 2000b). Cognitive–behavioral treatment provides an equivalent benefit without the side effects of drugs (Antonuccio et al., 1995; DeRubeis et al., 2005), and it may help prevent relapse (Hollon & Shelton, 2001; Hollon et al., 2005). The skills and tools learned during psychological treatment are likely to remain after treatment stops.

CBT may also help treat residual symptoms of depression following treatment with antidepressant medication (Paykel et al., 2005). This supplemental use of CBT lowers the relapse rate when medication is discontinued (Fava et al., 1998a; Otto et al., 2005). At a 6-year follow-up, those who had supplemental CBT were less likely to have had another episode of depression than those without CBT (Fava et al., 1998b). Similarly, a number of studies have found that medication and cognitive therapy combined may be more helpful than medication alone, even with severely depressed people (Macaskill & Macaskill, 1996; Thase et al., 1997), although not all studies have found an additional benefit of adding medication to CBT or IPT (Browne et al., 2002; Oei & Yeoh, 1999; Otto et al., 2005).

Anxiety Disorders

For a number of anxiety disorders, exposure appears to be particularly helpful. In comparison to medication, researchers have shown that particular types of psychotherapy (CBT and IPT) provide as much, if not more, long-term relief of symptoms (Gould et al., 1995; Otto et al., 2005). In the treatment of panic disorder, for instance, although medication and CBT work about equally well, CBT does a better job of preventing symptom relapse (Chambless & Gillis, 1993; Otto et al., 1994). And for OCD, one behavior therapy technique—exposure with response prevention—is as helpful as medication, and possibly more helpful over the long term (Foa et al., 2005). Moreover, combining the exposure treatment with medication isn't more beneficial than just using exposure. However, some researchers question whether these findings generalize to clients diagnosed with more than OCD alone (Kozak et al., 2000). In the treatment of social phobias, research shows that SSRIs and group CBT are equally helpful (Davidson et al., 2004; Heimberg et al., 1998). However, when medication is discontinued, the symptoms usually return; in contrast, the beneficial effects of CBT continue after treatment ends.

Although medication can work in treating social phobia, such as a fear of public speaking, it is not necessarily superior to CBT because symptoms often return after medication is stopped. CBT's benefits usually last after treatment ends.

Other Disorders

For the treatment of bulimia nervosa, CBT and IPT have been shown to have efficacy; the results are less conclusive for the treatment of anorexia nervosa. Meta-analytic studies of medication versus CBT for treating participants with bulimia nervosa have found CBT to be more effective (Whittal et al., 1999).

For the treatment of schizophrenia, family interventions are efficacious, but research results are not yet available to indicate whether cognitive therapy effectively treats delusions (Gaudiano, 2005). Medication for schizophrenia and bipolar disorder is clearly superior to therapy, although CBT can help decrease psychotic symptoms (Gould et al., 2001; Rector & Beck, 2001; Thase & Jindal, 2004). For people with these disorders, therapy can play a role in helping them to accept the need to take medication on a lifelong or long-term basis (Colom et al., 1998; Tohen & Grundy, 1999) and can provide an opportunity to learn new relationship skills after the medication has helped them to be more stable. Moreover, psychological treatment in conjunction with medication can help patients to identify any triggers of the psychotic, manic, or depressive episodes and can help prevent relapses (Buchkremer et al., 1997; Goldstein, 1992). Guidelines for the treatment of schizophrenia advocate behavioral and cognitive skills training to encourage compliance with the medication regimen and social skills training to help improve functioning (Lehman & Steinwachs, 1998). CBT can also be effective in helping to reduce positive symptoms in schizophrenic patients who are not helped by medication (Kuipers et al., 1997, 1998; Sensky et al., 2000; Tarrier et al., 1998). A meta-analysis of nonmedication treatments for schizophrenia found that those patients with more chronic symptoms were more responsive to psychotherapy than those whose symptoms were more transient (Mojtabai et al., 1998).

Caveat

We need to end this section with a caveat: As with all research that examines groups of people, the results of research on the efficacy or effectiveness of various treatments do not necessarily apply to a particular individual. Thus, for any particular person with a given disorder, one type of therapy may be more effective than another, which in turn may be more effective than medication. The opposite may be true for someone else with apparently identical symptoms. Moreover, a number of disorders have a moderately high rate of relapse. For instance, in some studies, as many as half of those who receive a psychological treatment for depression later have a relapse (Gortner et al., 1998; Westen & Morrison, 2001). For such individuals, a combination of therapy and medication may be most helpful (Thase & Jindal, 2004).

Treatment for an Ethnically Diverse Population

According to the 2000 census, 30% of the population of the United States are members of an ethnic minority, and this number continues to grow (Zane et al., 2004). As the composition of the American population changes, so too does the composition of the population seeking mental health services. At least until the early 1990s, most psychotherapy research did not include information about race, education, or economic status. However, these factors may influence the effectiveness of a given treatment for a particular client (Francis & Aronson, 1990). Psychotherapists are now more aware of the need to consider a client's background, cultural values, and attitudes about psychotherapy (McGoldrick et al., 1996; Ramirez, 1999). For instance, a client's immigrant or refugee experience creates a stressor that can affect mental health. And members of minority groups who are born and raised in the United States may experience prejudice and other hardships that can affect mental health.

Therapists try to be aware of unique ethnic and cultural factors that can play a role in treatment, such as the stressors related to being an immigrant, a refugee, or a member of a minority group.

An example of the importance of understanding a symptom's cultural context can be found in *ataques de nervios* (Spanish for "attack of nerves"), which some Puerto Rican women experience. This condition is a physical expression of strong emotions and includes trembling, heart palpitations, numbness, difficulty breathing, loss of consciousness, and a hyperkinetic (overactive) state (Rivera-Arzola & Ramos-Grenier, 1997). The context for this illness is a culture in which women are likely to endure great hardships, have little real power, and are actively discouraged from expressing anger. *Ataque de nervios* provides a culturally sanctioned way for them to express an inability to cope with a current situation, and the community responds (Rivera-Arzola & Ramos-Grenier, 1997).

It is clear that the most effective therapist is one who is aware of both the cultural and familial contexts of a client's disorder. It is part of a therapist's responsibility to be aware of cultural or racial issues that can affect all aspects of treatment—diagnosis, the process of the therapy, and its goals (Helms & Cook, 1999; Ramirez, 1999). The therapist should inquire about the client's understanding of the meaning of the problem, so that therapist and client can discuss and come to agreement on the nature of the problem, the interventions to be used, and the expected goals (Higgenbotham et al., 1988; Kleinman, 1978).

Although age, sex, and ethnicity do not appear to play a systematic role in therapy outcomes generally (Beutler et al., 1994; Lam & Sue, 2001), research suggests that some people (such as some Asian Americans) prefer a therapist from their own ethnic group, and such matching leads to better outcomes for them (Sue et al., 1994). In general, however, there is yet no clear-cut evidence that matching client and therapist by ethnicity results in better outcomes for clients of most ethnic groups (Garfield, 1994). Some attempts have been made to develop particular therapies for certain ethnic groups, with varying success; for example, *cuento therapy* (from the Spanish word for "fable"), which uses folktales or stories, has proved helpful with some Latino/Latina children (Sue et al., 1994).

How to Pick a Therapist and a Type of Therapy

Suppose you, like Beth, decide to seek psychotherapy. How do you pick a therapist? Keep several factors in mind when trying to find someone who could most effectively help you. If your problem is identifiable (such as depression or anxiety), it's a good idea to see someone who has experience in treating people with that problem. There are many state and national referral agencies and professional associations, such as the American Psychological Association, the National Association of Social Workers, and the American Psychiatric Association (see Chapter 1 for a discussion regarding different types of mental health practitioners). Regional organizations, such as the Massachusetts Eating Disorders Association or the Manic-Depressive and Depressive Association of Boston (MDDA-Boston), can also provide referrals for specific problems. These organizations all have national associations that can also supply the names of therapists with expertise in treating specific problems.

If a certain type of therapy seems as if it may be a good fit with your problem, you might want to obtain referrals for a therapist who is experienced at providing that type of treatment. National organizations such as those listed in Table 12.5 may be able to refer you to therapists in your local area.

It can be helpful to get the names of several therapists because any one therapist may not have compatible office hours, location, or available times. You can also ask friends, family members, teachers, and religious leaders for recommendations, as well as the counseling center at your college or university. Many insurance companies will authorize or reimburse treatment only if the provider is on their list. Thus, it's best to tell the therapists you are considering what insurance coverage you have and ask whether their services are reimbursed by that company; if they don't know, call the company and check. Alternatively, call your insurance company and ask for referrals to a therapist who is experienced in helping people with your problem or in a particular type of therapy.

It is important that you feel comfortable with your therapist. If you don't, you may be less likely to talk about what's on your mind or about how you are really doing. And if you aren't able to talk about these things, the therapy can't be as helpful. It's also important to feel that the therapist is trustworthy—if the therapist doesn't have your trust, you will find it easy to discount what he or she says if it is something that you don't want to hear. If after one or two sessions, you realize that you just don't feel comfortable, make an appointment with someone else and see whether the situation feels different. Therapists are used to this initial "try out" period, and you shouldn't worry about possibly hurting their feelings by switching to someone else.

Table 12.5

National Organizations for Specific Types of Therapy

- American Association for the Advancement of Behavior Therapy
- Beck Institute for Cognitive Therapy and Research
- Albert Ellis Institute
- American Institute for Cognitive Therapy
- International Society for Interpersonal Psychotherapy
- American Psychoanalytic Association

Looking at Levels

Treating Obsessive-Compulsive Disorder

We know that both behavior therapy and medication can help those with obsessive-compulsive disorder (OCD). But do the two types of treatments exert their beneficial effects in a similar way? And can we fully understand why these treatments work by considering only the level of the brain?

OCD is marked by intrusive, illogical thoughts and overpowering compulsions to repeat certain acts, such as hand-washing to get rid of germs (see Chapter 11). In some cases, OCD can be disabling. To study the effects of behavior therapy on this disorder, the brain activity of nine people with OCD was examined by PET scanning before and after behavior therapy (which included exposure with response prevention) (Baxter et al., 1992). In addition, to compare such therapy to medication, the brains of nine other people with OCD were also scanned, before and after they received the SSRI fluoxetine (Prozac), which suppresses some of the symptoms of OCD. The scans revealed that behavior therapy and Prozac both decrease activity in the right caudate (part of the basal ganglia involved in automatic behaviors). The drug also affected the anterior cingulate and thalamus, both of which are involved in attention. The effects of behavior therapy on the brain were replicated by Schwartz and colleagues (1996; see Figure 12.4) and Nakatani and colleagues (2003).

Figure 12.4

Brain PET Scans Before and After Behavior Therapy

These PET scans show the brain of someone with OCD before (left) and after (right) 2 months of behavior therapy. Note the changes in the right caudate after successful treatment.

But, as usual, considering the brain in isolation will not tell us the complete story. At the level of the person, researchers have also shown that trying new behaviors (not washing dirty hands or not rechecking a locked door) and testing the truth of automatic negative thoughts (that nothing catastrophic happened after leaving the hands dirty or not checking that the door was locked) encourage people to replace old, maladaptive thoughts and behaviors with more adaptive ones and provide a sense of mastery and hope (Emmelkamp, 2004). These events at the level of the person, in turn, lead the individuals to persist in engaging in the new behaviors. These events, in turn, affect events at the level of the brain: the functioning of specific brain circuits.

Events at the level of the group are also involved. It is interactions with another person—the therapist—that help to change the thoughts, feelings, and behaviors of the individual with OCD. And just like people with schizophrenia (see Chapter 11), people with OCD whose family members are high in expressed emotion—particularly in expressing hostile criticism—are more likely to relapse (Chambless & Steketee, 1999; Emmelkamp et al., 1992). People with OCD who were receiving behavior therapy were six times more likely to drop out of treatment if relatives provided hostile criticism (versus constructive criticism or support; Chambless & Steketee, 1999). Thus, although exposure with response prevention can be very helpful, events at the level of the group can influence whether clients relapse after the treatment or even stick with it.

Given that family members can sometimes play such an important role, treatment for OCD may also specifically target group-level events, changing family members' responses to the client's symptoms and to his or her newly learned strategies (Van Noppen & Steketee, 2003). For instance, prior to treatment, family members may have gone along with the client's wishes, for example, by not touching certain "contaminated" objects; such accommodation can inadvertently reinforce the client's maladaptive beliefs and behaviors. Alternatively, family members may become (understandably) angry and frustrated by the client's behavior, which leads them to be hostile; however, such a response usually increases the patient's anxiety and symptom severity. In such cases, psychoeducation or behavior therapy for the family members focuses on helping them not to accommodate the client's symptoms and instructs them in how to support the client's efforts at exposure with response prevention. Such family participation can help reduce the OCD symptoms (Grunes et al., 2001; Van Noppen & Steketee, 2003).

Moreover, as symptoms subside, the client's personal relationships often change. For example, some of the time and energy that was devoted to OCD rituals can now be spent on relationships. Thus, events at the three levels of analysis and their interactions are helpful in understanding different aspects of treatment for this disorder.

LOOKING BACK: *Review*

1. *What are other forms, or modalities, of therapy besides individual therapy?*
   As well as meeting with a therapist for individual therapy, a client can meet with a group (often a group of people with similar problems) led by a therapist; the client can be a family (usually working with a therapist who has a systems approach) or a couple. Self-help groups and bibliotherapy may also be beneficial.

2. *What are some innovations in psychotherapy?* In integrative psychother-apy, the therapist systematically integrates two or more different theoret-ical approaches and their techniques into a treatment regimen based on research and clinical factors. The use of protocol-based and brief treat-ments, including computer-assisted treatments, has increased and is the subject of ongoing research.

3. *What key issues should be kept in mind when reading research studies on psychotherapy?* Overall, therapy is more beneficial than no treatment. However, methodological issues have a bearing on what conclusions we can draw from a psychotherapy study, such as what has been measured and when it was measured. Studies should note the ethnic composition of the participants, and treatment should consider ethnic and cultural factors that may affect the treatment.

4. *What are good ways to find a therapist?* A therapist can be chosen by a re-ferral from a counseling center, family and friends, self-help organiza-tions, professional associations, and/or insurance companies. The therapist should be someone with whom the client feels comfortable; if trust is lacking, the person should seek another therapist.

⬤ LOOKING BEYOND: *Critical Thinking*

Suppose you were designing a treatment program for an ethnically diverse set of depressed clients. What would you want to know about these clients? How would you use that information? How would you design a study to test the effectiveness of your new program? Why would you do it that way?

LET'S SUM IT UP

I. Historical Influences on Psychotherapy: Insight-Oriented Therapies

A. Insight-oriented therapies rest on the belief that psy-chological problems are caused by emotional forces.

B. Such treatments focus on helping people gain in-sight into their problems and propose that such in-sight will lead to changes in thoughts, feelings, and behavior.

C. Examples of insight-oriented therapies are psycho-dynamic therapy and client-centered therapy.

D. Psychodynamic therapy focuses on unconscious con-flicts and sexual and aggressive drives. The goal of the therapy is to make unconscious conflict conscious.

E. Psychodynamic techniques include free associa-tion, dream analysis, interpretation, and the use of transference.

F. Client-centered therapy focuses on each client's unique experiences and potential for growth. The goal of the therapy is to unblock the client's poten-tial for growth by decreasing incongruence.

G. Client-centered techniques include showing empa-thy and unconditional positive regard toward the client.

II. Cognitive–Behavior Therapy

A. Behavior therapy is grounded in the idea that psychological problems are a product of a client's learning history. Treatment seeks to help the client develop more adaptive behaviors.

B. Behavioral techniques based on classical conditioning include exposure, stimulus control, systematic desensitization, and progressive muscle relaxation.

C. Behavioral techniques based on operant conditioning include behavior modification and self-monitoring.

D. Cognitive therapy is grounded in the idea that psychological problems are caused by faulty perceptions or interpretations. Treatments seek to help the client develop more realistic thoughts.

E. The REBT sequence of techniques (ABCDEF) may be used by a therapist in trying to persuade the client to give up his or her irrational beliefs.

F. Beck's cognitive therapy involves the identification of dysfunctional automatic thoughts and cognitive distortions and replacing them with more rational responses.

G. Both types of cognitive therapy generally focus on current problems and often assign between-session homework.

III. Biomedical Therapies

A. Medication is one type of biomedical therapy. Medications are used to treat schizophrenia and mood and anxiety disorders, as well as other disorders.

B. For schizophrenia and other psychotic disorders, traditional antipsychotic medications reduce positive symptoms but can cause serious side effects. Atypical antipsychotic medications can also reduce negative symptoms and have less serious side effects.

C. TCAs, MAOIs, SSRIs, and SNRIs can be used to treat depression. Mood stabilizers such as lithium can help alleviate symptoms of bipolar disorder.

D. Benzodiazepines may be used as a short-term treatment for anxiety disorders. For longer-term treatment, antidepressants can be helpful.

E. Electroconvulsive therapy is used with severely depressed people when other treatments have failed.

F. Treatment by transcranial magnetic stimulation is still considered experimental.

IV. Treatment Variations and Issues

A. Psychological treatment can be provided in a variety of forms, including individual, family, and group therapy; self-help resources include books and tapes, as well as groups such as AA.

B. Systems therapy views a client's symptoms in a family context; it seeks to reduce the symptoms by changing the family system.

C. Therapy protocols and brief therapy have been more widely used in recent years, partly because of the growth of managed care.

D. The answers to various questions about psychotherapy research determine what conclusions can be drawn from the results of a given study and how far the results generalize to other circumstances.

E. Research on psychotherapy shows that, overall, those who receive some type of psychotherapy fare better than those who don't receive any treatment.

F. For some disorders, symptoms can worsen when clients stop taking medication that had been helpful. Beneficial psychotherapies can continue to exert their positive influence after treatment ends.

G. Research shows that certain types of psychotherapy are more effective with certain disorders than with others; for example, exposure with response prevention is a particularly effective treatment for OCD.

H. It is also important to understand the ethnic and cultural factors related to a client's problems and goals.

Key Terms

antipsychotic medication, p. 537
behavior modification, p. 531
behavior therapy, p. 529
benzodiazepine, p. 539
bibliotherapy, p. 544
client-centered therapy, p. 525
cognitive–behavior therapy (CBT), p. 528
cognitive distortions, p. 533
cognitive restructuring, p. 535
cognitive therapy, p. 532
dream analysis, p. 523
electroconvulsive therapy (ECT), p. 540
exposure, p. 530
family therapy, p. 543
free association, p. 523

group therapy, p. 542
incongruence, p. 526
individual therapy, p. 542
insight-oriented therapy, p. 523
interpersonal therapy (IPT), p. 545
interpretation, p. 525
modality, p. 542
monoamine oxidase inhibitor (MAOI), p. 538
outcome research, p. 546
progressive muscle relaxation, p. 531
psychoanalysis, p. 523
psychodynamic therapy, p. 524
psychoeducation, p. 535
psychopharmacology, p. 537
psychotherapy integration, p. 544

resistance, p. 525
selective serotonin reuptake inhibitor (SSRI), p. 538
self-help group, p. 543
self-monitoring techniques, p. 531
serotonin/norepinephrine reuptake inhibitor (SNRI), p. 539
stimulus control, p. 530
systematic desensitization, p. 531
systems therapy, p. 543
tardive dyskinesia, p. 538
technical eclecticism, p. 544
token economy, p. 531
transference, p. 525
tricyclic antidepressant (TCA), p. 538

LOOKING ONLINE: *Enhance Your Learning*

MyPsychLab is an interactive and instructive multimedia resource that can be used to supplement a traditional lecture course or as an online course. It is an all-inclusive tool with a text-specific e-book plus multimedia tutorials, videos, simulations, animations, and controlled assessment to completely engage students and reinforce learning. MyPsychLab meets the individual learning needs of every student. Visit *www.mypsychlab.com* for more information!

Practice Test

For each of the following items, choose the single best answer.

1. During psychoanalysis,
   a. the patient lies on a couch.
   b. the analyst sits in a chair behind the couch, out of the patient's range of sight.
   c. the technique of free association, in which the patient says whatever comes into his or her mind, is often used.
   d. All of the above statements are true.

2. Humanistic therapy
   a. emphasizes the past, mental mechanisms, and the working through of conflictual impulses and feelings.
   b. assumes that problems arise because of a lack of a coherent, unified sense of self.
   c. focuses on the process of transference, in which patients may relate to therapists as they did to some important person in their lives.
   d. emphasizes that the therapist must provide conditional positive regard and unfocused empathy.

3. Behavior therapy
   a. focuses on changing observable, measurable behavior.
   b. emphasizes an unconscious "root cause."
   c. views depressive thoughts as producing depressive feelings and behaviors.
   d. uses a technique called *exposure* that relies on operant conditioning principles.

4. Exposure with response prevention
   a. is a planned, programmatic procedure that exposes the client to the anxiety-provoking object but prevents the usual maladaptive response.
   b. is as effective as medication for obsessive-compulsive disorder (OCD).
   c. can have longer-lasting benefits than medication for OCD.
   d. All of the above statements are true.

5. According to Albert Ellis, one process that interferes with healthy functioning is *low frustration tolerance*, in which a person

   a. is unkind to or critical of others for performing poorly.
   b. blames everyone and everything for "poor, dislikable conditions."
   c. is highly self-critical for "performing poorly or being rejected."
   d. develops logical and rational thoughts as a result of experiences.

6. Beth thinks that if she doesn't get an A on a test, she has failed in life. This is an example of the cognitive distortion called
   a. dichotomous thinking.   c. control beliefs.
   b. mental filtering.   d. mind reading.

7. The use of medication to treat psychological disorders and problems is known as
   a. psychopharmacology.
   b. tardive dyskinesia.
   c. cognitive restructuring.
   d. systematic desensitization.

8. Newer atypical antipsychotic drugs, such as Risperdal,
   a. increase the amount of free serotonin and dopamine available in the brain.
   b. counteract negative symptoms of schizophrenia, such as apathy and lack of interest.
   c. have more side effects than traditional antipsychotic medications.
   d. are not effective in improving cognitive functioning.

9. The tricyclic antidepressants (TCAs)
   a. affect serotonin levels and can take weeks to work.
   b. lead to decreased sexual interest as their most common side effect.
   c. are not as effective as the selective serotonin reuptake inhibitors (SSRIs) for treating depression.
   d. require users not to eat foods with tyramine (such as cheese and wine).

10. Electroconvulsive therapy (ECT)
    a. is most often used to treat anxiety disorders (including panic disorder and the panic symptoms of phobias).
    b. cures schizophrenia but is not a recommended treatment when medication does not work.

c. is particularly helpful in treating certain mood disorders, specifically psychotic depression and manic episodes of bipolar disorder.

d. is now less frequently administered to affluent patients than to those in publicly funded hospitals.

11. A person receiving transcranial magnetic stimulation

a. requires anesthesia.

b. needs to be hospitalized.

c. receives pulses of low-intensity magnetism in the brain in long bursts lasting 5 to 10 minutes.

d. may develop a slight headache, which is the most common short-term side effect.

12. A therapist using psychotherapy integration

a. relies on the use of self-help books and tapes for therapeutic purposes.

b. integrates specific techniques without regard for an overarching theory.

c. uses techniques from different theoretical orientations, with an overarching theory of how the integrated techniques will achieve the goals of treatment.

d. uses the 12-step approach.

13. What does research have to say about the effectiveness of cognitive–behavior therapy (CBT) versus medication for the treatment of panic disorder?

a. CBT is much more effective than medication.

b. Medication is generally more effective than CBT.

c. Medication and CBT work about equally well.

d. Medication does a better job of preventing symptom recurrence than does CBT.

14. *Cuento* therapy

a. uses folktales or stories.

b. has proved helpful with Latino/Latina children.

c. is an example of an attempt that has been made to develop particular therapies for different ethnic groups.

d. All of the above statements are true.

15. Which of the following statements best expresses the relationship between ethnicity and therapy outcome?

a. Ethnicity plays a systematic role in therapy outcomes generally.

b. Some people prefer a therapist from their own ethnic group, and such matching leads to better outcomes for them.

c. There is clear-cut evidence that matching therapist and client by ethnicity results in better outcomes for most ethnic groups.

d. None of the above statements is true.

Answers: 1. d **2.** b **3.** a **4.** d **5.** b **6.** a **7.** a **8.** b **9.** a **10.** c **11.** d **12.** c **13.** c **14.** d **15.** b

chapter 13

Social Psychology

Meeting of the Minds

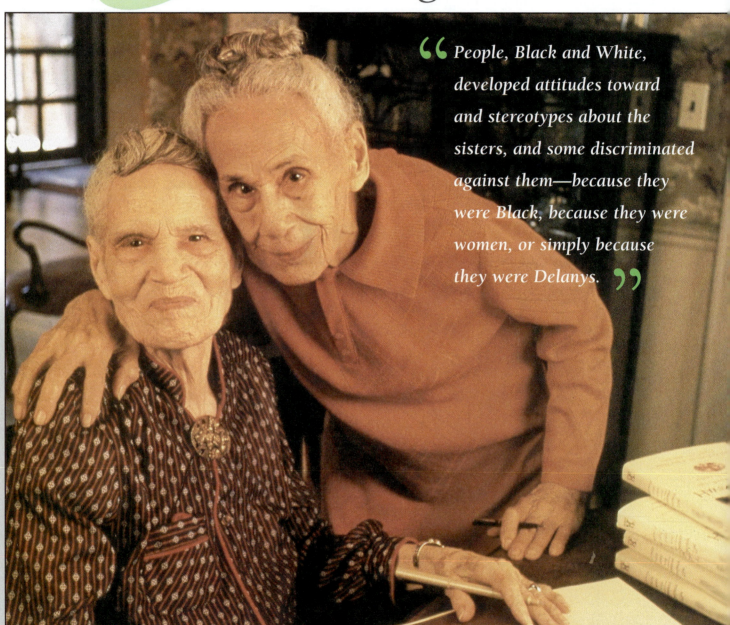

> " People, Black and White, developed attitudes toward and stereotypes about the sisters, and some discriminated against them—because they were Black, because they were women, or simply because they were Delanys. "

CHAPTER OUTLINE

IN 1993, SARAH DELANY, KNOWN AS SADIE, AND HER YOUNGER SISTER ELIZABETH, called Bessie, published their first book, *Having Our Say* (Delany et al., 1993). What's remarkable about these authors is that they were 104 and 102 at the time of publication. Their book recounts the story of their lives, their experiences as Black children and then as Black women during a century of American history. It was during their childhood that the South's Jim Crow laws came into effect, legalizing separate facilities— separate schools, separate water fountains, separate seats on the bus, separate toilets—for Blacks and Whites; it was during their adulthood that these laws were struck down.

Sadie and Bessie had 8 brothers and sisters. Their father, Henry, had been born a slave but was freed by emancipation. He became vice principal of St. Augustine's School (now St. Augustine's College), a Black college in Raleigh, North Carolina. Their mother, Nanny James, who had both Black and White grandparents, was light-skinned. In addition to managing her 10 children, she was the matron of the college, overseeing many of its daily functions. The Delany children were educated at "St. Aug's," where their father also taught.

All 10 Delany children became college-educated professional men and women—a remarkable feat for anyone of that era, regardless of race or sex. Sadie earned both a bachelor's and a master's degree from Columbia University and became a teacher. In 1926, she became the first Black woman appointed to teach home economics at the high school level in New York City. Bessie went to dental school at Columbia in 1923, where she was the only Black woman, and she was the second Black woman licensed to practice dentistry in New York City.

The Delany family, well known in Black society in North Carolina and in New York City's Harlem neighborhood, was considered to be part of an elite group of educated Blacks. But the road was not easy for the sisters. People, Black and White, developed attitudes toward and stereotypes about the sisters, and some discriminated against them—because they were Black, because they were women, or simply because they were Delanys.

Like the Delanys, we are all targets of other people's attitudes and stereotypes, and we have attitudes and stereotypes of our own about other people. And like the Delanys, we all feel pressure from others to behave in certain ways, and we exert pressure on others to behave in certain ways. How we think about other people and interact in relationships and groups is the focus of the subfield of psychology called **social psychology**.

Many of the phenomena psychology seeks to understand—sensation, learning, and memory, to name just a few—take place primarily at the levels of the brain and the person, but are influenced, as shown in the Looking at Levels features in this book, by the environment and the social world. In this chapter, the central emphasis is the level of the group. By definition, social psychology is about our relationships with other people. It focuses on two general topics: the way we think about others (*social cognition*) and the way we act toward them, individually and in groups (*social behavior*). And these interactions affect our thoughts, feelings, behaviors, even our brains. Are there psychological principles that underlie the ways we think about and behave toward other people? If so, what are they?

Social Cognition: Thinking About People

The Delany sisters' parents worked hard to protect their children as much as possible from prejudice, discrimination, and intimidation. They also tried to instill in their children a sense of dignity, self-respect, and respect for and support of others. They encouraged their children to think about the world and their places in it, in specific ways. For example, their parents called each other Mr. and Mrs. Delany in front of others, including their children. This was a conscious decision. It was common for Whites to call Blacks by their first names in instances in which they would use surnames for other Whites; therefore, Mr. and Mrs. Delany deliberately chose to use formal titles to convey respect for each other and the expectation of respect from others.

In this section, we focus largely on the ways people think about other people, in other words, on social cognition—*cognition* because it is about how we think, and *social* because the thoughts involve other people and the social world in general. **Social cognition** does not focus on the "objective" social world, but instead on how individuals perceive their social worlds and how they attend to, store, remember, and use information about other people and the social world.

LOOKING AHEAD: *Learning Objectives*

1. *What is the relationship between people's attitudes and their behaviors?*
2. *What are stereotypes? Why do people have them? What are the differences between stereotypes and prejudice?*
3. *How do we determine responsibility for events and behaviors, and what difference does it make?*

Attitudes and Behavior: Feeling and Doing

When you read or hear the news, your attitudes affect your interpretation of the events being reported. In a smaller arena, your attitudes about people from a particular ethnic group will determine how you feel about them. For instance, your attitude about Blacks will determine how you *feel* about Blacks, which will, in turn, affect how you feel when you read about the Delanys. And in your own circle, if a friend tells you that she's had an abortion, your attitude toward abortion will influence your feelings about your friend. An **attitude** is an overall evaluation about some aspect of the world—people, issues, or objects (Petty & Wegener, 1998). This evaluation has three components: affective, behavioral, and cognitive, summarized by the acronym ABC (Breckler, 1984):

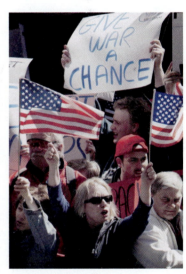

Attitudes can be positive, such as being in favor of energy conservation; negative, such as disliking speed limits on highways; or neutral, such as not being moved one way or the other by a political candidate. The same issue—for instance, whether the U.S. military should intervene in a foreign war—can evoke strong negative or strong positive attitudes. These different evaluations are accompanied by different changes in facial muscles (Cacioppo, Petty, Losch, et al., 1986).

- *Affective* refers to your feelings about the object or issue.
- *Behavioral* refers to your predisposition to act in a particular way toward the object or issue (note that this component does not refer to an actual behavior, but an inclination to behave in a certain way).
- *Cognitive* refers to what you believe or know about the object or issue.

Your attitudes can affect your behavior. The opportunity for the interplay of attitude and behavior can be seen in Sadie's father's comment to her: "Daughter, you are college material. You owe it to your nation, your race, and yourself to go. And if you don't go, then shame on you" (Delany et al., 1993, p. 91). His remarks reflected the components of his attitude toward higher education for Blacks: He was passionately positive about it (affective); his inclination to promote higher education was reflected in his comment to Sadie (behavioral); he had no doubt about the power of education to elevate the position of Blacks in American society (cognitive).

Social cognition: The area of social psychology that focuses on how people perceive their social worlds and how they attend to, store, remember, and use information about other people and the social world.

Attitude: An overall evaluation about some aspect of the world.

When an event is ambiguous, our attitudes can influence our cognitive processing of the event. A study of Princeton and Dartmouth students who watched a motion picture of a controversial Princeton–Dartmouth football game found that, although all students saw the same motion picture of the game, students from the different schools described different events (Hastorf & Cantril, 1954), such as which team started rough play.

Attitudes and Cognitions

Just as attention can play an important role in how we process and remember perceptual information in the physical world (see Chapters 3 and 5), attitudes play an important role in how we process information and remember events in our social world (Eagly & Chaiken, 1998). Particularly in ambiguous social situations, our attitudes help organize events and thus determine what information is attended to, processed, encoded, and remembered. This is one reason why people in the same social situation can come away with different versions of what occurred.

Our attitudes also affect how we shape our goals and expectations and how we interpret obstacles we encounter while trying to achieve our goals, perhaps inducing stress in ourselves through our interpretations. (As a general rule, it is not an event itself, but how it is perceived that determines whether it induces stress; see Chapter 10.) Our attitudes guide us as we selectively evaluate information; generally, we find information that is contrary to our attitudes to be unconvincing, and we may even try to disprove it (Eagly & Chaiken, 1998). As an example, consider the effect of socioeconomic class in the workplace (Gerteis & Savage, 1998). If you think that someone from a lower socioeconomic class will make a bad colleague, you will look for any evidence of shoddy work. You may not notice your colleague's well-performed tasks, and if you do notice them, you make up reasons that discount or discredit your colleague's abilities—perhaps, you say, those are easy tasks.

Predicting Behavior

Attitudes influence behavior, but they do not always lead to behavior that is consistent with them. Several factors determine how likely it is that an attitude toward a behavior will lead to the behavior's occurrence. An attitude is more likely to affect behavior when it is (Eagly & Chaiken, 1998):

- strong,
- relatively stable,
- directly relevant to the behavior,
- important, or
- easily accessed from memory.

For instance, suppose you strongly dislike eating Moroccan food—an attitude. Against your better judgment, you went to a Moroccan restaurant recently and only picked at the food. If a friend invites you today to a meal at a Moroccan restaurant, you are likely to suggest another place to go: Your attitude about Moroccan food is strong, stable, directly relevant to your behavior, and easily accessed from memory. But if you haven't eaten this type of food in years, don't feel that strongly about it now, and have almost forgotten why you ever disliked it, you would be less likely to object to your friend's choice of a Moroccan restaurant (Sanbonmatsu & Fazio, 1990). Attitudes based on indirect experience, such as hearsay, have less influence on behavior than those based on direct experience (Regan & Fazio, 1977).

Behavior Affects Attitudes

If a professor assigned an essay on a topic about which you didn't have very strong feelings (say, supporting curbside recycling versus recycling at a local center), do you think writing the essay would influence your subsequent views? Research has shown that it can: When people are asked repeatedly to assert an attitude on a given topic, thus priming that attitude and making it easier to access, they are more likely to behave in ways consistent with that attitude, compared with those who did not repeatedly express the attitude (Fazio et al., 1982; Powell & Fazio, 1984). In fact, repeatedly asserting an attitude can make the attitude more extreme (Downing et al., 1992).

Cognitive Dissonance

Attitudes and behavior don't always go hand in hand. But most people prefer that their attitudes and behavior are consistent (Snyder & Ickes, 1985). When an attitude and behavior—or two attitudes—are inconsistent, an uncomfortable state that psychologists refer to as **cognitive dissonance** arises. Cognitive dissonance is accompanied by heightened arousal (Losch & Cacioppo, 1990).

Creating Dissonance.   Festinger and Carlsmith's (1959) classic study on cognitive dissonance found that, counterintuitively, participants who were paid less to tell someone that a boring task was enjoyable reported afterward that they enjoyed the task more than those who were paid a greater amount (Figure 13.1). How can we understand this? By the effects of cognitive dissonance reduction. The participants who were paid less, only $1, could not have justified reporting that they enjoyed the task for that amount. To reduce the "dissonance" between what they did and what they received, they appear to have convinced themselves, unconsciously, that they really *did* enjoy the task, so much that they were willing to say that they enjoyed it even though they received little reimbursement. The participants who were paid more felt no such compulsion; the money they received, they apparently felt, adequately compensated them for telling someone that they liked the task. For these participants, there was no dissonance to be resolved. In general, research has shown that the less reason there is to engage in a behavior that is

Cognitive dissonance: The uncomfortable state that arises because of a discrepancy between an attitude and behavior or between two attitudes.

Figure 13.1 Cognitive Dissonance

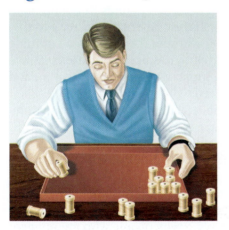

In Festinger and Carlsmith's classic 1959 study, participants were asked to perform a very boring, repetitive task: putting spools on a tray, then dumping them out, and starting all over again.

Participants were given either $1 or $20 (a lot of money in those days) and were then asked to tell another person that the task was, in fact, quite interesting.

After telling the other person about the task, the participants were asked to rate how much they liked the task. Those who were paid $1 to tell the other person that they liked the task reported actually liking the task more than those paid $20 to do so!

Cognitive dissonance can occur when our attitudes and our behavior are inconsistent, even though we have a choice about how to behave.

counter to an attitude, the stronger the dissonance. Cognitive dissonance does not occur with every inconsistency; it is experienced only by people who believe that they have a choice and that they are responsible for their course of action, and thus for any negative consequences (Cooper, 1998; Goethals et al., 1979).

Ask yourself these questions: Do you think that giving to charity (either money or time) is a good thing? Do you think that homeless people should be helped? If you answered "yes" to these questions, when was the last time you donated time or money to help a homeless person? Do you ignore homeless people on the street? You may feel uncomfortable after answering these questions. These feelings arise from the contradiction—the dissonance—between your attitudes about helping the homeless and your behavior related to this issue.

Reducing Dissonance.   Because cognitive dissonance creates an uncomfortable state, we try to decrease it. How do we minimize cognitive dissonance once it has occurred? We can use *indirect strategies*, such as trying to feel good about ourselves in other areas of life, or *direct strategies*, which involve actually changing our attitudes or behavior. Direct strategies also include attempts to obtain additional information supporting our attitude or behavior. Alternatively, we can trivialize an inconsistency between two conflicting attitudes (or between an attitude and a behavior) as being unimportant, and therefore less likely to cause cognitive dissonance (Simon et al., 1995). For example, suppose you really believe in, and talk about, the issue of homelessness and the need to help homeless people. Then a friend points out that you talk about this issue repeatedly but don't do anything about it. This observation would probably induce cognitive dissonance in you. To lessen it, you could use an indirect strategy by telling yourself what a good person you are, or by finding information about how hard it is for one individual to do anything about homelessness, or by simply saying, "Well, my heart's in the right place." Or, you could implement a direct strategy that has an impact on homelessness, such as volunteering to work in a shelter.

Attempts to reduce dissonance can also explain why people who are not generally immoral may act immorally (Tsang, 2002). These individuals can:

1. *change how they understand their immoral act,* in order to see it as having a higher moral purpose or as being less immoral than what some other people do;

2. *minimize their responsibility for it;*

3. *disregard the negative consequences* (by avoiding knowledge of the results or minimizing the harm); or

4. *blame and dehumanize the victims* (Bandura, 1999; Tsang, 2002).

For instance, those otherwise upstanding citizens who cheat on their taxes may tell themselves that it's not really cheating because they:

1. view their lessened tax payment as a protest against a government policy;

2. argue that it's not really their fault, they need the money because the cost of living is so high;

3. claim that the government collects so much money that the small amount they don't pay is totally inconsequential; or

4. blame the President or members of Congress for imposing "such a high income tax" while giving themselves high salaries, lots of perks, and even tax breaks.

Attitude Change: Persuasion

Walking to class, have you ever been approached by someone offering you a leaflet about an upcoming event, a political candidate, or a new product? If so, someone (or some company) was trying to encourage you to do something: go to the event, vote for the candidate, or buy the product. We are bombarded by attempts to change our attitudes about things, through advertisements, editorials, and conversations with friends. These efforts to change our attitudes are called <mark>persuasion</mark>.

Routes to Persuasion.   Petty and Cacioppo (1986), in their *elaboration likelihood model* of attitude change, propose two routes to persuasion: central and peripheral. You are being affected by the *central route* when you pay close attention to the content of the argument—when you carefully read the leaflet to decide whether to attend the event, vote for the candidate, or buy the product. If you already hold the opposite view from that expressed in the leaflet, you will likely only be persuaded by strong arguments. But people who try to persuade us know that we don't always have the time, energy, or expertise to use the central route. Therefore, they may rely instead on the *peripheral route* to persuade us. This route consists of attempts to sway us based not on the content of an argument, but rather on the attractiveness and expertise of the source (as in celebrity endorsements; Hovland & Weiss, 1951; Kiesler & Kiesler, 1969), the number of arguments presented (although not necessarily how "strong" we think they are), or information about how other people respond to the message. Furthermore, the <mark>mere exposure effect</mark> can change attitudes through the peripheral route: Simply becoming familiar with something (being exposed to it) can change your attitude toward it—generally, in a favorable way. And this attitude can generalize to similar objects or people (Zajonc, 2001).

Persuasive People.   Various characteristics of the person who tries to persuade us affect the peripheral route. Fast speakers are generally more persuasive than slow speakers (Miller et al., 1976). Not surprisingly, people who are perceived as honest are more persuasive (Priester & Petty, 1995).

If you've ever heard a Republican speaking to a group of Democrats (or vice versa), you may have noticed a persuasion technique used to convince people who hold the opposite view, whatever that view is: The would-be persuader uses a two-sided approach. That is, he or she presents both sides of an argument rather than only one side (as is common if the audience already agrees with the speaker).

After Katie Couric's colonoscopy was televised live into millions of homes, there was a 20% increase in the number of colonoscopy screenings performed (Dobson, 2002). Using both central and peripheral routes, this televised event undoubtedly persuaded more people to have the same procedure. Can you describe how the two routes to persuasion were used in this situation?

Persuasion: Attempts to change people's attitudes.

Mere exposure effect: The change—generally favorable—in attitude that can result from simply becoming familiar with something.

In an effort to persuade smokers to quit, this ad uses persuasion techniques. Which techniques are at work here?

Persuasive Message.   If an attempt at persuasion arouses strong emotions in you, particularly fear, it is more likely to work, especially if it includes specific advice about what you can do to bring about a more positive outcome (Leventhal et al., 1965). This technique is used in public service messages that try to scare people into behaving differently, such as ads that graphically describe how someone contracted AIDS by not using a condom and then strongly recommend condom use.

When Simplistic Arguments Work.   If you are not paying full attention to an attempt at persuasion, you are less likely to be persuaded by a rational argument that requires you to think deeply, but more likely to be persuaded by a simplistic argument; this comes about at least in part because your inattention makes you less able to develop a counterargument (Allyn & Festinger, 1961; Romero et al., 1996). So, if you are watching a TV commercial while sorting the laundry, you are more likely to be persuaded by it than if you're focused on it.

Social Cognitive Neuroscience

Attitudes are often unconscious, and therefore can be difficult to measure. As we've seen, one way to approach this thorny problem is to tap into unconscious processes by observing telltale behavioral signs (such as those measured by indirect measures). Another way to tap into unconscious processes is to examine the brain itself. **Social cognitive neuroscience** attempts to understand social cognition not only by specifying the cognitive mechanisms (such as those involved in memory, attention, and perception) that underlie it, but also by discovering how those mechanisms are rooted in the brain (Blakemore et al., 2004; D. T. Gilbert, 2002; Heatherton, 2004; Ochsner & Lieberman, 2001). Social cognitive neuroscience bridges cognitive neuroscience and social psychology. On the one hand, as we saw in Chapter 1, cognitive neuroscience rests on the idea that "the mind is what the brain does"—and thus focuses on how mental processes can be related to brain structure and function. On the other hand, the field of social cognition addresses how social events are related to cognitive function. Social cognitive neuroscience ties together the two fields, attempting to fathom how social cognition arises from cognitive processes that, in turn, arise from the brain. This approach allows researchers to use the methods of neuroscience to grapple with questions that cannot easily be answered in other ways.

Here's an example: Do you think that reduction of your cognitive dissonance depends on your consciously noticing the dissonance? The traditional view implies that you reason about the causes of cognitive dissonance in order to reduce this uncomfortable feeling. Lieberman and colleagues (2001) set out to test this idea. They studied patients with brain damage that produced amnesia; these patients could not consciously recall anything they had recently experienced. If you met the most severely affected of these patients, talked to him for 3 hours, and then left the room for 10 minutes, he would have no idea who you were when you returned (Schacter, 1996). Lieberman and colleagues realized that if cognitive dissonance reduction depends on recalling the events that led to the dissonance, then these patients should not experience such reduction. These researchers used a classic way to induce cognitive dissonance: If a researcher gives you two sets of stimuli that you like almost to the same degree and requires you to decide which one you like better, you will end up liking the set you choose even more than you did at first (and disliking the rejected set; Brehm, 1956). Because the two sets are in fact so similar, you can find reasons for liking either one—but when forced to choose, you need to reduce the dissonance that arises from rejecting one that you do in fact like (but a hair less than the other) by ex-

Social cognitive neuroscience: The subfield of psychology that attempts to understand social cognition not only by specifying the cognitive mechanisms that underlie it, but also by discovering how those mechanisms are rooted in the brain.

aggerating the differences between them. The question was, would amnesic patients behave the same way? The answer was yes: Even amnesic patients become more positive about the chosen set and more negative about the rejected one. Their attitudes toward the sets shifted even though these patients had no conscious memory of ever having chosen between the two almost equivalent sets! Thus, the traditional view is wrong: You don't need to be conscious of the causes of dissonance in order to try to reduce it.

The social cognitive neuroscience approach has been used to study a wide range of topics related to social cognition, such as the nature of moral disgust (Moll et al., 2005), empathy (Decety & Jackson, 2004; Ruby & Decety, 2003), and the self (Heatherton et al., 2004; Macrae et al., 2004), and it has even been used to investigate why people rack up credit card debt (Spinella et al., 2004). The examples go on and on.

Stereotypes: Seen One, Seen 'Em All

In the social world we inhabit, we could easily be overwhelmed by the torrent of information conveyed by other people—their words, postures, gestures, and facial expressions—to say nothing of what we can infer about their attitudes and goals, and even what other people have said about them. The world is full of information and stimuli, and if we had no way of organizing this input flying at us from all directions, assaulting our senses, we would live in chaos. In the physical realm, we organize all of this information by principles such as Gestalt groupings of visual stimuli (see Chapter 3). To avoid drowning in this sea of social information, we create stereotypes, which provide cognitive shortcuts for processing all of this information about the social world (Allport, 1954; Gilbert & Hixon, 1991; Macrae et al., 1994). A **stereotype** is a belief (or set of beliefs) about people in a particular category; the category can be defined by race, sex, social class, religion, ethnic background, hair color, sport, hobby, and myriad other characteristics. A stereotype may be positive (such as "women are nurturing"), neutral (such as "Mexicans eat spicy food"), or negative (such as "soccer fans drink too much").

When lawyers select a jury, they try to have certain potential jurors excluded because of stereotypes about how people of a certain race, sex, age, or profession are likely to view the case. But one study found that lawyers' stereotype-based expectations of whether jurors would be likely to convict were often incorrect (Olczak et al., 1991).

Stereotypes Affect Attention, Cognition, and Behavior

Like other types of classification, stereotypes can be useful shortcuts. But stereotypes are caricatures, not reasoned formulations, and they are often incorrect. The effect of errors we make when using stereotypes is anything but trivial. Perhaps because we often strive for cognitive efficiency, we prefer to read information consistent with our stereotypes, and we process such information more quickly (Hugenberg & Bodenhausen, 2004; Smith, 1998). As with attitudes, we are less likely to attend to, and therefore encode or remember, information inconsistent with our stereotypes (Johnston & Macrae, 1994), and, in fact, we may deny the truth of such information (O'Sullivan & Durso, 1984).

Once a stereotype is activated, we respond to a person's membership in the particular category, not to the characteristics of the individual person. Here's how this works. Suppose that you have a positive stereotype of New Englanders, believing them to be punctual and hard-working. When you meet someone from Maine, your "New Englander" stereotype is activated. You will then be more

Stereotype: A belief (or set of beliefs) about people in a particular category.

likely to notice aspects of her behavior that are consistent with your stereotype, and in thinking about her, you will be more likely to remember those aspects. You may not notice when she comes in late, or you will come up with plausible excuses for her tardiness and see it as the exception to the rule. The stereotype thus lives on and may shape your future thinking. One way this influence on thinking occurs is that information relevant to the stereotype is recalled faster than unrelated information (Dovidio et al., 1986). However, if you are motivated to be accurate and do *not* assume that a stereotype applies to a particular individual, you can minimize the impact of stereotypes (Wyer et al., 2000).

Sometimes the conflict between a stereotype and the actual behavior of someone from the stereotyped group is too great to be ignored—but rather than change the stereotype, we are more likely to create a new subtype within it (Anderson, 1983; Anderson et al., 1980). So, for example, if your New England acquaintance's chronic lateness and laziness are too great to ignore, you might create a subtype—"New Englander having a hard time coping." This allows you to preserve your stereotype of New Englanders as punctual and hard-working. Because of this psychological phenomenon—creating subtypes in order to preserve a stereotype—stereotypes can be extremely difficult to change or eliminate. However, under certain circumstances, stereotypes *can* change: when the exception is made to appear typical of its group and when we are encouraged to think that the person's behavior results from his or her characteristics, *not* the situation (Wilder et al., 1996).

Cognition and Prejudice

Stereotyping can lead to **prejudice**, which is an attitude, generally negative, toward members of a group (Arkes & Tetlock, 2004). Prejudice includes not only beliefs and expectations about the group but also an emotional component: Simply thinking about members of a disliked group can produce strong feelings about them (Bodenhausen et al., 1994). As is the case with attitudes and stereotypes, information inconsistent with a prejudice is less likely to be attended to and remembered accurately than is information consistent with a prejudice, making prejudice self-perpetuating.

Prejudice may be conscious and intentional; it may also be conscious and unintentional, or even unconscious and unintentional (Carter & Rice, 1997; Fazio et al., 1995; Greenwald & Banaji, 1995). And emotions can influence prejudice in two ways: The *presence of negative feelings* may account for conscious prejudice, whether intentional or unintentional. But even if someone does not have negative feelings toward a group, prejudice can also arise from the *absence of positive feelings* (Pettigrew & Meertens, 1995); in this case, the prejudice is unconscious (Banaji et al., 2004). Thus, someone can be prejudiced against a group with whom he or she has no experience; for instance, someone from an Asian country might have a prejudice against people with red hair that is engendered by the absence of any positive feelings toward or experiences with such people.

Processes Perpetuating Unconscious Prejudice

Some cognitive operations perpetuate unconscious prejudice. For example, *social categorization* leads people to divide the world automatically into categories of "us" and "them," both consciously and unconsciously. According to *social identity theory* (Tajfel, 1982), in an effort to enhance self-esteem, people usually think of their own group—the **ingroup**—favorably. The other group, the **outgroup**, is usually disliked and assumed to possess more undesirable traits (Brewer & Brown, 1998; Fiske, 1998; Judd et al., 1991; Lambert, 1995; Linville & Fischer, 1993;

Prejudice: An attitude (generally negative) toward members of a group.

Ingroup: An individual's own group.

Outgroup: A group other than an individual's own.

According to social identity theory, members from both of these high school groups view their own group as superior to the other, and these views (conscious or not) may lead to prejudicial behavior against those in the other group.

Rustemli et al., 2000; Vonk & van Knippenberg, 1995). When we identify with an ingroup, we are more inclined to like, trust, help, and cooperate with other ingroup members than we are to like, trust, help, and cooperate with outgroup members (Brewer & Brown, 1998). Our views of the ingroup and the outgroup can lead to unconscious prejudice (DeSteno et al., 2004; Fiske, 2002).

Discrimination

When Bessie Delany was in dental school, a White professor failed her on some work that she knew was good. A White girlfriend, also a dental student, offered to hand in Bessie's work as her own to see what grade the work would be given this time. Bessie's friend passed with the same work that had earned Bessie a failing grade.

Bessie's experience was one of *discrimination*; specifically, she suffered the effect of prejudiced behavior. Her professor's behavior was influenced by his prejudice against Bessie because of her race, her membership in a particular social category. As with stereotypes, people discriminate on the basis of just about anything that distinguishes groups: gender, race, social class, hair color, religion, college attended, height, and on and on. As with prejudice, discrimination may be subtle, and sometimes even unconscious.

Most Americans believe that discrimination is wrong; when their own discriminatory behavior is pointed out to them, they are uncomfortable (Devine & Monteith, 1993), and they may subsequently reduce such behavior (Monteith, 1996). This phenomenon provides another example of the way we act to reduce cognitive dissonance: Becoming aware of the discrepancy between attitudes and behavior leads to the discomfort of cognitive dissonance, which can be reduced through changing future behaviors.

Why Does Prejudice Exist?

The effects of prejudice are limiting, damaging, and painful. Why then does prejudice exist?

Realistic Conflict Theory.   The *realistic conflict theory* (Bobo, 1983) suggests a reason—competition for scarce resources such as good housing, jobs, and

Figure 13.2 The Creation and Dissolution of Prejudice: The Robber's Cave Study

Eleven-year-old boys at a special overnight summer camp (called the Robber's Cave) were the participants in this study. In the initial phase of the study, the boys were randomly divided into two groups and separated from each other for a week. During this time, activities fostered a sense of cohesion in each group.

During the 2-week-long second phase, the two groups competed for highly desired prizes such as pocket knives and medals. Conflict between the two groups quickly escalated from name calling to direct acts (destroying personal property). Negative attitudes as well as negative behavior developed, with each group labeling members of the other with pejorative terms such as "coward."

In the third phase, the two groups were brought together to work on a number of superordinate goals, such as restoring the camp's water supply. Tensions between the groups dissolved by the 6th day of this phase.

schools. As groups compete for these resources, increasingly negative views of the other groups take form, eventually becoming prejudice.

A classic experiment, the Robber's Cave study, showed how easily prejudice can be created from competition (see Figure 13.2; Sherif et al., 1961). A set of 11-year-old boys was divided into two groups, Eagles and Rattlers, at a special overnight camp called the Robber's Cave. The two groups competed for valued prizes. Conflict between the two groups quickly escalated into prejudice and discrimination, with boys from competing groups sometimes calling each other names and even destroying each other's property. However, such attitudes and behavior stopped when the two groups no longer competed for resources but cooperated for larger, mutually beneficial goals such as restoring the camp's water supply. Although the study has several limitations (it is unclear if the findings generalize to girls, non-White boys, or adults), it does illustrate how prejudice can both develop and dissipate (Sherif et al., 1961).

Social Categorization and Social Learning Theories. The Robber's Cave study supports the view of realistic conflict theory that competition between groups for scarce resources can produce prejudice. But are scarcity and competition necessary to produce prejudice? Apparently not. *Social categorization theory* provides one explanation for prejudice in the absence of scarcity or competition: In this view, the psychological forces leading to ingroup favoritism are so powerful that creating even an *arbitrary* "us" and "them" can lead to unconscious favoritism and discriminatory behavior (Feather, 1996; Perdue et al., 1990). This social categorization can lead to discrimination in two distinct ways: (1) The ingroup is actively favored, and (2) the outgroup is actively disfavored.

Although social categorization can perpetuate a skewed picture of other people, it is efficient because once we've made an "us" versus "them" distinction, we can then use our stereotypes about "us" and "them" to understand behavior, saving us the effort of paying close attention to other people and actively processing our observations of their behavior. Because we expect certain behaviors from outgroup members, just being in their presence can activate our stereotypes about them (Bargh et al., 1996). We may then behave in ways that elicit behavior from an outgroup member that is consistent with that stereotype, even if he or she wouldn't otherwise behave that way (Major & O'Brien, 2005; Snyder, 1984, 1992). This process thus becomes a self-fulfilling prophecy: The elicited behavior confirms our stereotype, and we regard the outgroup member's behavior as "proof" of the validity of our prejudices (Fiske, 1998). However, our goals in a given situation or interaction can lessen the use of these cognitive shortcuts: If it is important to be accurate in our view of an outgroup member, we are more motivated to think actively, and perhaps accurately, about that person (Fiske, 1998).

Once a prejudicial attitude is in place, *social learning theory* (see Chapter 4) explains how it can be spread and passed through generations as a learned stereotype. Parents, peers, television, movies, and other aspects of the culture provide models of prejudice (Pettigrew, 1969). When prejudice is translated into words and actions, it may be reinforced. Scarce resources, competition, natural cognitive mechanisms, and learning may all contribute to the development and maintenance of prejudice.

Changing Prejudice: Easier Said Than Done

Psychology has shown us how prejudice develops and deepens. Equally important, can psychology show us how to arrest the development of prejudice? The answer is yes, but the task is not easily accomplished.

Increased Contact. One method of decreasing prejudice is described by the *contact hypothesis*, which holds that increased contact between different groups will decrease prejudice between them (Pettigrew, 1981). Increased contact serves several purposes:

1. Both groups are more likely to become aware of similarities between the groups, which can enhance mutual attraction.
2. Even though stereotypes resist change, when stereotypic views are met with enough inconsistent information or exceptions, those views *can* change (Kunda & Oleson, 1995).
3. Increased contact can shatter the illusion that the outgroup is homogeneous (Baron & Byrne, 1997).

Increased contact does reduce prejudice (Emerson et al., 2002), particularly under certain conditions, as when people are working toward a shared goal and all of those involved are deemed to be equal.

Recategorization. Another way to decrease prejudice is through recategorization—that is, shifting the categories of "us" and "them" so that the two groups are no longer distinct entities. Examples of recategorization are familiar in everyday life. An assembly-line worker who is promoted to management experiences recategorization: The identity of "us" and "them" changes. When distinctions between groups are minimized so that different groups can be thought of as a single entity, recategorization can decrease prejudice. Working together toward a common goal facilitates recategorization, as occurred in the

Recategorization: A means of reducing prejudice by shifting the categories of "us" and "them" so that the two groups are no longer distinct entities.

Many science fiction stories rely on recategorization to shift the animosity from country against country to a united Earth defending against a common enemy—aliens. Recategorization may decrease prejudice toward the new members of the ingroup, but some outgroup will undoubtedly still be thought of negatively (Tajfel, 1982). In the movie *Men In Black*, humans are allied with some aliens—a new definition of "us"—against a different type of alien.

Robber's Cave study when, instead of being Eagles or Rattlers, all boys became simply campers who had no running water.

Mutual Interdependence. Social psychologist Eliot Aronson and his colleagues devised another way to decrease prejudice, which has been used in many American classrooms. This technique, called the *jigsaw classroom*, is a cooperative learning technique (Aronson & Osherow, 1980; Aronson & Patnoe, 1997). Integrated groups of five or six students from different backgrounds are formed and given an assignment, such as learning about the American War of Independence (see Figure 13.3). Each member of a jigsaw group researches a different aspect of the project (such as military strategy, George Washington's actions, women's roles); after doing their separate research, the students researching the same topic form a new group—an expert group—composed of one member from each jigsaw group. For instance, all students researching George Washington will meet together after doing their research; this is the "George Washington" expert group. These expert groups meet to share information and rehearse presentations. The expert groups then disband, and each member writes a report and reads it to his or her original jigsaw group. The only way that jigsaw group members can learn about all of the topics is to pay close attention to everyone's reports; as with a jigsaw puzzle, each member's contribution is a piece of the whole, and each person depends on the

Figure 13.3 The Jigsaw Classroom

The classroom is divided into groups of 5 or 6 children from different backgrounds (jigsaw groups), and each group studies the same general subject. The general subject has 5 or 6 separate research topics, and each group member is assigned a different topic to research.

After each student does his or her research, they reconfigure into expert groups, where one member from each jigsaw group meets with his or her counterparts from the other groups. Expert groups discuss the results of their research and practice their presentations. This is the "George Washington" expert group.

Each member of the jigsaw group presents his or her research to the rest of the group. Every student is tested on all of the information, so students must listen closely to every presentation. This method fosters interdependence and mutual respect and reduces prejudice.

others. The jigsaw classroom decreases prejudice (Aronson & Osherow, 1980; Walker & Crogan, 1998) in ways similar to other techniques: by increasing contact between individuals from different "groups" and creating new, integrated groups that require mutual interdependence in order to achieve a superordinate goal.

Attributions: Making Sense of Events

When you read about the Delany sisters' successes, how did you explain them? Did you say to yourself, "The sisters worked hard and persevered," or "They were lucky"? Whatever your reaction, it reflects not only your attitudes, stereotypes, and prejudices, but the attributions you make. **Attributions** are our explanations for the causes of events or behaviors.

What Is the Cause?

Usually, events and actions have many possible causes. An unreturned telephone call to a friend might be an indication that your friend is very busy, is annoyed at you, or is simply having problems with voice-mail. If a politician you admire changes position on an issue, do you explain the behavior as a sincere change of heart, a cave-in to heavy campaign contributors, or a calculated attempt to appeal to new supporters?

The particular attributions people make are of two broad types: internal and external. **Internal attributions** (also called *dispositional attributions*) explain a person's behavior in terms of that person's preferences, beliefs, goals, or other characteristics. For instance, if a friend leaves a math lecture very confused, you could attribute his confusion to internal factors: "I guess he's not very good at math." **External attributions** (also called *situational attributions*) explain a person's behavior in terms of the situation (Kelley, 1972; Kelley & Michela, 1980). If you make an external attribution for your friend's confusion, you might say, "The professor gave a really bad lecture today."

The attributions you make about events affect both you and other people (see Table 13.1): Blaming yourself for negative events (internal attribution) can suppress your immune system (Segerstrom et al., 1996; see Chapter 10). Blaming yourself or others affects behavior: Mothers who view their children's misbehavior as the children's fault are likely to discipline their children more harshly than mothers who attribute such misbehavior to other causes, such as their own parenting practices (Slep & O'Leary, 1998).

Taking Shortcuts: Attributional Biases

Like stereotypes, **attributional biases** are cognitive shortcuts for determining attributions that generally occur outside our awareness. They help lessen the cognitive load required to make sense of the world, but they can lead to errors. These errors have implications for social relationships, the legal system, and social policy.

Table 13.1 Examples of Types of Attributions

	Internal Attributions	External Attributions
Attributions About Oneself	*Positive*: I did a good job because I'm smart. *Negative*: I did a bad job because I'm inept.	*Positive*: I did a good job because the task was easy. *Negative*: I did a bad job because the time allotted for the task was too short.
Attributions About Others	*Positive*: She did a good job because she's smart. *Negative*: She did a bad job because she's inept.	*Positive*: She did a good job because the task was easy. *Negative*: She did a bad job because the time allotted for the task was too short.

Attribution: An explanation for the cause of an event or behavior.

Internal attribution: An explanation of someone's behavior that focuses on the person's preferences, beliefs, goals, or other characteristics; also called *dispositional attribution*.

External attribution: An explanation of someone's behavior that focuses on the situation; also called *situational attribution*.

Attributional bias: A cognitive shortcut for determining attribution that generally occurs outside of conscious awareness.

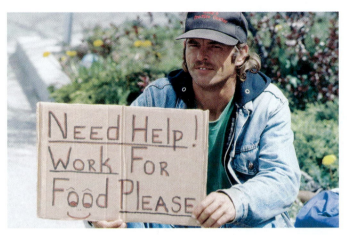

When you see a homeless person, to what do you attribute his or her homelessness? Chances are that the correspondence bias is at work if you assume that his or her plight is due to an internal trait such as laziness rather than to external factors such as a run of bad luck, a high unemployment rate, and a lack of affordable housing.

Correspondence bias: The strong tendency to interpret other people's behavior as due to internal (dispositional) causes rather than external (situational) ones.

Self-serving bias: A person's inclination to attribute his or her own failures to external causes and own successes to internal causes, but to attribute other people's failures to internal causes and their successes to external causes.

The Correspondence Bias. Suppose, for example, you are a member of a jury and hear that the defendant confessed to the crime. It turns out that the confession was extracted after many hours of tough, coercive questioning by police. The judge then throws out the confession, striking it from the record, and tells you, the jury, to ignore it. Would you? Could you? Researchers using mock juries found that jurors in this situation assume that the confession was heartfelt and vote guilty more often than jurors who do not hear about a confession (Kassin & Wrightsman, 1981). The jurors are demonstrating the **correspondence bias** (also called the *fundamental attribution error*; Ross et al., 1977), the strong tendency to interpret other people's behavior as caused by internal causes rather than external ones. In the courtroom example, jurors would thus be more likely to view the confession as evidence of guilt (an internal attribute) than coercion (an external attribute). You are even likely to assume that other people fall prey to the correspondence bias more than you do, at least if you are from an individualist culture (Van Boven et al., 2003).

The correspondence bias is one of the most common attributional biases and a frequent source of error. This bias is at work, for example, when the sight of a homeless man on a bench leads us to assume his plight is due to an internal trait such as laziness rather than external factors such as a run of bad luck, a high unemployment rate, and a lack of affordable housing, or when a driver cuts in front of you on the road, and you attribute his lack of road etiquette to his despicable personality traits rather than situational factors (J. S. Baxter et al., 1990). The correspondence bias helps perpetuate discrimination because fault is attributed to the person, not to the circumstances. Once the correspondence bias shapes how you understand a particular person's behavior, you are likely to ignore the context of future behavior (that is, the surrounding situation), and thus the effect of the initial error is multiplied.

Self-Serving Bias. Related to the correspondence bias is the **self-serving bias** (Brown & Rogers, 1991; Miller & Ross, 1975), the inclination to attribute your failures to external causes and your successes to internal ones, but to attribute other people's failures to internal causes and their successes to external causes. As a result, you consider the negative actions of others as arbitrary and unjustified, but perceive your own negative actions as understandable and justifiable (Baumeister et al., 1990). You are angry and slam things around because you've had a terrible day; your roommate throws tantrums because he or she has an awful temper. A culture, ethnic group, or nation as a whole may engage in this type of bias, attributing positive values and traits to its own group and negative values and traits to other groups, thereby sustaining ethnic or cultural conflict (Rouhana & Bar-Tal, 1998).

Not all cultures exhibit these various biases to the same degree. Just as different cultures promote different personality traits (see Chapter 8), they also lead people to use attributional biases somewhat differently. For example, accounts of

Because of the self-serving bias, you are likely to believe that you are kinder, more generous, and more selfless than other people. Research suggests that you probably overestimate your own generosity, rather than underestimating that of other people (Epley & Dunning, 2000).

crimes in Chinese-language newspapers are more likely to give external explanations for the criminals' behavior, whereas for the same offense, English-language newspapers are more likely to emphasize internal factors (Morris & Peng, 1994).

Belief in a Just World. Attributions can also be distorted by a **belief in a just world** (Lerner, 1980), the assumption that people get what they deserve; this contrasts with the assumption that untoward events can happen randomly and "justice" may not always prevail. Because most Americans are richer than most Egyptians, Colombians, or Bulgarians, they must, according to this bias, also be smarter or work harder. According to the belief in a just world, if you get what you deserve, you must have done something to deserve what you get—notice the circular reasoning here!

The belief in a just world can shape reactions to violent crime (particularly rape; Karuza & Carey, 1984), and it contributes to the practice of blaming the victim. For example, those who strongly believe in a just world are more likely than others to view AIDS as a deserved punishment for homosexual behavior (Glennon & Joseph, 1993) and to view the plight of a disadvantaged group, such as immigrants, as deserved (Dalbert & Yamauchi, 1994). The belief in a just world can maintain discriminatory behaviors (Lipkus & Siegler, 1993). However, when individuals identify with victims, as occurred for many Americans in the weeks and months after September 11, 2001, rather than blame the victims, the belief in a just world was associated with a desire for revenge 2 months after the attacks (Kaiser et al., 2004). People may make an attribution based on the belief in a just world when their sense of justice has been violated; in order restore a sense of order and justice, they seek to see the people hurt by the untoward event as somehow undeserving of their plight (Hafer & Bègue, 2005).

LOOKING BACK: *Review*

1. *What is the relationship between people's attitudes and their behaviors?* Attitudes affect how we process, encode, and remember information about the social world. Attitudes that are strong, stable, relevant, important, and readily accessible are likely to affect behavior. Attitudes and future behavior can change as a result of cognitive dissonance and persuasion. A persuader is more likely to facilitate attitude change if he or she is an expert, is attractive, speaks quickly, or is perceived as honest.

2. *What are stereotypes? Why do people have them? What are the differences between stereotypes and prejudice?* Stereotypes are beliefs or sets of beliefs about people in a particular social category; these beliefs help us to organize efficiently, though perhaps incorrectly, the large amount of information presented by the social world. These cognitive shortcuts can be outside of our awareness and are resistant to change. Prejudice is an attitude that contains a generally negative view toward members of a group; prejudice can be either conscious or unconscious, intentional or unintentional. Prejudice can arise from negative feelings or from the absence of positive feelings. Social categorization and other cognitive operations can account for the perpetuation of unconscious prejudice.

3. *How do we determine responsibility for events and behaviors, and what difference does it make?* Attributions are ways we explain the cause of events or behaviors. There are two types of attributions: internal (dispositional) and external (situational). The fundamental attribution error, the self-serving bias, and the belief in a just world can lead to incorrect attributions.

● *If you were to design an antismoking campaign based on your knowledge of persuasion and stereotypes, what strategies might you include?*

What psychological factors might explain the ways in which people attribute their success in quitting or their failure to quit smoking?

If you wanted to help people resist the pull of advertisements or political campaigns, what information would be particularly important to convey? Explain.

Social Behavior: Interacting With People

The Delanys had very definite ideas about how they were supposed to behave with people. Based on their ideas about marriage, both Sadie and Bessie decided early on not to marry. They both wanted careers, and women of that era often had to choose between a career and marriage. Moreover, their father instilled in them a sense of self-reliance, as evidenced in his advice to Sadie about going to Columbia University: He advised her not to take a scholarship because she might then feel indebted to the people who offered it. He encouraged her to pay for her own education.

The Delanys also had definite ideas about how other people should be treated. They were taught to help others, regardless of skin color; the family motto was "Your job is to help someone." The Delanys stuck by their beliefs, even when others did not agree. Bessie recounted a time she vacationed in Jamaica with a darker-skinned Jamaican-born friend. There, Bessie learned that there were two official classes of Jamaican Negroes: "White Negroes," who had more privileges in society, and "Black Negroes," who were considered to be in a lower social class. The young women stayed with the family of Bessie's friend, who was a "Black Negro." "White Negroes" extended invitations to Bessie (a lighter-skinned Black woman) and ignored her friend. Bessie refused all invitations until her friend was invited as well.

Whereas social cognition pertains to individuals' perceptions of the social world, social behavior pertains to diverse types of behavior—from intimate relationships to obedience—that occur in and are affected by social situations.

LOOKING AHEAD: *Learning Objectives*

1. *What psychological principles explain why we like certain people and not others?*

2. *Why do all groups have rules for social behavior and organization?*

3. *Why do we sometimes "go along with" or obey others even when we don't want to? What makes us able to refuse?*

4. *Does being part of a group change our behavior? How do groups make decisions?*

5. *Are some people more helpful than others? What makes us likely to help other people?*

Relationships: Having a Date, Having a Partner

Sadie and Bessie's White maternal great-great-grandmother had a liaison with a slave while her husband was away fighting in the War of 1812. This relationship produced two daughters, half-sisters to the seven children she had already had with her husband. When her husband returned home, he adopted the two girls as his own. No one knew exactly what happened to her lover, although it was rumored that he ran away on the husband's return. The relationship between the Delanys' great-great-grandmother and biological great-great-grandfather would appear to have been based on more than a passing interest, given that the relationship spanned a number of years. Why were they attracted to each other? Why are we attracted to certain people? Why do we like particular people, and love others?

As the Delany children's ancestors undoubtedly experienced almost two centuries ago, and you may be experiencing now, relationships are strong stuff. They can lead to our most positive emotions and, as you saw in Chapter 10, can help us cope with events outside the relationship (Berscheid & Reis, 1998). They can also be the source of negative emotions: When asked about the "last bad thing that happened to you," almost half the respondents reported conflict in a significant relationship (Cupach & Spitzberg, 1994).

Liking: To Like or Not to Like

Even though Sadie and Bessie decided not to marry, they did have boyfriends. Why were they attracted to certain men—why are you attracted to some people and not others?

Repeated Contact. First impressions play an initial role, as does *repeated contact*, which usually leads to a more positive evaluation of someone (Moreland & Zajonc, 1982; Zajonc, 1968). The Delany sisters recount that a lot of "racial mixing, especially after slavery days, was just attraction between people, plain and simple, just like happened in our family, on Mama's side. You know, when people live in close proximity, they can't help but get attracted to each other" (Delaney et al., 1993, p. 76).

Similarity. *Similarity* is a second factor in the development of liking; the more similar a stranger's attitudes are to your own, the more likely you are to be attracted (Montoya & Horton, 2004; Tesser, 1993). The adage "Opposites attract" has *not* been borne out by research. Similarity of preferred activities (Lydon et al., 1988), even similar ways of communicating, can lead to increased attraction and liking. For instance, we are more likely to be attracted to someone whose nonverbal cues are the same as those used in our own culture (Dew & Ward, 1993). In general, the greater the similarity, the more probable it is that our liking for another person will endure (Byrne, 1971).

Attraction. A third, and major, factor is *physical attraction* (Collins & Zebrowitz, 1995; Hatfield & Sprecher, 1986). In part, the role of physical attraction in liking may be influenced by our stereotypes about attractive people—such as that they are smarter and happier. Although the stereotype that people who are physically more attractive possess more desirable attributes is found in various cultures, what constitutes "more desirable" differs across cultures. For instance, in Korea, attractive people are thought to have greater integrity and concern for others—qualities more valued in that collectivist culture than in individualist

Recent research recognizes that physical distance may no longer be as important as it once was for defining "repeated contact": Internet chat rooms and interest groups make it possible for a couple to "meet" and have a relationship without any physical contact (Bargh et al., 2002; McKenna et al., 2002; Parks & Roberts, 1998).

Western ones (Wheeler & Kim, 1997; see Chapters 7 and 8 for discussion of collectivist versus individualist cultures).

Loving: How Do I Love Thee?

Despite all the poems and plays, novels and movies, that chronicle, celebrate, and analyze love, its mystery endures. Its variations, components, styles, and fate over time have all been examined by psychologists. Loving appears to be a qualitatively different feeling from liking, not simply very strong liking (Rubin, 1970). Moreover, attitudes about and experiences with love appear to be similar across cultures as diverse as those of Russia, Japan, and the United States (Sprecher, Aron, et al., 1994).

Types of Love. People talk about "loving" all sorts of things in all sorts of ways. You might say you love a pet, a friend, a parent, a mate, and pizza with anchovies; obviously you don't mean quite the same thing in each case. Love is usually studied in the context of relationships. **Passionate love**—the intense, often sudden feeling of being "in love"—involves sexual attraction, a desire for mutual love and physical closeness, arousal, and a fear that the relationship will end. **Companionate love** is marked by very close friendship, mutual caring, liking, respect, and attraction (Caspi & Herbener, 1990).

Dimensions of Love. What do the various sorts of love have in common, and how can we understand their differences? Robert Sternberg has proposed a **triangular model of love** (1986a, 1988a). Love, he says, has three dimensions:

1. *passion* (including sexual desire),
2. *intimacy* (emotional closeness and sharing), and
3. *commitment* (the conscious decision to be in the relationship).

Particular relationships reflect different proportions of each dimension, in amounts that are likely to vary over time (see Figure 13.4). According to Sternberg's theory, most types of love relationships involve two of the three components; only "consummate love" has passion, intimacy, *and* commitment.

Figure 13.4 Sternberg's Triangular Model of Love

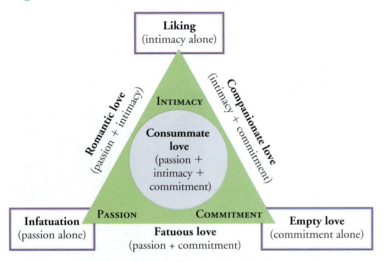

According to Sternberg's triangular theory of love, passion, intimacy, and commitment form three points of a triangle. Any given relationship may have only one component (at a point), two components (one of the sides of the triangle), or all three components (the center of the triangle).

Passionate love: An intense feeling that involves sexual attraction, a desire for mutual love and physical closeness, arousal, and a fear that the relationship will end.

Companionate love: A type of love marked by very close friendship, mutual caring, liking, respect, and attraction.

Triangular model of love: The theory that love has three dimensions: passion (including sexual desire), intimacy (closeness), and commitment.

Love: Attachment Styles. Attachment style is another way of thinking about different kinds of love relationships. As discussed in Chapter 8, the attachment style shown with a partner stems from the interaction pattern developed between parent and child (Waller & Shaver, 1994). For instance, adults who seek closeness and interdependence in relationships and are not worried about the possibility of the loss of the relationship, about 59% of an American sample, are said to have a *secure* style of attachment (Mickelson et al., 1997). Those who are uncomfortable with intimacy and closeness, about 25% of an American sample, have an *avoidant* style and structure their daily lives so as to avoid closeness (Tidwell et al., 1996). Those who want but simultaneously fear a relationship have an *anxious–ambivalent* style (Hazan & Shaver, 1990); about 11% of Americans have this style. Although these studies indicate that a majority of Americans have a secure attachment style (Hazan & Shaver, 1987), an anxious–ambivalent style is more common in Japan and Israel, and an avoidant style more common in Germany (Shaver & Hazan, 1994).

Mating Preferences: Your Cave or Mine?

Is love the reason people settle down and have children? According to evolutionary theory, those couples among our ancestors who were more closely bonded to each other and to their children were more likely to have offspring who survived. Thus, evolutionary theorists propose, humans today are genetically predisposed not only to search for sex but also to fall in love and to tend to their children (Trivers, 1972).

Evolutionary Reasons for Mate Selection.

Finding someone attractive and liking, or even loving, that person is different from choosing him or her as a mate; we may date people we wouldn't necessarily want to marry. Why do we view certain people as potential mates, and not others? Evolutionary theorists propose that a reason why men are attracted by a well-proportioned body and symmetrical features is that these characteristics, along with other features, signal fertility and health (Thornhill & Gangestad, 1993). This view is supported by research with identical female twins; the twin whose face was more symmetrical was rated as more attractive (Mealey et al., 1999). In contrast, women find men attractive who appear to be able to protect and nourish them and their children; in modern society, researchers translate this characteristic as having good earning potential (Buss, 1989, 1999; Sprecher et al., 1994).

Evolutionary psychologists have argued that characteristics associated with reproduction are particularly likely to have been shaped by natural selection. David Buss (1989) asked people in 37 countries to rank 18 different characteristics in order of how important those are in ideal mates. In most respects, men and women valued the characteristics similarly; everybody agreed, for example, that kindness and intelligence are of paramount importance, and that emotional stability, dependability, and a good disposition are important (similar findings are reported by Cramer et al., 1996; Li et al., 2002). Respondents also valued mutual attraction and love. However, men and women did not have identical desires: Men tended to focus on physical attractiveness, whereas women tended to focus on wealth and power. Basing his view on evolutionary theory (Trivers, 1972, 1985), Buss (1994) has argued that women seek characteristics in men that would direct resources to their children, whereas men seek characteristics in women that indicate high fertility.

Mate Selection: Not Just for Evolutionary Reasons.

Ann Speed and Steven Gangestad (1997) found slightly different results when they collected less subjective ratings. In their study, they asked members of a sorority and a fraternity to nominate other members whom they felt scored high on specific qualities such as physical attractiveness and likelihood of financial success. The investigators then examined which of these characteristics predicted the frequency with which those nominated were asked out on dates. Perhaps the most interesting results concerned the men. As expected, romantically popular men were seen by their peers as confident, outgoing, and "trend-setting." However, they were not seen as likely to succeed financially or as being the best leaders, both characteristics that

Evolutionary theorists propose that women are attracted to men who will be good providers, and men are attracted to women who have physical attributes associated with fertility. However, not all research supports this view: As women gain more economic power, they become more interested in a man's attractiveness.

What constitutes an "attractive" body type differs over time and across cultures. Women who today would be considered overweight or even obese in the United States have a body type that has been and continues to be attractive in some other cultures.

would seem to reflect the qualities that evolution is supposed to favor in males. Mate selection is not just about evolutionarily relevant characteristics.

Other studies have shown that as women come to have more economic power, their preference in mates becomes more similar to men's—that is, physical attractiveness becomes more important (Eagly & Wood, 1999; Gangestad, 1993). Women's preference for men who make good providers may reflect women's historic economic dependence on men rather than a true biological preference. In general, then, the sex differences are more pronounced in studies that use self-reports than in ones that measure actual behavior (Feingold, 1990) and in situations in which women have less economic power.

However, evolution is more than natural selection (see Chapters 1 and 2); we have inherited some characteristics not because they are adaptive in themselves but rather because they are associated with other characteristics that are adaptive. Nor are the brain's circuits all dictated from birth: Learning changes the brain's neural connections, and development itself allows the environment to shape the way the brain works. Moreover, culture obviously plays an important role in shaping mate preferences: What is deemed an attractive body type changes with time (Wolf, 1991). Also, the characteristics that make a man a good provider depend in part on the culture and the individual's role in it; the traits that make a man a good rancher are not necessarily those of a good stockbroker. In short, it would be a serious error to assume that what people find attractive or unattractive in a potential mate can be entirely explained by analyses of what might have been useful for mating among our distant ancestors.

The military tries to instill a sense of "groupness" in new recruits: The group's goal, such as a successful military action, is supposed to become more important than an individual's goal, such as staying alive.

Group: A social entity characterized by regular interaction among members, some emotional connection, a common frame of reference, and a degree of interdependence.

Social Organization: Group Rules, Group Roles

If you live with other people, in the same apartment or on the same dorm floor, you might agree that the people in your living unit constitute a group, even if you don't get along. But if you live in a building with a number of apartments, or a residence hall with many floors, would everyone living there be considered part of a group, even if they don't all know one another? What, exactly, constitutes a group? Social psychologists have long wrestled with such questions and have come up with a number of definitions. There are some commonalities, though, in the use of the term **group**: regular interaction among members, some type of social or emotional connection with one another, a common frame of reference, and some type of interdependence (Levine & Moreland, 1998). In a group, each of us may feel, think, and act less from the point of view of an individual and more from the point of view of a group member. Military training, such as boot camp, is a dramatic example of a situation that promotes the shift from feeling like an individual to feeling like a group member: Loyalties and actions are no longer driven by individual goals but by group goals.

At the other extreme of group experience is **deindividuation**, traditionally defined as the loss of sense of self that occurs when people in a group are literally *anonymous*—their identities are unknown to others in the group. This is often the situation in crowds. With deindividuation, attention is focused on external events, and a high level of arousal is experienced (Diener, 1977). When this occurs, people respond to external cues and immediate feelings and act on them without monitoring the appropriateness of their behaviors. Violence by fans at European soccer matches has usually been explained as arising from deindividuation. However, a meta-analytic study on deindividuation suggests that loss of self is not the precipitating cause of the behaviors attributed to deindividuation, as has traditionally been thought. Rather, the behaviors result from the sense, shared by members of the crowd, that certain behaviors are permissible in the particular circumstances that would not be acceptable otherwise (Postmes & Spears, 1998).

Disappointed fans riot at a European soccer game. Are they violent because they've become deindividuated? Probably not. In this case, they engage in situation-specific behaviors that are inconsistent with general expectations of appropriate behavior.

Norms: The Rules of the Group

The Delany sisters recount that in their hometown of Raleigh, North Carolina, even strangers passing on the street would nod and say good morning or good evening. But when Sadie and Bessie moved to New York City, they discovered that courteous behavior toward strangers did not always bring about a pleasant exchange, and they had to learn a new way of behaving in their new social context. Perhaps you, like them on their arrival in New York, have at one time or another been the "new kid on the block"—in school or college, in a new neighborhood, in an already established group of people. Chances are you didn't know the "rules"—how people were supposed to behave toward one another, and especially how you, a new member, were supposed to behave. Once you figured things out by watching other people (Gilbert, 1995)—an obvious case of observational learning—you probably felt more comfortable in the group. And, in fact, groups create such rules and structures to help the group function.

The rules that implicitly or explicitly govern members of a group are called **norms**. They are, in essence, shared beliefs that are enforced through the group's use of *sanctions*, or penalties (Cialdini & Trost, 1998). Just as individuals have attitudes, groups have norms (Wellen et al., 1998). Norms pervade our everyday experience, defining the behaviors that make us good family members, friends, neighbors, partners, employees, employers, students, teachers, and so on. Norms guide us in what we say—and don't say—in chat rooms and e-mail exchanges (Bargh & McKenna, 2004).

Although norms can endure over time, even if the members of the group change (Jacobs & Campbell, 1961), norms can also change. This is the case for the use of "Ms." When this form of address was introduced, it was seen as one that would be used only by radical feminists. Now, however, it is much more widely used and positively viewed (Crawford et al.,

Deindividuation: The loss of sense of self that occurs when people in a group are anonymous.

Norm: A shared belief that is enforced through a group's use of penalties.

Norms can affect all kinds of behavior, including a cold sufferer's willingness to wear a surgical mask when out in public. This Japanese woman is behaving according to one of her culture's norms: It is frowned on for a cold sufferer to go outside without a mask and spread cold germs to others.

1998). Another example of changing norms is found among adolescents in India who watch Western TV shows (and derive from them what they perceive of as Western norms). Their attitudes about drugs, alcohol, and sex change, and they reject the social norms of Indian society and become more Western (Varma, 2000).

Roles: Expected Behaviors

In contrast to norms, **roles** are the behaviors that members in different positions in a group are expected to perform. Groups often create different roles to fulfill different group functions. Sometimes roles are assigned officially, as when a group votes for a leader; sometimes roles are filled informally, without a specific election or appointment. Roles help a group delineate both responsibility *within* the group and responsibility *to* the group.

When Roles Become Reality: The Stanford Prison Experiment

In the summer of 1971, nine Stanford University students were apparently arrested in Palo Alto, some searched spread-eagle style against a city police car. They were read their Miranda rights, and thrown into prison. Despite the fact that all nine knew that they were innocent of the crime they were accused of—armed robbery and burglary—the group soon adopted a prisoner-like mentality. In fact, the nine prisoners, like the nine guards who watched over them, were all participants in a psychological study.

This study later became famous, and it is now known as the *Stanford Prison Experiment* (Haney et al., 1973; Haney & Zimbardo, 1976; Zimbardo et al., 2000). Earlier that August, Professor Philip Zimbardo had placed the following ad in the local newspaper, the *Palo Alto Times*: "Male college students needed for psychological study of prison life. $15 per day for 1–2 weeks. . . ." Some 70 people applied, and the 24 judged to be most healthy and "normal" (having no history of psychological problems or past problems with the police or drugs) were selected. Half of these students were randomly assigned (by flipping a coin) to be guards and half to be prisoners. Of these, 9 students actually played guards, and 9 played prisoners; the others were backups, in case they later were needed.

In the Stanford Prison Experiment, student guards fell into their new roles easily, exploring their power. Student prisoners, in turn, reacted to their new status by staging a rebellion.

Student prisoners received prison uniforms, stayed in cells, and were referred to only by a number—all of which served as regular reminders of their new status. The guards, on the other hand, were given uniforms, handcuffs, keys, whistles, and billy clubs. The guards had offices, which—unlike the prisoners' cells—they were free to enter and leave as they pleased. The guards habitually wore mirrored sunglasses, which were intended to disorient the prisoners by cutting them off from many common social cues. These students were not given any specific training or instructions, other than to maintain "law and order" and to behave in a way that would command the respect of the prisoners.

The purpose of the experiment was to observe how the relationships between prisoners and guards developed over time. In remarkably short order, prisoners behaved passively, as if they realized that since they had no control over what happened to them, they should stop trying. In contrast, the guards began to act as if they had genuine power over the prisoners and to explore the limits of that power. Some, but not all, of the guards taunted the prisoners and harassed them (such as by sliding their billy clubs across the bars, causing a click-clacking repetitive slapping sound). After a while, the prisoners became

Role: The behaviors that a member in a given position in a group is expected to perform.

active, staging a rebellion. The guards responded with force and put the rebellion's readers in solitary confinement.

Zimbardo later reported that he was shocked at how quickly and deeply the prisoners and guards slipped into opposing roles. He was so disturbed by the turn of events that he terminated the experiment early; the expected 2-week duration of the study shrank to only 6 days. The participants in this study were ordinary, middle-class, healthy students, who were randomly assigned to the different roles. The situation alone seems to have transformed not only their perceptions and behavior, but even aspects of their characters.

Zimbardo (2004) attributes the atrocities at Abu Ghraib prison in 2004 to the same situational factors that were at work during his Stanford study—roles, norms, and the status hierarchy. Others, however, point out that personality factors were likely at work at Abu Ghraib, but did not play a role in the Stanford Prison Experiment: Zimbardo's participants had been carefully screened to exclude those with a history of legal, substance, or psychological problems. Abu Ghraib's guards had no such screening, and one guard, at least, had several restraining orders against him by his ex-wife because of his history of violence (Saletan, 2004).

Yielding to Others: Going Along With the Group

In Raleigh when the Jim Crow laws were in effect, Black customers in a White-owned shoe store were supposed to sit in the back of the store to try on shoes. On one occasion when Sadie Delany shopped for shoes, she was asked by the White owner, Mr. Heller, to sit in the back. She asked, "Where, Mr. Heller?" And he gestured to the back saying, " 'Back there.' And I would say, 'Back *where?*' . . . Finally, he'd say, 'Just sit anywhere, Miss Delany.' And so I would sit myself down in the White section, and smile" (Delany et al., 1993, p. 84). What made Sadie able to resist Mr. Heller's request—or his order, backed by law? What made Mr. Heller give up his attempt to have Sadie comply with the law and social convention? What made him call her "Miss Delany" and not "Sadie"? What would you have done if you were Sadie? In what circumstances do we go along with the group, do what someone asks of us, obey orders? When do we resist?

Conformity and Independence: Doing What's Expected

Social norms tell us how we ought to behave, and sometimes we change our beliefs or behavior in order to follow these norms. This change in beliefs or behavior because of pressure from others is known as conformity. For example, immigrants must decide how much to conform to the norms of their new country and how much to retain the ways of their homeland (Lorenzo-Hernandez, 1998). Two types of social influence—informational and normative—can lead to conformity.

Informational Social Influence. One type of social influence is *informational social influence,* which occurs when we conform to others' views or behavior because we want to be right and we believe that they are correct (Cialdini & Goldstein, 2004). This type of conformity is most likely to occur when the situation is ambiguous, when there is a crisis, or when other people are experts. Suppose you are working in a study group that is trying to solve a complex engineering problem, or that you are part of a medical team trying to agree on a diagnosis of a particularly perplexing case. The majority agree on an answer that doesn't seem right to

Conformity: A change in beliefs or behavior in order to follow a group's norms.

you. What would make you more likely to go along with the majority view? Research indicates that *task difficulty* increases conformity: The harder the task, the more you are likely to conform—at least in part because you are less sure of yourself. *Social comparison theory* (Festinger, 1950) is consistent with this explanation: All people are driven to evaluate their abilities and opinions. When their abilities or views cannot be measured objectively, they seek out others, particularly people similar to themselves, to serve as a basis of comparison (Morris et al., 1976). Thus, even when we are initially certain, the disagreement of other members of our group can make us doubt (Orive, 1988).

Normative Social Influence. Informational social influence, however, cannot be the only explanation for conformity. Conformity can also arise from *normative social influence*, which occurs when we conform because we want to be liked or thought of positively, as demonstrated in pioneering research by Solomon Asch (1951, 1955). If you had been a participant in Asch's original study, you would have found yourself in a group with five to seven others and been asked to perform a task of visual perception. You are all shown a target line and asked to say which of three other lines matches the length of the target line. Each person gives an answer aloud; you are next to last. This sounds like an easy task, as you can see in Figure 13.5, but it soon becomes perplexing. For 12 of the 18 times you are shown the lines, everyone else gives the wrong answer! Will you agree with the answer everyone else is giving?

Figure 13.5 Asch's Conformity Study

Participants in Asch's classic study on conformity were shown lines similar to these and asked the following type of question: Here are three lines of different lengths and a fourth target line. Which of the three lines matches the target line?

Only two people have yet to give their opinions, but everyone else appears to have given the same incorrect answer. Which would you say was the correct line if you were next to answer? Asch (1951, 1955) created this situation with the use of confederates, and the true participant was the next-to-last person. Although 76% of participants conformed to the incorrect group response at least once, over the entire experiment, approximately two thirds of responses were independent of the majority.

In fact, in Asch's experiment, only one person in the group was the true participant; the others were confederates playing a role. Seventy-six percent of participants went along with the confederates at least once, and approximately one third of participants' total responses conformed with the obviously wrong majority.

Why would these people conform with the norm established by the group? Variations on Asch's original experiment showed that characteristics of the situation are part of the answer. When participants *wrote* their answers instead of announcing them to the group, they gave the correct response 98% of the time, reflecting the fact that participants accurately perceived the lines.

Social Support. *Social support* also influences conformity. If another group member openly disagrees with the group consensus, conformity is less likely (Morris & Miller, 1975). When Asch had one confederate disagree—that is, give the correct answer—91% of the real participants did not conform with the group answer. Furthermore, the more *cohesive* a group—the more attraction and commitment members have toward it—the more likely members are to conform, as are members who identify more strongly with a group's norms (Prapavessis & Carron, 1997; Schofield et al., 2001; Terry & Hogg, 1996). And when a member of a less powerful group, such as a social or political minority, is in a group with more powerful members, the minority member may be more likely to conform (Roll et al., 1996). In general, despite the pressure to conform to group norms, not everyone is equally affected (Trafimow & Finlay, 1996).

Were the people in Asch's study typical? All were men, but the results of later studies with women as participants were similar (Eagly & Carli, 1981). However, Asch's original participants may have been influenced by their culture. His experiment has been repeated by many researchers in many countries, and studies in countries with a more collectivist orientation, such as China, found higher levels of conformity than did those in individualistic countries (Bond & Smith, 1996). Furthermore, the findings of conformity studies over the years suggest that conformity has decreased since Asch's original work was done (Bond & Smith, 1996). Thus, characteristics of the individual, his or her relationship to the group, characteristics of the group, and the larger culture can all affect conformity and independence.

Compliance: Doing What You're Asked

Even if you don't want to go along with a group's norms, you may be willing to comply with a direct request, as occurs when someone asks, "Could you please tell me how to get to the library?" **Compliance** is a change in behavior brought about through a direct request rather than by social norms. When the driver of the car in the next lane gestures to you, asking to be let into your lane in front of you, you will either comply or not.

Principles of Compliance. Without realizing it, you are a target of multiple requests for compliance each day, from TV commercials, in conversations with friends, or through questions on a survey form. Skill at getting people to comply is key to success in many occupations, from sales and advertising to lobbying, politics, and health prevention programs. Psychologist Robert Cialdini decided to find out from "compliance professionals"—people in jobs such as advertising, fund-raising, and door-to-door sales—exactly what they know about the subject. He inferred that the essence of effective compliance technique lies in six principles (Cialdini, 1994; Cialdini & Goldstein, 2004):

1. *Friendship/liking.* People are more likely to comply with a request from a friend than from a stranger.

Compliance: A change in behavior prompted by a direct request rather than by social norms.

Foot-in-the-door technique: A technique that achieves compliance by beginning with an insignificant request, which is then followed by a larger request.

Lowball technique: A compliance technique that consists of getting someone to make an agreement and then increasing the cost of that agreement.

Door-in-the-face technique: A compliance technique in which someone makes a very large request and then, when it is denied, as expected, makes a smaller request (for what is actually desired).

2. *Commitment/consistency*. People tend to be more likely to comply when the request is consistent with a previous commitment.

3. *Scarcity*. People are more likely to comply with requests related to limited, short-term, rather than open-ended, opportunities.

4. *Reciprocity*. People tend to comply with a request that comes from someone who has provided a favor.

5. *Social validation*. People are more likely to comply if they think that others similar to themselves would comply.

6. *Authority*. People tend to comply with a request if it comes from someone who appears to be in authority.

Compliance Techniques. To see these principles at work, let's examine a few of the techniques most often used to win compliance. The commitment/consistency principle explains why a classic compliance technique, the **foot-in-the-door technique**, works so often. In this method, first you make an insignificant request; if you meet with compliance, you follow up with a larger request. Consider the study by Freedman and Fraser (1966), who had a male investigator phone housewives, asking what brand of soap they used. Three days later, the same man telephoned and asked if five or six people could perform a 2-hour inventory of everything in the housewife's cupboards, drawers, and closets. Fifty-three percent of the housewives who had agreed to the simple first request agreed to this much larger second request. In contrast, when housewives did not receive the first request but were asked to allow the inventory, only 22% complied.

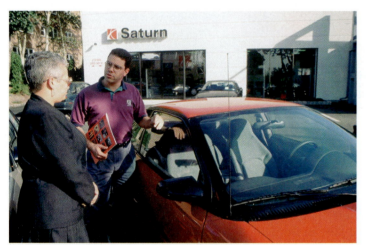

Car salespeople are notorious for using the lowball technique; however, some car makers have changed to a nonnegotiable pricing policy so that there is less opportunity for the lowball technique.

The foot-in-the-door technique appears to work, at least in part, because people want to seem consistent (Guadagno et al., 2001). If you agree to the first request, you are being a nice person; declining the second request would call this self-perception into question. The commitment/consistency principle also explains the success of an unethical sales technique, the **lowball technique**, which consists of first getting someone to make an agreement and then increasing the cost of that agreement. Suppose you see an advertisement for some shoes you've been eyeing—for a very low price. You go the store and are told that the shoes are no longer available at that price, but you can get them for a somewhat higher (although still discounted) price. What do you do? Many people would comply with the request to buy the shoes at the higher price.

Reversing the foot-in-the-door procedure also works; this is the **door-in-the-face technique**. You begin by making a very large request; when it is denied, as expected, you make a smaller request—for what you actually wanted in the first place. For instance, in one study (Cialdini et al., 1975), college students were stopped on campus and asked to serve as unpaid counselors to a group of juvenile delinquents for 2 hours a week for 2 years. Not surprisingly, no one agreed. Then the same students were asked to take the group on a 2-hour field trip. Fifty percent agreed. In contrast, when students were asked only to make the field trip without the larger, first request, only 17% agreed.

The door-in-the-face technique is a staple of diplomacy and labor–management negotiations. Why does it work? The reciprocity principle may hold the answer. If your first request is denied and you then make a smaller one, you appear to be making concessions, and the other party tries to reciprocate.

Obedience: Doing as You're Told

If people can be so obliging in response to a polite request, what happens when they receive an order? Compliance with an order is called **obedience**. The nature of obedience attracted intense study in the United States after World War II, when the world heard about atrocities apparently committed in the name of obedience.

The Milgram Study. The most famous study of obedience was carried out by Stanley Milgram (1963). Milgram expected that Americans would not follow orders to inflict pain on innocent people. In testing this hypothesis, his challenge was to design a study that gave the appearance of inflicting pain without actually doing so. He hit on the following procedure: Suppose you volunteered to participate in a study of memory. You are asked to act the part of "teacher" (see Figure 13.6). You are paired with a "learner" (a confederate), who, you are told, was asked to memorize a list of pairs of common words. You, the teacher, are to present one word from each pair and keep track of how well the learner does in correctly remembering the other word. If the learner makes a mistake, you are to administer a shock, increasing the voltage with each successive mistake. Although the shock generator is a phony and no shock at all is administered, you do not know this.

This is precisely what Milgram did; by prearrangement, at 120 volts, the learner shouted that the shocks were becoming too painful. At 150 volts, the learner asked to stop. At 180, he screamed that he couldn't stand the pain. At 300, he pounded on the wall and demanded to be set free. At 330 volts, there was only silence—an "incorrect response" according to the directions of the experimenter, who stood beside the teacher.

How far would you go in obeying the experimenter's instructions? If you were like the participants in Milgram's study, when the learner cried out in pain or refused to go on, you would turn to the experimenter for instructions, who would reply that the experiment had to proceed and that he would take full responsibility. Would you obey? When Milgram described the experiment to a group of psychiatrists, they predicted that only a "pathological fringe" of at most 2% of the population would go to the maximum shock level. In fact, much to Milgram's surprise, 65% of the participants went to the highest level. Some of the participants, but apparently not all, felt terrible about what they were doing. But they still continued to administer the shocks.

Understanding Milgram's Results. The willingness of so many of Milgram's participants to obey orders to hurt others disturbed many people. Was there

Figure 13.6 The Milgram Obedience Study

Each participant was paired with another man, having drawn lots to decide who would be the "teacher" and the "learner." In fact, the participant was always the teacher. The learner was always the same 47-year-old accountant who was a confederate in the study. The man who introduced himself as the experimenter was an actor. The learner was asked to memorize a list of pairs of common words; the teacher was to present the words, keep track of how well the learner did, and punish the learner for incorrect responses. The teacher watched as the learner was brought to a cubicle where the experimenter asked him to sit down and strapped him in a chair to "prevent excess movement." The experimenter attached shock electrodes to his wrist. Throughout the remainder of the study, the teacher could not see the learner, and all communication took place via an intercom.

The teacher was seated in front of the shock generator. The generator had 30 switches labeled in 15-volt increments from 15 to 450 volts. A description below each switch ranged from "Slight Shock" to "Danger: Severe Shock." The labels under the last two switches were ominous: "XXX." At the outset, the teacher was given a sample shock of 45 volts so that he could know what it felt like.

Obedience: Compliance with an order.

something distinctive about Milgram's participants that could explain the results? In the original studies, the participants were men. Later studies, however, found similar results with women (Milgram, 1965, 1974), as well as with people in Jordan, Germany, and Australia, and with children (Kilham & Mann, 1974; Shanab & Yahya, 1977).

Why did so many participants obey orders to hurt someone else? Were there particular characteristics of the situation that fostered obedience? Compliance research suggests two ways in which the study's design increased the likelihood of obedience. First, Milgram's experiment applied something like the foot-in-the-door-technique: Participants were first ordered to give a trivial amount of shock before going on to give apparently harmful ones. When participants were allowed to set the punishment voltage themselves, none ever went past 45 volts. Second, additional research indicated that people become more likely to comply with a request if it comes from someone in authority; the same holds true for obedience (Bushman, 1984, 1988). In a variant of the study (Milgram, 1974), when a college student was the one who gave a fellow student the order to shock, instead of an older, white-coated experimenter, obedience fell to only 20%. When the experimenters were two authority figures who disagreed with each other, no participants administered further shocks. It appears that the more authoritative the person who gives the order, the more likely it is to be obeyed; when someone in authority gives an order, the person obeying can deny responsibility for his or her actions.

Later variations of Milgram's original study point to other characteristics of the situation that have an important influence on obedience. *Proximity* to the learner is one. When teachers saw the learners while they were being shocked, and even held an electrode directly on the accomplice's skin (with a "special insulating glove"), 30% progressed to the maximum voltage, compared with 65% in the original design. Proximity to the experimenter also matters: When the experimenter telephoned his commands to the teacher instead of giving face-to-face instructions, obedience dropped to 21%.

As disturbing as Milgram's results were, it is important to remember that not all participants obeyed the experimenter, and in some conditions the great majority did not obey; it is the specifics of the situation (such as proximity to the learner) that influences an individual's willingness to obey an order to hurt someone else (Blass, 1999; Gibson, 1991; A. G. Miller et al., 1995).

Performance in Groups: Working Together

When Sadie and Bessie went to New York City, they moved into their brother Hubert's apartment, along with another brother and sister. Now there were five Delanys living in a three-room apartment. In such tight quarters, it helped to be very organized and to have clear rules and clear roles. Even though the apartment was Hubert's, and they all participated in making decisions, Sadie would have the final say because she was the oldest. How do groups make decisions? What are the advantages and disadvantages of working as a group?

Decision Making in Groups: Paths to a Decision

After living in Hubert's apartment for a while, Sadie and Bessie got a place of their own in New York, and their mother came to live with them. However, at some point, their mother's health began to fade, and it was no longer safe for her to be home alone all day while her daughters were at work. The situation required that one of the sisters leave her job to stay home with Mrs. Delany (it never occurred to them to hire someone to stay at home with their mother while they were out at work). How did they decide who would stay home? This question faces many families today, and the path to a solution often involves group decision making. Such decision making also occurs in other contexts: Political parties, military planners, and athletic teams must decide on strategies; clinical groups must decide who receives what medical treatment and for how long; college admissions officers decide who is accepted and who is not. How are decisions made in groups?

In general, if a group is not initially unanimous in favor of a particular decision, it is likely that the view favored by the majority will prevail (Levine & Moreland, 1998). The larger the majority, the more likely it is that their choice will "win." This path is known as the *majority-win rule*, and it works well when the decision involves judgments or opinions (Hastie & Kameda, 2005). But there are times—you may have been present at some—when what began as the minority position eventually "wins." When there is an objectively correct answer, the *truth-win rule* works well because its inherent worthiness is recognized by the group (Kirchler & Davis, 1986). In general, groups reach a better decision when one solution can be shown to be correct (Hastie, 1986; Hastie & Kameda, 2005; Laughlin & Ellis, 1986).

Group Polarization.   Group decision making does not always lead to the best decision. The opinion of a powerful member can shift others' opinions by might rather than right. Group decisions can also be marred by <mark>group polarization</mark>, the tendency of members of the group to take more extreme positions (with the same orientation as their initial opinions) after discussion (Isenberg, 1986; Levine & Moreland, 1998). This polarization of attitude can last well beyond the initial discussion (Liu & Latané, 1998).

One reason group polarization develops is that some members of the group may give very compelling reasons for their initial views, and more of them. In listening to these reasons, members who are in general agreement may become more convinced of the correctness of that initial assessment and more extreme in their views (Burnstein, 1982). This route to group polarization is more likely to be a factor when an intellectual issue is at stake or when the group's goal is to make a "correct" or task-oriented decision (Kaplan, 1987). Another reason behind group polarization is that, through discussion, members can figure out the group's consensus on the issue and may be tempted to increase their standing in the group (and improve their view of themselves) by taking a more extreme position in accordance with the group norm (Goethals & Zanna, 1979). This route to group polarization is likely to occur when the issue requires judgments and when the group is more focused on group harmony than on correctness (Kaplan, 1987).

Groupthink.   Groupthink is another means by which decision making can go awry. <mark>Groupthink</mark> refers to the tendency of people who try to solve problems together to accept one another's information and ideas without subjecting them to critical analysis. According to Janis (1982), members of a group are most likely to fall into groupthink when they are especially close. In such instances, rather than realistically thinking through a problem, members are more concerned with agreeing with one another. This tendency has been used to explain many real-life disasters, such as why NASA launched the space shuttle *Challenger* despite widespread concerns about its booster rockets. (The failure of the booster rockets ended up causing the shuttle to crash.) Although the evidence that groupthink leads to bad decisions is mixed (Aldag & Fuller, 1993), a meta-analysis revealed

Group polarization: The tendency of group members' opinions to become more extreme (in the same direction as their initial opinions) after group discussion.

Groupthink: The tendency of people who try to solve problems together to accept one another's information and ideas without subjecting them to critical analysis.

that cohesive groups tend to make poorer decisions if the cohesiveness grew out of "interpersonal attraction"—the members' feelings about one another (Mullen et al., 1994). In such groups, the members want to seem cooperative, and so refrain from asking questions or making comments that they otherwise would, potentially leading to a different outcome than would result if they did question or comment. Groups that have a norm of coming to consensus are more vulnerable to group-think than those that have a norm of minority dissent (Postmes et al., 2001).

Decision Making in Heterogeneous Versus Homogeneous Groups. The variety of people in a group may also affect its decision-making process and performance (Kerr & Tindale, 2004). In general, as a group becomes more heterogeneous, it communicates less effectively (Maznevski, 1994; Zenger & Lawrence, 1989), and subgroups of similar members may form, causing nonsimilar members to feel alienated (Jackson et al., 1991). Some of the negative effects of heterogeneous groups can be minimized in the following ways:

- educating members about their similarities and differences, leading to recategorization by increasing a sense of the group as a team (creating an "us");
- increasing social skills among members; and
- teaching members conflict resolution skills (Caudron, 1994).

Paradoxically, although heterogeneity can create some group conflict, it can also have a positive effect on the group's performance (McLeod & Lobel, 1992) because of the increased innovation and flexibility that diversity brings to a group (Levine & Moreland, 1998).

When a group as a whole is responsible for a task, some members may work less hard than they would if they were individually responsible for the task. This tendency toward social loafing can be countered by evaluating everyone's performance separately or by making the task attractive.

Social loafing: The tendency to work less hard when responsibility for an outcome is spread over a group's members.

Social facilitation: The increase in performance that can occur simply as a result of being part of a group or in the presence of other people.

Social Loafing

When responsibility for an outcome is spread among the members of a group, some members may be likely to let other members work harder (Latané et al., 1979), a phenomenon that has been called **social loafing**. One way to prevent social loafing is to instill a sense of importance and responsibility in each person, even if the work is boring or if the member's contribution is anonymous (Harkins & Petty, 1982; Rynes et al., 2005). Making the task attractive also reduces social loafing, as does knowing that individual as well as group performance will be evaluated (Harkins & Szymanski, 1989; Hoeksema-van Orden et al., 1998; Karau & Williams, 1993). If you have lived with other people, you may have experienced the effects of social loafing: When dishes pile up in the sink or the bathroom goes uncleaned for weeks, each member of the household is doing some social loafing, waiting for somebody else to do the work.

Social Facilitation: Everybody Loves an Audience

Sometimes being part of a group, or just being in the presence of other people, can increase performance; this effect is called **social facilitation**. However, usually the presence of others enhances performance only on well-learned, simple tasks; on complicated, less well-learned tasks, the presence of others can hinder performance (Guerin, 1993). The presence of others appears to increase arousal, which then facilitates the *dominant* response in that situation (Schmitt et al., 1986; Seta & Seta, 1992). Thus, well-learned responses are likely to come to the fore when you are aroused, and you will be less likely to execute complicated or recently learned behaviors. Hence, at a concert, a musician may perform an old song better than a new one, whereas when practicing at home that same day, she probably could play them both equally well.

Helping Behavior: Helping Others

When Bessie Delany began her dentistry practice in 1923, both cleanings and extractions were $2 each, and a silver filling cost $5. When she retired in 1950, she charged the same rates and was proud of it. In fact, she treated people regardless of their ability to pay. The Delany family ethic was to help others. This quality is called <mark>altruism</mark>, which has been defined as "the motivation to increase another person's welfare" (Batson, 1998, p. 282). What made Bessie so willing to help others? Why do we help other people? What circumstances encourage altruism?

New York City's firefighters displayed their altruism in September 2001, both when going into the burning World Trade Center towers to rescue people inside and when searching through the burning rubble for survivors.

Prosocial Behavior

Acting to benefit others, called <mark>prosocial behavior</mark>, includes sharing, cooperating, comforting, and helping (Batson, 1998). Whether or not we help someone depends on factors about us, about the situation, and about the person we could help.

Characteristics of the Helper.
We are more likely to help others if we have certain personality traits, such as a high need for approval, a predisposition to feeling personal and social responsibility, and an empathic concern for others (Batson et al., 1986; Eisenberg et al., 1989, 2002), or we are generally high on the personality dimension agreeableness (see Chapter 8; Carlo et al., 2005; Graziano et al., 2004). People who tend to be helpers also have a belief in a just world, an internal locus of control, and less concern for their own welfare (Bierhoff et al., 1991). Bessie Delany seemed to feel a sense of personal and social responsibility toward others and could empathize with their plights. She also appeared to have less concern for her own welfare; when she was in dental school, a White girl born with syphilis came to the dental clinic—only Bessie volunteered to help her.

Group identity also plays a role in prosocial behavior. We are more likely to help and cooperate with other members of our group (Hewstone et al., 2002; Stürmer et al., 2005). Principles of learning (see Chapter 4) are also influential. Through our learning history, we may have been reinforced for helping or punished for not helping (Grusec et al., 2002). Moreover, parents, teachers, and others are models for observational learning. Thus, in time, we come to reward ourselves for helping, feel good after helping, and punish ourselves or feel guilty when we don't (Batson, 1998). Being in a positive mood may also make us more likely to help others (Guéguen & De Gail, 2003).

Characteristics of the Person Being Helped and the Situation.
Some people in need of assistance are more likely to be helped than others. Who are they? First, we are more likely to help people we view as similar to ourselves (Park & Schaller, 2005). Consider an experiment in which Americans in three foreign cities asked for directions: Residents of those cities who were similar in age to the Americans requesting help were more likely to give directions (Rabinowitz et al., 1997). Second, we are more likely to help friends or people we like (remember, similarity facilitates liking). Third, we are more likely to help people we believe are not responsible for their predicaments, or those who give a socially acceptable justification for their plight (Weiner, 1980). In fact, the more justification the requester gives, the more likely he or she is to receive help (Bohm & Hendricks, 1997).

Altruism: The motivation to increase another person's welfare.

Prosocial behavior: Acting to benefit others.

How the act of helping is framed can also influence our prosocial behavior. We are more likely to help when:

- the "cost" of helping seems to decline, as when helping others is framed as an opportunity for personal development (Perlow & Weeks, 2002);

- the "rewards" of helping appear to increase (Guéguen & De Gail, 2003); and

- there appears to be an increased "cost" of *not* helping (Dovidio et al., 1991), such as a heightened sense of shame and guilt (Penner et al., 2005).

Figure 13.7 Bystander Intervention

Participants thought they were involved in a study of campus life but instead were exposed to an "emergency" with a varying number of bystanders. Participants went into a private cubicle and were told that they could all hear one another, but only one student would be able to speak during any 2-minute period; when all had spoken, the cycle would start again. They were also told that the experimenter would not be listening. Participants were led to believe that either four, one, or no other students ("bystanders") were listening. In fact, there was only one true participant at a time; the rest of the voices on the intercom were prerecorded tapes.

The crisis came after one (prerecorded) voice confessed to having seizures in stressful situations. This person subsequently seemed to be having a seizure, and asked for help.

I er think I need er … help because I er I'm er h-h-having a a a real problem … (choking sounds) … I'm gonna die er … seizure (chokes, then is quiet)

What should I do?

Would participants leave their cubicles to get help? Their responses depended greatly on the perceived number of bystanders. The great majority of participants went to get help when they thought they were the only ones aware of the problem, but they helped less often the more bystanders they thought were aware of the problem.

Bystander Intervention

A great deal has been learned about a specific type of prosocial behavior—bystander intervention—as a result of research inspired by one dreadful incident. At about 3 a.m. on March 13, 1964, a 28-year-old woman named Catherine Genovese—known to her neighbors as Kitty—was brutally murdered in Queens, a borough of New York City, only minutes from her own apartment building. She was coming home from her job as a manager of a bar. When her attacker first caught and stabbed her, she screamed for help. The lights came on in several apartments overlooking the scene of the crime, and a man yelled down to her attacker to leave her alone. Her attacker briefly stopped and walked away. The apartment lights went out. The attacker returned and stabbed her again, she screamed again, to no avail, although lights again came on in the surrounding apartments. The attacker left in a car, and Kitty Genovese dragged herself to the lobby of an apartment building near her own. The attacker returned again, and this time he kept stabbing her until she died. The gruesome ordeal took some 35 minutes and at least part of it was heard by no less than 38 neighbors. Only one person called the police (Rosenthal, 1964).

Darley and Latané (1968) hypothesized that if only a few of

those 38 neighbors had heard the attack, those few would have been more likely to help Kitty Genovese. This relationship is known as the <mark>bystander effect</mark>: As the number of bystanders increases, offers of assistance decrease. To test this relationship, Darley and Latané, with the aid of confederates, created the following situation. Imagine yourself as a participant in a study, taking part in a telephone conference about campus life with a number of others. Each participant speaks without interruption, and when everyone has spoken, the first person gets to speak again, and so on. Suppose another participant mentions that when stressed he gets seizures; then you hear that person stutter, start to choke, and ask for help. Would you get help? If you were like most participants in Darley and Latané's study (1968) (see Figure 13.7), and you believed that there were only two people in the telephone conference—you and the person with seizures—you would very likely seek help. But if you had been told that there were three participants, you would be less likely to seek help, and even less likely with a total of six participants. In short, attempts to help rose as the number of apparent bystanders dropped: When participants thought that they were the only one aware of the "emergency," 85% of them left the cubicle and got the experimenter within the first minute. When they thought there was one other bystander, 65% helped within the first minute. When participants thought there were four other bystanders, only 25% helped within the first minute. At the end of 4 minutes, all in the smallest group helped, as did 85% of those in the mid-sized group, but only 60% in the largest group.

From this and other studies, Darley and Latané (1970) described five steps, or "choice points," in bystander intervention (see Figure 13.8). At each step, various factors, such as the number of bystanders and characteristics of the bystanders, shape the likelihood that someone will help. For example, consider Step 2, perceiving the event as an emergency. If a situation is ambiguous, leaving you uncertain about whether the emergency is real, you may hesitate to offer help. If other bystanders are present, your hesitancy may be increased by *evaluation apprehension*—a fear that you might be embarrassed or ridiculed if you try to intervene because there may be no emergency after all. The number of bystanders also influences Step 3, assuming responsibility. The more bystanders there are, the less responsible each one feels for offering help, creating a <mark>diffusion of responsibility</mark>. Fortunately, once

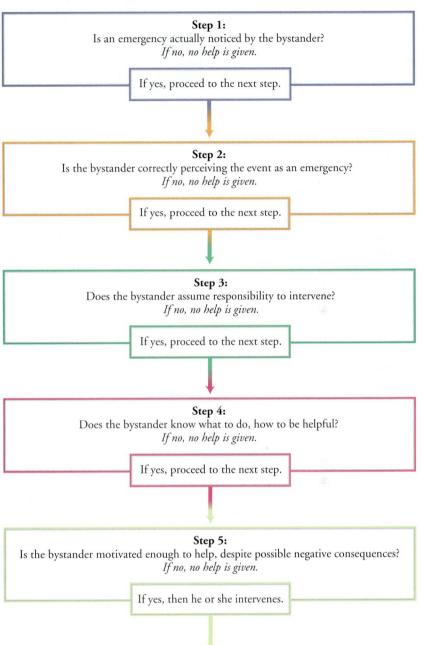

Figure 13.8 The Five Choice Points of Bystander Intervention

Step 1:
Is an emergency actually noticed by the bystander?
If no, no help is given.

If yes, proceed to the next step.

Step 2:
Is the bystander correctly perceiving the event as an emergency?
If no, no help is given.

If yes, proceed to the next step.

Step 3:
Does the bystander assume responsibility to intervene?
If no, no help is given.

If yes, proceed to the next step.

Step 4:
Does the bystander know what to do, how to be helpful?
If no, no help is given.

If yes, proceed to the next step.

Step 5:
Is the bystander motivated enough to help, despite possible negative consequences?
If no, no help is given.

If yes, then he or she intervenes.

Bystander effect: The decrease in offers of assistance that occurs as the number of bystanders increases.

Diffusion of responsibility: The diminished sense of responsibility to help that each person feels as the number of bystanders grows.

people have learned about the bystander effect, they are subsequently more likely to intervene (Beaman et al., 1978).

Looking at Levels

Cults

In 1997, members of the Heaven's Gate cult killed themselves in order to ascend to an alien spaceship that they believed was hidden behind the Hale–Bopp Comet; they believed that the spaceship would take them to the next level of existence. How is it that cults exert such a powerful influence on their members? We can best understand how cults function by looking at the phenomenon from the three levels of analysis and their interactions.

At the level of the brain, the bodily functions of cult members, such as eating, sleeping, and sexual relations (in those cults that permit them), are carefully monitored. New recruits in many cults are often physically and mentally exhausted after listening to music, chanting, or engaging in similar activities for hours on end (Schein, 1961; Streiker, 1984), which can induce a meditative or hypnotic-like state that alters brain function as well as the sense of reality.

At the level of the person, the initial immersion in many cults requires dramatic changes on the part of new recruits as the cult strives to eliminate members' experience of themselves as individuals (West, 1980; Williams, 2003). In the Heaven's Gate group, each day was structured down to the minute in order to minimize the sense of self and individual choice. Moreover, members were forbidden to trust their own judgments or to have "inappropriate" curiosity (Bearak, 1997). Members, particularly new ones, were not allowed to be alone, even in the bathroom. These measures, along with the altered state of consciousness and the exhaustion, can induce a sense of *depersonalization* (the experience of observing oneself as if from the outside) and *derealization* (the sense that familiar objects have changed or seem unreal; Singer, 1995). The goal of such changes in perception and consciousness is to influence and control the new recruit's attitudes, beliefs, and behavior (Gesy, 1993; Richmond, 2004). In such states, new recruits usually cannot rationally evaluate what they are being told (Walsh, 2001).

At the level of the group, new recruits are often asked to engage in behaviors that they would normally refuse to do, but cults may use the foot-in-the-door compliance technique, starting with small requests and progressing to larger, more outrageous, ones (T. W. Miller et al., 1999). In addition, performing actions at the behest of the group that would otherwise be refused, such as begging for money or having sexual relations, can induce cognitive dissonance; only a change in attitude can then resolve the discomfort aroused (Galanter, 2000). Moreover, members receive enormous amounts of attention and reinforcement, sometimes called "love-bombing," for behaving in desired ways—in other words, conforming to their expected role and to group norms (T. W. Miller et al., 1999). Group polarization and groupthink may affect the group's decision making. Perhaps these group processes led to the decision that group suicide was an effective way to join the alien spaceship. The norms and practices of a cult create a strong ingroup (with the rest of the world comprising the outgroup), increasing group cohesion.

Events at these levels of analysis interact: Recruits are often separated from their families and friends (Richmond, 2004; Singer & Lalich, 1995) to heighten their sense of belonging to the cult (level of the group). Moreover, the arousal and the unpleasant changes in perception and consciousness (levels of brain and person) are calmed by the positive response of group members after a recruit complies with the cult members' requests—or obeys their orders (level of the group). Such negative reinforcement (level of the person) leads to changes in self-concept and heightens the importance of, and dependence on, the group (Galanter, 2000).

LOOKING BACK: *Review*

1. *What psychological principles explain why we like certain people and not others?* Repeated contact, similarity to ourselves, and physical attraction all tend to make us like other people. Liking is not the same as loving, which can be passionate or companionate. According to Sternberg's triangular theory, love has three dimensions: passion, intimacy, and commitment. Relationships reflect different proportions of each dimension, and those proportions change over time. People's attachment styles—secure, avoidant, or anxious–ambivalent—also affect the pattern of relationships they will develop.

2. *Why do all groups have rules for social behavior and organization?* Social norms help a group function, defining appropriate and inappropriate behavior for some or all members; they also help new members learn how to function in the group.

3. *Why do we sometimes "go along" with or obey others even when we don't want to? What makes us able to refuse?* If we hold a minority position, we may come to doubt the correctness of our view; we tend to conform to the majority view when the task at hand is difficult. Furthermore, as Asch's studies showed, we are more likely to conform to the majority view when we are part of a cohesive group. In contrast, we are less likely to conform to the majority view if another member also does not conform to that position or if we have a strong desire to retain a sense of individuality. Compliance with a request can be maximized when the person making the request is a friend, someone who has provided a favor in the past, or someone in authority. We are also more likely to comply if we think people similar to ourselves would comply. A number of persuasion techniques make use of compliance principles, including the foot-in-the-door technique, the lowball technique, and the door-in-the-face technique. Obedience to a command with which we don't agree is more likely when the person issuing the command is authoritative and nearby. However, not everyone obeys such orders, and the specifics of the situation help determine the level of obedience.

4. *Does being part of a group change our behavior? How do groups make decisions?* Groups can make decisions according to the majority-win rule or the truth-win rule; the latter is more likely when one answer is objectively correct. Although more heterogeneous groups may communicate less effectively, they may also be more innovative and flexible because of their diversity. Reasons why group decision making can go awry include group polarization and groupthink. Being part of a group can cause people to do less than their share (social loafing). Moreover, just being in the presence of others can increase someone's performance of a well-learned task (social facilitation), but have the opposite effect on newly learned or complex skills.

5. *Are some people more helpful than others? What makes us likely to help other people?* People with certain personality traits are more likely to help others. Those traits include a high need for approval and a feeling of social responsibility. We are more likely to help people who seem similar to ourselves, people we like, or people who have a socially justifiable reason for needing help. The more bystanders on hand (diffusion of responsibility) or the more ambiguous the situation, the less likely we are to help.

LOOKING BEYOND: *Critical Thinking*

When Sadie Delany began her job as a New York high school teacher, how might she have learned the school's norms and students' and teachers' roles?

Imagine that you have started a new job working in a large corporation. Based on what you have learned, what colleagues are you likely to be attracted to and why? If your boss wants employees to do something "slightly illegal," what factors may make employees less likely to go along with this request (or order)? Will working as a group change the way the work is performed? Why or why not? If an employee is injured at work, what factors may make the employees who witness the incident more likely to help?

A Final Word: Ethics and Social Psychology

The researchers who conducted many of the studies described in this chapter did not tell participants about the true nature of the experiments at the outset, and several used confederates. Many of the classic social psychology studies were carried out before the discipline established rigorous ethical guidelines (see Chapter 1). In fact, some of the guidelines were formulated *because* these studies raised serious ethical concerns. Keep in mind, however, several issues related to the use of deception in psychology. First, many of the pioneering researchers did not expect to cause psychological distress. For example, Milgram initially did not expect participants to be willing to shock learners at higher "voltage" levels, although he did continue to perform variants of his study after he knew the results of his first study. Second, some psychological phenomena are extremely difficult, if not impossible, to study if the participant knows the true nature of the experiment. For example, could you think of a way to design a study on conformity *without* using deception? Third, at present, in order to receive approval for a study that uses deception, researchers must show that the deception is absolutely necessary (that the information could not be ascertained without deception), that the information is valuable and the deception minimal, and that at the conclusion of the study, the investigators will fully explain to the participants the nature of the study and the reasons for deception. (In fact, participants in Milgram's study were the first to be systematically and fully informed about the purposes and predictions of the study immediately after their participation; Blass, 2004.) In short, deception is now permitted in research only if it is crystal clear that the participants will not be harmed and that important knowledge will be gained.

LET'S SUM IT UP

I. Social Cognition: Thinking About People

A. Attitudes and stereotypes help reduce the cognitive effort required to understand the social world. Our attitudes, stereotypes, and attributions affect how we process, encode, and remember information.

B. Our attitudes can affect our behavior and are especially likely to do so when they are strong, stable, relevant, important, and/or easily accessible.

C. Conflict between an attitude and our behavior (or between two attitudes) can lead to cognitive dissonance, which we are then driven to reduce.

D. Efforts to change attitudes are attempts at persuasion. Central routes to persuasion require more time, energy, or expertise than peripheral routes.

E. Social cognitive neuroscience has helped reveal that cognitive dissonance and other social cognitive phenomena can occur outside conscious awareness.

F. The human process of categorizing objects (including people) leads to stereotypes, and our stereotypes of others affect our behavior toward them and the ways others behave toward us and can lead to prejudice and discrimination.

G. Because our stereotypes create biases in the way we process information, they often seem more accurate than they really are and thus are difficult to change.

H. Although we are driven to make attributions to understand events or behavior, our reasoning about the causes of these phenomena may rely on attributional biases, such as the correspondence bias, the self-serving bias, and the belief in a just world. Such biases can lead us to understand people's behavior inaccurately.

II. Social Behavior: Interacting With People

A. In our intimate relationships, we are more likely to be attracted to, and to like, people we view as similar to ourselves or with whom we have repeated contact.

B. Love can be understood by examining different types of love, by using Sternberg's triangular model of love's three dimensions, or by looking at different attachment styles.

C. All groups have norms and roles, which guide members' behaviors. Zimbardo's prison study provides an example of the power of group norms and roles within a group.

D. Conformity is affected by informational and normative social influences, depending on the situation. Asch's conformity experiment illustrates normative social influence.

E. The foot-in-the-door, lowball, and door-in-the-face techniques are used to increase compliance.

F. Obedience to an order can be affected by various factors, including the status and proximity of the person giving the order.

G. The style of a group's decision making depends on the group's goals and composition and on the ways in which members articulate their views before the group.

H. Being in a group can help or harm a given individual's performance.

I. Prosocial behavior is affected by characteristics of the helper, the person being helped, and the situation. Psychological principles, such as the bystander effect and diffusion of responsibility, also determine when and whom we help.

Key Terms

altruism, p. 591
attitude, p. 561
attribution, p. 573
attributional bias, p. 573
belief in a just world, p. 575

bystander effect, p. 593
cognitive dissonance, p. 563
companionate love, p. 578
compliance, p. 585
conformity, p. 583

correspondence bias, p. 574
deindividuation, p. 581
diffusion of responsibility, p. 593
door-in-the-face technique, p. 586
external attribution, p. 573

LOOKING ONLINE: *Enhance Your Learning*

MyPsychLab is an interactive and instructive multimedia resource that can be used to supplement a traditional lecture course or as an online course. It is an all-inclusive tool with a text-specific e-book plus multimedia tutorials, videos, simulations, animations, and controlled assessment to completely engage students and reinforce learning. MyPsychLab meets the individual learning needs of every student. Visit *www.mypsychlab.com* for more information!

Practice Test

For each of the following items, choose the single best answer.

1. The *affective* component of an attitude refers to
   a. your predisposition to act in a particular way toward the object or issue.
   b. your feelings about the object or issue.
   c. what you believe or know about the object or issue.
   d. your perception of the "objective" social world.

2. Our attitudes
   a. affect the way we shape our goals and expectations.
   b. affect how we interpret obstacles we encounter in trying to achieve our goals.
   c. guide us as we selectively evaluate information.
   d. All of the above statements are true.

3. Cognitive dissonance
   a. is an uncomfortable state that arises when an attitude and behavior—or two attitudes—are inconsistent.
   b. is accompanied by decreased arousal.
   c. occurs with every inconsistency and is experienced by people who do not believe that they have a choice.
   d. All of the above statements are true.

4. The mere exposure effect
   a. cannot change attitudes.
   b. can change attitudes through the central route to persuasion.
   c. can change attitudes through the peripheral route to persuasion.
   d. works only if close attention is paid to the content of the argument.

5. If a researcher gives you two sets of stimuli that you like almost to the same degree and requires you to decide which one you like better, then
   a. you later will end up liking the set you chose even more than you did at the outset.
   b. you later will end up liking the set you chose much less than you did at the outset.
   c. you later will end up disliking the rejected set much less than you did at the outset.
   d. None of the above statements is true.

6. Prejudice
   a. cannot arise if someone does not have negative feelings toward a group.
   b. cannot be both conscious and unintentional.
   c. can be both unconscious and unintentional.
   d. does not include an emotional component.

7. Methods of decreasing prejudice include
   a. increased contact, particularly under certain conditions, such as when working toward a shared goal and when all participants are deemed to be equal.
   b. recategorization—that is, shifting the categories of "us" and "them" so that the two groups are no longer distinct entities.
   c. the jigsaw classroom, a cooperative learning technique.
   d. All of the above are methods that can decrease prejudice.

8. Blaming yourself for negative events
   a. is a type of external attribution.
   b. can suppress your immune system.
   c. is a type of situational attribution.
   d. is a type of fundamental attribution error.

9. Why are you attracted to some people and not others?
   a. The adage "Opposites attract" has been borne out by research.
   b. Repeated contact usually leads to a more negative evaluation of someone.
   c. The more similar a stranger's attitudes are to your own, the more likely you are to be attracted.
   d. People prefer men and women's faces that reflect higher levels of male hormones.

10. According to Sternberg's triangular model of love, the dimension of intimacy
    a. is unlikely in "consummate love."
    b. does not occur during infatuation.
    c. is the conscious decision to be in the relationship.
    d. characterizes "fatuous love."

11. Speed and Gangestad found that romantically popular men were seen by their peers as
    a. confident and outgoing.
    b. the best leaders.
    c. likely to succeed financially.
    d. unlikely to be "trend-setting."

12. With deindividuation,
    a. attention is focused on internal events.
    b. a low level of arousal is experienced.
    c. people respond to immediate feelings and act on them after monitoring the appropriateness of their behaviors.
    d. the identities of people in a group are unknown to others in the group.

13. A member of a group is less likely to conform if
    a. another group member openly disagrees with the group consensus.
    b. participants in the group announce their answers to the group, rather than writing them down anonymously.
    c. the task is more difficult; the harder the task, the less likely members are to conform.
    d. the group is more cohesive—that is, members have more attraction and commitment toward it.

14. The essence of effective compliance techniques lies in six principles. According to the principle of _____, people are more likely to comply with requests related to limited, short-term, rather than open-ended, opportunities.
    a. reciprocity
    b. scarcity
    c. social validation
    d. commitment/consistency

15. Sometimes being part of a group, or just being in the presence of other people, can increase performance. This effect
    a. is called social loafing.
    b. decreases arousal.
    c. enhances performance only on well-learned, simple tasks.
    d. enhances performance only on complicated, less well-learned tasks.

Answers: 1. b 2. d 3. a 4. c 5. a 6. c 7. d 8. b 9. c 10. b 11. a 12. d 13. a 14. b 15. c

Appendix: Statistics

Mark Twain once said that there are three kinds of lies: "Lies, damn lies, and statistics." **Statistics** are numbers that summarize or indicate differences or patterns of differences in measurements. Twain's point was that statistics can be used to obscure the facts as easily as to illuminate them. For instance, although the divorce rate in the United States is about 50%, this does not necessarily mean that out of 10 couples only 5 will stay married. If 3 of those 10 couples divorce and remarry, and all 3 of those second marriages end in divorce, that makes 6 divorces out of 13 marriages; and if one of those ex-partners remarries a third time and divorces again, we now have 14 marriages and 7 divorces: a 50% divorce rate, even though 7 of the original 10 couples stayed married from the start. To understand and evaluate reports of psychological research—whether they are surveys in newspapers or on television or formal research reports in scientific publications—you need to know a few basics about statistics.

There are two major types of statistics: One type describes or summarizes data, whereas the other indicates which differences or patterns in the data are worthy of attention. This is the distinction between descriptive statistics and inferential statistics. **Descriptive statistics** are concise ways of summarizing properties of sets of numbers. You're already familiar with such statistics: They are what you see plotted in bar graphs and pie charts and presented in tables. Descriptive statistics include measures of *central tendency*, such as the familiar arithmetic average. But descriptive statistics are not limited to figures and tables. For example, in financial news, the Dow Jones Industrial Average is a descriptive statistic, as is the unemployment rate.

Inferential statistics, in contrast, are the results of tests that reveal whether differences or patterns in measurements reflect true differences in the population or just chance variations. For instance, if you toss a coin 10 times and it lands heads up 7 times, instead of the 5 you would expect purely by chance, does this mean that it is a "trick coin," or that an edge is worn away, or could this outcome also arise from just chance? Inferential statistics seek to address this question of whether patterns in a set of data are random, or if they reflect a true underlying phenomenon. A correlation (see Chapter 1) is an example of inferential statistics; if the correlation is high enough (we will discuss what "high enough" means later), it tells you that the scores on one variable do in fact vary systematically with the scores on another variable.

In this appendix, we consider both types of statistics, starting with descriptive statistics and the nature of variables and data, then turning to an overview of key inferential statistics. We conclude by exploring how statistics can be used to deceive you, both in printed numbers and in graphs, and how you can use statistics in everyday life.

Descriptive Statistics

You already know a lot about descriptive statistics, but you may not be aware you know it—and you may not be familiar with the technical vocabulary scientists use to discuss such statistics. This section provides a review of the essential points of descriptive statistics.

Statistics: Numbers that summarize or indicate differences or patterns of differences in measurements.

Descriptive statistics: Concise ways of summarizing properties of sets of numbers.

Inferential statistics: Results of tests that reveal which differences or patterns in the measurements reflect actual differences in a population, as opposed to those that merely reflect random variations.

Variables and Data

First, you need to learn about variables and data—what they are, how researchers obtain data, and how they use the data to answer the questions posed in their research.

In Chapter 1, a *variable* was defined as an aspect of a situation that is liable to change (or, in other words, that can *vary*). More precisely, a variable is a characteristic of a substance, quantity, or entity that is measurable. *Independent variables* are the characteristics manipulated, and *dependent variables* are those measured, whose values depend on the values of the independent variable. For example, in Chapter 1 you read about an experiment in which golfers were or were not asked to use mental practice between games (the independent variable), and their subsequent golfing performance (the dependent variable) was measured by their scores. *Data* are careful observations or numerical measurements of a phenomenon, such as golf scores. In other words, in an experiment, data are the measurements, the values of the dependent variable as it varies. Examples of dependent variables used in psychological research are response times (how fast it takes to press a button after perceiving a stimulus), scores on an intelligence test, and ratings of the severity of depression.

Values of variables can be described in two ways. For example, intelligence could be described numerically by a score (such as 104) or by the category in which a score falls (such as "average intelligence"). **Continuous variables** are those whose values can fall anywhere along the measurement scale, just as measures of length can fall anywhere along a ruler. Continuous variables allow you to perform mathematical operations such as adding or subtracting two or more values. For example, suppose you developed a drug that you think boosts memory. If your drug works as promised, it would be in great demand—from students in language-learning schools to brokers in Wall Street firms. To test the effectiveness of your drug, you ask people to learn a set of words either after taking the drug or, on another day, after taking a placebo. You are interested in whether the participants can later recall more words if they've taken your drug than if they took the placebo; the condition, drug versus placebo, is the independent variable, and the number of words recalled is the dependent variable. Half the participants get the drug first and half get an identical-looking and -tasting placebo first. You put the pills in coded envelopes so that your assistant doesn't know when she's giving the drug versus the placebo (nor do the participants, because you've used a *double-blind design*; see Chapter 1). The comparison, easily accomplished with values from a continuous scale, is expressed as the number of words remembered following the drug minus the number following the placebo. Ten participants' scores in each condition are shown in Table A.1.

Some data cannot be expressed as continuous variables, such as sex (male versus female), city of residence (Toledo versus Austin), or stage of sleep (Stage 2, 3, 4, or REM). These are examples of **categorical variables**, which assign measurements to discrete classes. Such variables do not change gradually from one to the other, and you can't perform mathematical operations on them. Commonly used categorical variables are sex, race, location, and political party. However, note that continuous measurements can also be classified as categorical variables, such as assigning an IQ score to an "average" category.

Frequency Distributions

It can be useful to treat continuous measures as categorical if you want to get a sense of the way scores are distributed in a population (such as how many college students have above average IQ scores). **Frequency distributions** indicate the

Table A.1
Fictional Participant Data from Drug and Placebo Conditions

Number of Words Remembered

Placebo	Memory Drug
15	27
12	34
18	21
21	17
22	31
38	47
28	31
15	23
14	40
17	19

Continuous variables: Variables whose values can fall anywhere along the measurement scale.

Categorical variables: Variables whose values are assigned to discrete classes.

Frequency distribution: A distribution that indicates the number of each type of case that was observed in a set of data.

number of each type of case that was observed in a set of data. For example, the number of people who voted for a Democratic versus a Republican candidate can be considered for different ages. You could group the ages (making a continuous variable, age, into a categorical variable), perhaps starting with ages 18–30, and then considering each subsequent decade. For each category, you would indicate the number of people who voted Democratic versus Republican. If you were a political strategist trying to determine how best to spend your candidate's campaign money, such a distribution would be helpful: You could decide to target the age ranges that had previously voted your way, or—alternatively—you could figure that those voters are relatively secure and instead target age ranges that previously were *not* in your camp.

Central tendency: A descriptive statistic that indicates the clustering of the most characteristic values, or scores, for a particular group or sample.

Mean: A measure of central tendency that is the arithmetic average of a set of scores or values.

Median: A measure of central tendency that is the midpoint score of the values for the group or sample; half the values fall above the median, and half fall below the median.

Mode: A measure of central tendency that is the most frequently occurring value in a group or sample.

Table A.2 Calculating the Mean

Number of Words Remembered

Placebo condition   Total: 200   **Memory drug condition**   Total: 290

Mean = Total number of words remembered ÷ Number of participants

Mean: 200 ÷ 10 = 20   Mean: 290 ÷ 10 = 29

Measures of Central Tendency

When individual measurements are directly presented, they are considered *raw data*; Table A.1 presents raw data. Descriptive statistics are used to summarize characteristics of a set of such data. It is the transformation of raw data into statistical terms that makes the data useful, allowing you to illustrate the relationships among the values or scores. One important type of descriptive statistic is the central tendency of the data: the clustering of the most characteristic values, or scores, for a particular group or sample. Central tendency can be expressed three ways. The most common, and probably the one with which you are most familiar, is the arithmetic average, or mean, of the scores or values. You calculate a mean by adding up the values in the group or sample, then dividing that sum by the total number of entries you summed. As shown in Table A.2, the mean for the placebo condition is 20 words remembered, and the mean for the drug condition is 29 words remembered.

A second way to specify central tendency is the median, which is the score that is the midpoint of the values for the group or sample; half the values fall above the median, and half fall below the median. It is easier to find the median if the data are arranged in order, as shown in Table A.3. The median in the placebo condition is 17.5, halfway between 17 and 18, the fifth and sixth ordered scores. In the memory drug condition, the median is 29.0, halfway between the fifth and sixth ordered scores of 27 and 31.

A third measure of central tendency is the mode, the value that appears most frequently in the group or sample. The mode

Table A.3 Fictional Data From Drug and Placebo Conditions, Arranged in Order

Number of Words Remembered

Placebo condition	Memory drug condition
12	17
14	19
15	21
15	23
17	27
----Median 17.5	----Median 29.0
18	31
21	31
22	34
28	40
38	47
Mode* = 15	Mode* = 31

*Mode = Value that appears most frequently.

can be any value, from the highest to the lowest. The mode in Table A.3 is 15 for the placebo condition and 31 for the memory drug condition. In addition, you can also use a mode for categorical scales, where the mode would be the most frequent category, such as "children" among all viewers of *Sesame Street*, or "Saturday night" as the evening most people go to bed the latest.

The mean is the measure of central tendency that is most sensitive to extreme values or scores; if you add a few values at the extreme end of the scale, the mean would change much more than the median (which often will not change at all). The mode does not generally change in response to an extreme score. If you changed the last score in Table A.3 in the placebo condition from 38 to 50, the mean would change from 20 to 21.2, but the median and mode would remain the same.

When a set of data has many scores near one extreme value and away from the center, it is said to have a **skewed distribution**. When a set of data has a skewed distribution, the median is often a more appropriate measure of central tendency than the mean (see Figure A.1).

Figure A.1 Skewed Distributions

In a positively skewed distribution, the bulk of the scores cluster on the low end of the graph and tail off on the high end.

In a negatively skewed distribution, the bulk of the scores cluster on the high end of the graph and tail off on the low end.

However, the three measures of central tendency generally yield similar results; this is especially likely as the number of observations (data points) becomes larger and if the data follow a normal distribution. As discussed in Chapter 6, the *normal distribution* is the familiar bell-shaped curve, in which most values fall in the midrange of the scale, and scores are increasingly less frequent as they taper off symmetrically toward the extremes (see Figure A.2). Normal curves occur many places in nature. For example, look at stone stairs in a very old building: You can usually see that they are worn more deeply in the center, and then less so as you move toward the sides. (If the building isn't old enough, you will see the beginnings of a normal curve, which over the generations will become deeper in the center until it resembles the shape of Figure A.2 upside down.) Or picture your classmates lined up according to height. Probably there are a few very tall or very short students on either end, with most clumping at an intermediate height. The same is true for many psychological qualities, such as scores on intelligence or personality tests.

Figure A.2 A Normal Distribution

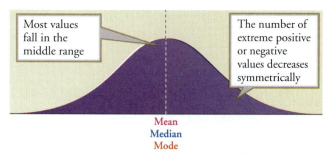

A NORMAL DISTRIBUTION

Most values fall in the middle range

The number of extreme positive or negative values decreases symmetrically

Mean
Median
Mode

Skewed distribution: A distribution of a set of data in which many scores are near one extreme value and away from the center.

Range: The difference obtained by subtracting the smallest score in a set of data from the largest; the simplest measure of variability.

Measures of Variability

Whereas measures of central tendency convey information about the most common values or scores, measures of *variability* convey information about the spread of the scores. **Range**, the difference obtained when you subtract the smallest score in a set of data from the largest, is the simplest measure of variability. For the data in Table A.3, for example, the range of scores in the placebo condition is 38 − 12, or 26. The range of scores for the drug condition is 47 − 17, or 30. But the range does not tell you how variable the scores are in general. Suppose you have developed two different drugs for improving memory, and participants who are given either one remember anywhere from 30 to 40 words; thus, both drugs have a range of 10. However, this measure of variability does not tell you that most participants who took drug A remember 37 or 38 words, whereas most of those who received drug B remember only 31 or 32 words. The range is the measure of variability most sensitive to extreme values.

Another method of assessing variability is the *standard deviation*, which is a kind of "average variability" in a set of measurements. In Chapter 6, you saw how important the standard deviation is for understanding IQ. Let's walk through how this important measure is computed:

Step 1: Calculate how much each score differs from the mean of the scores, as shown in Table A.4. Following this, it might be tempting to try to obtain an "average difference score" directly, by simply computing the average of the differences from the mean. But if you do this, you will get an average score of zero (each difference above the mean will be compensated by one below the mean; otherwise, it wouldn't be the mean!). Instead, before taking the average of the deviations from the mean, you square them, which eliminates the plus or minus signs.

Step 2: Find the total of these squared values. This number is often referred to as the *sum of squares*, or SS. As shown in Table A.4, the SS for the placebo condition data recorded in Table A.3 is 556.

Table A.4	Computing the Standard Deviation From the Placebo Condition Data in Table A.3

Step 1:

(Number of words remembered − Mean)^2 = Deviation score^2

$(12 - 20)^2 = -8^2 = 64$	$(18 - 20)^2 = -2^2 = 4$
$(14 - 20)^2 = -6^2 = 36$	$(21 - 20)^2 = 1^2 = 1$
$(15 - 20)^2 = -5^2 = 25$	$(22 - 20)^2 = 2^2 = 4$
$(15 - 20)^2 = -5^2 = 25$	$(28 - 20)^2 = 8^2 = 64$
$(17 - 20)^2 = -3^2 = 9$	$(38 - 20)^2 = 18^2 = 324$

Step 2: Sum of squares (SS) = Sum of squared deviation scores = 556

Step 3: Variance = SS ÷ Number of deviation scores = 556 ÷ 10 = 55.6

Step 4: Standard deviation = Square root of the variance = $\sqrt{55.6}$ = 7.46

Step 3: Divide the sum of squares by the total number of deviation scores that contributed to this sum. The resulting value is the *variance*. The variance for the placebo condition is 55.6.

Step 4: Finally, because the difference scores were squared in the first step, you need to "unsquare" variance to get a number that conveys meaningful information about the average variability of the scores. The square root of the variance is the *standard deviation*. The standard deviation of the placebo condition is 7.46.

Here is a simpler example. Say you want to know which of two Web search engines is likely to be consistently fastest. This means not just which engine has the fastest mean search time, or even the narrowest range of search times, but which has the least spread from the mean. The standard deviation is a measure of how consistently scores or values cluster near the mean, in this case how consistently fast a search engine can produce a list of hits for your query. The standard deviation is computed by taking each measured search time and subtracting it from the mean. Say, for simplicity's sake, that you measured the times for three searches by one search engine at 1, 3, and 5 seconds. The average (the mean) is 3 seconds. If you subtract each number from 3, you get −2, 0, and 2. Then, you square each of the differences from the mean (in this case, obtaining 4, 0, and 4), which gets rid of the plus and minus signs, and then sum these squared numbers and take their average (which gives you 8 divided by 3, or 2.67). If you then take the square root of this average (to undo the act of squaring), you have the standard deviation, a bit more than 1.6 seconds. You would do the same thing with the search times for the other engine and compare the results. A smaller standard deviation would mean that the searches are, in general, closer to the average search time. To do this right, however, you would perform many more than three trials with each search engine.

For values that are normally distributed, the standard deviation will tell you the percentage of values that fall at different points on the distribution. For instance, as noted in Chapter 6, about 68% of values fall between one standard deviation below the mean and one standard deviation above the mean. And about 95% of the values fall between two standard deviations below the mean and two standard deviations above the mean. Because 99.7% of values fall between three standard deviations below the mean and three standard deviations above the mean, you know that any value greater than three standard deviations is *really* different from the other values. The fact that standard deviations in a normal distribution always have these properties makes it easier to understand the relationship of standard deviations to the rest of the values in the data.

Let's go back to the earlier example of the placebo condition's standard deviation of 7.46 words (for simplicity's sake, we'll round this down to 7 words). What this means is that, with the placebo condition's mean of 20 words, roughly 68% of the participants in the placebo condition will remember somewhere between 13 and 27 words (20 − 7 to 20 + 7). At two standard deviations from the mean, roughly 95% of participants will remember between about 6 and 34 words.

Finally, it is well worth being familiar with the concept of a **confidence interval**, which specifies the range within which the mean of the actual population is likely to fall. The confidence interval is calculated like the standard deviation, but it is adjusted to reflect how the means of samples are distributed, not the individual data points (the details of this adjustment are not crucial here). You are probably already familiar with this concept, having heard it referred to in news broadcasts as the "margin of error" that accompanies poll results. For example, you might hear that "Smith is preferred by 51% of the voters and Jones by 47%, with a margin of error of 4—which puts them in a dead heat." A margin of error of 4 is a way of saying "plus or minus 4." That is, Smith is preferred by somewhere between 47% and 55% of the voters—51% plus or minus 4%. The confidence intervals can be set more or less stringently. For example, the most common confidence interval, set at 95%, means that 95% of the time the mean of the population would fall within the range of the upper and lower ends of that confidence interval.

Relative Standing

Sometimes you want to know where a particular score stands relative to other scores. For example, college admissions officers want to know how an applicant's SAT scores stand relative to other applicants' scores. One way to convey this information is in terms of measures of variability. For example, you could specify how many standard deviations a score is from the mean. (This is the way IQ scores are set up, with 15 points as a standard deviation for the WAIS.) However, this isn't very useful if you are interested in the specific number or percentage of other cases that fall above or below a particular one. Another way of conveying information about a value relative to other values in a set of measurements is to use a **percentile rank**: a number indicating the percentage of data that have values at or below a particular value. A value converted to a percentile rank of 50, for example, instantly tells you that 50% of the values in a sample fall at or below that

Confidence interval: The range within which the mean of a population is likely to occur.

Percentile rank: A number indicating the percentage of data that have values at or below a particular value.

particular score; the median is a percentile rank of 50. *Quartiles* are percentile ranks that divide the group into fourths (25th, 50th, 75th, and 100th percentiles); a score that is at the third quartile signifies that 75% of the group fall at or below that score. *Deciles* are percentile ranks that divide the group into tenths; a score at the sixth decile indicates that 60% of the scores fall at or below that value.

Inferential Statistics

So far the discussion has focused on descriptive statistics. But you now have the tools to understand common inferential statistics.

Correlation: The Relationship Between Two Variables

Suppose you want to know not just about the central tendency and variability of a set of scores, but whether two variables are related to each other. Is a change in one variable accompanied by a change in another? You saw in Chapter 1 that a *correlation* shows only that two variables vary together, not that a change in one causes a change in the other. A positive relationship (in which increases in one variable are accompanied by increases in another) is indicated by a correlation value that falls between 0 and 1.0; a negative relationship (in which increases in one variable are accompanied by decreases in another) is indicated by a correlation that is between 0 and −1.0. Zero indicates no relationship between the two variables; they do not vary together. The closer the correlation is to 1.0 or −1.0, the stronger the relationship. So, for instance, you may read that people who exercise moderately don't get as severely depressed as people who don't exercise at all. If this information is based on a correlation, it would be a negative correlation: Increasing exercise is associated with less severe depression. However, concluding that exercise helps prevent severe depression (exercise *causes* less severe depression) based on that correlation would be a mistake. Perhaps people who are severely depressed don't have the energy to exercise. If that is true, the direction of causation would be in the other direction (more severe depression *causes* less exercise). With correlation, we know only that the two variables are related, either positively or negatively, not the direction of causality. It is possible that some third variable affects the other two variables. It could be that regularly getting out of the house or office and going to a gym (and therefore having a change of scenery and being around other people) affects the severity of depression, and so it is not the exercise per se but interacting with people that is related to less severe depression.

To think about how the correlation value is calculated, go back to the idea of a standard deviation. But now, instead of computing the deviations relative to the mean of all the numbers, imagine that you have a line running through the data points (Figure A.3). The closer the data points hug the line, the higher the absolute value of correlation (that is, the higher the number—ignoring whether it is positive or negative). The *method of least squares* is a way to fit a line to a cloud of points. Again, squared numbers are used to eliminate the signs of the difference values. This method positions the line to minimize the square of the distance of each point from the line.

Correlations and other types of inferential statistics can be *significant* or *not significant*. What does "significant" mean? In statistics, it does not mean "important." Rather, it means that the measured relationship is not simply due to chance. If you correlate any two randomly selected sets of measurements, it is likely that the correlation will not be precisely zero. Say you correlated IQ with ear size and found a correlation of .12. Should you pay attention to this correlation, developing

Figure A.3 Strength of Correlation

ZERO CORRELATION

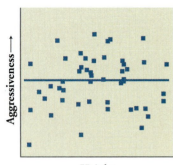

A zero correlation indicates no relationship between the two variables, height and aggressiveness here; they do not vary together. The closer the correlation is to 1.0 or −1.0, the stronger the relationship; visually, the more tightly the data points cluster around the line, the higher the correlation.

POSITIVE CORRELATION BETWEEN 0 AND 1.0

Here, increases in one variable (height) are accompanied by increases in another (weight); this is a positive correlation, indicated by a correlation value that falls between 0 and 1.0.

NEGATIVE CORRELATION BETWEEN 0 AND −1.0

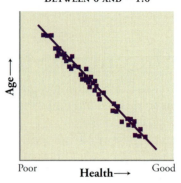

Here, increases in one variable (age) are accompanied by decreases in another (health); this is a negative correlation, indicated by a correlation value that is between 0 and −1.0.

a grand theory to explain it? The size of a correlation needed for statistical significance, to be taken as not just chance variation, depends on the number of pairs of values analyzed (each represented by a point in Figure A.3). As a general rule, the more observations considered when computing the correlation, the smaller the correlation value needs to be to achieve statistical significance. Why? Imagine that you were randomly throwing darts into a rectangular corkboard on the wall. It is possible that the first few on the left would be lower than those on the right. But as you tossed more and more darts, those initial quirks would be balanced out by quirks later in the process, so after 100 darts, there would no longer be any discernible pattern. The more observations you have, the less influence extreme values will have.

Statistical significance is expressed in terms of the probability (p) that a value (such as the size of a correlation) could be due to chance. For example, $p < .05$ means that the probability that the result was simply due to chance is less than 5 in 100; $p < .001$ means that the probability that it was due to chance is less than 1 in 1,000. By convention, any value with $p < .05$ or smaller is considered significant—not likely to be a result simply of chance variation in the data. You can look up a correlation value in a table to determine its significance, but most computer programs that compute correlation do this for you automatically.

Samples and Populations

Back to the memory-enhancing drug study. Did the drug work? If you had measured every person on the planet, all you would need to do is look at the descriptive statistics. Either the drug resulted in better remembering than the placebo or it didn't. But such all-inclusive testing isn't practical. Virtually all research in psychology relies on studying data from a *sample*—a group drawn from the population at large—and the goal is to generalize from the findings with the sample to the larger population. Inferential statistics let you *infer* that the difference found between your samples does, in fact, reflect a difference in the corresponding populations.

Here's a simple example: Say you wanted to know whether seniors are generally friendlier than freshmen (you theorize that as they gain confidence and a sense of independence, students *do* become friendlier). To find out, you administer a questionnaire your professor has just designed and validated to measure friendliness. If you administered the questionnaire to five freshmen and five seniors, you would probably find a difference. But if you had ten students from a single year and randomly assigned them to two groups of five, you would probably also find a difference between the groups! This difference would arise because of how you happened to assign students to groups. No matter how you did it, the groups would be likely to be different. Only if you had a large number of students would assigning them randomly to two groups be likely to result in groups that were very similar. When enough students from the same class have been tested, those who score particularly high or low will be assigned equally often to each group, on average, and thus their disproportionate contributions will cancel out. When you compare freshmen and seniors, you can't know for sure whether you've got enough participants so that any difference between them is "real"—reflecting actual differences between the two classes in general—or is due to ==sampling error==, a difference that arises from the luck of the draw, not because two samples are, in fact, representative of different populations. In this example, if differences between freshmen and seniors are due to sampling error, the two classes of students are not different. There are tests that can indicate whether a difference between two groups is due to sampling error or reflects a real difference, although details about such tests are beyond the scope of this appendix.

Generalizing From the Results

Say that a research study found that exercise by itself really does ward off severe depression. Does that mean that *you* should start exercising when you feel yourself getting depressed? Not necessarily. Generalizing from the results of a study should be done with caution. Consider the following questions before applying the results of this or any study to yourself or anyone else.

1. Are the results *valid*? If the study relied on an experimental design, were the participants randomly assigned? (See Chapter 1 for an explanation of why this is important.) If it used a correlational design, is the study implying that one variable causes another? If so, that conclusion isn't supported by the data. Do you think the researchers were appropriately assessing the variables they claimed to be assessing? For instance, if they measured depression by simply comparing how slowly participants spoke at the end of the study with their speech speed at the beginning, would that be a valid assessment of depression?

2. If the study involved a new treatment or method of improving some aspect of life, was this method compared with a control group, perhaps a group given a placebo?

3. Did the researchers try to control for possible confounds (see Chapter 1)?

4. Was the study performed with a wide cross-section of people or a small sample? For instance, if a positron emission tomography (PET) study found that people with attention-deficit/hyperactivity disorder (ADHD) had unusual activity levels in a particular part of the brain, you would want to ask the following questions before concluding that the findings generalize beyond the participants in the study: How many participants were involved? What was

Sampling error: A difference that arises by chance, not because the samples are representative of different populations.

the gender of the participants? Are there other factors about the participants that make it difficult to generalize to you, to North Americans, or to all people? If a study is restricted to people of a certain geographic region, ethnic group, or those with a particular medical, psychological, or social history, it may not be appropriate to generalize the results, depending on the variable being assessed.

Lying With Statistics

Statistics can be used or misused. In a famous book entitled *How to Lie with Statistics*, Derrell Huff (1954) demonstrated many ways that people use statistics to distort the pattern of results. This book played a valuable role in inoculating many people against these deceptive techniques, and some of its high points are summarized here. Be on the lookout for these manipulations whenever you see statistics.

Figure A.4 Number of Symptoms After Therapy for Acrophobia

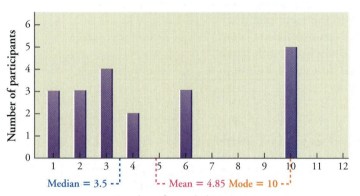

Number of acrophobic symptoms

Selective Reporting

Because different types of statistics convey different information, the same data can be manipulated to "say" different things. Look at Figure A.4 and Table A.5, which present fictitious data for the results of a new type of therapy for people with acrophobia—a fear of heights. Before the therapy, participants reported 9 symptoms of acrophobia on average; that is, before treatment, the mean number of symptoms was 9. After the therapy, the mean number of symptoms was 4.85, the median was 3.5, and the mode was 10. Proponents of the new therapy make the following claims: On average, symptoms decreased by almost half (based on the mean), and more than 50% of participants had substantial symptom reduction (based on the median). Opponents, however, convey the data differently. A spokeswoman from the pharmaceutical company that manufactures a medication to treat acrophobia makes several counterclaims when she promotes the superiority of her company's medication: The number of symptoms most frequently reported was 10, which shows that the therapy actually made people *more* symptomatic (based on the mode). Also, the therapy achieved mixed results, as indicated by the fact that the number of symptoms after treatment ranged from 1 to 10.

As you can see, both supporters and detractors of the new treatment are correct. They are just presenting different aspects of the data. Thus, when hearing or reading about research or survey results, you should ask several questions before taking the results too seriously.

1. What is the distribution of the results? If the scores or data points are normally distributed, the measures of central tendency will be similar. If the distribution is skewed, however, the measures of central tendency will convey different information, and the one presented will be the one that conveys the information the reporter wants you to know about. Do the other measures of central tendency paint a different picture of the results?

2. How variable are the data? What does it mean if the results vary a lot rather than a little?

Table A.5

Fictional Results of Therapy for Acrophobia

Mean number of symptoms after therapy for acrophobia

= Total number of symptoms ÷ Total number of participants

= 1 + 1 + 1 + 2 + 2 + 2 + 3 + 3 + 3 + 3 + 4 + 4 + 6 + 6 + 6 + 10 + 10 + 10 + 10 + 10

= 97 ÷ 20 = 4.85

Median = 3.5

Mode = 10

Figure A.5 Shortening the Y Axis Can Mislead

The graph on the left presents the actual numbers in a neutral way; the graph on the right exaggerates the difference.

Figure A.6 Lengthening the Y Axis Can Mislead

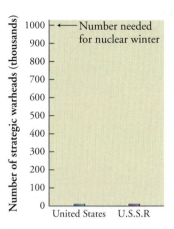

The graph on the left presents the actual numbers in a neutral way; the graph on the right minimizes the difference.

Lying With Graphs

Many results are presented in graph form. Graphs work largely because of a single principle: *More is more* (Kosslyn, 1994a). Larger bars, higher lines, or bigger wedges all stand for greater amounts than smaller bars, lines, or wedges. Our tendency to see more on the page as standing for more of a substance can lead us astray if graphs are constructed to deceive. Be alert to the following tricks.

- *Shortening the Y (vertical) axis to exaggerate a difference.* As you can see in the right-hand graph of Figure A.5, starting the Y axis at a high value and devoting the Y axis to a small part of the scale make what is in fact a small difference look like a large one. If a difference is significant, it should look that way (and thus shortening the axis may be appropriate). But if it's not, then shortening the axis to exaggerate the difference is deception.

- *Using an inappropriately large range of values to minimize a difference.* The flip side of the coin is illustrated in the right-hand graph of Figure A.6, in which a difference is made to appear smaller by using a large range in values on the Y axis.

- *Using three-dimensional graphics to exaggerate size.* As shown in Figure A.7 (on p. A-12), a designer can take advantage of our tendency to impose size constancy (see Chapter 3), so that a bar that is farther away will be seen as *much* larger than a same-size one that is closer. And even if an actual difference exists, this technique can exaggerate its magnitude.

- *Transforming the data before plotting.* Compare the two graphs in Figure A.8 (on p. A-12). The left-hand one shows the size of the stock market in three countries over 3 years; the right-hand one shows the percentage increase over two 5-year periods. If you saw only the graph on the right, you wouldn't realize that the increases in the U.S. stock market were

Figure A.7 Size Constancy Can Exaggerate Three-Dimensional Bar Size

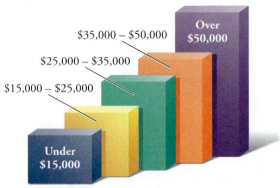

$35,000 – $50,000

$25,000 – $35,000

$15,000 – $25,000

Under $15,000

Over $50,000

INCOME IN WHITE FAMILIES (1991)

Size constancy leads us to see the bars that are farther away as larger than they are, thereby exaggerating a difference.

actually much greater than those in Japan. If the user is trying to sell Japanese stocks, you can bet which display will be preferred.

- *Changing width along with height.* As shown in Figure A.9, our visual system does not register height and width separately; instead, we see them simultaneously, as specifying area. So changing the width along with the height gives a much larger impression of amount than is conveyed by changing height alone.

Figure A.8 Transforming Data Can Distort the Conclusions

SIZE OF STOCK MARKET

PERCENT CHANGE IN SIZE OF STOCK MARKET

The graph on the left shows the actual dollar figures, and the one on the right shows the percentage change. Clearly, the message conveyed by the two displays is different. Which one is "more honest" depends on the purpose for which the graph is used.

Figure A.9 Changing Width With Height Exaggerates Size

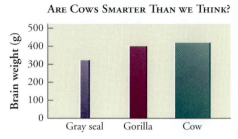

Expanding the bar width conveys the impression that more quantity is being represented than increasing the height alone signals.

Statistics in Daily Life

You can see that there is nothing magical or mysterious about statistics. Whenever you see a graph in the newspaper, you are seeing statistics; when you hear that a poll is accurate to "plus or minus 3 points," you know that you are being supplied with a confidence interval. The crucial ideas are that there are measures of central tendency (mean, median, and mode), measures of variability (range and standard deviation), and statistical tests that tell you the likelihood that a measured difference is due to chance alone. What you've learned here is enough to enable you to read and understand many reports of original research in psychology.

GLOSSARY

Absolute threshold: The smallest amount of a stimulus needed in order to detect that the stimulus is present.

Academic psychologist: The type of psychologist who focuses on teaching and conducting research.

Accommodation (in eye):   The phenomenon that occurs when muscles adjust the shape of the lens so that it focuses light on the retina from objects at different distances.

Accommodation (in Piaget's theory):   The process that results in schemas' changing as necessary to cope with a broader range of situations.

Acquisition: In classical conditioning, the initial learning of the conditioned response (CR).

Action potential: The shifting change in charge that moves down the axon.

Activation–synthesis hypothesis: The theory that dreams arise from random bursts of nerve cell activity, which may affect brain cells involved in hearing and seeing; the brain attempts to make sense of this hodgepodge of stimuli, resulting in the experience of dreams.

Active interaction: Occurs when people choose, partly based on genetic tendencies, to put themselves in specific situations and to avoid others.

Activity: A temperament dimension characterized by the general expenditure of energy, which has two components: vigor (intensity of the activity) and tempo (speed of the activity).

Acute stressor: A stressor of short-term duration.

Adaptation: A characteristic that increases an organism's fitness for an environment.

Adolescence: The period between the onset of puberty and, roughly, the end of the teenage years.

Adoption study: A study in which characteristics of children adopted at birth are compared to those of their adoptive parents or siblings versus their biological parents or siblings (often twins). These studies often focus on comparisons of twins who were raised in the same versus different households.

Affirming the consequent: A reasoning error that occurs because of the assumption that if a result has occurred, a specific cause must also be present.

Afterimage: The image left behind by a previous perception.

Aggression: Behavior that is intended to harm another living being who does not wish to be harmed.

Agonist: A chemical that mimics the effects of a neurotransmitter by activating a type of receptor.

Agoraphobia: A condition in which people fear or avoid places that might be difficult to leave should panic symptoms occur.

Alarm phase: The first phase of the GAS, in which a stressor is perceived and the fight-or-flight response is activated.

Alcohol myopia: The disproportionate influence of immediate experience on behavior and emotion due to the effects of alcohol use.

Algorithm: A set of steps that, if followed methodically, will guarantee the solution to a problem.

All-or-none law: States that if the neuron is sufficiently stimulated, it fires, sending the action potential all the way down the axon and releasing chemicals from the terminal buttons; either the action potential occurs or it doesn't.

Altruism: The motivation to increase another person's welfare.

Amnesia: A loss of memory over an entire time span, resulting from brain damage caused by accident, infection, or stroke.

Amphetamines: Synthetic stimulants.

Amplitude: The height of the peaks in a light wave.

Amygdala: A subcortical structure that plays a special role in fear and is involved in other sorts of emotions, such as anger.

Androgens: Sex hormones that cause many male characteristics such as beard growth and a low voice.

Anorexia nervosa: An eating disorder characterized by the refusal to maintain even a low normal weight, and an intense fear of gaining weight.

Antagonist: A chemical that interferes with the effect of a neurotransmitter (often by blocking a receptor).

Anterograde amnesia: Amnesia that leaves consolidated memories intact but prevents new learning.

Antipsychotic medication: Medication that reduces psychotic symptoms.

Antisocial personality disorder (ASPD):   A personality disorder characterized by a long-standing pattern of disregard for other people to the point of violating their rights.

Anxiety disorders: A category of disorders whose hallmark is intense or pervasive anxiety or fear, or extreme attempts to avoid these feelings.

Applied psychologist: The type of psychologist who studies how to improve products and procedures and conducts research to help solve specific practical problems.

Approach–approach conflict: The internal conflict that occurs when competing alternatives are equally positive.

Approach–avoidance conflict: The internal conflict that occurs when a course of action has both positive and negative aspects.

Assimilation: In Piaget's theory, the process that allows the use of existing schemas to take in new sets of stimuli and respond accordingly.

Atherosclerosis: A medical condition characterized by plaque buildup in the arteries.

Attachment: An emotional bond that leads a person to want to be with someone else and to miss him or her when separated.

Attention: The act of focusing on particular information, which allows it to be processed more fully than what is not attended to.

Attentional blink: A rebound period in which a person cannot pay attention to one thing after having just paid attention to another.

Attitude: An overall evaluation about some aspect of the world.

Attribution: An explanation for the cause of an event or behavior.

Attributional bias: A cognitive shortcut for determining attribution that generally occurs outside of conscious awareness.

Attributional style: A person's characteristic way of explaining life events.

Automatic processing: Processing that allows you to carry out a sequence of steps without having to pay attention to each one or to the relations between the steps.

Autonomic nervous system (ANS):   Controls the smooth muscles in the body, some glandular functions, and many of the body's self-regulating activities, such as digestion and circulation.

Availability heuristic: The tendency to judge objects or events as more likely, common, or frequent if they are easier to bring to mind.

Avoidance–avoidance conflict: The internal conflict that occurs when competing alternatives are equally unpleasant.

Avoidance learning: In classical conditioning, learning that occurs when a CS is paired with an unpleasant US that leads the organism to try to avoid the CS.

Axon: The sending end of the neuron; the long cablelike structure extending from the cell body.

B cell: A type of white blood cell that matures in the bone marrow.

Basal ganglia: Subcortical structures that play a role in planning and producing movement.

Base-rate rule: The rule stating that if something is chosen from a set at random, the chances that the thing will be of a particular type are directly proportional to the percentage of that type in the larger set.

Basic emotion: An innate emotion that is shared by all humans, such as surprise, happiness, anger, fear, disgust, or sadness.

Basic level: A level of specificity, which is usually the most likely to be applied to an object.

Behavior: The outwardly observable acts of an individual, alone or in a group.

Behavior modification: Any technique that brings about therapeutic change in behavior through the application of operant conditioning principles and the use of secondary reinforcers.

Behavior therapy: A type of therapy, based on well-researched learning principles, that focuses on changing observable, measurable behaviors.

Behavioral genetics: The field in which researchers attempt to determine the extent to which the differences among people are due to their genes or to the environment.

Behaviorism: The school of psychology that focuses on how a specific stimulus (object, person, or event) evokes a specific response (behavior in reaction to the stimulus).

Belief in a just world: An attributional bias that assumes that people get what they deserve.

Benzodiazepine: A type of antianxiety medication that affects the target symptoms within 36 hours and does not need to be taken for more than a week to be effective.

Bias (in experimental research): An effect that occurs when beliefs, expectations, or habits alter how participants in a study respond or affect how a researcher sets up or conducts a study, thereby influencing its outcome.

Bias (in signal detection theory): A person's willingness to report noticing a stimulus.

Bibliotherapy: The use of self-help books and tapes for therapeutic purposes.

Big Five: The five superfactors of personality—extraversion, neuroticism, agreeableness, conscientiousness, and openness—determined by factor analysis.

Binocular cues: Cues to the distance of an object that arise from both eyes working together.

Biological preparedness: A built-in readiness for certain conditioned stimuli to elicit particular conditioned responses, so less conditioning (training) is necessary to produce learning.

Bipolar disorder: A mood disorder marked by one or more episodes of either mania or hypomania, often alternating with periods of depression.

Bisexual: A person who is sexually attracted to members of both sexes.

Blackout: A period of time for which an alcoholic has no memory of events that transpired while he or she was intoxicated.

Bottom-up processing: Processing that is initiated by stimulus input.

Brain circuit: A set of neurons that affect one another.

Brainstem: The set of neural structures at the base of the brain, including the medulla and pons.

Breadth of processing: Processing that organizes and integrates information into previously stored information, often by making associations.

Bulimia nervosa: An eating disorder characterized by recurrent episodes of binge eating, followed by some attempt to prevent weight gain.

Bystander effect: The decrease in offers of assistance that occurs as the number of bystanders increases.

Case study: A scientific study that focuses on a single instance of a situation, examining it in detail.

Castration anxiety: A boy's anxiety-laden fear that, as punishment for loving mother and hating father, his father will cut off his penis (the primary zone of pleasure).

Categorical perception: Identifying sounds as belonging to distinct categories that correspond to the basic units of speech.

Categorical variables: Variables whose values are assigned to discrete classes.

Category: A grouping in which the members are specific cases of a more general type.

Cell body: The central part of a neuron (or other cell), which contains the nucleus.

Cell membrane: The skin of a cell.

Central executive: The set of processes that operates on information in one or another of two specialized STMs; part of working memory.

Central nervous system (CNS): The spinal cord and the brain.

Central tendency: A descriptive statistic that indicates the clustering of the most characteristic values, or scores, for a particular group or sample.

Cerebellum: A large structure at the base of the brain that is concerned in part with physical coordination, estimating time, and paying attention.

Cerebral cortex: The convoluted pinkish-gray outer layer of the brain, where most mental processes take place.

Cerebral hemisphere: A left or right half-brain, shaped roughly like half a sphere.

Chemical senses: Taste and smell, which rely on sensing the presence of specific chemicals.

Child-directed speech (CDS): Speech by caregivers to babies that relies on short sentences with clear pauses, careful enunciation, exaggerated intonation, and a high-pitched voice.

Chronic stressor: A stressor of long-term duration.

Chunk: A unit of information, such as a digit, letter, or word.

Circadian rhythms: The body's daily fluctuations in response to the cycle of dark and light, which occur with blood pressure, pulse rate, body temperature, blood sugar level, hormone levels, and metabolism.

Classical conditioning: A type of learning that occurs when a neutral stimulus becomes paired (associated) with a stimulus that causes a reflexive behavior and, in time, is sufficient to produce that behavior.

Client-centered therapy: A type of insight-oriented therapy that focuses on people's potential for growth and the importance of an empathic therapist.

Clinical psychologist: The type of psychologist who provides psychotherapy and is trained to administer and interpret psychological tests.

Cocktail party phenomenon: The effect of not being aware of other people's conversations until your name is mentioned, and then suddenly hearing it.

Code: A type of mental representation, an internal "re-presentation" (such as in words or images) of a stimulus or event.

Cognitive–behavior therapy (CBT): A type of therapy that aims to change problematic behaviors and irrational thoughts and provide new, more adaptive behaviors and beliefs to replace old, maladaptive ones.

Cognitive dissonance: The uncomfortable state that arises because of a discrepancy between an attitude and behavior or between two attitudes.

Cognitive distortions: Irrational thoughts that arise from a systematic bias in the way a person thinks about reality.

Cognitive learning: The acquisition of information that often is not immediately acted on but is stored for later use.

Cognitive neuroscience: A blending of cognitive psychology and neuroscience (the study of the brain) that aims to specify how the brain stores and processes information.

Cognitive psychology: The approach in psychology that attempts to characterize how information is stored and operated on internally.

Cognitive restructuring: The process of helping clients shift their thinking away from the focus on automatic, dysfunctional thoughts to more realistic ones.

Cognitive therapy: A type of therapy that focuses on the client's thoughts rather than his or her feelings or behaviors.

Collectivist culture: A culture that emphasizes the rights and responsibilities of the group over those of the individual.

Color blindness: An inability, either acquired (by brain damage) or inherited, to perceive certain hues.

Color constancy: Seeing objects as having the same color in different viewing situations.

Companionate love: A type of love marked by very close friendship, mutual caring, liking, respect, and attraction.

Complex inheritance: The joint action of combinations of genes working together.

Compliance: A change in behavior prompted by a direct request rather than by social norms.

Compulsion: A repetitive behavior or mental act that an individual feels compelled to perform in response to an obsession.

Computer-assisted tomography (CT, formerly CAT): A neuroimaging technique that produces a three-dimensional image of brain structures using X rays.

Concept: An unambiguous, sometimes abstract, internal representation that defines a grouping of a set of objects (including living things) or events (including relationships).

Concrete operation: In Piaget's theory, a (reversible) manipulation of the mental representation of an object that corresponds to an actual physical manipulation.

Conditioned emotional response (CER): An emotional response elicited by a previously neutral stimulus.

Conditioned response (CR): A response that depends, or is conditional, on pairings of the conditioned stimulus with an unconditioned stimulus; once learned, the conditioned response occurs when the conditioned stimulus is presented alone.

Conditioned stimulus (CS): An originally neutral stimulus that acquires significance through pairings with an unconditioned stimulus (US).

Conduction deafness: A type of deafness caused by a physical impairment of the external or middle ear.

Cones: Cone-shaped retinal cells that respond most strongly to one of three wavelengths of light; the combined outputs from cones that are most sensitive to different wavelengths play a key role in producing color vision.

Confidence interval: The range within which the mean of a population is likely to occur.

Confirmation bias: A tendency to seek information that will confirm a rule, and not to seek information that is inconsistent with the rule.

Conformity: A change in beliefs or behavior in order to follow a group's norms.

Confound (or confounding variable): An independent variable that varies along with the ones of interest, and could be the actual basis for what you are measuring.

Conservation: The Piagetian principle that certain properties, such as amount or mass, remain the same even when the appearance of the material or object changes, provided that nothing is added or removed.

Consolidation: The process of converting information stored dynamically in LTM into a structural change in the brain.

Continuous reinforcement: Reinforcement given for each desired response.

Continuous variables: Variables whose values can fall anywhere along the measurement scale.

Contrapreparedness: A built-in disinclination (or even an inability) for certain conditioned stimuli to elicit particular conditioned responses.

Control condition: A condition administered to the same participants who receive the experimental condition; this effectively makes the participants both the experimental and the control group.

Control group: A group that is treated exactly the same way as the experimental group, except that the one aspect of the situation being studied is not manipulated for this group. The control group holds constant—"controls"—all of the variables in the experimental group except the one of interest.

Controlled processing: Processing that requires paying attention to each step of an action and using working memory (WM) to coordinate the steps.

Convergence: The degree to which the eyes are crossed when a person fixates on an object.

Coping: Taking some course of action regarding the stressor, its effects, or the person's reaction to it.

Cornea: The transparent covering over the eye, which serves partly to focus the light onto the back of the eye.

Corpus callosum: The large band of nerve fibers that connects the two halves of the brain.

Correlation coefficient (or *correlation*): An index of how closely interrelated two sets of measured variables are, which ranges from -1.0 to $+1.0$. The higher the correlation (in either direction), the better we can predict the value of one type of measurement when given the value of the other.

Correspondence bias: The strong tendency to interpret other people's behavior as due to internal (dispositional) causes rather than external (situational) ones.

Cortisol: A hormone produced by the outer layer of the adrenal glands that helps the body cope with the extra energy demands of stress by breaking down and converting protein and fat to sugar.

Counseling psychologist: The type of psychologist who is trained to help people with issues that naturally arise during the course of life.

Crack: Cocaine in crystalline form, usually smoked in a pipe (free-basing) or rolled into a cigarette.

Creativity: The ability to produce something original of high quality or to devise an effective new way of solving a problem.

Critical period: A narrow window of time when a certain type of learning or some aspect of development is possible.

Cross-sectional study: A study in which different groups of people are tested, with each group composed of individuals of a particular age.

Crystallized intelligence: According to Cattell and Horn, the kind of intelligence that relies on knowing facts and having the ability to use and combine them.

Cues: Stimuli that trigger or enhance remembering; reminders.

Dark adaptation: The process whereby exposure to darkness causes the eyes to become more sensitive, allowing for better vision in the dark.

Data: Objective observations.

Debriefing: An interview after a study to ensure that the participant has no negative reactions as a result of participation and understands why the study was conducted.

Decay: The fading away of memories with time because the relevant connections between neurons are lost.

Decibel (dB): A measure of loudness on a base-10 logarithmic scale; the threshold for hearing is set at 0 dB.

Deductive reasoning: Reasoning that applies the rules of logic to a set of assumptions (stated as premises) to discover whether certain conclusions follow from those assumptions; deduction goes from the general to the particular.

Defense mechanism: An unconscious psychological means by which a person tries to prevent unacceptable thoughts or urges from reaching conscious awareness.

Deindividuation: The loss of sense of self that occurs when people in a group are anonymous.

Delayed reinforcement: Reinforcement given some period of time after the desired behavior is exhibited.

Delusions: Entrenched false beliefs that are often bizarre.

Dendrite: The treelike part of a neuron that receives messages from the axons of other neurons.

Deoxyribonucleic acid, or DNA: The molecule that contains genes.

Dependent variable: The aspect of the situation that is measured as an independent variable is changed; the value of the dependent variable depends on the independent variable.

Depressants: A class of substances, including barbiturates, alcohol, and antianxiety drugs, that depress the central nervous system, decreasing the user's behavioral activity and level of awareness; also called *sedative-hypnotic drugs.*

Deprived reward: Reward that occurs when a biological need is met.

Depth of processing: The number and complexity of the operations involved in processing information, expressed in a continuum from shallow to deep.

Descriptive statistics: Concise ways of summarizing properties of sets of numbers.

Diathesis–stress model: A way of understanding the development of a psychological disorder, in which a predisposition to a given disorder (diathesis) and specific factors (stress) combine to trigger the onset of the disorder.

Dichotic listening: A procedure in which participants hear stimuli presented separately to the two ears (through headphones) and are instructed to listen only to sounds presented to one ear.

Diffusion of responsibility: The diminished sense of responsibility to help that each person feels as the number of bystanders grows.

Discrimination: The ability to engage in a learned behavior in response to a particular stimulus but not in response to a similar one.

Discriminative stimulus: The cue that tells the organism whether a specific response will lead to the expected reinforcement.

Disinhibition: The inhibition of inhibitory neurons, which makes other neurons (the ones that are usually inhibited) more likely to fire and which usually occurs as a result of depressant use.

Display rule: A culture-specific rule that indicates when, to whom, and how strongly certain emotions can be shown.

Dizygotic: From different eggs and sharing only as many genes as any pair of brothers or sisters—on average, half.

Door-in-the-face technique: A compliance technique in which someone makes a very large request and then, when it is denied, as expected, makes a smaller request (for what is actually desired).

Double-blind design: The participant is "blind" to (unaware of) the predictions of the study (and so cannot consciously or unconsciously produce the predicted results), and the experimenter is "blind" to the condition assigned to the participant (and so experimenter expectancy effects cannot produce the predicted results).

Double pain: The sensation that occurs when an injury first causes a sharp pain, and later a dull pain; the two kinds of pain arise from different fibers sending their messages at different speeds.

Down syndrome: A type of mental retardation that results from the creation of an extra chromosome during conception; it is a genetic problem but not inherited.

Dream analysis: A technique used in psychoanalysis and psychodynamic therapy in which the therapist examines the content of dreams to gain access to the unconscious.

Drive: An internal imbalance that motivates animals (including humans) to reach a particular goal that will reduce the imbalance.

Eating disorders: A category of disorders involving a severe disturbance in eating behavior.

Effect: The difference in the dependent variable that is due to the changes in the independent variable.

Ego: A personality structure, proposed by Freud, that develops in childhood and tries to balance the competing demands of the id, superego, and reality.

Egocentrism: In Piaget's theory, the inability to take another person's point of view.

Elaborative encoding: Encoding that involves great breadth of processing.

Electroconvulsive therapy (ECT): Use of an electric current to induce a controlled brain seizure in people with certain psychological disorders such as psychotic depression or those for whom medication has not been effective or recommended.

Electroencephalogram (EEG): A recording from the scalp of electrical activity in the brain over time, which produces a tracing of pulses at different frequencies.

Electroencephalograph: A machine that records electrical current produced by the brain.

Embryo: A developing baby from the point where the major axis of the body is present until all major structures are present, spanning from about 2 weeks to 8 weeks after conception.

Emotion: A psychological state with four components: (1) a positive or negative subjective experience, (2) bodily arousal, (3) the activation of specific mental processes and stored information, and (4) characteristic overt behavior.

Emotion-focused coping: Coping focused on changing the person's emotional response to the stressor.

Emotional intelligence (EI): The ability to understand and regulate emotions effectively.

Emotionality: A temperament dimension characterized by an inclination to become aroused in situations in which the predominant emotion is distress, fear, or anger.

Enacted social support: The specific supportive behaviors provided by others.

Encoding: The process of organizing and transforming incoming information so that it can be entered into memory, either to be stored or to be compared with previously stored information.

Encoding failure: A failure to process to-be-remembered information well enough to begin consolidation.

Endogenous cannabinoids: Neuromodulators released by the receiving neuron that then influence the activity of the sending neuron.

Endorphins: Painkilling chemicals produced naturally in the brain.

Episodic memories: Memories of events that are associated with a particular context—a time, place, and circumstance.

Estrogen: The hormone that causes breasts to develop and is involved in the menstrual cycle.

Estrogens: Sex hormones that cause many female characteristics such as breast development and the bone structure of the female pelvis.

Evocative (or reactive) interaction: Occurs when genetically influenced characteristics draw out behaviors from other people.

Evolution: Gene-based changes in the characteristics of members of a species over successive generations.

Evolutionary psychology: The approach in psychology that assumes that certain cognitive strategies and goals are so important that natural selection has built them into our brains.

Exhaustion phase: The final stage of the GAS, in which the continued stress response itself becomes damaging to the body.

Expectancies: Expectations that have a powerful influence on thoughts, feelings, and behaviors and, in turn, on personality.

Experimental condition: A part of a study in which the participant receives the complete procedure that defines the experiment. Usually this is accompanied by a control condition, with the same participants receiving both experimental and control conditions.

Experimental group: A group that receives the complete procedure that defines the experiment.

Experimenter expectancy effects: Effects that occur when an investigator's expectations lead him or her (consciously or unconsciously) to treat participants in a way that encourages them to produce the expected results.

Explicit (or declarative) memories: Memories that can be retrieved at will and represented in STM; verbal and visual memories are explicit if they can be called to mind as words or images.

Exposure: A therapeutic technique based on classical conditioning that rests on the principle of habituation.

External attribution: An explanation of someone's behavior that focuses on the situation; also called *situational attribution*.

Extinction (in classical conditioning): The process by which a CR comes to be eliminated through repeated presentations of the CS without the presence of the US.

Extinction (in operant conditioning): The fading out of a response following an initial burst of that behavior after the withdrawal of reinforcement.

Extrasensory perception (ESP): The ability to perceive and know things without using the ordinary senses.

Facial feedback hypothesis: The idea that emotions arise partly as a result of the positioning of facial muscles.

Factor analysis: A statistical method that uncovers the particular attributes (factors) that make scores more or less similar; the more similar the scores, the more strongly implicated are shared underlying factors.

False memories: Memories of events or situations that did not, in fact, occur.

Family therapy: A therapy modality in which a family (or certain members of a family) is treated.

Fetal alcohol syndrome: A condition that includes mental retardation and is caused by excessive drinking of alcohol by the mother during pregnancy.

Fetus: A developing baby during the final phase of development in the womb, from about 8 weeks after conception until birth.

Figure: In perception, a set of characteristics (such as shape, color, texture) that corresponds to an object.

Fixed interval schedule: Reinforcement schedule in which reinforcement is given for a response emitted after a fixed interval of time.

Fixed ratio schedule: Reinforcement schedule in which reinforcement is given after a fixed number of responses.

Flashback: A hallucination that recurs without the use of a drug.

Flashbulb memory: An unusually vivid and detailed memory of a dramatic event.

Fluid intelligence: According to Cattell and Horn, the kind of intelligence that underlies the creation of novel solutions to problems.

Food aversion (taste aversion): A classically conditioned avoidance of a certain food or taste.

Foot-in-the-door technique: A technique that achieves compliance by beginning with an insignificant request, which is then followed by a larger request.

Forebrain: The cortex, thalamus, limbic system, and basal ganglia.

Forgetting curve: A graphic representation of the rate at which information is forgotten over time: Recent events are recalled better than more distant ones, but most forgetting occurs soon after learning.

Formal operation: In Piaget's theory, a mental act that can be performed (and reversed) even with an abstract concept.

Fovea: The small, central region of the retina with the highest density of cones and the highest resolution.

Free association: A technique used in psychoanalysis and psychodynamic therapy in which the patient says whatever comes to mind and the train of thought reveals the patient's issues and ways of dealing with them.

Frequency: The number of waves per second that move past a given point.

Frequency distribution: A distribution that indicates the number of each type of case that was observed in a set of data.

Frequency theory: The theory that higher frequencies produce higher rates of neural firing.

Frontal lobe: The brain lobe located behind the forehead; the seat of planning, memory search, motor control, and reasoning, as well as numerous other functions.

Functional fixedness: When solving a problem, getting stuck on one interpretation of an object or one part of the situation.

Functional magnetic resonance imaging (fMRI): A type of MRI that usually detects the amount of oxygen being brought to a particular place in the brain while a task is performed.

Functionalism: The school of psychology that sought to understand how the mind helps individuals *function*, or adapt to the world.

g: "General factor," a single intellectual capacity that underlies the positive correlations among different tests of intelligence.

Gate control (of pain): The top-down inhibition of interneurons that regulate the input of pain signals to the brain.

Gender roles: The culturally determined appropriate behaviors of males versus females.

Gene: A stretch of DNA that produces a specific protein.

General adaptation syndrome (GAS): The overall stress response that has three phases: alarm, resistance, and exhaustion.

Generalization: The ability to emit a learned behavior in response to a similar stimulus.

Generalized anxiety disorder: An anxiety disorder whose hallmark is excessive anxiety and worry that is not consistently related to a specific object or situation.

Genotype: The genetic code within an organism.

Gestalt laws of organization: A set of rules describing the circumstances—such as proximity, good continuation, similarity, closure, and good form—under which marks will be grouped into perceptual units.

Gestalt psychology: An approach to understanding mental processes that focuses on the idea that the whole is more than the sum of its parts.

Gifted: People who have IQs between 150 and 180.

Glial cell: A type of cell that surrounds neurons, influences the communication among neurons, and generally helps in the "care and feeding" of neurons.

Glucocorticoids: A group of hormones that are released when the stress response is triggered.

Grammar: The set of rules that determines how words can be organized into an infinite number of acceptable sentences in a language.

Ground: In perception, the background, which must be distinguished in order to pick out figures.

Group: A social entity characterized by regular interaction among members, some emotional connection, a common frame of reference, and a degree of interdependence.

Group polarization: The tendency of group members' opinions to become more extreme (in the same direction as their initial opinions) after group discussion.

Group therapy: A therapy modality in which a number of clients with compatible needs meet together with one or two therapists.

Groupthink: The tendency of people who try to solve problems together to accept one another's information and ideas without subjecting them to critical analysis.

Gyrus: A bulge between sulci in the cerebral cortex.

Habit: A well-learned response that is carried out automatically (without conscious thought) when the appropriate stimulus is present.

Habituation: The learning that occurs when repeated exposure to a stimulus decreases an organism's responsiveness to the stimulus.

Hair cells: The cells with stiff hairs along the basilar membrane of the inner ear that, when moved, produce nerve impulses that are sent to the brain; these cells are the auditory equivalent of rods and cones.

Hallucinations: Sensory images so vivid that they seem real.

Hallucinogen: A substance that induces hallucinations.

Health psychology: The field concerned with the promotion of health and the prevention and treatment of illness as it relates to psychological factors.

Heritability: The degree to which variability in a characteristic is due to genetics.

Heterosexual: A person who is sexually attracted to members of the opposite sex.

Heuristic: A strategy that does not guarantee the correct answer to a problem but offers a likely shortcut to it.

High expressed emotion: An emotional style in families that are critical, hostile, and overinvolved.

Hindbrain: The medulla, pons, cerebellum, and parts of the reticular formation.

Hippocampus: A subcortical structure that plays a key role in allowing new information to be stored in the brain's memory banks.

Homeostasis: The process of maintaining a steady state, in which bodily characteristics and substances are within a certain range.

Homosexual: A person who is sexually attracted to members of the same sex.

Hormone: A chemical that is produced by a gland and can act as a neuromodulator.

Hostile attribution bias: The propensity to misread the intentions of others as negative.

Hostility: The personality trait associated with heart disease and characterized by mistrust, an expectation of harm and provocation by others, and a cynical attitude.

Humanistic psychology: The school of psychology that assumes people have positive values, free will, and deep inner creativity, the combination of which leads them to choose life-fulfilling paths to personal growth.

Hypnogogic sleep: The initial stage of sleep, which lasts about 5 minutes and can include the sensation of gentle falling or floating or a sudden jerking of the body.

Hypothalamic-pituitary-adrenal (HPA) axis: The hypothalamus, pituitary gland, and adrenal glands, which work together to fight off infection.

Hypothalamus: A brain structure that sits under the thalamus and plays a central role in controlling eating and drinking and in regulating the body's temperature, blood pressure, and heart rate.

Hypothesis: A tentative idea that might explain a set of observations.

Id: A personality structure, proposed by Freud, that exists at birth and houses sexual and aggressive drives, physical needs, and simple psychological needs.

Immediate reinforcement: Reinforcement given immediately after the desired behavior is exhibited.

Implicit (or nondeclarative) memories: Memories that cannot be voluntarily called to mind, but nevertheless influence behavior or thinking.

Impulsivity: A temperament dimension characterized by the propensity to respond to stimuli immediately, without reflection or concern for consequences.

Incentive: A stimulus or event that draws animals (including humans) toward a particular goal in anticipation of a reward.

Incidental learning: Learning that occurs without intention.

Incongruence: According to client-centered therapy, a mismatch between a person's real self and his or her ideal self.

Independent variable: The aspect of the situation that is intentionally varied while another aspect is measured.

Individual therapy: A therapy modality in which an individual client is treated by a single therapist.

Individualist culture: A culture that emphasizes the rights and responsibilities of the individual over those of the group.

Inductive reasoning: Reasoning that uses examples to figure out a rule that governs them; induction goes from the particular (examples) to the general (a rule).

Inferential statistics: Results of tests that reveal which differences or patterns in measurements reflect actual differences in a population, as opposed to those that merely reflect random variations.

Informed consent: The requirement that a potential participant in a study be told what he or she will be asked to do and be advised of possible risks and benefits of the study before agreeing to take part.

Ingroup: An individual's own group.

Inhibitory conflict: An internal response when a behavior is both strongly instigated and inhibited.

Insight learning: Learning that occurs when a person or animal suddenly grasps what something means and incorporates that new knowledge into old knowledge.

Insight-oriented therapy: A type of therapy that aims to remove distressing symptoms by leading people to understand their causes through deeply felt personal insights.

Insomnia: Repeated difficulty falling asleep, difficulty staying asleep, or waking up too early.

Instinct: An inherited tendency to produce organized and unalterable responses to particular stimuli.

Insulin: A hormone that stimulates the storage of food molecules in the form of fat.

Intelligence: The ability to solve problems well and to understand and learn complex material.

Intelligence quotient (IQ): A score on an intelligence test, originally based on comparing mental age to chronological age, but later based on norms and used as a measure of general intelligence.

Intentional learning: Learning that occurs as a result of trying to learn.

Interference: The disruption of the ability to remember one piece of information by the presence of other information.

Internal attribution: An explanation of someone's behavior that focuses on the person's preferences, beliefs, goals, or other characteristics; also called *dispositional attribution*.

Internal conflict: The emotional predicament people experience when making difficult choices.

Interneuron: A neuron that is connected to other neurons, not to sense organs or muscles.

Interpersonal therapy (IPT): A type of researched, manual-based treatment that focuses on how issues that arise in the client's current relationships can affect mood.

Interpretation: A technique used in psychodynamic therapies in which the therapist deciphers the patient's words and behaviors, assigning unconscious motivations to them.

Interval schedule: Partial reinforcement schedule based on time.

Introspection: The process of "looking within."

Ion: An atom that has a positive or negative charge.

Iris: The circular muscle that adjusts the size of the pupil.

Just-noticeable difference (JND): The size of the difference in a stimulus property needed for the observer to notice that a change has occurred.

Kinesthetic sense: The sense that registers the movement and position of the limbs.

Language acquisition device (LAD): An innate mechanism, hypothesized by Chomsky, that contains the grammatical rules common to all languages and allows language acquisition.

Language comprehension: The ability to understand the message conveyed by words, phrases, and sentences.

Language production: The ability to speak or otherwise use words, phrases, and sentences to convey information.

Latent content: The symbolic content and meaning of a dream.

Latent learning: Learning that occurs without behavioral signs.

Law of Effect: Actions that subsequently lead to a "satisfying state of affairs" are more likely to be repeated.

Learned helplessness: The condition that occurs after an animal has an aversive experience in which nothing it does can affect what happens to it, and so it simply gives up and stops trying to change the situation or to escape.

Learning: A relatively permanent change in behavior that results from experience.

Lesion: A region of impaired tissue.

Level of the brain: Events that involve the structure and properties of the organ itself—brain cells and their connections, the chemical soup in which they exist, and the genes.

Level of the group: Events that involve relationships between people (such as love, competition, and cooperation), relationships among groups, and culture. Events at the level of the group are one aspect of the environment; the other aspect is the physical environment itself (the time, temperature, and other physical stimuli).

Level of the person: Events that involve the nature of beliefs, desires, and feelings—the *content* of the mind, not just its internal mechanics.

Limbic system: A set of brain areas, including the hippocampus, amygdala, and other areas, that have long been thought of as being involved in fighting, fleeing, feeding, and sex.

Linguistic relativity hypothesis: The idea that perceptions and thoughts are shaped by language, and thus people who speak different languages think differently.

Lobes: The four major parts of each cerebral hemisphere—occipital, temporal, parietal, and frontal.

Locus of control: The source a person perceives to be exerting control over life's events.

Logic: The process of applying the principles of correct reasoning to reach a decision or evaluate the truth of a claim.

Longitudinal study: A study in which the same group of people is tested repeatedly, at different ages.

Long-term memory (LTM): A memory store that holds a huge amount of information for a long time (from hours to years).

Loudness: The strength of a sound; pressure waves with greater amplitude produce the experience of louder sound.

Lowball technique: A compliance technique that consists of getting someone to make an agreement and then increasing the cost of that agreement.

Magnetic resonance imaging (MRI): A technique that uses magnetic properties of atoms to take sharp pictures of the structures of the brain.

Magnetoencephalography (MEG): A technique for assessing brain activity that relies on recording magnetic waves from outside of the head.

Major depressive disorder (MDD): A mood disorder characterized by at least 2 weeks of depressed mood or loss of interest in nearly all activities, along with sleep or eating disturbances, loss of energy, and feelings of hopelessness.

Manic episode: A period of at least 1 week during which an abnormally elevated, expansive, or irritable mood persists.

Manifest content: The obvious, memorable content of a dream.

Maturation: The developmental process that produces genetically programmed changes with increasing age.

Mean: A measure of central tendency that is the arithmetic average of a set of scores or values.

Median: A measure of central tendency that is the midpoint score of the values for the group or sample; half the values fall above the median, and half fall below the median.

Medulla: The lowest part of the lower brainstem, which plays a central role in automatic control of breathing, swallowing, and blood circulation.

Memory store: A set of neurons that serves to retain information over time.

Mendelian inheritance: The transmission of characteristics by individual elements of inheritance (genes), each acting separately.

Meninges: Membranes that cover the brain.

Mental images: Representations like those that arise during perception, but based on stored information rather than on immediate sensory input.

Mental processes: What the brain does when a person stores, recalls, or uses information or has specific feelings.

Mental set: A fixed way of viewing the kind of solution being sought.

Mentally retarded: People who have an IQ of 70 or less and significant limitations in at least two aspects of everyday life since childhood.

Mere exposure effect: The change—generally favorable—in attitude that can result from simply becoming familiar with something.

Meta-analysis: A statistical technique that allows researchers to combine results from different studies, which can determine whether there is a relationship among variables that transcends any one study.

Metabolism: The sum of the chemical events in each of the body's cells, events that convert food molecules to the energy needed for the cells to function.

Microelectrode: A tiny probe inserted into the brain to record the electrical activity of individual neurons.

Microenvironment: The environment created by a person's own presence, which depends partly on appearance and behavior.

Midbrain: Brainstem structures that lie between forebrain and hindbrain, including parts of the reticular formation.

Minnesota Multiphasic Personality Inventory-2 (MMPI-2): A personality inventory primarily used to assess psychopathology.

Misattribution of arousal: The failure to interpret signs of bodily arousal correctly, which leads to the experience of emotions that ordinarily would not arise in the particular situation.

Mnemonic devices: Strategies that improve memory, typically by using effective organization and integration.

Modality: A form of therapy.

Modality-specific memory stores: Memory stores that retain input from a single sense, such as vision or audition, or from a specific processing system, such as language.

Mode: A measure of central tendency that is the most frequently occurring value in a group or sample.

Monoamine oxidase inhibitor (MAOI): A type of antidepressant medication that requires strict adherence to a diet free of tyramine.

Monocular static cues: Information that specifies the distance of an object that can be picked up with one eye without movement of the object or eye.

Monozygotic: From the same egg and having identical genes.

Mood disorders: A category of disorders marked by persistent or episodic disturbances in emotion that interfere with normal functioning in at least one realm of life.

Moral dilemma: A situation in which there are moral pros and cons for each of a set of possible actions.

Morpheme: The smallest unit of meaning in a language.

Motion cues: Information that specifies the distance of an object on the basis of its movement.

Motivation: The set of requirements and desires that lead an animal (including a human) to behave in a particular way at a particular time and place.

Motor neuron: A neuron that sends signals to muscles to control movement.

Motor strip: The brain area, located immediately in front of the central sulcus, that controls fine movements and is organized by body part; also called *primary motor cortex*.

Myelin: A fatty substance that helps impulses travel down the axon more efficiently.

Narcotic analgesics: A class of strongly addictive drugs, such as heroin, that relieve pain.

Nativism (approach to language): The view that people are born with some knowledge.

Natural killer (NK) cell: A type of T cell that detects and destroys damaged or altered cells, such as precancerous cells.

Natural selection: Changes in the frequency of genes in a population that arise because genes allow an organism to have more offspring that survive.

Need: A condition that arises from the lack of a requirement; needs give rise to drives.

Need for achievement (nAch): The need to reach goals that require skilled performance or competence to be accomplished.

Negative punishment: Occurs when a behavior leads to the removal of a pleasant event or circumstance, thereby decreasing the likelihood of a recurrence of the behavior.

Negative reinforcement: Occurs when an unpleasant event or circumstance that follows a behavior is removed, thereby increasing the likelihood of a recurrence of the behavior.

Negative symptom: A diminution or loss of normal functions, such as a restriction in speech.

Nerve deafness: A type of deafness that typically occurs when the hair cells are destroyed by loud sounds.

Neuroendocrine system: The system, regulated by the CNS, that makes hormones that affect many bodily functions and that also provides the CNS with information.

Neuroimaging: Brain-scanning techniques that produce a picture of the structure or functioning of neurons.

Neuromodulator: A chemical that alters the effect of a neurotransmitter.

Neuron: A cell that receives signals from other neurons or sense organs, processes these signals, and sends the signals to other neurons, muscles, or organs; the basic unit of the nervous system.

Neurosis: An abnormal behavior pattern relating to a conflict between the ego and either the id or the superego.

Neurotransmitter: A chemical that carries a signal from the terminal button on one neuron to the dendrite or cell body of another.

Nocebo effect: A variation of the placebo effect in which the person expects a negative outcome instead of a positive outcome.

Nondeprived reward: Reward that occurs not when a need is being met, but rather when a want is being satisfied.

Norm: A shared belief that is enforced through a group's use of penalties.

Norming: The process of setting the mean and the standard deviation of a set of test scores, based on results from a standardized sample.

Obedience: Compliance with an order.

Object permanence: The understanding that objects (including people) continue to exist even when they cannot be immediately perceived.

Observational learning: Learning that occurs through watching others, not through reinforcement.

Obsession: A recurrent and persistent thought, impulse, or image that feels intrusive and inappropriate and is difficult to suppress or ignore.

Obsessive-compulsive disorder (OCD): An anxiety disorder marked by the presence of obsessions, and sometimes compulsions.

Occipital lobe: The brain lobe at the back of the head; concerned entirely with different aspects of vision.

Operant conditioning: The process by which a behavior becomes associated with its consequences.

Operational definition: A definition of a variable that specifies how it is measured or manipulated.

Opiate: A narcotic, such as morphine, derived from the opium poppy.

Opponent cells: Cells that pit the colors in a pair, most notably blue/yellow or red/green, against each other.

Opponent process theory of color vision: The theory that if a color is present, it causes cells that register it to inhibit the perception of the complementary color (such as red versus green).

Optic nerve: The large bundle of nerve fibers carrying impulses from the retina into the brain.

Outcome research: Research that asks whether, after psychotherapy, clients are feeling better, functioning better, living more independently, and experiencing fewer symptoms.

Outgroup: A group other than an individual's own.

Overextension: An overly broad use of a word to refer to a new object or situation.

Overregularization error: A mistake that occurs in speech because the child applies a newly learned rule even to cases where it does not apply.

Panic attack: An episode of intense fear or discomfort accompanied by physical and psychological symptoms such as palpitations, breathing difficulties, chest pain, fear of impending doom or of doing something uncontrollable, and a sense of unreality.

Panic disorder: An anxiety disorder whose hallmark is panic attacks or fear and avoidance of such attacks.

Paradoxical cold: The sensation of cold that occurs when certain nerves in the skin are stimulated by something hot.

Parasympathetic nervous system: Part of the ANS that is "next to" the sympathetic system and that tends to counteract its effects.

Parietal lobe: The brain lobe across the top part of the brain behind the ears, which is involved in registering spatial location, attention, and motor control.

Partial reinforcement: Reinforcement given only intermittently.

Passionate love: An intense feeling that involves sexual attraction, a desire for mutual love and physical closeness, arousal, and a fear that the relationship will end.

Passive interaction: Occurs when genetically shaped tendencies of parents or siblings produce an environment that is passively received by the child.

Perceived social support: The subjective sense that support is available should it be needed.

Percentile rank: A number indicating the percentage of data that have values at or below a particular value.

Perception: The act of organizing and interpreting sensory input as signaling a particular object or event.

Perceptual constancy: The perception of characteristics that occurs when an object or quality (such as shape or color) looks the same, even though the sensory information striking the eyes changes.

Perceptual set: The sum of your assumptions and beliefs that lead you to expect to perceive certain objects or characteristics in particular contexts.

Peripheral nervous system (PNS): The autonomic nervous system and the sensory-somatic nervous system.

Personality: A set of behavioral, emotional, and cognitive tendencies that people display over time and across situations and that distinguish individuals from each other.

Personality disorders: A category of disorders in which relatively stable personality traits are inflexible and maladaptive, causing distress or difficulty with daily functioning.

Personality inventory: A pencil-and-paper method for assessing personality that requires the test-takers to read statements and indicate whether each is true or false about themselves.

Personality trait: A relatively consistent characteristic exhibited in different situations.

Persuasion: Attempts to change people's attitudes.

Phenotype: The observable structure and behavior of an organism.

Pheromones: Chemicals that function like hormones but are released outside the body (in urine and sweat).

Phobia: A fear and avoidance of an object or situation extreme enough to interfere with everyday life.

Phoneme: The basic building block of speech sounds.

Phonology: The structure of the sounds that can be used to produce words in a language.

Pitch: How high or low a sound seems; higher frequencies of pressure waves produce the experience of higher pitches.

Pituitary gland: The "master gland" that regulates other glands but is itself controlled by the brain, primarily via connections from the hypothalamus.

Place theory: The theory that different frequencies activate different places along the basilar membrane.

Placebo: A medically inactive substance that is presented as though it has medicinal effects.

Plasticity: The brain's ability to be molded by experience.

Polygraph: A machine that monitors the activity of the sympathetic and parasympathetic nervous systems, particularly changes in skin conductance, breathing, and heart rate, in an attempt to detect lying.

Pons: A bridge between the brainstem and the cerebellum that plays a role in functions ranging from sleep to control of facial muscles.

Pop-out: Phenomenon that occurs when a stimulus is sufficiently different from the ones around it that it is immediately evident.

Population: The entire set of relevant people or animals.

Positive punishment: Occurs when a behavior leads to an undesired consequence, thereby decreasing the likelihood of a recurrence of that behavior.

Positive reinforcement: Occurs when a desired reinforcer is presented after a behavior, thereby increasing the likelihood of a recurrence of that behavior.

Positive symptom: An excess or distortion of normal functions, such as a hallucination.

Positron emission tomography (PET): A neuroimaging technique that uses small amounts of a radioactive substance to track blood flow or energy consumption in the brain.

Posttraumatic stress disorder (PTSD): An anxiety disorder experienced by some people after a traumatic event and whose symptoms include persistent re-experiencing of the trauma, avoidance of anything associated with the trauma, and heightened arousal.

Pragmatics: The way in which words and sentences in a language convey meaning indirectly, by implying rather than asserting.

Prediction: An expectation about specific events that should occur in particular circumstances if the theory or hypothesis is correct.

Prejudice: An attitude (generally negative) toward members of a group.

Primacy effect: Increased memory for the first few stimuli in a set, reflecting storage of information in LTM.

Primary mental abilities: According to Thurstone, seven fundamental abilities that are the components of intelligence and are not outgrowths of other abilities.

Primary reinforcer: An event or object, such as food, water, or relief from pain, that is inherently reinforcing.

Priming: The result of having just performed a task that facilitates repeating the same or an associated task.

Proactive interference: Interference that occurs when previous knowledge makes it difficult to learn something new.

Problem: An obstacle that must be overcome to reach a goal.

Problem-focused coping: Coping focused on changing the environment itself or the way the person interacts with the environment.

Prodigies: Children who demonstrate immense talent in a particular area, such as music or mathematics, but who are normal in other areas.

Progressive muscle relaxation: A relaxation technique whereby the person relaxes muscles sequentially from one end of the body to the other.

Projective test: A method used to assess personality and psychopathology that involves asking the test-taker to make sense of an ambiguous stimulus.

Propositional representation: A mental sentence that expresses the unambiguous meaning of an assertion.

Prosocial behavior: Acting to benefit others.

Prototype: The most typical example of a concept category.

Pruning: A process whereby certain connections among neurons are eliminated.

Pseudopsychology: Theories or statements that at first glance look like psychology, but are in fact superstition or unsupported opinion pretending to be science.

Psychiatric nurse: A nurse with a master's degree and a clinical specialization in psychiatric nursing who provides psychotherapy and works with medical doctors to monitor and administer medications.

Psychiatrist: A physician who focuses on mental disorders; unlike psychologists, psychiatrists can prescribe drugs, but they are not trained to administer and interpret psychological tests, nor are they trained to interpret and understand psychological research.

Psychoanalysis: An intensive form of therapy, originally developed by Freud, based on the idea that people's psychological difficulties are caused by conflicts among the id, the ego, and the superego.

Psychodynamic theory: A theory of how thoughts and feelings affect behavior; refers to the continual push-and-pull interaction among conscious and unconscious forces.

Psychodynamic therapy: A less intensive form of psychoanalysis.

Psychoeducation: The process of educating clients about therapy and research findings pertaining to their disorders or problems.

Psychological determinism: The view that all behavior, no matter how mundane or insignificant, has an underlying psychological cause.

Psychological disorder: The presence of a constellation of cognitive, emotional, and behavioral symptoms that create significant distress; impair work, school, family, relationships, or daily living; or lead to significant risk of harm.

Psychology: The science of mental processes and behavior.

Psychopharmacology: The use of medication to treat psychological disorders and problems.

Psychophysics: The study of the relation between physical events and the corresponding experience of those events.

Psychosexual stages: Freud's developmental stages based on erogenous zones; the specific needs of each stage must be met for its successful resolution.

Psychosis: An obvious impairment in the ability to perceive and comprehend events accurately, combined with a gross disorganization of behavior.

Psychosocial development: The effects of maturation and learning on personality and relationships.

Psychotherapy: The process of helping clients learn to change so they can cope with troublesome thoughts, feelings, and behaviors.

Psychotherapy integration: The use of techniques from different theoretical orientations with an overarching theory of how the integrated techniques will be used to achieve the goals of treatment.

Puberty: The time when hormones cause the sex organs to mature and secondary sexual characteristics, such as breasts for women and a beard for men, to appear.

Pupil: The opening in the eye through which light passes.

Random assignment: The technique of assigning participants randomly, that is, by chance, to the experimental and the control groups, so that no biases can sneak into the composition of the groups.

Range: The difference obtained by subtracting the smallest score in a set of data from the largest; the simplest measure of variability.

Ratio schedule: Partial reinforcement schedule based on a specified number of emitted responses.

Reality monitoring: An ongoing awareness of the perceptual and other properties that distinguish real from imagined stimuli.

Recall: The act of intentionally bringing explicit information to awareness, which requires transferring the information from LTM to STM.

Recategorization: A means of reducing prejudice by shifting the categories of "us" and "them" so that the two groups are no longer distinct entities.

Recency effect: Increased memory for the last few stimuli in a set, reflecting storage of information in STM.

Receptor: A site on a dendrite or cell body where a messenger molecule attaches itself; like a lock that is opened by one key, a receptor receives only one type of neurotransmitter or neuromodulator.

Recognition: The act of encoding an input and matching it to a stored representation.

Reflex: An automatic response to an event.

Rehearsal: The process of repeating information over and over to retain it in STM.

Reinforcement: The process by which consequences lead to an increase in the likelihood that the response will occur again.

Reinforcer: An object or event that comes after a response and that changes the likelihood of its recurrence.

Reliability: Data are reliable if the same results are obtained when the measurements are repeated.

REM rebound: The higher percentage of REM sleep that occurs following a night lacking the normal amount of REM.

REM sleep: Stage of sleep characterized by rapid eye movements and marked brain activity.

Repetition blindness: The inability to see the second occurrence of a stimulus that appears twice in succession.

Repetition priming: Priming that makes the same information more easily accessed in the future.

Replication: Collecting the same observations or measurements and finding the same results as were found previously.

Representation problem: The challenge of how best to formulate the nature of a problem.

Representativeness heuristic: The heuristic that the more similar something is to a prototype stored in memory, the more likely it is to belong to the prototype's category.

Repressed memories: Real memories that have been pushed out of consciousness because they are emotionally threatening.

Repression: A defense mechanism that occurs when the unconscious prevents threatening thoughts, impulses, and memories from entering consciousness.

Resistance: A reluctance or refusal to cooperate with the therapist, which can range from unconscious forgetting to outright refusal to comply with a therapist's request.

Resistance phase: The second phase of the GAS, in which the body mobilizes its resources to achieve equilibrium, despite the continued presence of the stressor; also called the *adaptation phase*.

Response bias: A tendency to respond in a particular way regardless of respondents' actual knowledge or beliefs.

Response contingency: The relationship that occurs when a consequence is dependent on the organism's emitting the desired behavior.

Resting potential: The negative charge within a neuron when it is at rest.

Reticular formation: A collection of small structures in the brainstem organized into two main parts: the "ascending" part plays a key role in keeping a person awake and alert; the "descending" part is important in producing autonomic nervous system reactions.

Retina: A sheet of tissue at the back of the eye containing cells that convert light to neural impulses.

Retinal disparity (also called *binocular disparity*): The difference between the images striking the retinas of the two eyes.

Retrieval: The process of accessing information stored in memory.

Retroactive interference: Interference that occurs when new learning impairs memory for something learned earlier.

Retrograde amnesia: Amnesia that disrupts previous memories.

Reuptake: The process by which surplus neurotransmitter is reabsorbed back into the sending neuron so that the neuron can effectively fire again.

Rods: Rod-shaped retinal cells that are very sensitive to light but register only shades of gray.

Role: The behaviors that a member in a given position in a group is expected to perform.

Rorschach test: A projective test consisting of a set of inkblots that people are asked to interpret.

s: "Specific factors," or aspects of performance that are particular to a given kind of processing—and distinct from *g*.

Sample: A group that is drawn from a larger population and measured or observed.

Sampling bias: A bias that occurs when the participants or items are not chosen at random, but instead are chosen so that one attribute is over- or underrepresented.

Sampling error: Any difference that arises by chance, not because the samples are representative of different populations.

Schema: In Piaget's theory, a mental structure that organizes perceptual input and connects it to the appropriate responses.

Schizophrenia: A psychotic disorder in which the patient's affect, behavior, and thoughts are profoundly altered.

Scientific method: The scientific method involves specifying a problem, systematically observing events, forming a hypothesis of the relation between variables, collecting new observations to test the hypothesis, using such evidence to formulate and support a theory, and finally testing the theory.

Secondary reinforcer: An event or object, such as attention, praise, money, a good grade, or a promotion, that is reinforcing but that does not inherently satisfy a physical need.

Selective attention: The process of picking out a particular quality, object, or event for relatively detailed analysis.

Selective serotonin reuptake inhibitor (SSRI): A type of antidepressant medication that has relatively few side effects and that acts by blocking the reuptake of the neurotransmitter serotonin at selective serotonin receptors.

Self-actualization: An innate motivation to attain the highest possible emotional and intellectual potential.

Self-concept: The beliefs, desires, values, and attributes that define a person to himself or herself.

Self-efficacy: The sense of being able to follow through and produce specific desired behaviors.

Self-help group: A group whose members focus on a specific disorder or event and do not usually have a clinically trained leader; also called a *support group*.

Self-monitoring techniques: Behavioral techniques that help the client identify the antecedents and consequences of a problematic behavior.

Self-serving bias: A person's inclination to attribute his or her own failures to external causes and own successes to internal causes, but to attribute other people's failures to internal causes and their successes to external causes.

Semantic memories: Memories of the meanings of words, concepts, and general facts about the world.

Semantics: The meaning of a word or sentence.

Sensation: The awareness of properties of an object or event that occurs when a type of receptor (such as those at the back of the eye, in the ear, on the skin) is stimulated.

Sensitivity: In signal detection theory, the threshold level for distinguishing between a stimulus and noise; the lower the threshold, the greater the sensitivity.

Sensory memory (SM): A memory store that holds a large amount of perceptual input for a very brief time, typically less than 1 second.

Sensory neuron: A neuron that responds to input from sense organs.

Sensory-somatic nervous system (SSNS): Part of the PNS that consists of neurons in the sensory organs (such as the eyes and ears) that convey information to the brain, as well as neurons that actually trigger muscles and glands.

Separation anxiety: Fear of being away from the primary caregiver.

Serotonin/norepinephrine reuptake inhibitor (SNRI): A newer type of antidepressant that affects both serotonin and norepinephrine neurotransmitter systems.

Set point: The particular body weight that is easiest for an animal (including a human) to maintain.

Sexual response cycle: The stages the body passes through during sexual activity, including sexual attraction, desire, excitement, and possibly performance (which includes full arousal, orgasm, and resolution).

Shape constancy: Seeing objects as having the same shape even when the image on the retina changes.

Shaping: The gradual process of reinforcing an organism for behavior that gets closer to the desired behavior.

Short-term memory (STM) (also called *immediate memory*): A memory store that holds relatively little information (typically 5 to 9 items) for only a few seconds (but perhaps as long as 30 seconds).

Signal detection theory: A theory explaining why people detect signals independently of bias; the theory is based on the idea that signals are always embedded in noise, and thus the challenge is to distinguish signal from noise.

Size constancy: Seeing an object as being the same size when viewed at different distances.

Skeletal system: Consists of nerves that are attached to striated muscles.

Skewed distribution: A distribution of a set of data in which many scores are near one extreme value and away from the center.

Sleep: The naturally recurrent experience during which normal consciousness is suspended.

Sleep apnea: A disorder characterized by a temporary cessation of breathing during sleep, usually preceded by a period of difficult breathing accompanied by loud snoring.

Sociability: A temperament dimension characterized by a preference for being in other people's company rather than alone.

Social causation: The chronic psychological and social stresses of living in an urban environment that may lead to an increase in the rate of schizophrenia (especially among the poor).

Social cognition: The area of social psychology that focuses on how people perceive their social worlds and how they attend to, store, remember, and use information about other people and the social world.

Social cognitive neuroscience: The subfield of psychology that attempts to understand social cognition not only by specifying the cognitive mechanisms that underlie it, but also by discovering how those mechanisms are rooted in the brain.

Social desirability: A source of bias in responding to questions on personality inventories that occurs when people try to make themselves "look good" even if it means giving untrue answers.

Social facilitation: The increase in performance that can occur simply as a result of being part of a group or in the presence of other people.

Social loafing: The tendency to work less hard when responsibility for an outcome is spread over a group's members.

Social phobia: A type of phobia involving fear of public humiliation or embarrassment and the ensuing avoidance of situations likely to arouse this fear.

Social psychology: The subfield of psychology that focuses on how people think about other people and interact in relationships and groups.

Social selection: The tendency of the mentally disabled to drift to the lower economic classes; also called *social drift*.

Social support: The help and support gained through interacting with others.

Social worker: A mental health professional who uses psychotherapy to help families (and individuals) and teaches clients to use the social service systems in their communities.

Somasthetic senses: Senses that have to do with perceiving the body and its position in space—specifically, kinesthetic sense, vestibular sense, touch, temperature sensitivity, pain sense, and possibly magnetic sense.

Somatosensory strip: The brain area, located immediately behind the central sulcus, that registers sensation on the body and is organized by body part.

Specific phobia: A type of phobia involving persistent and excessive or unreasonable fear triggered by a specific object or situation, along with attempts to avoid the feared stimulus.

Speech-segmentation problem: The problem of organizing a continuous stream of speech into separate parts that correspond to individual words.

Spinal cord: The flexible rope of nerves that runs inside the backbone, or spinal column.

Split-brain patient: A person whose corpus callosum has been severed for medical reasons, so that neuronal impulses no longer pass from one hemisphere to the other.

Spontaneous recovery (in classical conditioning): The event that occurs when the CS again elicits the CR after extinction has occurred.

Spontaneous recovery (in operant conditioning): The process by which an old response reappears if there is a period of time after extinction.

Standardized sample: A random selection of people, drawn from a carefully defined population.

State-dependent retrieval: Recall that is better if it occurs in the same psychological state that was present when the information was first encoded.

Statistics: Numbers that summarize or indicate differences or patterns of differences in measurements.

Stereotype: A belief (or set of beliefs) about people in a particular category.

Stimulants: A class of substances that excite the central nervous system, leading to increases in behavioral activity and heightened arousal.

Stimulus control: A behavior therapy technique that involves controlling the exposure to a stimulus that elicits a conditioned response, so as to decrease or increase the frequency of the response.

Stimulus discrimination: The ability to distinguish among stimuli similar to the CS and to respond only to the actual CS.

Stimulus generalization: A tendency for the CR to be elicited by neutral stimuli that are like, but not identical to, the CS; in other words, the response generalizes to similar stimuli.

Storage: The process of retaining information in memory.

Strategy: An approach to solving a problem, determined by the type of representation used and the processing steps to be tried.

Stress: The general term describing the psychological and physical response to a stimulus that alters the body's state of equilibrium.

Stress response: The bodily changes that occur to help a person cope with a stressor; also called the *fight-or-flight response*.

Stressor: A stimulus that throws the body's equilibrium out of balance.

Stroke: A source of brain damage that occurs when blood (with its life-giving nutrients and oxygen) fails to reach part of the brain, causing neurons in that area to die.

Structuralism: The school of psychology that sought to identify the basic elements of experience and to describe the rules and circumstances under which these elements combine to form mental *structures*.

Subcortical structures: Parts of the brain located under the cerebral cortex and beneath the ventricles.

Substance abuse: Drug or alcohol use that causes distress or trouble with functioning in major areas of life, occurs in dangerous situations, or leads to legal difficulties.

Substance dependence: Chronic substance abuse that is characterized by seven symptoms, the two most important being tolerance and withdrawal.

Successive approximations: The series of smaller behaviors involved in shaping a complex behavior.

Sulcus: A crease in the cerebral cortex.

Superego: A personality structure, proposed by Freud, that is formed during early childhood and houses the sense of right and wrong, based on the internalization of parental and cultural morality.

Suprachiasmatic nucleus (SCN): A small part of the hypothalamus just above the optic chiasm that registers changes in light, leading to production of hormones that regulate various bodily functions.

Survey: A set of questions, typically about beliefs, attitudes, preferences, or activities.

Sympathetic nervous system: Part of the ANS that readies an animal to fight or to flee by speeding up the heart, increasing breathing rate to deliver more oxygen, dilating the pupils, producing sweat, increasing salivation, inhibiting activity in the stomach, and relaxing the bladder.

Synapse: The place where an axon of one neuron can send signals to the membrane (on a dendrite or cell body) of another neuron.

Synaptic cleft: The gap between the axon of one neuron and the membrane of another, across which communication occurs.

Syntax: The internal structure of a sentence, determined by a set of rules (grammar) for combining different parts of speech into acceptable arrangements.

Systematic desensitization: A behavior therapy technique that teaches people to be relaxed in the presence of a feared object or situation.

Systems therapy: A type of therapy that views a client's symptoms as occurring in a larger context, or system (the family and subculture), and holds that a change in one part of the system affects the rest of the system.

T cell: A type of white blood cell that matures in the thymus.

Tardive dyskinesia: An irreversible movement disorder in which the person involuntarily smacks his or her lips, displays facial grimaces, and exhibits other symptoms; caused by traditional antipsychotic medication.

Taste buds: Microscopic structures on the bumps on the tongue surface, at the back of the throat, and inside the cheeks; different types of taste buds are sensitive to sweet, sour, salty, and bitter tastes and to glutamate.

Technical eclecticism: The use of specific techniques that may benefit a particular client, without regard for an overarching theory.

Telegraphic speech: Speech that packs a lot of information into a few words, typically omitting words such as *the*, *a*, and *of*.

Temperament: Innate inclinations to engage in a certain style of behavior.

Temporal lobe: The brain lobe under the temples, in front of the ears, where sideburns begin to grow down; among its many functions are visual memory and hearing.

Teratogen: Any external agent, such as a chemical, virus, or type of radiation, that can cause damage to the zygote, embryo, or fetus.

Terminal button: A structure at the end of a branch of an axon that, when the neuron is triggered, releases chemicals into the space between neurons.

Test bias: Features of test items or design that lead a particular group to perform well or poorly and that thus invalidate the test.

Testosterone: The hormone that causes males to develop facial hair and other sex characteristics and to build up muscle volume.

Texture gradient: Progressive change in texture that signals distance.

Thalamus: A subcortical structure that receives inputs from sensory and motor systems and plays a crucial role in attention; often thought of as a switching center.

Thematic Apperception Test (TAT): A projective test consisting of a set of detailed black-and-white drawings, various elements of which people are asked to explain.

Theory: An interlocking set of concepts or principles that explain a set of observations.

Theory of multiple intelligences: Gardner's theory of eight distinct forms of intelligence, which can vary separately for a given individual.

Thought suppression: The coping strategy that involves purposefully trying not to think about something emotionally arousing or distressing.

Threshold: The point at which stimulation is strong enough to be noticed.

Token economy: A treatment program that uses secondary reinforcers (tokens) to bring about behavior modification.

Tolerance: The condition of requiring more of a substance to achieve the same effect (because the usual amount provides a diminished response).

Top-down processing: Processing that is guided by knowledge, expectation, or belief.

Transcranial magnetic stimulation (TMS): A technique in which the brain is stimulated from outside by putting a wire coil on a person's head and delivering a magnetic pulse. The magnetic fields are so strong that they make neurons under the coil fire.

Transduction: The process whereby physical energy is converted by a sensory neuron into neural impulses.

Transfer appropriate processing: Processing used to retrieve material that is the same type as was used when the material was originally studied, which improves memory retrieval.

Transference: The process by which patients may relate to their therapists as they did to some important person in their lives.

Triangular model of love: The theory that love has three dimensions: passion (including sexual desire), intimacy (closeness), and commitment.

Trichromatic theory of color vision: The theory that color vision arises from the combinations of neural impulses from three different kinds of sensors, each of which responds maximally to a different wavelength.

Tricyclic antidepressant (TCA): A type of antidepressant medication named for the three rings in the chemical structure.

Twin study: A study that compares identical and fraternal twins to determine the relative contribution of genes to variability in a trait or characteristic.

Typicality: The degree to which an entity is representative of its concept category.

Unconditional positive regard: Acceptance without any conditions.

Unconditioned response (UR): The reflexive response elicited by a particular stimulus.

Unconditioned stimulus (US): A stimulus that elicits an automatic response (UR), without requiring prior learning.

Unconscious: Outside conscious awareness and not able to be brought to consciousness at will.

Underextension: An overly narrow use of a word to refer to a new object or situation.

Validity: A measure is valid if it does in fact measure what it is supposed to measure.

Variable: An aspect of a situation that can vary, or change; specifically, a characteristic of a substance, quantity, or entity that is measurable.

Variable interval schedule: Reinforcement schedule in which reinforcement is given for a response emitted after a variable interval of time.

Variable ratio schedule: Reinforcement schedule in which reinforcement is given after a variable number of responses.

Vestibular sense: The sense that provides information about the body's orientation relative to gravity.

Want: A condition that arises when you have an unmet goal that will not fill a requirement; wants turn goals into incentives.

Wavelength: The distance between the arrival of peaks of a light wave (measured in nanometers); shorter wavelengths correspond to higher frequencies.

Weber's law: The rule that a constant percentage of a magnitude change is necessary to detect a difference.

Wechsler Adult Intelligence Scale (WAIS): The most widely used intelligence test; consists of both verbal and performance subtests.

Withdrawal symptoms: The onset of uncomfortable or life-threatening effects when the use of a substance is stopped.

Working memory (WM): The system that includes two specialized STMs (auditory loop and visuospatial sketchpad) and a central executive that operates on information in them to plan, reason, or solve a problem.

Zygote: A fertilized ovum (egg).

REFERENCES

Aalto, S., Naatanen, P., Wallius, E., Metsahonkala, L., Stenman, H., Niem, P. M., & Karlsson, H. (2002). Neuroanatomical substrata of amusement and sadness: A PET activation study using film stimuli. *Neuroreport: For Rapid Communication of Neuroscience Research*, 13, 67–73.

Aartsen, M. J., van Tilburg, T., Smits, C. H. M., & Knipscheer, K. C. P. M. (2004). A longitudinal study of the impact of physical and cognitive decline on the personal network in old age. *Journal of Social & Personal Relationships*, 21, 249–266.

Abdollahi, P., & Mann, T. (2001). Eating disorder symptoms and body image concerns in Iran: Comparisons between Iranian women in Iran and in America. *International Journal of Eating Disorders*, 30, 259–268.

Abel, T., Martin, K. C., Bartsch, D., & Kandel, E. R. (1998). Memory suppressor genes: Inhibitory constraints on the storage of long-term memory. *Science*, 279, 338–341.

Abraham, H. D. (1983). Visual phenomenology of the LSD flashback. *Archives of General Psychiatry*, 40, 884–889.

Abrams, L. R., & Jones, R. W. (1994, August). *The contribution of social roles to psychological distress in businesswomen*. Paper presented at the 102nd annual convention of the American Psychological Association, Los Angeles, CA.

Abramson, L. Y., Seligman, M. E., & Teasedale, J. D. (1978). Learned helplessness in humans: Critique and reformulation. *Journal of Abnormal Psychology*, 87, 49–74.

Achter, J., Lubinski, D., & Benbow, C. P. (1996). Multipotentiality among the intellectually gifted: "It was never there and already it's vanishing." *Journal of Counseling Psychology*, 43, 65–76.

Adams, J. (1967). *Human memory*. New York: McGraw-Hill.

Adams, S. J., & Pitre, N. (2000). Who uses bibliotherapy and why? A survey from an underserviced area. *Canadian Journal of Psychiatry*, 45, 645–649.

Addis, D. R., & Tippett, L. J. (2004). Memory of myself: Autobiographical memory and identity in Alzheimer's disease. *Memory*, 12, 56–74.

Addis, M. E. (1997). Evaluating the treatment manual as a means of disseminating empirically validated psychotherapies. *Clinical Psychology: Science & Practice*, 4, 1–11.

Ader, R. (1976). Conditioned adrenocortical steroid elevations in the rat. *Journal of Comparative and Physiological Psychology*, 90, 1156–1163.

Ader, R., & Cohen, N. (1975). Behaviorally conditioned immunosuppression. *Psychosomatic Medicine*, 37, 333–340.

Adler, A. (1964). *Social interest: A challenge to mankind*. New York: Capricorn Books. (Original work published 1933)

Adolph, K. E. (2000). Specificity of learning: Why infants fall over a veritable cliff. *Psychological Science*, 11, 290–295.

Adolphs, R. (2002). Neural systems for recognizing emotion. *Current Opinion in Neurobiology*, 12, 169–177.

Adolphs, R., Damasio, H., Tranel, D., & Damasio, A. R. (1996). Cortical systems for the recognition of emotion in facial expressions. *Journal of Neuroscience*, 16, 7678–7687.

Agency for Health Care Policy and Research. (1999). Newer antidepressant drugs are equally as effective as older-generation drug treatments, research shows. AHCPR Pub. No. 99-E013. Rockville, MD: Author.

Aguilar-Alonso, A. (1996). Personality and creativity. *Personality and Individual Differences*, 21, 959–969.

Ahadi, S., & Diener, E. (1989). Multiple determinants and effect size. *Journal of Personality and Social Psychology*, 56, 398–406.

Ainsworth, M. D. S., Blehar, M. C., Waters, E., & Wahl, S. (1978). *Patterns of attachment: A psychological study of the Strange Situation*. Hillsdale, NJ: Erlbaum.

Ajzen, I. (2002). Perceived behavioral control, self-efficacy, locus of control, and the theory of planned behavior. *Journal of Applied Social Psychology*, 32, 665–683.

Akhtar, N., & Tomasello, M. (1996). Two-year-olds learn words for absent objects and actions. *British Journal of Developmental Psychology*, 14, 79–93.

Akiskal, H. S. (1996). The prevalent clinical spectrum of bipolar disorders: Beyond DSM–IV. *Journal of Clinical Psychopharmacology*, 16(Suppl. 1), 4S–14S.

Alberini, C. (2004) Mechanisms of memory destabilization: Are consolidation and reconsolidation similar or distinct processes? *Trends in Neuroscience*, 28, 51–56.

Albert, M., & Ayres, J. J. B. (1997). One-trial simultaneous and backward excitatory fear conditioning in rats: Lick suppression, freezing, and rearing to CS compounds and their elements. *Animal Learning & Behavior*, 25, 210–220.

Albert, M. S., Duffy, F. H., & McAnulty, G. B. (1990). Electrophysiologic comparisons between two groups of patients with Alzheimer's disease. *Archives of Neurology*, 47, 857–863.

Albert, M. S., & Moss, M. B. (1996). Neuropsychology of aging: Findings in humans and monkeys. In E. L. Schneider, J. W. Rowe, T. E. Johnson, N. J. Holbrook, & J. H. Morrison (Eds.), *Handbook of the biology of aging* (4th ed.). San Diego, CA: Academic Press.

Alcock, J. E. (1987). Parapsychology: Science of the anomalous or search for the soul? *Behavioral and Brain Sciences*, 10, 553–565.

Aldag, R. J., & Fuller, S. R. (1993). Beyond fiasco: A reappraisal of the groupthink phenomenon and a new model of group decision processes. *Psychological Bulletin*, 113, 533–552.

Alexander, D. (1991). Keynote address. In *President's Committee on Mental Retardation, Summit on the National Effort to Prevent Mental Retardation and Related Disabilities*.

Alexander, F., & French, T. (1946). *Psychoanalytic theory*. New York: Ronald.

Allen, J. J. B., & Iacono, W. G. (1997). A comparison of methods for the analysis of event-related potentials in deception detection. *Psychophysiology*, 34, 234–240.

Allen, L. S., & Gorski, R. A. (1992). Sexual orientation and the size of the anterior commissure in the human brain. *Proceedings of the National Academy of Sciences of the United States of America*, 89, 7199–7202.

Allport, G. (1954). *The nature of prejudice*. Oxford, England: Addison-Wesley.

Allport, G. W. (1937). *Personality: A psychological interpretation*. New York: Holt.

Allyn, J., & Festinger, L. (1961). The effectiveness of unanticipated persuasive communications. *Journal of Abnormal and Social Psychology*, 62, 35–40.

Almli, C. R., Ball, R. H., & Wheeler, M. E. (2001). Human fetal and neonatal movement patterns: Gender differences and fetal-to-neonatal continuity. *Developmental Psychobiology*, 38, 252–273.

Alonso, P., Pujol, J., Cardoner, N., Benlloch, L., Deus, J., Menchon, J. M., et al. (2001). Right prefrontal repetitive transcranial magnetic stimulation in obsessive-compulsive disorder: A double-blind, placebo-controlled study. *American Journal of Psychiatry*, 158, 1143–1145.

Alonzo, M., & Aiken, M. (2004). Flaming in electronic communication. *Decision Support Systems*, 36(3), 205–221.

Altshuler, L. L., Bartzokis, G., Grieder, T., Curran, J., & Mintz, J. (1998). Amygdala enlargement in bipolar disorder and hippocampal reduction in schizophrenia: An MRI study demonstrating neuroanatomic specificity. *Archives of General Psychiatry*, 55, 663–664.

Aluja-Fabregat, A., Colom, R., Abad, F., & Juan-Espinosa, M. (2000). Sex differences in general intelligence defined as g among young adolescents. *Personality & Individual Differences*, 28, 813–820.

Amabile, T. M. (1983). *The social psychology of creativity*. New York: Springer-Verlag.

Amabile, T. M. (1998, September–October). How to kill creativity. *Harvard Business Review*, pp. 76–87.

Amabile, T. M. (2001). Beyond talent: John Irving and the passionate craft of creativity. *American Psychologist*, 56, 333–336.

American Association for Mental Retardation (1992). *Mental retardation: Definition, classification, and systems of supports* (9th ed.). Washington, DC: Author.

American Psychiatric Association. (1994). *Diagnostic and statistical manual of mental disorders* (4th ed.). Washington, DC: Author.

American Psychiatric Association. (2000a). *Diagnostic and statistical manual of mental disorders* (4th ed., text revision). Washington, DC: Author.

American Psychiatric Association. (2000b). Practice guideline for the treatment of patients with major depressive disorder (revision). *American Journal of Psychiatry*, 157(Suppl.), 1–45.

Amsterdam, B. (1972). Mirror self-image reactions before age two. *Developmental Psychology*, 5, 297–305.

Anastasi, A. (1988). *Psychological testing* (6th ed.). New York: Macmillan.

Anch, A. M., Bowman, C. P., Mitler, M. M., & Walsh, J. K. (1988). *Sleep: A scientific perspective*. Englewood Cliffs, NJ: Prentice-Hall.

Andersen, A. E., & DiDomenico, L. (1992). Diet vs. shape content of popular male and female magazines: A dose response relationship to the incidence of eating disorders? *International Journal of Eating Disorders*, 11, 283–287.

Andersen, B. (1997, July). Psychological interventions for individuals with cancer. *Clinician's Research Digest*, 16(Suppl.), 1–2.

Andersen, B. L., Kiecolt-Glaser, K. K., & Glaser, R. (1994). A biobehavioral model of cancer stress and disease course. *American Psychologist*, 49, 389–404.

Anderson, A. K., & Phelps, E. A. (2002). Is the human amygdala critical for the subjective experience of emotion? Evidence of intact dispositional affect in patients with amygdala lesions. *Journal of Cognitive Neuroscience*, 14, 709–720.

Anderson, C. A. (1983). Abstract and concrete data in the perseverance of social theories: When weak data lead to unshakable beliefs. *Journal of Experimental Social Psychology*, 19, 930–1108.

Anderson, C. A., & Bushman, B. J. (1997). External validity of "trivial" experiments: The case of laboratory aggression. *Review of General Psychology*, 1, 19–41.

Anderson, C. A., Lepper, M. R., & Ross, L. (1980). Perseverance of social theories: This role of explanation in the persistence of discredited information. *Journal of Personality and Social Psychology*, 39, 1037–1049.

Anderson, I. M. (2000). Selective serotonin reuptake inhibitors versus tricyclic antidepressants: A meta-analysis of efficacy and tolerability. *Journal of Affective Disorders*, 58, 19–36.

Anderson, J. R. (2000). *Cognitive psychology and its implications* (5th ed.). New York: Worth.

Anderson, J. R., & Betz, J. (2001). A hybrid model of categorization. *Psychonomic Bulletin & Review*, 8, 629–647.

Anderson, M. C., Ochsner, K. N., Kuhl, B., Cooper, J., Robertson, E., Gabrieli, S. W., Glover, G. H., and Gabrieli, J. D. E. (2004). Neural systems underlying the suppression of unwanted memories. *Science*, 303, 232–235.

Anderson, N. B. (1998). Levels of analysis in health science: A framework for integrating sociobehavioral and biomedical research. In S. M. McCann, J. M. Lipton, et al. (Eds.), *Annals of the New York Academy of Sciences: Vol. 840, Neuroimmunomodulation: Molecular aspects, integrative systems, and clinical advances* (pp. 563–576). New York: New York Academy of Sciences.

Anderson, N. B., & Nickerson, K. J. (2005). Genes, race, and psychology in the genome era. *American Psychologist, 60,* 5–8.

Anderson, V. L., Levinson, E. M., Barker, W., & Kiewra, K. R. (1999). The effects of meditation on teacher perceived occupational stress, state and trait anxiety, and burnout. *School Psychology Quarterly, 14,* 3–25.

Andreasen, N. C. (1987). Creativity and mental illness: Prevalence rates in writers and their first-degree relatives. *American Journal of Psychiatry, 144,* 1288–1292.

Andreasen, N. C., Nasrullah, H., Dunn, V., Olson, S., Grove, W., Erhardt, J., et al. (1986). Structural abnormalities in the frontal system in schizophrenia. *Archives of General Psychiatry, 43,* 136–144.

Andreasen, N. C., Nopoulos, P., O'Leary, D. S., Miller, D. D., Wassink, T., & Flaum, M. (1999). Defining the phenotype of schizophrenia: Cognitive dysmetria and its neural mechanisms. *Biological Psychiatry, 46,* 908–920.

Andreasen, N. C., Rezai, K., Alliger, R., Swayze, V., Flaum, M., Kirchner, P., et al. (1992). Hypofrontality in neuroleptic-naïve patients and in patients with chronic schizophrenia: Assessment with xenon-133 single proton emission computed tomography and the Tower of London. *Archives of General Psychiatry, 49,* 943–958.

Andrews, H. B., & Jones, S. (1990). Eating behaviour in obese women: A test of two hypotheses. *Australian Psychologist, 25,* 351–357.

Angleitner, A., Riemann, R., & Strelau, J. (1995). A study of twins using the self-report and peer-report NEO-FFI scales. Paper presented at the seventh meeting of the International Society for the Study of Individual Differences, July 15–19, Warsaw, Poland.

Anglin, J. M. (1993). Vocabulary development: A morphological analysis. *Monographs of the Society for Research in Child Development, 58*(10, Serial No. 238).

Angst, J. (1998). The emerging epidemiology of hypomania and bipolar II disorder. *Journal of Affective Disorders, 50,* 143–151.

Anisman, H., Zaharia, M. D., Meaney, M. J., & Merali, Z. (1998). Do early-life events permanently alter behavioral and hormonal responses to stressors? *International Journal of Developmental Neuroscience, 16,* 149–164.

Anonymous. (1970). Effects of sexual activity on beard growth in man. *Nature, 226,* 867–870.

Antoch, M. P., Song, E. J., Chang, A. M., Vitaterna, M. H., Zhao, Y., Wilsbacher, L. D., et al. (1997, May 16). Functional identification of the mouse circadian Clock gene by transgenic BAC rescue. *Cell, 89*(4), 655–667.

Antonuccio, D. O., Danton, W. G., & DeNelsky, G. Y. (1995). Psychotherapy versus medication for depression: Challenging the conventional wisdom with data. *Professional Psychology: Research & Practice, 26,* 574–585.

Antony, M. M., & Barlow, D. H. (2002). Specific phobias. In D. H. Barlow (Ed.), *Anxiety and its disorders* (2nd ed., pp. 380–417). New York: Guilford Press.

Arana, G. W., & Rosenbaum, J. F. (2000). *Handbook of Psychiatric Drug Therapy.* Philadelphia: Lippincott Williams & Wilkins.

Aranda, M. P., & Knight, B. G. (1997). The influence of ethnicity and culture on the caregiver stress and coping process: A socio-cultural review and analysis. *Gerontologist, 37,* 342–354.

Archer, J. (2004). Sex differences in aggression in real-world settings: A meta-analytic review. *Review of General Psychology, 8,* 291–322.

Argyle, M. L., & Lu, L. (1990). Happiness and social skills. *Personality & Individual Differences, 11,* 1255–1261.

Arkes, H. R., & Tetlock, P. E. (2004). Attributions of implicit prejudice, or "Would Jesse Jackson 'fail' the Implicit Association Test?" *Psychological Inquiry, 15,* 257–278.

Arias, E., Anderson, R. S., Kung, H.-C., Murphy, S. L., & Kochanek, K. D. (2003). Deaths: Final data for 2001. National Vital Statistics Reports. National Center for Health Statistics, Centers for Disease Control and Prevention, U.S. Dept. of Health and Human Services. DHHS Publication Number (PHS) 2001-1120 PRS

03-0436. Retrieved from: http://www.cdc.gov/nchs/about/major/dvs/mortdata.htm; pdf file nvsr52_09p9.pdf

Armstrong, S. L., Gleitman, L. R., & Gleitman, H. (1983). What some concepts might not be. *Cognition, 13,* 263–308.

Arnell, K. M., & Jolicoeur, P. (1999). The attentional blink across stimulus modalities: Evidence for central processing limitations. *Journal of Experimental Psychology: Human Perception and Performance, 25,* 630–648.

Arnett, J. (1992). Reckless behavior in adolescence: A developmental perspective. *Developmental Review, 12,* 339–373.

Arnett, J. J. (1999). Adolescent storm and stress, reconsidered. *American Psychologist, 54,* 317–326.

Arnsten, A. F. T. (1998). The biology of being frazzled. *Science, 280,* 1711–1712.

Aronson, E., & Osherow, N. (1980). Cooperation, prosocial behavior, and academic performance: Experiments in the desegregated classroom. *Applied Social Psychology Annual, 1,* 163–196.

Aronson, E., & Patnoe, S. (1997). *The jigsaw classroom: Building cooperation in the classroom* (2nd ed.). New York: Addison Wesley Longman.

Aronson, J., Fried, C. B., & Good, C. (2002). Reducing the effects of stereotype threat on African American college students by shaping theories of intelligence. *Journal of Experimental Social Psychology, 38,* 113–125.

Arterberry, M. E., & Yonas, A. (2000). Perception of three-dimensional shape specified by optic flow by 8-week-old infants. *Perception & Psychophysics, 62,* 550–556.

Asch, S. E. (1951). Effects of group pressure upon the modification and distortion of judgment. In H. Guetzkow (Ed.), *Groups, leadership, and men* (pp. 177–190). Pittsburgh: Carnegie.

Asch, S. E. (1955). Opinions and social pressure. *Scientific American, 193,* 31–35.

Asendorpf, J. B., Warkentin, V., & Baudonniere, P.-M. (1996). Self-awareness and other-awareness: II. Mirror self-recognition, social contingency awareness, and synchronic imitation. *Developmental Psychology, 32,* 313–321.

Ashton, C. H. (2001). Pharmacology and effects of cannabis: A brief review. *British Journal of Psychiatry, 178,* 101–106.

Aspinwall, L. G., & Taylor, S. E. (1997). A stitch in time: Self-regulation and proactive coping. *Psychological Bulletin, 121,* 417–436.

Association of SIDS and Infant Mortality Programs (2002). Infant sleep positioning and SIDS. Retrieved from http://www.asip1.org/isp.html

Athanasiou, M. S. (2000). Current nonverbal assessment instruments: A comparison of psychometric integrity and test fairness. *Journal of Psychoeducational Assessment, 18,* 211–229.

Atienza, M., Cantero, J. L., & Stickgold, R. (2004). Posttraining sleep enhances automaticity in perceptual discrimination. *Journal of Cognitive Neuroscience, 16,* 53–64.

Atkinson, R. C., & Shiffrin, R. M. (1968). Human memory: A proposed system and its control processes. In K. W. Spence & J. T. Spence (Eds.), *The psychology of learning and motivation: Advances in research and theory* (Vol. 2, pp. 89–195). New York: Academic Press.

Atkinson, R. C., & Shiffrin, R. M. (1971). The control of short-term memory. *Scientific American, 225,* 82–90.

Atre-Vaidya, N., & Hussain, S. M. (1999). Borderline personality disorder and bipolar mood disorder: Two distinct disorders or a continuum? *Journal of Mental and Nervous Disorders, 187,* 313–315.

Auden, W. H. (1989). *Van Gogh: A self-portrait.* New York: Marlowe.

Avorn, J., & Langer, E. (1982). Induced disability in nursing home patients: A controlled trial. *Journal of the American Geriatrics Society, 30,* 397–400.

Ayton, P., & Wright, G. (1994). Subjective probability: What should we believe? In G. Wright & P. Ayton (Eds.), *Subjective probability* (pp. 163–183). New York: Wiley.

Azar, B. (1995). Timidity can develop in the first days of life. *APA Monitor, 26*(11), 23.

Baccus, J. R., Baldwin, M. W., & Packer, D. J. (2004). Increasing implicit self-esteem through classical conditioning. *Psychological Science, 15,* 498–502.

Bachen, E. A., Manuck, S. B., Cohen, S., Muldoon, M. F., Raible, R., Herbert, T. B., & Rabin, B. S. (1995). Adrenergic blockage ameliorates cellular immune responses to mental stress in humans. *Psychosomatic Medicine, 57,* 366–372.

Baddeley, A. (1986). *Working memory.* Oxford, England: Clarendon Press.

Baddeley, A. (1992). Working memory: The interface between memory and cognition. *Journal of Cognitive Neuroscience, 4,* 281–288.

Baddeley, A. (1994). The magical number seven: Still magic after all these years? *Psychological Review, 101,* 353–356.

Baeck, E. (2002). The neural networks of music. *European Journal of Neurology, 9,* 449–456.

Baenninger, M., & Newcombe, N. (1989). The role of experience in spatial test performance: A meta-analysis. *Sex Roles, 20,* 327–344.

Bahrick, L. E., Moss, L., & Fadil, C. (1996). Development of visual self-recognition in infancy. *Ecological Psychology, 8,* 189–208.

Bailey, J. M., & Pillard, R. C. (1991). A genetic study of male sexual orientation. *Archives of General Psychiatry, 48,* 1089–1096.

Bailey, M., Engler, H., Hunzeker, J., & Sheridan, J. F. (2003). The hypothalamic-pituitary-adrenal axis and viral infection. *Viral Immunology, 16,* 141–157.

Baillargeon, R. (1993). The object concept revisited: New directions in the investigation of infants' physical knowledge. In C. E. Granrud (Ed.), *Visual perception and cognition in infancy* (pp. 265–315). Hillsdale, NJ: Erlbaum.

Baillargeon, R. (2004). Infants' physical world. *Current Directions in Psychological Science, 13,* 89–94.

Baily, C. H., & Chen, M. (1989). Time course of structural changes at identified sensory neuron synapses during long-term sensitization in Aplysia. *Journal of Neuroscience, 9,* 1774–1781.

Baird, A., Kagan, J., Gaudette, T., Walz, K., Hershlag, N., & Boas, D. (2002). Frontal lobe activation during object permanence: Data from near-infrared spectroscopy. *NeuroImage, 16,* 1120–1126.

Baker, F. (2001). The effects of live, taped, and no music on people experiencing posttraumatic amnesia. *Journal of Music Therapy, 38,* 170–192.

Baker, R. R. (1980). Goal orientation by blindfolded humans after long-distance displacement: Possible involvement of a magnetic sense. *Science, 210,* 555–557.

Bakermans-Kranenburg, M. J., van IJzendoorn, M. H., & Kroonenberg, P. M. (2004). Differences in attachment security between African-American and white children: Ethnicity or socio-economic status? *Infant Behavior & Development, 27,* 417–433.

Ball, K., Berch, D. B., Helmers, K. F., Jobe, J. B., Leveck, M. D., Marsiske, M., et al. (2002). Effects of cognitive training interventions with older adults: A randomized controlled trial. *JAMA: Journal of the American Medical Association, 288,* 2271–2281.

Ball, S. A. (2002). Big Five, alternative five, and seven personality dimensions: Validity in substance-dependent patients. In P. T. Costa, Jr., & T. A. Widiger (Eds.), *Personality disorders and the five-factor model of personality* (2nd ed., pp. 177–201). Washington, DC: American Psychological Association.

Ballus, C. (1997). Effects of antipsychotics on the clinical and psychosocial behavior of patients with schizophrenia. *Schizophrenia Research, 28,* 247–255.

Baltes, P. B. (1987). Theoretical propositions of life-span developmental psychology: On the dynamics between growth and decline. *Developmental Psychology, 23,* 611–626.

Banaji, M. R., Nosek, B. A., & Greenwald, A. G. (2004). No place for nostalgia in science: A response to Arkes and Tetlock. *Psychological Inquiry, 15,* 279–310.

Bandura, A. (1976). Self-reinforcement: Theoretical and methodological considerations. *Behaviorism, 4,* 135–155.

Bandura, A. (1977a). *Social learning theory.* Englewood Cliffs, NJ: Prentice-Hall.

Bandura, A. (1977b). Self-efficacy: Toward a unifying theory of behavior change. *Psychological Review, 84,* 191–215.

Bandura, A. (1986). *Social foundations of thought and action: A social-cognitive theory.* Englewood Cliffs, NJ: Prentice-Hall.

Bandura, A. (1999). Moral disengagement in the perpetration of inhumanities. *Personality & Social Psychology Review, 3,* 193–209.

Bandura, A. (2001). Social cognitive theory: An agentic perspective. *Annual Review of Psychology, 52,* 1–26.

Bandura, A. (2004). Health promotion by social cognitive means. *Health Education & Behavior, 31,* 143–164.

Bandura, A., Grusec, J. E., & Menlove, F. L. (1967). Vicarious extinction of avoidance behavior. *Journal of Personality & Social Psychology, 5,* 16–23.

Bandura, A., Ross, D., & Ross, S. A. (1961). Transmission of aggression through imitation of aggressive models. *Journal of Abnormal and Social Psychology, 63,* 575–582.

Bandura, A., Ross, D., & Ross, S. A. (1963). Imitation of film-mediated aggressive models. *Journal of Abnormal & Social Psychology, 66,* 3–11.

Banks, M. S., & Bennett, P. J. (1988). Optical and photoreceptor immaturities limit the spatial and chromatic vision of human neonates. *Journal of the Optical Society of America, 5,* 2059–2079.

Bao, S., Chen, L., & Thompson, R. F. (2000). Learning- and cerebellum-dependent neuronal activity in the lateral pontine nucleus. *Behavioral Neuroscience, 114,* 254–261.

Bar, M., Tootell, R. B., Schacter, D. L., Greve, D. N., Fischl, B., Mendola, J. D., et al. (2001). Cortical mechanisms specific to explicit visual object recognition. *Neuron, 29,* 529–535.

Barañano, D. E., Ferris, C. D., & Snyder, S. H. (2001). Atypical neural messengers. *Trends in Neurosciences, 24,* 99–106.

Barbarich, N. (2002). Is there a common mechanism of serotonin dysregulation in anorexia nervosa and obsessive compulsive disorder? *Eating & Weight Disorders, 7,* 221–231.

Barber, J. (1997). Hypnosis and memory: A cautionary chapter. In G. A. Fraser (Ed.), *The dilemma of ritual abuse: Cautions and guides for therapists* (pp. 17–29). Washington, DC: American Psychiatric Press.

Barclay, J. R., Bransford, J. D., Franks, J. J., McCarrell, N. S., & Nitsch, K. (1974). Comprehension and semantic flexibility. *Journal of Verbal Learning and Verbal Behavior, 13,* 471–481.

Barefoot, J. C., Dahlstrom, W. G., & Williams, R. B. (1983). Hostility, CHD incidence, and total mortality: A 25-year follow-up study of 255 physicians. *Psychosomatic Medicine, 45,* 59–63.

Barefoot, J., Dodge, K., Peterson, B., Dahlstrom, W., & Williams, R. (1989). The Cook-Medley Hostility Scale: Item content and ability to predict survival. *Psychosomatic Medicine, 51,* 46–57.

Barger, L. K., Cade, B. E., Ayas, N. T., Cronin, J. W., Rosner, B., Speizer, F. E., & Czeisler, C. A. (Harvard Work Hours, Health, and Safety Group). (2005). Extended work shifts and the risk of motor vehicle crashes among interns. *New England Journal of Medicine, 352,* 125–134.

Bargh, J. A., Chen, M., & Burrows, L. (1996). Automaticity of social behavior: Direct effects of trait construct and stereotype activation on action. *Journal of Personality & Social Psychology, 71,* 230–244.

Bargh, J. A., & McKenna, K. Y. A. (2004). The Internet and social life. *Annual Review of Psychology, 55,* 573–590.

Bargh, J. A., McKenna, K. Y. A., & Fitzsimons, G. M. (2002). Can you see the real me? Activation and expression of the "true self" on the Internet. *Journal of Social Issues, 58,* 33–48.

Barinaga, M. (2001). How cannabinoids work in the brain. *Science, 291,* 2530–2531.

Barkham, M., & Shapiro, D. A. (1990). Brief psychotherapeutic interventions for job-related distress: A pilot study of prescriptive and exploratory therapy. *Counseling Psychology Quarterly, 3,* 133–147.

Barkham, M., Shapiro, D. A., Hardy, G. E., & Rees, A. (1999). Psychotherapy in two-plus-one sessions: Outcomes of a randomized controlled trial of cognitive-behavioral and psychodynamic-interpersonal therapy for subsyndromal depression. *Journal of Consulting and Clinical Psychology, 67,* 201–211.

Barkow, J. H., Cosmides, L., & Tooby, J. (Eds.). (1992). *The adapted mind: Evolutionary psychology and the generation of culture.* New York: Oxford University Press.

Barnes, V. A., Davis, H. C., Murzynowski, J. B., & Treiber, F. A. (2004). Impact of meditation on resting and ambulatory blood pressure and heart rate in youth. *Psychosomatic Medicine, 66,* 909–914.

Barnet, R. C., Arnold, H. M., & Miller, R. R. (1991). Simultaneous conditioning demonstrated in second-order conditioning: Evidence for similar associative structure in forward and simultaneous conditioning. *Learning & Motivation, 22,* 253–268.

Bar-On, R., Brown, J. M., Kirkcaldy, B. D., & Thome, E. P. (2000). Emotional expression and implications for occupational stress: An application of the emotional quotient inventory (EQ-i). *Personality and Individual Differences, 28,* 1107–1118.

Bar-On, R., & Parker, J. (Eds.). (2000). *The handbook of emotional intelligence.* San Francisco: Jossey-Bass.

Baron, R. A., & Byrne, D. (1997). *Social psychology* (8th ed.). Needham Heights, MA: Allyn & Bacon.

Baron, R. A., & Richardson, D. (1994). *Human aggression* (2nd ed.). New York: Plenum.

Barone, P. (2003). Clinical strategies to prevent and delay motor complications. *Neurology, 61,* S12–S16.

Barrett, L. F. (2006). Solving the emotion paradox: Categorization and the experience of emotion. *Personality and Social Psychology Review, 10,* 20–46.

Barrantes-Vidal, N. (2004). Creativity & madness revisited from current psychological perspectives. *Journal of Consciousness Studies, 11,* 58–78.

Barrett, L. F., & Niedenthal, P. M. (2004). Valence focus and the perception of facial affect. *Emotion, 4,* 266–274.

Barrett, L. F., Ochsner, K. N., & Gross, J. J. (in press). Automaticity and emotion. In J. Bargh (Ed.), *Automatic processes in social thinking and behavior.* New York: Psychology Press.

Barsky, A. J., Saintfort, R., Rogers, M. P., & Borus, J. F. (2002). Nonspecific medication side effects and the nocebo phenomenon. *JAMA: Journal of the American Medical Association, 287,* 622–627.

Barth, J., Schumacher, M., & Herrmann-Lingen, C. (2004). Depression as a risk factor for mortality in patients with coronary heart disease: A meta-analysis. *Psychosomatic Medicine, 66,* 802–813.

Bartoshuk, L. M., & Beauchamp, G. K. (1994). Chemical senses. *Annual Review of Psychology, 45,* 419–449.

Baruch, D. E., Swain, R. A., & Helmstetter, F. J. (2004). Effects of exercise on Pavlovian fear conditioning. *Behavioral Neuroscience, 118,* 1123–1127.

Basic Behavioral Science Task Force of the National Advisory Mental Health Council (1996). Basic behavioral science research for mental health. *American Psychologist, 51,* 722–731.

Bast, T., Zhang, W., & Feldon, J. (2003). Dorsal hippocampus and classical fear conditioning to tone and context in rats: Effects of local NMDA-receptor blockade and stimulation. *Hippocampus, 13,* 657–675.

Bastien, C. H., Morin, C. M., Ouellet, M., Blais, F. C., & Bouchard, S. (2004). Cognitive-behavioral therapy for insomnia: Comparison of individual therapy, group therapy, and telephone consultations. *Journal of Consulting & Clinical Psychology, 72,* 653–659.

Batsell, W. R., Jr., & Brown, A. S. (1998). Human flavor-aversion learning: A comparison of traditional aversions and cognitive aversions. *Learning & Motivation, 29,* 383–396.

Batshaw, M., & Perret, Y. (1992). *Children with disabilities: A medical primer.* Baltimore: Brookes.

Batson, C. D. (1998). Altruism and prosocial behavior. In D. T. Gilbert, S. T. Fiske, & G. Lindzey (Eds.), *The handbook of social psychology* (4th ed., pp. 282–316). New York: McGraw-Hill.

Batson, C. D., Bolen, M. H., Cross, J. A., & Neuringer-Benefiel, H. E. (1986). Where is the altruism in the altruistic personality? *Journal of Personality & Social Psychology, 50,* 212–220.

Baumeister, R. F., & Boden, J. M. (1998). Aggression and the self: High self-esteem, low self-control, and ego threat. In R. G. Geen & E. Donnerstein (Eds.), *Human aggression: Theories, research, and implications for social policy* (pp. 111–137). San Diego, CA: Academic Press.

Baumeister, R. F., Smart, L., & Boden, J. M. (1996). Relation of threatened egotism to violence and aggression: The dark side of high self-esteem. *Psychological Review, 103,* 5–33.

Baumeister, R. F., Stillwell, A., & Wotman, S. R. (1990). Victim and perpetrator accounts of interpersonal conflict: Autobiographical narratives about anger. *Journal of Personality and Social Psychology, 59,* 994–1003.

Baxendale, S. (2004). Memories aren't made of this: Amnesia at the movies. *British Medical Journal, 329,* 1480–1483.

Baxter, J. S., Macrae, C. N., Manstead, A. S. R., Stradling, S. G., & Parker, D. (1990). Attributional biases and driver behavior. *Social Behaviour, 5,* 185–192.

Baxter, L. R., Schwartz, J. M., Bergman, K. S., Szuba, M. P., Guze, B. H., Mazziota, J. C., et al. (1992). Caudate glucose metabolic rate changes with both drug and behavior therapy for obsessive-compulsive disorder. *Archives of General Psychiatry, 49,* 681–689.

Baxter, M. G., Parker, A., Lindner, C. C. C., Izquierdo, A. D., & Murray, E. A. (2000). Control of response selection by reinforcer value requires interaction of amygdala and orbital prefrontal cortex. *Journal of Neuroscience, 20,* 4311–4319.

Bayley, P. J., Hopkins, R. O., & Squire, L. R. (2003). Successful recollection of remote autobiographical memories by amnesic patients with medial temporal lobe lesions. *Neuron, 38,* 135–144.

Beach, F. A. (1956). Characteristics of masculine "sex drive." In M. Jones (Ed.), *Nebraska Symposium on Motivation* (pp. 1–32). Lincoln: University of Nebraska Press.

Beals, J., Novins, D. K., Spicer, P., Orton, H. D., Mitchell, C. M., Barón, A. E., et al. (2004). Challenges in operationalizing the DSM-IV clinical significance criterion. *Archives of General Psychiatry, 61,* 1197–1207.

Beaman, A., Barnes, P., Kletz, B., & McQuirk, B. (1978). Increasing helping rates through information dissemination: Teaching pays. *Personality and Social Psychology Bulletin, 4,* 406–411.

Bearak, B. (1997, March 29). Time of puzzles, heartbreak binds relatives left behind. *New York Times,* 1.

Beatty, J. (1995). *Principles of behavioral neuroscience.* Dubuque, IA: Brown & Benchmark.

Beaumont, M., Batejat, D., Pierard, C., Van Beers, P., Denis, J., Coste, O., Doireau, P., Chauffard, F., French, J., & Lagarde D. (2004). Caffeine or melatonin effects on sleep and sleepiness after rapid eastward transmeridian travel. *Journal of Applied Physiology, 96,* 50–58.

Beauregard, M., Levesque, J., & Bourgouin, P. (2001). Neural correlates of conscious self-regulation of emotion. *Journal of Neuroscience, 21,* 6993–7000.

Bechara, A., Damasio, H., Tranel, D., & Damasio, A. R. (1997). Deciding advantageously before knowing the advantageous strategy. *Science, 275,* 1293–1294.

Bechara, A., Tranel, D., & Damasio, H. (2000). Characterization of the decision-making deficit of patients with ventromedial prefrontal cortex lesions. *Brain, 123,* 2189–2202.

Bechara, A. & Van der Kooy, D. (1992). A single brain stem substrate mediates the motivational effects of both opiates and food in nondeprived rats but not in deprived rats. *Behavioral Neuroscience, 106,* 351–363.

Beck, A. T. (1967). *Depression: Causes and treatment.* Philadelphia: University of Pennsylvania Press.

Beck, A. T., Emery, G., & Greenberg, R. L. (1985). *Anxiety disorders and phobias: A cognitive perspective.* New York: Basic Books.

Beck, J. G., Ohtake, P. J., & Shipherd, J. C. (1999). Exaggerated anxiety is not unique to CO2 in panic disorder: A comparison of hypercapnic and hypoxic challenges. *Journal of Abnormal Psychology, 108,* 473–482.

Beck, R., & Fernandez, E. (1998). Cognitive-behavioral therapy in the treatment of anger: A meta-analysis. *Cognitive Therapy & Research, 22,* 63–74.

Becker, A., & Hamburg, P. (1996). Culture, the media, and eating disorders. *Cross-Cultural Psychiatry, 4,* 163–167.

Becker, A. E., Burwell, R. A., Herzog, D. B., Hamburg, P., & Gilman, S. E. (2002). Eating behaviours and attitudes following prolonged exposure to television among ethnic Fijian adolescent girls. *British Journal of Psychiatry, 180,* 509–514.

Beevers, C. G., & Meyer, B. (2004). Thought suppression and depression risk. *Cognition & Emotion, 18,* 859–867.

Behrens, R. R. (2003). Thinking outside of the box: On Karl Duncker, functional fixedness, and the adaptive value of engaging in purposely deviant acts. *Gestalt Theory, 25,* 63–70.

Behrmann, M. (2000). The mind's eye mapped onto the brain's matter. *Current Directions in Psychological Science, 9,* 50–54.

Beilin, H. (1996). Mind and meaning: Piaget and Vygotsky on causal explanation. *Human Development, 39,* 277–286.

Belkin, M. & Rosner, M. (1987). Intelligence, education, and myopia in males, *Archives of Opthamology, 105,* 1508–1511.

Bell, A. E. (1977). Heritability in retrospect. *Journal of Heredity, 68,* 297–300.

Bell, J. H., & Bromnick, R. D. (2003). The social reality of the imaginary audience: A ground theory approach. *Adolescence, 38,* 205–219.

Beller, M., & Gafni, N. (1996). The 1991 international assessment of educational progress in mathematics and sciences: The gender differences perspective. *Journal of Educational Psychology, 88,* 365–377.

Bem, D. J., & Honorton, C. (1994). Does psi exist? Replicable evidence for an anomalous process of information transfer. *Psychological Bulletin, 115,* 4–18.

Benbow, C. P., & Minor, L. L. (1990). Cognitive profiles of verbally and mathematically precocious students: Implications for identification of the gifted. *Gifted Child Quarterly, 34,* 21–26.

Benedetti, F., Pollo, A., Lopiano, L., Lanotte, M., Vighetti, S., & Rainero, I. (2003). Conscious expectation and unconscious conditioning in analgesic, motor, and hormonal placebo/nocebo responses. *Journal of Neuroscience, 23,* 4315–4323.

Bensafi, M., Tsutsui, T., Khan, R., Levenson, R. W., & Sobel, N. (2004). Sniffing a human sex-steroid derived compound affects mood and autonomic arousal in a dose-dependent manner. *Psychoneuroendocrinology, 29,* 1290–1299.

Ben-Shakhar, G., & Furedy, J. J. (1990). *Theories and applications in the detection of deception: A psychophysiological and international perspective.* New York: Springer-Verlag.

Benson, D. F., & Greenberg, J. P. (1969). Visual form agnosia: A specific deficit in visual recognition. *Archives of Neurology, 20,* 82–89.

Berenbaum, S. A. (1999). Effects of early androgens on sex-typed activities and interests in adolescents with congenital adrenal hyperplasia. *Hormones & Behavior, 35,* 102–110.

Berg, S. (1996). Aging, behavior, and terminal decline. In J. E. Birren & K. W. Schaie (Eds.), *Handbook of the psychology of aging* (4th ed., pp. 323–337). New York: Academic Press.

Bergeman, C. S., Plomin, R., Pederson, N. L., McClearn, G. E., & Nesselroad, J. R. (1990). Genetic and environmental influences on social support: The Swedish Adoption/Twin Study of Aging (SATSA). *Journal of Gerontology: Psychological Sciences, 45,* P101–P106.

Berkman, L. F., & Syme, S. L. (1979). Social networks, host resistance, and mortality: A nine year follow-up study of Alameda Country residents. *American Journal of Epidemiology, 109,* 186–204.

Berko, J. (1958). The child's learning of English morphology. *Word, 14,* 150–177.

Berkowitz, L. (1998). Affective aggression: The role of stress, pain, and negative affect. In R. G. Geen & E. Donnerstein (Eds.), *Human aggression: Theories, research, and implications for social policy* (pp. 49–72). San Diego, CA.: Academic Press.

Berkowitz, L., & Harmon-Jones, E. (2004). Toward an understanding of the determinants of anger. *Emotion, 4,* 107–130.

Berlyne, D. E. (1960). *Conflict, arousal, and curiosity.* New York: McGraw-Hill.

Berlyne, D. E. (Ed.). (1974). *Studies in the new experimental aesthetics: Steps toward an objective psychology of aesthetic appreciation.* Washington, DC: Hemisphere.

Berman, J. D., & Straus, S. E. (2004). Implementing a research agenda for complementary and alternative medicine. *Annual Review of Medicine, 55,* 239–254.

Berman, S. M., & Noble, E. P. (1995). Reduced visuospatial performance in children with the D2 dopamine receptor A1 allele. *Behavior Genetics, 25,* 45–58.

Bermond, B. N., Fasotti, L., & Schuerman, J. (1991). Spinal cord lesions, peripheral feedback, and intensities of emotional feelings. *Cognition & Emotion, 5,* 201–220.

Berridge, K. C. (1996). Food reward: Brain substrates of wanting and liking. *Neuroscience and Biobehavioral Reviews, 20,* 1–20.

Berridge, K. C. (2003). Pleasures of the brain. *Brain and Cognition, 52,* 106–128.

Berridge, K. C. (2004). Motivation concepts in behavioral neuroscience. *Physiology and Behavior, 81,* 179–209.

Berscheid, E., & Reis, H. T. (1998). Attraction and close relationships. In D. T. Gilbert, S. T. Fiske, & G. Lindzey (Eds.), *The handbook of social psychology* (4th ed., pp. 193–281). New York: McGraw-Hill.

Berson, D. M., Dunn, F. A., & Takao, M. (2002). Phototransduction by retinal ganglion cells that set the circadian clock. *Science, 295,* 1070–1073.

Berthoud, H. R. (2002). Multiple neural systems controlling food intake and body weight. *Neuroscience and Biobehavioral Reviews, 26,* 393–428.

Beutler, L. E., & Hodgson, A. B. (1993). Prescriptive psychotherapy. In G. Stricker & J. R. Gold (Eds.), *Comprehensive handbook of psychotherapy integration* (pp. 151–164). New York: Plenum Press.

Beutler, L. E., Machado, P. P., & Neufeldt, S. A. (1994). Therapist variables. In A. E. Bergin & S. L. Garfield (Eds.), *Handbook of psychotherapy and behavior change* (4th ed., pp. 229–269). New York: Wiley.

Beyers, J. M., & Loeber, R. (2003). Untangling developmental relations between depressed mood and delinquency in male adolescents. *Journal of Abnormal Child Psychology, 31,* 247–266.

Bhatt, R. S., & Bertin, E. (2001). Pictorial cues and three-dimensional information processing in early infancy. *Journal of Experimental Child Psychology, 80,* 315–332.

Biedenkapp, J. C., & Rudy, J. W. (2004). Context memories and reactivation: Constraints on the reconsolidation hypothesis. *Behavioral Neuroscience, 118,* 956–964.

Biederman, I. (1987). Recognition-by-components: A theory of human image understanding. *Psychological Review, 94,* 115–147.

Biederman, I., & Shiffrar, M. M. (1987). Sexing day-old chicks: A case study and expert systems analysis of a difficult perceptual-learning task. *Journal of Experimental Psychology: Learning, Memory, and Cognition, 13,* 640–645.

Biederman, J., Hirshfeld-Becker, D. R., Rosenbaum, J. F., Hérot, C., Friedman, D., Snidman, N., et al. (2001). Further evidence of association between behavioral inhibition and social anxiety in children. *American Journal of Psychiatry, 158,* 1673–1679.

Bierhoff, H. W., Klein, R., & Kramp, P. (1991). Evidence for the altruistic personality from data on accident research. *Journal of Personality, 59,* 263–280.

Bihrle, A. M., Brownell, H. H., Powelson, J. A., & Gardner, H. (1986). Comprehension of humorous and non-humorous materials by left and right brain-damaged patients. *Brain and Cognition, 5,* 399–411.

Bilukha, O. O., & Utermohlen, V. (2002). Internalization of Western standards of appearance, body dissatisfaction and dieting in urban educated Ukrainian females. *European Eating Disorders Review, 10,* 120–137.

Bindra, D. (1968). Neuropsychological interpretation of the effects of drive and incentive motivation on general activity and instrumental behavior. *Psychological Review, 75,* 1–22.

Bird, H., Howard, D., & Franklin, S. (2000). Why is a verb like an inanimate object? Grammatical category and semantic category deficits. *Brain & Language, 72,* 246–309.

Birkenhäger, T. K., Renes, J. W., & Pluijms, E. M. (2004). One-year follow-up after successful ECT: A naturalistic study in depressed inpatients. *Journal of Clinical Psychiatry, 65,* 87–91.

Birnbaum, S. G., Yuan, P. X., Wang, M., Vijayraghavan, S., Bloom, A. K., Davis, D. J., et al. (2004). Protein kinase C overactivity impairs prefrontal cortical regulation of working memory. *Science 306,* 882–884.

Birren, J. E., Riegel, K. F., & Morrison, D. F. (1962). Age differences in response speed as a function of controlled variations of stimulus conditions: Evidence of a general speed factor. *Gerontologia, 6,* 1–18.

Bishop, G. D. (1994). *Health psychology: Integrating mind and body.* Boston, MA: Allyn & Bacon.

Biswas-Diener, R., Diener, E., & Tamir, M. (2004). The psychology of subjective well-being. *Daedalus, 133,* 18–24.

Bjork, E. L., & Bjork, R. A. (2003). Intentional forgetting can decrease residual influences of to-be-forgotten information. *Journal of Experimental Psychology: Learning, Memory, & Cognition, 29,* 524–531.

Bjork, R. A. (1972). Theoretical implications of directed forgetting. In A. W. Melton & E. Martin (Eds.), *Coding processes in human memory* (pp. 217–235). Washington, DC: Winston.

Black, D. W., Noyes, R., Goldstein, R. B., & Blum, N. (1992). A family study of obsessive-compulsive disorder. *Archives of General Psychiatry, 49,* 362–368.

Black, J. E., Jones, T. A., Nelson, C. A., & Greenough, W. T. (1998). Neuronal plasticity and the developing brain. In N. E. Alessi, J. T. Coyle, S. I. Harrison, & S. Eth (Eds.), *Handbook of child and adolescent psychiatry: Vol 6. Basic psychiatric science and treatment* (pp. 31–53). New York: Wiley.

Blais, M. A., Hilsenroth, M. J., & Castlebury, F. D. (1997). Psychometric characteristics of the Cluster B personality disorders under DSM-III–R and DSM-IV. *Journal of Personality Disorders, 11,* 270–278.

Blakemore, S., Winston, J., & Frith, U. (2004). Social cognitive neuroscience: Where are we heading? *Trends in Cognitive Sciences, 8,* 216–222.

Blalock, E. M., Chen, K, Sharrow, K., Herman, J. P., Porter, N. M., Foster, T. C., & Landfield, P. W. (2003). Gene microarrays in hippocampal aging: Statistical profiling identifies novel processes correlated with cognitive impairment. *Journal of Neuroscience, 23,* 3807–3819.

Blanchard, R. (2001). Fraternal birth order and the maternal immune hypothesis of male homosexuality. *Hormones & Behavior, 40,* 105–114.

Blanck, H. M., Marcus, M., Tolbert, P. E., Rubin, C., Henderson, A. K., Hertzberg, V. S., et al. (2000). Age at menarche and Tanner stage in girls exposed *in utero* and postnatally to polybrominated biphenyl. *Epidemiology, 11,* 641–647.

Blascovich, J., & Tomaka, J. (1996). The biopsychosocial model of arousal regulation. *Advances in Experimental Social Psychology, 28,* 1–51.

Blass, T. (1999). The Milgram Paradigm after 35 years: Some things we now know about obedience to authority. *Journal of Applied Social Psychology, 29,* 955–978.

Blass, T. (2004). *The man who shocked the world: The life and legacy of Stanley Milgram.* New York: Basic Books.

Blatt, S. J., Zuroff, D. C., Bondi, C. M., & Sanislow, C. A., III. (2000). Short- and long-term effects of medication and psychotherapy in the brief treatment of depression: Further analyses of data from the NIMH TDCRP. *Psychotherapy Research, 10,* 215–234.

Bleiberg, K. L., & Markowitz, J. C. (2005). A pilot study of interpersonal psychotherapy for posttraumatic stress disorder. *American Journal of Psychiatry, 162,* 181–183.

Block, N. (1995). How heritability misleads about race. *Cognition, 56,* 99–128.

Bloom, B. L. (1997). *Planned short-term psychotherapy: A clinical handbook* (2nd ed.). Boston, MA: Allyn & Bacon.

Bloom, B. S. (1985). Generalizations about talent development. In B. S. Bloom (Ed.), *Developing talent in young people* (pp. 507–549). New York: Ballantine Books.

Blumenthal, J. A., Babyak, M., Wei, J., O'Connor, C., Waugh, R., Eisenstein, E., et al. (2002). Usefulness of psychosocial treatment of mental stress-induced myocardial ischemia in men. *American Journal of Cardiology, 89,* 164–168.

Blundell, J. E. (1977). Is there a role for 5-hydroxytryptamine in feeding? *International Journal of Obesity, 1,* 15–42.

Blundell, J. E. (1984). Serotonin and appetite. *Neuropharmacology, 23,* 1537–1551.

Blundell, J. E. (1986). Serotonin manipulations and the structure of feeding behaviour. *Appetite, 7,* 39–56.

Blundell, J. E., & Halford, J. C. G. (1998). Serotonin and appetite regulation: Implications for the pharmacological treatment of obesity. *CNS Drugs, 9,* 473–495.

Bly, B. M., & Kosslyn, S. M. (1997). Functional anatomy of object recognition in humans: Evidence from PET and fMRI. *Current Opinion in Neurology, 10,* 5–9.

Bobo, L. (1983). Whites' opposition to busing: Symbolic racism or realistic group conflict? *Journal of Personality and Social Psychology, 45,* 1196–1210.

Bochner, S., & Jones, J. (2003). *Child language development: Learning to talk.* London: Whurr.

Bodenhausen, G. V., Kramer, G. P., & Susser, K. (1994). Happiness and stereotypic thinking in social judgment. *Journal of Personality and Social Psychology, 66,* 621–632.

Bogaert, A. F. (1996). Volunteer bias in human sexuality research: Evidence for both sexuality and personality differences in males. *Archives of Sexual Behavior, 25,* 125–140.

Bohm, J. K., & Hendricks, B. (1997). Effects of interpersonal touch, degree of justification, and sex of participant on compliance with a request. *Journal of Social Psychology, 137,* 460–469.

Boivin, D. B., Czeisler, C. A., Dijk, D., Duffy, J. F., Folkard, S., Minors, D. S., et al. (1997). Complex interaction of the sleep-wake cycle and circadian phase modulates mood in healthy subjects. *Archives of General Psychiatry, 54,* 145–152.

Bokhorst, C. L., Bakermans-Kranenburg, M. J., Fearon, R. M. P., van IJzendoorn, M. H., Fonagy, P., & Schuengel, C. (2003). The importance of shared environment in mother-infant attachment security: A behavioral genetic study. *Child Development, 74,* 1769–1782.

Bolton, P., Bass, J., Neugebauer, R., Verdeli, H., Clougherty, K. F., Wickramaratne, P., Speelman, L., Ndogoni, L., & Weissman, M. (2003). Group interpersonal psychotherapy for depression in rural Uganda: A randomized controlled trial. *Journal of the American Medical Association, 289,* 3117–3124.

Bonanno, G. A. (2004). Loss, trauma, and human resilience: Have we underestimated the human capacity to thrive after extremely aversive events? *American Psychologist, 59,* 20–28.

Bonanno, G. A. (2005). Clarifying and extending the construct of adult resilience. *American Psychologist, 60,* 265–267.

Bonanno, G. A., Papa, A., Lalande, K., Westphal, M., & Coifman, K. (2004). The importance of being flexible: The ability to both enhance and suppress emotional expression predicts long-term adjustment. *Psychological Science, 15,* 482–487.

Bond, M., Gardiner, S. T., Christian, H., & Sigel, J. J. (1983). Empirical study of self-rated defense styles. *Archives of General Psychiatry, 40,* 333–338.

Bond, R., & Smith, P. B. (1996). Culture and conformity: A meta-analysis of studies using Asch's (1952b, 1956) line judgment task. *Psychological Bulletin, 119,* 111–137.

Bontempo, D. E., & D'Augelli, A. R. (2002). Effects of at-school victimization and sexual orientation on lesbian, gay, or bisexual youths' health risk behavior. *Journal of Adolescent Health, 30,* 364–374.

Borg, E., & Counter, S. A. (1989). The middle ear muscles. *Scientific American, 261,* 74–80.

Boring, E. G. (1950). *A history of experimental psychology* (2nd ed.). New York: Appleton-Century-Crofts.

Borman, W. C., Hanson, M. A., & Hedge, J. W. (1997). Personnel selection. *Annual Review of Psychology, 48,* 299–337.

Bornstein, M. H., DiPietro, J. A., Hahn, C. S., Painter, K., Haynes, O. M., & Costigan, K. A. (2002). Prenatal cardiac function and postnatal cognitive development: An exploratory study. *Infancy, 3,* 475–494.

Bornstein, M. H., Tal, J., Rahn, C., Galperin, C. Z., et al. (1992). Functional analysis of the contents of maternal speech to infants of 5 and 13 months in four cultures: Argentina, France, Japan, and the United States. *Developmental Psychology, 28,* 593–603.

Bornstein, S. R., & Chrousos, G. P. (1999) Clinical review 104. Adrenocorticotropin (ACTH)- and non-ACTH-mediated regulation of the adrenal cortex: Neural and immune inputs. *Journal of Clinical Endocrinology and Metabolism, 84,* 1729–1736.

Boroditsky, L. (2001). Does language shape thought? Mandarin and English speakers' conceptions of time. *Cognitive Psychology, 43,* 1–22.

Bosch, J. A., Brand, H. S., Ligtenberg, A. J. M., Bermond, B., Hoogstraten, J., & Nieuw Amgerongen, A. V. (1998). The response of salivary protein levels and S-IgA to an academic examination are associated with daily stress. *Journal of Psychophysiology, 12,* 384–391.

Bosson, J. K., Haymovitz, E. L., & Pinel, E. C. (2004). When saying and doing diverge: The effects of stereotype threat on self-reported versus non-verbal anxiety. *Journal of Experimental Social Psychology, 40,* 247–255.

Bosworth, H. B., & Siegler, I. C. (2002). Terminal change in cognitive function: An updated review of longitudinal studies. *Experimental Aging Research, 28,* 299–315.

Bottini, G., Corcoran, R., Sterzi, R., Paulesu, E., Schenone, P., Scarpa, P., et al. (1994). The role of the right hemisphere in the interpretation of figurative aspects of language: A positron emission tomography activation study. *Brain, 117,* 1241–1253.

Botwinick, J. (1984). *Aging and behavior: A comprehensive integration of research findings.* New York: Springer.

Bouchard, T. J., Jr. (1994). Genes, environment, and personality. *Science, 264,* 1700–1701.

Bouchard, T. J., Jr. (2004). Genetic influence on human psychological traits: A survey. *Current Directions in Psychological Science, 13,* 148–151.

Bouchard, T. J., Jr., Lykken, D. T., McGue, M., Segal, N. L., & Tellegen, A. (1990). Sources of human psychological differences: The Minnesota Study of Twins Reared Apart. *Science, 250,* 223–228.

Bouchard, T. J., & McGue, M. (1981). Familial studies of intelligence: A review. *Science, 212,* 1055–1059.

Bouton, M. (1993). Context, time and memory retrieval in the interference paradigms of Pavlovian conditioning. *Psychological Bulletin, 114,* 80–99.

Bouton, M. (1994). Context, ambiguity and classical conditioning. *Current Directions in Psychological Science, 3,* 49–52.

Bouton, M. E. (2000). A learning theory perspective on lapse, relapse, and the maintenance of behavior change. *Health Psychology, 19,* 57–63.

Bouton, M. E. (2002). Context, ambiguity, and unlearning: Sources of relapse after behavioral extinction. *Biological Psychiatry, 52,* 976–979.

Bouton, M. E., Mineka, S., & Barlow, D. H. (2001). A modern learning theory perspective on the etiology of panic disorder. *Psychological Review, 108,* 4–32.

Bowdle, B. F., & Gentner, D. (2005). The career of metaphor. *Psychological Review, 112,* 193–216.

Bower, G. H. (1972). Mental imagery and associative learning. In L. Gregg (Ed.), *Cognition and learning and memory* (pp. 51–88). New York: Wiley.

Bower, G. H. (1981). Mood and memory. *American Psychologist, 36,* 129–148.

Bower, G. H. (1992). How might emotions effect learning? In S-Å. Christianson (Ed.), *The handbook of emotion and memory: Research and theory* (pp. 3–31). Hillsdale, NJ: Erlbaum.

Bower, G. H., Clark, M. C., Lesgold, A. M., & Winzenz, D. (1969). Hierarchical retrieval schemes in recall of categorized word lists. *Journal of Verbal Learning and Verbal Behavior, 8,* 323–343.

Bowlby, J. (1969). *Attachment and loss: Vol. 1, Attachment.* New York: Basic Books.

Bowlby, J. (1973). *Separation: Anxiety & anger.* Vol. 2 of *Attachment and loss.* London: Hogarth Press.

Bowman, E. S., & Nurnberger, J. I. (1993). Genetics of psychiatry diagnosis and treatment. In D. L. Dunner (Ed.), *Current psychiatric therapy* (pp. 46–56). Philadelphia: Saunders.

Brach, J. S., Simonsick, E. M., Kritchevsky, S., Yaffe, K., & Newman, A. B. (2004). The association between physical function and lifestyle activity and exercise in the health, aging and body composition study. *Journal of the American Geriatrics Society, 52,* 502–509.

Bradburn, N. M. (1969). *The structure of psychological well-being.* Chicago: Aldine.

Braden, J. P. (2000). Editor's introduction: Perspectives on nonverbal assessment of intelligence. *Journal of Psychoeducational Assessment, 18,* 204–220.

Bradley, M. M., Greenwald, M. K., Petry, M. C., & Lang, P. J. (1992). Remembering pictures: Pleasure and arousal in memory. *Journal of Experimental Psychology: Learning, Memory, and Cognition, 18,* 379–390.

Bradley, M. T., MacLaren, V. V., & Carle, S. B. (1996). Deception and nondeception in Guilty Knowledge and Guilty Actions Polygraph Tests. *Journal of Applied Psychology, 81,* 153–160.

Bradley, M. T., & Warfield, J. F. (1984). Innocence, information, and the Guilty Knowledge Test in the detection of deception. *Psychophysiology, 21,* 683–689.

Bradshaw, G. L., & Anderson, J. R. (1982). Elaborative encoding as an explanation of levels of processing. *Journal of Verbal Learning & Verbal Behavior, 21,* 165–174.

Brainard, G. C., Hanifin, J. P., Greeson, J. M., Byrne, B., Glickman, G., Gerner, E., & Rollag, M. D. (2001). Action spectrum for melatonin regulation in humans: Evidence for a novel circadian photoreceptor. *Journal of Neuroscience, 21,* 6405–6412.

Brannon, L. (1996). *Gender: Psychological perspectives.* Needham Heights, MA: Simon & Schuster.

Bransford, J. D., & Franks, J. J. (1971). The abstraction of linguistic ideas. *Cognitive Psychology, 2,* 331–350.

Brashers-Krug, T., Shadmehr, R., & Bizzi, E. (1996). Consolidation in human motor memory. *Nature, 382,* 252–254.

Brasiek, R. J., & Roberts, D. J. (2002). Amusement park injuries and deaths. *Annals of Emergency Medicine, 39,* 65–72.

Braun, K. A., Ellis, R., & Loftus, E. F. (2002). Make my memory: How advertising can change our memories of the past. *Psychology & Marketing, 19,* 1–23.

Breckler, S. J. (1984). Empirical validation of affect, behavior, and cognition as distinct components of attitude. *Journal of Personality and Social Psychology, 47,* 1191–1205.

Bregman, A. S. (1990). *Auditory scene analysis: The perceptual organization of sound.* Cambridge, MA: MIT Press.

Bregman, A. S. (1993). Auditory scene analysis: Hearing in complex environments. In S. McAdams & E. Bigand (Eds.), *Thinking in sound: The cognitive psychology of human audition* (pp. 10–36). New York: Oxford University Press.

Bregman, E. O. (1934). An attempt to modify the emotional attitudes of infants by the conditioned response technique. *Journal of Genetic Psychology, 45,* 169.

Brehm, J. W. (1956). Post-decision changes in the desirability of alternatives. *Journal of Abnormal and Social Psychology*, 52, 384–389.

Breiter, H. C., Rauch, S. L., Kwong, K. K., Baker, J. R., Weisskoff, R. M., Kennedy, D. N., et al, (1996). Functional magnetic resonance imaging of symptom provocation in obsessive-compulsive disorder. *Archives of General Psychiatry*, 53, 595–606.

Bremner, J. D., Narayan, M., Anderson, E. R., Staib, L. H., Miller, H. L., & Charney, D. S. (2000). Hippocampal volume reduction in major depression. *American Journal of Psychiatry*, 157, 115–117.

Bremner, J. D., Steinberg, M., Southwick, S. M., Johnson, D. R., & Charney, D. S. (1993). Use of the structured clinical interview for DSM-IV dissociative disorders for systemic assessment of dissociative symptoms in posttraumatic stress disorder. *American Journal of Psychiatry*, 150, 1011–1014.

Bremner, J. D., Vythilingam, M., Vermetten, E., Southwick, S. M., McGlashan, T., Nazeer, A., Khan, S., Vaccarino, L. V., Soufer, R., Garg, P. K., Ng, C. K., Staib, L. H., Duncan, J. S., & Charney, D. S. (2003). MRI and PET study of deficits in hippocampal structure and function in women with childhood sexual abuse and posttraumatic stress disorder. *American Journal of Psychiatry*, 160, 924–932.

Breslau, N., Kessler, R. C., Chilcoat, H. D. Schultz, L. R., Davis, G. C., & Andreski, P. (1998). Trauma and posttraumatic stress disorder in the community: The 1996 Detroit Area Survey of Trauma. *Archives of General Psychiatry*, 55, 626–632.

Brewer, A. A., Press, W. A., Logothetis, N. K., & Wandell, B. A. (2002). Visual areas in Macaque cortex measured using functional magnetic resonance imaging. *Journal of Neuroscience*, 22, 10416–10426.

Brewer, J. B., Zhao, Z., Desmod, J. E., Glover, G. H., & Gabrielli, J. D. E. (1998). Making memories: Brain activity that predicts how well visual experience will be remembered. *Science*, 281, 1185–1187.

Brewer, K. R., & Wann, D. L. (1998). Observational learning effectiveness as a function of model characteristics: Investigating the importance of social power. *Social Behavior & Personality*, 26, 1–10.

Brewer, M. B., & Brown, R. J. (1998). Intergroup relations. In D. T. Gilbert, S. T. Fiske, & G. Lindzey (Eds.), *The handbook of social psychology* (4th ed., pp. 554–594). New York: McGraw-Hill.

Brian, D. (1996). *Einstein: A life*. New York: John Wiley & Sons.

Brickman, P., & Campbell, D. T. (1971). Hedonic relativism and the good society. In M. H. Appley (Ed.), *Adaptation-level theory: A symposium* (pp. 215–231). New York: Academic Press.

Broadbent, D. E. (1971). The magic number seven after fifteen years. In A. Kennedy & A. Wilkes (Eds.), *Studies in long-term memory* (pp. 2–18). New York: Wiley.

Brody, J. (1998, April 6). Dealing with sleep deprivation. *International Herald Tribune*, 9.

Brody, N. (2003a). Construct validation of the Sternberg triarchic abilities test: Comment and reanalysis. *Intelligence*, 31, 319–329.

Brody, N. (2003b). What Sternberg should have concluded. *Intelligence*, 31, 339–342.

Brooks-Gunn, J., Graber, J. A., & Paikoff, R. L. (1994). Studying links between hormones and negative affect: Models and measures. *Journal of Research on Adolescence*, 4, 469–486.

Brosschot, J. F., & Thayer, J. F. (2003). Heart rate response is longer after negative emotions than after positive emotions. *International Journal of Psychophysiology*, 50, 181–187.

Brown, A. S., Cohen, P., Harkavy-Friedman, J., & Babulas, V. (2001). Prenatal rubella, premorbid abnormalities, and adult schizophrenia. *Biological Psychiatry*, 49, 473–486.

Brown, A. S., van Os, J., Driessens, C., Hoek, S. W., & Susser, E. S. (1999). Prenatal famine and the spectrum of psychosis. *Psychiatric Annals*, 29, 145–150.

Brown, B. (1999). Optimizing expression of the common human genome for child development. *Current Directions in Psychological Science*, 8, 37–41.

Brown, B. B., Clasen, D., & Eicher, S. (1986a). Perceptions of peer pressure, peer conformity dispositions, and self-reported behavior among adolescents. *Developmental Psychology*, 22, 521–530.

Brown, B. B., Lohr, M. J., & McClenahan, E. L. (1986b). Early adolescents' perceptions of peer pressure. *Journal of Early Adolescence*, 6, 139–154.

Brown, D. E. (1991). *Human universals*. Philadelphia: Temple University Press.

Brown, I., Jr., & Inouye, D. K. (1978). Learned helplessness through modeling: The role of perceived similarity in competence. *Journal of Personality and Social Psychology*, 36, 900–908.

Brown, J. D., & Rogers, R. J. (1991). Self-serving attributions: The role of physiological arousal. *Personality and Social Psychology Bulletin*, 17, 501–506.

Brown, P. L., & Jenkins, H. M. (1968). Auto-shaping of the pigeon's key peck. *Journal of the Experimental Analysis of Behavior*, 68, 503–507.

Brown, R. (1989). Roger Brown. In G. Lindzey (Ed.), *A history of psychology in autobiography* (Vol. 8, pp. 37–60). Stanford, CA: Stanford University Press.

Brown, R., & Kulik, J. (1977). Flashbulb memories. *Cognition*, 5, 73–99.

Brown, R. P., & Pinel, E. C. (2003). Stigma on my mind: Individual differences in the experience of stereotype threat. *Journal of Experimental Social Psychology*, 39, 626–633.

Browne, C. A., Colditz, P. B., & Dunster, K. R. (2000). Infant autonomic function is altered by maternal smoking during pregnancy. *Early Human Development*, 59, 209–218.

Browne, G., Steiner, M., Roberts, J., Gafni, A., Byrne, C., Dunn, E., et al. (2002). Sertraline and/or interpersonal psychotherapy for patients with dysthymic disorder in primary care: 6-month comparison with longitudinal 2-year follow-up of effectiveness and costs. *Journal of Affective Disorders*, 68, 317–320.

Brownell, H. H., Potter, H. H., Michelow, D., & Gardner, H. (1984). Sensitivity to lexical denotation and connotation in brain-damaged patients: A double dissociation. *Brain and Language*, 22, 253–265.

Brownell, K. D., & Rodin, J. (1992). *Medical, metabolic, and psychological effects of weight cycling*. Unpublished manuscript, Yale University.

Brugger, P., Landis, T., & Regard, M. (1990). A "sheep-goat effect" in repetition avoidance: Extrasensory perception as an effect of subjective probability? *British Journal of Psychology*, 81, 455–468.

Brummett, B. H., Mark, D. B., Siegler, I. C., Williams, R. B., Babyak, M. A., Clapp-Channing, N. E., & Barefoot, J. C. (2005). Perceived social support as a predictor of mortality in coronary patients: Effects of smoking, sedentary behavior, and depersssive symptoms. *Psychosomatic Medicine*, 67, 40–45.

Brunner, D. P., Dijk, D. J., Tobler, I., & Borbely, A. A. (1990). Effect of partial sleep deprivation on sleep stages and EEG power spectra: Evidence for non-REM and REM sleep homeostasis. *Electroencephalogr. Clin. Neurophysiol.*, 75, 492–499.

Brussoni, M. J., Jang, K. L., Livesley, W. J., & MacBeth, T. M. (2000). Genetic and environmental influences on adult attachment styles. *Personal Relationships*, 7, 283–289.

Bryan, R. N., Wells, S. W., Miller, T. J., Elster, A. D., Jungreis, C. A., Poirier, V. C., et al. (1997). Infarctlike lesions in the brain: Prevalence and anatomic characteristics at MR imaging of the elderly—data from the Cardiovascular Health Study. *Radiology*, 202, 47–54.

Bryant, R. A., & Barnier, A. J. (1999). Eliciting autobiographical pseudomemories: The relevance of hypnosis, hypnotizability, and attributions. *International Journal of Clinical & Experimental Hypnosis*, 47, 267–283.

Buchanan, C. M., Eccles, J., & Becker, J. (1992). Are adolescents the victims of raging hormones? Evidence for activational effects of hormones on moods and behavior at adolescence. *Psychological Bulletin*, 111, 62–107.

Buchkremer, G., Klingberg, S., Holle, R., Schulze-Moenking, H., & Hornung, W. P. (1997). Psychoeducational psychotherapy for schizophrenic patients and their key relatives or care-givers: Results of a 2-year follow-up. *Acta Psychiatrica Scandinavica*, 96, 483–491.

Buck, L., & Axel, R. (1991). A novel multigene family may encode odorant receptors: A molecular basis for odor recognition. *Cell*, 65, 175–187.

Buckalew, L. W., & Ross, S. (1981). Relationship of perceptual characteristics to efficacy of placebos. *Psychological Reports*, 49, 955–961.

Buckner, R. L., Kelley, W. M., & Petersen, S. E. (1999). Frontal cortex contributes to human memory formation. *Nature Neuroscience*, 2, 311–314.

Buda, R., & Elsayed-Elkhouly, S. M. (1998). Cultural differences between Arabs and Americans: Individualism-collectivism revisited. *Journal of Cross-Cultural Psychology*, 29, 487–492.

Buehler, R., Griffin, D., & Ross, M. (1994). Exploring the "planning fallacy": Why people underestimate their task completion times. *Journal of Personality and Social Psychology*, 67, 366–381.

Buka, S. L., Goldstein, J. M., Seidman, L. J., Zornberg, G. L., Donatelli, J. A., Denny, L. R., & Tsuang, M. T. (1999). Prenatal complications, genetic vulnerability, and schizophrenia: The New England Longitudinal Studies of Schizophrenia. *Psychiatric Annals*, 29, 151–156.

Bulik, C. M., Tozzi, F., Anderson, C., Mazzeo, S. E., Aggen, S., & Sullivan, P. F. (2003). The relation between eating disorders and components of perfectionism. *American Journal of Psychiatry*, 160, 366–368.

Bunce, S. C., Bernat, E., Wong, P. S., & Shevrin, H. (1999). Further evidence for unconscious learning: Preliminary support for the conditioning of facial EMG to subliminal stimuli. *Journal of Psychiatric Research*, 33, 341–347.

Bunney, W. E., & Garland, B. L. (1983). Possible receptor effects of chronic lithium administration. *Neuropharmacology*, 22, 367–372.

Burish, T. G., & Carey, M. P. (1986). Conditioned aversive responses in cancer chemotherapy patients: Theoretical and developmental analysis. *Journal of Counseling and Clinical Psychology*, 54, 593–600.

Burnstein, E. (1982). Persuasion as argument processing. In H. Brandstatter, J. H. Davis, & G. Stocker-Krechgauer (Eds.), *Group decision making* (pp. 103–124). London: Academic Press.

Burton, L. M. (1990). Teenage childbearing as an alternative life-course strategy in multigeneration Black families. *Human Nature*, 1, 123–143.

Burton, L. M. (1996). Age norms, the timing of family role transitions, and intergenerational caregiving among aging African American women. *Gerontologist*, 36, 199–208.

Burton, M. J., Rolls, E. T., & Mora, F. (1976). Effects of hunger on the responses of neurons in the lateral hypothalamus to the sight and taste of food. *Experimental Neurology*, 51, 668–677.

Bushman, B. J. (1984). Perceived symbols of authority and their influence on compliance. *Journal of Applied Social Psychology*, 14, 501–508.

Bushman, B. J. (1988). The effects of apparel on compliance: A field experiment with a female authority figure. *Personality and Social Psychology Bulletin*, 14, 459–467.

Bushman, B. J. (1998). Threatened egotism, narcissism, self-esteem, and direct and displaced aggression: Does self-love or self-hate lead to violence? *Journal of Personality and Social Psychology*, 75, 219–229.

Bushman, B. J., Baumeister, R. F., & Phillips, C. M. (2001). Do people aggress to improve their mood? Catharsis beliefs, affect regulation opportunity, and aggressive responding. *Journal of Personality and Social Psychology*, 81, 17–32.

Bushman, B. J., Bonacci, A. M., van Dijk, M., & Baumeister, R. F. (2003). Narcissism, sexual refusal, and aggression: Testing a narcissistic reactance model of sexual coercion. *Journal of Personality & Social Psychology*, 84, 1027–1040.

Bushman, B. J., & Cooper, H. M. (1990). Effects of alcohol on human aggression: An integrative research review. *Psychological Bulletin*, 107, 1–14.

Bushman, B. J., & Wells, G. L. (1998). Trait aggressiveness and hockey penalties: Predicting hot tempers on the ice. *Journal of Applied Psychology, 83,* 969–974.

Buss, A. H. (1995). *Personality: Temperament, social behavior, and the self.* Needham Heights, MA: Allyn & Bacon.

Buss, A. H., & Plomin, R. (1984). *Temperament: Early developing personality traits.* Hillsdale, NJ: Erlbaum.

Buss, D. M. (1989). Sex differences in human mate preferences: Evolutionary hypotheses tested in 37 cultures. *Behavioral and Brain Sciences, 12,* 1–49.

Buss, D. M. (1994). *The evolution of desire: Strategies of human mating.* New York: Basic Books.

Buss, D. M. (1995). Psychological sex differences: Origins through sexual selection. *American Psychologist, 50,* 164–168.

Buss, D. M. (1998). The psychology of human mate selection: Exploring the complexity of the strategic repetoire. In C. B. Crawford & D. L. Krebs (Eds.), *Handbook of evolutionary psychology: Ideas, issues, and applications* (pp. 405–429). Mahwah, NJ: Erlbaum.

Buss, D. M. (1999). *Evolutionary psychology: The new science of the mind.* Boston: Allyn & Bacon.

Buss, D. M., Larsen, R. J., Western, D., & Semmelroth, J. (1992). Sex differences in jealousy: Evolution, physiology, and psychology. *Psychological Science, 3,* 251–255.

Busse, E. W. (1969). Theories of aging. In E. W. Busse & E. Pfeiffer (Eds.), *Behavior and adaptation in later life* (pp. 11–32). Boston: Little, Brown.

Butcher, J. N., & Rouse, S. V. (1996). Personality: Individual difference and clinical assessment. *Annual Review of Psychology, 47,* 87–111.

Butler, E. A., Egloff, B., Wilhelm, F. H., Smith, N. C., Erickson, E. A., & Gross, J. J. (2003). The social consequences of expressive suppression. *Emotion, 3,* 48–67.

Butzlaff, R. L., & Hooley, J. M. (1998). Expressed emotion and psychiatric relapse: A meta-analysis. *Archives of General Psychiatry, 55,* 547–552.

Byrne, D. (1971). *The attraction paradigm.* New York: Academic Press.

Cabeza, R., & Nyberg, L. (1997). Imaging cognition: An empirical review of PET studies with normal subjects. *Journal of Cognitive Neuroscience, 9,* 1–26.

Cabeza, R., & Nyberg, L. (2000). Imaging cognition II: An empirical review of 275 PET and fMRI studies. *Journal of Cognitive Neuroscience, 12,* 1–47.

Cabeza, R., Prince, S. E., Daselaar, S. M., Greenberg, D. L., Budde, M., Dolcos, F., LaBar, K. S., & Rubin, D. C. (2004). Brain activity during episodic retrieval of autobiographical and laboratory events: An fMRI study using a novel photo paradigm. *Journal of Cognitive Neuroscience, 16,* 1583–1594.

Cacioppo, J. T., Berntson, G. G., Larsen, J. T., Poehlmann, K. M., & Ito, T. A. (2000). The psychophysiology of emotion. In R. Lewis & J. M. Haviland-Jones (Eds.), *The handbook of emotion* (2nd ed., pp. 173–191). New York: Guilford Press.

Cacioppo, J. T., Gardner, J. T., & Berntson, W. L. (1997). Beyond bipolar conceptualizations and measures: The case of attitudes and evaluative space. *Personality & Social Psychology Review, 1,* 3–25.

Cacioppo, J. T., Petty, R. E., Losch, M. E., & Kim, H. S. (1986). Electromyographic activity over facial muscle regions can differentiate the valence and intensity of affective reactions. *Journal of Personality and Social Psychology, 50,* 260–268.

Cadinu, M., Maass, A., Frigerio, S., Impagliazzo, L., & Latinotti, S. (2003). Stereotype threat: The effect of expectancy on performance. *European Journal of Social Psychology, 33,* 267–285.

Cahan, S., & Cohen, N. (1989). Age versus schooling effects on intelligence development. *Child Development, 60,* 1239–1249.

Cahill, L., Haier, R. J., Fallon, J., Alkire, M. T., Tang, C., Keator, D., et al. (1996). Amygdala activity at encoding correlated with long-term free recall of emotional information. *Proceedings of the National Academy of Sciences, USA, 93,* 8016–8021.

Cahill, L., Haier, R. J., White, N. S., Fallon, J., Kilpatrick, L., Lawrence, C., et al. (2001). Sex-related differences in amygdala activity during emotionally in-

fluenced memory storage. *Neurobiology of Learning & Memory, 75,* 1–9.

Cahill, L., Prins, B., Weber, M., & McGaugh, J. L. (1994). Adrenergic activation and memory for emotional events. *Nature, 371,* 702–704.

Cailliet, R. (1993). *Pain: Mechanisms and management.* Philadelphia: Davis.

Cain, W. S. (1973). Spatial discrimination of cutaneous warmth. *American Journal of Psychology, 86,* 169–181.

Cain, W. S. (1979). To know with the nose: Keys to odor identification. *Science, 203,* 467–470.

Cain, W. S. (1982). Odor identification by males and females: Predictions and performance. *Chemical Senses, 7,* 129–141.

Cain, W. S., & Gent, J. F. (1991). Olfactory sensitivity: Reliability, generality, and association with aging. *Journal of Experimental Psychology: Human Perception and Performance, 17,* 382–391.

Cajochen, C., Knoblauch, V., Wirz-Justice, A., Kräuchi, K., Graw, P., & Wallach, D. (2004). Circadian modulation of sequence learning under high and low sleep pressure conditions. *Behavioural Brain Research, 151,* 167–176.

Caldera, Y. M., & Sciaraffa, M. A. (1998). Parent-toddler play with feminine toys: Are all dolls the same? *Sex Roles, 39,* 657–668.

Calvocoressi, L., Lewis, B., Harris, M., Trufan, S. J., et al. (1995). Family accommodation in obsessive-compulsive disorder. *American Journal of Psychiatry, 152,* 441–443.

Cameron-Faulkner, T., Lieven, E., & Tomasello, M. (2003). A construction based analysis of child directed speech. *Cognitive Science, 27,* 843–873.

Campos, J. J., Langer, A., & Krowitz, A. (1970). Cardiac responses on the visual cliff in prelocomotor human infants. *Science, 170,* 196–197.

Canli, T., Zhao, Z., Desmond, J. E., Kang, E., Gross, J., & Gabrieli, J. D. E. (2001). An fMRI study of personality influences on brain reactivity to emotional stimuli. *Behavioral Neuroscience.*

Cannon, T. D. (1997). On the nature and mechanisms of obstetric influences in schizophrenia: A review and synthesis of epidemiologic studies. *International Review of Psychiatry, 9,* 387–397.

Cannon, W. B. (1927). The James-Lange theory of emotions: A critical examination and an alternative theory. *American Journal of Psychology, 39,* 106–124.

Cannon, W. B. (1932). *The wisdom of the body.* New York: Norton.

Cannon, W. B. (1942). Voodoo death. *American Anthropologist, 44,* 169–181.

Canter, S. (1973). Personality traits in twins. In G. Claridge, S. Canter, & W. I. Hume (Eds.), *Personality differences and biological variations* (pp. 21–51). New York: Pergamon.

Cantor, J. M., Blanchard, R., Paterson, A. D., & Bogaert, A. F. (2002). How many gay men owe their sexual orientation to fraternal birth order? *Archives of Sexual Behavior, 31,* 63–71.

Cappa, S. F., & Grafman, J. (2004). Neuroimaging of higher cognitive function. *Cortex, 40,* 591–592.

Caprara, G. V., Barbaranelli, C., Pastorelli, C., & Cervone, D. (2004). The contribution of self-efficacy beliefs to psychosocial outcomes in adolescence: Predicting beyond past behavior and global dispositional tendencies. *Personality and Individual Differences, 37,* 751–763.

Caprara, G. V., Steca, P., Cervone, D., & Artistico, D. (2003). The contribution of self-efficacy beliefs to dispositional shyness: On social cognitive systems and the development of personality dispositions. *Journal of Personality, 71,* 943–970.

Cardinal, R. N., Parkinson, J. A., Hall, J., & Everitt, B. (2002). Emotion and motivation: The role of the amygdala, ventral striatum, and prefrontal cortex. *Neuroscience and Biobehavioral Reviews, 26,* 321–352.

Cardinal, R. N., Parkinson, J. A., Marbini, H. D., Toner, A. J, Bussey, T. J., Robbins, T. W., & Everitt, B. J. (2003). The role of the anterior cingulate cortex in the control over behavior by Pavlovian conditioned stimuli in rats. *Behavioral Neuroscience, 117,* 566–587.

Carey, M. P., & Burish, T. G. (1988). Etiology and treatment of the psychological side effects associated with cancer chemotherapy: A critical review and discussion. *Psychological Bulletin, 104,* 307–325.

Carey, S. (1978). The child as word learner. In J. Bresnan, G. Miller, & M. Halle (Eds.), *Linguistic theory and psychological reality* (pp. 264–293). Cambridge, MA: MIT Press.

Carlbring, P., Westling, B. E., Ljungstrand, P., Ekselius, L., & Andersson, G. (2001). Treatment of panic disorder via the Internet: A randomized trial of a self-help program. *Behavior Therapy, 32,* 751–764.

Carlo, G., Okun, M. A., Knight, G. P., & de Guzman, M. T. (2005). The interplay of traits and motives on volunteering: Agreeableness, extraversion and prosocial value motivation. *Personality and Individual Differences, 38,* 1293–1305.

Carlsson, C. P. O., & Sjoelund, B. H. (2001). Acupuncture for chronic low back pain: A randomized placebo-controlled study with long-term follow-up. *Clinical Journal of Pain, 17,* 296–305.

Carlyon, R. P. (2004). How the brain separates sounds. *Trends in Cognitive Sciences, 8,* 465–471.

Carmines, E. G., & Zeller, R. A. (1979). *Reliability and validity assessment.* Beverly Hills, CA: Sage.

Carney, R. M., Freeland, K. E., Veith, R. C., Cryer, P. E., Skala, J. A., Lynch, T., & Jaffe, A. S. (1999). Major depression, heart rate, and plasma norepinephrine in patients with coronary heart disease. *Biological Psychiatry, 45,* 458–463.

Carroll, J. (1993). *Human cognitive abilities: A survey of factor-analytic studies.* New York: Cambridge University Press.

Carrothers, R. M., Gregory, S. W., Jr., & Gallagher, T. J. (2000). Measuring emotional intelligence of medical school applicants. *Academic Medicine, 75,* 456–463.

Carstensen, L. L. (1991). Socioemotional selectivity theory: Social activity in life-span context. In K. W. Schaie & M. P. Lawton (Eds.), *Annual review of gerontology and geriatrics* (Vol. 11, pp. 195–217). New York: Springer.

Carstensen, L. L. (1992). Social and emotion patterns in adulthood: Support for socioemotional selectivity theory. *Psychology & Aging, 7,* 331–338.

Carstensen, L. L., & Charles, S. T. (1998). Emotion in the second half of life. *Current Directions in Psychological Science, 7,* 144–149.

Carstensen, L. L., Gottman, J. M., & Levenson, R. W. (1995). Emotional behavior in long-term marriage. *Psychology & Aging, 10,* 140–149.

Carstensen, L. L., Pasupathi, M., Mayr, U., & Nesselroade, J. R. (2000). Emotional experience in everyday life across the adult life span. *Journal of Personality & Social Psychology, 79,* 644–655.

Carter, C., & Rice, C. L. (1997). Acquisition and manifestation of prejudice in children. *Journal of Multicultural Counseling and Development, 25,* 185–194.

Carter, C. S. (2004). Oxytocin and the prairie vole: A love story. In J. T. Cacioppo & G. G. Berntson (Eds.), *Essays in social neuroscience* (pp. 53–63). Cambridge, MA: MIT Press.

Cartford, M. C., Gemma, C., & Bickford, P. C. (2002). Eighteen-month-old Fischer 344 rats fed a spinach-enriched diet show improved delay classical eyeblink conditioning and reduced expression of tumor necrosis factor α (TNF α) and TNF β in the cerebellum. *Journal of Neuroscience, 22,* 5813–5816.

Caruso, S., Grillo, C., Agnello, C., Maiolino, L., Intelisano, G., & Serra, A. (2001). A prospective study evidencing rhinomanometric and olfactometric outcomes in women taking oral contraceptives. *Human Reproduction, 16,* 2288–2294.

Carver, C. S., Meyer, B., & Antoni, M. H. (2000). Responsiveness to threats and incentives expectancy of recurrence and distress and disengagement: Moderator effects in early-stage breast cancer patients. *Journal of Consulting and Clinical Psychology, 68,* 965–975.

Carver, C. S., Scheier, M. F., & Weintraub, J. K. (1989). Assessing coping strategies: A theoretically based approach. *Journal of Personality and Social Psychology, 56,* 267–283.

Carver, C. S., & White, T. L. (1994). Behavioral inhibition, behavioral activation, and affective responses to impending reward and punishment: The BIS/BAS scales. *Journal of Personality and Social Psychology, 67,* 319–333.

Casbon, T. S., Burns, A. B., Bradbury, T. N., & Joiner, T. E., Jr. (2005). Receipt of negative feedback is related to increased negative feedback seeking among individuals with depressive symptoms. *Behaviour Research and Therapy, 43,* 485–504.

Case, R. (1977). Responsiveness to conservation training as a function of induced subjective uncertainty, M-space, and cognitive style. *Canadian Journal of Behavioral Sciences, 9,* 12–25.

Case, R. (1978). Intellectual development from birth to adulthood: A neo-Piagetian approach. In R. S. Siegler (Ed.), *Children's thinking: What develops?* (pp. 37–71). Hillsdale, NJ: Erlbaum.

Case, R. (1992a). *The mind's staircase.* Hillsdale, NJ: Erlbaum.

Case, R. (1992b). The role of the frontal lobes in the regulation of cognitive development. *Brain and Cognition, 20,* 51–73.

Caspi, A. (2000). The child is father of the man: Personality continuities from childhood to adulthood. *Journal of Personality and Social Psychology, 78,* 158–172.

Caspi, A., Begg, D., Dickson, N., Harrington, H., Langley, J., Moffitt, T. E., & Silva, P. A. (1997). Personality differences predict health-risk behaviors in young adulthood: Evidence from a longitudinal study. *Journal of Personality and Social Psychology, 73,* 1052–1063.

Caspi, A., & Herbener, E. S. (1990). Continuity and change: Assortative marriage and the consistency of personality in adulthood. *Journal of Personality and Social Psychology, 58,* 250–258.

Caspi, A., Moffitt, T. E., Morgan, J., Rutter, M., Taylor, A., Arseneault, L., et al. (2004). Maternal expressed emotion predicts children's antisocial behavior problems: Using monozygotic-twin differences to identify environmental effects on behavioral development. *Developmental Psychology, 40,* 149–161.

Castellà, J., & Pérez, J. (2004). Sensitivity to punishment and sensitivity to reward and traffic violations. *Accident Analysis & Prevention, 36,* 947–952.

Cattell, R. B. (1943). The description of personality: Basic traits resolved into clusters. *Journal of Abnormal and Social Psychology, 38,* 476–506.

Cattell, R. B. (1971). *Abilities: Their structure, growth, and action.* Boston: Houghton Mifflin.

Cattell, R. B., Eber, H. W., & Tatsuoka, M. M. (1970). *Handbook for the Sixteen Personality Factor Questionnaire (16PF).* Champaign, IL: Institute for Personality and Ability Testing.

Caudron, S. (1994). Diversity ignites effective work teams. *Personnel Journal, 73,* 54–63.

Cavallaro, S., Schreurs, B. G., Zhao, W., D'Agata, V., & Alkon, D. L. (2001). Gene expression profiles during long-term memory consolidation. *European Journal of Neuroscience, 13,* 1809–1815.

Cave, C. B. (1997). Very long-lasting priming in picture naming. *American Psychological Society, 8,* 322–325.

Cave, C. B., & Kosslyn, S. M. (1993). The role of parts and spatial relations in object identification. *Perception, 22,* 229–248.

Ceci, S. J. (1991). How much does schooling influence general intelligence and its cognitive components? A reassessment of the evidence. *Developmental Psychology, 27,* 703–722.

Ceci, S. J., & Williams, W. M. (1997). Schooling, intelligence, and income. *American Psychologist, 52,* 1051–1058.

Center for the Advancement of Health (1998). Facts of life: An issue briefing for health reporters, 3(3), 2.

Centers for Disease Control and Prevention (2003). National Center for Health Statistics, National Health Interview Survey, family core and sample adult questionnaires. Table 65.

Centers for Disease Control and Prevention. (2004). *Health, United States, 2004: With chartbook on trends in the health of Americans.* Washington, DC: U.S. Department of Health and Human Services.

Cerella, J. (1990). Aging and information-processing rate. In J. E. Birren & K. W. Schaie (Eds.), *Handbook of the psychology of aging* (3rd ed., pp. 201–221). San Diego, CA: Academic Press.

Cervone, D. (2005). Personality architecture: Within-person structures and processes. *Annual Review of Psychology, 56,* 423–452.

Chamberlain, K., & Zika, S. (1990). The minor events approach to stress: Support for the use of daily hassles. *British Journal of Psychology, 81,* 469–481.

Chambless, D. L., & Gillis, M. M. (1993). Cognitive therapy of anxiety disorders. *Journal of Consulting and Clinical Psychology, 61,* 248–260.

Chambless, D. L., & Steketee, G. (1999). Expressed emotion and behavior therapy outcome: A prospective study with obsessive-compulsive and agoraphobic outpatients. *Journal of Consulting & Clinical Psychology, 67,* 658–665.

Chan, J., & Yang, J. (1999). *I am Jackie Chan.* New York: Ballantine Books.

Chang, R. C., Blaisdell, A. P., & Miller, R. R. (2003). Backward conditioning: Mediation by the context. *Journal of Experimental Psychology: Animal Behavior Processes, 29,* 171–183.

Changizi, M. A., McGehee, R. M. F., & Hall, W. G. (2002). Evidence that appetitive responses for dehydration and food-deprivation are learned. *Physiology & Behavior, 75,* 295–304.

Chao, L. L., & Martin, A. (1999). Cortical regions associated with perceiving, naming, and knowing about colors. *Journal of Cognitive Neuroscience, 11,* 25–35.

Chapman, C. R., & Nakamura, Y. (1999). A passion of the soul: An introduction to pain for consciousness researchers. *Consciousness and Cognition, 8,* 391–422.

Chapman, J. K. (2000). Developmental outcomes in two groups of young children: Prenatally cocaine exposed and noncocaine exposed: Part 2. *Infant-Toddler Intervention, 10,* 81–96.

Chapman, R. S., & Hesketh, L. J. (2000). Behavioral phenotype of individuals with Down syndrome. *Mental Retardation & Developmental Disabilities Research Reviews, 6,* 84–95.

Chase, W. G., & Ericsson, K. A. (1981). Skilled memory. In J. R. Anderson (Ed.), *Cognitive skills and their acquisition.* Hillsdale, NJ: Erlbaum.

Chaudhari, N., Landin, A. M., & Roper, S. D. (2000). A metabotropic glutamate receptor variant functions as a taste receptor. *Nature Neuroscience, 3,* 113–119.

Cheour-Luhtanen, M., Alho, K., Sainio, K., Rinne, T., & Reinikainen, K. (1996). The ontogenetically earliest discriminative response of the human brain. *Psychophysiology, 33,* 478–481.

Cherry, E. C. (1953). Some experiments on the recognition of speech with one and two ears. *Journal of the Acoustical Society of America, 25,* 975–979.

Chess, S., & Thomas, A. (1987). *Know your child.* New York: Basic Books.

Chess, S., & Thomas, A. (1996). *Temperament: Theory and practice.* New York: Brunner/Mazel.

Chilcoat, H. D., & Breslau, N. (1998). Posttraumatic stress disorder and drug disorders testing causal pathways. *Archives of General Psychiatry, 55,* 913–917.

Child, I. L. (1985). Psychology and anomalous observations: The question of ESP in dreams. *American Psychologist, 40,* 1219–1230.

Chipuer, H. M., Rovine, M. J., & Plomin, R. (1990). LISREL modeling: Genetic and environmental influences on IQ revisited. *Intelligence, 14,* 11–29.

Choderow, N. (1978). *The reproduction of mothering.* Berkeley: University of California Press.

Chomsky, N. (1957). *Syntactic structures.* Mouton: The Hague.

Chomsky, N. (1972). *Language and mind.* New York: Harcourt Brace.

Christensen, A. J., Benotsch, E. G., Wiebe, J. S., & Lawton, W. J. (1995). Coping with treatment-related stress: Effects on patient adherence in hemodialysis. *Journal of Consulting & Clinical Psychology, 63,* 454–459.

Christensen, K. A., Stephens, M. A. P., & Townsend, A. L. (1998). Mastery in women's multiple roles and well-being: Adult daughters providing care to impaired parents. *Health Psychology, 17,* 163–171.

Christian, K. M., & Thompson, R. F. (2003). Neural substrates of eyeblink conditioning: Acquisition and retention. *Learning & Memory, 10,* 427–455.

Christmann, C., & Leuthold, H. (2004). The attentional blink is susceptible to concurrent perceptual processing demands. *Quarterly Journal of Experimental Psychology: Human Experimental Psychology, 57,* 357–377.

Chumlea, W. C., Schubert, C. M., Roche, A. F., Kulin, H. E., Lee, P. A., Himes, J. H., & Sun, S. S. (2003). Age at menarche and racial comparisons in U.S. girls. *Pediatrics, 111,* 110–113.

Chun, M. M. (1997). Types and tokens in visual processing: A double dissociation between the attentional blink and repetition blindness. *Journal of Experimental Psychology: Human Perception and Performance, 23,* 738–755.

Chun, M. M. (2000). Contextual cueing of visual attention. *Trends in Cognitive Sciences, 4,* 170–177.

Church, T. A., & Katigbak, M. S. (2000). Trait psychology in the Philippines. *American Behavioral Scientist, 44,* 73–94.

Cialdini, R. B. (1994). Interpersonal influence. In N. S. Shavitt & T. C. Brock (Eds.), *Persuasion: Psychological insights and perspectives* (pp. 195–218). Boston: Allyn & Bacon.

Cialdini, R. B., Eisenberg, N., Green, B. L., Rhoads, K., & Bator, R. (1998). Undermining the undermining effect of reward on sustained interest. *Journal of Applied Social Psychology, 28,* 249–263.

Cialdini, R. B., & Goldstein, N. J. (2004). Social influence: Compliance and conformity. *Annual Review of Psychology, 55,* 591–621.

Cialdini, R. B., & Trost, M. R. (1998). Social influence: Social norms, conformity, and compliance. In D. T. Gilbert, S. T. Fiske, & G. Lindzey (Eds.), *The handbook of social psychology* (4th ed., pp. 151–192). New York: McGraw-Hill.

Cialdini, R. B., Vincent, J. A., Lewis, S. K., Catalan, J., Wheeler, D., & Darby, B. L. (1975). Reciprocal concessions procedure for inducing compliance: The door-in-the-face technique. *Journal of Personality and Social Psychology, 31,* 206–215.

Ciarrochi, J., Forgas, J. P., & Mayer, J. D. (2001). Emotional intelligence in everyday life. Philadelphia: Psychology Press.

Citron, M., Solomon, P., & Draine, J. (1999). Self-help groups for families of persons with mental illness: Perceived benefits of helpfulness. *Community Mental Health Journal, 35,* 15–30.

Claar, R. L., & Blumenthal, J. A. (2003). The value of stress-management interventions in life-threatening medical conditions. *Current Directions in Psychological Science, 12,* 133–137.

Clancy, S. A., Schacter, D. L., McNally, R. J., & Pitman, R. K. (2000). False recognition in women reporting recovered memories of sexual abuse. *Psychological Science, 11,* 26–31.

Clark, D. M., Ball, S., & Pape, D. (1991). An experimental investigation of thought suppression. *Behaviour Research and Therapy, 29,* 253–257.

Clark, E. V. (1983). Meanings and concepts. In P. H. Mussen (Ed.), *Handbook of child psychology: Vol. 3, Cognitive development* (pp. 787–840). New York: Wiley.

Clark, E. V. (1993). *The lexicon in acquisition.* Cambridge: Cambridge University Press.

Clark, L. F., & Collins, J. E. (1993). Remembering old flames: How the past affects assessments of the present. *Personality & Social Psychology Bulletin, 19,* 399–408.

Clark, R. W. (1971). *Einstein: The life and times.* New York: World Publishing.

Claxton, L. J., Keen, R., & McCarty, M. E. (2003). Evidence of motor planning in infant reaching behavior. *Psychological Science, 14,* 354–356.

Clay, R. (1995). Working mothers: Happy or haggard? *The APA Monitor, 26*(11), 1, 37.

Cleary, A. M., & Greene, R. L. (2002). Paradoxical effects of presentation modality on false memory. *Memory, 10,* 55–61.

Cleveland, H. H., Jacobson, K. C., Lipinski, J. J., & Rowe, D. C. (2000). Genetic and shared environmental contributions to the relationship between the HOME environment and child and adolescent achievement. *Intelligence, 28*, 69–86.

Clifford, D. B. (2000). Human immunodeficiency virus-associated dementia. *Archives of Neurology, 57*, 321–324.

Cloninger, R., Svarkic, D. M., & Prysbeck, T. R. (1993). Psychobiological model of temperament and character. *Archives of General Psychiatry, 50*, 975–990.

Clopton, N. A., & Sorell, G. T. (1993). Gender differences in moral reasoning: Stable or situational? *Psychology of Women Quarterly, 17*, 85–101.

Coffey, C. E., Saxton, J. A., Ratcliff, G., Bryan, R. N., & Lucke, J. F. (1999). Relation of education to brain size in normal aging: Implications for the reserve hypothesis. *Neurology, 53*, 189–196.

Cohen, J. D., Peristein, W. M., Braver, T. S., Nystrom, L. E., Noll, D. C., Jonides, J., & Smith, E. E. (1997). Temporal dynamics of brain activation during a working memory task. *Nature, 386*, 604–608.

Cohen, M. R., & Newsome, W. T. (2004). What electrical microstimulation has revealed about the neural basis of cognition. *Current Opinion in Neurobiology, 14*, 169–177.

Cohen, S., & Herbert, T. B. (1996). Health Psychology: Psychological factors and physical disease from the perspective of human psychoneuroimmunology. *Annual Review of Psychology, 47*, 113–142.

Cohen, S., & Wills, T. (1985). Stress, social support and the buffering hypothesis. *Psychological Bulletin, 98*, 310–357.

Cohen-Kerem, R., & Koren, G. (2003). Antioxidants and fetal protection against ethanol teratogenicity I. Review of the experimental data and implications to humans. *Neurotoxicology & Teratology, 25*, 1–9.

Colado, M. I., O'Shea, E., & Green, A. R. (2004). Acute and long-term effects of MDMA on cerebral dopamine biochemistry and function. *Psychopharmacology, 173*, 249–263.

Cole, G. G., Heywood, C., Kentridge, R., Fairholm, I., & Cowey, A. (2003). Attentional capture by colour and motion in cerebral achromatopsia. *Neuropsychologia, 41*, 1837–1846.

Cole, M. (1990). Cognitive development and formal schooling: The evidence from cross-cultural research. In L. C. Moll (Ed.), *Vygotsky and education* (pp. 89–110). New York: Cambridge University Press.

Cole, M., & Wertsch, J. V. (1996). Beyond the individual-social antinomy in discussions of Piaget and Vygotsky. *Human Development, 39*, 250–256.

Coleman, P., & Flood, D. (1986). Dendritic proliferation in the aging brain as a compensatory repair mechanism. *Progress in Brain Research, 70*, 227–236.

Collins, M. A., & Zebrowitz, L. A. (1995). The contributions of appearance to occupational outcomes in civilian and military settings. *Journal of Applied Social Psychology, 25*, 129–163.

Collins, N. L. (1996). Working models of attachment: Implications for explanation, emotion, and behavior. *Journal of Personality & Social Psychology, 71*, 810–832.

Collins, N. L., & Feeney, B. C. (2004). Working models of attachment shape perceptions of social support: Evidence from experimental and observational studies. *Journal of Personality & Social Psychology, 87*, 363–383.

Colom, F., Vieta, E., Martinez, A., Jorquera, A., & Gasto, C. (1998). What is the role of psychotherapy in the treatment of bipolar disorder? *Psychotherapy & Psychosomatics, 67*, 3–9.

Colombo, J., & Richman, W. A. (2002). Infant timekeeping: Attention and temporal estimating in 4-month-olds. *Psychological Science, 13*, 475–479.

Comery, T. A., Shah, R., & Greenough, W. T. (1995). Differential rearing alters spine density on medium-sized spiny neurons in the rat corpus striatum: Evidence for association of morphological plasticity with early response gene expression. *Neurobiology of Learning & Memory, 63*, 217–219.

Comings, D. E., Muhleman, D., Johnson, J. P., & MacMurray, J. P. (2002). Parent-daughter transmission of the androgen receptor gene as an explanation of the effect of father absence on age of menarche. *Child Development, 73*, 1046–1051.

Compas, B. E., Haaga, D. A. F., Keefe, F. J., Leitenberg, H., & Williams, D. A. (1998). Sampling of empirically supported psychological treatments from health psychology, *Journal of Consulting and Clinical Psychology, 66*, 89–112.

Cone, E. J. (1995). Pharmacokinetics and pharmacodynamics of cocaine. *Journal of Analytical Toxicology, 19*, 459–477.

Conger, R. D., Neppl, T., Kim, K. J., & Scaramella, L. (2003). Angry and aggressive behavior across three generations: A prospective, longitudinal study of parents and children. *Journal of Abnormal Child Psychology, 31*, 143–160.

Connell, M. W., Sheridan, K., Gardner, H., & Sternberg, R. J. (Eds.). (2003). *The psychology of abilities, competencies, and expertise*. New York: Cambridge University Press.

Connor, C. E. (2002). Reconstructing a 3D world. *Science, 298*, 376–377.

Conway, A. R. A., Cowan, N., & Bunting, M. F. (2001). The cocktail party phenomenon revisited: The importance of working memory capacity. *Psychonomic Bulletin & Review, 8*, 331–335.

Conway, M. A., & Rubin, D. C. (1993). The structure of autobiographical memory. In A. F. Collins, S. E. Gathercole, M. A. Conway & P. E. Morris (Eds.), *Theories of memory* (pp. 103–137). Hillsdale, NJ: Erlbaum.

Conyers, C., Miltenberger, R., Romaniuk, C., Kopp, B., & Himle, M. (2003). Evaluation of DRO schedules to reduce disruptive behavior in a preschool classroom. *Child & Family Behavior Therapy, 25*, 1–6.

Cook, E. W., III, Hawk, L. W., Davis, T. L., Stevenson, V. E. (1991). Affective individual differences and startle reflex modulation. *Journal of Abnormal Psychology, 100*, 5–13.

Cooper, J. (1998). Unlearning cognitive dissonance: Toward an understanding of the development of dissonance. *Journal of Experimental Social Psychology, 34*, 562–575.

Cooper, M. L., Shapiro, C. M., & Powers, A. M. (1998). Motivations for sex and risky sexual behavior among adolescents and young adults: A functional perspective. *Journal of Personality and Social Psychology, 75*, 1528–1558.

Cooper, M. L., Wood, P. K., Orcutt, H. K., & Albino, A. (2003). Personality and the predisposition to engage in risky or problem behaviors during adolescence. *Journal of Personality and Social Psychology, 84*, 390–410.

Cooper, R. P., Abraham, J., Berman, S., & Staska, M. (1997). The development of infants' preference for motherese. *Infant Behavior & Development, 20*, 477–488.

Coplan, J. D., Goetz, R., Klein, D. F., Papp, L. A., Fyer, A. J., Liebowitz, M. R., et al. (1998). Plasma cortisol concentrations preceding lactate-induced panic: Psychological, biochemical, and physiological correlates. *Archives of General Psychiatry, 55*, 130–136.

Corbetta, M., & Shulman, G. L. (2002). Control of goal-directed and stimulus-driven attention in the brain. *Nature Reviews Neuroscience, 3*, 201–215.

Coren, S. (1996). *Sleep thieves: An eye-opening exploration into the science and mysteries of sleep*. New York: Free Press.

Corkin, S. (2002). What's new with the amnestic patient H. M.? *Nature Reviews Neuroscience, 3*, 153–160.

Cornblatt, B., Obuchowski, M., Schnur, D. B., & O'Brien, J. (1997). Attention and clinical symptoms in schizophrenia. *Psychiatric Quarterly, 68*, 343–359.

Cornelius, M. D., & Day, N. L. (2000). The effects of tobacco use during and after pregnancy on exposed children. *Alcohol Research & Health, 24*, 242–249.

Corr, P. J., & Kumari, V. (1997). Sociability/impulsivity and attenuated-dopaminergic arousal: Critical flicker/fusion frequency and procedural learning. *Personality and Individual Differences, 22*, 805–815.

Corr, P. J., Pickering, A. D., & Gray, J. A. (1995). Sociability/impulsivity and caffeine-induced arousal: Critical flicker/fusion frequency and procedural learning. *Personality and Individual Differences, 18*, 713–730.

Cosmides, L., & Tooby, J. (1996). Are humans good intuitive statisticians after all? Rethinking some conclusions from the literature on judgment under uncertainty. *Cognition, 58*, 1–73.

Costa, P. T., Jr., Herbst, J. H., McCrae, R. R., & Siegler, I. C. (2000). Personality at midlife: Stability, intrinsic maturation, and response to life events. *Assessment, 7*, 365–378.

Costa, P. T., & McCrae, R. R. (1988). Personality in adulthood: A six-year longitudinal study of self-reports and spouse ratings on the NEO personality inventory. *Journal of Personality and Social Psychology, 54*, 853–863.

Costa, P. T., & McCrae, R. R. (1995). Primary traits of Eysenck's P-E-N System: Three- and five-factor solutions. *Journal of Personality and Social Psychology, 69*, 308–317.

Costa, P. T., McCrae, R. R., & Dye, D. A. (1991). Facet scales for agreeableness and conscientiousness: A revision of the NEO Personality Inventory. *Personality and Individual Differences, 12*, 887–898.

Costa, P. T., Terracciano, A., & McCrae, R. R. (2001). Gender differences in personality traits across cultures: Robust and surprising findings. *Journal of Personality and Social Psychology, 81*, 322–331.

Costela, C., Tejedor-Real, P., Mico, J. A., & Gilbert-Rahola, J. (1995). Effect of neonatal handling on learned helplessness model of depression. *Physiology and Behavior, 57*, 407–410.

Cotman, C. (1990). The brain: New plasticity/new possibility. In R. N. Butler, M. R. Oberlink, & M. Schechter (Eds.), *The promise of productive aging: From biology to social policy* (pp. 70–84). New York: Springer.

Cotman, C. W., & Berchtold, N. C. (2002). Exercise: A behavioral intervention to enhance brain health and plasticity. *Trends in Neurosciences, 25*, 295–301.

Cotter, D. R., Pariante, C. M., & Everall, I. P. (2001). Glial cell abnormalities in major psychiatric disorders: The evidence and implications. *Brain Research Bulletin, 55*, 585–595.

Coupland, N. J., Singh, A. J., Sustrik, R. A., Ting, P., & Blair, R. J. (2003). Effects of diazepam on facial emotion recognition. *Journal of Psychiatry & Neuroscience, 28*, 452–463.

Cowan, N. (2001). The magical number 4 in short-term memory: A reconsideration of mental storage capacity. *Behavioral and Brain Sciences, 24*, 87–114.

Cowan, W. M., Fawcett, J. W., O'Leary, D. D. M., & Stanfield, B. B. (1984). Regressive events in neurogenesis. *Science, 225*, 1258–1265.

Cowey, A., & Stoerig, P. (1995). Blindsight in monkeys. *Nature, 373*, 247–249.

Coyne, J. C. (1976). Toward an interactional description of depression. *Psychiatry, 39*, 28–40.

Coyne, J. C., & Downey, G. (1991). Social factors in psychopathology: Stress, social support, and coping processes. *Annual Review of Psychology, 42*, 401–425.

Coyne, J. C., Kessler, R. C., Tal, M., Turnbull, J., Wortman, C., & Greden, J. (1987). Living with a depressed person: Burden and psychological distress. *Journal of Clinical and Consulting Psychology, 55*, 347–352.

Crago, M., & Crago, H. (1983). *Prelude to literacy*. Carbondale: Southern Illinois University Press.

Craik, F. I., & McDowd, J. M. (1987). Age differences in recall and recognition. *Journal of Experimental Psychology: Learning, Memory, & Cognition, 13*, 474–479.

Craik, F. I. M., Anderson, N. D., Kerr, S. A., & Li, K. Z. H. (1995). Memory changes in normal aging. In A. D. Baddeley, B. A. Wilson, & F. N. Watts (Eds.), *Handbook of memory disorders* (pp. 211–241). New York: Wiley.

Craik, F. I. M., & Lockhart, R. S. (1972). Levels of processing: A framework for memory research. *Journal of Verbal Learning and Verbal Behavior, 11*, 671–684.

Craik, F. I. M., & Tulving, E. (1975). Depth of processing and the retention of words in episodic memory. *Journal of Experimental Psychology: General, 104*, 268–294.

Cramer, R. E., Abraham, W. T., Johnson, L. M., & Manning-Ryan, B. (2001–2002). Gender differences in subjective distress to emotional and sexual infidelity: Evolutionary or logical inference explanation? *Current Psychology: Developmental, Learning, Personality, Social, 20,* 327–336.

Cramer, R. E., Schaefer, J. T., & Reid, S. (1996). Identifying the ideal mate: More evidence for male-female convergence. *Current Psychology: Developmental, Learning, Personality, Social, 16,* 157–166.

Crawford, M., Stark, A. C., & Renner, C. H. (1998). The meaning of Ms.: Social assimilation of a gender concept. *Psychology of Women Quarterly, 22,* 197–208.

Crawford Solberg, E., Diener, E., Wirtz, D., Lucas, R. E., & Oishi, S. (2002). Wanting, having, and satisfaction: Examining the role of desire discrepancies in satisfaction with income. *Journal of Personality & Social Psychology, 83,* 725–734.

Crick, F., & Mitchison, F. (1983). The function of dream sleep. *Nature, 304,* 111–114.

Crick, F., & Mitchison, G. (1986). REM sleep and neural nets. *Journal of Mind and Behavior, 7,* 229–250.

Crick, N. R., & Grotpeter, J. K. (1995). Relational aggression, gender, and social-psychological adjustment. *Child Development, 66,* 710–722.

Crist, R. E., Li, Wu, & Gilbert, C. D. (2001). Learning to see: Experience and attention in primary visual cortex. *Nature Neuroscience, 4,* 519–525.

Crits-Christoph, P. (1992). The efficacy of brief dynamic psychotherapy: A meta-analysis. *American Journal of Psychiatry, 149,* 151–158.

Croen, L. A., Grether, J. K., Hoogstrate, J., & Selving, S. (2002). The changing prevalence of autism in California. *Journal of Autism & Developmental Disorders, 32,* 207–215.

Croizet, J., Després, G., Gauzins, M., Huguet, P., Leyens, J., & Méot, A. (2004). Stereotype threat undermines intellectual performance by triggering a disruptive mental load. *Personality & Social Psychology Bulletin, 30,* 721–731.

Croizet, J.-C., & Claire, T. (1998) Extending the concept of stereotype and threat to social class: The intellectual underperformance of students from low socio-econimic backgrounds. *Personality & Social Psychology Bulletin, 24,* 588–594.

Cronbach, L. J. (1990). *Essentials of psychology testing* (5th ed.). New York: HarperCollins.

Crowe, R., Noyes, R., Pauls, D., & Slyman, D. (1983). A family study of panic disorder. *Archives of General Psychiatry, 40,* 1065–1069.

Crowther, J. H., Kichler, J. C., Shewood, N. E., & Kuhnert, M. E. (2002). The role of familial factors in bulimia nervosa. *Eating Disorders: The Journal of Treatment & Prevention, 10,* 141–151.

Culbertson, F. M. (1997). Depression and gender: An international review. *American Psychologist, 52,* 25–31.

Cullen, M. J., Hardison, C. M., & Sackett, P. R. (2004). Using SAT-grade and ability-job performance relationships to test predictions derived from stereotype threat theory. *Journal of Applied Psychology, 89,* 220–230.

Cupach, W. P., & Spitzberg, B. H. (1994). *The dark side of interpersonal communication.* Hillsdale, NJ: Erlbaum.

Curtius, M. (1996, July 3). Man won't be retried in repressed memory case murder: Prosecutor says there is not enough evidence to re-convict him of crime daughter recalled years later. *Los Angeles Times,* pg. 1.

Czeisler, C. A., Duffy, J. F., Shanahan, T. L., Brown, E. N., Mitchell, J. F., Rimmer, D. W., et al. (1999). Stability, precision, and near-24-hour period of the human circadian pacemaker. *Science, 284,* 2101–2103.

Dabbs, J. M., Jr., Riad, J. K., & Chance, S. E. (2001). Testosterone and ruthless homicide. *Personality & Individual Differences, 31,* 599–603.

Dabbs, J. M., Jr., Strong, R., & Milun, R. (1997). Exploring the mind of testosterone: A beeper study. *Journal of Research in Personality, 31,* 577–587.

Dackis, C. A., & O'Brien, C. P. (2001). Cocaine dependence: A disease of the brain's reward centers. *Journal of Substance Abuse Treatment, 21,* 111–117.

Dadds, M. R., Bovberg, D. H., Redd, W. H., & Cutmore, T. R. H. (1997). Imagery in human classical conditioning. *Psychological Bulletin, 122,* 89–103.

Dahloef, P., Norlin-Bagge, E., Hedner, J., Ejnell, H., Hetta, J., & Haellstroem, T. (2002). Improvement in neuropsychological performance following surgical treatment for obstructive sleep apnea syndrome. *Acta Oto-Laryngologica, 122,* 86–91.

Dai, X. Y., & Lynn, R. (1994). Gender differences in intelligence among Chinese children. *The Journal of Social Psychology, 134,* 123–125.

Dalbert, C., & Yamauchi, L. (1994). Belief in a just world and attitudes toward immigrants and foreign workers: A cultural comparison between Hawaii and Germany. *Journal of Applied Social Psychology, 24,* 1612–1626.

Damasio, A. R. (1994). *Descartes' error: Emotion, reason, and the human brain.* New York: Grosset/Putnam.

D'Angelo, B., & Wierzbicki, M. (2003). Relations of daily hassles with both anxious and depressed mood in students. *Psychological Reports, 92,* 416–418.

Dannon, P. N., Dolberg, O. T., Schreiber, S., & Grunhaus, L. (2002). Three and six-month outcome following courses of either ECT or rTMS in a population of severely depressed individuals—Preliminary report. *Biological Psychiatry, 51,* 687–690.

Dannon, P. N., Lowengrub, K., Amiaz, R., Grunhaus, L., & Kotler, M. (2004). Comorbid cannabis use and panic disorder: Short term and long term follow-up study. *Human Psychopharmacology, 19(2),* 97–101.

Dansinger, M. L., Gleason, J. A., Griffith, J. L., Selker, H. P., & Schaefer, E. J. (2005). Comparison of the Atkins, Ornish, Weight Watchers, and Zone diets for weight loss and heart disease risk reduction: A randomized trial. *Journal of the American Medical Association, 293,* 43–53.

Dar, Y., & Kimhi, S. (2001). Military service and self-perceived maturation among Israeli youth. *Journal of Youth & Adolescence, 30,* 427–448.

Darley, J. M., & Latané, B. (1968). Bystander intervention in emergencies: Diffusion of responsibility. *Journal of Personality and Social Psychology, 10,* 202–214.

Darley, J. M., & Latané, B. (1970). Norms and normative behavior: Field studies of social interdependence. In J. Macauley & L. Berkowitz (Eds.), *Altruism and helping behavior* (pp. 83–101). New York: Academic Press.

Darwin, C. (1872). *The expression of the emotions in man and animals.* Chicago: University of Chicago Press, 1965.

Dauncey, K., Giggs, J., Baker, K., & Harrison, K. (1993). Schizophrenia in Nottingham: Lifelong residential mobility of a cohort. *British Journal of Psychiatry, 163,* 613–619.

Davey, G. C. L. (1992). Classical conditioning and the acquisition of human fears and phobias: A review of synthesis of the literature. *Advances in Behavior Research and Therapy, 14,* 29–66.

David, J. P., & Suls, J. (1999). Coping efforts in daily life: Role of Big Five traits and problem appraisals. *Journal of Personality, 67,* 265–294.

Davidson, J. R. T., Foa, E. B., Huppert, J. D., Keefe, F. J., Franklin, M. E., Compton, J. S., Zhao, N., Connor, K. M., Lynch, T. R., & Gadde, K. M. (2004). Fluoxetine, comprehensive cognitive behavioral therapy, and placebo in generalized social phobia. *Archives of General Psychiatry, 61,* 1005–1013.

Davidson, R. J. (1992a). Emotion and affective style: Hemispheric substrates. *Psychological Science, 3,* 39–43.

Davidson, R. J. (1992b). A prolegomenon to the structure of emotion: Gleanings from neuropsychology. *Cognition and Emotion, 6,* 245–268.

Davidson, R. J. (1993). Parsing affective space: Perspectives from neuropsychology and psychophysiology. *Neuropsychology, 7,* 464–475.

Davidson, R. J. (1994). Honoring biology in the study of affective style. In P. Ekman & R. J. Davidson (Eds.), *The nature of emotion: Fundamental questions* (pp. 321–328). New York: Oxford University Press.

Davidson, R. J. (1998). Affective style and affective disorders: Perspectives from affective neuroscience. *Cognition and Emotion, 12,* 307–330.

Davidson, R. J. (2001). Toward a biology of personality and emotion. *Annals of the New York Academy of Sciences, 935,* 191–207.

Davidson, R. J. (2002). Anxiety and affective style: Role of prefrontal cortex and amygdala. *Biological Psychiatry, 51,* 68–80.

Davidson, R. J. (2004). What does the prefrontal cortex "do" in affect: Perspectives on frontal EEG asymmetry research. *Biological Psychology, 67,* 219–233.

Davidson, R. J., Abercrombie, H., Nitschke, J. B., & Putnam, K. (1999). Regional brain function, emotion and disorders of emotion. *Current Opinion in Neurobiology, 9,* 228–234.

Davidson, R. J., Jackson, D. C., & Kalin, N. H. (2000a). Emotion, plasticity, context, and regulation: Perspectives from affective neuroscience. *Psychological Bulletin, 126,* 890–909.

Davidson, R. J., Pizzagalli, D., Nitschke, J. B., & Putnam, K. M. (2002). Depression: Perspectives from affective neuroscience. *Annual Review of Psychology, 53,* 545–574.

Davidson, R. J., Putnam, K. M., & Larson, C. L. (2000b). Dysfunction in the neural circuitry of emotion regulation—A possible prelude to violence. *Science, 289,* 591–594.

Davies, P. G., Spencer, S. J., & Steele, C. M. (2005). Clearing the air: Identity safety moderates the effects of stereotype threat on women's leadership aspirations. *Journal of Personality & Social Psychology, 88,* 276–287.

Davis, B. E., Moon, R. Y., Sachs, H. C., & Ottolini, M. C. (1998). Effects of sleep position on infant motor development. *Pediatrics, 102,* 1135–1140.

Davis, C., Ralevski, E., Kennedy, S. H., & Neitzert, C. S. (1995). The role of personality factors in the reporting of side effect complaints to moclobemide and placebo. *Journal of Clinical Psychopharmacology, 15,* 347–352.

Davis, D., Shaver, P. R., & Vernon, M. L. (2003). Physical, emotional, and behavioral reactions to breaking up: The roles of gender, age, emotional involvement, and attachment style. *Personality & Social Psychology Bulletin, 29,* 871–884.

Davis, J. D., & Campbell, C. S. (1973). Peripheral control of meal size in the rat: Effects of sham feeding on meal size and drinking rate. *Journal of Comparative & Physiological Psychology, 83,* 379–387.

Davis, J. D., & Levine, M. W. (1977). A model for the control of ingestion. *Psychological Review, 84,* 379–412.

Davis, M. (1992). The role of the amygdala in conditioned fear. In J. P. Aggleton (Ed.), *The amygdala: Neurobiological aspects of emotion, memory, and mental dysfunction* (pp. 255–306). New York: Wiley-Liss.

Davis, M., & Whalen, P. J. (2001). The amygdala: Vigilance and emotion. *Molecular Psychiatry, 6,* 13–34.

Davis, M. C., Matthews, K. A., & McGrath, C. E. (2000). Hostile attitudes predict elevated vascular resistance during interpersonal stress in men and women. *Psychosomatic Medicine, 62,* 17–25.

Dawda, D., & Hart, S. D. (2000). Assessing emotional intelligence: Reliability and validity of the Bar-On Emotional Quotient Inventory (EQ-i) in university students. *Personality and Individual Differences, 28,* 797–812.

Dean, W., Morgenthaler, J., & Fowkes, S. W. (1993). *Smart drugs: II. The next generation: New drugs and nutrients to improve your memory and increase your intelligence (Smart Drug Series, Vol. 2).* Petaluma, CA: Smart Publications.

Deary, I. J. (2000). *Looking down on human intelligence: From psychometrics to the brain.* Oxford, UK: Oxford University Press.

Deary, I. J., Whiteman, M. C., Starr, J. M., Whalley, L. J., & Fox, H. C. (2004). The impact of childhood intelligence on later life: Following up the Scottish mental surveys of 1932 and 1947. *Journal of Personality & Social Psychology, 86,* 130–147.

De Beni, R., & Palladino, P. (2004). Decline in working memory updating through ageing: Intrusion error analyses. *Memory, 12,* 75–89.

DeCasper, A. J., & Fifer, W. P. (1980). On human bonding: Newborns prefer their mothers' voices. *Science, 208,* 1174–1176.

De Castro, J. M. (1990). Social facilitation of duration and size but not rate of the spontaneous meal intake of humans. *Physiology & Behavior, 47*, 1129–1135.

Decety, J., & Jackson, P. L. (2004). The functional architecture of human empathy. *Behavioral and Cognitive Neuroscience Reviews, 3*, 406–412.

Deci, E. L., Koestner, R., & Ryan, R. M. (1999). The undermining effect is a reality after all—Extrinsic rewards, task interest, and self-determination: Reply to Eisenberger, Pierce, and Cameron (1999) and Lepper, Henderlong, and Gingras (1999). *Psychological Bulletin, 125*, 692–700.

DeClue, G. (2003). The polygraph and lie detection. *Journal of Psychiatry and Law, 31*, 361–368.

Deese, J. (1959). On the prediction of occurrence of particular verbal intrusions in immediate recall. *Journal of Experimental Psychology, 58*, 17–22.

Deffenbacher, J. L., Oetting, E. R., Huff, M. E., Cornell, G. R., & Dalleger, C. J. (1996). Evaluation of two cognitive-behavioral approaches to general anger reduction. *Cognitive Therapy & Research, 20*, 551–573.

Degarrod, L. N. (1990). Coping with stress: Dream interpretation in the Mapuche family. *Psychiatric Journal of the University of Ottawa, 15*, 111–116.

Dehaene-Lambertz, G., & Dehaene, S. (1994). Speed and cerebral correlates of syllable discrimination in infants. *Nature, 370*, 292–295.

Dehaene-Lambertz, G., & Pena, M. (2001). Electrophysiological evidence for automatic phonetic processing in neonates. *Neuroreport, 12*, 3155–3158.

De Houwer, J., Thomas, S., & Baeyens, F. (2001). Associative learning of likes and dislikes: A review of 25 years of research on human evaluative conditioning. *Psychological Bulletin, 127*, 853–869.

de la Chica, R. A., Ribas, I., Giraldo, J., Egozcue, J., & Fuster, C. (2005). Chromosomal instability in amniocytes from fetuses of mothers who smoke. *JAMA: Journal of the American Medical Association, 293*, 1212–1222.

Delany, S. L., Delany, A. E., & Hearth, A. H. (1993). *Having our say: The Delany sisters' first 100 years.* New York: Delta.

Delk, J. L., & Fillenbaum, S., (1965). Difference in perceived color as a function of characteristic color. *American Journal of Psychology, 78*, 290–293.

DeLongis, A., Coyne, J. C., Dakof, G., Folkman, S., & Lazrus, R. S. (1982). Relationship of daily hassles, uplifts, and major life events to health status. *Health Psychology, 1*, 119–136.

DeMann, J. A. (1994). First person account: The evolution of a person with schizophrenia. *Schizophrenia Bulletin, 20*, 579–582.

Dement, W. C. (1974). *Some must watch while some must sleep.* San Francisco: W. H. Freeman.

Demetriou, A., Christou, C., Spanoudis, G., & Platsidou, M. (2002). The development of mental processing: Efficiency, working memory, and thinking. *Monographs of the Society for Research in Child Development, 67*, vii-154.

de Muinck Keizer-Schrama, S. M. P. F., & Mul, D. (2001) Trends in pubertal development in Europe. *Human Reproduction Update, 7*, 287–291.

Denis, M., & Kosslyn, S. M. (1999). Scanning visual images: A window on the mind. *Current Psychology of Cognition, 18*, 409–465.

Dennis, W. (1966). Goodenough scores, art experience, and modernization. *Journal of Social Psychology, 68*, 211–228.

DePaulo, B. M., Charlton, K., Cooper, H., Lindsay, J. J., & Muhlenbruck, L. (1997). The accuracy-confidence correlation in the detection of deception. *Personality & Social Psychology Review, 1*, 346–357.

DePaulo, B. M., Lindsay, J. J., Malone, B. E., Muhlenbruck, L., Charlton, K., & Cooper, H. (2003). Cues to deception. *Psychological Bulletin, 129*, 74–118.

De Renzi, E. (1982). *Disorders of space exploration and cognition.* New York: Wiley.

De Renzi, E., Liotti, M., & Nichelli, P. (1987). Semantic amnesia with preservation of autobiographical memory. A case report. *Cortex, 23*, 575–597.

Derryberry, D., & Reed, M. A. (1994). Temperament and the self-organization of personality. *Development & Psychopathology, 6*, 653–676.

DeRubeis, R. J., Hollon, S. D., Amsterdam, J. D., Shelton, R. C., Young, P. R., Salomon, R. M., O'Reardon, J. P., Lovett, M. L., Gladis, M. M. Brown, L. L., & Gallop, R. (2005). Cognitive therapy vs. medications in the treatment of moderate to severe depression. *Archives of General Psychiatry, 62*, 409–416.

D'Esposito, M., Detre, J. A., Alsop, D. C., Shin, R. K., Atlas, S., & Grossman, M. (1995). The neural basis of the central executive system of working memory. *Nature, 378*, 279–281.

DeSteno, D., Dasgupta, N., Bartlett, M. Y., Cajdric, A. (2004). Prejudice from thin air: The effect of emotion on automatic intergroup attitudes. *Psychological Science, 15*, 319–324.

DeSteno, D. A., & Salovey, P. (1996). Evolutionary origins of sex differences in jealousy? Questioning the "fitness" of the model. *Psychological Science, 7*, 367–372.

Deutsch, J. A., Young, W. G., & Kalogeris, T. J. (1978). The stomach signals satiety. *Science, 201*, 165–167.

De Valois, R. L., & De Valois, K. K. (1975). Neural coding of color. In E. C. Carterette & M. P. Friedman (Eds.), *Handbook of perception* (pp. 117–166). New York: Academic Press.

De Valois, R. L., & De Valois, K. K. (1993). A multi-stage color model. *Vision Research, 33*, 1053–1065.

de Villiers, P. A., & de Villiers, J. G. (1992). Language development. In M. H. Bornstein & M. E. Lamb (Eds.), *Developmental psychology: An advanced textbook* (3rd ed., pp. 337–418). Hillsdale, NJ: Erlbaum.

Devine, P. G., & Monteith, M. J. (1993). The role of discrepancy-associated affect in prejudice reduction. In D. M. Mackie, D. L. Hamilton, et al. (Eds.), *Affect, cognition, and stereotyping: Interactive processes in group perception* (pp. 317–344). San Diego, CA: Academic Press.

Devlin, B., Daniels, M., & Roeder, K. (1997). The heritability of IQ. *Nature, 388*, 468–471.

Dew, A. M., & Ward, C. (1993). The effects of ethnicity and culturally congruent and incongruent nonverbal behaviors on interpersonal attraction. *Journal of Applied Social Psychology, 23*, 1376–1389.

de Wijk, R. A., & Cain, W. S. (1994). Odor identification by name and by edibility: Life-span development and safety. *Human Factors, 36*, 182–187.

de Wijk, R. A., Schab, F. R., & Cain, W. S. (1995). Odor identification. In F. R. Schab & R. G. Crowder (Eds.), *Memory for odors* (pp. 21–37). Mahwah, NJ: Erlbaum.

Dhume, V. G., Agshikar, N. V., & Diniz, R. S. (1975). Placebo-induced side effects in healthy volunteers. *Clinician, 39*, 289–290.

Diamond, L. M., & Dube, E. M. (2002). Friendship and attachment among heterosexual and sexual-minority youths: Does the gender of your friend matter? *Journal of Youth & Adolescence, 31*, 155–166.

Diamond, M. C., Rosenzweig, M. R., Bennett, E. L., Lindner, B., & Lyon, L. (1972). Effects of environmental enrichment and impoverishment on rat cerebral cortex. *Journal of Neural Biology, 3*, 47–64.

DiBlasio, F. A., & Benda, B. B. (1990). Adolescent sexual behavior: Multivariate analysis of a social learning model. *Journal of Adolescent Research, 5*, 449–466.

Dick, F., Bates, E., Wulfeck, B., Utman, J. A., Dronkers, N., & Gernsbacher, M. A. (2001). Language deficits, localization, and grammar: Evidence for a distributive model of language breakdown in aphasic patients and neurologically intact individuals. *Psychological Review, 108*, 759–788.

Dickerson, S. S., & Kemeny, M. E. (2002). Acute stressors and cortisol responses: A theoretical integration and synthesis of laboratory research. *Psychological Bulletin, 130*, 355–391.

Diehm, R., & Armatas, C. (2004). Surfing: An avenue for socially acceptable risk-taking, satisfying needs for sensation seeking and experience seeking. *Personality & Individual Differences, 36*, 663–677.

Diener, E. (1977). Deindividualtion: Causes and consequences. *Social Behavior and Personality, 5*, 143–155.

Diener, E. (2000). Subjective well-being: The science of happiness and a proposal for a national index. *American Psychologist, 55*, 34–43.

Diener, E., & Biswas-Diener, R. (2002). Will money increase subjective well-being? *Social Indicators Research, 57*, 119–169.

Diener, E., & Emmons, R. A. (1984). The independence of positive and negative affect. *Journal of Personality and Social Psychology, 47*, 1105–1117.

Dienstfrey, H. (1991). *Where the mind meets the body.* New York: HarperCollins.

Dietrich, A. (2004). The cognitive neuroscience of creativity. *Psychonomic Bulletin & Review, 11*, 1011–1026.

DiGiuseppe, R., & Tafrate, R. C. (2003). Anger treatment for adults: A meta-analytic review. *Clinical Psychology: Science and Practice, 10*, 70–84.

Digman, J. M. (1990). Personality structure: Emergence of the five-factor model. *Annual Review of Psychology, 41*, 417–440.

Dill, P. L., & Henley, T. B. (1998). Stressors of college: A comparison of traditional and nontraditional students. *Journal of Psychology, 132*, 25–32.

Dimberg, J., Thunberg, M., & Elmehed, K. (2000). Unconscious facial reactions to emotional facial expressions. *Psychological Science, 11*, 86–89.

Dinges, D., Pack, F., Williams, K., Gillen, K., Powell, J., Ott, G., et al. (1997). Cumulative sleepiness, mood disturbance, and psychomotor vigilance performance decrements during a week of sleep restricted to 4–5 hours per night. *Sleep, 20*, 267–277.

Dion, K., Berscheid, E., & Walster, E. (1972). What is beautiful is good. *Journal of Personality & Social Psychology, 24*, 285–290.

DiPietro, J. A. (2004). The role of prenatal maternal stress in child development. *Current Directions in Psychological Science, 13*, 71–74.

DiPietro, J. A., Costigan, K. A., & Gurewitsch, E. D. (2003). Fetal response to induced maternal stress. *Early Human Development, 74*, 125–138.

DiPietro, J. A., Hodgson, D. M., Costigan, K. A., Hilton, S. C., & Johnson, T. R. B. (1996). Fetal neurobehavioral development. *Child Development, 67*, 2553–2567.

Di Pietro, M., Laganaro, M., Leemann, B., & Schnider, A. (2004). Receptive amusia: Temporal auditory processing deficit in a professional musician following a left temporo-parietal lesion. *Neuropsychologia, 42*, 868–877.

Dittrich, W. H., Troscianko, T., Lea, S., & Morgan, D. (1996). Perception of emotion from dynamic point-light displays represented in dance. *Perception, 25*, 727–738.

Dixon, M. R., Rehfeldt, R. A., & Randich, L. (2003). Enhancing tolerance to delayed reinforcers: The role of intervening activities. *Journal of Applied Behavior Analysis, 36*, 263–266.

Dobson, M., & Markham, R. (1993). Imagery ability and source monitoring: Implications for eyewitness memory. *British Journal of Psychology, 32*, 111–118.

Dobson, R. (2002, May 11). Broadcast of star's colonoscopy puts up screening by 20%. *British Medical Journal, 324*, 1118.

Dodge, K. A., & Newman, J. P. (1981). Biased decision-making processes in aggressive boys. *Journal of Abnormal Psychology, 90*.

Dodge, K. A., & Pettit, G. S. (2003). A biopsychosocial model of the development of chronic conduct problems in adolescence. *Developmental Psychology, 39*, 349–371.

Doheny, M. (1993). Effects of mental practice on performance of a psychomotor skill. *Journal of Mental Imagery, 17*(3–4), 111–118.

Dohnanyiova, M., Ostatnikova, D., & Laznibatova, J. (2001). Spatial imagery, testosterone and anthropometric characteristics in intellectually gifted and control children. *Homeostasis in Health & Disease, 41*, 53–55.

Dohrenwend, B. P., Levav, I., Shrout, P. E., Schwartz, S., Naveh, G., Link. B. G., Skodol, A. E., & Stueve, A.

(1992). Socioeconomic status and psychiatric disorders: The causation-selection issue. *Science, 255*, 946–952.

Dohrmann, R. J., & Laskin, D. M. (1978). An evaluation of electromyographic biofeedback in the treatment of myofascial pain-dysfunction syndrome. *Journal of the American Dental Association, 96*, 656–662.

Dolan, B. (1991). Cross-cultural aspects of anorexia nervosa and bulimia: A review. *International Journal of Eating Disorders, 10*, 67–79.

Dominey, P. F., & Dodane, C. (2004). Indeterminacy in language acquisition: The role of child directed speech and joint attention. *Journal of Neurolinguistics, 17*, 121–145.

Domjan, M., Cusato, B., & Krause, M. (2004). Learning with arbitrary versus ecologically conditioned stimuli: Evidence from sexual conditioning. *Psychonomic Bulletin and Review, 11*, 232–246.

Doty, R. L., Bartoshuk, L. M., & Snow, J. B., Jr. (1991). Causes of olfactory and gustatory disorders. In T. V. Getchell, R. L. Doty, L. M. Bartoshuk, & J. B. Snow, Jr. (Eds.), *Smell and taste in health and disease* (pp. 449–462). New York: Raven.

Double, D. (2002). The limits of psychiatry. *British Medical Journal, 324*, 900–904.

Dovidio, J. F., Evans, N., & Tyler, R. B. (1986). Racial stereotypes: The contents of their cognitive representations. *Journal of Experimental Social Psychology, 22*, 22–37.

Dovidio, J. F., Piliavin, J. A., Gaertner, S. L., Schroeder, D. A., & Clark, R. D., III. (1991). The arousal: Cost-reward model and the process of intervention: A review of the evidence. In M. S. Clark (Ed.), *Prosocial behavior* (pp. 86–118). Thousand Oaks, CA: Sage Publications.

Dowling, J. E. (1992). *Neurons and networks: An introduction to neuroscience.* Cambridge, MA: Harvard University Press.

Downing, J. W., Judd, C. M., & Brauer, M. (1992). Effects of repeated expressions on attitude extremity. *Journal of Personality and Social Psychology, 63*, 17–29.

Dozier, M., & Kobak, R. R. (1992). Psychophysiology in attachment interviews: Converging evidence for deactivating strategies. *Child Development, 63*, 1473–1480.

Draycott, S. G., & Kline, P. (1995). The Big Three or the Big Five—the EPQ-R vs the NEO-PI: A research note, replication and elaboration. *Personality & Individual Differences, 18*, 801–804.

Drevets, W. C., Price, J. L., Bardgett, M. E., Reich, T., Todd, R. D., & Raichle, M. E. (2002). Glucose metabolism in the amygdala in depression: Relationship to diagnostic subtype and plasma cortisol levels. *Pharmacology, Biochemistry & Behavior, 71*, 431–447.

Drid, M. D., Raybaud, F., De Lunardo, C., Iacono, P., & Gustovic, P. (1995). Influence of the behavior pattern on the nocebo response of healthy volunteers. *British Journal of Clinical Pharmacology, 39*, 204–206.

Driskell, J., Copper, C., & Moran, A. (1994). Does mental practice enhance performance? *Journal of Applied Psychology, 79*(4), 481–492.

Druckman, D., & Swets, J. A. (Eds.). (1988). *Enhancing human performance: Issues, theories, and techniques.* Washington, DC: National Academy Press.

Drummond, S. P. A., Brown, G. G., Gillin, J. C., Stricker, J. L., Wong, E. C., & Buxton, R. B. (2000). *Nature, 403*, 655–657.

Druss, B. G., Schlesinger, M., & Allen, H. M., Jr. (2001). Depressive symptoms, satisfaction with health care, and 2-year work outcomes in an employed population. *American Journal of Psychiatry, 158*, 731–734.

Duclaux, R., Feisthauer, J., & Cabanac, M. (1973). The effects of eating on the pleasantness of food and non-food odors in man. *Physiology & Behavior, 10*, 1029–1033.

Duclos, S. E., Laird, J. D., Schneider, E., Sexter, M., Stern, L., & Van Lighten, O. (1989). Emotion-specific effects of facial expressions and postures on emotional experience. *Journal of Personality and Social Psychology, 57*, 100–108.

Duman, R. S., Heninger, G. R., & Nestler, E. J. (1997). A molecular and cellular theory of depression. *Archives of General Psychiatry, 54*, 597–606.

Duncan, H. F., Gourlay, N., & Hudson, W. (1973). *A study of pictorial perception among Bantu and White primary school children in South Africa.* Johannesburg, South Africa: Witwatersrand University Press.

Duncker, K. (1945). On problem solving. *Psychological monographs, 58* (No. 270).

Dunnett, S. B., Lane, D. M., & Winn, P. (1985). Ibotenic acid lesions of the lateral hypothalamus: Comparison with 6-hydroxydopamine-induced sensorimotor deficits. *Neuroscience, 14*, 509–518.

Dupuy, B., & Krashen, S. D. (1993). Incidental vocabulary acquisition in French as a foreign language. *Applied Language Learning, 4*, 55–63.

Dusek, D., & Girdano, D. A. (1980). *Drugs: A factual account.* Reading, MA: Addison Wesley.

Eacott, M. J., & Crawley, R. A. (1999). Childhood amnesia: On answering questions about very early life events. *Memory, 7*, 279–292.

Eagly, A. (1987). *Sex differences in social behavior: A social-role interpretation.* Hillsdale, NJ: Erlbaum.

Eagly, A. H. (1995). The science and politics of comparing women and men. *American Psychologist, 50* 145–158.

Eagly, A. H., & Carli, L. (1981). Sex of researchers and sex-typed communications as determinants of sex differences in influence-ability: A meta-analysis of social influence studies. *Psychological Bulletin, 90*, 1–20.

Eagly, A. H., & Chaiken, S. (1998). Attitude structure and function. In D. T. Gilbert, S. T. Fiske, & G. Lindzey (Eds.), *The handbook of social psychology* (4th ed., pp. 269–322). New York: McGraw-Hill.

Eagly, A. H., & Steffen, V. J. (1986). Gender and aggressive behavior: A meta-analytic review of the social psycholgical literature. *Psychological Bulletin, 100*, 309–330.

Eagly, A. H., & Wood, W. (1999). The origins of sex differences in human behavior: Evolved dispositions versus social roles. *American Psychologist, 54*, 408–423.

Eaker, E. D., Pinsky, J., & Castelli, W. P. (1992). Myocardial infarction and coronary death among women: psychosocial predictors from a 20-year follow-up of women in the Framingham Study. *American Journal of Epidemiology, 135*, 854–864.

Eakin, E. (2000, January 15). Bigotry as mental illness or just another norm. *New York Times*, p. A21.

Eals, M., & Silverman, I. (1994). The hunter-gatherer theory of spatial sex differences: Proximate factors mediating the female advantage on recall of object arrays. *Ethology and Sociobiology, 15*, 95–105.

Earle, T. L., Linden, W., & Weinberg, J. (1999). Differential effects of harassment on cardiovascular and salivary cortisol stress reactivity and recovery in women and men. *Journal of Psychosomatic Research, 46*, 125–141.

Ebbinghaus, H. (1885/1964). *Memory: A contribution to experimental psychology.* New York: Dover.

Eberman, C., & McKelvie, S. J. (2002). Vividness of visual imagery and source memory for audio and text. *Applied Cognitive Psychology, 16*, 87–95.

Ebstein, R. P., Benjamin, J., & Belmaker, R. H. (2002). Behavioral genetics, genomics, and personality. In R. Plomin, J. C. DeFries, I. W. Craig, & P. McGuffin (Eds.), *Behavioral genetics in the postgenomic era* (pp. 365–388). Washington, DC: American Psychological Association.

Ebstein, R. P., Novick, O., Umansky, R., Priel, B., Osher, Y., Blaine, D., et al. (1996). Dopamine D4 receptor (D4DR) exon III polymorphism associated with the human personality trait of Novelty Seeking. *Nature Genetics, 12*, 78–80.

Eby, K. K. (2004). Exploring the stressors of low-income women with abusive partners: Understanding their needs and developing effective community responses. *Journal of Family Violence, 19*, 221–232.

Edelstein, R. S., Alexander, K. W., Shaver, P. R., Schaaf, J. M., Quas, J. A., Lovas, G. S., & Goodman, G. S. (2004). Adult attachment style and parental responsiveness during a stressful event. *Attachment & Human Development, 6*, 31–52.

Eder, R. A. (1989). The emergent personologist: The structure and content of 3-, 5-, and 7-year-olds' concepts of themselves and other persons. *Child Development, 60*, 1218–1228.

Edgerton, R. B., & Cohen, A. (1994). Culture and schizophrenia: The DOSMD challenge. *British Journal of Psychiatry, 164*, 222–231.

Egbert, L. D., Battit, G. E., Welch, C. E., & Barlett, M. K. (1964). Reduction of postoperative pain by encouragement and instruction of patients. *New England Journal of Medicine, 270*, 825–827.

Ehlers, A., Mayou, R. A., & Bryant, B. (1998). Psychological predictors of chronic posttraumatic stress disorder after motor vehicle accidents. *Journal of Abnormal Psychology, 107*, 508–519.

Eich, E. (1989). Theoretical issues in state dependent memory. In H. L. Roediger, III, & F. I. M. Craik (Eds.), *Varieties of memory and consciousness: Essays in honour of Endel Tulving* (pp. 331–354). Hillsdale, NJ: Erlbaum.

Eich, E. (1995). Searching for mood dependent memory. *Psychological Science, 6*, 67–75.

Eimas, P. D., & Corbit, J. D. (1973). Selective adaptation of linguistic feature detectors. *Cognitive Psychology, 4*, 99–109.

Einstein, A. (1945). A testimonial from Professor Einstein (Appendix II). In J. Hadamard, *An essay on the psychology of invention in the mathematical field* (pp. 142–143). Princeton, NJ: Princeton University Press.

Eisenberg, N., Fabes, R. A., & Murphy, B. (1995). The relations of shyness and low sociability to regulation and emotionality. *Journal of Personality & Social Psychology, 68*, 505–517.

Eisenberg, N., Guthrie, I. K., Cumberland, A., Murphy, B. C., Shepard, S. A., Zhou, Q., & Carlo, G. (2002). Prosocial development in early adulthood: A longitudinal study. *Journal of Personality & Social Psychology, 82*, 993–1006.

Eisenberg, N., Miller, P. A., Schaller, M., Fabes, R. A., Fultz, J., Shell, R., & Shea, C. L. (1989). The role of sympathy and altruistic personality traits in helping: A reexamination. *Journal of Personality, 57*, 41–67.

Eisenberger, R., & Cameron, J. (1996). Detrimental effects of reward: Reality or myth? *American Psychologist, 51*, 1153–1166.

Ekman, P. (1980). Biological and cultural contributions to body and facial movement in the expression of emotion. In A. O. Rorty (Ed.), *Explaining emotions.* Berkeley: University of California Press.

Ekman, P. (1984). Expression and the nature of emotion. In K. R. Scherer & P. Ekman (Eds.), *Approaches to emotion* (pp. 319–343). Hillsdale, NJ: Erlbaum.

Ekman, P. (1985). *Telling lies: Clues to deceit in the marketplace, marriage, and politics.* New York: Norton.

Ekman, P. (1992). Facial expressions of emotion: New findings, new questions. *Psychological Science, 3*, 34–38.

Ekman, P., & Davidson, R. J. (1993). Voluntary smiling changes regional brain activity. *Psychological Science, 4*, 342–345.

Ekman, P., Davidson, R. J., & Friesen, W. V. (1990). The Duchenne smile: Emotional expression and brain psychology II. *Journal of Personality & Social Psychology, 58*, 342–353.

Ekman, P., & Friesen, W. (1971). Constants across cultures in the face and emotion. *Journal of Personality & Social Psychology, 17*, 124–129.

Ekman, P., & Friesen, W. V. (1975). *Unmasking the face.* Englewood Cliffs, NJ: Prentice-Hall.

Ekman, P., O'Sullivan, M., & Frank, M. G. (1999). A few can catch a liar. *Psychological Science, 10*, 263–266.

Elaad, E. (2003). Effects of feedback on the overestimated capacity to detect lies and the underestimated ability to tell lies. *Applied Cognitive Psychology, 17*, 349–363.

Elber, T., Pantev, C., Wienbruch, C., Rockstroh, B., & Taub, E. (1995). Increased cortical representation of the fingers of the left hand in string players. *Science, 270*, 305–307.

Eley, T. C., Deater-Deckard, K., Fombone, E., Fulker, D. W., & Plomin, R. (1998). An adoption study of depressive symptoms in middle childhood. *Journal of Child Psychology & Psychiatry & Allied Disciplines, 39*, 337–345.

Elfenbein, H. A., & Ambady, N. (2002). On the universality and cultural specificity of emotion recognition: A meta-analysis. *Psychological Bulletin, 128*, 203–235.

El-Islam, M. F. (1991). Transcultural aspects of schizophrenia and ICD-10. *Psychiatria Danubina, 3*, 485–494.

Elkin, I., Shea, M. T., Watkins, J. T., Imber, S. D., Sotsky, S. M., Collins, J. F., Glass, D. R., Pilkonis, P. A., Leber, W. R., Docherty, J. P., Fiester, S. J., & Parloff, M. B. (1989). National Institute of Mental Health Treatment of Depression Collaborative Research Program: General effectiveness of treatments. *Archives of General Psychiatry, 46*, 971–982.

Elkind, D. (1967). Egocentrism in adolescence. *Child Development, 38*, 1025–1034.

Elkind, D., & Bowen, R. (1979). Imaginary audience behavior in children and adolescence. *Developmental Psychology, 15*, 33–44.

Elliott, D., Huizinga, D., & Ageton, S. S. (1985). *Multiple problem youth: Delinquency, substance use, and mental health problems*. New York: Springer-Verlag.

Ellis, A. (1994a). The treatment of borderline personalities with rational emotive behavior therapy. *Journal of Rational-Emotive & Cognitive Behavior Therapy, 12*, 101–119.

Ellis, A. (1994b). Rational emotive behavior therapy approaches to obsessive-compulsive disorder (OCD). *Journal of Rational-Emotive & Cognitive Behavior Therapy, 12*, 121–141.

Ellis, A. W., & Young, A. W. (1987). *Human cognitive neuropsychology*. Hillsdale, NJ: Lawrence Erlbaum.

Ellis, B. J., Bates, J. E., Dodge, K. A., Fergusson, D. M., Horwood, L. J., Pettit, G. S., & Woodward, L. (2003). Does father absence place daughters at special risk for early sexual activity and teenage pregnancy? *Child Development, 74*, 801–821.

Ellis, H. C. (1973). Stimulus encoding processes in human learning and memory. In G. H. Bower (Ed.), *The psychology of learning and motivation* (Vol. 7, pp. 124–182). New York: Academic Press.

Ellis, H. C., & Hunt, R. R. (1993). *Fundamentals of cognitive psychology* (5th ed.). Dubuque, IA: Brown Communications.

Ellis, L., & Blanchard, R. (2001). Birth order, sibling sex ratio, and maternal miscarriages in homosexual and heterosexual men and women. *Personality & Individual Differences, 30*, 543–552.

Elman, J. L., Bates, E. A., Johnson, M. H., Karmiloff-Smith, A., et al. (1996). *Rethinking innateness: A connectionist perspective on development*. Cambridge: MIT Press.

Emerson, M. O., Kimbro, R. T., & Yancey, G. (2002). Contact theory extended: The effects of prior racial contact on current social ties. *Social Science Quarterly, 83*, 745–761.

Emmelkamp, P. M. G. (2004). Behavior therapy with adults. In M. J. Lambert (Ed.), *Bergin and Garfield's handbook of psychotherapy and behavior change*, 5th ed. (pp. 393–446). New York: Wiley and Sons.

Emmelkamp, P. M. G., Bruynzeel, M., Drost, L., & Van Der Mast, C. A. P. G. (2001). Virtual reality treatment in acrophobia: A comparison with exposure in vivo. *CyberPsychology & Behavior, 4*, 335–339.

Emmelkamp, P. M. G., Kloek, J., & Blaauw, E. (1992). Obsessive-compulsive disorders. In P. H. Wilson (Ed.), *Principles and practice of relapse prevention* (pp. 213–234). New York: Guilford Press.

Emmelkamp, P. M. G., Krijn, M., Hulsbosch, A. M., de Vries, S., Schuemie, M. J., & van der Mast, C. A. P. G. (2002). Virtual reality treatment versus exposure in vivo: A comparative evaluation in acrophobia. *Behaviour Research & Therapy, 40*, 509–516.

Engel, S. A., Glover, G. H., & Wandell, B. A. (1997). Retinotopic organization in human visual cortex and the spatial precision of functional MRI. *Cerebral Cortex, 7*, 181–192.

Engelberg, E., & Sjöberg, L. (2004). Emotional intelligence, affect intensity, and social adjustment. *Personality and Individual Differences, 37*, 533–542.

Entwisle, D. R. (1972). To dispel fantasies about fantasy-based measures of achievement motivation. *Psychological Bulletin, 77*, 377–391.

Epley, N., & Dunning, D. (2000). Feeling "holier than thou": Are self-serving assessments produced by errors in self- or social prediction? *Journal of Personality & Social Psychology, 79*, 861–875.

Epstein, C. M., Figiel, G. S., McDonald, W. M., Amazon-Leece, J., & Figiel, L. (1998). Rapid rate transcranial magnetic stimulation in young and middle-aged refractory depressed patients. *Psychiatric Annals, 28*, 36–39.

Epstein, H. T. (1980). EEG developmental stages. *Developmental Psychobiology, 13*, 629–631.

Eranti, S. V., & McLoughlin, D. M. (2003). Changing use of ECT: Author's reply. *British Journal of Psychiatry, 183*, 173.

Erickson, K., Drevets, W., & Schulkin, J. (2003). Glucocorticoid regulation of diverse cognitive functions in normal and pathological emotional states. *Neuroscience & Biobehavioral Reviews, 27*, 233–246.

Erikson, D. H., Beiser, M., & Iacono, W. G. (1998). Social support predicts 5-year outcome in first-episode schizophrenia. *Journal of Abnormal Psychology, 107*, 681–685.

Ernst, C., & Angst, J. (1983). *Birth order: Its influence on personality*. Berlin: Springer-Verlag.

Ernst, M. O., & Bülthoff, H. H. (2004). Merging the senses into a robust percept. *Trends in Cognitive Sciences, 8*, 162–169.

Eskenazi, B. (1993). Caffeine during pregnancy: Grounds for concern? *Journal of the American Medical Association, 270*, 2973–2974.

Eskenazi, B., Stapleton, A. L., Kharrazi, M., & Chee, W. Y. (1999). Associations between maternal decaffeinated and caffeinated coffee consumption and fetal growth and gestational duration. *Epidemiology, 10*, 242–249.

Etcoff, N. L., Ekman, P., Magee, J. J., & Frank, M. G. (2000). Lie detection and language comprehension. *Nature, 405*, 139.

Evans, G. W. (2003). A multimethodological analysis of cumulative risk and allostatic load among rural children. *Developmental Psychology, 39*, 924–933.

Evans, J. J., Floyd, R. G., McGrew, K. S., & Leforgee, M. H. (2002). The relations between measures of Cattell-Horn-Carroll (CHC) cognitive abilities and reading achievement during childhood and adolescence. *School Psychology Review, 31*, 246–262.

Exner, J. E. (1974). *The Rorschach: A comprehensive system*. Oxford, UK: John Wiley.

Exner, J. E., Jr. (2002). A new nonpatient sample for the Rorschach Comprehensive System: A progress report. *Journal of Personality Assessment, 78*, 391–404.

Eyferth, K. (1961). Ein Vergleich der Beurteilung projektiver Tests durch verschiedene Berteiler [A comparison of judging projective tests by different judges]. *Zeitschrift fuer Experimentelle und Angewandte Psychologie, 8*, 329–338.

Eysenck, H. J. (1977). *Crime and personality*, St. Albans, England: Paladin Frogmore.

Eysenck, H. J. (1979). The conditioning model of neurosis. *Behavioral and Brain Sciences, 2*, 155–199.

Eysenck, H. J. (1990a). Genetic and environmental contributions to individual differences: The three major dimensions of personality. *Journal of Personality, 58*, 245–261.

Eysenck, H. J. (1990b). Biological dimensions of personality. In L. A. Pervin (Ed.), *Handbook of personality: Theory and research* (pp. 244–276). New York: Guilford.

Eysenck, H. J. (1992). Four ways five factors are *not* basic. *Personality and Individual Differences, 13*, 667–673.

Eysenck, H. J. (1993). The structure of phenotypic personality traits: Comment. *American Psychologist, 48*, 1299–1300.

Eysenck, H. J. (1995). *Genius: The natural history of creativity*. Cambridge, England: Cambridge University Press.

Eysenck, H. J., & Gudjonsson, G. (1989). *The causes and cures of criminality*. New York: Plenum Press.

Eysenck, S. B. G., & Eysenck, H. J. (1967). Salivary response to lemon juice as a measure of introversion. *Perceptional and motor skills, 24*, 1047–1053.

Fabbro, F. (2001). The bilingual brain: Bilingual aphasia. *Brain & Language, 79*, 201–210.

Faber, S. (1981). *Identical twins reared apart*. London: Blackwell.

Fagan, J. L., & Holland, C. R. (2002). Equal opportunity and racial differences in IQ. *Intelligence, 30*, 361–387.

Fairburn, C. G., Cooper, Z., Doll, H. A., & Welch, S. L. (1999). Risk factors for anorexia nervosa: Three integrated case-control comparisons. *Archives of General Psychiatry, 56*, 468–476.

Fairburn, C. G., Stice, E., Cooper, Z., Doll, H. A., Norman, P. A., & O'Connor, M. E. (2003). Understanding persistence in bulimia nervosa: A 5-year naturalistic study. *Journal of Consulting & Clinical Psychology, 71*, 103–109.

Farroni, T., Csibra, G., Simion, F., & Johnson, M. H. (2002). Eye contact detection in humans from birth. *Proceedings of the National Academy of Sciences USA, 99*, 9602–9605.

Farthing, G. (1992) *The psychology of consciousness*. Englewood Cliffs, NJ: Prentice-Hall.

Fast, K., & Fujiwara, E. (2001). Isolated retrograde amnesia. *Neurocase, 7*, 269–272.

Fatt, I., & Weissman, B. A. (1992). *Physiology of the eye: An introduction to the vegetative functions* (2nd ed.). Boston: Butterworth-Heinemann.

Fava, G. A. Rafanelli, C., Grandi, S., Conti, S., & Belluardo, P. (1998a). Prevention of recurrent depression with cognitive behavioral therapy: Preliminary findings. *Archives of General Psychiatry, 55*, 816–820.

Fava, G. A., Rafanelli, C., Grandi, S., Canestrari, R., & Morphy, M. A. (1998b). Six-year outcome for cognitive behavioral treatment of residual symptoms in major depression. *American Journal of Psychiatry, 155*, 1443–1445.

Fawzy, F. I., Kemeny, M. E., Fawzy, N. W., Elashoff, R., Morton, D., Cousins, N., & Fahey, J. L. (1990). A structured psychiatric intervention for cancer patients: II. Changes over time in immunological measures. *Archives of General Psychiatry, 47*, 729–735.

Fay, R. E., Turner, C. F., Klassen, A. D., & Gagnon, J. H. (1989). Prevalence and patterns of same-gender sexual contact among men. *Science, 243*, 338–348.

Fazio, R. H., Chen, J., McDonel, E. C., & Sherman, S. J. (1982). Attitude accessibility and the strength of the object-evaluation association. *Journal of Experimental Psychology, 18*, 339–357.

Fazio, R. H., Jackson, J. R., Dunton, B. C., & Williams, C. J. (1995). Variability in automatic activation as an unobstrusive measure of racial attitudes: A bona fide pipeline? *Journal of Personality and Social Psychology, 69*, 1013–1027.

Feather, N. T. (1996). Social comparisons across nations: Variables relating to the subjective evaluation of national achievement and to personal and collective self-esteem. *Australian Journal of Psychology, 48*, 53–63.

Febbraro, G. A. R. (in press). Investigation into the effectiveness of bibliotherapy and minimal contact interventions in the treatment of panic attacks. *Journal of Clinical Psychology*.

Feigenson, L., & Halberda, J. (2004). Infants chunk object arrays into sets of individuals. *Cognition, 91*, 173–190.

Feingold, A. (1990). Gender differences in effects of physical attractiveness on romantic attraction: A comparison across five research paradigms. *Journal of Personality and Social Psychology, 59*, 981–993.

Feingold, A. (1994). Gender differences in personality: A meta-analysis. *Psychological Bulletin, 116*, 429–456.

Feldman, D. H., & Goldsmith, L. T. (1991). *Nature's gambit: Child prodigies and the development of human potential*. New York: Teachers College Press.

Feldman, R. S., Coats, E. J., & Spielman, D. A. (1996). Television exposure and children's decoding of nonverbal behavior. *Journal of Applied Social Psychology, 26*, 1718–1733.

Fell, J., Klaver, P., Elger, C. E., & Guillén, F. (2002). Suppression of EEG Gamma activity may cause the attentional blink. *Consciousness and Cognition, 11*, 114–122.

Felleman, D. J., & Van Essen, D. C. (1991). Distributed hierarchical processing in the primate cerebral cortex. *Cerebral Cortex, 1*, 1–47.

Fergusson, D., Doucette, S., Glass, K. C., Shapiro, S., Healy, D., Hebert, P., & Hutton, B. (2005). Association between suicide attempts and selective serotonin reuptake inhibitors: Systematic review of randomised controlled trials. *British Medical Journal, 330,* 396.

Ferketich, A. K., Schwartzbaum, J. A., Frid, D. J., & Moeschberger, M. L. (2000). Depression as an antecedent to heart disease among women and men in the NHANES I study. National Health and Nutrition Examination Survey. *Archives Internal Medicine, 160,* 1261–1268.

Fernald, A., Taeschner, T., Dunn, J., Papousek, M., Boysson-Bardies, B., & Fukui, I. (1989). A cross-language study of prosodic modifications in mothers' and fathers' speech to infants. *Child Development, 64,* 637–656.

Ferrier, S., & Brewin, C. R. (2005). Feared identity and obsessive-compulsive disorder. *Behaviour Research and Therapy, 43,* 1363–1374.

Ferveur, J.-F., Stoertkuhl, K. F., Stocker, R. F., & Greenspan, R. J. (1995). Genetic feminization of brain structures and changed sexual orientation in male *Drosophila. Science, 267,* 902–905.

Festinger, L. (1950). Informed social communication. *Psychological Review, 57,* 271–282.

Festinger, L., & Carlsmith, J. M. (1959). Cognitive consequences of forced compliance. *Journal of Abnormal and Social Psychology, 58,* 203–210.

Ficker, J. H. I., Wiest, G. H., Lehnert, G., Meyer, M., & Hahn, E. G. (1999). Are snoring medical students at risk of failing their exams? *Sleep, 22,* 205–209.

Field, A. E., Camargo, C. A., Jr., Taylor, B., Berkey, C. S., & Colditz, G. A. (1999). Relation of peer and media influences to the development of purging behaviors among preadolescent and adolescent girls. *Archives of Pediatric Adolescent Medicine, 153,* 1184–1189.

Field, A. P., Psychol, C., & Morgan, J. (2004). Post-event processing and the retrieval of autobiographical memories in socially anxious individuals. *Journal of Anxiety Disorders, 18,* 647–663.

Field, T., Schanberg, S., Scarfidi, F., Bauer, C., Vega-Lahr, N., Garcia, R., et al. (1986). Tactile/kinesthetic stimulation effects on preterm neonates. *Pediatrics, 77,* 654–658.

Field, T. M. (1998). Touch therapy effects on development. *International Journal of Behavioral Development, 22,* 779–797.

Field, T. M., Woodson, R., Greenberg, R., & Cohen, D. (1982). Discrimination and imitation of facial expressions by neonates. *Science, 218,* 179–181.

Fields, R. D., & Stevens-Graham, B. (2002). New insights into neuron-glia communication. *Science, 298,* 556–562.

Figiel, G. S., Epstein, C., McDonald, W. M., Amazon-Leece, J., Figiel, L., Saldivia, A., & Glover, S. (1998). The use of rapid-rate transcranial magnetic stimulation (rTMS) in refractory depressed patients. *Journal of Neuropsychiatry & Clinical Neurosciences, 10,* 20–25.

Fink, B., Grammer, K., & Thornhill, R. (2001). Human (*Homo sapiens*) facial attractiveness in relation to skin texture and color. *Journal of Comparative Psychology, 115,* 92–99.

Finkel, D., Pedersen, N. L., McGue, M., & McClearn, G. E. (1995). Heritability of cognitive abilities in adult twins: Comparison of Minnesota and Swedish data. *Behavioral Genetics, 25,* 421–432.

Finlay, F. O., Jones, R., & Coleman, J. (2002). Is puberty getting earlier? The views of doctors and teachers. *Child: Care, Health & Development, 28,* 205–209.

Finn, J., & Banach, M. (2000). Victimization online: The down side of seeking services for women on the Internet. *CyberPsychology & Behavior, 3,* 243–254.

Fiorentine, R. (1999). After drug treatment: Are 12-step programs effective in maintaining abstinence? *American Journal of Drug and Alcohol Abuse, 25,* 93–116.

Fiorillo, C. D. (2004). The uncertain nature of dopamine. *Molecular Psychiatry, 9,* 122–123.

Fischer, C., Hatzidimitriou, G., Wlos, J., Katz, J., & Ricaurte, G. (1995). Reorganization of ascending 5-HT axon projections in animals previously exposed to recreational drug 3,4-methelenedioxymetham-pheta-mine (MDMA, "Ecstasy"). *Journal of Neuroscience, 15,* 5476–5485.

Fisher, P. J., Turic, D., Williams, N. M., McGuffin, P., Asherson, P., Ball, D., et al. (1999). DNA pooling identifies QTLs on Chromosome 4 for general cognitive ability in children. *Human Molecular Genetics, 8,* 915–922.

Fisher, R. P., & Craik, F. I. M. (1977). The interaction between encoding and retrieval operations in cued recall. *Journal of Experimental Psychology: Human learning and Perception, 3,* 153–171.

Fisher, R. P., & Geiselman, R. E. (1992). *Memory enhancing techniques for investigative interviewing: The cognitive interview.* Springfield: Charles C. Thomas.

Fisher, R. P., Geiselman, R. E., & Amador, M. (1989). Field test of the cognitive interview: Enhancing the recollection of actual victims and witnesses of crime. *Journal of Applied Psychology, 74,* 722–727.

Fiske, S. (1998). Stereotyping, prejudice, and discrimination. In D. T. Gilbert, S. T. Fiske, & G. Lindzey (Eds.). *The handbook of social psychology* (4th ed., pp. 357–411). New York: McGraw-Hill.

Fiske, S. T. (2002). What we know about bias and intergroup conflict, the problem of the century. *Current Directions in Psychological Science, 11,* 123–128.

Fitch, R. H., & Bimonte, H. A. (2002). Hormones, brain, and behavior: Putative biological contributions to cognitive sex differences. In A. McGillicuddy-De Lisi & R. De Lisi (Eds), *Biology, society, and behavior: The development of sex differences in cognition* (pp. 55–91). Westport, CT: Ablex.

Fitton, A., & Heel, R. C. (1990). Clozapine: A review of its pharmacological properties and therapeutic use for schizophrenia. *Drugs, 40,* 722–747.

Fivush, R., & Edwards, V. J. (2004). Remembering and forgetting childhood sexual abuse. *Journal of Child Sexual Abuse, 13,* 1–19.

Flas, W., Dupont, P., Reynvoet, B., & Orban, G. A. (2002). The quantitative nature of a visual task differentiates between ventral and dorsal stream. *Journal of Cognitive Neuroscience, 14,* 646–658.

Flaten, M. A., Simonsen, T., & Olsen, H. (1999). Drug-related information generates placebo and nocebo responses that modify the drug response. *Psychosomatic Medicine, 61,* 250–255.

Fleischman, D. A., Wilson, R. S., Gabrieli, J. D. E., Bienias, J. L., & Bennett, D. A. (2004). A longitudinal study of implicit and explicit memory in old persons. *Psychology and Aging, 19,* 617–625.

Fletcher, A. C., Elder, G. H., Jr., & Mekos, D. (2000). Parental influences on adolescent involvement in community activities. *Journal of Research on Adolescence, 10,* 29–48.

Floyd, M., Scogin, F., McKendree-Smith, N. L., Floyd, D. L., & Rokke, P. D. (2004). Cognitive therapy for depression: A comparison of individual psychotherapy and bibliotherapy for depressed older adults. *Behavior Modification, 28,* 297–318.

Floyd, R. L., Rimer, B. K., Giovino, G. A., Mullen, P. D., & Sullivan, S. E. (1993). A review of smoking in pregnancy: Effects on pregnancy outcomes and cessation efforts. *Annual Review of Public Health, 14,* 379–411.

Flynn, J. R. (1991). *Asian Americans: Achievement beyond IQ.* Hillsdale, NJ: Erlbaum.

Flynn, J. R. (1999a). Massive IQ gains in fourteen nations: What IQ tests really measure. *Psychological Bulletin, 101,* 171–191.

Flynn, J. R. (1999b). Searching for justice: The discovery of IQ gains over time. *American Psychologist, 54,* 5–20.

Foa, E. B., Liebowitz, M. R., Kozak, M. J., Davies, S., Campeas, R., Franklin, M. E., Huppert, J. D., Kjernisted, K., Rowan, V., Schmidt, A. B., Simpson, H. B., & Tu, X. (2005). Randomized, placebo-controlled trial of exposure and ritual prevention, clomipramine, and their combination in the treatment of obsessive-compulsive disorder. *American Journal of Psychiatry, 162,* 151–161.

Foa, E. B., Steketee, G., & Olasov-Rothbaum, B. O. (1989). Behavioral/cognitive conceptualization of post-traumatic stress disorder. *Behavior Therapy, 20,* 155–176.

Fodor, J. A. (1968). *Psychological explanation: An introduction to the philosophy of psychology.* New York: Random House.

Fodor, J. A. (1983). *The modularity of mind.* Cambridge, MA: MIT Press.

Folkman, S., & Moskowitz, J. T. (2004). Coping: Pitfalls and promise. *Annual Review of Psychology, 55,* 745–774.

Fones, C. S. L., Manfro, G. G., & Pollack, M. H. (1998). Social phobia: An update. *Harvard Review of Psychiatry, 5,* 247–259.

Forbes, E. J., & Pekala, R. J. (1993). Psychophysiological effects of several stress management techniques. *Psychological Reports, 72,* 19–27.

Ford, C. S., & Beach, F. (1951). *Patterns of sexual behavior.* New York: Harper & Row.

Ford, K., & Norris, A. E. (1997). Effects of interviewer age on reporting of sexual and reproductive behavior of Hispanic and African American youth. *Hispanic Journal of Behavioral Sciences, 19,* 369–376.

Ford, T. E., Ferguson, M. A., Brooks, J. L., & Hagadone, K. M. (2004). Coping sense of humor reduces effects of stereotype threat on women's math performance. *Personality & Social Psychology Bulletin, 30,* 643–653.

Foster, G. D., Wyatt, H. R., Hill, J. O., McGuckin, B. G., Brill, C., Mohammed, B. S., et al. (2003). A randomized trial of a low-carbohydrate diet for obesity. *New England Journal of Medicine, 348,* 2082–2090.

Fox, C. H. (1994). Cocaine use in pregnancy. *Journal of the American Board of Family Practice, 7,* 225–228.

Fox, E., Russo, R., Bowles, R., & Dutton, K. (2001). Do threatening stimuli draw or hold attention in subclinical anxiety? *Journal of Experimental Psychology General, 130,* 681–700.

Fox, E., Russo, R., & Dutton K. (2002). Attentional bias for threat: Evidence for delayed disengagement from emotional faces. *Cognition & Emotion, 16,* 355–379.

Fox, N. A., Henderson, H. A., Marshall, P. J., Nichols, K. E., & Ghera, M. M. (2005). Behavioral inhibition: Linking biology and behavior within a developmental framework. *Annual Review of Psychology, 56,* n.p.

Fox, W. M. (1982). Why we should abandon Maslow's Need Hierarchy Theory. *Journal of Humanistic Education and Development, 21,* 29–32.

Fozard, J. (1990). Vision and hearing in aging. In J. E. Birren & K. W. Schaie (Eds.), *Handbook of the psychology of aging* (3rd ed., pp. 150–170). San Diego: Academic Press.

Fraley, R. C., Garner, J. P., & Shaver, P. R. (2000). Adult attachment and the defensive regulation of attention and memory: Examining the role of preemptive and postemptive defensive processes. *Journal of Personality & Social Psychology, 79,* 816–826.

Fraley, R. C., & Shaver, P. R. (1997). Adult attachment and the suppression of unwanted thoughts. *Journal of Personality & Social Psychology, 73,* 1080–1091.

Fraley, R. C., & Spieker, S. J. (2003). Are infant attachment patterns continuously or categorically distributed? A taxometric analysis of strange situation behavior. *Developmental Psychology, 39,* 387–404.

Frances, A. (1998). Problems in defining clinical significance in epidemiological studies. *Archives of General Psychiatry, 55,* 119.

Francis, J. R., & Aronson, H. (1990). Communicative efficacy of psychotherapy research. *Journal of Consulting and Clinical Psychology, 58,* 368–370.

Francis, M. E., & Pennebaker, J. W. (1992). Putting stress into words: The impact of writing on physiological, absentee, and self-reported emotional well-being measures. *American Journal of Health Promotion, 6,* 280–286.

Frasure-Smith, N., Lesperance, F., Juneau, M., Talajic, M., & Bourassa, M. G. (1999). Gender, depression, and one-year prognosis after myocardial infarction. *Psychosomatic Medicine, 61,* 26–37.

Fredrickson, B. L. (2001). The role of positive emotions in positive psychology: The broaden-and-build theory of positive emotions. *American Psychologist, 56,* 218–226.

Fredrickson, B. L., & Joiner, T. (2002). Positive emotions trigger upward spirals toward emotional well-being. *Psychological Science, 13,* 172–175.

Freedman, J. L., & Fraser, S. C. (1966). Compliance without pressure: The foot-in-the-door technique.

Journal of Personality and Social Psychology, 4, 195–202.

Freedman, M. R., King, J., & Kennedy, E. (2001). Popular diets: A scientific review. *Obesity Research, 9,* 1S–40S.

Freedman, M. S., Lucas, R. J., Soni, B., von Schantz, M., Muñoz, M., David-Gray, Z., & Foster, R. (1999). Regulation of mammalian circadian behavior by non-rod, non-cone, ocular photoreceptors. *Science, 284,* 502–504.

Freeman, H. (1994). Schizophrenia and city residence. *British Journal of Psychiatry, 164*(Suppl. 23), 39–50.

Freeman, J. H., Jr., & Nicholson, D. A. (2001). Ontogenetic changes in the neural mechanisms of eye-blink conditioning. *Integrative Physiological & Behavioral Science, 36,* 15–35.

Freeman, W. J. (1991). The psychology of perception. *Scientific American, 264,* 78–85.

Freese, J., Powell, B., & Steelman, L. C. (1999). Rebel without a cause or effect: Birth order and social attitudes. *American Sociological Review, 64,* 207–231.

Freud, A. (1958). Adolescence. *Psychoanalytic Study of the Child, 15,* 255–278.

Freud, S. (1900/1958). *The interpretation of dreams.* New York: Basic Books.

Freud, S. (1910). The origin & development of psychoanalysis. *American Journal of Psychology, 21,* 181–218.

Freud, S. (1937/1964). Analysis terminable and interminable. In J. Strachey (Ed. and Trans.), *The standard edition of the complete psychological works of Sigmund Freud* (Vol. 23, pp. 209–253). London: Hogarth Press.

Freud, S. (1938). *The basic writings of Sigmund Freud.* New York: Modern Library (Random House).

Fridlund, A. J. (1994). *Human facial expression: An evolutionary view.* San Diego, CA: Academic Press.

Fried, P. A., & Makin, J. E. (1987). Neonatal behavioral correlates of prenatal exposure to marijuana, cigarettes, and alcohol in a low risk population. *Neurobehavioral Toxicology and Teratology, 9,* 1–7.

Fried, P. A., & Watkinson, B. (2000). Visuoperceptual functioning differs in 9- to 12-year-olds prenatally exposed to cigarettes and marihuana. *Neurotoxicology & Teratology, 22,* 11–20.

Friedler, G. (1996). Paternal exposures: Impact on reproductive and developmental outcome: An overview. *Pharmacology, Biochemistry & Behavior, 55,* 691–700.

Friedman, M., & Rosenman, R. (1974). *Type A behavior and your heart.* New York: Knopf.

Friedman, M. I. (1991). Metabolic control of calorie intake. In M. T. Friedman, M. G. Tordoff, & M. R. Kare (Eds.), *Chemical senses.* New York: Marcel Dekker.

Friedman, M. I., Tordoff, M. G., & Ramirez, I. (1986). Integrated metabolic control of food intake. *Brain Research Bulletin, 17,* 855–859.

Friedrich, R. W. (2004). Odorant receptors make scents. *Nature, 430,* 511–512.

Fryer, R. G., & Levitt, S. D. (2004). Understanding the Black-White test score gap in the first two years of school. *The Review of Economics and Statistics, 86,* 447–464.

Fryers, T. (1993). Epidemiological thinking in mental retardation: Issues in taxonomy and population frequency. In N. W. Bray (Ed.), *International review of research in mental retardation* (Vol. 19). Novato, CA: Academic Therapy Publication.

Fulker, D. W., Eysenck, S. B., & Zuckerman, M. (1980). A genetic and environmental analysis of sensation seeking. *Journal of Research in Personality, 14,* 261–281.

Funder, D. C. (2001). *The personality puzzle* (2nd ed.). New York: Norton.

Funder, D. C., & Colvin, C. R. (1991). Explorations in behavioral consistency: Properties of persons, situations, and behaviors. *Journal of Personality and Social Psychology, 60,* 773–794.

Fung, H. H., Carstensen, L. L., & Lang, F. R. (2001). Age-related patterns in social networks among European Americans and African Americans: Implications for socioemotional selectivity across the life span. *International Journal of Aging & Human Development, 52,* 185–206.

Funtowicz, M. N., & Widiger, T. A. (1999). Sex bias in the diagnosis of personality disorders: An evaluation of

the *DSM-IV* criteria. *Journal of Abnormal Psychology, 108,* 195–201.

Furnham, A., Shahidi, S., & Baluch, B. (2002). Sex and culture differences in perceptions of estimated multiple intelligence for self and family: A British-Iranian comparison. *Journal of Cross-Cultural Psychology, 33,* 270–285.

Fuster, J. M. (1997). Network memory. *Trends in Neuroscience, 20,* 451–459.

Gabbard, G. O. (1990). *Psychodynamic psychiatry in clinical practice.* Washington, DC: American Psychiatric Press.

Gabrieli, J. D. E. (1996). Memory systems analyses of mnemonic disorders in aging and age-related diseases. *Proceedings of the National Academy of Sciences, USA, 93,* 13534–13540.

Gabrieli, J. D. E., Desmond, J. E., Demb, J. B. Wagner, A. D., Stone, M. V., Vaidya, C. J., & Glover, G. H. (1996). Functional magnetic resonance imaging of semantic memory processes in the frontal lobes. *Psychological Science, 7,* 278–283.

Gabrieli, J. D. E., Fleischman, D. A., Keane, M. M., Reminger, S. L., & Morrell, F. (1995). Double dissociation between memory systems underlying explicit and implicit memory in the human brain. *American Psychological Society, 6,* 76–82.

Gagliese, L., & Katz, J. (2000). Medically unexplained pain is not caused by psychopathology. *Pain Research & Management, 5,* 251–257.

Gagné, F., & St Père, F. (2001). When IQ is controlled, does motivation still predict achievement? *Intelligence, 30,* 71–100.

Galanaki, E. (2001). The "imaginary audience" and the "personal fable" in relation to risk behavior and risk perception during adolescence. *Psychology: The Journal of the Hellenic Psychological Society, 8,* 411–430.

Galanter, M. (2000). Cults. In A. E. Kazdin (Ed.), *Encyclopedia of psychology* (Vol. 2, pp. 380–382). Washington, DC: American Psychological Association.

Galdzicki, Z., Siarey, R., Pearce, R., Stoll, J., & Rapoport, S. I. (2001). On the cause of mental retardation in Down syndrome: Extrapolation from full and segmental trisomy 16 mouse models. *Brain Research Reviews, 35,* 115–145.

Gandour, J., & Baum, S. R. (2001). Production of stress retraction by left- and right-hemisphere-damaged patients. *Brain & Language, 79,* 482–494.

Gangestad, S. W. (1993). Sexual selection and physical attractiveness: Implications for mating dynamics. *Human Nature, 4,* 205–235.

Gangestad, S. W., Thornhill, R., & Garver, C. E. (2002). Changes in women's sexual interests and their partners' mate-retention tactics across the menstrual cycle: Evidence for shifting conflicts of interest. *Proceedings of the Royal Society of London: B, Biological Sciences, 269,* 975–982.

Ganis, G., Kosslyn, S. M., Stose, S., Thompson, W. L., & Yurgelun-Todd, D. (2003). Neural correlates of different types of deception: An fMRI investigation. *Cerebral Cortex, 13,* 830–836.

Ganis, G., Thompson, W. L., & Kosslyn, S. M. (2004). Brain areas underlying visual imagery and visual perception: An fMRI study. *Cognitive Brain Research, 20,* 226–241.

Garb, H. N. (1997). Race bias, social class bias, and gender bias in clinical judgment. *Clinical Psychology: Science & Practice, 4,* 99–120.

Garb, H. N., Wood, J. M., Lilienfeld, S. O., & Nezworski, M. T. (2002). Effective use of projective techniques in clinical practice: Let the data help with selection and interpretation. *Professional Psychology: Research & Practice, 33,* 454–463.

Garcia, J., Ervin, F. R., & Koelling, R. A. (1966). Learning with prolonged delay of reinforcement. *Psychonomic Science, 5,* 121–122.

Garcia, J., & Koelling, R. (1966). Relation of cue to consequence in avoidance learning. *Psychonomic Science, 4,* 123–124.

Garcia-Arraras, J. E., & Pappenheimer, J. R. (1983). Site of action of sleep-inducing muramyl peptide isolated

from human urine: Microinjection studies in rabbit brains. *Journal of Neurophysiology, 49,* 528–533.

Gardner, H. (1985). *The mind's new science: A history of the cognitive revolution.* New York: Basic Books.

Gardner, H. (1993a). *Creating minds: An anatomy of creativity as seen through the lives of Freud, Einstein, Picasso, Stravinsky, Eliot, Graham, and Gandhi.* New York: Basic Books.

Gardner, H. (1993b). *Frames of mind: The theory of multiple intelligences.* New York: Basic Books. (Original work published 1983)

Gardner, H. (1995, November). Reflections on multiple intelligences: Myths and messages. *Phi Delta Kappan,* pp. 200–209.

Gardner, H. (1999). *Intelligence reframed: Multiple intelligences for the 21st century.* New York: Basic Books.

Gardner, H. (2002). Three distinct meanings of intelligence. In R. J. Sternberg, J. Lautrey, & T. I. Lubart (Eds.), *Models of intelligence: International perspectives* (pp. 43–45). Washington, DC: American Psychological Association.

Gardner, H., Kornhaber, M. L., & Wake, W. K. (1996). *Intelligence: Multiple perspectives.* Ft. Worth, TX: Harcourt Brace.

Garfield, S. L. (1994). Research on client variables in psychotherapy. In A. E. Bergin & S. L. Garfield (Eds.), *Handbook of psychotherapy and behavior change* (4th edition, pp. 190–228). New York: John Wiley & Sons.

Garfield, S. L., & Bergin, A. E. (1994). Introduction and historical overview. In A. E. Bergin & S. L. Garfield (Eds.), *Handbook of psychotherapy and behavior change* (4th edition, pp. 3–18). New York: John Wiley & Sons.

Garfinkel, P. E., Goldbloom, D., David, R., Olmsted, M. P., Garner, D. M., & Halmi, K. A. (1992). Body dissatisfaction in Bulimia Nervosa: Relationship to weight and shape concerns and psychological functioning. *International Journal of Eating Disorders, 11,* 151–161.

Garner, D. M. (1997). Psychoeducational principles in treatment. In D. M. Garner & P. E. Garfinkel (Eds.), *Handbook of treatment for eating disorders* (2nd ed.). New York: Guilford Press.

Garrard, P., Lambon, R. M. A., Hodges, J. R., & Patterson, K. (2001). Prototypicality, distinctiveness, and intercorrelation: Analyses of the semantic attributes of living and nonliving concepts. *Cognitive Neuropsychology, 18,* 125–174.

Garrido, E., Masip, J., & Herrero, C. (2004). Police officers' credibility judgments: Accuracy and estimated ability. *International Journal of Psychology, 39,* 254–275.

Garrigue, S., Bordier, P., Jais, P., Shah D. C., Hocini M., Raherison C., Tunon De Lara, M., Haïssaguerre, M., & Clementy, J. (2002). Benefit of atrial pacing in sleep apnea syndrome. *New England Journal of Medicine, 346,* 404–412.

Garry, M., & Polaschek, D. L. L. (2000). Imagination and memory. *Current Directions in Psychological Science, 9,* 6–10.

Gaser, C., & Schlaug, G. (2003). Brain structures differ between musicians and non-musicians. *Journal of Neuroscience, 23,* 9240–9245.

Gaster, B., & Holroyd, J. (2000). St. John's Wort for depression: A systematic review. *Archives of Internal Medicine, 160,* 152–156.

Gater, R., Tansella, M., Korten, A., Tiemens, B. G., Mavreas, V. G., & Olatawura, M. O. (1998). Report from the World Health Organization collaborative study on psychological problems in general health care. *Archives of General Psychiatry, 55,* 405–413.

Gaudiano, B. A. (2005). Cognitive behavior therapies for psychotic disorders: Current empirical status and future directions. *Clinical Psychology: Science & Practice, 12,* 33–50.

Gazzaniga, M. S. (1995). Consciousness and the cerebral hemispheres. In M. S. Gazzaniga (Ed.), *The cognitive neurosciences* (pp. 1391–1400). Cambridge, MA: MIT Press.

Gazzaniga, M. S., (Ed.). (2004). *The cognitive neurosciences III.* Cambridge, MA: MIT Press.

Gazzaniga, M. S., & LeDoux, J. E. (1978). *The integrated mind.* New York: Plenum.

Geary, D. C. (1996). Sexual selection and sex differences in mathematical abilities. *Behavioral and Brain Sciences, 19,* 229–284.

Geddes, J. R., Freemantle, N., Mason, J., Eccles, M., & Boynton, J. (2000). SSRIs versus alternative antidepressants in depressive disorder. *Cochrane Database System Review (2):* CD001851.

Geddes, J. R., & Lawrie, S. M. (1995). Obstetric complications and schizophrenia: A meta-analysis. *British Journal of Psychiatry, 67,* 786–793.

Gega, L., Marks, I., & Mataix-Cols, D. (2004). Computer-aided CBT self-help for anxiety and depressive disorders: Experience of a London clinic and future directions. *Journal of Clinical Psychology, 60,* 147–157.

Geiselman, R. E., Fisher, R. P., MacKinnon, D. P., & Holland, H. L. (1985). Eyewitness memory enhancement in the police interview. *Cognitive Journal of Applied Psychology, 70,* 401–412.

Gelfand, S. A. (1981). *Hearing.* New York: Marcel Dekker.

Gelman, R. (1972). Logical capacity of very young children: Number invariance rules. *Child Development, 43,* 75–90.

Gentner, D., & Bowdle, B. F. (2001). Convention, form, and figurative language processing. *Metaphor & Symbol, 16,* 223–247.

Gentner, D., & Gunn, V. (2001). Structural alignment facilitates the noticing of differences. *Memory & Cognition, 29,* 565–577.

George, M. S., Lisanby, S. H., & Sackheim, H. A. (1999). Transcranial magnetic stimulation: Applications in neuropsychiatry. *Archives in General Psychiatry, 56,* 300–311.

Gerhardstein, P., Adler, S. A., & Rovee-Collier, C. (2000). A dissociation in infants' memory for stimulus size: Evidence for the early development of multiple memory systems. *Developmental Psychobiology, 36,* 123–135.

Gerlai, R. (1996). Gene-targeting studies of mammalian behavior: Is it the mutation of the background genotype? *Trends in Neuroscience, 19,* 177–181.

German, T. P., & Barrett, H. C. (2005). Functional fixedness in a technologically sparse culture. *Psychological Science, 16,* 1–5.

Gerteis, J., & Savage, M. (1998). The salience of class in Britain and America: A comparative analysis. *British Journal of Sociology, 49,* 252–274.

Gerwig, M., Dimitrova, A., Kolb, F. P., Maschke, M., Brol, B., Kunnel, A., Böring, D., Thilmann, A. F., Forsting, M., Diener, H. C., & Timmann, D. (2003). Comparison of eyeblink conditioning in patients with superior and posterior inferior cerebellar lesions. *Brain, 126,* 71–94.

Gesell, A., & Thompson, H. (1938). *The psychology of early growth including norms of infant behavior and a method of genetic analysis.* New York: Macmillan.

Gesy, L. J. (Ed.). (1993). *Today's destructive cults and movements.* Huntington, IN: Our Sunday Visitor Publications.

Gibson, J. J. (1966). *The senses considered as perceptual systems.* Boston: Houghton Mifflin.

Gibson, J. J., & Walk, R. D. (1960). The "visual cliff." *Scientific American, 202,* 64–71.

Gibson, J. T. (1991). Training people to inflict pain: State terror and social learning. *Journal of Humanistic Psychology, 31,* 72–87.

Gick, M. L., & Holyoak, K. J. (1980). Analogical problem solving. *Cognitive Psychology, 12,* 306–355.

Gick, M. L., & Holyoak, K. J. (1983). Schema induction and analogical transfer. *Cognitive Psychology, 15,* 1–38.

Gick, M. L., & Thompson, W. G. (1997). Negative affect and the seeking of medical care in university students with irritable bowel syndrome. *Journal of Psychosomatic Research, 43,* 535–540.

Gidron, Y., Davidson, K., & Bata, I. (1999). The short-term effects of a hostility-reduction intervention on male coronary heart disease patients. *Health Psychology, 18,* 416–420.

Giesbrecht, B., & Kingstone, A. (2004). Right hemisphere involvement in the attentional blink: Evidence from a split-brain patient. *Brain & Cognition, 55,* 303–306.

Gigerenzer, G. (1996). On narrow norms and vague heuristics: A reply to Kahneman & Tversky (1996). *Psychological Review, 103,* 592–596.

Gigerenzer, G., & Goldstein, D. G. (1996). Reasoning the fast and frugal way: Models of bounded rationality. *Psychological Review, 103,* 650–669.

Gigerenzer, G., Hell, W., & Blank, H. (1988). Presentation and content: The use of base rates as a continuous variable. *Journal of Experimental Psychology: Human Perception and Performance, 14,* 513–525.

Gilbert, D. T. (1995). Attribution and interpersonal perception. In A. Tesser (Ed.), *Advanced social psychology* (pp. 99–147). New York: McGraw-Hill.

Gilbert, D. T. (2002). Are psychology's tribes ready to form a nation? *Trends in Cognitive Sciences, 6,* 3.

Gilbert, D. T., & Hixon, J. G. (1991). The trouble of thinking: Activation and application of stereotypic beliefs. *Journal of Personality and Social Psychology, 60,* 509–517.

Gilbert, S. (2002, June 25). When brain trauma is at the other end of the thrill ride. *New York Times,* D5.

Gilligan, C. (1982). *In a different voice.* Cambridge, MA: Harvard University Press.

Gilmore, J. H., Sikich, L., & Lieberman, J. A. (1997). Neuroimaging, neurodevelopment, and schizophrenia. *Child & Adolescent Psychiatric Clinics of North America, 6*(2), 325–341.

Gladwell, M. (1998, February 2). The Pima paradox. *New Yorker,* pp. 44–57.

Glaser, R., & Kiecolt-Glaser, J. K. (1998). Stress-associated immune modulation: Relevance to viral infections and chronic fatigue syndrome. *American Journal of Medicine, 105,* 35S–42S.

Glass, R. M. (2001). Electroconvulsive therapy: Time to bring it out of the shadows. *Journal of the American Medical Association, 285,* n.p.

Glennon, F., & Joseph, S. (1993). Just world belief, self-esteem, and attitudes towards homosexuals with AIDS. *Psychological Reports, 72,* 584–586.

Gloaguen, V., Cottraux, J., Cucherat, M., & Blackburn, I. (1998). A meta-analysis of the effects of cognitive therapy in depressed patients. *Journal of Affective Disorders, 49,* 59–72.

Gluck, M., & Myers, C. (2000). *Gateway to memory: An introduction to neural network modeling of the hippocampus and learning.* Cambridge, MA: MIT Press.

Glucksberg, S., Newsome, M. R., & Goldvarg, Y. (2001). Inhibition of the literal: Filtering metaphor-irrelevant information during metaphor comprehension. *Metaphor & Symbol, 16,* 277–293.

Glutting, J. J., Oh, H-J., Ward, T., & Ward, S. (2000). Possible criterion-related bias of the WISC-III with a referral sample. *Journal of Psychoeducational Assessment, 18,* 17–26.

Glynn, S. M. (1990). Token economy approaches for psychiatric patients: Progress and pitfalls over 25 years. *Behavior Modification, 14,* 383–407.

Goedde, H. W., & Agarwal, D. P. (1987). Aldehyde hydrogenase polymorphism: Molecular basis and phenotypic relationship to alcohol sensitivity. *Alcohol & Alcoholism* (Suppl. 1), 47–54.

Goel, V., & Dolan, R. J. (2003). Explaining modulation of reasoning by belief. *Cognition, 87,* B11–B22.

Goetestam, K. G., & Berntzen, D. (1997). Use of the modelling effect in one-session exposure. *Scandinavian Journal of Behaviour Therapy, 26,* 97–101.

Goethals, G. R., Cooper, J., & Naficy, A. (1979). Role of foreseen, foreseeable, and unforeseeable behavioral consequences in the arousal of cognitive dissonance. *Journal of Personality and Social Psychology, 37,* 1179–1185.

Goethals, G. R., & Zanna, M. P. (1979). The role of social comparison in choice shifts. *Journal of Personality and Social Psychology, 37,* 1469–1485.

Goff, D. C., & Coyle, J. T. (2001). The emerging role of glutamate in the pathophysiology and treatment of schizophrenia. *American Journal of Psychiatry, 158,* 1367–1377.

Goldapple, K., Segal, Z., Garson, C., Lau, M., Bieling, P., Kennedy, S., & Mayberg, H. (2004). Modulation of cortical-limbic pathways in major depression. *Archives of General Psychiatry, 61,* 34–41.

Goldberg, E. (2001). *The executive brain: Frontal lobes and the civilized mind.* New York: Oxford University Press.

Goldberg, L. R. (1981). Language and individual differences: The search for universals in personality lexicons. In L. Wheeler (Ed.), *Review of personality and social psychology* (Vol. 2, pp. 141–165). Beverly Hills, CA: Sage.

Goldstein, A. (1994). *Addiction: From biology to drug policy.* New York: Freeman.

Goldstein, D. S. (1995). *Stress, catecholamines, and cardiovascular disease.* New York: Oxford University Press.

Goldstein, D. S. (2000). *The autonomic nervous system in health and disease.* New York: Marcel Dekker.

Goldstein, D. S., & McEwen, B. (2002). Allostasis, homeostats, and the nature of stress. *Stress: International Journal on the Biology of Stress, 5,* 55–58.

Goldstein, J. M., Goodman, J. M., Seidman, L. J., Kennedy, D. N., Makris, N., Lee, H., et al. (1999). Cortical abnormalities in schizophrenia identified by structural magnetic resonance imaging. *Archives of General Psychiatry, 56,* 537–547.

Goldstein, M. D., & Strube, M. J. (1994). Independence revisited: The relation between positive and negative affect in a naturalistic setting. *Personality & Social Psychology Bulletin, 20,* 57–64.

Goldstein, M. J. (1992). Psychosocial strategies for maximizing the effects of psychotropic medications for schizophrenia and mood disorder. *Psychopharmacology Bulletin, 28,* 237–240.

Goodale, M. A., & Milner, A. D. (1992). Separate visual pathways for perception and action. *Trends in Neurosciences, 15,* 20–25.

Goode, E. (1999, November 2). New clues to why we dream. *New York Times,* p. D1.

Goodfellow, P. N., & Lovell-Badge, R. (1993). SRY and sex determination in mammals. *Annual Review of Genetics, 27,* 71–92.

Goodwin, F. K., & Ghaemi, S. N. (1998). Understanding manic–depressive illness. *Archives of General Psychiatry, 55,* 23–25.

Goodwin, F. K., & Jamison, K. R. (1990). *Manic-depressive illness.* New York: Oxford University Press.

Goodwin, R. D., & Gotlib, I. H. (2004). Gender differences in depression: The role of personality factors. *Psychiatry Research, 126,* 135–142.

Gorman, J. M., & Kent, J. M. (1999). SSRIs and SNRIs: Broad spectrum of efficacy beyond major depression. *Journal of Clinical Psychiatry, 60*(Suppl. 4), 33–39.

Gorman, J. M., Liebowitz, M. R., Fyer, A. J., & Stein, J. (1989). A neuroanatomical hypothesis for panic disorder. *American Journal of Psychiatry, 146,* 148–161.

Gortner, E. T., Gollan, J-K., Dobson, K. S., & Jacobson, N. S. (1998). Cognitive-behavioral treatment for depression: Relapse prevention. *Journal of Consulting & Clinical Psychology, 66,* 377–384.

Gotlib, I. H., & Robinson, L. A. (1982). Responses to depressed individuals: Discrepancies between self-report and observer rated behavior. *Journal of Abnormal Psychology, 91,* 231–240.

Gottesman, I. I. (1991). *Schizophrenia genesis: The origins of madness.* New York: Freeman.

Gottesman, I. I., & Moldin, S. O. (1998). Genotypes, genes, genesis, and pathogenesis in schizophrenia. In M. F. Lenzenweger & R. H. Dworkin (Eds.), *Origins and development of schizophrenia: Advances in experimental psychopathology* (pp. 5–26). Washington, DC: American Psychological Association.

Gottfredson, L. (1997). Why "g" matters: The complexity of everyday life. *Intelligence, 24,* 79–132.

Gottfredson, L. S. (2003a). Dissecting practical intelligence theory: Its claims and evidence. *Intelligence, 31,* 343–397.

Gottfredson, L. S. (2003b). Discussion: On Sternberg's "Reply to Gottfredson." *Intelligence, 31,* 415–424.

Gottfredson, M. R., & Hirschi, T. (1990). *A general theory of crime.* Stanford, CA: Stanford University Press.

Gottfried, J. A., & Dolan, R. J. (2003). The nose smells what the eye sees—crossmodal visual facilitation of human olfactory perception. *Neuron, 39,* 375–386.

Gottlieb, G. (1998). Normally occurring environmental and behavioral influences on gene activity: From central dogma to probabilistic epigenesis. *Psychological Review, 105*, 792–802.

Gould, E., Tanapat, P., Hastings, N. B., & Shors, T. J. (1999). Neurogenesis in adulthood: A possible role in learning. *Trends in Cognitive Sciences, 3*, 186–192.

Gould, J. L. (1998). Sensory bases of navigation. *Current Biology, 8*, R731–R738.

Gould, R. (1978). *Transformations.* New York: Simon & Schuster.

Gould, R. A., & Clum, G. A. (1993). A meta-analysis of self-help treatment approaches. *Clinical Psychology Review, 13*, 169–186.

Gould, R. A., Mueser, K. T., Bolton, E., Mays, V., & Goff, D. (2001). Cognitive therapy for psychosis in schizophrenia: An effect size analysis. *Schizophrenia Research, 48*, 335–342.

Gould, R. A., Otto, M. W., & Pollack, M. H. (1995). A meta-analysis of treatment outcome for panic disorder. *Clinical Psychology Review, 15*, 819–844.

Gould, S. J., & Lewontin, R. C. (1979). The spandrels of San Marco and the Panglossian paradigm: A critique of the adaptationist programme. *Proceedings of the Royal Society of London, Series B, 205*, 581–598.

Grammer, K. (1990). Strangers meet: Laughter and non-verbal signs of interest in opposite-sex encounters. *Journal of Nonverbal Behavior, 14*, 209–236.

Granhag, P. A., & Strömwall, L. A. (2001). Deception detection: Interrogators' and observers' decoding of consecutive statements. *Journal of Psychology: Interdisciplinary & Applied, 135*, 603–620.

Grant, B. F., & Dawson, D. A. (1997). Age at onset of alcohol use and its association with DSM-IV alcohol abuse and dependence: Results from the National Longitudinal Alcohol Epidemiologic Survey. *Journal of Substance Abuse, 9*, 103–110.

Grant, B. F., Stinson, F. S., Dawson, D. A., Chou, S. P., Dufour, M. C., Compton, W., Pickering, R. P., & Kaplan, K. (2004). Prevalence and co-occurrence of substance use disorders and independent mood and anxiety disorders: Results from the National Epidemiologic Survey on Alcohol and Related Conditions. *Archives of General Psychiatry, 61*, 807–816.

Grant, I., Marcotle, T. D., Heaton, R. K., & HNRC Group, San Diego, CA, USA. (1999). Neurocognitive complications of HIV disease. *Psychological Science, 10*, 191–195.

Gray, J. A. (1982). Précis of the neuropsychology of anxiety: An enquiry into the functions of the septo-hippocampal system. *Behavioral & Brain Sciences, 5*, 469–534.

Gray, J. A. (1987). Perspectives on anxiety and impulsiveness: A commentary. *Journal of Research in Personality, 21*, 493–509.

Gray, J. A. (1991). The neuropsychology of temperament. In J. Strelau & A. Angleitner (Eds.), *Explorations in temperament: International perspectives on theory and measurement* (pp. 105–128). New York: Plenum Press.

Gray, J. R. (1999). A bias toward short-term thinking in threat-related negative emotional states. *Personality and Social Psychology Bulletin, 25*, 65–75.

Gray, J. R. (2001). Emotional modulation of cognitive control: Approach-withdrawal states double-dissociate spatial from verbal two-back task performance. *Journal of Experimental Psychology: General, 130*, 436–452.

Gray, J. R., Braver, T. S., & Raichle, M. E. (2002). Integration of emotion and cognition in the lateral prefrontal cortex. *Proceedings of the National Academy of Sciences USA, 99*, 4115–4120.

Gray, J. R., & Thompson, P. M. (2004). Neurobiology of intelligence: Science and ethics. *Nature Reviews Neuroscience, 5*, 471–482.

Gray, P. B., Kahlenberg, S. M., Barrett, E. S., Lipson, S. F., & Ellison, P. T. (2002). Marriage and fatherhood are associated with lower testosterone in males. *Evolution & Human Behavior, 23*, 193–201.

Graziano, W. G., Habashi, M., Sheese, B. E., & Tobin, R. (2004). Feeling compassion and helping the unfortu-

nate: A social motivational analysis. Manuscript submitted for publication.

Graziano, W. G., Jensen-Campbell, L. A., & Sullivan-Logan, G. M. (1998). Temperament, activity, and expectations for later personality development, *Journal of Personality and Social Psychology, 74*, 1266–1277.

Green, A. R. (2004). MDMA: Fact and fallacy, and the need to increase knowledge in both the scientific and popular press. *Psychopharmacology, 173*, 231–233.

Green, A. R., Cross, A. J., & Goodwin, G. M. (1995) Review of the pharmacology and clinical pharmacology of 3,4-methylenedioxymethamphetamine (MDMA or "Ecstasy"). *Psychopharmacology, 119*, 247–260.

Green, D. M. (1976). *An introduction to hearing.* Hillsdale, NJ: Erlbaum.

Green, D. M., & Swets, J. A. (1966). *Signal detection theory and psychophysics.* New York: Wiley.

Green, J. P., Lynn, S. J., & Malinoski, P. (1998). Hypnotic pseudomemories, prehypnotic warnings, and malleability of suggested memories. *Applied Cognitive Psychology, 12*, 431–444.

Green, M. F., Kern, R. S., Braff, D. L., & Mintz, J. (2000). Neurocognitive deficits and functional outcome in schizophrenia: Are we measuring the "right stuff"? *Schizophrenia Bulletin, 26*, 119–136.

Green, M. F., Nuechterlein, K. H., Breitmeyer, B., & Mintz, J. (1999). Backward masking in unmedicated schizophrenic patients in psychotic remission: possible reflection of aberrant cortical oscillation. *American Journal of Psychiatry, 156*, 1367–1373.

Greenberg, B. D., Altemus, M., & Murphy, D. L. (1997). The role of neurotransmitters and neurohormones in obsessive-compulsive disorder. *International Review of Psychiatry, 9*, 31–44.

Greenberg, D. L., & Rubin, D. C. (2003). The neuropsychology of autobiographical memory. *Cortex, 39*, 687–728.

Greenberg, J. R., & Mitchell, S. A. (1983). *Object relations in psychoanalytic theory.* Cambridge, MA: Harvard University Press.

Greenberg, R. P., & Fisher, S. (1989). Examining antidepressant effectiveness: Findings, ambiguities and some vexing puzzles. In S. Fisher & R. P. Greenberg (Eds.), *The limits of biological treatments for psychological distress* (pp. 1–37). Hillsdale, NJ: Erlbaum.

Greene, K., Krcmar, M., Rubin, D. L., Walters, L. H., & Hale, J. L. (2002). Elaboration in processing adolescent health messages: The impact of egocentrism and sensation seeking on message processing. *Journal of Communication, 52*, 812–831.

Greenough, W. T., Black, J. E., & Wallace, C. S. (1987). Experience and brain development. *Child Development, 58*, 539–559.

Greenough, W. T., & Chang, F.-L. F. (1985). Synaptic structural correlates of information storage in mammalian nervous systems. In C. W. Cotman (Ed.), *Synaptic plasticity* (pp. 335–372). New York: Guilford.

Greenwald, A. G., & Banaji, M. R. (1995). Implicit social cognition: Attitudes, self-esteem, and stereotypes. *Psychological Review, 102*, 4–27.

Greenwald, A. G., Spangenberg, E. R., Pratkanis, A. R., & Eskenazi, J. (1991). Double-blind tests of subliminal self-help audiotapes. *Psychological Science, 2*, 119–122.

Gregg, V. R., Winer, G. A., Cottrell, J. E., Hedman, K. E., & Fournier, J. S. (2001). The persistence of a misconception about vision after educational interventions. *Psychonomic Bulletin and Review, 8*, 622–626.

Gregory, R. L. (1974). *Concepts and mechanisms of perception.* New York: Scribner's.

Gregory, R. L., & Harris, J. P. (1984). Real and apparent movement nulled. *Nature, 307*, 729–730.

Gregory, R. J., Schwer Canning, S., Lee, T. W., & Wise, J. C. (2004). Cognitive bibliotherapy for depression: A meta-analysis. *Professional Psychology: Research & Practice, 35*, 275–280.

Grézes, J., & Decety, J. (2001). Functional anatomy of execution, mental simulation, observation, and verb generation of actions: A meta-analysis. *Human Brain Mapping, 12*, 1–19.

Grice, H. P. (1975). Logic and conversation. In P. Cole & J. L. Morgan (Eds.), *Syntax and semantics: Vol. 3, Speech acts* (pp. 41–58). New York: Seminar Press.

Grice, J. W., & Seely, E. (2000). The evolution of sex differences in jealousy: Failure to replicate previous results. *Journal of Research in Personality, 34*, 348–356.

Griffiths, T. D., Warren, J. D., Dean, J. L., & Howard, D. (2004). "When the feeling's gone": A selective loss of musical emotion. *Journal of Neurology, Neurosurgery & Psychiatry, 75*, 344–345.

Grillo, C., La Mantia, I., Triolo, C., Scollo, A., La Boria, A., Intelisano, G., & Caruso, S. (2001). Rhinomanometric and olfactometric variations throughout the menstrual cycle. *Annals of Otology, Rhinology & Laryngology, 110*, 785–789.

Grill-Spector, K. (2003). The neural basis of object perception. *Current Opinion in Neurobiology, 13*, 159–166.

Grill-Spector, K., Kushnir, T., Hendler, T., Edelman, S., Itzchak, Y., & Malach, R. (1998). A sequence of object-processing stages revealed by fMRI in the human occipital lobe. *Human Brain Mapping, 6*, 316–328.

Grilly, D. (1994). *Drugs and human behavior* (2nd ed.). Boston: Allyn & Bacon.

Grimes, K., & Walker, E. F. (1994). Childhood emotional expressions, educational attainments, and age at onset of illness in schizophrenia. *Journal of Abnormal Psychology, 103*, 784–790.

Grimshaw, G. M., Adelstein, A., Bryden, M. P., & MacKinnon, G. E. (1998). First-language acquisition in adolescence: Evidence for a critical period for verbal language development. *Brain & Language, 63*, 237–255.

Grisaru, N., Amir, M., Cohen, H., & Kaplan, Z. (1998). Effect of transcranial magnetic stimulation in posttraumatic stress disorder: A preliminary study. *Biological Psychiatry, 44*, 52–55.

Grisaru, N., Chudakov, B., Yaroslavsky, Y., & Belmaker, R. H. (1998). Transcranial magnetic stimulation in mania: A controlled study. *American Journal of Psychiatry, 155*, 1608–1610.

Gross, J., & Levenson, R. W. (1997). Hiding feelings: The acute effects of inhibiting negative and positive emotion. *Journal of Abnormal Psychology, 106*, 95–103.

Gross, J. J. (2001). Emotion regulation in adulthood: Timing is everything. *Current Directions in Psychological Science, 10*, 214–219.

Gross, J. J. (2002). Emotion regulation: Affective, cognitive, and social consequences. *Psychophysiology, 39*, 281–291.

Gross, J. J., Carstensen, L. L., Pasupathi, M., Tsai, J., Goetestam Skorpen, C., & Hsu, A. Y. C. (1997). Emotion and aging: Experience, expression, and control. *Psychology & Aging, 12*, 590–599.

Grossarth-Maticek, R., Eysenck, H. J., Boyle, G. J., Heeb, J., Costa, C. D., & Diel, I. J. (2000). Interaction of psychosocial and physical risk factors in the causation of mammary cancer, and its prevention through psychological methods of treatment. *Journal of Clinical Psychology, 56*, 33–50.

Grossman, R. P., & Till, B. D. (1998). The persistence of classically conditioned brand attitudes. *Journal of Advertising, 27*, 23–31.

Gruber, A. J., Pope, H. G., Hudson, H. I., & Yurgelun-Todd, D. (2003). Attributes of long-term heavy cannabis users: A case control study. *Psychological Medicine, 33*, 1415–1422.

Grunes, M. S., Neziroglu, F., & McKay, D. (2001). Family involvement in the behavioral treatment of obsessive-compulsive disorder: A preliminary investigation. *Behavior Therapy, 32*, 803–820.

Grusec, J. E., Davidov, M., & Lundell, L. (2002). Prosocial and helping behavior. In P. K. Smith & C. H. Hart (Eds.), *Blackwell handbook of childhood social development* (pp. 457–474). Malden, MA: Blackwell Publishers.

Guadagno, R. W., Asher, T., Demaine, L. H., & Cialdini, R. B. (2001). When saying yes leads to saying no: Preference for consistency and the reverse foot-in-the-door effect. *Personality & Social Psychology Bulletin, 27*, 859–867.

Guéguen, N., & De Gail, M. (2003). The effect of smiling on helping behavior: Smiling and Good Samaritan behavior. *Communication Reports, 16*, 133–140.

Guerin, B. (1993). *Social facilitation*. Paris: Cambridge University Press.

Guilford, J. P. (1967). *The nature of human intelligence*. New York: McGraw-Hill.

Gunewardene, A., Huon, G. F., & Zheng, R. (2001). Exposure to westernization and dieting: A cross-cultural study. *International Journal of Eating Disorders, 29*, 289–293.

Gunnell, D., Saperia, J., Ashby, D. (2005). Selective serotonin reuptake inhibitors (SSRIs) and suicide in adults: meta-analysis of drug company data from placebo controlled, randomised controlled trials submitted to the MHRA's safety review. *British Medical Journal, 330*, 385–388.

Gureje, O., Mavreas, V., Vazquez-Barquero, J. L., & Janca, A. (1997). Problems related to alcohol use: A cross-cultural perspective. *Culture, Medicine, and Psychiatry, 21*, 199–211.

Gustafsson, J.-E. (1984). A unifying model for the structure of mental abilities. *Intelligence, 8*, 179–203.

Gutchess, A. H., Welsh, R. C., Hedden, T., Bangert, A., Minear, M., Liu, L. L., & Park, D. C. (2005). Aging and the neural correlates of successful picture encoding: Frontal activations compensate for decreased medial-temporal activity. *Journal of Cognitive Neuroscience, 17*, 84–96.

Guthrie, G. M., Guthrie, H. A., Fernandez, T. L., & Esterea, N. O. (1982). Cultural influences and reinforcement stratifies. *Behavior Therapy, 13*, 624–637.

Guthrie, R. M., & Bryant, R. A. (2005). Auditory startle response in firefighters before and after trauma exposure. *American Journal of Psychiatry, 162*, 283–290.

Guttmann, C. R. G., Jolesz, F. A., Kikinis, R., Killiany, R. J., Moss, M. B., Sandor, T., & Albert, M. S. (1998). White matter changes with normal aging, *Neurology, 50*, 972–978.

Gyulai, L., Abass, A., Broich, K., & Reilley, J. (1997). I-123 lofetamine single-photon computer emission tomography in rapid cycling bipolar disorder: A clinical study. *Biological Psychiatry, 41*, 152–161.

Haaga, D. A., & Davison, G. C. (1989). Slow progress in rational-emotive therapy outcome research: Etiology and treatment. *Cognitive Therapy & Research, 13*, 493–450.

Haapasalo, J., & Pokela, E. (1999). Child-rearing and child abuse antecedents of criminality. *Aggression & Violent Behavior, 4*, 107–127.

Habra, M. E., Linden, W., Anderson, J. C., & Weinberg, J. (2003). Type D personality is related to cardiovascular and neuroendocrine reactivity to acute stress. *Journal of Psychosomatic Research, 55*, 235–245.

Hafer, C. L., & Bègue, L. (2005). Experimental research on just-world theory: Problems, developments, and future challenges. *Psychological Bulletin, 131*, 128–167.

Hahn, R. A. (1995). *Sickness and healing: An anthropological perspective*. New Haven, CT: Yale University Press.

Hahn, R. A. (1997). The nocebo phenomenon: Scope and foundations. In A. Harrington (Ed.), *The placebo effect: An interdisciplinary exploration*. Cambridge, MA: Harvard University Press.

Hahn, R. A. (1999). Expectations of sickness: Concept and evidence of the nocebo phenomenon. In I. Kirsch (Ed.), *How expectancies shape experience* (pp. 333–356). Washington, DC: American Psychological Association.

Haier, R. J., et al. (1984) Evoked potential augmenting-reducing and personality differences. *Personality & Individual Differences, 5*, 293–301.

Hakuta, K., Bialystok, E., & Wiley, E. (2003). Critical evidence: A test of the critical-period hypothesis for second-language learning. *Psychological Science, 14*, 31–38.

Halari, R., Hines, M., Kumari, V., Mehrotra, R., Wheeler, M., Ng, V., & Sharma, T. (2005). Sex differences and individual differences in cognitive performance and their relationship to endogenous gonadal hormones and gonadotropins. *Behavioral Neuroscience, 119*, 104–117.

Hall, D. T., & Nougaim, K. E. (1968). An examination of Maslow's need hierarchy in an organizational setting. *Organizational Behavior and Human Performance, 3*, 12–35.

Hall, J., Thomas, K. L., & Everitt, B. J. (2001) . Cellular imaging of *zif268* expression in the hippocampus and amygdala during contextual and cued fear memory retrieval: Selective activation of hippocampal CA1 neurons during the recall of contextual memories. *Journal of Neuroscience, 21*, 2186–2193.

Hall, J. A. (1978). Gender effects in decoding nonverbal cues. *Psychological Bulletin, 85*, 845–857.

Hall, J. A. (1987). On explaining gender differences: The case of nonverbal communication. In P. Shaver & C. Hendrick (Eds.), *Sex and gender*. Newbury Park, CA: Sage.

Hall, J. A., & Matsumoto, D. (2004). Gender differences in judgments of multiple emotions from facial expressions. *Emotion, 4*, 201–206.

Hall, J. F. (1984). Backward conditioning in Pavlovian type studies: Reevaluation and present status. *Pavlovian Journal of Biological Science, 19*, 163–168.

Halle, M. (1990). Phonology. In D. N. Osherson & H. Lasnik (Eds.), *An invitation to cognitive science: Vol. 1, Language* (pp. 43–68). Cambridge, MA: MIT Press.

Hallem, E. A., Ho, M. G., & Carlson, J. R. (2004) The molecular basis of odor coding in the *Drosophila* antenna. *Cell, 117*, 965–979.

Halmi, K. (1995). Basic biological overview of eating disorders. In F. E. Bloom & D. J. Kupfer (Eds.), *Psychopharmacology: The fourth generation of progress*. New York: Raven Press.

Halmi, K. (1996). The psychobiology of eating behavior in anorexia nervosa. *Psychiatry Research, 62*, 23–29.

Halpern, D. F. (1992). *Sex differences in cognitive ability*. Hillsdale, NJ: Erlbaum.

Halpern, D. F. (1997). Sex differences in intelligence: Implications for education. *American Psychologist, 52*, 1091–1102.

Halpern, D. F. (2000). *Sex differences in cognitive abilities* (3rd ed.). London: LEA.

Hamann, S., & Mao, H. (2002). Positive and negative emotional verbal stimuli elicit activity in the left amygdala. *Neuroreport: For Rapid Communication of Neuroscience Research, 13*, 15–19.

Hamer, D. H., Hu, S., Magnuson, V. L., Hu, N., & Pattatucci, A. M. (1993). A linkage between DNA markers on the X chromosome and male sexual orientation. *Science, 261*, 321–327.

Hamilton, M. E., Voris, J. C., Sebastian, P. S., Singha, A. K., Krejci, L. P., Elder, I. R., et al. (1998). Money as a tool to extinguish conditioned responses to cocaine in addicts. *Journal of Clinical Psychology, 54*, 211–218.

Hampson, E. (1990). Estrogen-related variations in human spatial and articulatory motor skills. *Psychoneuroendocrinology, 15*, 97–111.

Hampson, E., & Kimura, D. (1988). Reciprocal effects of hormonal fluctuations on human motor and perceptual-spatial skills. *Behavioral Neuroscience, 102*, 456–459.

Haney, C., Banks, W. C., & Zimbardo, P. G. (1973). Interpersonal dynamics in a simulated prison. *International Journal of Criminology and Penology, 1*, 69–97.

Haney, C., & Zimbardo, P. G. (1976). Social roles and role-playing: Observations from the Stanford prison study. In E. P. Hollander & R. G. Hunt (Eds.), *Current perspectives in social psychology* (4th ed., pp. 266–274). New York: Oxford University Press.

Haney, M., Ward, A. S., Comer, S. D., Foltin, R. W., & Fischman, M. W. (1999). Abstinence symptoms following smoked marijuana in humans. *Psychopharmacology, 141*, 395–404.

Hansenne, M., Pinto, E., Pitchot, W., Reggers, J., Scantamburlo, G., Moor, M., & Ansseau, M. (2002). Further evidence on the relationship between dopamine and novelty seeking: A neuroendocrine study. *Personality & Individual Differences, 33*, 967–977.

Hapidou, E. G., & De Catanzaro, D. (1988). Sensitivity to cold pressor pain in dysmenorrheic and non-dysmenorrheic women as a function of menstrual cycle phase. *Pain, 34*, 277–283.

Hardy, J. D., & Smith, T. W. (1988). Cynical hostility and vulnerability to disease: Social support, life stress, and physiological response to conflict. *Health Psychology, 7*, 447–459.

Hare, R. D. (1993). *Without conscience: The disturbing world of the psychopaths among us*. New York: Pocket Books.

Hariri, A. R., Mattay, V. S., Tessitore, A., Kolachana, B., Fera, F., Goldman, D., et al. (2002). Serotonin transporter genetic variation and the response of the human amygdala. *Science, 297*, 400–403.

Harkins, S., & Szymanski, K. (1989). Social loafing and group evaluation. *Journal of Personality and Social Psychology, 56*, 934–941.

Harkins, S. G., & Petty, R. E. (1982). Effects of task difficulty and task uniqueness on social loafing. *Journal of Personality & Social Psychology, 43*, 1214–1229.

Harlow, H. F. (1958). The nature of love. *American Psychologist, 13*, 573–685.

Harris, C. R. (2000). Psychophysiological responses to imagined infidelity: The specific innate modular view of jealousy reconsidered. *Journal of Personality & Social Psychology, 78*, 1082–1091.

Harris, C. R. (2002). Sexual and romantic jealousy in heterosexual and homosexual adults. *Psychological Science, 13*, 7–12.

Harris, J. R. (1998). *The nurture assumption: Why children turn out the way they do*. New York: Free Press.

Hart, B., & Risley, T. R. (1995/2002) *Meaningful differences in everyday parenting and intellectual development in young American children*. Baltimore: Paul H. Brookes.

Hart, H. C., Palmer, A. R., & Hall, D. A. (2003). Amplitude and frequency-modulated stimuli activate common regions of human auditory cortex. *Cerebral Cortex, 13*, 773–781.

Hart, J., Berndt, R. S., & Caramazza, A. (1985). Category-specific naming deficit following cerebral infarction. *Nature, 316*, 439–440.

Hart, K. E., & Hope, C. W. (2004). Cynical hostility and the psychosocial vulnerability model of disease risk: Confounding effects of neuroticism (negative affectivity) bias. *Personality & Individual Differences, 36*, 1571–1582.

Hartman, B. J. (1982). An exploratory study of the effects of disco music on the auditory and vestibular systems. *Journal of Auditory Research, 22*, 271–274.

Hartung, C. M., & Widiger, T. A. (1998). Gender differences in the diagnosis of mental disorders: Conclusions and controversies of the DSM-IV. *Psychological Bulletin, 123*, 260–278.

Hasegawa, I., Fukushima, T., Ihara, T., & Miyashita, Y. (1998). Callosal window between prefrontal cortices: Cognitive interaction to retrieve long-term memory. *Science, 281*, 814–818.

Hasler, G., Drevets, W. C., Manji, H. K., & Charney, D. S. (2004). Discovering endophenotypes for major depression. *Neuropsychopharmacology, 29*, 1765–1781.

Hastie, R. (1986). Review essay: Experimental evidence on group accuracy. In B. Grofman & G. Guillermo (Eds.), *Information pooling and group decision making* (Vol. 2, pp. 129–157). Greenwich, CT: JAI Press.

Hastie, R., & Kameda, T. (2005). The robust beauty of majority rules in group decisions. *Psychological Review, 112*, 494–508.

Hastorf, A. H., & Cantril, H. (1954). They saw a game; a case study. *Journal of Abnormal and Social Psychology, 49*, 129–134.

Hatfield, E., & Sprecher, S. (1986). Men's and women's preferences in marital partners in the United States, Russia, and Japan. *Journal of Cross-Cultural Psychology. 26*, 728–750.

Hauser, M. (1996). *The evolution of communication*. Cambridge, MA: MIT Press.

Hausmann, M., Slabbekoorn, D., Van Goozen, S. H. M., Cohen-Kettenis, P. T., & Guenteurkuen, O. (2000). Sex hormones affect spatial abilities during the menstrual cycle. *Behavioral Neuroscience, 114*, 1245–1250.

Havinghurst, R. (1953). *Human development and education*. New York: Longmans, Green.

Hawkins, J. R. (1994). Sex determination. *Human Molecular Genetics, 3,* 1463–1467.

Haxby, J. V., Gobbini, M. I., Furey, M. L., Ishai, A., Schouten, J. L., & Pietrini, P. (2001). Distributed and overlapping representations of faces and objects in ventral temporal cortex. *Science, 293,* 2425–2430.

Haxby, J. V., Grady, C. L., Horowitz, B., Ungerleider, L. G., Mischkin, M., Carson, R. E., et al. (1991). Dissociation of object and spatial visual processing pathways in human extrastriate cortex. *Proceedings of the National Academy of Sciences, USA, 88,* 1621–1625.

Haxby, J. V., Horowitz, B., Ungerleider, L. G., Maisog, J. M., Pietrini, P., & Grady, C. L. (1994). The functional organization of human extrastriate cortex: A PET-rCBF study of selective attention to faces and locations. *Journal of Neuroscience, 14,* 6336–6353.

Hayashi, T., Yamaguchi, T., Kitahara, K., Sharpe, L. T., Jägle, H., Yamade, S., Ueyama, H., Motulsky, A. G., & Deeb, S. S. (2001). The importance of gene order in expression of the red and green visual pigment genes and in color vision. *Color Research & Application, 26,* S79–S83.

Hazan, C., & Shaver, P. R. (1987). Romantic love conceptualized as an attachment process. *Journal of Personality and Social Psychology, 52,* 511–524.

Hazan, C., & Shaver, P. R. (1990). Love and work: An attachment-theoretical perspective. *Journal of Personality and Social Psychology, 59,* 270–280.

Heath, A. C., & Martin, N. G. (1990) Psychoticism as a dimension of personality: A multivariate genetic test of Eysenck and Eysenck's Psychoticism construct. *Journal of Personality and Social Psychology, 58,* 11–121.

Heatherton, T. F. (2004). Introduction to special issue on social cognitive neuroscience. *Journal of Cognitive Neuroscience, 16,* 1681–1682.

Heatherton, T. F., Macrae, C. N., & Kelley, W. M. (2004). What the social brain sciences can tell us about the self. *Current Directions in Psychological Science, 13,* 190–193.

Hebert, L. E., Scherr, P. A., Bienias, J. L., Bennett, D. A., & Evans, D. A. (2003). Alzheimer disease in the US population: Prevalence estimates using the 2000 census. *Archives of Neurology, 60,* 1119–1122.

Hecker, M., Chesney, M. N., Black, G., & Frautsch, N. (1988). Coronary-prone behaviors in the Western Collaborative Group Study. *Psychosomatic Medicine, 50,* 153–164.

Heilman, K. M., Nadeau, S. E., & Beversdorf, D. O. (2003). Creative innovation: Possible brain mechanisms. *Neurocase, 9,* 369–379.

Heimberg, R. G., Liebowitz, M. R., Hope, D. A., Schneier, F. R., Holt, C. S., Welkowitz, L. A., et al. (1998). Cognitive behavioral group therapy vs. phenelzine therapy for social phobia: 12-week outcome. *Archives of General Psychiatry, 55,* 1133–1141.

Heinssen, R. K., Perkins, D. O., Appelbaum, P. S., & Fenton, W. S. (2001). Informed consent in early psychosis research: NIMH workshop, November 15, 2000. *Schizophrenia Bulletin, 27,* 571–584.

Heisel, M. J., & Mongrain, M. (2004). Facial expressions and ambivalence: Looking for conflict in all the right faces. *Journal of Nonverbal Behavior, 28,* 35–52.

Heit, G., Smith, M. E., & Halgren, E. (1988). Neural encoding of individual words and faces by the human hippocampus and amygdala. *Nature, 333,* 773–775.

Held, J. D., Alderton, D. L., Foley, P. P., & Segall, D. O. (1993). Arithmetic reasoning gender differences: Explanations found in the Armed Services Vocational Aptitude Battery. *Learning and Individual Differences, 5,* 171–186.

Hellige, J. B. (1993). *Hemispheric asymmetry: What's right and what's left.* Cambridge, MA: Harvard University Press.

Hellige, J. B., & Michimata, C. (1989). Categorization versus distance: Hemispheric differences for processing spatial information. *Memory & Cognition, 17,* 770–776.

Helms, J. E., & Cook, D. A. (1999). *Using race and culture in counseling and psychotherapy: Theory and process.* Needham Heights, MA: Allyn & Bacon.

Helson, H. (1964). *Adaptation-level theory: An experimental and systematic approach to behavior.* New York: Harper & Row.

Hemsley, D. R. (1994). Perceptual and cognitive abnormalities as the bases for schizophrenic symptoms. In A. S. David & J. C. Cutting (Eds.), *The neuropsychology of schizophrenia* (pp. 97–116). Hillsdale, NJ: Lawrence Erlbaum Associates.

Henderlong, J., & Lepper, M. R. (2002). The effects of praise on children's intrinsic motivation: A review and synthesis. *Psychological Bulletin, 128,* 774–795.

Henley, N. M. (1977). *Body politics: Power, sex, and nonverbal communication.* Englewood Cliffs, NJ: Prentice-Hall.

Henry, B., Caspi, A., Moffitt, T. E., & Silva, P. A. (1996). Temperamental and familial predictors of violent and nonviolent criminal convictions: Age 3 to Age 18. *Developmental Psychology, 32,* 614–623.

Henry, J. P. (1977). *Stress, health, and the environment.* New York: Springer-Verlag.

Henry, W. P., Strupp, H. H., Schacht, T. E., & Gaston, L. (1994). Psychodynamic approaches. In A. E. Bergin & S. L. Garfield (Eds.), *Handbook of psychotherapy and behavior change* (4th ed., pp. 467–508). New York: John Wiley & Sons.

Hensel, H. (1982). *Thermal sensations and thermoreceptors in man.* Springfield, IL: Thomas.

Henslin, J. M. (1999). *Sociology: A down-to-earth approach* (4th ed.). Needham Heights, MA: Allyn & Bacon.

Henson, R., Shallice, T., & Dolan, R. (2000). Neuroimaging evidence for dissociable forms of repetition priming. *Science, 287,* 1269–1272.

Heponiemi, T., Keltikangas-Järvinen, L., Puttonen, S., & Ravaja, N. (2003). BIS/BAS sensitivity and self-rated affects during experimentally induced stress. *Personality & Individual Differences, 34,* 943–957.

Herbst, J. H., McCrae, R. R., Costa, P. T., Jr., Feaganes, J. R., & Siegler, I. C. (2000). Self-perceptions of stability and change in personality at midlife: The UNC Alumni Heart Study. *Assessment, 7,* 379–388.

Herman, C. P., Roth, D. A., & Polivy, J. (2003). Effects of the presence of others on food intake: A normative interpretation. *Psychological Bulletin, 129,* 873–886.

Herman-Giddens, M. E., Slora, E. J., Wasserman, R. C., Bourdony, C. J., Bhapkar, M. V., Koch, G. G., & Hasemeier, C. M. (1997). Secondary sexual characteristics and menses in young girls seen in office practice: A study from the Pediatric Research in Office Settings Network. *Pediatrics, 99,* 505–512.

Herman-Giddens, M. E., Wang, L., & Koch, G. (2001). Secondary sexual characteristics in boys: Estimates from the National Health and Nutrition Examination Survey III, 1988–1994. *Archives of Pediatric Adolescent Medicine, 155,* 1022–1028.

Hermann, J. A., deMontes, A. I., Dominguez, B., Montes, F., & Hopkins, B. L. (1973). Effects of bonuses for punctuality on the tardiness of industrial workers. *Journal of Applied Behavior Analysis, 4,* 267–272.

Hernandez, P. J., & Kelley, A. E. (2004). Long-term memory for instrumental responses does not undergo protein synthesis-dependent reconsolidation upon retrieval. *Learning & Memory, 11,* 748–754.

Herrera, H. (1983). *Frida: Biography of Frida Kahlo.* New York: Harper and Row.

Herrnstein, R. J., & Murray, C. (1994). *The bell curve: Intelligence and class structure in American life.* New York: Free Press.

Hershman, D. J., & Lieb, J. (1988). *The key to genius/manic-depression and the creative life.* New York: Prometheus Books.

Hershman, D. J., & Lieb, J. (1998). *Manic depression and creativity.* New York: Prometheus Books.

Hertzog, C., & Schaie, K. W. (1988). Stability and change in adult intelligence: 2. Simultaneous analysis of longitudinal means and covariance structures. *Psychology and Aging, 3,* 122–130.

Herxheimer, A., & Petrie, K. J. (2002). Melatonin for the prevention and treatment of jet lag. *Cochrane Library,* disk issue 4: CD001520.

Herz, R. S., & Schooler, J. W. (2002). A naturalistic study of autobiographical memories evoked by olfactory and visual cues: Testing the Proustian hypothesis. *American Journal of Psychology, 115,* 21–32.

Hess, T. M., Auman, C., Colcombe, S. J., & Rahhal, T. A. (2003). The impact of stereotype threat on age differences in memory performance. *Journals of Gerontology: Series B: Psychological Sciences & Social Sciences, 58,* P3–P11.

Hewstone, M., Rubin, M., & Willis, H. (2002). Intergroup bias. *Annual Review of Psychology, 51,* 575–604.

Hierholzer, R., Munson, J., Peabody, C., & Rosenberg, J. (1992). Clinical presentation of PTSD in World War II combat veterans. *Hospital and Community Psychiatry, 43,* 816–820.

Higgenbotham, H. N., West, S., & Forsyth, D. (1988). *Psychotherapy and behavior change: Social, cultural and methodological perspectives.* New York: Pergamon.

Higgens, S. T., & Morris, E. K. (1984). Generality of free-operant avoidance conditioning to human behavior. *Psychological Bulletin, 96,* 247–272.

Hill, J. O., & Peters, J. C. (1998). Environmental contributions to the obesity epidemic. *Science, 280,* 1371–1374.

Hill, L., Chorney, M. J., Jubinski, D., Thompson, L. A., & Plomin, R. (2002). A quantitative trait locus not associated with cognitive ability in children: A failure to replicate. *Psychological Science, 13,* 561–562.

Hill, L., Craig, I. W., Asherson, P., Ball, D., Eley, T., Ninomiya, T., et al. (1999). DNA pooling and dense marker maps: A systematic search for genes for cognitive ability. *Neuroreport, 10,* 843–848.

Hines, M. (2004). *Brain gender.* New York: Oxford University Press.

Hinton, D., Um, K., & Ba, P. (2001). Kyol goeu ("wind overload") Part I: A cultural syndrome of orthostatic panic among Khmer refugees. *Transcultural Psychiatry, 38,* 403–432.

Hirokawa, E. (2004). Effects of music listening and relaxation instructions on arousal changes and the working memory task in older adults. *Journal of Music Therapy, 41,* 107–127.

Hirsch, J. (1971). Behavior-genetic analysis and its biosocial consequences. In R. Cancro (Ed.), *Intelligence: Genetic and environmental influences* (pp. 88–106). New York: Grune & Stratton.

Hirsch, J. (1997). The triumph of wishful thinking over genetic irrelevance. *Cahiers de Psychologie Cognitive/Current Psychology of Cognition, 16,* 711–720.

Hobson, J. A. (1989). *Sleep.* New York: Scentific American Library.

Hobson, J. A. (1995). *Sleep.* New York: Scientific American Library.

Hobson, J. A., & McCarley, R. W. (1977). The brain as a dream state generator: An activation-synthesis hypothesis of the dream process. *American Journal of Psychiatry, 134,* 1335–1348.

Hobson, J. A., Pace-Schott, E., & Stickgold, R. (2000). Dreaming and the brain: Toward a cognitive neuroscience of conscious states. *Behavioral and Brain Sciences, 23.*

Hochman, D. W. (2000). Optical monitoring of neuronal activity: Brain-mapping on a shoestring. *Brain & Cognition, 42,* 56–59.

Hochschild, A. (1989). *The second shift: Working parents and the revolution at home.* New York: Viking.

Hockemeyer, J., & Smyth, J. (2002). Evaluating the feasibility and efficacy of the self-administered manual-based stress management intervention for individuals with asthma: Results from a controlled study. *Behavioral Medicine, 27,* 161–172.

Hoeksema-van Orden, C. Y. D., Gaillard, A. W. K., & Buunk, B. P. (1998). Social loafing under fatigue. *Journal of Personality and Social Psychology, 75,* 1179–1190.

Hoffman, D. D., & Richards, W. A. (1984). Parts of recognition. *Cognition, 18,* 65–96.

Hoffman, L. W. (1991). The influence of the family environment on personality: Accounting for sibling differences. *Psychological Bulletin, 110,* 187–203.

Hoffman, M. L. (2000). *Empathy and moral development: Implications for caring and justice.* New York: Cambridge University Press.

Hoffman, R. E., Hawkins, K. A., Gueorguieva, R., Boutros, N. N., Rachid, F., Carroll, K., & Krystal, J. H. (2003). Transcranial magnetic stimulation of left temporal cortex and medication-resistent auditory hallucinations. *Archives of General Psychiatry, 60,* 49–56.

Hofstede, G., & McCrae, R. R. (2004). Personality and culture revisited: Linking traits and dimensions of culture. *Cross-Cultural Research: The Journal of Comparative Social Science, 38,* 52–88.

Hohlstein, L. A., Smith, G. T., & Atlas, J. G. (1998). An application of expectancy theory to eating disorders: Development and validation of measures of eating and dieting expectancies. *Psychological Assessment, 10,* 49–58.

Hohman, G. W. (1966). Some effects of spinal cord lesions on experienced emotional feelings. *Psychophysiology, 3,* 143–156.

Holden, C. (1980). Identical twins reared apart. *Science, 207,* 1323–1328.

Holland, A. J., Sicotte, N., & Treasure, J. (1988). Anorexia nervosa: Evidence for a genetic basis. *Journal of Psychosomatic Research, 32,* 561–571.

Hollerman, J. R., & Schultz, W. (1998). Dopamine neurons report an error in the temporal prediction of reward during learning. *Nature Neuroscience, 1,* 304–309.

Hollis, K. L. (1997). Contemporary research on Pavlovian conditioning: A "new" functional analysis. *American Psychologist, 52,* 956–965.

Hollon, S. D., & Beck, A. T. (1994). Cognitive and cognitive-behavioral therapies. In A. E. Bergin & S. L. Garfield (Eds.), *Handbook of psychotherapy and behavior change* (4th ed., pp. 428–466). New York: John Wiley & Sons.

Hollon, S. D., DeRubeis, R. J., Shelton, R. C., Amsterdam, J. D., Salomon, R. M., O'Reardon, J. P., Lovett, M. L., Young, P. R., Haman, K. L., Freeman, B. B., & Gallop, R. (2005). Prevention of relapse following cognitive therapy vs. medications in moderate to severe depression. *Archives of General Psychiatry, 62,* 417–422.

Hollon, S. D., & Shelton, R. C. (2001). Treatment guidelines for major depressive disorder. *Behavior Therapy, 32,* 235–258.

Holmes, T. H., & Rahe, R. H. (1967). The social readjustment rating scale. *Journal of Psychosomatic Research, 11,* 213–218.

Honig, A., Hofman, A., Rozendaal, N., & Dingemans, P. (1997). Psycho-education in bipolar disorder: Effect on expressed emotion. *Psychiatry Research, 72,* 17–22.

Honorton, C. (1997). The Ganzfeld novice: Four predictors of initial ESP performance. *Journal of Parapsychology, 61,* 143–158.

Hooley, J. M., & Licht, D. M. (1997). Expressed emotional and causal attributions in the spouses of depressed patients. *Journal of Abnormal Psychology, 106,* 298–306.

Hooper, C. J., Luciana, M., Conklin, H. M., & Yarger, R. S. (2004). Adolescents' performance on the Iowa gambling task: implications for the development of decision making and ventromedial prefrontal cortex. *Developmental Psychology, 40,* 1148–1158.

Hooper, F. H., Hooper, J. O., & Colbert, K. K. (1984). *Personality and memory correlates of intellectual functioning: Young adulthood to old age.* Basel, Switzerland: Karger.

Horn, J. (1985). Remodeling old models of intelligence. In B. B. Wolman (Ed.), *Handbook of intelligence* (pp. 267–300). New York: Wiley.

Horn, J. (1989). Models of intelligence. In R. L. Linn (Ed.), *Intelligence: Measurement, theory, and public policy* (pp. 29–73). Urbana: University of Illinois Press.

Horn, J., & Cattell, R. B. (1966). Refinement and test of the theory of fluid and crystallized general intelligences. *Journal of Educational Psychology, 57,* 253–270.

Horn, J. L. (1986). Intellectual ability concepts. In R. J. Sternberg (Ed.), *Advances in the psychology of human intelligence* (Vol. 3, pp. 35–77). Hillsdale, NJ: Erlbaum.

Horn, J. L. (1994). Theory of fluid and crystallized intelligence. In R. J. Sternberg (Ed.), *The encyclopedia of human intelligence* (Vol. 1, pp. 443–451). New York: Macmillan.

Horn, J. L., & Masunaga, H. (2000). New directions for research into aging and intelligence: The development of expertise. In T. J. Perfect & E. A. Maylor (Eds.), *Models of cognitive aging* (pp. 125–159). Oxford, UK: Oxford University Press.

Horn, J. L., & Noll, J. (1994). A system for understanding cognitive capabilities: A theory and the evidence on which it is based. In D. K. Detterman (Ed.), *Current topics in human intelligence, Vol. 4: Theories of intelligence.* Norwood, NJ: Ablex.

Horn, J. L., & Noll, J. (1997). Human cognitive capabilities: Gf-Gc theory. In D. P. Flanagan, J. L. Genshaft, & P. L. Harrison (Eds.), *Contemporary intellectual assessment: Theories, tests and issues* (pp. 53–91). New York: Guilford.

Horowitz, M. J. (1998). Personality disorder diagnoses. *American Journal of Psychiatry, 155,* 1464.

Horvath, P., & Zuckerman, M. (1993). Sensation seeking, risk appraisal and risky behavior. *Personality & Individual Differences, 14,* 41–52.

Horwath, E., & Weissman, M. M. (2000). The epidemiology and cross-national presentation of obsessive-compulsive disorder. *Psychiatric Clinics of North America, 23,* 493–507.

Hoshi, Y., Oda, I., Wada, Y., Ito, Y., Yamashita, Y., Oda, M., et al. (2000). Visuospatial imagery is a fruitful strategy for the digit span backward task: A study with near-infrared optical tomography. *Cognitive Brain Research, 9,* 339–342.

House, J., Landis, K., & Umberson, D. (1988). Social relationships and health. *Science, 241,* 540–545.

Hovland, C. I., & Weiss, W. (1951). The influence of source credibility on communication effectiveness. *Public Opinion Quarterly, 15,* 635–650.

Howard, R. W. (2001). Searching the real world for signs of rising population intelligence. *Personality & Individual Differences, 30,* 1039–1058.

Hsee, C. K., Elaine, H., Carlson, J. G., & Chemtob, C. (1990). The effect of power on susceptibility to emotional contagion. *Cognition & Emotion, 4(4),* 327–340.

Hu, K., Ivanov, P., Hilton, M. F., Chen, Z., Ayers, R. T., Stanley, H. E., & Shea, S. A. (2004). Endogenous circadian rhythm in an index of cardiac vulnerability independent of changes in behavior. *Proceedings of the National Academy of Science, 101,* 18223–18227

Hu, W. (1990, Nov. 2–3). *The pragmatic motivation behind the use of the inverted sentence in the Beijing dialect.* Paper presented at Midwest Conference on Asian Affairs, Bloomington, IN.

Hu, W. (1995). Verbal semantics of presentative sentences. *Yuyan Yanjiu (Linguistic Studies), 29,* 100–112.

Hubacek, J. A., Pitha, J., Skodova, Z., Adamkova, V., Lanska, V., & Poledne, R. (2001). A possible role of apolipoprotein E polymorphism in predisposition to higher education. *Neuropsychobiology, 43,* 200–203.

Hubel, D. H., & Wiesel, T. N. (1962). Receptive fields, binocular interaction and functional architecture in the cat's visual cortex. *Journal of Physiology, 160,* 106–154.

Hubel, D. H., & Wiesel, T. N. (1974). Sequence regularity and orientation columns in the monkey striate cortex. *Journal of Comparative Neurology, 158,* 295–306.

Huen, K. F., Leung, S. S., Lau, J. T., Cheung, A. Y., Leung, N. K., & Chiu, M. C. (1997). Secular trend in the sexual maturation of southern Chinese girls. *Acta Paediatrica, 86,* 1121–1124.

Huerta, P. T., Scearce, K. A., Farris, S. M., Empson, R. M., & Prusky, G. T. (1996). Preservation of spatial learning in fyn tyrosine kinase knockout mice. *Neuroreport, 7,* 1685–1689.

Huff, D. (1954). *How to lie with statistics.* New York: Norton.

Hugdahl, K. (1995a). Classical conditioning and implicit learning: The right hemisphere hypothesis. In R. J. Davidson & K. Hugdahl (Eds.), *Brain asymmetry* (pp. 235–267). Cambridge, MA: MIT Press.

Hugdahl, K. (1995b). *Psychophysiology: The mind-body perspective.* Cambridge, MA: Harvard University Press.

Hugdahl, K. (2001). *Psychophysiology: The mind-body perspective* (2nd ed.). Cambridge, MA: Harvard University Press.

Hugdahl, K., & Davidson, R. J. (Eds.) (2003). *The asymmetrical brain.* Cambridge, MA: MIT Press.

Hugenberg, K., & Bodenhausen, G. V. (2003). Facing prejudice: Implicit prejudice and the perception of facial threat. *Psychological Science, 14,* 640–643.

Hugenberg, K., & Bodenhausen, G. V. (2004). Ambiguity in social categorization: The role of prejudice and facial affect in race categorization. *Psychological Science, 15,* 342–345.

Hui, C. H., & Triandis, H. C. (1986). Individualism-collectivism: A study of cross-cultural researchers. *Journal of Cross-cultural psychology, 17,* 225–248.

Hultman, C. M., Wieselgren, I., & Oehman, A. (1997). Relationships between social support, social coping and life events in the relapse of schizophrenic patients. *Scandinavian Journal of Psychology, 38,* 3–13.

Hummel, J. E., & Biederman, I. (1992). Dynamic binding in a neural network for shape recognition. *Psychological Review, 99,* 480–517.

Hummel, J. E., & Holyoak, K. J. (1997). Distributed representations of structure: A theory of analogical access and mapping. *Psychological Review, 104,* 427–466.

Humphreys, G. W., Riddoch, M. J., & Price, C. J. (1997). Top-down processes in object identification: Evidence from experimental psychology, neuropsychology and functional anatomy. *Philosophical Transactions of the Royal Society, London, 352,* 1275–1282.

Hunt, E. (2001). Multiple views of multiple intelligence. *Contemporary Psychology, 46,* 5–7.

Hunter, J. E. (1983). A casual analysis of cognitive ability, job knowledge, job performance, and supervisor ratings. In F. Landy, S. Zedeck, & J. Cleveland (Eds.), *Performance measurement and theory* (pp. 257–266). Hillsdale, NJ: Erlbaum.

Huppert, J. D., Bufka, L. F., Barlow, D. H., Gorman, J. M., Shear, M. K., & Woods, S. W. (2001). Therapists, therapist variables and cognitive-behavioral therapy outcome in a multicenter trial for panic disorder. *Journal of Consulting and Clinical Psychology, 69,* 747–755.

Hur, Y., & Bouchard, T. J., Jr. (1997). The genetic correlation between impulsivity and sensation seeking traits. *Behavior Genetics, 27,* 455–463.

Hurvich, L. M., & Jameson, D. (1957). An opponent-process theory of color vision. *Psychological Review, 64,* 384–404.

Husain, M., & Jackson, S. R. (2001). Vision: Visual space is not what it appears to be. *Current Biology, 11,* R753–R755.

Husain, M. M., Rush, A. J., Fink, M., Knapp, R., Petrides, G., Rummans, T., Biggs, M. M., O'Connor, K., Rasmussen, K., Litle, M., Zhao, W., Bernstein, H. J., Smith, G., Mueller, M., McClintock, S. M., Bailine, S. H., & Kellner, C. H. (2004). Speed of response and remission in major depressive disorder with acute electroconvulsive therapy (ECT): A consortium for research in ECT (CORE) report. *Journal of Clinical Psychiatry, 65,* 485–491.

Huttenlocher, P. (2002). *Neural plasticity.* Cambridge, MA: Harvard University Press.

Hyde, T. S., & Jenkins, J. J. (1973). Recall for words as a function of semantic, graphic, and syntactic orientation tasks. *Journal of Verbal Learning and Verbal Behavior, 12,* 471–480.

Hyman, A., Mentzer, T., & Calderone, L. (1979). The contribution of olfaction to taste discrimination. *Bulletin of Psychonomic Society, 13,* 359–362.

Iansek, R., & Porter, R. C. (1980). The monkey globus pallidus: Neuronal discharge properties in relation to movement. *Journal of Physiology, 301,* 439–455.

Ingledew, D. K., Hardy, L., & Cooper, C. L. (1997). Do resources bolster coping and does coping buffer stress? An organizational study with longitudinal aspect and control for negative affectivity. *Journal of Occupational Health Psychology, 2,* 118–133.

Inlow, J. K., & Restifo, L. L. (2004). Molecular and comparative genetics of mental retardation. *Genetics, 166*, 835–881.

Inman, D. J., Silver, S. M., & Doghramji, K. (1990). Sleep disturbance in post-traumatic stress disorder: A comparison with non-PTSD insomnia. *Journal of Traumatic Stress, 3*, 429–437.

Insel, T. R. (1992). Toward a neuroanatomy of obsessive-compulsive disorder. *Archives of General Psychiatry, 49*, 739–744.

Insel, T. R. (2000). Toward a neurobiology of attachment. *Review of General Psychology, 4*, 176–185.

Ione, A. (2003). Examining Semir Zeki's "Neural concept formation and art: Dante, Michelangelo, Wagner." *Journal of Consciousness Studies, 10*, 58–66.

Ironson, G., Wynings, C., Schneiderman, N., Baum, A., Rodriguez, M., Greenwood, D., et al. (1997). Posttraumatic stress symptoms, intrusive thoughts, loss, and immune function after Hurricane Andrew. *Psychosomatic Medicine, 59*, 128–141.

Isenberg, D. J. (1986). Group polarization: A critical review and meta-analysis. *Journal of Personality & Social Psychology, 50*, 1141–1151.

Itkowitz, N. I., Kerns, R. D., & Otis, J. D. (2003). Support and coronary heart disease: The importance of significant other responses. *Journal of Behavioral Medicine, 26*, 19–30.

Ivry, R. B., & Robertson, L. C. (1998). *The two sides of perception.* Cambridge, MA: The MIT Press.

Ivry, R. B., & Spencer, R. M. C. (2004). The neural representation of time. *Current Opinion in Neurobiology, 14*, 225–232.

Ivy, G., MacLeod, C., Petit, T., & Markus, E. (1992). A physiological framework for perceptual and cognitive changes in aging. In F. I. M. Craik & T. A. Salthouse (Eds.), *The handbook of aging and cognition* (pp. 273–314). Hillsdale, NJ: Erlbaum.

Izard, C. E. (1971). *The face of emotion.* New York: Appleton-Century-Crofts.

Jackson, N., & Butterfield, E. (1986). A conception of giftedness designed to promote research. In R. J. Sternberg & J. E. Davidson (Eds.), *Conceptions of giftedness* (pp. 151–181). New York: Cambridge University Press.

Jackson, S. E., Brett, J. F., Sessa, V. I., Cooper, D. M., Julin, J. A., & Peyronnin, K. (1991). Some differences make a difference: Individual dissimilarity and group heterogeneity as correlates of recruitment, promotion, and turnover. *Journal of Applied Psychology, 76*, 675–689.

Jacobs, G. D., Pace-Schott, E. F., Stickgold, R., & Otto, M. W. (2004). Cognitive behavior therapy and pharmacotherapy for insomnia: A randomized controlled trial and direct comparison. *Archives of Internal Medicine, 164*, 1888–1896.

Jacobs, N., Van Gestel, S., Derom, C., Thiery, E., Vernon, P., Derom, R., & Vlietinck, R. (2001). Heritability estimates of intelligence in twins: Effect of chorion type. *Behavior Genetics, 31*, 209–217.

Jacobs, R. C., & Campbell, D. T. (1961). The perpetuation of an arbitrary tradition through several generations of a laboratory microculture. *Journal of Abnormal and Social Psychology, 62*, 649–648.

Jacobsen, L. K., Mencl, W. E., Pugh, K. R., Skudlarski, P., & Krystal, J. H. (2004). Preliminary evidence of hippocampal dysfunction in adolescent MDMA ("ecstasy") users: Possible relationship to neurotoxic effects. *Psychopharmacology, 173*, 383–390.

Jacobsen, L. K., Southwick, S. M., & Kosten, T. R. (2001). Substance use disorders in patients with posttraumatic stress disorder: A review of the literature. *American Journal of Psychiatry, 158*, 1184–1190.

Jacobsen, T., Schröger, E., & Alter, K. (2004). Preattentive perception of vowel phonemes from variable speech stimuli. *Psychophysiology, 41*, 654–659.

Jadack, R. A., Hyde, J. S., Moore, C. F., & Keller, M. L. (1995). Moral reasoning about sexually transmitted diseases. *Child Development, 66*, 167–177.

Jaffee, S., Caspi, A., Moffitt, T. E., Belsky, J., & Silva, P. (2001). Why are children born to teen mothers at risk for adverse outcomes in young adulthood? Results from a 20-year longitudinal study. *Development & Psychopathology, 13*, 377–397.

Jakobson, R., & Halle, M. (1956). *Fundamentals of language.* The Hague: Mouton.

James, L. E., Burke, D. M., Austin, A., & Hulme, E. (1998). Production and perception of "verbosity" in younger and older adults. *Psychology and Aging, 13*, 355–367.

James, T. W., Culham, J., Humphrey, G. K., Milner, A. D., & Goodale, M. A. (2003). Ventral occipital lesions impair object recognition but not object-directed grasping: An fMRI study. *Brain, 126*, 2463–2475.

James, W. (1884). What is emotion? *Mind, 9*, 188–205.

Jameson, K. A., Highnote, S. M., & Wasserman, L. M. (2001). Richer color experience in observers with multiple photopigment opsin genes. *Psychonomic Bulletin & Review, 8*, 244–261.

Jamison, K. R. (1989). Mood disorders and patterns of creativity in British writers and artists. *Psychiatry, 52*, 125–134.

Jamison, K. R. (1993). *Touched with fire: Manic-depressive illness and the artistic temperament.* New York: Free Press.

Jamison, K. R. (1995). *An unquiet mind: A memoir of moods and madness.* New York: Vintage Books, p. 67.

Jamison, K. R., Gerner, R. H., Hammen, C., & Padesky, C. (1980). Clouds and silver linings: Positive experiences associated with primary affective disorders. *American Journal of Psychiatry, 137*, 198–202.

Janicak, P. G., Dowd, S. M., Martis, B., Alam, D., Beedle, D., Krasuski, J., et al. (2002). Repetitive transcranial magnetic stimulation versus electroconvulsive therapy for major depression: Preliminary results of a randomized trial. *Biological Psychiatry, 51*, 659–667.

Janis, I. L. (1982). *Victims of groupthink* (2nd ed.). Boston: Houghton Mifflin.

Janowsky, J. S., Oviatt, S. K., & Orwoll, E. S. (1994). Testosterone influences spatial cognition in older men. *Behavioral Neuroscience, 108*, 325–332.

Jansen, A., Nederkoorn, C., & Mulkens, S. (2005). Selective visual attention for ugly and beautiful body parts in eating disorders. *Behaviour Research and Therapy, 43*, 183–196.

Jason, L. A., & Fries, M. (2004). Helping parents reduce children's television viewing. *Research on Social Work Practice, 14*, 121–131.

Jeannerod, M. (1994). The representing brain: Neural correlates of motor intention and imagery. *Behavioral & Brain Sciences, 17*, 187–245.

Jeannerod, M. (1995). Mental imagery in the motor context. *Neuropsychologia, 33*, 1419–1432.

Jeannerod, M., & Frak, V. (1999). Mental imaging of motor activity in humans. *Current Opinion in Neurobiology, 9*, 735–739.

Jenike, M. (1984). Obsessive-compulsive disorder: A question of a neurologic lesion. *Comprehensive Psychiatry, 25*, 298–304.

Jenkins, J. M., Rasbash, J., & O'Connor, T. G. (2003). The role of the shared family context in differential parenting. *Developmental Psychology, 39*, 99–113.

Jenkins-Hall, K., & Sacco, W. P. (1991). Effects of client race and depression on evaluations by white therapists. *Journal of Social Clinical Psychology, 10*, 322–333.

Jenner, P. (2002). Pharmacology of dopamine agonists in the treatment of Parkinson's disease. *Neurology, 58*, S1–S8.

Jensen, A. R. (1980). *Bias in mental testing.* New York: Free Press.

Jensen, A. R. (1998). *The g factor: The science of mental ability.* Westport, CT: Praeger.

Jerome, E. M., & Liss, M. (2005). Relationships between sensory processing style, adult attachment, and coping. *Personality & Individual Differences, 38*, 1341–1352.

Jewett, D. L., Fein, G., & Greenberg, M. H. (1990). A double-blind study of symptom provocation to determine food sensitivity. *New England Journal of Medicine, 323*, 429–433.

Ji, L-J., Nisbett, R. E., & Su, Y. (2001). Culture, change, and prediction. *Psychological Science, 12*, 450–456.

Johansson, B., Hofer, S. M., Allaire, J. C., Maldonado-Molina, M. M., Piccinin, A. M., Berg, S., et al. (2004). Change in cognitive capabilities in the oldest old: The effects of proximity to death in genetically related individuals over a 6-year period. *Psychology and Aging, 19*, 145–156.

Johnson, J. D., Noel, N. E., & Sutter, J. (2000). Alcohol and male sexual aggression: A cognitive disruption analysis. *Journal of Applied Social Psychology.*

Johnson, M. H. (2001). Functional brain development in humans. *Nature Reviews Neuroscience, 2*, 475–483.

Johnson, M. K., Hashtroudi, S., & Lindsy, D. S. (1993). Source monitoring. *Psychological Bulletin, 114*, 3–28.

Johnson, M. K., Nolde, S. F., Mather, M., Kounios, J., Schacter, D. L., & Curran, T. (1997). The similarity of brain activity associated with true and false recognition memory depends on test format. *Psychological Science, 8*, 250–257.

Johnson, M. K., & Raye, C. L. (1981). Reality monitoring. *Psychological Review, 88*, 67–85.

Johnson, M. R., & Lydiard, B. (1995). Personality disorders in social phobia. *Psychiatric Annals, 25*, 554–563.

Johnson, S. C., Leslie, C., Baxter, L. C., Lana S., Wilder, L. S., Pipe, J. G., Heiserman, J. E., & Prigatano, G. P. (2002). Neural correlates of self-reflection. *Brain, 125*, 1808–1814.

Johnson, S. L., & Miller, I. (1997). Negative life events and time to recovery from episodes of bipolar disorder. *Journal of Abnormal Psychology, 106*, 449–457.

Johnson, S. L., Turner, R. J., & Iwata, N. (2003). BIS/BAS levels and psychiatric disorder: An epidemiological study. *Journal of Psychopathology & Behavioral Assessment, 25*, 25–36.

Johnson, S. M., & Roberts, J. E. (1995). Life events and bipolar disorder: Implications from biological theories. *Psychological Bulletin, 117*, 434–449.

Johnson, S. P., Bremner, J. G., Slater, A., Mason, U., Foster, K., & Cheshire, A. (2003). Infants' perception of object trajectories. *Child Development, 74*, 94–108.

Johnson, W., Bouchard, T. J., Jr., Krueger, R. F., McGue, M., & Gottesman, I. I. (2004). Just one g: Consistent results from three test batteries. *Intelligence, 32*, 95–107.

Johnson, W., McGue, M., & Krueger, R. F. (2005). Personality stability in late adulthood: A behavioral genetic analysis. *Journal of Personality, 73*, 523–551.

Johnston, L. C., & Macrae, C. N. (1994). Changing social stereotypes: The case of the information seeker. *European Journal of Social Psychology, 24*, 581–592.

Johnston, L. D., O'Malley, P. M., & Bachman, J. G. (1994). *National survey results on drug use from the Monitoring the Future study, 1975–1993* (NIH Publication No. 94–3810). Washington, DC: U.S. Government Printing Office.

Joiner, T. E. (1994). Contagious depression: Existence, specificity to depressed symptoms, and the role of reassurance seeking. *Journal of Personality and Social Psychology, 67*, 287–296.

Jolicoeur, P. (1998). Modulation of the attentional blink by on-line response selection: Evidence from speeded and unspeeded Task 1 decisions. *Memory & Cognition, 26*, 1014–1032.

Jones, D. (1996). *Physical attractiveness and the theory of sexual selection: Results from five populations.* Museum of Anthropology: University of Michigan.

Jones, N. A., Field, T., & Davalos, M. (1998). Massage therapy attenuates right frontal EEG asymmetry in one-month-old infants of depressed mothers. *Infant Behavior & Development, 21*, 527–530.

Jones, T. A., & Greenough, W. T. (1996). Ultrastructural evidence for increased contact between astrocytes and synapses in rats reared in a complex environment. *Neurobiology of Learning and Memory, 65*, 48–56.

Jonides, J., Lacey, S. C., & Nee, D. E. (2005). Processes of working memory in mind and brain. *Current Directions in Psychological Science, 14*, 2–5.

Jorm, A. F., Anstey, K. J., Christensen, H., & Rodgers, B. (2004). Gender differences in cognitive abilities: The mediating role of health state and health habits. *Intelligence, 32*, 7–23.

Joseph, J. (2001). Separated twins and the genetics of personality differences: A critique. *American Journal of Psychology, 114*, 1–30.

Joseph, S., Williams, R., & Yule, W. (1995). Psychosocial perspectives on post-traumatic stress disorder. *Clinical Psychology Review, 15,* 515–544.

Josephs, R. A., Newman, M. L., Brown, R. P., & Beer, J. M. (2003). Status, testosterone, and human intellectual performance: Stereotype threat as status concern. *Psychological Science, 14,* 158–163.

Joubert, S., Barbeau, E., Walter, N., Ceccaldi, M., & Poncet, M. (2003). Preservation of autobiographical memory in a case of pure progressive amnesia. *Brain & Cognition, 53,* 235–238.

Judd, C. M., Ryan, C. S., & Parke, B. (1991). Accuracy in the judgment of in-group and out-group variability. *Journal of Personality and Social Psychology, 61,* 366–379.

Judd, L. L., Akiskal, H. S., Maser, J. D., Zeller, P. J., Endicott, J., Coryell, W., et al. (1998). A prospective 12-year study of subsyndromal and syndromal depressive symptoms in unipolar major depressive disorders. *Archives of General Psychiatry, 55,* 694–700.

Judge, T. A., Erez, A., Bono, J. E., & Thoresen, C. J. (2002). Are measures of self-esteem, neuroticism, locus of control, and generalized self-efficacy indicators of a common core construct? *Journal of Personality and Social Psychology, 83,* 693–710.

Julesz, B. (1971). *Foundations of cyclopean perception.* Oxford, UK: University of Chicago Press.

Jusczyk, P. W. (1995). Language acquisition: Speech sounds and phonological development. In J. L. Miller & P. D. Eimas (Eds.), *Handbook of perception and cognition: Vol. 11. Speech, language, and communication* (pp. 263–301). Orlando, FL: Academic Press.

Kac, G., Auxiliadora de Santa Cruz Coel, & Velasquez-Melendez, G. (2000). Secular trend in age at menarche for women born between 1920 and 1979 in Rio de Janeiro, Brazil. *Annals of Human Biology, 27,* 423–428.

Kagan, J. (1989a). Temperamental contributions to social behavior. *American Psychologist, 44,* 668–674.

Kagan, J. (1989b). *Unstable ideas: Temperament, cognition, and self.* Cambridge, MA: Cambridge University Press.

Kagan, J. (1994). On the nature of emotion. *Monographs of the Society for Research in Child Development, 59,* 7–24, 250–283.

Kagan, J., Reznick, J. S., & Snidman, N. (1988). Biological bases of childhood shyness. *Science, 240,* 167–171.

Kagan, R. M., & Reid, W. J. (1986). Critical factors in the adoption of emotionally disturbed youths. *Child Welfare, 65,* 63–73.

Kahneman, D. (2003). A perspective on judgment and choice. *American Psychologist, 58,* 697–720.

Kahneman, D., Fredrickson, B. L., Schreiber, C. A., & Redelmeier, D. A. (1993). When more pain is preferred to less: Adding a better end. *Psychological Science, 4,* 401–405.

Kahneman, D., Krueger, A. B., Schkade, D. A., Schwarz, N., & Stone, A. A. (2004). A survey method for characterizing daily life experience: The day reconstruction method. *Science. 306,* 1776–1780.

Kahneman, D., & Tversky, A. (1996). On the reality of cognitive illusions: A reply to Gigerenzer's critique. *Psychological Review, 103,* 582–591.

Kaiser, C. R., Vick, S. B., & Major, B. (2004). A prospective investigation of the relationship between just-world beliefs and the desire for revenge after September 11, 2001. *Psychological Science, 15,* 503–506.

Kalivas, P. W., & Nakamura, M. (1999). Neural systems for behavioral activation and reward. *Current Opinion in Neurobiology, 9,* 223–227.

Källén, B. (2004). Use of folic acid supplementation and risk for dizygotic twinning. *Early Human Development, 80,* 143–151.

Kamin, L. (1969). Predictability, surprise, attention and conditioning. In B. A. Campbell and R. M. Church (Eds.), *Punishment and aversive behavior.* New York: Appleton-Century-Crofts.

Kamins, M. L., & Dweck, C. S. (1999). Person versus process praise and criticism: Implications for contingent self-worth and coping. *Developmental Psychology, 35,* 835–847.

Kanaya, T., Scullin, M. H., & Ceci, S. J. (2003). The Flynn effect and U.S. policies: The impact of rising IQ scores on American society via mental retardation diagnoses. *American Psychologist, 58,* 778–790.

Kandel, E. R., Schwartz, J. H., & Jessell, T. M. (2000). *Principles of neural science.* New York: McGraw-Hill/Appleton & Lange.

Kaniasty, K., & Norris, F. H. (1992). Social support and victims of crime: Matching event, support, and outcome. *American Journal of Community Psychology, 20,* 211–241.

Kaniasty, K. Z., Norris, F. H., & Murrell, S. A. (1990). Received and perceived social support following natural disaster. *Journal of Applied Psychology, 20,* 85–114.

Kanner, A. D., Coyne, J. C., Schaefer, C., & Lazarus, R. S. (1981). Comparison of two modes of stress management: Daily hassles and uplifts versus major life events. *Journal of Behavioral Medicine, 4,* 1–39.

Kanwisher, N. (1991). Repetition blindness and illusory conjunctions: Errors in binding visual types with visual tokens. *Journal of Experimental Psychology: Human Perception and Performance, 17,* 404–421.

Kanwisher, N. G. (1987). Repetition blindness: Type recognition without token individuation. *Cognition, 27,* 117–143.

Kaplan, M. F. (1987). The influencing process in group decision making. In C. Hendrick (Ed.), *Review of personality and social psychology* (Vol. 8, pp. 189–212). Newbury Park, CA: Sage.

Kaplowitz, P. B., Slora, E. J., Wasserman, R. C., Pedlow, S. E., & Herman-Giddens, M. E. (2001). Earlier onset of puberty in girls: Relation to increased body mass index and race. *Pediatrics, 108,* 347–353.

Karacan, I., Goodenough, D. R., Shapiro, A., & Starker, S. (1966). Erection cycle during sleep in relation to dream anxiety. *Archives of General Psychiatry, 15,* 183–189.

Karau, S. J., & Williams, K. D. (1993). Social loafing: A meta-analytic review and theoretical integration. *Journal of Personality and Social Psychology, 65,* 681–706.

Karkowski, L. M., & Kendler, K. S. (1997). An examination of the genetic relationship between bipolar and unipolar illness in an epidemiological sample. *Psychiatric Genetics, 7,* 159–163.

Karlamangla, A. S., Singer, B. H., McEwen, B. S., Rowe, J. W., & Seeman, T. E. (2002). Allostatic load as a predictor of functional decline. MacArthur studies of successful aging. *Journal of Clinical Epidemiology, 55,* 696–710.

Karni, A., & Sagi, D. (1993). The time course of learning a visual skill. *Nature, 365,* 250–252.

Karni, A., Tanne, D., Rubenstein, B. S., Askenasi, J. J. M., & Sagi, D. (1994). Dependence on REM sleep of overnight improvement of a perceptual skill. *Science, 265,* 679–682.

Karon, B. J. (2000). The clinical interpretation of the Thematic Apperception Test, Rorschach, and other clinical data: A reexamination of statistical versus clinical prediction. *Professional Psychology: Research and Practice, 31,* 230–233.

Karpov, Y. V., & Haywood, H. C. (1998). Two ways to elaborate Vygotsky's concept of mediation. *American Psychologist, 53,* 27–36.

Karuza, J., & Carey, T. O. (1984). Relevance preference and adaptiveness of behavioral blame for observers of rape victims. *Journal of Personality, 52* 249–262.

Kasch, K. L., Rottenberg, J., Arnow, B. A., & Gotlib, I. H. (2002). Behavioral activation and inhibition systems and the severity and course of depression. *Journal of Abnormal Psychology, 111,* 589–597.

Kasper, S., & Resinger, E. (2001). Panic disorder: The place of benzodiazepines and selective serotonin reuptake inhibitors. *European Neuropsychopharmacology, 11,* 307–321.

Kassin, S. M., & Wrightsman, L. S. (1981). Coerced confessions, judicial instruction, and mock juror verdicts. *Journal of Applied Social Psychology, 11,* 489–506.

Katigbak, M. S., Church, A. T., & Akamine, T. X. (1996). Cross-cultural generalizability of personality dimensions: Relating indigenous and imported dimensions in two cultures. *Journal of Personality and Social Psychology, 70,* 99–114.

Katigbak, M. S., Church, A. T., Guanzon-Lapena, M., Angleres, C., Annadaisy, J., & del Pilar, G. H. (2002). Are indigenous personality dimensions culture specific? Philippine inventories and the five-factor model. *Journal of Personality & Social Psychology, 82,* 89–101.

Katona, I., Sperlagh, B., Magloczky, Z., Santha, E., Kofalvi, A., Czirjak, S., et al. (2000). GABAergic interneurons are the targets of cannabinoid actions in the human hippocampus. *Neuroscience, 100,* 797–804.

Katz, J., Beach, S. R. H., & Joiner, T. E. (1999). Contagious depression in dating couples. *Journal of Social & Clinical Psychology, 18*(1), 1–13.

Katz, J., & Joiner, T. E., Jr. (2001). The aversive interpersonal context of depression: Emerging perspectives on depressotypic behavior. In R. M. Kowalski (Ed.), *Behaving badly: Aversive behaviors in interpersonal relationships* (pp. 117–147). Washington, DC: American Psychological Association.

Kauffmann, C. D., Cheema, M. A., & Miller, B. E. (2004). Slow right prefrontal transcranial magnetic stimulation as a treatment for medication-resistant depression: A double-blind, placebo-controlled study. *Depression & Anxiety, 19,* 59–62.

Kaufman, M. H. (1997). The teratogenic effects of alcohol following exposure during pregnancy, and its influence on the chromosome constitution of the pre-ovulatory egg. *Alcohol & Alcoholism, 32,* 113–128.

Kavanagh, D. J. (1992). Recent developments in expressed emotion in schizophrenia. *British Journal of Psychiatry, 148,* 601–620.

Kay, D. A., & Anglin, J. M. (1982). Overextension and underextension in the child's expressive and receptive speech. *Journal of Child Language, 9,* 83–98.

Kaye, W. H. (1995). Neurotransmitters and anorexia nervosa. In K. D. Brownell & C. G. Fairburn (Eds.), *Eating disorders and obesity: A comprehensive handbook* (pp. 255–260). New York: Guilford Press.

Kazdin, A. E. (1994). Methodology, design, and evaluation in psychotherapy research. In A. E. Bergin & S. L. Garfield (Eds.), *Handbook of psychotherapy and behavior change* (4th ed., pp. 19–71). New York: John Wiley & Sons.

Keane, T. M., Zimering, R. T., & Caddell, J. M. (1985). A behavioral formulation of post-traumatic stress disorder in Vietnam veterans. *Behavior Therapist, 8,* 9–12.

Keefe, R. S. E., Silva, S. G., Perkins, D. O., & Lieberman, J. A. (1999). The effects of atypical antipsychotic drugs on neurocognitive impairment in schizophrenia: A review and meta-analysis. *Schizophrenia Bulletin, 25,* 201–222.

Keith, P. M., & Schafer, R. B. (1991). *Relationships and well-being over the life stages.* New York: Praeger.

Keith, S. J., Regier, D. A., & Rae, D. S. (1991). Schizophrenic disorders. In L. N. Robins & D. A. Regier (Eds.), *Psychiatric disorders in America: The Epidemiologic Catchment Area Study* (pp. 33–52). New York: Free Press.

Keitner, G. I., Solomon, D. A., Ryan, C. E., Miller, I. W., & Mallinger, A. (1996). Prodromal and residual symptoms in bipolar I disorder. *Comprehensive Psychiatry, 37,* 362–367.

Keller, A., Ford, L. H., & Meacham, J. A. (1978). Dimensions of self-concept in preschool children. *Developmental Psychology, 14,* 483–489.

Keller, J., & Dauenheimer, D. (2003). Stereotype threat in the classroom: Dejection mediates the disrupting threat effect on women's math performance. *Personality & Social Psychology Bulletin, 29,* 371–381.

Kelley, H. H. (1972). Attribution in social interaction. In E. E. Jones, D. E. Kanouse, H. H. Kelley, R. E. Nisbett, S. Vahns, & B. Weiner (Eds.), *Attribution: Perceiving the causes of behavior.* Morristown, NJ: General Learning Press.

Kelley, H. H., & Michela, J. L. (1980). Attribution theory and research. *Annual Review of Psychology, 31,* 57–501.

Kelley, W. M., Macrae, C. N., Wyland, C. L., Caglar, S., Inati, S., & Heatherton, T. F. (2002). Finding the self?

An event-related fMRI study. *Journal of Cognitive Neuroscience, 14,* 785–794.

Kelley, W. M., Miezin, F. M., McDermott, K. B., Buckner, R. L., Raichle, M. E., Cohen, N. J., et al. (1998). Hemispheric specialization in human dorsal frontal cortex and medial temporal lobe for verbal and nonverbal memory encoding. *Neuron, 20,* 927–936.

Kellogg, R. T. (2001). Presentation modality and mode of recall in verbal false memory. *Journal of Experimental Psychology: Learning, Memory, & Cognition, 27,* 913–919.

Keltner, D., & Haidt, J. (2001). Social functions of emotions. In T. J. Mayne & G. A. Bonanno (Eds.), *Emotions: Current issues and future directions* (pp. 192–213). New York: Guilford Press.

Keltner, D., & Shiota, M. N. (2003). New displays and new emotions: A commentary on Rozin and Cohen (2003). *Emotion, 3,* 86–91.

Kemp, D. T. (1978). Stimulated acoustic emissions from within the human auditory system. *Journal of the Acoustical Society of America, 64,* 1386–1391.

Kemp, D. T. (1979). Evidence of mechanical nonlinearity and frequency selective wave amplification in the cochlea. *Archives of Otology, Rhinology, and Laryngology, 224,* 37–45.

Kempermann, G., & Gage, F. H. (1999). Experienced-dependent regulation of adult hippocampal neurogenesis: Effects of long-term stimulation and stimulus withdrawal. *Hippocampus, 9,* 321–332.

Kempermann, G., Kuhn, H. G., & Gage, F. H. (1998). Experience-induced neurogenesis in the senescent dentate gyrus. *Journal of Neuroscience, 18,* 3206–3212.

Kempermann, G., Wiscott, L., & Gage, F. H. (2004). Functional significance of adult neurogenesis. *Current Opinion in Neurobiology, 14,* 186–191.

Kendler, K. S., & Diehl, S. R. (1993). The genetics of schizophrenia: A current genetic-epidemiologic perspective. *Schizophrenia Bulletin, 19,* 87–112.

Kendler, K. S., Gardner, C. O., & Prescott, C. A. (1999). Clinical characteristics of major depression that predict risk of depression in relatives. *Archives of General Psychiatry, 56,* 322–327.

Kendler, K. S., Jacobsen, K. C., Myers, J., & Prescott, C. A. (2002). Sex differences in genetic and environmental risk factors for irrational fears and phobias. *Psychological Medicine, 32,* 209–217.

Kendler, K. S., MacLean, C., Neale, M., Kessler, R. C., Heath, A. C., & Eaves, L. J. (1991). The genetic epidemiology of bulimia nervosa. *American Journal of Psychiatry, 148,* 1627–1637.

Kendler, K. S., Myers, J., Prescott, C. A., & Neale, M. C. (2001). The genetic epidemiology of irrational fears and phobias in men. *Archives of General Psychiatry, 58,* 257–265.

Kendler, K. S., Neale, M. C., Kessler, R. C., Heath, A. C., & Eaves, L. J. (1992). The genetic epidemiology of phobias in women: The interrelationship of agoraphobia, social phobia, situational phobia and simple phobia. *Archives of General Psychiatry, 49,* 273–281.

Kennedy, S. H., Javanmard, M., Franco, J., & Vaccarino, F. J. (1997). A review of functional neuroimaging in mood disorders: Positron emission tomography and depression. *Canadian Journal of Psychiatry, 42,* 467–475.

Kenrick, D. T., & Funder, D. C. (1988). Profiting from the controversy: Lessons from the person-situation debate. *American Psychologist, 43,* 23–34.

Kerr, N. L., & Tindale, R. S. (2004). Group performance and decision making. *Annual Review of Psychology, 55,* 623–655.

Kessler, R. C., Berglund, P., Demler, O., Jin, R., Koretz, D., Merikangas, K. R., et al. (2003). The epidemiology of major depressive disorder: Results from the National Comorbidity Survey Replication (NCS-R). *JAMA: Journal of the American Medical Association, 289,* 3095–3105.

Kessler, R. C., & Frank, R. G. (1997). The impact of psychiatric disorders on work loss days. *Psychological Medicine, 27,* 861–873.

Kessler, R. C., McGonagle, K. A., Zhao, S., Nelson, C. B., Hughes, M., Eshelman, S., et al. (1994). Lifetime and 12-month prevalence of DSM-III–R psychiatric

disorders in the United States: Results from the National Comorbidity Study. *Archives of General Psychiatry, 51,* 8–19.

Kessler, R. C., Stein, M. B., & Berglund, P. (1998). Social phobia subtypes in the National Comorbidity Survey. *American Journal of Psychiatry, 155,* 613–619.

Kiecolt-Glaser, J., Glaser, R., Strain, E., Stout, J., Tarr, K., Holliday, J., & Speicher, C. (1986). Modulation of cellular immunity in medical students. *Journal of Behavioral Medicine, 9,* 5+.

Kiecolt-Glaser, J. K., & Glaser, R. (2002). Depression and immune function: Central pathways to morbidity and mortality. *Journal of Psychosomatic Research, 53,* 873–876.

Kiecolt-Glaser, J. K., Marucha, P. T., Atkinson, C., & Glaser, R. (2001). Hypnosis as a modulator of cellular immune dysregulation during acute stress. *Journal of Consulting and Clinical Psychology, 69,* 674–682.

Kiecolt-Glaser, J. K., Marucha, P. T., Malarky, W. B., Mercado, A. M., & Glaser, R. (1995). Slowing of wound healing by psychological stress. *Lancet, 346,* 1194–1196.

Kiecolt-Glaser, J. K., & Newton, T. L. (2001). Marriage and health: His and hers. *Psychological Bulletin, 127,* 472–503.

Kiecolt-Glaser, J. K., Page, G. G., Marucha, P. T., MacCallum, R. C., & Glaser, R. (1998). Psychological influences on surgical recovery perspectives from psychoneuroimmunology. *American Psychologist, 53,* 1209–1218.

Kiesler, C. A., & Kiesler, S. B. (1969). *Conformity.* Reading, MA: Addison-Wesley.

Kiffel, C., Campanella, S., & Bruyer, R. (2005). Categorical perception of faces and facial expressions: The age factor. *Experimental Aging Research, 31,* 119–147.

Kihlstrom, J. F. (1985). Hypnosis. *Annual Review of Psychology, 36,* 385–418.

Kilham, W., & Mann, L. (1974). Level of destructive obedience as a function of transmitter and executant roles in the Milgram obedience paradigm. *Journal of Personality and Social Psychology, 29,* 696–702.

Kim, J., Lim, J., & Bhargava, M. (1998). The role of affect in attitude formation: A classical conditioning. *Journal of the Academy of Marketing Science, 26,* 143–152.

Kim, K. H. S., Relkin, N. R., Lee, K., & Hirsch, J. (1997). Distinct cortical areas associated with native and second languages. *Nature, 388,* 171–174.

Kim, M., & Kim, H. (1997). Communication goals: Individual differences between Korean and American speakers. *Personality & Individual Differences, 23,* 509–517.

Kimata, H. (2003). Kissing reduces allergic skin wheal responses and plasma neurotrophin levels. *Physiology & Behavior, 80,* 395–398.

Kimble, G. A. (1981). Biological and cognitive constraints of learning. In L. T. Benjamin, Jr. (Ed.), *The G. Stanley Hall Lecture Series* (Vol. 1). Washington, DC: American Psychological Association.

Kimura, D. (1994). Body asymmetry and intellectual pattern. *Personality and Individual Differences, 17,* 53–60.

King, A. C., Oman, R. F., Brassington, G. S., Bliwise, D. L., & Haskell, W. L. (1997). Moderate-intensity exercise and self-rated quality of sleep in older adults: A randomized controlled trial. *Journal of the American Medical Association, 277,* 32–37.

King, L. A., King, D. W., Fairbank, J. A., Keane, T. M., & Adams, G. A. (1998). Resilience-recovery factors in post-traumatic stress disorder among female and male Vietnam veterans: Hardiness, postwar social support, and additional stressful life events. *Journal of Personality and Social Psychology, 74,* 420–434.

Kingdom, F. A. A., Beauce, C., & Hunter, L. (2004). Colour vision brings clarity to shadows. *Perception, 33,* 907–914.

Kirchler, E., & Davis, J. H. (1986). The influence of member status differences and task type on group consensus and member position change. *Journal of Personality & Social Psychology, 51,* 83–91.

Kirsch, I. (2004). Conditioning, expectancy, and the placebo effect: Comment on Stewart-Williams and Podd (2004). *Psychological Bulletin, 130,* 341–343.

Kirsch, I., & Lynn, S. J. (1999). Automaticity in clinical psychology. *American Psychologist, 54,* 504–515.

Kirsch, I., Lynn, S. J., Vigorito, M., & Miller, R. R. (2004). The role of cognition in classical and operant conditioning. *Journal of Clinical Psychology, 60,* 369–392.

Kirsch, I., Moore, T. J., Scoboria, A., & Nicholls, S. S. (2002a). The emperor's new drugs: An analysis of antidepressant medication data submitted to the U.S. Food and Drug Administration. *Prevention and Treatment, 5,* n.p.

Kirsch, I., & Sapirstein, G. (1998). Listening to Prozac but hearing placebo: A meta-analysis of antidepressant medication. *Prevention & Treatment, 1,* Article 0002a.

Kirsch, I., Scoboria, A., & Moore, T. J. (2002b). Antidepressants and placebos: Secrets, revelations, and unanswered questions. *Prevention & Treatment, 5,* n.p.

Kirschvink, J. L., Walker, M. M., & Diebel, C. E. (2001). Magnetite-based magnetoreception. *Current Opinion in Neurobiology, 11,* 462–467.

Kisilevsky, B. S., Hains, S. M. J., Jacquet, A. Y., Granier-Deferre, C., & Lecanuet, J. P. (2004). Maturation of fetal responses to music. *Developmental Science, 7,* 550–559.

Kisilevsky, B. S., & Low, J. A. (1998). Human fetal behavior: 100 years of study. *Developmental Review, 18,* 1–29.

Kitayama, S., Markus, H. R., Matsumoto, H., & Norasakkunkit, V. (1997). Individual and collective processes in the construction of the self: Self-enhancement in the United States and self-criticism in Japan. *Journal of Personality & Social Psychology, 72,* 1245–1267.

Kitchener, R. F. (1996). The nature of the social for Piaget and Vygotsky. *Human Development, 39,* 243–249.

Kitzmann, K. M. (2000). Effects of marital conflict on subsequent triadic family interactions and parenting. *Developmental Psychology, 36,* 3–13.

Kivlighan, D. M., Jr., Multon, K. D., & Patton, M. J. (2000). Insight and symptom reduction in time-limited psychoanalytic counseling. *Journal of Counseling Psychology, 47,* 50–58.

Kleemeier, R. W. (1962). Intellectual changes in the senium. *Proceedings of the American Statistical Association, 1,* 290–295.

Klein, D. F. (1993). False suffocation alarms, spontaneous panics, and related conditions: An integrative hypothesis. *Archives of General Psychiatry, 50,* 306–317.

Klein, E., Kreinin, I., Chistyakov, A., Koren, D., Mecz, L., Marmur, S., et al. (1999). Therapeutic efficacy of right prefrontal slow repetitive transcranial magnetic stimulation in major depression: A double-blind controlled study. *Archives of General Psychiatry, 56,* 315–320.

Kleinknecht, R. A., & Lenz, J. (1989). Blood/injury fear, fainting and avoidance of medical treatment: A family correspondence study. *Behaviour Research and Therapy, 27,* 537–547.

Kleinman, A. (1978). Clinical relevance of anthropological and cross-cultural research: Concepts and strategies. *American Journal of Psychiatry, 135,* 427–431.

Klerman, E. B., Davis, J. B., Duffy, J. F., Dijk, D., & Kronauer, R. E. (2004). Older people awaken more frequently but fall back asleep at the same rate as younger people. *Sleep: Journal of Sleep & Sleep Disorders Research, 27,* 793–798.

Klinkenborg, V. (1997, January 5). Awakening to sleep. *New York Times Magazine, 26.*

Klinteberg, B., Andersson, T., Magnusson, D., & Stattin, H. (1993). Hyperactive behavior in childhood as related to subsequent alcohol problems and violent offending: A longitudinal study of male subjects. *Personality and Individual Differences, 15,* 381–388.

Klosko, J. S., Barlow, D. H., Tassinari, R., & Cerny, J. A. (1990). A comparison of alprazolam and behavior therapy in treatment of panic disorder. *Journal of Consulting and Clinical Psychology, 58,* 77–84.

Knox, S. S., Weidner, G., Adelman, A., Stoney, C. M., & Ellison, R. C. (2004). Hostility and physiological risk in the National Heart, Lung, and Blood Institute Family Heart Study. *Archives of Internal Medicine, 1642,* 2442–2448.

Knutson, B., Adams, C. M., Fong, G. W., & Hommer, D. (2001). Anticipation of increasing monetary reward selectively recruits nucleus accumbens. *Journal of Neuroscience, 21:RC159,* 1–5.

Kochanska, G., DeVet, K., Goldman, M., Murray, K., & Putman, S. P. (1994). Maternal reports of conscience development and temperament in young children. *Child Development, 65,* 852–868.

Koffka, K. (1935). *Principles of Gestalt psychology.* New York: Harcourt Brace.

Koga, H., Yuzuriha, T., Yao, H., Endo, K., Hiejima, S., Takashima, Y., et al. (2002). Quantitative MRI findings and cognitive impairment among community dwelling elderly subjects. *Journal of Neurology, Neurosurgery & Psychiatry, 72,* 737–741.

Kohlberg, L. (1969). Stage and sequence: The cognitive-developmental approach to socialization. In D. S. Goslin (Ed.), *Handbook of socialization theory and research* (pp. 347–480). Chicago: Rand McNally.

Kohler, P. F., Rivera, V. J., Eckert, E. D., Bouchard, T. J., Jr., & Heston, L. (1985). Genetic regulation of immunoglobulin and specific antibody levels in twins reared apart. *Journal of Clinical Investigation, 75,* 883–888.

Kohler, S., Kapur, S., Moscovitch, M., Winocur, G., & Houle, S. (1995). Dissociation of pathways for object and spatial vision: A PET study in humans. *Neuroreport, 6,* 1865–1868.

Kohn, M. L., & Schooler, C. (1973). Occupational experience and psychological functioning: An assessment of reciprocal effects. *American Sociological Review, 38,* 97–118.

Kohut, H. (1977). *The restoration of self.* New York: International Universities Press.

Kolata, G. (1997, January 14). Which comes first: Depression or heart disease? *New York Times,* C1.

Kondo, T., Zakany, J., Innis, J. W., & Duboule, D. (1997). Of fingers, toes and penises. *Nature, 390,* 185–198.

Konishi, M. (1993). Listening with two ears. *Scientific American, 268,* 66–73.

Konishi, S., Nakajima, K., Uchida, I., Kikyo, H., Kameyama, M., & Miyashita, Y. (1999). Common inhibitory mechanism in human inferior prefrontal cortex revealed by event-related functional MRI. *Brain, 122,* 981–991.

Kop, W. J. (2003). The integration of cardiovascular behavioral medicine and psychoneuroimmunology: New developments based on converging research fields. *Brain, Behavior & Immunity, 17,* 233–237.

Koren, D., Norman, D., Cohen, A., Berman, J., & Klein, E. M. (2005). Increased PTSD risk with combat-related injury: A matched comparison study of injured and uninjured soldiers experiencing the same combat events. *American Journal of Psychiatry, 162,* 276–282.

Kosslyn, S. M. (1975). On retrieving information from visual images. In R. Schank & B. Nash-Webber (Eds.), *Theoretical issues in natural language processing.* Arlington, VA: Association for Computational Linguistics.

Kosslyn, S. M. (1976). Can imagery be distinguished from other forms of internal representation? Evidence from studies of information retrieval times. *Memory and Cognition, 4,* 291–297.

Kosslyn, S. M. (1978). Measuring the visual angle of the mind's eye. *Cognitive Psychology, 10,* 356–389.

Kosslyn, S. M. (1980). *Image and mind.* Cambridge, MA.: Harvard University Press.

Kosslyn, S. M. (1987). Seeing and imagining in the cerebral hemispheres: A computational approach. *Psychological Review, 94,* 148–175.

Kosslyn, S. M. (1994a). *Elements of graph design.* New York: Freeman.

Kosslyn, S. M. (1994b). *Image and brain: The resolution of the imagery debate.* Cambridge, MA: MIT Press.

Kosslyn, S. M. (2006). *Graph design for the eye and mind.* New York: Oxford University Press.

Kosslyn, S. M., Digirolamo, G. J., Thompson, W. L., & Alpert, N. M. (1998). Mental rotation of objects versus hands: Neural mechanisms revealed by positron emission tomography. *Psychophysiology, 35,* 151–161.

Kosslyn, S. M., Ganis, G., & Thompson, W. L. (2001). Neural foundations of imagery. *Nature Reviews Neuroscience, 2,* 635–642.

Kosslyn, S. M., & Koenig, O. (1995). *Wet mind: The new cognitive neuroscience.* New York: Free Press.

Kosslyn, S. M., Koenig, O., Barrett, A., Cave, C. B., Tang, J., & Gabrieli, J. D. E. (1989). Evidence for two types of spatial representations: Hemispheric specialization for categorical and coordinate relations. *Journal of Experimental Psychology: Human Perception and Performance, 15,* 723–735.

Kosslyn, S. M., Pascual-Leone, A., Felician, O., Camposano, S., Keenan, J. P., Thompson, W. L., et al. (1999). The role of area 17 in visual imagery: Convergent evidence from PET and rTMS. *Science, 284,* 167–170.

Kosslyn, S. M., Segar, C., Pani, J., & Hillger, L. A. (1990). When is imagery used in everyday life? A diary study. *Journal of Mental Imagery. 14,* 131–152.

Kosslyn, S. M., & Thompson, W. L. (2003). When is early visual cortex activated during visual mental imagery? *Psychological Bulletin, 129,* 723–746.

Kosslyn, S. M., Thompson, W. L, & Ganis, G. (2006). *The case for mental imagery.* New York: Oxford University Press.

Kosslyn, S. M., Thompson, W. L., Kim, I. J., & Alpert, N. M. (1995). Topographical representations of mental images in primary visual cortex. *Nature, 378,* 496–498.

Koster, E. H. W., Rassin, E., Crombez, G., & Näring, G. W. B. (2003). The paradoxical effects of suppressing anxious thoughts during imminent threat. *Behaviour Research & Therapy, 41,* 1113–1120.

Kozak, M. J., Liebowitz, M. R., & Foa, E. B. (2000). Cognitive behavior therapy and pharmacotherapy for obsessive-compulsive disorder: The NIMH-sponsored collaborative study. In W. K. Goodman, M. V. Rudorfer, & J. D. Masur (Eds.). *Obsessive-compulsive disorder: Contemporary issues in treatment* (pp. 501–530). Mahwah, NJ: Erlbaum.

Kozel, F. A., Padgett, T. M., & George, M. S. (2004). A replication study of the neural correlates of deception. *Behavioral Neuroscience, 118,* 852–856.

Kozel, F. A., Revell, L. J., Lorberbaum, J. P., Shastri, A., Elhai, J. D., Horner, M. D., et al. (2004). A pilot study of functional magnetic resonance imaging brain correlates of deception in healthy young men. *Journal of Neuropsychiatry and Clinical Neurosciences, 16,* 295–305.

Kozhevnikov, M., Kosslyn, S. M., & Shephard, J. M. (2005). Spatial versus object visualizers: A new characterization of visual cognitive style. *Memory and Cognition, 33(4),* 710–726.

Kraepelin, E. (1921). Ueber Entwurtzelung [Depression]. *Zietschrift fuer die Gasamte Neurologie und Psychiatrie, 63,* 1–8.

Kramer, M. S., Cutler, N., Feighner, J., Shrivastava, R., Carman, J., Sramek, J. J., et al. (1998). Distinct mechanism for antidepressant activity by blockade of central substance P receptors. *Science, 281,* 1640–1645.

Krause, N. (2004). Stressors arising in highly valued roles, meaning in life, and the physical health status of older adults. *Journals of Gerontology: Series B: Psychological Sciences and Social Sciences, 59B,* S287–S291.

Kreitzer, A. C., & Regehr, W. G. (2001a). Retrograde inhibition of presynaptic calcium influx by endogenous cannabinoids at excitatory synapses onto Purkinje cells. *Neuron, 29,* 717–727.

Kreitzer, A. C., & Regehr, W. G. (2001b). Cerebellar depolarization-induced suppression of inhibition is mediated by endogenous cannabinoids. *Journal of Neuroscience, 21,* RC174.

Krieger, S., Lis, S., & Gallhofer, B. (2001). Cognitive subprocesses and schizophrenia: A reaction time decomposition. *Acta Psychiatrica Scandanavia Supplement, 104,* 18–27.

Kringelbach, M. L., Araujo, I., & Rolls, E. T. (2001). Face expression as a reinforcer activates the orbitofrontal cortex in an emotion-related reversal task. *Neuroimage 13(6),* S433.

Kritchevsky, M., Chang, J., & Squire, L. R. (2004). Functional amnesia: Clinical description and neuropsychological profile of 10 cases. *Learning and Memory, 11,* 213–226.

Kruglanski, A. W., & Webster, D. M. (1996). Motivated closing of the mind: "Seizing" and "freezing." *Psychological Review, 103,* 263–283.

Krummenacher, J., Müller, H. J., & Heller, D. (2002). Visual search for dimensionally redundant pop-out targets: Parallel-coactive processing of dimensions is location specific. *Journal of Experimental Psychology: Human Perception & Performance, 28,* 1303–1322.

Kubzansky, L. D., & Kawachi, I. (2000). Going to the heart of the matter: Do negative emotions cause coronary heart disease? *Journal of Psychosomatic Research, 48,* 323–337.

Kubzansky, L. D., Kawachi, I., Weiss, S. T., & Sparrow, D. (1998). Anxiety and coronary heart disease: A synthesis of epidemiological, psychological, and experimental evidence. *Annals of Behavioral Medicine, 20,* 47–58.

Kuhl, P. K. (1989). On babies, birds, modules, and mechanisms: A comparative approach to the acquisition of vocal communication. In R. J. Dooling & S. H. Husle (Eds.), *The comparative psychology of audition: Perceiving complex sounds* (pp. 379–419). Hillsdale, NJ: Erlbaum.

Kuhl, P. K., Williams, K. A., Lacerda, F., Stevens, K. N., et al. (1992). Linguistic experience alters phonetic perception in infants by 6 months of age. *Science, 255,* 606–608.

Kuipers, E., Fowler, D., Garety, P. Chisholm, D., Freeman, D., Dunn, G., et al. (1998). London–East Anglia randomised controlled trial of cognitive-behavioural therapy for psychosis. III: Followup and economic evaluation at 18 months. *British Journal of Psychiatry, 173,* 61–68.

Kuipers, E., Garety, P., Fowler, D., Dunne, G., Bebbington, P., Freeman, D., & Hadley, C. (1997). London–East Anglia randomised controlled trial of cognitive-behavioural therapy for psychosis. I: Effects of the treatment phase. *British Journal of Psychiatry, 171,* 319–327.

Kulhara, P., & Chakrabarti, S. (2001). Culture and schizophrenia and other psychotic disorders. *Psychiatric Clinics of North American, 24,* 449–464.

Kuncel, N. R., Hezlett, S. A., & Ones, D. S. (2004). Academic performance, career potential, creativity, and job performance: Can one construct predict them all? *Journal of Personality and Social Psychology, 86,* 148–161.

Kunda, Z., & Oleson, K. C. (1995). Maintaining stereotypes in the face of disconfirmation: Constructing grounds for subtyping deviants. *Journal of Personality and Social Psychology, 68,* 565–579.

Kung, J., Su, N., Fan, R., Chai, S., & Shyu, B. (2003). Contribution of the anterior cingulate cortex to laser-pain conditioning in rats. *Brain Research, 970,* 58–72.

Kuntze, M. F., Stoermer, R., Mager, R., Roessler, A., Mueller-Spahn, F., & Bullinger, A. H. (2001). Immersive virtual environments in cue exposure. *CyberPsychology & Behavior, 4,* 497–501.

Kunz, G., Beil, D., Deiniger, H., Einspanier, A., Mall, G., & Leyendecker, G. (1997). The uterine peristaltic pump. Normal and impeded sperm transport within the female genital tract. *Advances in Experimental Medicine and Biology, 424,* 267–277.

Kuperberg, G., & Heckers, S. (2000). Schizophrenia and cognitive function. *Current Opinion in Neurobiology, 10,* 205–210.

Kushner, M., Riggs, D., Foa, E., & Miller, S. (1992). Perceived controllability and the development of posttraumatic stress disorder (PTSD) in crime victims. *Behaviour Research and Therapy, 31,* 105–110.

Kvale, G., & Hugdahl, K. (1994). Cardiovascular conditioning and anticipatory nausea and vomiting in cancer patients. *Behavioral Medicine, 20,* 78–83.

Kwong, M. J., Bartholomew, K., Henderson, A. J. Z., & Trinke, S. J. (2003). The intergenerational transmission of relationship violence. *Journal of Family Psychology, 17,* 288–301.

Lachman, M. E., & Weaver, S. L. (1998). The sense of control as a moderator of social class differences in health and well-being. *Journal of Personality and Social Psychology, 74,* 763–773.

Lacks, P., & Morin, C. M. (1992). Recent advances in the assessment and treatment of insomnia. *Journal of Consulting & Clinical Psychology, 60,* 586–594.

Laeng, B., Chabris, C. F., & Kosslyn, S. M. (2003). Asymmetries in encoding spatial relations. In K. Hugdahl & R. J. Davidson (Eds.), *The asymmetrical brain* (pp. 303–339). Cambridge, MA: MIT Press.

Lafuente, M. J., Grifol, R., Segarra, J., Soriano, J., Gorba, M. A., & Montesinos, A. (1997). Effects of the Firstart method of prenatal stimulation on psychomotor development: The first six months. *Pre- & Peri-Natal Psychology Journal, 11,* 151–162.

Laird, J. D. (1974). Self-attribution of emotion: The effects of expressive behavior on the quality of emotional experience. *Journal of Personality & Social Psychology, 29,* 475–486.

Laird, J. D. (1984). The real role of facial response in the experience of emotion: A reply to Tourangeau and Ellsworth, and others. *Journal of Personality & Social Psychology, 47,* 909–917.

Lakey, B., & Dickenson, L. G. (1994). Antecedents of perceived support: Is perceived family environment generalized to new social relationships? *Cognitive Therapy and Research, 18,* 39–53.

Lakey, B., & Heller, K. (1988). Social support from a friend, perceived support, and social problem solving. *American Journal of Community Psychology, 16,* 811–824.

Lalumiere, M. L., & Quinsey, L. (1998). Pavlovian conditioning of sexual interests in human males. *Archives of Sexual Behavior, 27,* 241–252.

Lam, A. G., & Sue, S. (2001). Client diversity. *Psychotherapy: Theory, Research, Practice, Training, 38,* 479–486.

Lam, R. W., Bartley, S., Yatham, L. N., Tam, E. M., & Zis, A. P. (1999). Clinical predictors of short-term outcome in electroconvulsive therapy. *Canadian Journal of Psychiatry, 44,* 158–163.

Lambert, A. J. (1995). Stereotypes and social judgment: The consequences of group variability. *Journal of Personality and Social Psychology, 68,* 388–403.

Lambert, M. J. (1983). Introduction to assessment of psychotherapy outcome: Historical perspective and current issues. In M. J. Lambert, E. R. Christensen, & S. S. De-Julio (Eds.), *The assessment of psychotherapy outcome* (pp. 3–32). New York: Wiley-Interscience.

Lamm, C., Windischberger, C., Leodolter, U., Moser, E., & Bauer, H. (2001). Evidence for premotor cortex activity during dynamic visuospatial imagery from single-trial functional magnetic resonance imaging and event-related slow cortical potentials. *NeuroImage, 14,* 268–283.

Land, E. H. (1959). Experiments in color vision. *Scientific American, 200,* 84–99.

Land, E. H. (1977). The retinex theory of color vision. *Scientific American, 237,* 108–128.

Land, E. H. (1983). Recent advances in retinex theory and some implications for cortical computations: Color vision and the natural image. *Proceedings of the National Academy of Sciences, USA, 80,* 5163–5169.

Landrigan, C. P., Rothschild, J. M., Cronin, J. W., Kaushal, R., Burdick, E., Katz, J. T., Lilly, C. M., Stone, C. M., Lockley, S. W., Bates, D. W., & Czeisler, C. A. (Harvard Work Hours, Health and Safety Group). (2004). Effect of reducing interns' work hours on serious medical errors in intensive care units. *New England Journal of Medicine, 351,* 1838–1848.

Lang, F. R., & Carstensen, L. L. (2002). Time counts: Future time perspective, goals, and social relationships. *Psychology & Aging, 17,* 125–139.

Lang, P. J. (1994). The varieties of emotional experience: A meditation on the James-Lange theory. *Psychological Review (Special Issue: The Centennial Issue), 101,* 211–221.

Lang, P. J. (1995). The emotion probe: Studies of motivation and attention. *American Psychologist, 50,* 372–385.

Lang, P. J., Bradley, M. M., Cuthbert, B. N. (1990). Emotion, attention, and the startle reflex. *Psychological Review, 97,* 377–395.

Lange, C. (1887). *Uber gemuthsbewegungen.* Leipzig: Theodor Thomas.

Langer, E. J., & Rodin, J. (1976). The effects of choice and enhanced personal responsibility for the aged: A field experiment in an institutional setting. *Journal of Personality & Social Psychology, 34,* 191–198.

Lansford, J. E., Sherman, A. M., & Antonucci, T. C. (1998). Satisfaction with social networks: An examination of socioemotional selectivity theory across cohorts. *Psychology & Aging, 13,* 544–552.

Lapsley, D. K. (1990). Egocentrism theory and the "new look" at the imaginary audience and personal fable in adolescence. In R. M. Lerner, A. C. Petersen, & J. Brooks-Gunn (Eds.), *The encyclopedia of adolescence* (pp. 281– 286). New York: Garland.

Lapsley, D. K., Jackson, S., Rice, K., & Shadid, G. (1988). Self-monitoring and the "new look" at the imaginary audience and personal fable: An ego-developmental analysis. *Journal of Adolescent Research, 3,* 17–31.

Larsen, J. T., McGraw, A. P., & Cacioppo, J. T. (2001). Can people feel happy and sad at the same time? *Journal of Personality & Social Psychology, 81,* 684–696.

Larson, J. A. (1932). *Lying and its detection: A study of deception and deception tests.* Chicago: University of Chicago Press.

Larson, R., & Richards, M. H. (1994). *Divergent realities: The emotional lives of mothers, fathers, and adolescents.* New York: Basic Books.

Larson, S. A., Lakin, K. C., Anderson, L., Kwak, N., Lee, J., & Anderson, D. (2001). Prevalence of mental retardation and developmental disabilities: Estimates from the 1994/1995 National Health Interview Survey Disability Supplements. *American Journal on Mental Retardation, 106,* 231–252.

Laruelle, M., Kegeles, L. S., & Abi-Dargham A. (2003). Glutamate, dopamine, and schizophrenia: from pathophysiology to treatment. *Annals of the New York Academy of Sciences, 1003,* 138–158.

Latané, B., Williams, K., & Harkins, S. (1979). Many hands make light the work: The causes and consequences of social loafing. *Journal of Personality and Social Psychology, 37,* 822–832.

Laughlin, P. R., & Ellis, A. L. (1986). Demonstrability and social combination processes in mathematical intellectual tasks. *Journal of Experimental Social Psychology, 22,* 177–189.

Laursen, B., Coy, K. C., & Collins, W. A. (1998). Reconsidering changes in parent-child conflict across adolescence: A meta-analysis. *Child Development, 69,* 817–832.

Lawless, H. T. (1984). Oral chemical irritation: Psychophysical properties. *Chemical Senses, 9,* 143–155.

Lazarus, R. S. (1984). On the primacy of cognition. *American Psychologist, 39,* 124–129.

Lazarus, R. S., & Folkman, S. (1984). *Stress, appraisal, and coping.* New York: Springer.

Lazev, A. B., Herzog, T. A., & Brandon, T. H. (1999). Classical conditioning of environmental cues to cigarette smoking. *Experimental and Clinical Psychopharmacology, 7,* 56–63.

Lê, S., Cardebat, D., Boulanouar, K., Hénaff, M., Michel, F., Milner, D., Dijkerman, C., Puel, M., & Démonet, J. (2002). Seeing, since childhood, without ventral stream: A behavioural study. *Brain, 125,* 58–74.

Leavitt, F. (1997). False attribution of suggestibility to explain recovered memory of childhood sexual abuse following extended amnesia. *Child Abuse & Neglect, 21,* 265–272.

LeBihan, D., Jezzard, P., Turner, R., Cuenod, C. A., Pannier, L., & Prinster, A. (1993). Practical problems and limitations in using Z-maps for processing of brain function MR images. *Abstracts of the 12th Meeting of the Society of Magnetic Resonance in Medicine, 1,* 11.

Leccese, A. P. (1991). *Drugs and society: Behavioral medicines and abusable drugs.* Englewood Cliffs, NJ: Prentice-Hall.

LeDoux, J. E. (1996). *The emotional brain: The mysterious underpinnings of emotional life.* New York: Simon & Schuster.

LeDoux, J. E., Wilson, D. H., & Gazzaniga, M. S. (1977). A divided mind: Observations on the conscious properties of the separated hemispheres. *Annals of Neurology, 2,* 417–421.

Lee, A. M., & Lee, S. (1996). Disordered eating and its psychosocial correlates among Chinese adolescent females in Hong Kong. *International Journal of Eating Disorders, 20,* 177–183.

Lee, E. S. (1951). Negro intelligence and selective migration: A Philadelphia test of the Klineberg hypothesis. *American Sociological Review, 16,* 227–233.

Lee, J. L. C., Everitt, B. J., & Thomas, K. L. (2004). Independent cellular processes for hippocampal memory consolidation and reconsolidation. *Science, 304,* 339–343.

Lee, S. (1996). Clinical lessons from the cross-cultural study of anorexia nervosa. *Eating Disorders Review, 7*(3), 1.

Lee, S., & Lee, A. M. (2000). Disordered eating in three communities of China: A comparative study of female high school students in Hong Kong, Shenzhen, and rural Hunan. *International Journal of Eating Disorders, 27,* 317–327.

Lehman, A. F., & Steinwachs, D. M. (1998). Translating research into practice: The Schizophrenia Patients Outcome Research Team (PORT) Treatment Recommendations. *Schizophrenia Bulletin, 24,* 1–10.

Leibowitz, H. W. (1971). Sensory, learned and cognitive mechanisms of size perception. *Annals of the New York Academy of Sciences, 188,* 47–62.

Leichsenring, F. (2001). Comparative effects of short-term psychodynamic psychotherapy and cognitive-behavioral therapy in depression: A meta-analytic approach. *Clinical Psychology Review, 21,* 401–419.

Leichsenring, F., Rabung, S., & Leibing, E. (2004). The efficacy of short-term psychodynamic psychotherapy in specific psychiatric disorders: A meta-analysis. *Archives of General Psychiatry, 61,* 1208–1216.

Lemme, B. H. (1995). *Development in adulthood.* Needham Heights, MA: Allyn & Bacon.

Lennon, R., & Eisenberg, N. (1987). Gender and age differences in empathy and sympathy. In N. Eisenberg & J. Strayer (Eds.), *Empathy and its development* (pp. 195–217). New York: Cambridge University Press.

Lensvelt-Mulders, G., & Hettema, J. (2001a). Analysis of genetic influences on the consistency and variability of the Big Five across different stressful situations. *European Journal of Personality, 15,* 355–371.

Lensvelt-Mulders, G., & Hettema, J. (2001b). Genetic analysis of autonomic reactivity to psychologically stressful situations. *Biological Psychology, 58,* 25–40.

Lepper, M. R., Greene, D., & Nisbett, R. E. (1973). Undermining children's intrinsic interest with extrinsic reward: A test of the "overjustification" hypothesis. *Journal of Personality and Social Psychology, 28,* 129–137.

Leproult, R., Copinschi, G., Buxton, O., & Van Cauter, E. (1997). Sleep loss results in an elevation of cortisol levels the next evening. *Sleep, 20,* 865–870.

Leproult, R., Van Reeth, O., Byrne, M. M., Sturis, J., & Van Cauter, E. (1997). Sleepiness, performance, and neuroendocrine function during sleep deprivation: Effects of exposure to bright light or exercise. *Journal of Biological Rhythms, 12,* 245–258.

Lerner, M. J. (1980). *The belief in a just world: A fundamental illusion.* New York: Plenum Press.

Lesch, K. P. (2003). Neuroticism and serotonin: A developmental genetic perspective. In R. Plomin, J. C. DeFries, et al. (Eds.), *Behavioral genetics in the postgenomic era* (pp. 389–423). Washington, DC: American Psychological Association.

Lester, B. M. (2000). Prenatal cocaine exposure and child outcome: A model for the study of the infant at risk. *Israel Journal of Psychiatry & Related Sciences, 37,* 223–235.

Lester, B. M., LaGasse, L. L., & Seifer, R. (1998). Cocaine exposure and children: The meaning of subtle effects. *Science, 282,* 633–634.

Leuchter, A. F., Cook, I. A., Witte, E. A., Morgan, M., & Abrams, M. (2002). Changes in brain function of depressed subjects during treatment with placebo. *American Journal of Psychiatry, 159,* 122–129.

LeVay, S. (1991). A difference in hypothalamic structure between heterosexual and homosexual men. *Science, 253,* 1034–1037.

LeVay, S., & Hamer, D. (1994). Evidence for a biological influence in male homosexuality. *Scientific American, 270,* 44–49.

Levenson, R. W., Ekman, P., & Friesen, W. V. (1990). Voluntary facial action generates emotion-specific autonomic nervous system activity. *Psychophysiology, 27,* 363–384.

Leventhal, G. S., Singer, R., & Jones, S. (1965). The effects of fear and specificity of recommendation upon attitudes and behavior. *Journal of Personality and Social Psychology, 2,* 20–29.

Levie, W. H., & Lentz, R. (1982). Effects of text illustrations: A review of research. *Educational Communication and Technology Journal, 30,* 195–232.

Levin, J. R., Anglin, G. J., & Carney, R. N. (1987). On empirically validating functions of pictures in prose. In D. M. Willows & H. A. Houghton (Eds.), *The psychology of illustration: I. Basic research* (pp. 51–85). New York: Springer-Verlag.

Levin, R. J. (1994). Human male sexuality: Appetite and arousal, desire and drive. In C. R. Legg & D. Booth (Eds.), *Appetite: Neural and behavioral bases* (pp. 127–164). New York: Oxford University Press.

Levin, R. S. (1980). The physiology of sexual function in women. *Clinics in Obstetrics and Gynaecology, 7,* 213–252.

Levine, A. S., & Billington, C. J. (1997). Why do we eat? A neural systems approach. *Annual Review of Nutrition, 17,* 597–619.

Levine, B. (2004). Autobiographical memory and the self in time: Brain lesion effects, functional neuroanatomy, and lifespan development. *Brain & Cognition, 55*(1), 54–68.

Levine, B., Turner, G. R., Tisserand, D., Hevenor, S. J., Graham, S. J., & McIntosh, A. R. (2004). The functional neuroanatomy of episodic and semantic autobiographical remembering: A prospective functional MRI study. *Journal of Cognitive Neuroscience, 16,* 1633–1646.

Levine, D. N. (1982). Visual agnosia in monkey and man. In D. J. Ingle, M. A. Goodale, & R. J. W. Mansfield (Eds.), *Analysis of visual behavior* (pp. 629–670). Cambridge: MIT Press.

Levine, J. M., & Moreland, R. L. (1998). Small groups. In D. T. Gilbert, S. T. Fiske, & G. Lindzey (Eds.), *The handbook of social psychology* (4th ed., pp. 415–469). New York: McGraw-Hill.

Levine, L. J., & Bluck, S. (2004). Painting with broad strokes: Happiness and the malleability of event memory. *Cognition & Emotion, 18,* 559–574.

Levine, R. L., & Bluni, T. D. (1994). Magnetic field effects on spatial discrimination learning in mice. *Physiology and Behavior, 55,* 465–467.

Levitt, A. G., & Wang, Q. (1991). Evidence for language-specific rhythmic influences in the reduplicative babbling of French- and English-learning infants. *Language and Speech, 34,* 235–249.

Levitt, M. J., Weber, R. A., & Guacci, N. (1993). Convoys of social support: An intergenerational analysis. *Psychology and Aging, 8,* 323–326.

Levy, B., Ashman, O., & Dror, I. (1999–2000). To be or not to be: The effects of aging stereotypes on the will to live. *Omega: Journal of Death & Dying, 40,* 409–420.

Levy, S. M., Herberman, R. B., Lippman, M. N., & d'Angelo, T. (1987). Correlation of stress factors with sustained depression of natural killer cell activity and predicted prognosis in patients with breast cancer. *Journal of Clinical Oncology, 5,* 348–353.

Levy, S. M., Herberman, R. B., Maluish, A. M., Schlien, B., & Lippman, M. (1985). Prognostic risk assessment in primary breast cancer by behavioral and immunological parameters. *Health Psychology, 4,* 99–113.

Levy, S. M., Lee, J., Bagley, C., & Lippman, M. (1988). Survival hazards analysis in first year recurrent breast cancer patients: Seven-year follow-up. *Psychosomatic Medicine, 50,* 520–528.

Lewinsohn, P. M., Allen, N. B., Seeley, J. R., & Gotlib, I. H. (1999). First onset versus recurrence of depression: Differential processes of psychosocial risk. *Journal of Abnormal Psychology, 108,* 483–489.

Lewinsohn, P. M., Rohde, P., Seeley, J. R., & Fischer, S. A. (1993). Age-cohort changes in the lifetime occurrence of depression and other mental disorders. *Journal of Abnormal Psychology, 102,* 110–120.

Lewis, M., & Brooks-Gunn, J. (1979). *Social cognition and the acquisition of self.* New York: Plenum.

Lewontin, R. C. (1976a). Further remarks on race and the genetics of intelligence. In N. J. Block & G. Dworkin (Eds.), *The IQ controversy* (pp. 107–112). New York: Pantheon Books.

Lewontin, R. C. (1976b). Race and intelligence. In N. J. Block & G. Dworkin (Eds.), *The IQ controversy* (pp. 78–92). New York: Pantheon Books.

Li, D., Chokka, P., & Tibbo, P. (2001). Toward an integrative understanding of social phobia. *Journal of Psychiatry & Neuroscience, 26,* 190–202.

Li, N. P., Bailey, J. M., Kenrick, D. T., & Linsenmeier, J. A. W. (2002). The necessities and luxuries of mate preferences: Testing the tradeoffs. *Journal of Personality & Social Psychology, 82,* 947–955.

Li, S-C., Lindenberger, U., & Sikström, S. (2001). Aging cognition: From neuromodulation to representation. *Trends in Cognitive Science, 5,* 479–486.

Li, S-C., Lindenberger, U., Hommel, B., Aschersleben, G., Prinz, W., & Baltes, P. B. (2004). Transformations in the couplings among intellectual abilities and constituent cognitive processes across the life span. *Psychological Science, 15,* 155–163.

Libby, L. K., Eibach, R. P., & Gilovich, T. (2005). Here's looking at me: The effect of memory perspective on assessments of personal change. *Journal of Personality & Social Psychology, 88,* 50–62.

Liben, L. S., Susman, E. J., Finkelstein, J. W., Chinchilli, V. M., Kunselman, S., Schwab, J., et al. (2002). The effects of sex steroids on spatial performance: A review and an experimental clinical investigation. *Developmental Psychology, 38,* 236–253.

Lickliter, R., & Honeycutt, H. (2003a). Developmental dynamics: toward a biologically plausible evolutionary psychology. *Psychological Bulletin, 129,* 819–835.

Lickliter, R., & Honeycutt, H. (2003b). Developmental dynamics and contemporary evolutionary psychology: Status quo or irreconcilable views? Reply to Bjorklund (2003), Krebs (2003), Buss and Reeve (2003), Crawford (2003), and Tooby et al. (2003). *Psychological Bulletin, 129,* 866–872.

Liddell, C. (1997). Every picture tells a story—or does it? Young South African children interpreting pictures. *Journal of Cross-Cultural Psychology, 28,* 266–282.

Lieberman, J. A., Tollefson, G. D., Charles, C., Zipursky, R., Sharma, T., Kahn, R. S., Keefe, R. S. E., Green, A. I., Gur, R. E., McEvoy, J., Perkins, D., Hamer, R. M., Gu, H., & Tohen, M., for the HGDH Study Group (2005). Antipsychotic drug effects on brain morphology in first-episode psychosis. *Archives of General Psychiatry, 62,* 361–370.

Lieberman, M. D., Ochsner, K. N., Gilbert, D. T., & Schacter, D. L. (2001). Attitude change in amnesia and under cognitive load. *Psychological Science, 12,* 135–140.

Light, L. (1991). Memory and aging: Four hypotheses in search of data. *Annual Review of Psychology, 42,* 333–376.

Lilenfeld, L. R., Kaye, W. H., Greeno, C. G., Merikangas, K. R., Plotnicov, K., Pollice, C., et al. (1998). A controlled family study of anorexia nervosa and bulimia nervosa: Psychiatric disorders in first-degree relatives and effects of proband comorbidity. *Archives of General Psychiatry, 55,* 603–610.

Lilienfeld, S. O., Wood, J. M., & Garb, H. N. (2000). The scientific status of projective techniques. *Psychological Science in the Public Interest, 1,* 27–66.

Lindblom, K. (2001). Cooperating with Grice: A cross-disciplinary metaperspective on uses of Grice's cooperative principle. *Journal of Pragmatics, 33,* 1601–1623.

Linden, M., Zubraegel, D., Baer, T., Franke, U., & Schlattmann, P. (2005). Efficacy of cognitive behaviour therapy in generalized anxiety disorders. *Psychotherapy & Psychosomatics, 74,* 36–42.

Lindsay, D. S., & Johnson, M. K. (1989). The eyewitness suggestibility effect and memory for source. *Memory & Cognition, 17,* 349–358.

Lindsay, S., Hagen, L., Read, J. D., Wade, K. A., & Garry, M. (2004). True photographs and false memories. *Psychological Science, 15,* 149–154.

Linley, P. A., & Joseph, S. (2004). Positive change following trauma and adversity: A review. *Journal of Traumatic Stress, 17,* 11–21.

Linner, B. (1972). *Sex and society in Sweden.* New York: Harper Colophon.

Linnoila, M., Virkkunen, M., Scheinin, M., Nuutila, A., Romin, R., & Goodwin, F. K. (1983). Low cerebrospinal fluid 5-hydroxindoleacetic acid concentration differentiates impulsive from non-impulsive violent behavior. *Life Sciences, 33,* 2609–2614.

Linville, P. W., & Fischer, G. W. (1993). Exemplar and abstraction models of perceived group variability and stereotypicality. *Social Cognition, 11,* 92–125.

Liotti, M., Mayberg, H. S., McGinnis, S., Brannan, S. L., & Jerabek, P. (2002). Unmasking disease-specific cerebral blood flow abnormalities: Mood challenge in patients with remitted unipolar depression. *American Journal of Psychiatry, 159,* 1830–1840.

Lipkus, I. M., & Siegler, I. C. (1993). The belief in a just world and perceptions of discrimination. *Journal of Psychology, 127,* 465–474.

Lissek, S., Powers, A. S., McClure, E. B., Phelps, E. A., Woldehawariat, G., Grillon, C., & Pine, D. S. (2005). Classical fear conditioning in the anxiety disorders: A meta-analysis. *Behaviour Research and Therapy, 43,* 1391–1424.

Lisspers, J., Sundin, Ö., Öhman, A., Hofman-Bang, C., Rydén, L., & Nygren, A. (2005). Long-term effects of lifestyle behavior change in coronary artery disease: Effects on recurrent coronary events after percutaneous coronary intervention. *Health Psychology, 24,* 41–48.

Liu, D., Diorio, J., Tannenbaum, B., Caldji, C., Francis, D., Freedman, A., et al. (1997). Maternal care, hippocampal glucocorticoid receptors, and hypothalamic-pituitary-adrenal responses to stress. *Science, 277,* 1659–1662.

Liu, J. H., & Latané, B. (1998). Extremitization of attitudes: Does thought- and discussion-induced polarization cumulate? *Basic & Applied Social Psychology, 20,* 103–110.

Livesley, W. J. (1998). Suggestions for a framework for an empirically based classification of personality disorder. *Canadian Journal of Psychiatry 43,* 137–147.

Livesley, W. J. (Ed.). (2001). *Handbook of personality disorders: Theory, research, and treatment.* New York: Guilford Press.

Livesley, W. J., Jang, K. L., & Vernon, P. A. (2003). Genetic basis of personality structure. In T. Millon & M. J. Lerner (Eds.), *Handbook of psychology: Personality and social psychology* (Vol. 5, pp. 59–83). New York: John Wiley.

Lobaugh, N. J., Cole, S., & Rovet, J. F. (1998). Visual search for features and conjunctions in development. *Canadian Journal of Experimental Psychology, 52,* 201–212.

Locke, S. E., Kraus, L., Leserman, J., Hurst, M. W., Heisel, J. S., & Williams, R. M. (1984). Life change stress, psychiatric symptoms, and natural killer-cell activity. *Psychosomatic Medicine, 46,* 441–453.

Lockley, S. W., Cronin, J. W., Evans, E. E., Cade, B. E., Lee, C. J., Landrigan, C. P., Rothschild, J. M., Katz, J. T., Lilly, C. M., Stone, P. H., Aeschbach, D., & Czeisler, C. A. (2004). Effect of reducing interns' weekly work hours on sleep and attentional failures. *New England Journal of Medicine, 351,* 1829–1837.

Loehlin, J. C. (1989). Partitioning environmental and genetic contributions to behavioral development. *American Psychologist, 44,* 1285–1292.

Loehlin, J. C. (1992). *Genes and environment in personality development.* Newbury Park, CA: Sage.

Loehlin, J. C., Horn, J. M., & Willerman, L. (1981). Personality resemblance in adoptive families. *Behavior Genetics, 11,* 309–330.

Loftus, E. F. (1993). The reality of repressed memories. *American Psychologist, 48,* 518–537.

Loftus, E. F. (2004). Memories of things unseen. *Current Directions in Psychological Science, 13,* 145–147.

Loftus, E. F., & Pickrell, J. E. (1995). The formation of false memories. *Psychiatric Annals, 25,* 720–725.

Long, J. M., Mouton, P. R., Jucker, M., & Ingram, D. K. (1999). What counts in brain aging? Design-based stereological analysis of cell number. *Journals of Gerontology: Series A: Biological Sciences & Medical Sciences, 54A,* B407–B417.

Lonky, M. L. (2003). Human consciousness: A systems approach to the mind/brain interaction. *Journal of Mind & Behavior, 24,* 91–118.

Looren de Jong, H. (1996). Levels: Reduction and elimination in cognitive neuroscience. In C. W. Tolman, F. Cherry, et al. (Eds.), *Problems of theoretical psychology* (pp. 165–172). North York, ON, Canada: Captus Press.

Loori, A. A. (2005). Multiple intelligences: A comparative study between the preferences of males and females. *Social Behavior & Personality, 33,* 77–88.

Lopes, P. N., Salovey, P., Côté, S., & Beers, M. (2005). Emotion regulation abilities and the quality of social interaction. *Emotion, 5,* 113–118.

Lopes, P. N., Salovey, P., & Straus, R. (2003). Emotional intelligence, personality, and the perceived quality of social relationships. *Personality and Individual Differences, 35,* 641–658.

Lorenzo-Hernandez, J. (1998). How social categorization may inform the study of Hispanic immigration. *Hispanic Journal of Behavioral Sciences, 20,* 39–59.

Losch, M., & Cacioppo, J. (1990). Cognitive dissonance may enhance sympathetic tonus, but attitudes are changed to reduce negative effect rather than arousal. *Journal of Experimental Social Psychology, 26,* 289–304.

Lott, B. (1996) Politics or science? The question of gender sameness/difference. *American Psychologist, 51,* 153–164.

Lou, H. C., Hansen, D., Nordentoft, M., Pryds, O., et al. (1994). Prenatal stressors of human life affect fetal brain development. *Developmental Medicine & Child Neurology, 36,* 826–832.

Lowe, C. F. (1979). Determinants of human operant behaviour. In M. D. Zeiler & P. Harzem (Eds.), *Advances in analysis of behavior (Vol. 1): Reinforcement and the organization of behavior.* New York: Wiley.

Lowe, P. (1999, May 2). Alike and different. *Denver Post.*

Lowe, S. M. (1995). Essay. In F. Kahlo, *The diary of Frida Kahlo: An intimate self-portrait* (pp. 25–29). New York: Abradale Press.

Lu, L. (1999). Personal or environmental causes of happiness: A longitudinal analysis. *Journal of Social Psychology, 139,* 79–90.

Lu, L., Shih, J. B., Lin, Y. Y., & Ju, L. S. (1997). Personal and environmental correlates of happiness. *Personality & Individual Differences, 23,* 453–462.

Lubin, A. J. (1972). *Stranger on the earth: Vincent van Gogh.* New York: Da Capo Press.

Lubinski, D. (2000). Scientific and social significance of assessing individual differences: Sinking shafts at a few critical points. *Annual Review of Psychology, 51,* 405–444.

Lubinski, D. (2004). Introduction to the special section on cognitive abilities: 100 years after Spearman's (1904) " 'General intelligence,' objectively determined and measured." *Journal of Personality and Social Psychology, 86,* 96–111.

Lucas, R. J., Freedman, M. S., Muñoz, M., Garcia-Fernandez, J-M., & Foster, R. G. (1999). Regulation of the mammalian pineal by non-rod, non-cone, ocular photoreceptors. *Science, 284,* 505–507.

Luce, G. G. (1971). *Biological rhythms in human and animal physiology.* New York: Dover.

Luck, S. J., Vogel, E. K., & Shapiro, K. L. (1996). Word meanings can be accessed but not reported during the attentional blink. *Nature, 383,* 616–618.

Luckow, A., Reifman, A., & McIntosh, D. N. (1998, August). *Gender differences in coping: A meta-analysis.* Poster session presented at the 106th Annual Convention of the American Psychological Association, San Francisco, CA.

Luna, B. (2004). Algebra and the adolescent brain. *Trends in Cognitive Sciences, 8,* 437–439.

Luna, B., Garver, K. E., Urban, T. A., Lazar, N. A., & Sweeney, J. A. (2004). Maturation of cognitive processes from late childhood to adulthood. *Child Development, 75,* 1357–1372.

Lunzer, E. A. (1978). Formal reasoning: A reappraisal. In B. Z. Presseisen, D. Goldstein, & M. H. Appel (Eds.), *Topics in cognitive development: Vol. 2. Language and operational thought* (pp. 47–76). New York: Plenum.

Luria, A. R. (1968). *The mind of a mnemonist: A little book about a vast memory* (L. Solotaroff, Trans.). Cambridge, MA: Harvard University Press. (Original work published 1887)

Lush, J. L. (1937). *Animal breeding plans.* Ames, IA: Collegiate Press.

Lydon, J. E., Jamieson, D. W., & Zanna, M. P. (1988). Interpersonal similarity and the social and intellectual dimensions of first impressions. *Social Cognition, 6,* 269–286.

Lykken, D., & Tellegen, A. (1996). Happiness is a stochastic phenomenon. *Psychological Science, 7,* 186–189.

Lykken, D., Bouchard, T. J., Jr., McGue, M., & Tellegen, A. (1993). Heritability of interests: A twin study. *Journal of Applied Psychology, 78,* 649–661.

Lykken, D. T. (1959). The GSR in the detection of guilt. *Journal of Applied Psychology, 43,* 385–388.

Lykken, D. T. (1960). The validity of the guilty knowledge technique: The effects of faking. *Journal of Applied Psychology, 44,* 258–262.

Lynn, R. (1998). Has the black-white intelligence difference in the United States been narrowing over time? *Personality and Individual Differences, 25,* 999–1002.

Lynn, R., & Irwing, P. (2004). Sex differences on the progressive matrices: A meta-analysis. *Intelligence, 32,* 481–498.

Lynn, R., & Martin, T. (1997). Gender differences in extraversion, neuroticism, and psychoticism in 37 nations. *Journal of Social Psychology, 137,* 369–373.

Lyon, H. M., Startup, M., & Bentall, R. P. (1999). Social cognition and the manic defense: Attributions, selective attention, and self-schema in bipolar affective disorder. *Journal of Abnormal Psychology, 108,* 273–282.

Lyons, E. A., & Levi, C. S. (1994). Sperm are not like salmon: Altered myometrial contractility is significant in unexplained infertility rates. *Radiology, 193[P],* 144.

Lyons, M. J., Goldberg, J., Eisen, S. A., True, W., Tsuang, M. T., Meyer, J. M., & Henderson, W. G. (1993). Do genes influence exposure to trauma: A twin study of combat. *American Journal of Medical Genetics (Neuropsychiatric Genetics), 48,* 22–27.

Lytton, H., & Romney, D. M. (1991). Parents' differential socialization of boys and girls: A meta-analysis. *Psychological Bulletin, 109,* 267–296.

Lyubomirsky, S. (2001). Why are some people happier than others? The role of cognitive and motivational processes in well-being. *American Psychologist, 56,* 239–249.

Maas, J. B. (1998). *Power sleep.* New York: Harper Perennial.

Macaskill, N. D., & Macaskill, A. (1996). Rational-emotive therapy plus pharmacotherapy versus pharmacotherapy alone in the treatment of high cognitive dysfunction depression. *Cognitive Therapy & Research, 20,* 575–592.

Maccoby, E. E. (1988). Gender as a social category. *Developmental Psychology, 26,* 755–765.

Maccoby, E. E. (1990). Gender and relationships: A developmental account. *American Psychologist, 45,* 513–520.

Maccoby, E. E. (1991). Gender and relationships: A reprise. *American Psychologist, 46,* 538–539.

Maccoby, E. E., & Jacklin, C. N. (1987). Gender segregation in childhood. In H. W. Reese (Ed.), *Advances in child development and behavior* (Vol. 20, pp. 239–288). New York: Academic Press.

MacDonald, J. A., & Balakrishnan, J. D. (in press). Signal detection theory. *Encyclopedia of Cognitive Science.*

MacGregor, A. J., Griffiths, G. O., Baker, J., & Spector, T. D. (1997). Determinants of pressure pain threshold in adult twins: Evidence that shared environmental influences predominate. *Pain, 73,* 253–257.

Macht, M., Roth, S., & Ellgring, H. (2002). Chocolate eating in healthy men during experimentally induced sadness and joy. *Appetite, 39,* 147–158.

Macklin, M. L., Metzger, L. J., Litz, B. T., McNally, R. J., Lasko, N. B., Orr, S. P., & Pitman, R. K. (1998). Lower precombat intelligence is a risk factor for posttraumatic stress disorder. *Journal of Consulting & Clinical Psychology, 66,* 323–326.

Macmillan, M. (1992). Inhibition and the control of behavior: From Gall to Freud via Phineas Gage and the frontal lobes. *Brain & Cognition, 19,* 72–104.

Macmillan, M. B. (1986). A wonderful journey through skull and brains: The travels of Mr. Gage's tamping iron. *Brain & Cognition, 5,* 67–107.

MacPhillamy, D. J., & Lewinsohn, P. M. (1974). Depression as a function of levels of desired and obtained pleasure. *Journal of Abnormal Psychology, 83,* 651–657.

Macrae, C. N., Bodenhausen, G. V., Milne, A. B., & Jetten, J. (1994). Out of mind but back in sight: Stereotypes on the rebound. *Journal of Personality and Social Psychology, 67,* 808–817.

Macrae, C. N., Moran, J. M., Heatherton, T. F., Banfield, J. F., & Kelley, W. M. (2004). Medial prefrontal activity predicts memory for self. *Cerebral Cortex, 14,* 647–654.

Madden, K. S. (2003). Catecholamines, sympathetic innervation, and immunity. *Brain, Behavior & Immunity, 17,* S5–S10.

Madill, A., & Holch, P. (2004). A range of memory possibilities: The challenge of the false memory debate for clinicians and researchers. *Clinical Psychology & Psychotherapy, 11,* 299–310.

Magee, W. L., & Davidson, J. W. (2002). The effect of music therapy on mood states in neurological patients: A pilot study. *Journal of Music Therapy, 39,* 20–29.

Magnusson, D. (2003). The person approach: Concepts, measurement models, and research strategy. *New Directions in Child Adolescent Development, 101,* 3–23.

Maher, B. A. (1966). *Principles of psychopathology: An experimental approach.* New York: McGraw-Hill.

Maier, K. J., Waldstein, S. R., & Synowski, S. J. (2003). Relation of cognitive appraisal to cardiovascular reactivity, affect, and task engagement. *Annals of Behavioral Medicine, 26,* 32–41.

Major, B., & O'Brien, L. T. (2005). The social psychology of stigma. *Annual Review of Psychology, 56,* 393–421.

Malan, D. H. (1976). *The frontier of brief psychotherapy: An example of the convergence of research and clinical practice.* New York: Plenum Medical.

Maletzky, B. M. (2004). The first-line use of electroconvulsive therapy in major affective disorders. *Journal of ECT, 20,* 112–117.

Malik, M. L., Beutler, L. E., Alimohamed, S., Gallagher-Thompson, D., & Thompson, L. (2003). Are all cognitive therapies alike? A comparison of cognitive and noncognitive therapy process and implications for the application of empirically supported treatment. *Journal of Consulting & Clinical Psychology, 71,* 150–158.

Malina, R. M., & Bouchard, C. (1991). *Growth, maturation, and physical activity.* Champaign, IL: Human Kinetics.

Mandler, G. (1967). Organization in memory. In K. W. Spence & J. T. Spence (Eds.), *The psychology of learning and motivation* (Vol. 1, pp. 327–372). San Diego, CA: Academic Press.

Manfro, G. G., Otto, M. W., McArdle, E. T., Worthington, J. J., III, Rosenbaum, J. F., & Pollack, M. H. (1996). Relationship of antecedent stressful life events to childhood and family history of anxiety and the course of panic disorder. *Journal of Affective Disorders, 41,* 135–139.

Mann, S., Vrij, A., & Bull, R. (2004). Detecting true lies: Police officers' ability to detect suspects' lies. *Journal of Applied Psychology, 89,* 137–149.

Manns, J. R., Hopkins, R. O., & Squire, L. R. (2003). Semantic memory and the human hippocampus. *Neuron, 38,* 127–133.

Manto, M., & Pandolfo, M. (Eds.) (2001). *Cerebellum and its disorders.* New York: Cambridge University Press.

Manuck, S. B., Cohen, S., Rabin, B. S., Muldoon, M. F., & Bachen, E. A. (1991). Individual differences in cellular immune response to stress. *Psychological Science, 2,* 111–115.

Marcus, G. F., Vijayan, S., Rao, S. B., & Vishton, P. M. (1999). Rule learning by 7-month-old infants. *Science, 283,* 77–80.

Mareschal, D., & Johnson, M. H. (2003). The "what" and "where" of object representations in infancy. *Cognition, 88,* 259–276.

Marica, James E. (1993). The status of the statuses: Research review. In J. E. Marica, A. S. Waterman, D. R. Matteson, S. L. Archer, & J. L. Orlofsky (Eds.), *Ego identity: A handbook for psychosocial research* (pp. 22–41). New York: Springer.

Marini, P., Ramat, S., Ginestroni, A., & Paganini, M. (2003). Deficit of short-term memory in newly diagnosed untreated Parkinsonian patients: Reversal after L-dopa therapy. *Neurological Sciences, 24,* 184–185.

Marinova-Todd, S., Marshall, D., & Snow, C. (2000). Three misconceptions about age and L2 learning. *TESOL Quarterly, 34,* 9–34.

Markham, R., & Wang, L. (1996). Recognition of emotion by Chinese and Australian children. *Journal of Cross-Cultural Psychology, 27,* 616–643.

Markovits, C. (2003). *The un-Gandhian Gandhi: The life and afterlife of the Mahatma.* London: Anthem Press.

Marks, I. (1997). Behaviour therapy for obsessive-compulsive disorder: A decade of progress. *Canadian Journal of Psychiatry, 42,* 1021–1027.

Marks, I. M. (1969). *Fears and phobias.* New York: Academic Press.

Markson, L., & Bloom, P. (1997). Evidence against a dedicated system for word learning in children. *Nature, 385,* 813–815.

Markus, H. R., & Kitayama, S. (1991). Culture and the self: Implications for cognition, emotion, and motivation. *Psychological Review, 98,* 224–253.

Markus, S. J. (2002). *Neuroethics: Mapping the field.* New York: Dana Press.

Maroun, M., & Richter-Levin, G. (2003). Exposure to acute stress blocks the induction of long-term potentiation of the amygdala-prefrontal cortex pathway in vivo. *Journal of Neuroscience, 23,* 4406–4409.

Marr, D. (1982). *Vision: A computational investigation into the human representation and processing of visual information.* New York: Freeman.

Martin, C. L., & Ruble, D. (2004). Children's search for gender cues: Cognitive perspectives on gender development. *Current Directions in Psychological Science, 13,* 67–70.

Martin, R. A., & Dobbin, J. P. (1988). Sense of humor, hassles, and immunoglobulin A: Evidence for a stress-moderating effect of humor. *International Journal of Psychiatry in Medicine, 18,* 93–105.

Martindale, C. (1989). Personality, situation, and creativity. In J. A. Glover, R. R. Ronning, & C. R. Reynolds (Eds.), *Handbook of creativity* (pp. 211–228). New York: Plenum.

Martindale, C. (2001). Oscillations and analogies: Thomas Young, M.D., F.R.S., genius. *American Psychologist, 56,* 342–345.

Martinez, C., Rietbrock, S., Wise, L., Ashby, D., Chick, J., Moseley, J., Evans, S., & Gennell, D. (2005). Antidepressant treatment and the risk of fatal and non-fatal self harm in first episode depression: Nested case-control study. *British Medical Journal, 330,* 389–393.

Martínez-Miranda, J., & Aldea, A. (2005). Emotions in human and artificial intelligence. *Computers in Human Behavior, 21,* 323–341.

Marucha, P. T., Kiecolt-Glaser, J. K., & Favagehi, M. (1998). Mucosal wound healing is impaired by examination stress. *Psychosomatic Medicine, 60,* 362–365.

Marx, D. M., Stapel, D. A., & Muller, D. (2005). We can do it: The interplay of construal orientation and social comparisons under threat. *Journal of Personality & Social Psychology, 88,* 432–446.

Masataka, N. (1996). Perception of motherese in a signed language by 6-month-old deaf infants. *Developmental Psychology, 32,* 874–879.

Maschke, M., Schugens, M., Kindsvater, K., Drepper, J., Kolb, F. P., Diener, H., Daum, I., & Timmann, D. (2002). Fear conditioned changes of heart rate in patients with medial cerebellar lesions. *Journal of Neurology, Neurosurgery & Psychiatry, 72,* 116–118.

Maslow, A. H. (1970). *Motivation and personality* (2nd ed.). New York: Harper & Row.

Masters, W. H., & Johnson, V. E. (1966). *Human sexual response.* Boston: Little, Brown.

Matarazzo, J. D. (1972). *Wechsler's measurement and appraisal of adult intelligence.* Baltimore: Williams & Wilkins.

Mather, M., Henkel, L. A., & Johnson, M. K. (1997). Evaluating characteristics of false memories: Remember/know judgments and memory characteristics questionnaire compares. *Memory & Cognition, 25,* 826–837.

Matthews, B. A., Shimoff, E., Catania, A. C., & Sagvolden, T. (1977). Uninstructed human responding: Sensitivity to ratio and interval contingencies. *Journal of the Experimental Analysis of Behavior, 27,* 453–467.

Matthews, G., & Amelang, M. (1993). Extraversion, arousal theory and performance: A study of individual differences in the EEG. *Personality and Individual Differences, 14,* 347–363.

Matthews, G., & Gilliland, K. (1999). The personality theories of H. J. Eysenck and J. A. Gray: A comparative review. *Personality and Individual Differences, 26,* 583–626.

Matthews, G., Zeidner, M., & Roberts, R. D. (2002). *Emotional intelligence: Science and myth.* Cambridge, MA: MIT Press.

Mauch, D. H., Nägler, K., Schumacher, S., Göritz, C., Müller, E. C., Otto, A., & Pfrieger, F. W. (2001). CNS synaptogenesis promoted by glia-derived cholesterol. *Science, 294,* 1354–1357.

Mayer, D. M., & Hanges, P. J. (2003). Understanding the stereotype threat effect with "culture-free" tests: An examination of its mediators and measurement. *Human Performance, 16,* 207–230.

Mayer, J. D., Caruso, D. R., & Salovey, P. (2000). Emotional intelligence meets traditional standards for an intelligence. *Intelligence, 27,* 267–298.

Mayer, J. D., Salovey, P., & Caruso, D. (2001a). *The Mayer-Salovey-Caruso Emotional Intelligence Test (MSCEIT).* Toronto: Multi-Health Systems.

Mayer, J. D., Salovey, P., Caruso, D. R., & Sitarenios, G. (2001b). Emotional intelligence as a standard intelligence. *Emotion, 1,* 232–242.

Mayer, J. D., Salovey, P., Caruso, D. R., & Sitarenios, G. (2003). Measuring emotional intelligence with the MSCEIT V2.0. *Emotion, 3,* 97–105.

Mayer, R. E. (1997). *Thinking, problem solving, cognition.* New York: Freeman.

Mayes, A. R., & Downes, J. J. (Eds.). (1997). *Theories of organic amnesia.* Hove, England: Psychology Press/Erlbaum (UK) Taylor & Francis.

Maynard, R. A. (Ed.). (1996). *Kids having kids: A Robin Hood Foundation special report on the costs of adolescent childbearing.* New York: Robin Hood Foundation.

Maznevski, M. L. (1994). Understanding our differences: Performance in decision-making groups with diverse members. *Human Relations, 47,* 531–552.

McAdams, D. P., & de St. Aubin, E. (1992). A theory of generativity and its assessment through self-report, behavioral acts, and narrative themes in autobiography. *Journal of Personality & Social Psychology, 62,* 1003–1015.

McAdams, D. P., de St. Aubin, E., & Logan, R. L. (1993). Generativity among young, midlife, and older adults. *Psychology & Aging, 8,* 221–230.

McAdams, D. P., Reynolds, J., Lewis, M., Patten, A. H., & Bowman, P. J. (2001). When bad things turn good and good things turn bad: Sequences of redemption and contamination in life narrative and their relation to psychosocial adaptation in midlife adults and in students. *Personality & Social Psychology Bulletin, 27,* 474–485.

McArdle, J. J., Ferrer-Caja, E., Hamagami, F., & Woodcock, R. W. (2002). Comparative longitudinal structural analyses of the growth and decline of multiple intellectual abilities over the life span. *Developmental Psychology, 38,* 115–142.

McBride, J. (1999). *Steven Spielberg: A biography.* New York: Da Capo.

McCarley, R. W., & Hobson, J. A. (1975). Neuronal excitability modulation over the sleep cycle: A structural and mathematical model. *Science, 189,* 58–60.

McCartney, K., Harris, M. J., & Bernieri, F. (1990). Growing up and growing apart: A developmental meta-analysis of twin studies. *Psychological Bulletin, 107,* 226–237.

McClelland, D. C., & Atkinson, J. W. (1953). *The achievement motive.* New York: Appleton-Century-Crofts.

McClelland, D. C., Koestner, R., & Weinbereger, J. (1989). How do self-attributed and implicit motives differ? *Psychological Review, 96,* 690–702.

McClure, E. B. (2000). A meta-analytic review of sex differences in facial expression processing and their development in infants, children, and adolescents. *Psychological Bulletin, 126,* 424–453.

McCornack, S. A., & Parks, M. R. (1990). What women know that men don't: Sex differences in determining the truth behind deceptive messages. *Journal of Social and Personal Relationships, 7,* 107–118.

McCoy, N. L., & Pitino, L. (2002). Pheromonal influences on sociosexual behavior in young women. *Physiology and Behavior, 75,* 367–375.

McCrae, R. H., & Costa, P. T., Jr. (1987). Validation of the five-factor model of personality across instruments and observers. *Journal of Personality and Social Psychology, 52,* 81–90.

McCrae, R. H., & Costa, P. T., Jr. (1997a). Conceptions and correlates of Openness to Experience. In R. Hogan, J. Johnson, & S. Briggs (Eds.), *Handbook of personality psychology* (pp. 825–847). San Diego, CA: Academic Press.

McCrae, R. H., & Costa, P. T., Jr. (1997b). Personality trait structure as a human universal. *American Psychologist, 52,* 509–516.

McCrae, R. H., Costa, P. T., Jr., DelPilar, G. H., Rolland, J. P., & Parker, W. D. (1998). Cross-cultural assessment of the five-factor model: The revised NEO personality inventory. *Journal of Cross-Cultural Psychology, 29,* 171–188.

McCrink, K., & Wynn, K. (2004). Large-number addition and subtraction by 9-month-old infants. *Psychological Science, 15,* 776–781.

McDaniel, M. A., & Einstein, G. O. (1986). Bizarre imagery as an effective memory aid: The importance of distinctiveness. *Journal of Experimental Psychology: Learning, Memory, & Cognition, 12,* 54–65.

McDaniel, M. A., Einstein, G. O., DeLosh, E. L., & May, C. P. (1995). The bizarreness effect: It's not surprising, it's complex. *Journal of Experimental Psychology: Learning, Memory, & Cognition, 21,* 422–435.

McDermott, K. B., & Roediger, H. L., III. (1998). Attempting to avoid illusory memories: Robust false recognition of associates persists under conditions of explicit warnings and immediate testing. *Journal of Memory and Language, 39,* 508–520.

McDougall, W. (1908/1960). *Introduction to social psychology.* New York: Barnes & Noble.

McEwen, B. S. (1997). Possible mechanisms for atrophy of the human hippocampus. *Molecular Psychiatry, 2,* 255–262.

McEwen, B. S. (1998). Stress, adaptation, and disease: Allostasis and allostatic load. In S. M. McCann, J. M. Lipton, E. M. Sternberg, et al. (Eds.), *Annals of the New York Academy of Sciences: Neuroimmunomodulation: Molecular aspects, integrative systems, and clinical advances* (Vol. 840, pp. 33–44). New York: New York Academy of Sciences.

McEwen, B. S. (2000). Allostasis and allostatic load: Implications for neuropsychopharmacology. *Neuropsychopharmacology, 22,* 108–124.

McEwen, B. S. (2003). Mood disorders and medical illness: Mood disorders and allostatic load. *Biological Psychiatry, 54*, 200–207.

McEwen, B. S., Biron, C. A., Brunson, K. W., Bulloch, K., Chambers, W. H., Dhabhar, F. S., et al. (1997). The role of adrenocorticoids as modulators of immune function in health and disease: Neural, endocrine and immune interactions. *Brain Research Review, 23*, 79–133.

McEwen, B. S., & Schmeck, H. M., Jr. (1994). *The hostage brain*. New York: Rockefeller University Press.

McEwen, B. S., & Wingfield, J. C. (2003). Response to commentaries on the concept of allostasis. *Hormones & Behavior, 43*, 28–30.

McFadden, D., & Pasanen, E. G. (1999). Spontaneous otoacoustic emissions in heterosexuals, homosexuals, and bisexuals. *Journal of the Acoustical Society of America, 105*, 2403–2413.

McFarland, L. A., Lev-Arey, D. M., & Ziegert, J. C. (2003). An examination of stereotype threat in a motivational context. *Human Performance, 16*, 181–205.

McGaugh, J. L. (2000). Memory—a century of consolidation. *Science, 287*, 248–251.

McGaugh, J. L., & Herz, M. J. (1972). *Memory consolidation*. San Francisco: Albion.

McGillicuddy-De Lisi, A., & De Lisi, R. (Eds.). (2002). *Biology, society, and behavior: The development of sex differences in cognition*. Westport, CT: Ablex.

McGoldrick, M., Giordano, J., & Pearce, J. K. (Eds.). (1996). *Ethnicity and family therapy* (2nd ed.). New York: Guilford Press.

McGraw, K., Hoffman, R. I., Harker, C., & Herman, J. H. (1999). The development of circadian rhythms in a human infant. *Sleep, 22*, 303–310.

McGraw, M. B. (1943). *The neuromuscular maturation of the human infant*. New York: Columbia University Press.

McGue, M., Bouchard, T. J., Jr., Iacono, W. G., & Lykken, D. T. (1993). Behavioral genetics of cognitive ability: A life-span perspective. In R. Plomin & G. E. McClearn (Eds.), *Nature, nurture & psychology* (pp. 59–76). Washington, DC: American Psychological Association.

McGue, M., & Lykken, D. T. (1992). Genetic influence on the risk of divorce. *Psychological Science, 3*, 368–373.

McGuffin, P., & Gottesman, I. I. (1985). Genetic influences on normal and abnormal development. In M. Rutter & L. Hersov (Eds.), *Child and adolescent psychiatry: Modern approaches* (2nd ed., pp. 17–33). Oxford, England: Blackwell Scientific.

McGuffin, P., & Katz, R. (1993). Genes, adversity and depression. In R. Plomim & G. E. McClearn (Eds.), *Nature, nurture, and psychology* (pp. 217–230). Washington, DC: American Psychological Association.

McGuffin, P., Katz, R., Aldrich, J., & Bebbington, P. (1988). The Camberwell Collaborative Depression Study. II. Investigation of family members. *British Journal of Psychiatry, 152*, 766–774.

McIntyre, R. B., Paulson, R. M., & Lord, C. G. (2003). Alleviating women's mathematics stereotype threat through salience of group achievements. *Journal of Experimental Social Psychology, 39*, 83–90.

McKay, P. F., Doverspike, D., Bowen-Hilton, D., & Martin, Q. D. (2002). Stereotype threat effects on the Raven Advanced Progressive Matrices scores of African-Americans. *Journal of Applied Social Psychology, 32*, 767–787.

McKellar, P. (1965). The investigation of mental images. In S. A. Bartnet & A. McLaren (Eds.), *Penguin science survey B (biological sciences)* (pp. 79–94). New York: Penguin.

McKelvie, S. J. (2000). Quantifying the availability heuristic with famous names. *North American Journal of Psychology, 2*, 347–356.

McKenna, K. Y. A., Green, A. S., & Gleason, M. E. J. (2002). Relationship formation on the Internet: What's the big attraction? *Journal of Social Issues, 58*, 9–31.

McKenna, R. J. (1972). Some effects of anxiety level and food cues on the eating behavior of obese and normal subjects: A comparison of the Schachterian and psychosomatic conceptions. *Journal of Personality and Social Psychology, 22*, 311–319.

McKnight, J., & Malcolm, J. (2000). Is male homosexuality maternally linked? *Psychology, Evolution & Gender, 2*, 229–239.

McLaughlin, S., & Margolskee, R. F. (1994). The sense of taste. *American Scientist, 82*, 538–545.

McLean, D. E., Hatfield-Timajchy, K., Wingo, P. A., & Floyd, R. L. (1993). Psychosocial measurement: Implications of the study of preterm delivery in black women. *American Journal of Preventive Medicine, 9*, 39–81.

McLeod, P. L., & Lobel, S. A. (1992). The effects of ethinic diversity on idea generation in small groups. *Academy of Management Best Paper Proceedings, 22*, 227–231.

McNally, R. J. (2003). *Remembering trauma*. Cambridge, MA: Harvard University Press.

McNally, R. J. (2004). Is traumatic amnesia nothing but psychiatric folklore? *Cognitive Behaviour Therapy, 33*, 97–101.

McNally, R. J., & Clancy, S. A. (2005). Sleep paralysis, sexual abuse, and space alien abduction. *Transcultural Psychiatry, 42*, 113–122.

McNally, R. J., Lasko, N. B., Clancy, S. A., Macklin, M. L., Pitman, R. K., & Orr, S. P. (2004). Psychophysiological responding during script-driven imagery in people reporting abduction by space aliens. *Psychological Science, 15*, 493–497.

McNally, R. J., & Shin, L. M. (1995). Association of intelligence with severity of posttraumatic stress disorder symptoms in Vietnam combat veterans. *American Journal of Psychiatry, 152*, 936–938.

McNeil, T. F., Cantor-Graae, E., & Weinberger, D. R. (2000). Relationship of obstetric complications and differences in size of brain structures in monozygotic twin pairs discordant for schizophrenia. *American Journal of Psychiatry, 157*, 203–212.

Mealey, L., Bridgestock, R., & Townsend, G. C. (1999). Symmetry and perceived facial attractiveness: A monozygotic co-twin comparison. *Journal of Personality and Social Psychology, 76*, 151–158.

Meaney, M. J., Mitchell, J. B., Aitken, D. H., Bhatnagar, S., Bodnoff, S. R., Iny, L. J., & Sarrieau, A. (1991). The effects of neonatal handling on the development of the adrenocortical response to stress: Implications for neuropathology and cognitive deficits in later life. *Psychoneuroendocrinology, 16*, 85–103.

Medin, D. L., Lynch, E. B., & Solomon, K. O. (2000). Are there kinds of concepts? *Annual Review of Psychology, 51*, 121–147.

Medin, D. L., & Schaffer, M. M. (1978). A context theory of classification learning. *Psychological Review, 85*, 207–238.

Mednick, S. (1962). The associative basis of the creative process. *Psychological Review, 69*, 220–232.

Mednick, S. A., Gabrielli, W. F., & Hutchings, B. (1984). Genetic factors in criminal behavior: Evidence from an adoption cohort. *Science, 224*, 891–893.

Mednick, S. A., Watson, J. B., Huttunen, M., Cannon, T. D., Katila, H., Machon, R., et al. (1998). A two-hit working model of the etiology of schizophrenia. In M. F. Lenzenweger & R. H. Dworkin (Eds.), *Origins and development of schizophrenia: Advances in experimental psychopathology* (pp. 27–66). Washington, DC: American Psychological Association.

Mednick, S., Nakayama, K., & Stickgold, R. (2003). Sleep-dependent learning: A nap is as good as a night. *Nature Neuroscience, 6*, 697–698.

Meehl, P. (1960). The cognitive activity of the clinician. *American Psychologist, 15*, 19–27.

Meeter, M., & Murre, J. M. J. (2004). Consolidation of long-term memory: Evidence and alternatives. *Psychological Bulletin, 130*, 843–857.

Meister, I. G., Krings, T., Foltys, H., Boroojerdi, B., Müller, M., Töpper, R., & Thron, A. (2004). Playing piano in the mind—an fMRI study on music imagery and performance in pianists. *Cognitive Brain Research, 19*, 219–228.

Mellet, E., Petit, L., Mazoyer, B., Denis, M., & Tzourio, N. (1998). Reopening the mental imagery debate: Lessons from functional neuroanatomy. *NeuroImage, 8*, 129–139.

Mello, C. V., Vicario, D. S., & Clayton, D. F. (1992). Song presentation induces gene expression in the songbird forebrain. *Proceedings of the National Academy of Science, USA, 89*, 6818–6822.

Meltzoff, A. N., & Moore, M. K. (1977). Imitation of facial and manual gestures by human neonates. *Science, 198*, 75–78.

Melzack, R., & Wall, P. D. (1982). *The challenge of pain*. New York: Basic Books.

Menyuk, P., Liebergott, J. W., & Schultz, M. C. (1995). *Early language development in full-term and premature infants*. Hillsdale, NJ: Erlbaum.

Merchant, H., Battaglia-Mayer, A., & Georgopoulos, A. P. (2003). Functional organization of parietal neuronal responses to optic-flow stimuli. *Journal of Neurophysiology, 90*, 675–682.

Merlo, A., & Schotter, A. (2003). Learning by not doing: An experimental investigation of observational learning. *Games & Economic Behavior, 42*, 116–136.

Merrick, E. N. (1995). Adolescent childbearing as career "choice": Perspective from an ecological context. *Journal of Counseling & Development, 73*, 288–295.

Messinger, S. M. (1998). Pleasure and complexity: Berlyne revisited. *Journal of Psychology, 132*, 558–560.

Meston, C. M., & Frohlich, P. F. (2000). The neurobiology of sexual function. *Archives of General Psychiatry, 57*, 1012–1030.

Meyer, B., Olivier, L., & Roth, D. A., (2005). Please don't leave me! BIS/BAS, attachment styles, and responses to a relationship threat. *Personality and Individual Differences, 38*, 151–162.

Meyer, G. J. (2002). Exploring possible ethnic differences and bias in the Rorschach Comprehensive System. *Journal of Personality Assessment, 78*, 104–129.

Meyer, G. J., & Archer, R. P. (2001). The hard science of Rorschach research: What do we know and where do we go? *Psychological Assessment, 13*, 486–502.

Micallef, J., & Blin, O. (2001). Neurobiology and clinical pharmacology of obsessive-compulsive disorder. *Clinical Neuropharmacology, 24*, 191–207.

Michael, T., Ehlers, A., Halligan, S. L., & Clark, D. M. (2005). Unwanted memories of assault: What intrusion characteristics are associated with PTSD? *Behaviour Research and Therapy, 43*, 613–628.

Michalski, R. L., & Shackelford, T. K. (2002). An attempted replication of the relationships between birth order and personality. *Journal of Research in Personality, 36*, 182–188.

Mickelson, K. D., Kessler, R. C., & Shaver, P. R. (1997). Adult attachment in a nationally representative sample. *Journal of Personality & Social Psychology, 73*, 1092–1106.

Miklowitz, D. J., Goldstein, M. J., Nuechterlein, K. H., Snyder, K. S., & Mintz, J. (1988). Family factors and the course of bipolar affective disorder. *Archives of General Psychiatry, 45*, 225–231.

Mikulincer, M. (1994). *Human learned helplessness: A coping perspective*. New York: Plenum.

Mikulincer, M., & Horesh, N. (1999). Adult attachment style and the perception of others: The role of projective mechanisms. *Journal of Personality and Social Psychology, 76*, 1022–1034.

Mikulincer, M., & Orbach, I. (1995). Attachment styles and repressive defensiveness: The accessibility and architecture of affective memories. *Journal of Personality & Social Psychology, 68*, 917–925.

Miles, L. E. M., Raynal, D. M., & Wilson, M. A. (1977). Blind man living in normal society has circadian rhythms of 24.9 hours. *Science, 198*, 421–423.

Milgram, S. (1963). Behavioral study of obedience. *Journal of Abnormal and Social Psychology, 67*, 371–378.

Milgram, S. (1965). Some conditions of obedience and disobedience to authority. *Human Relations, 18*, 57–76.

Milgram, S. (1974). *Obedience to authority: An experimental view*. New York: Harper & Row.

Miller, A. G., Collins, B. E., & Brief, D. E. (1995). Perspectives on obedience to authority: The legacy of the Milgram experiments. *Journal of Social Issues, 51*, 1–19.

Miller, E. M. (1992). On the correlation of myopia and intelligence. *Genetic, Social and General Psychology Monographs 118*, 361–383.

Miller, G. A. (1956). The magical number seven, plus or minus two: Some limits on our capacity for processing information. *Psychological Review, 63*, 81–97.

Miller, G. E., Cohen, S., & Ritchey, A. K. (2002). Chronic psychological stress and the regulation of pro-inflammatory cytokines: A glucocorticoid resistance model. *Health Psychology, 21*, 531–541.

Miller, G. E., Dopp, J. M., Stevens, S. Y., & Fahey, J. L. (1999). Psychosocial predictors of natural killer cell mobilization during marital conflict. *Health Psychology, 18*, 262–271.

Miller, I. W., Keitner, G. E., Whisman, M. A., Ryan, C. E., Epstein, N. B., & Bishop, D. S. (1992). Depressed patients with dysfunctional families: Description and course of illness. *Journal of Abnormal Psychology, 101*, 637–646.

Miller, J. M., Boudreaux, M. C., & Regan, F. A. (1995). A case-control study of cocaine use in pregnancy. *American Journal of Obstetrics and Gynecology, 172*, 180–185.

Miller, L. C., Putcha-Bhagavatula, A., & Pedersen, W. C. (2002). Men's and women's mating preferences: Distinct evolutionary mechanisms? *Current Directions in Psychological Science, 11*, 88–93.

Miller, M. G., & Ross, M. (1975). Self-serving biases in attribution of causality: Fact or fiction? *Psychological Bulletin, 82*, 313–325.

Miller, N. E. (1959). Liberalization of basic S-R concepts: Extensions to conflict behavior, motivation, and social learning. In S. Koch (Ed.), *Psychology: A study of science* (Vol. 2). New York: McGraw-Hill.

Miller, N., Maruayama, G., Beaber, R. J., & Valone, K. (1976). Speed of speech and persuasion. *Journal of Personality and Social Psychology, 34*, 615–624.

Miller, T. Q., Smith, T. W., Turner, C. W., Guijarro, M. L., & Hallet, A. J. (1996). A meta-analytic review of research on hostility and physical health. *Psychological Bulletin, 119*, 322–348.

Miller, T. W., Veltkamp, L. J., Kraus, R. F., Lane, T., & Heister, T. (1999). An adolescent vampire cult in rural America: Clinical issues and case study. *Child Psychiatry & Human Development, 29*, 209–219.

Miller, W. B., Pasta, D. J., MacMurray, J., Chiu, C., Wu, H., & Comings, D. E. (1999). Dopamine receptor genes are associated with age at first sexual intercourse. *Journal of Biosocial Science, 31*, 43–54.

Millet, B., Leclaire, M., Bourdel, M. C., Loo, H., Tezcan, E., & Kuloglu, M. (2000). Comparison of sociodemographic, clinical and phenomenological characteristics of Turkish and French patients suffering from obsessive-compulsive disorder. *Canadian Journal of Psychiatry, 45*, 848.

Millon, T. (1975). Reflections on Rosenhan's "On being sane in insane places." *Journal of Abnormal Psychology, 84*, 456–461.

Milner, A. D., & Goodale, M. A. (1995). *The visual brain in action.* New York: Oxford University Press.

Milner, B., Corkin, S., & Teuber, H. L. (1968). Further analysis of the hippocampal amnesic syndrome: 14-year followup study of H. M. *Neuropsychologia, 6*, 215–234.

Mineka, S., Davison, M., Cook, M., & Keir, R. (1984). Observational conditioning of snake fear in Rhesus monkeys. *Journal of Abnormal Psychology, 93*, 355–372.

Mischel, W. (1984). Convergences and challenges in the search for consistency. *American Psychologist, 39*, 351–364.

Mischel, W. (2004). Toward an integrative science of the person. *Annual Review of Psychology, 55*, 1–22.

Mischel, W., & Peake, P. K. (1982). Beyond déjà vu in the search for cross-situational consistency. *Psychological Review, 90*, 394–402.

Mischel, W., & Shoda, Y. (1995). A cognitive-affective system theory of personality: Reconceptualizing situations, dispositions, dynamics, and invariance in personality structure. *Psychological Review, 102*, 246–268.

Mischel, W., Shoda, Y., & Rodriguez, M. L. (1989). Delay of gratification in children. *Science, 244*, 933–938.

Mitchell, J. E., Halmi, K., Wilson, G. T., Agras, W. S., Kraemer, H., & Crow, S. (2002). A randomized secondary treatment study of women with bulimia nervosa who fail to respond to CBT. *International Journal of Eating Disorders, 32*, 271–281.

Modell, J. (1996). Family niche and intellectual bent. [Review of *Born to Rebel* by F. J. Sulloway]. *Science, 275*, 624.

Modell, J., Mountz, J., Curtis, G., & Greden, J. (1989). Neurophysiologic dysfunction in basal ganglia/limbic striatal and thalamocortical circuits as a pathogenetic mechanism of obsessive-compulsive disorder. *Journal of Neuropsychiatry, 1*, 27–36.

Mojtabai, R., Nicholson, R. A., & Carpenter, B. N. (1998). Role of psychosocial treatments in management of schizophrenia: A meta-analytic review of controlled outcome studies. *Schizophrenia Bulletin, 24*, 569–587.

Moll, J., de Oliveira-Souza, R., Moll, F. T., Ignácio, F. A., Bramati, I. E., Caparelli-Dáquer, E. M., & Eslinger, P. J. (2005). The moral affiliations of disgust: A functional MRI study. *Cognitive & Behavioral Neurology, 18*, 68–78.

Moller, J., Theorell, T., de Faire, U., Ahlbom, A., & Hallqvist, J. (2005). Work related stressful life events and the risk of myocardial infarction. Case-control and case-crossover analyses within the Stockholm Heart Epidemiology Programme (SHEEP). *Journal of Epidemiological Community Health, 59*, 23–30.

Monk, T. H., Buysse, D. J., Reynolds, C. F., Berga, S. L., Jarrett, D. B., Begley, A. E., & Kupfer, D. J. (1997). Circadian rhythms in human performance and mood under constant conditions. *Journal of Sleep Research, 6*, 9–18.

Monnier, P. (2003). Redundant coding assessed in a visual search task. *Displays, 24*, 49–55.

Monroe, S. M., & Depue, R. A. (1991). Life stress and depression. In J. Becker & A. Kleinman (Eds.), *Psychosocial aspects of depression* (pp. 101–130). Hillsdale, NJ: Erlbaum.

Montague, P. R., Hyman, S. E., & Cohen, J. D. (2004). Computational roles for dopamine in behavioural control. *Nature, 431*, 760–767.

Monteith, M. J. (1996). Affective reactions to prejudice-related discrepant responses: The impact of standard salience. *Personality and Social Psychology Bulletin, 22*, 48–59.

Montoya, R. M., & Horton, R. S. (2004). On the importance of cognitive evaluation as a determinant of interpersonal attraction. *Journal of Personality & Social Psychology, 86*, 696–712.

Moody, D. B., Stebbins, W. C., & May, B. J. (1990). Auditory perception of communication signals by Japanese monkeys. In W. C. Stebbins & M. A. Berkley (Eds.), *Comparative perception: Complex signals* (pp. 311–343). New York: Wiley.

Moran, P. (1999). The epidemiology of antisocial personality disorder. *Social Psychiatry & Psychiatric Epidemiology, 34*, 231–242.

Moreland, R. L., & Zajonc, R. B. (1982). Exposure effects in person perception: Familiarity, similarity, and attraction. *Journal of Experimental Social Psychology, 18*, 395–415.

Morf, C. C., & Rhodewalt, F. (2001). Unraveling the paradoxes of narcissism: A dynamic self-regulatory processing model. *Psychological Inquiry, 12*, 177–196.

Morgan, J. L., & Demuth, K. D. (1996). *Signal to syntax: Bootstrapping from speech to grammar in early acquisition.* Hillsdale, NJ: Erlbaum.

Morgan, M. J., McFie, L., Fleetwood, L. H., & Robinson, J. A. (2002). Ecstasy (MDMA): Are the psychological problems associated with its use reversed by prolonged abstinence? *Psychopharmacology, 159*, 294–303.

Morgane, P. J., Austin-LaFrance, R., Bronzino, J., Tonkiss, J., Diaz-Cintra, S., Cintra, L., et al. (1993). Prenatal malnutrition and development of the brain. *Neuroscience and Biobehavioral Reviews, 17*, 91–128.

Mori, H., Kamada, M., Maegawa, M., Yamamoto, S., Aono, T., Futaki, S., et al. (1998). Enzymatic activation of immunoglobulin binding factor in female reproductive tract. *Biochemical and Biophysical Research Communications, 246*, 409–413.

Morling, B., Kitayama, S., & Miyamoto, Y. (2003). American and Japanese women use different coping strategies during normal pregnancy. *Personality & Social Psychology Bulletin, 29*, 1533–1546.

Morris, A. L., & Harris, C. L. (2004). Repetition blindness: Out of sight or out of mind? *Journal of Experimental Psychology: Human Perception & Performance, 30*, 913–922.

Morris, C. D., Bransford, J. D., & Franks, J. J. (1977). Levels of processing versus transfer-appropriate processing. *Journal of Verbal Learning and Verbal Behavior, 16*, 519–533.

Morris, J., & Dolan, R. (2002). The amygdala and unconscious fear processing. In B. de Gelder, E. de Haan, & C. Heywood (Eds.), *Out of mind: Varieties of unconscious processes* (pp. 185–204). London: Oxford University Press.

Morris, M. W., & Peng, K. (1994). Culture and cause: American and Chinese attributions for social and physical events. *Journal of Personality and Social Psychology, 67*, 949–971.

Morris, R. (1984). Developments of a water-maze procedure for studying spatial learning in the rat. *Journal of Neuroscience Methods, 11*, 47–60.

Morris, W. N., Worchel, S., Bois, J. L., Pearson, J. A., Rountree, C. A., Samaha, G. M., et al. (1976). Collective coping with stress: Group reactions to fear, anxiety, and ambiguity. *Journal of Personality and Social Psychology, 33*, 674–679.

Morris, W., & Miller, R. (1975). The effects of consensus-breaking and consensus preempting partner on reduction in conformity. *Journal of Experimental Social Psychology, 11*, 215–223.

Mortensen, P. B., Pedersen, C. B., Westergaard, T., Wohlfahrt, J., Ewald, H., Mors, O., et al. (1999). Effects of family history and place and season of birth on the risk of schizophrenia. *New England Journal of Medicine, 340*, 603–608.

Moscovitch, M., & Craik, F. I. M. (1976). Depth of processing, retrieval cues, and uniqueness of encoding as factors in recall. *Journal of Verbal Learning and Verbal Behavior, 15*, 447–458.

Moser, M., Lehofer, M., Hoehn-Saric, R., McLeod, D. R., Hildebrandt, G., Steinbrenner, B., et al. (1998). Increased heart rate in depressed subjects in spite of unchanged autonomic balance. *Journal of Affective Disorders, 48*, 115–124.

Moskowitz, D. S. (1993). Dominance and friendliness: On the interaction of gender and situation. *Journal of Personality, 61*, 387–409.

Mowrer, O. H. (1939). A stimulus-response analysis of anxiety and its role as a reinforcing agent. *Psychological Review, 46*, 553–565.

Mroczek, D. K., & Almeida, D. M. (2004). The effect of daily stress, personality, and age on daily negative affect. *Journal of Personality, 72*, 355–378.

Muehlenhard, C. L., & Linton, M. A. (1987). Date rape and sexual aggression in dating situations: Incidence and risk factors. *Journal of Counseling Psychology, 34*, 186–196.

Mullen, B., Anthony, T., Salas, E., & Driskell, J. E. (1994). Group cohesiveness and quality of decision making: An integration of tests of the groupthink hypothesis. *Small Group Research, 25*, 189–204.

Mulvany, F., O'Callaghan, E., Takei, N., Byrne, M., Fearson, P., & Larkin, C. (2001). Effect of social class at birth on risk and presentation of schizophrenia: Case control study. *British Medical Journal, 323*, 1398–1401.

Mumford, M. D. (2001). Something old, something new: Revisiting Guilford's conception of creative problem solving. *Creativity Research Journal, 13*, 267–276.

Münte, T. F., Kohlmetz, C., Nager, W., & Altenmüller, E. (2001). Superior auditory spatial tuning in conductors. *Nature, 409*, 580.

Murata, K., Weihe, P., Renzoni, A., Debes, F., Vasconcelos, R., Zino, F., et al. (1999). Delayed evoked potentials in children exposed to methylmercury from seafood. *Neurotoxicology & Teratology, 21*, 343–348.

Muris, P., & Meesters, C. (2002). Attachment, behavioral inhibition, and anxiety disorder symptoms in normal adolescents. *Journal of Psychopathology & Behavioral Assessment, 24*, 97–106.

Murphy, C. (1986). Taste and smell in the elderly. In H. L. Meiselman & R. S. Rivlin (Eds.), *Clinical measurement of taste and smell* (pp. 343–371). New York: Macmillan.

Murphy, F. C., Nimmo-Smith, I., & Lawrence, A. D. (2003). Functional neuroanatomy of emotions: A meta-analysis. *Cognitive, Affective & Behavioral Neuroscience, 3,* 207–233.

Murray, C. J. L., & Lopez, A. D. (Eds.). (1996). *The global burden of disease. A comprehensive assessment of mortality and disability from diseases, injuries, and risk factors in 1990 and projected to 2020.* Cambridge, MA: Harvard School of Public Health.

Myers, C. E., McGlinchey-Berroth, R., Warren, S., Monti, L., Brawn, C. M., & Gluck, M. A. (2000). Latent learning in medial temporal amnesia: Evidence for disrupted representational but preserved attentional processes. *Neuropsychology, 14,* 3–15.

Myers, D. G. (2000). The funds, friends, and faith of happy people. *American Psychologist, 55,* 56–67.

Nader, K., Bechara, A., & van der Kooy, D. (1997). Neurobiological constraints on behavioral models of motivation. *Annual Review of Psychology, 48,* 85–114.

Nadler, J., Thompson, L., & van Boven, L. (2003). Learning negotiation skills: Four models of knowledge creation and transfer. *Management Science, 49,* 529–540.

Nagel, E. (1979). *The structure of science: Problems in the logic of scientific explanation* (2nd ed.). Indianapolis, IN: Hackett.

Nagy, Z., Westerberg, H., & Klingberg, T. (2004). Maturation of white matter is associated with the development of cognitive functions during childhood. *Journal of Cognitive Neuroscience, 16,* 1227–1233.

Naito, M., & Lipsitt, L. P. (1969). Two attempts to condition eyelid responses in human infants. *Journal of Experimental Child Psychology, 8,* 263–270.

Nakai, Y., Fujita, T., Kuboki, T., Nozoe, S., Kubo, C., Yoshimasa, Y., et al. (2001). Nationwide survey of eating disorders in Japan. *Seishin Igaku (Clinical Psychiatry), 43,* 1373–1378.

Nakatani, E., Nakgawa, A., Ohara, Y., Goto, S., Uozumi, N., Iwakiri, M., Yamamotob, Y., Motomura, K., Iikura, Y., & Yamagami, T. (2003). Effects of behavior therapy on regional cerebral blood flow in obsessive-compulsive disorder. *Psychiatry Research: Neuroimaging, 124,* 113–120.

Nakayama, K., He, Z. J., & Shimojo, S. (1995). Visual surface representation: A critical link between lower-level and higher-level vision. In S. M. Kosslyn & D. N. Osherson (Eds.), *Visual cognition: An invitation to cognitive science, Vol. 2* (2nd ed., pp. 1–70). Cambridge, MA: MIT Press.

Nakayama, K., & Mackeben, M. (1989). Sustained and transient components of focal visual attention. *Vision Research, 29,* 1631–1647.

Nanda, S. B. R. (1987). *Mahatma Gandhi: His life in pictures.* [Online edition]. Delhi, India: Central Electric Press. Retrieved June, 2005 from http://www.mkgandhi.org/bio5000/birth.htm

Nasby, W., Hayden, B., & DePaulo, B. M. (1979). Attributional bias among aggressive boys to interpret unambiguous social stimuli as displays of hostility. *Journal of Abnormal Psychology 89,* 459–468.

Nathawat, S. S., Singh, R., & Singh, B. (1997). The effect of need for achievement on attributional style. *Journal of Social Psychology, 137,* 55–62.

National Admissions to Substance Abuse Treatment Services, November 2001, funded by the Substance Abuse and Mental Health Service Administration, DHHS. The latest data are available at 1-800-729-6686 or online at www.samhsa.gov

National Heart, Lung, and Blood Institute. (2003). Who gets obstructive sleep apnea? Retrieved August 13, 2005, from http://www.nhlbi.nih.gov/health/dci/Diseases/SleepApnea/SleepApnea_WhoIsAtRisk.html

National Institute for Occupational Safety and Health. (1998). *Criteria for a recommended standard: Occupational noise exposure.* Cincinnati, OH: Author.

National Institute on Drug Abuse (1998). Slide Teaching Packet I, For Health Practitioners, Teachers and Neuroscientists. Section III: Introduction to Drugs of Abuse: Cocaine, Opiates (Heroin) and Marijuana (THC).

National Institute on Drug Abuse, (2003). InfoFax: Drug Addiction treatment methods. Retrieved from http://www.drugabuse.gov/infofax/treatmeth.html

National Institute on Drug Abuse. (2004, September). NIDA InfoFacts: Crack and cocaine. Retrieved August, 2005, from http://www.drugabuse.gov/DrugPages/Cocaine.html

National Science Foundation (2001). National survey of recent college graduates. Washington, DC: National Science Foundation, Division of Science Resources Statistics.

National Sleep Foundation. (1998). Omnibus sleep in America poll. Retrieved 2002, from http://www.sleepfoundation.org/publications

National Sleep Foundation. (2002). "Sleep in America" poll. Retrieved from www.sleepfoundation.org/2002poll.html

National Sleep Foundation. (2004). Sleep in America poll. Retrieved August 13, 2005, from http://www.sleepfoundation.org/hottopics/index.php?secid=16&id=143

Nawrot, M., Nordenstrom, B., & Olson, A. (2004). Disruption of eye movements by ethanol intoxication affects perception of depth from motion parallax. *Psychological Science, 15,* 858–865.

Nayatani, Y. (2001). Some modifications to Hering's opponent-colors theory. *Color Research & Application, 26,* 290–304.

Nayatani, Y. (2003). A modified opponent-colors theory considering chromatic strengths of various hues. *Color Research & Application, 28,* 284–297.

Neel, R. G., Tzeng, O. C., & Baysal, C. (1986). Need achievement in a cross-cultural contact study. *International Review of Applied Psychology, 35,* 225–229.

Neisser, U. (1967). *Cognitive psychology.* New York: Appleton-Century-Crofts.

Neisser, U., Boodoo, G., Bouchard, T. J., Jr., Boykin, A. W., Brody, N., Ceci, S. J., et al. (1996). Intelligence: Knowns and unknowns. *American Psychologist, 51,* 77–101.

Neisser, U., & Harsch, N. (1992). Phantom flashbulbs: False recollections of hearing news about *Challenger.* In E. Winograd & U. Neisser (Eds.), *Affect and accuracy in recall: Studies of "flashbulb memories"* (pp. 9–31). Cambridge, UK: Cambridge University Press.

Neitz, J., Neitz, M., & Kainz, P. M. (1996). Visual pigment gene structure and the severity of color vision defects. *Science, 274,* 801–804.

Nelson, C. A. (1999). Human plasticity and human development. *Current Directions in Psychological Science, 8,* 42–45.

Nelson, C. B., Heath, A. C., & Kessler, R. C. (1998). Temporal progression of alcohol dependence symptoms in the U.S. household population: Results from the National Comorbidity Survey. *Journal of Consulting & Clinical Psychology, 66, 3,* 474–483.

Nelson, K. (1981). Individual differences in language development: Implications for development and language. *Developmental Psychology, 17,* 170–187.

Nemec, P., Altmann, J., Marhold, S., Burda, H., & Oelschläger, H. H. A. (2001). Neuroanatomy of magnetoreception: The superior colliculus involved in magnetic orientation in a mammal. *Science, 294,* 366–368.

Nemeroff, C. J., Stein, R., Diehl, N. S., & Smilach, K. M. (1994). From the Cleavers to the Clintons: Role choices and body orientation as reflected in magazine article content. *International Journal of Eating Disorders, 16,* 167–176.

Nemeroff, C., & Rozin, P. (1989). "You are what you eat": Applying the demand-free "impressions" technique to an unacknowledged belief. *Ethos, 17,* 50–69.

Nestler, E. J. (1997). Schizophrenia: An emerging pathophysiology. *Nature, 385,* 578–579.

Neugebauer, R., Hoek, H. W., & Susser, E. (1999). Prenatal exposure to wartime famine and development of antisocial personality disorder in early adulthood. *JAMA: Journal of the American Medical Association, 282,* 455–462.

Neumann, C., & Walker, E. F. (1996). Childhood neuromotor soft signs, behavior problems, and adult psychopathology. In T. Ollendick & R. Prinz (Eds.), *Advances in clinical child psychology.* New York: Plenum Press.

Nevid, J., Rathus, S., & Rubenstein, H. (1998). *Health in the new millennium.* New York: Worth.

Newcombe, N. S., Drummey, A. B., Fox, N. A., Lie, E., & Ottinger-Alberts, W. (2000). Remembering early childhood: How much, how, and why (or why not). *Current Directions in Psychological Science, 9,* 55–58.

Newcomer, J. W., Selke, G., Melson, A. K., Hershey, T., Craft, S., Richards, K., & Alderson, A. L. (1999). Decreased memory performance in healthy humans induced by stress-level cortisol treatment. *Archives of General Psychiatry, 56,* 527–533.

Newman, L. S., Duff, K. J., & Baumeister, R. F. (1997). A new look at defensive projection: Thought suppression, accessibility, and biased person perception. *Journal of Personality and Social Psychology, 72,* 980–1001.

Newman, M. G., Kenardy, J., Herman, S., & Taylor, C. B. (1997). Comparison of palmtop-computer-assisted brief cognitive-behavioral treatment to cognitive-behavioral treatment for panic disorder. *Journal of Consulting and Clinical Psychology, 65,* 178–183.

Newsome, G. L., III. (2000). A review of some promising approaches to understanding and improving thinking skills. *Journal of Research & Development in Education, 33,* 199–222.

Ng, V. W. K., Bullmore, E. T., de Zubicaray, G. I., Cooper, A., Suckling, J., & Williams, S. C. R. (2001). Identifying rate-limiting nodes in large-scale cortical networks for visuospatial processing: An illustration using fMRI. *Journal of Cognitive Neuroscience, 13,* 537–545.

Nichols, R. C. (1978). Twin studies of ability, personality, and interests. *Homo, 29,* 158–173.

Nickerson, R. S., & Adams, M. J. (1979). Long-term memory for a common object. *Cognitive Psychology, 11,* 287–307.

Niedenthal, P. M., Brauer, M., Halberstadt, J. B., & Innes-Ker, A. H. (2001). When did her smile drop? Facial mimicry and the influences of emotional state on the detection of change in emotional expression. *Cognition & Emotion, 15,* 853–864.

Niedenthal, P. M., Brauer, M., Robin, L., & Innes-Ker, H. (2002). Adult attachment and the perception of facial expression of emotion. *Journal of Personality & Social Psychology, 82,* 419–433.

Nielsen, T. A. (2000). A review of mentation in REM and NREM sleep: "Covert" REM sleep as a possible reconciliation of two opposing models. *Behavioral Brain Science, 23(6),* 851–866.

Nigg, J. T., & Goldsmith, H. H. (1994). Genetics of personality disorders: Perspectives from personality and psychopathology research. *Psychological Bulletin, 115,* 346–380.

NIH Technology Assessment Panel. (1996). Integration of behavioral and relaxation approaches into the treatment of chronic pain and insomnia. *Journal of the American Medical Association, 276,* 313–318.

Niles, S. (1998). Achievement goals and means: A cultural comparison. *Journal of Cross-Cultural Psychology, 29,* 656–667.

Nilsson, L., & Hamberger, L. (1990). *A child is born.* New York: Delacorte.

Nilsson, T., Ericsson, M., Poston, W. S. C., Linder, J., Goodrick, G. K., & Foreyt, J. P. (1998). Is the assessment of coping capacity useful in the treatment of obesity? *Eating Disorders: The Journal of Treatment & Prevention, 6,* 241–251.

Nisbett, R. E. (1972). Hunger, obesity, and the ventromedial hypothalamus. *Psychological Review, 79,* 433–453.

Nisbett, R. E. (1996). Race, genetics, and IQ. In C. Jencks & M. Phillips (Eds.), *The black-white test score gap* (pp. 86–102). Washington, DC: Brookings Institution.

Nodelmann, P. (1988). *Words about pictures.* Athens: University of Georgia Press.

Nolan, S. A., & Mineka, S. (1997, November). Verbal, nonverbal, and gender-related factors in the interpersonal consequences of depression and anxiety. Presented at the annual meeting of the Association for the Advancement of Behavior Therapy, Miami Beach, FL.

Nolen-Hoeksema, S. (1987). Sex differences in unipolar depression: Evidence and theory. *Psychological Bulletin, 101,* 259–282.

Nolen-Hoeksema, S. (2000). The role of rumination in depressive disorders and mixed anxiety/depressive symptoms. *Journal of Abnormal Psychology, 109,* 504–511.

Nolen-Hoeksema, S., & Morrow, J. (1993). Effects of rumination and distraction on naturally occurring depressed mood. *Cognition & Emotion, 7,* 561–570.

Norman, K. A., & Schacter, D. L. (1997). False recognition in younger and older adults: Exploring the characteristics of illusory memories. *Memory & Cognition, 25,* 838–848.

Nowakowski, R. S. (1987). Basic concepts of CNS development. *Child Development, 58,* 568–595.

Nuechterlein, K. H. (1991). Vigilance in schizophrenia and related disorders. In S. R. Steinhauer, J. H. Gruzelier, & J. Zubin (Eds.), *Neuropsychology, psychophysiology, and information processing* (pp. 397–433). New York: Elsevier Science.

Núñez, J. P., & de Vincente, F. (2004). Unconscious learning. Conditioning to subliminal visual stimuli. *Spanish Journal of Psychology, 7,* 13–28.

Nyberg, L., McIntosh, A. R., Houle, S., Nilsson, L. G., & Tulving, E. (1996). Activation of medial temporal structures during episodic memory retrieval. *Nature, 380,* 715–717.

Nye, R. D. (1992). *Three psychologies: Perspectives from Freud, Skinner, and Rogers.* Pacific Grove, CA: Brooks-Cole.

O'Brien, L. T., & Crandall, C. S. (2003). Stereotype threat and arousal: Effects on women's math performance. *Personality & Social Psychology Bulletin, 29,* 782–789.

Ochsner, K. N., & Gross, J. J. (2005). The cognitive control of emotion. *Trends in Cognitive Sciences, 9,* 242–249.

Ochsner, K. N., & Lieberman, M. D. (2001). The emergence of social cognitive neuroscience. *American Psychologist, 56,* 717–734.

O'Conner, T. G., Marvin, R. S., Rutter, M., Olrick, J. T., & Britner, P. A. (2003). Child-parent attachment following early institutional deprivation. *Development & Psychopathology, 15,* 19–38.

O'Connor, D. B., & Shimizu, M. (2002). Sense of personal control, stress and coping style: A cross-cultural study. *Stress & Health: Journal of the International Society for the Investigation of Stress, 18,* 173–183.

O'Doherty, J., Winston, J., Critchley, H., Perrett, D., Burt, D. M., & Dolan, R. J. (2003). Beauty in a smile: The role of medial orbitofrontal cortex in facial attractiveness. *Neuropsychologia, 41,* 147–155.

Oei, T. P. S., & Yeoh, A. E. O. (1999). Pre-existing antidepressant medication and the outcome of group cognitive-behavioural therapy. *Australian & New Zealand Journal of Psychiatry, 33,* 70–76.

O'Grady, W., & Lee, M. (2005). A mapping theory of agrammatic comprehension deficits. *Brain & Language, 92,* 91–100.

Öhman, A. (2002). Automaticity and the amygdala: Nonconscious responses to emotional faces. *Current Directions in Psychological Science, 11,* 62–66.

Öhman, A., Fredrikson, M., Hugdahl, K., & Rimmo, P.-A. (1976). The premise of equipotentiality in human classical conditioning: Conditioned electrodermal responses to potentially phobic stimuli. *Journal of Experimental Psychology: General, 105,* 313–337.

Ojemann, G. A. (1983). Brain organization for language from the perspective of electrical stimulation mapping. *Behavioral and Brain Sciences, 6,* 189–230.

Ojemann, G. A., Ojemann, J., Lettich, E., & Berger, M. (1989). Cortical language localization in left, dominant hemisphere. *Journal of Neurosurgery, 71,* 316–326.

Okello, E. J., Savelev, S. U., & Perry, E. K. (2004). In vitro anti-beta-secretase and dual anti-cholinesterase activities of *Camellia sinensis* L. (tea) relevant to treatment of dementia. *Phytotherapy Research, 18,* 624–627.

Olczak, P. V., Kaplan, M. F., & Penrod, S. (1991). Attorneys' lay psychology and its effectiveness in selecting jurors: Three empirical studies. *Journal of Social Behavior and Personality, 6,* 431–452.

Olds, J., & Milner, P. (1954). Positive reinforcement produced by electrical stimulation of septal area and other regions of rat brain. *Journal of Comparative & Physiological Psychology, 47,* 419–427.

Olson, C. R. (2001). Object-based vision and attention in primates. *Current Opinion in Neurobiology, 11,* 171–179.

Olson, I. R., & Chun, M. M. (2002). Perceptual constraints on implicit learning of spatial context. *Visual Cognition, 9,* 273–302.

Olson, J. M., Vernon, P. A., Harris, J. A., & Jang, K. L. (2001). The heritability of attitudes: A study of twins. *Journal of Personality & Social Psychology, 80,* 845–860.

Olsson, A., & Phelps, E. A. (2004). Learned fear of "unseen" faces after Pavlovian, observational, and instructed fear. *Psychological Science, 15,* 822–828.

O'Regan, J. K. (1992). Solving the "real" mysteries of visual perception: The world as an outside memory. *Canadian Journal of Psychology, 46,* 461–488.

Orive, R. (1988). Social projection and social comparison of opinions. *Journal of Personality and Social Psychology, 54,* 953–964.

Ornish, D., Scherwitz, L. W., Billings, J. H., Gould, K. L., Merritt, T. A., Sparler, S., et al. (1998). Intensive lifestyle changes for reversal of coronary heart disease. *Journal of the American Medical Association, 280,* 2001–2007.

Orth-Gomér, K., Wamala, S. P., Horsten, M., Schenck-Gustafsso, K., Schneiderman, N., & Mittleman, M. A. (2000). Marital stress worsens prognosis in women with coronary heart disease: The Stockholm female coronary risk study. *Journal of the American Medical Association, 284,* 3008–3014.

Osborn, D. R. (1996). Beauty is as beauty does? Makeup and posture effects on physical attractiveness judgments. *Journal of Applied Social Psychology, 26,* 31–51.

Ost, J. (2003). Seeking the middle ground in the "memory wars." *British Journal of Psychology, 94,* 125–139.

Ostatnikova, D., Laznibatova, J., Putz, Z., Mateseje, A., Dohnanyiova, M., & Pastor, K. (2000). Salivary testosterone levels in intellectually gifted and non-intellectually gifted preadolescents: An exploratory study. *High Ability Studies, 11,* 41–54.

Ostatnikova, D., Laznibatova, J., Putz, Z., Mateseje, A., Dohnanyiova, M., & Pastor, K. (2002). Biological aspects of intellectual giftedness. *Studia Psychologica, 44,* 3–13.

O'Sullivan, C. S., & Durso, F. T. (1984). Effects of schema-incongruent information on memory for stereotypical attributes. *Journal of Personality and Social Psychology, 47,* 55–70.

Otto, M. W., Gould, R. A., & Pollack, M. H. (1994). Cognitive-behavioral treatment of panic disorder: Considerations for the treatment of patients over the long term. *Psychiatric Annals, 24,* 307–315.

Otto, M. W., Smits, J. A. J., & Reese, H. E. (2005). Combined psychotherapy and pharmacotherapy for mood and anxiety disorders in adults: Review and analysis. *Clinical Psychology: Science & Practice, 12,* 72–86.

Ouimette, P. C. (1997). Psychopathology and sexual aggression in nonincarcerated men. *Violence & Victims, 12,* 389–395.

Overmier, J. B., & Seligman, M. E. P. (1967). Effects of inescapable shock upon subsequent escape and avoidance responding. *Journal of Comparative and Physiological Psychology, 63,* 28–33.

Overmier, J. B. (2002). On learned helplessness. *Integrative Physiological & Behavioral Science, 37,* 4–8.

Owens, L., Shute, R., & Slee, P. (2000). "I'm in and you're out . . . " Explanations for teenage girls' indirect aggression. *Psychology, Evolution & Gender, 2,* 19–46.

Oyserman, D., Coon, H. M., & Kemmelmeier, M. (2002). Rethinking individualism and collectivism: Evaluation of theoretical assumptions and meta-analyses. *Psychological Bulletin, 128,* 3–72.

Ozer, D. J., Best, S. R., Lipsey, T. L., & Weiss, D. S. (2003). Predictors of posttraumatic stress disorder and symptoms in adults: A meta-analysis. *Psychological Bulletin, 129,* 52–73.

Pacak, K., & Palkovits, M. (2001). Stressor specificity of central neuroendocrine responses: Implications for stress-related disorders. *Endocrine Review, 22,* 502–548.

Páez, D., Velasco, C., & González, J. L. (1999). Expressive writing and the role of alexythimia as a dispositional deficit in self-disclosure and psychological health. *Journal of Personality and Social Psychology, 77,* 630–641.

Pagnoni, G., Zink, C. F., Montague, P. R., & Berns, G. S. (2002). Activity in human ventral striatum locked to errors of reward prediction. *Nature Neuroscience, 5,* 97–98.

Paivio, A. (1971). *Imagery and verbal processes.* New York: Holt, Rinehart & Winston.

Palace, E. M. (1999). Response expectancy and sexual dysfunction. In I. Kirsch (Ed.), *How expectancies shape experience* (pp. 173–196). Washington, DC: American Psychological Association.

Palmer, S. E. (1992a). Modern theories of Gestalt perception. In G. W. Humphreys (Ed.), *Understanding vision: An interdisciplinary perspective* (pp. 39–70). Oxford, England: Blackwell.

Panksepp, J. (1998). *Affective neuroscience: The foundations of human and animal emotions.* London: Oxford University Press.

Panksepp, J. (2005). Affective consciousness: Core emotional feelings in animals and humans. *Consciousness and Cognition: An International Journal, 14,* 30–80.

Pantev, C., Roberts, L. E., Schulz, M., Engelien, A., & Ross, B. (2001). Timbre-specific enhancement of auditory cortical representations in musicians. *Neuroreport: For Rapid Communication of Neuroscience Research, 12,* 169–174.

Papp, L. A., Klein, D. F., & Gorman, J. M. (1993). Carbon dioxide hypersensitivity, hyperventilation, and panic disorder. *American Journal of Psychiatry, 150,* 1149–1157.

Papp, L. A., Martinez, J. M., Klein, D. F., Coplan, J. D., Norman, R. G., Cole, R., et al. (1997). Respiratory psychophysiology of panic disorder: Three respiratory challenges in 98 subjects. *American Journal of Psychiatry, 154,* 1557–1565.

Paquette, V., Lévesque, J., Mensour, B., Leroux, J. M., Beaudoin, G., Bourgouin, P., & Beauregard, M. (2003). "Change the mind and you change the brain": Effects of cognitive-behavioral therapy on the neural correlates of spider phobia. *Neuroimage, 18,* 401–409.

Paradis M. (1990). Language lateralization in bilinguals: Enough already! *Brain and Language, 39,* 576–586.

Paradis M. (1992). The Loch Ness monster approach to bilingual language lateralization: A response to Berquier and Ashton. *Brain and Language, 43,* 534–537.

Park, C. L., & Fenster, J. R. (2004). Stress-related growth: Predictors of occurrence and correlates with psychological adjustment. *Journal of Social & Clinical Psychology, 23,* 195–215.

Park, D. C., Polk, T. A., Park, R., Minear, M., Savage, A., & Smith, M. R. (2004). Aging reduces neural specialization in ventral visual cortex. *Proceedings of the National Academy of Sciences USA, 101,* 13091–13095.

Park, J. H., & Schaller, M. (2005). Does attitude similarity serve as a heuristic cue for kinship? Evidence of an implicit cognitive association. *Evolution & Human Behavior, 26,* 158–170.

Parker, G., Cheah, Y.-C., & Roy, K. (2001). Do the Chinese somatize depression? A cross-cultural study. *Social Psychiatry & Psychiatric Epidemiology, 36,* 287–293.

Parkin, A. J. (1987). *Memory and amnesia: An introduction.* Oxford, England: Blackwell.

Parks, M. R., & Roberts, L. D. (1998). "Making MOOsic": The development of personal relationships on line and a comparison to their off-line counterparts. *Journal of Social & Personal Relationships, 15,* 517–537.

Parsons, L. M. (1987). Imagined spatial transformation of one's body. *Journal of Experimental Psychology: General, 116*, 172–191.

Parsons, L. M. (1994). Temporal and kinematic properties of motor behavior reflected in mentally simulated action. *Journal of Experimental Psychology: Human Perception & Performance, 20*, 709–730.

Parsons, L. M., & Fox, P. T. (1998). The neural basis of implicit movements used in recognising hand shape. *Cognitive Neuropsychology, 15*, 583–615.

Pascual-Leone, A., Grafman, J., Cohen, L. G., Roth, B. J., & Hallett, M. (1997). Transcranial magnetic stimulation. A new tool for the study of higher cognitive functions in humans. In J. Grafman & F. Boller (Eds.), *Handbook of neuropsychology* (Vol. 11). Amsterdam: Elsevier.

Pascual-Leone, A., Tormos, J. M., Keenan, J., Tarazona, F., Cañete, C., & Catalá, M. D. (1998). Study and modulation of human cortical excitability with transcranial magnetic stimulation. *Journal of Clinical Neurophysiology, 15*, 333–343.

Pascual-Leone, J. (1970). A mathematical model for the transition rule in Piaget's developmental stages. *Acta Psychologica, 32*, 301–345.

Passingham, D., & Sakai, K. (2004). The prefrontal cortex and working memory: Physiology and brain imaging. *Current Opinion in Neurobiology, 14*, 163–168.

Pasupathi, M. (2003). Emotion regulation during social remembering: Differences between emotions elicited during an event and emotions elicited when talking about it. *Memory, 11*, 151–163.

Patel, S., Cravatt, B. F., & Hillard, C. J. (in press). Synergistic interactions between cannabinoids and environmental stress in the activation of the central amygdala. *Neuropsychopharmacology*.

Patel, V., Abas, M., Broadhead, J., Todd, C., & Reeler, A. (2001). Depression in developing countries: Lessons from Zimbabwe. *British Medical Journal, 322*, 482–484.

Pato, M. T., Pato, C. N., & Pauls, D. L. (2002). Recent findings in the genetics of OCD. *Journal of Clinical Psychiatry, 63*, 30–33.

Patterson, G. R. (1986). Performance models for antisocial boys. *American Psychologist, 41*, 432–444.

Patterson, G. R., DeBaryshe, B. D., & Ramsey, E. (1989). A developmental perspective on antisocial behavior. *American Psychologist, 44*, 329–335.

Patterson, T. L., Semple, S. J., Shaw, W. S., Yu, E., He, Y., Zhang, M. Y., et al. (1998). The cultural context of caregiving: A comparison of Alzheimer's caregivers in Shanghai, China and San Diego, California. *Psychological Medicine, 28*, 1071–1084.

Pauli-Pott, U., Mertesacker, B., Bade, U., Haverkock, A., & Beckmann, D. (2003). Parental perceptions and infant temperament development. *Infant Behavior & Development, 26*, 27–48.

Paunonen, S. V. (1998). Hierarchical organization of personality and prediction of behavior. *Journal of Personality and Social Psychology, 74*, 538–556.

Paunonen, S. V., & Ashton, M. C. (1998). The structured assessment of personality across cultures. *Journal of Cross-Cultural Psychology, 29*, 150–170.

Paunonen, S. V., Haddock, G., Forsterling, F., & Keinonen, M. (2003). Broad versus narrow personality measures and the prediction of behaviour across cultures. *European Journal of Personality, 17*, 413–433.

Paunonen, S. V., Zeidner, M., Engvik, H. A., Oosterveld, P., & Maliphant, R. (2000). The nonverbal assessment of personality in five cultures. *Journal of Cross-Cultural Psychology, 31*, 220–239.

Pavlov, I. P. (1927). *Conditioned reflexes* (G. V. Anrep, Trans.). London: Oxford University Press.

Paykel, E. S., Scott, J., Cornwall, P. L., Abbott, R., Crane, C., Pope, M., & Johnson, A. L. (2005). Duration of relapse prevention after cognitive therapy in residual depression: Follow-up of controlled trial. *Psychological Medicine, 35*, 59–68.

Payne, B. R., & Lomber, S. G. (2001). Reconstructing functional systems after lesions of cerebral cortex. *Nature Reviews Neuroscience, 2*, 911–919.

Payne, D. L. (1992). *Pragmatics of word order flexibility*. Amsterdam: John Benjamins.

Pedersen, W. C., Miller, L. C., Putcha-Bhagavatula, A. D., & Yang, Y. (2002). Evolved sex differences in the number of partners desired? The long and short of it. *Psychological Science, 13*, 157–161.

Pederson, C. L., Maurer, S. H., Kaminski, P. L., Zander, K. A., Peters, C. M., Stokes-Crowe, L. A., & Osborn, R. E. (2004). Hippocampal volume and memory performance in a community-based sample of women with posttraumatic stress disorder secondary to child abuse. *Journal of Traumatic Stress, 17*, 37–40.

Pederson, N. L., Plomin, R., McClearn, G. E., & Friberg, L. (1988) Neuroticism, extraversion and related traits in adult twins reared apart and reared together. *Journal of Personality and Social Psychology, 55*, 950–957.

Pedreira, M. E., Perez-Cuesta, L. M., & Maldonado, H. (2004) Mismatch between what is expected and what actually occurs triggers memory reconsolidation or extinction. *Learning and Memory, 11*, 579–585.

Pelletier, C. L. (2004). The effect of music on decreasing arousal due to stress: A meta-analysis. *Journal of Music Therapy, 41*, 192–214.

Penfield, W. (1955). The permanent record of the stream of consciousness. *Acta Psychologica, 11*, 47–69.

Penfield, W., & Perot, P. (1963). The brain's record of auditory and visual experience. *Brain, 86*, 595–696.

Penfield, W., & Rasmussen, T. (1950). *The cerebral cortex of man: A clinical study of localization of function*. New York: Macmillan.

Pengilly, J. W., & Dowd, E. T. (1997). Hardiness and social support as moderator of stress in college students. Paper presented at the annual convention of the Association for the Advancement of Behavior Therapy, Miami Beach, FL.

Penn, D. L., Corrigan, P. W., Bentall, R. P., Racenstein, J. M., & Newman, L. (1997). Social cognition in schizophrenia. *Psychological Bulletin, 121*, 114–132.

Pennebaker, J. W. (1989). Confession, inhibition and disease. In L. Berkowitz (Ed.), *Advances in experimental social psychology* (Vol. 22, pp. 211–244). New York: Academic Press.

Pennebaker, J. W., Colder, M., & Sharp, L. K. (1990). Accelerating the coping process. *Journal of Personality and Social Psychology, 58*, 528–537.

Pennebaker, J. W., & Francis, M. E. (1996). Cognitive, emotional, and language processes in disclosure. *Cognition & Emotion, 10*, 601–626.

Penner, L. A. Dovidio, J. F., Piliavin, J. A., & Schroeder, D. A. (2005). Prosocial behavior: Multilevel perspectives. *Annual Review of Psychology, 56*, np

Penton-Voak, I. S., & Perrett, D. I. (2000). Female preference for male faces changes cyclically: Further evidence. *Evolution & Human Behavior, 21*, 39–48.

Perdue, C. W., Dovidio, J. F., Gurtman, M. B., & Tyler, R. B. (1990). Us and them: Social categorization and the process of intergroup bias. *Journal of Personality and Social Psychology, 59*, 475–486.

Peretz, I., Blood, A. J., Penhune, V., & Zatorre, R. (2001). Cortical deafness to dissonance. *Brain, 124*, 928–940.

Perlow, L., & Weeks, J. (2002). Who's helping whom? Layers of culture and workplace behaviour. *Journal of Organizational Behavior, 23*, 345–361.

Perna, F. M., Antoni, M. H., Baum, A., Gordon, P., & Schneiderman, N. (2003). Cognitive behavioral stress management effects on injury and illness among competitive athletes: A randomized clinical trial. *Annals of Behavioral Medicine, 25*, 66–73.

Perrett, D. I., Lee, K. J., Penton-Voak, I., Rowland, D., Yoshikawa, S., Burt, D. M., et al. (1998). Effects of sexual dimorphism on facial attractiveness. *Nature, 394*, 884–887.

Peters, A., Von Klot, S., Heier, M., Trentinaglia, I., Hörmann, A., Wichmann, H. E., & Löwel, H. (Cooperative Health Research in the Region of Augsburg Study Group). (2004). Exposure to traffic and the onset of myocardial infarction. *New England Journal of Medicine, 351*, 1721–1730.

Peters, M. L., Godaert, G. L. R., Ballieux, R. E., & Heijnen, C. J. (2003). Moderation of physiological stress responses by personality traits and daily hassles: Less flexibility of immune system responses. *Biological Psychology, 65*, 21–48.

Petersen, A. C., Compas, B. E., Brooks-Gunn, J., Stemmler, M., Ey, S., & Grant, K. E. (1993). Depression in adolescence. *American Psychologist, 48*, 155–168.

Petersen, R. C. (1977, July). Marihuana research findings: 1976. Summary. *NIDA Research Monograph, 14*, 1–37.

Petersen, R. C. (1979). Importance of inhalation patterns in determining effects of marihuana use. *Lancet, 31*, 727–728.

Peterson, C. (2000). The future of optimism. *American Psychologist, 55*, 44–55.

Peterson, C., & Seligman, M. E. (1984). Causal explanations as a risk factor for depression: Theory and evidence. *Psychological Review, 91*, 347–374.

Petitto, L. A., & Marentette, P. F. (1991). Babbling in the manual mode: Evidence for the ontogeny of language. *Science, 251*, 1493–1496.

Petrides, K. V., & Furnham, A. (2000). Gender differences in measured and self-estimated trait emotional intelligence. *Sex Roles, 42*, 449–461.

Petrides, K. V., & Furnham, A. (2003). Trait emotional intelligence: Behavioural validation in two studies of emotion recognition and reactivity of mood induction. *European Journal of Personality, 17*, 39–57.

Petrie, K. J., Booth, R. J., & Pennebaker, J. W. (1998). The immunological effects of thought suppression. *Journal of Personality and Social Psychology, 75*, 1264–1272.

Petrie, K. J., Booth, R. J., Pennebaker, J. W., Davison, K. P., & Thomas, M. G. (1995). Disclosure of trauma and immune response to a hepatitis B vaccination program. *Journal of Consulting and Clinical Psychology, 63*, 787–792.

Petrill, S. A., Plomin, R., McClearn, G. E., Smith, D. L., Vignetti, S., Chorney, M. J., et al. (1997). No association between general cognitive ability and the A1 allele of the D2 dopamine receptor gene. *Behavior Genetics, 27*, 29–31.

Petrovic, P., Kalso, E., Petersson, K. M., & Ingvar, M. (2002). Placebo and opioid analgesia—imaging a shared neuronal network. *Science, 295*, 1737–1740.

Pettigrew, T. F. (1969). Racially separate or together? *Journal of Social Issues, 24*, 43–69.

Pettigrew, T. F. (1981). Extending the stereotype concept. In D. L. Hamilton (Ed.), *Cognitive processes in stereotyping and intergroup behavior* (pp. 303–331). Hillsdale, NJ: Erlbaum.

Pettigrew, T. F., & Meertens, R. W. (1995). Subtle and blatant prejudice in western Europe. *European Journal of Social Psychology, 25*, 57–75.

Petty, R. E., & Cacioppo, J. T. (1986). The elaboration likelihood model of persuasion. In L. Berkowitz (Ed.), *Advances in experimental social psychology* (Vol. 19, pp. 123–205). New York: Academic Press.

Petty, R. E., & Krosnick, J. A. (1996). *Attitude strength: Anetecedents and consequences*. Hillsdale, NJ: Erlbaum.

Petty, R. E., & Wegener, D. T. (1998). Attitude change: Multiple roles for persuasion variables. In D. T. Gilbert, S. T. Fiske, & G. Lindzey (Eds.), *The handbook of social psychology* (4th ed., pp. 323–390). New York: McGraw Hill.

Pezdek, K., Finger, K., & Hodge, D. (1997). Planting false childhood memories: The role of event plausibility. *Psychological Science, 8*, 437–441.

Pfaffmann, C. (1978). The vertebrate phylogeny, neural code, and integrative processes of taste. In E. C. Carterette & M. P. Friedman (Eds.), *Handbook of perception* (pp. 51–123). New York: Academic Press.

Pfrieger, F. W. (2002). Role of glia in synapse development. *Current Opinion in Neurobiology, 12*, 486–490.

Phan, K. L., Wager, T., Taylor, S. F., & Liberzon, I. (2002). Functional neuroanatomy of emotion: A meta-analysis of emotion activation studies in PET and fMRI. *Neuro-Image, 16*, 331–348.

Phan, K. L., Wager, T., Taylor, S. F., & Liberzon, I. (2004). Functional neuroimaging studies of human emotions. *CNS Spectrums, 9*, 258–266.

Phelps, J. A., Davis, J. O., & Schartz, K. M. (1997). Nature, nurture, and twin research strategies. *Current Directions in Psychological Science, 6*, 117–121.

Philipson, T. J., & Posner, R. A. (2003). The long-run growth in obesity as a function of technological change. *Perspectives in Biology and Medicine, 46,* S87–S107.

Phillips, D. P., & Smith, D. G. (1990). Postponement of death until symbolically meaningful occasions. *Journal of the American Medical Association, 263,* 1947–1951.

Phillips, D. P., Van Voorhees, C. A., & Ruth, T. E. (1992). The birthday: Lifeline or deadline. *Psychosomatic Medicine, 54,* 532–542.

Phillips, K., & Matheny, A. P., Jr. (1995). Quantitative genetic analysis of injury liability in infants and toddlers. *American Journal of Medical Genetics (Neuropsychiatric Genetics), 60,* 64–71.

Phillips, S. D., & Imhoff, A. R. (1997). Women and career development: A decade of research. *Annual Review of Psychology, 48,* 31–59.

Piaget, J. (1962). *Play, dreams, and imitation in childhood.* New York: W. W. Norton.

Piaget, J. (1969). *The mechanisms of perception* (G. N. Seagrim, Trans.). New York: Basic Books.

Pickles, J. O. (1988). *An introduction to the physiology of hearing* (2nd ed.). London: Academic Press.

Pietromonaco, P. R., Manis, J., & Frohardt-Lane, K. (1986). Psychological consequences of multiple social roles. *Psychology of Women Quarterly, 10,* 373–381.

Pihl, R. O., Paylan, S. S., Gentes-Hawn, A., & Hoaken, P. N. S. (2003). Alcohol affects executive cognitive functioning differentially on the ascending versus descending limb of the blood alcohol concentration curve. *Alcoholism: Clinical & Experimental Research, 27,* 773–779.

Pine, D. S., Cohen, P., & Brook, J. (2001). Adolescent fears as predictors of depression. *Biological Psychiatry, 50,* 721–724.

Pinel, J. P. J. (1993). *Biopsychology* (2nd ed.). Boston: Allyn & Bacon.

Pinker, S. (1994). *The language instinct: How the mind creates language.* New York: Morrow.

Pinker, S. (1997). *How the mind works.* New York: Norton.

Pinker, S. (1999). *Words and rules: The ingredients of language.* New York: Basic Books, Inc.

Pinker, S. (2002). *The blank slate: The modern denial of human nature.* New York: Viking Press.

Pinker, S., & Jackendoff, R. (2005). The faculty of language: What's special about it? *Cognition, 95,* 201–236.

Pinkerman, J. E., Haynes, J. P., & Keiser, T. (1993). Characteristics of psychological practice in juvenile court clinics. *American Journal of Forensic Psychology, 11,* 3–12.

Pirke, K. M. (1995). Physiology of bulimia nervosa. In K. D. Brownell & C. G. Fairburn (Eds.), *Eating disorders and obesity: A comprehensive handbook* (pp. 261–265). New York: Guilford Press.

Pitman, D. L., Natelson, B. H., Ottenmiller, J. E., McCarty, R., Pritzel, T., & Tapp, W. N. (1995). Effects of exposure to stressors of varying predictability on adrenal function in rats. *Behavioral Neuroscience, 109,* 767–776.

Plehn, K., & Peterson, R. A. (2002). Anxiety sensitivity as a predictor of the development of panic symptoms, panic attacks, and panic disorder: A prospective study. *Journal of Anxiety Disorders, 16,* 455–474.

Ploghaus, A., Tracey, I., Gati, J. S., Clare, S., Menon, R. S., Matthews, P. M., & Rawlins, J. N. P. (1999). Dissociating pain from its anticipation in the human brain. *Science, 284,* 1979–1981.

Plomin, R. (1988). The nature and nurture of cognitive abilities. In R. J. Sternberg (Ed.), *Advances in the psychology of human intelligence* (Vol. 4, pp. 1–33). Hillsdale, NJ: Erlbaum.

Plomin, R. (1990). *Nature and nurture: An introduction to human behavioral genetics.* Pacific Grove, CA: Brooks/Cole.

Plomin, R. (1995). Genetics and children's experiences in the family. *Journal of Child Psychology and Psychiatry, 36,* 33–68.

Plomin, R., & Bergeman, C. S. (1991). The nature of nurture: Genetic influences on "environmental" measures. *Behavioral and Brain Sciences, 14,* 373–427.

Plomin, R., & DeFries, J. C. (1998). The genetics of cognitive abilities and disabilities: Investigations of specific cognitive skills can help clarify how genes shape the components of intellect. *Scientific American, 278,* 40–47.

Plomin, R., DeFries, J. C., Craig, I. W., & McGuffin, P. (Eds.). (2003). *Behavioral genetics in the postgenomic era.* Washington, DC: APA Books.

Plomin, R., DeFries, J. C., McClearn, G. E., & Rutter, M. (1997). *Behavioral genetics* (3rd ed.). New York: Freeman.

Plomin, R., Fulker, D. W., Corley, R., & DeFries, J. C. (1997). Nature, nurture, and cognitive development from 1 to 16 years: A parent-offspring adoption study. *Psychological Science, 8,* 442–447.

Plomin, R., & Kosslyn, S. M. (2001). Genes, brain and cognition. *Nature Neuroscience, 4,* 1153–1155.

Plomin, R., Pedersen, N. L., Lichtenstein, P., & McClearn, G. E. (1994). Variability and stability in cognitive abilities are largely genetic later in life. *Behavior Genetics, 24*(3), 207–215.

Plomin, R., & Spinath, F. M. (2004). Intelligence: Genetics, genes and genomics. *Journal of Personality and Social Psychology, 86,* 112–129.

Plotkin, H. (1994). *The nature of knowledge: Concerning adaptations, instinct and the evolution of intelligence.* New York: Allen Lane/Viking Penguin.

Plotkin, H. (1997). *Evolution in mind: An introduction to evolutionary psychology.* Cambridge, MA: Harvard University Press.

Ployhart, R. E., Ziegert, J. C., & McFarland, L. A. (2003). Understanding racial differences on cognitive ability tests in selection contexts: An integration of stereotype threat and applicant reactions research. *Human Performance, 16,* 231–259.

Plutchik, R., & Kellerman, I. (Eds.). (1980). *Emotion: Theory, research, and experience. Vol. 1. Theories of emotion.* New York: Academic Press.

Poldrack, R. A., & Wagner, A. D. (2004). What can neuroimaging tell us about the mind? Insights from prefrontal cortex. *Current Directions in Psychological Science, 13,* 177–181.

Polivy, J., & Herman, C. P. (1993). Etiology of binge eating: Psychological mechanisms. In C. G. Fairburn & G. T. Wilson (Eds.), *Binge eating: Nature, assessment, and treatment* (pp. 173–205). New York: Guilford Press.

Pollack, H. A. (2001). Sudden infant death syndrome, maternal smoking during pregnancy, and the cost-effectiveness of smoking cessation intervention. *American Journal of Public Health, 91,* 432–436.

Pollock, V. E., Briere, J., Schneider, L., Knop, J., Mednick, S. A., & Goodwin, D. H. (1990). Childhood antecedents of antisocial behavior: Parental alcoholism and physical abusiveness. *American Journal of Psychiatry, 147,* 1290–1293.

Pope, K. S. (1996). Memory, abuse, and science: Questioning claims about the false memory syndrome epidemic. *American Psychologist, 51,* 957–974.

Porter, R. H., Makin, J. W., Davis, L. B., & Christensen, K. M. (1992). An assessment of the salient olfactory environment of formula-fed infants. *Physiology & Behavior, 50,* 907–911.

Posner, M. I., & Raichle, M. (1994). *Images of mind.* New York: Freeman.

Post, R. M. (1992). Transdirection of psychosocial stress into the neurobiology of recurrent affective disorder. *American Journal of Psychiatry, 149,* 999–1010.

Postmes, T., & Spears, R. (1998). Deindividuation and antinormative behavior: A meta-analysis. *Psychological Bulletin, 123,* 238–259.

Postmes, T., Spears, R., & Cihangir, S. (2001). Quality of decision making and group norms. *Journal of Personality & Social Psychology, 80,* 918–930.

Poston, W. S. C., Ericsson, M., Linder, J., Nilsson, J., Goodrick, G. K., & Foreyt, J. P. (1999). Personality and the prediction of weight loss and relapse in the treatment of obesity. *International Journal of Eating Disorders, 25,* 301–309.

Poulet, E., Brunelin, J., Bediou, B., Bation, R., Forgeard, L., Dalery, J., D'Amato, T., & Saoud, M. (2005). Slow transcranial magnetic stimulation can rapidly reduce resistant auditory hallucinations in schizophrenia. *Biological Psychiatry, 57,* 188–191.

Poulton, R., & Menzies, R. G. (2002). Non-associative fear acquisition: A review of the evidence from retrospective and longitudinal research. *Behaviour Research & Therapy, 40,* 1227–1249.

Powell, M. C., & Fazio, R. H. (1984). Attitude accessibility as a function of repeated attitudinal expression. *Personality and Social Psychology Bulletin, 10,* 139–148.

Prapavessis, H., & Carron, A. V. (1997). Sacrifice, cohesion, and conformity to norms in sport teams. *Group Dynamics: Theory, Research, and Practice, 1,* 231–240.

Prasada, S. (2000). Acquiring generic knowledge. *Trends in Cognitive Science, 4,* 66–72.

Prescott, C. A., Johnson, R. C., & McArdle, J. J. (1991). Genetic contributions to television viewing. *Psychological Science, 2,* 430–431.

Pressley, M., Brown, R. El-Dinary, P. B., & Allferbach, P. (1995). The comprehension instruction that students need: Instruction fostering constructively responsive reading. *Learning Disabilities Research & Practice, 10,* 215–224.

Pressman, E. K., DiPietro, J. A., Costigan, K. A., Shupe, A. K., & Johnson, T. R. B. (1998). Fetal neurobehavioral development: Associations with socioeconomic class and fetal sex. *Developmental Psychobiology, 33,* 79–91.

Prien, R. F., & Kocsis, J. H. (1995). Long term treatment of mood disorders. In F. E. Bloom & D. J. Kupfer (Eds.), *Psychopharmacology: The fourth generation of progress* (pp. 1067–1080). New York: Raven Press.

Priester, J. R., & Petty, R. E. (1995). Source attributions and persuasion: Perceived honesty as a determinant of message scrutiny. *Personality and Social Psychology Bulletin, 21,* 637–654.

Privette, G., & Landsman, T. (1983). Factor analysis of peak performance: The full use of potential. *Journal of Personality and Social Psychology, 44,* 195–200.

Proctor, R. W., & Van Zandt, T. (1994). *Human factors in simple and complex systems.* Boston: Allyn & Bacon.

Przeworski, A., & Newman, M. G. (2004). Palmtop computer-assisted group therapy for social phobia. *Journal of Clinical Psychology, 60,* 179–188.

Pujol, R., Lavigne-Rebillard, M., & Uziel, A. (1990). Physiological correlates of development of the human cochlea. *Seminars in Perinatology, 14,* 275–280.

Puka, B. (Ed.). (1994). *Kohlberg's original study of moral development.* New York: Garland.

Putnam, H. (1973). Reductionism and the nature of psychology. *Cognition, 2,* 131–146.

Qin, Y., Carter, C. S., Silk, E. M., Stenger, V. A., Fissell, K., Goode, A., & Anderson, J. R. (2004). The change of the brain activation patterns as children learn algebra equation solving. *Proceedings of the National Academy of Sciences USA, 101,* 5686–5691.

Quay, H. C. (1965). Psychopathic personality as pathological stimulus-seeking. *American Journal of Psychiatry, 122,* 180–183.

Quigley, K. S., Barrett, L. F., & Weinstein, S. (2002). Cardiovascular patterns associated with threat and challenge appraisals: A within-subjects analysis. *Psychophysiology, 39,* 292–302.

Quinn, P. C., Bhatt, R. S., Brush, D., Grimes, A., & Sharpnack, H. (2002). Development of form similarity as a Gestalt grouping principle in infancy. *Psychological Science, 13,* 320–328.

Raag, T., & Rackliff, C. L. (1998). Preschoolers' awareness of social expectations of gender: Relationships to toy choices. *Sex Roles, 38,* 685–700.

Rabin, M. D., & Cain, W. S. (1986). Determinants of measured olfactory sensitivity. *Perception & Psychophysics, 39,* 281–286.

Rabinowitz, F. E., Sutton, L., Schutter, T., Brow, A., Krizo, C., Larsen, J., et al. (1997). Helpfulness to lost tourists. *Journal of Social Psychology, 137,* 502–509.

Rachman, S. (1997). A cognitive theory of obsessions. *Behaviour Research & Therapy, 35,* 793–802.

Radvansky, G. A. (1999). Aging, memory, and comprehension. *Current Directions in Psychological Science, 8,* 49–53.

Rahman, Q., Wilson, G. D., & Abrahams, S. (2004). Sex, sexual orientation, and identification of positive and negative facial affect. *Brain & Cognition, 54,* 179–185.

Räikkönen, K., Matthews, K. A., Flory, J. D., & Owens, J. F. (1999). Effects of hostility on ambulatory blood pressure and mood during daily living in healthy adults. *Health Psychology, 18,* 44–53.

Räikkönen, K., Pesonen, A. K., Järvenpää, A. L., & Strandberg, T. E. (2004). Sweet babies: Chocolate consumption during pregnancy and infant temperament at six months. *Early Human Development, 76,* 139–145.

Raine, A., Reynolds, C., Venables, P. H., & Mednick, S. A. (2002). Stimulation seeking and intelligence: A prospective longitudinal study. *Journal of Personality & Social Psychology, 82,* 663–674.

Raine, A., Venables, P. H., & Wiliams, M. (1990). Relationships between central and autonomic measures of arousal at age 15 years and criminality at age 24 years. *Archives of General Psychiatry, 47,* 1003–1007.

Rainville, P., Duncan, G. H., Price, D. D., Carrier, B., & Bushnell, M. C. (1997). Pain affect encoded in human anterior cingulate but not somatosensory cortex. *Science, 277,* 968–971.

Rajaram, S., Srinivas, K., & Roediger, H. L., III. (1998). A transfer-appropriate processing account of context effects in word fragment completion. *Journal of Experimental Psychology: Learning, Memory, & Cognition, 24,* 993–1004.

Rakic, P. (1975). Timing of major ontogenetic events in the visual cortex of the rhesus monkey. In N. Buchwald & M. Brazier (Eds.), *Brain mechanisms in mental retardation* (pp. 3–40). New York: Academic Press.

Ramirez, M., III. (1999). *Multicultural psychotherapy: An approach to individual and cultural differences* (2nd ed.). Needham Heights, MA: Allyn & Bacon.

Rankinen, T., Pérusse, L., Weisnagel, S. J., Snyder, E. E., Chagnon, Y. C., & Bouchard, C. (2002). The human obesity gene map: The 2001 update. *Obesity Research, 10,* 196–243.

Rao, H., Zhou, T., Zhuo, Y., Fan, S., & Chen, L. (2003). Spatiotemporal activation of the two visual pathways in form discrimination and spatial location: A brain mapping study. *Human Brain Mapping, 18,* 78–89.

Rao, S. C., Rainer, G., & Miller, E. K. (1997). Integration of what and where in the primate prefrontal cortex. *Science, 276,* 821–834.

Rassin, E. (2003). The White Bear Suppression Inventory (WBSI) focuses on failing suppression attempts. *European Journal of Personality, 17,* 285–298.

Ratliff-Schaub, K., Hunt, C. E., Crowell, D., Golub, H., Smok-Pearsall, S., Palmer, P., et al. (2001). Relationship between infant sleep position and motor development in preterm infants. *Journal of Developmental & Behavioral Pediatrics, 22,* 293–299.

Rauch, S. L., Jenike, M. A., Alpert, N. M., Baer, L., Breiter, H. C. R., Savage, C. R., & Fischman, A. J. (1994). Regional cerebral blood flow measured during symptom provocation in obsessive-compulsive disorder using oxygen 15–labeled carbon dioxide and positron emission tomography. *Archives of General Psychiatry, 51,* 62–70.

Rauch, S. L., van der Kolk, B. A., Risler, R. E., Alpert, N. M., Orr, S. P., Savage, C. R., et al. (1996). A symptom provocation study of posttraumatic stress disorder using positron emission tomography and script-driven imagery. *Archives of General Psychiatry, 53,* 380–387.

Rauch, S. L., Whalen, P. J., Shin, L. M., McInerney, S. C., Macklin, M. L., Lasko, N. B., et al. (2000). Exaggerated amygdala response to masked facial stimuli in posttraumatic stress disorder: A functional MRI study. *Biological Psychiatry, 47,* 769–776.

Ravussin, E., & Bouchard, C. (2000). Human genomics and obesity: Finding appropriate target drugs. *European Journal of Pharmacology, 410,* 131–145.

Raymond, J. E., Shapiro, K. L., & Arnell, K. M. (1992). Temporary suppression of visual processing in an RSVP task: An attentional blink? *Journal of Experimental Psychology: Human Perception and Performance, 18,* 849–860.

Raz, N., Gunning, F. M., Head, D., Dupuis, J. H., McQuain, J. M., Briggs, S. D., et al. (1997). Selective aging of human cerebral cortex observed in vivo: Differential vulnerability of the prefrontal gray matter. *Cerebral Cortex, 7,* 268–282.

Razran, G. H. S. (1940). Conditioned response changes in rating and appraising sociopolitical solutions. *Psychological Bulletin, 37,* 481.

Reber, P. J., Siwiec, R. M., Gitleman, D. R., Parrish, T. B., Mesulam, M.-M., & Paller, K. A. (2002). Neural correlates of successful encoding identified using functional magnetic resonance imaging. *Journal of Neuroscience, 22,* 9541–9548.

Rechtschaffen, A., Gilliland, M. A., Bergmann, B. M., & Winter, J. B. (1983). Physiological correlates of prolonged sleep deprivation in rats. *Science, 221,* 182–184.

Rector, N. A., & Beck, A. T. (2001). Cognitive behavioral therapy for schizophrenia: An empirical review. *Journal of Nervous & Mental Disease, 189,* 278–287.

Redd, W. H., Dadds, M. R., Futterman, A. D., Taylor, K. L., & Bovbjerg, D. J. (1993). Nausea induced by mental images of chemotherapy. *Cancer, 72,* 629–636.

Redelmeier, D. A., & Kahneman, D. (1996). Patients' memories of painful medical treatments: Real-time and retrospective evaluations of two minimally invasive procedures. *Pain, 66,* 3–8.

Reese, H. W., Lee, L.-J., Cohen, S. H., & Puckett, J. M., Jr. (2001). Effects of intellectual variables, age, and gender on divergent thinking in adulthood. *International Journal of Behavioral Development, 25,* 491–500.

Regan, D. T., & Fazio, R. H. (1977). On the consistency between attitudes and behavior: Look to the method of attitude formation. *Journal of Experimental Psychology, 13,* 38–45.

Regan, P. C. (1996). Rhythms of desire: The association between menstrual cycle phases and female sexual desire. *Canadian Journal of Human Sexuality, 5,* 145–156.

Regier D. A., & Kaelber, C. T. (1995). The Epidemiologic Catchment Area (ECA) program: Studying the prevalence and incidence of psychopathology. In M. T. Tsuang, M. Tohen, & G. E. P. Zahner (Eds.), *Textbook in psychiatric epidemiology* (pp. 133–157). New York: John Wiley & Sons.

Regier, D. A., Narrow, W. E., Rae, D. S., Manderscheid, R. W., Locke, B. Z., & Goodwin, F. K. (1993). The de facto US mental and addictive disorders service system. Epidemiologic Catchment Area prospective 1-year prevalence rates of disorders and services. *Archives of General Psychiatry, 50,* 85–94.

Reid, J. E. (1947). A revised questioning technique in lie-detection tests. *Journal of Criminal Law & Criminology, 37,* 542–547.

Reid, R. C. (1999). Vision. In M. J. Zigmond, F. E. Bloom, S. C. Landis, J. L. Roberts, & L. R. Squire (Eds.), *Fundamental neuroscience* (pp. 821–851). New York: Academic Press.

Reif, A., & Lesch, K. (2003). Toward a molecular architecture of personality. *Behavioural Brain Research, 139,* 1–20.

Reifman, A., & Windle, M. (1995). Adolescent suicidal behaviors as a function of depression, hopelessness, alcohol use, and social support: A longitudinal investigation. *American Journal of Community Psychology, 23,* 329–354.

Reinisch, J. M., & Sanders, S. A. (1992). Prenatal hormonal contributions to sex differences in human cognitive and personality development. In A. A. Gerall, H. Moltz, & I. I. Ward (Eds.), *Sexual differentiation: Vol. II. Handbook of behavioral neurobiology* (pp. 221–243). New York: Plenum.

Reis, V. A., & Zaidel, D. W. (2001). Brain and face: Communicating signals of health in the left and right sides of the face. *Brain & Cognition, 46,* 240–244.

Reisenzein, R., Meyer, W., & Schützwohl, A. (1995). James and the physical basis of emotion: A comment on Ellsworth. *Psychological Review, 102,* 757–761.

Rende, R., & Plomin, R. (1992). Diathesis-stress models of psychopathology: A quantitative genetic perspective. *Applied & Preventative Psychology. 1,* 177–182.

Rensink, R. A., O'Regan, J. K., & Clark, J. J. (1997). To see or not to see: The need for attention to perceive changes in scenes. *Psychological Science, 8,* 368–373.

Rescorla, R. A. (1967). Pavlovian conditioning and its proper control procedures. *Psychological Review, 74,* 71–80.

Resnick, H. S., Kilpatrick, D. G., Dansky, B. S., Saunders, B., & Best, C. L. (1993). Prevalence of civilian trauma and posttraumatic stress disorder in a representative national sample of women. *Journal of Consulting and Clinical Psychology, 61,* 984–991.

Resnick, S. M., Pham, D. L., Kraut, M. A., Zonderman, A. B., & Davatzikos, C. (2003). Longitudinal magnetic resonance imaging studies of older adults: A shrinking brain. *Journal of Neuroscience, 23,* 3295–3301.

Rest, J. R. (1979). *Development in judging moral issues.* Minneapolis: University of Minnesota Press.

Reynolds, C. F., III, Frank, E., Perel, J. M., Imber, S. D., Cornes, C., Miller, M. D., et al. (1999). Nortriptyline and interpersonal psychotherapy as maintenance therapies for recurrent major depression: A randomized controlled trial in patients older than 59 years. *Journal of the American Medical Association, 281,* 39–45.

Rice, G., Anderson, C., Risch, N., & Ebers, G. (1999). Male homosexuality: Absence of linkage to microsatellite markers at Xq28. *Science, 284,* 665–667.

Rice, M. E., & Grusec, J. E. (1975). Saying and doing: Effects on observer performance. *Journal of Personality and Social Psychology, 32,* 584–593.

Rich, A. N., & Mattingley, J. B. (2002). Anomalous perception in synaesthesia: A cognitive neuroscience perspective. *Nature Reviews Neuroscience, 3,* 43–52.

Richards, J. M. (2004). The cognitive consequences of concealing feelings. *Current Directions in Psychological Science, 13,* 131–134.

Richards, J. M., Butler, E. A., & Gross, J. J. (2003). Emotion regulation in romantic relationships: The cognitive consequences of concealing feelings. *Journal of Social & Personal Relationships, 20,* 599–620.

Richards, J. M., & Gross, J. J. (2000). Emotion regulation and memory: The cognitive costs of keeping one's cool. *Journal of Personality & Social Psychology, 79,* 410–424.

Richert, E. S. (1997). Excellence with equity in identification and programming. In N. Colangelo & G. A. Davis (Eds.), *Handbook of gifted education* (2nd ed., pp. 75–88). Boston: Allyn & Bacon.

Richmond, L. J. (2004). When spirituality goes awry: Students in cults. *Professional School Counseling, 7,* 367–375.

Riddoch, M. J., Humphreys, G. W., Jacobson, S., Pluck, G., Bateman, A., & Edwards, M. (2004). Impaired orientation discrimination and localisation following parietal damage: On the interplay between dorsal and ventral processes in visual perception. *Cognitive Neuropsychology, 21,* 597–623.

Rinaldi, M. C., Marangolo, P., & Baldassarri, F. (2004). Metaphor comprehension in right brain-damaged patients with visuo-verbal and verbal material: A dissociation (re)considered. *Cortex, 40,* 479–490.

Rips, L. (2001). Necessity and natural categories. *Psychological Bulletin, 127,* 827–852.

Rips, L. J., Shoben, E. J., & Smith, E. E. (1973). Semantic distance and the verification of semantic relations. *Journal of Verbal Learning and Verbal Behavior, 12,* 1–20.

Rivas-Vazques, R. A. (2001). Antidepressants as first-line agents in the current pharmacotherapy of anxiety disorders. *Professional Psychology: Research and Practice, 32,* 101–104.

Rivera, G., & Colle, M.-P. (1994). *Frida's fiestas: Recipes and reminiscences of life with Frida Kahlo* (K. Krabbenhoft, Trans.). New York: Clarkson N. Potter.

Rivera-Arzola, M., & Ramos-Grenier, J. (1997). Anger, ataques de nervios, and la mujer puertorriquena: Sociocultural considerations and treatment implications. In J. G. Garcia & M. C. Zea (Eds.), *Psychological interventions and research with Latino populations.* Boston, MA: Allyn & Bacon.

Robbins, T. W., & Everitt, B. J. (1998). Motivation and reward. In M. J. Zigmond, F. E. Bloom, S. C. Landis, J. L. Roberts, & L. R. Squire (Eds.), *Fundamental neuroscience* (pp. 1245–1260). New York: Academic Press.

Robbins, T. W., & Everitt, B. J. (1999). Interaction of the dopaminergic system with mechanisms of associative learning and cognition: Implications for drug abuse. *Psychological Science, 10,* 199–202.

Roberson, D., Davidoff, J., Davies, I. R. L., & Shapiro, L. R. (2004). The development of color categories in two languages: A longitudinal study. *Journal of Experimental Psychology: General, 133,* 554–571.

Roberti, J. W., Storch, E. A., & Bravata, E. A. (2004). Sensation seeking, exposure to psychosocial stressors, and body modifications in a college population. *Personality & Individual Differences, 37,* 1167–1177.

Roberts, A. H., Kewman, D. G., Mercier, L., & Hovell, M. (1993). The power of nonspecific effects in healing: Implications for psychosocial and biological treatments. *Clinical Psychology Review, 13,* 375–391.

Roberts, B. W., Caspi, A., & Moffitt, T. E. (2001). The kids are alright: Growth and stability in personality development from adolescence to adulthood. *Journal of Personality & Social Psychology, 81,* 670–683.

Roberts, B. W., & DelVecchio, W. F. (2000). The rank-order consistency of personality traits from childhood to old age: A quantitative review of longitudinal studies. *Psychological Bulletin, 126,* 3–25.

Roberts, R. D., Zeidner, M., & Matthews, G. (2001). Does emotinal intelligence meet traditional standards for an intelligence? Some new data and conclusions. *Emotion, 1,* 196–231.

Robins, L. N., & Regier, D. A. (1991). *Psychiatric disorders in America: The epidemiological catchment area study.* New York: Free Press.

Robinson, L. C. (2000). Interpersonal relationship quality in young adulthood: A gender analysis. *Adolescence, 35,* 775–784.

Robinson, N. M., Abbott, R. D., Berninger, V. W., & Busse, J. (1996). The structure of abilities in math-precocious young children: Gender similarities and differences. *Journal of Educational Psychology, 88,* 341–352.

Robinson, N. M., Zigler, Z., & Gallagher, J. J. (2000). Two tails of the normal curve: Similarities and differences in the study of mental retardation and giftedness. *American Psychologist, 55,* 1413–1424.

Robinson, S. J., & Manning, J. T. (2000). The ratio of the 2nd to 4th digit length and male homosexuality. *Evolution and Human Behaviour, 21,* 333–345.

Robinson, T. E., & Berridge, K. C. (2001). Incentive-sensitization and addiction. *Addiction, 96,* 103–114.

Rochat, P., & Hespos, S. J. (1997). Differential rooting response by neonates: Evidence for an early sense of self. *Early Development & Parenting, 6,* 105–112.

Rodier, P. (1980). Chronology of neuron development. *Developmental Medicine and Child Neurology, 22,* 525–545.

Rodin, J., & Langer, E. J. (1977). Long-term effects of a control-relevant intervention with the institutionalized aged. *Journal of Personality & Social Psychology, 35,* 897–902.

Roediger, H. L., III. (1980). Memory metaphors in cognitive psychology. *Memory & Cognition, 8,* 231–246.

Roediger, H. L., III, & McDermott, K. B. (1993). Implicit memory in normal human subjects. In F. Bohler & J. Grafman (Eds.), *Handbook of neuropsychology* (Vol. 8, pp. 63–131). Amsterdam: Elsevier.

Roediger, H. L., III, & McDermott, K. B. (1995). Creating false memories: Remembering words not presented in lists. *Journal of Experimental Psychology: Learning, Memory, and Cognition, 21,* 803–814.

Roediger, H. L., III, Meade, M. L., & Bergman, E. T. (2001). Social contagion of memory. *Psychonomic Bulletin & Review, 8,* 365–371.

Roediger, H. L., III, & Thorpe, L. A. (1978). The role of recall time in producing hypermnesia. *Memory & Cognition, 6,* 296–305.

Rohde, P. A., Atzwanger, K., Butovskayad, M., Lampert, A., Mysterud, I., Sanchez-Andres, A., & Sulloway, F. J. (2003). Perceived parental favoritism, closeness to kin, and the rebel of the family: The effects of birth order and sex. *Evolution & Human Behavior, 24,* 261–276.

Rojas, I. G., Padgett, D. A., Sheridan, J. F., & Marucha, P. T. (2002). Stress-induced susceptibility to bacterial infection during cutaneous wound healing. *Brain, Behavior, and Immunity, 16,* 74–84.

Roll, S., McClelland, G., & Abel, T. (1996). Differences in susceptibility to influence in Mexican American and Anglo females. *Hispanic Journal of Behavioral Sciences, 18,* 13–20.

Rollman, G. B. (1991). Pain responsiveness. In M. A. Heller & W. Schiff (Eds.), *The psychology of touch* (pp. 91–114). Hillsdale, NJ: Erlbaum.

Rollman, G. B., & Harris, G. (1987). The detectability, discriminality, and perceived magnitude of painful electrical shock. *Perception & Psychophysics, 42,* 257–268.

Rolls, B. J., Rowe, E. A., Rolls, E. T., Kingston, B., Megson, A., & Gunary, R. (1981). Variety in a meal enhances food intake in man. *Physiology & Behavior, 26,* 215–221.

Rolls, E. T., & Cooper, S. J. (1974). Connection between the prefrontal cortex and pontine brain-stimulation reward sites in the rat. *Experimental Neurology, 42,* 687–699.

Romero, A. A., Agnew, C. R., & Insko, C. A. (1996). The cognitive mediation hypothesis revisited: An empirical response to methodological and theoretical criticism. *Personality & Social Psychology Bulletin, 22,* 651–665.

Romero, L., & Sapolsky, R. (1996). Patterns of ACTH secretagog secretion in response to psychological stimuli. *Journal of Neuroendocrinology, 8,* 243–258.

Roozendaal, B. (2003). Systems mediating acute glucocorticoid effects on memory consolidation and retrieval. *Progress in Neuro-Psychopharmacology & Biological Psychiatry, 27,* 1213–1223.

Rosch, E. (1973). Natural categories. *Cognitive Psychology, 4,* 328–350.

Rosch, E. (1975). The nature of mental codes for color categories. *Journal of Experimental Psychology: Human Perception and Performance, 1,* 303–322.

Rosch, E. (1978). Principles of categorization. In E. Rosch, & B. B. Lloyd (Eds.), *Cognition and categorization* (pp. 27–48). Hillsdale, NJ: Erlbaum.

Rosch, E., Mervis, C. B., Gray, W. D., Johnson, D. M., & Boyes-Braem, P. (1976). Basic objects in natural categories. *Cognitive Psychology, 8,* 382–439.

Rosen, A. C., Prull, M. W., Gabrieli, J. D. E., Stoub, T., O'Hara, R., Friedman, L., et al. (2003). Differential associations between entorhinal and hippocampal volumes and memory performance in older adults. *Behavioral Neuroscience, 117,* 1150–1160.

Rosen, C. M. (1987). The eerie world of reunited twins. *Discover, 8,* 36–46.

Rosenberg, M. (1979). *Conceiving the self.* New York: Basic Books.

Rosengren, A., Hawken, S., Ôunpuu, S., Sliwa, K., Zubaid, M., Almahmeed, W. A., et al. (2004). Association of psychosocial risk factors with risk of acute myocardial infarction in 11119 cases and 13648 controls from 52 countries (the INTERHEART study): Case-control study. *Lancet, 364,* 953–962.

Rosenhan, D. L. (1973). On being sane in insane places. *Science, 179,* 250–258.

Rosenheim, M. K., & Testa, M. F. (Eds.). (1992). *Early parenthood and coming of age in the 1990s.* New Brunswick, NJ: Rutgers University Press.

Rosenkranz, M. A., Jackson, D. C., Dalton, K. M., Dolski, I., Ryff, C. D., Singer, B. H., et al. (2003). Affective style and in vivo immune response: Neurobehavioral mechanisms. *Proceedings of the National Academy of Sciences, USA, 100,*11148–11152.

Rosenthal, A. M. (1964). *Thirty-eight witnesses.* New York: McGraw-Hill.

Rosenthal, R. (1976). *Experimenter effects in behavioral research.* New York: Irvington.

Rosenthal, R. (1991). *Meta-analytic procedures for social research.* Beverly Hills, CA: Sage.

Rosenzweig, P., Brohler, S., & Zipfel, A. (1993). The placebo effect in healthy volunteers: Influence of experimental conditions on the adverse events profile during phase I studies. *Clinical Pharmacological Therapy, 54,* 579–583.

Roskill, M. (1963). *The letters of Vincent van Gogh.* London: William Collins.

Ross, C. A. (1991). Epidemiology of multiple personality disorder and dissociation. *Psychiatric Clinics of North America, 14,* 503–517.

Ross, C. E. (1995). Reconceptualizing marital status as a continuum of social attachment. *Journal of Marriage & the Family, 57,* 129–140.

Ross, L., Greene, D., & House, P. (1977). The false consensus effect: An egocentric bias in social perception and attribution processes. *Journal of Experimental Social Psychology, 13,* 279–301.

Roth, A., & Fonagy, P. (2005). *What works for whom: A critical review of psychotherapy research* (2nd ed.). New York: Guilford.

Rothbaum, B. O., Hodges, L., Anderson, P. L., Price, L., & Smith, S. (2002). Twelve-month follow-up of virtual reality and standard exposure therapies for the fear of flying. *Journal of Consulting & Clinical Psychology, 70,* 428–432.

Rothbaum, B. O., Hodges, L., Smith, S., Lee, J. H., & Price, L. (2001). A controlled study of virtual reality exposure therapy for the fear of flying. *Journal of Consulting & Clinical Psychology, 68,* 1020–1026.

Rotter, J. B. (1966). Generalized expectancies for internal versus external control of reinforcement. *Psychological Monographs, 80*(1, Whole No. 609).

Rouhana, N. N., & Bar-Tal, D. (1998). Psychological dynamics of intractable ethnonational conflicts: The Israeli-Palestinian case. *American Psychologist, 53,* 761–770.

Rouillon, F. (1997). Epidemiology of panic disorder. *Human Psychopharmacology Clinical & Experimental, 12*(Suppl. 1), S7–S12.

Rovee-Collier, C. (1997). Dissociations in infant memory: Rethinking the development of implicit and explicit memory. *Psychological Review, 104,* 467–498.

Rowe, J. W., & Kahn, R. L. (1998). *Successful aging.* New York: Pantheon.

Roy, R., Benenson, J. F., & Lilly, F. (2000). Beyond intimacy: Conceptualizing sex differences in same-sex relationships. *Journal of Psychology, 134,* 93–101.

Royet, J., & Plailly, J. (2004). Lateralization of olfactory processes. *Chemical Senses, 29,* 731–745.

Roysamb, E., Harris, J. R., Magnus, P., Vitterso, J., & Tambs, K. (2002). Subjective well-being: Sex-specific effects of genetic and environmental factors. *Personality & Individual Differences, 32,* 211–223.

Rozin, P. (1982). "Taste-smell confusions" and the duality of the olfactory sense. *Perception and Psychophysics, 31,* 397–401.

Rozin, P., Ashmore, M., & Markwith, M. (1996). Lay American conceptions of nutrition: Dose insensitivity, categorical thinking, contagion, and the monotonic mind. *Health Psychology, 15,* 438–447.

Rozin, P., & Fallon, A. (1986). The acquisition of likes and dislikes for foods. In National Research Council et al. (Eds.), *What is America eating? Proceedings of a symposium.* Washington, DC: National Academy Press.

Rozin, P., & Jonides, J. (1977). Mass reaction time: Measurement of the speed of the nerve impulse and the duration of mental processes in class. *Teaching of Psychology, 4,* 91–94.

Rozin, P., Lowery, L., & Ebert, R. (1994). Varieties of disgust faces and the structure of disgust. *Journal of Personality & Social Psychology, 66,* 870–881.

Rubin, K., & Borwick, D. (1984). The communication skills of children who vary with regard to sociability. In H. Sypher & J. Applegate (Eds.), *Social cognition and communication.* Hillsdale, NJ: Erlbaum.

Rubin, K. H., Burgess, K. B., & Coplan, R. J. (2002). Social withdrawal and shyness. In P. K. Smith & C. H. Hart (Eds.), *Blackwell handbook of childhood social development* (pp. 330–352). Malden, MA: Blackwell Publishers.

Rubin, L. J. (1996). Childhood sexual abuse: False accusations of "false memory"? *Professional Psychology Research and Practice, 27,* 447–451.

Rubin, Z. (1970). Measurement of romantic love. *Journal of Personality and Social Psychology, 16,* 265–273.

Ruby, P., & Decety, J. (2003). What you believe versus what you think they believe: A neuroimaging study of conceptual perspective-taking. *European Journal of Neuroscience, 17,* 2475–2480.

Ruiz, C. J., Wray, K., Delay, E. R., Margolskee, R. F., & Kinnamon, S. C. (2003). Behavioral evidence for a role of α-gustducin in glutamate taste. *Chemical Senses, 28,* 573–579.

Runco, M. A., & Albert, R. S. (1986). The threshold theory regarding creativity and intelligence: An empirical test with gifted and nongifted children. *Creative Child & Adult Quarterly, 11,* 212–218.

Rush, A. N., Robinette, B. L., & Stanton, M. E. (2001). Ontogenetic differences in the effects of unpaired stimulus preexposure on eyeblink conditioning in the rat. *Developmental Psychobiology, 39,* 8–18.

Rushton, J. P. (1975). Generosity in children: Immediate and long-term effects of modeling, preaching, and moral judgement. *Journal of Personality and Social Psychology, 31,* 459–466.

Rushton, J. P. (1995). *Race, evolution and behavior: A life-history perspective*. New Brunswick, NJ: Transaction.

Russell, J. A. (2003). Core affect and the psychological construction of emotion. *Psychological Review, 110,* 145–172.

Russell, J. A., Bachorowski, J.-A., & Fernández-Dols, J.-M. (2003). Facial and vocal expressions of emotion. *Annual Review of Psychology, 54,* 329–349.

Russell, R. (2003). Sex, beauty, and the relative luminance of facial features. *Perception, 32,* 1093–1107.

Rustemli, A., Mertan, B., & Ciftci, O. (2000). In-group favoritism among native and immigrant Turkish cypriots: Trait evaluations of in-group and out-group targets. *Journal of Social Psychology, 140,* 26–34.

Rutledge, T., Reis, S. E., Olson, M., Owens, J., Kelsey, S. F., Pepine, C. J., et al. (2004). Social networks are associated with lower mortality rates among women with suspected coronary disease: The National Heart, Lung, and Blood Institute-Sponsored Women's Ischemia Syndrome Evaluation Study. *Psychosomatic Medicine, 66,* 882–888.

Ryan, K. E., & Ryan, A. M. (2005). Psychological processes underlying stereotype threat and standardized math test performance. *Educational Psychologist, 40,* 53–63.

Ryan, R. M., & Deci, E. L. (2000). Self-determination theory and the facilitation of intrinsic motivation, social development, and well-being. *American Psychologist, 55,* 68–78.

Ryner, L. C., Goodwin, S. F., Castrillon, D. H., Anand, A., Villella, A., Baker, B. S., et al. (1996). Control of male sexual behavior and sexual orientation in Drosophila by the fruitless gene. *Cell, 87,* 1079–1089.

Rynes, S. L., Gerhart, B., & Parks, L. (2005). Personnel psychology: Performance evaluation and pay-for-performance. *Annual Review of Psychology, 56,* 561–600.

Ryska, T. A. (1998). Cognitive-behavioral strategies and precompetitive anxiety among recreational athletes. *Psychological Record, 48,* 697–708.

Sachs, J. S. (1967). Recognition memory for syntactic and semantic aspects of connected discourse. *Perception and Psychophysics, 2,* 437–442.

Sackeim, H. A., Devanand, D. P., & Nobler, M. S. (1995). Electroconvulsive therapy. In F. E. Bloom & D. J. Kupfer (Eds.), *Psychopharmacology: The fourth generation of progress* (pp. 1123–1141). New York: Raven Press.

Sackeim, H. A., Haskett, R. F., Mulsant, B. H., Thase, M. E., Mann, J. J., Pettinati, H. M., et al. (2001). Continuation pharmacotherapy in the prevention of relapse following electroconvulsive therapy: A randomized controlled trial. *Journal of the American Medical Association, 285,* 1299–1307.

Sackett, P. R., Schmitt, N., Ellingson, J. E., & Kabin, M. B. (2001). High-stakes testing in employment, credentialing, and higher education: Prospects in a post-affirmative-action world. *American Psychologist, 56,* 302–318.

Sacks, O. (1995). *An anthropologist on Mars: Seven paradoxical tales.* New York: Knopf.

Saffran, J. R. (2001). Words in a sea of sounds: The output of infant statistical learning. *Cognition, 81,* 149–169.

Saggino, A. (2000). The Big Three or the Big Five? A replication study. *Personality & Individual Differences, 28,* 879–886.

Sagi, A., Koren-Karie, N., Gini, M., Ziv, Y., & Joels, T. (2002). Shedding further light on the effects of various types and quality of early child care on infant-mother attachment relationship: The Haifa Study of Early Child Care. *Child Development, 73,* 1166–1186.

Sagi, A., van IJzendoorn, M. H., Scharf, M., Joels, T., Mayseless, O., & Aviezer, O. (1997). Ecological constraints for intergenerational transmission of attachment. *International Journal of Behavioral Development, 20,* 287–299.

Sagie, A., Elizur, S., & Hirotsugu, Y. (1996). The structure and strength of achievement motivation: A cross-cultural comparison. *Journal of Organization Behavior, 17,* 431–444.

Saha, L. J. (Ed.). (2004). Levels of analysis in the social psychology of education [Editorial]. *Social Psychology of Education, 7,* 253–255.

Sakai, N., Kobayakawa, T., Gotow, N., Saito, S., & Imada, S. (2001). Enhancement of sweetness ratings of aspartame by a vanilla odor presented either by orthonasal or retronasal routes. *Perceptual & Motor Skills, 92,* 1002–1008.

Saldana, H. N., & Rosenblum, L. D. (1993). Visual influences on auditory pluck and bow judgments. *Perception & Psychophysics, 54,* 406–416.

Saletan, W. (2004, May 12). Situationist ethics: The Stanford Prison Experiment doesn't explain Abu Ghraib. *Slate Magazine.* Retrieved from http://slate.msn.com/id/2100419/

Salkovskis, P. M. (1985). Obsessional-compulsive problems: A cognitive-behavioral analysis. *Behaviour Research and Therapy, 23,* 571–583.

Salkovskis, P. M., Wroe, A. L., Gledhill, A., Morrison, N., Forrester, E., Richards, C., et al. (2000). Responsibility attitudes and interpretations are characteristic of obsessive–compulsive disorder. *Behaviour Research and Therapy, 38,* 347–372.

Salmon, C. A. (1998). The evocative nature of kin terminology in political rhetoric. *Politics and the Life Sciences, 17,* 51–57.

Salmon, C. A. (1999). On the impact of sex and birth order on contact with kin. *Human Nature, 10,* 183–197.

Salmon, C. A., & Daly, M. (1998). Birth order and familial sentiment: Middleborns are different. *Evolution and Behavior, 19,* 299–312.

Salovey, P., & Mayer, J. D. (1990). Emotional intelligence. *Imagination, Cognition, and Personality, 9,* 185–211.

Salthouse, T. A. (1985). Speed of behavior and its implications for cognition. In J. E. Birren & K. W. Schaie (Eds.), *Handbook of the psychology of aging* (2nd ed., pp. 400–426). New York: Van Nostrand Reinhold.

Salthouse, T. A. (1991a). Cognitive facets of aging well. *Generations, 15*(1), 35–38.

Salthouse, T. A. (1991b). *Theoretical perspectives on cognitive aging.* Hillsdale, NJ: Erlbaum.

Salthouse, T. A. (1996). The processing-speed theory of adult age differences in cognition. *Psychological Review, 103,* 403–428.

Samoluk, S. B., & Stewart, S. H. (1998). Anxiety sensitivity and situation-specific drinking. *Journal of Anxiety Disorders, 12,* 407–419.

Sanbonmatsu, D. M., & Fazio, R. H. (1990). The role of attitudes in memory-based decision making. *Journal of Personality and Social Psychology, 59,* 614–622.

Sanudo-Pena, M., Tsou, K., Romero, J., Mackie, K., & Walker, J. M. (2000). Role of the superior colliculus in the motor effects of cannabinoids and dopamine. *Brain Research, 853,* 207–214.

Sapolsky, R. M. (1992). *Stress, the aging brain, and the mechanisms of neuron death.* Cambridge, MA: MIT Press.

Sapolsky, R. M. (1996). Why stress is bad for your brain. *Science, 273,* 749–750.

Sapolsky, R. M. (1997). *Why zebras don't get ulcers.* New York: Freeman.

Sargent, J. D., Beach, M. L., Dalton, M. A., Mott, L. A., Tickle, J. J., Ahrens, M. B., & Heatherton, T. L. (2001). Effect of seeing tobacco use in films on trying smoking among adolescents: Cross sectional study. *British Medical Journal, 323,* 1394–1397.

Sargent, P. A., Sharpley, A. L., Williams, C., Goodall, E. M., & Cowen, P. J. (1997). 5-HT-sub(2C) receptor activation decreases appetite and body weight in obese subjects. *Psychopharmacology, 133,* 309–312.

Saroglou, V., & Fiasse, L. (2003). Birth order, personality, and religion: A study among young adults from a three-sibling family. *Personality & Individual Differences, 35,* 19–29.

Satcher, D. (1999). *Mental health: A report of the Surgeon General.* Washington, DC: Department of Health and Human Services.

Saxe, G. B. (1988). Candy selling and math learning. *Educational Research. 17,* 14–21.

Saxena, S., & Rauch, S. L. (2000). Functional neuroimaging and the neuroanatomy of obsessive-compulsive disorder. *Psychiatric Clinics of North America, 23,* 563–586.

Scarr, S., & McCartney, K. (1983). How people make their own environments: A theory of genotype-environment effects. *Child Development, 54,* 424–435.

Scarr, S., & Weinberg, R. A. (1983). The Minnesota Adoption Studies: Genetic differences and malleability. *Child Development, 54,* 260–267.

Schachter, S., & Latané, B. (1964). Crime, cognition, and the autonomic nervous system. In D. Levine (Ed.), *Nebraska Symposium on Motivation* (Vol. 12, pp. 221–273). Lincoln: University of Nebraska Press.

Schachter, S., & Singer, J. (1962). Cognitive, social and physiological determinants of emotional state. *Psychological Review, 69,* 379–399.

Schacter, D. L. (1987). Implicit memory: History and current status. *Journal of Experimental Psychology: Learning, Memory, and Cognition, 13,* 501–518.

Schacter, D. L. (1996). *Searching for memory: The brain, the mind, and the past.* New York: Basic Books.

Schacter, D. L. (1999). The seven sins of memory: Insights from psychology and cognitive neuroscience. *American Psychologist, 54,* 182–203.

Schacter, D. L., & Badgaiyan, R. D. (2001). Neuroimaging of priming: New perspectives on implicit and explicit memory. *Current Directions in Psychological Science, 10,* 1–4.

Schacter, D. L., Cendan, D. L., Dodson, C. S., & Clifford, E. R. (2001). Retrieval conditions and false recognition: Testing the distinctiveness heuristic. *Psychonomic Bulletin & Review, 8,* 827–833.

Schacter, D. L., Reiman, E., Curran, T., Yun, L. S., Bandy, D., McDermott, K. B., & Roediger, H. L., III. (1996). Neuroanatomical correlates of veridical and illusory recognition memory: Evidence from positron emission tomography. *Neuron, 2,* 267–274.

Schaefer, S. M., Jackson, D. C., Davidson, R. J., Aguirre, G. K., Kimberg, D. Y., & Thompson-Schill, S. L. (2002). Modulation of amygdalar activity by the conscious regulation of negative emotion. *Journal of Cognitive Neuroscience, 14,* 913–921.

Schaffner, K. F. (1967). Approaches to reduction. *Philosophy of Science, 34,* 137–147.

Schaie, K. W., Willis, S. L., & Caskie, G. I. L. (2004). The Seattle longitudinal study: Relationship between personality and cognition. *Aging, Neuropsychology, & Cognition, 11,* 304–324.

Scheflin, A., & Brown, D. (1996). Repressed memory or dissociative amnesia: What science says. *Journal of Psychiatry and Law, 24,* 143–188.

Schein, E. H. (1961). *Coercive persuasion.* New York: W. W. Norton.

Schifano, F. (2004). A bitter pill. Overview of ecstasy (MDMA, MDA) related fatalities. *Psychopharmacology, 173,* 242–248.

Schiffman, S. S., Graham, B. G., Sattely-Miller, E. A., & Warwick, Z. S. (1999). Orosensory perception of dietary fat. *Current Directions in Psychological Science, 7,* 137–144.

Schlaepfer, T. E., Kosel, M., & Nemeroff, C. B. (2003). Efficacy of repetitive transcranial magnetic stimulation (rTMS) in the treatment of affective disorders. *Neuropsychopharmacology, 28,* 201–205.

Schlaug, G., Jancke, L., Huang, Y., & Steinmetz, H. (1995). In vivo evidence of structural brain asymmetry in musicians. *Science, 267,* 699–701.

Schmader, T. (2002). Gender identification moderates stereotype threat effects on women's math performance. *Journal of Experimental Social Psychology, 38,* 194–201.

Schmader, T., & Johns, M. (2003). Converging evidence that stereotype threat reduces working memory capacity. *Journal of Personality & Social Psychology, 85,* 440–452.

Schmajuk, N. A. (2001). Hippocampal dysfunction in schizophrenia. *Hippocampus, 11,* 599–613.

Schmid, W., & Aldridge, D. (2004). Active music therapy in the treatment of multiple sclerosis patients: A matched control study. *Journal of Music Therapy, 41,* 225–240.

Schmidt, F. L., & Hunter, J. (2004). General mental ability in the world of work: Occupational attainment and job performance. *Journal of Personality and Social Psychology, 86,* 162–173.

Schmidt, N. B., Lerew, D. R., & Jackson, R. J. (1997). The role of anxiety sensitivity in the pathogenesis of panic: Prospective evaluation of spontaneous panic attacks during acute stress. *Journal of Abnormal Psychology, 106,* 355–364.

Schmidt, N. B., Lerew, D. R., & Jackson, R. J. (1999). Prospective evaluation of anxiety sensitivity in the pathogenesis of panic: Replication and extension. *Journal of Abnormal Psychology, 108,* 532–537.

Schmitt, B. H., Gilovich, T., Goore, N., & Joseph, L. (1986). Mere presence and social facilitation: One more time. *Journal of Experimental Social Psychology, 22,* 242–248.

Schmitt, D. P. (2002). How shall I compare thee? Evolutionary psychology viewed as a psychological science. *Psychology, Evolution & Gender, 4,* 219–230.

Schmolck, H., Buffalo, E. A., & Squire, L. R. (2000). Memory distortions develop over time: Recollections from the O. J. Simpson trial verdict after 15 and 32 months. *Psychological Science, 11,* 39–45.

Schneider, W., & Chein, J. M. (2003). Controlled and automatic processing: Behavior, theory, and biological mechanisms. *Cognitive Science, 27,* 525–559.

Schneider, M., & Koch, M. (2002). The cannabinoid agonist WIN 55,212-2 reduces sensorimotor gating and recognition memory in rats. *Behavioural Pharmacology, 13,* 29–37.

Schofield, P. E., Pattison, P. E., Hill, D. J., & Borland, R. (2001). The influence of group identification on the adoption of peer group smoking norms. *Psychology & Health, 16,* 1–16.

Schrof, J. M., & Schultz, S. (1999, March 8). Melancholy nation. *U.S. News and World Report,* pp. 56–63.

Schul, R., Slotnick, B. M., & Dudai, Y. (1996). Flavor and the frontal cortex. *Behavioral Neuroscience, 110,* 760–765.

Schwartz, J. M., Stoessel, P. W., Baxter, L. R., Martin, K. M., & Phelps, M. E. (1996). Systematic changes in cerebral glucose metabolic rate after successful behavior modification treatment of obsessive-compulsive disorder. *Archives of General Psychiatry, 53,* 109–113.

Schwarz, N. (1999). Self-reports: How the questions shape the answers. *American Psychologist, 54,* 93–105.

Schwarzer, R., & Knoll, N. (2003). Positive coping: Mastering demands and searching for meaning. In S. J. Lopez & C. R. Snyder (Eds.), *Positive psychological assessment: A handbook of models and measures* (pp. 393–409). Washington, DC: American Psychological Association.

Schweiger, A., & Parducci, A. (1981). Nocebo: The psychologic induction of pain. *Pavlovian Journal of Biological Science, 16,* 140–143.

Schyns, P. (1998). Crossnational differences in happiness: Economic and cultural factors explored. *Social Indicators Research, 43,* 3–26.

Scott, B., & Melin, L. (1998). Psychometric properties and standardised data for questionnaires measuring negative affect, dispositional style and daily hassles: A nationwide sample. *Scandinavian Journal of Psychology, 39,* 301–307.

Scott, J., Stanton, B., Garland, A., & Ferrier, I. N. (2000). Cognitive vulnerability in patients with bipolar disorder. *Psychological Medicine, 30,* 467–472.

Scott, T. R., & Plata-Salaman, C. R. (1991). Coding of taste quality. In T. V. Getchell, R. L. Doty, L. M. Bartoshuk & J. B. Snow, Jr. (Eds.), *Smell and taste in health and disease* (pp. 345–368). New York: Raven.

Sears, R., Maccoby, E., & Levin, H. (1957). *Patterns of child rearing.* New York: Harper & Row.

Sedikides, C., Gaertner, L., & Toguchi, Y. (2003). Pancultural self-enhancement. *Journal of Personality & Social Psychology, 84,* 60–79.

Seeman, R. E., Berkman, L. F., Blazer, D., & Rowe, J. W. (1994). Social ties and support and neuroendocrine function: The MacArthur studies of successful aging. *Annals of Behavioral Medicine, 16,* 95–106.

Seeman, T. E. (2000). Health promoting effects of friends and family on health outcomes in older adults. *American Journal of Health Promotion, 14,* 362–370.

Seeman, T. E., Singer, B. H., Rowe, J. W., Horwitz, R. I., & McEwen, B. S. (1997). Price of adaptation—allostatic load and its health consequences: MacArthur stud-

ies of successful aging. *Archives of Internal Medicine, 157,* 2259–2268.

Segal, N. L. (1999). *Entwined lives: Twins and what they tell us about human behavior.* New York: Dutton/Penguin.

Segerstrom, S. C., Taylor, S. E., Kemeny, M. E., Reed, G. M., & Visscher, B. R. (1996). Causal attributions predict rate of immune decline in HIV-seropositive gay men. *Health Psychology, 15,* 485–493.

Segrin, C., & Abramson, L. Y. (1994). Negative reactions to depressive behaviors: A communication theory analysis. *Journal of Abnormal Psychology, 103,* 655–668.

Segrin, C., & Dillard, J. P. (1992). The interactional theory of depression: A meta-analysis of the research literature. *Journal of Social & Clinical Psychology, 11*(1), 43–70.

Seith, R. (2000). Back sleeping may delay infant crawling. CWK Network. Retrieved from http://www.kidsmd.com/Tipsheets/21_may2301/crawling.html

Sekiyama, K., Kanno, I., Miura, S., & Sugita, Y. (2003). Auditory-visual speech perception examined by fMRI and PET. *Neuroscience Research, 47,* 277–287.

Seligman, M. E., & Csikszentmihalyi, M. (2000). Positive psychology: An introduction. *American Psychologist, 55,* 5–14.

Seligman, M. E. P. (1971). Phobias and preparedness. *Behavior Therapy, 2,* 307–320.

Seligman, M. E. P., & Pawelski, J. O. (2003). Positive psychology: FAQs. *Psychological Inquiry, 14,* 159–163.

Selye, H. (1976). *The stress of life.* New York: McGraw-Hill.

Semenov, L. A., Chernova, N. D., & Bondarko, V. M. (2000). Measurement of visual acuity and crowding effect in 3–9-year-old children. *Human Physiology, 26,* 16–20.

Sensky, T., Turkington, D., Kingdon, D., Scott, J. L., Scott, J., Siddle, R., et al. (2000). A randomized controlled trial of cognitive-behavioral therapy for persistent symptoms in schizophrenia resistant to medication. *Archives of General Psychiatry, 57,* 165–172.

Serpell, R. (1979). How specific are perceptual skills? A cross-cultural study of pattern reproduction. *British Journal of Psychology, 70,* 365–380.

Seta, J. J., & Seta, C. E. (1992). Increments and decrements in mean arterial pressure as a function of audience composition: An averaging and summation analysis. *Personality and Social Psychology Bulletin, 18,* 173–181.

Setliff, A. E., & Marmurek, H. H. C. (2002). The mood regulatory function of autobiographical recall is moderated by self-esteem. *Personality and Individual Differences, 32,* 761–771.

Seuling, B. (1976). *The loudest screen kiss and other little-known facts about the movies.* New York: Doubleday.

Seuling, B. (1978). *The last cow on the White House lawn and other little-known facts about the presidency.* New York: Doubleday.

Shalev, A. Y., Peri, T., Brandes, D., Freedman, S., Orr, S. P., & Pitman, R. K. (2000). Auditory startle response in trauma survivors with posttraumatic stress disorder: A prospective study. *American Journal of Psychiatry, 157,* 255–261.

Shalev, A. Y., Sahar, T., Freedman, S., Peri, T., Glick, N., Brandes, D., et al. (1998). A prospective study of heart rate response following trauma and the subsequent development of posttraumatic stress disorder. *Archives of General Psychiatry, 55,* 553–559.

Shallenberger, R. S. (1993). *Taste chemistry.* New York: Blackie Academic.

Shallice, T., Fletcher, P., Frith, C. D., Grasby, P., Frackowiak, R. S. J., & Dolan, R. J. (1994). Brain regions associated with acquisition and retrieval of verbal episodic memory. *Nature, 368,* 633–635.

Shanab, M. E., & Yahya, K. A. (1977). A behavioral study of obedience in children. *Journal of Personality and Social Psychology, 35,* 530–536.

Shapira, B., Tubi, N., Drexler, H., Lidsky, D., Calev, A., & Lerer, B. (1998). Cost and benefit in the choice of ECT schedule: Twice versus three times weekly ECT. *British Journal of Psychiatry, 172,* 44–48.

Shapiro, A. K. (1964). Factors contributing to the placebo effect: Their significance for psychotherapy. *American Journal of Psychotherapy, 18,* 73–88.

Shapiro, A. K., & Morris, L. A. (1978). The placebo effect in medical and psychological therapies. In S. L. Garfield & A. E. Bergin (Eds.), *Handbook of psychotherapy and behavior change: An empirical analysis* (2nd ed.). New York: Wiley.

Shapiro, D. H., Jr., Schwartz, C. E., & Astin, J. A. (1996). Controlling ourselves, controlling our world: Psychology's role in understanding positive and negative consequences of seeking and gaining control. *American Psychologist, 51,* 1213–1230.

Shaver, P. R., & Hazan, C. (1994). Attachment. In A. L. Weber & J. H. Harvey (Eds.), *Perspectives on close relationships.* Boston: Allyn & Bacon.

Shaw, P. J., Bergmann, B. M., & Rechtschaffen, A. (1998). Effects of paradoxical sleep deprivation on thermoregulation in the rat. *Sleep, 21,* 7–17.

Shaywitz, B. A., Shaywitz, S. E., Pugh, K. R., Constable, R. T., Skudlarski, P., Fulbright, R. K., et al. (1995). Sex differences in the functional organization of the brain for language. *Nature, 373,* 607–611.

Sheehan, P. W. (1988). Memory distortion in hypnosis. *International Journal of Clinical Experimental Hypnosis, 36,* 296–311.

Sheehan, T. P., Chambers, R. A., & Russell, D. S. (2004). Regulation of affect by the lateral septum: Implications for neuropsychiatry. *Brain Research Reviews, 46,* 71–117.

Sheehy, R., & Horan, J. J. (2004). Effects of stress inoculation training for 1st-year law students. *International Journal of Stress Management, 11,* 41–55.

Sheen, M., Kemp, S., & Rubin, D. (2001). Twins dispute memory ownership: A new false memory phenomenon. *Memory & Cognition, 29,* 779–788.

Sheese, B. E., Brown, E. L., & Graziano, W. G. (2004). Emotional expression in cyberspace: Searching for moderators of the Pennebaker disclosure effect via e-mail. *Health Psychology, 23,* 457–464.

Sheinberg, D. L., & Logothetis, N. K. (2001). Noticing familiar objects in real world scenes: The role of temporal cortical neurons in natural vision. *Journal of Neuroscience, 21,* 1340–1350.

Shekim, W. O., Bylund, D. B., Frankel, F., Alexson, J., Jones S. B., Blue, L. D., et al. (1989). Platelet MAO activity and personality variations in normals. *Psychiatry Research, 27,* 81–88.

Sheldon, K. M., Ryan, R., & Reis, H. T. (1996). What makes for a good day? Competence and autonomy in the day and in the person. *Personality & Social Psychology Bulletin, 22,* 1270–1279.

Sheline, Y. I., Gado, M. H., & Kraemer, H. C. (2003). Untreated depression and hippocampal volume loss. *American Journal of Psychiatry, 160,* 1516–1518.

Shepard, R. N., & Cooper, L. A. (1982). *Mental images and their transformations.* Cambridge, MA: MIT Press/Bradford Books.

Shepherd, M. (1993). The placebo: From specificity to the non-specific and back. *Psychological Medicine, 23,* 569–578.

Shepherd, M. D., Schoenberg, M., Slavich, S., Wituk, S., Warren, M., & Meissen, G. (1999). Continuum of professional involvement in self-help groups. *Journal of Community Psychology, 27,* 39–53.

Sherif, M., Harvey, O. J., White, B. J., Hood, W. R., & Sherif, C. W. (1961). *Intergroup conflict and cooperation: The robber's cave experiment.* Norman, OK: University Book Exchange.

Shibahara, H., Shigeta, M., Toji, H., & Koyama, K. (1995). Sperm immobilizing antibodies interfere with sperm migration from the uterine cavity through the fallopian tubes. *American Journal of Reproductive Immunology, 34,* 120–124.

Shields, S. A. (1987). Women, men, and the dilemma of emotion. In P. Shaver & C. Hendrick (Eds.), *Sex and gender* (pp. 229–250). Newbury Park, CA: Sage.

Shiffrin, R. M. (1999). 30 years of memory. In C. Izawa (Ed.), *On human memory: Evolution, progress, and reflections on the 30th anniversary of the Atkinson-Shiffrin model* (pp. 17–33). Hillsdale, NJ: Erlbaum.

Shin, L. M., Kosslyn, S. M., McNally, R. J., Alpert, N. M., Thompson, W. L., Raush, S. L., et al. (1997). Visual imagery and perception in posttraumatic stress disorder: A positron emission tomographic investigation. *Archives of General Psychiatry, 54*, 233–241.

Shin, L. M., Orr, S. P., Carson, M. A., Rauch, S. L., Macklin, M. L., Lasko, N. B., et al. (2004). Regional cerebral blood flow in the amygdala and medial prefrontal cortex during traumatic imagery in male and female Vietnam veterans with PTSD. *Archives of General Psychiatry, 61*, 168–176.

Shioiri, S., Cavanagh, P., Miyamoto, T., & Yaguchi, H. (2000). Tracking the apparent location of targets in interpolated motion. *Vision Research, 40*, 1365–1376.

Shiraishi, T., Oomura, Y., Sasaki, K., & Wayner, M. J. (2000). Effects of leptin and orexin-A on food intake and feeding related hypothalamic neurons. *Physiology & Behavior, 71*, 251–261.

Shoda, Y., & LeeTiernan, S. (2002). What remains invariant? Finding order within a person's thoughts, feelings, and behaviors across situations. In D. Cervone & W. Mischel (Eds.), *Advances in personality science* (pp. 241–270). New York: Guilford Press.

Shulman, S., Elicker, J., & Sroufe, L. A. (1994). Stages of friendship growth in preadolescence as related to attachment history. *Journal of Social & Personal Relationships, 11*, 341–361.

Siegel, A. M., Andersen, R. A., Freund, H., & Spencer, D. D. (Eds.). (2003). The parietal lobes. Philadelphia: Lippincott Williams & Wilkins.

Siegel, D. J. (1999). *The developing mind: Toward a neurobiology of interpersonal experience*. New York: Guilford Press.

Siegel, J. L., & Longo, D. L. (1981). The control of chemotherapy induced emesis. *Annals of Internal Medicine, 95*, 352–359.

Siegel, M., Brisman, J., & Weinshel, M. (1988). *Surviving an eating disorder: Strategies for family and friends*. New York: Harper and Row.

Siegel, S. (1988). State dependent learning and morphine tolerance. *Behavioral Neuroscience, 102*, 228–232.

Siegel, S., Baptista, M. A. S., Kim, J. A., McDonald, R. V., & Weise-Kelly, L. (2000). Pavlovian psychopharmacology: The associative basis of tolerance. *Experimental & Clinical Psychopharmacology, 8*, 276–293.

Siegel, S., & Ramos, B. M. C. (2002). Applying laboratory research: Drug anticipation and the treatment of drug addiction. *Experimental & Clinical Psychopharmacology, 10*, 162–183.

Sifneos, P. E. (1992). *Short-term anxiety-provoking psychotherapy: A treatment manual*. New York: Basic Books.

Silverman, L. (1976). Psychoanalytic theory: The reports of my death are greatly exaggerated. *American Psychologist, 31*, 621–637.

Silverman, L. K. (1993a). Counseling families. In L. K. Silverman (Ed.), *Counseling the gifted and talented* (pp. 43–89). Denver: Love.

Silverman, L. K. (1993b). A developmental model for counseling the gifted. In L. K. Silverman (Ed.), *Counseling the gifted and talented* (pp. 51–78). Denver, CO: Love.

Simcock, G., & Hayne, H. (2002). Breaking the barrier? Children fail to translate their preverbal memories into language. *Psychological Science, 13*, 225–231.

Simmons, J. A., & Chen, L. (1989). The acoustic basis for target discrimination by FM echo-locating bats. *Journal of the Acoustical Society of America, 86*, 1333–1350.

Simon, L., Greenberg, J., & Brehm, J. (1995). Trivialization: The forgotten mode of dissonance reduction. *Journal of Personality and Social Psychology, 68*, 247–260.

Simons, D. J. (2000). Current approaches to change blindness. *Visual Cognition, 7*, 1–15.

Simons, D. J., & Ambinder, M. S. (2005). Change blindness. *Current Directions in Psychological Science, 14*, 44–48.

Simon-Thomas, E. R., Role, K. O., & Knight, R. T. (2005). Behavioral and electrophysiological evidence of a right hemisphere bias for the influence of negative emotion on higher cognition. *Journal of Cognitive Neuroscience, 17*, 518–529.

Simonton, D. K. (1984). *Genius, creativity, and leadership: Historiometric inquiries*. Cambridge, MA: Harvard University Press.

Simonton, D. K. (1988). Creativity, leadership, and chance. In R. J. Sternberg (Ed.), *The nature of creativity* (pp. 386–436). New York: Cambridge University Press.

Simonton, D. K. (1994). *Greatness: Who makes history and why*. New York: Guilford.

Simonton, D. K. (1997). Creative productivity: A predictive and explanatory model of career trajectories and landmarks. *Psychological Review, 104*, 66–89.

Simos, P. G. (2001). *Vision in the brain*. The Netherlands: Swets & Zeitlinger.

Singer, L. T., Arendt, R., Minnes, S., Farkas, K., Salvator, A., Kirchner, H. L., & Kliegman, R. (2002a). Cognitive and motor outcomes of cocaine-exposed infants. *Journal of the American Medical Association, 287*, 1952–1960.

Singer, L. T., Salvator, A., Arendt, R., Minnes, S., Farkas, K., & Kliegman, R. (2002b). Effects of cocaine/polydrug exposure and maternal psychological distress on infant birth outcomes. *Neurotoxicology & Teratology, 24*, 127–135.

Singer, M. T. (1995). Cults: Implications for family therapists. In R. H. Mikesell et al. (Eds.), *Integrating family therapy: Handbook of family psychology and systems theory* (pp. 519–527). Washington, DC: American Psychological Association.

Singer, M. T., & Lalich, J. (1995). *Cults in our midst*. San Francisco: Jossey-Bass.

Singh, V. N. (1995). Human uterine amylase in relation to infertility. *Hormone and Metabolic Research, 27*, 35–36.

Sinha, B. K., Willson, L. R., & Watson, D. C. (2000). Stress and coping among students in India and Canada. *Canadian Journal of Behavioral Sciences, 32*, 218–225.

Sireteanu, R. (2000). Texture segmentation, "pop-out," and feature binding in infants and children. In C. Rovee-Collier & L. P. Lipsitt (Eds.), *Progress in infancy research* (Vol. 1, pp. 183–249). Mahwah, NJ: Erlbaum.

Skinner, B. F. (1953). *Science and human behavior*. New York: Macmillan.

Skinner, B. F. (1956). A case history in scientific method. *American Psychologist, 11*, 221–233.

Skinner, N. F. (2003). Birth order effects in dominance: Failure to support Sulloway's view. *Psychological Reports, 92*, 387–388.

Skowronski, J. J., Gibbons, J. A., Vogl, R. J., & Walker, W. R. (2004). The effect of social disclosure on the intensity of affect provoked by autobiographical memories. *Self & Identity, 3*, 285–309.

Skowronski, J. J., & Walker, W. R. (2004). How describing autobiographical events can affect autobiographical memories. *Social Cognition, 22*, 555–590.

Slep, A. M. S., & O'Leary, S. G. (1998). The effects of maternal attributions on parenting: An experimental analysis. *Journal of Family Psychology, 12*, 234–243.

Slimp, J. C., Hart, B. L., & Goy, R. W. (1978). Heterosexual, autosexual and social behavior of adult male rhesus monkeys with medial preoptic-anterior hypothalamic lesions. *Brain Research, 142*, 105–122.

Slotnick, S. D., Moo, L. R., Tesoro, M. A., & Hart, J. (2001). Hemispheric asymmetry in categorical versus coordinate spatial processing revealed by temporary cortical deactivation. *Journal of Cognitive Neuroscience, 13*, 1088–1096.

Small, B. J., & Bäckman, L. (2000). Time to death and cognitive performance. *Current Directions in Psychological Science, 6*, 168–172.

Small, B. J., Fratiglioni, L., von Strauss, E., & Backman, L. (2003). Terminal decline and cognitive performance in very old age: Does cause of death matter? *Psychology and Aging, 18*, 193–202.

Small, D. M., Zatorre, R. J., Dagher, A., Evans, A. C., & Jones-Gotman, M. (2001). Changes in brain activity related to eating chocolate: From pleasure to aversion. *Brain, 124*, 1720–1733.

Smeets, M. A. M., Smit, F., Panhuysen, G. E. M., & Ingleby, J. D. (1997). The influence of methodological differences on the outcome of body size estimation studies in anorexia nervosa. *British Journal of Clinical Psychology, 36*, 263–277.

Smith, C. A., & Kirby, L. D. (2000). Consequences require antecedents: Toward a process model of emotion elicitation. In J. P. Forgas (Ed.), *Feeling and thinking: The role of affect in social cognition* (pp. 83–106). New York: Cambridge University Press.

Smith, D. (1982). Trends in counseling and psychotherapy. *American Psychologist, 37*, 802–809.

Smith, D. E., Roberts, J., Gage, F. H., & Tuszynski, M. H. (1999). Age-associated neuronal atrophy occurs in the primate brain and is reversible by growth factor gene therapy. *Proceedings of the National Academy of Sciences U.S.A., 96*, 10893–10898.

Smith, D. V., & Frank, M. E. (1993). Sensory coding by peripheral taste fibers. In S. A. Simon & S. D. Roper (Eds.), *Mechanisms of taste transduction* (pp. 295–338). Boca Raton, FL: CRC Press.

Smith, E. E. (2000). Neural bases of human working memory. *Current Directions in Psychological Science, 9*, 45–49.

Smith, E. E., & Jonides, J. (1999). Storage and executive processes in the frontal lobes. *Science, 283*, 1657–1661.

Smith, E. E., & Medin, D. L. (1981). *Categories and concepts*. Cambridge, MA: Harvard University Press.

Smith, E. E., Patalano, A. L., & Jonides, J. (1998). Alternative strategies of categorization. *Cognition, 65*, 167–196.

Smith, E. R. (1998). Mental representation and memory. In D. T. Gilbert, S. T. Fiske, & G. Lindzey (Eds.), *The handbook of social psychology* (4th ed., Vol. 1, pp. 391–445). New York: McGraw-Hill.

Smith, J. C., & Joyce, C. A. (2004). Mozart versus New Age music: Relaxation states, stress, and ABC Relaxation Theory. *Journal of Music Therapy, 41*, 215–224.

Smith, J. L., & White, P. H. (2002). An examination of implicitly activated, explicitly activated, and nullified stereotypes on mathematical performance: It's not just a woman's issue. *Sex Roles, 47*, 179–191.

Smith, S. M., & Blankenship, S. E. (1989). Incubation effects. *Bulletin of the Psychonomic Society, 27*, 311–314.

Smith, S. M., & Blankenship, S. E. (1991). Incubation and the persistence of fixation in problem solving. *American Journal of Psychology, 104*, 61–87.

Smith, T. W., & Ruiz, J. M. (2002). Psychosocial influences on the development and course of coronary heart disease: Current status and implications for research and practice. *Journal of Consulting & Clinical Psychology, 70*, 548–568.

Smyth, J. M., Stone, A. A., Hurewitz, A., & Kaell, A. (1999). Effects of writing about stressful experiences on symptom reduction in patients with asthma or rheumatoid arthritis. *Journal of the American Medical Association, 281*, 1304–1329.

Snidman, N., Kagan, J., Riordan, L., & Shannon, D. C. (1995). Cardiac function and behavioral reactivity during infancy. *Psychophysiology, 32*, 199–207.

Snodgrass, S. E. (1985). Women's intuition: The effect of subordinate role on interpersonal sensitivity. *Journal of Personality and Social Psychology, 49*, 146–155.

Snow, C. E. (1991). The language of the mother–child relationship. In M. Woodhead & R. Carr (Eds.), *Becoming a person* (pp. 195–210). London: Routledge.

Snow, C. E. (1999). Social perspectives on the emergence of language. In B. MacWhinney (Ed.), *The emergence of language* (pp. 257–276). Mahwah, NJ: Erlbaum.

Snow, C. E. (2002). Second language learners' contributions to our understanding of languages of the brain. In A. M. Galaburda, S. M. Kosslyn, & Y. Christen (Eds.), *Languages of the brain* (pp. 151–165) Cambridge, MA: Harvard University Press.

Snow, R. E. (1994). A person-situation interaction theory of intelligence in outline. In A. Demetriou & A. Efklides (Eds.), *Intelligence, mind, and reasoning: Structure and development* (pp. 11–28). Amsterdam: Elsevier.

Snow, R. E. (1996). Aptitude development and education. *Psychology, Public Policy, and Law, 3/4*, 536–560.

Snow, R., & Yalow, R. (1982). Education and intelligence. In R. J. Sternberg (Ed.), *Handbook of human intelligence* (pp. 493–585). New York: Cambridge University Press.

Snowdon, D. A., Greiner, L. H., & Markesbery, W. R. (2000). Linguistic ability in early life and the neuropathology of Alzheimer's disease and cerebrovascular disease: Findings from the nun study. *Annals of the New York Academy of Sciences, 903*, 34–38.

Snyder, M. (1984). When belief creates reality. In L. Berkowitz (Ed.), *Advances in experimental social psychology* (Vol. 25, pp. 67–114). San Diego, CA: Academic Press.

Snyder, M. (1992). Motivational foundations of behavioral confirmation. In M. P. Zanna (Ed.), *Advances in experimental social psychology* (Vol. 18, pp. 248–306). New York: Academic Press.

Snyder, M., & Ickes, W. (1985). Personality and social behavior. In G. Lindzey & E. Aronson (Eds.), *Handbook of social psychology* (3rd ed., Vol. 2, pp. 883–947). New York: Random House.

Snyderman, M., & Herrnstein, R. J. (1983). Intelligence tests and the Immigration Act of 1924. *American Psychologist, 38,* 986–995.

Soli, S. D. (1994). Hearing aids: Today and tomorrow. *Echoes: The newsletter of the Acoustical Society of America, 4,* 1–5.

Solms, M. (1997). *The neuropsychology of dreams: A clinico-anatomical study.* Mahwah, NJ: Erlbaum.

Solomon, D. A., Keller, M. B., Leon, A. C., Mueller, T. I., Lavori, P. W., Shea, M. T., et al. (2000). Multiple recurrences of major depressive disorder. *American Journal of Psychiatry, 157,* 229–233.

Solomon, R. L., & Corbit, J. D. (1974). An opponent-process theory of motivation: I. Temporal dynamics of affect. *Psychological Review, 78,* 3–43.

Sommer, F. G., & Ling, D. (1970). Auditory testing of newborns using eyeblink conditioning. *Journal of Auditory Research, 10,* 292–295.

Soper, B., Milford, G. E., & Rosenthal, G. T. (1995). Belief when evidence does not support the theory. *Psychology & Marketing, 12,* 415–422.

Soto-Faraco, S., & Spence, C. (2001). Spatial modulation of repetition blindness and repetition deafness. *Quarterly Journal of Experimental Psychology: Human Experimental Psychology, 54,* 1181–1202.

Sowell, E. R., Thompson, P. M., Holmes, C. J., Jernigan, T. L., & Toga, A. W. (1999). In vivo evidence for post-adolescent brain maturation in frontal and striatal regions. *Nature Neuroscience, 2,* 859–861.

Spangler, W. D. (1992). Validity of questionnaire and TAT measures of need for achievement: Two meta-analyses. *Psychological Bulletin, 112,* 140–154.

Spearman, C. (1927). *The abilities of man.* New York: Macmillan.

Speed, A., & Gangestad, S. (1997). Romantic popularity and mate preferences: A peer-nomination study. *Personality & Social Psychology Bulletin, 23,* 928–935.

Speisman, J. C., Lazarus, R. S., Mordkoff, A., & Davison, L. (1964). Experimental reduction of stress based on ego-defense theory. *Journal of Abnormal and Social Psychology, 68,* 367–380.

Spelke, E. S. (1991). Physical knowledge in infancy: Reflections on Piaget's theory. In S. Carey & R. Gelman (Eds.), *The epigenesis of mind: Essays on biology and cognition* (pp. 133–169). Hillsdale, NJ: Erlbaum.

Spelke, E. S., Breinlinger, K., Jacobson, K., & Phillips, A. (1993). Gestalt relations and object perception: A developmental study. *Perception, 22,* 1483–1501.

Spelke, E. S., Breinlinger, K., Macomber, J., & Jacobson, K. (1992). Origins of knowledge. *Psychological Review, 99,* 605–632.

Sperling, G. (1960). The information available in brief visual presentations. *Psychological Monographs, 74,* 1–29.

Spiers, H. J., Maguire, E. A., & Burgess, N. (2001). Hippocampal amnesia. *Neurocase, 7,* 357–382.

Spinella, M., Yang, B., & Lester, D. (2004). Prefrontal system dysfunction and credit card debt. *International Journal of Neuroscience, 114,* 1323–1332.

Spitzer, R. L. (1975). On pseudoscience in science, logic in remission, and psychiatric diagnosis: A critique of Rosenhan's "On being sane in insane places." *Journal of Abnormal Psychology, 84,* 442–452.

Sprecher, S., Aron, A., Hatfield, E., Cortese, A., Potapova, E., & Levitskaya, A. (1994). Love: American style, Russian style and Japanese style. *Personal Relationships, 1,* 349–369.

Sprecher, S., Sullivan, Q., & Hatfield, E. (1994). Mate selection preferences: Gender differences examined in a national sample. *Journal of Personality and Social Psychology, 66,* 1074–1080.

Sprock, J., & Yoder, C. Y. (1997). Women and depression: An update on the report of the APA Task Force. *Sex Roles, 36,* 269–303.

Squire, L. R. (1987). *Memory and the brain.* New York: Oxford University Press.

Squire, L. R. (2004). Memory systems of the brain: A brief history and current perspective. *Neurobiology of Learning and Memory, 82,* 171–177.

Squire, L. R., Clark, R. E., & Knowlton, B, J. (2001). Retrograde amnesia. *Hippocampus, 11,* 50–55.

Squire, L. R., & Kandel, E. R. (1999). *Memory: From mind and molecules.* New York: Scientific American Books.

Squire, L. R., Ojemann, J. G., Miezin, F. M., Petersen, S. E., Videen, T. O., & Raichle, M. E. (1992). Activation of the hippocampus in normal humans: A functional anatomical study of memory. *Proceedings of the National Academy of Sciences, USA, 89,* 1837–1841.

Squire, L. R., & Schacter, D. L. (Eds.). (2002). *Neuropsychology of memory* (3rd ed.). New York: Guilford Press.

Sroufe, L. A., & Fleeson, J. (1986). Attachment and the construction of relationships. In W. W. Hartup & Z. Rubin (Eds.), *Relationships and development* (pp. 51–71). Hillsdale, NJ: Erlbaum.

Stack, S., & Eshleman, J. R. (1998). Marital status and happiness. *Journal of Marriage and the Family, 60,* 527–536.

Staddon, J. E. R., & Cerruti, D. T. (2003). Operant conditioning. *Annual Review of Psychology, 54,* 115–144.

Stager, C. L., & Werker, J. F. (1997). Infants listen for more phonetic detail in speech perception than in word-learning tasks. *Nature, 388,* 381–382.

Stallone, D. D., & Stunkard, A. J. (1994). Obesity. In A. Frazer & P. B. Molinoff (Eds.), *Biological bases of brain function and disease* (pp. 385–403). New York: Raven Press.

Stanley, M. A., & Turner, S. M. (1995). Current status of pharmacological and behavioral treatment of obsessive-compulsive disorder. *Behavior Therapy, 25,* 153–186.

Starker, S. (1988). Psychologists and self-help books: Attitudes and prescriptive practices of clinicians. *American Journal of Psychotherapy, 42,* 448–455.

Steele, C., & Josephs, R. A. (1990). Alcohol myopia: Its prized and dangerous effects. *American Psychologist, 45,* 921–933.

Steele, C. M. (1997). A threat in the air: How stereotypes shape intellectual identity and performance. *American Psychologist, 52,* 613–629.

Steele, C. M., & Aronson, J. (1995). Stereotype threat and the intellectual test performance of African Americans. *Journal of Personality & Social Psychology, 69,* 797–811.

Steele, C. M., & Southwick, L. (1985). Alcohol and social behavior I: The psychology of drunken excess. *Journal of Personality and Social Psychology, 48,* 18–34.

Steketee, G., & White, K. (1990). *When once is not enough: Help for obsessive-compulsives.* Oakland, CA: New Harbinger.

Stelmack, R. M. (1990). Biological bases of extraversion: Psychophysiological evidence. *Journal of Personality, 58,* 293–311.

Stephan, W. G., Stephan, C. W., & de Vargas, M. C. (1996). Emotional expression in Costa Rica and the United States. *Journal of Cross-Cultural Psychology, 27,* 147–160.

Sterling-Smith, R. S. (1976). A special study of drivers most responsible in fatal accidents. Summary for Management Report, Contract DOT HS 310-3-595. Washington, DC: Department of Transportation.

Stern, P. C., & Carstensen, L. L. (Eds.). (2000). *The aging mind: Opportunities in cognitive research.* Washington, DC: National Academy Press.

Sternbach, R. A. (1978). Psychological dimensions and perceptual analyses, including pathologies of pain. In E. C. Carterette & M. P. Friedman (Eds.), *Handbook of perception* (pp. 231–261). New York: Academic Press.

Sternberg, R. J. (1985). *Beyond IQ: A triarchic theory of human intelligence.* Cambridge, England: Cambridge University Press.

Sternberg, R. J. (1986a). A triangular theory of love. *Psychological Review, 93,* 119–135.

Sternberg, R. J. (1986b). *What is intelligence?* Norwood, NJ: Ablex.

Sternberg, R. J. (1988a). *The triangle of love.* New York: Basic Books.

Sternberg, R. J. (1988b). *The triarchic mind: A new theory of human intelligence.* New York: Viking.

Sternberg, R. J. (1990). *Metaphors of mind: Conceptions of the nature of intelligence.* New York: Cambridge University Press.

Sternberg, R. J. (2003a). Issues in the theory and measurement of successful intelligence: A reply to Brody. *Intelligence, 31,* 331–337.

Sternberg, R. J. (2003b). Our research program validating the triarchic theory of successful intelligence: Reply to Gottfredson. *Intelligence, 31,* 399–413.

Sternberg, R. J. (Ed.). (2000). *Handbook of intelligence.* New York: Cambridge University Press.

Sternberg, R. J., & Detterman, D. K. (Eds.). (1986). *What is intelligence? Contemporary viewpoints on its nature and definition.* Norwood, NJ: Ablex.

Sternberg, R. J., Nokes, C., Geissler, P. W., Prince, R., Okatcha, F., Bundy, D. A., & Grigorenko, E. L. (2001). The relationship between academic and practical intelligence: A case study in Kenya. *Intelligence, 29,* 1–18.

Sternberg, R. J., & Wagner, R. K. (1993). The g-ocentric view of intelligence and job performance is wrong. *Current Directions in Psychological Science, 2,* 1–5.

Sternberg, R. J., Wagner, R. K., & Okagaki, L. (1993). Practical intelligence: The nature and role of tacit knowledge in work. In J. M. Puckett, H. W. Reese, et al. (Eds.), *Mechanisms of everyday cognition.* Hillsdale, NJ: Erlbaum.

Stevens, L. E., & Fiske, S. T. (1995). Motivation and cognition in social life: A social survival perspective. *Social Cognition, 13,* 189–214.

Stevenson, H., Lee, S., & Stigler, J. (1986). Mathematics achievement of Chinese, Japanese, and American children. *Science, 231,* 693–699.

Stewart, W. F., Ricci, J. A., Chee, E., Hahn, S. R., & Morganstein, D. (2003). Cost of lost productive work time among US workers with depression. *JAMA: Journal of the American Medical Association, 289,* 3135–3144.

Stewart-Williams, S., & Podd, J. (2004). The placebo effect: Dissolving the expectancy versus conditioning debate. *Psychological Bulletin, 130,* 324–340.

Stice, E., Presnell, K., & Spangler, D. (2002). Risk factors for binge eating onset in adolescent girls: A 2-year prospective investigation. *Health Psychology, 21,* 131–138.

Stickgold, R. (1998). Sleep: Off-line memory reprocessing. *Trends in Cognitive Science, 2,* 484–492.

Stickgold, R., Fosse, R., & Walker, M. P. (2002). Linking brain and behavior in sleep-dependent learning and memory consolidation. *Proceedings of the National Academy of Science, 99,* 16519–16521.

Stickgold, R., Malia, A., Maguire, D., Roddenberry, D., & O'Connor, M. (2000). Replaying the game: Hypnagogic images in normals and amnesics. *Science, 290,* 350–353.

Stickgold, R., Rittenhouse, C. D., & Hobson, J. A. (1994). Dream splicing: A new technique for assessing thematic coherence in subjective reports of mental activity. *Consciousness & Cognition: An International Journal, 3,* 114–128.

Stickgold, R., Whidbee, D., Schirmer, B., Patel, V., & Hobson, J. A. (2000). Visual discrimination task improvement: A multi-step process occurring during sleep. *Journal of Cognitive Neuroscience, 12,* 246–254.

Stoel-Gammon, C., & Otomo, K. (1986). Babbling development of hearing-impaired and normally hearing subjects. *Journal of Speech and Hearing Disorders, 51,* 33–41.

Stokes, J. P., Damon, W., & McKirnan, D. J. (1997). Predictors of movement toward homosexuality: A longitudinal study of bisexual men. *Journal of Sex Research, 34,* 304–312.

Stone, J. (2002). Battling doubt by avoiding practice: The effects of stereotype threat on self-handicapping in white athletes. *Personality & Social Psychology Bulletin, 28,* 1667–1678.

Stoolmiller, M. (1999). Implications of the restricted range of family environments for estimates of heritability and nonshared environment in behavior-genetic adoption studies. *Psychological Bulletin, 125,* 392–409.

Strack, F., Martin, L. L., & Stepper, S. (1988). Inhibiting and facilitating conditions of the human smile: A nonobtrusive test of the facial feedback hypothesis. *Journal of Personality & Social Psychology, 54,* 768–777.

Strakowski, S. M., Adler, C. M., & DelBello, M. P. (2002). Volumetric MRI studies of mood disorders: Do they distinguish unipolar and bipolar disorder? *Bipolar Disorders, 4,* 80–88.

Strakowski, S. M., Lonczak, H. S., Sax, K. W., West, S. A., Crist, R. M., & Thienhaus, O. J. (1995). The effects of race on diagnosis and disposition from a psychiatric emergency service. *Journal of Clinical Psychiatry, 56,* 101–107.

Strakowski, S. M., Shelton, R. C., & Kolbrener, M. L. (1993). The effects of race and comorbidity on clinical diagnosis in patients with psychosis. *Journal of Clinical Psychiatry, 54,* 96–102.

Straus, M. A. (1980). Social stress and marital violence in a national sample of American families. *Annals of the New York Academy of Sciences, 347,* 229–250.

Straus, M. A. (2000). Corporal punishment and primary prevention of physical abuse. *Child Abuse & Neglect, 24,* 1109–1114.

Straus, M. A., & Gelles, R. J. (1980). *Behind closed doors: Violence in the American family.* New York: Anchor/Doubleday.

Straus, M. A., & McCord, J. (1998). Do physically punished children become violent adults? In S. Nolen-Hoeksema (Ed.), *Clashing views on abnormal psychology: A Taking Sides custom reader* (pp. 130–155). Guilford, CT: Dushkin/McGraw-Hill (1998).

Straus, M. A., Sugarman, D. B., & Giles-Sims, J. (1997). Spanking by parents and subsequent antisocial behavior of children. *Archives of Pediatrics & Adolescent Medicine, 151,* 761–767.

Streiker, L. D. (1984). *Mind-bending: Brainwashing, cults, and deprogramming in the '80s.* Garden City, NY: Doubleday.

Streissguth, A. P., Barr, H. M., Bookstein, F. L., Sampson, P. D., & Olson, H. C. (1999). The long-term neurocognitive consequences of prenatal alcohol exposure: A 14-year study. *Psychological Science, 10,* 186–190.

Streissguth, A. P., Barr, H. M., Sampson, P. D., Darby, B. L., & Martin, D. C. (1989). IQ at age 4 in relation to maternal alcohol use and smoking during pregnancy. *Developmental Psychology, 25,* 3–11.

Streufert, S., & Swezey, R. W. (1986). *Complexity, managers, and organizations.* Orlando, FL: Academic Press.

Stricker, E. M., Swerdloff, A. F., & Zigmond, M. J. (1978). Intrahypothalamic injections of kainic acid produce feeding and drinking deficits in rats. *Brain Research, 158,* 470–473.

Stricker, G. (1993). The current status of psychotherapy integration. In G. Stricker & J. R. Gold (Eds.), *Comprehensive handbook of psychotherapy integration* (pp. 533–545). New York: Plenum Press.

Stricker, L. J., & Ward, W. C. (2004). Stereotype threat, inquiring about test takers' ethnicity and gender, and standardized test performance. *Journal of Applied Social Psychology, 34,* 665–693.

Striegel-Moore, R. H. (1993). Etiology of binge eating: A developmental perspective. In C. G. Fairburn & G. T. Wilson (Eds.), *Binge eating: Nature, assessment, and treatment* (pp. 144–172). New York: Guilford Press.

Strike, P. C., Magid, K., Brydon, L., Edwards, S., McEwan, J. R., & Steptoe, A. (2004). Exaggerated platelet and hemodynamic reactivity to mental stress in men with coronary artery disease. *Psychosomatic Medicine, 66,* 492–500.

Strober, M. (1995). Family-genetic perspective on anorexia nervosa and bulimia nervosa. In C. G. Fairburn & K. Brownell (Eds.), *Comprehensive textbook of eating disorders and obesity* (pp. 212–218). New York: Guilford Press.

Strom, S. (2000, January 4). Tradition of equality fading in new Japan. *New York Times.*

Strömwall, L. A., Granhag, P. A., & Jonsson, A. (2003). Deception among pairs: "Let's say we had lunch and

hope they will swallow it!" *Psychology, Crime and Law, 9,* 109–124.

Strupp, J. J., & Binder, J. L. (1984). *Psychotherapy in a new key: A guide to time-limited dynamic psychotherapy.* New York: Basic Books.

Stunkard, A. J. (1982). Anorectic agents lower a body weight set point. *Life Science, 30,* 2043–2055.

Stürmer, S., Snyder, M., & Omoto, A. M. (2005). Prosocial emotions and helping: The moderating role of group membership. *Journal of Personality & Social Psychology, 88,* 532–546.

Suarez, E. C., Kuhn, C. M., Schanberg, S. M., Williams, R. B., Jr., & Zimmermann, E. A. (1998). Neuroendocrine, cardiovascular, and emotional responses of hostile men: The role of interpersonal challenge. *Psychosomatic Medicine, 60,* 78–88.

Suarez, E., & Williams, R. (1989). Situational determinants of cardiovascular and emotional reactivity in high and low hostile men. *Psychosomatic Medicine, 51,* 404–418.

Subrahmanyam, K., & Greenfield, P. M. (1994). Effect of video game practice on spatial skills in girls and boys. *Journal of Applied Developmental Psychology, 15*(special issue), 13–32.

Sue, S., Zane, N., & Young, K. (1994). Research on psychotherapy with culturally diverse populations. In A. E. Bergin & S. L. Garfield (Eds.), *Handbook of psychotherapy and behavior change* (4th ed., pp. 783–820). New York: John Wiley & Sons.

Suga, N. (1990). Biosonar and neural computation in bats. *Scientific American, 262,* 60–68.

Sugita, Y. (2004). Experience in early infancy is indispensable for color perception. *Current Biology, 14,* 1267–1271.

Sullins, E. S. (1991). Emotional contagion revisited: Effects of social comparison and expressive style on mood convergence. *Personality & Social Psychology Bulletin, 17*(2), 166–174.

Sullivan, H. S. (1953). *The interpersonal theory of psychiatry.* Oxford, England: Norton.

Sullivan, R. (1999, June). Dad again. *Life,* pp. 66–68.

Sulloway, F. J. (1996). *Born to rebel: Birth order, family dynamics, and creative lives.* New York: Vintage.

Sulloway, F. J. (1999). Birth order. In M. A. Runco & S. R. Pritzken (Eds.), *Encyclopedia of creativity* (Vol. 1, pp. 189–202). San Diego: Academic Press.

Suomi, S. J. (2003). Gene-environment interactions and the neurobiology of social conflict. *Annals of the New York Academy of Sciences, 1008,* 132–139.

Surguladze, S. A., Young, A. W., Senior, C., Brébion, G., Travis, M. J., & Phillips, M. L. (2004). Recognition accuracy and response bias to happy and sad facial expressions in patients with major depression. *Neuropsychology, 18,* 212–218.

Susser, E., Neugebauer, R., Hoek, H. W., Brown, A. S., Lin, S., Lanbovitz, D., & Gorman, J. M. (1996). Schizophrenia after prenatal famine: Further evidence. *Archives of General Psychiatry, 53,* 25–31.

Suzuki, L. A., & Valencia, R. R. (1997). Race-ethnicity and measured intelligence: Educational implications. *American Psychologist, 52,* 1103–1114.

Svanborg, P., Gustavsson, J. P., & Weinryb, R. M. (1999). What patient characteristics make therapists recommend psychodynamic psychotherapy or other treatment forms? *Acta Psychiatrica Scandinavica, 99,* 87–94.

Svartberg, M., & Stiles, T. C. (1991). Comparative effects of short-term psychodynamic psychotherapy: A meta-analysis. *Journal of Consulting & Clinical Psychology, 59,* 704–714.

Swaab, D. F. (2003). *The human hypothalamus: Basic and clinical aspects. Part 1: Nuclei of the human hypothalamus.* Amsterdam: Elsevier.

Swanson, K., Beckwith, L., & Howard, J. (2000). Intrusive caregiving and quality of attachment in prenatally drug-exposed toddlers and their primary caregivers. *Attachment & Human Development, 2,* 130–148.

Syvalathi, E. K. G. (1994). Biological factors in schizophrenia: Structural and functional aspects. *British Journal of Psychiatry, 164* (Suppl. 23), 9–14.

Szasz, T. S. (1961). *The myth of mental illness: Foundations of a theory of personal conduct.* New York: Hoeber-Harper.

Tacón, A. M., Caldera, Y. M., & Ronaghan, C. (2004). Mindfulness-based stress reduction in women with breast cancer. *Families, Systems & Health, 22,* 193–203.

Tafarodi, R. W., & Smith, A. J. (2001). Individualism-collectivism and depressive sensitivity to life events: The case of Malaysian sojourners. *International Journal of Intercultural Relations, 25,* 73–88.

Tafarodi, R. W., & Swann, W. B., Jr. (1996). Individualism-collectivism and global self-esteem: Evidence for a cultural trade-off. *Journal of Cross-Cultural Psychology, 27,* 651–672.

Tajfel, H. (1982). *Social identity and intergroup relations.* Cambridge, England: Cambridge University Press.

Takahashi, K. (1990). Are the key assumptions of the "Strange Situation" procedure universal? A view from Japanese research. *Human Development, 33,* 23–30.

Takahashi, T., Sasaki, M., Itoh, H., Yamadera, W., Ozone, M., Obuchi, K., Hayashida, K., Matsunaga, N., & Sano, H. (2002). Melatonin alleviates jet lag symptoms caused by an 11-hour eastward flight. *Psychiatry & Clinical Neurosciences, 56,* 301–302.

Talarico, J. M., Rubin, D. C. (2003). Confidence, not consistency, characterizes flashbulb memories. *Psychological Science, 14,* 455–461.

Tan, H., Zhong, P., & Yan, Z. (2004). Corticotropin-releasing factor and acute stress prolongs serotonergic regulation of GABA transmission in prefrontal cortical pyramidal neurons. *Journal of Neuroscience, 24,* 5000–5008.

Tanabe, S., Ichikawa, K., Hukami, K., & Nakashima, S. (2001). A family with protanomaly and deuteranomaly. *Color Research & Application, 26,* S93–S95.

Tangrea, J. A., Adrianza, M. E., & Helzer, W. E. (1994). Risk factors for the development of the placebo adverse reactions in a multicenter clinical trial. *Annals of Epidemiology, 4,* 327–331.

Tanner, J. M. (1990). *Foetus into man* (2nd ed.). Cambridge, MA: Harvard University Press.

Tarabulsy, G. M., Bernier, A., Provost, M. A., Maranda, J., Larose, S., Moss, E., et al. (2005). Another look inside the gap: Ecological contributions to the transmission of attachment in a sample of adolescent mother-infant dyads. *Developmental Psychology, 41,* 212–224.

Taris, T. W. (2000). Dispositional need for cognitive closure and self-enhancing beliefs. *Journal of Social Psychology, 140,* 35–50.

Tarrier, N., Yusupoff, L., Kinney, C., McCarthy, E., Gledhill, A., Haddock, G., & Morris, J. (1998). Randomised controlled trial of intensive cognitive behaviour therapy for patients with chronic schizophrenia. *British Medical Journal, 317,* 303–307.

Tarter, R. E., Jones, B. M., Simpson, C. D., & Vega, A. (1971). Effects of task complexity and practice on performance during acute alcohol intoxication. *Perceptual & Motor Skills, 33,* 307–318.

Tavares, C. H., Haeffner, L. S., Barbieri, M. A., Bettiol, H., Barbieri, M. R., & Souza, L. (2000). Age at menarche among schoolgirls from a rural community in Southeast Brazil. *Cad Saude Publica, 16,* 709–715.

Tavris, C. (1991). The mismeasure of woman: Paradoxes and perspective in the study of gender. In J. D. Goodchilds (Ed.), *Psychological perspectives on human diversity in America* (pp. 89–136). Washington, DC: American Psychological Association.

Taylor, S. E., Klein, L. C., Lewis, B. P., Gruenewald, T. L., Gurung, R. A. R., & Updegraff, J. A. (2000). Biobehavioral responses to stress in females: Tend-and-befriend, not fight-or-flight. *Psychological Review, 107,* 411–429.

Taylor, S. E., Lewis, B. P., Gruenewald, T. L., Gurung, R. A. R., Updegraff, J. A., & Klein, L. C. (2002). Sex differences in biobehavioral responses to threat: Reply to Geary and Flinn (2002). *Psychological Review, 109,* 751–753.

Taylor, S. E., Sherman, D. K., Kim, H. S., Jarcho, J., Takagi, K., & Dunagan, M. S. (2004). Culture and social support: Who seeks it and why? *Journal of Personality & Social Psychology, 87,* 354–362.

Taylor, S. W., Repetti, R. L., & Seeman, T. (1997). Health psychology: What is an unhealthy environment and how does it get under the skin? *Annual Review of Psychology, 48,* 411–447.

Tecott, L. H., Sun, L. M., Akana, S. F., Strack, A. M., Lowenstein, D. H., Dallman, M. F., & Julius, D. (1995). Eating disorder and epilepsy in mice lacking 5-HT2C serotonin receptors. *Nature, 374,* 542–546.

Tedlock, B. (1992). The role of dreams and visionary narratives in Mayan cultural survival. *Ethos, 20,* 453–476.

Teigen, K. H. (1994). Variants of subjective probabilities: Concepts, norms, and biases. In G. Wright & P. Ayton (Eds.), *Subjective probability.* New York: Wiley.

Teilmann, G., Juul, A., Skakkebaek, N. E., & Toppari, J. (2002). Putative effects of endocrine disrupters on pubertal development in the human. *Best Practice & Research Clinical Endocrinology & Metabolism, 16,* 105–121.

Tein, J. Y., Sandler, I. N., & Zautra, A. J. (2000). Stressful life events, psychological distress, coping, and parenting of divorced mothers: A longitudinal study. *Journal of Family Psychology, 14,* 27–41.

Telch, M. J., Lucas, J. A., & Nelson, P. (1989). Nonclinical panic in college students: An investigation of prevalence and symptomatology. *Journal of Abnormal Psychology, 98,* 300–306.

Tellegen, A., Lykken, D. T., Bouchard, T. J., Wilcox, K. J., Segal, N. L., & Rich, S. (1988). Personality similarity in twins reared apart and together. *Journal of Personality and Social Psychology, 54,* 1031–1039.

Tentori, K., Osherson, D., Hasher, L., & May, C. (2001). Wisdom and aging: Irrational preferences in college students but not older adults. *Cognition, 81,* B87–B96.

Teri, L., & Lewinsohn, P. M. (1985). Group intervention for unipolar depression. *Behavior Therapist, 8,* 109–111, 123.

Terry, D. J., & Hogg, M. A. (1996). Group norms and the attitude-behavior relationship: A role for group identification. *Personality & Social Psychology Bulletin, 22,* 776–793.

Terry, D. J., & Hynes, G. J. (1998). Adjustment to a low-control situation: Reexamining the role of coping responses. *Journal of Personality and Social Psychology, 74,* 1078–1092.

Tesser, A. (1993). The importance of heritability of psychological research: The case of attitudes. *Psychological Review, 100,* 129–142.

Tesser, A., Whitaker, D., Martin, L., & Ward, D. (1998). Attitude heritability, attitude change and physiological responsivity. *Personality & Individual Differences, 24,* 89–96.

Tew, J. D., Jr., Mulsant, B. H., Haskett, R. F., Prudic, J., Thase, M. E., Crowe, R. R., et al. (1999). Acute efficacy of ECT in the treatment of major depression in the old-old. *American Journal of Psychiatry, 156,* 1865–1870.

Thalbourne, M. A. (1989). Psychics and ESP: A reply to Grimmer and White. *Australian Psychologist, 24,* 307–310.

Thapar, A., & McGuffin, P. (1996). Genetic influences on life events in childhood. *Psychological Medicine, 26,* 813–820.

Thase, M. E., Greenhouse, J. B., Frank, E., Reynolds, C. F., III, Pilkonis, P. A., Hurley, K., et al. (1997). Treatment of major depression with psychotherapy or psychotherapy-pharmacotherapy combinations. *Archives of General Psychiatry, 54,* 1009–1015.

Thase, M. E., & Jindal, R. D. (2004). Combining psychotherapy and psychopharmacology for treatment of mental disorders. In M. J. Lambert (Ed.), *Bergin and Garfield's handbook of psychotherapy and behavior change,* 5th ed. (pp. 743–766). New York: Wiley and Sons.

Thatcher, R. W. (1994). Cyclic cortical reorganization: Origins of human cognitive development. In G. Dawson & K. W. Fischer (Eds.), *Human behavior and the developing brain* (pp. 232–266). New York: Guilford.

Thelen, E. (1995). Motor development: A new synthesis. *American Psychologist, 50,* 79–95.

Thelen, E., & Ulrich, B. D. (1991). Hidden skills: A dynamic systems analysis of treadmill stepping during the first year. *Monographs of the Society for Research in Child Development, 56*(1, Serial No. 223).

Thesen, T., Vibell, J. F., Calvert, G. A., & Österbauer, R. A. (2004). Neuroimaging of multisensory processing in vision, audition, touch, and olfaction. *Cognitive Processing, 5,* 84–93.

Thomas, A., & Chess, S. (1996). *Temperament: Theory and practice.* New York: Brunner/Mazel.

Thompson, J. K., & Stice, E. (2001). Thin-ideal internalization: Mounting evidence for a new risk factor for body-image disturbance and eating pathology. *Current Directions in Psychological Science, 10,* 181–183.

Thompson, P. M., Cannon, T. D., Narr, K. L., van Erp, T., Poutanen, V. P., Huttunen, M., et al. (2001). Genetic influences on brain structure. *Nature Neuroscience, 12,* 1253–1258.

Thompson, P. M., Giedd, J. N., Woods, R. P., MacDonald, D., Evans, A. C., & Toga, A. W. (2000). Growth patterns in the developing brain detected by using continuum mechanical tensor maps. *Nature, 404,* 190–193.

Thompson, R. F., Bao, S., Chen, L., Cipriano, B. D., Grethe, J. S., Kim, J. J., Thompson, J. K., Tracy, J. A., Weninger, M. S., & Krupa, D. J. (1997). Associative learning. *International Review of Neurobiology, 41,* 151–189.

Thorn, B. L., & Gilbert, L. A. (1998). Antecedents of work and family role expectations of college men. *Journal of Family Psychology, 12,* 259–267.

Thorndike, E. L. (1927). The law of effect. *American Journal of Psychology, 39,* 212–222.

Thorndike, E. L. (1949). The law of effect. In *Selected writings from a connectionist's psychology* (pp. 13–26). New York: Appleton-Century-Crofts. (Original work published 1933)

Thornhill, R., & Gangestad, S. W. (1993). Human facial beauty: Averageness, symmetry, and parasite resistance. *Human Nature, 4,* 237–269.

Thornhill, R., & Gangestad, S. W. (1999). Facial attractiveness. *Trends in Cognitive Sciences, 3,* 452–460.

Thurstone, L. L. (1938). *Primary mental abilities.* Chicago: University of Chicago Press.

Thurstone, L. L., & Thurstone, T. G. (1941). *Factorial studies of intelligence.* Chicago: University of Chicago Press.

Tidwell, M. O., Reis, H. T., Shaver, P. R. (1996). Attachment, attractiveness, and social interaction: A diary study. *Journal of Personality & Social Psychology, 71,* 729–745.

Tiernari, P. (1991). Interaction between genetic vulnerability and family environment: The Finnish adoptive family study of schizophrenia. *Acta Psychiatrica Scandinavica, 84,* 460–465.

Till, B. D., & Priluck, R. L. (2000). Stimulus generalization in classical conditioning: An initial investigation and extension. *Psychology & Marketing, 17,* 55–72.

Timmerman, I. G. H., Emmelkamp, P. M. G., & Sanderman, R. (1998). The effects of a stress-management training program in individuals at risk in the community at large. *Behaviour Research & Therapy, 36,* 863–875.

Tingey, H., Kiger, G., & Riley, P. J. (1996). Juggling multiple roles: Perceptions of working mothers. *Social Science Journal, 33,* 183–191.

Tinker, J. E., & Tucker, J. A. (1997). Motivations for weight loss and behavior change strategies associated with natural recovery from obesity. *Psychology of Addictive Behaviors, 11,* 98–106.

Tohen, M., & Grundy, S. (1999). Management of acute mania. *Journal of Clinical Psychology, 60*(Suppl. 5), 31–34.

Tolman, E. C., & Honzik, C. H. (1930a). Degrees of hunger, reward and non-reward, and maze learning in rats. *University of California Publications in Psychology, 4,* 241–256.

Tolman, E. C., & Honzik, C. H. (1930b). Introduction and removal of reward, and maze performance in rats. *University of California Publications in Psychology, 4,* 257–275.

Tomaka, J., Blascovich, J., Kibler, J., & Ernst, J. M. (1997). Cognitive and physiological antecedents of threat and challenge appraisal. *Journal of Personality & Social Psychology, 73,* 63–72.

Tomkins, S. S. (1962). *Affect, imagery, consciousness, Vol I. The positive affects.* New York: Springer-Verlag.

Tootell, R. B. H., Mendola, J. D., Hadjikhani, N. K., Ledden, P. J., Liu, A. K., Reppas, J. B., et al. (1997). Functional analysis of V3A and related areas in human visual cortex. *Journal of Neuroscience, 17,* 7060–7078.

Tootell, R. B., Silverman, M. S., Switkes, E., & de Valois, R. L. (1982). Deoxyglucose analysis of retinotopic organization in primate striate cortex. *Science, 218,* 902–904.

Torgersen, S. G. (1983). Genetic factors in anxiety disorders. *Archives of General Psychiatry, 40,* 1085–1089.

Torrey, E. F. (1988). *Nowhere to go: The tragic odyssey of the homeless mentally ill.* New York: Harper & Row.

Tovée, M. J., & Cornelissen, P. L. (2001). Female and male perceptions of female physical attractiveness in front-view and profile. *British Journal of Psychology, 92,* 391–402.

Tractinsky, N., & Meyer, J. (1999). Chartjunk or goldgraph? Effects of presentation objectives and content desirability on information presentation. *MIS Quarterly, 23,* 397–420.

Tracy, J. L., & Robins, R. W. (2004). Show your pride: Evidence for a discrete emotion expression. *Psychological Science, 15,* 194–197.

Trafimow, D., & Finlay, K. (1996). The importance of subjective norms for a minority of people: Between-subjects and within-subjects analyses. *Personality and Social Psychology Bulletin, 22,* 820–828.

Treisman, A. M. (1964a). Monitoring and storage of irrelevant messages in selective attention. *Journal of Verbal Learning and Verbal Behavior, 3,* 449–459.

Treisman, A. M. (1964b). Selective attention in man. *British Medical Bulletin, 20,* 12–16.

Treue, S. (2003). Climbing the cortical ladder from sensation to perception. *Trends in Cognitive Sciences, 7,* 469–471.

Trevethan, S. D., & Walker, L. J. (1989). Hypothetical versus real-life moral reasoning among psychopathic and delinquent youth. *Development and Psychopathology, 1,* 91–103.

Triandis, H. C., Bontempo, R., Villareal, M. J., Asai, M., & Lucca, N. (1988). Individualism and collectivism: Cross-cultural perspectives on self-ingroup relationships. *Journal of Personality and Social Psychology, 54,* 323–338.

Triandis, H. C., McCusker, C., & Hui, C. H. (1990). Multimethod probes of individualism and collectivism. *Journal of Personality and Social Psychology, 59,* 1006–1020.

Trimpop, R., & Kirkcaldy, B. (1997). Personality predictors of driving accidents. *Personality & Individual Differences, 23,* 147–152.

Trivedi, M. A., & Coover, G. D. (2004). Lesions of the ventral hippocampus, but not the dorsal hippocampus, impair conditioned fear expression and inhibitory avoidance on the elevated T-maze. *Neurobiology of Learning & Memory, 81,* 172–184.

Trivedi, N., & Sabini, J. (1998). Volunteer bias, sexuality, and personality. *Archives of Sexual Behavior, 27,* 181–195.

Trivers, R. (1972). Parental investment and sexual selection. In B. Campbell (Ed.), *Sexual selection and the descent of man, 1871–1971* (pp. 136–179). Chicago: Aldine.

Trivers, R. (1985). *Social evolution.* Menlo Park, CA: Benjamin/Cummings.

True, W. R., Rice, J., Eisen, S. A., Heath, A. C., Phil, D., Goldberg, J., et al. (1993). A twin study of genetic and environmental contributions to liability for posttraumatic stress symptoms. *Archives of General Psychiatry, 50,* 257–264.

Tsai, G., & Coyle, J. T. (2002). Glutamatergic mechanisms in schizophrenia. *Annual Review of Pharmacology and Toxicology, 42,* 165–179.

Tsai, J. L., Levenson, R. W., & Carstensen, L. L. (2000). Autonomic, subjective, and expressive responses to emotional films in older and younger Chinese Americans and European Americans. *Psychology & Aging, 15,* 684–693.

Tsai, S.-J., Hong, C.-H., Yu, W-Y. Y., & Chen, T.-J. (2004). Association study of a brain-derived neurotrophic factor (BDNF) Val66Met polymorphism and personality trait and intelligence in healthy young females. *Neuropsychobiology, 49,* 13–16.

Tsai, S-J., Yu, Y. W.-Y., Lin, C-H., Chen, T-J., Chen, S-P., & Hong, C-J. (2002). Dopamine D2 receptor and N-methyl-D-aspartate receptor 2B subunit genetic variants and intelligence. *Neuropsychobiology, 45,* 128–130.

Tsang, J. (2002). Moral rationalization and the integration of situational factors and psychological processes in immoral behavior. *Review of General Psychology, 6,* 25–50.

Tsao, D. Y., Freiwald, W. A., Knutsen, T. A., Mandeville, J. B., & Tootell, R. B. H. (2003). Faces and objects in macaque cerebral cortex. *Nature Neuroscience, 6,* 989–995.

Tsekhmistrenko, T. A., Vasil'eva, V. A., Shumeiko, N. S., & Vologirov, A. S. (2004). Quantitative changes in the fibroarchitectonics of the human cortex from birth to the age of 12 years. *Neuroscience and Behavioral Physiology, 34,* 983–988.

Tucker, G. J. (1998). Putting DSM-IV in perspective. *American Journal of Psychiatry 155*(2), 159–161

Tucker, P. (2003). The impact of rest breaks upon accident risk, fatigue and performance: A review. *Work & Stress, 17,* 123–137.

Tugade, M. M., & Fredrickson, B. L. (2004). Resilient individuals use positive emotions to bounce back from negative emotional experiences. *Journal of Personality and Social Psychology, 86,* 320–333.

Tugade, M. M., Fredrickson, B. L., & Barrett, L. F. (2004). Psychological resilience and positive emotional granularity: Examining the benefits of positive emotions on coping and health. *Journal of Personality, 72,* 1161–1190.

Tuna, S., Tekcan, I., & TopÁuoglu, V. (2005). Memory and metamemory in obsessive-compulsive disorder. *Behaviour Research and Therapy, 43,* 15–27.

Turkheimer, E., Haley, A., Waldron, M., D'Onofrio, B., & Gottesman, I. I. (2003). Socioeconomic status modifies heritability of IQ in young children. *Psychological Science, 14,* 623–628.

Turkheimer, E., & Waldron, M. (2000). Nonshared environment: A theoretical, methodological, and quantitative review. *Psychological Bulletin, 126,* 78–108.

Turner, A. M., & Greenough, W. T. (1985). Differential rearing effects on rat visual cortex synapses. I. Synaptic and neuronal density and synapses per neuron. *Brain Research, 329,* 195–203.

Tversky, A., & Kahneman, D. (1974). Judgment under uncertainty: Heuristics and biases. *Science, 185,* 1124–1131.

Twenge, J. M. (1997). Changes in masculine and feminine traits over time: A meta-analysis. *Sex Roles, 36,* 305–325.

Twenge, J. M. (2000). The age of anxiety? Birth cohort change in anxiety and neuroticism, 1952–1993. *Journal of Personality and Social Psychology, 79,* 1007–1021.

Twenge, J. M. (2001a). Changes in women's assertiveness in response to status and roles: A cross-temporal meta-analysis, 1931–1993. *Journal of Personality & Social Psychology, 81,* 133–145.

Twenge, J. M. (2001b). Birth cohort changes in extraversion: A cross-temporal meta-analysis, 1966–1993. *Personality & Individual Differences, 30,* 735–748.

Twenge, J. M., & Campbell, W. K. (2003). "Isn't it fun to get the respect that we're going to deserve?" Narcissism, social rejection, and aggression. *Personality & Social Psychology Bulletin, 29,* 261–272.

Twenge, J. M., Zhang, L., & Im, C. (2004). It's beyond my control: A cross-temporal meta-analysis of increasing externality in locus of control, 1960–2002. *Personality & Social Psychology Review, 8,* 308–319.

Twisk, J. W. R., Snel, J., Kemper, H. C. G., & van Mechelen, W. (1999). Changes in daily hassles and life events and the relationship with coronary heart disease risk factors: A 2-year longitudinal study in 27–29-yr-old males and females. *Journal of Psychosomatic Research, 46,* 229–240.

Tyrka, A. R., Waldron, I., Graber, J. A., & Brooks-Gunn, J. (2002). Prospective predictors of the onset of anorexic and bulimic syndromes. *International Journal of Eating Disorders, 32,* 282–290.

Tzschentke, T. M., & Schmidt, W. J. (2000). Functional relationship among medial prefrontal cortex, nucleus accumbens, and ventral tegmental area in locomotion and reward. *Critical Reviews in Neurobiology, 14,* 131–142.

Ubell, E. (1995, January 15). New devices can help you hear. *Parade Magazine,* pp. 14–15.

Ullian, E. M., Sapperstein, S. K., Christopherson, K. S., & Barres, B. A. (2001). Control of synapse number by glia. *Science, 291,* 657–661.

Ullman, M. T. (2001). The neural basis of lexicon and grammar in first and second language: The declarative/procedural model. *Bilingualism: Language & Cognition, 4,* 105–122.

Ullman, S. (1996). *High-level vision.* Cambridge: MIT Press.

Ungerleider, L. G. (1995). Functional brain imaging studies of cortical mechanisms for memory. *Science, 270,* 769–775.

Ungerleider, L. G., & Haxby, J. V. (1994). "What" and "where" in the human brain. *Current Opinion in Neurology, 4,* 157–165.

Ungerleider, L. G., & Mishkin, M. (1982). Two cortical visual systems. In D. J. Ingle, M. A. Goodale, & R. J. W. Mansfield (Eds.), *Analysis of visual behavior* (pp. 549–586). Cambridge, MA: MIT Press.

Urbszat, D., Herman, C. P., & Polivy, J. (2002). Eat, drink, and be merry, for tomorrow we diet: Effects of anticipated deprivation on food intake in restrained and unrestrained eaters. *Journal of Abnormal Psychology, 111,* 396–401.

Vaillant, G. (1977). *Adaptation to life.* Boston: Little, Brown.

Vajk, F. C., Craighead, W. E., Craighead, L. W., & Holley, C. (1997, November). Risk of major depression as a function of response styles to depressed mood. Poster presented at the annual meeting of the Association for the Advancement of Behavior Therapy, Miami Beach, FL.

Valins, S. (1966). Cognitive effects of false heart-rate feedback. *Journal of Personality & Social Psychology, 4,* 400–408.

van Boven, L., White, K., Kamada, A., & Gilovich, T. (2003). Intuitions about situational correction in self and others. *Journal of Personality & Social Psychology, 85,* 249–258.

Van Cauter, E., Leproult, R., & Plat, L. (2000). Age-related changes in slow wave sleep and REM sleep and relationship with growth hormone and cortisol levels in healthy men. *Journal of the American Medical Association, 284,* 861–868.

van den Heuval, O. A., van de Wetering, B. J., Veltman, D. J., & Pauls, D. L. (2000). Genetic studies of panic disorder: A review. *Journal of Clinical Psychiatry, 61,* 756–766.

Vanderlinden, J., Grave, R. D., Vandereycken, W., & Noorduin, C. (2001). Which factors do provoke binge-eating? An exploratory study in female students. *Eating Behaviors, 2,* 79–83.

Van Goozen, S. H. M, Cohen-Kettenis, P. T., Gooren, J. J. G., Frijda, N. H., & Van De Poll, N. E. (1995). Gender differences in behaviour: Activating effects of cross-sex hormones. *Psychoneuroendocrinology, 20,* 343–363.

van Honk, J., Tuiten, A., Hermans, E., Putnam, P., Koppeschaar, H., Thijssen, J., Verbaten, R., & van Doornen, L. (2001). A single administration of testosterone induces cardiac accelerative responses to angry faces in healthy young women. *Behavioral Neuroscience, 115,* 238–242.

van Honk, J., Tuiten, A., van den Hout, M., Koppeschaar, H., Thijssen, J., de Haan, E., & Verbaten, R. (2000). Conscious and preconscious selective attention to social threat: Different neuroendocrine response patterns. *Psychoneuroendocrinology, 25,* 577–591.

van IJzendoorn, M. (1995). Adult attachment representations, parental responsiveness, and infant attachment: A meta-analysis on the predictive validity of the Adult Attachment Interview. *Psychological Bulletin, 117,* 387–403.

Van Noppen, B., & Steketee, G. (2003). Family responses and multifamily behavioral treatment for obsessive-compulsive disorder. *Brief Treatment & Crisis Intervention, 3,* 231–247.

van Praag, H., Kempermann, G., & Gage, F. H. (1999). Running increases cell proliferation and neurogenesis in the adult mouse dentate gyrus. *Nature Neuroscience, 2,* 266–270.

Van Rooy, D. L., Alonso, A., & Viswesvaran, C. (2005a). Group differences in emotional intelligence scores: theoretical and practical implications. *Personality and Individual Differences, 38,* 689–700.

Van Rooy, D. L., Viswesvaran, C., & Pluta, P. (2005b). A meta-analytic evaluation of construct validity: What is this thing called emotional intelligence? *Human Performance, 18,* 445–462.

van Zoest, W., & Donk, M. (2004). Bottom-up and top-down control in visual search. *Perception, 33,* 927–937.

Varma, A. (2000). Impact of watching international television programs on adolescents in India. *Journal of Comparative Family Studies, 31,* 117–126.

Vartanian, L. R. (2001). Adolescents' reactions to hypothetical peer group conversations: Evidence for an imaginary audience? *Adolescence, 36,* 347–380.

Vasterling, J., Jenkins, R. A., Tope, D. M., & Burish, T. G. (1993). Cognitive distraction and relaxation training for the control of side effects due to cancer chemotherapy. *Journal of Behavioral Medicine, 16,* 65–80.

Vaughn, C., & Leff, J. (1976). Measurement of expressed emotion in the families of psychiatric patients. *British Journal of Social and Clinical Psychology, 15,* 1069–1177.

Vazire, S., & Gosling, S. D. (2004). e-Perceptions: Personality impressions based on personal Websites. *Journal of Personality & Social Psychology, 87,* 123–132.

Vehmanen, L., Kaprio, J., & Loennqvist, J. (1995). Twin studies on concordance for bipolar disorder. *Psychiatria Fennica, 26,* 107–116.

Ventura, J., Nuechterlein, K. H., Lukoff, D., & Hardesty, J. P. (1989). A prospective study of stressful life events and schizophrenic relapse. *Journal of Abnormal Psychology, 98,* 407–411.

Vermetten, E., & Brenner, J. D. (2002). Circuits and systems in stress. I. Preclinical studies. *Depression & Anxiety, 15,* 126–147.

Viereck, G. S. (1929, October 26). What life means to Einstein: An interview by George Sylvester Viereck. *Saturday Evening Post.*

Vieweg, R., & Shawcross, C. R. (1998). A trial to determine any difference between two and three times a week ECT in the rate of recovery from depression. *Journal of Mental Health (UK), 7,* 403–409.

Villringer, A., & Chance, B. (1997). Non-invasive optical spectroscopy and imaging of human brain function. *Trends in Neurosciences, 20,* 435–442.

Vinar, O. (2001). Neurobiology of drug dependence. *Homeostasis in Health & Disease, 41,* 20–34.

Viney, W. (1993). *A history of psychology: Ideas and context.* Needham Heights, MA: Allyn & Bacon.

Vogel, E. K., & Luck, S. J. (2002). Delayed working memory consolidation during the attentional blink. *Psychonomic Bulletin & Review, 9,* 739–743.

Vogel, G. (1996). School achievement: Asia and Europe top in the world, but reasons are hard to find. *Science, 274,* 1296.

Vogel, G. (1997). Cocaine wreaks subtle damage on developing brains. *Science, 278,* 38–39.

Volkow, N. D., Chang, L., Wang, G., Fowler, J. S., Franceschi, D., Sedler, M. J., et al. (2001). Higher cortical and lower subcortical metabolism in detoxified methamphetamine abusers. *American Journal of Psychiatry, 158,* 383–389.

Vonk, R., & van Knippenberg, A. (1995). Processing attitude statements from in-group and out-group members: Effects of within-group and within-person inconsistencies on reading times. *Journal of Personality and Social Psychology, 68,* 215–227.

von Zerssen, D., Leon, C. A. Moller, H., Wittchen, H., Pfister, H., & Sartorius, N. (1990). Care strategies for schizophrenic patients in a transcultural comparison. *Comprehensive Psychiatry, 31,* 398–408.

Voth, H. M., & Orth, M. H. (1973). *Psychotherapy and the role of the environment.* New York: Behavioral Press.

Voudouris, N. J., Peck, C. L., & Coleman, G. (1985). Conditioned placebo responses. *Journal of Personality and Social Psychology, 48,* 47–53.

Vrana, S. R. & Lang, P. J. (1990). Fear imagery and the startle-probe reflex. *Journal of Abnormal Psychology, 99*, 181–189.

Vrana, S. R., Spence, E. L., & Lang, P. J. (1988). The startle probe response: A new measure of emotion? *Journal of Abnormal Psychology, 97*, 487–491.

Vranas, P. B. M. (2000). Gigerenzer's normative critique of Kahneman and Tversky. *Cognition, 76*, 179–193.

Vrij, A. (2004). Why professionals fail to catch liars and how they can improve. *Legal and Criminological Psychology, 9*, 159–181.

Vrij, A., & Mann, S. (2001). Telling and detecting lies in a high-stake situation: The case of a convicted murderer. *Applied Cognitive Psychology, 15*, 187–203.

Vuilleumier, P., & Sagiv, N. (2001). Two eyes make a pair: Facial organization and perceptual learning reduce visual extinction. *Neuropsychologia, 39*, 1144–1149.

Vurpillot, E. (1968). The development of scanning strategies and their relation to visual differentiation. *Journal of Experimental Child Psychology, 6*, 632–650.

Vygotsky, L. S. (1978). *Mind in society: The development of higher mental processes.* Cambridge, MA: Harvard University Press. (Original works published 1930, 1933, 1935)

Vygotsky, L. S. (1986). *Thought and language* (A. Kozulin, Trans.). Cambridge, MA: MIT Press. (Original work published 1934)

Vythilingam, M., Vermetten, E., Anderson, G. M., Luckenbaugh, D., Anderson, E. R., Snow, J., Staib, L. H., Charney, D. S., & Bremner, J. D. (2004). Hippocampal volume, memory, and cortisol status in Major Depressive Disorder: Effects of treatment. *Biological Psychiatry, 56*, 101–112.

Wade, T., Martin, N. G., & Tiggemann, M. (1998). Genetic and environmental risk factors for the weight and shape concerns characteristic of bulimia nervosa. *Psychological Medicine, 28*, 761–771.

Waelti, P., Dickinson, A., & Schultz, W. (2001). Dopamine responses comply with basic assumptions of formal learning theory. *Nature, 412*, 43–48.

Wager, T. D., Phan, K. L., Liberzon, I., & Taylor, S. F. (2003). Valence, gender, and lateralization of functional brain anatomy in emotion: A meta-analysis of findings from neuroimaging. *NeuroImage. 19*, 513–531.

Wager, T. D., Rilling, J. K., Smith, E. E., Sokolik, A., Casey, K. L., Davidson, R. J., et al. (2004). Placebo-induced changes in fMRI in the anticipation and experience of pain, *Science, 303*, 1162–1167.

Wagner, A. D., Schacter, D. L., Rotte, M., Koutstaal, W., Maril, A., Dale, A. M., et al. (1998). Building memories: Remembering and forgetting of verbal experiences as predicted by brain activity. *Science, 281*, 1188–1191.

Wagner, R. K. (1997). Intelligence, training, and employment. *American Psychologist, 52*, 1059–1069.

Wahba, M. A., & Bridwell, L. G. (1976). Maslow reconsidered: A review of research on the need hierarchy theory. *Organizational Behavior & Human Decision Processes, 15*, 212–240.

Wahlbeck, K., Forsén, T., Osmond, C., Barker, D. J. P., & Eriksson, J. G. (2001). Association of schizophrenia with low maternal body mass index, small size at birth, and thinness during childhood. *Archives of General Psychiatry, 58*, 48–52.

Walach, H., & Maidhof, C. (1999). Is the placebo effect dependent on time? A meta-analysis. In I. Kirsch (Ed.), *How expectancies shape experience* (pp. 321–332). Washington, DC: American Psychological Association.

Walder, D., Walker, E., & Lewine, R. J. (2000). The relations among cortisol release, cognitive function and symptom severity in psychotic patients. *Biological Psychiatry, 48*, 1121–1132.

Waldron, V. R., Lavitt, M., & Kelley, D. (2000). The nature and prevention of harm in technology-mediated self-help settings: Three exemplars. *Journal of Technology in Human Services, 17*, 267–293.

Walker, E. F., & Diforio, D. (1997). Schizophrenia: A neural diathesis-stress model. *Psychological Review, 104*, 667–685.

Walker, E. F., Grimes, K. E., Davis, D., & Smith, A. (1993). Childhood precursors of schizophrenia: Facial expressions of emotion. *American Journal of Psychiatry, 150*, 1654–1660.

Walker, E. F., Logan, C. B., & Walder, D. (1999). Indicators of neurdevelopmental abnormality in schizotypal personality disorder. *Psychiatric Annals, 29*, 132–136.

Walker, E. F., Savoie, T., Davis, D. (1994). Neuromotor precursors of schizophrenia. *Schizophrenia Bulletin, 148*, 661–666.

Walker, E., Kestler, L., Bollini, A., & Hochman, K. M. (2004). Schizophrenia: Etiology and course. *Annual Review of Psychology, 55*, 401–430.

Walker, I., & Crogan, M. (1998). Academic performance, prejudice, and the Jigsaw Classroom: New pieces of the puzzle. *Journal of Community & Applied Social Psychology, 8*, 381–393.

Walker, L. J. (1995). Sexism in Kohlberg's moral psychology? In W. M. Kurtines & J. L. Gewirtz (Eds.), *Moral development: An introduction* (pp. 83–107). Boston: Allyn & Bacon.

Walker, M. P., Brakefield, T., Hobson, J. A., & Stickgold, R. (2003). Dissociable stages of human memory consolidation and reconsolidation. *Nature, 425*, 616–620.

Walker, M. P., Brakefield, T., Seidman, J., Morgan, A., Hobson, J. A., & Stickgold, R. (2003). Sleep and the time course of motor skill learning. *Learning & Memory, 10*, 275–284.

Walker, M. P., & Stickgold, R. (2004). Sleep-dependent learning and memory consolidation. *Neuron, 44*, 121–133.

Walker, W. R., Skowronski, J. J., Gibbons, J. A., Vogl, R. J., & Thompson, C. P. (2003). On the emotions that accompany autobiographical memories: Dysphoria disrupts the fading affect bias. *Cognition & Emotion, 17*, 703–723.

Walker, W. R., Skowronski, J. J., & Thompson, C. P. (2003). Life is pleasant—and memory helps to keep it that way! *Review of General Psychology, 7*, 203–210.

Wall, P. (2000). *Pain: The science of suffering.* New York: Columbia University Press.

Waller, N. G., Kojetin, B. A., Bouchard, T. J., Jr, Lykken, D. T., & Tellegen, A. (1990). Genetic and environmental influences on religious interests, attitudes, and values: A study of twins reared apart and together. *Psychological Science, 1*, 138–142.

Waller, N. G., & Shaver, P. R. (1994). The importance of non-genetic influences on romantic love styles: A twin family study. *Psychological Science, 5*, 268–274.

Walsh, V., & Pascual-Leone, A. (2003). *Transcranial magnetic stimulation: A neurochronometrics of mind.* Cambridge, MA: MIT Press.

Walsh, Y. (2001). Deconstructing "brainwashing" within cults as an aid to counselling psychologists. *Counselling Psychology Quarterly, 14*, 119–128.

Walster, E., Walster, G. W., & Berscheid, E. (1978). *Equity: Theory and research.* Needham Heights, MA: Allyn & Bacon.

Walters, J., & Gardner, H. (1985). The development and education of intelligences. In F. Link (Ed.), *Essays on the intellect* (pp. 1–21). Washington, DC: Curriculum Development Association/Association for Supervision and Curriculum Development.

Wang, Q., & Conway, M. A. (2004). The stories we keep: Autobiographical memory in American and Chinese middle-aged adults. *Journal of Personality, 72*, 911–938.

Wang, X., Trivedi, R., Trieber, F., & Snieder, H. (2005). Genetic and environmental influences on anger expression, John Henryism, and stressful life events: The Georgia cardiovascular twin study. *Psychosomatic Medicine, 67*, 16–23.

Wareing, M., Murphy, P. N., & Fisk, J. E. (2004). Visuospatial memory impairments in users of MDMA ("ectasy"). *Psychopharmacology, 173*, 391–397.

Wark, G. R., & Krebs, D. L. (1996). Gender and dilemma differences in real-life moral judgment. *Developmental Psychology, 32*, 220–230.

Warren, R. M., & Warren, R. P. (1970). Auditory illusions and confusions. *Scientific American, 223*, 30–36.

Warrington, E. K., & McCarthy, R. A. (1988). The fractionation of retrograde amnesia. *Brain and Cognition, 7*, 184–200.

Washburne, C. (1956). Alcohol, self and the group. *Quarterly Journal of Studies on Alcohol, 17*, 108–123.

Wason, P. C., & Johnson-Laird, P. N. (1972). *Psychology of reasoning: Structure and content.* Cambridge, MA: Harvard University Press.

Wässle, H. (2004). Parallel processing in the mammalian retina. *Nature Reviews Neuroscience, 5*, 747–757.

Watkins, L. R., Milligan, E. D., & Maier, S. F. (2001). Glial activation: A driving force for pathological pain. *Trends in Neuroscience, 24*, 450–455.

Watkins, P. C., Grimm, D. L., & Kolts, R. (2004). Counting your blessings: Positive memories among grateful persons. *Current Psychology: Developmental, Learning, Personality, Social, 23*, 52–67.

Watson, D., & Hubbard, B. (1996). Adaptation style and dispositional structure: Coping in the context of the five-factor model. *Journal of Personality, 64*, 737–774.

Watson, J. B. (1913). Psychology as a behaviorist views it. *Psychological Review, 20*, 158–177.

Watson, J. M., Bunting, M. F., Poole, B. J., & Conway, A. R. A. (2005). Individual differences in susceptibility to false memory in the Deese-Roediger-McDermott paradigm. *Journal of Experimental Psychology: Learning, Memory, & Cognition, 31*, 76–85.

Watson, J., & Rayner, R. (1920). Conditioned emotional reactions. *Journal of Experimental Psychology, 3*, 1–14.

Watson, M., Greer, S., Rowden, L., Gorman, C., Robertson, B., Bliss, J. M., & Tunmore, R. (1991). Relationships between emotional control, adjustment to cancer, and depression and anxiety in breast cancer patients. *Psychological Medicine, 21*, 51–57.

Watt, C. A., & Morris, R. L. (1995). The relationship among performance on a prototype indicator of perceptual defence/vigilance, personality, and extrasensory perception. *Personality and Individual Differences, 19*, 635–648.

Watt, D. F. (2005). Panksepp's common sense view of affective neuroscience is not the commonsense view in large areas of neuroscience. *Consciousness and Cognition: An International Journal, 14*, 81–88.

Waugh, N. C., & Norman, D. A. (1965). Primary memory. *Psychological Review, 72*, 89–104.

Weaver, I. C. G., Cervoni, N., Champagne, F. A., D'Alessio, A. C., Sharma, S., Seckl, J. R., et al. (2004). Epigenetic programming by maternal behavior. *Nature Neuroscience, 7*, 847–854.

Wechsler, D. (1958). *The measurement and appraisal of adult intelligence* (5th ed.). Baltimore: Williams & Wilkins.

Weerasinghe, J., & Tepperman, L. (1994). Suicide and happiness: Seven tests of the connection. *Social Indicators Research, 32*, 199–233.

Wegner, D. M., Schneider, D. J., Carter, S. R., & White, T. L. (1987). Paradoxical effects of thought suppression. *Journal of Personality & Social Psychology, 53*, 5–13.

Wegner, D. M., Wenzlaff, R. M., & Kozak, M. (2004). Dream rebound: The return of suppressed thoughts in dreams. *Psychological Science, 15*, 232–236.

Wehr, T. A., Turner, E. H., Shimada, J. M., Clark, C. H., Barker, C., & Liebenluft, E. (1998). Treatment of a rapidly cycling bipolar patient by using extended bedrest and darkness to stabilize the timing and duration of sleep. *Biological Psychiatry, 43*, 822–828.

Weinberger, J. (1995). Common factors aren't so common: The common factors dilemma. *Clinical Psychology: Science and Practice, 2*, 45–69.

Weiner, B. (1980). A cognitive (attribution) emotion-action model of motivated behavior: An analysis of judgments of help-giving. *Journal of Personality and Social Psychology, 39*, 186–200.

Weiner, B., & Kukla, A. (1970). An attributional analysis of achievement motivation. *Journal of Personality & Social Psychology, 15*, 1–20.

Weingarten, H. P., Chang, P., & McDonald, T. J. (1985). Comparison of the metabolic and behavioral disturbances following paraventricular- and ventromedial-hypothalamic lesions. *Brain Research Bulletin, 14*, 551–559.

Weinstein, S. (1968). Intensive and extensive aspects of tactile sensitivity as a function of body part, sex, and laterality. In D. R. Kenshalo (Ed.), *The skin senses* (pp. 195–218). Springfield, IL: Thomas.

Weinstock, M. (1997). Does prenatal stress impair coping and regulation of hypothalamic-pituitary-adrenal axis? *Neuroscience & Biobehavioral Reviews, 21,* 1–10.

Weiskrantz, L. (1986). *Blindsight: A case study and implications.* New York: Oxford University Press.

Weiss, R. S. (1986). Continuities and transformations in social relationships from childhood to adulthood. In W. W. Hartup & Z. Rubin (Eds.), *Relationships and development* (pp. 95–110). Hillsdale, NJ: Erlbaum.

Weisskirch, R. S., & Murphy, L. C. (2004). Friends, porn, and punk: Sensation seeking in personal relationships, Internet activities and music preference among college students. *Adolescence, 39,* 189–201.

Weissman, M. M., Bland, R. C., Canino, G. J., Greenwald, S., Hwu, H., Lee, C. K., et al. (1994). The cross national epidemiology of obsessive compulsive disorder: The Cross National Collaborative Group. *Journal of Clinical Psychiatry, 55*(3, Suppl.), 5–10.

Weissman, M. M., Bruce, M. L., Leaf, P. J., Florio, L., & Holzer, C. (1991). Affective disorders. In L. N. Robins & D. A. Regier (Eds.), *Psychiatric disorders in America* (pp. 53–80). New York: Free Press.

Weissman, M. M., Wickramaratne, P., Nomura, Y., Warner, V., Verdeli, H., Pilowsky, D. J., et al. (2005). Families at high and low risk for depression: A 3-generation study. *Archives of General Psychiatry, 62,* 29–36.

Welberg, L. A., & Seckl, J. R. (2001). Prenatal stress, glucocorticoids and the programming of the brain. *Journal of Neuroendocrinology, 2,* 113–128.

Wellen, J. M., Hogg, M. A., & Terry, D. J. (1998). Group norms and attitude-behavior consistency: The role of group salience and mood. *Group Dynamics: Theory, Research, and Practice, 2,* 48–56.

Wender, P. H., Kety, S. S., Rosenthal, D., Schulsinger, F., Ortmann, J., & Luhde, I. (1986). Psychiatric disorders in the biological and adoptive families of adopted individuals with affective disorders. *Archives of General Psychiatry, 43,* 923–929.

Wenzlaff, R. M., & Luxton, D. D. (2003). The role of thought suppression in depressive rumination. *Cognitive Therapy & Research, 27,* 293–308.

Werner, C., Brown, B., & Altman, I. (1997). Environmental psychology. In J. W. Berry, M. H. Segall, & C. KagitÁibasi (Eds.), *Handbook of cross-cultural psychology, Vol. 3: Social behavior and applications* (pp. 255–290). Needham Heights, MA: Allyn & Bacon.

Wertheimer, M. (1912). Experimentelle Studien über das Sehen Bewegung. *Zeitschrift für Psychologie, 61,* 247–250.

Wertheimer, M. (1923). Untersuchungen zur Lehre von der Gestalt, II (Laws of organization in perceptual forms, II). In W. D. Ellis (Ed.), *A source book of Gestalt psychology* (pp. 71–88). London: Routledge & Kegan Paul.

Wessel, I., & Wright, D. B. (2004). Emotional memory failures: On forgetting and reconstructing emotional experiences. *Cognition & Emotion, 18,* 449–455.

West, L. J. (1980). Persuasive techniques in contemporary cults. In M. Galanter (Ed.), *Cults and new religious movements* (pp. 165–192). Washington, DC: American Psychiatric Press.

Westen, D. (1998). The scientific legacy of Sigmund Freud. Toward a psychodynamically informed psychological science. *Psychological Bulletin, 124,* 333–371.

Westen, D. (1999). The scientific status of unconscious processes: Is Freud really dead? *Journal of the American Psychoanalytic Association, 47*(Suppl.), 1–45.

Westen, D., & Morrison, K. (2001). A multidimensional metaanalysis of treatments for depression, panic, and generalized anxiety disorder: An empirical examination of the status of empirically supported therapies. *Journal of Consulting and Clinical Psychology, 60,* 875–899.

Wetsman, A., & Marlowe, F. (1999). How universal are preferences for female waist-to-hip ratios? Evidence from the Hadza of Tanzania. *Evolution and Human Behavior, 20,* 219–228.

Wetzstein, C. (2002, June 7). U.S. teens' birthrate lowest in 6 decades. *Washington Times.*

Whalen, P. J., Rauch, S. L., Etcoff, N. L., McInerney, S. C., Lee, M. B., & Jenike, M. A. (1998). Masked presentations of emotional facial expressions modulate amygdala activity without explicit knowledge. *Journal of Neuroscience, 18,* 411–418.

Wheeler, B. L., Shiflett, S. C., & Nayak, S. (2003). Effects of number of sessions and group or individual music therapy on the mood and behavior of people who have had strokes or traumatic brain injuries. *Nordic Journal of Music Therapy, 12,* 139–151.

Wheeler, L., & Kim, Y. (1997). What is beautiful is culturally good: The physical attractiveness stereotype has different content in collectivistic cultures. *Personality and Social Psychology Bulletin, 23,* 795–800.

Wheeler, M. D. (1991). Physical changes of puberty. *Endocrinology and Metabolism Clinics of North America, 20,* 1–14.

White, A., & Hardy, L. (1995). Use of different imagery perspectives on the learning and performance of different motor skills. *British Journal of Psychology, 86*(2), 169–180.

White, J. M., & Ryan, C. F. (1996). Pharmacological properties of ketamine. *Drug & Alcohol Review, 15,* 145–155.

White, T. G. (1982). Naming practices, typicality, and underextension in child language. *Journal of Experimental Child Psychology, 33,* 324–346.

Whittal, M. L., Agras, W. S., & Gould, R. A. (1999). Bulimia nervosa: A meta-analysis of psychosocial and pharmacological treatments. *Behavior Therapy, 30,* 117–135.

Whorf, B. (1956). *Language, thought, and reality.* Cambridge, MA: MIT Press.

Wickramasekera, I., Davies, T. E., & Davies, S. M. (1996). Applied psychophysiology: A bridge between the biomedical model and the biopsychosocial model in family medicine. *Professional Psychology: Research & Practice, 27,* 221–233.

Wiesbeck, G. A., Mauerer, C., Thome, J., Jakob, F., & Boening, J. (1995). Neuroendocrine support for a relationship between "novelty seeking" and dopaminergic function in alcohol-dependent men. *Psychoneuroendocrinology, 20,* 755–761.

Wigfield, A., Battle, A., Keller, L. B., & Eccles, J. S. (2002). Sex differences in motivation, self-concept, career aspiration, and career choice: Implications for cognitive development. (pp. 93–124) In A. McGillicuddy-De Lisi & R. De Lisi (Eds.), *Biology, society, and behavior: The development of sex differences in cognition.* Westport, CT: Ablex.

Wiggins, J. S. (1992). Have model, will travel. *Journal of Personality, 60,* 527–532.

Wigram, T., Pedersen, I. N., & Bonde, L. O. (2002). *A comprehensive guide to music therapy: Theory, clinical practice, research and training.* London, UK: Jessica Kingsley Publishers.

Wilder, D. A., Simon, A. F., & Faith, M. (1996). Enhancing the impact of counter-stereotypic information: Dispositional attributions for deviance. *Journal of Personality and Social Psychology, 71* 276–287.

Wildman, D. E., Grossman, L. I., and Goodman, M. (2002). Functional DNA in humans and chimpanzees shows they are more similar to each other than either is to other apes. In M. Goodman & A. S. Moffat (Eds.), *Probing human origins* (pp. 1–10). Cambridge, MA: American Academy of Arts and Sciences.

Wilkinson, R. B. (2004). The role of parental and peer attachment in the psychological health and self-esteem of adolescents. *Journal of Youth and Adolescence, 33,* 479–493.

Willer, J. C., Le, B. D., & De, B. T. (1990). Diffuse noxious inhibitory controls in man: Involvement of an opioidergic link. *European Journal of Pharmacology, 182,* 347–355.

Williams, C. N. (2003). America's opposition to new religious movements: Limiting the freedom of religion. *Law & Psychology Review, 27,* 171–182.

Williams, J. E., Paton, C. C., Eigenbrodt, M. L., Nieto, F. J., & Tyroler, H. A. (2000). Anger proneness predicts coronary heart disease risk: Prospective analysis from the atherosclerosis risk in communities (ARIC) study. *Circulation, 101,* 2034–2039.

Williams, L. M. (1994). Recall of childhood trauma: A prospective study of women's memories of child sexual abuse. *Journal of Consulting and Clinical Psychology, 62,* 1167–1176.

Williams, R., Barefoot, J., Califf, R., Haney, T., Saunders, E., Pryor, D., et al. (1992). Prognostic importance of social and economic resources among patients with angiographically documented coronary artery disease. *Journal of the American Medical Association, 267,* 520+.

Williams, S. M., Sanderson, G. F., Share, D. L., & Silva, P. A. (1988). Refractive error, IQ and reading ability: A longitudinal study from age seven to 11. *Developmental Medicine & Child Neurology, 30,* 735–742.

Williams, T. J., Pepitone, M. E., Christensen, S. E., Cooke, B. M., Huberman, A. D., Breedlove, N. J., et al. (2000). Finger length patterns and human sexual orientation. *Nature, 404,* 455–456.

Wilson, G. T., & Fairburn, C. G. (2002). Treatments for eating disorders. In P. E. Nathan & J. M. Gorman (Eds.), *A guide to treatments that work* (2nd ed., pp. 559–592). London: Oxford University Press.

Wilson, R. I., & Nicoll, R. A. (2001). Endogenous cannabinoids mediate retrograde signalling at hippocampal synapses. *Nature, 410,* 588–592.

Wilson, R. I., & Nicoll, R. A. (2002). Endocannabinoid signaling in the brain. *Science, 296,* 678–682.

Winer, G. A., & Cottrell, J. E. (1996). Does anything leave the eye when we see? Extramission beliefs of children and adults. *Current Directions in Psychological Science, 5,* 137–142.

Winer, G. A., Cottrell, J. E., Gregg, V., Fournier, J. S., & Bica, L. A. (2002). Fundamentally misunderstanding visual perception: Adults' belief in visual emissions. *American Psychologist, 57,* 417–424.

Winer, G. A., Cottrell, J. E., Gregg, V., Fournier, J. S., & Bica, L. A. (2003). Do adults believe in visual emissions? *American Psychologist, 58,* 495–496.

Winer, G. A., Cottrell, J. E., Karefilaki, K. D., & Gregg, V. R. (1996). Images, words and questions: Variables that influence beliefs about vision in children and adults. *Journal of Experimental Child Psychology, 63,* 499–525.

Winkelman, M. (2003). Complementary therapy for addiction: "drumming out drugs." *American Journal of Public Health, 93,* 647–651.

Winner, E. (1996). *Gifted children: Myths and realities.* New York: Basic Books.

Winner, E. (1997). Exceptionally high intelligence and schooling. *American Psychologist, 52,* 1070–1081.

Winner, E. (2000a). Giftedness: Current theory and research. *Current Directions in Psychological Science, 9,* 153–156.

Winner, E. (2000b). The origins and ends of giftedness. *American Psychologist, 55,* 159–169.

Winnicott, D. W. (1958). *Collected papers: Through paediatrics to psychoanalysis.* London: Tavistock.

Winzelberg, A., & Humphreys, K. (1999). Should patients' religiosity influence clinicians' referral to 12-step self-help groups? Evidence from a study of 3,018 male substance abuse patients. *Journal of Consulting and Clinical Psychology, 67,* 790–794.

Wise, P. M., Krajnak, K. M., & Kashon, M. L. (1996). Menopause: The aging of multiple pacemakers. *Science, 273,* 67–70.

Wise, R. A. (1996). Addictive drugs and brain stimulation reward. *Annual Review of Neuroscience, 19,* 319–340.

Wise, R. A. (2004). Dopamine, learning and motivation. *Nature Reviews Neuroscience, 5,* 483–494.

Witt, S. D. (1997). Parental influence on children's socialization to gender roles. *Adolescence, 32,* 253–259.

Witter, M. P., Wouterlood, F., & Witter, M. (2002). *The parahippocampal region: Organization and role in cognitive functions.* New York: Oxford University Press.

Wittstein, I. S., Thiemann, D. R., Lima, J. A. C., Baughman, K. L., Schulman, S. P., Gerstenblith, G., et al. (2005). Neurohumoral features of myocardial stunning due to sudden emotional stress. *New England Journal of Medicine, 352,* 539–548.

Wixted, J. T., & Ebbesen, E. B. (1991). On the form of forgetting. *Psychological Science, 2,* 409–415.

Wixted, J. T., & Ebbesen, E. B. (1997). Genuine power curves in forgetting: A quantitative analysis of individual subject forgetting functions. *Memory & Cognition, 25,* 731–739.

Wolf, N. (1991). *The beauty myth*. New York: Anchor/Doubleday.

Wolf, O. T., Preut, R., Hellhammer, D. H., Kudielka, B. M., Schuermeyer, T. H., & Kirschbaum, C. (2000). Testosterone and cognition in elderly men: A single testosterone injection blocks the practice effect in verbal fluency, but has no effect on spatial or verbal memory. *Biological Psychiatry, 47*, 650–654.

Wolpe, J. (1997). Thirty years of behavior therapy. *Behavior Therapy, 28*, 633–635.

Wolsko, P. M., Eisenberg, D. M., Davis, R. B., & Phillips, R. S. (2004). Use of mind-body medical therapies: Results of a national survey. *Journal of General Internal Medicine, 19*, 43–50.

Wood, J. J., McLeod, B. D., Sigman, M., Hwang, W., & Chu, B. C. (2003). Parenting and childhood anxiety: Theory, empirical findings, and future directions. *Journal of Child Psychology & Psychiatry, 44*, 134–151.

Wood, J. M., Lilienfeld, S. O., Nezworski, M. T., & Garb, H. N. (2001). Coming to grips with negative evidence for the comprehensive system for the Rorschach: A comment on Gacono, Loving, and Bodholdt; Ganellen; and Bornstein. *Journal of Personality Assessment, 77*, 48–70.

Wood, J. M., Nezworski, M. T., Garb, H. N., & Lilienfeld, S. O. (2001). Problems with the norms of the comprehensive system for the Rorschach: Methodological and conceptual considerations. *Clinical Psychology: Science & Practice, 8*, 397–402.

Woods, S. C., Schwartz, M. W., Baskin, D. G., & Seeley, R. J. (2000). Food intake and the regulation of body weight. *Annual Review of Psychology, 51*, 255–277.

World Health Organization (2001). *The world health report 2001. Mental health: New understanding, new hope*. Geneva, Switzerland: Author.

Worthington, T. S. (1979). The use in court of hypnotically enhanced testimony. *International Journal of Clinical & Experimental Hypnosis, 27*, 402–416.

Wraga, M. J., Thompson, W. L., Alpert, N. M., & Kosslyn, S. M. (2003). Implicit transfer of motor strategies in mental rotation. *Brain and Cognition, 52*, 135–143.

Wurtzel, E. (1995). *Prozac nation: A memoir*. New York: Riverhead.

Wyatt, R. J., Green, M. F., & Tuma, A. H. (1997). Long-term morbidity associated with delayed treatment of first admission schizophrenic patients: A re-analysis of the Camarillo State Hospital data. *Psychological Medicine, 27*, 261–268.

Wyer, N. A., Sherman, J. W., & Stroessner, S. J. (2000). The roles of motivation and ability in controlling the consequences of stereotype suppression. *Personality & Social Psychology Bulletin, 26*, 13–25.

Wyvell, C. L., & Berridge, K. C. (2000). Intra-accumbens amphetamine increases the conditioned incentive salience of sucrose reward: Enhancement of reward "wanting" without enhanced "liking" or response reinforcement. *Journal of Neuroscience, 20*, 8122–8130.

Yagueez, L., Nagel, D., Hoffman, H., Canavan, A., Wist, E., & Hoemberg, V. (1998). A mental route to motor learning: Improving trajectory kinematics through imagery training. *Behavioral and Brain Research, 90*, 95–106.

Yang, K., & Bond, M. H. (1990). Exploring implicit personality theories with indigenous or imported constructs: The Chinese case. *Journal of Personality and Social Psychology, 58*, 1087–1095.

Yazigi, R. A., Odem, R. R., & Polakoski, K. L. (1991). Demonstration of specific binding of cocaine to human spermatozoa. *Journal of the American Medical Association, 266*, 1956–1959.

Yehuda, R. (2002a). Post-traumatic stress disorder. *New England Journal of Medicine, 346*, 108–114.

Yehuda, R. (2002b). Clinical relevance of biologic findings in PTSD. *Psychiatric Quarterly, 73*, 123–133.

Yehuda, R. (2003). Adult neuroendocrine aspects of PTSD. *Psychiatric Annals, 33*, 30–36.

Yehuda, R., Golier, J. A., Yang, R., & Tischler, L. (2004). Enhanced sensitivity to glucocorticoids in peripheral

mononuclear leukocytes in posttraumatic stress disorder. *Biological Psychiatry, 55*, 1110–1116.

Yeomans, M. R., & Gray, R. W. (1997). Effects of naltrexone on food intake and changes in subjective appetite during eating: evidence for opioid involvement in the appetizer effect. *Physiology & Behavior, 62*, 15–21.

Yeshurun, Y., & Carrasco, M. (1998). Attention improves or impairs visual performance by enhancing spatial resolution. *Nature, 396*, 72–75.

Yeshurun, Y., & Carrasco, M. (1999). Spatial attention improves performance in spatial resolution tasks. *Vision Research, 39*, 293–306.

Yost, W. A., & Dye, R. H. (1991). Properties of sound localization by humans. In R. A. Altschuler, R. P. Bobbin, B. M. Clopton, & D. W. Hoffman (Eds.), *Neurobiology of hearing: The central auditory system* (pp. 389–410). New York: Raven.

Yu, D. W., & Shepard, G. H. (1998). Is beauty in the eye of the beholder? *Nature, 396*, 321–322.

Zacks, J., & Tversky, B. (1999). Bars and lines: A study of graphic communication. *Memory & Cognition, 27*, 1073–1079.

Zaharia, M. D., Kulczycki, J., Shanks, N., Meaney, M. J., & Anisman, H. (1996). The effects of early postnatal stimulation on Morris water-maze acquisition in adult mice: Genetic and maternal factors. *Psychopharmacology, 128*, 227–239.

Zaidel, E., & Iacoboni, M. (2003). *The parallel brain: The cognitive neuroscience of the corpus callosum*. Cambridge, MA: MIT Press

Zajicek, J. (2004). Primary progressive multiple sclerosis. *Cognitive Neuropsychology, 21*, 2784–2785.

Zajonc, R. B. (1968). Attitudinal effects of mere exposure. *Journal of Personality & Social Psychology, 9(2, Pt. 2)*, 1–27.

Zajonc, R. B. (2001). Mere exposure: A gateway to the subliminal. *Current Directions in Psychological Science, 10*, 224–228.

Zakowski, S., Hall, M. H., & Baum, A. (1992). Stress, stress management, and the immune system. *Applied and Preventative Psychology, 1*, 1–13.

Zalla, T., Koechlin, E., Pietrini, P., Basso, G., Aquino, P., Sirigu, A., & Grafman, J. (2000). Differential amygdala responses to winning and losing: A functional magnetic resonance imaging study in humans. *European Journal of Neuroscience, 12*, 1764–1770.

Zane, N., Hall, G. C. N., Sue, S., Young, K., & Nunez, J. (2004). Research on psychotherapy with culturally diverse populations. In M. J. Lambert (Ed.), *Bergin and Garfield's handbook of psychotherapy and behavior change*, 5th ed. (pp. 805–821). New York: Wiley and Sons.

Zane, N. W. S., Sue, S., Hu, L., & Kwon, J. H. (1991). Asian-American assertion: A social learning anyalsis of cultural differences. *Journal of Counseling Psychology, 38*, 63–70.

Zeki, S. (2002). Neural concept formation and art: Dante, Michelangelo, Wagner. *Journal of Consciousness Studies, 9*, 53–76.

Zeki, S. M. (1978). Functional specialisation in the visual cortex of the rhesus monkey. *Nature, 274*, 423–428.

Zeki, S. M. (1993). *Vision of the brain*. London: Blackwell.

Zenger, T. R., & Lawrence, B. S. (1989). Organizational demography: The differential effect of age and tenure distributions on technical communication. *Academy of Management Journal, 32*, 353–376.

Zentner, M. R., & Kagan, J. (1998). Infants' perception of consonance and dissonance in music. *Infant Behavior & Development, 21*, 483–492.

Zhang, Q., & Zhu, Y. (2001). The relationship between individual differences in working memory and linear reasoning. *Journal of Psychology in Chinese Societies, 2*, 261–282.

Zhdanova, I., & Wurtman, R. (1996, June). "How does melatonin affect sleep? *Harvard Mental Health Newsletter*, p. 8

Zhengyan, W., Huichang, C., & Xinyin, C. (2003). The stability of children's behavioral inhibition: A longitu-

dinal study from two to four years of age. *Acta Psychologica Sinica, 35*, 93–100.

Ziegler, D. J., & Leslie, Y. M. (2003). A test of the ABC model underlying rational emotive behavior therapy. *Psychological Reports, 92*, 235–240.

Zihl, J., von Cramon, D., & Mai, N. (1983). Selective disturbance of movement vision after bilateral brain damage. *Brain, 106*, 313–340.

Zimbardo, P. G. (2004, May 9). Power turns good soldiers into "bad apples." *Boston Globe*. Retrieved June, 2006 from http://www.boston.com/news/globe/ editorial_opinion/oped/articles/2004/05/09/

Zimbardo, P. G., Maslach, C., & Haney, C. (2000). Reflections on the Stanford Prison Experiment: Genesis, transformations, consequences. In T. Blass (Ed.), *Obedience to authority: Current perspectives on the Milgram paradigm* (pp. 193–237). Mahwah, NJ: Erlbaum.

Zimmer, E. Z., Fifter, W. P., Young-Ihl, K., Rey, H. R., Chao, C. R., & Myers, M. M. (1993). Response of the premature fetus to stimulation by speech sounds. *Early Human Development, 33*, 207–215.

Zlotnick, C. (1999). Antisocial personality disorder, affect dysregulation and childhood abuse among incarcerated women. *Journal of Personality Disorders, 13*, 90–95.

Zoccolillo, M., Price, R., Ji, T., & Hwu, H. (1999). Antisocial personality disorder: Comparisons of prevalence, symptoms, and correlates in four countries. In P. Cohen, C. Slomkowski, et al. (Eds.), *Historical and geographical influences on psychopathology* (pp. 249–277). Mahwah, NJ: Erlbaum.

Zornberg, G. L., Buka, S. L., & Tsuang, M. T. (2000). Hypoxic-ischemia-related fetal/neonatal complications and risk of schizophrenia and other nonaffective psychoses: A 19-year longitudinal study. *American Journal of Psychiatry 157*, 196–202.

Zuckerman, M. (1979). *Sensation seeking: Beyond the optimal level of arousal*. Hillsdale, NJ: Erlbaum.

Zuckerman, M. (1989). Personality as a third dimension: A psychobiological approach. *Personality & Individual Differences, 10*, 391–418.

Zuckerman, M. (1991). *Psychobiology of personality*. Cambridge, England: Cambridge University Press.

Zuckerman, M. (1994). *Behavioral expressions and biosocial bases of sensation seeking*. New York: Cambridge University Press.

Zuckerman, M. (1995). Good and bad humors: Biochemical bases of personality and its disorders. *Psychological Science, 6*, 325–332.

Zuckerman, M. (2003). Biological bases of personality. In T. Millon & M. J. Lerner (Eds.), *Handbook of psychology: Personality and social psychology* (Vol. 5, pp. 85–116). New York: John Wiley.

Zuckerman, M., & Cloninger, C. R. (1996). Relationships between Cloninger's, Zuckerman's, and Eysenck's dimensions of personality. *Personality & Individual Differences, 21*, 283–285.

Zuckerman, M., Joireman, J., Kraft, M., & Kuhlman, D. M. (1999). Where do motivational and emotional traits fit within three factor models of personality? *Personality & Individual Differences, 26*, 487–504.

Zuckerman, M., & Kuhlman, D. M. (2000). Personality and risk-taking: Common biosocial factors. *Journal of Personality, 68*, 999–1029.

Zuckerman, M., Kuhlman, D. M., & Camac, C. (1988). What lies beyond E and N? Factor analyses of scales believed to measure basic dimensions of personality. *Journal of Personality and Social Psychology, 54*, 96–107.

Zurek, P. M. (1981). Spontaneous narrowband acoustic signal emitted by human ears. *Journal of Acoustical Society of America, 69*, 514–523.

Zurek, P. M. (1985). Acoustic emissions from the ear: A summary of results from humans and animals. *Journal of the Acoustical Society of America, 78*, 340–344.

Zweigenhaft, R. L. (2002). Birth order effects and rebelliousness: Political activism and involvement with marijuana. *Political Psychology, 23*, 219–233.

Zwicker, E., & Schloth, E. (1984). Interrelation of different oto-acoustic emissions. *Journal of the Acoustical Society of America, 75*, 1148–1154.

NAME INDEX

Aalto, S., 298
Aartsen, M. J., 417
Abdollahi, P., 508
Abel, T., 213
Abraham, H. D., 462
Abrams, L. R., 466
Abramson, L. Y., 487, 488
Adams, J., 213
Adams, M. J., 191
Adams, S. J., 544
Addis, D. R., 204
Addis, M. E., 545
Ader, R., 157
Adler, A., 338, 362
Adolph, K. E., 385
Adolphs, R., 73, 302
Agarwal, D. P., 88
Agency for Health Care Policy and Research, 539
Aguilar-Alonso, A., 279
Ahadi, S., 343
Aiken, M., 351
Ainsworth, M. D. S., 398
Ajzen, I., 361
Akhtar, N., 389
Akiskal, H. S., 486
Alberini, C., 193
Albert, M., 148
Albert, M. S., 215, 412
Albert, R. S., 264
Alcock, J. E., 136
Aldag, R. J., 589
Aldea, A., 250
Aldridge, D., 76
Alexander, D., 277
Alexander, F., 524
Allen, J. J. B., 304
Allen, L. S., 325
Allport, G., 342, 567
Allyn, J., 566
Almeida, D. M., 433
Almli, C. R., 379
Alonso, P., 541
Alonzo, M., 351
Altshuler, L. L., 487
Aluja-Fabregat, A., 273
Amabile, T. M., 279
Ambady, N., 291, 300
Ambinder, M. S., 119
Amelang, M., 352
American Association for Mental Retardation, 276

American Psychiatric Association, 456, 477, 483, 493, 504, 505, 513, 548
American Psychological Association, 23, 41, 490
Amir, M., 541
Amsterdam, B., 399
Anastasi, A., 347
Anch, A. M., 439
Andersen, A. E., 508
Andersen, B., 464
Andersen, B. L., 437
Anderson, A. K., 298
Anderson, C. A., 455, 568
Anderson, J. R., 194, 242, 538
Anderson, M. C., 19, 214
Anderson, N. B., 8, 271
Anderson, V. L., 464
Andreasen, N. C., 280, 501, 502
Andrews, H. B., 319
Angleitner, A., 355
Anglin, J. M., 389, 390
Angst, J., 362, 486
Anisman, H., 384
Antoch, M. P., 446
Antonuccio, D. O., 548
Antony, M. M., 494
Arana, G. W., 459
Aranda, M. P., 466
Archer, J., 364
Archer, R. P., 347
Argyle, M. L., 299
Arkes, H. R., 568
Arlas, E., 485
Armatas, C., 351
Armstrong, S. L., 242
Arnell, K. M., 119
Arnett, J. J., 408
Arnold, M., 293
Arnsten, A. F. T., 275
Aron, A., 578
Aronson, E., 572, 573
Aronson, H., 549
Aronson, J., 274, 275
Arterberry, M. E., 386
Asch, S. E., 584, 585
Asendorpf, J. B., 399
Ashton, C. H., 57
Ashton, M. C., 366
Aspinwall, L. G., 451

Association of SIDS and Infant Mortality Programs, 385
Athanasiou, M. S., 258
Atienza, M., 443
Atkinson, J. W., 312
Atkinson, R. C., 187
Atre-Vaidya, N., 512
Auden, W. H., 504
Avorn, J., 411, 418
Axel, R., 131
Ayres, J. J. B., 148
Ayton, P., 249
Azar, B., 350

Baccus, J. R., 154
Bachen, E. A., 436
Bäckman, L., 411, 417
Badgaiyan, R. D., 201
Baddeley, A., 189, 190
Baeck, E., 76
Baenninger, M., 274
Bahrick, L. E., 399
Bailey, J. M., 325
Bailey, M., 75
Baillargeon, R., 395
Baily, C. H., 213
Baird, A., 396
Baker, F., 76, 136
Bakermans-Kranenburg, M. J., 399
Balakrishnan, J. D., 102
Ball, K., 418
Ball, S. A., 354
Ballus, C., 538
Baltes, P. B., 413
Banaji, M. R., 568
Bandura, A., 177, 178, 179, 361
Banks, M. S., 386
Bao, S., 153
Bar, M., 114
Barañano, D. E., 56
Barbarich, N., 507
Barber, J., 208
Barclay, J. R., 207
Bard, P., 293
Barefoot, J., 434
Barger, L. K., 442
Bargh, J. A., 571, 577, 581
Barinaga, M., 57
Barkham, M., 527, 545
Barkow, J. H., 17, 18, 307
Barlow, D. H., 494

Barnes, V. A., 464
Barnet, R. C., 148
Barnier, A. J., 208
Bar-On, R., 260
Baron, R. A., 453, 571
Barone, P., 59
Barrantes-Vidal, N., 280
Barrett, H. C., 244
Barrett, L. F., 294, 295, 296, 298, 302
Barsky, A. J., 467, 468
Bar-Tal, D., 574
Barth, J., 438
Bartoshuk, L. M., 133
Basic Behavioral Science Task Force, 479
Bast, T., 152
Bastien, C. H., 448, 449
Batsell, W. R., Jr., 317
Batshaw, M., 276
Batson, C. D., 591
Baum, S. R., 233
Baumeister, R. F., 301, 339, 455, 456, 574
Baxendale, S., 214, 215
Baxter, J. S., 574
Baxter, L. R., 551
Baxter, M. G., 311
Bayley, P. J., 215
Beach, F., 121
Beach, F. A., 309
Beals, J., 480
Beaman, A., 594
Bearak, B., 594
Beatty, J., 104
Beauchamp, G. K., 133
Beaumont, M., 446
Beauregard, M., 301
Bechara, A., 250, 309, 311
Bechterev, V., 148
Beck, A. T., 487, 491, 492, 532, 533, 534, 535, 549
Beck, R., 434
Becker, A. E., 508, 509
Beevers, C. G., 453
Bègue, L., 575
Behrens, R. R., 244
Behrmann, M., 240
Beilin, H., 397
Belkin, M., 31
Bell, A. E., 266
Bell, J. H., 407
Beller, M., 273

Bellugi, U., 23
Bem, D. J., 137
Benbow, C. P., 278
Benda, B. B., 324
Benedetti, F., 468
Bennett, P. J., 386
Bensafi, M., 132
Ben-Shakhar, G., 303
Benson, D. F., 51
Berchtold, N. C., 418
Berenbaum, S. A., 365
Berg, S., 411
Bergeman, C. S., 355, 357
Bergin, A. E., 546
Berkman, L. F., 463
Berko, J., 390
Berkowitz, L., 454
Berlyne, D. E., 308
Berman, J. D., 464
Berman, S. M., 266
Bermond, B. N., 294
Berntzen, D., 532
Berridge, K. C., 311
Berscheid, E., 577
Berson, D. M., 105, 446
Berthold, A., 321
Bertin, E., 387
Betz, J., 242
Beutler, L. E., 544, 550
Beyers, J. M., 408
Bhatt, R. S., 387
Biedenkapp, J. C., 193
Biederman, I., 111, 115
Biederman, J., 494
Bierhoff, H. W., 591
Bihrle, A. M., 71
Billington, C. J., 318
Bilukha, O. O., 508
Bimonte, H. A., 273
Binder, J. L., 545
Bindra, D., 309
Binet, A., 253, 392
Bird, H., 242
Birkenhäger, T. K., 540
Birnbaum, S. G., 275
Birren, J. E., 411
Bishop, G. D., 430
Biswas-Diener, R., 298
Bjork, E. L., 214
Bjork, R. A., 214
Black, D. W., 495
Black, J. E., 86
Blais, M. A., 481
Blakemore, S., 18, 566

White, J. M., 462
White, P. H., 275
White, T. G., 390
White, T. L., 351
Whittal, M. L., 548
Whorf, B., 236
Wickramasekera, I., 464
Widiger, T. A., 489, 512
Wierzbicki, M., 433
Wiesbeck, G. A., 354
Wiesel, T. N., 110
Wigfield, A., 274
Wiggins, J. S., 343
Wigram, T., 76
Wilder, D. A., 568
Wilkinson, R. B., 408
Willer, J. C., 135
Williams, C. N., 594
Williams, J. E., 434
Williams, K. D., 590
Williams, L. M., 216
Williams, R., 433, 463
Williams, S. M., 31
Williams, T. J., 326

Williams, W. M., 267
Wills, T., 463
Wilson, G. T., 545
Wilson, R. I., 56, 462
Windle, M., 485
Winer, G. A., 103
Wingfield, J. C., 429
Winkelman, M., 76
Winner, E., 277, 278
Winnicott, D. W., 524
Winzelberg, A., 544
Wise, P. M., 411
Wise, R. A., 309, 311
Witt, S. D., 400
Witter, M. P., 67
Wittstein, I. S., 438
Wixted, J. T., 212
Wolf, N., 580
Wolf, O. T., 273
Wolpe, J., 529, 531
Wolsko, P. M., 464
Wood, J. J., 350
Wood, J. M., 347
Wood, W., 580

Woods, S. C., 317
World Health
    Organization, 475
Worthington, T. S., 208
Wraga, M. J., 240
Wright, D. B., 216
Wright, G., 249
Wrightsman, L. S., 574
Wundt, W., 10–11, 18, 23
Wurtman, R., 446
Wurtzel, E., 484
Wyatt, R. J., 538
Wyer, N. A., 568
Wynn, K., 395
Wyvell, C. L., 311

Yagueez, L., 26
Yahya, K. A., 588
Yalow, R., 256
Yamauchi, L., 575
Yang, J., 143, 145, 146,
    161, 164, 175, 179
Yang, K., 366
Yazigi, R. A., 380

Yehuda, R., 497, 498
Yeoh, A. E. O., 548
Yeomans, M. R., 315,
    316
Yeshurun, Y., 117
Yoder, C. Y., 489
Yonas, A., 386
Yost, W. A., 128
Young, A. W., 71
Young, T., 106
Yu, D. W., 121

Zacks, J., 43
Zaharia, M. D., 384
Zaidel, D. W., 120
Zaidel, E., 69
Zajicek, J., 54
Zajonc, R. B., 565, 577
Zakowski, S., 465
Zalla, T., 298
Zane, N., 549
Zane, N. W. S., 343
Zanna, M. P., 589
Zebrowitz, L. A., 577

Zeki, S. M., 113, 279
Zeller, R. A., 34
Zenger, T. R., 590
Zentner, M. R., 387
Zhang, Q., 189
Zhdanova, I., 446
Zhengyan, W., 350
Zhu, Y., 189
Ziegler, D. J., 532
Zihl, J., 113
Zika, S., 433
Zimbardo, P. G., 582,
    583
Zimmer, E. Z., 379
Zlotnick, C., 514
Zoccolillo, M., 513
Zornberg, G. L., 502
Zuckerman, M., 30, 345,
    351, 352, 353, 354,
    355, 358, 364
Zurek, P. M., 124
Zweigenhaft, R. L., 363
Zwicker, E., 124

SUBJECT INDEX

Page numbers followed by f indicate figures; page numbers followed by t indicate tables; **boldface** type indicates key terms and the pages on which they are defined.

Clairvoyance, 136
Classical conditioning, 146–147, 147f
   acquisition in, 147, 150f
   and advertising, 155
   biological preparedness for, 148–149
   and chemotherapy, 156
   cognition and, 151–152
   and drug overdoses, 154
   of emotions, 148
   extinction and spontaneous recovery in,
      150–151, 150f
   of eye-blink, 153
   of fear, 152–153, 297
   of food (taste) aversions, 148, 155–156,
      156f, 157
   generalization and discrimination in, 151
   implicit memory as, 199, 201f
   of immune system, 156–157
   incentives and, 309
   mechanisms of, 152–153
   operant conditioning versus, 171–172,
      171f
   Pavlov's experiments on, 146–148, 146f
   personality and, 359
   of phobias, 148, 149f, 494
   posttraumatic stress disorder and, 498
   psychological disorders and, 478
   in therapy, 154–155, 530–531
Clever Hans, 37, 39
Client-centered therapy, 15, 340, **525–527**
Clinical neuropsychologists, 19–20, 23t
Clinical psychologist, 19–20, 23t
Clomiprimine, 540
Cloninger's theory of personality dimensions,
   353–354
Close Encounters of the Third Kind, 376
Closure, Gestalt law of, 110
CNS. *See* Central nervous system
Cobain, Kurt, 279
Cocaethylene, 460
Cocaine, 57t, 380, 460
   attachment and, 399
Cochlea, 125f, 126f
Cocktail party phenomenon, 129
Code, 191–192, 191f
Codeine, 461
Cognition. *See also* Social cognition;
      Thought
   in adulthood, 411–414
   attitude and, 562
   prejudice and, 568
Cognitive appraisal, 430, 431f
Cognitive–behavior therapy (CBT), 528,
   535–536, 536t, 547, 548
Cognitive development
   in adolescence, 406–407
   in infancy and childhood, 392–397
   and neural development, 396–397
   Piaget's theory of, 392–395
   self-concept and, 399–400

Vygotsky's sociocultural theory of, 397
Cognitive dissonance, 563–565, 563f, 566
Cognitive distortions, 487, **533,** 533t
Cognitive illusion, 249
Cognitive learning, 175–176
Cognitive map, 176
Cognitive neuroscience, 16, 18, 18t, 19
Cognitive psychologist, 21, 23t, 29
Cognitive psychology, 15–16, 18, 18t, 19
Cognitive restructuring, 535, 536t
Cognitive taste aversion, 317
Cognitive theory of emotion, 293, 293f, 298
Cognitive therapy, 532–535, 533t, 534f, 549
Collective unconscious, 338
Collectivist culture, 313, 366, 466
Color blindness, 108
Color constancy, 111
Color mixing, 106–107, 107f
Color Purple, The, 376
Color vision, 105–108
Columbus, Christopher, 103
Communication. *See also* Language
   nonverbal, 300–302
   sign language as, 389
Companionate love, 578, 578f
Complex inheritance, 85
Compliance, 585–587
Compulsion, 494–495
Computer-assisted tomography (CT, for-
      merly CAT), 81
Computers
   in brief therapy, 546
   as model for mental processes, 15–16
Concealed information test, 303
Concept, 240–243
   of self, 366–367, 399–400
Conception, 377
Conclusion, 247
Concrete operation, 395
Concrete operations period, 393t, 394–395
Conditioned compensatory responses, 154
Conditioned emotional response (CER),
      148, 149f, 154, 352
Conditioned response (CR), 147, 147f, 148,
   149f, 150f, 151, 155, 156, 156f, 494
Conditioned stimulus (CS), 147, 147f, 148,
   149, 149f, 150, 150f, 151, 152, 154,
   155, 156, 156f, 157, 494
Conditioning. *See* Classical conditioning;
      Operant conditioning
Conditions of worth, 340
Conduction deafness, 126
Cones, 104, 105f, 106, 108
Confederate, 296, 585
Confidence interval, A-6
Confirmation bias, 248
Conflict, 432. *See also* Realistic conflict
      theory
   between adolescents and parents, 408
   inhibitory, 457

Conformity, 583–585, 584f
Confound (confounding variable), 31, 32f
Conscience, 402
Conscientiousness, 344, 345t, 353, 354, 451
Conscious, 335, 335f
Consciousness, 10, 12
Consequence(s)
   in ABCDEF technique, 534, 534f
   in behavior therapy, 529, 529t
Conservation, 394, 394f, 396
Consolidation, 192–193
Constancy, perceptual, 111, 113f, A-11
Construct validity, 35t
Consummate love, 578f
Contact hypothesis, 571
Content validity, 35t
Continuity, 110
Continuous Positive Airway Pressure
      (CPAP), 449
Continuous reinforcement, 168
Continuous variables, A-2, A-2t
Contraception, 320, 409
Contrapreparedness, 149–150
Control
   eating disorders and, 508
   of emotions, 301–302
   locus of, 360, 365
   perceived, 431–432, 437, 452
   stimulus, 530, 531, 536t
Control beliefs, 533t
Control condition, 32
Control group, 31–32
Control question technique (CQT), 303
Controlled processing, 200, 200t
Conventional level, of moral development,
   402
Convergence, 112
Convergent thinking, 278
Cooperative learning, 572
Coordinate spatial relations, 117, 117f
Coping, 299, 430, 451, 451t
   aggression as, 453–456
   allostatic load and, 429, 452
   cultural differences in, 466
   drug and alcohol use as, 456–462
   gender differences in, 465–466
   social support and, 462–464
   thought suppression as, 453
Core affect, 294
Cornea, 104
Corpus callosum, 64, 65f, 69
Correlation, A-1, A-7–A-8, A-8f
Correlation coefficient, 29–30, 30f, 33t
Correspondence bias, 574
Cortisol, 75, 381
   and posttraumatic stress disorder, 498
   and schizophrenia, 502, 504
   and sleep deprivation, 442
   and stress response, 202, 428, 429, 433
Counseling psychologist, 20, 23t

L-Dopa, 59
Dopamine, 57t, 59, 311
  antipsychotic medication and, 538
  and cocaine use, 460
  MDMA and, 460
  novelty seeking and, 353, 354
  Parkinson's disease and, 73, 354
  and schizophrenia, 502
Dopamine-based reward system, 171, 172, 353, 460, 461
Double-blind design, 37, 465, A-2
Double pain, 135
Down syndrome, 277
Drapetomania, 476
Dream analysis, 13, 523
Dreams, 440
  activation-synthesis hypothesis of, 444
  brain damage and, 445
  latent and manifest content of, 444
  reasons for, 443–445, 445t
  REM rebound and, 441
Drinking. *See* Alcohol
Drive(s), 308, 311, 312f
Drive theory, 308
Drugs. *See also* Alcohol; Medications; *specific drugs*
  agonist, 59
  antagonist, 59
  classical conditioning and overdose of, 154
  in pregnancy, 380
DSM. See Diagnostic and Statistical Manual of Mental Disorders
Dual codes, 191
Dynamic memory, 192
Dysfunctional beliefs, 535, 535f

e, 190, 460
E.T., The Extra-Terrestrial, 376
Ear
  anatomy of, 125–126, 125f
  emitted sound from, 325
Eardrum, 125
Eating behavior, 311, 315–319
Eating disorders, 19, 57t, 504, 505–510, 506f, 508f, 530, 548
Ebbinghaus's forgetting curve, 213f
Echoic memory, 188
Eclecticism, technical, 544
Ecstasy (or e), 190, 460
ECT (electroconvulsive therapy), 540
Edges, inserting, 109f
Educational psychologist, 22, 23t
EEG. *See* Electroencephalogram
Effect, 31
Effect (effective new philosophy), in ABCDEF technique, 534, 534f
Effexor, 539
Egg (ovum), 377
Ego, 335, 336, 337, 523

Ego ideal, 335
Egocentrism, 394
  in adolescence, 407
Einstein, Albert, 226, 227, 228, 229, 232, 235, 247, 250, 251, 252, 265, 276
Elaboration likelihood model, of attitude change, 565
Elaborative encoding, 194
Elavil, 57t
Electra complex, 337
Electroconvulsive therapy (ECT), 540
Electroencephalogram (EEG), 80, 292, 439, 439f, 440
Electroencephalograph, 79–80, 80f, 439
Electromagnetic radiation, 103, 103f
Ellis's rational-emotive behavior therapy (REBT), 532
Embryo, 378
Emerging synthesis theory of emotion, 293–294, 293f
Emotion, 289
  aging and, 416
  amygdala and, 294, 297–298, 301
  basic, 290–291, 290f
  body language and, 300–301
  causes of, 292–300
  classical conditioning of, 148
  cognitive interpretation of, 296–297
  culture and expression of, 300
  decision making and, 250–251
  fear as, 297–298
  happiness as, 298–299
  high expressed, 503
  homeostasis and, 308
  memory and, 194–196
  odors and, 131
  perceiving, 302–305
  physiological profiles and, 294–295
  prejudice and, 568
  regulation of, 301–302
  sleep deprivation and, 442
  stress and, 438
  theories of, 292–294
  types of, 289–292
Emotion-focused coping, 451, 451t
Emotional development. *See* Social and emotional development
Emotional intelligence (EI), 260–261, 260t
Emotionality, 344, 345t, 349
Empathy, 402–403, 526
Empty love, 578f
Enacted social support, 463
Encoding, 186, 217–220
Encoding failure, 212
Endocrine glands, 75, 75f
Endogenous cannabinoids, 56, 57t
Endorphin receptors, 461
Endorphins, 135, 427
Enkephalins, 427

Environment
  of adoptive households, 267–268
  aggression and, 454
  aging brain and, 417, 418
  criminality and, 353
  family, 357, 488
  influence on genes by, 86–88, 89–90
  intelligence and, 266–269, 272
  mental retardation and, 277
  obesity and, 319
  perceived, 268
  personality and, 357, 362–369
  prenatal, 379–382
  shyness and, 350
Epilepsy, 57t, 69, 72
Epinephrine, 296, 296f, 428
Episodic memories, 198, 201f, 203–204, 215, 412
Erikson's psychosocial stages, 414–415, 414t
Eroticism, 322
Error
  margin of, A-6
  overregularization, 390–391
  in reasoning, 247–248
  sampling, A-9
ESP. *See* Extrasensory perception
Estrogen(s), 75, 322
Ethic of care, 402
Ethics
  in clinical practice, 41–42, 41t
  neuroethics, 42–43
  in research, 39–41, 596
Evaluative conditioning, 155
Event, 25, 27f
Evocative (or reactive) interaction, 88
Evolution, 11, 90
  brain and, 90–92
  and natural selection, 90–92, 91f
Evolutionary psychology, 16, 17–18, 18t, 19
  and mating preferences, 323–324, 579–580
  and motivation, 307
  and personality, 365
  and sleep function, 443
Excitatory effects, on neuron, 58
Excitement phase, of sexual response cycle, 321
Exhaustion phase, 428f, 429
Existential intelligence, 262t
Expectancies, 360–361
Expectancy effects, 364
Experimental condition, 32
Experimental group, 31–32
Experimental research, 31–32, 33t
Experimenter expectancy effects, 37
Explicit (declarative) memories, 198, 199, 201f, 234, 391–392
Exposure, 530, 548
Exposure with response prevention, 530, 536t, 548

Good form, Gestalt law of, 110
Gourmand syndrome, 316
Graduate Record Examination (GRE), 274
Grain, in mental space, 238–239, 240
Grammar, 390–391
Graphs, 43–44, A-11–A-13
Gray matter, 64, 266, 412
Ground, 109
Group(s), 580–583. *See also* Level of the
    group
    compliance with, 585–587
    conformity to, 583–585, 584f
    decision making in, 588–590
    differences within versus between,
        269–271
    obedience in, 587–588
    roles in, 582–583
    rules of, 581–582
    self-help, 543–544
Group polarization, 589
Group therapy, 542–543
Groupthink, 589–590
Growth, during adolescence, 405–406
Guilt, 294, 305, 335
Guilty actions test, 303
Guilty knowledge technique (GKT), 303,
    304
Gyrus, 65

Habit, 73, 199–200, 201f
Habituation, 145, 199
Habituation technique, 386, 387f
Hair cells, 125f, **126,** 126f
Halcion, 57t
Haldol, 538
Hallucinations, 476, 500, 538
Hallucinogen, 461–462
Hammer, 125, 125f
Happiness, 295, 298–299, 300
Harlow's attachment studies, 398
Harm avoidance, 353, 354t
Harris, Eric, 455
Hassles, 433
Having Our Say (Delaney, Delaney, and
    Hearth), 559
Health maintenance organization (HMO),
    476
Health psychology, 426
Hearing, 123–129
    aging and, 412
    in infancy, 387–388
    locating sounds in, 128
    temporal lobes and, 67
    thalamus in, 72
Heart attack, 411, 437–438
Heart disease, type A personality and,
    433–434
Heaven's Gate cult, 594
Helplessness, learned, 310, 310f, 431,
    488

Hemispheres, of brain, 69–71, 70f. *See also*
    Cerebral hemisphere
Heritability, 89
    of intelligence, 266
    of personality, 355, 356f
    of specific behaviors, 355–358
Heroin, 380, 461
Hertz (Hz), 124
Heterosexual, 324
Heuristic(s), 244, 246f
    availability, 249–250
    culture and, 249
    representativeness, 248–249
Hierarchical organization, as mnemonic de-
    vice, 217–218
High blood pressure, 438
High expressed emotion, 503
Highly charged emotional consequence,
    534, 534f
Hiking monk problem, 244f
Himba language, 237
Hindbrain, 71f, **74**
Hippocampus, 72–73
    aging and, 412
    amnesia and, 215
    depression and, 487, 547
    emotional memory and, 195
    false memories and, 211
    fear and, 152, 153
    memory and, 202–203, 214
    memory consolidation and, 192
    and posttraumatic stress disorder, 498
    and schizophrenia, 501
Histrionic personality disorder, 512t
HIV, 380
HMO, 476
Homeobox genes, 326
Homeostasis, 308, 427
Homosexual, 324, 476
Homosexuality, biology of, 324–326
Hormone(s), 75. *See also specific hormones*
    attractiveness and female, 120
    brain and, 74
    glucocorticoids as, 428
    in puberty, 405, 406, 408
    sex, 322
    and sexual behavior, 321–323
Horney, Karen, 338
Hostile attribution bias, 454
Hostility, 433–434
    and rage, 532
Hot flashes, 411
How to Lie with Statistics (Huff), A-10
Hox genes, 326
HPA axis, 75, 428, 487
Hue, 106
Human factors psychologist, 22, 23t
Human genome project, 202
Human immunodeficiency virus, 380
Human serotonin transporter gene, 297

Humanistic psychology, 15, 18t, 339–340
Humanistic therapy, 525–527
Humor, 233
Humors, 477
Hunch, 250
Hunger
    as drive, 308
    eating behavior and, 315–317
    overeating and, 317–319
Huntington's disease, 57t
Hypercolumn, 109–110
Hypnic jerk, 439
Hypnogogic sleep, 439
Hypnosis, 464t
    memory and, 208
    pain and, 135
Hypomania, 485
Hypothalamic-pituitary-adrenal (HPA) axis,
    75, 428, 487
Hypothalamus, 72, 321
    eating and, 316
    emotion and, 301
    fear and, 297
    homosexuality and, 324–325
    stress and, 428
Hypothesis, 25, 26, 27f

Iconic memory, 188
Id, 335, 336, 337, 523
Identical twins, 89, 267f, 478
    body language of, 301
    cancer and, 437
    mood disorders in, 487
    obesity in, 319
    personality of, 355, 356
    schizophrenia and, 501
Identity versus role confusion, 414t
Illusions, 101f, 249
Images
    interactive, 218–219
    mental, 11, 233, 237–240, 238f
Imaginal exposure, 530
Imaginary audience, 407
Imagination, 246
Imaging, optical, 82
Imitation
    by infants, 395
    of perceived emotion, 302
Immediate memory. *See* Short-term memory
Immediate reinforcement, 166
Immigration Act of 1924, 269
Immune system, 435–436, 437
    classical conditioning of, 156–157
    mind-body interventions and, 464–465
    placebo and, 465
    sleep deprivation and, 441
    social support and, 463
    stress and, 428
Impairment, as element of psychological
    disorder, 475

Neuron(s), 53
    action potential and, 54, 55f, 56f
    communication between, 56–59
    glial cells and, 60
    motor, 53
    of primary visual cortex, 109–110
    pruning of, 86
    sensory, 53
    stimulation of, 82–83
    structure of, 53–54, 53f
Neuropsychologist, 29
Neuroscience, cognitive, 16, 18, 18t, 19
Neurosis, 336
Neuroticism, 344, 345t, 346, 351, 352–353, 354, 354t, 355, 364
Neuroticism-anxiety, in alternative five, 354, 354t
Neurotransmitter(s), 56–59, 56f, 57t, 58f
    aging and, 412
    and bipolar disorder, 487
    and depression, 487
    eating disorders and, 507
    personality dimensions and, 353, 357–358
    and psychological disorders, 477–478
    and schizophrenia, 502
    sleep and, 446
    and stress response, 428
Newborn, 382–383
Newton, Sir Isaac, 10, 279
Nicotine, 461
Nitric oxide, as neurotransmitter, 56
NK cell. See Natural killer cell
Nocebo effect, 467–468
Noise, 102
Nonassociative learning, 145, 199, 201f
Nonconformity, 345
Nondeclarative memories. See Implicit memories
Nondeprived reward, 311, 312f
Nonpurging type, of bulimia nervosa, 506
Nonsense syllables, 191
Nonspecific side effects, 467
Nonverbal communication, 300–302
Nonviolent resistance, 288
Noradrenaline (norepinephrine), 57t
    and bipolar disorder, 487
    and cocaine use, 460
    depression and, 487
    emotion and, 195
    and sleep, 446
    and stress response, 428
Norm, 581
Normal curve, 256f
Normal distribution, 256, A-4, A-4f
Normative social influence, 584–585, 584f
Norming, 255
Novelty seeking, 353, 354t, 355
NREM sleep, 443

Obedience, 587–588, 587f

Obesity, 318–319
Object permanence, 393, 395, 396
Observation
    in assessing personality, 346
    naturalistic, 28, 33t
    personality development and, 359
Observational learning, 177–178, 178f, 179, 180
    in behavior therapy, 532, 536t
    of phobias, 494
    of prosocial behavior, 591
    psychological disorders and, 478
Obsession, 494
Obsessive-compulsive disorder (OCD), 494–496, 512t
    neurotransmitters and, 507
    serotonin and, 57t
    treatment for, 530, 548, 551–552
Occipital lobe, 64, 66–67
Occlusion cue, 112
OCD. See Obsessive-compulsive disorder
OCEAN, 344
Odor receptors, 131, 131f
Oedipus complex, 336
Olfaction, 130–132, 131f, 133
Olfactory bulb, 131f
Olfactory receptor cells, 131f
One Flew Over the Cuckoo's Nest, 540
Openness to experience, 344, 345t, 346, 362
Operant conditioning, 158–166, 159f
    behavior therapy techniques using, 531–532
    brain in, 171–172
    classical conditioning versus, 171–172, 171f
    dopamine in, 171
    extinction and spontaneous recovery in, 167
    generalization and discrimination in, 166–167
    obsessive-compulsive disorder and, 496
    personality and, 359
    of phobias, 494
    posttraumatic stress disorder and, 498
    psychological disorders and, 478
    reinforcement schedules for, 168–170, 170f
    shaping in, 167–168
Operational definition, 26
Opiate, 461
Opioid receptors, 461
Opioids, appetite and, 316
Opponent cells, 107
Opponent process theory of color vision, 107–108
Optic chiasm, 446f
Optic nerve, 104
Optical imaging, 82
Oral stage, 336, 336t
Orbital frontal cortex, 120

Organic amnesia, 214, 215
Orgasm phase, of sexual response cycle, 321
Osteoporosis, 411
Outcome research, 546
Outer ear, 125f
Outgroup, 568
Oval window, 125f, 126f
Overeating, 317–319
Overextension, 390
Overregularization error, 390–391
Ovulation, 322
Ovum, 377
Owls, 447
Oxycodone, 461
Oxytocin, 323

Pain, 57t, 135–136
Panic attack, 491
Panic disorder, 491–493, 492f, 548
Papillae, 133f
Paradoxical cold, 135
Paranoid personality disorder, 512t
Paranoid schizophrenia, 500–501, 500t
Parasympathetic nervous system, 62f, 63, 303, 428
Parental investment, theory of, 323
Parents. See Family
Parietal lobe, 64, 68
    false memories and, 21
    music and, 76
    visual pathways and, 114f
Parkinson's disease, 57t, 73, 354
Paroxetine, 547f
Partial reinforcement, 168
Passionate love, 578
Passive interaction, 87–88
Pavlov's conditioning experiments, 146–148, 146f, 151
Paxil, 59, 538, 547
PCP (phencyclidine), 461, 462
PDAs, in brief therapy, 546
Peak experience, 340
Peer group, gender roles and, 400–401
Peer relationships, in adolescence, 408–409
Pegword system, 219
Penis envy, 337
Pentecostals, 477
Perceived control, 431–432, 437, 452
Perceived environment, 268
Perceived social support, 463
Percentile rank, A-6–A-7
Perception, 101. See also Hearing; Vision
    in adulthood, 411–412
    brain activation during, 239
    categorical, 127–128
    cultural conventions and, 112–113
    depth, 386
    of distance, 111–113
    extrasensory, 38–39
    motion cues in, 113

Profile of intelligences, 262
Progressive muscle relaxation, 531
Project A, 174, 175
Projection, 337t
Projective test, 347
Propositional representation, 231, 232f
Prosocial behavior, 591–592
Protein kinase C, 275
Proteins, and memory, 202
Prototype, 241–242
Proximity, 110
Prozac, 57t, 59, 495–496, 538, 551, 552
Prozac Nation, 484
Pruning, 86
Pseudopsychology, 38–39
Psi, 136
Psilocybin, 461
Psychiatric nurse, 20
Psychiatrist, 20
Psychoanalysis, 523–524
Psychodynamic theory, 13, 18t, 19
  of obesity, 318–319
  of personality, 334–339
Psychodynamic therapy, 523, 524–525, 527
Psychoeducation, 535, 536t
Psychokinesis (PK), 136
Psychological determinism, 334
Psychological disorder(s), 475. *See also specific disorders*
  Axis I, 482–510
  Axis II, 511–514
  categorizing, 480–482, 481t
  creativity and, 278–279
  identifying, 474–482
Psychologist(s)
  ethical principles and code of conduct for, 41t
  types of, 19–22, 23t, 29, 376
Psychology, 4–6. *See also specific schools and subfields*
  ethics in, 39–41
  history of, 9–19
  interpretation in, 34–39
  levels of analysis in, 6–8
  research in, 21–22, 24–34
Psychometric approach, to analyzing intelligence, 257–260
Psychoneuroimmunology, 436
Psychopharmacology, 537–540
Psychophysics, 101–102
Psychosexual stages, 336–337, 336t
Psychosis, 336, 476
Psychosocial development, 414–415, 414t
Psychotherapy, 19–20. *See also* Therapy
  research in, 546, 547t
Psychotherapy by Reciprocal Inhibition (Wolpe), 529
Psychotherapy integration, 544–545
Psychoticism, 345, 353, 354, 354t
PTSD. *See* Posttraumatic stress disorder

Puberty, 404–406, 405f
Punch-drunk, 74
Punctuation, 232f
Punishment, 14, 163–165, 163f, 351, 352
  facial expressions as, 172–173
  negative, 162f, 164
  physical, 164
  positive, 162f, 163
Pupil, 104, 105, 412
Purging, 506
Purging type, of bulimia nervosa, 506

Quartiles, A-6
Quasi-experimental design, 32, 33t

Race differences, in IQ scores, 271–273
Racial bias, 479
Radiation, classically conditioned taste aversion to, 155–156, 156f
Random assignment, 32
Range, A-4–A-5
Rape, date, 458
Rapid-eye movement (REM), 440
RAS, 73
Ratio schedule, 169
Rational-emotive behavior therapy (REBT), 532–533, 534, 534f
Rationalization, 337t
Raw data, A-2t, A-3
Reaction formation, 337t
Reactive coping, 451
Realistic conflict theory, 569–570, 570f
Reality monitoring, 211–212
Reality principle, 335
Reasoning, 247–248, 247f
  spatial, 273, 274
Rebound effect, 453
REBT. *See* Rational-emotive behavior therapy
Recall, 206–208, 412
Recategorization, 571–572
Recency effect, 191
Receptor(s), 57–59, 58f
  glucocorticoid, 498
  light, 446
  odor, 131, 131f
  opioid, 461
Recognition, 206–207
Recognition test, 206, 207
Reconsolidation, 193
Recovered memory, 216
Recreational sex, 320
Reflex(es), 64, 382
Refractory period, in sexual response cycle, 321
Rehearsal, 189, 190
Reinforcement, 14, **160**
  in behavior modification, 531
  continuous, 168
  delayed, 166

drive theory and, 308
expectations of, 309
facial expressions as, 172–173
immediate, 166
negative, 161–163, 162f, 163f
partial, 168
positive, 161, 162f, 163f
Reinforcement schedules, 168–170, 170f
Reinforcer, 160
  primary, 165
  secondary, 165–166, 530, 531
Relational aggression, 455
Relationships
  adolescent peer, 408–409
  in adulthood, 416–417
  liking, 577–578
  loving, 578–579
Relative standing, A-6–A-7
Relevant/irrelevant technique (RIT), 303
Reliability, 34
  of IQ scores, 256
  of projective tests, 347
REM rebound, 441
REM sleep, 440, 442, 443, 444, 446
Remembering, 206, 207–208, 207f
Remeron, 539
Repeated contact, liking with, 577
Repetition blindness, 119, 120
Repetition deafness, 119
Repetition priming, 201
Replication, 25
Representation problem, 243–244
Representativeness heuristic, 248–249
Repressed memories, 216–217
Repression, 337t, 338
Reproductive sex, 320
Research, 21–22
  with animals, 40–41
  ethics in, 39–41, 596
  with humans, 39–40
  interpretation of, 34–39
  outcome, 546
  psychotherapy, 546, 547t
  scientific method in, 24, 25–28, 27f
  split-brain, 69–70, 70f
  techniques of, 28–34, 33t
Resilience, 299
Resistance, 525
Resistance phase, 428–429, 428f
Resistant attachment, 398
Resolution phase, of sexual response cycle, 321
Response. *See* Conditioned emotional response; Conditioned response; Ruminative response; Unconditioned response
Response bias, 36, 321
Response contingency, 160, 531
Responsibility, diffusion of, 593
Resting potential, 54

CREDITS

Text and Illustrations

Figure 1.3, p. 30: From *Introduction to the Practice of Statistics* by David S. Moore and George P. McCabe. © 1989, 1993, and 1999 by W. H. Freeman and Company. Used with permission. **Table 1.6, p. 41:** Excerpts from Principles A through E, pages 1062–1063, from "Ethical principles of psychologists and code of conduct," *American Psychologist*, 2002, 57, 1067–1073. Copyright © 2002 by the American Psychological Association. Adapted with permission. **Figure 2.1, p. 53:** From Goodenough, Judith A.; McGuire, Betty A.; Wallace, Robert A., *Biology of Humans: Concepts, Applications, and Issues*, 1st edition, © 2005, Figure 7.2. Adapted by Permission of Pearson Education, Inc., Upper Saddle River, NJ. **Figure 2.2, p. 55:** From Goodenough, Judith A.; McGuire, Betty A.; Wallace, Robert A., *Biology of Humans: Concepts, Applications, and Issues*, 1st edition, © 2005, Figure 7.5. Adapted by Permission of Pearson Education, Inc., Upper Saddle River, NJ. **Figure 2.4, p. 56:** From Goodenough, Judith A.; McGuire, Betty A.; Wallace, Robert A., *Biology of Humans: Concepts, Applications, and Issues*, 1st edition, © 2005, Figure 7.7. Adapted by Permission of Pearson Education, Inc., Upper Saddle River, NJ. **Figure 2.5, p. 59:** From Goodenough, Judith A.; McGuire, Betty A.; Wallace, Robert A., *Biology of Humans: Concepts, Applications, and Issues*, 1st edition, © 2005, Figure 7.2. Adapted by Permission of Pearson Education, Inc., Upper Saddle River, NJ. **Figure 2.6, p. 62:** From Goodenough, Judith A.; McGuire, Betty A.; Wallace, Robert A., *Biology of Humans: Concepts, Applications, and Issues*, 1st edition, © 2005, Figure 8.10. Adapted by Permission of Pearson Education, Inc., Upper Saddle River, NJ. **Figure 2.9, p. 68:** From Goodenough, Judith A.; McGuire, Betty A.; Wallace, Robert A., *Biology of Humans: Concepts, Applications, and Issues*, 1st edition, © 2005, Figure 8.7. Adapted by Permission of Pearson Education, Inc., Upper Saddle River, NJ. **Figure 2.11, p. 70:** From Gazzaniga, M. S. and LeDoux, J. E. *The Integrated Mind*. New York: Plenum Press, 1978. Reprinted with kind permission from Springer Science and Business Media. **Figure 2.12, p. 71:** From Goodenough, Judith A.; McGuire, Betty A.; Wallace, Robert A., *Biology of Humans: Concepts, Applications, and Issues*, 1st edition, © 2005, Figure 7.2. Adapted by Permission of Pearson Education, Inc., Upper Saddle River, NJ. **Figure 2.13, p. 72:** From Goodenough, Judith A.; McGuire, Betty A.; Wallace, Robert A., *Biology of Humans: Concepts, Applications, and Issues*, 1st edition, © 2005, Figure 8.8. Adapted by Permission of Pearson Education, Inc., Upper Saddle River, NJ. **Figure 2.16, p. 81:** From Goodenough, Judith A.; McGuire, Betty A.; Wallace, Robert A., *Biology of Humans: Concepts, Applications, and Issues*, 1st edition, © 2005, Figure 8.6. Adapted by Permission of Pearson Education, Inc., Upper Saddle River, NJ. **Figure 2.17, p. 85:** From Goodenough, Judith A.; McGuire, Betty A.; Wallace, Robert A., *Biology of Humans: Concepts, Applications, and Issues*, 1st edition, © 2005, Figures 21.1 and 21.2. Adapted by Permission of Pearson Education, Inc., Upper Saddle River, NJ. **Figure 3.4, p. 104:** From Goodenough, Judith A.; McGuire, Betty A.; Wallace, Robert A., *Biology of Humans: Concepts, Applications, and Issues*, 1st edition, © 2005, Figure 9.4. Adapted by Permission of Pearson Education, Inc., Upper Saddle River, NJ. **Figure 3.5, p. 105:** From Goodenough, Judith A.; McGuire, Betty A.; Wallace, Robert A., *Biology of Humans: Concepts, Applications, and Issues*, 1st edition, © 2005, Figure 9.5. Adapted by Permission of Pearson Education, Inc., Upper Saddle River, NJ. **Figure 3.17, p. 118:** From *Psychology* by Peter Gray. © 1991, 1994, 1999, and 2002 by Worth Publishers. Used with permission. **Figure 3.19, p. 125:** From Goodenough, Judith A.; McGuire, Betty A.; Wallace, Robert A., *Biology of Humans: Concepts, Applications, and Issues*, 1st edition, © 2005, Figures 9.11 and 9.13. Adapted by Permission of Pearson Education, Inc., Upper Saddle River, NJ. **Figure 3.23, p. 131:** From Goodenough, Judith A.; McGuire, Betty A.; Wallace, Robert A., *Biology of Humans: Concepts, Applications, and Issues*, 1st edition, © 2005, Figure 9.15. Adapted by Permission of Pearson Education, Inc., Upper Saddle River, NJ. **Figure 3.24, p. 133:** From Goodenough, Judith A.; McGuire, Betty A.; Wallace, Robert A., *Biology of Humans: Concepts, Applications, and Issues*, 1st edition, © 2005, Figure 9.16. Adapted by Permission of Pearson Education, Inc., Upper Saddle River, NJ. **Figure 4.13, p. 170:** Figure from "Teaching Machines" by B. F. Skinner, *Scientific American*, 1961. Reprinted by permission of the estate of Mary E. and Dan Todd. **Figure 5.4, p. 190:** Adapted from *Working Memory* by Alan Baddeley, Clarendon Press (1986). **Figure 5.5, p. 191:** Adapted from M. Glanzer and A. R. Cunitz, "Two storage mechanisms in free recall," *Journal of Verbal Learning and Verbal Behavior*, 5, 351–360, 1996. **Table 5.1, p. 200:** Based on Schneider and Chein (2003). **Figure 5.7, p. 201:** Adapted from L. R. Squire and S. Zola-Morgan, "The medial temporal lobe memory system," *Science*, 253, 1380–1386. **Figure 5.8, p. 207:** Adapted from Barclay et al., 1974. Comprehension and semantic flexibility. *Journal of Verbal Learning and Verbal Behavior*, 13, 471–481. **Figure 6.2, p. 238:** From Kosslyn, S. M., Ball, T. M., and Reiser, B. J., "Visual images preserved metric spatial information: Evidence from studies of image scanning," *Journal of Experimental Psychology: Human Perception and Performance*, 4, 47–60. Copyright © 1978 by the American Psychological Association. Reprinted with permission. **Figure 6.6, p. 245:** From *Cognition: Exploring the Science of the Mind* by Daniel Reisberg. Copyright © 1997 by W. W. Norton & Company, Inc. Used by permission of W. W. Norton & Company, Inc. **Figure 6.7, p. 246:** From *Cognition: Exploring the Science of the Mind* by Daniel Reisberg. Copyright © 1997 by W. W. Norton & Company, Inc. Used by permission of W. W. Norton & Company, Inc. **Table 6.2, p. 254:** Actual WAIS test items cannot be published; part of the table was adapted from Gardner et al., 1996, pp. 80–81. **Table 6.3, p. 259:** Adapted from information on the website of the Institute for Applied Psychometrics at www.iapsych.com **Table 6.4, p. 261:** Adapted from Mayer, Salovey, Caruso, & Sitarenios (2001, Table 2, p. 235). **Table 6.7, p. 278:** From

http://thearc.org/faqs/mrqa.html **Figure 7.2, p. 293:** From Lester A. Lefton, *Psychology*, 7/e. Published by Allyn and Bacon, Boston, MA. © 2000 by Pearson Education. Reprinted by permission of the publisher. **Table 7.1, p. 304:** Based on DePaulo, Stone and Lassiter (1985); DePaulo et al. (2003); Ekman (1985); Zuckerman et al. (1981). **Figure 7.8, p. 323:** Figure from Cooper, M. L., Shapiro, C. M., and Powers, A. M., "Motivations for sex and risky behavior among adolescents and young adults: A functional perspective," *Journal of Personality and Social Psychology*, 75, 1528–1558. Copyright © 1998 by the American Psychological Association. Reprinted with permission. **Figure 8.1, p. 335:** From Lester A. Lefton, *Psychology*, 8/e. Published by Allyn and Bacon, Boston, MA. © 2003 by Pearson Education. Reprinted by permission of the publisher. **Table 8.2, p. 337:** From Freud (1933/1965), p. 70. **Figure 8.3, p. 344:** Adapted from Cattell, Eber, and Tatsuoka. Copyright © 1970 by the Institute for Personality and Ability Testing, Inc. Reproduced by permission. "16PF" is a trademark belonging to IPAT, Inc. **Table 8.4, p. 354:** Based on Cloninger & Zuckerman (1966); Ebstein et al. (2002); Gomez & Gomez (2005); Zuckerman, Joireman, et al. (1999); Zuckerman & Kuhlman (2000). **Figure 8.5, p. 356:** From H. J. Eysenck, *The Biological Basis of Personality*, 1967. Courtesy of Charles C. Thomas Publisher, Ltd., Springfield, Illinois. **Figure 8.6, p. 360:** Adapted from Mischel & Shoda, 1995, p. 262. **Table 8.6, p. 368:** Percentages of three attachment styles in second column from Michelson et al. (1997); first-person descriptions in third column from Lopez (2003, p. 288). **Figure 9.2, p. 385:** Based on LaRossa (2000). **Figure 9.4, p. 389:** Adapted from Reznick, J. S., and Goldfield, B. A., "Rapid change in lexical development in comprehension and production," *Developmental Psychology*, 28, 406–413. **Figure 9.7, p. 396:** From Renee Baillargeon, "How do infants learn about the physical world?" *Current Directions in Psychological Science*, 3, 5, 133–140, 1994. Reprinted with permission from Blackwell. **Figure 10.1, p. 428:** From Hans Selye, *The Stress of Life*, Second edition, 1978. Reproduced with permission of The McGraw-Hill Companies. **Figure 10.5, p. 440:** From *Sleep* by J. Allan Hobson. Copyright © 1989 by J. Allan Hobson. M.D. Reprinted by permission of Henry Holt and Company, LLC. **Table 10.3, p. 451:** From Carver, C. S., Scheier, M. F., and Weintraub, J. K. "Assessing Coping Strategies," *Journal of Personality and Social Psychology*, 56, 267–83, 1989. Copyright © 1989 by the American Psychological Association. Adapted with permission. **Table 10.4, p. 456:** Reprinted with permission from the *Diagnostic and Statistical Manual of Mental Disorders, Fourth Edition, Text Revision* (Copyright 2000). American Psychiatric Association. **Figure 10.8, p. 460:** From Goodenough, Judith A.; McGuire, Betty A.; Wallace, Robert A., *Biology of Humans: Concepts, Applications, and Issues*, 1st edition, © 2005, Figure 7.7. Adapted by permission of Pearson Education, Inc., Upper Saddle River, NJ. **Table 11.1, p. 481:** Reprinted with permission from the *Diagnostic and Statistical Manual of Mental Disorders, Fourth Edition, Text Revision*, (Copyright 2000). American Psychiatric Association. **Table 11.2, p. 484:** Reprinted with permission from the *Diagnostic and Statistical Manual of Mental Disorders, Fourth Edition, Text Revision*, (Copyright 2000). American Psychiatric Association. **Table 11.3, p. 485:** Adapted from Suicide awareness/Voices of Education (SA/VE), PO Box 24507, Minneapolis, MN 55424; Phone: (612) 946-7998; Internet: http://www.save.org; E-mail: save@winternet.com **Figure 11.3, p. 488:** Based on Lewinsohn et al., 1999, Table 1. **Table 11.4, p. 493:** Reprinted with permission from the *Diagnostic and Statistical Manual of Mental Disorders, Fourth Edition, Text Revision*, (Copyright 2000). American Psychiatric Association. **Table 11.5, 499:** Reprinted with permission from the *Diagnostic and Statistical Manual of Mental Disorders, Fourth Edition, Text Revision*, (Copyright 2000). American Psychiatric Association. **Table 11.6, p. 500:** Reprinted with permission from the *Diagnostic and Statistical Manual of Mental Disorders, Fourth Edition, Text Revision*, (Copyright 2000). American Psychiatric Association. **Table 11.7, p. 512:** Reprinted with permission from the *Diagnostic and Statistical Manual of Mental Disorders, Fourth Edition, Text Revision*, (Copyright 2000). American Psychiatric Association. **Figure 11.4, p. 492:** From Goodenough, Judith A.; McGuire, Betty A.; Wallace, Robert A., *Biology of Humans: Concepts, Applications, and Issues*, 1st edition, © 2005, p. 137. Adapted by permission of Pearson Education, Inc., Upper Saddle River, NJ. **Figure 11.5, p. 506:** Adapted from Thompson, J. K. (1990). *Body Image Disturbance: Assessment and Treatment*, p. 11. **Figure 11.6, p. 508:** Adapted from Jansen et al., 2005, p. 190. **Table 12.2, p. 533:** Based on Beck (1967). **Figure 12.2, p. 535:** Format adapted from Beck et al. (1979). **Table 12.4, p. 547:** Based on Kazdin (1994). **Figure 12.4, p. 551:** Based on Schwartz, *Archives of General Psychiatry*, 53(2), February 1996. 109–113. **Figure 13.1, p. 563:** Based on Festinger & Carlsmith (1959). **Figure 13.4, p. 578:** Sternberg's Triangular Theory of Love. Reprinted by permission of Robert Sternberg. **Figure 13.8, p. 593:** Based on Darley and Latané (1970). **Figure A.3, p. A-8:** From *Introduction to the Practice of Statistics* by David S. Moore and George P. McCabe. © 1989, 1993, and 1999 by W. H. Freeman and Company. Used with permission. **Figure A.5, p. A-11:** From Kosslyn, 1994a, pp. 209 and 211. Data for illustration on left from Natural Resources Defense Council. **Figure A.6, p. A-11:** From Kosslyn, 1994a, pp. 209 and 211. Data for illustration on left from Natural Resources Defense Council. **Figure A.7, p. A-12:** From Kosslyn, 1994a, p. 227. Data from Hacker, 1992, p. 98, cited in *Newsweek*, March 23, 1992, p. 61. **Figure A.8, p. A-12:** From Kosslyn, 1994a, p. 219. Data from Morgan Stanley Capital International, cited in *The Economist World Atlas and Almanac*, 1989, p. 90. **Figure A.9, p. A-13:** From Kosslyn, 1994a, p. 225. Data from Weisberg, 1980, cited in Chambers et al., 183, p. 371.

Photos and Cartoons

Chapter 1 2 © Leo Mason/CORBIS; 5 (left) © Roger Tully/Getty Images/Stone; 5 (center) © David Young-Wolff/PhotoEdit; 5 (right) © Royalty Free/CORBIS; 10 Archives of the History of American Psychology; 11 (top) Archives of the History of American Psychology; 11 (middle) © 2000 North Wind Picture Archives; 12 © Kelly-Mooney Photography/CORBIS; 13 © Mary Evans/Sigmund Freud Copyrights; 14 THE FAR SIDE® by Gary Larson © 1986 Farworks, Inc. All Rights Reserved. The Far Side® and the Larson® signature are registered trademarks of FarWorks, Inc. Used with permission; 16 © Bettmann/CORBIS; 17 (left) AP Images/Carlos Osorio; 17 (right) © Louise Gubb/The Image Works; 20 © Michael Newman/PhotoEdit; 21 © Brian Smith/Stock Boston, LLC; 22 (top) © Bob Daemmrich/The Image Works; 22 (bottom) Courtesy of Wellesley College; 28 (top) AP Images/Jay LaPrete; 28 (bottom) © Dennis MacDonald/PhotoEdit; 29 © Michael Newman/PhotoEdit; 30 © Terje Rakke/Getty Images/The Image Bank; 32 © Richard Lord/PhotoEdit; 38 DILBERT: © Scott Adams/Dist. by United Feature Syndicate, Inc.; 40 © 1996 Jane Tyska/Stock Boston, LLC; 42 Center for Cognitive Liberty and Ethics; 43 © SuperStock, Inc.; 43 (inset) © Volker Steger/Photo Researchers, Inc.

Chapter 2 50 © Leif Skoogfors/CORBIS; 59 © Ron Sachs/CORBIS Sygma; 65 © A. Glaublerman/Photo Researchers, Inc.; 69 Damasio H, Grabowski T, Frank R, Galaburda AM, Damasio AR: The return of Phineas Gage: Clues about the brain from a famous patient. *Science*, 264:1102-1105, 1994. Department of Neurology and Image Analysis Facility, University of Iowa; 73 © Victoria Pearson/Getty Images/Taxi; 76 © Pablo Corral V/CORBIS; 76 (inset) © Digital Art/CORBIS; 79 © Getty Images/The Image Bank/Ataboy; 80 © Will and Deni McIntyre/Science Source/Photo Researchers, Inc.; 81 (top left) © Susie Levines/Photo Researchers, Inc.; 81 (top right) © Neil Borden/Photo Researchers, Inc.; 81 (bottom) © Will and Deni McIntyre/Photo Researchers, Inc.; 86 © Karen Huntt/CORBIS; 87 (top) Dorling Kindersley Media Library; 87 (bottom) ALPHAVILLE/IMOHOTEP PROD/THE KOBAL COLLECTION/HAMSHERE, KEITH; 88 (top left) © Laura Dwight/PhotoEdit, Inc.; 88 (top center) © Getty Images/Zen Sekizawa/Taxi; 88 (top right) © Getty Images/Siri Stafford/Taxi; 88 (middle) © The Philadelphia Museum of Art/Art Resource, NY; 89 © PhotoDisc/Getty Images

Chapter 3 98 © Condé Nast Archive/CORBIS; 100 The Art Archive/Museum of Modern Art Mexico/Dagli Orti. 2005 Banco de Mexico Diego Rivera & Frida Kahlo Museums Trust. Av. Cinco de Mayo No. 2, Col. Centro, Del Cuauhtemoc 06059, Mexico, D.F.; 103 © North Wind Picture Archives; 106 © David Young-Wolff /PhotoEdit; 108 © Robert Harbison; 109 (top) Pintos © 2006 Bev Doolittle®; 109 (bottom) © Erich Lessing/Art Resource, NY; 110 Reprinted with permission from Tootell, RBH, Silverman, MS, Switkes, E, and DeValors, RL 1982. Deoxyglucose analysis of retinotopic organization in primate striate cortex. *Science*, Vol. 218, 26 November 1982. pg. 902. © 1982 American Association for the Advancement of Science; 112 © Bill Lyons Photography; 113 © Baron Wolman/Woodfin Camp & Associates; 115 © CORBIS Sygma; 119 (left and right) Corel, Courtesy of Ron Rensink/Rensink, O'Regan, and Clark, 1997. *Psychology Science*. Vol. 8, No. 5, September 1997. Need for Attention to See Change; 120 © Leland Bobbe/Getty Images/Photographer's Choice; 120 (inset) © Volker Steger/Photo Researchers, Inc.; 121 Perrett, DI, et al. (1998). *Nature*, vol. 394, August 27, 1998, pg. 885. Effects of Sexual Dimorphism on Facial Attractiveness. 884-887; 126 © Mark Richards/PhotoEdit; 128 © Jack K Clark/The Image Works; 134 © Addison Geary/Stock Boston, LLC; 135 © TEK Image/Photo Researchers, Inc.

Chapter 4 142 GOLDEN PORT PROD./TRI-STAR/THE KOBAL COLLECTION/CHAN KAM TSEUN; 148 © Getty Images/Brand X Pictures/Andersen/Ross; 152 © Richard Prideaux/Photo Researchers, Inc.; 155 © Barbara Alper/PhotoEdit; 157 © Andreas von Einsiedel; Elizabeth Whiting & Associates/CORBIS; 165 "Illustrations" by Kimberley Ann Coe, from SIBLINGS WITHOUT RIVALRY: HOW TO HELP YOUR CHILDREN LIVE TOGETHER SO YOU CAN TOO by Adele Faber and Elaine Mazlish; 166 © Dennis MacDonald/PhotoEdit; 169 (top) © Getty Images/Photodisc Red/Andersen/Ross; 169 (middle) DynamicGraphics/Inmagine, LLC; 169 (bottom) © Robert Harbison; 170 © Bonnie Kamin/PhotoEdit; 172 © C. Lyttle/zefa/CORBIS; 172 (inset) © Digital Art/CORBIS; 175 © Getty Images/Blend Images; 177 DILBERT: © Scott Adams/Dist. by United Feature Syndicate, Inc.; 179 (top) © James A. Sugar/CORBIS; 179 (bottom) © Michael Newman/PhotoEdit

Chapter 5 190 Reprinted with permission from Smith, EE, & Jonides, J, Storage and executive processes in the frontal lobes, *Science*, Vol. 283, 12 March 1999. pp 1657–1661. © 1999 American Association for the Advancement of Science; 195 AP Images; 199 (left) © David Young Wolff/PhotoEdit; 199 (right) © Marko Haggerty/Getty Images/The Image Bank; 203 © Royalty-Free/CORBIS; 203 (inset) © GJLP/Photo Researchers, Inc.; 208 (top) Getty Images/Photodisc Red; 208 (bottom) © Michael Newman/PhotoEdit; 211 (top) DILBERT: © Scott Adams/Dist. by United Feature Syndicate, Inc.; 211 (middle) © Tony Hopewell/Getty Images/Taxi; 212 © David Butow/CORBIS SABA; 214 COLUMBIA/THE KOBAL COLLECTION; 215 (top) © Paul Conklin/PhotoEdit; 215 (bottom) Getty Images/Photodisc; 218 © Bob Daemmrich/Stock Boston, LLC; 219 © PhotoDisc/Getty Images; 221 © Tony Freeman/PhotoEdit

Chapter 6 226 © Bettmann/CORBIS; 230 © Paul Barton/CORBIS; 233 © Getty Images/Stockdisc Premium; 236 © CORBIS; 239 Brain areas underlying visual mental imagery and visual perception: An fMRI study, Giorgio Ganis, William L. Thompson, Stephen M. Kosslyn. *Cognitive Brain Research* 20 (2004), 226-241; 249 © Kelly-Mooney Photography/CORBIS; 250 © Getty Images/Image Source; 253 © Bob Daemmrich Photography; 257 © Owen Franken/CORBIS; 259 © 1994 David J Sams/Stock Boston, LLC; 262 (middle) © Jonathan Nourok/PhotoEdit, Inc.; 262 (bottom) © Lawrence Migdale/Stock Boston, LLC; 268 (left) © Cleo Photography/PhotoEdit; 268 (right) © Robert Ginn/PhotoEdit; 269 © Michael S. Yamashita/CORBIS; 272 © Material World/Kirk McCoy; 274 (top) © T. Zuidema/The Image Works; 274 (bottom) © Richard Hutchings/PhotoEdit; 274 (bottom inset) © Digital Art/CORBIS; 277 Reprinted with permission from Streissguth, A.P., Landesman-Dwyer, S., Martin, J.C., & Smith, D.W. (1980). Teratogenic effects of alcohol in humans and laboratory animals. *Science*, 209 (18): 353-362. © 1980 American Association for the Advancement of Science; 278 © Marianne Barcellona/Time Life Pictures/Getty Images; 279 © S. Evertson; 280 AP Images

Chapter 7 286 © Hulton-Deutsch Collection/CORBIS; 290 Reprinted by permission of the Human Interaction Laboratory/Japanese and Caucasian Facial Expressions of Emotion, Matsimoto & Ekman, 1988; 295 © Roger Ressmeyer/CORBIS; 297 Whalen, P.J., et al., Masked presentations of emotional facial expressions modulate amygdala activity without explicit knowledge. *J. Neurosci*. 18:411-418. Used with Permission; 299 © Ariel Skelley/CORBIS; 300 © Dwayne Newton/PhotoEdit; 303 © Stewart Cohen/Getty Images/Stone; 303 (inset) © Digital Art/CORBIS; 304 © Mark C. Burnett/Photo Researchers, Inc.; 307 (left) © Doug Martin/Stock Boston, LLC; 307 (center) © Syracuse Newspapers/Steve Ruark/The Image Works; 307 (right) AP Images/Shizuo Kambayashi; 309 © Royalty-Free/CORBIS; 312 © M. Granitsas/The Image Works; 316 © Dana White/PhotoEdit; 317 © Reuters NewMedia Inc./CORBIS; 318 © Bob Daemmrich/Stock Boston, LLC; 319 AP Images; 320 AP Images; 322 © Getty Images/Photodisc Green; 324 © David Young-Wolff/PhotoEdit

Chapter 8 332 © Bill Ross/CORBIS; 338 (left) © Hulton/Archive/Getty Images; 338 (center and right) © Bettmann/CORBIS; 340 © Cindy Charles/PhotoEdit; 342 © The Everett Collection; 343 © Mark Richards/PhotoEdit; 345 © Colin Young-Wolff/PhotoEdit, Inc.; 347 © Lew Merrim/Photo Researchers, Inc.; 349 (left) © Bill Bachmann/Stock Boston, LLC; 349 (right) © Jose Carrillo/Stock Boston, LLC; 351 (top) © Robert Aschenbrenner/Stock Boston, LLC; 351 (bottom) © Mary Steinbacher/PhotoEdit; 352 © Ted Soqui/CORBIS; 354 © Fujofotos/The Image Works; 356 © Bob Sacha Photography; 361 © Mark Richards/PhotoEdit; 364 © Spencer Grant/PhotoEdit; 366 © Joe Cavanaugh/DDB Stock Photo; 367 © Myrleen Ferguson Cate/PhotoEdit; 367 (inset) © Digital Art/CORBIS

Chapter 9 374 © Rufus F. Folkks/CORBIS; 377 © Dr. Yorgos Nikas/Science Photo Library/Photo Researchers, Inc.; 379 (left and right) Photo Lennart Nilsson/Albert Bonniers Forlag AB; 381 © Getty Images/Digital Vision; 382 (top left) © Renee Lynn/Getty Images/Stone; 382 (top right) © David Young-Wolff/PhotoEdit; 382 (bottom) © Paul Conklin/PhotoEdit; 383 © John Ficara/Woodfin Camp & Associates; 386 © Mark Richards/PhotoEdit; 389 © Michael Newman/PhotoEdit; 391 Courtesy of Carolyn Rovee-Collier; 392 © Bill Anderson/PhotoResearchers, Inc.; 393 © Michael Newman/PhotoEdit; 395 Reprinted with permission from A. N. Meltzoff & M. K. Moore, 1977. Imitation of facial and manual gestures by human neonates. *Science*, 198, p. 75 © 1977 American Association for the Advancement of Science; 397 © Nik Wheeler/CORBIS; 398 Harlow Primate Laboratory; 399 (top) © Mark Wexler/Woodfin Camp Associates, Inc.; 399 (bottom) © Cathy Melloan/PhotoEdit; 400 (left) © Frank Siteman; 400 (right) © Mary Kate Denny/PhotoEdit; 402 © Joe Carini/PacificStock.com; 406 © Bob Daemmrich/Stock Boston, LLC; 407 © Brand X Pictures/Alamy; 411 (top) © Steven Peters/Getty Images/Stone; 411 (bottom) © Tom Prettyman/PhotoEdit; 412 Resnick, S.M., Pham, D.L., Kraut, M.A., Zonderman, A.B., Davatzikos, C.: Longitudinal magnetic resonance imaging studies of older adults: A shrinking brain. *J. Neurosci*. 23(8): 3295-3301, 2003. © 2003 by the Society for Neuroscience; 413 © Jose Carillo/PhotoEdit; 414 © Timothy Greenfield-Sanders; 415 AP Images/Louis Lanzano; 416 © 1997 Erin Moroney LaBelle/The Image Works; 417 © David Young-Wolff/PhotoEdit; 417 (inset) © Volker Steger/Photo Researchers, Inc.; 418 © David Young-Wolff/PhotoEdit

Chapter 10 424 © Bill Varie/Alamy; 430 © B. Stitzer/PhotoEdit; 431 © B. Deconinck/The Image Works; 433 (top) © Rachel Epstein/PhotoEdit; 433 (bottom) Getty Images/image100; 435 © Meckes/Ottawa/Photo Researchers, Inc.; 436 (top) © Franco Vogt/CORBIS; 436 (bottom) © Jason Reed/Reuters/CORBIS; 437 © SPL/Photo Researchers, Inc.; 439 © Michael Heron/Woodfin Camp & Associates; 441 © Mark Richards/PhotoEdit; 442 © Jose Luis Pelaez, Inc./CORBIS; 443 AP Images/Richard Drew; 445 © Jeremy Horner/CORBIS; 447 © David Lees/CORBIS; 448 © Jon Feingersh/CORBIS; 452 © Mark Romanelli/Getty Images/The Image Bank; 453 AP Images/Mike Fiala; 455 © Mark Leffingwell/Boulder Daily Camera; 457 © ImageDJ/Index Stock; 458 © Cathrine Wessel/CORBIS; 461 © blickwinkel/Alamy; 463 (top) © Getty Images/Stockbyte; 463 (bottom) © Network Productions/The Image Works; 464 © George D. Lepp/CORBIS; 466 © Henning Christoph/DAS FOTOARCHIV/Peter Arnold; 466 (inset) © Digital Art/CORBIS

Chapter 11 472 © Erich Lessing/Art Resource, NY; 476 (top) © Erich Lessing/Art Resource, NY; 476 (middle, left and right) © Reuters/CORBIS; 478 © Myrleen Ferguson/PhotoEdit, Inc.; 484 Painting by Kate Monson, Courtesy of Sarah Mentock; 486 © WDCN/Univ. College London/Photo Researchers, Inc.; 488 © Richard Pasley/Stock Boston, LLC; 489 © Chung Sung-Jun/Getty Images; 491 © The Everett Collection; 493 © Getty Images/Stockdisc; 494 © Ingo Arndt/Nature Picture Library; 495 © Margaret Ross/Stock Boston, LLC; 497 (middle) © Culver Pictures, Inc.; 497 (bottom) © Arnold Gold/New Haven Register/The Image Works; 501 (left and right) National Institute of Mental Health; 502 Courtesy of Edna Morlock; 504 © Sean Sprague/The Image Works; 508 (top) © The Everett Collection; 508 (bottom) © Chet Gordon/The Image Works; 509 © Photodisc Red/Getty Images; 509 (inset) © Volker Steger/Photo Researchers, Inc.; 513 © Getty Images/Tim Boyle/Des Plaines Police Department

Chapter 12 520 © Gabe Palmer/CORBIS; 524 (top) © Rhoda Sidney/Stock Boston, LLC; 524 (bottom) © Zigy Kaluzny/Getty Images/Stone; 526 © Amy Etra/PhotoEdit; 530 (left and right) © Bob Mahoney/The Image Works; 531 © Getty Images/Photodisc Red; 539 © Michael P. Gadomski/Photo Researchers, Inc.; 541 Julian Keenan; 542 © Bob Daemmrich/Stock Boston, LLC; 544 © James Marshall/The Image Works; 545 © Stuart Cohen/The Image Works; 546 © David Young-Wolff/PhotoEdit; 547 Goldapple, K., Segal, Z., Garson, C., Lau, M., Bieling, P., Kennedy, S., Mayberg, H. (2004). Modulation of Cortical-Limbic Pathways in Major Depression. *Archives of General Psychiatry*, 61, 34-41; 548 © David Young-Wolff/PhotoEdit; 550 © Chuck Fishman/Woodfin Camp & Associates; 551 (middle) © Amy Etra/PhotoEdit; 551 (middle, inset) © Digital Art/CORBIS; 551 (bottom) Baxter et al., 1992

Chapter 13 558 © Marianne Barcellona/Time Life Pictures/Getty Images; 561 (left) AP Images/Daniel Bersak; 561 (right) © Reuters/Mike Segar/CORBIS; 562 © Bettmann/CORBIS; 564 DILBERT: © Scott Adams/Dist. by United Feature Syndicate, Inc.; 565 © Mario Tama/Getty Images; 566 © Jeff Greenberg/juno.com/Photo Researchers, Inc.; 567 © John Neubauer/PhotoEdit; 569 (left) © Michael Newman/PhotoEdit; 569 (right) © Stephen Simpson/Getty Images/Taxi; 572 © Columbia Pictures/courtesy Everett Co./Everett Collection; 574 (top) © David Wells/The Image Works; 581 (top) © Reuters/Oleg Popov/CORBIS; 581 (bottom) © Burbank/The Image Works; 582 Philip G. Zimbardo, Inc.; 586 © Rhonda Sidney/The Image Works; 587 From the film *Obedience* copyright 1965 by Stanley Milgram and distributed by Penn State Media Sales; 590 © James Nubile/The Image Works; 591 © SHANNON STAPLETON/REUTERS/Landov; 594 © Ariel Skelley/CORBIS; 594 (inset) © GJLP/Photo Researchers, Inc.